Ind. Notre Dame

Ave Maria

January-June, 1860

Ind. Notre Dame

Ave Maria

January-June, 1860

ISBN/EAN: 9783742840875

Manufactured in Europe, USA, Canada, Australia, Japa

Cover: Foto ©Andreas Hilbeck / pixelio.de

Manufactured and distributed by brebook publishing software (www.brebook.com)

Ind. Notre Dame

Ave Maria

THE AVE MARIA.

A Journal devoted to the Honor of the Blessed Virgin.

HENCEFORTH ALL GENERATIONS SHALL CALL ME BLESSED.—St. Luke, i, 48.

'Beth's Promise.

BY MRS. ANNA HANSON DORSEY.

CHAPTER I.
BETWEEN SUNRISE AND SUNSET.

"I AM going to make a white mark for this day, mamma; it has been altogether the happiest one I ever knew! First of all, a long letter from dear papa; then, shopping with you, to buy my lovely silk dress,—my first young lady's dress, mamma; then the sky so clear and blue, and the sunshine so bright and pleasant after the storm! Oh, dearest mamma, haven't we enjoyed ourselves, and won't papa be glad when I write and tell him what a nice time we've had!" exclaimed 'Beth Morley, as she tripped up the marble steps to the hall door of their house, her sweet, clear voice ringing with the gladness of her young life, her cheeks dimpling with smiles.

"Yes, it has been a very happy day, 'Beth; I don't know when I have enjoyed myself more," answered Mrs. Morley, with a fond look at the bright, eager face smiling into hers.

"That's because *I* was with you, Lady-Bird; you know it was," said 'Beth, tossing back the stray golden curls that the wind was blowing over her face; "and oh, mamma, did you notice in papa's letter, all through, how proud he is of his ship, and how satisfied he is with his officers, —'a nice, gentle, manly, brave set of fellows,' he says?"

"Yes, I noticed," said Mrs. Morley, while a shadow flitted over her face, and her mouth grew hard and stern for a moment, but only for a moment. "Ring again, 'Beth; I am very tired, and quite ready for my lunch. I hope Andrew has thought to make me a cup of tea."

"Here he is, mamma. Now, Andy, have you got a cup of nice hot tea for mamma?" said 'Beth, as the servant man opened the door—a grave, respectable-looking person, who had been with Captain Morley on most of his cruises, and had followed him through the perils of the war, serving him with rare and affectionate fidelity under all circumstances until, owing to a hurt he had received from a spent-ball at the storming of a fort on the Mississippi, he was ordered home, and was only reconciled to the separation from his captain by being placed by him in charge of his family, and the assurance that he should go with him on his next cruise. He did not answer 'Beth; there was a preoccupied and almost frightened look in his dusky face, as he took up the card-tray from the hall table and held it towards Mrs. Morley. There was but a single large card on it.

"The Secretary's been here, madam," he said, as she glanced at it and tossed it back in the tray, and was passing on towards the dining-room. "He came back ag'in, madam, and when he found you wasn't in yet, he left word—and told me to be sure and tell you—he'd be back here at 4 o'clock," said Andrew, following his mistress, and placing a chair for her.

"What," exclaimed Mrs. Morley, in a startled tone, "what could have brought him here? Did he leave no message, Andrew?"

"Nothing but what I told you, madam; he only seemed bent upon seeing you, and he looked glummer 'n he does in general."

"Come, 'Beth, I won't wait; I cannot wait for him a whole hour! It is so strange! I must know at once what it all means. Come: I am going straight to his house; I don't want him to come here again—particularly if he has any ill news to tell me," exclaimed Mrs. Morley, in an agitated tone.

"Oh, mamma, rest a little first, and get a cup of tea. I expect papa has been promoted, and he only wanted to be the first to tell you," said 'Beth. "Oh, Andy, you should not have worried mamma with this until she had got rested and had refreshed herself. Yes, dear mamma, I am coming," she answered, as her mother, already in the hall, called to her.

"I was afeard there was news from the captain that she ought to know, Miss," said Andrew, humbly; but 'Beth had left the room, and he heard the front door shut after them. "I know there's bad news; something or other's gone wrong with the captain, and I not there to stand by him!" Andrew covered his face with his hands, and a great sob burst from his lips.

The Secretary of the Navy, himself a distinguished naval officer, lived quite near; they had only a square to walk and a corner to turn to reach his elegant residence. And 'Beth growled all the way, full of indignation. "He might have known how tired you'd be, mamma, and that you would not be glad to see him; he needn't have come so often, taking people's breath away with his messages! After all, I expect it's some stupid nonsense about buoys and torpedoes and those everlasting sand-banks he's always talking about."

Mrs. Morley did not utter a word, but walked very fast, her previous fatigue and aching feet quite forgotten in the strange, indefinable dread that had taken possession of her. A few minutes brought them to Secretary Ashton's door; and the porter, seeing their approach through the lace blinds that covered the vestibule glass, admitted them instantly, ushered them into one of the closed drawing-rooms, opened a shutter, and went to hand in Mrs. Morley's card.

"I hope he won't make a mistake, and take my card to Mrs. Ashton."

"They're all in New York, mamma; Lillian Gray told me so yesterday," said 'Beth. "But sit down in this great cushioned chair, mamma dear; you are so tired!"

"'Beth, do not talk; just let me alone, my child; I cannot, I would not sit down in this house, were I ever so weary. I am so restless, it relieves me to keep walking. Oh, I wish he would come!"

"I think I hear him in the hall now, mamma—yes—those are his footsteps; do try to be calm, mamma."

No need to tell her that. By the time Secretary Ashton entered the room, she was standing as still and white as marble, not even seeking to veil the scorn and dislike expressed in her sensitive face; she was only intent on concealing every trace of the agitation and dread that he had caused her by his unusual visits and his message; he should not triumph so far as to know they had in the least disturbed her. He offered her his hand, which she barely touched, and invited her to be seated. She could but observe that there was a troubled, worried look in his sallow face.

"You called twice at my house, Mr. Secretary, while I was out, and left word with my servant that you would come again at half-past four o'-clock. Imagining that your business with me must be very urgent, although I have just got home I came right away, to see what it might be, as well as to relieve you of the necessity of calling again." She remained standing, and spoke in a calm, proud tone, which he appeared not to notice—or, if he did, he was indifferent to it.

"Sit down, my dear lady; my errand was urgent; but sit down. I can tell you nothing until you sit down," he said, drawing forward a chair.

"Excuse me: I prefer standing, and I wish to hear at once what I have to know," she answered, quietly.

"But, madam—for God's sake sit down!"

"Admiral Ashton," she said, fixing her eyes steadily on his, "you have news of my husband. What is it?"

"I have, madam; but sit down, I beg of you; here on the sofa—"

"Sir, this is the merest trifling. I will not sit down under your roof, and you know the reason why. I can forgive injuries done to myself, but injustice to my husband—my brave, noble husband —never. You understand me. Now tell me your news; had it been good news, you would not, probably, have been so zealous to impart it."

"Madam—Mrs. Morley—indeed you wrong me! I was always his friend—"

"Was! That is the way people speak of the dead. Admiral Ashton, is my husband dead?"

He was silent; he covered his face for an instant with his hand; how could he tell her here, away from her own home? By this time 'Beth was at her side, her strong arm around her, her face very pale.

"Tell me, is my husband dead?" she asked again—in that high-strung, concentrated key always expressive of keen agony.

"Be composed, madam; bear up now—but—but —I am pained to say, it is so; your brave husband, the most gallant officer in the service, is dead."

A wild shriek burst from her lips, and she dropped to the floor in a dead faint. 'Beth, in a tumult of grief and terror, half wild at seeing her thus prostrate upon the floor, and perhaps dead, exclaimed: "What did you send him away for? What made you break your promise, and send him away from us—off to sea again, when his time would not be up where he was for two years? Oh, you cruel, wicked man! Oh, mamma! mamma!" she screamed, throwing her arms around her mother and lifting her head to her breast; "Oh, my mamma! come back to me!" But minutes passed before she showed any sign of life. At last she opened her eyes, shuddered violently for a minute, and attempted to rise. "We must go —go home," she whispered. "Help me, 'Beth."

"Yes, darling, you shall go. Lean on me; I am strong, you know," said 'Beth, while torrents of tears drenched her cheeks.

The Secretary offered wine, and would have aided her to rise; but she would accept nothing, and shrunk from his touch as if it had given her severe physical pain.

"My carriage is at the door, madam; let me prevail on you to use it; you are really in no condition to walk home," he said, stung bitterly by the whole scene, yet trying to show kindness, although he felt guilty and miserable.

"No, sir. Had you kept faith with my husband, I should not now be desolate, and his child fatherless. I will ask you no questions; *his* friend and mine, Captain Brandt, will hear all that you may have to tell—about—about—oh, my God!" she cried, striking her forehead—"about all that has happened. Come, my child. Oh, can it—can it be true?"

They left the house together, the grief-stricken mother and daughter, and hastened homeward, frightening those they passed by the wild, woebegone expression of their pallid faces, and the unusually rapid haste they made. Andrew awaited them at the door, and as it closed Mrs. Morley once more fell to the floor, unconscious.

"Oh, Andy, papa is dead! Oh, help mamma! lift her up and carry her to her own room, then run and tell Captain Brandt to come," cried the poor young creature, into whose life no sorrow had ever come before. Trembling and sobbing, his face an ashen gray, the faithful servant obeyed, muttering all the way: "If I had been there he wouldn't ha' died. But here I am; and he, worth ten thousand like me, gone!"

He laid Mrs. Morley upon the bed as tenderly as if she had been an infant; the sight of her still, white face, set with the anguish that had so suddenly wrung her heart, redoubled his grief; and, weeping and moaning aloud, he hastened to send the house-keeper to her assistance with restoratives, then went with the dreadful news to Captain Brandt. Poor 'Beth, nearly wild between her sorrow for her father and her dread lest her mother should never wake to life again, filled the house with her cries, and wrung her hands as she hung over her, kissing her white lips and drenching her unconscious face with the hot tears, that, happily for her, nature did not refuse to give.

And so in one little hour the bright sunshine had gone out of their lives; their gladness had suffered a sudden and dark eclipse, and to that fair young girl just on the threshold of life had come a bitter and heavy loss, the loss of a fond, affectionate father, a man whose nature was truly noble; who with the highest courage had the tenderness of a woman for the suffering, the weak, and the oppressed; whose record was bright with heroic acts in the service of his country, and upon whose pages not even the shadow of a stain had ever fallen.

On his way to Captain Brandt's, Andrew had rushed into the office of the family physician, who happened to be in, and begged him to go without delay to Mrs. Morley. "If you don't find her dead, sir, it'll be be mor'n I expect," he said, then rushed out again before Dr. Milner found an opportunity to make a single inquiry. Knowing Andrew to be a grave, steady fellow, the doctor imagined that something extraordinary must have happened to have thrown him into such a panic, and without more ado he sprang into his carriage, and in a few minutes was by Mrs. Morley's bedside, where he learned from the housekeeper, in broken sentences, all that had happened. Moved by the deepest sympathy, and with a pang of deep distress at the loss of so old and dear a friend, he lost no time in doing all that his skill suggested for the recovery of the grief-stricken woman; finally, when he almost thought the shock had killed her, he felt her pulse faintly quiver under his finger, and then with a shudder and a moan life struggled back to her heart. Captain and Mrs. Brandt now came, almost speechless with agitation, for he who was dead had been the dearest and most intimate friend they had in the world. Choking back their own sorrow, they exerted every effort to soothe Mrs. Morley; to attempt to console her would be vain, they knew, for such grief must have its way, and they only "uttered words of endearment" and the deepest sympathy, "when words of consolation availed not." At last, when floods of tears gushed from her burning eyes, giving relief to her overwrought heart and brain, they felt comforted.

"Let her cry, let her cry; it will save her," whispered Dr. Milner. "My God! it was a terrible blow to fall upon a sensitive heart like hers. Poor fellow! how did it happen, Brandt? and when? He was the bravest officer in the navy. How did it happen? was he drowned, or wrecked, or what?"

The doctor and Captain Brandt were on their way down-stairs, and stood together for a moment in the hall.

"I have heard no particulars. The first word I heard of it was a half hour ago, when Andrew came to my house with the news. I am going now to see the Secretary—who, I suppose, received the telegram—to ask the particulars. I have a faint hope that there may be a mistake somewhere. Morley was my best friend on earth; I loved him more than if he were a brother!" said the old officer, over whose bronzed cheeks fell heavy tears.

"Don't go, Milner, until I get back; you may be needed upstairs. That poor little girl! did you notice how brave she is trying to be for her mother's sake, and how much she looked like her father? I'll be back presently."

Captain Brandt went to the Secretary's, sent in his card, and was admitted. He found the functionary wrapped in a fur cloak, lying upon a lounge beside a wood fire, completely unnerved by the scene be had passed through, and toning himself up with frequent draughts of hot whiskey punch.

Captain Brandt's hope was vain. There was no mistake; the news was strictly official, and came by telegraph. A violent hurricane had swept the Gulf, and every ship and vessel in its track had been nearly or quite wrecked except the "Portland," Captain Morley's, which he had by almost superhuman exertions finally saved by running her out to sea in the teeth of such a wind as was scarcely ever known before. A night and day, aided by officers and crew, he battled with wind and waves, never for one instant relaxing his personal vigilance, or sparing the use of his own arms at the ropes or elsewhere, if need be, until, at last, when drenched and exhausted, his ship safe, he threw himself upon his cot, and fell asleep. His servant passing through, saw him lying there in his wet clothes, threw his heavy cloak over him, and was careful not to awake him, knowing that sailors laugh at the idea of salt water ever giving any one a cold. But when Captain Morley awoke out of his ten hours' sleep, he had congestion of the lungs, and was in a high fever. All that human skill suggested was done by the ship's surgeon for his relief; he did not leave the captain's bedside for a moment, administered every remedy himself, and when one failed had another at hand; but all to no avail; the brave sailor breathed his last just as the ship dropped her anchors at Key West.

That was the substance of what Captain Brandt gathered from the telegram, and he rose to go.

"Please offer my sympathy to Mrs. Morley," said the Secretary, shaking hands. "She blames me, I know, for sending poor Morley to sea, but she doesn't understand how it was. Any way, Brandt, assure her that I am at her service, and that I particularly wish—when the remains come —the funeral to be of the most imposing character the service allows, to show honor to the memory of a brave, heroic man."

"When Mrs. Morley is more composed, Admiral,"—so the other officers, forgetting his new rank, sometimes called him—"I will deliver your message. Good day, sir." Captain Brandt marched out, giving vent to his bitter indignation, when he got on the pavement, by one or two imprecations in the emphatic vernacular of the sea, which sailors declare mean no harm, and as necessary to their relief when under high pressure as "blowing" off water is to a whale. When he got back to Mrs. Morley's, the doctor was waiting for him, eager to hear if there might be a faint hope gleaned from the telegram: but, as he soon learned, there was not; the sad news was too briefly and distinctly told to be misunderstood.

"I will say nothing to her about it to-night," added Captain Brandt. "To-morrow I shall undoubtedly get a letter from Commander Brooke, the executive officer of the 'Portland,' who knows all about the old friendship between Morley and myself. I'm sure he'll write. But how is she, doctor?"

"Apparently calm; but every nerve is strung, and every emotion suppressed as by a will of iron: unnatural all of it. I thought she'd go on crying and moaning as other women do, but her tears didn't last long. It seems as if there were a sense of wrong mingled with her grief. God help her!

"So there is!" growled the captain, his gray eyes scintillating wrathful sparkles.

"I am sorry to hear it; her loss is bitter enough without any other sting. I tried to get her to swallow a composing draught, but she said: 'It would only make my awakening more bitter; it will be best for me to look my sorrow in the face, doctor,' so piteously that I did not insist upon it; and I don't know but she is right."

The doctor went away, and Captain Brandt was about going upstairs, when, in the dusky hall, for it was twilight and the hall lamp not yet lighted, he felt some one touch his arm, and heard a hoarse whisper. "Tell me 'bout it, Cap'n; for God's sake, sir, tell me how it happened." It was poor Andrew, bowed and trembling, his old heart broken for the friend he had lost.

"Andrew, my poor fellow," said Captain Brandt, wringing his hand, while his eyes were for the moment blinded with tears, "I'll tell you all I know. But come into the dining-room; she might hear us, and I don't want her to be troubled any more to-night."

"Oh, didn't I say so! didn't I know it!" exclaimed the old negro, wringing his hands; "didn't I say if I had been there it wouldn't ha' happened! Do you think I'd ha' let him lay there in his wet clothes! No: I'd ha' waked him up an' made him put on dry ones, an' made him drink hot coffee, if he had pitched me overboard for it. He wouldn't ha' died if I had bin there to take care of him. Captain, please to shoot me right through my head; I can't live, sir, arter this; I can't indeed, sir!"

"See here, Andy, confound you! stop such foolishness or I'll break your head instead of putting a ball into it. Is that the way to show your love for your captain, wanting to put yourself out of the way, when you've got his wife and child to serve and watch over for his sake. Cry, old fellow; cry your eyes out, if it will do you any good, —the Lord knows we've all got enough to make us cry; but no more such foolishness as that."

"Aye, master, you're right. I'll try. I'll try to do what he would 'spect me to do; yes, sir, he's my cap'n yet, if he is dead. Oh, sir, if you'd seen them two, how happy they was over his letter this morning, and heard them talking and laughing over it, and calling me to hear his messages, and all 'bout his ship, that he seemed so proud of—

and if you only knowed how pretty and how glad they both looked when they comed home in the sunshine to-day, up to the minute I told her that Sec'tary Ashton had been here twice!—oh, Lord! what grief to come between sunrise and sunset!"

"Sit down there, Andy," said Captain Brandt, deeply touched, pushing Andy into a corner of the sofa, "sit there and cry it out, old fellow; only keep as quiet as you can, for the sake of those upstairs; and, mind you! no more of that foolishness you spoke of just now." And there, when Captain Brandt had left the room, closing the door after him, the poor old soul sobbed himself to sleep.

(TO BE CONTINUED.)

[For the "Ave Maria."]
First Friday Flowers.

(INSCRIBED TO MISS ELEANOR C. DONNELLY.)

I.

WHERE shall we look for flowers to-day,
  Fair and fresh for the altar-throne?
Summer blooms are hidden away
  Deep 'neath the snowy circling zone.

II.

Faded the blossoms that sweetly lent
  Their beauty to brighten the resting-place
Of the ever-Adorable Sacrament,—
  Departed all their fragrant grace!

III.

The mountain's side is swept with hail,
  Where the ling'ring lilies drooped and died;
Deep is the snow in the shady vale,
  Where the sweet sky pansies loved to hide.

IV.

Naught remains of the roses bright
  That clambered about the chapel-door;
Only the thorn-crown greets our sight,
  —The roses, alas! are ours no more.

V.

Those festal buds of the Sacred Heart,
  Red and warm like Its wondrous love
(Which burns Its graces to impart
  To those that soul's devotion prove),—

VI.

Oh! where shall we look for their bloom to-day?
  The earth's sweet charms are dead and drear;
Turn not, in tears, good friends, away,
  There are other blossoms to offer here.

VII.

Dear children! bring your lilies pure
  Of innocence, and roses warm
Of heart's fond love, that doth endure
  When coldly wails life's wintry storm.

VIII.

Ah! suff'ring hearts, your garland bring,
  The thorns (of life's sweet roses robb'd),
—Dear is the gift to the thorn-crowned King,
  Whose Heart thro' the woful Passion throbb'd.

IX.

Contrite souls! ye may offer here
  Purple pansies of penance true,
Gemm'd with affliction's heart-wrung tear,
  Dripping with Mercy's plenteous dew.

X.

O Sacred Heart of our God and King!
  We place these buds on Thy winter-shrine;
Dear Lord! accept our offering,
  And make our hearts like unto Thine!

JOSEPH W. S. NORRIS.

A Lover of the Beautiful.

BY KATHLEEN O'MEARA, AUTHOR OF "IZA'S STORY," "ROBIN REDBREAST," "LIFE OF FREDERIC OZANAM," "PEARL," ETC., ETC.

THERE is nothing so wonderful as the variety of God's works in nature, unless it be the diversity of His likeness in souls. Sanctity, while it faithfully adheres to the essential lines of the divine Model, reveals itself by characteristics as distinctive and manifold as the features of the human face, or the leaves of the forest; and just as star differeth from star in brightness, without the variety of their splendor disturbing the music of the spheres, or as one voice in a well ordered choir will rise in sweet predominance above the rest, without marring the harmony of the whole, so does one predominant virtue, one divine characteristic, strike, as it were, the key-note to the soul where all are singing in unison. The key-note of Henry Perreyve's soul was his love of beauty. It drew him like a magnet to God, to that Beauty ever ancient and ever new of which he would seem to have been born enamored. On the day of his First Communion it revealed itself to his young heart with the clearness of a vision, enshrining itself in his soul for ever after, to the exclusion of all earthly loves. On that blessed morning, kneeling on the red velvet *prie-dieu* in the old church of St. Sulpice, Henry heard the voice of the Beautiful One calling him to His service, and he answered, unhesitatingly, "Yes, Lord, I come!" But, though he never wavered in his allegiance to that divine call, his vocation was to be put to a long test before he finally embraced it.

The Perreyve family were of Lyonnese origin. Henry was born in Paris (April 11th, 1831), but a great part of his childhood was spent in the old home at Lyons, where his grandfather continued to reside after his son had gone to Paris and started in the practice of the law. M. Perreyve, Henry's father, was a distinguished Latiniat, as well as an able jurisconsult, and he intended his son to adopt the bar as a profession. Out of deference to the wishes of his parents, the boy followed the classes of the Lycée St. Louis, and then entered on a course of law at home, working hard at the study of philosophy at the same time. Just as he reached his seventeenth year, the Revolution of July broke out (1848), and the peaceful life of the young student was for a moment swept into the current of national excitement. Monsieur Perreyve, sharing the patriotic enthusiasm that moved the worthiest of his fellow-citizens, enrolled himself in the National Guard, and went out to his duty in the streets of Paris; and Henry insisted on shouldering a musket and accompanying his father in spite of his mother's fears and expostulations. He relates the result himself in a letter dated the 7th of July, 1848.

"My father and I were on duty every day, and even every night, of the insurrection, without getting a single wound. Yet it was not for lack of opportunities. Every moment we saw soldiers of the line and Gardes Mobiles falling around us. . . . . . M. Barch told me he was quite put out at coming home without some honorable wound. No doubt, if one might guide the ball oneself, a wound after such a fight would be very precious. But if we got off safe, Paris has suffered terribly. There was nothing to be seen last week but funerals; yesterday the public ceremony took place. An immense altar, draped in black and silver, supported by high pillars and surmounted by a veiled cross, was erected in the Place de la Concorde. All the great bodies of the State, several regiments, legions of the National Guard, all covered the vast square, and the day's silence and recollection were only broken by the muffled roll of the drums and the solemn chaunts of a large orchestra. The sun shone magnificently: the day was splendid. At the elevation of the Host, the entire multitude knelt, the drums beat, the choruses sang out, all the bells of the city rang in joyous peals: it was a sublime spectacle. We must admit that if our metropolis is terrible to behold in the day of its wreck, it is great and beautiful on the day of victory and triumph. . . . . To-day the funeral of Monseigneur Affre takes place. . . . . . Does not God mean, by that awful blow, to awake our country from the lethargy in which it has slept so long? M. de Lamartine says that a nation should not regret the blood it sheds in order to make eternal truths blossom forth! You see, I take our epoch very philosophically, thereby anticipating a little on the lectures I am to give next year. If they should see fit to refuse me the right to teach philosophy this year, I will always have religion—that better philosophy—to fall back on."

Meantime, he began to teach the "better philosophy" to a gathering of poor children in one of the worst quarters of Paris. A group of young men had joined together for the purpose of instructing these young pariahs in the elementary sciences, and their religious instruction devolved on Henry. His health, always delicate, was not equal to the strain this work and study put upon it. He burst a blood-vessel, and, for the next year, his life was in danger, all study was suspended, and he was condemned to practice the philosophy he had hoped to teach, thus graduating in the school which alone can lead to the highest kind of success. He was ordered to Italy, a banishment in which he was to find many compensations for the interruption of his studies. On his way thither, he writes from Lyons:

"I gazed up at the steeple of Notre Dame on the green slopes that had echoed to the merry laughter of my childhood. . . . I seemed to see my mother leading me by the hand up the steep steps of the mountain; I heard my grandfather calling to me from the garden gate; there was the field where the cow used to be; but all this is of the past. . . . My beloved Madonna of Fourvières is still here, still the same with her pretty créob face, and her little Child looks down on us poor sinners with His sweet smile as of old; the little sanctuary is warm with the lights which pilgrims burn here in great quantities, and its trembling silver tinkle rises still above the din of mingled sounds from the busy city. . . ."

Amongst the earliest notes of his Italian tour, we find one on Plato's bust, the beauty of which delights him: "What a soul! what immaterial life! The strength and purity of the mind reflected as in a mirror. On the brow, the calm effort telling of the soul's wealth, beaming with purity. On every feature the harmony of beauty—physical beauty, the expression of moral beauty, one revealing the other,—both symbolizing the eternal beauty of God."

This keen appreciation of the highest beauty made him quick to discern the true beauty from the false, and he was intolerant of the mutilated ideal which appeals to the senses only. True beauty is strength clothed in grace; where this fundamental element of strength is lacking, Henry Perreyve with heaven-born instinct, turns from it in disgust and disappointment.

"I came to Naples," he says, "full of fine theories and illusions; I had shed tears over the oppressed nation, and dreamed of liberty coming to bless the shores of this beautiful gulf; one day sufficed to undeceive me; the people are unworthy of independence. Let us come out of this city. When humanity disgusts us, we must lift up our eyes to heaven, to the high mountains, to the God who sustains the beauty of the earth."

He consoled himself in the spectacle of ideal beauty which he found reigning in undiminished splendor at Monte Cassino, and declares to his father that he was very near taking up his abode definitively in one of the cells of this magnificent monastery.

"The monks are men of the highest intelligence, to whom unceasing mental labor has given that free and independent air which is the mark of true elevation."

His feelings on first entering Rome were almost too deep for expression. Here he beheld strength everywhere triumphant in beauty, even amidst decay; the ruins of the past grander in their cyclopean fragments than the mightiest efforts of the present. "Time! time! it is here that one learns to recognize this terrible power," exclaims the traveller, ... "everything testifies to its resistless force. . . . Yet, owing to a providence, which has, no doubt, its philosophical reason, the efforts of the mighty enemy seem to have no power against the relics of the old Roman world: these ruins are eternal, and cannot be destroyed. It is because of the great lesson which they teach humanity? God has set them side by side with the radiant monuments of the true religion, in order that we may by constant comparison choose between what is dead and what lives with an imperishable life. The Roman world is incredible in its grandeur; it is almost the idea of the Infinite, which a pagan people, not being able to conceive as an immaterial existence, strove to embody here below. One is struck by the idea of power and strength which prevails in the construction of public edifices."

But Rome had far deeper attractions for him than these noble ruins, which spoke louder to his imagination than to his soul. His heart was with his Treasure, and that was in the sanctuary. No delight in the beauty of this world, of art or nature, could draw away his mind from that first and supreme object of his life, the priesthood. He had broken the matter to his father, who received the appeal reverently—exacting, however, that Henry should pass his examinations for the law, which would involve a year's delay. Meantime, he continued that distant preparation for the higher vocation which is comprised in the conquest of self and the practice of all virtue. The news of one of his young friends, Adolphe Perraud,* having decided on becoming a priest, throws him into an extacy of joy.

"I cannot remain silent. . . . I must embrace you as a brother in Jesus Christ; that is, with all conceivable tenderness. . . . Courage, blessed friend! courage! You carry our vocation in yours! We congratulate you for being the first to reach the goal. We give you joy; we follow you with pride; for, again I say, your victory is ours, and we shall be saved with you. You may tremble, you may be sorrowful unto death, you may even weep in the solitude of your heart. It is ever so, and the combat between God and man is not a thing of yesterday. But don't take these things for hesitation. I am certain you do not hesitate. . . . Take courage; give yourself with strength, and don't mistake for doubt and uncertainty the weakness of a heart overcome by its own glory and sinking beneath the weight of its happiness. Our kings wept on the day of their coronation; on taking your first step in the "Royal Highway," it is natural that you should feel the same emotion in your soul. Go forth! Our pride and joy should reassure you. We salute you from afar, and pray God to give you strength interiorly to bear the burden of so great an honor."

With such bold and glowing wisdom did Henry cheer on his friends to the service of the sanctuary. If this should be a surprise to some, let them remember that in his eyes this vocation was not alone the most sublime prerogative, but the greatest joy—humanly and divinely—that God could bestow upon a soul. The world expresses no surprise when a young artist or a young soldier endeavors to recruit his friends to the camp or the studio, and represents the career of his choice as the most delightful that a man can embrace; it has a smile of indulgence for the rash enthusiasm which exaggerates the glories of war and the delights of art, ignoring, with a treachery that is partly unconscious, the hardships, humiliations and deceptions with which the road is strewn; but if a soldier of the Cross endeavors to gain over a comrade to the service of the Divine Master, this same world is scandalized at his imprudence and loudly condemns his ill-advised zeal. Yet may we not all say with Père Gratry, "I know of no wiser enthusiasm than that which excites men to become the workmen of God!"

On the Tombs of the Apostles, Henry made a vow "to renounce all that we call happiness, tranquillity, the interests of this world, in order to embrace a life of toil and struggle. Shall I have strength to do it? I hope so, for I have rested my hopes in God alone."

Writing to a friend who hesitated about entering the religious life, he says: "I dwell rather much on this point, that you may find happiness, real happiness, in the religious state; because it seems to me that D——'s letter exaggerates the austere and sad side of such a resolution. The love of God is to me far more the *expression of life than the expression of death.*"

On his return from Italy, Henry made the acquaintance of Père Lacordaire. He had followed the conferences of the illustrious orator at Notre Dame, and conceived for his genius that passionate admiration which it awoke in the noblest minds of the age. This excess of admiration, however, inspired the young man with a certain awe, which made him fly from the great Dominican when he met him out of the pulpit. One day, a friend, who sometimes rallied him on the point,

---

* Afterwards Père Perraud, of the Oratory.

carried him off to see Père Lacordaire in his convent, Rue Vauzirard. There were visitors in the room, and Père Lacordaire, who was very busy, divided between all the few minutes he had to give; and as Henry had no questions to ask, no notice was taken of him, and he left the room without having exchanged a word with the great man. But Lacordaire had seen him, and, with that unerring instinct which enabled him to recognize at once "one of God's conquests," he read the beauty of the young man's soul upon his face. A few days later, Henry was at work in his room, when a knock came to his door, and Père Lacordaire walked in.

"*Mon enfant!*" he said, holding out his hand, "I received you badly the other day. I have come to beg your pardon, and to have a chat with you."

Thus did the great master who was to give him so many noble lessons, begin by giving him one of humility and kindness. Few men possessed in a higher degree than Père Lacordaire that seeing eye which discerns the true ideal and detects the least flaw in its perfection. In these first days of their intercourse, he pointed out to Henry the mistake he made in separating beauty from goodness, a divorce which, he declared, was absolutely fatal to the former.

"Take a face," he says to him, "where the regularity of the lines and the softness of the contours are perfect, but without any expression of goodness in the eyes, or on the lips, and you will have the head of a Medusa."

Henry took the lesson to heart, and grew, says, Père Gratry, "in goodness and beauty, before God and man, to the last day of his life."

But death was the teacher, above all others, which sounded the *Sursum corda!* that kept his eyes uplifted to the eternal Beauty, towards which he was fast journeying. The thought that he might soon be called away from amidst men, inclined his heart to a tender indulgence which is seldom characteristic of holiness in the young. "The habit of being dangerously ill," he says himself, "has inclined me to love men. I feel that as life is so short, we ought not to waste it in hating each other; and as death is at our heels, we ought to be ready to leave the world on friendly terms."

The grim professor kept faithful watch by him. His health, which had improved during his visit to Italy, again alarmed his family, and he was obliged to spend the winter at Pau. He worked hard to make up for lost time in view of the approaching examinations, and found in the beauty of nature some compensation for the absence of his friends.

. . . . "The weather is superb, the mountains more beautiful on account of the snow, the torrents are white with foam, the pastures green and rich with herds and flocks; the mountaineers are swift-footed, the songs from the valley are plaintive, the solitary hours full of memories, and I am always your friend."

Early in January (1852) he went up for his examination at Toulouse, and announced the results to his parents on the 19th. "I don't wait to doff my cap and gown to embrace you. . . . I have had almost a success. . . . I held forth *à la méridionale*, and, with God's help, came pretty well out of it."

This was a modest report of an ordeal which won for the competitor the applause of all present, and flattering congratulations from the examiners. While Henry was quietly engaged in these intellectual combats, France was passing through a crisis from which the ardent heart of the young student could not hold aloof in indifference. The *Coup d'Etat*, so variously judged by opposing parties, had sent a thrill of horror through the country, and many who had hailed the advent of Napoleon III as that of the heaven-sent minister who was to rescue the nation from anarchy, now recoiled in dismay, their confidence shaken, or changed to indignation and hostility. "It seems to me," writes Henry, "that liberty is dead. Too much applause, too many hurrahs greeted, throughout our unfortunate France, what I must call the violation of the fatherland. I feel as if there were nothing to do, nothing to hope for; shame and humiliation are all that remain to us in such depths of degradation. We must seek a Master and a fatherland above, and no longer waste our hopes on a phantom who has proved false to himself."

Henry formed one of that aspiring youthful band who called Ozanam their leader, and who, having lost all confidence in the old monarchical rule, looked for the salvation of France in the reign of free democracy as it consists in America. The violence which ushered in the empire did not tend to check their admiration for the republican form of government. "What is to be done?" exclaims Henry. "What I believed before, I believe still—if the happiness of humanity is in the application of the widest democratic system, the democratic system is only possible on condition of being founded upon Christian virtues. We are not Christians, consequently we shall be slaves. That is all."

He continued faithful to his principle of democracy when many of his friends had rallied to the Empire, now surrounded with the prestige of success, and about to enter on the brilliant military phase of its career. "I should like to know what you think of this war" (the Crimean), he writes to Père Lacordaire; "it seems to me that it is a fine war. How much finer it would be if it were undertaken in the name of democracy! But now it must inevitably be the triumph of egotism and tyranny. And yet that odious Russian Empire is so near Constantinople, and

Constantinople is so near Rome, that from the Catholic point of view the question seems to me one of appalling gravity. Does not the prophecy of Napoleon I appear astounding? 'France will be Republican or Cossack.' How many Frenchmen are likely to perish for not having believed in these words! But there is so little enthusiasm! Everything is so dead! I am not very old, and yet what hours and days I spent in bed crying out to M. de Lamartine under the balconies of the Hotel de Ville—'War for Poland! The deliverance of Poland!' There was life in those days, anyhow; but now...."

Even to the last, when life was fast ebbing away and the eternal frontiers within sight, Henry clung to his ideal republic, and we shall find him under the green trees at Lorège, dreaming again the dream of his ardent youth, and building up with his beloved master, Lacordaire, "a new form government, which shall constitute an alliance between Christianity and liberty, where men shall love God without hating one another."

He looked to this alliance of God and liberty alone for the regeneration of France. While that old bugbear of Europe, the Eastern problem, was being solved with cannon on the shores of the Black Sea, and eyes of the West were watching for the external signs of conquest or defeat, Henry was steadily awaiting the one result whose consequence would endure, and whose victory would outlive the din of battle and the triumph of despotism. "A day will come," he writes to Adolphe Perraud, "when we must speak out, for words will then be actions, and it will be a duty for us even more than for others, because we have received from God two treasures seldom united in the same breast—the love of Jesus Christ and the love of liberty."

Bewailing the decay of these generous aspirations in the nation, he says to a friend on his return from the South: "I could not have conceived such a change in the public mind in so short a time; the sleep of indifference has paralyzed everything, and people speak of liberty as a thing that has been sold! After all, it is folly to think of founding a democracy when there is no longer a people...."

But instead of dwelling in morbid despair on the political mistakes of France, he turned his eyes to more consoling subjects, and found consolation in the beauty of souls, the triumph of virtue and the splendor of genius; above all, in his love for God. His health, improved by the winter in the South, was not much to be trusted, as he playfully tells us in describing a concert given for the benefit of a night-school which he had founded, and where he played the part of *cavalière servience* to one of the lady collectors.

"There were about fifteen hundred persons present, and it was dreadfully hot; I might have passed on the duty to some one else—but the desire to play the dandy, etc., prevailed; so I took the lady by the hand, and gallantly made my *grèle;* dress-coat, pumps, light gloves, etc. The result was that next day the dandy was in his bed with a cotton night-cap pulled over his his ears, his nose swollen and his throat on fire. . . . *Vanitas, vanitatum!*"

The friend to whom he makes this abject confession was himself in very bad health, and Henry was full of anxiety about him. "You have a cough, and you are not sure of going to the Eaux Bonnes. You must go, dear M. l'Abbé. You simply must. My little savings are at your disposal with all my heart; I have some time still to increase them, and by the end of August they may amount to 100 francs. You have called me your friend so often, that I expect you will behave *generously* to me on this occasion."

The little hoard so lovingly offered was not, however, enough to pay for the journey to Eaux Bonnes, and Henry was amazed and shocked to find that other friends did not run as eagerly as himself to offer their savings to the sick priest. He determined to apply to the minister for the extra 300 francs that were necessary. He tells the adventure with characteristic *verve*.

.... "I made *grande toilette* and hurried off to the Administration des Cultes at the Minister of Justice's. I won't tell you what a happiness it was to approach such a big-wig. After two hours' hard labor I succeeded! I held forth—I explained, I argued. All in vain. The sum was too large, and, above all, I suspect, the patronage too small. I grew red in the face; I stood up; I *prayed to* my imperturbable director. I don't know what I said, for I was a trifle excited by his refusal ... The great man stared at me, and then all of a sudden he said, '*Allons, Monsieur.* I have not the heart to hold out against you any longer!' With that he rose, conducted me to his secretary and ordered him to draw up at once an order for the sum in question. The secretary was for putting it off, but he said: 'No: I wish it done immediately, signed to-morrow by the minister, and despatched forthwith. I hold to this being done.' ... I embrace you joyfully. It is so seldom we have a chance of proving to our friends that we really love them."

A scheme for resuscitating the ancient Congregation of the Oratory had for some time been germinating in the minds of a few fervent souls, and Henry Perreyve was one of those on whom they based their hopes for its accomplishment. He himself entered into it with delight.

"We are going to undertake a great work," he says; "three or four Bishops are in the plot, and the Abbé Gratry is at the head of it. . . . It is a great work—it is enormous, and we are so little and so weak! This is what is capable of moving the mercy of God."

He relates in a touching page of his Souvenirs of Frederic Ozanam, how he first opened his heart on the subject to that gentle master. It was at the Eaux Bonnes, and Henry was just going to start on a trip to Spain. "Before leaving, I went to dine with M. Ozanam. That evening we were sitting over the fire together, intimately conversing about things. I thought the moment had come for confiding to that noble heart the secret of my religious vocation. I did it simply, easily, with joy, and yet with a kind of shyness.... That night I learned what M. Ozanam's heart was. There were tears of affection, of fatherly indulgence, of holy enthusiasm in the voice that answered me. Our wish to serve God in the cultivation of sciences and literature, our scheme of reunion with M. l'Abbé Gratry, and of a studious congregation to be called 'The Oratory,' all these hopes, all these dreams, which might turn out to be illusions, quickly took a living form in that soul which believed so readily in all that was beautiful.... He followed me with words of encouragement that night, he strained me to his heart, and we parted. I walked quickly home, inebriated with joy and hope and strength. I could not go in. I wanted to taste my happiness in solitude, far from men. It was very late; but I could not resist the longing, so I struck into a road that led to the heights. I walked on, beside myself with joy, not looking before me, but looking up to heaven. Suddenly, I arrested my step, and an unconscious impulse made me start back; I was on the edge of a precipice. One step more and I had fallen into the abyss. I was frightened, and gave up my nocturnal promenade."

Before crossing over the Pyrenees, Henry wrote to a cousin of his, announcing the visit of a lady whose acquaintance he wished her to make.

.... "I have spoken of you to her, and she is very anxious to make friends with you. She is kind and good and gracious and simple, although enjoying enormous wealth and launched into the very first society, where she occupies with distinction a high position; but in spite of her aristocracy, she is charming in every way.... She will present herself at your door on Wednesday, between one and two o'clock. She will most likely take her little son with her; he is about three years old, and a little angel of beauty. Tell him from me that I don't forget the sweet smiles he gave me during my visits here. You may talk of him to his mother, who *adores* him, and you will present my respectful homage to her. Now, good bye. Don't let this visit alarm you, and make no preparations to receive her. I am quite sure you will be delighted to have made an acquaintance which may one day prove most valuable to you...."

At the hour and on the day named, his cousin received a box containing a lovely statue of Our Lady of Betharram.

The dream of the restoration of the Oratory was destined, unlike Henry's ideal Republic, to take in reality that living form which it at once assumed in the breast of Frederic Ozanam.

The history of the early days of its existence reads like a page from the records of the first Christians, so full of mutual love and joy and enthusiasm were the young brotherhood. They lived in a small house, big enough to hold seven, and here, under the guidance of a saintly and learned priest, the days flew swiftly in study and meditation on divine things. They were halcyon days to Henry Perreyve, for he found here, joined with him in the bonds of a divine fraternity, the friends he had loved best from his childhood. "I cannot sufficiently admire the councils of God!" he exclaims; "He prepared us by friendship before confiding His work to us; we had the same heart before being joined in the same priesthood. The will of God has but to communicate itself to one, in order to burst out in hearts that are all so deeply united."

The moment the fact of his vocation became known amongst his general circle of friends, Henry had to endure that trial which awaits most souls under the same circumstances—the lamentations of the world over his cruel lot. He could laugh so long as it was only the world that followed him to the sanctuary, with its stupid pity, but it was hard to bear patiently the commiseration of good Christians, who, instead of giving him joy, openly bewailed and expostulated with him on thus throwing away his life. "It passes my comprehension how people who believe in the grandeur of the priesthood can be in despair at seeing a young man receive the favor of it! Can you bear to be pitied, M. l'Abbé? For my part, *I have a horror of it!*" he cries.

Eight days after his entrance into the Oratory (Nov. 8, 1853), he writes to an old friend: "You are right, Stephen, in thinking that the new life on which I am entering will diminish nothing of the warm affection God has given me for you. I am renouncing fully and absolutely all the joys and ambitions which at our age allure the soul; but there is one that I still cling to—that of being loved. It is a great deal; but it seems to me this sacrifice is not required of me."

(TO BE CONTINUED.)

———

PACIFICUS, who lived about the ninth century, is thought to have been the inventor of clocks worked by wheels.

THE oldest printed book to be found is a Latin Bible called the Mazarin Bible, supposed to have been printed between the years 1452 and 1456.

The Bridal Ring of Our Lady at Perugia.

BY "ARTHUR."

I.

THE city of Perugia is the city of Mary by excellence. Its title alone attests this: *Augusta Perusia civitas Mariæ*—August Perugia, the city of Mary. Perugia was always august. Its very aspect, as seen from the neighboring plains and hillsides, is serene and majestic. Its lofty position rendered it unassailable in the olden times; its beetling walls were impregnable; its warriors redoubtable; its clergy irreproachable; its magistrates styled, from time out of mind, "magnificent"; its men of learning numerous, profound, and honored abroad; its artists incomparable; it gave a Pier Vannucci (the Perugino) to art, and he taught a Raphael; its people staid and severe, but withal delightfully urbane. Perugia merited, and still merits, its title of August.* Not less deserving is it of the title of City of Mary, bestowed upon it centuries ago by a devout and grateful Signiory and people. Its devotion to the Mother of God was proverbial from the days of its first Bishop, St. Herculanus. The love of Mary was essential and integral with their faith, and their love did not go unrewarded. In the year 1473, Perugia became the possessor of the nuptial Ring with which, it is piously and reasonably believed, St. Joseph espoused the immaculate daughter of Joachim and Anna. Perugia from that date became still more august, still more deserving of the name, City of Mary. Magistrates and people vied with one another in showing their devout appreciation of the treasure which had providentially come into their possession,—those by voting generous subsidies and making ample provisions for its preservation and honor; these by a devotion to the relic, and an increasing love for her (whose marriage keepsake it had been), at once enthusiastic and rational. Perugia became almost as attractive a cynosure to pilgrims from abroad as Loreto. The good Perugini asked no questions as to the authenticity of the relic. Had it not been for a thousand years previous the object of great veneration to the people of Chiusi? Nor did they question the motives of the German monk, Brother Winter, who stole it from that city and gave it to Perugia. The Madonna's Ring had fallen into their possession, and they were content and grateful.

Yet the Ring has its history, and this I will attempt to narrate briefly, and on the authority of historic documents. I would, in the outset, offer two observations for the behoof of those who might object that the bestowing of a ring

---
* Perugia is really styled August in honor of the Emperor Augustus, who rebuilt it after it had been totally destroyed.

---

upon the spouse was not included in the ancient Jewish rite as prescribed by Moses. The first is, all the erudite writers on Jewish antiquities agree that at the time of the Machabees the Jews *followed the example of other nations in their marriage ceremonies.* The other nations used a nuptial ring. The second is, that the onyx Ring of Perugia, rude and large as it is, suited the lowly condition of Mary and Joseph, it being a material abounding in the East, especially in Arabia, consequently easy of acquisition even by the priest.

I begin with two important quotations, which will form the basis of my narrative. The Siennese Diary, compiled by Gigli, contains the following: "*The Ring of the most holy Spouse was preserved in ancient times in the city of Chiusi, in the dominion of Sienna, where it was left by St. Mustiola, martyred there.*" And in the *Libro di Memorie* of the city of Chiusi, under the date of August 3, 1473, we read the following official indenture: "*On the 3d day of the month of August,* 1473. *Mention is here made by me, Leonetto, undersigned Chancellor, for the memory of the present and future: Whereas the Signiors Priors, wishing, in observance of the laudable custom of the Commune of the City of Chiusi, to show to the people, who came from remote parts through devotion, the glorious and devout Relic, the Ring of our Glorious Lady, the Virgin Mary, placed and preserved in the aforesaid City of Chiusi for more than a thousand years past, they found it had been stolen.*" The Bollandists place the martyrdom of St. Mustiola in the reign of the Emperor Aurelian, who ruled from A. D. 270 till A. D. 275. Deducting the medium of these two dates from that of the indenture just quoted, we find that the Ring of Our Lady had been in the possession of the city of Chiusi 1200 years before it was stolen by the German friar.

These premises have established a very important point in our narrative, the fact, to wit, that the Ring of Our Lady was brought to Chiusi by St. Mustiola. Who was St. Mustiola, and how did the ring come into her possession? She was a noble Roman matron, and the cousin of the Emperor Marcus Aurelius Claudius—*Matrona nobilissima, Claudii consobrina.* (Bolland., sub die ter., Jul. 3.) Cavallucci, and after him, Adamo Rossi, both of whom published very creditable dissertations on this relic, conjecture that it was first brought to Rome from Ephesus by St. John the Evangelist, who, it is most natural to suppose, inherited and preserved with religious solicitude every souvenir of his adopted mother; that when the Apostle was cast into the caldron of boiling oil at Rome, it passed into the hands of the devout Christians who eagerly sought the relics and souvenirs of the martyrs, and finally, after the lapse of a century and a half, became the possession of Mustiola, who then resided in Rome, with her cousin. The successor of Marcus Aurelius, the cruel Aurelian, inaugurated the eighth persecution, and Mustiola fled from Rome to Chiusi, where we read of her ministering to the Christians who suffered persecution. "She used to come at night and give money to the jailers, and entering, consoled them (the Christians), and washed and anointed the feet of those who were wounded by the chains, and administered food and clothing to all during the night." (Bolland., loco cit.) Finally, by order of Turcius, she was beaten to death with leaden plummets, and "a servant of God, by name Marcus, took up her body and buried it near the walls of the city of Chiusi." That the ring of Our Lady was religiously preserved, we know from the fact that when in the eighth century two citizens of Chiusi, Gregory and Aresibutus, erected a temple over the remains of St. Mustiola, the canons of the church caused the image of the Saint to be depicted holding the ring of our Lady,—even as we see St. Helen represented with the instruments of the Passion, which she discovered and preserved for posterity: "*In aede S. Musthiolae etiamnum contra temporis injurias eiusdem S. Musthiolae conspicitur Imago depicta cum eodem Mariae Annulo pendente.*" (Ex. Genealog. Seraph. Hil.) There the ring remained in great veneration until the middle of the thirteenth century, when it was transferred to the Church of S. Secondiano within the walls of Chiusi. (See letter of the Signiors of Sienna to the Bishop of Chiusi—April 12, 1421.)

The fame of the relic spread all over Italy and went beyond the Alps; and when the great Indulgence of the Portiuncula was opened at the request of the humble Francis, and pilgrims flocked to Assisi, Chiusi became an essential part of the itinerary because of its treasure. Charles IV, King of Bohemia, on his way back from Rome where he had been crowned as Emperor, passed purposely by Chiusi, (April 17, 1355,) in order to venerate the holy relic. Meanwhile, the canons of St. Mustiola began to dispute the possession of the Ring with those of St. Secondiano. The Bishop, Pietro Paolo Bertini, cut the dissension short by causing the Ring to be transferred to the Church of S. Francesco of the Minors Conventual on the Pentecost of 1420. There it was solemnly exposed to public veneration twice a year—on the Monday after Pentecost, and on the 3rd of August, for the behoof of the pilgrims who returned from Assisi. The fame of its miraculous efficacy in restoring sight to those who were afflicted with diseases of the eye, was so great that the city of Sienna tendered a formal request, in November, 1430, to the Commune of Chiusi, for a loan of the Ring. Though the request was endorsed by the Bishop himself of Chiusi, it was firmly refused, so jealous was the city of its treasure. With equal firmness did the Priors of the city of Chiusi refuse a similar request of Filippo Maria Visconti, Duke of Milan. Being on the point of losing his sight, and having tried every human remedy to no purpose, he resolved to recommend himself to our Lady through the means of this relic. He was not daunted by the first refusal. He invoked the intermediation of Pope Eugene IV. That Pontiff immediately addressed a Brief—dated Feb. 17, 1444—to the Priors and people of Chiusi, in behalf of the Duke. (I will explain further on in what sense this and similar Papal documents affecting the Ring are to be accepted in connexion with the formal approbation thereof.) The intercession of the Pope was successful. The Priors of Chiusi consented to let the Ring go to Milan. The Duke of Milan was to deposit 200,000 florins in the bank of Sienna as security for its safe return. The Magnificent Signiors of Sienna were to pay the expenses of the voyage, besides 1,000 florins to the city of Chiusi until the Ring was returned. The Bishop of Chiusi, provided with six horses, and attended by ten knights, was to carry the Ring to the Duke of Milan. A general safe-conduct was to be given to himself and escort, and, finally, the clergy and people of Milan were to go out of the city to meet the relic, and receive it with honors.

The chronicles are silent as to the issue. We know not whether the Ring left Chiusi or not. But the fact that the Duke became hopelessly blind the following year induces the historian Rossi to believe that the relic was not carried to Milan.

Among the monks who inhabited the Convent of St. Fransis at Chiusi in the year 1570 was a German, "lofty of stature," says Matthæus of Insula, "of hair curly, fat of body." He was an eye-sore to the community, for having been suspected of making away with some chalices belonging to the Franciscans of Castello della Pieve. He was on that occasion subjected to the torture, and afterwards manacled in prison for forty days. But he remained constant and silent, something which was regarded as a sure evidence of innocence in those days. Returning to his convent, he found his brethren less favorably disposed to him than before. They gave out that he had furtive designs on the treasure of their church and of Chiusi, the Ring of our Lady. The citizens began to suspect and dislike him. Brother Winter became provoked. He would have ample revenge on his brethren by turning against them the wrath of the citizens of Chiusi. On the night of July 23d, 1473, by the aid of false keys he perpetrated the act of which he had been suspected. Knowing that the Ring would not be missed until the 8d of August, when it should be shown to the people, he returned to his cell, with the treasure. The Indulgence of the Portiuncula afforded him a legitimate excuse for leaving the convent. He took the road towards Perugia, skirting Lake Thrasimene,—the very road traversed by the Blessed Mustiola with the self-same treasure a thousand year before.

It was not until he arrived within the walls of proud Perugia that Fra Winter began to reflect that he carried with him a very dangerous treasure. He had a friend in Perugia, one Luca di Francesco delle Mine. He sought him out, confided to him under an oath of secrecy the whole affair, and then asked him to present the Ring to the community of Perugia. Delle Mine consented. He repaired to Matteo Francesch Montesperelli, then Prior and first Merchant of Perugia, to whom he imparted the secret. The Prior at first regarded the matter as an imposture. When Delle Mine showed him the Ring, he replied, "The one I saw at Chiusi seemed larger." They resolved to await further proof, and the monk betook himself to Assisi, leaving the relic with Delle Mine.

The 3d of August, 1473, was a sad day for Chiusi, and especially for the poor Franciscans. The Ring was gone. The pilgrims were disappointed, stricken with consternation. People spoke of impending calamities. A cloud was upon the city. Chiusi was prostrate. It was noon before any action was taken. Then was the absence of Fra Winter coupled with the catastrophe. Messengers were dispatched in every direction with orders to bring back the fugitive. He had, in the mean time, made the pilgrimage to Assisi and returned to Assisi on the 5th of August. There he ran against a messenger of Chiusi, Fra Andrea. The messenger first endeavored to induce the monk to return with him to Chiusi on some pretense quite foreign to the great matter at issue. Finding he did not succeed, he had recourse to the Cardinal Legate of St. Sisto, and procured the immediate arrest of Brother Winter. And a long time elapsed before the unscrupulous or perhaps weakminded monk again breathed the air of liberty.

Meanwhile the events that had occurred removed every doubt from the mind of Montesperelli as to the identity of the relic. He convened a council of the Signiors of Perugia, and recounted to them how the precious relic came into his possession. It was unanimously resolved to keep it; a solemn act of donation by Luca delle Mine to the August city of Perugia was drawn up by the municipal notary, and filed in the municipal archives. This was on the 6th of August, 1473. On that day the holy Ring was shown publicly thrice to the people of Perugia amid shouts of joy and acclamations. The Decemviri then bethought themselves of the unfortunate monk, and tried, but in vain, to obtain his liberation. But here begins the struggle between Sienna and its fief Chiusi on the one side, and Perugia on the other,—a matter that will be treated in another chapter.

(CONCLUSION NEXT WEEK.)

A Strange Occurrence.

HOW AN ACT OF UNCHARITABLENESS WAS PUNISHED.

"THE poor you have always with you," says our Blessed Redeemer. But who are oftener poorer than those helpless little children who have been deprived of their dear parents and thrown upon a cold, heartless, and selfish world! God's holy Church, like a tender, loving Mother, however, has always had their spiritual and temporal welfare near at heart, and the many beautiful, spacious, sometimes even over-costly homes for such children, speak well of the charity of those that have understood the words of our Blessed Lord and acted accordingly.

The Christmas holidays have come, and with them in many dioceses, in many congregations, offerings are made for the support of the orphans. To show how God sometimes visits those who have no heart for the fatherless, let me narrate an event which took place but a few years ago, and under the immediate observation of the writer.

On the Sunday previous to the great Festival of Christmas, the pastor of a certain congregation announced, according to the regulation of the diocese, the annual orphan collection, appealing to the charity of the rich for the poor and fatherless orphans. One individual, however, after holy Mass, was heard to be very noisy in protesting against such collections, and asserting that money collected for the orphans was never used for them; that it went somewhere else; adding that each man should provide for his own children, then there would be no need for orphan asylums or orphan collections.

Christmas came. After the last Solemn High Mass, while the whole congregation chanted the beautiful hymn "*Te Deum*" in thanksgiving for the blessings of Christmas, the pastor took up the collection. The individual referred to above stood at the door, inside of the church; but when the collection plate came nearer, he sneeringly left the church.

Not one respectable Catholic had followed his bad example; but before God's eye stood chronicled the deed of a cold and black heart. A few weeks passed. It is a frosty, boisterous and dark February night; not a star to be seen; the wind blows fiercely through the leafless trees; deep silence reigns over the city; the streets are deserted, but here and there a dim light glimmers from a window and tells of some one watching at the bedside of a dear one. Yes, so it is. Bleak and dreary as is the night, the faithful shepherd may be seen making his way abroad to bring consolation to some dying one among the flock entrusted to his care. Who can it be? Be still! It is the oldest son of that heartless Christian father, a pious youth of thirteen summers, who the year previous had been seen approaching the holy altar for the first time to receive his God in the Eucharistic Bread. But now? Behold the weak and broken body! The last rites of Holy Church have been administered; bathed in tears stood the parent, looking on the dying face of the family's hope. It is all over; the corpse is laid in its last resting-place here on earth, and the funeral procession has wended its way homeward, while weeping parents linger around the grave of their good boy.

The tears have not dried, and the sound of the funeral bell still lingers in our ears, when again the pastor is hurriedly summoned to bring once more the last Sacraments to the dying—this time to the mother of the lately buried child. And while the priest of God speaks words of consolation to the slowly-sinking mother, the father of that son, the husband of this wife, is breathing heavily in an adjoining room, evidently suffering from a severe cold. The physician, too, makes his appearance; he walks from one room to the other, looking at one, then at the other, and from his countenance can be seen that he has *no hope for either*. And so it is! Within a fortnight he too must die and leave his three helpless little children—*fatherless, motherless, homeless—orphans!*

And what became of the three poor little orphans? The oldest son, the fond hope of the parents, whom they hoped would be for them and the rest of the children a help and a support, was dead. Strange fact! This father and mother had to see God take him *first*. The three that were left were now thrown upon the charity of others. It is true the parents had left a small farm, but this land would not give the children bread. Kind friends and relatives came to their rescue. The orphan asylum was mentioned, and proposed to them; but no: the relatives thought they should be kept by other families. So things went on. For a few years the helpless little ones were shifted from one place to another, from one home to another, from one family to another, until finally the youngest one had to be taken to the orphans' home. The second child died shortly after her first holy Communion, well prepared. God forbid that we should constitute ourselves judges in the matter, but we think the reader will exclaim: *Digitus Dei est hic!*—" The finger of God is here!"

The remaining child, the last member of that unfortunate family, still lives, as if to keep the facts we have related fresh in the memory of all who are cognizant of them.

MORAL.—Let all who are blessed with temporal goods be charitable to the orphans, to the poor and needy, and such works of mercy will be sure to draw down the blessings of God upon them.

M.

Catholic Missions Among the Indian Tribes of the Northwest.

F. N. B. in the "Catholic Sentinel."

As the Vicariate of Idaho (which also contains that part of Montana Territory lying west of the Rocky Mountains) has been under the administration of Archbishop Blanchet, since the resignation of its Vicar-Apostolic—July 16, 1876; and as the Coadjutor to Archbishop Blanchet will visit that region first, I send for insertion in the columns of your valuable Catholic weekly the following historical facts concerning the establishment of Catholic missions in that region. The missions to be visited are those of Northern Idaho, Montana, and Southern Idaho, in the order named. The Vicariate contains four Indian Missions, which are still under the Jesuit Fathers, whose Order first founded them, and seven other Missions for the whites. The Indian Missions still retain the names given to the tribes by the French Canadians employed as voyagers by the various early expeditions to this coast, and as traders among the Indians by the Northwest and Hudson's Bay Companies.

The Missions of Northern Idaho are known as the *Nez Perces* (Pierced Noses) and the *Cœurs d'Alenes* (Hearts Awls or Pointed Hearts.) Those of Montana are the *Pendants d'Oreille* (Ear Rings) of St. Ignatius. Their cognomen, for abbreviation sake, is written not *Pen* but *Pend' d'Oreille*. The other tribe is the *Tetes Plates* (Flat Heads) of St. Mary's Mission.

In the order of conversion to the Faith the *Tetes Plates* are the first, and the manner of their becoming Catholics is worthy of finding a record in the archives of history. In the year 1812, twenty-four Catholic Iroquois Indians from Canada deserted from the expedition organized by Captain Hunt in 1811, and took up their abode among the Flat Head nation, where they intermarried and raised numerous families. During their daily intercourse the Iroquois naturally spoke to the *Tetes Plates* of their religion, their priests, ceremonies, churches and festivals. This information made the Flat Heads desire to learn more about the Christian religion; accordingly, in 1830, they sent a deputation to St. Louis, Missouri, in order to secure missionaries to teach them the truths of Christianity. The delegation arrived safely, but shortly afterwards its members fell sick; they called for the priest, were baptized, and expired kissing the crucifix. Two years later the Indians sent an Iroquois to seek for the Blackgowns. He arrived safely at St. Louis, had his children baptized, and was returning with the glad tidings, when he was murdered by Sioux Indians on his route. A third delegation of the two Iroquois was sent in 1839, which also reached St. Louis, leaving in the fall of that year, filled with the hope that some Catholic Missionaries would visit them the ensuing year. This hope was fulfilled by the appearance among them in 1840 of Father P. J. de Smet S. J., who founded the Flat Head Mission of St. Mary's in 1841. It is related by Bishop Rosati of St. Louis, Missouri, that some Protestant missionaries, who had left the Eastern States with great *eclat*, were anxious to settle among the *Tetes Plates*, but the Iroquois told their Indian relatives that "these men were not the priests about whom they had spoken to them. They were not the priests with long black gowns, who have no wives, who say Mass, and who bear a crucifix upon their hearts." The Mission of St. Ignatius among the Pend' d'Oreille Indians was established in 1842. It has a boarding and day school for the Indians, established many years ago, attended by five Sisters of the House of Providence, Montreal. That of the Cœur d'Alenes, in 1843. The Cœur d'Alene Mission also has schools for the Indian children, attended by three Sisters of the House of Providence, Vancouver; that of the Nez Perces in 1875. The Cœur d'Alene Indians were very wicked; the name Pointed Hearts signifies their true character, but the Catholic Church—the true civilizer of pagan nations—changed, in a short time, these wolves of the forest into lambs of the fold. Far different was the result in the case of the Nez Perces Indians of Lapwai, and of the Cayuse Indians of Wailatpu, under the rule of Protestant preachers. The Presbyterian minister Spalding settled among the Nez Perces in 1836; Dr. Whitman, also a Presbyterian minister, started during the same year an extensive mission among the Cayuses, a mile distant from old Fort Walla Walla, Washington Territory. But the labors of both these representatives of sectarianism were almost entirely fruitless, if we may judge from the fact that after laboring among them assiduously for eleven years —from 1836 to 1847—Dr. Whitman was murdered by his neophytes, and Mr. Spalding would have shared a similar fate had he not been rescued from their hands by Peter S. Ogden, Chief Factor of the Hudson's Bay Co., in January, 1848. Mr. Spalding returned to the Nez Perces in 1862, and remained until 1877 (fifteen years) with no better success, as he had not sufficient influence over them to keep them from joining the forces of Joseph on the war-path against the whites in 1877. The mission of the Cœur d'Alene Indians, was about eighty miles north of the Nez Perces; the latter Indians had heard much of the manner in which the Catholic missionaries instructed and assisted the Indians among whom they labored. Many of them, therefore, embraced the Catholic faith, and, their number increasing, they asked that a priest might reside among them so as to be able to give them the consolations of the Sacraments. Accordingly, Father Cataldo, S. J., yielded to their petitions, and took up his residence among them in 1875. Assisted by the generosity of the citizens of Lewiston, Idaho, he was enabled to erect a church and establish a school, the beneficial effects of which were discovered when, in 1877, it was found that not a single Catholic Indian under his teaching was hostile to the whites, but, on the contrary, both they and the Cœurs d'Alenes thoroughly proved their fidelity to Catholic teaching by using their influence among other Indian tribes to keep them from joining the ranks of those who were hostile; they, also aided the soldiers by acting as scouts and doing all in their power to bring the war to a close.

Of the several missions for the whites, two are in Montana, and the other five in Southern Idaho, called by the early Canadian traders, Boise, in English "woody" from Bois, wood. This name was given to Fort Boise in consequence of the density of the woods in its immediate vicinity.

Missoula City, Montana, is in charge of one of the Jesuit Fathers. It has a day school and a boarding school, also an hospital attended by six Sisters of Providence from Montreal.

Deer Lodge City, Montana, is in charge of a secular priest, Rev. R. de Ryckere, who was sent there in 1867 by the Bishop of Nesqualy. In 1873 Father de Ryckere erected a hospital which was opened in the October following under charge of five Sisters of Charity from the mother-house at Leavenworth, Kansas. A stone church, 26x60, with a residence in the rear, was completed in 1876, having cost $4,000. This mission extends over a circumference of sixty miles.

The discovery of gold in the Boise Basin of Idaho in 1861-2 having induced a large immigration, Archbishop Blanchet appointed the following year Rev. A. Z. Poulin and Rev. T. Mesplie to attend to the spiritual wants of Catholics. Three churches were built in 1863; the first, at Idaho City, was blessed on the 15th of November; the second, at Placerville, on December 20th; and the third, at Centreville, on Christmas Day.

During subsequent years, spacious churches were erected at Granite Creek, Silver City and Boise City. On December 13th, 1867, three Sisters of the Holy Name, from the mother-house in this city, took their departure for Idaho City to open a day and boarding school which they conducted for two years, but the transitory character of the settlement forced them to abandon the enterprise.

In accordance with the recommendations of the Second Plenary Council of Baltimore, in 1866, the eastern portions of the Diocese of Oregon City and Nesqualy were erected into the Vicariate Apostolic of Idaho March 3d, 1868, with Rt. Rev. Louis Lootens of California for its Vicar Apostolic. Having been consecrated by the Most Rev. Archbishop of San Francisco, August 9th, 1868, he took possession of his Vicariate early in 1869. Bishop Lootens obtained his resignation July 16th, 1876.

The Southern Missions of Idaho are now attended by two secular priests, Rev. A. J. A. Archambault and Rev. Joseph Pickl. Both the priests and faithful in Idaho have long and earnestly desired the Episcopal visitation of the Coadjutor Archbishop; and as a matter of interest to Catholics, I desire to append the following itinerary of Archbishop Seghers' visit, now being made.

I.—From Portland to Lewiston, Idaho, a mile from the Nez Perces Catholic mission—401 miles by steamboat, in three days, two days on the Columbia and one day on the Snake River. II.—From Lewiston North to Pine Creek—the new Mission to which the Cœur d'Alene Indians were removed a few years since— 60 miles on horseback in two days. III.—East to St. Ignatius' Mission among the Pend' d'Oreille Indians, 250 miles over mountain roads rendered difficult through fallen timber. Time: six to eight days on horseback. IV.—Thence south to the Mission of St. Mary's among the Flat Head Indians, seventy miles on horseback in two or three days (Missoula City is half way between the two). V.—From St. Mary's southeast to Deer Lodge, 120 miles on horseback, or by stage from Missoula. VI.—Deer Lodge south to Ogden, 475 miles, by stage. VII.—From Ogden west to Kelton, 70 miles by railroad, in three hours. VIII.—From Kelton north to Boise City, 300 miles by stage. IX.—Thence northwest to Baker City, the farthest eastern mission of the Archdiocese (350 miles from Portland), by stage in two days. X.—Thence southwest to Canyon City, 90 miles by stage. XI.—Thence southwest to Jacksonville by stage. XII.—From Jacksonville to Portland, visiting the intermediate missions and stations at Roseburg, the Coast, from Gardiner City to Ellensburg; Corvallis, Salem, Gervais, St. Louis, St. Paul, and Oregon City.

The performance of this episcopal tour will occupy

nearly three months. Let us all pray that Archbishop Seghers may have a safe and prosperous journey. Upon his return he will subsequently visit the missions at Grand Round Agency, McMinville, Cornelius, Astoria, Dalles and Umatill Agency.

Catholic Notes.

——NOTRE DAME had the honor and pleasure during the holidays of a visit from Rt. Rev. Bishop Dufal and Very Rev. Father Chambodut, V. G. of Galveston.

——The Governor-General has presented bronze medals for competition to the Notre Dame Convent, Kingston, and the Ottawa Institute.—*Catholic Record*, (*London, Ont.*)

——PADRE CHELINI.—A monument to Padre Chelini, the great mathematician, of the Order of St. Joseph Calasanctius, was recently unveiled by the Rector of the University of Rome.

——ORDINATION.—On the 12th of December, Rev. Messrs. Anthony Kroeger and Henry M. Plaster were ordained priests in the Cathedral of Fort Wayne by Rt. Rev. Bishop Dwenger.

——MONSIGNOR DE GOESBRIAND, Bishop of Burlington, United States, is now in Rome, and intends, before returning to his diocese, to pay a visit to the Holy Land.—*London Tablet.*

——MISS MARY STANLEY, the well-known Catholic lady who died recently in England, was a convert and a sister of the famous Dean of Westminster. Her life was one of rare devotedness to various works of charity. She was greatly beloved by all who knew her. R. I. P.

——"PRELUDES," the new volume of poems by Maurice F. Egan, and published to aid in the rebuilding of the University of Notre Dame, is a very handsomely printed and elegantly bound book of 96 pages. It is a beautiful volume, and admirably suited for a holiday gift. The price is $1. It is published by Messrs. Peter F. Cunningham & Sons, 817 Arch St., Philadelphia. We are compelled to keep over a notice of "Preludes" till next week.

——WÜRTEMBERG.—Whilst everywhere in Germany the Church is more or less persecuted, peace and tranquillity reign in the little kingdom of Würtemberg. A new proof of this was lately given at Stuttgart, the capital of the realm, on the occasion of the solemn dedication of St. Mary's Church, one of the most magnificent, by the way, in Southern Germany. The King and Queen—both non-Catholics—accompanied by the entire court, assisted at the impressive ceremony, which was presided over by Rt. Rev. Bishop Hefee.

——THE CATHEDRAL OF COLOGNE.—The *Cologne Gazette* states that, although unfinished, the towers of the Cologne Cathedral are the highest buildings in the world, measuring 157 and 160 metres respectively in altitude, as compared with the Nicolai Tower in Hamburg, measuring 144.20; St. Peter's at Rome, which measures 143; the Münster at Strasburg, 145; the Pyramid of Cheops, 137; St. Stephen's Cathedral at Vienna, 135.20; the Cathedral of Antwerp, 123.40; the Duomo of Florence, 119; and St. Paul's in London, which measures 111.30 metres.

——A DISPLAY OF ENLIGHTENMENT.—Another London journal has at last been educated sufficiently up to the mark to find out that only for the Catholic Church the knowledge of the present day would be in a sadly backward condition. A London newspaper has positively said that England's debt of gratitude to the Benedictines ought to be very deep, inasmuch as they preserved, in written integrity, the Latin tongue long after it ceased to be a living language, during the centuries when all but a few churchmen were plunged in ignorance, and when printing and Protestantism had yet to be invented. This is refreshing, and no mistake. The leaders of public thought in England are of late displaying a large amount of enlightenment. Almost time. God be praised!—*London Universe.*

——POPE LEO XIII AND CATHOLIC JOURNALISM.—At the Catholic Congress of Modena, Professor Brunelli, chief editor of the Catholic journal *Paces*, of Perugia, related that his Holiness, when Bishop of that city, had encouraged him to establish a Catholic paper in his episcopal city. "You could not," said Mgr. Pecci on that occasion, "tell me of anything that would give me greater pleasure to hear. I look upon a good Catholic journal as really a perpetual mission in my diocese." And the holy Bishop aided in every possible way the establishment of the newspaper—by handsome donations of money, as well as by earnest recommendations to the clergy and laity to become subscribers, and to use all their influence to promote the circulation of the journal. "And," added Signor Brunelli, "the Pope has, as you as are all aware, since his accession, spoken to the effect at the public audience which he granted to the representatives of the Catholic journals of the whole world. The Pope loves the Catholic press. He well knows their difficulties, their trials, their labors, and their discouragements."

——A REMINISCENCE OF MARQUETTE.—A very interesting and instructive paper on Early Illinois, by E. G. Mason, Esq., was read at the annual meeting of the Chicago Historical Society held in that city on the 17th ult. Mr. Mason related that "when Father Marquette returned from his adventurous voyage on the Mississippi in 1678 by the way of the Illinois, he found in that region an Illinois town called Kaskaskia, composed of seventy-four cabins. Its inhabitants received him well, and obtained from him a promise to return and instruct them. He kept that promise faithfully, undaunted by disease and toilsome journeys and inclement weather, and, after a rude wintering by the Chicago River, reached the Illinois town again, April 8th, 1675. Its site has since been identified with the great meadow south of the modern village of Utica, and nearly opposite the tall cliff soon after known as Fort St. Louis of the Illinois, and in later times as Starved Rock. He instructed the chiefs and the people, established a mission there, and gave it the name of the Immaculate Conception of the Blessed Virgin."

——THE PRONUNCIATION OF LATIN AND GREEK.—We see from the notices of new books in the *Tablet*, that an Oxonian M. A., Mr. F. M. Wyndham, has published a short pamphlet on the pronunciation of Latin and Greek. We thought that a conference of educational authorities had been held some years ago to devise ways and means of changing our barbarous English pronunciation of these dead languages. If we remember rightly, it was unanimously agreed that the English mode was indefensible, but the members of the conference could not agree as to the model to be adopted in its stead. Some were for calling the great Roman orator "Chichero," others "Kikero," while others stuck to "Sissero"; and evidently the conference broke up *re infecta*—or, as the Englishman says, *ree infectay*. Mr. Wyndham thinks the most practical plan would be to pronounce Latin as the Italians, and Greek as the modern Greeks pronounce it. But a reference to "Rome's Recruits" shows us that Mr. Wyndham is a convert. Protestantism should be on the alert. Here is a Papist brewing a dark plot to inveigle Protestants into pronouncing Latin as the Pope pronounces it!—*Indo-European Correspondence.*

—A BRAVE SOLDIER'S END.—Not long ago there died at the Trappist monastery in France a venerable religious, distinguished for his tender devotion to the Blessed Virgin. It was known that he had formerly been a soldier of the Grand Army; but few suspected that beneath his calm exterior beat the heart of a hero. On one occasion during the Russian campaign, after marching for many weary hours through deep snow, and almost fainting from fatigue, the regiment to which Brother —— belonged found itself face to face with a small though strong Russian battery. Death seemed inevitable. Terror seized upon every heart: both officers and men laid down their arms in token of surrender. One brave officer, however, quickly changed his resolution, and, seizing his sword, called out: "Follow me, my braves." There was no one to obey the command but Brother ——, who replied, "I will go forward with you alone." He laid down his gun, and, after making the sign of the Cross devoutly, recited the *Pater, Ave* and *Credo*, and made a fervent act of contrition. Then rising quickly and seizing his gun, he bounded towards the foe accompanied by the intrepid officer. Two terrible volleys were fired at them from the guns, but they escaped unharmed, as if by magic. Fearing some stratagem, the Russians suddenly took to their heels, leaving everything behind. At the sight of this unexpected movement the Colonel of Brother ——'s regiment rushed towards him and said: "My brave comrade, you are more deserving of my cross than I am"; and suiting the action to the words, he took the military cross of the Legion of Honor from his breast and presented it to the brave soldier, who drew back, simply remarking, "Colonel, I only did my duty." And later, when he embraced the austere life of a Trappist, he said to his friends, "I am only doing what I feel to be a duty."

New Publications.

THE ENGLISH IN IRELAND; or, People who Live in Glass Houses, etc. A Reply to "The Turks in Europe, by Edward A. Freeman, D.C. L., LL. D.," by Thomas Adolphus. Philadelphia: Robinson & Co. 1879.

This is a little 24mo. book of ninety pages, written by one who is evidently well posted in Irish and English history, and who takes a great interest in the wrongs of that much-wronged country, Ireland. For those who have read Mr. Freeman's "Turks in Europe," the scope of Thomas Adolphus's little book needs no explanation, and even to others the double title will no doubt convey a sufficiently clear idea. It must not be supposed, however, that Thomas Adolphus (a *nom de plume* of course) wishes, no matter how just cause there may be, to intensify further the feelings of the Irish people against the oppressors of their country. He divides his work into five sections, as follows: Introduction—Who and What are the English?—Who and What are the Irish?—What Have the English Done in Ireland?—What is to be Done with the English? After a general view, the writer sums up by drawing in his lines parallel with those of Mr. Freeman, concluding with the statement that if the Turks should be driven out of Europe, so also should the English landlord be driven out of his unjustly acquired possessions in Ireland. We see that Thomas Adolphus shares the general impression that Pope Adrian, misled by the false representations of Henry II of England as to the state of Ireland, granted him a Bull empowering him to enter that country and subdue it to law, order, and religion; whereas late historical researches have clearly proved Henry's alleged Bull to be a *forgery*—"a thumping English lie," as Father Burke emphatically expresses it. We have neither the time nor space at present to enter into details on this matter; suffice it to say that all necessary information regarding the forged Bull can be found in the learned letter of Dr. Moran, Bishop of Ossory, published a few years ago in many of the papers, and lately republished by a few others.

APPARITIONS OF OUR LADY OF LOURDES, AND PARTICULARS CONCERNING THE LIFE OF BERNADETTE, AND THE PILGRIMAGE SINCE THE APPARITIONS. Translated from the French of Rev. Father Marcel Bouix, of the Society of Jesus, by Thomas Layton, A. M., M. D., P., Knight of St. Gregory. New Orleans: T. Fitzwilliam & Co., Printers, 76 Camp St. 1879.

"What can be said of Our Lady of Lourdes that is not contained in that valuable and exhaustive work on the same subject by M. Henri Lasserre?" said we to ourselves, as we took up this most interesting and edifying work by Father Bouix, S. J., of which Chevalier Layton has given us an enjoyable translation. We confess that we were most agreeably surprised in our perusal of this work. From beginning to end, we found it intensely interesting. In this instance particularly we see strikingly verified the words of the great St. Augustine, as appositely quoted by the author in the preface, "That it is useful that certain books, even when they treat of the same questions, should be written by many authors, each in his own style, the faith of all being the same, in order that the subject with which they deal should reach the greatest number, its meaning coming home to some by one channel, and to others by another." The work is divided into two parts. The first treats of the apparition of Our Blessed Lady, and the second contains a narrative of the life of Bernadette at Lourdes and Nevers, as also of the pilgrimages made to Lourdes from all parts of the world, with an account of the principal sanctuaries of Our Lady of Lourdes in the Old and the New World. In addition to the above, there are also several interesting and instructive chapters on the teaching of the fathers and doctors of the Church regarding the prerogatives of the Immaculate Virgin that will make this volume doubly welcome to all devout clients of our Blessed Mother.

—Messrs. Benziger Bros. have published a German translation of Mr. Henri Lasserre's admirable biography of Bernadette Soubirous.

RECEIVED.—Parts 21 and 22 of The Life of Our Lord and Saviour Jesus Christ and of His Blessed Mother. Translated and adapted from the original of Rev. L. C. Businger, by Rev. Richard Brennan, LL. D. Benziger Bros., Publishers.

For Rebuilding Notre Dame University.

A Friend, $5; Miss Ellen O'Neil, $1; Mrs. Ellen Fitzpatrick, $1; Mrs. Cecilia Donovan, 50 cts.; Peter Murphy, $5; Anne Murphy, $5; Thomas Murphy, $5; Patrick Murphy, $5; Mrs. William Mullen, 50 cts.; A Friend, $15; Anne McCraren, $2; Benedictine Sisters, $2.50; F. X. Kast, $2; Michael Loughman, $1; Thomas J. Relihan, $2; Miss Annie Burns, $1.

Confraternity of the Immaculate Conception
(Or of Our Lady of Lourdes).

REPORT FOR THE WEEK ENDING DECEMBER 24TH.

The following petitions have been received: Recovery of health for 46 persons and 3 families,—change of life for 15 persons and 3 families,—conversion to the Faith for 20 persons and 7 families,—special graces for 2 priests, 5 religious, 8 clerical students, and 3 persons aspiring to the religious state,—temporal favors for 33 persons and 5 families,—spiritual favors for 45 persons and 3 families,—the spiritual and temporal welfare of 5 communities, 2 congregations, and 4 schools. Also 36 particular intentions, and 5 thanksgivings for favors received.

Specified intentions: Light to know one's vocation,—change of life for a family,—prevention of a scandalous lawsuit between near relatives,—cure of defective sight and hearing,—safe return and spiritual welfare of the pupils of Catholic colleges and academies away for the holidays,—vocations to the priesthood for several young men,—preservation of 3 schools from the diseases prevailing in some parts of the country,—consolation for a sorrowing mother,—increase of pupils in a school.

FAVORS OBTAINED.

We continue with pleasure to record a number of favors obtained through the patronage of our Blessed Mother: "Last week," writes a correspondent, "I asked prayers for the conversion of a young lady; thanks to our Heavenly Queen, she is now a good Catholic and happily married to a Catholic." ... "It is with praise and thanksgiving," says another, "that I write these few lines: I completed a novena yesterday, and I now feel a decided change for a religious vocation, and enjoy peace of mind." .... A grateful wife writes: "I thank you for sending the Water of Lourdes to my husband, and I return thanks to our Lady for the benefit he has received from it. He had broken and bruised his hand in a frightful manner. A few applications of the blessed water cured it perfectly, and he is now able to work again."

OBITUARY.

Of your charity pray for the following deceased persons: Mrs. MARY KELLY, a devout client of Mary, who departed this life at Emmittsburg, Md., on the 21st of November, in the sixty-third year of her age. SISTER AURELIA (McSherry) of the Order of St. Joseph, at McSherrystown, Pa., who went to her heavenly Spouse on the 12th inst. Mr. JOHN HENRY BURNS, an ecclesiastical student, at Troy, N. Y., deceased on the 5th inst. His death is much regretted by all who knew him. Mr. WM. GIBBONS, who was lately killed by a boiler explosion at Newton, Iowa. Mr. JOSEPH REAUME, of Indianapolis, Ind.; Mr. JAMES LYNCH, of Chicago, Ill.; Miss NELLIE TRAINOR, of Boston, Mass.; MARGARET MURPHY, of Charlestown, Mass.; MARTHA GREENWOOD, of Webster, Ky.; Mr. JAMES CONLIN, Mrs. HAND, Mr. PETER FAGAN, Mr. EDWARD NOLAN, Mr. JOHN MCCANN, Mrs. MARIA DONNELLY, and PETER SINNOT, whose deaths are of recent occurrence. Mrs. MARY DORAN, Altoona, Pa. MICHAEL, MARY and JOSEPH FERRALL, JOHN TORMEY, DOMINICK MCGUIRE, ELIZABETH BAKER, Mrs. EMELINE KERRICK, Mrs. MILDRED STAPLES, Mr. STEPHEN MILLS, Mr. PIUS ELDER, JAMES and MARY MATTINGLY, EDWARD N. CANNON, and WINEFRED CANNON, all of whom died some time ago. And several others whose names have not been given.

Requiescant in pace.

A. GRANGER, C. S. C., Director.

Youths' Department.

For the "Ave Maria."
Tribute of the Months to Mary.

BY ELEANOR C. DONNELLY.

I.

HAUNTS the ice-crown'd January:
"I within my bosom bear
Thine Espousals, pure and fair,
Virgin Bride! I hail thee, Mary!"

Moans the shiv'ring February:
"Candlemas, amid the snow,
Bids the blesséd tapers glow,
Bids them burn for thee, O Mary!"

II.

Cries the boisterous March: "I see
Early snow-drops in the way;
Sweet Annunciation Day
Blooms, O sinless Maid, for thee!"

April stands and weeps: "Ah! me,
Ne'er was sorrow like to thine;
Mother, 'neath the Cross divine,
Let me stand and mourn with thee!"

III.

May, among her violets airy,
Sings exultant hymns of praise:
"All my nights and all my days
Are thy very own, dear Mary!"

June, the rosy, radiant fairy,
Murmurs: "Oh! how fair thou art!
Lady of the Sacred Heart!
Summer's sweets are thine, sweet Mary!"

IV.

Flowers in her tangled hair,
Pants the beautiful July:
"Visitation Day is nigh,
Mary's happy journey share!"

August sinking, flush'd and fair,
In the harvest fields to rest:
"Welcome!" (cries) "*L'Assunta*, blest,
Queen of heaven! hear our prayer!"

V.

Beauteous babe, her arms, between,—
Sweet September seems to say:
"Hither haste, and homage pay
To the little new-born Queen!"

Floats thro' russet fields (once green),
Brown October's plaintive plea:
"Lady of the Rosary!
Hear our *Aves*, Maid serene!"

VI.

Pale November, at the door,
Kneels in mystic contemplation:

"'Tis Our Lady's Presentation,
Zealous souls! her help implore."

Raptur'd, cries December hoar,
"Queen conceived without the stain
Of the sin of Adam,—reign
O'er our hearts for evermore!"

The Story of a Revenge.

BY ELIZA ALLEN STARR.

WEEPING, wailing, and terrible threats of vengeance, were all that could be heard in one of the noble palaces in Florence on a certain night in the year 1020. Death had entered; but in a way so violent, that grief did not seem to be the sentiment of the house so much as revenge. The youthful features of the dead had a beauty as noble as if cut in marble. A wonderful repose had settled down upon them, leaving no trace of the tumult and struggle in which life had been lost. The death wound in his breast was covered, and he lay as if in a trance, rather than a sleep, from which none but an angel would dare to wake him. But around the couch on which he rested were heard no prayers,—no *De profundis*, no *Miserere*. Armed men, instead of monks, kept the watch of death. The blaze of the tall tapers of unbleached wax flared on the young, dead face, as the huge doors swung to and fro on their hinges; but there were no beads of holy water on the forehead, and no crucifix had been laid in the hands, so white and so shapely. Instead of the sigh of prayer, fierce menaces against a youth, "Luigi," were whispered from one to another, and not always under the breath. The hours of that terrible night wore on, and every now and then the fierce old count would exclaim to his son, Giovanni: "The blood of thy brother Hugo will call out to thee from the ground, until he is avenged. See to it: that blood answers for blood!" Then, with a horrible imprecation for the curse of God on the hand which had dealt the death blow, he would bewail his son stricken down in the very flower of his age. Yet the one on whose head these imprecations were called down, was not older than the son whom he mourned. Both were young, and hot tempered. The strife, begun hardly in earnest, became a quarrel for life or death, and Hugo fell. From that moment, the young nobleman who had been Hugo's companion and friend, was like one sure to be hunted down, sooner or later, by bloodhounds. The count, still in the vigor of manhood, Giovanni, in all the pride of a military career, swore upon their swords, in the presence of the dead, to give themselves no rest from the pursuit of the murderer. It was not the law which should mete out to him its slow justice, but their own hands, "swift to shed blood." The funeral of Hugo, if it brought peace to the dead, certainly brought none to the living. All Florence sided with the count in his stormy grief, and looked upon the avenging of the murder as a point of honor.

In the midst of this tumult, only one voice was heard on the side of mercy. It was that of the Abbot of San Miniato, the old Benedictine convent overlooking Florence, with her river Arno, and her circle of beautiful hills. The Florence of 1020 was not the Florence of to-day nor of the year 1500. Of her three most renowned churches—Santa Maria Novella, Santa Croce,* and her Cathedral, or Santa Maria in Fiore,†—not one was in existence. Her venerable Baptistery, built by Theolinda, Queen of the Lombards, before the year 600, and dedicated to Saint John Baptist, was indeed standing; but without those bronze doors which Michael Angelo declared were "fit to be the gates of Paradise." Neither had Franciscans or Dominicans been thought of, excepting in the forecasting mind of God. The Benedictines, under one form or another of their rule, were the monks and the priests of Florence; and San Miniato was their beloved home as well as the venerated shrine of one of the oldest patrons of Florence. Saint Minias, from whom the lofty hill takes its name, was in the Roman army under Decius, in the year 251. While this Emperor was carrying on in Florence the seventh great persecution against the Christians, the soldiers under him were called upon to sacrifice to the gods. Then it was that the Armenian prince, Minias, was found as brave in facing death for the true God, as he had been in facing death for his emperor. This death for the "God of the Christians" was one of such torment as had never come before the imagination of the soldier. To be thrown to a panther, only to have the panther lick his feet; to be thrown into a caldron of boiling oil, and to come forth refreshed; to be suspended from a gallows, then stoned, then pierced with javelins, was the way by which the soldier Minias won heaven, and the crown and palm of the martyr. Hundreds of years—yea, a thousand years, after all this, the Florentine painters loved to picture him in a scarlet robe, crowned, like a prince, with a javelin, a lily and a palm in his hand. But before these painters were born, San Miniato and its Benedictines made a home for the heart of every Florentine; and the Abbot of San Miniato could reprove prince or count as well as peasant. It was this

---

* Holy Cross.

† Saint Mary of the Flower, or of the *Lily*, which is the emblem of the city of Florence. This lily is like our wild flag or iris, only a little deeper in hue.

abbot who raised his voice against the vindictive wrath of Count Gualberto. "'Vengeance is Mine; I will repay,' saith the Lord," he repeated to the count, while the body of Hugo still lay in his father's palace. "Beware, my son, how you bring down upon yourself the malediction of the Most High by any act of revenge on your own part; but, more than all, by stirring up your son to any deed of violence. At your door will lie the sin," insisted the abbot.

Count Gualberto heard the abbot, but paid no attention to his admonition: hearing him, in fact, as one hears in a dream—too much absorbed with the idea of vengeance to realize its sin. Again the abbot breathed a word of tender admonition into the ear of Giovanni, but was shocked to find that the son considered himself bound to carry out the will of his father.

Yet there was one in the old Florentine palace who mourned not only for the dead but the living, and this was the mother, Laurina. One son had fallen, in the first beauty of manhood, a victim to the passion of anger; and now another son, as noble as Hugo, and with a grandeur about him which spurned all fear of consequences, was given up to the pursuit and utter destruction of the young man who had killed his brother instead of being killed by him. In vain had she put in a plea for mercy. She only saw the flames of revenge leap higher. She prayed for the dead; but, with an agony as keen, she prayed for the living. In her distress, she found the way, known to all the Florentines, to San Minias, and to the feet of its abbot. How could she know that the hand which had been raised against Hugo might not, in sheer self-defence, be raised against Giovanni? The mother's heart was broken. The abbot heard her story, and said: "Expostulation is useless. Your only safety, and the only safety of your surviving son, lies in prayer." And prayer became her sole occupation. Day after day, week after week, she was seen haunting the churches, one after another. Especially she lingered in the old Church of San Zenobia,* which stood on the very spot where the Tower of Giotto now stands. But, above all, she lingered around the shrine of San Miniato, where a soldier as brave as Giovanni had, for centuries, drawn souls to God.

Meanwhile, the youth Luigi was hiding from the very light of day. He knew there was no mercy for him at the hand of Count Gualberto or of Giovanni. With the instinct of faith, he, too, like Laurina, threw himself at the feet of the Abbot of San Miniato, and the same reply came from the same inspired lips: "Pray, my son.

---
* The same Saint Zenobia, Bishop of Florence, whose dead body borne against an elm tree long leafless and dry, restored it to life; and upon whose shrine the sculptor Ghiberti modelled a garland of elm-leaves in memory of the miracle.

You have a great wrong to expiate. Let penance be your occupation, and prayer and penance will win for you the special protection which you desire. Lay aside your arms; so that, if attacked, your reliance may be upon God, not upon weapons, which, indeed, wrought death for Hugo, but a still more terrible death for your own soul." The admonition which had fallen unheeded upon the ear of Count Gualberto and upon the ear of Giovanni, was drunk in as a most healing draught by the hunted fugitive of an unpitying enemy.

(TO BE CONTINUED.)

Charity Rewarded.

AT the time of a great famine, on a cold winter's day, a poor woman came to a village and began to beg. Her clothes were very clean, but torn, and patched in many, many places. The snow was falling fast: her head was wrapped in a handkerchief; in one hand she had a stick, and with the other she carried a basket. From most of the houses she received only a very scanty succor; even some rich persons drove her away with harsh words. There was but one poor peasant who invited her into his house, where there was a good fire in the grate; and his wife took a cake out of the oven and gave the poor woman a large slice of it.

The next day all from whom this stranger had asked for charity were invited, quite unexpectedly, to sup at a distant castle. When all the guests were arrived, they proceeded to the dining-room, where they saw two tables laid out. One was very small, but upon it were many exquisite dishes. The other was large and magnificent, and had a great number of plates, but they held but scanty nourishment, such as a piece of half musty bread, a couple of potatoes, a handful of bran, and some held nothing at all. Whilst the guests were wondering what this meant, the lady of the castle spoke thus: "The beggar who passed through your village was myself; I was disguised in order to judge, myself, of your charity in this time of need. The two poor people whom you see here, took me in and treated me as best they could. They will eat at my table to-day, and I will give them a pension besides. As to you, regale yourselves with the offerings which you gave me yesterday, and which you see here upon your plates."

WE all have two secretaries: the demon, who writes our bad actions, to accuse us; and our good angel, who writes our good ones, to justify us on the day of judgment.—*Curé of Ars.*

THE AVE MARIA.

A Journal devoted to the Honor of the Blessed Virgin.

HENCEFORTH ALL GENERATIONS SHALL CALL ME BLESSED.—St. Luke, i, 48.

Vol. XVI. NOTRE DAME, INDIANA, JANUARY 10, 1880. No. 2.

[Copyright: Rev. D. E. Hudson, C. S. C.]

The Bridal Ring of Our Lady at Perugia.

BY "ARTHUR."

II.

(CONCLUSION.)

THE all-absorbing solicitude of the Perugini now was to make sure and stable the possession of the treasure which had, in their estimation, been given to them providentially. They immediately dispatched two ambassadors to Pope Sixtus IV to represent to His Holiness how on the 6th of August, the Feast of the Saint whose name he had taken as Pontiff, heaven had favored his faithful Perugini by bestowing upon them the nuptial Ring of Mary, a most precious and famous relic: and that as he, as Vicar of Christ, had faculty over all sacred things, he would vouchsafe by an Apostolic Brief to confirm them in the possession thereof. (Annal Xvir. 1473, 8 Aug. F. 70–71). No sooner had the ambassadors set out on their mission, than the magnificent Signiors of Perugia set about the formation of a law which would insure the permanent possession of the treasure, no matter what the will of the Pontiff might be. It was ordained that "if any one of any state and condition whatever be so rash, perfidious and wicked as to dare, directly or indirectly, tacitly or expressly, under any color whatsoever, to propose to harangue or moot in any council of Perugia or elsewhere, or to consent or impose in any way that the most sacred relic of the Blessed and glorious Virgin Mary be given, permuted, granted to any person, ecclesiastic or secular, to college or community, or endeavored to make it leave the city, he, in virtue of the present to be held good forever, together with his children and posterity, shall be regarded as a rebel to the commune of Perugia, and with the rebels esteemed, and his goods shall be, *ipso jure*, adjudicated to that community, and he himself be marked with infamy," etc., etc. The reader will perceive from this extract that Perugia meant no trifling in what concerned the Ring. A box of solid iron, was ordered for the safe custody of the Ring. To this box there were seven locks, the keys of which were distributed as follows: one to the Bishop, one to the Chapter of San Lorenzo, one to the Priors of the Arts, one to the Consuls of the Mercers, one to the Auditors of the Cambro, one to the College of Doctors, and one to the Association of the Notaries. This box was enclosed in a grating of iron, which was secured by four locks, the keys of which were consigned to the four principal convents of the city, to wit. San Domenico, Sant' Agostino, Santa Maria de' Servi, and San Francesco. It was resolved, moreover, to show the Ring to the people three times a year, viz.: on the third of August, on All-Saints Day, and on Easter Tuesday—and this should be done by the hands of the most worthy cleric in Perugia; that the Ring should be carried from the town-hall to the church with magnificent pomp, and back again; that it be locked in the box in the presence of all; that the Notary of the Priors draw up an act attesting the same, and the Communal Chancellor make mention thereof in his books and protocols. (Annal. Xvir. 1473, F. 75.)

In the mean time Chiusi sent an embassy to Sienna, acquainting the Signiors of that Republic with its loss, and asking justice. The Siennese lords immediately wrote to the Cardinal Legate of Perugia demanding the restoration of the Ring. Not content with this, the Bishop of Chiusi set out for Perugia with the intention of making a personal appeal to the honesty and sense of justice of the Perugini. He was kindly received by the Magnificent Signiors, but no sooner had he touched the subject of the Ring than he was interrupted by Montesperelli, who informed him that the matter could not be spoken of save before a general assembly. The Bishop saw that further parley was useless, and left the city. Two days later the official ambassador of Sienna arrived in Perugia. He made known his mission in a general assembly, was listened to de'erentially, but informed that the Ring, having come to Perugia by Divine favor, there it should remain. Seeing the Perugini immovable, the Siennese also appealed to the Pope. For months after, the Signiors of Perugia held no assembly in which some measure was not adopted concerning the Ring. A gratification of 200 florins was voted to Lucca delle Mine for having presented the Ring to the city, and a yearly pension of 16 florins awarded to himself and children unto the third generation. They were also exempted from all taxes, ordinary and extraordinary. Besides this, the sum of 40,000 florins was voted for the eventuality of a war with the Siennese. These last had already made an appropriation of 50,000 florins to be spent in the recovery of the Ring—while little Chiusi made preparations for war.

The Annals do not tell us the precise tenor of the Pope's reply to the ambassadors of Perugia. The Siennese ambassadors became indignant in Rome when they were answered that the Pope would institute a commission of five Cardinals to discuss the question. "But how can there be any discussion?" said they; "we only claim our own, which is unjustly and obstinately withheld by the Perugini." They left Rome in disgust, alleging that the Pope would soon hear from the Doge of Venice, the King of Naples and the Duke of Milan, whose mediation Sienna had already invoked. In the heat of the contention, the Signiors of Perugia did not forget the unfortunate Brother Winter. They bestowed upon him a gratuity of five pounds, and afterwards voted him an annuity of twenty-five florins. His trial took place in the fall of 1474. He confessed frankly that he stole the Ring with the mere and only intention of avenging himself on his brethren. Accomplices and instigators he had none. In a solemn assembly of the Priors and Chamberlains of Perugia it was unanimously resolved that the German friar should be set at liberty. But after three days he was again imprisoned by order of the Archbishop of the city, who alleged that the Decemvirs had gone beyond their prerogatives. He was, however, well disposed to the friar, and freely gave permission to the Chamberlains of the following year (1475) to deliberate anew on his liberation. His final release took place on the 18th of January. He was assigned the ministry of the chapel of the palace in which the Ring was preserved, and lodged in a little apartment next door to the famous Sala del Cambio, where he saw the great Pietro Perugino at work on his frescoes. There he led a quiet, uneventful life, and died a happy death in the year 1509. The holy Ring had already been transferred to the chapel of the Duomo, where it still remains. Under this chapel they gave him honorable sepulture, over which they placed an inscription (no longer extant), to the effect that Perugia was as grateful to him for his "fortuitous gift" as if he had given it freely and righteously—wherefore he merited repose before the very altar which was dedicated to Mary and Joseph.

In disposing of Fra Winter, I have been carried unconsciously through a lapse of years of struggles and reprisals to an epoch of peace. I must needs retrace my steps to observe how the magnificent city of Sienna, ill brooking the delayed restitution of the Ring, published a formidable edict of reprisal against every citizen of Perugia found within the territory of Sienna. Acting, moreover, at the instigation of unhappy Chiusi, it was furthermore declared that every Perugino found within the dominions, either resident or otherwise, should be regarded as an enemy to the state, his goods should be confiscated, and he himself confined in prison. Perugia of course retorted in kind by confiscating the estates of the Bishop of Chiusi, which lay within its territory. Ambassadors were sent in the meanwhile by each of the litigants in turn to the Sovereign Pontiff, without any definite results. At one time the Pope desired to have the friar and Luca delle Mine sent to Rome, in order to examine them personally. At another, he proposed that the Ring itself should be sent to the Eternal City, to be deposited in one of the great Basilicas. In vain. Perugia invariably replied, "It has pleased God to bestow the Ring upon your faithful subjects—here it shall remain." The hostilities continued. The Siennesi captured Perugini. The Chiusini captured Perugini; and the Perugini avenged themselves on both by frequent raids on their territory. Still they smarted under the reprisals. Matters went on thus for thirteen years, and, becoming more complicated daily, a war was deemed inevitable.

At last, in the year 1486, another ambassador was sent to Rome by the Perugini, in the person of the "respectable Knight, Antonio degli Acerbi." His first thought was to secure the sympathy and influence of Cardinal Francesco Picolomini, a Siennese by birth, but educated in Perugia. Innocent VIII had already deputed the Cardinal as arbiter in the matter. It was finally decided that Perugia should keep the Ring, and a Brief to that effect was drawn up. The contending parties were bound to make mutual restitution for the damages inflicted. Thus peace was restored, and Perugia remained the happy possesser of the treasure.

The reader has doubtless come to the conclusion that the conduct of Perugia was most unjust, not to say dishonest. I would request him to remember the old historic maxim: *Distingue tempora, et omnia concordabis*. Let him remember that we are dealing with the Middle Ages, when a great, unquestioning, childlike faith preponderated in every sphere of life; when local pride was an element that made of the Hundred Cities of Italy the glorious monuments we witness to-day; when popular passions were not so easy of control.

The want of space deters me from submitting other and pertinent considerations on the purloining of the Ring, on its retention by the Perugini, on the means adopted by all three of the contending parties to gain their object, and finally, on the decision of the Sovereign Pontiff, which was, by the way, dictated *pro bono pacis*. But would the Sienna and Chiusi of to-day appropriate 50,000 florins for a war towards the recovery of a relic? Would Perugia suffer reprisals and submit to fabulous expenses (the sums at issue during the struggle were fabulous for those times) to preserve a religious treasure? Knowing that your answer will be far from flattering, I pass on to more agreeable matters appertinent to the Ring of Our Lady. In that same year of 1486 Fra Bernardino of Feltre, a famous Franciscan preacher who gave the Lenten sermons that year, proposed to the Perugini that an apposite chapel for the custody of the Ring should be erected in the Duomo, where it could always be venerated by the people. The proposal was received favorably. A chapel was constructed on the left-hand side of the principal entrance, and dedicated to Mary and Joseph. The Ring was carried there with great pomp. The great Pietro Perugino was engaged to paint the altar-piece, and he produced that famous picture known as the "Espousal." For this immortal masterpiece—now in Caen, France, stolen by the French and never returned,—Pietro received the sum of *fifteen florins!* The actual picture over the altar, a fair production, is by Wicar. The rest of the history of this remarkable relic effects the further embellishment of the chapel, the devotions practised therein, and the solemn processions in which the Ring was carried, at one time to stay the oncoming pestilence, at another, famine, at another for rain, at another for the cessation of rain, and again against earthquakes. Leo X granted a plenary Indulgence to all who, having confessed and communicated, should visit this relic with pious intentions. It is to obtain this Indulgence that pilgrims flock hither in shoals on the last day of July. Among the illustrious visitors who came to venerate this relic may be mentioned Popes Paul III, Pius VII, and Gregory XVI. Pius III wished with his own hand to touch the Fisherman's Ring with it, and when some one spoke of other rings of Our Lady existing elsewhere, he replied, "We know but this one." Gregory XVI exclaimed on beholding it, "O wonderful, O great relic!"

A word about the material and form of the Ring. It is now a settled conclusion that it is made of white onyx. It is very thick,—indeed clumsy, as compared with similar modern ornaments—with a slight depression in the part where the seal is usually inserted. The irregularity of the indenture would lead one to suppose that it was once an intaglio. But the eye can discover nothing definite. Allusion has been made to other rings of the Blessed Virgin. Gerson mentions two that were venerated at Paris in his time. Ferreol Locre speaks of two more which existed at Semur, in Burgundy. Another was venerated in a Benedictine Church of the diocese of Arras, in Belgium. But no trace or memory of any of them exists at present.

In conclusion, I will fulfil my promise of explaining how far the Briefs of the Sovereign Pontiffs concerning this Ring effect the approbation of its authenticity. I cannot better do so than in the words of Cardinal Lambertini, afterwards better known as Pope Benedict XIV, probably the most rigid and intelligent critic in matters appertaining to the Sacred Congregation of Rites that ever sat in the Chair of Peter: "They preserve in Perugia the Ring with which, it is piously believed, St. Joseph espoused the Virgin. A certain Gio. Battisti Lauri, a Perugini, has published its history. Its finding is supposed to be in the time of Gregory V, that it was preserved in the city of Chiusi 484 years (according to Lauri's version), that it then passed into the hands of the Perugini, that its possession was disputed before the Pontiff Sixtus IV, who ordered the Perugini to restore it to those of Chiusi, having given the order to Cardinal Giovanbattista Savelli, his Legate: and the said order not having had execution, and the above mentioned Sixtus IV being dead, that a sentence favorable to the Perugini was pronounced by his sucessor, Innocent VIII. In the work of Lauri there is a letter written to him by Abramo Bzovio, which speaks of this relic of the Holy Ring as of something verisimilar. In lib. 2 of his *Apologia pro Sancta Maria*, there is a good deal of noise raised against this Holy Ring by Riveto, a heterodox author. But as nothing else is pretended beyond piously believing what is narrated about the said Ring, and that for it there is a certain moral certainty which is sufficient in such matters, all his bitter criticism goes for nothing. Pompeo Pellini speaks at length of the relic of the Holy Ring. And, lastly, there is a discourse published on this matter of the Holy Ring and dedicated to the magistrate of Perugia, in which there are various arguments in favor of this presumption; regarding which it is not out of place to observe, that, always supposing, and admitting with due piety the veneration for this holy relic, it cannot however be from the acts published before by Sixtus IV and Innocent VIII that judgment has been pronounced by the Apostolic See on the truth and identity of the Holy Ring, the principal purpose of the controversy being to see to whom did it belong, that is, to those of Chiusi, or those of Perugia. And though in such judgment the truth and identity of the relic be supposed, everybody knows, that it is one thing to suppose, and another to declare or define; and that many things are disposed by the Popes which regard some particular relics, but with the clause expressed, or always to be understood, of leaving the judgment on the identity and truth in that degree in which it is of pure probability, without carrying the matter farther; as is demonstrated by us in our Work *De Canonizzatione Sanctorum*—on the Canonization of Saints—when we spoke of the identity of the identity of relics, and of the clausule which is often put by the Sacred Congregation of Rites in its rescript, *citra tamen approbationem reliqiae*—leaving out the question of the approbation of the relic."

Rosary Rhymes.

BY THE REV. MATTHEW RUSSELL, S. J., AUTHOR OF "EMMANUEL."

SOME of the Indulgences granted to the Rosary require meditation on the mysteries. Many are in the habit of mentioning in each "Hail Mary" the mystery commemorated in each decade, thus: "Blessed is the Fruit of thy womb, Jesus, who was crowned with thorns, etc." This breaks too much the flow of the "Hail Mary," and might at most be confined to the first "Hail Mary" of each decade. The announcement of the mysteries as given in prayer-books may readily be learned by heart. The following verses may be of use to some for this purpose.

It is easy to keep in mind that the Joyful, Sorrowful, and Glorious Mysteries are assigned in this same order to the first three days of each week and then to the last three, so that the Joyful Mysteries are thought of while saying the beads on Monday and Thursday, the Sorrowful on Tuesday and Friday, the Glorious on Wednesday and Saturday. As for the Sundays, the season of the year determines which of the three sets of mysteries is appropriate: after Christmas, the Nativity and other Joyful Mysteries; after Easter, the Resurrection and other Glorious Mysteries; in the penitential times of Lent and Advent, the Sorrowful Mysteries.]

In the Name of Father and of Son
And Holy Ghost, God Three in One,
And Mary, for the love of thee,
We say the holy Rosary.

I.—THE JOYFUL MYSTERIES.

1.—*The Annunciation.*

"Hail, full of grace! The Holy One,
The Son of God, shall be thy Son."
Low spake the handmaid of the Lord:
"Be it according to Thy word!"

2.—*The Visitation.*

O'er the bleak hills in March she sped,
Comfort and grace around to shed.
"God's Mother cometh thus to me!
Blest amongst women shalt thou be."

3.—*The Nativity.*

Glory to God on high! for low
Hath He stooped down to heal our woe.
Glory to Christ our Lord for aye,
Who shivering in the manger lay.

4.—*The Presentation.*

Clasp Him, old Simeon, to thy breast,
Then ask of God to let thee rest.
But ah! hast thou no gentler word
For that young Mother than the sword?

5.—*The Finding in the Temple.*

He's lost! to those fond hearts what pain!
He's lost—but joy! He's found again.
"We've sought for Thee with tears, my Son!"
"My Father's work must needs be done."

II.—THE SORROWFUL MYSTERIES.

1.—*The Agony in the Garden.*

Crushed down, O Jesus, 'neath my sins,
Thy Heart Its agony begins.
"Father, Thy will, not Mine, be done!"
Thou prayest, as the red streams run.

2.—*The Scourging.*

Shudder, my soul, with grief and awe,
As if ear heard, as if eye saw,
How, thick as hail, the lashes fell
On Him who "hath done all things well."

3.—*The Crowning with Thorns.*

Unmoved shall I behold Thy woe,
Because endured so long ago?
Thou lovest me as truly now
As when the rude thorns rent Thy Brow.

4.—*The Carrying of the Cross.*

While up the mount His Cross He bore,
His Mother tracked Him by His gore,
Till, tottering 'neath the weight He fell—
That Mother's anguish who could tell?

5.—*The Crucifixion.*

Nailed to the cruel, shameful Tree
For three long hours, thy Saviour see.
Go stand with Mary near the Cross,
Nor shrink from shame or pain or loss.

III.—THE GLORIOUS MYSTERIES.

1.—*The Resurrection.*

The gloom hath passed from earth away,
Arise, O Sun! whose smile is day.
He who was dead hath eager flown
To where His Mother mourneth lone,

2.—*The Ascension.*

The pageant fadeth up from sight;
The gazers, tranced in meek delight,
Hear white-robed angels chide their pain:
"He who is gone will come again."

3.—*The Descent of the Holy Ghost.*

With patient longings deep, serene,
The Twelve are waiting with their Queen,
Till God fulfil their souls' desire—
And see! they flash, those tongues of fire.

4.—*The Assumption.*

Say, who is she who upward soars,
Leaning on Him her soul adores?
The King of Heaven has whispered "Come!"
And bids His Mother welcome home.

5.—*The Coronation.*
Joy in the courts of Sion! Bow,
Saints, angels! as on Mary's brow
Gleams bright yon crown of dazzling sheen,
And Heaven exultant greets it Queen.

The blessed beads are numbered all,
"Hail, holy Queen!" on thee we call
To hallow all our pilgrim-days
Into a rosary of praise.

'Beth's Promise.

BY MRS. ANNA HANSON DORSEY.

CHAPTER II.
"OUT OF THE DEPTHS."

The next day's mail brought the letter that Captain Brandt had hoped for from his friend. It was brief, written immediately after Captain Morley's death, in substance the same as the telegram, except a few details which made it infinitely more satisfactory and precious. Commander Brooke concludes as follows:

"He realized his danger from the very first; he told the surgeon that weak lungs was a family failing of his people. He spoke to me several times of his wife and daughter, in the fondest tones; and when he saw how much we were affected by his sufferings, he rallied, and his voice rang out in its old cheerful way as he waved his hand and said: 'What's the odds! I die, but the ship is saved.' He fixed his eyes on the crayon portrait of his wife that always hung in his state-room and murmured, 'My wife!—my poor little 'Beth!' After this his mind wandered; the words: 'Ship saved!' 'Duty before all,' were the last he uttered, and the gallant fellow's life ebbed as gently away as the going out of a summer's tide. Our surgeon was in constant attendance, doing everything that skill and kindness could suggest for his relief. All of us feel the deepest sorrow; the sailors, who idolized him, gather in groups, talk of his courage, and how good he was to them, 'if he *was* strict,' and don't care to hide the tears that roll over their rough faces. But I must stop; the mail-boat is waiting. I will see that all of the Captain's effects are forwarded to your care by the first opportunity, and will send the remains on as soon as the weather gets cold. Offer my respectful services and sympathies to Mrs. Morley, and tell her that her loss is also ours, and that we grieve with her. He was the purest of men, the bravest of officers.

"In haste yours,
"CHARLES BROOKE."

That was all. Shutting himself in his library, Captain Brandt gave way to his grief, and read the letter over and over again; then, recollecting the duty that lay before him, he controlled his emotion, blew his nose with a trumpet note, dashed some cold water into his eyes, swallowed a glass of brandy and water, got his overcoat and hat on, and was on his way out, but turned to call to his wife and tell her not to go out—that he would be back soon; he had got a letter from Brooke, and was on his way to Mrs. Morley's to read it to her. "There's no mistake: he's dead." He did not wait to answer questions; he shrank from his painful task, and thought the sooner it was over the better. The hall door was closed with a bang, and he was gone.

Captain Brandt found Mrs. Morley quite calm, with not a vestige of color in her face except the dark purple rings under her eyes, which she had not closed all night. He told her of the letter; she started, and fixed her eyes questioningly on him, as if, after all, there lingered a hope that the news of the telegram had proved false. Captain Brandt understood the mute appeal.

"Have courage, my dear lady," he said. "Yesterday's news is confirmed. Shall I read you Brooke's letter, or would you prefer reading it yourself?" He hoped that she would choose the latter, for he felt his courage oozing away.

"Read it to me, if you please," she answered, closing her eyes.

He read every word, and, except a quivering of the nerves of her face, she showed no sign of how it was wringing her heart.

"I suppose I know all now," she said, when he finished, holding out her hand for the letter, which he gave her. Reading and pondering every word, as if there might be some deeper meaning under it all, which the Captain had failed to understand, she went over it twice; but there it was, in black and white,—he was dead; they would never meet again on earth.

"I ought to cry. I wish I could, but my eyes burn, and every thing is benumbed. It is not heartlessness, Captain Brandt; you know how I loved him, and how proud I was of him; but it is strange that, knowing he is dead, I am not frenzied with grief. The hurt is so deep that I think it has killed me, in a way. It is not courage—or resignation; it is all so unreal, so strange, that—that—perhaps it is a horrible dream, from which I shall awake and find everything as it was. Don't you wish it was a dream, Captain Brandt?"

"I'd give my own life to make it so, dear lady. But come; you must try and bear it; bear it, you know, as he would like to see his wife bear affliction; you must do it for his sake," said the Captain, smoothing her cold hand, and wishing he could say something about heaven and the consolations of religion, but he was all at sea on such topics as those. "Then, you know, there's poor 'Beth, poor little girl! you must think of her; indeed you must now," he added, almost at his wits' end.

"Yes; 'Beth must be thought of. You mean well, my friend, and I'm glad you spoke. Will you write—to—to my husband's aunt, Mrs. Elizabeth Morley, for me, and tell her all that has happened, and ask her to come to us? 'Beth must have some one to comfort her—I can't. You have been very kind, Captain Brandt—you and your wife; and I thank you—thank you. Ah, I know how you loved him!"

"Certainly I'll write, with the greatest—I mean at once. What is Miss Morley's address?" answered the Captain. "That or anything else I can do—I am at your service day or night, madam."

"Alton Post-Office, Seneca County, New York. I accept your friendly offer; for oh! there's so much to be done before all is finished!" she said, thinking of the time in the near future, when the remains of her husband would be brought home for burial.

A servant came in with two cards on the tray. "I can see no one. Why did you bring them up? Tell every one that I do not see visitors," said Mrs. Morley, turning away from the cards.

"So I do, ma'am; the hall table's filled with cards—so many keeps on comin' to inquire how you does, an' if they can do anything for you an' Miss 'Beth."

"They are very kind; but what is it all to me since he can never come again?" she murmured.

"But, my dear lady, look here," said Captain Brandt, glancing at the cards, "it is the parson and his wife; maybe they might be able to comfort you; indeed, I think you'd better see them!" said the Captain, thanking his stars that they would know how to say all those pious things to her which good people, women especially, found comfort in when under affliction.

"Invite them up, Nelly—but no one else, remember. Not that I expect to be comforted by anything Mr. Haller can say," she added to Captain Brandt, after the servant had left the room; "but he means kindly, and I would not wound him by refusing to see him and Mrs. Haller. What is there on earth, who is there left to comfort me? It seems like mockery even to think of comfort."

"Have courage, have courage!" said the Captain; "Mrs. Brandt and I will be here this evening. I'll write to Miss Morley as soon as I get home. But here they are," he said as the door opened to admit the pastor and his wife, giving him the opportunity to slip out unobserved.

Mr. and Mrs. Haller were overflowing with sympathy, nor were their tears withheld as they expressed it in kindly words; he offered the prescribed consolations of his creed, and read the touching prayers of its liturgy for those who are in affliction; but in the presence of such white, silent anguish as that before him, he forbore insisting upon a resignation which would stifle the human cry of a broken heart. Thinking it best not to weary her, the gentleman and his wife soon took their leave, but returned daily, sparing no effort to win the bereaved woman to a consideration of things which would give her peace of mind.

But in vain all these well-meant ministrations. White and silent, Mrs. Morley's heart was filled only with her loss—a loss which had aroused other regrets known only to herself, which stung her like adders, leaving her nothing on which to lean in this great tribulation. To 'Beth, Mrs. Haller proved a comforting, kindly friend, and many a time she sobbed out the grief which for her mother's sake she sought to repress in her presence, upon her breast. Later on, the pastor again attempted in a more emphatic manner to admonish and console the grief-stricken woman, who dared not think of her happy past, while she turned away from the future with almost terror, bearing the indescribable anguish of the present without a hope beyond it. Her husband was dead, and nothing they could say or do could bring him back to her; nothing that they said or did could help him where he was, or give her a hope that death had not broken every tie between them.

"No, no, Mr. Haller," she exclaimed one day; "don't talk to me any more of resignation and the will of God! I can't bear it! I am no more resigned to-day than I was at first; and words, words, are just empty sounds. Nor will I ever believe that God was cruel enough to will that my true, noble, brave husband should die like that. No! had Admiral Ashton kept faith with him, I should not be desolate this day. He—after his long sea-services—after all that he did so gloriously in the war—after being separated from his family year after year, seeing us only now and then—he was placed in command at the Naval Academy with Admiral Ashton's pledged word that there he should remain for four years,—'deserving such rest,' he said, 'after his long and gallant sea-service.' And yet in less than two years he was ordered to the 'Portland.' Our home was broken up in midwinter, and an officer who was a favorite at court—whose record could show no war service, he having been kept on a foreign station on account of ill-health until the war was over—was apppointed to the place. And this is the end of it; this, this, oh, my God! it was not Thy ordering that my husband went to his death; it was a mean intrigue, the breaking of a promise that he had accepted in good faith, that led to it!"

"But it must comfort you," said Mr. Haller, in slow, solemn tones, "to know that the renown of his valuable services rests like a halo around his name; and that dying as he did, at the post of duty, is a worthy close to a life like his."

Poor Mr. Haller had offered all the religious consolation at his command to assuage her grief; and, finding how useless it seemed to be, fell back upon the human, as a pagan might have done when comforting a friend by speaking of the approaching apotheosis of the dead hero they mourned. But this also failed, like the rest.

"Comfort!" she said, bitterly. "No! I take comfort in nothing, since all his renown, all his splendid fame cannot bring him back to me; and I pray—yes, I pray that the curse of a widowed heart may fall upon the man by whose capricious will my husband went to his death. Let the world smirk and smile when they talk about their dead hero—he is not theirs, that's why they can do it,—but mine, mine,—but dead,—and what do I care for empty honors! There's only one thing that could comfort me in the least."

"And what may that be, Mrs. Morley," said the pastor, pricking up his ears for something that he could at last take hold of.

"To pray for him—*now*—as I do. Yes! it is all I can do. I pray for him as Catholics pray for their dead; it is the only prayer I utter; and the only grief I can think of that was greater than mine, was that of the Mother of Jesus, who pities the sorrowful, and helps them, too."

"My dear friend," said Mr. Haller, greatly shocked, "trust in God! Peace will come to your sorely troubled heart after a season, when, leaning upon the immeasurable mercy and promise of the Almighty Disposer of events, you will find solace in Him, and rest in His will. Meantime, hope is His gift, and as He judges not as men judge, let us hope largely for the eternal rest of those who pass before us, beyond the veil."

"That does not satisfy me. My only comfort is to pray for him, to feel that I am somehow in communion with him, and can help him, if—if such prayers as mine can be heard in heaven," she exclaimed, wringing her pale hands.

The pastor had many arguments against such things as this. Where had she, one of his own flock, got such a heresy into her head as a belief in purgatory, a downright "Romish" belief! He could have told her a great deal that was believed by his Church about a place called Paradise, which was held to be the intermediate place for the departed, and many other things besides, but he did not think she was in a condition of mind to be harassed with arguments, so he only knelt down and read some of the prayers for those under trial, and asking God's blessing upon her when he finished, took leave, fearing in his own mind that the shock she had sustained had unsettled Mrs. Morley's mind.

'Beth's youth, and the elasticity of her nature, joined to the fact that she had never seen very much of her father, he having been on sea-service ever since she could remember, coming home for a short time every three or four years, although she loved him tenderly, prevented her from suffering the sharp anguish that her mother endured. The cloud lay heavy upon her young life, however. The sense that she was left fatherless was one of bitter loss, while her mother's grief was so absorbing that she felt shut out from the old warm place in her heart.

"She just looks at me, and speaks to me, as she does to anybody else. Oh, Aunt 'Beth, do you think she will ever love me again?" cried 'Beth, throwing herself in a passion of tears upon the breast of her aunt, Miss Morley, who had arrived that morning. She had come from her own beautiful home in the hop-growing region of New York; packed up, and left everything as soon as she got Captain Brandt's letter informing her of her nephew's death; had come full of kindly, loving thoughts for the bereaved ones, sorrowing herself, yet putting self aside to do all she could to comfort them, and hoping to take them back with her, if she could prevail upon them to go.

Miss Elizabeth Morley was a small, spare, alert woman, a little past middle age, with keen blue eyes, gray hair which hung in three short curls over each temple, a somewhat frosty nose but well shaped, and a white, sound set of teeth, which sometimes, on occasion, she had a way of snapping together like castanets; she was clear-headed and brusque, with a pleasant voice of very decided and incisive tones.

"Love you!" she answered. "Of course she will. This won't last. It would be contrary to human nature. By-and-by, when time blunts her grief a little, she'll open her arms to you, my poor baby."

"When? How soon, Aunt 'Beth? Do you think by next week?"

"No: nor by next month. You must be patient, my dear, and wait; that is woman's life, to wait and by-and-by the mother-love that has been beaten down by this dreadful blow will lift up its head and open its blossoms again, and you will have it all back, 'full measure, pressed together, and running over.'"

"Oh, Aunty 'Beth, if I thought so, I would wait so patiently! Are you sure, though?"

"As sure as that I am living," answered Aunt 'Beth, as, drawing the fair tear-stained face to her own, she kissed it tenderly.

Aunt 'Beth, strong, active and practical, looked quietly and keenly about her, and soon discovered how she could be most useful. Putting her own sorrow out of sight, she brought things to order without fuss, or offence to Mrs. Morley's old servants. Jealousy is a failing of their class; they hate what they call "meddling," even though it be the mildest suggestion, or the most indulgent show of authority exercised by one when the master or mistress of the house is, from some cause or other, unable to see after their own affairs; but Aunt 'Beth was one of those fortunate beings who are endowed with a masterful spirit. She had what New-England folk call "faculty;" she always seemed to know exactly what to do, and she did it with a will. And now when she gave directions about this or that, they were so clear, simple, and methodical, that her right, or authority, was never questioned. The poor creatures, who had grown old in the service of the family, felt the sorrow that had so suddenly come upon it with that emotional grief which is a peculiarity of their race; consequently, ever since the sad news had arrived, things had been going at 'sixes and sevens.' But now, with Aunt 'Beth to the fore, they felt the same kind of relief that a ship's crew might whose captain had by some casualty of the tempest lost his life, leaving them, without guide or compass, to drift to destruction, should some one appear to take his place and guide them into port. Everything was brought into perfect order; and 'Beth, who was much with her aunt, was learning lessons of practical use. "She couldn't," thought Aunt 'Beth, "be diverted from brooding over her sorrows in a better way than by learning to be useful." Captain Brandt, and his amiable wife came daily to see Mrs. Morley; they were the only persons she saw except Mr. and Mrs. Haller, who were evidently discouraged in their attempts to impart consolation to one who seemed to reject all solace, and devoted herself only to vain regrets. Crowds of friends called daily to inquire, leaving messages, flowers, and notes of condolence for Mrs. Morley and 'Beth, among them Mrs. Secretary Ashton and the Misses Ashton, whose cards Andrew put into his pocket, out of sight. It did his old heart good to see such attentions, and when the President himself, and the general of the army called, making the kindest inquiries as to Mrs. Morley's health, and leaving cards of condolence, he felt somewhat more reconciled; for with his race the "pomp of woe" smooths the rugged edges of the sharpest griefs.

Captain Brandt came one evening to tell Aunt 'Beth that Captain Morley's chests and other effects had arrived, and ask her what he should do.

"Send them here, captain, of course; there's nothing else to be done. It's a new trial to face," —her voice and lip quivered. "Whenever his chests had come before, he was with them. But I will tell Anne; God only knows how she'll stand it; possibly it may rouse her to a more natural sort of condition. She takes no interest in anything; she answers if she is spoken to, and looks all the time as white and motionless as stone, or as if she were dreaming. And she doesn't sleep, and positively refuses narcotics."

"You're right, Miss Morley; she'll go 'melancholy mad' if this continues, and perhaps, as you say, the sight of poor Morley's things will set her to crying and screaming as other women do when they're in trouble. I wish I could help you; if I can, send Andrew right off for me," said Captain Brandt, rising to go.

But they were both mistaken. Aunt 'Beth went upstairs, and sat down beside Mrs. Morley, and, taking her hand, began smoothing it gently between both her own. "How do you feel? Is the room comfortable? Your fingers are very cold," she said.

"I am very well, and I do not feel cold," she answered, gently.

"Anne, Captain Brandt has just been here to tell me that poor Will's chests and things have arrived," said Aunt 'Beth. "Shall you wish to see them, or what?"

But Mrs. Morley closed her eyes; a spasm of anguish ran shuddering through her from head to feet, and she did not speak. Aunt 'Beth waited in tearful silence, her eyes fixed with tender pity on the white woebegone face.

"Anne, my child, I must know your wishes," she said at last, speaking very gently.

"Are you here yet, Aunt 'Beth? How patient every one is with me! I heard what you said, and you don't know how everything that has happened rose up before me all at once; when I thought of *his not coming*, that he would never come again. Senseless things, worthless by comparison. Oh! the jealous anger I feel that *they* should be brought back safe to the home he will never enter again. Put them all somewhere out of sight, Aunt 'Beth. The hall room up-stairs will be a good place—perhaps—some day 'Beth may like to see her father's things."

"I will do as you wish, Anne; but do, do try and bear up! Indeed, my child, this will never do; you must have courage," spoke Aunt 'Beth.

"You don't know," was the low-toned reply; "you mean well, but you don't know."

Aunt 'Beth was on the eve of saying "Don't know what?" but she held her tongue; leaning over, she kissed Mrs. Morley's pale forehead and went out of the room, closing the door very gently. She and 'Beth talked affairs over, and did each her best to comfort the other.

The sea-chests came the next day and were taken up to the room named by Mrs. Morley; Aunt 'Beth shut herself in with them, and, Captain Brandt having sent her the keys, she proceeded to examine and arrange their contents in her usual methodical way. The battle-worn uniform, discolored by the smoke of cannon; his clothing, his full dress-uniform, his sword, his papers, all the pretty curiosities and presents he had collected for his wife and 'Beth at the ports his ship had visited, were sprinkled with tears as Miss Morley assorted them, folding and refolding everything, making separate packages of letters and journals, wrapping fine linen towels around the delicate fabrics he had got for dresses, and laying each article just where it could be found without confusion. In one of the boxes she found his battle-flag. This she folded up, intending to take it to her own room, knowing that later on it would be needed. The best part of two days were thus occupied, an inventory made, and the battered sea-chests were relocked, and the door closed upon them. There was only one thing she did not return—a pearl locket and heavy gold chain which he had bought in Havana—which he had intended, as written upon the box with his own hand, for a "Christmas gift for my dear daughter, 'Beth."

"She shall have it as he meant," said Aunt 'Beth to herself, "but I will wait until all is over, before I give it to her." And it was hidden away in the recesses of her trunk.

The last duty was the most trying of all to Aunt 'Beth, but she remained to attend to it. Captain Morley's remains arrived soon after winter set in, and by Captain Brandt's advice they were deposited in Mr. Haller's church, instead of being brought to the house. Mrs. Morley insisted on visiting them, and with her daughter and Aunt 'Beth, all clad in the deepest mourning, they drove to the church, where they remained until near midnight, feeling in all its bitterness that unutterable sense of grief, the deep desolation of "being so near yet so far apart," that no response of look or word, but only silence, can come to the aching heart.

The *Requiem* was sung, the burial service was read, and under the old trees of Oak Hill Cemetery the brave sailor was laid to rest. All that could be done had been arranged to honor his memory on that sad occasion: the newspapers were filled with eulogy of his heroic career, the Navy Department was draped in mourning, and an order issued directing officers to wear crape on their arm for thirty days. The President and the higher officers of the Government, officers of the army and navy, and hundreds of private citizens, reverently followed the casket, which was draped with the torn battle-flag of the dead hero, his sword, now sheathed forever, rested upon its smoke-stained folds. A shield of white flowers, on which was written in violets the words: "I die, but the ship is saved," was upon the casket, its only floral ornament. It was lowered into the grave, the earth was shovelled in, and all was over. Mrs. Morley was borne fainting to her carriage, and Aunt 'Beth held her on her breast until they got home. She made no moan when consciousness returned; a gasping sob, now and then, without tears, and a face as white as marble attested her woe. She answered when spoken to, but otherwise kept silence.

"What shall I do? What can I do?" thought Aunt 'Beth wringing her hands. "Why can't she grieve as other women do? She must have a cup of hot tea." She brought the tea herself—a hot, steaming, fragrant cup—the only panacea that can be thought of when everything else fails—and Mrs. Morley tried to drink it; but she had difficulty in swallowing it, and Aunt 'Beth took it away. The minister and Dr. Milner were down-stairs, but she declined seeing them.

"I must fight it out alone, Aunt 'Beth; they can't help me. I thank them for all their kindness. My sin has found me out," she moaned as Miss Morley left the room, "and who shall comfort me?"

(TO BE CONTINUED.)

A Lover of the Beautiful.

BY KATHLEEN O'MEARA, AUTHOR OF "IZA'S STORY," "ROBIN REDBREAST," "LIFE OF FREDERIC OZANAM," "PEARL," ETC., ETC.

(CONTINUED.)

ST. Theresa said of the devil—"Poor wretch! he does not love." Henry's idea of heaven was a place where everyone loved. "It is Arnaud, I think, who says that we shall have all eternity to rest; this notion of heaven does not smile on me at all; the idea of rest is fatiguing and inadequate, but if you were to say, 'We shall have all eternity to love,' ah, then I should agree with you!"

Nor was it only that purest and most sublime love which possessed his own soul that he could admire and sympathize with. Whatsoever was holy, whatsoever was pure, whatsoever was brave and of good report, found an echo in his heart. He writes from the Oratory to a friend about to embrace the marriage state. . . . "Ah, Stephen, do not laugh at love, I implore of you, like those fools who are incapable of feeling it. Do not laugh at love. There is no more sacred word amongst men. Love is not pleasure, it is not selfish enjoyment, nor passion. The aim and end of love is sacrifice. . . . You should sacrifice yourself in marriage as the priest sacrifices himself in the priesthood, with devotion, with entire self-surrender, with joy, if you will, but with a sober joy which is akin to resignation and accepts sorrow beforehand."

How sincere was his own self-surrender to the Crucified Spouse, who had chosen him, is touchingly manifested in a note which we find in his private memorandum about this time: "I have scarcely put on the blessed livery of Thy service, Lord, and I have already received a stone for Thy sake. It was yesterday in the street. The stone was aimed by a strong hand, for it made a rent in the wall where I was passing. I cannot describe the sensation of pride and gratitude that thrilled my soul. O, my Lord, to suffer for Thee! I was not worthy of it. I have done nothing yet to deserve the honor!"

On the day that he entered the Oratory, Henry received a letter from a poor man whom he had been in the habit of visiting in the prison of Ste. Pélagie. This is his answer:

"No, I don't forget you. Your letter was the first that greeted me in this solitude to which the voice of God has conducted me. What you say to me, even your praise, unmerited as it is, did me good, and was very precious to me just that day, for I was a little cowardly and frightened, and I wanted some one to give me a helping hand to cross the threshold of the life I was entering on. .... See how well Providence arranges things! You have so often said that you never could do anything for me, and already you have done me a great service. Be assured of one thing: we all want each other, and no one but a fool can say, 'That man will never be of any use to me!' . . . . . Here I am, a prisoner like yourself—my wings clipped, and if there is one thing I have loved all my life, it is liberty—in theory and in practice." And through several pages, he continues in this tone of delicate and tender grace, drawing a parallel between his own position and that of the poor victim of human justice, encouraging him to imitate in humility and fortitude the Prisoner of Love, who made Himself a slave that we might be made free; the letter closes with these words: " . . . . Don't weary of blessing God for your misfortunes, and if there does not come a moment when, in the full acceptance of the cross, the springs of consolation are suddenly opened to you, and a heaven of interior joy expands your soul until you are forced to cry out: 'what is this, my God, that my tears are changed to smiles, and I feel actually happy!' If this moment does not come, then I will confess that I do not know my God, and that I understand nothing of His promises."

This "interior heaven of joy" was already given to him, who so boldly announced it as the inevitable reward of "the cross accepted," and this possession enabled him to speak with the irresistible force of experience and conviction. "I will confess anything you like, madame," he says to a lady whom he was trying to convert to the faith, "but there still remains the fact that *I am happy*. The certainty of being where God wishes me to be, places my soul on a solid foundation of peace and calm. There are, no doubt, memories tinged with sadness; but there are no regrets. . . . There is, moreover, an indescribable charm in certain moods of the soul when it has just enough of *tristesse* to taste the full value of divine consolations. So, I beg of you, don't pity me! That would be very unjust, and very ungrateful to God, who has done and is doing so much for me."

He was never tired impressing upon the souls who drew near him that suffering was the road to all true consolation, that joy was to be reached only through the cross, and that they only who had learned this lesson could teach it to others.

"Let me remind you," he says to a broken-hearted mother, "that great grief, accepted as becomes a Christian, gives to the soul a kind of unction, very fit to console the sufferings of others. You believe in *les graces d'état*, dear lady? Well, the state of resigned sorrow has a special grace for communicating resignation. He who has not suffered is nearly always incapable of consoling others. . . . Use this grace which has cost you so dear, and seek the company of those who are in sorrow."

One who was so richly endowed with spiritual gifts as Henry Perreyve, could not remain unnoticed by those whose mission it is to discover and employ them. He had been about a year at the Oratory, when he was invited by the Dominicans, on the Feast of St. Dominick, to a banquet at which the Archbishop of Paris presided. After paying a tribute to the various religious orders represented amongst the guests, Monseigneur Sibour fixed his eyes steadily on Henry, and said in a very significant manner that he built hopes on him in the future. "That is one of my little ones!" said Père Pététot, Superior of the Oratorians.

"Let him be," replied his grace, "he will grow to be a big one." Then turning to the young man, who sat overpowered with confusion: "My child," he added, "preserve in your heart what I have been saying until the will of God shall be accomplished in you."

Writing to Père Lacordaire next day, Henry says: "I am still full of our beautiful *fête* of yesterday. . . . One ought to die after a beautiful Christian festival. It is like a glimpse of heaven that makes the wings of one's soul beat, then the vision vanishes, and the veil drops, and to those strong interior lights which our Lord gives to His friends, there succeeds the dim twilight in which small souls dwell. I am one of them. . . . Father, I should so like to know if I am not deceiving myself in the love I have for the thought of death? I find in this thought treasures of joy, and it seems to me that there is not a moment in my life in which, were the choice given me to live or die, I should not choose death. And yet I am so happy! . . . "

His holidays this year (1854) were passed with the Dominican Fathers in their beautiful Convent of Chalais, and the visit was like one of those Christian festivals which Henry loved. The monks welcomed him "with a great fire and a great meal, the two forms of perfect hospitality. . . . . O, my friend," he writes, "I am transported. There is in this nature, regenerated by the habitation of saints, such an indescribable influence of prayer, and chastity, and peace. . . . Yesterday we climbed to the top of one of the highest mountains of Dauphine; we saw the Alps with their chain of glaciers and snows sparkling against the sky, and, towering above them all, Mont Blanc surrounded by its peaks, like a monarch by his guards and knights. I bethought me that at that hour you were perhaps contemplating the horizon of the sea, and I wondered which of us had the finest spectacle. But I was wrong: The greatness of God is in the sea and His grandeur in the mountains. The sound of the waves is like the sound of the wind amongst the pine trees; the roll of the mountains is like the surging of the billows: they echo the same voice, and invite to the same prayer: *Mirabiles elationes maris, mirabilis in altis Dominus.*"

The beauty of the visible world was to him a reflexion of the invisible beauty of God which it shadows forth to the pure in heart. "I know not why it is," he says, "that in contemplating the beauty of the mountains with a young Dominican monk, we were led to admire the beauty of the Blessed Virgin. Perhaps there is something more than a mere chance and indirect relation between them. If physical nature is made according to the image of God, and on the plans of the Eternal Word, the human soul is still more truly His likeness, His mirror; and of all souls that of the Blessed Virgin is the most perfect likeness to the Divine soul. It is not, therefore, strange that the incomplete beauty of nature should remind us of the beauty of the most perfect of creatures, and lead us to the contemplation of God, the term of all beauty."

The desire of communicating to souls this knowledge of their own beauty, and thus hastening on the coming of God's reign, possessed his heart with ever-increasing ardor.

"What a mission is ours, Adolphe!" he cries. "I say it in trembling, in unutterable happiness— we are a few chosen from amongst so many, and we have received from God the *Divine secret*. The more I see of souls, the more convinced I am that these grand ideas of social and political progress by the rigorous application of the evangelical doctrines are rare, and rarely granted. It is astounding how little these blessed ideas have touched hearts, and how little they have penetrated the hard, dry soil of egotism! . . . Yet they alone can save France, they alone can save Christian civilization."

Henry returned from his visit to Chalais feeling refreshed in body, and stimulated to new ardor in the pursuit of his ideal. He resumed his work with great zest, but it was very soon brusquely interrupted. He was seized one morning in the street with a violent congestion of the lungs; he had burst a blood-vessel, and his life was once more in jeopardy. Skilful care and complete rest restored him for the time, but he felt that recovery was doubtful, and likely, at best, to be but partial.

"The moment I felt myself stricken," he writes to Père Lacordaire in the first days of convalescence, "the idea of a broken, useless life presented itself to me; but the very danger of my position brought a sort of consolation with it. I thought I was going to die, I waited for death, I hoped for it, I asked for it. It so happened I had been meditating on death lately a good deal; I had looked over my will, and made a good retreat, during which I felt for the first time perhaps, the joy of an unbounded abandonment to the will of God, and the hope of a life sacrificed for the service of truth and justice. In fact, I felt ready to go, and I was waiting for death, full of consolation and spiritual joy. But God would not have me. He flung me back into this world, and now I have got to live in it with the dread before me of a future without strength, disarmed, useless. . . . . Father, can you imagine what such a life must be for a soul that hoped to work and to fight? A life of ease and cowardice, fictitiously supported, of no use to anyone or anything. This prospect has given me more pain than all the rest. I try to turn away from it, but in vain; it is an *idée fixe* that devours me."

The allied armies were suffering gloriously in the east, and Henry's heart swelled with grief at not being able to go and solace his countrymen, "instead of taking care of himself and lying quiet."

"If I were a priest now, I would beg leave to go out as chaplain to the Crimea," he cries. "What is to become of me this winter? And my theology only just begun! . . . Pray for me. I know I must accept the will of God; but can I accept as such a life contrary to all He wills me to do? If He means me to be in His service, can He mean me to be an invalid, useless, sterile in works? . . . . I cannot, I *ought* not to believe this. I will do what God wishes me to do or I will die. Is it not so, Father?"

If the voice of the natural will is too clearly heard in this passionate appeal, it will serve to show later on how perfectly the triumph of the Divine will had been accomplished in a soul, as yet not entirely purified from self, but whose whole energies were bent upon the noble conquest. Henry regained sufficient strength to resume a certain amount of work, and the following letter shows us something of the spirit in which it was performed, and the rewards which it brought him.

"I had a nice day yesterday. . . . I had the happiness of coming in contact with one or two beautiful souls. The first was the soul of a child, a little soul of twelve years old. You never saw anything so beautiful! Imagine the most sparkling diamond, the most limpid crystal, and yet you have not even the symbol of this soul. I went to see the child in a convent where she is being brought up. God withdrew her, almost by a miracle, from the most dangerous surroundings, and placed her in this atmosphere of light and peace. The little creature feels His hand upon her soul. Her heart is a perpetual thanksgiving. She talks already of the religious life; I said to her, 'Marie, you must not think of that yet awhile; you are only a child now'; but I said interiorly to God—'Take her Lord. She is worthy of You!'... Another soul—a friend of my childhood, a poor young fellow of my own age, brilliant, rich, launched in the world, and lost, unless God saves him. He has faith, but.... well, he has a beautiful soul, for all that. But what a different kind of beauty from the first! It is beautiful as a ruin; beautiful, because it suffers.... I cannot tell you the compassion I feel for that soul. Nothing can be more beautiful, cast down and broken as it is.... This has taught me many things, and how our Lord could give His Blood for such an object of love."

We cannot wonder that one who was so keen to feel the beauty and value of souls should have suffered in no small degree from seeing these likenesses of God debased and blurred, even when not utterly broken, by the unhealthy influences of society, of life in general.

"The life of souls here below is a sad and curious spectacle," he says. "Take a bird, tie its wings so that it cannot fly, gag its throat so that it cannot sing, put a bandage round its eyes so that it may not see. Then shut it up in a narrow wooden cage in company with an immense number of other poor birds arranged in the same way. Then watch the awkward movements, the discomfort, the clumsy, blundering ways, the misery of this crowd of prisoners, without sight, or voice, or power of flying. I think you will have a very fair representation of the life of souls in human society."

A feeling that he was himself maimed and cramped in his power of working for these souls whom he loved so dearly, awoke in his heart an intense desire to at least suffer something for them. Prompted by this feeling, in a moment of extraordinary fervor he asked God to send him a humiliation. The prayer was answered almost immediately. Let him relate the incident himself.

"A circumstance in which I had acted rather giddily, out of kindness and to oblige another, brought me in contact with a personage whom I will not name, but who was the offended party. This man treated me as a wretch; he overpowered me with the most unjust reproaches and imposed silence on me when I tried to answer. I (naturally so quick and hasty) felt crushed by his violence, and incapable of defending myself. The next day I knew what a wound was. I had a fever, a thirst for reparation that was like a physical suffering. I had utterly forgotten my prayer and my promises, and I demanded the reparation. It was no sooner done *than I remembered!* It was rather late. I did what I could, and I forgave. But the whole thing has left in me a sort of interior soreness which is dreadful.... All this is cowardly. I am not a man. Forgive me. I hope to become one."

He was blessed with a natural gaity which added a great charm to his spiritual graces and intellectual gifts; he prized it himself, even in the spiritual order, and was on the watch to guard against the depression which bodily suffering is so apt to engender. He combated in himself and in others a tendency to melancholy, as the result of embittered self-love, and unworthy of a Christian.

"What do I hear of you being constantly in tears?" he writes to a relative. "I have never read anywhere that the Blessed Virgin had a *maladie noire* (blue devils) and, yet the Blessed Virgin had terrible trials! And, for that matter, is not everybody's malady a black malady? Do you imagine mine is rose-colored? When I see myself incapable of doing anything, whilst all my friends are working away, and that I am 'becoming a dunce,' as my old *bonne* says, do you suppose this is not black to me? But instead of crying over it, I try to laugh, and when one has said resolutely, 'No, I *won't* be cast down; God does not try us above our strength; there are thousands in Paris more to be pitied than I am.'... and such like thoughts, courage returns, and we find ourselves on our feet."

Speaking of himself in a moment of great physical suffering and prolonged inaction, he says; "It would grieve me if I were to grow sad; people don't like sad priests. I hope to get back my gaity."

And so he did; or rather, he never lost it; the sadness which he fought against so unselfishly was never more than a passing cloud which lent a sweeter charm to the brightness that soon returned. He got through the winter without any serious accident, but the warm weather was the signal for his departure again to Eaux Bonnes. After the usual course of waters, he went for a time to Biarritz (August 7, 1855.)

"I have been visiting a community of nuns extraordinarily edifying—holy women, who devote their lives to directing poor penitent girls. These latter are admirable; they dig the earth, they possess nothing, give themselves up to the most rigorous penance and for their reward aspire to become *Bernardines*. And this is what a Bernardine is, a holy soul who lives on the sands of the sea-shore, like the early anchorites of the deserts of Africa. She eat black bread and drinks water; she *never speaks*,... mind, *never!* (The Chartreux speak once a week; she, never), she dies after this long martyrdom, in which she has regained more honor and innocence than she has lost in her wanderings. The last who died—they showed me the new made grave—expired saying: 'How joyful it is to die when one loves God!' That is what I call a happy death. Will our's be like it?"

The effect of the waters, though beneficial, was

far from being entirely reassuring, and his friends, more uneasy than they dared confess, proposed to make a great, general novena for his recovery. The invalid heard of it and was grateful; but he had made long strides in the way of the cross since that passionate appeal to be allowed "to do what God meant him to do, or die."

"I don't ask for deliverance from this trial," he writes to an anxious friend, "I have seen too clearly how much the road to truth is shortened by passing through suffering to recoil from being led that way. I have a horror of it, a natural horror, for there does not exist a being less fit to suffer than I, nor one more easily frightened, more restive, more liable to exaggerate the evil, more accessible to anguish of soul; but I offer even this want of strength, this faint-heartedness, these childish fears, this weariness of spirit, to Him who in the Garden of Olives "began to tremble and to be sorrowful unto death."

(TO BE CONTINUED.)

Death of Rev. Father Edward I. Lilly, C. S. C.

On Tuesday evening, the 30th ult., Rev. Father Lilly departed this life at Notre Dame, after a protracted illness borne with edifying resignation to the Divine will. Though conscious to the last, he died without a struggle, just at the conclusion of the prayers for the dying. He had the happiness of being assisted in his last hours by his mother and sister, both religious. The funeral took place on New Year's day, and was attended by all the members of the Community, and numerous friends. The body was first conveyed to the Church of Our Lady of the Sacred Heart, where Vespers for the Dead were chanted, and then carried in procession to the graveyard, where it was laid to rest beside the other deceased priests of the Congregation.

Rev. Father Lilly came to Notre Dame a mere child, his heart still fresh with baptismal dews; here he passed his life, dying as he had lived, and bearing the white robe of innocence unspotted to the grave. He remained for some years with his venerable grandmother, still a resident at the neighboring convent, and attended class at the College. When he had attained his fifteenth year, he manifested a desire to enter the Community, and was received. After completing the usual term of probation he made his religious profession. On the Feast of Pentecost, 1872, having gone through the necessary studies, he was elevated to the priesthood. Possessed of musical talents of such a high order as to be considered a prodigy when only a little boy, he might have acquired world-wide fame had he been so disposed, and left a record that would be enduring. But ambition had no place in his heart. He was for many years a teacher of music at the University, and latterly director of that department.

The deceased was one of the most simple, unworldly men we have ever known; his faults were the faults of a little child, without malice and without heed, and he seemed quite unconsious of the beautiful virtues which adorned his soul. A characteristic little incident of his last illness may be related. About a week before his death he called the writer to his bedside and expressed a wish to have an old habit procured for his burial, so that there might be *no waste*. Nothing would satisfy him but a promise to see that his commission was fulfilled. Death seemed to have no terrors for him; he prepared himself as calmly as if for a journey.

Father Lilly died in the flower of his age, not having completed his thirty-fifth year.

> Death takes us by surprise,
> And stays our hurrying feet;
> The great design unfinished lies,
> Our lives are incomplete.
>
> But in the dark unknown
> Perfect their circles, seem,
> Even as a bridge's arch of stone
> Is rounded in the stream.

MR. SAMUEL HUDSON.

We beg the charitable prayers of the readers of THE AVE MARIA for our father, who died suddenly at his home near Boston, last Saturday. Though not a Catholic he was a God-fearing man and led a blameless life. The Blessed Virgin sang: "And His mercy is from generation unto generation to them that fear him."

Requiescant in pace.

Letter from Rome.

AVE GRATIA PLENA!

I.
Pulchra nites
Virgo
Radianti solis amictu
Praecincta et serto
Tempora
Sidereo.

II.
Undique inextinctus
Ambita nitoribus
Eos
Ceu roseum fundens
Ardua ab axe
Jubar.

III.
Solve igitur terras
Stygia caligine
Mersas
Nueis miseram abduntur
Lucida templa
Poli.

IV.
Pulsa redde diem
Nocte
Urbi rursus et orbi
Ah! redeant soles
Candidi et usque
Micent.

ROME, Dec. 11, 1879.

DEAR "AVE MARIA": This epigraph is by Prof. David Farabulini. I have selected it from the many that have been written on this occasion of the twenty-fifth anniversary of the definition of the Immaculate Conception, because it struck me as being the most beautiful, and, at the same time, prayerful. Let me paraphrase the last paragraph: Ah! yes, dearest Mother, putting the night to flight, give back the glorious day, both to the Eternal City and to the world. Let the bright Sun return and shine on!

And it did return on last Monday, careering through the cold blue heaven that overcircled Rome. And this was the orb of day. But the orb of faith gleamed with even greater brightness, certainly with greater warmth. Was it that heaven came down nearer to the dear old city? or did the dear old city lift up its broken heart at the jubilant *SURSUM CORDA* of its happy children, who vied with each other in celebrating their great Mother's Twenty-Fifth Immaculate Anniversary? Somewhat of both, methinks. Thousands, aye, tens o of thousands, of faithful souls united in His name and in her name. Their hearts went upwards, and He fulfilled the old promise and came down amongst them, and with Him came His Mother. And what was that I said about the Twenty-Fifth Immaculate anniversary? she was always Immaculate, *ab initio et ante sæcula!* It is a dogma as old as Christianity—yes, older—going back to that day in Eden when an angry yet merciful God vowed that He would put enmities between the wily Serpent and the Woman. *Inimicitias ponam inter te et Mulierem.* To the glorious Pius IX was reserved the glory of giving formality to the dogma *always believed.* He it was who at last gave definite signification to that enmity between the Woman and the Serpent, showing what crushing his head meant. There could not be enmity between Her and the devil, if it were possible to tempt her. Hence she was conceived Immaculate. And so it fell out that Rome seemed to celebrate a feast likewise in honor of the "Pontiff of the Immaculate Conception."

Pardon me if, in speaking of the celebration of the great event, I use the trite figure, it beggared description. This is literal. Every church and chapel in Rome solemnized the day. But particular notice may be made of the patriarchal Basilicas,—St. Mary Major's especially—and of the churches of the Holy Apostles, the Gesù, and that of the Immaculate Conception, where the Capuchins officiate. The churches of the Holy Apostles and that of the Gesù vied with each other in the magnificence of the decorations and ceremonies. A solemn novena of preparation was celebrated in both churches, and both churches were crowded to excess each day. But I would speak of the Gesù. The Gesù has always been the darling church of the old Roman aristocracy. Until 1873 it was the church of the Jesuits. So it brought back old times to hear the silver-tongued Father Gallerain, S. J., hold forth in his familiar pulpit. How can I describe the effect in a magnificent church of thirty thousand lights resplendant amid a forest of chandeliers of rock crystal? The splendid decorations? The music that lifted the soul hence and sent it quivering with pure delight through a welkin warmed with the presence of God? I must be prosaic, stating, by way of information, that the entire expense—and it must have been fabulous—of the celebration at the Gesù was borne by a wealthy Italian lady.

The greatest feature of the occasion was the arrival in Rome, and reception at the Vatican, of the Sixth Italian Pilgrimage, organized by the *Gioventù Cattolica*—Young Men's Catholic Association—of Bologna. The pilgrimage numbered 700, and represented as many as 100 dioceses of Italy. On Sunday morning, the 7th, they all met at an early hour in St. Peter's, where they heard Mass and received Holy Communion from the hands of Cardinal Oreglia, protector of the Catholic Associations of Rome. After the Mass they chaunted the *Miserere*, and then went in a body and knelt before the tomb of Pius IX. Many of them wept while kneeling there, for they remembered that voice which time and again thrilled them in the hall of the Consistory, above in the Vatican. In the evening, a reception was tendered them in the Conservatory of the Arcadians by the Circle of St. Peter. Discourses proper to the occasion were delivered by several orators, chief of whom was the great ecclesiastical historian, Don Pietro Balan, now Sub-Archivist of the Holy See.

On the joyful morrow at noon, they were all assembled in the Consistorial Hall. They represent flower of the Italian aristocracy. A glorious contrast they presented to the popular assemblages which boast that they represent the Italian nation. It was an assemblage of grave, gentle-mannered, educated gentlemen, of tranquil-visaged matrons, of beautiful maidens and modest children. They presented a true picture of Catholic Italy. The Pope appeared, surrounded by seventeen cardinals, by his entire household, and by many prelates, native and foreign. A cheer of *Evviva Leone XIII* rang through the hall. The Pope mounted the steps of his throne; but before seating himself he glanced comprehensively over the assembly, while a smile of joy radiated his countenance. When he had seated himself, Commendatore Acquaderni, President of the Superior Council of the *Gioventù Cattolica*, approached the throne, and read a noble address, which may be briefly characterized as an act of faith in the dogma of the Immaculate Conception. When he had concluded, himself, Chev. Ugo Flandoli, and other gentlemen of the Young Men's Catholic Association, together with Prof. Filippo Tolli, President of the Circle of St. Peter in Rome, presented to the Holy Father offerings in Peter's Pence in the name of different dioceses of Italy.

Arising to his feet, the Holy Father said: "On this most joyous day in which is consummated the fifth lustrum since the proclamation of the Immaculate Conception of Mary, it is just in sooth, O dearest children, that your hearts and those of all the faithful should expand with unusual gladness, the fruit of the dearest memories. Twenty-five years have already passed since our glorious predecessor, Pius IX of happy memory, for whom Providence had reserved the lot of giving to the Virgin a most splendid gem and of associating with her's his own glories, promulgated to the Catholic world, obedient and applauding, the dogmatic decree of the Immaculate Conception of Mary, and soon the faithful, moved by a most fervent love of their Mother, tender in what concerned her greatness, full of sweet hopes, devoted themselves then and in subsequent years to celebrating everywhere with magnificent pomp her singular prerogative.

At the approach of the first jubilee of that memorable day, on the occasion of the Fifth Pilgrimage to Rome, you manifested in our presence the intention of wishing to celebrate more solemnly the twenty-fifth anniversary of the dogmatic definition; and we,—it is pleasant to remember it—finding that this holy idea corresponded perfectly with our own wishes, praised it highly, and with our all our heart blessed it, being disposed to open more widely the heavenly treasure of Indulgences.

In such a happy circumstance, the Bishops of the Catholic world, in their pastoral zeal were solicitous in appealing to the devotion of their diocesans; and these responded willingly to the invitation, so that in a short time an ardent desire sprang up everywhere, and a noble emulation, to honor with splendid demonstrations of religious piety the Virgin without a stain. And while you, wisely placing under her auspices your Sixth Pilgrimage, assembled near the tomb of the Prince of the Apostles, in the august Basilica whence was proclaimed to the world the wonderful privilege, and confirmed to-day by a new and solemn protestation your obedience to the Vicar of Jesus Christ; in all Italy, or better, throughout the whole world, there has been but one thought common to the true believers, to give honor to the Virgin Immaculate, to exalt her glories, to recommend to her the Church and the Visible Head who now governs it.

This outburst of piety, of devotion, so ardent, so universal, so unanimous, consoles us greatly: in the midst of the fight which now wages fiercely against the Church, it revives the hope of a complete triumph over error and hell. In fact, the error which sums up all, and which most of all renders delirious the proud minds of our age, is that cold and base naturalism which has finally invaded all the orders of public and private life, substituting human for divine reason, nature for grace, and ignoring the Redeemer. Now the Virgin by her Immaculate Conception opportunely reminds the faithful that by the fall of the first father the whole human race lay for many ages weak and infirm, the slave of error and the passions; that only from Jesus is derived in abundance grace, truth, salvation, life; that without Him there is no dignity for man, no greatness, no real good: that, finally, whoever tries to withdraw himself from the beneficent influence of the Redeemer, remains in darkness, falls into the mire, meets with certain ruin. Besides this, the Immaculate Conception reveals to us the secret and the first cause of the great power of Mary over the common enemy, who, by means of his trusty ministers, wages so fierce a war against the Church. Because faith therein teaches us that Mary from the beginning of the world was destined to exercise against the demon and his seed implacable and eternal enmity: *Inimicitias ponam inter te et mulierem:* and that from the first instant of her being, she victoriously crushed his proud head: *Ipsa conteret caput tuum.* This thought inspires confidence in her, who, strong in the power of her Son, extinguished all heresies, and was in the most critical moments the shield and immediate help of Christians. This thought inspires in hearts the certainty that this time, too, the final victory will be Mary's.

You, dearest children, and with you all believing people, in the frank and open profession of your faith, by the practice of virtuous works, by sincere devotion to the Virgin, hasten the desired moment in which the human family will again rejoice in the signal benefits of the Redemption of Christ; hasten the desired moment in which the storm being quieted through the intercession of the great Mother of God, days of prosperity, of peace, of glory, will shine again upon the Church.

Meanwhile, to increase your piety, to confirm your holy resolutions, as a pledge of our paternal affection, receive, dearest children, the Apostolic Benediction, which from the bottom of our heart we liberally bestow upon you, your families, your works. *Benedictio,*" etc.

After this discourse, many of the pilgrims were admitted into the Holy Father's presence in order to present their individual offerings. Finally he descended from his throne and walked through the hall amid the pilgrims, stopping to converse affably with those who manifested a desire to speak to him. As he left the hall it rang anew with lusty cheers of *Evviva Leone XIII!*

Nor did these good pilgrims forget the spot where the remains of Pius IX will repose ultimately. In the afternoon, a deputation repaired to the quiet but sumptuous Basilica of San Lorenzo, outside the city walls, and appended near the tomb of the glorious martyr-deacon a garland, in the midst of which was the following inscription:

ON THIS DAY, THE 8TH OF DECEMBER, 1879,
WHICH MARKS
THE TWENTY-FIFTH ANNIVERSARY
SINCE PIUS IX, SOVEREIGN PONTIFF,
PROCLAIMED MARY CONCEIVED WITHOUT ORIGINAL
SIN,
THE PILGRIMS OF CATHOLIC ITALY
TO THE SACRED MEMORY
OF THE GREAT PONTIFF INSPIRED BY GOD
THIS GARLAND,
SYMBOL OF ETERNITY AND GLORY,
DEPOSITED.

It is evening. Let us return to the Gesù. But it is impossible to enter. Nay, we cannot even mount the steps. The square itself is crowded. We can only see a firmament of brilliant lights gleaming over the surging yet reverent throng. We can hear the music of the *Tantum Ergo.* We can get a glimpse of the old congregation of the Roman Nobles moving up to the high altar bearing torches. Then there is silence. We kneel down in the street, for Jesus is held aloft in Sacramental benison,—and then a mighty voice—a voice of thousands blending into one—chants responsively to the intonation of the great pæan of the great Ambrose, *Te Dominum Confitemur!* Then three choirs sing the alternate verses to the music of the immortal Terziani. But what is musical harmony compared with that great, all-hushing unison of the Plain Chant? A great jubilant heart is uplifted to God, and its music re-echoes even to the summit of the Capitol.

All disperse in perfect order. The city is illuminated. Catholic Rome has asserted herself.

A Decree, *Urbis et Orbis,* of the Sacred Congregation of Rites, bearing the date of November 30th, has been published, which, in gracious consideration of the petitions of many Bishops, elevates the Feast and Office of the Immaculate Conception to the rank of a Double of the First Class for the whole world, establishing also a *Missa Vigiliæ* as enjoyed hitherto by several dioceses.

ARTHUR.

Catholic Notes.

——The Index, with title-page of Vol. XV of THE AVE MARIA, is nearly ready. It will be sent to those who desire it, on application.

——The eldest daughter of Paul Feval, the distinguished Catholic writer, has taken the resolution to become a member of the Visitation Order.

——DOM CLEMENT PAGNANI, of the Order of St. Benedict, has been appointed Vicar-Apostolic of Columba, in place of Mgr. Silani, deceased last March.

——The Little Sisters of the Poor in Brooklyn have one room in their building for women over one hundred years of age. There were recently five inmates of the room.

——At the conclusion of the annual retreat of the Young Men's Sodality of St. Francis Xavier's Church, St. Louis, Mo., last month, over one thousand men received Holy Communion.

——RT. REV. WILLIAM HENRY ELDER, D. D., the great and good Bishop of Natchez, Miss., from Nov. 15 to Dec. 15 of last year confirmed forty converts in his episcopal visits through that State.—*Catholic Universe.*

——HISTORY OF THE VATICAN COUNCIL.—Three

more volumes of the History of the Vatican Council, edited by His Grace the Archbishop of Florence, have just been completed. The work is sent to all the Fathers of the Council free of cost.

—We learn that a Church History of West Virginia will soon appear. An old pioneer of this State, a ready and fluent writer, who has been gathering the particulars for many years in various localities, has almost completed his work. The history, we hear, will commence with the early Indian Missions, and ending with the year 1880.—*Catholic Messenger.*

—REV. FATHER COONEY, C. S. C., concluded a very successful mission last week in St. Andrew's Church, New York. There was an immense number of confessions, and a great many took the pledge at the closing exercises. Father Cooney gave a lecture on "The Church and the Bible," for the benefit of the poor of the parish, after the mission.

—THE MOST REV. ARCHBISHOP OF CORDOVA has offered a price of 1,500 reals to any Catholic writer for the best essay on the duties of Catholic workmen, refuting the popular errors now so widely spread among the laboring classes of society. The proceeds of the sale of the volume are intended for the benefit of the Catholic associations of workingmen established in the diocese.

—MOTHER M. JEROME, on the late festival of the Immaculate Conception of the Blessed Virgin, was re-elected Superioress of the Sisters of Charity. Her life is not one of the least remarkable among the record of those who have devoted themselves to the service of the Church in this country. Stretching far back over more than half a century, her religious career forms a glorious link between the humble beginnings of the Church in New York and the wonderful growth it has now attained.—*New York Tablet.*

—DISCOURAGING RESULTS.—A committee of the Park Street Church, Boston, reported lately that it had made patient investigation among the converts of the recent revival meetings in that city, and found a marked falling from grace among those who had been most earnest in religious professions a year ago. The Rev. Dr. Withrow, in reading the report from his pulpit, said that with few exceptions the converts had relapsed into a condition worse than that in which they were previous to their professed change of heart.

—ARCHBISHOP M'HALE.—The following letter has been addressed to Mr. E. D. Gray, M. P., by the illustrious Archbishop of Tuam: "My dear Dwyer Gray,—After the very many obligations which the *Freeman's Journal* has laid me under for more than threescore years by publications of relief in those seasons of distress which have been so frequent, I did hope that we should be spared any recurrence of those duties of gratitude which seasonable relief requires. Within those few days an English clergyman sent me for the poor £2; Michael Campbell, Esq., £5; Edward Lucas, £5. I have the honor to remain your faithful servant, "✠ JOHN, Archbishop of Tuam."

—MGR. MASSAJA, VICAR-APOSTOLIC OF THE GALLAS MISSION, who was lately arrested, and confined in the fortress Devra Tabor, is a native of Piova in Italy, and a member of the Capuchin Order. Since 1846, he has been engaged in the Abyssinian mission, of which he has been Vicar-Apostolic since May 4th of the same year. He has a coadjutor, Mgr. Taurin. Considerable anxiety is felt about the fate of Mgr. Massaja, although, according to Mr. Bianchi, an influential and wealthy Italian merchant residing at the court of King Johannes, nothing more forcible than a transportation to Europe is likely to ensue. The missionary district under Mgr. Massaja was formerly independent of the Abyssinians. Mgr. Taurin has been obliged by the hostile attitude of the new *regime* to abandon three stations in the northren part of the mission, and to retire to the south-eastern region, where the Gallas and other tribes still maintain their independence.

—THE CONDITION OF THE CHURCH IN ARMENIA is slowly but steadily improving. Here, as in many other places, the real mischief makers are the freethinkers and freemasons. Seeing themselves disappointed lately, in so many of their nefarious schemes the grandmaster of the Armenian lodge assembled a band of forty young men from among the neo-schismatics and repaired to the Nestorian Patriarch at Koum Kapon. This opened the eyes of the well-meaning Christians among the neo-schismatics, and caused them to enter at once into negotiations with the Armenian Catholics, to whom they belonged before their defection. The best results are hoped from these negotiations. Mgr. Kupelian, the former leader of these erring people, who made a solemn recantation of his errors and asked pardon of the Holy Father at Rome last year in person, has been laboring with great zeal since his return to Constantinople for the conversion of his former adherents. Other Armenian Catholic priests are working with much success for the conversion of the Gregorian Armenians, who for centuries have held to the Nestorian heresy.

—THE 25TH ANNIVERSARY OF THE DEFINITION OF THE IMMACULATE CONCEPTION was celebrated throughout the entire Catholic world with the greatest splendor. Italy, France, Spain, Poland and Catholic Germany, all Catholic peoples in the Old and the New World vied with each other in honoring our heavenly Queen. The centre of the Universal Church, the Eternal City of Rome, welcomed on that day pilgrims from all parts of the globe, prominent among whom was a band from England. There was also a procession of Spanish pilgrims, who had set out from Barcelona on the 20th of November. They continued their journey to the Holy Land, after the celebration in Rome. In some of the Spanish republics of South America, too, where for half a century secret societies have held sway, the glorious memory of our Immaculate Mother revived the old Catholic spirit. On the day of the feast the Pia Union de la Immaculata, an association founded in 1602, was solemnly reorganized in the Church of San Francisco at Buenos Ayres. The pastoral letters issued by so many Bishops and Archbishops in different countries on the occasion formed a sublime concert of praise to our Immaculate Mother.

New Publications.

PRELUDES. By Maurice F. Egan. Published to Aid in the Rebuilding of the University of Notre Dame. Philadelphia: Peter P. Cunningham & Son, 817 Arch street. 1880. Price, $1 (post free).

Poetry! aye, the pure gold of true poesy! It is a long time since we have enjoyed reading verse like this. Not that it is all equal, but there are poems here bathed through and through with the limpid light of Keats,—that sweet intellectual Greek light which shone only upon Keats and perhaps Mrs. Browning, of English poets, and upon no American poet before Mr. Egan. If we substitute Grecian for pagan in his poem on Maurice de Guérin we shall, with a change or two more, well describe our poet himself, for

A Grecian heart, a Christian soul has he

He follows Christ, yet beauteous nature loves,
Till earth and heaven meet within his breast.

It is easy to discover the authors in whom he delights,—Keats, Shakspeare, Chaucer, the De Guérins Dante and the Grecian poets. What an exalted company! and yet our author is worthy of that companionship. Were we asked to point out the poems that justify this criticism, we should name the poem already referred to "Theocritus," "November," "Of Flowers," and others. Of a higher rank are "Fra Angelico," "Raphael," "Frederic Ozanam," "Arière Pensée," "A Pierced Heart," "Troubled Souls," "The Lesson of a Season," "Consolation," "After Lent," and the "Workers." Whoever is capable of appreciating these noble verses will surely have a more exalted sense of life and duty after reading them. The Sonnets in memory of O'Connell are fine pieces, especially the first and the third. There is a bitter strength in the third which comes from the heart—alas, it is the truth but too well uttered. Some of the lighter pieces are very pretty, though a vein of sadness runs through them all—all true poetry, 'tis said, is written in tears. "Apple Blossoms," "A Rhapsody," "Drifting," are excellent in this way. Well, have we no fault to find with this youthful genius? None with the poems we have mentioned and others, and very little with any. Occasionally a little over labor, occasionally a little incompleteness, at times a little that may seem commonplace. That is what we think, even if we mistake. For instance, how poor is "Cervantes" compared to the superb pieces that precede and follow it? Is not "Marguerite" too near what Goethe wrote himself? At least two poems, so it seems to us, are spoiled by the "morals" tacked to them, "Illusion" and "Hylas,"—there is nothing more unpoetical than explaining poetry. That should be left to poor critics, like ourselves. The poet should not unlock his own doors, kindred spirits can pass into his most guarded temple, even to the veiled shrine, and none else should be admitted.

But we might write of this little book for hours. It stands the tone test of good Composition—it is suggestive. Every poem fills one brim full of thought. We lay it down delighted, flattering ourselves that we have poetical thoughts, when in truth it is the genius of the poet that has inspired us. Our readers will find many a beautiful poem which we have not mentioned. We trust all fair ladies will read the story of Dona Inez, who "was a lady," and profit thereby. Mr. Egan has done a pleasant thing for his readers in reserving one of his finest poems for the last. Too often the last pages of a book are used merely as "a stow-a-way" for useless lumber; but one of the finest and most characteristic poems of this volume is the concluding one. In conclusion, we know not how to express our appreciation of the honor and service the poet has done Notre Dame in the manner in which his volume has been given to the public. "Published to aid in the rebuilding of the University of Notre Dame," and dedicated to the Rev. Editor of THE "AVE MARIA." We hope that every one that loves Notre Dame and our Lady's Journal will buy, read and love these poems as we do.

The book is elegantly gotten up, and reflects credit on the publishers.   T. E. H.

FIVE-MINUTE SERMONS for Low Masses on all the Sundays of the Year. By Priests of the Congregation of St. Paul. Vol. I. New York: The Catholic Publication Society.

We receive with welcome the first volume of these excellent and well-known sermons. Their special merit is thoughtfulness and concentration; and they are eloquent in the sense of being thoroughly earnest. We cannot help feeling, as we read, not only that the preacher feels and means what he says, but that he has endeavored to say it in the most direct and forcible manner. There is more real substance in these little sermons than in many other collections of greater pretension; and if they do not possess eloquence of language they, have what is of much greater value, eloquence of thought.

THE FOUR ANTIPHONS OF THE BLESSED VIRGIN For two or three Voices, with Accompaniment for Organ or Melodeon. By Prof. John Singenberger, President of the American St. Cecilia Society. Price, 30 cts. a Copy; 12 Copies for $3. New York, Pustet, L. B. 3627; Chicago, Mühlbaur & Behrle; St. Louis. B. Herder, 19 South 5th st.

The composer of these pieces is already favorably known in church-music circles, having composed several Masses and a number of smaller pieces, motetts, etc., which are sung wherever the Cecilian reform has made its way. These four antiphons—*Alma Redemtoris, Ave Regina Cœlorum, Regina Cœli,* and *Salve Regina*—will prove a most acceptable addition to Prof. Singenberger's other musical compositions; the arrangement—soprano and alto, with the privilege of leaving out the bass—will save choir-leaders in our academies and convent schools a great deal of trouble. Thus filling a special want, they will no doubt be appreciated by many an overworked choir-leader and musician. The pieces are not difficult of execution, and are, moreover, devotional and pleasing. They are stitched together in a neat blue paper cover. The collection is dedicated to the venerable Mother Mary Caroline, Superior of the School Sisters of Notre Dame at Milwaukee, Wis.

THE IRISH AMERICAN ALMANAC FOR 1880. New York: Lynch, Cole & Meehan.

The present number of this popular Almanac is the best we have seen. The publishers are the proprietors of the newspaper of the same name, much prized by Irish priests in this country as an antidote to the *Irish World,* of which the less said the better.

PEARL. By Kathleen O'Meara, author of "Life of Frederic Ozanam," "Are You My Wife?" etc., etc. New York: The Catholic Publication Society Co., No. 9 Barclay St.

Those who have read the other beautiful stories of Miss O'Meara know beforehand what to expect in "Pearl"; whilst those who have not read any of them can be assured that they have a rich treat in store. As a biographer or a writer of fiction Miss O'Meara succeeds admirably though not equally well, and she well richly deserves the place assigned her in the front rank of Catholic writers. To those who love a tale well told, who delight in characters and incidents well described, we say, get a copy of "Pearl." It will be read with pleasure, and recommended to fiction-loving friends.

THE STORY OF JESUS SIMPLY TOLD FOR THE YOUNG By Rosa Mulholland. With a Preface by Rev. Richard Brennan, LL. D. New York, Cincinnati, and St. Louis: Benziger Brothers.

A handsome little volume, in which the story of our Saviour's Life and the lessons—ever old and ever new—which it inculcates, are related in charming simplicity. At this season of gift-making, there are very few books so appropriate for presents to children as this,

Confraternity of the Immaculate Conception
(Or of Our Lady of Lourdes).

"We fly to thy patronage, O Holy Mother of God!"
REPORT FOR THE WEEK ENDING DECEMBER 31ST.

The following petitions have been received: Recovery of health for 72 persons and 2 families,—change of life for 37 persons and 4 families,—conversion to the Faith for 55 persons and 35 families,—special graces for 6 priests, 8 religious, 7 clerical students, and 4 persons aspiring to the religious state,—temporal favors for 17 persons and 5 families,—spiritual favors for 36 persons and 2 families,—the spiritual and temporal welfare of 5 communities, 2 congregations, 4 schools, and 2 orphan asylums,—also 24 particular intentions, and 5 thanksgivings for favors received.

Specified Intentions: Conversion, protection and safe return for several young men who have left their homes and their aged parents, some of whom are poor widows,—reconciliation of husband and wife,—change of life for several wayward girls,—an aged widow in trouble on account of an unjust lawsuit,—the payment of lawful debts, to needy creditors,—preservation of eyesight for a poor woman,—conversion of a Protestant in the last stage of consumption, and of a infidel on his death-bed,—several fathers and mothers of families in ill-health,—reconciliation of several families at variance, either among themselves or with other families.

FAVORS OBTAINED.

A grateful parent relates that his daughter, twenty-one years old, while returning home in a wagon was accidentally thrown out, and under the wheels, which had to be lifted before she could be released from her perilous situation. We thought she would have to stay in bed for some time; but some water of Lourdes was applied to the bruises, and she was able to go to her work next morning as if nothing had happened. Another correspondent writes: "I have the pleasure to inform you of a cure attributed to the water of Lourdes. One is that of a young girl, who has been delicate for eighteen months. Her mother was afraid of her going into consumption, and employed doctors and medicines to no purpose. I gave her some water of Lourdes, and, after making two novenas she was cured."

OBITUARY.

The prayers of the members of the Confraternity are requested for the following deceased persons: Rev. EDWARD LILLY, C. S. C., who died a happy death last week at Notre Dame. Mr. JOHN CASEY, of Erie, Pa., an estimable Catholic gentleman of whose death the sad news has just been received. [In the death of Mr. Casey, Erie has lost one of its most worthy and prominent citizens, and THE AVE MARIA a noble and generous friend.—Ed. A. M.] Mrs. M. MITCHELL, of Grand Rapids, Mich., deceased last August. JOSEPH MCENTEGART, of Liverpool, England, who was lately drowned at sea. SISTER MARY OF ST. ALEXANDER, (Mary Quinn) who slept in the Lord the 28th ult., at St. Mary's Academy, Notre Dame, Ind. Mr. PIERRE WHALEN, of Ashland, Ill., who met death by drowning. Rev. MOTHER MARY XAVIER, SISTERS MARY JOHN, EDWARD and BLANCHE, members of the Sisterhood of the Holy Child Jesus. WILLIAM GORMAN and KATE GORMAN, of Fredonia, Wis., Mrs. ELIZABETH DODDS, GEORGE and CATHARINE DODDS, THOMAS and MARY FORD, who died some time ago. And several others, whose names have not been given.

Requiescant in pace.

A. GRANGER, C. S. C., Director.

Youths' Department.

To Our Blessed Lady.

MOTHER of Mercy! day by day
My love of thee grows more and more;
Thy gifts are strewn upon my way,
Like sands upon the ocean's shore.

But scornful men have coldly said,
Thy love was leading me from God;
And yet in this I did but tread
The very path my Saviour trod.

They know but little of thy worth
Who speak these heartless words to me;
For what did Jesus love on earth
One half so tenderly as thee?

Procure me grace to love thee more,
Jesus will give, if thou wilt plead;
And, Mother! when life's cares are o'er
O, I shall love thee then, indeed!

Jesus, when His three hours were run,
Bequeathed thee from the Cross to me;
And O, how can I love thy Son,
Sweet Mother! if I love not thee?

The Story of a Revenge.

BY ELIZA ALLEN STARR.

(CONTINUED.)

THE mild winter of Florence is over, but not a day has been unadorned by some rose blooming in the open air. The holy Lenten season of penance has come, and with it there is a quickening of sap through the forests, a tinge of green in the grass, and the almond trees are putting forth buds. It would seem as if nature, in this charming clime, could not wait for the sacred drama of Redemption and the Resurrection to be duly acted out; but she anticipates the Passion of her Lord, and calls on her fragrant violets to leave their hiding places and to shed their chaste perfumes over His feet as did once St. Mary Magdalene. But while all this is going on under the rays of the early vernal sun, souls are quickening under the touch of heavenly grace. The Florentines, so gay on a festival, know the meaning of penance, and how to practice it. One of their favorite devotions is the *Via Crucis*, or Way of the Cross. In 1020 the people were not accustomed to make this devotion before pictures. A simple cross marked the stations on this way of sorrows, and the minds of the people were not slow to picture for themselves the various acts of our Lord on His weary walk to Calvary. Neither did they need books to read from. Familiar as they were with the incidents commemorated by each of these stations, they had only to imagine them for a moment, and our Lord was in the hall of Pilate, bore His Cross, fell under its grievous weight, met His Blessed Mother, consoled Saint Veronica by leaving the image of His Face on her linen veil, was stripped of His garments, nailed to a Cross, laid in the sepulchre—all the same as if He had been actually before them; and they followed after Him with the holy women, pitying and bewailing Him, without ever looking into a book. But it was not in the churches that these Stations of the Cross were most to the public mind. It was into the open air, on the side of some hill where the winding path gave them time to meditate between each station, that the people flocked during Lent for the stations. San Miniato seemed to have been made expressly for these stations of the Cross, and nothing could have been more touching than the devotion of the people to this pious practice. Laurina, however, was not satisfied with following along with the crowd at the appointed time. Whenever her burden seemed too great for her to bear, she joined her Lord on the way to Calvary, and helped Him to bear His Cross who had accepted it for her sake. The tender blue of the vernal skies, the breath of new blown violets, the faint odor from the cypress trees, the coo of the ring-doves in the deep groves, seemed to have lost their charm for the senses of Laurina. To her the wet days and sunny were all alike, and she was found making this painful journey to Calvary in the open air in all weathers. "See," the people would whisper to each other, as they saw her flitting from one station-cross to another, "see how the signora * prays for the soul of young Hugo, cut off in the beauty of life, without even an absolution spoken over him!" And the patrician mothers, as they watched her growing daily thinner and thinner, yet never leaving the station-crosses unvisited, would sigh: "Poor Laurina! young Hugo's death sits heavily on her soul"; and then they would remember how many old feuds and sharp quarrels were among their own sons and lords, and they trembled lest a blow as cruel as the one dealt by Luigi might not fall on some of their households. Hugo indeed needed his mother's prayers, and he had them; but the abbot of San Miniato knew that Giovanni was not forgotten at the stations.

Count Gualberto and Giovanni spurned the idea of becoming devotees themselves, but were still very glad to have the poor Countess Laurina win suffrages for Hugo. It never entered their minds that their schemes for vengeance made the burden of Laurina's petitions. "Honor," they said, "claimed the life of Luigi." But the countess still prayed on, and at last, a sort of awe took possession of Giovanni whenever he saw his mother kneeling at those stations of the cross on the steeps of San Miniato. For some reason, and, it was guessed, for some reason which would bear hard upon Luigi, Count Gualberto left his palace in the city and lived in his villa some distance from the gates. But this distance was easily gone over by the Count or by Giovanni, mounted on their steeds fit for war horses. As to Laurina, her feet now seemed to crave penance and she would always walk the distance.

The gayest festival of the year did not draw the Florentines from their homes like the last Friday of Lent, or Good Friday. It would seem as if the city rose up like one man; and sinner as well as saint was sure to join the throngs that pressed into every church to hear the Passion of our Lord sung by the monks. Not however in chorus, like the psalms, where every monk is in his stall,* but by three voices; one taking the part of Pilate and of the Jews, which is done by a voice on a very high key; and another that of our Lord, in a low, but O, how sweet a key! while a third takes the part of the narrator and tells the story as it is given in the Gospels. How real is the scene thus recalled to the eye and ear! That awful shout from the multitude: "Crucify Him, crucify Him!" strikes horror to the soul of whoever listens; coming, as it seems to do by that high voice, from some far-off host of malignant spirits. And the horror only changes to a heart-breaking compassion when the low, sweet voice of our Redeemer utters, painfully, one of the seven words spoken on the Cross. Strong men weep during this singing of the Passion, and when we hear it for the first time, for the first time do we realize the awful scenes in the hall of Pontius Pilate, on the road to Calvary and on the Cross.

Giovanni might be vindictive, implacable; but he was not one of the youths to turn his back upon our Lord. Therefore, on the morning of Good Friday he mounted his steed and rode swiftly from the villa to Florence and to the Church of San Zenobia, which was then the Cathedral, as the church which is built on the spot is still. Never, Giovanni thought, had he heard the Passion sung as on that day. He forgot the monks; forgot to note the quality of each voice, and to pronounce on its excellence. He was no longer in one of the churches in Florence,

---

* Lady.

* The *stalls* of the monks are seats arranged along the walls of the sanctuary, on each side of the Abbot; the altar standing in front of them.

but in the Judgment hall of Pilate, with the crowd below the balcony where our Lord comes forth clad in a scarlet cloak, crowned with thorns, a reed for a sceptre, while Pilate calls forth, *Ecce Homo!*—Behold the Man! And then he was one of the crowd crying out: "Crucify Him!" heard, too, the horrible blasphemies spoken against Him, heard the whips as they scourged this Man who had "gone about doing good." And again he was one of the crowd jostling each other, pressing upon the steps of the sinless Lamb led forth to be sacrificed. He saw the Cross rise on Mount Calvary bearing its precious load, and the white figure, so meek in its agony, shone out before his eyes against the blackness of that three hours' eclipse. He saw the thieves who were crucified with Him, one on each side; the one who reviled, the one too who said in his repentance: "Remember me, Lord, when Thou comest into Thy Kingdom;" and the divine answer: "This day thou shalt be with Me in Paradise." He heard the "Vah! vah!" of the mocking scribes and pharisees, and then, sweeter, tenderer, meeker, lower than all, that prayer, "Father, forgive them, for they know not what they do!" The whole passed before him, was heard by him, not as a drama but as a reality; and the strong young man bent his head to the very ground in the fulness of his compassion.

The Mass was over; the crucifix had been kissed by weeping crowds; Giovanni's lips were among the first to touch the image of his crucified Lord, and now, young and old pour forth into the street. What was it that Giovanni saw or heard which suddenly changed the whole temper of his mind? No one can say; but, mounted on his swift charger, he has passed through the city gate and is making his way along the narrow forest road among the ravines and short turns of Mount San Miniato, or San Miniato of the Mount, while his sole meditation is on the surest means to snare young Luigi and to stab him to the heart without one moment of preparation, one moment in which to make an act of contrition. With this picture firing his brain, he dashes along the steep bridle-path, the boughs touching him on either hand, till he enters a well-known ravine, sombre, shut in by high rocks, and so narrow as to give barely a footing for his horse. Suddenly, with a turn of the road, a figure stands before him, pale, haggard, the undressed hair falling around his face to his shoulder. "Can it be!" and at the moment, as the eyes of both meet, "Luigi!" he cries, with a fierce cry: "Luigi at last!"

Swift as lightning Giovanni's sword is drawn from its scabbard and flashes in the sunlight of the forest over his foe. But that foe no longer meets his sword with a sword. No cry of supplication even comes from the pale lips; but throwing himself on his knees he extends his arms as our Lord extended His on the Cross, and a voice as low, as tender, as agonizing as that which Giovanni had heard only an hour before, conjured him: "By the Passion of Christ, this day celebrated, spare the life which God has given into thy hands!"

The outspread arms, the pallid, suffering face, the voice so meek in its supplication, the sacred Name by which it entreats, overwhelms the soul of Giovanni. The lips which had but just now kissed the crucifix, what could they speak, unless words of forgiveness? The sword dropped at his side. Leaping from his horse, he throws himself on his knees beside Luigi, embracing him while the tears streamed down his cheeks. "Forgive me," he cried, "O Luigi, my friend, for whom Christ died! What am I, that I should lift my sword against thee? And from what an awful crime has not the Crucified One withheld my hand? Henceforth be to me more than a friend, as a dear brother!"

Laurina, has not thy prayer been answered? But what suffrage of thine ever won for Hugo what the fierce Giovanni now offers for the soul of his brother?

(TO BE CONTINUED.)

Anecdote of Cardinal Viviers.

JOHN de Brogni, Cardinal of Viviers, who presided at the Council of Constance, as dean of the Cardinals, had been a hog driver in his youth. Some monks passing by the place where he was busied in that employment, and observing his wit and vivacity, offered to take him to Rome, and give him a chance to study. He accepted their offer, and went straight to a shoemaker to buy a pair of shoes for his journey; the shoemaker trusted him for part of the price, and told him, smiling, he might pay him the rest whenbe was a Cardinal. He became a Cardinal in reality, and did not forget his former low condition; in a chapel which he built at Geneva, he caused this adventure to be carved in a stone. He was represented young and without shoes, to express the favor he had received from the shoemaker.

A beautiful story is told of a poor crazy man who was in the habit of following St. Antony about when he was preaching, and disturbing him by his cries. The Saint gently begged him to be quiet. "I cannot," he said, "unless you give me your girdle." Antony immediately came down from the pulpit, and gave it to him. The man kissed it, and put it on. And as he did so, his reason was fully restored to him.

THE AVE MARIA.

A Journal devoted to the Honor of the Blessed Virgin.

HENCEFORTH ALL GENERATIONS SHALL CALL ME BLESSED.—*St. Luke, 1, 48.*

VOL. XVI. NOTRE DAME, INDIANA, JANUARY 17, 1880. No. 3.

[Copyright: Rev. D. E. Hudson, C. S. C.]

Saint Agnes, Virgin and Martyr.

THE devotion to Saint Agnes is most ancient; and Saint Jerome, in a letter to the holy virgin Demetrias, represents it as already in his time universal in all the churches. Her glories have been sung by the poet Prudentius, and her virtues and martyrdom were held up as conspicuous examples by such Pontiffs and Doctors as Saints Augustine, Ambrose, Martin, Damasus, Maximus of Turin, and Gregory the Great.

Agnes was a Roman, the child of a noble family. Born of Christian parents, hers was the proud illustration of being (according to a phrase of early Christian epigraphy) *Fidelis ex Fidelibus*,* —that is, one who was not a convert, but sprung from a line of Christian ancestors.

She consecrated her virginity to God from a tender age; and when a wealthy young man, son of the Prefect of the city, sought to obtain her hand in marriage, she steadily refused him. Baffled in his passion, the youth denounced her as a Christian. To break her constancy, it was ordered by the impious judge that she should be exposed in a place of ill-repute to lose her precious virginity unless she would consent to the importunities of her pagan lover. Many wonders of divine protection saved her from dishonor; and after a vain attempt to burn her alive—the fire refusing to encircle so chaste a body—she was struck with the sword. Her martyrdom took place in the year 304, the second of Diocletian's persecution, when she had not yet completed her thirteenth year. Her body was deposited by her parents on a property which they owned about one mile from the city, along the Nomentan Way and the crypt containing her sacred remains is the chief object of devotion in one of Rome's most famous Catacombs. Her Feast is celebrated on the 21st of January, the anniversary of her death; and another Feast is kept on the 28th of the same month, to commemorate a vision in which she appeared to her parents and consoled them. Saint Ambrose, in an epistle addressed to consecrated virgins, thus narrates the event: "It so happened that the parents of blessed Agnes, who kept a perpetual watch at her tomb, had a vision at the dead of night in which they saw a company of virgins, all dressed in queenly robes embroidered with gold, pass slowly before them surrounded by a great effulgence of light, and in their midst walked the holy Agnes as richly clad as they, but distinguished from the rest by a milk-white lamb which stood at her right hand. This sight surprised them; but Agnes, asking her sisters to tarry awhile, spoke to her parents, and said: 'Weep not for me as though I were dead; but rather rejoice with me and be glad, for with these others I have been admitted to the realms of perpetual splendor, and am united in heaven to Him whom I loved with my whole heart on earth.' This spoken, she disappeared."

The lamb seen in this vision has furnished Christian artists with the special iconographic sign of Saint Agnes, and has also given rise to the curious and ancient custom of blessing two lambkins on her Feast-day, after Pontifical Mass celebrated in her basilica by the Lord Abbot of the adjoining monastery. From their wool the archiepiscopal pallia are made. The name of Agnes is inscribed in the Canon of the Mass, and is found in all the oldest sacramentaries—a liturgical honor accorded to but very few holy women. There are two churches in Rome dedicated in honor of this illustrious Saint. One is the beautiful little basilica built over her tomb by the Emperor Constantine at the pious request of his daughter Constantia, who had been cured of a malignant disease by the prayers of St. Agnes; the other is a magnificent edifice put up in the

---

* This peculiar phrase, *Fidelis ex Fidelibus*—literally, a "Christian born of Christians," seems to have been adopted by those who composed those early inscriptions to insinuate that the True Faith, although its professors were despised, and debarred from attaining in the usual course to the distinctions in the state to which they might otherwise be entitled by reasons of their social eminence and talents, was the highest nobility of all, and to offset the pompous boast of the great patrician families of pagan Rome, among which a distinguished member was so often described as *Consul ex Consulibus*—"a Consul born of Consuls."

17th century, on the site of part of an ancient circus, and over one of the arches in which the holy virgin was exposed to the insults of ribald youth. The Sovereign Pontiffs used formerly to go every year to visit her basilica on the 21st of January, and two Homilies of Saint Gregory the Great were preached there. In one of them he unfavorably compares the degeneracy of his times with the faith and fervor of other days. "This Saint," he says, "whose festival we celebrate to-day, could not have died for God in her body, if first she were not dead to earthly desires in her mind. Her soul, erect in the perfection of virtue, blandishments and pain alike despised; and standing before armed kings and rulers she was stronger than the striker, greater than the judge who sentenced. What say we—bearded weaklings—whom anger conquers, pride inflates, ambition vexes, and lust defiles, at the sight of maidens who go to heaven by the *sword*? If we cannot reach the heavenly kingdom by the ways of persecution, we should be ashamed not to seek God in times of peace at least. In these days He says to no one: Die for Me; but only: Kill in yourself unlawful desires. If we will not refuse in time of peace the demands of the flesh, would we sacrifice in war the whole body for God?"

Good Catholics should cultivate a personal devotion to the saints, and take an interest in learning whatever can be known about them. We thereby obtain their intercession, and have our faith strengthened and our fervor excited.

We can also acquire great knowledge of sacred antiquities from the lives of the early saints—the martyrs particularly. The following words of Thomas à Kempis, who was a religious in the Monastery of Mount Saint Agnes and nourished a great affection for his conventual patroness, should arouse us from sloth to spiritual activity in the service of God, and may well be pondered beside the extract which we have given from the XIth Homily of St. Gregory: "Behold these are the saints and friends of God, who, at the price of their blood, and by the crown of their martyrdom, have merited eternal life. Read with pleasure the recital of their labors and sufferings, and thou wilt be consoled in thine own toil and slight affliction; for whatever thou mayest do or suffer, it is as nothing in comparison with that which the martyrs and all the blessed have done and undergone for Christ in the service of God." (*Valley of Lilies*, ch. xxxiii).

The name Agnes (from the Greek word *agnos*) means 'chaste,' 'pure,' whence the early panegyrists of our Saint remark that it perfectly corresponded to her virginity. She is a special patroness of holy purity; in which connection James de Voragine, a good and learned Dominican, who was Archbishop of Genoa in the year 1292, tells a story in his Golden Legend, as follows: "There was once upon a time a certain man named Paulinus who was employed in the service of a church dedicated in honor of Saint Agnes, but who was troubled with the most vehement temptations. As, however, he would not offend against his vows, he went to the Pope and asked permission to return to the world. The Pontiff, observing his simplicity and good dispositions, gave him an emerald ring off his own finger and told him to go to a beautiful image of the Saint that was in his church and command her by Papal authority to let herself be espoused to him. When the simple-minded man returned to his monastery, and going into the church approached the image, the annular finger of the right hand was miraculously extended, and he slipped thereon the nuptial ring. From that instant all his temptations ceased." (*Apud Bolland die* 21, *Jan*)

Saint Agnes is variously represented in sacred art; but the two great divisions of art on this subject are classed under the heads of *ancient* and *modern* conography. In the oldest representations the distinctive marks are the virginal veil on her head, falling gracefully upon her shoulders, while the hair is covered by a little mitre—*Mitella*—which was a sort of diadem used by noble unmarried females to hide their tresses, which were modestly braided and gathered up in a knot. A learned antiquarian, our dear friend Father Garucci, S. J., whom we knew at Rome, has described no fewer than fourteen representations of Saint Agnes, in his work on the Gilded Glasses of the Catacombs. A proof of the veneration in which she was held is found, also, rather in the peculiar circumstances in which she is represented than in the number (although comparatively great) of portraits on these painted glasses that have come down to us. Only the two Apostles Saints Peter and Paul, have been oftener represented than she on the Gilded Glasses used in the *Agapæ* (or Love Feasts) of the early Christians, which were celebrated over the tombs of the martyrs buried in the Catacombs. These circumstances in which she is painted are highly indicative of the popular devotion and esteem. In one case the Saint, richly attired, stands between two doves, either of which bears in its beak a crown in allusion to her double merit of virginity and martyrdom; in another she is even more splendidly dressed, and with hands uplifted in prayer for the Romans, she stands between her Divine Spouse Jesus Christ and the famous deacon Saint Laurence; in which connection there would seem to be indicated more than the fact that Saint Laurence was her countryman. The artist intended, we believe, to convey the idea not only that her holy purity had disposed her for the grace of martyrdom, but to illustrate a point in her personal history, viz., that her vow of virginity was not a merely private one, but a solemn and perpetual vow accepted by the Church through the minister of the Sacraments and custodian of discipline—who in her case was the Pope—for a deacon was *ex-officio* to assist the Bishop in the ceremony of giving the veil to females in their mystical espousals to Christ our Lord. Agnes has the high honor of being four times represented between the Apostles Peter and Paul, whom ancient art proclaim the introducers of the souls of the elect into the realms of bliss. Twice she is represented with another female figure, designated by the sweet name *Maria*, to teach us that by her holy virginity she became an imitator of and a child of Blessed Mary. (*St. Max. of Turin Serm.* 51 *in Nat. S. Agn.*) In a less ancient but still very interesting representation of the Saint, in the mosaic put up in her basilica by Pope Honorius I about the year 630, she holds in her hands a volume—the "Book of Life of the Lamb" (Apoc., xxi, 27), in which are written the names of the elect.

Modern art generally represents Saint Agnes either in rich garments with a lamb clasped to her bosom, or in an attitude of prayer, on a burning pyre, as Guercino has depicted her in his exquisite painting now in the Doria Gallery at Rome; or naked, but sufficiently draped by a profusion of long hair, that by the hands of angels was miraculously unloosed and spread out, to fall from her head to her feet, and cover her person when exposed to the lust of profligates by order of the wicked judge. A celebrated sculptor of the first half of the 17th century, Alexander Algardi, has thus chastely represented her in his wonderful bas-relief over the altar of the subterranean chapel in her church on the Piazza Navona at Rome.

We had written thus far, dear and indulgent Ave Maria, when, instead of closing as in duty bound to your valuable space (and out of shame for our pen), we are impressed by a couple of lines in the *Peristephanon* of Prudentius to write a little more on the subject. Prudentius, having in mind the representations of Saint Agnes as an *Orante i. e.*, in attitude of prayer as mentioned above—says (xiv, 3, 194) that standing before the towers of the city, this virgin protects [her countrymen] the Romans:

Conspectu in ipso condita turrium
Servat salutem virgo Quiritium.

Now, to use one of those *rapprochements* of history (so much affected, although not always in a good sense, by French writers), we may see the finger of Divine Providence setting at naught the designs of men, and working out the destinies of nations in a different, but far more perfect manner than natural courses could do; setting up Saint Agnes with her profession of virginity—by which Rome is peopled again and again, through the force of her example, by countless nuns and virgins;—(far exceeding in the lapse of ages Rome's original population) and the strength of her intercession—by which Rome's walls are more securely protected than by legions of soldiers—as the type of Christian woman who does more for her native city than did the Sabine woman, whose valor and forgiving spirit made peace between her countrymen and the Romans, and acquiescing in the violence of rape, peopled the city with a race of heroes. Those in fact who have studied with Saint Augustin and Orosius, his disciple, the philosophy of Roman history, are convinced that there is an analogy, although often of *contraries*, between the leading incidents of the city before the coming of our Lord and the principal events after the introduction of Christianity. Rome is the *Eternal* City: and her history is a *mysterious* one. Certain it is, that the tomb and basilica of Saint Agnes are on the great road leading from the country of the Sabines—Rome's earliest enemies—to Rome, and which was followed by the Sabine maidens going to the treacherous holiday of the unwedded Romans—and subsequently by their fathers, brothers and husbands bent on avenging the sudden and inhospitable crime. "All the rich among the people shall entreat thy countenance" (Ps. 44). The wealthiest and most powerful patricians of Rome have looked up to Saint Agnes and sought her favor; thus the Princess Constantia coming humbly to pray at her tomb, was healed of her malady; the Emperor Constantine lavished his resources upon the magnificent basilica which he erected; the Sovereign Pontiff Liberius sought a refuge and protection beside her remains during the schism of the antipope Felix; and his successor Pius IX (of immortal memory) experienced there her miraculous aid on the memorable 12th of April in the year 1855.

"After her shall virgins be brought to the King." This is amply verified in Saint Agnes, whose example of chastity was imitated in succeeding generations, and will continue in the Church until the end of the world to draw many Catholic maidens to renounce the vanities of life and choose the better part in the espousals of the Great King—*for Behold the Bridegroom cometh.* Already in his age Saint Ambrose wrote: "And whereas Faith dies not, even to this day many Roman virgins watch beside the much abused Agnes as though she were yet living in the body; and thereunto moved by her example, they courageously continue in their vows, being firmly persuaded that if they persevere to the end, they shall obtain the unfading palm of victory." "Her neighbors," the psalm continues, "shall be brought to Thee in gladness and rejoicing." Thus many who before blasphemed the God and

Saviour of the Christians were converted to the true Faith at the sight of her constancy, so that her Greek Acts (July 5th) record that "she induced many women of bad lives to turn aside from their evil ways, and believe in Christ the Lord."

The readers of THE AVE MARIA will perhaps recall the touching conclusion of Cardinal Wiseman's *Fabiola*, the heroine of which is St. Agnes.

To Sister Felix, of the Sisters of Charity, on her Golden Jubilee.

BY ELEANOR C. DONNELLY.

I.

WHY do the clouds of Advent
To-day with sunlight blaze?
Why do the heights of Heaven
Re-echo psalms of praise?
And why these strains of gladness
That float through old St. John's,
From lips of happy Sisters,
From joyous little ones?

II.

Ah! ask the thronging angels
That viewless fill the air,
With pearly, perfum'd pinions,
And sunny, floating hair;
Ask but those shining spirits,
And they will answer thee,
"To-day our Sister Felix
Keeps her Golden Jubilee!"

III.

Weigh well that simple answer
('Mid mingled smiles and tears),
'Tis fraught with all the glory,
All the grace of fifty years;
Fifty years of shade and sunshine,
Fifty years of toil and care,
Fifty years of self-renouncement,
Fifty years of constant prayer.

IV.

In the Past's resplendent mirror
We gaze (with eye-lids wet)
On a youthful novice-Sister
In her habit and cornette;
We see her at the altar,
We hear her breathe her vows,
Take the Cross, her chosen portion,
With Christ, her chosen Spouse.

V.

Then forth upon her mission,
She goes with willing feet,—
The angels counting every step
With rapture pure and sweet.
Friend of the sick and suff'ring,—
The orphans' loving stay,—
In high and noble duties,
Her brave life wears away.

VI.

But while the busy seasons
Are passing swift as light,
Celestial hands are weaving
A crown of blossoms bright;
A wreath of radiant roses,
Fit for the fields above,
Whose ev'ry seed hath found its root
In some pure deed of love!

VII.

Bring hither, then, ye angels!
Your Garland, heaven-worn,
And crown the mistress of our *fête*,
This glad December morn.
Rejoice! dear friends and Sisters,
O children! shout for glee!
The very saints in heaven share
Our Golden Jubilee!

VIII.

Joy to thee, Sister Felix!
Well-chosen was thy name,—
For *happy* is that favor'd soul
Who Christ, as spouse, can claim;
But *happier* still that spirit
Which bravely perseveres
Thro' all the cares and changes
Of fifty faithful years!

IX.

Dear Daughter of Saint Vincent!
May it be thine, one day,
(Before the solemn Judgment-seat),
To hear our dear Lord say:
"O blessed of My Father!
Come up and dwell with Me,
And we shall keep for evermore
An endless Jubilee!"

'Beth's Promise.

BY MRS. ANNA HANSON DORSEY.

CHAPTER III.
AUNT 'BETH MAKES UP HER MIND.

"IT will never do to let her go on in this way," said Aunt 'Beth to herself, one night after she had left Mrs. Morley's room, where she had been doing her best to awaken in her some interest in the affairs of life, things that required attention, that involved pecuniary loss and no end of disagreeable complications if neglected, but all in vain. She listened to all Aunt 'Beth said, but it was with benumbed faculties; she expressed no wish, no opinion; her white face did not relax its rigid expression, nor her eyes their heavy, woebegone look.

"I *do* wish you would say something, Anne; you can't live on like this, you know," Aunt 'Beth blurted out.

"Oh, Aunt 'Beth! don't, don't! you hurt me!" she cried, in such piteous accents, that Aunt 'Beth drew her head to her bosom and held it there, fondling with gentlest touches her forehead and cheek, while her tears sprinkled the once beautiful tresses, which within a few weeks had shown many a white thread. Then kissing her "good-night," she sought her own room, feeling a strange mixture of grief and anger at the unreasonableness of any human beings' giving away so utterly to an event which no earthly power could change, when the business of life demanded the exercise of every energy. Miss Morley did not look at the matter from a Christian point of view; she had never professed to be religious, she had never even been baptized; in fact she gave herself no concern about questions which, as she curtly expressed it, only set people by the ears, and made them think every one was going wrong except themselves. She was willing they should fight it out between themselves, but made up her mind to attend to the duties devolving upon her through providence or chance—she did not inquire which—to do what good she could to others, and, in short, to live a useful, common-sense, unselfish life; judging none, and allowing no one to force their doctrines, their uncharitableness, or bickerings upon her. She used to say sometimes: " If I undertook to be a Christian like some I know, I should grow fanatical and lose what little human kindness there is in my nature. I believe in God, and thank Him for all His mercies; that is enough; and when I die He will know that I have done the best I could." With such sentiments of belief, Miss Morley took a very commonsense view of her niece's inordinate sorrow, and was convinced that she only required the *will* to arouse herself from the apathy she was in, to be able to do it, and she felt it to be her duty to begin with a tonic form of treatment which would literally set her on her feet again. "Too much sympathy, and too much giving up to her," thought Aunt 'Beth, "is injudicious and cruel. It will never do, and she must and shall shake it off for the sake of my poor little 'Beth, whom she seems to have forgotten, and who is breaking her heart over it. Bless my soul! I loved Hugh—dear, noble fellow!—I brought him up, and loved him as if he had been my own son. I was proud of him—yes, he was very near to me—and his death has hurt me sorely, too; and if I were to give myself time to brood over it I should cry my eyes out"; and here she buried her face in her hands and wept bitterly for several minutes. "But what would be the good of it," she added, wiping her eyes. "Did the greatest grief ever known bring back the dead? I must do all that I think my brave boy would best like to be done,—that is while I stay here,—for I must be hurrying home very soon now. All my winter arrangements are at a stand-still; in fact, there's nothing done; servants all idle, through not knowing how to manage; but that might all go to the mischief if Anne would only be natural." Then Aunt 'Beth prepared with her usual energy for bed, but after putting out her light she dropped upon the rug before the fire now smouldering redly among the white ashes, and embracing her knees, leaned her forehead upon them, remaining so motionless that one would have supposed she was asleep, but she was never more wide awake in her life.

"I'll do it! she will think it cruel, no doubt, but she will live to thank me for it, I know," she said, getting up and plunging into bed, where, having settled herself upon her pillow, she added: "I'll tell her in plain words what I think is her duty!"

Aunt 'Beth meant all that she said; and, the next day, after the domestic affairs of the house were wound up like a clock to running order, when all outside calls and messages had been attended to, and 'Beth sent out to walk, she went into Mrs. Morley's room, seated herself opposite to her, asked her how she felt, and how she had passed the night, and if she had eaten her breakfast. "She was well," she said, "but had not slept much, and could eat nothing."

"I suppose you know, Anne, that if you go on in this way you'll simply kill yourself," said Aunt 'Beth, in a firm, hard voice. "It is not grief but suicide, and not at all what poor Hugh—could he speak to us from where he is—would wish. Here are his affairs, which to be neglected would dishonor his memory; and his child, who is breaking her heart because you have put her aside—"

"Oh, Aunt 'Beth, don't! don't! I can't bear it!"

"Yes, you can, and must, Anne. All of us can bear more than we think, if we only try. You must throw off this morbid grief; it is not a true or right sort of grief; it is more like pagan despair. You must rouse yourself for the sake of your child, who is fretting herself into typhoid fever—the doctor says so."

"Is 'Beth ill?" she asked hurriedly.

"She will be, if you don't let her come in to you, and let her see that you feel some interest in her existence. I awoke the other night, and hearing a strange sound in her room, I went in, and there she was lying upon the floor, as cold as death, and sobbing as if her heart would break. I brought her into my bed and held her in my arms, doing all I could to comfort her; but it is you Anne—*you*, her mother—that she wants, and must have, or she'll die."

"Oh, Aunt 'Beth, can it be that she grieves so sorely?"

"Yes: just think of it: a young thing like her, who has been as happy as a lark all her life, to lose father and mother at one blow!"

"Oh no! only one! How can you be so unkind, and say such things to me!"

"I am only telling you the truth, Anne. Your husband used to call you a brave woman: be brave now for the love of him. You must grieve for him, it is only natural, but for God's sake be rational. I must go home next week,—I am needed there; but how can I leave you in this condition, and 'Beth desolate and pining for her mother's breast to lay her poor head upon?"

Mrs. Morley rose from her chair, and walked up and down the room. "That," thought Aunt

'Beth, watching her while she pretended to knit, "that is a good beginning."

At last she stopped, and stood before her, her pale hands clasped and her face wrung with anguish: "Aunt 'Beth, I thought you loved my husband!" she cried.

"Loved him! I fairly idolized him, Anne; didn't I bring him up from the cradle? No mother ever loved her first-born as I loved him; and if I gave way to my sorrow, I should not cease my moan day or night," cried Aunt 'Beth, in trembling tones. "But life is too short, Anne, too crowded with duties to the living, for me to waste it by nursing my grief. I'll do my duty, as he did, and when death comes it shall find me, as it did him, with his work accomplished; my hero! my boy!"

Aunt 'Beth covered her face with her hands, tears gushed through her fingers, and her form shook with emotion; nature demands, and will have compensation, when her laws, given for the relief of human beings are violated; and this good pagan, who imagined that by her strong will she could overcome all mundane weakness, felt all the better for this spontaneous outburst of a really deep-seated sorrow. Mrs. Morley knelt by her side, folded her arms about her, and leaning her head upon her breast, whispered: "Aunt 'Beth, let me love you, let me share *his* place in your heart. Grief is selfish, but such a loss, such a grief as mine! coming like a bolt out of a clear sky, crushing me so suddenly as it did, I find very hard to bear. But I'll try; I'll try, dear Aunt 'Beth; I don't know if I can, but I will make the effort to rouse myself, and take up my life-work again; but don't, don't leave me; for how can I do it alone! You do not know—ah! Aunt 'Beth! my soul, my *very soul*, cries out for help."

"Anne, my love, I cannot give you any comfort about religious matters; my ideas, you know, are peculiar, and while they satisfy me, would be no solace to you. Send for Mr. Haller, lay open your heart to him; he knows all about the doctrines that people pin their faith to, and find consolation in. I think Mr. Haller's a good man, and is really in earnest in all that he teaches," answered Miss Morley.

"He has been very kind, but he cannot help me, Aunt 'Beth; my need is far beyond anything that Mr. Haller can do. But don't leave me," said Mrs. Morley.

"I shall have to go; but why not come with me, you and 'Beth?"

"No, that is impossible *now;* later, perhaps, she and I will come."

"I hope so. Now, I'm going to send you a nice lunch, and 'Beth shall bring it; I heard her come in just now, and, my dear, you will see that in trying to comfort her—even just a little at first—you'll find comfort for your own aching heart."

"She is right," said Mrs. Morley, with a moan which bespoke the anguish of her heart; "but how little indeed does she understand the bitter sting that makes my sorrow so unendurable! that it is the consolations of that faith which I so weakly and sinfully abandoned, that I now, in the hour of supreme sorrow, crave and hunger for! Alas! alas! what is there to save me from despair in this bitter hour!"

She had resolved, and she determined to make an effort to shake off the morbid lethargy of grief from which Aunt 'Beth had partially aroused her. It would give her heart a great wrench to bury her woe, and come back to the ways of life; dead to the world, she was nearer to him she mourned; living among its petty concerns again would remove them farther and farther apart. Oh, that she might go on grieving and grieving, satisfying her sorrow until death released her, and reunited her with her lost love! Such were the outcries of her poor, undisciplined heart; but she had promised to "try"; and, hurt her as it might, she would keep her word. All these thoughts were rushing through her brain when, raising her eyes, she caught sight of her dishevelled hair, the dark purple rings under her eyes, and her pallid, woe-begone face, in a mirror opposite her. It was the ghost of herself that she saw, and she gazed upon it as upon the face of a stranger. She turned away, bathed her eyes, and smoothed her hair, thinking of 'Beth, and how it would pain her if she found her looking like that, not knowing that she had looked thus for many days.

'Beth came in timidly with the tray, placing it upon the table. "Mamma!" she said, gently, "I fixed your lunch myself; I even made the chocolate with my own hands; won't you please try and eat just a little?"

"Thank you, my child," said Mrs. Morley, folding her arms about her, and kissing her. "It seems so long since we have been together; draw that *tabouret* here and sit by me while I try to eat." And 'Beth, leaning upon her mother's knee, taken to her heart once more, was filled with a serene consciousness of peace, almost of gladness. But she was afraid she might weary her if she remained too long, and not be permitted to come in again; and seeing that she had finished her lunch, she gathered the things together to take them away, when Mrs. Morley drew her face down and kissed her, telling her to come in whenever she wished.

"That will be always, dear mamma! We have never been parted before, you know," answered 'Beth, with quivering lip.

"Let it be always, then, 'Beth. We will not be parted again so long as we both live."

"Oh, mamma! how happy you make me!" she exclaimed, as leaning over she kissed her mother's head. Then she ran down to tell the good news to Aunt 'Beth, who felt comforted. "There's nothing," she thought, "after all, like plain, practical common sense."

After that, Mrs. Morley, who was neither intellectually weak nor naturally deficient in will and energy, took up once more the burden of life, determined to endure her sorrow, and, like her brave husband, fulfil her duties as strength might be given her. No more wild outcries of anguish must burst from her heart; there must be no more speechless woe, or benumbed inactivity; her husband used to call her "brave," and for his sake she would collect all her powers to be so.

But, alas! alas! while nerves, muscles, and brain, while every faculty may be brought under discipline, where shall help be found for the poor heart, which under its mask is eating itself away, stung to death by its secret pain? On earth? No! Earth has no balm of healing for such wounds, and if help is not sought of God, if He touches them not with His divine chrisms, there is left for it only despair. Like the precious sandal-wood tree, the faithful heart when wounded almost beyond human endurance gives back the sweet aroma of resignation and trust, for every blow as when

"——the generous wood
Perfumes with its own sweets the cruel blade":

and He who pities His suffering ones as a "father pitieth his children," gives healing and peace, treasuring up, for the day of eternal compensation, every pang that has been patiently endured for the love of Him, and turning their grief into songs of rejoicing, while He crowns them with everlasting recompense.

But this afflicted woman had forfeited by her own faithlessness and almost apostasy, all claim to the consolations which she so much needed; she had by her long neglect of those Divine Sacraments, which would have given her supernatural strength, "trampled them," as it were, "under her feet." She had, by making her faith of so small account, caused her husband to be satisfied with his own errors of belief, and indifferent to religion generally; and last of all, had shut out from the one true fold her innocent child, who, now grown to womanhood, had no knowledge of the religion, to which she—at least by Baptism—belonged. Is it any wonder that grief, stung to remorse like this, should be unendurable? Is it any wonder that 'out of the depth' her soul lifted its despairing cry for help, or that she shrank with terror from seeking reconciliation with that holy faith she had so many years ago betrayed?

(TO BE CONTINUED.)

HE who reforms himself has done much toward reforming others.

A Lover of the Beautiful.

BY KATHLEEN O'MEARA, AUTHOR OF "IZA'S STORY," "ROBIN REDBREAST," "LIFE OF FREDERIC OZANAM," "PEARL," ETC., ETC.

(CONTINUED.)

BEFORE returning to Paris, Henry paid a visit to Lorège, "a delicious week in the constant society of Père Lacordaire, who spoiled me more than ever," he says; and he goes on to relate an episode of the visit which affected him deeply. "One of my great delights here, as been hearing the Father read his notice on M. Ozanam.... Fancy, he quotes two whole pages of the little *memoires** I sent him six months ago! I was quietly listening to the reading, when suddenly I recognized the thoughts, then the author..... I grew scarlet, and the drops stood on my forehead. I protested—honestly—but to no purpose. So I shall be printed in the works of Père Lacordaire. It is enough to confound me and make me sink into the earth..... Don't tell this to anybody." .... The improvement which he brought back from Eaux Bonnes did not seem to warrant his spending the winter in Paris. The doctors decided that he must return to Italy. His hopes of receiving the subdiaconate at Christmas in the venerable old Church of St. Sulpice where he had made his First Communion, were thus disappointed. Henry bowed his head unmurmuringly, but the pang was none the less bitter.

On the 3d of November, he writes from Nice, ... "On All Saints' morning, after Communion, I renewed the pledges to which when taking the habit two years ago, we committed ourselves. I was very happy, full of consolation and strength, and I am still walking in the light of the graces given me in that Communion..... The rest of the day I spent at the great military hospital at Marseilles, where our wounded soldiers from the east daily disembark. It is one of the deepest impressions of my life. I felt proud and happy, amazed and humbled by the confidence which these brave fellows showed me; many amongst them were dying, some were in their agony. If I had been a priest I might have confessed over thirty of them. Their wounds are dreadful, and their accounts of the winter and the taking of Sebastopol are awful. We have no idea of what they have suffered. You can't think how sad it is to hear these tales of glory and battle on the lips of poor young fellows, who for three months and more have been lying on a bed of pain, weakened by fever, with wounds that have festered in the long and painful journey, and who, after their great labors have before them nothing but a broken and useless career.... I wish I

---
* These two pages, the most tenderly poetic perhaps of any that H. Perreyve has left us, are quoted in full by the present writer in the Life of Frederic Ozanam.

could give you an idea of the really *holy* look with which many of them said to me—'I have done my duty, M. l'Abbé; may the will of God be done.' This word *duty* is in every mouth. I was much struck by it, and it has filled me with an immense hope for France. Such foretastes of the divine consolations which await the priest in his ministry only made Henry hunger the more for the day when his life should be filled with them; but he was learning in the school of the Cross to be more worthy of them. His life had become a daily, nay, hourly, struggle between the too willing spirit and the fainting flesh. "I am not sure," he says, "if there is not a new source of energy and vigor for thought in the constant effort of the mind struggling against the hindrances of disease. One works somewhat as one fights. So I am satisfied with my condition until the next break-down, and perhaps you will read some day an essay entitled *La Liberté de l'Eglise*, which may be born of the struggle I describe. Ah! the liberty of the Church. Let us love it, Eugène! Let us two swear to love it, to love it always, to serve it always."

One of the first consolations which awaited him in Rome was receiving Holy Communion from the hands of Pius IX. It was on the Feast of St. Agnes. The spectacle of the pomp with which the Church celebrates the glory of the humble maiden martyred seventeen centuries ago, woke deep emotions in Henry's soul.

"... Two little white lambs, ornamented with flowers and streamers, are blessed by the Pope, and their wool is used for weaving the palliums. Ah, how true it is that the most beautiful vestment of her church is that which is woven for her by pure hearts, by the innocence of her virgins, and the chastity of her priests?"

A few days later he "had the happiness of being presented" to Cardinal (then Dr.) Newman, by F. Ambrose St. John.

"F. Newman is a man of infinite sweetness and kindness, with none of the English stiffness, and full of the loftiest ideas concerning the religious future of England. He gave me precious details as to what one may hope for in that noble country, so naturally pious and earnest. F. Newman said to me: 'We only want priests.' Alas! ..... Our conversation was of the funniest; he understands French, and answers in Italian; I consequently spoke to him in French; then I had to speak Italian to F. St. John, who does not speak French; finally, they spoke English to one another. The ideas made their way through this Babel, and I don't think one went astray."

Another distinguished personage whose acquaintance Henry made in Rome was Cardinal Villecourt, who became his patron, and opened every door to him.

"... I reminded him, as you told me," he writes to his father, "of the old servant who used to say at Fourvières: 'Little Villecourt will be a priest.' He laughed heartily, and bade me remember him to you. He makes great fun of me, in the gentlest way, and says to me: 'Do you suppose that because I am a Cardinal, and sixty-eight years old, I have not the right to laugh?' He leads the life of a hermit in Rome, and cannot accustom himself to the grand ways of the purple. When he was named Cardinal, he never slept for eight days; but as the intention of the Pope was still a secret, he could not confide his trouble to anyone. His old servant, John, used to say to him—'Monsignor has some trouble that he won't tell me.' And he would reply, 'What will you, my poor John? such an unlikely thing has befallen us!' 'If it is in a case of going to the ends of the earth, why can you not tell me? you know well that I will follow you.' At last the day came, and the good Bishop said to John: 'My poor John, I am a Cardinal!' John did not know whether to laugh or cry; but since he has been *laquais* in the anteroom and has become himself the majordomo of a large establishment, they say he makes the best of being a Cardinal. Is there not something very touching and of ancient times about it all?... Good-bye, dear father; your son embraces you, and his mother, and his good old Rose,* who is his *vieux Jean*, and prays God to bless you."

Cardinal Villecourt obtained for his young protégé an audience of the Holy Father, which Henry thus describes to Père Gratry—"That quarter of an hour's conversation was so sweet to me that I know not what to say of it. Ah, I pity from my heart the man who, kneeling at the feet of Pius IX, does not feel his heart overpowered with love. I entered with the three usual genuflexions, and the Holy Father, not being in official audience, but busy working at his bureau, held out his hand to me to kiss. Then I wanted to kiss his foot, for I hold that there is a great significance of love and obedience in the complete prostration of Catholics at the feet of the Pope. The Holy Father smiled, and said, laughingly, 'Ah, he wants the foot too; well, he must have it. ...' And he turned towards me and put out the slipper.... He made me tell him how I had left the world, and I at once mentioned the Oratory. This is what he said, word for word: 'The Oratory of Paris? The one directed by the Abbé Pététot, former Curé of St. Roch? Ah, my son, there is a priest that is good, that is excellent, that is sacerdotal; that seeks to make no noise, does good for God alone, and makes no fuss in the newspapers; but God sees hearts.' And the Holy Father went on from this to make

---

* The old servant who had brought him up.

me a most admirable exhortation to priestly zeal, to devotion to souls. He quoted several texts from Scripture, but my heart was so full that I heard without hearing, and I don't remember them. . . ."

The question of his being admitted to orders had been discussed since his arrival in Rome, and after a good deal of hesitation, his health being the great, the only obstacle, it was decided that he should be ordained subdeacon on Trinity Sunday. His joy on receiving this sentence is not easily described, but it flows from his heart with an eloquence that gives some idea of its intensity: "O, what a heart I ought to have! A new heart! My friend, as you love Jesus Christ ask Him to change my heart for *that day*. I cannot bear the thought of offering Him on that beloved day of our spiritual nuptials a heart so poor in virtue, so small, so full of self! Ask to obtain for me that which I have not. Commend me to the prayers of holy souls. I tell you I am unworthy of this unspeakable honor. In pity for me, ask of God to build Himself the temple in which He is to dwell, and to purify His own tabernacle." And, a few days later, to another friend: ". . . . Eugène, pray for me. . . . Let our joy be full. . . . Let us lift up our hearts; let us look at the beauty of the divine plan. It is all too beautiful! Who has made the advances in this mystery of love wherein Jesus and we are but one soul? Who has never grown weary of loving with infinite delicacy, and, alas! with infinite patience! Who but Jesus, our Master, our Lord! . . . . We are not worth the trouble of saying that we are worth nothing. Let us only speak of Jesus. . . . Friend, I embrace Thee at His feet. God forbid we should be priests, you and I, if it were not to love Jesus unto death! Amen."

That day which was waited for with such transports of joy came at last. On the Feast of the Holy Trinity, Henry Perreyve was ordained subdeacon at the Church of St. John of Lateran.

"What shall I say to thee, my mother?" he writes home, the next day . . . "It is all over; or, rather, it is *begun*. The blessed ceremony was more imposing, more full of grace and sweet emotions than I had hoped. I prostrated myself with a willing heart on the pavement of the *Mother of Churches* to promise to God that immortal fidelity that your prayers will enable me to keep. The ordination was performed by Cardinal Patrizi, whom you will see one of these days in Paris for the imperial christening. . . . . After this grand morning, we received our kind neighbors, who made our feast theirs. Need I say how much I missed thee, mother dear, and my father, and my old Rose! My sister was very happy and gave me some compensation for your absence. . . . Sunday I saw the Holy Father, and presented him with a copy of the unpublished part of my work on the Immaculate Conception. The binding was splendid, at any rate, and the Holy Father promised me to have the inside examined. . . .

A great many people came to my ordination. M. Ampère remained the whole time, and coming out he pressed my hands with tears in his eyes. What a beautiful soul! He brought a young French painter with him, who seemed deeply impressed by the ceremony."

About a month later the young deacon made his usual pilgrimage to Eaux Bonnes, stopping at Lorège on his way thither, for the *fête* of P Lacordaire. He was called upon suddenly to make a speech at the dinner table before two hundred and fifty persons, and was surprised to find that his voice had regained something of its former power and sonority. "I was greatly moved," he writes to his mother, "which was a reason for moving others; but what encourages me is that this emotion, instead of crushing, sustained and carried me with it. I tell you this in all filial simplicity. Père Lacordaire said to me afterwards, *en tête-à-tête*, 'My dear friend, you will be a speaker.' But for this, one must have lungs, and this is what has brought me again to Eaux Bonnes."

During his stay at the waters, he met M. Cousin, and he informs P. Gratry of his glad surprise in discovering how near that noble mind had come to Catholic ideas. Let us pray for these souls," he says, "and above all let us not make the doors of the Church bristle with razors, and pike-staffs, and pitch-forks, and bundles of thorns."

The waters proved so beneficial to the invalid this season that on his return to Paris he writes to P. Lacordaire: "I feel wonderfully better this year, and the doctors protest that they believe seriously in my cure." But notwithstanding this protest, they insisted on his returning to Rome for the winter, and his stay there was more of an exile this year, as his sister did not accompany him.

". . . Dear one," he writes to her, "I cannot understand why I should not set off to go to the *Via della Vite* in half an hour from this, and sit warming myself with you over the fire. Yesterday evening, I could not resist going to look up at the house; there was light in the windows, and I could fancy. . . . . but all that is swept away with the shadows of the past. . . . Life has assumed a graver aspect for me, I am tasting the life of the poor lonely student in Paris. I am not sorry for this. One ought to learn what those ordeals are. Up to the present, I should not have known how to confess those poor young fellows who are ill at ease in a hotel by themselves; to-morrow, I should know better how to go about it. One only knows really the various conditions of the soul by experiencing them one's self."

He found delights in his solitary life which soon made it dear to him. "I have a little apartment rather far from all my acquaintances," he writes to a friend in Paris. "I fly from visits as much as I can, for I love my solitude. I suffer now and then, when souvenirs crowd upon me; but I have a horror of people who want to divert my mind (*me distraire*.) Divert it from what? Good heavens! From that ardent, living, interior life with God, where I dwell with the souls I love. Ah, how infinitely I prefer to all the diversions of the world, the hours, mayhap a little shaded with regret, which I pass in this dear company!"

On the Feast of St. Gregory he tells P. Gratry— "I have just served the venerable Doctor Manning's Mass in the fine church of the great Saint who rests under the shadow of the Coliseum.... The famous Doctor Palmer had come to fetch us, and went to Communion with us. His is one of those souls conquered by the irresistible violence of the Lamb, and who have broken all their ties rather than let go the hand of Jesus Christ. I can't tell you what I feel in seeing these English converts in the sanctuaries of Rome; they bear on their brow the glory of the great sacrifices they have consummated, and of a conscience satisfied at any cost; exiled, and yet returned to their true country; having lost all, and yet found all...."

He was hard at work, meantime, and engaged, amidst his studies and active spiritual life, on a treatise entitled "Entretiens sur l'Eglise Catholique," which appeared on his return to Paris. He made a retreat at the Jesuit Novitiate, before leaving Rome, and some of his meditations during those days of silence with God have been preserved to us by P. Gratry.* One, headed "La Mort Sacerdotale," is so characteristic of the state of his soul, that we cannot refrain from quoting a few passages from it.... "A priest should desire death as Thou didst desire Thy Passion *in spite of the anguish and the terrors that Thou didst foresee*.... What would it be, Lord, if instead of thus looking at death, Thy priests were to fear it, to fly from it? to dread its approach, as an intolerable vision?.... And yet, when I look into myself, I find the dregs of this same cowardly, stupid, pagan fear..... Lord, this is what I implore of Thee this day to exterminate in me. And thou wilt do it, Lord, if I ask Thee with sufficient fervor, and faith, and trust. O God! take out of my heart all fear of death. For this fear of death is the great enemy, the great obstacle, the great weight which crushes down all generous virtues. Teach me to break this chain. In whatsoever danger Thou dost place me, in the midst of an epidemic, of political revolutions; in those days of trouble and terror when all presence of mind is lost, and when fear conspires so basely with evil, grant that I may take refuge in the full and courageous acceptance of death..... But this is not enough, and I dare ask Thee for more. It is hard not to fear death, if one looks at it by its appalling side, and we may look at it from this side. It is easier to love it, because it has its adorably beautiful side. I dare ask Thee, therefore, Lord, the grace to love death...."

On coming out of retreat, he announces to a friend that his ordination as deacon is fixed for the end of May, on his return to Paris.

"I was very happy in my retreat, Charles.... Ah! What a friend we have in Jesus Christ! What indulgence! What a drawing near of His Heart to ours at the foot of the altar!... I shall embrace you, on the eve of the day when we two shall prostrate ourselves together at the feet of our Lord to receive the holy order of deacon. We will share our prayers, our graces, our meditations; we will share everything.... I embrace you at the feet of Jesus...."

His birthday came round before he left Rome. "I am six-and-twenty to-day! It is dreadful! And with that I have discovered that I know nothing, and that I have done nothing!... Alas! how I do burn with impatience to do something for souls in the name of Jesus Christ! You are in the secret of this interior fire, which so wore me out at Eaux Bonnes, and which follows me everywhere. Where are the souls I am to teach and to love? Where are the ears of that sheaf which the priest gleans amidst tears and anguish? Where are my children? I see no sign of their coming yet. You talk of my writings.... It is a hundred times better worth while to confess a rag-and-bone man than to write a fine article in a fashionable magazine; but where is my rag-and-bone man? It is always him I am in search of."

His return to Paris, and impending ordination, seemed to bring him nearer to this object of his search, but the cross of the divine will once more placed itself between him and the cross, that he so thirsted to embrace. On the second day of his retreat at St. Sulpice, preparatory to his ordination, he was seized with congestion of the lungs and a cough that racked him day and night. He kept up by sheer stress of will till the Saturday when, during the solemn prostration, he drew his handkerchief from his mouth soaked with blood.

"That day so longed for," he says, relating the incident to a friend when all was over, "that day of special graces of the Lord, was also a day of great fatigue. The ceremony was barely over when I had just time to get home, and the doctor was sent for. They bled me, and since then I have been from one remedy to another. I am now better; but here is another trial, a fresh proof of my uselessness, a new humiliation for

---

* See "Henri Perreyve," by P. Gratry. P. 209.

my soul.... But God sees that it is not pure enough since He does not accept it.... Ah! how true it is what you say, Eugène, that we should give our whole heart to Him who gives always more love than He receives. How is it that we do not understand that His incomparable love is the one thing necessary!..... What madness it is to hold in our hands the supreme Beauty, the supreme Good, Love without end, and yet.... to go on suffering and complaining, and never to be done with it!"

The complaint was not that of those who murmur and are destroyed. Joy was the strong cry of his soul, despite the blow which love had again dealt at him.

"Well, at last I am deacon!" he says to Père Gratry; "and you will see if, by dint of good will, I don't arrive, little by little, at the priesthood. *Introibo ad altare Dei!* I hope to bring to it a heart inebriated with the love of God and souls!"

"I asked our Lord to take my *whole* heart in this ordination," he says; "and I hope He did. The Abbé B——, a beautiful soul, with gifts and lights of inconceivable richness, preached the sermon. As a sermon, it was faulty; but what a living soul! what a heart! what rays of light! It produced on me the effect of a warm, glowing atmosphere. Eugène, let us love. If we mean ever to speak to souls of men, let us love...."

The first break of winter was the signal for his departure to the South. He rested a little while at Lorège, and came in while there for the great *fête* of the school on St. Cecilia's day. All the notabilities of the town were present, and Henry was called on for a speech. He felt more sure of himself on this occasion than he had done the preceding year. "I don't know how it was that I felt sufficiently master of myself to taste even *the pleasure* of the thing," he says to his friend, Charles Perraud. "Verily, I can understand that it must be an immense delight, above all when one speaks for the salvation of souls, for God. But what perils lurk in the exercise of this gift! How deeply it penetrates the heart, agitating us, thrilling us with a sense of power, even when it has done nothing, or next to nothing.... What must it be in the case of successful effort, of an oratorical triumph! Ah, let us prepare our souls to receive these shocks without weakness, without betraying the cause of our Master, to whom alone and always praise and honor are due."

He was now beginning to count the days till the dawn of that day to which he had aspired unceasingly since his First Communion. His health was still very precarious, and he was spitting blood again; but the more the body flagged, the more the spirit burned. What did anything matter so long as he arrived at saying Mass! "The one thing serious amidst all this," he says, exultingly, "is that in six months I am going to be a priest! Alas, how I ought to shake with fear before this awful prerogative, so overpowering to my weak nature!.... In deed and in truth I blush as I write these lines, so conscious am I of my unworthiness to guide souls for the glory of Jesus Christ.... You will pray for me, will you not? and get all the holy souls you can to pray for me."

His friend Charles Perraud was ordained during his absence, and Henry thus greets the young priest on the morning of his divine espousals: ".... May the Lord be with thee, dear brother! With thee this morning at the altar of thy first Mass, to accept thy nuptial vows, to answer them with that reciprocity of love which passes all love!... With thee to-morrow to make thee feel that the joy of God, unlike the joys of this world, is perpetual, and to be tasted forever, while never satiating! With thee soon, when, after these sacred inebriations, thou wilt feel what it is to be a priest for men, and to descend from Thabor to go to those who suffer, to those who are ignorant, to those who hunger and thirst after light and life! With thee in thy sorrows, to console thee! With thee in thy joys, to sanctify them! With thee, my Charles, if thou art to be left alone in life, with only the arm of the divine Friend to lean on! With thee in thy young priesthood! With thee, grown old in the service of God and men!... May the Lord be with thee! Charles, bless me. I embrace thee on the Heart of the beloved divine Master."

The heart which uttered this sweet canticle of love had now come too near that of "the divine beloved Master" to have a wish, however holy, that was not in perfect conformity to His will. Henry had reached that point where the soul, called upon to make the sacrifice of its sacrifice, answers with unhesitating fidelity: "Behold the servant of the Lord!"

"Listen to me, my Charles," he writes to the newly-anointed priest a few days later; "listen to me. This morning amidst those burning desires for the priesthood which have possessed me lately, a feeling stronger than all this seemed to pervade my soul. I felt that I was ready to sacrifice even *that joy of joys, that sole aim of my whole life* (cette unique raison de toute ma vie) to the will of God, and I accepted to die to-morrow without having gone up to the altar, notwithstanding that this death would be to me *a sacrifice of a thousand lives, a sorrow of a thousand deaths*."

(TO BE CONTINUED.)

THERE ought to be in every Catholic house a picture of the Blessed Virgin, an image of a saint, or some other symbol of Catholic faith, and such symbols will always be found where Catholic faith has taken deep root, or has not been partially smothered.—*Dr. Mahar.*

Motives of Forgiveness.

AT first it may seem a hard saying, the command of our Lord to love those who hate us, and to pray for those who persecute and calumniate us. To obey this command through the fear of eternal torments or the hope of an eternal reward is perhaps the more general way, but it is not the easiest or the best. Look in the face of your neighbor, and beneath the shades cast upon it by passion behold a fellow-creature, one, like yourself, made to the image and likeness of God. Behold within him a soul to be lost or saved, like to your own, and beholding that soul a slave to the world, the flesh, or the devil, is not that neighbor more deserving of your pity than your hatred? Notwithstanding the many sins that disfigure his soul in the sight of God—each and every one of which sins, as also your own, was present to our Lord when He endured cold in the manger, and when He sweated blood in the Garden of Olives—yet our Divine Saviour loved that soul so much that He offered Himself a voluntary sacrifice to redeem it; naked, bruised and bleeding, His limbs dislocated, His Head crowned with thorns, parched with a burning thirst, His sacred body given over to the most intense suffering, our Divine Lord lays down His life to redeem the soul of that neighbor, of that enemy whom you think you are justified in hating, whom you fancy you cannot forgive! Looking away from the hope of reward or the fear of punishment—looking away from the callous, or darkened, or passion-suffused face of him or her who has wronged you in your character, your property, or your affections—turning from all these to the thorn-crowned Head and blood besmeared Face of our Lord—beholding every pore sweating blood for all mankind in the garden—beholding Him bound, naked, to a pillar, and cruelly scourged for our sakes—beholding Him buffeted, spat upon, insulted and blasphemed—beholding His sacred shoulder gored with the heavy weight of the cross on the painful journey to Calvary—and, lastly, beholding Him die a shameful and ignominious death on the Cross, between two thieves—*forgiving His enemies* (yourself and your neighbor among them) with His last breath—seeing all this, can you still find it in your heart to hate your enemy, to wish him evil, to refuse to palliate his conduct, or to return him good for evil, in word or in act, when occasion presents? Should you, not rather, seek opportunities to return good for evil?

WHAT can be more pleasing than a family picture? But yet one disagreeable feature casts a shade over the happiness of all! Every member of a family has, in his keeping, the happiness of all.

A Non-Catholic's Testimony to the Excellence of Catholic Conventual Schools.

A gentleman or lady who has recently been making a tour of the United States and Canada, and who thinks Washington and Ottawa two of the most beautiful cities he (or, more, probably *she*) had seen, gives the following impressions, in a letter to the Chicago *Daily Tribune* of Jan. 2, of the conventual schools of Canada, which are an exact counterpart of those in the United States:

"I have for years wondered why the convent system of education flourished so successfully and had such a hold upon the people of Canada as I knew it had, but I have in this visit solved the question to my satisfaction. I think it is because they have no such common-school system as in the States for general education. It may be that the common-school system is discouraged there for religious reasons. However that may be, I have, after repeated visits to many of these institutions, and rigid investigation into their systems of management, become most favorably impressed with all I have seen, and am convinced that, with the same expenditure of money, parents can obtain a more practical, and fully as fashionable, an education for their daughters at these institutions as in our most popular educational institutions in the States. Nothing seems to be neglected. The morals of the pupils are most rigidly guarded. They are taught musical and fashionable accomplishments, and also taught to take the most scrupulous care of their own rooms and clothing, and in the culinary department.

"I am more especially pleased with what I saw at two of the most aristocratic educational establishments of Canada—Hochelaga Convent, some three miles north of Montreal, and the Villa Maria, two miles south of it. The Hochelaga Convent is under the immediate direction of Mother Scholastique, Lady Superior. She has some 300 pupils of all ages under her care, and is a real mother to them all. They are educated in all branches and accomplishments, and for all necessities. Each branch of the school was in perfect discipline. Some of the most wonderful specimens of ladies' handiwork were shown me. In one circular music-room were fifteen pianos ranged around it, and the pupils played upon them with such perfect harmony that it seemed as if I heard but one.

"The Villa Maria is in charge of the Sisters of the Congregation of Notre Dame. One of the buildings was the former residence of Governor-General Monk. The institution could not be more favorably or elegantly situated, overlooking Lachine Rapids on the west, and down upon a beautiful city east. Immense additions are being made to it, as it is to be the 'Mother House,' the home of those Sisters who have distinguished themselves by long lives of devotion and sacrifices, and at last become incapacitated for more severe labor."

THE object of God has been to perfect the heart of man rather than his mind. Perfect light would indeed help his mind, but would check his feelings. There is nothing in the world that does not show either the wretchedness of man or the mercy of God; either the impotence of man without God, or the power of man with God.

A Unique Charity.

THE following interesting communication appeared in a recent number of *Macmillan's Magazine*. We thank the friend who has kindly sent it to us for publication in THE AVE MARIA.

Passing out one day by the river-side gate of the Exhibition Gardens, my eye was caught by a woman perched on a high chair fronting the spectators, in a small kiosk, and knitting vigorously in the off-hand fashion of a German, who can read or look about without dropping a stitch. Behind her a man was busy folding up linen, but above and around them hung wooden legs and hands of that primitive description which one sees offered up as *Ex-votos* in foreign village churches. A crowd stood around; in fact, every passer-by was attracted like myself to the sight—common in some respects, but most uncommon from its position; and as each left, I heard the clink of money in a box hard by. Approaching, I found it to belong to the "Society for Aiding the Maimed Poor." Soon, too, I noticed that the woman's thumb alone moved, the man's likewise, and that both wore gloves. These, then, were some of the "maimed poor," enabled to work with rough-looking, apparently unfinished, substitutes for their lost members, the same as those which hung around. A sad, touching spectacle amidst so many proofs of industry and joy! and no wonder that poor men in blouses, young and old, never left without throwing a mite into the box. But the man and woman looked happy, almost proud of their activity, and less helpless than many who have full use of their limbs. Of the Society and its noble-minded founder, the Comte de Beaufort, I had, no doubt, previously heard, but my interest naturally deepened on viewing its productions, thus witnessing its marvellous effects, and becoming thoroughly acquainted with the secret of its success, which lies in its cheapness and utility.

So far back as 1847—even earlier—the Comte de Beaufort, so well known, so pre-eminent in France for his devoted philanthropy, his disinterested character, his labors for the sick and wounded societies, and various inventions for their benefit, felt a secret longing to invent something to relieve laborers and others of the poorest classes whom he so often saw forced to become burdens to their families, or reduced to beggary, not only by those severe accidents to which they are so much more exposed than the rich, but also from their inability to purchase artificial limbs, in consequence of their high price and complicated nature. He first directed his attention to the old-fashioned wooden stump, and very soon his meditations produced a great improvement. Having noticed the slight support afforded by the straight peg, and, above all, by its pointed end, he made one of ash in the shape of the natural leg and placed it in a shoe, by which the base at once grew wide and firm. But this was not enough. He made the shoe convex, the front and back rising in a slight curve. By this simple means a man, getting up to walk, leans and finds support on his heel, while bending forward on the toe his step is lengthened as with his ordinary gait. Moreover, the Comte invented jointed legs of the most simple, efficacious kind, one-tenth the expense of those better finished, but more useful for work. From the first, Paris surgeons, such as Drs. Nélaton and Larrey, approved of them; after the Crimean War more than fifty soldiers whose legs had been amputated were provided with the "Beaufort leg" at the Val de Grâce, the great military hospital of Paris, and nothing could prove more satisfactory, the patients as well as the doctors preferring them to all others.

Next he gave his mind to hands and arms. Here especially the complicated "articulated" fingers seemed to him to impede rather than facilitate work; for, being flexible, they gave way at every movement, and the difficulty of holding anything with a firm grasp became immense. For this purpose a flexible thumb alone is necessary, and the stiffer the other joints are on which the thumb rests the better. Consequently in the wooden hands invented by him, the four fingers and the palm are simply worked into a shape indicating a hand, so that they require no expensive cutting, while the thumb alone moves in a socket. The power of moving this, moreover, is regulated in the easiest and most effective manner by a band which, passing round the chest and back to the opposite shoulder, is there worked by the mere action of the arm. The same system holds good even for amputations above the elbow, for which he has also invented simple joints without the usual steel bands and costly springs, the thumb of the hand being worked in the same way from the opposite arm. Even two false hands can thus be made available. With this system, the hold obtained is so firm that heavy work can be undertaken when the hand only is amputated, and even field labor is not uncommon, aided by additional contrivances of the Comte de Beaufort's for fastening on to these solid blocks cheap agricultural instruments designed by him. Even if the operation has been performed above the elbow, lighter work is quite possible, such as knitting, and the like. At this moment the "Beaufort hand" is adopted by many besides the very poorest, being found much more useful than the costlier ones; and, so universally acknowledged is this quality, that his inventions are popularly christened "the useful." In an interesting work lately published by the Comte are three letters beautifully written with the wooden hand by officers of rank; one who, having lost his hand in the Crimea, has used this Beaufort one since 1862; another who lost his at Gravelotte, and the third by General Zumpt, present "Commandant" at the "Invalides," whose two hands, when he was Colonel on the Staff at Sedan, were carried away by a shell.

The Comte de Beaufort's leading thought, however, had from the first been for the poor; and in the hope of widening his circle of usefulness, and interesting all classes in the work, he founded the above-named Society in 1868. The President Bonjean, murdered by the Communists, was its first chief; the great Dr. Nélaton, its second President; Baron Larrey, Doctor and Member of the Institute, acts in that capacity at present, while the Comte himself continues to be its indefatigable, benevolent secretary. It has spread in various directions throughout France, prefects and sous-prefects gladly acting as its correspondents and intermediates in the rural districts. To aid the rural population especially, and to restore the power of work to common laborers, is a main object of the Society; one in which it has eminently succeeded, for amongst other instances we hear of a carter, able to return to his occupation, walking sixteen miles with his wooden leg and shoe, without the slightest symptom of fatigue. Since the Exhibition, they have supplied one hundred individuals with legs and arms; no authenticated case of poverty is refused; nay, more, they do not even reject foreign applications, and not long since sent an arm to a poor sufferer in Italy. It would not be fair, however for foreigners to trespass too much on such kindness. The Comte de Beaufort's only desire, in his unbounded charity, is that similar societies should be founded else where, and his models copied. For these, neither he nor his manufacturer, who is also a disinterested character, have been willing to take any privileges, such as patents, assistance to the poor being their sole object. At present, however, none so good or so cheap can be obtained elsewhere; and by a system of measurement, everything can be sent from Paris to any distance. The Comte himself never rejoices so much as at the establishment of some new branch of the Society, and he is always willing and happy to give information to inquirers either by letter or otherwise, at No. 43 Rue de Verneuil, Paris. Those who have seen the good effected privately by this benevolent Christian, and now by the Society he has founded, can alone estimate its value, or wish it as heartily as we do, Godspeed in its noble undertaking, and rapid adoption in other countries.

A Suggestion.

WE gladly comply with the request to publish the following letter in reference to the distress in Ireland:

10 POWER SQUARE, BAYSWATER,
LONDON (ENGLAND), December 17, 1879.
To the Editor:

DEAR SIR:—Will you kindly make room for and ventilate in your columns a suggestion that nearly concerns Ireland? Not only have troubles come upon the old country, but others, I fear, are are *on the way;* and a little money-assistance given at this moment, though needful, can only be a half-measure of relief. Why? Because our people (thank God!) will neither beg, nor submit to be pauperized; and yet, the spring is coming, when the poor farmer fears that he must lose his land because he has neither money, nor money's worth, as a prospective harvest. Well, I only ask our six millions of Irish citizens in America to give, out of their abundance, not cash, but grain. Send home to the old people the seeds that may be most suitable for the soil of Ireland—pour them, as into a treasury, into the hands of the priesthood, to be distributed by those unpaid agents among the most needy and the most deserving,—and don't forget to tell your friends to do likewise; and God will send a blessed harvest to Ireland and to you!

I am, dear sir,
Yours faithfully,
GEORGE NOBLE PLUNKETT.

Individuals and local (American) committees can find no difficulty in communicating with the clergy and local committees in Ireland; but the need is pressing, so set your hands to the task of relieving it at once, and God bless your work! G. N. P.

THE God of the Christians is a God who makes the soul feel that He is its only good; that it can only rest in Him; that it can have no gladness but in loving Him: and who, at the same time, makes it hate the hindrances which keep it back and weaken its love. The self-love and lusts which clog its upward flight are hateful to it. God Himself makes it feel that it is clogged by this self-love, and that He only can cure it.—*Pascal.*

Catholic Notes.

——The *Catholic Mirror's* excellent Christmas Supplement must have greatly pleased all its patrons.

——It looks strange to see laudatory notices of such publications as *Puck's Annual* in Catholic papers.

——Our subscribers will kindly excuse the delay in sending out last week's issue, occasioned by the holyday.

——The Society of St. Vincent de Paul in France has resolved to have a special collection in each of its Conferences to relieve the distress in Ireland.

——THE SACRED COLLEGE.—There are now six Cardinal-archbishops, 50 Cardinal-priests, and 12 Cardinal-deacons; two Cardinals still survive who received their hats from Gregory XVI, the predecessor of Pope Pius IX.

——THE NEW GENERAL OF THE DOMINICANS.—Rev. Father La Rocca, O. S. D., a Spaniard, has been chosen Superior-General of his Order. It has been without a head since 1872. The former Superior-General was Père Jandel.

——Mr. Charles Condert, once a Lieutenant in the Guard of Honor of the First Napoleon, died at South Orange, N. J., on the 31st ult. at the advanced age of 84. He was a devout Catholic, and greatly respected by all who knew him. R. I. P.

——THE KING AND QUEEN OF SPAIN while driving through Madrid recently, met a priest who was taking the last Sacraments to a dying man. Their majesties immediately alighted from their carriage and resigned it to the priest, following on foot.

——The death is announced from Paris, at the age of 61, of M. Dominique Alexandre Denuelle, a distinguished French decorative painter. In May, 1856, he was appointed to decorate Notre Dame for the christening of the late Prince Imperial. R. I. P.

——A PRECIOUS RELIC.—From times immemorial a precious and remarkable relic, the right hand of St. Anne, has been preserved in the Cathedral of Carcassonne, France. It was lately exposed for public veneration in a neighboring church. The shrine is of giltwood, and forms the frame of four crystal panes through which the relic is visible.

——ESTABLISHMENT OF A CATHOLIC COLLEGE AT CAIRO, IN EGYPT.—With the approval of the Propaganda and the Very Rev. Custodian of the Holy Land, a College has been established by the Jesuits, at Cairo, in Egypt. The President, Very Rev. Alexis de Villeneuve, has been a professor in the Oriental colleges of the Order for a long time, and is thoroughly acquainted with the manners and spirit of the different peoples dwelling in Syria, Egypt, etc.

——THE INAUGURATION OF THE PALESTRINA MONUMENT at Rome is likely to be celebrated with great magnificence, and to assume, in fact, an almost international character. Signor Verdi is known to be engaged in the task of setting to music Dante's "Ave Maria" for the occasion. Besides the great composer, and Signors Ponchielli and Marchetti, a number of foreign authors will probably be present, personal invitations having already been addressed to MM. Gounod, Ambroise Thomas, Liszt, and Richard Wagner.

——BOSTON BEHIND.—Boston has been outrun by Rome in the race of public schools. In 1870, the last year of Rome under the Popes, there were, according to an authoritative work, *Carità in Roma*, 23,905 young persons receiving gratuitous instruction. At the same time the whole city of Boston, according to Superintendent Philbrick's report, had only an average attendance of 32,463, which will not compare with Rome, in proportion to population. In the higher educational works, Rome has still further surpassed Boston.—*The Pilot.*

—MORE AID FOR SUFFERING IRELAND.—Right Rev. Bishop Dwenger, of Fort Wayne, has addressed a circular to the clergy of his diocese, saying: "You have heard of the great want and distress in Ireland owing to the wet and unfavorable season. At all times there are in that land of faith many very poor people, who became poor for the sake of their Holy Religion; now many are absolutely starving. We recommend, therefore, that in all churches, where it can be done without interfering with your own absolute wants, a collection be taken up on a Sunday, and the amount forwarded to the Bishop of the Diocese, who will send it to some Bishops in Ireland where the greatest suffering is reported. You will perceive the expediency of taking up this collection as soon as possible."

—COUNT LADISLAUS PLATER has sent the following communication to the Editor of the *Missions Catholiques*: "There is not the least sign of any improvement in the condition of our poor exiles. The excess of the evil is the only reason we have to hope that it cannot last much longer. Even in Warsaw, the authorities are concerned about the Polish prayers in the churches, and demand them to be translated into Russian. A seminary directed and maintained by the Government, has just been officially inaugurated at St. Petersburg. It will be the nursery of the Polish clergy. The Polish language is excluded in this institution, to give way to the Russian. This measure, so hurtful to the Catholic orthodoxy, is to pave the way for the Greco-Russian schism. In the midst of these calamities, however, the Catholics of Poland do not give themselves up to despair: they are turning their tearful eyes towards Heaven."

—THE ORDER OF THE ELEPHANT.—At the recent visit of the royal couple from Denmark to Berlin, the German Emperor wore the Order of the Elephant, the highest order of the kingdom of Denmark. It may be interesting to our readers to learn that the origin of this famous order dates from the Ages of Faith, and was thoroughly Catholic in the beginning. At the time of its foundation, which occured most likely in 1190 under Canute IV, it was called the Confraternity of the Holy Virgin Mary. The badge was formerly a gold medal, representing on one side the image of the Immaculate Conception, and on the other an elephant. Later on it was a collar, with a golden elephant standing upon roses in a field of white enamel, and carrying a tower of ivory. As a coat of arms it was represented, in a chain of elephants, to which a medal of the Immaculate Conception was attached. It is interesting to know that the Immaculate Conception was already in the XIIth century an object of devotion among Catholic chivalry, in a country far remote from Rome. The ivory of the elephant, signifying both strength and purity, typifies the "*Turris eburnea*," one of the titles of Our Lady.

—A PRINCELY CHRISTMAS GIFT.—On Christmas eve the Right Rev. Bishop left his confessional in the church at a late hour, intending to take a short rest, as previous arrangements required that he should be again at his post before 4 a. m. Christmas morning. Before retiring, however, he was handed a letter, which on opening he found to be from a former Mayor of this city, and learning that the messenger had left without asking for an answer, he concluded, after hastily glancing over its contents, that the writer was about to consummate one of those acts so characteristic of Hon. W. L. Scott. Having celebrated Pontifical Mass, the Bishop again turned his attention to the letter, and after reading it through carefully, found that Mr. Scott desired to know in whose name he should register one hundred shares of the Erie & Pittsburgh Railroad Company stock, guaranteed at 7 per cent. for 999 years by the Pennsylvania Railroad Company, the principle to be held in trust, and the income to be applied towards the support of the orphans in the Catholic Orphan Asylum of this city. The par value of one hundred shares is five thousand dollars. The necessary information having been given Mr. Scott, that gentleman has had the stock registered in the name of the proper party, and thus secured to the orphans a gift which will go a good way in providing them with a competent support, and in completing improvements at the Asylum, which hitherto could not have been made for want of the necessary funds. As a business man, Hon. W. L. Scott's success has been great, but not greater than the munificence with which he dispenses his charities. At the same time that he exhibited his good will for our orphans, he made a similar donation to the Home of the Friendless in this city. May the prayers of the orphans secure for him a happy life and a blissful eternity!—*Lake-Shore Visitor (Erie, Pa.)*

Answers to Correspondents.

N. N.—The book you refer to is utter rubbish. What it was published for is past finding out.

THOMAS.—Our advice is to consult your confessor, and to abide by his decision.

J. McN., New York.—We will gladly receive donations for the suffering poor in Ireland. Yes: the need is a pressing one. In all such emergencies, to give quickly is to give twice.

J. A. C.—A postal card will answer the purpose.

MISS N.—You surely oughtn't to dance round dances. Be sure of it, that St. Francis de Sales ("the misquoted" Saint," we are tempted to term him) would be horrified at the dance you mention. No priest who knows what it is, will have any hesitancy in condemning it.

M.—We haven't had time to examine your MS. yet.

HENRY A——.—We are sorry, but we have no encouragement to give you. Poetry is not your forte. Stick to your present employment.

N. N.—You oughtn't to write anonymous letters. Our knowledge of the commodity you are interested in amounts to 0.

A READER, England.—We prefer the old way.

LIZZIE.—Very good; but try again.

"IGNORANCE."—St. Mary Magdalene died in Provence. The cave in which she lived for thirty years is still seen. We have an interesting account of a pilgrimage to the Shrine of St. Mary Magdalene to be published after a while.

For Rebuilding Notre Dame University.

Miss Maggie Crowley, 30 cts.; Miss Louise Gallagher, 40 cts.; A Friend, 80 cts.; Miss Mary Cullen, $1; A Friend, 50 cts.; Daniel Kavanagh, $10; Sam Ready. $5; A Subscriber, $1; W. P. Dodds, $1; Mrs. Elizabeth Claus, $5; A Friend, 25 cts.; A Friend, 2.50; Mr. Henry Grine, $1; Mrs. Catharine Kalmes, $1; Mr. John Magnet, $1; Mrs. Catharine Claus, $2; Rosalie Southwick, $2.

New Publications.

PSYCHOLOGICAL ASPECTS OF EDUCATION. A Paper read before the University Convocation of the State of New York, at Albany, July 11, 1877. By Brother Azarias, of the Brothers of the Christian Schools. New York: E. Steiger. 1879.

An interesting and instructive disquisition on one of the great subjects of the day, by one who is favorably known both as a writer and an educator.

SEED ANNUAL FOR 1880. D. M. Ferry & Co., Detroit, Michigan.

We take pleasure in recommending this excellent and elegant pamphlet to those of our readers in need of an illustrated, descriptive and priced catalogue of garden, flower and agricultural seeds.

VICK'S FLORAL GUIDE FOR 1880.

This is certainly one of the most beautiful publications of the day, and one of the cheapest. It is full of useful and reliable information regarding flowers, plants, vegetables, seeds, etc. Those charged with the decoration of altars, etc., will find it of great service. Price, five cents. Address James Vick, Rochester, N. Y.

THE LIFE OF OUR LORD AND SAVIOUR JESUS CHRIST AND OF HIS BLESSED MOTHER. Translated and Adapted from the Original of Rev. L. C. Businger, by Rev. Richard Brennan, LL. D. Parts 23, 24. Benziger Bros., Publishers.

We are glad to notice that there is no deterioration in this popular work, now nearing its completion. A very good chromo-lithograph of the Good Shepherd accompanies the present instalment. The history is brought down to the Passion and Death of Christ.

Confraternity of the Immaculate Conception

(Or of Our Lady of Lourdes).

"We fly to thy patronage, O Holy Mother of God!"

[Every week, numerous petitions for spiritual and temporal favors come to us from various parts of the country. Continual prayers are offered to Almighty God for all these intentions, including a weekly Mass (on Saturday), two novenas every month, and some hours of adoration before the Blessed Sacrament at night, etc. To these must be added the prayers solicited from the members of the Confraternity, and we like to believe they are fervent and numerous. We would suggest that each member recite every day a fervent "Hail Mary," with this invocation: "O Mary conceived without sin, pray for us who have recourse to Thee," for the intentions recommended.]

REPORT FOR THE WEEK ENDING JANUARY 7TH.

The following petitions have been received: Recovery of health for 61 persons and 5 families,—change of life for 16 persons and 2 families,—conversion to the Faith for 29 persons and 5 families,—special graces for 6 priests, 4 religious, 3 clerical students, and 3 persons aspiring to the religious state,—temporal favors for 36 persons and 11 families,—spiritual favors for 53 persons and 14 families,—the spiritual and temporal welfare of 3 communities, 4 congregations, 2 schools, 1 hospital, and 2 orphan asylums. Also 39 particular intentions, and 7 thanksgivings for favors received.

Specified intentions: Conversion of a well-meaning Protestant, hopelessly ill,—return of some absent children,—the favorable settlement of some unjust lawsuits,—conversion of the Protestant children of a Western district school,—protection against accidents and sudden deaths,—the acquittal of a man accused of a crime, and the removal of the scandal occasioned thereby,—opportunity and will for the parents of 5 families to bring up their children good Catholics,—cure and conversion of several Protestants using the water of Lourdes,—conversion and happy death of several non-Catholics in a precarious state of health,—recovery of health, or a happy death, for several persons. —a Bishop and his diocese,—restoration of hearing for a religious,—the spiritual and temporal welfare of all the members of the Confraternity, and others, during this new year,—restoration of hearing for a nun of the Sacred Heart.

FAVORS OBTAINED.

Thanks are offered to our Immaculate Mother for the following favors ascribed to her powerful intercession: "The very first drops of the holy water of Lourdes," says a correspondent, "cured me of an ailment that had lasted over one year. During that time I never breathed a natural breath; now, I am perfectly relieved. A friend of mine was also cured of a severe pain by the application of the water of Lourdes."

.... "I have obtained a miraculous cure of ear-ache," a pious client of Mary writes, "which was driving me almost insane, and could not be cured by earthly means. I had been suffering from this complaint since I was two years old, and I am now eighteen. After a month of intolerable pain I commenced a novena to Our Lady of Lourdes. Up to the 8th night I was no better; but on the 9th I slept for the first time free from pain. Since then I have been able to face the winds and fogs of our Pacific coast. The worst gales have no effect on me, while previous to my cure I could not leave one room for another. Few of my friends would believe me at first, but facts cannot be contradicted."

.... Another grateful correspondent says: "We received the Lourdes water. My brother was dying, having been given up by two doctors. After using the water he was able to go to Mass on the Feast of the Immaculate Conception, and has been out since." Other cures have also been made known to us, which, for want of space, we cannot make mention of.

OBITUARY.

We recommend the following deceased persons to the prayers of the Confraternity: Mrs. MARY QUINN, of Cresco, Iowa, who departed this life on the 30th of November. DR. ALEXIS W. SULLIVAN, of Charlestown, Mass., who was relieved of a protracted and painful illness by a happy death on the 6th ult. Mrs. MARGARET WELLIN, whose death occurred at Philadelphia, Pa., on the 26th of November. Mr. GEORGE STEWART, of Washington, D. C., who breathed his last on the 17th ult. Miss MARY BRENHAM, whose happy death took place on the same day. Mr. P. MURPHY, deceased November 29th. Mr. M. O'NEILL, who died on the 18th of December. Mrs. MARGARET T. HACKETT, of Watertown, Mass., who departed for heaven last July. SISTER MARY BASILLA (Donahoe), of the Sisters of the Holy Cross, who was called to her eternal reward on the 5th of January. Mrs. MARY A. HARDY, of Cincinnati, Ohio, who rested in peace on the 17th ult. Mr. JOHN COMBER, of Philadelphia, Pa., recently deceased. Miss ANN MOLLOY, of N. Y. EDWARD COGAN, THOMAS MEANEY, and RICHARD DOWNEY, of Washington, D. C. Mrs. MARY KELLY, of Evansville, Ind. PATRICK HOGAN and Mrs. BRIDGET FIELDING, of Clontarf, Minn. Miss KATE BOLGER, of New York. Miss M. WHITAKER, of Fort Wayne, Ind. Mrs. J. D. COOK, of Schenectady, N. Y. Mr. CALDWELL, his daughter and son, of Ashland, Ill.

Requiescant in pace.

A. GRANGER, C. S. C., Director.

Youths' Department.

St. Agnes.

HOLY Roman Maiden
  With the gentle name,
Noble was thy lineage,
  Spotless is thy fame.
Next to Mother Mary,
  Thee we choose to be
Patroness and guardian
  Of our purity.

In thy youth so tender,
  Thou didst gladly die,
Rather than surrender
  Thy virginity.
Fair and peerless treasure!
  Pearl beyond all price!
In whose rich possession
  Chosen souls rejoice!

To thy young heart dearer
  Than all else beside,
Since it brought thee nearer
  Jesus crucified!
Nearer to His Mother—
  She of whom we sing:
"After her shall virgins
  Come unto the King."

Threats, nor chains, nor dungeon,
  Could thy soul appal,
For the love of Jesus
  Thou didst suffer all!
Till the sword descending,
  Severing thy head,
Numbered thee, sweet Agnes,
  With the sainted dead.

And thy blood's pure fragrance
  Mounting to the sky,
Rose as sweetest inscense
  To thy Spouse on high;
For thy noble vict'ry
  Over death and pain,
How hath He repaid thee
  O'er and o'er again!

"*Veni sponsa Mea!*"
  Lovingly He cried;
"Thou for Me hast conquered,
  Thou for Me hast died.
Wreaths of fadeless flowers
  Shall adorn thy brow,
For a spotless lily
  In My sight art thou!"

Holy, happy Martyr,
  Blissful now above,
In the sweet possession
  Of thy Lord and Love;
We thy humble clients,
  Thy protection claim,
Thy appeals to Jesus
  Ne'er can be in vain.

Pray that we may never
  Lose our holy faith;
That our souls may ever
Be prepared for death;
And, oh! dearest sister,
  Pray still more that we
May behold thy glory
  In eternity.

B. M. J. KERNAN.

The Story of a Revenge.

BY ELIZA ALLEN STARR, AUTHOR OF "PATRON SAINTS," ETC.

(CONCLUSION.)

IT was late in the afternoon of the same Good Friday when a young knight threw himself from his horse on the open space just outside the enclosure of San Miniato. The sun was near its setting, and wonderful was the panorama spread out before his eyes. Florence —the city of flowers, above all of that flower which typifies the Virgin of virgins, the tripetaled lily, which Florence carries on her shield—lay at his feet, cradled among hills which are to be the delight of artists and the inspiration of poets to the end of time: and these hills dotted by towns and cities and monasteries which were already famous, but which were to become still more so by the triumphs of genius in the age then called future, and which we call past. And over this city, and over these beauteous hills, and over this Arno flowing full between its banks, was a heaven of such splendor that the eye which looked up to it would seem to have a foresight of celestial glory. Rose-tints from the palest blush to the deepest crimson; gorgeous purples edged with living gold; shifting clouds, melting, then flushing again to die at last into tender greys; tinges of pale green among these tints, or fading off into the blue sky: such were the glories of that hour from the summit of San Miniato. The Italian eye is naturally alive to such gorgeous effects: but this evening the young patrician did not raise his eyes when he threw his bridle rein to one of half-a-dozen who stood ready to hold it and to catch the small coin which he flung with the rein, as if both were matters of mere habit. The colors flushed or paled as they might, without notice from him; and striding past the old fortified tower which crowned the height, he made his way straight through the arched gateway of masonry into the church, by a door always open. Without one look at the church itself, or a thought of the beauty of its proportions or the pale green of its precious columns, or of the choir resting on its twenty-eight pillars with its windows of translucent marble; without a thought of who might be near him or who might think him singular or even quite beside himself, the young knight prostrated himself like a penitent at the foot of the high altar. Nor was this for merely one moment or for many. During one long hour the head of that proud young knight had not been raised from the pavement of the church. The monks went to and fro from the cloister to the choir; devout worshippers passed the prostrate figure in silence, awed by the sighs and sobs which seemed to come from a soul broken with anguish. The shadows of evening had begun to settle upon the church, but through the dim twilight could be seen the crucifix above the altar. At three o'clock of the afternoon this crucifix had been laid on a cushion before the altar railing, in order that the faithful performing their devotions to the Passion of our Lord should kiss His sacred Wounds. While the knight still kept his place, it had been put again over the high altar. As he looked up and saw those arms extended, the head raised as if saying, "My God, My God, why hast Thou forsaken Me!" a sudden anguish seized him, a temptation to despair; when the raised head of the Crucified bent sweetly towards him, as if to say, "My son, this day all thy sins are forgiven thee!" Transported by the look of tender compassion on this face, altogether divine in Its anguish, his tears and his sighs ceased. A peace profound, altogether supernatural, took possession of his soul. The world, and all it had hitherto possessed that was precious, suddenly passed from his mind. There was a combat more difficult than with any foe to Florence or to his family, which suddenly called for his courage and his perseverance; it was the combat with himself and his fierce passions. How near had he not come to committing the crime of murder! His hand had been mercifully checked, but he knew how often he had committed murder in his heart. Worldly maxims, about honor and military glory, ceased to have any meaning for him. Before that image of our crucified Lord, all desire for glory died out of him, and before that Head bowed in meek submission, the desire to command his fellow-men utterly ceased. A sudden resolution had sprung up in his heart. He would lay aside his sword forever; he would exchange his spurs as a knight for the cowl of a Benedictine. To think was to act. He knew well the door to the monastery, and knocked for admission with such humility that it was hard to refuse him. "But," said the abbot, "remember your father will never forgive us for receiving you."

"I know," replied Giovanni, "but, at least, allow me to come within your doors and to find peace. You would not deny this to a beggar; why then to the son of Count Gualberto?" Every objection was met by a plea which no heart could resist, and that night saw him within the walls of San Miniato. Nothing could be more docile than the spirit of this knight longing to be a monk. But when the time came for him to receive the habit and the tonsure,* no one was found who would bestow them upon him. Count Gualberto was there, ready to visit his indignation on the whole community. There was but one way open to him. "Since you will not give me the habit and tonsure," he said, "I will even take them for myself." With a razor he shaved his own head, and then exchanged his worldly garments for the coarse habit of a Benedictine novice. The abbot, the monks kept the silence of death. And Count Gualberto? As water quenches the burning brand, all the fire of his rebellious pride, of his self-will, of his revengeful anger, was quenched by this one act of his son Giovanni. When it was all over, instead of burning the monastery as he had threatened to do if they dared to give the habit and tonsure to the heir of the house of Gualberto, a little child could have led him. Knocking quietly at the door of the monastery, he asked to see his son, fell on his neck and kissed him, while tears rained down his cheeks.

Laurina, had not thy prayer been fully and altogether answered?

. . . .

Twenty miles from Florence, among the wilds of the Apennine mountains, was a valley deeply shaded by trees. Among others, the weeping willow grew to a great size and beauty along the margins of the brooks which coursed down the mountain sides to the valley. A tender gloom pervaded the whole spot and inclined the soul to meditation. Giovanni had often come upon this valley on his long rides over the country in the days of his knighthood, and never without saying he would like to make his home there. The remembrance of it came back to him, in the peaceful routine of life at San Miniato; and when the good abbot died, and Giovanni was named as one worthy to succeed him, he begged instead to be allowed to retire to this shaded valley with one companion, and there to live out the rule of Saint Benedict in all its strictness. His request was granted, and he made a little hut for himself and the brother-monk, calling the place Vallambrosa, the shaded valley, or valley of shadows. But no sooner had he begun to live out the perfect rule of Saint Benedict, choosing the coarsest garments, the plainest food, than the luxurious youth of Florence flocked around him, eager to share his privations; so that he was obliged to build a small convent of the trunks of trees plastered with mud. From this small beginning grew a powerful community, which took the name of this valley, and were called Monks of Vallambrosa; another strong branch on the tree of Saint Benedict. From this community went forth others, each one carrying with it the spirit of heroic penitence which char-

---
* The crown of the head was shaved when a monk received the habit.

acterized their abbot, Giovanni, or John, of Gualbert. One day, however, when he went to visit a monastery of his Vallambrosans, he found that the prior, Rudolphe, instead of keeping two plain buildings suited to hard-working monks, had raised buildings fit for colleges or houses for the rich. "Alas, my brother," said the abbot, "in your vain ambition to do great things, you have spent the means which should have been given to the poor, in raising houses of luxury for poor religious, where they are to live like lords; but it will come to naught. God knows how to use small means to work great results."

Hardly had the abbot left them than the brook near by suddenly rose to a wild torrent which roared against the foundations of the new buildings until they were mere wrecks. The monks, seized with affright, wished to leave the place: but the abbot assured them that the stream had merely wrought the will of God. And so long as their buildings remained suited to their wants, they had nothing to fear.

But the dread of luxury made him always on the alert. He heard that in some of the monasteries a novice had been received who had immense wealth; and that the whole of this wealth had been made over to the community, without any regard to his family. This was enough to cause a visit to the community. He asked them to show him the deeds by which so much wealth had been secured to them. The deeds were handed to him; but no sooner were they in his possession than he tore them into shreds.

In the year 1073, at the age of seventy-two, this soldier who had fought his battle against sin so bravely, died peacefully, among his fellow-soldiers trained so zealously by him.

The pilgrims who now visit San Miniato, on the hill overlooking Florence, not only venerate there the memory of St. Minias, the soldier Saint, but of John, the son of the vindictive Count Gualberto, under the name of "Saint John Gualbert." For a long time the Benedictines at San Miniato guarded as one of their most precious treasures the crucifix over the high altar which had bent its head towards the repentant young knight in token of forgiveness. But at length they parted with this dear relic, in favor of the Vallambrosa monks in the Convent of the Trinity, in Florence. There it is still venerated; and before it the fiery young nobles of Florence have learned not only the story of John Gualbert, but how to forgive an enemy. To realize how grace changes even the outer man, one must go to the gallery of *Belle Arte* in Florence. There is the grand picture of the Assumption of the Blessed Virgin, painted by Perugino for the monks at Vallambrosa. Sitting upon the clouds in the midst of an almond-shaped glory edged with cherubs' heads, she is borne upward in an ecstasy of solemn delight, to her Divine Son. Angels, vested like acolythes, playing their viols and harps and cithems, accompany her, while others from above are hastening to welcome her to the courts of heaven. But below this celestial vision, and as if wholly absorbed in contemplating it, while standing on the earth, are four saints rapt into such a trance of bliss that they have been named in art the *ambrosial* saints. One of these, to the right of the spectator, is Saint Michael, Archangel, in all the splendor of his celestial attributes. Plumes from birds of paradise float from his helmet; but while cased in his shining armor, the shield and unsheathed sword are held as if resting a moment from combat. At the extreme left of the picture is Saint Bernard of Uberti, in his Cardinal's hat; and who, besides his dignity of Cardinal, was a celebrated Abbot of Vallambrosa, which gave him his place in this picture. The middle of the space left is taken up, first by Saint Benedict as Patriarch of the Order from which sprang the Vallambrosans, and opposite to him, and like him fixedly gazing into heaven, stands our Saint John Gualberto, bearing in his hand a crucifix. To none of the four saints has been given a mien of such profound peace as to this once vindictive son of a vindictive father. Every fold of the garments discloses a rest of the soul which comes only from a perfect submission of the will to the law of love. It is the story of the transformation of the young knight bent on revenge into this serene contemplater of heavenly joys, which San Miniato cherishes as one of her choicest flowers.

And let us take one more look into this old church, which dates back to the 4th century of our Christian era. It had been rebuilt by Bishop Hildebrand of Florence only a few years before our story of Saint John Gualberto opens. To him we owe its admirable proportions, the nave with its twelve beautiful columns (some of them antique, and doubtless belonging to the first church) of white and also polished green marble. To him, also, we owe the beautiful choir for the monks, raised on twenty-eight columns above the worshippers from the world, in order to sing God's praises all the better; and to him we owe the five windows of the apse or choir, or sanctuary as we should say; not in painted glass or in stained glass, but in translucent marble. But we must date still later than his time, which was 1013, the precious carved marble which encrusts, like frost-work, the choir with its altar and pulpit. How mysterious that sanctuary looks from below, so carefully adorned yet almost beyond the sight of the visitor, and lighted so dimly by its marble windows! But the eagle of Saint John the Evangelist, and the symbols of all the other Evangelists, gleam out from its pulpit in spite of the gloom. To the right of the sanctuary is the chapter-room of the monastery, adorned by the great Signorelli, with frescoes telling the story of Saint Benedict, and worthy to be studied, long after, by Michael Angelo. Above the high altar before which John Gualberto prostrated himself on the afternoon of that Good Friday in 1020, are represented the Annunciation, Passion, Resurrection and Ascension of our Lord. Below these we see, of life-size, the early patroness of Florence, Saint Reparata, with her crown and palm and lilies; and at the other end of the altar, our Saint John Gualberto, with his crucifix. Between these are small pictures, representing scenes from the life of this favorite Saint among the Florentines, while the front of the altar bears a large marble tablet (1) giving the story of Saint John Gualbert, and telling us where we can see the crucifix which gave him so sweet a token of forgiveness, in return for his merciful forgiveness of his brother's murderer.

(1) NOTE.—"Cosmas Medici, by a decree of the Supreme Pontiff, built and consecrated this noble chapel to the honor of the most holy image of Jesus hanging upon the cross, which in this ancient Church of Saint Miniatis inclined its head at the prayer of the brave soldier. John Gualbert—afterward founder of the monks of Vallis-Umbrosal—when granting him pardon for his crime of fratricide, which he implored with his very life. From here it was, in the year 1671, transferred with befitting pomp to Florence, by Leopold Medici, a most illustrious Cardinal of the Holy Roman Church; and the abbot and monks, consulting both the piety and convenience of the faithful, there placed it upon the principal altar of the Church and Monastery of the Most Holy Trinity. Which has been done by King Cosmas III out of love towards the blessed in heaven, and that the memory of these things might not perish."

"I'll Keep My Eyes Shut."

LITTLE Henry had been quite sick. When he was slowly recovering, and just able to be up and go about, he was left alone for a short time, when his sister came in, eating a piece of cake. Henry's mother had told him that he must eat nothing but what she gave him, and that it would not be safe for him to have what the other children did until he was stronger.

His appetite was coming back, and the cake looked inviting; he wanted very much to take a bite of it, and his kind sister would gladly have given it to him.

"Jennie," said he, "you must run right out of the room, away from me, with that cake, and *I'll keep my eyes shut* while you go, so that I shan't want it."

Was not that a good way for a little boy of seven years to get out of temptation? I think so. And when I heard of it, I thought that there are a great many times when children, and grown people too, if they would remember little Henry's way, would escape from sin and trouble.

"Turn away mine eyes from beholding vanity, and quicken Thou me in Thy way," was the Psalmist's prayer, and it is also a good one for each of us.

The Cardinal and the Jew.

A YOUNG Jew had been sent out by his father on a peddling errand, and on his arrival at Gran he found to his dismay that he had lost his bundle. A gentleman who happened to hear of this, advised the youth to apply to the Archbishop of Gran, Mgr. Scitovsky von Nagy-Kér, Primate of Hungary, for relief. The Jew drew up a petition to the Cardinal, and presented it at the palace. Mgr. Scitovsky thereupon sent for the youth, received him with the utmost kindness, and handing him thirty florins, the value of the "notions," said to him: "There, my son, God speed you; be more careful in future that you don't bring any loss on your old father."

The next day the young Jew called again at the palace. "What! have you met with another misfortune?" said the Prelate.

"No," replied the Jew; "I have found my bundle again, and have come to return the money to your Eminence."

The Cardinal replied, "Keep the money, my son, and take my blessing too," and dismissed him with some sound advice. The thirty florins turned out a source of prosperity to the youth, and he became one of the wealthiest men of the land.

A version of the Bible appeared in Spain in 1478, before Luther was thought of, and almost before he was born. In Italy, the country most peculiarly under the sway of Papal dominion, the Scriptures were translated into Italian by Malermi, at Venice, in 1471; and this version was republished seventeen times before the conclusion of that century, and twenty-three years before that of Luther appeared. A second version, of parts of Scripture, was published in 1472; a third at Rome in 1471; a fourth at Venice in 1522; and a corrected edition, in 1538; two years after Luther had completed his. And every one of these came out, not only with the approbation of the ordinary authorities, but with that of the Inquisition, which approved of their being published, distributed and promulgated.—*Dr. Wiseman.*

THE AVE MARIA.

A Journal devoted to the Honor of the Blessed Virgin.

HENCEFORTH ALL GENERATIONS SHALL CALL ME BLESSED.—St. Luke, i, 48.

VOL. XVI.   NOTRE DAME, INDIANA, JANUARY 24, 1880.   No. 4.

(Copyright: Rev. D. E. Hudson, C. S. C.)

[For the "Ave Maria."]

Alma Redemptoris Mater.

BY CHARLES KENT.

HAIL, Mother pure of our Redeeming Lord!
Hail, open gate, to holiest heaven restored!
Sweet Star of ocean, beacon in the sky
To lift our sinking souls to God on high!
Thou who thy Holy One by marvel rare
Didst in thy sinless, stainless bosom bear!
Virgin before and after Gabriel's "Hail!"
With God, for sinners, make thy prayers prevail!

St. Francis de Sales, Doctor of the Church.

BY "ARTHUR."

THE natural, unperverted bent of human nature is towards perfection. This is a psychological fact. We are made to the image and likeness of the All-Perfect. To reproduce Him, so to speak, in our own measure, is our purpose here below; to enjoy Him forever, our destiny above. The Scriptures confirm this; Jesus Christ preached it. "Be ye perfect as your heavenly Father is perfect." And this injunction was delivered to every living being: not to priest and religious exclusively, as is not uncommonly believed in this our day,—an unpardonable error, because contradictory of common sense. The refutation of this error, thereby showing the necessity and means of perfection to every Christian, was the glory of St. Francis de Sales,—the having clearly shown how we *can* and *ought* to walk with God, "not hanging on precariously to His skirts," to use Father Faber's expression. For this, principally, has the Church, in two recent monuments, confirmed and proclaimed St. Francis de Sales a Doctor of the universal Church. And he may be particularly styled the Doctor of Devotion, just as St. Athanasius has been called the Doctor of the Divinity of Christ; St. Jerome, the Doctor of the Scriptures; St. Augustine, the Doctor of Grace; St. Thomas the Doctor of the Schools; and St. Alphonsus, the Doctor of Moral Theology. Just a word or two on the significance of this declaration.

When the Church gives the title of Doctor of the Church to a saint, she places him in the category of those sages according to God's own Heart whose wisdom guides the clergy and the people, whose doctrines are the aids of Popes and Councils in teaching truths, and whose opinions are accepted as the essence of faith in matters of dogma and morals. Prior to the decree (July 10th, 1877,) which proclaimed St. Francis de Sales a Doctor of the Church, his doctrines obtained a very high reputation—simply, however, on the authority of the writer, and the strength of his arguments; but now, that he is placed in the canon of Doctors by the supreme authority of the Church, his writings are supported by doctoral authority, into the possession of which he has entered periodically. Hence, any proposition of his, even if not demonstrated, assumes an authoritative degree of probability, just the same as an opinion of St. Jerome, [St. Augustine, or St. Thomas. The second confirmatory Brief *ad perpetuam rei memoriam*, dated November 16, 1877, defines this as follows: "By our Apostolic Authority, and in virtue of these presents, we confirm the title of Doctor in honor of St. Francis de Sales; or, insomuch as it may be necessary, we give and impart it to him anew, so that he will be considered as Doctor in the universal Catholic Church. We decree, moreover, that the books, commentaries, and, finally, all the works, of the same Doctor, like those of other Doctors of the Church, be cited, adduced, and used as necessity requires, not only privately, but also publicly, in Gymnasiums, Academies, Schools, Colleges, Lessons, Disputations, Sermons, and other ecclesiastical studies and Christian exercises."*

---

* Auctoritate nostra Apostolica, tenore presentium, titulum Doctoris in honorem Sancti Francisci Salesii confirmamus, seu, quatenus opus sit, denuo et tribuimus, impertimus, ita ut in universali Catholica Ecclesia semper ipse Doctor habeatur. Præterea, ejusdem Doctoris libros, commentaria, opera denique omnia, ut aliorum Ecclesiæ Doctorum, non modo privatim, sed et publice in Gymnasiis, Academiis, Scholis, Collegiis,

We need scarcely comment on the pleasure, which has already greeted this declaration throughout the Church. It is the realization of a unanimous desire, not only of the faithful in general, who read the works of the sainted Bishop of Geneva, but, in particular, of the express petitions of many illustrious personages and of six theological universities: the Sorbonne, those of Bologna, Vienna, Pesht, Louvain, and the Seminary of Baltimore. To these add the Bollandist writers of Brussels, and the *Civiltà Cattolica* of Florence. This, however, is but a tithe of the demonstration in favor of the final decree. Thirty Cardinals of the Vatican Council, seven Patriarchs, seventy-four Archbishops, three hundred and twenty Bishops, and fifteen Superiors of religious Orders subscribed to another petition to the same effect. All this, though the embodiment of the universal sentiment of the Church on the matter, did not move his Holiness to publish the decree. He submitted the question, according to the custom of the Church, to the Sacred Congregation of Rites, and allowed it to be treated with that rigor *pro*, and *con*, which no civil tribunal on earth can equal. For seven years has the case been before that council, and we are far from exaggerating in saying that never did salaried and misanthropic hypercritic lacerate a work with more purpose and less remorse than did the "Devil's Advocate" in this case the works of the sweet St. Francis de Sales. Astute though the objections, yet still more learned and convincing were the explanations, else the decree would not have been promulgated.

St. Francis de Sales was naturally a genius. Not on this account did he study the less assiduously. He was a hard worker in the college of the Jesuits in Paris, where he studied philosophy, a hard worker in the theological University of the Sorbonne, then in its glory, for Genebrardus and Maldonatus were in the rostra. At Padua he won the laureate in jurisprudence under the famous and rigorous Panceroli. Here, too, he had for his master and friend Father Possevinus, who taught him to love St. Thomas and Bellarmine, his invincible weapons years after in his disputations with the heretics. His library, by the way, on his missions, was very limited: the Bible, the *Summa* of St. Thomas, and the Moral Theology of Reginaldus. He also devoted himself assiduously to profane sciences, and, besides being regarded as one of the most famous jurisconsults of his day, his reputation as a classical scholar and a sweet-spoken Frenchman extended over all Europe. He had the greatest saints and scholars of the time for his friends; Blessed Peter Canisius, Cardinal du Perron, the Venerable Baronius, the Venerable Bellarmine, Lipsius, and others. Pope Paul V consulted him on the great question *De Auxiliis*, which then agitated the Catholic academies of Europe, and settled it according to his opinion—so that the great scholars of the day proclaimed him a living oracle of science, and compared him with the great ancient Doctors of the Church. But his wisdom and doctrine still live in his works. He has left to the Church seventeen works on theology and sacred polemics. In one of these last, there is a glorious vindication of the Papal Infallibility, as defined by the Vatican Council. There are three splendid works on the Scriptures, one of which is a mystical commentary on the Canticle of Canticles; seven on Moral Theology, seventeen containing directions to his clergy, twelve on Canon Law and ecclesiastical discipline, two on history, and twelve others on various subjects. His letters are another treasure.

His masterpieces, however, in which the scholar and the saint rise before us, and which alone are sufficient title to the sacred Doctorate, are the *Philothea*, or *Introduction to a Devout Life*, and the *Theotime*, or *Treatise on the Love of God*. All his other works are the productions of a great genius. These pass the borderland of human science—they seem inspirations of Heaven. Such was the judgment of his contemporaries, such the opinion set forth in the Lessons of the Office on his Feast, *Suis scriptis cælesti doctrina refertis Ecclesiam illustravit, quibus iter ad Christianam perfectionem tritum et planum demonstrat*—by his writings, teeming with heavenly doctrine, in which he shows the road to Christian perfection easy and clear; he brought glory on the Church. Let the reader remember, too, that such a judgment was pronounced upon the works of St. Francis at a time when the Church was most prolific in ascetic writers. Blosius, in neighboring France, had just breathed his last. In Italy, the remembrance of St. Charles Borromeo was still fresh; and Lorenzo Scupoli, the disciple of St. Andrew of Avellino, and the author of the *Spiritual Combat*, was still alive. This little work was a great favorite with St. Francis himself. Spain was then in her glory, for she had just given to the Church men,—saints like Peter of Alcantara, Ignatius, John of the Cross, Venerable Avila, Alvarez de Paz, Louis of Granada, Francesco Arias, Rodriguez, and a woman like Theresa. All these wrote on Christian and religious perfection. Yet Francis was a sun among these luminaries. His *Philothea* was received as an event in the Catholic world, and—a rare occurrence in those days—was translated into seventeen different languages and dialects.

The purpose of this book was to propagate the highest Christian perfection among all classes.

---

lectionibus, disputationibus, concionibus, aliisque ecclesiasticis studiis Christianisque exercitationibus, citari, proferri, et prout res postulaverit, adhiberi decernimus.

In it, the Saint proposes rules and maxims adapted to every state of life. The idea was not a new one. The *Estote perfecti* was a well-known maxim to all Christians. The Fathers had commented upon it, and ministers were certainly not wanting who preached upon it, and with fruit too, as the history of the confessors of the Church attests. Yet no one had hitherto written a systematical work on a devout life, enriched with apposite evangelical maxims, suitable to all classes of people. This glory was reserved for the Bishop of Geneva. The *Theotimen* may be termed the complement of the *Philothea*. Therein he guides the soul through that heaven of earth, the unitive state. Both works form a code of devotion.

Observe, too, how providential their appearance, at a time when Protestantism blasphemously preached against the necessity of good works, denied the liberty of the will in acting, and held forth predestination in its most terrible form. Moreover, even within the Church, there was a general tendency among spiritual directors to associate almost exclusively, the highest perfection, with a religious life and its austerities. This prejudice, almost amounted to a heresy, and St. Francis was the hero whom God raised up to vanquish it, and remove the interdict, so to speak, to the highest perfection which had been attached to all conditions of life outside the sanctuary and the cloister. The *Philothea* and the *Theotime* were also a complete restraint upon the excesses of the Quietists, and the exaggerated piety of those pseudo-ascetics of Port Royal. They refuted triumphantly the dangerous maxims of Sanciranus, of D'Andilly, of Arnauld, of Quesnell, and of Paschal, whom the *Civilta Cattolica* aptly terms Calvinists in the garb of reformers. This of itself was no trifling merit in the writings of St. Francis. And now, the Church, provident for the wants of this age, and grieving for its spiritual inertia, recommends anew the works of the sweet Saint of Annecy to our study, investing them with her own authority. Nor is she unmindful of the fact, that the age is to be moved not by comminations, but by sweet persuasion supported by convincing reasons, whereof St. Francis was acknowledged, the perfect master, even by the most noted heretics of his own day.

It is a custom with all nations to solemnize great festivals with magnificent banquets. If this be true, he certainly is not of the number of those who are affectionate to Mary who does not honor her festivals with that heavenly banquet, which the Immaculate Lamb of God has prepared for us in His own Flesh upon our altars.

'Beth's Promise.

BY MRS. ANNA HANSON DORSEY.

CHAPTER IV.
RETROSPECTION.

AUNT 'BETH had, in her quaint positive way, done a good work in awakening Mrs. Morley from the morbid state she was in, to the actual duties of life; although it was slow work coming back to them, owing to the sense of her twofold loss, ever present with her. An unblest cross is a heavy load to carry, but when the stings and reproaches of conscience are added to it, who can sustain the burden?

One day, when searching through her work-box —an elaborate, elegant affair, that her husband had, in their early married life, sent her from China—for a certain receipt Aunt 'Beth had called for, Mrs. Morley opened one of its several small compartments and saw within it a small, twisted package of tissue paper, evidently containing a ring or locket, as the outline of whatever it was had impressed itself on the wrapping. She started, and drew back the hand stretched out to take it up, whispering, "I dare not"; then, suddenly, another impulse moved her—"But it is said," she murmured, "that the worst of sinners never asked her help in vain. O clement, O sweet Mother of Jesus! abandon me not in the end, as I have abandoned thee!" She opened the parcel she had placed there years before. It was a medal of the Blessed Virgin, attached to a silken cord. How well she remembered the night, when dressing for a ball, she had taken it off and hidden it away here, to make place for a jewelled necklace! She had put it away carefully; she had even pressed it to her lips before putting it out of sight,—and there it had lain ever since. She looked at this symbol, this link between the days of her strong, trusting faith, and the dark, hopeless present; she held it for a moment in her folded hands, pressed closely against her heart, then slipped the cord over her head, and once more the blest image of "Our Lady conceived without sin" rested upon her bosom. Not that she had any definite purpose or pious resolve in view in doing so; it was an instinct, as one might grasp at something long lost, and suddenly cast up by the waves at their feet. But the involuntary cry of her heart had gone forth; and she to whom it was addressed, listened, watchful and waiting, ready to stretch out her pitying hand, to save the soul her Son had redeemed from the wreck made by its own faithlessness. But, after all, her own will, her own act, must win back the graces she had cast from her. It is a thought full of tremendous meaning, that no human being can be saved without the consent of his own will.

"Have you found that paper, Anne?" said Aunt 'Beth, coming in, in a flurry.

"Not yet, Aunt 'Beth; perhaps, if you will be so kind——"

"Certainly, Anne. Push the box round! You never found anything you started to look for in your life," answered Aunt 'Beth, snapping her white teeth, little imagining how Mrs. Morley had been occupied; or that she had forgotten, as she really had, all about the receipt she had opened her box to hunt for.

"Thank goodness! here it is," exclaimed the energetic little woman, holding up the paper, after turning everything topsy-turvy. "All right! you're as good at hiding things as a magpie. It will do you good, my dear, to put that box to rights; only, try and remember where you place things, to save trouble"; and Aunt 'Beth whisked out as abruptly as she had entered, leaving Mrs. Morley occupied for the next hour, secretly delighted to know that it would interest her sufficiently to prevent her brooding over her griefs for a little while at least.

And now, while a degree of calmness has begun to reign over the afflicted household, and things have resumed something of their old routine; when the gloom of the rooms is dispelled by throwing open the shutters to the sunlight, and a few intimate friends are admitted, and 'Beth has got back to her old place in her mother's heart, who begins to need and depend upon her more and more every day, and each one is helping to bear the other's burden, we will leave them, for a brief retrospection of their previous history, explanatory of certain things not yet quite clear to the reader.

Mrs. Morley was the only daughter of Col. and Mrs. Hamilton, natives of Maryland, and both of them devout members of that one true Faith which they had inherited from a long line of Catholic ancestors. Their two younger children were boys, bright, handsome lads, who with their sister, had been taught from their earliest years, by example as well as by precept, the divine lessons of their holy Faith; having for their spiritual guide the good priest who had baptized them. Col. Hamilton was an officer of the regular army, who had only his pay for a support, but this, with economy—as he had no expensive vices—was sufficient for every moderate need. He had expectations, however, which he had good sense enough not to rely upon, as it was entirely adverse to his principles "to wait for dead people's shoes," although his stepmother—from whom these expectations came—had publicly announced that he was to inherit her fortune; in fact, she had made a will to that effect. She was a worldly, kind-hearted, narrow-minded woman, who imagined that New England was the pivot on which the world revolved, and Boston the Olympus of the modern gods, whose nod was glory or destruction to aspiring mortals. She met Mr. Hamilton at Newport, one summer, whither he had gone for his health, and after a few months of agreeable intercourse they were married, the only condition she insisted on, b. ing that he would spend the rest of his life in New England, where her elegant home was located, and her money invested. His being a Catholic did not in the least disturb her, as she had no fixed religious ideas of her own; and, altogether, he was made quite happy and comfortable by her wifely devotion and the luxuries with which she surrounded him. The first time his son, a handsome, manly lad of fourteen, came home from the old college in Maryland to spend the vacation, Mrs. Hamilton took him at once into high favor, and treated him with so much affection and kindness that he was not only grateful, but came to the conclusion that all he had ever heard about the traditionary stepmother was simply slander, and after a little while he grew to have quite an affection for her. There was one point of difference between them, however. She wanted him to change his college and go to Harvard, but he was very decided not to do so, as his heart clung to the old Catholic *alma mater* up there in the hill-country of Maryland, which had not only been the nursing-mother of faith and learning, but also of faithful priests and of Bishops, and Archbishops, whose names and lives reflect a glory on the American hierachy. The boy loved his Faith, and not for the world would he have gone among aliens who despised it. Mrs. Hamilton showed no displeasure, although she regretted his determination, because, as she told him, "he would have surer prospects of a brilliant career if educated at Harvard, than at the obscure college he preferred"; she gave him a check for fifty dollars, kissed him affectionately, and bade him write often and let her know whenever he wanted anything; waited to see him off on the train, then drove home to comfort her husband, who had become suddenly possessed of a shadowy idea that he and his boy would never meet again. The rigors of a New England climate proved too severe for Mr. Hamilton's delicate lungs, and before the winter was half gone, an acute attack of pneumonia terminated his life so suddenly that there was not time for his son to reach him before he breathed his last. He received the last Sacraments from a devoted priest of apostolic life, who had been his spiritual guide from the time he settled in New England to the hour of his death. Hugh arrived only in time to attend his father's funeral, deeply grieved by his loss, as may be imagined. After the sad ceremonies were over, Mrs. Hamilton again offered her stepson every inducement not only to change his college but to take his place in her home as her son and heir. Again he gratefully thanked her for all her goodness and kind attention, and told her that he had determined upon his career: that as soon as he graduated, which would be soon, he was going to West Point, an old friend of his father's in the United States Senate having promised him an appointment. She told him, knowing it was no use to argue with him, that he was the most obstinate youngster she had ever met, and she did not know but that she respected him the more for being so independent. There was another kindly parting; more money and gifts were pressed upon him, and he went away with a saddened heart, feeling in its very depths that since his father was dead he had no claim to any earthly home. Time passed. He graduated with honor from his college, afterwards at West Point, and received his commission, by virtue of the high number he had passed, as a lieutenant in the engineer corps, that being considered the highest and most desirable branch of the service. Mrs. Hamilton was very proud of the noble-looking young soldier; she had him fitted out with the handsomest and most expensive equipments that could be procured, and took him home with her to spend part of the usual furlough after graduation, where she *fêted* and exhibited him, and saw him addressed and courted to her heart's content. Her next ambitious plan for him was a splendid marriage with an accomplished and beautiful young lady, a daughter of one of the merchant princes of Boston, who had shown open admiration for him; "such a marriage," she thought, "will give him *prestige;* his place in society will be assured, and with such a companion he'll get some of his rusty Popish ideas taken out of him." But again were Mrs. Hamilton's good intentions for her stepson to be frustrated: he told her frankly that he was engaged to a fair young girl in Maryland, whom he had known ever since she was born, and whom he intended to marry within the year; that she was not rich, neither showy nor dashing; but that she was a pious Catholic, lovely in her character, intelligent and accomplished, and he hoped that when he brought his bride to see her, she would approve of his choice. It was too late to argue with him—the affair had gone too far, and she was really too fond of him to quarrel over it; so she made the best of it, and when Hugh went away to spend the rest of his leave with his betrothed, Mrs. Hamilton wrote her an affectionate, womanly letter, and sent her by him a costly present. "I cannot give him up, though he has thwarted me in every way; I love him as if he were my own son, and I cannot afford to lose him."

Years, into which a world of changes had come, passed by. Hugh Hamilton married the fair object of his choice, and the union proved all that he had hoped for. Two sons, and a daughter were born to them, and he had won promotion by signal acts of bravery in several serious outbreaks among the Indians on the western frontier. Seldom separated from his family after this, being stationed at posts where he could have them with him, his greatest pleasure was found in watching over and directing the mental and religious education of his children, a work which Mrs. Hamilton had faithfully devoted herself to, not allowing even the extreme delicacy of her health to interfere with or interrupt it. But the exigencies of the service interrupted once more this happy domestic intercourse; the Seminole war broke out, and Major Hamilton was ordered to the field with his regiment, where his bravery and military skill won for him special mention in the despatches sent to the War Department by his commanding General. Seeking only to do his duty, loving his profession with a noble enthusiasm, and brave by nature, he was not conscious of having done anything worthy of special notice in the dangerous and savage warfare in which he had been engaged, and it was a surprise to him, as well as a proud satisfaction, when among other promotions he received his own. Colonel now, he returned home, without "scratch or scar," to resume his happy family relations, and was more than pleased to find that he was assigned to command at Fort McHenry, near Baltimore; for there, near at hand, in that almost Catholic city, were all the advantages that he desired: church, Catholic schools for his children, and religious privileges for them —all which we may be sure they devoutly availed themselves of. The brave soldier was a true knight of the Blessed Virgin; he wore her medal, and recited the rosary daily, and ever commended himself and his dear ones to her loving care. Sometimes, when occasion had offered, at the mess-table, or in the midnight *bivouac,* when the gay young officers sought to while away the tedious hours of waiting, by jest, song, and story, bringing in her sacred name in ribald speeches, mocking and sneering at her holy virginity, he defended her cause with such eloquence and dignity that these frivolous spirits, who were ignorant of her great holiness and her high claims to the veneration of mankind, were ever after silent on this theme, at least in his presence. "What," said they, "if he does hold the Virgin Mary's honor as sacred as that of his mother and wife? It's his belief, and none of our business. We would not speak lightly of them, and we've no right to speak lightly of *her.* Gad! I don't believe he'd ask much to fight for her!"

"They do sometimes," said another. "Count D'Orsey challenged an officer at a mess dinner in France who spoke disrespectfully of the Virgin, and they fought a duel with small swords, and his antagonist fell. When D'Orsey was dying, he pointed to that sword which hung over his bed under a picture of the Virgin, and told the old Capuchin who was with him that it was his proudest trophy, for with it he had defended the Virgin."

"Hamilton's another sort of a man from D'Orsey: he's what I call a Christian gentleman, though, it is true, I know very little about such matters; I can only see that he seems to live up to his belief," answered one, to which the rest agreed. This is but one instance of how the influence of the brave Christian soldier was felt, even by the unbelieving and thoughtless.

Col. Hamilton's boys were now twelve and fourteen, and Anne—the Mrs. Morley of our story —ten years of age. Frank and Harry were handsome, well-grown lads, and bade fair to walk in their father's footsteps. They required no urging to practice their religious duties, seeing his example, and having instilled into their minds from their earliest recollection the most pious sentiments and principles. Their intellectual advancement was beyond their years, and their parents had good reason to look forward to a bright and successful future for them. Anne, the youngest, was a fair, sunny-haired, tripping little fairy, the pet of the household, and as full of life and joy as a lark is of song, thinking that the world was bounded by the love that surrounded her. "I misdoubt sometimes if we are not spoiling Anne," said Col. Hamilton one night after the nurse had taken the child away; "she's a vain little elf."

"I'm afraid she is," said Mrs. Hamilton, gently. "But what I fear for her is an inconstancy of will, traits of which I have noticed frequently in her little plays, for 'straws show which way the wind blows,' and she is fond of finery beyond measure. It is all very amusing *now*, but I'm afraid it bodes trouble in the future for my pretty darling."

"We must do all we can without violence: she is under the protection of our Blessed Lady,—in fact, consecrated to her; then she is so very young, that you will be able to give her mind and heart the right direction, with God's help," he replied.

"Mamma Hamilton makes such a pet of her whenever she pays us a visit, and gives her so many beautiful presents as to quite turn her little head for the time: it is '*Bonne-Mère* says I am to have this,' and '*Bonne-Mère* says I looks boo'ful in that,' and *Bonne-Mère* says I'm her own dear pitty baby,' all the time; and indeed she is so kind to us all, Hugh, that I cannot find heart to say a word."

"Yes, she is very kind and generous. But Anne has you to watch over her; and I think, dear, you'll be able to counteract all dangerous influences. Who in the world, though, taught the children to call her *Bonne-Mère*? Grandmamma is good English, and sounds better for American children."

"She did," said Mrs. Hamilton, laughing; "she has bribed and drilled them into it whenever she has visited us; and I really didn't mind, it seemed to give her such pleasure."

"When is she coming again?"

"I can't tell; not, I hope, until after the boys are confirmed; she would give them no end of distractions, without meaning the least harm on earth."

"That makes it no better for them; the result is all the same as if her intentions were bad," said Col. Hamilton, with a sigh.

How little did they know what was coming! they had not even felt a vague shadow of the cloud that was approaching to break up once more their peaceful home, and separate them, this time forever. Rumors of war with Mexico filled the papers the next day, and in a short time hostilities actually commenced. Mrs. Hamilton's heart grew sick with expectation and dread; there was almost silence in the house, usually so full of merry voices and pleasant sounds; but several weeks having passed without a sign from the War Department, she began to take "heart of grace," that, after all her fears, her husband would not be ordered to join the army then on its way to Mexico. She said the Rosary every evening with her children that this trial might be averted; every breath, almost, was a prayer that he might remain with t em. But one day his orderly brought him at the breakfast-table a large, ominous official envelope, which contained orders for him to join his regiment, and, without delay, unite with General Scott's army in Mexico. His noble face grew pale and his lips rigid; but only for an instant. Crowding back into his own brave heart the pain that he felt in the separation from all that was most dear to him on earth, he imparted the news to his wife and children; reminding them that he was a soldier, and that to remain in inglorious ease at such a time would be a dishonor. He then fortified his courage by receiving the adorable Sacrament of the Altar, and put on a cheerful front. When the time came, after having seen them pleasantly situated in a house near the Cathedral in Baltimore, he embraced them tenderly, commending them to the protection of Heaven; and pausing on his way only to collect his regiment together from the various posts to which portions of it had been assigned, he made his way as rapidly as possible to the army in Mexico. He reported at headquarters, and was immediately ordered to the front with his men. One or two severe battles followed, in which the enemy was—after fighting desperately— repulsed and routed. Hundreds of gallant privates, many brave officers of the United States Army fell, but Scott was marching towards the capital; he must hold the proud city of the Montezumas in his victorious grasp to make his conquest complete, so what mattered a few more lives, and rivers of blood, with such an object in view? Col. Hamilton, as usual, distinguished himself, and was so far unhurt. At length a day dawned on which another terrible battle was to be fought, the battle of Cherubusco. Knowing the frightful chances of war, and with a feeling that was almost a presentiment, Col. Hamilton went to the tent of the army chaplain, a venerable and devout Jesuit Father, and, waiting his opportunity—for since before midnight he had been up hearing confessions, and there was a crowd still waiting—he approached the tribunal of penance, and afterwards, with many other faithful souls, received the Bread of Life, received it with humble intention as his viaticum. Returning to his tent, he wrote an affectionate and consoling letter to his wife and children, and one to his stepmother, thanking her for all her kindness, and begging her for his sake to investigate and seek the true Faith; penned a tender adieu, then sealed and left them on his desk with directions for their delivery in case he fell.

He had scarcely swallowed some hot coffee and ate a biscuit when the bugle rang out the signal 'to arms'; and ere the sun was fairly risen over that beautiful tropical land, glorious with the richest blooms, a fierce assault on the Mexican lines filled the air with clouds of smoke, the thundering of artillery, and all the deadly sounds of tumult and dread that make the bravest heart quail when a battle rages. In storming a redoubt, —the enemy's last defence,—Col. Hamilton fell, shot through the head, just as his men gained the works, driving the enemy in rout and confusion, into wild flight. Did he hear their shout of victory? What then to him were the illusive glories of the earth, its fame, or its honors? *He was crowned with other, and eternal rewards.*

(TO BE CONTINUED.)

"THE waters saw their God and blushed," is a translation of a Latin epigram. It is often quoted, *Vidit et erubuit lympha pudica Deum*, and has been attributed to Dryden. It has also been claimed as the production of an Eton boy who was required to make a Latin verse on the miracle of turning the water into wine, but it is really from an epigram by Crashaw, an English poet of the time of Charles I, who was converted to the Roman Catholic faith, and died a canon of the Church of Loretto, in 1650. The original is as follows: *Nympha pudica Deum vidit et erubuit.* In one of Bishop Heber's poems we find the following line: "The conscious water saw its God and blushed." But the idea seems to have originated with Crashaw.—*N. Y. World.*

A Lover of the Beautiful.

BY KATHLEEN O'MEARA, AUTHOR OF "IZA'S STORY," "ROBIN REDBREAST," "LIFE OF FREDERIC OZANAM," "PEARL," ETC., ETC.

(CONTINUED.)

THE God whom Henry had come to love with this entire generosity was not likely to rob His servant of "that joy of joys." In spite of his sufferings, his strength seemed renovated so as to enable him to compass the work demanded by the final examinations.

"I rise at a quarter to six," he writes from Hyères to his father, "and serve Père Gratry's Mass in the neighboring chapel at half-past six; we come in and work from half-past seven till half-past eleven. This is a good pull. After breakfast, promenade from half-past twelve till three; from three to six work again; at six we meet to discuss some subject of religion or controversy; then comes supper, *soirée* till half-past eight, breviary at nine, and the curfew bell."

A severe relapse interrupted the even tenor of the student's programme, but nothing could disturb the peace of perfect conformity which the sufferer's soul had attained. ... "I was in bed, ill, far from my own people, tended by a kind Sister of Charity, in that state of union with Jesus on the Cross which tempers the soul so vigorously when one accepts it with faith and love. I made the sacrifice for both of us; and from that moment, every time I kiss my crucifix I place you with myself in the Heart of the Divine Master. There is nothing, *nothing* for us now in this world but complete and boundless abandonment into the arms of Jesus Christ. ... We are His. Let us love His rights, and defend them against the miserable faint-heartedness of our own will. ... No more cowardice—no more weakness. Whatever God wills!"

Père de Ravignan's death, which occurred at this time (on the 4th March, 1858), drew a tribute of tender regret and reverence from the kindred soul of Henry. ... "What a death!" he cries; "if we can call death a sigh somewhat fainter, which marks the entrance of a saint into his triumph! What words on that death-bed, round which shone the halo of a whole life of sacrifice! He kept repeating with the ardor of a wounded soldier; 'Fight, fight, fight the battles of the Lord!' And when in the middle of the night, the friend who was watching by him, Père de Ponlevoy, seeing by certain signs that death was at hand, said to him, 'Come, brother, you are going to die,' the holy religious, with that austere smile that you know so well, said: 'Ah! at last, *merci!*' And we call this dying? And we fear death? ...."

The departure of Père Gratry was a trial to

Henry, not merely in the loss of his companionship, but because it deprived him of daily Mass. He was now only able to assist at the Holy Sacrifice three times a week, and then in the face of a biting cold wind. Nevertheless, he managed to continue his theological studies without a break; although his health "threatens ruin from day to day, from one cause or another." " What I shall be able to do in the diocese with this fine instrument I knew not," he says laughingly; "I am in a state of uncertainty, and I must remain in it until our Lord passes this way and says to me, 'Arise and come!' Meanwhile, I am learning not to despise small efforts and small results, as probably my life is destined to be spent amongst such. I have often said that nothing would give me more real joy than to teach the catechism to children, and should the day come when I am called on to renounce all high projects, I will readily console myself in these lowly tasks, for not having achieved the ambitions of my boyhood."

The infirm state of health which threatened to shut him out from the larger action of the ministry did not prevent him from exercising a very active and salutary kind of priesthood around him. His holiness made him an object of general veneration, and his counsel and presence were sought for by numbers, especially amongst those higher classes against whom he entertained strong prejudices. Like most prejudices, they were the result of inexperience; he had not as yet come in contact with the society which he judged so severely; but he was quick in acknowledging his error as soon as he recognized it.

"... Just fancy me launched in spite of myself amongst the very highest aristocracy! I was requested to go to the Duke and Duchess de —— to give religious instructions to a little child of theirs. Other acquaintances grew out of this one, and it is high time I left this place, for I am in the midst of dukes, marquises and viscounts. These people are all good, at least those of them that I see. Their faults are different from the faults of our class; but they have qualities that I did not know of. Men misjudge each other half the time for want of knowing each other, and this is what happened me with regard to the aristocracy. I have found amongst them women who are modest, pious and charitable, and much less haughtiness than I thought. The malady of these people is idleness. The young men are all in danger of having their youth blighted by pleasure and the abuse of fortune. For this reason many families are now endeavoring to give them a career, and thus render them more useful to themselves and their country. A wise and excellent tendency. This is the result of my *aristocratic* observations."

But while ready to make the full *amends honorable* to the class whom he had judged in ignorance, Henry's sympathies remained true to the lowly ones whom his Master loved. Writing to a soul whom he was helping to pass through a great sorrow, he says: "I am glad to find that you are not confining yourself to a school for poor children; God has endowed you with gifts which will enable you to do for young girls of distinction what many others are incapable of doing; but for the benefit as well as the consolation of your soul, I advise you to devote yourself chiefly to the care of the poorer classes. What we do for well-bred, intelligent, amiable children is a source of pleasure; we reap the fruits of it easily, and often it becomes a source of vanity; whereas, what we do for the poor is generally devoid of any pleasure, and has no earthly reward; it is much easier to do it purely for the love of Jesus Christ, and therefore to derive great merit from it. At least, this is what I have always felt when I have been charged with the instruction of the children of the rich and of the poor."

The month of May arrived, and Henry was back in Paris, trying to realize the stupendous joy that was now fast advancing. The ordination was to take place on the 29th. Before entering on retreat, he writes to one friend: "Pray for me. *I am actually going to be a priest!* I can hardly believe it, the weight of my unworthiness seems so to draw me away from this grace. Yet, God has so willed it! O, abyss of mercy! .... Dear friend, if I have ever scandalized, or pained, or disedified you, in the course of my life, I humbly ask your pardon. Oh, in days like these how one longs to have been always good, always pure! How the memory of faults weighs us down! We have nothing for it but to take refuge in the abyss of infinite mercy, and to recall those words of the Master: *Non vos me elegistis, sed ego elegi vos.* .... "

To another friend he says: "I come to announce to you my priestly consecration. Let me repeat to your heart this astounding fact, which I scarcely believe in myself: '*I am going to be a priest!*' I tremble. Who would not tremble before such an honor! But I, above all others, for I know my weakness, my unworthiness.... Pray for me. I have often told you, and now I repeat it to you with special joy: all this dates from my First Communion. That day Jesus proposed to me to follow Him, and I had the happiness of answering Him: Yes, beloved Jesus, I am Thine forever! .... O, abyss of divine mercy! Unfathomable depths of the eternal decrees! ... Give thanks to God with me for having kept me faithful to the promises of my First Communion! ...."

An old family servant, named Micol, is not forgotten in the midst of his overflowing joy: "I wish you, my dear Micol, and your family to share in this blessed *fête* of my first Mass. I send you with my affectionate remembrances, a post-office order for ten francs. You will buy something for the children or for the *ménage*, and you will say, 'This is a souvenir of the Abbé Henry's first Mass.' I regret very much that I can't make it more, but I confess to you that you have the end of my purse, and that there remains to me at this moment *thirty-six sous*. Adieu, pray for me. Above all, I ask for the prayers of your children. So it is true that next Saturday I shall be a priest, and that on Sunday I shall celebrate Mass! Ah, if you knew how unworthy I am of this excess of honor! . . . ."

After eight days' of solitary communion with God, the morning of this day of awful and magnificent grace dawned. On the 29th of May, 1858, in the Church of St. Sulpice, Henry Perreyve was ordained a priest. The next day he went up to the altar.

"My first Mass was beautiful," he says; "Père Lacordaire was faithful to the rendezvous. He came from Lorège to assist me at the altar and to protect me before God by his great sacerdotal virtues. . . . Now I belong solely and absolutely to God, and I wait to know from Him in what way He means to make use of me. I have but one desire in my soul—to be a good priest, chaste and humble, to serve our beloved Master as He wills, in obscurity, before the world, in active ministry, in study, by my pen or by my speech. *A son bon plaisir!* The obstacle to everything still is my health. I assure you it is only a vigorous act of blind faith that enables me to think of remaining here next winter and undertaking a fixed service."

He set out to the Eaux Bonnes in July, by way of bracing himself for the winter campaign. On his way to the Pyrenees he stayed a week at Lorège, where a great but startling grace awaited him.

He writes in his private memorandum: "Yesterday, one of the most beautiful days of my life, I performed the first act of my ministry. I confessed a soul, a great soul. This soul, the first that has humbled itself at my feet, and laid its secrets in my breast, is the same that raised me up in the first days of my youth, Père Lacordaire. He wanted to do it for several days; he said to me, 'Henry, you must confess me.' I hesitated; I felt myself so little! I prayed God to enlighten me, and I came to see that it was a great design, worthy of two souls who loved each other in God. So yesterday I went to him and said: 'I am ready.' He laid bare his whole life to me from the age of six to his conversion, and from his conversion up to the present day. Lord what dost Thou will? For it is not like Thee to reveal these great things to a soul from whom Thou willest nothing. . . . . May these souvenirs, so beautiful in themselves, fertilized by Thy grace, make of my life one long oblation, one sacrifice!"

His next sacramental function was performed in the service of a soul, very different, but also dear, that of an aged relative who was much attached to him.

". . . . "I must tell you," he writes from Eaux Bonnes, "that in the midst of my present utter vacuity God has granted me a great grace. I was enabled to reconcile to God on his death-bed one of my uncles who has heard nothing about religion since his childhood. They ran to fetch me when he was dying; the poor man would have nobody but me, and I had to do everything. Certainly it is an honor a hundred-thousandfold too great for me that Jesus should make use of me to bring back one soul to Him. But these are baits which excite one's hunger for the apostolate, instead of appeasing it. . . . Pray for me. I don't forget that it is through prayers, through the Masses that were said for me, that I obtained the grace to live, against all appearances, until I became a priest. I firmly believe that God, by a positive and extraordinary miracle, may communicate to a natural remedy, such as the waters, a special efficacy for one person, and bless the remedy so as to give it a sovereign power. Pray, that if the little strength I may regain is to serve to the glory of God it may be given me. If not, I ask for nothing but peace of mind and a speedy end."

The latter prayer seemed the one that was to be granted. On his return to Paris, the Abbé Perreyve writes, after a serious relapse: "I am a little better, but the improvement is almost imperceptible, and the effects of the illness will last a long time. God's will be done; I even confess to you that I consider this illness one of the greatest graces I have received for a long time, and I wanted it badly. It has made a great impression on me, and has shown me by the light of the eternal frontiers what the priesthood really is, and what God has a right to expect of a priest."

The death of his old nurse, 'Ma vieille Rose,' occurred soon after, and the regrets that it draws forth from the young priest reveal the tenderness of his human affections, and present a charming picture of what is fast becoming an extinct type in the domestic relations of these days of progress.

". . . I have sad news for you. Our dear old Rose died on Monday, almost suddenly, from an attack of apoplexy. It is a sorrow to me; I feel that I have buried my childhood with her. She had the old souvenirs of by-gone days, and all the free-and-easy ways of the good old times, with the right of loving bluntly that which one earns by six and thirty years of a life of faithful and tender devotion. I held to her funeral being respectable, like that of an aged relative or friend. All our family were present, and I was greatly moved by the eagerness that our friends showed in doing honor to a poor *bonne*. I trust that God has found her worthy of eternal rest in Him. Simple souls have easy ways to salvation. I seem to see a blessed future in the life of this poor girl, who arrives in Paris from the depths of Silesia to find a Catholic family in place of the one she had left, becomes a convert, puts her whole heart into loving a little child who becomes a priest, receives Holy Communion several times from his hand, and finally the last Sacraments on her death-bed. There is something grand and sweet in it all, even to the *minutiæ* of the details, which shows the kind hand of God."

The energy of his will, or rather of the faith which strengthened it, enabled him now to undertake and carry on a life of active ministry that amazed his friends. But this was the apostolate that he was sent on; this was the lesson he was to teach his generation—the power of the soul to command and compel the body, the example of a lifelong struggle in which the spirit, even when beaten, remained triumphant. He was justified in speaking confidently, as he did, of the power of the soul to overrule the weak vessel of clay, for he was himself a living, we might say a miraculous witness of the truth of this power. In his *Livre des Malades* he says: "The soul carries the body, and makes it live and breathe as it wills. .... Happy the souls whom this passion (love of work) possesses to the exclusion of all others. ... The joys of work—I speak of Christian work, accomplished with sacrifice—done unto God, under His eye and in His company, who shall describe them, even when he has known them long? Such work, conquered in the first instance over the repugnance of the body, is not long in turning to a remedy."

Alas! he used the remedy with too little discretion, and it killed him. He was charged with teaching catechism in the Church of St. Clothilde, a labor specially delightful to him, but cruelly trying to his wounded lungs. Over and above the ordinary works of his ministry, in the confessional, his attendance on the sick, and his writing, he was in constant demand for preaching, addressing meetings of young men, etc. He was borne through the winter, however, without any serious illness, and the strength of the battle nerved him for fresh efforts. "What a perpetual struggle life is!" he exclaimed, when a truce in the battle sent him to recruit himself at Eaux Bonnes; "nothing without fighting, everything at the cost of blood! It is frightful, but how beautiful it is, too! Why should such strength and ardor have been given to souls, if they were never to fight? Let us then feel towards the struggle like good soldiers, who hold it a grievance to be badly placed in a battle, and grow impatient for action."

This military instinct, which is so often felt in common by the priest and the soldier, prompted the Abbé Perreyve to apply for the post of chaplain to the troops going to China. God, however, had a mission for him nearer home for which his gifts more especially adapted him. We get a glimpse of the life he was now leading from a letter to a near relative, written on New Year's day (1861): ". . . It seems that you are angry with a certain unfortunate chaplain to the Lycée St. Louis, late Vicar at St. Thomas d'Aquin, who has to preach, write books, direct a college, hear confessions, and who is so overpowered with work that he is often days and days without embracing his father or mother, and who has not even the time to be ill. And I hear that you reproach this wretched man with not writing letters! .... It is quite true that I have been installed chaplain to a great college. It is far too weighty a charge for me; but it was imposed upon me, so to speak, by the Cardinal.* I was for a long time a pupil of this Lyceum, a circumstance which they are in hopes may incline the hearts of the young ones toward me."

These hopes were not belied. The Abbé Perreyve possessed in a rare degree that "gift of prophecy" what St. Paul places first amongst the gifts of the Holy Spirit, and which he describes as the power of speaking to every man in his own tongue. All men understood him: the cultivated student, the unlettered workman, the little child. Each, as he listened, saw the "secrets of his heart made manifest," and fell down and believed. The potency of this divine gift was nowhere so strikingly displayed as in the sway which it exercised over that most critical and exacting of audiences, the youth of the Paris Lyceums. The secret of his power lay in a great measure in the reverence which he had for these young souls, in the timid respect with which he approached them. P. Gratry relates a characteristic incident of one of the conferences at the Lycée St. Louis.

". . . . The subject was one of the most delicate which words can deal with. It was only a narrative. He related a death that he had witnessed, and the crime which had led thereto. Those who heard that story will remember it through life. They will never forget the gentle and innocent victim, and those two creatures, killed by one of those crimes which our laws ought but do not reach, which those of America can and do. And when he cried out, "Yet this man, it appears, is a well-bred man, a gentleman full of honorable sentiments, who knows? perhaps even a religious man! Messieurs, will this be your honor? Is this the religion you will profess?" There followed one of those effects that thrill to the very centre of souls. Tears flowed from the eyes of those young

---

* Cardinal Morlot.

men, and when he had done, many drew near and said to him, "*Merci, monsieur!* you have enlightened us forever!"

His influence over the turbulent young population of St. Barbe was equally powerful. The director of the college requested him to give a conference every other Sunday morning. The arrangement retarded by half an hour the departure of the boys to their homes, and those who know anything of boys will commiserate the preacher who came to address them under such circumstances. Between the grand college and the preparatory school, the audience, aggrieved and sullen, numbered nearly one thousand, when the Abbé Perreyve stood up to address them. He had not, however, spoken five minutes when their grievance disappeared; they listened with interest, finally with delight, and two days later they wrote to the prefect, entreating him to let them have a conference every Sunday, instead of every fortnight. "Perhaps," concluded the letter, "the health and multitudinous occupations of M. Abbé Perreyve may prevent his acceding to our desires; but, come what may, he has earned a right to count on the gratitude that we owe him for his devotedness, and for an eloquence so remarkable in itself and so sympathetic to youth." Here follow the signatures.

His sermons in the church of the Sorbonne met with the same enthusiastic response from an audience recruited from the most distinguished men in Paris. M. de Montalembert, coming out one day from one of these impassioned discourses, hurried to the preacher's house, and, being denied admittance, left a card at his door with these words in pencil: "My friend, they won't let me in; but I want to tell you that I am moved, enchanted, as I have never been, since, twenty years ago, he whose worthy successor you are, inebriated my youth at Notre Dame."

This flame, which communicated itself to all who approached him, was nevertheless consuming the temple in which it burned. There was no concealing the fact,—the days of the young priest were numbered. But this only goaded his energies to more strenuous effort. He was named professor at the Sorbonne, with a chair of ecclesiastical history in the Faculty of Theology, to which heavy addition to his work he thus playfully alludes in a letter: "How are your good nuns? My firm belief is, that they have more sound theology in their little finger than I have in my square cap of Doctor of the Sorbonne. Beg their prayers for a poor priest who fusses a great deal but does very little good work."

"I have meet with more success at the Sorbonne than I should have ventured to hope for," he says by-and-by; "the hall is full, and my audience give even too much of that intoxicating reward, *applause*. But it is sad enough too. How long will they applaud me? Whom did they applaud last in this chair, and whom will they applaud next? If this were the sole aim of life, alas! what a pitiable recompense for the vigils and labors and efforts of a year would a momentary thrill be! . . ."

Although he owned to a sense of alarming exhaustion, he continued without a single break in his enormous accumulation of work to the close of the scholastic year. "I have been able to carry on my lectures at the Sorbonne," he says, "and to preach frequently, and the number of young men gathering around me has increased very much. Their confidence confounds me. I only hope it may contribute in some little degree to God's glory."

(TO BE CONTINUED.)

[For the "Ave Maria."]
The Angelus.
BY M. J. C.

AVE MARIA! It is morn,
The dawn hath chased the shades of night;
New duties with each day are born,
New cares with every morning's light;
For grace to guide our steps that stray,
O Mother-Maid! we turn to thee,
For wisdom to direct our way,
Hear, Mary! hear thy children's plea.
Ave Maria!

Ave Maria! At the hour
Of busy noontide let us pray;
For aid to foil the tempter's power,
We seek, and at thy feet we lay
The wants, the woes, the weariness,
The daily struggle, oft in vain;
Thy balm-like presence giveth rest,
And near thee we forget our pain.
Ave Maria!

Ave Maria! Lo! the bells
From their aerial homes declare,
As on the air their cadence swells,
The hour of rest, the hour of prayer,
The evening hour; and twilight falls
Like a soft veil on land and sea:
Oh, guard thy helpless child who calls,
Mother beloved! again on thee.
Ave Maria!

LET us honor, revere, respect, and love, with a special love, the most holy and glorious Virgin Mary. Let us have recourse to her, and, like little children, cast ourselves into her arms with perfect confidence. Let us implore her protection, invoke her maternal love, and try to imitate her virtues, thus testifying that we have toward her a truly filial heart.—*St. Francis de Sales.*

A Double Miracle.

AT the siege of Constantine in Africa, in the year 1837, a young French officer was stricken down by a ball, which hit him directly in the chest. Surprised at finding himself still alive after such a blow, he touched with his hand the spot where he was struck, and found to his joy that he was not in the least injured. Hardly able to divine the meaning of such a happy escape, he examined all around his body, and found at last between his clothes the ball by which he had been struck. Grasping it affectionately as a precious relic, and, deeply moved, he returned to the strife with renewed ardor. Soon afterwards, however, another ball struck him in the thigh. This time the wound was serious. He was carried from the field, and his recovery became so tedious, that he was permitted to return to France on furlough for the recovery of his health. He now examined the first ball, and was startled to see the exact print of a medal engraved in the lead, as if a seal had been imprinted in soft wax. The ball had struck against a medal which a pious mother had suspended on his neck, to shield him from danger.

The medal had done its part well, but how it happened that its image could be imprinted on the metal after it had passed through his clothing, seemed rather mysterious; and after pondering a while over the matter, he was satisfied to have profited by it, without paying any more attention to the fact.

When his furlough was nearly ended, he went to Paris. It was in the last weeks of Lent, and besides the desire of seeing once more the capital, the young man was rather pleased to get rid of the abstinence and austerity rigorously observed under his paternal roof.

One evening, surprised by a heavy rain-storm in the neighborhood of Notre Dame des Victoires, he sought shelter from the rain by entering this church. A priest was in the pulpit, relating some extraordinary facts, and pointing out some miraculous cures obtained through the intercession of our Blessed Lady. The walls of this temple are literally covered with *ex-votos* and tablets of commemoration, of which it would fill volumes to relate the circumstances.

The officer, who at first listened in a careless manner, soon became more attentive, as these stories reminded him of his own adventure. Smiling, he said to himself: "If his reverence knew what happened to me, what would he say?"

At the end, as if moved by a mysterious power, when the priest was going into the sacristy, he went to meet him, saying: "Does your reverence really believe in all you have just told?"

"Yes, sir: certainly. All these facts are proved to be perfectly true. I have witnessed several of them myself, and I have the others from reliable parties."

"And you call these miracles?"

"They are, at least, very extraordinary facts, in which it seems impossible not to see the divine power, due to the intercession of the Blessed Virgin."

"But is that which has happened to me also a miracle?"

And the young warrior now relates the history of his ball, showing it to the priest, with the medal, which he always carried about him. The priest then explained to the soldier that a bone, no matter how solid, could by no means, resist a ball, especially if it had force enough to flatten itself against a tiny leaf of metal. And again, that this inexplicable impression, made in spite of the interposition of the clothing, could hardly be considered as something natural. Finally, that the very circumstance, so natural in appearance, which had led him at this hour into the church, as it were in spite of himself, justly deserved to be considered as a special grace.

To be brief, the officer felt himself conquered; he falls on his knees and makes his confession. Soon afterwards he quitted the service and went to Rome. Here he entered the French Seminary, and a few years afterwards was ordained priest. Once more he returned to the African soil, already moistened by his blood. But it is no more with sword in hand, to establish by force the dominion of the French; his weapon is now a crucifix, and he carries to the poor negroes, to the most savage and degraded tribes of the earth, the welcome news of peace and redemption.

The young officer, wounded at Constantine and decorated with the cross of the Legion of Honor, is no other than the venerable Father Papetart, late Vicar-General of the African Missions, who died at Nice not long ago. His Superiors had sent him there to recruit his health, which had been broken down by severe labors, sufferings and fatigues.

THE Church honors the Blessed Virgin, because God Himself, who directs the Church, wills that she should be honored exactly in this manner: *Thus shall she be honored, whom the King hath a mind to honor.* And, in order that all may know that this is really the will of God Himself, He has so arranged, that to honor her thus has always been to the Church a source of the greatest blessings. Hence the Sovereign Pontiffs, who are the chief interpreters of the Divine will, have taught us by their own example that in all public and universal calamities to honor Mary is the most efficacious and the surest means of obtaining prompt assistance from Heaven.

The Beauty and Eloquence of the Church's Prayers.

THE Prefaces, Collects, Graduals, Prayers, and Litanies of the Catholic Church are not only perfect expressions of Christian needs, desires and aspirations, not only exact precatory statements of Christian doctrine, but are also possessed in an eminent degree of literary merit, replete with plaintive tenderness, well-poised harmonies, touching epithets, sublime descriptions and deep feeling. Anglicans are wont to boast of their "beautiful liturgy," and beautiful, no doubt, it is when taken from ours, but even then so curtailed in regard both of doctrine and devotional language as to bear no comparison with the rich and solemn notes of the Latin services whence it was in a great measure derived. Not even the liturgical devotions of the Greek Church can be compared for beauty with those of the Western, and it is only in the inspired prayers contained in Scripture that we can find the language of supplication rising to the same height of devotion as in the Missal, Breviary, and Office Books of the Church. A great traveller and missionary in the East once said to us: "When I meet with a new nation or tribe and speak to them on the subject of religion, they commonly ask me, 'How do you pray?'" And, indeed, it is certain that the character of the prayers of a community are a sure index of its right-mindedness, orthodoxy, and mental cultivation. It is another glory of the second Latin Literature, in addition to those we have already mentioned, that it has lavished on us with so liberal a hand devotions which cannot but elevate the mind and take fast hold on the heart and memory. Their great merit, considered merely as compositions, consists in the directness of their appeals and the condensation of thought which saves them from the poverty of diffuseness. Let the Litanies of the Holy Trinity, the Name of Jesus, the Holy Ghost, the Blessed Virgin, the Life and Passion of Jesus Christ, the Litany of the Saints and of the Blessed Sacrament be examined from this point of view, and they will be found to fail in nothing that contributes to form majesty of language and plenitude of meaning. They blaze and sparkle in every direction with spiritual light. The same may be said of many favorite devotions of saints, consecrated by the use of many ages. Such are the "Anima Christi, Sanctifica me," of St. Ignatius,* and the "Domine Jesu, noverim me, noverim Te," of St. Augustine, the "Salve Regina," and the "Memorare." Even what in worldly compositions would be called conceits, are hallowed by the use of the Church in Latin prayers by saintly writers. Thus in a prayer of St. Francis of Assisi in common use we read:

"Absorbeat, quæsumus, Domine Jesu Christe, mentem meam ignita et melliflua vis amoris Tui ab omnibus quæ sub cœlo sunt, ut amore amoris Tui mundo moriar, qui amore amoris mei dignatus es in ligno crucis mori."

In some instances passages from fathers and saints have been inwoven into the services of the Church, which glow with a perfect passion of devotion, and of these none is more remarkable than that outburst of St. Augustine in the "Paschale Præconium," or blessing of the paschal candle:

"O mira circa nos tuæ pietatis dignatio! O inestimabilis dilectio charitatis! ut servum redimeres, filium tradidisti. O certè necessarium Adæ peccatum, quod Christi morte deletum est! O felix culpa, quæ talem ac tantum meruit habere Redemptorem. O verè beata nox, quæ sola meruit scire tempus et horam in quâ Christus ab inferis resurrexit!"

Surely here, if anywhere, we find that nobility of expression, that all but divine grace of words which turns prose into poetry. There is a French proverb which, duly considered, will enhance the value of our Latin Prefaces, Collects and Litanies: "Simplicity is charming but there is nothing so difficult." It is the perfection of art to produce those imitations of the cries of regenerate nature with which the Latin devotions of the Church abound, nor is it too much to say that the most faultless compositions in the world, even in a literary point of view, the most eloquent, sublime, profound, and pathetic, will be found laid up in the Latin Treasury of the Church, in her Vulgate, Creeds, Liturgies and Hymns. Subjected as we are to many scoffs and sneers on the score of a supposed debasement of pure Latin for the service of religion, it may be well occasionally to call the attention of so-called scholars to the facts here mentioned, and to throw down before them a glove of defiance in support of a thesis we could confidently defend.

If the inspiration of the Holy Ghost is as much a reality as the awakening of the breath of morn, or the wafting of odors, or the passing of sweet music over seas and plains, then it might be expected that the prayers, whether in prose or verse, addressed to Him simultaneously by Christians throughout the world would be especially marked by elevation of thought and felicity of expression. If we desired to exhibit at a glance to an intelligent inquirer—say, for example, a monotheistic Buddhist or Hindoo—what is the spirit that prevails, or at least is supposed to prevail, in the Catholic Church, we would open the *Officium Sti. Spiritus* and bid him read attentively the Litany of the Holy Ghost and the Hymns "Veni Creator" and

---

* We think it has been shown that this famous prayer was not composed by St. Ignatius, as is commonly supposed.—ED. A. M.

"Veni, Sancte Spiritus." Nothing can be imagined capable of exhibiting in a smaller compass the multiform gifts of the Spirit and the Blessedness of His presence in the Church and in each individual of it. Affecting beyond measure are the exquisitely chosen epithets, with the ever and anon recurring references to the language of Scripture; such for instance, are "Spiritus adoptionis filiorum Dei; Spiritus reddens testimonium spiritu nostro, quod simus filii Dei; Spiritus suavis, benigne, super mel dulcis; Spiritus principalas; Spiritus pignus hereditatis nostræ." Nor should we fail to remark how the accuracy of doctrinal statement is often blended with a rhapsody of devotion which surpasses poetry, as when in the Litanies the Almighty Father, the Son, and the Holy Ghost are implored to shower down Their gifts of grace for the sake of causes and reasons of the utmost potency lovingly and fondly pleaded. The preposition "per" is generally in these cases the key-note of a bar full of music, meaning, and revealed truths; as, for example, in adressing the Holy Spirit: "Per supereffluentem sanctitatis abyssum, quâ inconceptione Verbi matrem Dei inundare fecisti." The pleasure and profit a devout Catholic may derive from using habitually a Latin prayer-book is worth years of study, nor indeed will it be a smattering of Latin, as is frequently supposed, suffice. No: it is those whose lamps have shed their lonely beams over the pages of ancient Latin historians, philosophers, and poets, who will best appreciate the surpassing loveliness of the devotional department of the second Latin Literature. Take the *Modus juvandi Morientes*, for example, and see whether Cicero in his *Somnium Scipionis* and *De Senectute* has ever approached to the divine eloquence of the divine commendation of the departing soul to God, beginning with the words: "Commendo te omnipotenti Deo, charissime frater." Surely it would be no unhallowed imagination which should discern angels incensing prayers and devotions such as these, even as the two angels said to have been seen by B. Herman of Steinfeld incensing the choir during the "Benedictus."

"When thou readest," says St. Augustine, "God talks with thee; when thou prayest thou talkest with God." The Church has carefully provided that the language employed in her public services shall be suited to the gravity of the occasion, and not left to the mood, temper or passions of priests or people. Nor could she have employed any language so convenient for this sacred and solemn purpose as that of the mistress of the world. Though not quite universal even among ecclesiastics, it comes nearer to it than any other tongue, and retains its quasi-universality though the world has grown so much older. Majestic yet flexible, it adapts itself yet admirably to solemn intonation, chant and hymn, and, aided by the music of voice and instrument, it expresses the finest shades and touches of prayer under its varied aspects of adoration, oblation, sacrifice, invocation, praise and giving of thanks. The Church, moreover, puts into the lips of her worshippers in choicest Latin the prayers of the greatest saints and seers, the "ipsissima verba," which have been most prevalent with God, the prayers of Moses on Mount Horeb, and of Joshua when he prevailed over Amalek, of Jeremiah consoled in his dungeon, Daniel exultant even in the lions' den, Job naked on his dunghill, Susanna pure among the impure, and the penitent thief finding paradise on the Cross. All these and many more plead through our voices with the might of words hallowed by the use of ages and the success of countless militant souls. If Religion could forgive the Reformation all its sins, Literature could never forgive it half its folly when it mutilated and mangled the Church's Latin and turned what remained of it into the shifting dialects and uncouth vernaculars of modern centuries.—*London Tablet.*

Approbation of Rt. Rev. Bishop Vertin.

WE have much pleasure in adding to the numerous other approbations of THE AVE MARIA the following of the Rt. Rev. Bishop of Marquette:

Your excellent Catholic family journal being sound in doctrine and very instructive for all, and suited to the different grades of Catholics and stations in life, I most cheerfully approve of its publication, and recommend it to the Catholics of my Diocese.

✠ JOHN VERTIN,
BP. SAULT-STE. MARIE AND MARQUETTE.
MARQUETTE, MICH., Jan. 13, 1880.

Catholic Notes.

——Rev. Father J. E. Hogan, of Galena, Ill., has our best thanks for kind favors to the AVE MARIA.

——Rt. Rev. Bishops Elder and O'Hara, and the Archbishops of Boston and Philadelphia, have ordered collections for the starving poor in Ireland.

——Americans visiting Spain always find bull-fighting, the national sport of that country, a disgusting spectacle. What of the women's walking-matches at home?

——Cardinal Nina is causing catalogues to be compiled and printed of all the artistic collections in the Vatican and Lateran palaces. They will be obtainable by the general public.

——Messrs. Diepenbrock and Steinback, agents in this country for the house of F. Pustet, of Ratisbon, have been admitted to partnership. The firm will be known henceforth as F. Pustet & Co.

——The Advent sermons this year at the chapel of St. Eugénie at Biarritz, France, were preached by the zealous Father Toner, pastor of St. Vincent's Church, Plymouth, Pa., who is abroad for his health.

——The Belgians have a pious custom of carrying blessed candles, when they are on a journey, to use in their bedrooms in hotels as a method of invoking Divine protection against the perils of travel, and of blessing their room for the night.

——We learn with pleasure that the Rev. Dr. Bernard O'Reilly, so favorably known as the author of "*Mirror of True Womanhood*," "*Heroic Women of the Bible*," etc., is engaged upon a new work entitled "*St. Angela de Merici and the Ursuline Order.*" It will be ready in May.

——The zouave who saved the life of the late General Lamoriciere at the siege of Constantine about forty years ago, has just died in the hospital at Avignon, France (his native city), in the sixty-eighth year of his age. His name was Joseph Roussel. He left his little savings, amounting to about 700 francs, to the hospital He enjoyed an annuity from the family of the Christian hero whose life he preserved.

——The great Prussian field-marshal Moltke relates that during the plague in Constantinople in 1837 he became acquainted with a priest in the French hospital at Pera who not only administered to the spiritual but also to the temporal necessities of the poor victims of the scourge, washing their wounds, nursing them, and burying them, after their death, with his own hands. "I must confess," Gen. Moltke says, "I esteemed and admired the courage of that noble man, whose bravery infinitely surpasses the most brilliant feat of arms."

——A COLONY OF LEPERS was founded by the Government of the Sandwich Islands at the Island of Molokai in 1865. Up to the 31st of March, 1878, no less than 6,827 lepers had been transported thither. Of this number 2,235 soon found relief in death. For some years a French priest has been living among these unfortunates to assuage their lot and minister to their spiritual needs, devoting a fortune to their cause. Of late years a salary of $3,000 a year has been offered to any able physician who would attend the lepers; but it is doubtful if anyone will even be found to brave the horrors of a living tomb at Molokai. Heroic acts are demanded of priests by their very profession.

——REAPING THE WHIRLWIND.—The Berlin correspondent of the *Osservatore Romano* says that Emperor William on hearing of the attempt against the life of his nephew, Alexander II, remained for some time in profound silence, and then exclaimed: "If we do not change the direction of our politics, if we do not make it our duty to give a sound instruction to our youth, if we do not grant the first place to religion, but, on the contrary, remain satisfied with ephemeral expedients, our thrones will fall to the ground, and society will soon become a prey to the most terrible disorders. There is no time to be lost; it will be a most lamentable thing if all Governments do not soon come to an understanding, and co-operate in the work of repelling the evil."—*Et nunc reges intelligite; erudimini qui judicatis terram. Ps.*

——THE ILLUSTRATED CATHOLIC AMERICAN.—A welcome addition to the Catholic press of the United States is the *Illustrated Catholic American*, the first issue of which made its appearance last week. It is a handsome 16-page paper, similar in form to the other illustrated journals of the country, and is published by the enterprising firm of Hickey & Co., No. 11 Barclay St., New York. The subscription price is $3 a year, post-paid. To our mind, one of the most consoling signs in the horizon of the Church in the United States is the multiplication of Catholic papers and books; prejudice is thereby dispelled in the minds of non-Catholics, and those of the household of the faith receive information and encouragement. *The Illustrated Catholic American* is sure to effect much good. The first number is excellent; the illustrations are good, but better are promised; the reading-matter is entertaining and instructive, and the general "make up" very attractive. Everything about it, too, is thoroughly Catholic. None of our periodicals have begun with brighter prospects. It only remains now for the Catholic reading public to give their support to the project of Messrs. Hickey & Co., to which we cordially wish the greatest success.

——CATHOLIC ART SOCIETY.—A circular from Rev. C. Fauquerey's, giving the aim of his Art Society, viz.: the furnishing of religious pictures, statues, and ecclesiastical decorations to Churches, Convents, and families, has been received; and not only from the intention named, but also from the list of clerical gentlemen to whom he refers, we may reasonably expect his society to be one for the benefit and actual consolation of Catholics in the country. The custom of furnishing religious objects, such as the Stations, statues of the Blessed Virgin, of St. Joseph, and the Sacred Heart, from some manufactory across the water, is one which the Catholic Church in the United States may well have outgrown. With chromos which challenge the admiration of Europeans, and every facility for reproducing whatever is needed in the sanctuary, all that is now wanted is a pure Catholic taste, well imbued with the best traditions, to enable us to supply all our wants from among ourselves. The enterprise in which Father Fauquerey is embarked, is one which should be encouraged; at least, until it is found not to answer the requirements; and we hope this encouragement will be given generously. Mr. A. Beaumont, 69 South Third Street, Brooklyn, E. D. New York, the Secretary of the society, will be glad to furnish any information that may be desired.

——THE NECESSITY OF A CHRISTIAN EDUCATION.—Rt. Rev. Bishop Hedley, in the course of an address delivered at the opening of a Catholic school at Aberkenfig, Glamorganshire, England, last May, and which has lately been published in pamphlet form by Messrs. Burns and Oates, makes use of the following strong arguments in favor of a Christian education for children. The truth could hardly have been expressed more forcibly. "As the child is, so the man or woman will be. Religion is the same, in its essentials, for little ones and for grown up people. The same God, the same heart, the same hindrances, the same responsibility, the same life eternal. But unless the seeds have been sown in childhood, there will be little fruit in mature years. Indeed, with all our teaching and all our schooling, we see too many grow up irreligious and immoral, regardless of decency and forgetful of God. Therefore, the Christian parent, and pastor, and teacher, are anxious and busy about Christian education. Some say, 'Let the child choose its religion for itself when it can think and look about the world.' This is like saying, 'Straighten the tree,' after it has grown crooked for years. You cannot do it. The crook is in the very fibre. You can only break it. A child not brought up religiously sucks in irreligion; because the absence of the knowledge and love of God is, not only the absence of religion, but the opposite of religion. If a thing is not white, it must be some other color. You cannot have a thing no color at all. If you take a child no older than ten, or eleven, or twelve, which has had hitherto no religious teaching, you will not find its mind a blank, or its heart an empty chamber; far from it. Its mind will be all written over, and the writing there will be: Thou shalt love thyself the first; Thou shalt labor and strive for this world alone; Thou shalt measure good and evil only by pleasure and pain; Thou shalt have no heed for the things that are unseen. And its heart will be full of rank weeds of selfishness; of unworthy interests; of evil passions, growing up strong and vicious, like vipers in their nest; of anger, hatred, and ill-will. Even the love of parents, of family, of neighbors, —even justice, and sweetness, and kindness,—even these will be dwarfed, in a heart that knows not God, to the smallness of human feelings, with no elevation to heaven, with no tinge of the grace of Calvary, with no brightness from the life to come. When you bring God and the Gospel to a heart like this, you are too late."

New Publications.

THE AMERICAN CATHOLIC QUARTERLY REVIEW. January, 1880.

This number opens with a long article on the "Pretended Unity of Modern Philosophy," in which the learned author, Rev. J. Ming, S. J., reviews the salient points of the Philosophy of Descartes, Kant, Fichte, Schelling, and Hegel. Rt. Rev. Thomas A. Becker, D. D., contributes a short article on "Vocations to the Priesthood," with especial reference to our present needs and circumstances, both spiritual and temporal. "The ordinary vocation to the ecclesiastical state may generally and readily be known when young people, or even those of riper years, show a real desire for their own advancement in all that is good and devout, when they add thereto an inclination for serious studies, and direct them in such a manner as to be subservient to the great end of creation. When they have not only a desire for their own advancement in virtue, but also a zeal for the salvation of others; when they show an aptitude for the ceremonies of the Church, and a degree of fondness for all that pertains to the decency of Divine worship." . . . . And towards the end, the writer says: "We are prepared to assert that whatever there be of scholarship in Latin and Greek culture, may be found in our colleges and seminaries, but we could wish that the latter study were more rigidly insisted upon, as well as mathematics and sciences." We will add that a correct, if not critical knowledge of the English tongue should be insisted upon. We know at least one director of ecclesiastical studies who considers it a mere loss of time for young men to devote themselves to the acquisition of a fluent use of our common language. "Socialism at the Present Day," by Rev. Aug. J. Thebaud, S. J., reveals the alarming proportions which this bane of modern society has now reached, especially in Russia. "That the conspiracy has taken deep root in Europe, and has even invaded this country cannot be denied; and it would be most imprudent on the part of those who are conservative to close their eyes to it, and to act as if it did not exist, merely because its ulterior aims and true character are systematically concealed. Dr. Daniel Gans, a recent convert, discusses "The Necessity for Infallibility." We commend this article to those whose notions in regard to this great question of the day are not clear. The writer explains what Infallibility is not, and what it is. It is not inerrancy in the private opinions of its subject; it is not inspiration; it is not impeccability; but "Infallibility is a supernatural gift secured by the Divine Spirit to him who occupies the office of Vicegerent of Christ on earth; so that when in this office, and teaching the whole Church in matters of faith and morals . . . . he is so guided and guarded by the promised light and grace of the Holy Ghost that he cannot but teach the truth in the most absolute accordance with revelation." Then he goes on to prove that without some infallible authority, revelation would be for us as if it were not—would be as the sun to one without eyes. He asks: "Where is this necessary Infallibility to be found? Is it in Episcopalianism? Is it in Presbyterianism? Is it in Methodism?—No, no, no. Still it must be somewhere—and the Catholic Church is the only claimant of this high and necessary prerogative. "Archbishop Gibbons, and his Episcopalian critic, Dr. Stearns," by A. de G., is a scorching review of Dr. Stearns's "Faith of Our Forefathers," written in refutation of the "Faith of Our Fathers." "English Manners," by A. Featherstone Marshall, B. A., Oxon., is a readable article. "Is Froude a Historian?" by J. Gilmary Shea, LL. D., is another deserved rebuke to a writer who proverbially disregards historical truths. Meline exposed him as a garbler in the case of Mary Queen of Scots. Father Burke silenced him for a time. Agnes Strickland is arrayed against him for his disregard of documentary evidence in regard to the part "Good Queen Bess" took in ordering the execution of the same unfortunate Mary. And now he is brought to court and convicted of utter ignorance and inexcusable misrepresentation in his late article on "Romanism and the Irish Race in the United States" (*North American Review*, Dec., 1879). Why does Mr. Froude still deceive himself? He was never cut out for a historian. He has never yet given to the public any work called "a history" which has not been proved a romance. His "Henry VIII" is a romance; his "Thomas à Becket" is a romance. Why does not Mr. Froude devote his talents to novel-writing, pure and simple? We are sure that the reader will enjoy the castigation Mr. Shea administers to this would-be historian.

The next article, "Insanity a Plea for Criminal Acts; Insanity as Emotional or Affective; and whether Insanity can be of the Will Alone," by Rev. Walter H. Hill, S. J.," calls attention to a point of jurisprudence becoming every day more and more obscured by the many conflicting doctrines of the medical profession on the physiological and psychological aspects of crime. There is no doubt that the plea of insanity as an excuse for crime is too common, and too easily admitted nowadays, especially in this country. Those who take interest in this question we refer to Father Hill's essay.

The last article is the "Stack-O'Hara Case," by S. L. M., which is a review of the case itself and the principles involved in the final judgment rendered by Judge Gamble. While implicitly admitting that the Rev. Mr. Stack had no case against the Bishop, this gamboling judge nevertheless condemns the Bishop to pay all the expenses incident to the suit. The glaring injustice of this decision is so evident that the New York *Observer* (Oct. 23d, 1879), a Presbyterian journal of much influence, said: "The opinion thus rendered is *not* consistent with religious liberty, nor in harmony with the fundamental idea of American relations between the Church and State. . . . When the civil power steps in and says that, because a priest draws a salary, therefore the civil power has the right to determine whether or not he has been properly inducted or extruded, it is an invasion of the religious freedom of the Church, which ought to be intelligently, but firmly, resisted."

In the "Book Notices," Dr. Stearns receives some farther attentions and compliments for his "Faith of Our Forefathers."

Confraternity of the Immaculate Conception
(Or of Our Lady of Lourdes).

"We fly to thy patronage, O Holy Mother of God!"
REPORT FOR THE WEEK ENDING JANUARY 13TH.
The following petitions have been received: Recovery of health for 79 persons and 3 families,—change of life for 49 persons and 12 families,—conversion to the faith for 52 persons and 13 families,—special graces for 6 priests, 7 religious, 2 clerical students, and 1 person aspiring to the religious state,—temporal favors for 43 persons and 8 families,—spiritual favors for 50 persons and 7 families,—the spiritual and temporal welfare of 7 communities, 6 congregations, 9 schools, and 2 orphan asylums. Also 15 particular intentions, and 12 thanksgivings for favors received.

Specified intentions: Restitution of a piece of land belonging to a church,—grace of perseverance for a young man, who is in danger of being led from the path of virtue by an evil companion,—the grace of a good confession,—the prevention of a mixed marriage,—a good crop,—the removal of some scandal and dissensions,—several insane persons and others in great spiritual danger,—and all the specified intentions recommended in previous reports.

FAVORS OBTAINED.

We continue to the record of favors obtained through the intercession of the Blessed Virgin and the use of the water of Lourdes. A grateful father writes: "The holy water which you sent has entirely cured the children of hooping cough.". . . "Mrs. B's. child," writes a pious lady, "became blind two days after birth. After numerous visits the doctor pronounced him blind in both eyes. But his mother who had faith in our Lady, made a novena, used the water of Lourdes, and the infant is now perfectly cured.". . . Another grateful correspondent writes: "A little girl, whose name I sent to be enrolled last spring, was at that time unable to stand, having to be held up. But now she is able to walk around the house; and yet the doctor had given her up, saying she was paralyzed. A year ago last fall I also sent the name of a young woman who had the inflammatory rheumatism so badly that she could not move or be moved, nor even touched. On a certain Sunday, when I was in the house, I gave her some of the water of Lourdes, and the next Tuesday she was able to ride *seven miles*, and she has never been troubled with rheumatism since."

OBITUARY.

The following deceased persons are recommended to the charitable prayers of the members: MR. MATTHEW O'CONNELL, who departed this life last November at East Boston, Mass. MR. THOMAS MAGEE, of Philadelphia, Pa., who was killed by a railroad train on the 30th ult. MISS MARY MULLEN, of Antioch, Cal., whose death occured on the 1st inst. JOHN J. DENNY, of New Orleans, La., who breathed his last on the 31st of December. MRS. CATHARINE QUINN, of Cresco, Iowa, deceased last June. MRS. ELLEN CASSIDY (*née* Dwyer), a native of Ennis, Co. Clare, Ireland, whose happy death took place at the Mission San José, Cal., on the 25th of November. MRS. P. SARSFIELD, and MISS MARGARET SARSFIELD, of Revere, Mass., who died last year. MR. THOMAS HANNING, of New Brunswick, N. J., who slept in the Lord on the 4th of January. MRS. ELIZA SOUTHWARD, of Boston, Mass., and MRS. THOMPSON, recently deceased. And several others whose names have not been given.

Requiescant in pace.

A. GRANGER, C. S. C., Director.

Youths' Department.

Mildred's Prize.

BY THE AUTHOR OF "TYBORNE," "FEAST OF FLOWERS," ETC., ETC.

CHAPTER I.

THE CROSS.

"YOU don't really mean it, Maggie: you *can't!* it is not possible such a thing can have happened; it is too bad!" exclaimed Rosa Birkett as she stood in the garden of St. Agatha's convent-school, looking with startled eyes into the face of her schoolmate.

"Well, you'll soon find out it is true," rejoined Maggie. "Sister Theodora has taken her to the dormitory, and is showing her about the place; and I heard Sister say, as they went upstairs, 'So you are Rosa Birkett's cousin?'"

"Tell me, Rosa, is she a *very* disagreeable girl?"

But she received no answer, for Rosa, pushing her aside with a vehement gesture, rushed towards the convent, and burst into, rather than entered, a small room on the ground-floor, where a nun was sitting at a table, writing.

"My dear child," said the religious, looking up, "what is the matter? are you ill?"

"I am heart-broken; I'm miserable; I've no hope left!" exclaimed Rosa, throwing herself on her knees by Sister Veronica's side, leaning her arms upon the table. The Sister could not help smiling.

"This is a terrible state of affairs; Rosa, again I ask what is the matter?"

"Maggie Ryan just told me that my cousin Mildred has come to this school; I think it is *too bad* that I have been kept in the dark all this time; if I had only known she was coming I could have *begged* mamma to take me away"; and Rosa gave her head an angry toss.

Sister Veronica took up her pen. "If you have only come here," she said, gravely, "to criticize Rev. Mother's conduct, *I* had better continue my writing; *I* should never dream of supposing she could not admit whom she pleases into the school, so we should not be likely to agree."

"Sister, you are *very* unkind," replied Rosa, bursting into tears. "You know I don't mean to be impertinent, and you don't know how very, *very* hard it is for me to have my cousin here."

"Tell me all about it," said Sister Veronica, turning towards her and speaking in her usual gentle voice; "what is the reason you dislike her so?"

"Sister, she has always been in my way ever since I can remember anything; neither of us had any sister, and Aunt Bessie lives close to our house at home; so we were always together. I was always naughty, and she always good. Her name was continually dinned into my ears. 'Just look at Miss Millie!' nurse would say; '*she* never tears her dresses'; and then, 'Oh, my dear, if you would only be like Mildred!' mamma would sigh. Sister, I do assure you it was because of *this*, because of *her*, I asked mamma to let me go to school, and you know how hard it was on me when first I came here; and now that I am at home, and happy with you all, she is to come and upset me. Oh, it is too—*too* hard!" and Rosa sobbed violently.

Sister Veronica waited till the passion had spent itself; meanwhile a prayer went up from her soul that she might have light and grace to guide this troubled heart. Then she spoke: 'Rosa dear, indeed I feel for you,—for you have real suffering to bear; such a passion as you have allowed to grow within you is a suffering in itself. But now, with God's grace, you are going to overcome it."

"I can't, Sister," sobbed Rosa.

"Oh yes, you can; for though you have many faults, you have, at least, one good quality."

"What is that, Sister?" said poor Rosa, looking up with a gleam of hope in her tear-stained face.

"You are brave," answered the nun; "you have courage, and thus I feel sure you will overcome yourself. I am going to give you a motto—some words of Father Faber's that I am very fond of: '*A cross is a crown begun.*' Now, here has poor Mildred come to be your cross; but she is also going to be your crown some day."

"Oh, never, Sister!" said Rosa in a tone of dejection, sitting down on the ground; "I never can like her."

"Well, my child, if she is never to be your crown in this world—if you can never cry 'Victory' over this weakness—so long as you are trying and fighting, God will not ask more, and the cross will turn into a crown in a bright eternity. But now let us go and get help. Come with me," and taking the child by the hand, the nun led her through a door at the end of the room, into a pretty oratory, called the Chapel of the Children of Mary. A beautiful Image of the Virgin Mother was in the centre. How many childish griefs were brought to its feet, how many struggles fought and victories won in this little oratory can only be known by the records of the angels. And now, kneeling at the feet of this loved image, Sister Veronica prayed in these words of Holy Church, which so wonderfully meet the needs of aching hearts: "*To thee do we cry, weeping and mourning in this valley of tears!*" And the words that have calmed so many aching hearts did their work in that of Rosa, and her last sobs died away before the feet of her heavenly Mother.

CHAPTER II.
TRYING HARD.

On leaving the oratory, Sister Veronica sent Rosa to bathe her red eyes, and when she returned they went into the garden; there it was that Rosa met her cousin Mildred.

Sister Veronica felt a little curious to see the child who had excited so strong a feeling of aversion in Rosa's breast. When she saw the cousins meet she could not help smiling at the contrast, Rosa's figure was short and square; her hair, which was nearly black, having a tendency to curl, and obstinately refusing to be brushed into shape, had earned for its owner among her companions the *sobriquet* of mop-head. Her complexion was a mixture of dark red tan and freckles, and her round brown eyes were full of mischief. But they were also full of truth, and if her face was not handsome it was open and honest.

Mildred was very pretty; tall and slender, with long chestnut hair smoothly brushed back and tied with ribbon; bright blue eyes, and fair skin. She had a pleasant voice and manner, neither too shy nor too forward; but Sister Veronica's keen eyes read in her face a little too much self-satisfaction and confidence in her own goodness. She greeted Rosa with the greatest affection: "I am so pleased to be at the same school with you," she said. "Mamma made up her mind to send me, and I begged her to fix on this convent, that I might be with you."

Rosa made no answer, but Sister Veronica began to ask Mildred questions, and rapidly drew the conversation away to other subjects.

Rosa was not mistaken in supposing that Mildred's arrival would be the source of trials to her. The cousins were the same age, having been born on the same day, and therefore it naturally excited surprise and comment that one should be so much behind the other. Mildred was in a higher class than Rosa in every branch except drawing, and this not from want of ability on Rosa's part, but from her want of application. German she declared was one of the "unknown tongues"; French, gibberish; geography, tiresome; history, stupid; and so on through the catalogue. For music, she really had no ear, and the only talent she seemed to possess was for drawing. In the drawing-class, the cousins were together, and though Mildred had not near so much natural genius as Rosa, she was so painstaking that some of the nuns predicted that in a long race between the two, Mildred would prove the tortoise, and Rosa the hare.

Mildred soon became a great favorite in the school, and had it not been for the unceasing vigilance of the nuns the cousins would have headed two parties.

The nuns of St. Agatha's were an enclosed Order, and their grounds were very large,—two miles in extent, and comprising several large meadows, and an extensive wood through which ran a brook. On half-holidays, Rosa headed whatever prank it was possible to play. While Mildred spent part of the time "drawing from nature," Rosa and her band would be off to see what feats in the way of climbing, jumping, running and shouting could be accomplished, regardless of Sister De Chantal or Sister Stanislaus threatening to appeal to higher authority. To tear her dress in the brambles, or wet her shoes in the brook, were delightful incidents of the day; while Mildred and her followers ran races on the smooth grass, tossed each other in the swing, played at reasonable games, and read story-books.

Sister Veronica was first mistress of the school. She did not teach much herself, but trained the younger Sisters as they left the novitiate for their new duties, superintended the school, and kept a careful watch over the children. She was much beloved, a little feared, and entirely trusted. She was sometimes thought severe by those who could not have their own way with her, but when in real trouble the children all flew to her, as birds fly to their nests.

One half-holiday the rain poured in such torrents that even Rosa felt it would be useless to ask to go out, and amusement must be sought within the walls of the school-room. It was cold and chilly also, and a fire was lighted. Near this, Mildred and the "quiet ones" seated themselves with their fancy work, each in turn reading aloud a new story-book that Mildred's mamma had sent her; while Rosa and her companions were having a furious game of battledore and shuttlecock. After it had lasted some time, Agnes Doyle fell down and hurt herself. This brought the game to an end, and the party wandered towards the fire-place where they found Mildred and her group in eager argument over the story.

"Well, I do think, Milly, you are hard upon her," said Fanny Dean. "She was dreadfully afraid of her uncle, and that made her tell the lie."

"Afraid!" said Mildred, scornfully; "the idea of anyone being afraid to do right!"

"Oh, Sister, what do you say?" exclaimed Maggie Ryan, catching sight of Sister Veronica who had come in unperceived and stood listening with an amused smile on her face. "You know the story—*Frederica and her Sisters*. Don't you think it was very hard on her to live with that dreadfully severe uncle?"

"It was her duty," said Mildred, solemnly. "Sister, ought she not to have done it? I can never like her, or feel any interest in her again."

"And, pray, do *you* never do anything wrong yourself, Milly?" cried Rosa, reddening. "I am sure you could be naughty enough when you chose at home, when nobody was by, for all you are so prim and stuck up now."

"Rosa!" said Sister Veronica, severely; and Rosa retreated with a black face, mumbling something to herself.

"Well," said the Sister, going on with the conversation, "I think, Mildred, that while we love the truth and the right, we must be very merciful to those who fail. We fail ourselves in many things; we all do."

Mildred drew up her head: "Sister, it is a mean, base thing to tell a lie."

"Yes, dear, but remember this child underwent strong temptation. You, who have always been with kind parents, can hardly understand the depth of her temptation," and, so saying, Sister Veronica turned away.

She mused as she went along, "Mildred has the elements of a noble character; she is as true and sincere as Rosa. I don't think her vanity goes very deep, but I should like to get that hardness towards others out of her."

The nun now went in search of Rosa, whom she found as she expected, in a fit of despair.

"It is no use, Sister," she wailed, "I shall never do it; I only get worse. She is always vexing me."

"For shame, Rosa; be up and doing. Don't you know this despondency is only a form of pride? *You* can do nothing,—but our Lord, and, through Him, Our Lady and your angel can do all things. Look up,"—as she pointed to a picture of the Angel Guardian,—"there is your true friend. And now, kneel at his feet and say bravely:

"Beautiful Angel, forgive me the past,
And help me to love and obey you at last;
And to think when I'm tempted to sadness or fear,
That God and His angels are watching and near."
ELLEN DOWNING.

CHAPTER III.

One day Sister Veronica was told the Rev. Mother wished her to go to the parlor. She accordingly went, and found there Rosa and Mrs. Birkett; Mildred, and her mother, Mrs. Luny. The latter had her arm around Mildred, and a look of proud, fond satisfaction on her face. Mrs. Birkett was trying to smooth Rosa's hair, with an expression of wistful disappointment on her features. Both ladies greeted Sister Veronica warmly.

"I thank you so much, Sister," began Mrs. Luny, "for the pains you are taking with Mildred. I find her much improved. She tells me she loves her school so much."

"Ah, dear Sister," sighed Mrs. Birkett, "I fear my wild madcap gives you much trouble. If she were only like her cousin!"

"I would much rather have her like herself," replied the nun, smiling.

"Really!" said Mrs. Birkett, in a tone of relief; "she is improving, then?"

"I do not like giving my children's characters before their faces," said Sister Veronica, brightly; "what I meant was that I like variety. I do not wish to lose my wild Rose only to have her a second Mildred; I want her to bloom as God intends her; and—yes, I think I may say she is improved."

Big tears of joy stood in Rosa's brown eyes: "Do you really think, Sister, she will get on? She does look rather untidy," and Mrs. Birkett's eyes wandered to the spot where Mildred, trim and neat, was seated by her mother's side, talking eagerly, in a low voice.

"Indeed, Mrs. Birkett," said the nun, "I hope Rosa will improve in that respect, but I do not think she can ever look like Mildred; the one has a natural taste for neatness, the other has to acquire it. In fact, I don't want her to imitate Mildred, but to aim at something higher."

"My dear Louisa," broke in Mrs. Birkett, "we must be off, or we shall lose the train"; and after hasty adieus and a shower of kisses the two ladies departed.

Rosa sprang down the steps into the garden, and danced along the walk in the exultation of her heart. She was like one who has got rid of a burden, or who has been set free from a chain. It was astonishing to see the effect this conversation between Sister Veronica and Mrs. Birkett had upon her; and as time passed on, the latter came often to the convent, took Sister Veronica's advice concerning Rosa—took also fresh heart about her, and totally left off the habit of comparing her with Mildred.

Two years passed away, and the rivalry between the cousins was almost, if not quite imperceptible. Both had improved: Mildred gave promise of growing into a very charming woman, if it were not for the little harshness in her character, against which Sister Veronica often fought, but had never wholly subdued. Rosa was less wild, and more attentive to her lessons. Both were pious; they had made their First Communion fervently, and had been Confirmed. They went often to Confession and Communion, and had the medal of the Children of Mary, but still could not be said to be really fond of each other. Rosa was still behindhand in her studies, and had never carried off a single prize.

About a month before the commencement of the summer vacation, the Rev. Mother came into the school-room one day, accompanied by a lady and gentleman. She asked Sister de Chantal to call out the drawing-class. This was done, and the children exhibited their drawings. It then transpired that the gentleman was Sir Edward Claridge, the celebrated artist, a relative of the Rev. Mother's, and that he was going to give a prize for drawing. After some discussion, six pupils only—among whom were Rosa and Mildred—were chosen to compete. The others were Henrietta Jackson, Margaret Ryan, Fanny Dean, and Agnes Doyle. Each pupil had a subject to copy, and these were supplied by a series of sketches made during a journey along the Corniche Road, that beautiful route from Genoa to Marseilles, by Sir Edward himself.

To Mildred fell a distant view of the white marble mountains of Carrara, while Rosa had one where pale olive groves and gardens of orange trees sloped down to the bright blue Mediterranean.

The prize was to be given on the Examination Day, when the Bishop, some of the clergy, and many other visitors would be present. Each pupil was to have extra time allowed for her drawing, and was also permitted to work unseen by her other competitors. It was to be a strict rule that no one was to see the other's work until the public exhibition, and no one was to have the slightest help from any quarter.

Sir Edward and Lady Claridge took leave, and next day the contest for the prize fairly began.

For the first fortnight Rosa worked hard at her water-color sketch, and then pronounced it finished. Sister Veronica did not agree with her.

"If I were you, Rosa," she said, "I should work longer at it. I can hardly say what it wants, but as you work on you will see for yourself. Your olives are not gray enough, I think."

"Yes, Sister; I mean to go over it again before the day comes. I always get an inspiration at the last moment. I can't do any more now; I don't feel in the humor for it."

The Sister looked grave. "The others are working steadily," she said.

Rosa tossed her head: "Yes, Sister; I know how Mildred plods away; but I can catch her. You know," she continued, coloring a little, "I could not help hearing Sir Edward say to Rev. Mother, 'There is the artist's touch here,' as he looked at my drawing of Keswick."

"Well," said the Sister, "what then?"

"I mean," said Rosa, "I have always heard that artists work by fits and starts, and that is what I mean to do; and, Sister, I mean to be an artist when I grow up, and exhibit my pictures and grow famous," and Rosa swelled herself out a little with conscious pride. She was saying to herself: "I shall excel Mildred at last!" and her angel was looking sorrowful.

"Well, Rosa," said the Sister, "I can't spend time arguing with you; you must run away now"; and when she was alone, Sister Veronica said to herself: "Poor child! I fear Sir Edward's praise has turned her head; and I should not wonder after all if it were the hare and tortoise in the end. *Pride goeth before a fall*"; and, as usual, Sister Veronica prayed.

(TO BE CONTINUED.)

THE AVE MARIA.

A Journal devoted to the Honor of the Blessed Virgin.

HENCEFORTH ALL GENERATIONS SHALL CALL ME BLESSED.—St. Luke, i, 48.

VOL. XVI.   NOTRE DAME, INDIANA, JANUARY 31, 1880.   NO. 5.

[Copyright: Rev. D. E. Hudson, C. S. C.]

Fra Angelico.

FROM "PRELUDES," BY MAURICE F. EGAN.

ART is true art when art to God is true,
And only then: to copy Nature's work
Without the chains that run the whole world through
Gives us the eye without the lights that lurk
In its clear depths: no soul, no truth is there.
Oh, praise your Rubens and his fleshly brush!
Oh, love your Titian and his carnal air!
Give me the trilling of a pure-toned thrush,
And take your crimson parrots. Artist—saint!
O Fra Angelico, your brush was dyed
In hues of opal, not in vulgar paint;
You showed to us pure joys for which you sighed.
Your heart was in your work, you never feigned:
You left us here the Paradise you gained!

The Purification of Our Lady.

ONE by one the days of enforced exemption from duty, the forty days of repose enjoined by the Law of Moses, had glided by; and now Mary and Joseph were wending their way to the Temple of the Most High, apparently to perform an act of humility, but in reality to bring the only offering worthy to be presented to the Godhead.

Those forty days, what were they? According to the law, days of humiliation, to be terminated by an act of obedience and sacrifice—seemingly a hard law, and yet one full of fatherly kindness, at once raising a barrier to protect the health of the people from the avarice of man, and the household ambition of woman. So it is with all humiliations that come from the hand of God: they carry their blessings with them. What were those forty days to the people of Bethlehem, whilst they had their Redeemer in their midst? Not what they might have been, had they recognized the fact; and yet, undoubtedly, they were fraught with wonderful blessings for all the inhabitants of that favored town. Why did they not know that their Redeemer was with them,—had heaven neglected to tell them? Hardly; there were the prophets, who had foretold all; but doubtless there would have been many to inform us that it was much more important to attend to the ordinary duties of life than to trouble one's mind with that department of religion. The vision seen by the shepherds was to them what visions are to the world nowadays, and so it was forty days of laughter and revelry, of buying and selling—and God was in their midst. Truly "He came unto His own, and His own received him not."

What were those forty days to Mary? Ah, here the loving soul beholds the compensation for man's coldness and neglect. Little heeded she the humiliation of the law, rather she rejoiced in it; for its observance gave her more leisure to bestow those caresses, and perform those services which in her were not only evidences of maternal affection, but more than that,—acts of perfect adoration. Oh happiest of the daughters of Eve! to thee alone was it given to love thy Creator with a mother's love,—the deepest, the most enduring, and the most self-forgetful love that possesses the human heart.

Now these days were accomplished; and she was going to the temple to fulfil the law, and afterwards to pick up the thread of daily life; to learn and to practice new duties; to learn to leave God to do God's work. Her uninterrupted communion with her Divine Child was at an end: now it was to be mingled—first, with the performance of her household occupations, and in later years to be disturbed by His ministry among men. Full of Grace was she when the angel appeared to her, nine months had the Eternal Word dwelt within her, for yet another month and more He had been her sole occupation; and, as St. Catharine of Genoa tells us, grace increases in proportion as man makes use of it; and as we know that Mary's co-operation was most faithful, we can see that the ordinary mind cannot fathom the ocean of grace that filled the soul of Mary on the morning of her purification.

At the dedication of Solomon's Temple, the Glory of the Lord came down like a luminous cloud into the sanctuary, at the sound of praise from voice and instrument (II Paralip, v, 13,)—and not even the priests could stand in the presence; but to the second Temple, its Master comes in silence, in meekness, and penance. How apparently contradictory are the ways of the Most High! and yet they seem so to us only, because the human mind is too finite to grasp the unity of plan displayed by Infinite Wisdom.

Jesus, Mary, and Joseph, how their apparition would gladden the eyes of many a fervent soul! yet there they stood unmarked amid the crowd which was gathered in the outer court of the Temple on an apparently like errand; or if noticed, it was to observe how the family of David had fallen. Doubtless, those of low origin deduced therefrom, that a long line of noble ancestry was of no importance; others thought that St. Joseph had no right to degrade the nation in the eyes of the Romans by becoming a carpenter; and some we may reasonably suppose, exclaimed at the turtle doves, the offering of the poor, "They might have endeavored to present a lamb"; yet of all her ancestresses, the queens and princesses of the house of Juda, who, surrounded with regal pomp, had presented in the Temple possible heirs to the throne, there was none to equal that Mother who was not only queen, but priest, as she is called by St. Epiphanius. Those who have studied deeply the Mystery of the Maternity of Mary, tell us that her consent was necessary, not only to the Incarnation, but also to all the other mysteries of the Redemption; and that it was by her compliance with the law regarding the presentation of the first-born in the Temple, that she signified her willingness to sacrifice her Son. Thus the turtle doves had more than one signification: not only did they show how thoroughly Mary and Joseph accepted the conditions of poverty; not only were they an exhortation to the world at large not to spend beyond its means even for praiseworthy objects, but they also signified that He whom Mary offered was the True Lamb,—the Lamb without spot, slain from the beginning, who therefore should not be ransomed.

Yet, though many of those who surrounded Our Lady on this morning of her Purification were ignorant of her high office, and were thus emblematic of the world,—who when God has chosen to confound its strength with the weakness of His instruments, goes its ways, not knowing that it has been confounded;—there must have been some who knew of the vision of the shepherds, and who accepted it as true, little caring that their piety was called by some, devoid of common sense, and spoken of as arising from an unhealthy tone of mind. Those would say with St. Epiphanius: "*Virginem appello velut Sacredotem*," for they knew that, whereas their purification was real and their sacrifice apparent, Mary's Sacrifice was real and her purification impossible, because she was stainless.

We may imagine these lingering to the last to gaze as long as possible on the long expected Redeemer. Other parents had carried their children away, little dreaming how irrevocably their destinies were bound up with those of that Child of the unpretentious pair from Nazareth. Yet those children were His contemporaries, all linked with Him. Some of them would be His disciples; some would carry palms to welcome Him, some would shout "Crucify Him!" and the children of Bethlehem would give their lives for His. Well rewarded were those who remained, for they heard from the lips of Simeon, that canticle which comes like a prolonged sequence to those words which brought the Glory of the Lord into Solomon's Temple. "Give praise to the Lord for He is good, and His mercy endureth forever," so chanted Solomon's choir; and Simeon responds with his sublime death song, which he utters not for himself alone, but also for the Law of Moses which the Divine Infant fulfilling, had dismissed in peace.

How grand was Simeon's act of faith! he had besought the Lord to be allowed to behold while yet on earth the desired One; he had entreated that his departure might be delayed until then; and when the wished-for moment came, he saw a helpless Infant: yet his believing gaze pierced veils scarcely less dense than those which screen the Eucharistic Presence, and he testified, that his eyes had seen that Salvation which was a light to the revelation of the Gentiles, and a glory to the people of Israel.

"A light to the revelation of the Gentiles": Remembering these words, the Church celebrates this festival with peculiar ceremonies; and in memory of the entrance of the Light of the world into His Temple, she makes this a day on which to bless and sanctify light. Let us accept from her hands these lights, emblematic of the True Light which enlighteneth every man; let us bear these sanctified tapers reverently to our homes, let them be among our household treasures, and should the angel of death surprise us before the year passes away, we may go forth to the unending wedding feast with our lamps ready and trimmed.

"A glory to the people of Israel": but they were to esteem Him their shame! and we are like them, when we neglect or despise the graces which the Church offers to us through her Sacraments and Sacramentals, which we should consider as glorious prerogatives of the children of salvation!

"Thy own soul a sword shall pierce." Filled

and replenished with grace, Mary entered the Temple, and yet she left it with another grace greater than all: a blood-red rose petal resting on the transparent liquid filling to the brim the crystal vase, and this was the grace of an added dolor, the clearer view of the sword that should pierce her heart on that day when Calvary would complete the oblation which she had just made before the sanctuary of the Holy of Holies.

'Beth's Promise.

BY MRS. ANNA HANSON DORSEY.

CHAPTER V.
THE YOUNG HAMILTONS.

MRS. HAMILTON, always fragile, and threatened for years with consumption, felt the shock so severely, that though she bore her cross with calm resignation, the disease so long dreaded rapidly developed itself, and after a few months of severe suffering, it was evident that she was sinking. Many and sad misgivings disturbed the mind of the dying mother as to the future temporal and spiritual welfare of her helpless and orphaned children,—all of them, at that impressionable and critical age, when youth most needs a steady and judicious influence to guide and control them. They had no near relatives, and the small fortune that she could leave would be barely sufficient to educate and support them. She could only commend them to the care of Almighty God, trusting in His promises, and with devout faith implore for them the protection of "Our Blessed Lady of Perpetual Help." Bonne Mère Hamilton, as she was now known in the family, had hastened to them, filled with the kindest intentions, as soon as the sad news of her stepson's death, and his farewell letter reached her. Her grief, her unfeigned sympathy and her efforts to be of use, were all of that fussy sort, far from tranquillizing to the poor invalid; but the well-meaning motive made her patient. As the end approached, both were conscious that words must be spoken which could not be left unsaid; and one night, after the Sacrament of Extreme Unction, and the holy Viaticum had been administered to the dying one, who, as is often the case, rallied and seemed stronger than she had been for some days, Mrs. Hamilton told her of her wish to adopt the children, promising in the most solemn manner, not only to be a mother to them, but never in any way to interfere with their religious faith, or practice, or seek to influence their belief.

"You will be kind to them, I know; you will make them happy; but, Mamma Hamilton, their souls are above all price: better they should be beggars than lose their faith," she said, faintly, clasping her crucifix to her heart.

"They need not lose their faith or be beggars either, my dear child. I will do as I have promised,' so help me God!'" answered Mrs. Hamilton, meaning all that she said.

"May He deal with you as you deal with them," came the low, falling voice. "Take them; be a mother in deed by trying to become one in Faith with them, as he, speaking, as it were, from the grave, besought you to do." Then closing her eyes, she lay so quiet and calm that Mrs. Hamilton thought she was sleeping, until the day dawned through the windows; then she saw the white, still change, which meant death and eternal freedom from human pangs.

Mrs. Hamilton meant to keep her promise, and devote herself henceforth to her stepson's children; they should be as her very own, and inherit her money when she died. But what were their best interests? How could she bring up these souls in the doctrines of their holy Faith?—she who had no settled ideas of faith, who was an unbeliever in revealed religion as taught by Jesus Christ who founded it; who had but one idea, viz., that all were to be saved—the wicked as well as the good—because, if there was a God, He would not condemn to eternal punishments those He created, let their sins be what they might. A Catholic would have known at once what the best interests of these children meant. With neither mind nor judgment matured; at an age when impressions are most indelibly printed on the soft clay of their nature, whether for good or evil, Catholic schools and Catholic influences with all their safeguards of Faith and practice, were what they needed above all. But Mrs. Hamilton, without the faintest idea that her plans for them would be the very course to undermine their faith, thought only of a brilliant future for them, and determined after the first six months of mourning had passed, to send the boys to Harvard, and Anne when a year older, to a fashionable French boarding-school in New York. Remaining in Baltimore until Col. Hamilton's affairs were all settled and placed under safe guardianship, and a beautiful and expensive monument was erected to the memory of himself and his wife in Greenmount Cemetery, she returned, accompanied by the almost inconsolable children, to her elegant home in one of the most picturesque nooks among the Berkshire hills, where the novelty of their surroundings, their delightful drives, the boating on a romantic lake near by in the valley, the trout-fishing and various other amusements, began to divert their minds from constantly brooding over their great loss. It was not Mrs. Hamilton's fault that there was not a Catholic church within fifty miles; she would have been glad had there been for their sakes, but she told them to read their prayers as they had been taught, until they should come to her elegant home in Boston, where "they could go to church every day if they wished." She invited two or three bright young persons of their own age—boys and girls, full of fun and frolic—to spend a few weeks with them; she loaded them with presents; provided all sorts of amusements she could think of to interest them, until they began to think that the world was a much happier place than they had ever dreamed of; and their sorrowful and dejected memories began to fade away in the new brightness that had come into their lives. When the first snow fell, Mrs. Hamilton moved her family to Boston; and once more, Frank and Harry, with their sister, attended Mass. The coachman, who was an Irish Catholic, always accompanied them to and from the church; and the boys, being old enough, received the Sacraments. It was a poor, dim, miserable edifice, so unlike the spacious cathedral and elegant churches of Baltimore, that the boys, who were very observant, noticed the contrast, and also that the devout congregation that filled it seemed to belong to the laboring class; but when the candles were lit upon the altar; when the soft strains of the organ stole upon the ear; when the acolytes and the priest entered and the Holy Sacrifice began; these Catholic children felt themselves at home, their hearts pulsed with happiness, and their minds were filled with tender memories of those loved and lost, for whose repose they prayed. Never had they felt so near them since they died as now; it was like home to be there, and they were more than comforted. Mrs. Hamilton did not relish their going among "all those low people," as she styled them, but there was no help for it; she had inquired, and learned that the two other Catholic churches had the same sort of congregations; it was the New Bethlehem —this Athens of America—where Jesus deigned to dwell in lowly abodes, and be worshipped and tended by the poor, and the simple of heart. She was glad to see "her children," as she called them, happy, and—true to her word—interposed no obstacle to their going to Mass and Vespers. After Christmas they were to be sent away to school, and she did not know exactly what difficulties they might have to encounter then, therefore they should be free to go as often and whenever they pleased to their church, the only proviso being that Patrick was to be always in attendance, a thing he did not very much relish, and therefore usually went to sleep; for although he would have fought and died for his Faith if necessary, his practice of its sacred precepts was of that kind which barely saved him from excommunication.

The boys, and especially Anne, with her fair silken curls and her great brown eyes, loved the *Bonne Mère* very much; she was always thinking of their comfort and amusement, and never let their purses go empty, and on Christmas day unveiled for the first time large three-quarter portraits of their father and mother, which she had been at great trouble and expense to have painted by a first-class artist, who made it a specialty to get faithful likenesses from photographs of persons he had never seen. Col. Hamilton's was wreathed with laurel, that of his gentle wife with violets. How could they help loving her more than ever now, since she had brought *them* almost living, and breathing, back to them? They embraced and thanked her, and wept upon her bosom, wondering how they could ever repay all her kindness.

The day came at last when *Bonne Mère* took them to school, the two lads to Harvard, and Anne to the celebrated and fashionable French boarding-school of Madame de Villiers, where the intellectual and æsthetic faculties of the pupils were cultivated as if it were the end and aim of their creation; where they were superficially crammed with the 'onomies and the 'ologies and the 'isms; where they were drilled in the accomplishments, and polished and instructed in worldly usages and the arts of social success, to prepare them for a *début* into fashionable life with an eclat which would reflect credit upon the establishment from which they emerged. Both at Harvard, and at Madame De Villiers' Mrs. Hamilton stated that her children were Catholics, and must be allowed to attend their own Church—to which no objection was offered, and during the first year they did so quite regularly, though under petty difficulties of one sort or another. At last vacation came, and they went back with *Bonne Mère* to the beautiful old home among the Berkshire hills, where they knew that unlimited delights awaited them. Thoughts of those who would never brighten their home-life again; sweet, tender memories, sometimes made them thoughtful and sad, and it was their habit, in accordance with a promise made to their dying mother, to find time every day, generally at twilight, to say the rosary. *Bonne Mère* Hamilton observed that they either slipped off by themselves, or remained very quiet about this time every evening, and at last discovered what it meant by a conversation she accidentally overheard between the boys, one of whom reminded the other that they had not yet said their beads, and that some frolic that was a-foot must wait until they did. "It is too bad," thought she, "for children full of life and frolic as these are, to be hampered and made gloomy by such superstitions, but I'll try and make it up to them, poor things." And so she did in her own good-natured way. She bought a pretty phæton, and a sure-footed, handsome pony for Anne; she changed her black dresses and crape hats and trimmings, for the most beautiful white, and daintily shaded organdies, made up by her own French dressmaker; and jaunty hats, decorated with graceful plumes, or humming-birds and flowers, with gay sashes and everything to correspond, which could possibly awaken a passion for dress in a young heart naturally vain. The boys had each their own pony, and with their boat and picnics and numerous other sports, their time was happily, and apparently harmlessly, filled up. But time that leaves no tithes for God's service cannot be harmlessly filled up; and this was the case with these Catholic children, removed from all the sacred influences of their faith, and constantly diverted from the very thought of it by pleasures and excitements that left no room for reflection. At first, they used to read their Mass-prayers on Sundays and holydays of obligation, whenever they could do so uninterruptedly; but the house was full of young company now, and there were such constant demands upon them, that they had scarcely a minute to spare; and gradually, thinking they could not help themselves, they grew so indifferent about it, that they scarcely knew when Sunday came, so much alike were all the days in that jolly pagan household. We say this under our breath, for Bonne Mère Hamilton fancied herself a very good, rational Christian, and would have resented any doubt expressed to the contrary. She thought moreover, that she had fulfilled in good faith, the promises she had so solemnly made to the dying mother when she committed her children to her care, and took great credit to herself for her liberality in not opposing their going to Mass when their church was within reach, and in making it a condition at the schools where she had placed them that they were to be allowed the same privilege. What did she know of the vital principles of the Catholic religion, of its importance above all earthly things? Literally nothing. She believed that one religion was as good as another, and that no special form of faith or creed was necessary to salvation. There are thousands like her in this enlightened land of ours; where then's the wonder that materialism and infidelity grow apace with nursing mothers like these?

Conscience was not always silent, however, in the heart of the young Hamiltons. Sometimes after the lights were extinguished and they were in bed, with no external sound to distract their attention, "the still small voice" would be heard reproaching them for their neglect, reminding them of the example of their parents, and their Christian training; then, filled with compunction, they would shed bitter tears, say the rosary, resolve to do better, and fall asleep, to awake only to another merry hilarious day. Their surroundings were too much for uncried minds like theirs, and in their better moments, they could only hope that a time would come when it would be convenient for them to practice their religion.

Years passed by. Harry and Frank Hamilton graduated creditably at Harvard, and at their earnest desire, appointments were procured for Harry to the West Point Military School, and for Frank to the Naval Academy. Each of them passed through the usual course with honor to themselves, received their commisions and were assigned to duty—Frank to a ship on the North Atlantic Station, Harry to a regiment in the far west. Bonne Mère Hamilton felt a proud satisfaction in having educated them according to their station, and given them every enjoyment within the range of her means and ability, and above all, that they had grown up without any of those prim, starched ideas which would have made them think they were too good for the world they lived in. They had steadily through these years called themselves Catholics, and never failed to make at least an Easter Communion; otherwise their religion sat lightly on their shoulders, and they were known among classmates and comrades as being *liberal* in their belief.

Anne had grown to be a rarely beautiful woman; highly accomplished, and quite finished in all those well bred, polished ways, which go so far towards social success. She had not yet made her *début*, and Mrs. Hamilton thought it would be of the highest advantage to her to go abroad for a year. The idea was a delightful one to Anne, who had often heard her school-mates that had been to Europe speak of the delights of Paris and other famed cities, and observed that it gave them a certain prestige quite unattainable to those who had not been so fortunate. Their preparations were made, and Mrs. Hamilton, although she loved her old home among the Berkshire hills, and felt a pang at leaving it, went away with Anne, and her two servants, towards the lands she had never expected to see. They had a prosperous voyage across, and things went well with them after their arrival. Friends to whom they had letters, showed them every attention. Bankers to whom they had letters of credit, facilitated their movements by every means in their power; the very weather was in their favor, and the season was known as one of the most delightful that had been experienced for years.

We have no idea of describing their tour and its various delights. The beauty of the young American girl, and the wealth and dignity of her *chaperone*, attracted admiration and respect everywhere: never in her whole life had Mrs. Hamilton felt so supremely happy and satisfied with herself and all the world. After spending the summer in the Swiss, and Austrian Tyrol, Mrs Hamilton determined to winter in Naples, where she had friends in the American colony resident there. Shortly after they had settled in their delightful quarters, an American man-of-war arrived, and the officers were the recipients of many attentions from their fair countrywoman, who gave entertainments and made everything pleasant for them. Then a ball was given by the officers on the flag-ship, which surpassed anything of the kind ever known there before. Royal and noble guests accepted the hospitalities of the admiral and his officers, and mingled good naturedly and without formality with the Americans present, which was highly flattering to their republican hearts. Mrs. Hamilton was led in to supper by a Duke, who was attracted by the beauty and grace of her *protégée* and desired an introduction, little imagining how easy a thing it would have been, without all that conventional circumlocution: for American girls thinking no harm, and accustomed to the chivalry of the men at home, never dream of giving social offence by little friendly freedom of manner, things absolutely insignificant in themselves, but which out there in the Old World are considered disreputable. Mrs. Hamilton was in a state of exalted bliss, and when she turned to present her granddaughter to his highness, she discovered that she had slipped away, and was engaged in an animated chat with an American officer whom she had been introduced to and met at several entertainments in Naples—a Lieut. Morley, who had one of those grand figures and noble faces that always command admiration wherever seen, and who had about him none of that foppishness, affectation, or littleness, too often exhibited by handsome men. Mrs. Hamilton saw at a glance the delicate flush of pleasure on Anne's face, and the brightening of her eyes, as she listened to the agreeable things that Lieut. Morley was saying to her with such a deferential, graceful air. She could not catch her eye—she could not call her—it would not do to send for her, and Anne saw presently, to her great delight, *Bonne Mère* being led back to the ball-room in great state by her royal friend. That night, after they got home, Anne received a lecture on the proprieties and etiquette ruling good society abroad, which she was told she must be very careful to observe unless she wished to be entirely excluded from it. Then *Bonne Mère* kissed her and went to bed, where she dreamed of princes and dukes, and lords and ladies the live-long night; and Anne, of Lieut. Morley.

It was whispered all through the American colony that Lieut. Morley was paying his addresses to Miss Hamilton, which report had more truth in it than rumors of this sort usually have, and every one's curiosity was gratified in a few weeks by the announcement that they were really engaged. Mrs. Hamilton had seen it all, and though she made no remark, she quietly and prudently set to work to learn all she could about Lieut. Morley's antecedents and family. Fortunately this was not difficult, as Admiral Irwin an old friend of the Morley's, was able to give her all the information that she required, which was, that Lieut. Morley belonged to a good family of northern New York, that his record was without stain, his standing in the service excellent, and his means independent of his pay; therefore, when he formally proposed for Anne's hand, *Bonne Mère* had no reasonable objection to interpose, except that she thought she was too young to assume the duties and responsibilities of married life, and, having seen so little of the world, she was afraid that she did not know her own mind. Besides, did he know that Anne was a Roman Catholic? and was he aware that if children were born of this marriage they would have to be brought up Catholics? *Bonne Mère* was sublime in carrying out to the last her promise to look after the religious interests of her children, and she imagined that she was doing it in this case; but another motive, which she scarcely acknowledged, mingled strongly with her intention: she had ambitious designs for Anne; she had hoped to see her married to a serene highness, or, at the very least, to a coronet, and not unreasonably, for the fair young Amercan had made a great sensation by her rare beauty and accomplishments, in addition to which it was understood that there would be generous "settlements" if she married to please Mrs. Hamilton, to whom it now occurred that Lieut. Morley might possibly object to the conditions she had named, and the match might, after all, be broken off; but she was mistaken.

"Yes," he replied, "I knew she was a Catholic. She told me so at first. I belong to no creed myself, and am, therefore, quite willing to subscribe to any conditions required by hers. Be assured that her happiness will be too precious to interfere with a principle so vitally necessary to it."

Then Mrs. Hamilton, knowing Anne's sentiments towards her lover,—she having confessed her preference when questioned,—gave her consent, not too graciously, to the marriage. "I must confess," she said afterwards, in confidence, to a friend, "the affair is not altogether agreeable to me. I do not like those amphibious creatures!"—meaning navy officers. "Why could not the child fall in love with a civilian, if she must fall in love at all? There was that Roman Count, the most romantic-looking creature I ever saw, with a pedigree as long as my arm, and old palaces and things; then, too, he was a Catholic, like herself, but she only laughed at him, and said he looked like a bandit. I was so provoked! Then there was that handsome young Englishman, and he a lord; and that splendid fellow from Boston, worth millions, one of the best matches in the United States! But there is no use in fretting: it is fate, I suppose, and I shall have to make the best of it."

Here in this Catholic land, Anne Hamilton attended Mass regularly at one or another of the grand old churches; it was good form to do so, her foreign friends and associates—people of rank and fashion—were all Catholics, and it gave her a certain *prestige* which she unconsciously enjoyed, to be known as an American Catholic. Frequenting these ancient basilicas and cathedrals where the altars were like thrones—where the light, rich and subdued, streamed through storied windows, only shadowed by banners, whose gorgeous blazonry tarnished by time, and sprinkled with the dust of centuries, told of conquest and glory; where clouds of incense wreathed themselves about columns of rare marble, whose wonderful carving was wrought by the cunning fingers of the masters of art, and half veiled the marvellous pictures in which the triumphs of Christ and His martyrs, and the tender, touching mysteries of His holy Mother, were delineated with such perfect skill as to thrill the very souls of those who gazed upon them; where the mellow organ breathed such strains that it would not have been impossible to fancy they were floating out of heaven; where the glimmer of hundreds of waxen tapers made a halo to crown the spot where the "King of kings" offered Himself an unbloody oblation in the Divine Sacrifice of the Altar, for the salvation of His creatures; it is not strange that the earliest and best associations of Anne Hamilton's life were revived, that the memory of her mother and the pious training she had received came thronging into her heart, filling it with emotions she had never experienced before. One day during Holy Week, when Mrs. Hamilton and a party of Americans and English were going the round of the churches, to see what they called "the strange Catholic performances," they entered one less celebrated than others they had visited, in which the ceremonies had taken place at an earlier hour than the rest, and from which the crowds that had thronged it had surged away, leaving only a few devout groups around the confessionals and before the shrines of the Virgin and the Saints, who all seemed to be engaged in devout recollection and prayer. Even Mrs. Hamilton and her irreverent party were impressed by the solemnity and devout silence that reigned; it was not agreeable to them to feel that indefinable sensation of awe, as of a Presence invisible to them, which so many of those who are separated from the Faith experience on entering a Catholic church; and they sought to return as soon as possible into the sunshine and air. But something suddenly attracted Mrs. Hamilton's notice, and she whispered to the others to go without her, as she was very much fatigued. "She's suddenly struck," they said, laughing, after they got out; "the next thing we know she'll turn Papist, and the pious soul will think it a miracle due to the relics of the saints preserved there."

But Mrs. Hamilton, unfortunately, was not "struck" in that way. She had only seen a figure very like Anne's enter one of the confessionals, and she determined to wait until she came out, to assure herself whether or not she had made a mistake. She had to wait for some time, and was beginning to feel very restive, when, hearing a slight stir, she turned her eyes towards the spot, and saw that it was indeed Anne, her countenance grave, and her eyes bedewed with tears—those tears more precious in the sight of Heaven than the richest gems that earth holds—but she did not see *Bonne Mère*, and, approaching the shrine of "Our Lady of Dolors," she knelt, and, bowing her head, she drew out a rosary and began to recite the Sorrowful Mysteries. "Well!" thought Mrs. Hamilton, "I had no idea she cared for her religion like this! I'm sure her poor mother would be glad to know that I have brought her up to be a good Catholic." Laying this flattering unction to her soul, the good lady rustled out, gave alms to an old beggar at the church door, and hurried away to join her friends at an elegant lunch at the house of one of them, to which she had been invited.

"Excuse me for saying 'good-night' so early, *Bonne Mère*," said Anne Hamilton that evening. Mrs. Hamilton was expecting quite a number of friends to drop in, and knowing that Anne was the attraction which brought many of the younger and gayer ones thither, she looked up with a displeased countenance, and asked if she was not feeling well.

"Perfectly well; but I wish to be alone, and retire early this evening. I am going to the first Mass in the morning, and I'm afraid of over-sleeping myself if I sit up as late as usual."

"Anne Hamilton, do you intend to try and kill yourself, going out so early when you know the air is reeking with malaria? The next thing we know you'll be down with Roman fever."

"Do not be alarmed, dear *Bonne Mère:* it is not the season for fevers yet. I have never made my First Communion, and shall do so in the morning," the young girl answered, in a low, but very determined tone.

"I thought all that was attended to at Madame De Villier's. I gave them instructions to see that you were given time and opportunity to attend your church," said *Bonne Mère*, with dignity, so far was she from comprehending all that was required to instil into the minds of the young the true principles of faith and religion.

"Had I been a little older," answered Anne, with confusion; "or had there been some one to have reminded me—but I blame no one, I should have remembered all that I had been taught by my mother! But I was thoughtless, and, at last, indifferent. Now I am going to do better. Kiss me good-night, *Bonne Mère*."

"And what am I to say to Lieut. Morley? he'll be here with the rest, presently," said Mrs. Hamilton, kissing the fair young face bent down to hers.

"Excuse me to him; he'll understand," she replied, as she hastened out of the drawing-room to avoid some guest whom she heard coming up the marble stairs.

Whenever Mrs. Hamilton's friends alluded, as they sometimes did, to the strangeness of her grand-daughter's being a Catholic, her reply was: "Oh, yes, Anne is a Roman Catholic, of course. I had her brothers and herself brought up in that religion because their father and mother were Catholics, and I promised them to do so." And Mrs. Hamilton believed what she said. She imagined that because she had not persecuted or been unkind to them, and had made it a condition with those who had charge of their education, that they were to attend their own Church, she had done all that was incumbent upon her in their regard, and quite plumed herself on her liberality. To be complimented on this point, as she frequently was, gave her the highest satisfaction. Occasionally, some of her high-toned Puritanical friends ventured to expostulate with her, and disapprove of her having allowed the children to grow up in such an erroneous and idolatrous belief as the Romanists taught, instead of having them trained in the doctrines of Calvin, to be simple Bible Christians! It made *Bonne Mère* wince a little, but she was generally sufficient for the emergency, and with something of the air of a martyr to circumstances, would answer: "It was not a matter of choice with me. The case was a peculiar one. But taking everything into consideration, I think it is a good thing for Anne to have a religion of some sort you know, for she's young and very impulsive, and it will help to steady her now that she's going to be married"; then, thinking her more to be pitied than blamed, they held their peace.

Lieut. Morley had written to his only living near relative at home—an aunt—informing her of his approaching marriage, and describing the object of his choice with all a lover's enthusiasm. After speaking of her family and position, a thing which he knew Miss Elizabeth Morley would deem it essential to be informed about, he added: "She is a Roman Catholic, to which I do not in the least object; what right should I have to do so, professing no belief of any sort myself? I find her liberal in sentiment, and her religion seems to suit her, somehow, and it would be strange for her to be other than she is, she is so full of æsthetic tastes and fancies which find ample gratification in a faith whose history and ceremonials are romance, poetry, splendor and mysticism combined." This was the young fellow's idea of the Catholic religion, and of what he understood as liberality of sentiment on his own part.

Trusting him with all the confiding faith of a first love, which could imagine no earthly danger ahead; proud of him in every sense, and not at all unwilling to be envied for her conquest of so noble a nature, Anne Hamilton was very happy—so entirely happy that she gave herself no concern about the elegant and costly trousseau *Bonne Mère* was having prepared for her, or the diamonds and rare ornaments which were to form a portion of it. She valued a spray of wild flowers, or a cluster of field daisies gathered by her lover, beyond all the jewels in creation. He used to go with her every afternoon to one or another of the churches, to watch her while she told her beads—not knowing in the least the deep meaning of the devotion—to look down at her beautiful face slightly uplifted, with the light of the blessed tapers resting upon her golden hair like an aureole, while the soft tones of the organ rolled through the dim arches overhead, and the voices of the choristers chanted the Litany of Loretto. "So she will look in heaven," he used to think; "God forbid that I should ever interfere with a belief that appears to make her so happy."

(TO BE CONTINUED.)

A Lover of the Beautiful.

BY KATHLEEN O'MEARA, AUTHOR OF "IZA'S STORY," "ROBIN REDBREAST," "LIFE OF FREDERICK OZANAM," "PEARL," ETC., ETC.

LIKE Frederick Ozanam, Henry exercised, indeed, a marvellous fascination over the minds and hearts of the young, his own youth establishing a kind of equality which removed all barriers to perfect sympathy; but the true key to his power was the love he bore them, the deep respect he felt for the beauty of their souls, and his burning desire to win them to their own salvation. This thirst for God's souls was perhaps not sufficiently controlled by prudence, for he squandered with reckless prodigality the little stock of strength which, prudently hoarded, might have carried him safely to middle age.

No doubt the demand made upon him was great, and the pressure hard to resist. "The work of ten priests was thrust upon him," says P. Gratry. "I said to him: 'But why do you not refuse all these things?'' 'I am always refusing,' was his reply. And so he was; but when he had refused five or seven times, the work of five or three still remained to him."

Over and above his lecture at the Sorbonne,—task enough in itself to keep him fully occupied, and this daily work of three or five priests—he was producing an incredible amount of literary work.* Those who saw him thus prodigal of himself, were urgent in entreaty and remonstrance. P. Gratry wrote him the following letter one morning: "My child, I cannot keep silence. I feel it my duty to warn you,—to save your life, perhaps. It was agreed eight months ago—by the advice of the doctor—that you should take complete rest for several years. You know this is the steady conviction of P. Lacordaire. What has he not said about it to yourself! If, in spite of your friends, you persist in the life you are leading, it will be almost a guilty blindness. You are in danger of a relapse; who knows? perhaps within a few weeks of it. Forgive me. It is the voice of profound affection that speaks in this warning. If, from imprudence, you become quite useless, or lifeless before the time, we should feel that we were all maimed." Another Oratorian Father signed his name to this note under that of P. Gratry. P. Lacordaire's expostulations came to strengthen these remonstrances. "This must not go on," he said to P. Gratry; "he ought to have three years' rest, not only for the body, but for the mind and the soul. If he goes on with this active, scattered life, in the first place it will kill him, and in the next, he will not acquire the strength and depth and greatness that God means him to attain. Let him come and spend three years with me at Sorèze."

But it was no use. The voice of friendship was as of one crying in the wilderness, "In vain do ye spread nets before the feet of those who have wings." It requires some weightier motive than personal considerations of health, or even of life, to induce a priest so consumed with zeal as the Abbé Perreyve was, to rest from his labors while the power of working remains. The rest, in itself, would have been exquisite enjoyment, had he been able to conciliate it with the work. Writing to an invalid friend just then banished on a holiday to Rome, he says: "I guess what you must suffer in the ambulance, whilst we are in the field. . . . . but, dear friend, I implore of you, don't study. Look and listen; listen to the silence of Rome, along the ruins of the Appian Way, at the Villa Volkouski, on the Pincio of a morning when the dome of St. Peter's rising afar from the mists of the dawn, is lighted up with the first rays of the sun. This *informs* the soul for the rest of one's life. . . . . Lounge about, then, and let your thoughts wander through the ages; it is easy enough to do this in Rome." But these dreamy wanderings were a luxury in which the Abbé Perreyve himself was not to indulge. His constant prayer was, "Lord, give me strength to work!" The year 1864 opens with these words written in his memorandum: "Never complain of fatigue when God sends us a soul to console. . . . . Pray to God to increase my courage and leave me my sufferings." . . . . . "Ask God to give me back life and strength if I am to do good to souls and to serve His glory; otherwise let things go their way," he writes to a penitent, who was alarmed by the reports that reached her.

He had come almost to the end of his strength, when he was requested to give a course of conferences to the pupils of St. Barbe, that indocile, but ardent young audience whose sympathies he had so quickly gained and now firmly held. He consented unhesitatingly. He had refused everything else this year. "But for the conferences at St. Barbe," he said to Père Gratry, "if I knew they were to kill me the day the last one was delivered, I should accept them all the more readily. Any non-commissioned officer does the same when he is ordered to a post of danger." There was no gainsaying the justice of this assertion, but the fictitious strength which the exceptional effort created, enticed him to undertake others less imperative, and less self-supporting. His lectures at the Sorbonne were exhausting him utterly; he knew this, but it did not induce him to give them up. "You are wearing yourself out," said a brother-in-arms who met him coming out from a lecture one morning. "Well," was the quiet rejoinder, "and what is a priest good for but to be worn out?" The most severe trial which ill health had brought him, so far, was having compelled him to leave the Oratory. This step, which had been long foreseen as unavoidable, had been postponed to the very last; but it failed to induce the worn-out worker to take the rest which, even then, might have postponed the evil day. His sufferings increased with his weakness; but this only fanned the flame of his soul. "Suffering!" he exclaims, writing from his lonely room, scarcely now a home, in the midst of the great city, "suffering! How strange that we must always come back to this, while all our aspirations, all the instincts of our nature tend towards a happiness of which it seems almost unjust to deprive us! And what a strange contradiction to so many elements and *beginnings of happiness* in us! We feel so strongly, so deeply that happiness is possible, close to us—only a step, and it would be ours! But no, there comes that grain of dust, that slight hold, that poverty, that nothing-at-all which spoils everything and plunges us into the miseries of a heart betrayed. . . . . All would be irreparable if the eternal hopes were vain, and I confess that then there would

---

* During the seven years of his priesthood he published: "*Meditations sur le Chemin de la Croix*," "*La Journée des Malades*;" "*Les Lettres du P. Lacordaire à des Jeunes Gens*," with a beautiful preface. "*Les Entretiens sur l'Eglise Catholique*," being the substance of his lectures at the Sorbonne, St. Barbe and the Lycée St. Louis. "*Une Station à la Sorbonne*"; "*La Pologne*," which was his last work, the death-cry of his soul, protesting against the triumph of cruelty and barbarism over patriotism and faith; and a number of short essays and biographies: "*Hermann de Jouffay*," "*Jeanne Vare*," "*Rose Ferucci*," etc.

be nothing for us but disgrace and indignation. Happily it is not so; there lies in wait for us after this period of struggle and contradiction a substantial and blessed reality, which will be peace, understanding, perfect union, and the certainty of possession without decay and without end. Let us learn to wait, to be courageous, and to merit what we hope for."

He was so alarmingly ill that after the water-cure the doctor ordered him south for the winter. The separation from his friends and the enforced inaction were a terrible trial; but the invalid bore it uncomplainingly.

"They say I am pretty well," he writes on New-year's-eve. "The other day, the doctor—a worthy man—after examining me, sat down and said, 'Oh! since Eaux Bonnes, it has progressed; decidedly it has progressed'; I, believing that he alluded to the progress of the disease, replied very cordially: 'My dear sir, I thank you for your frankness; I had much rather know the truth at once.' The poor man bounded on his chair, and protested that the progress was in an opposite direction, which I was willing to believe: but he kept on repeating with his *Béarnais* accent: 'What do you take me for? Do you think I would tell you the truth if it had been unpleasant?'" It was a comical scene, and shows, as you perceive, that there are two meanings to the word progress, according as we apply it to good or evil; a luminous distinction, and as simple as it is necessary."

The exile hails the year 1865 with a tender invocation to the Consolation of the Afflicted: "Virgin most blessed, amidst thy glory forget not the sorrows of the world. Cast a glance of pity on those who are suffering, struggling. . . . Have pity on those who love and are separated! Have pity on the isolation of the heart! Have pity on the weakness of our faith! Have pity on the objects of our tenderness! Have pity on those who weep, on those who pray, on those who tremble. . . . Give to all hope and peace."

From afar, he watched over the souls confided to him. "I bless you, Madame, for so generously taking on yourself the care of those two poor souls. . . . Do not abandon B——. She is in peril, alone in the world, and with her heart! these good works occupy your soul. . . . You will find the remedy to vain and imaginary sorrows in charity, and devotion to real misery. People who suffer from the ideal should lodge near a hospital, and when their heart is bruised and over full, they should cross the street and go into the cancer ward, or the ward of chronic diseases, or the ward of the amputated. I speak from experience when I declare this to be a sovereign remedy."

As Lent drew near, the longing to resume the active functions of the ministry increased, and a wail of regret, too resigned to be called a lamentation, escapes the captive now and then. "It would be false if I pretended that the approach of Lent is not filling me with sorrow," he writes from Pau to the Chaplain of St. Barbe. "I had hoped that a return of strength might have enabled me to make a bold venture,—but it is too clear that my health would not bear the brunt of the battle, and that I must linger on sorrowfully in the ambulance. Will you convey my regrets to the directors of St. Barbe? . . . I say nothing to *cette chère Jeunesse*, whom God confided to me for a while. I feel too keenly the strength of such bonds; for I own to you that this is to me a real grief, just as the greatest joy I ever knew was being able to address those young fellows. I desire with all my heart that my successor may inherit the sympathy they gave me, and nothing would be more painful to me than to think that their kindness towards me might make the least difficulty in the way of the priest who will address them this year. This is not the kind of success I aspired to in speaking to them of God; and I hope and trust, while remaining true to a souvenir that is precious to me, they will welcome my successor as they welcomed me. You have seen yourself how the reception I met with at St. Barbe used to revive my courage and renew the strength that was failing me. Everything is in that for the poor man who speaks, and it is in truth the audience that makes the discourse." A month later, he says: ". . . . The thought of my dear St. Barbe leaves me no rest. It is a something that goes from the head to the heart, and back again. My doctor can't understand this, and I forgive him. He is not a priest, and never preached three Lents at St. Barbe, with the prospect of the fourth."

Henry was hard at work on "La Pologne," which was to be sold for the profit of the poor Poles, whose cause he had so deeply at heart. This was his death-song. His strength was wearing rapidly, and when the spring came with the leaves and flowers that he loved, the sands were fast running down. They took him to Epinoy at the beginning of April, and he spent a few weeks with his father and mother, and that sister whom he called the tutelary angel of his life. "I am very tired," he writes from the midst of them in May; "I can hardly hold my pen. . . . . My friends are beginning a novena for me after tomorrow, to end on Ascension Day. Adieu! storms and sunshine, clouds, blue skies and songs of birds. . . . . Poor little speck of this world, struggling to protest that it is not heaven, but that it awaits that eternal day, of which here and there it catches a stray prophetic beam!"

(CONCLUSION NEXT WEEK.)

LET us have no fear of science, for God is the author of all the sciences.—*Leo XIII.*

In Memoriam.

MISS MARY BRENHAM.

RESPECTFULLY INSCRIBED TO HER MOTHER.

THESE lines were suggested by the sad but most consoling and beautiful *Requiem* Mass offered at the funeral of this singularly pure and gifted young lady, who died recently in this city, at the early age of 17. *Requiescat in pace.*

Ah! be Love's clean oblation-rite
Her memory's fitting shrine,
Where altar-wreathes of lilies white
In fragrant beauty twine.

Where tapers show, by emblem-glow,
Her glorious realm of rest,
And requiems echo, soft and low,
The angel-greetings blest.

Aye! where the "Blessèd Blood of God"
Her bridal robe doth lave,
Cleansing each stain of earthly sod,
Within Its wondrous wave.

And where the rich, abundant dower
Of Life's Immortal Bread,
In strength-bestowing manna-shower,
On mourning souls is shed.

Ah, on the heart of her
Who bore that blossom fair,
The Food of Angels shall confer
Celestial graces rare.

In fadeless visions she shall see
Her stainless lily-flower
Encrowned with immortality,
In heaven's unfading bower.

Her bright crown-jewel she shall know,
Amid each glorious gem,
That shines with rare and radiant glow,
In Love's own diadem.

And on her blest, enraptured ear,
'Mid heav'nly choirs, shall fall
One well-loved voice, in echoes clear,
Resounding over all.

And, sure that now her lily-bloom
No "serpent-trail" can blight,
That ne'er the shadow of the tomb
Shall dim its stainless white—

That demon grasp can never tear
From out its fitting shrine
Her peerless gem, that Love doth wear
In diadem divine.

And ne'er the voice whose blissful tones
Her ear enraptured hails,
Can sink to pain's low, weary moans,
Or sorrow's hopeless wails.

That mother-heart its grief doth still,
And, "passing 'neath the rod,"
Bows meekly to the loving will,
And chast'ning hand of God.

MARIE.

SAN FRANCISCO.

The School Question Fairly Stated by a Non-Catholic.

WE consider the following article on religious education, which appeared in the Boston *Sunday Herald* of the 18th inst., the fairest statement of the case we have ever seen from a non-Catholic pen. Putting aside prejudice, the writer examines carefully the objections raised by Catholics to the public schools, proves them to be well founded, and then draws his conclusions. The article does credit to his candor and judgment. We are under obligations to the kind friend in Boston who sent us the paper:

Our forefathers came to this country not only to live where they could worship God according to the dictates of their own consciences, but where they could educate their children in their own religious faith. No people ever believed more thoroughly in the importance of secular education, but it must always be subordinate to moral and religious education. Therefore the schools which they established were, from the first, under the especial charge of the clergy. The Bible was the standard reading-book, and the catechism a constant text-book. In my father's day the Westminster Catechism was taught in the schools; and when my mother taught, 70 years ago, the children were all required to meet the clergyman in the church at stated times to recite the catechism. When the first primary schools were established in Boston in 1820, the "rules and regulations" required the teachings of religion, and the teachers were expected to open and close the schools with prayer. No pupil in the second class could be advanced to the first who could not recite the Commandments and Lord's Prayer; and none could graduate into the grammar school who could not read fluently in the New Testament.

The Unitarian controversy put an end to the teaching of the Westminster Catechism, but the Bible still remained the principal reader for many years. As most of the teachers took sides in this theological strife, and interpreted the passages read from the Bible according to their sectarian tendencies, a law was passed requiring the reading to be without note or comment. As extemporaneous prayers were often made the medium of doctrinal instruction, this was given up and the Lord's Prayer substituted. It was almost a universal custom for the clergymen of the place to be on the school committee. They examined the teachers and the school, opening and closing the terms with exhortation and prayers. The late Joseph Allen, D. D., of Northboro, did this for 40 years in succession. A teacher who did not attend church regularly would hardly be tolerated in the town. The above statement will be sufficient to show the importance which our forefathers attached to religious instruction in the public schools. In thus considering it of the first importance, they only maintained what educators and religionists of all ages had done before.

De Tocqueville says: "Religion is no less than the companion of liberty in all its battles and its triumphs—the cradle of liberty—the divine source of its claims. The safeguard of morality is religion; and morality is the best security of law, as well as the surest pledge of freedom." Prof. Huxley says in his lay sermons: "I would rather the children of the poor should grow up ignorant of both the mighty arts of reading and writing, than that they should remain ignorant of that knowledge to which these arts are means."

Washington, in his farewell address, says: "Let us with caution indulge the supposition that morality can be maintained without religion. Reason and experience both forbid us to expect that national morality can prevail in exclusion of religious principles."

Through sectarian quarrels among Protestants, and protests from Catholics, religious instruction has gradually dropped out from the public schools, so that now this most important part of a child's education is wholly ignored in our great system of public instruction. It may well be considered a hazardous experiment, when we reflect that it is contrary to the custom in every country in Europe. In England—a country more nearly like our own than any other—the new educational act of 1870 makes careful provision for Biblical and religious instruction. With the exception of Birmingham, where the disorderly class is large, and a few small towns in Wales, every school board approved the act. Only a short time since the school board sent a circular to all the teachers, asking them to give more attention to this matter. It says: "The committee hope that, during the Bible lesson, the teachers will keep this object before [them, and that every opportunity will be used earnestly and sympathetically to bring home to the minds of the children these moral and religious principles on which the right conduct of their future lives must necessarily depend."

It is now 100 years since Robert Raikes of Glasgow opened the first Sunday school, and about fifty years since any considerable number were established in this country. These schools have been depended upon to give the Biblical and religious instruction formerly given in the public schools, and thought by many to be sufficient. It was thought so by some in England, and used as an argument against having religion taught in the public schools. The subject was thoroughly discussed and statistics taken. The following extract from a late report will show with what result: "It has been found that Sunday schools do but little, comparatively, in teaching the knowledge of religious duties and of the Bible." In one town when the giving of religious instruction in the schools was opposed on the ground that the Sunday schools of the place made it unnecessary, the chairman of the board examined personally 200 children between 9 and 13, of whom 80 per cent. attended Sunday schools. He put to each the following questions: Who was Adam? Who was Jesus Christ? Only 86 knew who Adam was, and but 98 who Jesus Christ was. In examining two Sunday schools in the vicinity of London—one connected with the Church of England—not one could be found who could explain whom he meant to address as "Our Father" in the Lord's Prayer.

It is thought by many that the Sunday schools in this country might make a similar appearance under examination, especially in the more liberal denominations, where so many object to any doctrinal teaching whatever. It may be considered fair to conclude that but little is done in our Sunday schools to compare with the regular daily religious instruction formerly given in the public school, and little to be compared with the secular instruction given.

Many persons think that the public schools teach morality, and, no doubt, they do to some degree. But a prominent teacher said to me not long since: "We do not meddle with a pupil's habits outside of school; we do not feel that it is our duty, more than any other person's, to speak to a boy for lying or stealing, if not done in school." According to this, teachers are not doing more in this direction than is done by overseers in any large manufactory for those in their employ. There is a general feeling in the community, probably, that intellectual education has a great moral influence, and, in part, takes the place of moral and religious education. Herbert Spencer says: "The belief in the moralizing effects of intellectual culture, flatly contradicted by facts is absurd." Any one who has read and considered a prize essay, written by Rev. Cyrus Pierce, for the American Institute of Instruction, entitled "Crime; Its Cause and Cure," will never expect people to be made good by cultivating their intellectual faculties. It was formerly said that ignorance was the great cause of crime, but probably our jails and prisons contain as large a per cent. of educated persons as the community from which they come. Mere intellectual culture, then, cannot be depended upon to make good men or citizens. All religious denominations believe that moral and religious instruction is of the highest importance, yet, as things are, it cannot be given in the public schools, and the Sunday schools, under the best of circumstances, can accomplish but little in the short time the children are under instruction, and as most parents are incompetent to give it, and those competent often neglectful, how shall this, the most important thing, be done—this, without which no nation can long endure? We pay tithes of mint, anise and cummin, and have omitted the weightier matter of the law, judgment, mercy and faith. We know the greater, but seek the less. To this important question the Catholics say: "Let each denomination teach religion to its own children without interference in connection with secular instruction in the public schools, under such rules and regulations as experience shall prove convenient. Either set apart a time when the clergymen can meet the children and give this instruction, or let them have separate schools and their share of the school money, subject to the same supervision and requirements as all the other schools." If no better answer can be given, something like the above should without doubt be done, not only in justice to them, but for the good of all. It is not safe to jump at conclusions and decide that a certain state of things results from this or that cause. One thing, however, cannot be denied—all crime, and especially juvenile crime, has increased to an alarming extent during the last half century, much faster than the population. Our oldest reform school was established less than forty years ago, and was built to accommodate but 200. This now would not be sufficient for the juvenile criminals of Boston alone.

Many have inherited such a prejudice against the Catholics that they can scarcely discuss educational or religious questions with them with fairness. They seem to feel that Catholics have no right that they are bound to respect. How often have I heard it said, "If the Catholics do not like this country, let them go back to Ireland"—as though they had not as good right here as we, and that our laws will not, in the end, protect all in their rights, without regard to race, color or religion. Even Washington, in 1751, to qualify himself for a certain office, had to take an oath that he did not believe in transubstantiation. In prisons and reformatories in Massachusetts, until very lately, a Catholic priest would hardly be allowed to see the sick and dying of his own Church.

We have assumed that Catholics were enemies of education, because they find fault with the sectarian teachings in our schools; because they prefer the Douay Bible to that of King James—because they prefer to teach their own children their own religion, in connection with secular instruction.

Are not some school-books justly offensive to the Catholics? Do not our children get the idea from the geographies that the people of Spain and the South American countries are ignorant, quarrelsome and poor because under Catholic control? How would the opinions obtained in our histories of Luther and the Reformation agree with Catholic histories of the same? Are not the children taught, directly or indirectly, that the Catholic Church has opposed all advance in scientific knowledge, and do they not neglect to tell that other sects have done and are doing the same things?

It is hard to be just to our opponents, especially in religious matters. The Catholics and some others oppose the teaching of religion in the public schools, under present circumstances, as friends of religion; but many, like some Communists, Socialists, etc., are enemies of religion itself. It is very significant that Catholics are rarely connected with these secret societies, which threaten the future peace of the country. Should serious trouble arise from them, the whole Catholic population will be arraigned in opposition, a conservative power not to be despised. A very wise and attentive observer of these things said to me not long ago, that, in California, society could hardly have held together two years since against the Sand-hillers and their dangerous associates had it not been for the Catholics, who stood as a unit against them for law and order.

The Catholics, though mostly poor, maintain over two thousand parochial schools in the United States, with an attendance of upward of 200,000 pupils, and pay their school tax besides. This proves that they are friends of education, and also that they will secure religious instruction for their children at much trouble and expense. Their schools are patronized by many of the most intelligent Protestants in the country, especially schools for girls. The late Rev. Samuel J. May, an eminent educator, said that of all the schools he visited in Europe, those under the Catholic Brothers in the North of Ireland were the best.

An article written by Edmond About, in speaking of the Brothers' schools in France, contains the following: "A very legitimate ambition spurs them on to contend for all the prizes which the administration offers for competition, and the statistics do not err in registering their victories. As the Brothers have no families to support, their teaching must, necessarily, be less expensive than the lay teachers. In one place, the cost of each pupil is less than ten francs at the Brothers' school, and 100 at the lay schools."

Should the Catholics open parochial schools, they would have no difficulty in finding competent teachers for a small fraction of what the teachers in the public schools receive. The principle of self-sacrifice seems to be more active among Catholics than Protestants, especially in matters pertaining to their religion. Therefore, should a division of the school money be made, they would be able to compete, successfully, with the public or other schools, and save something for other purposes. The following quotation from a late number of *The Catholic World* will give their views of education: "All are agreed that education is necessary. It is of the highest interest to the state to see that its citizens should be sufficiently educated. In no country in the world is this necessity for education more deeply felt than in our own, for in no country do the people enjoy so large a share in the Government. Universal suffrage demands universal education, else it might be a curse rather than a blessing." In regard to some plan of giving religious instruction in the schools, it says: "If these persons come forward who offer to give such education and to guarantee that the instruction (secular) shall be quite as satisfactory as that given in the public schools at a less cost, we maintain that the state is bound, in the interest of its citizens, to accept their offer." The remarks of Father O'Brien before the school committee of Cambridge, of which he is a member, will be interesting in this connection:

"You will allow me just a word or two in regard to my position on the school question. Those who have known me, both Protestant and Catholic, know that I am not satisfied with our present system of education; that I believe a better system is awaiting our cool and dispassionate consideration, and that I am strongly of the opinion that such a consideration will eventually result in adopting what is known as the religious system of education, or, at least, its adoption by those who do believe in it will receive the sanction of law and excite no unfavorable criticism. In this system the most important of all studies, the knowledge of God and of man's duties to God, will receive the attention it deserves. Now I believe that the interests of Protestants and Catholics alike, as well as the interests of civil society, demand more attention in our schools to this at present neglected branch of study, and I also believe that passion and prejudice alone stands in the way of adopting this system to-day. There is no good reason, in my opinion, why the city of Cambridge may not to-day grant the reasonable demands of Catholics and many Protestants in this matter. It would then give some of its schools to Catholics, pay teachers of ascertained ability to teach these schools, see that the work of the schools be up to the proper standard, and exercise such reasonable control over them as the interests of the community may demand. This course would, I am sure, contribute to the material, intellectual and moral welfare of its citizens."

The more I have thought of these great problems, affecting as they do the welfare of the whole people, the more I am convinced that it will require the united wisdom of our wisest and best men to find a satisfactory solution, a solution that shall recognize all parental rights and obligations, and provide in some manner for the moral and religious education of all our children.

A.

The Rosary is a source of consolation and light; a vital element of strength in the practice of virtue, and a powerful weapon in our conflicts against the devil, the world and the flesh. The prayers of which it is composed constitute a heavenly manna, which, though always the same, is endued with a variety of flavors, and amply satisfies all the wants of the soul.

Catholic Notes.

——The Irish Relief Fund instituted by the Duchess of Marlborough now amounts to $95,000.

——The death is announced of the Countess Ida von Hahn Hahn, the famous Catholic poetess and novelist. R. I. P.

——On the 17th inst. the venerable Father Alexander, of the Congregation of the Most Holy Redeemer, celebrated the golden jubilee of his ordination, at New Orleans, La., where he has been stationed for many years.

——We are requested by Very Rev. Father Strub, C. SS. Sp., to state that the drawing of his lottery, of which mention was made in THE AVE MARIA some time ago, will positively take place on the day named, March 19th.

——The Abbé Bourgeat, licentiate of physical and natural sciences, has been named "Master of Conferences of Geology" at the Catholic University of Lille, and the alumni rejoice in the acquisition of so profoundly learned a priest.

——We are indebted to Rev. Father Burke and Mr. Henry Spain, of Springfield, Ill., also to Rev. Father Heidemann, O. M. C., of Terre Haute, and Mr. M. Duggan, of Dubuque, Iowa, for a number of new subscribers, and for kind favors to our travelling agents.

——A cable despatch from Rome to the New York *Freeman's Journal* for this week states that on the 15th instant His Holiness Pope Leo XIII approved the appointment of the Right Rev. Dr. Elder, heretofore Bishop of Natchez, to be Coadjutor, with right of succession, to the Archbishop of Cincinnati, and to be Administrator of the Archdiocese.

——A beautiful statue of the Sacred Heart was lately blessed by Very Rev. Father Rouxel, V. G. of New Orleans, for the new Church of the Sacred Heart on Canal St., of which Rev. Father Mariné, C. S. C., is the beloved pastor. An eloquent sermon was preached on the occasion by Rev. Father Free, S. J. A great concourse of people was present, and a number of clergymen.

——Our American brethren are going ahead, as is their custom. Though they have already one able and attractive illustrated Catholic paper, in *McGee's Weekly*, another has appeared under the title of *The Illustrated Catholic American*, and is to be devoted to general literature and engravings. They now only need a daily paper to be wholly independent of the secular press.—*Liverpool Catholic Times*.

——AN INTERESTING MEDIÆVAL RELIC.—According to St. *Luke*, a Ritualistic organ, a very interesting relic of the past, has just come to light in Patcham, Sussex, England,—viz., a large fresco, over the chancel arch, representing "The Souls in Purgatory being liberated by the intercession of the Blessed Virgin." The fresco, it is said, is an excellent drawing, well-colored, and somewhat elaborate, the central compartment alone containing eighteen figures. "It is to be hoped," says the St. *Luke*, gravely, "that *Protestant* zeal will not be busy with the whitewash pail in consequence; and that if any such disposition shows itself, it will be promptly extinguished by the action of the Society for the Preservation of Ancient Buildings." It is the unkindest cut of all to intimate to a Ritualist that he has anything of Protestantism about him.

——DESECRATION OF CHURCHES IN ITALY.—*Apropos* to the desecration of Catholic churches in Italy, and their deliverance to the sects, *The Catholic Times* aptly remarks: "Since the days of that cataclysm known as the Reformation, which overwhelmed the renaissant growth of civilization and set it back two or three centuries, Protestants have had a good easy way of getting fine churches, viz.: Seizing those built by Catholics and desecrating them into mere conventicles. It was this inherent thirst of Protestant sectaries for power and property in no way belonging to them, that often brought punishments, which their abettors call persecutions, upon them. Italy has no more right to give away those churches to sectaries than Satan had to dispose of the kingdoms of the earth, as he assumed to do in a certain famous instance, and as he actually does in numberless instances testified to by such perverting of power to his worship as we have noted."

——NOT PEACE-MAKERS.—Commenting on the disgraceful part taken by the Protestant ministers of Maine in the recent political troubles in that State, the New York *Sun* says bitterly: "Apparently the Maine preachers have gotten themselves a new gospel, or a new and different version of the old one, in which the text reads: 'Blessed are the war-makers.' With honorable exceptions, they have behaved very much as the priests of Mars or the Druids would have behaved in the like case. Instead of seeking to quench public passion, they have fed and fanned it. Their sermons and prayers have been fuel to the fire of civil discord. No thanks to them that it has not flamed up into disastrous conflagration. No thanks to them that Maine snows are not even now reddening with Maine blood. What body of Christians will be the first to send missionaries to convert the Maine preachers to Christianity?" As a contrast to this, we refer the reader to what is said about Catholics always being on the side of law and order, in the excellent article, "The School Question Fairly Stated by a Non-Catholic," published elsewhere.

——THE APPARITIONS IN IRELAND.—An affair of less local importance, unconnected with religion, than the apparitions which have now, on three occasions, been seen by numbers of persons of all sexes and of all ages, would long before this have occupied a very prominent place in the columns of the press. All that may be said in the following lines is an expression of the feelings and the judgment which the ecclesiastical Superiors may express upon the facts, of which they are already cognizant. The chapel of Knock, at which the apparitions have occurred, is about five miles from Claremorris, and its gilt cross which ornaments the lofty tower can be seen for miles around. The priest who so worthily presides over the parish is the venerable Archdeacon of the diocese, the Very Rev. Bartholomew Cavanagh. The chapel is of cruciform shape. The sacristy occupies the upper and lower shaft, and is immediately behind the high altar. In the gable of the sacristy there is a Gothic window about five feet high by two broad; its lowest part is about twelve feet from the ground. The remainder of the gable is plain, and was covered outside by a good substantial coating of cement, to protect the wall from the rains, which beat with great violence, especially from this side. On this gable wall of the sacristy were seen the extraordinary lights, in the midst of which the Blessed Virgin, accompanied by St. Joseph and St. John the Evangelist, appeared. On Wednesday last, on arriving at the place, there were a great number of people on their knees before the scene of the apparition, and around were already many *ex votos* in the shape of a crutch, walking sticks, and statues, sent by those who believe that they have been miraculously cured through the intercession of the Blessed Virgin by the application of some of the cement and dust taken from the wall, the greater part of which is disfigured by persons breaking off portions of the cement, some of which, following the example of the pious people, we also carried off with us. Tuesday evening, the 21st of August last, the eve of the octave day of the Assumption of the Blessed Virgin Mary, was accompanied by a blinding drizzle of rain, which continued till the next day. As some persons were hurriedly going along the road which leads by the chapel, at about 7.30, they perceived the wall beautifully illuminated by a white flickering light, through which could be perceived brilliant stars, twinkling as on a fine, frosty night. The first person who saw it passed on, but others soon came and remained, and these saw, covering a large portion of the gable end of the sacristy, an altar, and on its Gospel side the figures of St. John the Evangelist, the Blessed Virgin, and St. Joseph. On the altar, which stood about eight feet from the ground, and immediately under the window, a lamb stood, and rising up behind the lamb was a crucifix with the figure of our Lord upon it. The altar was surrounded by a brilliant white light, through which, up and down, angels seemed to be flitting. Near the altar, and immediate to its Gospel side, but nearer the ground, was St. John, having a mitre on his head, and holding the book of the Gospels open in his left hand, as if reading from it. He held his right hand raised, and in the act of blessing, the index and middle fingers being extended after the manner adopted by Bishops. To St. John's right stood the Blessed Virgin, having her hands extended and raised toward her shoulders, the palms of her hands turned toward the people, and her eyes raised up toward heaven. To the Blessed Virgin's right was St. Joseph, turned toward her, and in an inclined posture. The figures remained visible from 7½ to 10 o'clock, witnessed during that time by about 20 persons, who forgot all about the heavy rain that was then falling, and which drenched them thoroughly. The light at the chapel was seen by people living near by. The Blessed Virgin appeared a second time on New Year's Day between the hours of 1 and 2 o'clock, just immediately after Mass. On Monday evening last, the eve of the Epiphany, a bright light was again visible, and from 11 o'clock, p. m., until 2, a. m., was seen by a very large number, of whom two were members of the Royal Irish Constabulary, who were on patrol duty that evening. One of them said that up to that time he did not believe in it, but he was really startled by the brightness of the light which he saw. Many cures have been already worked through the intercession of the Blessed Virgin Mary and by the application of the cement taken from the chapel wall. We have heard from the mouths of most trustworthy witnesses an account of nearly a dozen cures of which the narrators themselves were eye-witnesses. In addition to what we have already written regarding the visions seen at the chapel of Knock, two remarkable miracles, witnessed by hundreds of persons, were performed yesterday, namely, sight restored to two girls, one of whom had, on the testimony of her mother, not seen anything from her birth. She had been several times with physicians in Dublin, but all to no purpose. Yesterday, in the presence of hundreds, she received the use of her sight, having visited three times the spot where the Blessed Virgin Mary is said to have appeared, and after praying three times in honor of the Mother of God.—*Tuam Times.*

New Publications.

SADLIER'S EXCELSIOR STUDIES IN THE HISTORY OF THE UNITED STATES FOR SCHOOLS. By the Author of "Sadlier's Elementary History." New York: William H. Sadlier.

As the author very properly remarks in the preface: "It is simply wonderful how the part enacted by Catholics on our soil, from the days of Columbus to the present time, has been persistently and coolly ignored by writers of text-books." This negligence the excellent little work before us does much to repair. It must not be imagined, however, that the book is denominational in its character. On the contrary, it puts the leading events of the history of our country into such a shape as to render them easily memorized by those for whom it is written. In narrating the history of the Civil War, it is admirably free from all expressions and terms that would tend to stir up sectional animosity. It is characterized throughout by a spirit of good feeling, evidently believing the best of all the actors in the scenes which it describes. Moreover, it narrates simply, without philosophizing. The topics upon which it dwells particularly are those connected with military and naval engagements, which, after all, although they may constitute little of the true history of a nation, are the events that make the most striking impression and take the firmest hold upon the memory, where they set up a series of guide-posts, so to speak, from which the other events of history take their bearings. The little book is embellished with cuts and maps of a superior style of finish, and its whole apparel is attractive. The history comes down to the year 1879 inclusive, and the text is enriched with copious foot-notes, and supplemented by questions for review. The Declaration of Independence, the Constitution of the United States, and Useful Tables of the Presidents and States conclude the whole. We heartily recommend it to parents and teachers.

THE ART AMATEUR. For October, November, and December. Montague Marks, Publisher, No. 571 Broadway, New York.

The Art Amateur deserves a friendly notice at our hands. In the first place, it "sticks to its text,"—is exactly what it purports to be—an assistant to the amateur in bringing the principles of art, all the charms of decoration by great original masters, into the daily and hourly service of us human beings of to-day; into the arrangements of the house, into the furniture,—everything into which enters taste as well as comfort. The articles which have especially pleased us in these three numbers, are those on "house and home" adornment. In the October number, "An Artist's Suburban House"; the first sentence only of "Mantel-piece Decoration" (for we confess to no love of velvet mantelcovers when there is so much beautiful wood to be used; but the open fireplace *versus* "the hideous old black stove," and the still newer inventions of furnaces and steam-pipes for sitting-rooms, compels us to rescue the first sentence from oblivion) and "Country-Table Decorations" are all of a sort to encourage genuine taste, inexpensive taste, and artistic taste. In the November number, "A Homelike House," in which we see specimens of a gentleman's handiwork, and of laces and embroideries from the hand of his wife,—and in the December number, "Drawing-Room Fashions" and "Novel Dinner-Table Decorations," have the same drift—the drift towards variety of ideas instead of expensive upholstery and heavy carpets taken up only once, or at most twice, a year; lolling-chairs, and whatever else belongs to indolence in comfort and a lavishly barbarous taste; and there is even a delicate compliment to Parisian patterns in "rag rugs," which will console some woman of taste with a rag-bag better filled than her purse.

The needle-work and embroidery articles are still of the right sort. But while looking over the choice designs for needle-work which come with every number, we were sensible of one lack which may not have occurred to the accomplished editors; and this is, designs for ecclesiastical vestments. This lack once brought to mind, was confirmed by receiving a letter from a lady in New York, asking us to make a design for a Lent chasuble. She had read our articles, written and printed in THE AVE MARIA several years ago, upon "Catholic Industries for Catholic Women," in which we suggested certain designs for vestments according to the seasons and principal feasts, and wished us to furnish these designs. We thought immediately of our friend *The Art Amateur*, and wondered if the editors would not be more than pleased to meet this want of a class of Catholic ladies here in America, who, having leisure, wish to use it for the sanctuary? With this hint to the *Amateur*, we hastily wish it success throughout the year. E. A. S.

ANNOUNCEMENTS.

——Besides Father Moriarty's book, "STUMBLING-BLOCKS MADE STEPPING-STONES ON THE ROAD TO THE CATHOLIC FAITH," announced as in press last month, the Catholic Publication Society Co. have in press and will publish early in Lent:

——"THE CHURCH OF THE PARABLES, AND TRUE SPOUSE OF THE SUFFERING SAVIOUR." By Rev. Joseph Prachensky, S. J.

——"THE LAST JOURNEY AND MEMORIALS OF THE REDEEMER; or, Via Crucis as it is in Jerusalem. With Topographical, Archæological, Historical, Traditional, and Scriptural Notes." By Rev. J. J. Begel, Pilgrim to the Holy Places. With numerous engravings.

——"THE ELOCUTIONIST. A Practical Method of Teaching and Studying Elocution. Adapted for Schools and Colleges by Brother Frank."

——The fifth edition of Father O'Brien's book on "THE HOLY MASS," has just appeared.

——After the most unceasing labors, the venerable Abbé Leverrière, founder of the *Missions Catholiques*, has withdrawn from the direction of the *Missions* and from the management of the *Annales de la Propagation de la Foi*, his declining health admonishing him to seek rest from his labors. For the last fifteen years has this venerated priest devoted his intelligence, his energies and his heart to the Society of the Propagation of the Faith. Week after week he showed modern savants that the apostles of Catholicity, while gaining souls for Jesus Christ, were enriching science with their discoveries. But now his strength is unequal to his courage. May his sweetest reward in the silence of his retreat, with the regrets and kind wishes of all, be the words which Pius IX, of holy memory, gave him as a device for his journal: "In lending efficient aid to the labors of our missionaries, you earn for yourself a large share of their merit." —*N. Y. Freeman's Journal.*

Confraternity of the Immaculate Conception (Or of Our Lady of Lourdes).

"We fly to thy patronage, O Holy Mother of God!" REPORT FOR THE WEEK ENDING JANUARY 20TH.

Recovery of health for 104 persons and 6 families,—change of life for 51 persons and 5 families,—conversion to the Faith for 59 persons and 6 families,—special graces for 6 priests, 10 religious, 5 clerical students, and 7 persons aspiring to the religious state,—temporal favors for 93 persons and 20 families,—spiritual favors for 128 persons and 19 families,—the spiritual and temporal welfare of 9 communities, 4 congregations, 8 schools, 1 sodality, 3 orphanages, and 4 hospitals,—also 50 particular intentions, and 8 thanksgivings for favors received.

Specified intentions: Conversion of a young man unwilling to go to confession,—means to establish 3 religious houses in California,—the support of two children,—prevention of an unjust lawsuit, and a favorable decision of others previously recommended,—success in business for several persons,—the safe return of a family,—some priests and religious in ill-health,—the speedy appointment of a zealous priest for a certain mission,—the rental of several pieces of property,—conversion to the Faith, and change of life for a number of persons at the point of death,—success of a lawsuit in favor of a religious community,—a young orphan girl possessed of some wealth in danger of being deceived by an unscrupulous suitor,—the conversion of all infidels, also of the Indians in the diocese of Quebec,—recovery of health and use of limbs for one person.

FAVORS OBTAINED.

We gladly comply with a request to make known the following favors: "In October 1878," says our correspondent, "I wrote a letter to convey to your Reverence the statement that I had been cured of a very annoying sore by the use of the holy water of Lourdes. But on reflection I laid aside my letter, to wait a few more seasons, in order to see whether the cure would be permanent. For over ten years I had been troubled with severe chilblains on both my feet, and the many remedies resorted to during that period had been of no avail. On several occasions the affected parts became open sores, and the itching was frequently almost beyond endurance. During one of these periods I resolved to ask relief from Our Immaculate Lady of Lourdes. Having received some of the water from Notre Dame, I accordingly said a few prayers, promising at the same time to join the Rosary Society. I then applied the holy water to the part affected. This was in the fall of 1877; since that time, thanks to God and His Blessed Mother, I have not been troubled with either chilblains or sore feet, and now I deem it my duty to publish this great favor, to the truth of which I am ready to give the most emphatic testimony." . . . .

Another person writes: "At the time I received the water of Lourdes, I was suffering terribly with pains in my head, so much so that I feared my reason might be impaired; but thanks to the almighty God and His Blessed Mother, after using the blessed water the pain ceased. A lady had an abscess on her face, and tried every remedy without any apparent relief. I told her about the water of Lourdes and gave her what I had left. She said some prayers, and used the water at night. The next morning all the swelling had disappeared, and in three days she was as well as ever. The same person thanks God for having been deterred from marrying a young man addicted to drink."

OBITUARY.

Of your charity pray for the following deceased persons: CAPT. JOHN POWER, of Terre Haute, Ind., who died last April. Miss MARGARET MORAN, who was taken away in the bloom of youth on the 17th of December. Mr. PATRICK WALSH, who, after a long illness, slept peacefully in the Lord on Christmas-eve. Miss ELIZABETH PHELAN, whose death occurred last April, at Lawrence, Mass. Mr. WILLIAM HOLLYWOOD, of Benicia, Cal., deceased on the 5th inst. Mrs. EULALIA T. BARRON, of Washington, D. C., who departed this life last December. MISS AMELIA DORMER, of Galena, Ill., who had a happy death on Christmas day. Miss MARY ANNE MOYKES, of Loretto, Pa., who rested in peace on the 31st ult. Mrs. ELLEN MCGEE, of Baltimore, Md., who breathed her last on the 3d inst. Mrs. EMMA HOEG, a zealous convert, whose death took place on the Feast of the Immaculate Conception. Mrs. ANNE JANE STRICKLAND, who died on the 1st of January, at Malden, Mass. Mr. FITZPATRICK, who closed his life at South Boston, Mass., on the 5th inst. Mrs. THOMAS DAVEY, of Stillwater, Minn. MOTHER LUCY IGNATIA and MOTHER HELEN, of the Community of the Holy Child Jesus. Mr. GEORGE HUGHES. MR. JAMES BOYLE, of Lytle City, Iowa. EDWARD N. CANNON, WINEFRED CANNON, MRS. SUSAN BOYLAN, Mr. JAMES and Mrs. MARY MULLEN, Mrs. ROSE HANAHAN, JOHN, CATHARINA, and JOHN T. HANAHAN, who died some time ago. And others, whose names have not been given.

Requiescant in pace.

A. GRANGER, C. S. C., Director.

Papal Collection—Diocese of Fort Wayne, 1879.

Ft. Wayne Cathedral..	$134.00
" St. Mary's...	85.00
" Paul's...	38.90
" Peter's..	14.00
Huntington	61.85
Lafayette, St. Mary's...	74.25
" Bonifface...	34.00
Peru..............	47.50
St. John's, Lake Co...	45.25
Michigan City	34.00
Avilla and Mission....	20.00
" for 1878..........	24.00
New Haven	32.50
Decatur	24.00
Kentland...........	30.65
H se Cassel	25.00
Logansport, Saint Joseph's	21.00
Otys..............	20.00
Crawfordsville......	17.00
Shererville	16.00
Kluasville	19.00
Dyer	18.25
Notre Dame........	17.00
Trinity, Benton Co...	17.00
Bluffton Roads......	14.50
Lagro..............	12.65
St. Michael's, Allen Co	3.57
Areola.............	$14.50
South Bend, Lowell...	12.00
Columbia City.......	11.85
Fowler, St. Bridget's..	10.00
Girardot...........	10.50
Wabash	12.00
St. Anthony's, Benton Co	13.50
Auburn and Missions.	10.00
Moureoville	9.00
Turkey Creek.......	9.75
Cedar Lake	15.00
Covington	0.20
Mary's Home	8.40
Piereceton..........	7.17
Lebanon............	8.36
Colfax	8.00
Attica	7.80
Laporte, St. Joseph's.	7.00
Monterey	7.07
Leo	5.69
Winnamac	5.50
Clark's Hill........	4.80
Crown Point.......	5.00
Marshfield.........	3.15
Albion	4.00
Chesterton.........	3.51
Lowell, Lake Co	2.00

Sent to Rome, December 3, 5,586 francs. Since received, and on hand, $25.15.

✠ JOSEPH DWENGER,
BP. FT. WAYNE.

For Rebuilding Notre Dame University.

Mrs. M. E. McQuaid, $5; W. Kennedy, $1; Annie McCauley, 1.50; Bridget McCormick, 50 cts. Mrs. M. C. Ross, $2; Patrick Geirty, $1; James Shannessey, $1; John Pfeiffer, 50 cts.; A Friend, $2.50; Cathrine Young, $1; Eliza Young, $1; Richard Bracken, $1; Catharine Bracken, $1; Bridget Shortle, $1; William Shortle, $1; Elizabeth Manly, $1; Mary McGlynn, $1; Margaret Murray, $1; Laurence Murray, $1.

Youths' Department.

Mildred's Prize.

BY THE AUTHOR OF "TYBORNE," "FEAST OF FLOWERS," ETC., ETC.

(CONCLUSION.)

CHAPTER IV.

THE morning of the examination day had come, and some degree of bustle necessarily prevailed. The large school-room had to be decorated. Pieces of music were practised again for the last time, and everyone was very busy. Rosa sat alone in one of the small class-rooms, with her drawing before her. A girl named Laura Simmonds, who had lately come to the school and was not much esteemed by the teachers or pupils, came in. "Oh, Rosa!" she said, "I've been looking for you. I can tell you something you'll like to hear. I heard Rev. Mother and Sister Veronica talking in the corridor about the drawings—they did not see me."

Conscience told Rosa not to receive information thus unfairly and meanly obtained, but she would not listen to the angelic voice, and exclaimed: "Well, Laura, what did they say?"

"That the whole thing was between you and Mildred; none of the others can come near you. Rev. Mother said: 'Rosa has real talent: she is an artist; but Mildred's hard work and diligent study tell very much.'

"'Yes, it does,' answered Sister Veronica; 'but Rosa will gain the prize if she has done what she declared she would—give her drawing the finishing touches. She may spoil all by some neglect or blunder; but I shall not say anything to her, as it would be against the rule laid down.'"

"Thank you, Laura," said Rosa, in a tone of exultation.

"Rosa, will you lend me a pair of gloves? mine are so shabby, and you have lots."

"I have only one new pair," said Rosa, feeling vexed,—"but, yes; I'll make my second best do. You can have the new pair," and as Laura, with a delighted, face departed, Rosa felt the keen pang of one who has accepted and given a bribe. But Rosa had no time to reflect. She eagerly scanned her drawing; "Yes—Sister is right," she said to herself; "that clump of olives is not gray enough; I'll tone it down. And in a frantic manner she seized her palette and dipped her brush unfortunately in the blue, and the clump of olives became the same color as the Mediterranean. She stamped her foot with anger at her own folly, and snatching up a clean brush, dipped it in water and effaced the offending clump altogether. "Now," she said, "I must wait till the paper dries, and then I will make it all right"; and with an eager desire to get rid of half an hour she began to walk round the room and then bethought herself she might as well see how the decorations were going on.

Out she dashed to the school-room. Busy hands were putting up garlands and arranging seats. Rosa's eye fell on a small table pushed right behind the platform and quite out of the sight of the nuns and children decorating the room. On that table lay five portfolios, the topmost being Mildred's. Instantly Rosa remembered Rev. Mother's order that the portfolios were to be in their place by twelve, when all things should be in readiness. A quarter to twelve, said the clock.

Back flew Rosa to the class-room. "Oh, I am sure it is dry enough now!" she said, and sitting down before her drawing-board, she took up her brush, but the hanging sleeve of her dress caught the cup of water which stood beside her; it was upset and its whole contents discharged upon her drawing. Alas! olives, oranges and blue sea were all blurred over, the picture was spoilt.

As Rosa looked on the easel, a feeling of actual fury took possession of her. Here was the only chance of distinction in her school life snatched from her when it was actually within her grasp. She thought of her mother's tearful delight, of her father's look of pride, and all was lost—and gained by whom? Mildred! Mildred who had been always in her way,—who had carried off prizes for music, for German, for needlework,—who would have many other prizes this very day,—and now she would have also the drawing prize, the *only* one that Rosa coveted. "No," said the tempter, "let it not be so—it is not too late; let *neither* gain the prize; let her not triumph over you—it is unjust and cruel that she should; it is *too* hard—it must not be."

Is that really Rosa who flies along the corridor and gains the school-room? Yes: the table is still in its corner, far away from the merry group now ornamenting the Bishop's chair of state. The work of a minute, and Rosa has Mildred's portfolio in her hand. She opens it—she looks. Yes: it is beautiful! the pure masses of white marble and the soft pink glow over the landscape. Is it her evil angel who jogs her elbow and lets her see an ink bottle which has been used for writing some tickets and has been put away quite safely under the platform. Another moment and the marble mountains are a mass of inky darkness and the wet sketch is shut up in its portfolio.

Rosa turns hurriedly away, and meets Mildred face to face.

Mildred looks keenly at Rosa's flushed features and says in an icy tone: "It is forbidden to look at each other's drawing."

"I know that as well as you," said Rosa sharply; "mind your own business, Miss Milly!" and she rushed away.

Mildred went up to the table and counted the portfolios. Rosa's was not there. A vague suspicion crossed her mind. Surely she had not left her portfolio-strings untied. She opened it and she gazed. . . .

After a few minutes, when the clock struck twelve, and Sister Francesca came to put the table and portfolios in their places; "Of course," she said, "that unpunctual little Rosa has not brought hers." So she went to bring it, and found it all ready in the class-room, tied up neatly; but Rosa was not there. Two hours later the pupils were marshalled into their places and the company began to arrive.

A telegram had come with the news that Mrs. Luuy was indisposed, and neither she nor Mrs. Birkett could be present. It was this, the children thought, that made Mildred look so pale, and Rosa so odd. A strange storm was raging in both of these young hearts. Rosa's soul was drowned in a sea of dark misery—not sorry for her fault, yet consumed by gnawing pain. No act of contrition had passed her lips, and her angel's face was still hidden in his wing. Mildred had resolved to denounce Rosa when the time should come. The memory of sharp words, of rude slights, of stinging reproaches rose up before her, and she felt the cup was full. It was mere justice; her aunt was not coming: it was as well. Rosa should be exposed. Those who did such mean things *ought* to be punished.

The Bishop entered and took his place, and the Sisters were all seated near him. Sir Edward and Lady Claridge had not arrived, but that did not matter, for the drawing prize was to be the last.

"Are you ill, Rosa?" said Sister Veronica anxiously, as she saw the frequent changes of color and the look of pain that every now and then overspread the child's face.

"Of course not, Sister, I'm quite well; how silly you are?" said Rosa, in a hard, defiant, almost insolent tone, while her face darkened.

Sister Veronica felt what the French call a tightening of the heart. She loved all her children,—and, perhaps, wild, impetuous, but openhearted Rosa had a special warm corner in her large heart. She felt sure something was wrong. However, she moved away, and, according to her life-long habit, her soul when in pain cast its grief into the Heart of perfect love, of boundless pity, and she prayed for Rosa. Swift came the answer, and Rosa's angel came nearer to her.

Rosa sat as if in a dream. The music sounded like a confused jingle; and as to the French, German and English, it was all to her as the tongues of Babel. She saw the prizes given, the happy faces, the shining medals, the pretty books and pictures. Deep and dark indeed was her misery. There was a little pause; all the prizes had been given. Rev. Mother told the Bishop that Sir Edward had not arrived, but would be there in a few minutes. So the Bishop began to speak, and then Rosa's senses were unlocked and she listened. His lordship spoke of the pleasure it gave him to see the progress the pupils had made in their studies, and he exhorted them to further industry in the future; and it gave him comfort, he said, to know that while their secular education was attended to, the *one thing necessary was not forgotten.* "I hear with joy from Rev. Mother," he said, "that the tone of the school is high, and has grown higher lately; that you do not need a strict surveillance to keep you in the right path, but that the older set an example to the younger. I hear," the Bishop continued, "that there is among you a great regard for truth, a real horror of meanness and deceit, and that there is a kindly feeling one towards the other; for, my children, remember those words of St. Teresa—which one of you has so prettily illuminated:

"'All passes away;
God only shall stay.'

"We must learn these secular studies—and we should learn them well, for has not God said, 'Whatsoever thy hand is able to do, do it earnestly'? but we must ever remember that they are only means to an end, and our end is to glorify God, and that meekness and truth, charity and obedience are ten million times more precious in His eyes than the sweetest music or the finest painting. And, my children, our examinations and our prizes should remind us of the one great examination which we all must go through one day, for all one's life is but a school-time; we are all going home to our Father's house, and we hope to gain a prize from Him—a prize that will never grow old nor decay nor pass away, for the prize will be God Himself, and

"'All passes away;
God only shall stay.'"

The Bishop sat down, and Rosa grasped the rail of the bench on which she sat, for it seemed to her that the earth had opened under her feet. Sir Edward Claridge had entered now, and with him two men-servants carrying the prize, which was placed on an easel near the Bishop. It was a beautiful oil-painting of the Sacred Heart, a copy of the celebrated one in the Gesù at Rome. Rosa looked at it, and shuddered from head to foot. The eyes of the picture seemed fixed on her with a sad, reproachful gaze. Mildred looked at it, and the tears came into her eyes. Was she worthy to possess it—she who was so far from copying the "meek and humble Heart"?

A few minutes passed while the picture was being admired, and then Sir Edward proceeded to the portfolios. Margaret Ryan's drawing came first and was pronounced very creditable; so also were those of Fanny Dean, Agnes Doyle, and Henrietta Jackson. Then came Rosa's. "Oh, dear, what a pity!" exclaimed the examiner; "an accident has befallen this; it *has been* very good. I can see real talent in this."

Sister Veronica's eyes travelled towards Rosa. Was this the explanation of her odd manner and looks? and why had she not been told? But she found nothing. Rosa's face was hard set as a rock.

Mildred's portfolio-strings are undone. Oh, what is this? it sticks—it cracks—*what is this?* a mass of ink-stained paper, half stuck to the portfolio and half falling in shreds. Dismay and astonishment kept everyone silent, but one instantly divined the secret. Two people looked at Rosa and saw in the pale, sullen face, the confirmation of the truth. Those two were Sister Veronica and Mildred. Mildred turned red and pale by turns; a burning indignation filled her soul. She *would* stand and denounce her enemy; but she would not have her prize snatched from her. She looked up—the words trembling on her lips; they were arrested. She saw two things—the picture of the Sacred Heart, and Sister Veronica who was gazing at it. She saw those sweet, sad eyes that seemed to say, "*Do good to them that hate you*"; "*Forgive, and you shall be forgiven*"; and she saw Sister Veronica's face, the eager look of supplication for the child that had erred, and Mildred realized for the first time the wonderful power of a love for souls. Willingly would the nun have borne disgrace and shame rather than her child should thus have sinned.

"Mildred Luny, come forward," said Rev. Mother; "how did this happen?"

"I don't know, Mother; I did not spill any ink over it."

The discussion went on. Sister Francesca came forward. The portfolios had been in a safe place; no one had touched them, and she had fetched Rosa's herself. The mystery remained a mystery, and Sir Edward and the Bishop agreed the picture had better remain in the charge of the nuns and be competed for again.

Meanwhile Rosa had looked on in astonishment. She had perfectly understood Mildred's glance of indignation; she had expected to hear herself denounced every minute; and now all was over. The Bishop was standing up to go. Mildred had not spoken. No suspicion rested on her. She was free, and Mildred had lost her prize, and the white wings of Rosa's angel were folded about her and his voice was whispering in her ear. The strong and mighty angels bring us strength and help, else why does Rosa go forward and mount the platform and kneel before the Bishop? Why, in that hushed silence, while the pupils held their very breath, did Rosa speak so calmly: "My lord, it was I. Let Mildred have her prize—for it was I who spoilt her picture."

"You, Rosa,—you!" said the Bishop.

"Yes, my lord!" and Rosa told her tale, and strange to say that as she was kneeling there disgraced before them all and owning her fault, she felt a peace come into her soul which, after the storm of rage, hatred, revenge, and despair she had passed through, was sweet; for true shame has its sweetness, and when we wrap its folds around us we rest upon Him who *made Himself our shame.*

The Bishop spoke a few kind words—not lessening the fault, but bidding Rosa take courage, for she had made a reparation that must be pleasing to God.

Sister Veronica had found a corner to hide in and to let the tears she could no longer keep back have their flow. When she saw the child's action, when she saw that after the long storm and the defeat there had come victory, she could not but think of another assembly, and of one who had knelt at other Feet and had been forgiven, and had gained grace to become worthy to stand beneath the Cross.

The scene was over, the visitors departed, and the children were set free to talk over the extraordinary events of the day. Rosa was in Sister Veronica's room; she saw no one that evening but Mildred. The two cousins met, and in one long embrace the rivalry of their childhood has ended.

. . . .

It is many years ago since the events I have related took place, and Sister Veronica, who told me of them, has gone to her eternal rest.

"Both my children," said she, "gained that day a great grace. Mildred's act of forgiveness was rewarded by the gift of mercy and forbearance, which up to that time was lacking in her character." She is Lady Claridge now; she married Sir Edward's son. She is a good and happy wife and mother, and I hear she is the patient friend of the erring and the sinful. And Rosa, my Rosa! very soon indeed after her school-days she became a Sister of Charity of St. Vincent de Paul; and after she had made her vows she was sent to some charge in a large convict prison in France. Soon after she went, a virulent fever broke out. The governor of the prison was a military officer. He said to Sister Madelene (that was Rosa's name): "You are too young for this, Sister; better go back to your convent."

She answered with a smile: "Why, Colonel, do soldiers run away in time of war? this is a Sister of Charity's battle-field." *

They say she did wonders during that fever.

---

* These words were really spoken in similar circumstances.

Hardened sinners could not resist her voice; she gathered in a great harvest of souls, and then she lay down to die. "Well, I always think," said Sister Veronica, "it was that act of great humility that won for her the crown of a martyr of charity."

The Accusing Birds.

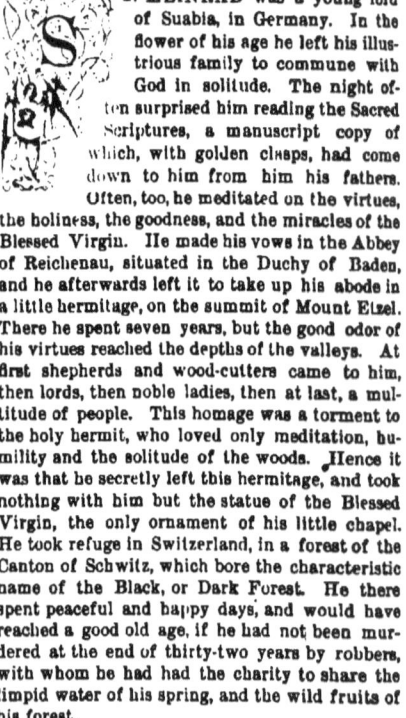

ST. MEINRAD was a young lord of Suabia, in Germany. In the flower of his age he left his illustrious family to commune with God in solitude. The night often surprised him reading the Sacred Scriptures, a manuscript copy of which, with golden clasps, had come down to him from his fathers. Often, too, he meditated on the virtues, the holiness, the goodness, and the miracles of the Blessed Virgin. He made his vows in the Abbey of Reichenau, situated in the Duchy of Baden, and he afterwards left it to take up his abode in a little hermitage, on the summit of Mount Etzel. There he spent seven years, but the good odor of his virtues reached the depths of the valleys. At first shepherds and wood-cutters came to him, then lords, then noble ladies, then at last, a multitude of people. This homage was a torment to the holy hermit, who loved only meditation, humility and the solitude of the woods. Hence it was that he secretly left this hermitage, and took nothing with him but the statue of the Blessed Virgin, the only ornament of his little chapel. He took refuge in Switzerland, in a forest of the Canton of Schwitz, which bore the characteristic name of the Black, or Dark Forest. He there spent peaceful and happy days, and would have reached a good old age, if he had not been murdered at the end of thirty-two years by robbers, with whom he had had the charity to share the limpid water of his spring, and the wild fruits of his forest.

But God did not permit this atrocious crime to remain long unknown and unpunished. The murderers had been seen by no one, but they were betrayed by two crows, who harrassed them continually, even in Zurich. They followed the robbers everywhere with incredible fury; they penetrated into the city, and made their way through the windows of the inn where the murderers had taken refuge, and never left them until they were arrested. The ruffians confessed their crime, and suffered the extreme penalty of the law. In memory of this singular event, which took place in the year 861, the Abbey of Reichenau, of whose community St. Meinrad had been a member, placed the figure of two crows on its arms and on its seal.

THE AVE MARIA.

A Journal devoted to the Honor of the Blessed Virgin.

HENCEFORTH ALL GENERATIONS SHALL CALL ME BLESSED.—St. Luke, i, 48.

VOL. XVI.   NOTRE DAME, INDIANA, FEBRUARY 7, 1880.   No. 6.

[Copyright: Rev. D. E. Hudson, C. S. C.]

The Seed of Life.

A SONNET FOR ASH-WEDNESDAY.

BOW down, O flesh of mine! for dust thou art,
 And into dust must soon return again:
Then, till these blessed Forty Days depart,
Stretched, victim-like, beneath the soul's disdain,
Right cheerfully thy peevish whims restrain,
Endure the fast, the penitential smart.
O comrade frail! I bid thee not complain,
But keep a hidden gladness in thy heart.
And why? Because this heart, at Paschal-tide,
Shall be of Life Itself the living nest;—
Within this breast, by penance purified,
The Pledge of Immortality will rest.
A fleeting doom those ashes typified—
"Who eats, shall live"; so runs the Promise blest.
           ETHEL TANE.

A Lover of the Beautiful.

BY KATHLEEN O'MEARA, AUTHOR OF "IZA'S STORY," "ROBIN REDBREAST," "LIFE OF FREDERICK OZANAM," "PEARL," ETC., ETC.

(CONCLUSION.)

THE end of the novena brought new peace, but not the gift which had been asked for. The dying man spent long hours in his room alone, communing with God. He was too weak to bear for any length of time the society of those dearest and most congenial to him; but at his lowest ebb he could rise up to meet a soul that needed him. One day, a pupil from the military school of St. Cyr came to Epinay and knocked at his door. It was opened at once; the intruder was one of those young men who had gathered round the Abbé Perreyve at St. Barbe, and had come to make his confession. This was the last sacramental function his old professor performed. A few days later, he was taken back to Paris. No notable change occurred until the middle of June, when a long fainting fit, of which he himself knew nothing, caused great alarm to those about him. The Abbé Bernard, his life-long friend and brother-almoner at the Lycée St. Louis, was sent to warn M. and Mme. Perreyve that the danger had now become imminent. Mme. Perreyve, who was detained at her husband's sick-bed, charged the Abbé Bernard with the solemn mission of announcing the truth to her beloved son. He tells us himself how the mission was fulfilled: "However strong a soul may be, it is a hard and painful task to bring it suddenly face to face with death; but I was resolved to do my duty as a priest and a friend, and I went straight to the Abbé Perreyve's room. It was at a moment when he was suffering from great exhaustion; and he said, on seeing me: 'Only a few minutes to-day, my dear friend.' A few minutes! It was very little to tell him so grave a truth. I called up my courage, nevertheless, and began by stating very distinctly that the disease had made alarming progress within the last two weeks. But to every word I said, he had a reassuring answer, which betrayed a confidence that I could not share. I prayed God interiorly to come to my help; He sent me this help through the sick man himself, who, becoming suddenly affected, said to me, without anything in his previous remarks having led to it: 'Ah! one of the things I feel most in going away, is having to leave you alone in life.' I wept with him, but I had strength to add: 'My dear friend, since you speak to me so openly, I must tell you that we have now cause for most serious anxiety about you.' He looked at me simply, and said: 'You think so?'

"'Yes, this is our impression; you had a very alarming fainting fit this morning.'

"'Ah! I own you surprise me; I thought I was very ill, but not so near death. It is well; so much the better; then you must give me Extreme Unction.'

"'That is what I was thinking of. Whom do you wish me to ask to do you this service?'

"'You, of course,—only you must let Charles know; I want him to be present at this great act of my life.'

"'He is outside, waiting for the issue of our conversation.'

"'Ah!'—with another look of surprise—'then let it be done at once.'"

Père Charles Perrand came in, and the Abbé Perreyve clasped him in a long embrace. M. Bernard hurried off to fetch the holy oils from St. Sulpice—St. Sulpice, where as children the friends had prayed side by side, where they had made their First Communion, where they had been ordained, and whence one of the three now went for the last succors for the brother who was being taken from them. Just as he returned, P. Gratry arrived. The dying man, weak as he was, had risen, and dressed himself carefully, wearing only his soutane, as if he were going to say Mass and clothe himself in the sacerdotal vestments. He then passed into an adjoining room, where an altar had been prepared.

"This was the last time I saw him standing up," says P. Gratry. "He had known for about an hour that he was condemned to death. I see him still, energetic and gracious as ever, smiling as usual. 'I am full of peace, Father; full of peace,' he said to me. While I live I will keep that picture in my heart: that soutane worn with such an air of proud joy, that noble bearing, that blanched face, those dilated dark eyes with their large, tender glance, and those last words, 'full of peace!'"

The last beautiful rite was performed, the anointed Christian joining in the magnificent responses with seraphic fervor, like one standing at the gates of pearl, not in fear, but in humble exultation. Before receiving the Holy Viaticum, the Abbé Bernard asked him to make his profession of faith, as it is customary for a dying priest to do, and he recited the *Credo* in a clear voice, without faltering, and with deep emotion. Then, making a sign that he wished to speak, he said: "I ask pardon of my parents—whose absence I bitterly regret at this moment—for any pain I have ever caused them. I ask pardon of my friends for the faults they have seen me commit; I thank them for their constant affection, and I beg of them to continue to pray for me long after my death. Let them not say, as too many do, and too quickly, 'He is in heaven'; let them pray much and long for me, I implore of them! And you, my servant Theodore, I beg your pardon for all the scandal I have given you; you have seen me closely; it is a bad way for men to be seen; I commend myself to your prayers."

The *Te Deum* was then recited, and the Viaticum administered. When the Abbé Perreyve had received the Body of the Lord, his face shone with a celestial brightness. He remained wrapt in God during his thanksgiving, and when it was terminated, he said to the Abbé Bernard: "*You can't conceive what a state of interior joy I am in since you told me I was going to die!*"

The Archbishop of Paris came the next day to see him. The moment his grace entered the room, and before he could prevent it, the dying man raised himself from the bed on which he lay dressed in his soutane, and flung himself on his knees to receive the blessing. Friends came in numbers to bid him farewell, to ask his prayers and a last word of counsel. He was touched and full of grateful surprise at these proofs of tender affection; but though he responded to them with grateful love, it was manifest that his soul was already dwelling above all earthly ties, and yearning to be left to undisturbed communion with God. His old friend and brother, P. Adolphe Perrand, came to see him, exclaiming with tears: "I come to bid you farewell, Henry!"

"Ah!" replied Henry, "we shall not cease to work *together* for the cause of God and His Church—shall we? I ought to be greatly troubled because of my sins, and nevertheless I am full of peace. Before we part, give my your blessing."

"With all my heart," replied Père Perrand, "but on condition that you give me yours."

They blessed one another, each kissing the consecrated hands of the other, and then parted; never to meet again in this world.

The Abbé Perreyve had said when he first felt that death was advancing towards him, though he knew not how fast: "As I have always done everything quickly in my life, so I hope through the kindness of God to be able to die quickly." God was kind to him in this as in everything else. To the last he retained the *élan* which had given to his soul, to his whole life, the impetus of a bird on the wing. It was a grand holocaust, the sacrifice of his young life that he was about to make with this same generous *élan*. He had meant to do such great things with it! "To do something for God and souls" had been a thirst with him, as with other men to achieve fortune and position, and all things had conspired to promise him the fulfilment of his noble ambition. "Our country is lost unless it returns to the faith. . . . and you, my child, are called to work at this regeneration," wrote Lacordaire; and Henry Perreyve answered to the call with the prompt enthusiasm of a crusader. None of us can, probably, form an idea of what it must have been to such a soul, sent forth on such a mission, magnificently endowed for it, to be suddenly arrested, and ordered away from the plough just as the smoke began to ascend from the fresh-made furrows. He did not see—this was what made the sacrifice—that he had already sown the seed, and that a harvest would be gathered by those who came after him.

Three days after he had received the last Sacraments he lapsed into a silence so deep and solemn that those friends, who, like guardian angels, hovered round his death-bed, knew not how to interpret it. Had that perfect peace, which the Viaticum had brought with It, passed away to be followed by the taste of the bitterness of death? Was the soldier, struck down in his youthful ardor, casting a look of rebellious regret on the battle-field that he was leaving behind him? The Abbé Bernard had seen many a brave and beautiful soul pass through the valley of the shadow, and he feared that his friend was suffering from one of those temptations against which the bravest are not always proof. He questioned him. "No," replied the dying man, "God in His mercy still keeps me in the same state of resignation to His will; but I own to you it was a disappointment and a pang to me not to have died when you told me I was going to die. Now and then the fear comes to me that my patience may fail if this state of waiting lasts much longer. Oh! how I bless God now for having given me a simple faith that goes straight to Jesus Christ, and is summed up in that one word of His agony, *Fiat!* ... When my heart is heavy, I repass in spirit the grand platonic ideas of Eternal Beauty, and thus philosophy, too, helps me in its turn, and brings me back to piety."

It was only fair that the Eternal Beauty, whose worship had been the key-note of his life, should shed its divine rays upon the parting struggle of the soul that was about to enter Its presence. On the Feast of Corpus Christi, to which he had a special devotion, he was lying on his bed, dressed, when the Abbé Bernard came in, and, at his request, read to him the 8th chapter of the Epistle to the Romans, that he had always loved, and used to meditate upon at the foot of the Cross in the Coliseum. When they came to the 30th verse, "*And whom He predestinated, them He also called. And whom He called, them He also justified; and whom He justified, them He also glorified,*" the Abbé Bernard looked up to see what impression these words.— which moved him deeply—had made upon his friend; their eyes met, both were full of tears. The reader went on. Each sentence flooded their souls with a new and fuller emotion. Like the disciples on the road to Emmaus, Jesus was with them, and made their hearts burn within them at the inspired words. When they came to the last verse, ". . . Neither life nor death, nor angels, ... nor things present, nor things to come. . . . nor any creature, shall be able to separate us from the love of God," . . . . their full hearts brimmed over, they sobbed aloud, and pressed each other's hands. "Leave me alone with God," said the Abbé Perreyve after a long silence. Then as his friend was leaving the room, he called out: "Stay! bring me Holy Communion first." The Abbé Bernard brought It to him, and withdrew, full of awe, as from the presence of a great mystery.

They thought he would have gone home that night; but he did not, and again gently expressed his disappointment, adding quickly an act of conformity to the divine will. "I represent to myself the will of God under the form of a citadel on a high rock," he said to P. Charles Perrand; "here I take refuge, and I say: 'I know nothing but this.'"

But though the delay seemed long to his impatient soul, the end was very near. On Sunday evening, the Sister who was watching him saw symptoms which made her fear for the night. The next morning his father and mother were sent for. Meantime the Abbé Bernard, who had said Mass for him at daybreak, came in and said he would not leave him, but remain by his side, or in the next room. "Am I much worse?" enquired his friend, calmly.

"Perhaps you may wish to confess, or to receive Communion; besides, I promised the Sister not to leave you till she returned."

"Ah! I understand. Then it is to be for to-day. We must make ready for the great combat. Go at once and bring me the Viaticum." He remained alone for a long thanksgiving.

His father and mother arrived later in the day. The moment he saw them entering the room, he called out: "We must take courage! Love is strength; God above all! It is He who upholds us in the hour of anguish; I know it more than ever at this hour." They knelt beside him, and he blessed them; he, their son, but also the Lord's anointed. Then he asked the Sister for the crucifix, that he might kiss it.

"Give me yours," he said, "not my own; yours that has been pressed by so many dying lips."

Presently he said to his mother: "If I die to-morrow, it will be the anniversary of my First Communion."

"Dear child," replied the mother, through her tears, "I was very happy that day!"

"Well, and you must be happy to-morrow, too," was the reply. He then called his sister to him, and told her of some changes that were to be made in the family vault, and in a clear, unfaltering voice dictated his epitaph to her: "*Satiabor cum apparuerit gloria Tua.*" (Ps., xvi, 15.) After this his agony may be said to have begun. Consciousness remained unclouded, and the soul in full possession of itself. He held the crucifix, pressing it to his lips with tender invocations: "Come quickly, my Lord! . . . Soon, Jesus, soon." . . . . He was as peaceful as a child in its mother's arms, and the mourners who knelt round him felt moved rather to give thanks than to grieve at this blessed going home of their loved one. The afternoon wore on; the long shadows of the summer's evening gathered in the death-chamber. Towards seven o'clock the dying man suddenly made an effort to raise himself on his pillows;

his face grew livid, his large, dark eyes fixed themselves with an expression of terror on some object present, but invisible, and he cried out twice, in a strong voice: "*I am afraid! I am afraid!*" The Abbé Bernard flew to his side. "Don't be afraid of God," he said; "cast yourself into the arms of his mercy. *In Te, Domine, speravi.*"....

The other looked at him, and said: "It is not God I am afraid of. Oh no! I am afraid ..... *that they won't let me die!*"

They gave him the crucifix to kiss—Père Lacordaire's crucifix, that he had had all day—and the Abbé Bernard pronounced slowly the words: "My God, I love Thee with all my heart, for time and for eternity."

"Oh! yes ..... *with all my heart!*" repeated his friend, imprinting a long kiss upon the wounded feet of his Saviour. These were his last words. He grew oppressed; his breath came fast and thick; by degrees the breathing grew faint, then inaudible; the shades of death closed round him, and Henry Perreyve faded into life.

'Beth's Promise.

BY MRS. ANNA HANSON DORSEY.

CHAPTER VI.
THE WEDDING.

ANNE HAMILTON'S wedding day rose fair and lovely over the beautiful Bay of Naples, its picturesque classic shores, and the old city, so famous in song and story. The golden light tinted the feathery plume of smoke that sprang gracefully skyward from the mysterious depths of Vesuvius; the ruined temples of Paestum gleamed upon their lonely height among the olives and roses; isles, and grottoes, and scenes that seemed like dream-land—so thronged were they with the fables of antiquity—emerged from the soft purple mists which night had thrown around them, kindling into new life and brightness as the sunbeams touched their dew-gemmed vines and flowers. Above all, the morning *Angelus*, chiming in silvery tones, floated out from the campaniles of the convents and monasteries that nestled among the wooded heights that skirted the bay, answering and blending with each other, until they filled the air like an anthem in honor of the holy Virgin and the wondrous incarnation of her divine Son.

At her anchorage, throwing graceful shadows as she gently rocked upon the sparkling waves, lay the old "Cumberland," from whose peak floated the "Stars and Stripes" like a messenger of peace and hope from the New World to lands already hoary, and tottering with the weight and changes of centuries. Boats loaded with flowers directed their course towards her, and fragrant flowers of every hue, and garlands full of rich odors, and vines starred with white and golden blossoms, were trailed up her grim side by the peasants who had brought them, in overflowing wicker baskets and by the armful, while they chattered and laughed, making the air musical. Presently the sound of hammers disturbed the harmony of the scene, and carpenters were seen busily at work, erecting an arch on the quarter-deck of the old line-of-battle ship, which was wreathed with flowers and draped with flags. Then masts and rigging were made gay with bunting, and the spacious deck was carpeted with leaves and flowers.

"A great *festa!*" said the peasants, as they lay upon their oars at a little distance, watching all that was going on. They had at first thought that an execution was at hand.

"Americans," said one, "love beautiful things; look at their flags! how gay!"

"And look at the big black guns grinning there like teeth that know how to bite! aha!" said an old fellow who had scars upon him, and knew something.

"They won't bite to-day; and we'll wait and see the end of it," they answered, gaily.

The end of it was the wedding of Anne Hamilton and Lieut. Morley, about which the fashionable circles of society in Naples had been gossiping for weeks. They had wished to be married in the grand old Basilica which Anne usually attended, but this was impossible, as Lieut. Morley was not a Catholic; then it was ascertained that they could not even be married by a priest at their own apartments, because the ecclesiastical laws forbid the clergy to officiate at mixed marriages, when no dispensation has been given. Anne, being a Catholic herself, had not dreamed of such difficulties,—in fact, she knew very little of her religion beyond the Sacraments, and was deeply mortified; but she declared that she would be married only by one of her own clergy, even if the wedding had to be deferred until after her return to the United States, where the regulations on this point were not so strict. Then the question arose of Lieut. Morley's being detached from his ship, his cruise not being up for two years. As hard as it was, he felt in honor bound to remain; even had he wished to be detached, he was too proud to ask favors of the Department at home. It was evident that the affair must be postponed, and quite a shadow settled over the usually gay household. The affianced pair tried to put a brave front on their disappointment, but they felt it none the less keenly. Mrs. Hamilton was furious; her plans were thrown into confusion by what she called "an arbitrary act of Popish fanaticism," after all the trouble and expense she had been at to make the wedding a distinguished affair. The matter was discussed in every circle. The Americans and English were very bitter, and did not hesitate to ventilate their sentiments concerning the intolerant bigotry which had been exercised by the Catholic clergy on the occasion. On the other hand, the Neapolitans were nettled and indignant at the bitter and insulting speeches that were made against their holy faith by these strangers who knew nothing about it. In the midst of all this commotion and ill-feeling, an intimation was conveyed to Mrs. Hamilton from the highest ecclesiastical authority in Naples, "that existing difficulties would be obviated if the marriage ceremony could be permitted to take place on board the American ship, then in the harbor, that being foreign ground, over which the existent ecclesiastical laws had no control; a priest would be permitted to perform the ceremony there as a *civil rite*, but not as a Sacrament, as there was a difference of faith in the contracting parties. It was not unusual," the message went on to explain, "in the United States for a Catholic and Protestant to be married by a Catholic priest, but not in church. On their ship, they would be as it were at home—under their own flag, and the same custom might be observed."*

Mrs. Hamilton returned a gracious answer, and proceeded to announce to all concerned the turn that affairs had taken. The idea was hailed with delight. Admiral Irwin cordially assented to the plan, and entered with zest into the arrangements, determined that on his part there should be nothing wanting that could give brilliancy to the occasion. "It shall be as grand," he said, with nautical exuberance, "as when the Doge of Venice used to go out in the *Bucentaur* to wed the Adriatic."

As if to crown everything, a Southern Bishop from the United States, on his way to Rome, arrived at Naples, bringing letters to some of the people with whom the Hamiltons were intimate. He was, after being frankly informed by Lieut. Morley of everything that had happened, invited to perform the marriage ceremony; and having ascertained from the proper source that his doing so would involve no ecclesiastical censure, he willingly consented. An early day was appointed, and invitations issued to attend the wedding of Miss Hamilton and Lieut. Morley on the United States flag-ship, the "Cumberland." Everyone immediately smoothed down their ruffled feathers; society, native and foreign, was delighted; such a sensation had never been known; it was unique, novel and delightful; a wedding on ship-board with flags flying, splendid music, and all the officers in full uniform. What

* A marriage under the same circumstances and difficulties took place a few years ago on board the flag-ship of the American squadron in the Mediterranean at a Catholic port.
A. H. D.

could be more enchanting! And all to be followed by a magnificent entertainment at Mrs Hamilton's superb apartments! Mrs. Hamilton was in her element; what could be more distinguished, after all, so out of the ordinary beaten track as the whole affair—including the American Bishop—would be, she really felt almost reconciled to Anne's marrying so far below her own ambitious expectations. The good lady had never been so supremely happy in all her life; she was delighted with everything and everybody around her.

The wedding *cortège* came off from shore in barges; the admiral received the bride at the gangway, and led her, followed by Mrs. Hamilton and Lieut. Morley and the train of invited guests, towards the flag-draped, flower-decorated arch, under which the Bishop, in company with a priest, awaited them. The band of the "Cumberland" filled the air with the music of the "Wedding March." Lieut. Morley received his bride—who looked very lovely in her rich, spotless attire, her veil of rare lace just shading her fair countenance and falling in diaphanous folds to her very feet—received her from the admiral, and the ceremony began. It was very simple and brief; it was not a solemn marriage, you know; therefore the more beautiful and impressive portions of the nuptial service were, as is usual under such circumstances, omitted.

They both knelt when it was over, and the good Bishop blessed them. "It seems very like home here, under our old flag," he said to them a moment afterwards. "Be as faithful, my child, to your holy religion, as you are loyal to your native land, and God will bless this union by the conversion of your spouse," he added to Anne, aside. "Wear this in memory of to-day"; and he placed in her hand a small gold medal of the Blessed Virgin, which she wore ever after until the night we have told of. All surrounded the newly-wedded pair with hearty congratulations; the band once more filled the air with triumphal strains, and every one would have gladly remained longer, but Mrs. Hamilton gave the signal to move, and the party left the ship, full of glee and merriment. A loud, irrepressible cheer arose from the sailors, who had provided themselves with flowers which they now showered down upon the bride until her barge was nearly full. Lieut. Morley stood up and waved his cap, and the ladies their handkerchiefs, until the barge shot out of range, leaving the sailors in the rigging, up which they had scampered to get the last view of a spectacle which had delighted them. The admiral had ordered a double allowance of grog to be served out to them, in which to drink a health to their favorite officer and his bride, which increased their hilarity to the very verge of insubordination. The admiral conveyed the Bishop ashore in his own barge, the attendant priest followed with the officer next in command, and the procession was closed by the officers of the "Cumberland" in full uniform, all of whom joined the wedding party at Mrs. Hamilton's, where a magnificent entertainment awaited them, and where the rank and fashion of Naples, and its foreign society, were assembled. Mrs. Hamilton was complimented to her heart's content, and was made more than happy by being told that everyone said "it was the most beautiful and *recherché* affair ever seen in Naples," meaning of course in private life, for the king, and other royalties, held court there with great magnificence.

A month or so passed, and one day Lieutenant Morley received a letter from his aunt—to whom he had written describing the wedding, and explaining why it had taken place on shipboard—in which she referred to it in brief and emphatic words: "I'd rather have had you married there, on American oak and under the American flag, than in the grandest cathedral of them all, by the Pope himself!" But the truth is, Miss Morley, not comprehending the matter from a Catholic standpoint, was deeply offended. She was firmly convinced that the clerical authorities out there were a benighted set, more given to "straining at gnats" than was good for them, and that it was an insult to the flag of his country not to allow a brave young American officer to be married in one of their old dingy cathedrals, to say nothing of his bride, who was not only an American, but a Roman Catholic. But these were her private opinions, and snapping her fine white teeth upon them, she kept them to herself, hoping that the marriage would turn out happily. Miss Morley was not a religionist, she had never been baptized, and had seen so much bickering and uncharitableness among the various sects around her that she had no desire to be one. "If there's a God," she used to say to her nephew sometimes in their confidential talks, when he was at home for a short time, "He's a God of Truth and not of discord and lies. If He says one thing, He doesn't mean another, as the various sects make out among themselves. I shall steer clear of them all, my boy, and follow St. Paul's advice; mind my own business, unless I can find a religion that seems to have a perfect and divine spirit to guide and govern it. I may never find it; if I don't—well, I'll do my work, and help my fellow-creatures all I can. I can do no more." Again, she laid down her newspaper one day, after having read of certain difficulties and disputations between two of the leading denominations, in which the bitterest acrimony prevailed, and each charged the other with false doctrine; and, taking off her spectacles, she wiped them carefully, sighed, and then after thinking it over a little while, she said: "They all think everybody wrong except themselves, and they've got Scripture to bolster up their different beliefs out of the same Bible. I don't know what to make of it, my boy; so I shall let them fight and scratch it out among themselves, without making myself miserable." And this was Miss Morley's creed, which she lived up to faithfully; she "gave her goods to the poor"; wherever there was calamity, destitution and sickness she spared neither herself nor her means —aye, she would have "given her very body to be burned," if by so doing she could have benefitted her fellow-creatures; but she was a stranger to that one true Faith which, through perfect charity, brings man as near to God as the angels themselves; a stranger to that higher motive, which would have sanctified her good works, and given her soul all that it blindly desired. There are many scattered through our land like Miss Morley; people who are by nature noble and good, and possessed of virtues which many professing to be Christians are devoid of, but who by the errors of education and training, are far off from the truth as revealed by Almighty God through His Divine Son to the Church which He founded and established through all time, which holds one Faith, one Lord, one Baptism, and an infallible authority to teach and defend its doctrines; who are withheld from investigation and a nearer approach to this only safe Fold by the belief that has been instilled into them from the dawn of their earliest reason, that it is a system worse than paganism itself, built up of idolatry and priestcraft, of pomp and ceremony, which entrap and delude the weak and ignorant; and of learning and sophistry to dazzle and confound the wiser and more intelligent. Hence, many outside the Church, looking upon it as antichrist, while finding no rest in their own troubled waters, and longing for a safe port for their weary souls, never imagine that it is there, and only there, that what they seek is to be found. Sometimes by accidental association with Catholics, and by the grace of God, their eyes are opened; sometimes it happens—as our story shows—that Catholic children who, by the force of circumstances, are placed under the guardianship or influence of unbelievers, almost make shipwreck of their Faith, if not by direct means, by the ignorant indifference to their religious interests of those having them in charge. Mrs. Hamilton did the best that could have been expected, and she believed firmly that she had done her whole duty to the children so solemnly committed to her care by their dying mother; and Mrs. Hamilton represents a large class in this country of untenable and contending beliefs.

Lieutenant Morley, when the "Cumberland" went into winter quarters at Nice, got a month's leave, and took his wife to Rome, where they explored together the wonders of art and the crumbling relics of the past; he did not hesitate to kneel with her in their audience with the Pope, to receive his blessing. Not even a distant shadow appeared to threaten their happiness. Lieutenant Morley, ever mindful of the pledge he had given, sought neither by word, nor look nor act to interfere with his wife's religion; on the contrary he attended her to Mass, and to the very door of the confessional, and to the festival devotions which she sometimes desired to take part in; he liked to see her devout—it was part of the pictured harmony around them, and he thought her never so lovely as when the pale radiance of the blessed tapers shone tenderly down upon her fair, finely cut face. How happy, how proud she was of her husband's deference to her faith, his toleration, his liberality! In fact, it was the wonder of every one who knew them, and nothing pleased her better than having it noticed. Indeed she was so touched by it that when they returned to Nice she offered to go with him occasionally to the English chapel; but he, belonging to no creed or sect, had not the least desire to go where the bare, cold worship of the Protestant religion had nothing to offer for the gratification of his æsthetic tastes. As to religion itself, he was perfectly indifferent: his honor was his god; his duty to the service, his only dogma. "I wish that he *could* be convinced," his wife said to a friend; "of course it would be a great happiness to me if he were to become a Catholic; but he is so good, why should I worry myself if he doesn't?" And there she rested quite satisfied, only that she sometimes offered "*Aves*" for his conversion.

Mrs. Hamilton had gone with a fashionable and distinguished party to visit Egypt and the Holy Land; the idea of seeing the pyramids, of riding on camels, and meeting actual Bedouins, proved too great a temptation for her to resist; besides, it was quite the thing to make this journey. "I have nothing to keep me tied down," said *Bonne Mère;* "Anne is very happily married, and letters from my two boys tell me they are doing well, so there's no earthly reason why I should not begin to enjoy myself. She took an affectionate leave of Anne, crammed a check for a large amount into her hand, embraced Lieutenant Morley, and started on her journey in fine spirits. Could she only have looked into the future, would she have gone with so light a heart to meet what was yet afar off, but coming slowly to meet her?

(TO BE CONTINUED.)

ON the eventful day of the passing of the Emancipation Act, the great O'Connell was seen pacing up and down outside the House of Commons saying his beads.

Sancta Maria.

MOTHER Immaculate, we pray thee hear us!
O may our humble prayers to thee arise!
We pray, sweet Mother, that thou'lt be near us
In death's dark hour—receive our parting sighs.
Then lift in silent prayer our hearts to thee,
As we are wafted to eternity.

Oh, Queen of Heaven, thy sorrows should have taught us
To bear our cares with fortitude and love.
By Precious Blood on Calvary He bought us,
Christ, the Redeemer, God of peace and love.
Sancta Maria, star forever bright,
Guard us and watch o'er us by day and night.
McN.

A Martyr of Charity.[*]

FATHER ANNE DE NOUÉ, S. J., MISSIONARY IN CANADA IN THE 17TH CENTURY.

ON the 30th of January, 1646, Father Anne de Noué left the mission-station of Three Rivers, which had been for a time his home, and, accompanied by two French soldiers and a converted Huron Indian, started for the fort built by the French near the mouth of the River Richelieu (now known as the Sorel), to say Mass and administer the Sacraments. This fort was situated about thirty-six miles from Three Rivers, and was held by but a scanty handful of French soldiers, aided by a number of converted Huron Indians. A weakness of memory had prevented Father Noué from acquiring the native languages, hence he confined his ministrations to the French soldiers and settlers, and the few Indians who had partially acquired the French tongue.

In this winter month, and this wild northern wilderness, every river and lake was a sheet of ice, and the earth was covered with snow, sometimes two or three feet deep. Father Noué and his companions, though equipped with snowshoes, could barely make eighteen miles each day, and this with great difficulty, dragging their luggage upon small sledges. At night their only resource was to build impromptu snow huts by scraping the deep snow from the ground and heaping it up on the side next to the wind, having no roof but the sky; in which toil Father Noué worked like the others. Then, after build-

---

[*] This is the first of a series of biographical sketches of those saintly missionaries of the early time, whose deeds of heroism and devotedness form one of the most thrilling pages in the history of North America. It is translated, adapted, and elaborated from the French. The series will include Fathers Jogues, Brebœuf, Garnier, and numerous others. We feel sure that these sketches will delight every reader, and many perhaps will learn for the first time that examples of heroic sanctity have not been wanting to the American Church.

ing a scanty fire on the ground to warm their perishing limbs, and partaking of such food as they had brought with them, they lay down to rest. About two hours after midnight, Father Nouë awoke, and pitying his weary companions, he resolved to precede them on their journey to Fort Richelieu, and, by arriving a few hours in advance, send back some soldiers from there to succor their comrades. Inspired to renewed energy by this charitable thought—which, alas! finally cost him his life—he roused his companions, told them his intentions, and cheered their failing hearts by promises of speedy relief. Advising them to start by daybreak, and follow his foot-prints in the snow, he then departed, and confiding in his knowledge of the route, and expecting to reach the fort before the next night, he left his flint and steel, and even his blanket, taking with him as his only provisions a little bread and five or six dried plums. Those were found upon his corpse. Calling upon his companions to join him once more in saying the rosary—his favorite devotion,—and commending them to the protection of that "Help of Christians," whom they had just invoked, Father Nouë calmly set forth upon his last mission of charity on earth.

Aided by the moonlight, and, as he trusted, still more efficaciously guided by his Guardian Angel, the saintly priest and destined martyr pursued his way; but before daybreak the clouds thickened; dimming the moonlight, and aided by a blinding snow-storm which just then set in, caused him to lose his way entirely. Father Nouë found himself in utter darkness, knowing nothing of the direction in which he was going, yet he toiled on, praying fervently as he went. The route by which they had travelled was the ice-covered surface of the St. Lawrence, and their camp at night had been made at St. Peter's Lake, an expansion of the great river.

Father Nouë, having lost the points of the compass in the darkness, instead of pursuing the direct route by the river, wandered far out upon the lake, circling round and round, and often retracing his own steps. When the day broke dimly through darkening clouds and ever thickening flakes of snow, the weary priest knew not where he was, nor what to do. Confiding in the care of his holy and powerful protectress, he still pursued his way, hoping soon to arrive at the fort. As night fell, he dug a hole in the snow near the shore of an island, and lay down to rest, without food, fire, or blanket.

In the mean time his companions, the two soldiers and the Huron Indian, had started at daybreak, as he had bidden them, and though they could not discover his footprints, covered as they were by the snow, they succeeded after great difficulties in reaching the fort. They had lost their way repeatedly, and wandered far from the track, for the Frenchmen knew nothing of the country, and the Huron was unskilled as a guide. At night they encamped by the shore of the Island of St. Ignatius, and made a small fire. The Indian, more accustomed to hardship than the white men, now proposed to set out by himself in search of the fort. Trusting to his instinct rather than to any knowledge of their locality, he started, and after a few hours' travel found himself near the palisades. It was but a feeble little fort, consisting of a few small buildings, surrounded by a palisade, and guarded by a mere handful of men; yet, such as it was, it kept at bay the ferocious Iroquois, the most terrible enemy of France and of the missions in this part of Nort America. On arriving at Richelieu, and asking after Father Nouë, the Huron was astonished to hear that he had not arrived there, and the captain of the fort was as much surprised to learn that their party had in all that time traversed only eighteen miles. Every one was filled with anxiety about the fate of Father Nouë. As it was night, nothing could then be done, but at daybreak they divided themselves into several parties, and went by different routes, some on the north bank of the river, and some on the south. They searched everywhere, called loudly, fired their muskets; but though they soon found the two soldiers, the search for Father Nouë was in vain; no response came to their repeated shouts, and at night they returned sadly to the fort.

On the 2d of February, a soldier, taking with him two of the converted Hurons, set forth anew in search of the saintly priest, or at least of his corpse. They went first to the spot whence Father Nouë had departed, on leaving his companions. Having found it, the Indians tracked with great care the hidden footprints, covered by the falling snow; yet they managed to uncover them, and so, step by step, they followed them, observing how often they had returned upon themselves, until at length they arrived at a spot near the shore of St. Ignatius, where Father Nouë had made his last camp, and which was about three miles from the place where his body was finally found. He had evidently passed the fort more than once during that last terrible night, yet could not see it in the darkness. At last, as the second night fell, he had scraped away the snow with feeble, failing hands, and here, alone and far from earthly succors—destitute of food—without shelter from the piercing, icy wind—without even a blanket over his thin, worn soutane, this holy martyr knelt upon the ground and prayed. Who cannot divine the language of that prayer when we see still clasped in the stiffened fingers his beloved rosary? Oh, how precious, how enviable a death! How poor, how utterly destitute, yet how sublimely possessed of all things! The snow-shoes and hat on the ground by his side, and the worn clothing upon his person, all he died possessed of. Yet the inheritor of infinite riches, of eternal glory! And thus they found him. His eyes were uplifted to heaven, his arms crossed on his breast, and a smile of ineffable peacefulness dwelt upon his lips. Penetrated with a sacred awe at this sight, the soldier knelt beside the venerable body, and murmured a prayer; then arising, he cut a cross upon one of the nearest trees, to mark the spot; and, wrapping the cold, stiff body in a cloak they had brought with them, placed it upon a sledge in order to carry it, first to Richelieu, and afterwards to Three Rivers, where they thought he ought to rest.

Father Nouë had been granted the consoling privilege of dying upon the day on which the Church honors the Feast of the Purification of the Blessed Virgin; to the truly devout child of Mary one of her sweetest festivals. And Father Nouë's whole life was marked by a most profound devotion to this Queen of Apostles and Martyrs. He not only honored her by many special devotions, such as fasting every Saturday in her honor, and reciting every day the Little Office of her Immaculate Conception, but throughout his life he could never speak of Mary except in tones of heartfelt emotion, and in terms which evinced the fervor of his soul. We may well believe that this tender and faithful Mother, as the reward of his devotedness, obtained for Father Nouë the favor of this death, so pure, so saintly, so far removed from all earthly succors or consolations, so calm on the Cross with his Divine Master. Father Nouë's own special children at Three Rivers, and even the rude soldiers at Fort Richelieu, felt their hearts divided between admiring awe at such a death, and bitter grief at the loss of such a father and friend—one who had never considered his own comfort for a moment, in comparison with their welfare. He was buried at Three Rivers, and his grave was surrounded by a great concourse, composed not only of all the French in that region, but also of all the Indians, converted or not, who had shared his ministrations. Few indeed were they, even among the stolid savages, who could refrain from the tribute of tears at the burial of this saintly priest and missionary. They remembered his unwearied zeal for their souls' welfare; they had witnessed his holy and consecrated life; and, melted by these memories, and their great loss, many approached the tribunal of penance; saying that they felt as if their dear lost Father constrained them to do so; many also, instead of praying for the repose of Father Nouë's soul, rather implored him, whom they regarded as both saint and martyr, to intercede for them. Thus was this saintly life crowned with a holy death; and thus, though dead, he yet spoke to the hearts of his beloved children for whom he lived and died—the poor, ignorant, yet loving natives of the North American forests.

Father de Nouë was of noble birth; son of the lord of Villers en Priere, which is a chateau and village situated six or seven leagues from the city of Rheims, in Champagne. In early youth he was a page at court; and exposed though he was to every corrupting influence, he still preserved his virginal purity of body and soul, and by constantly imploring the succor of his Immaculate Mother, and by the continual practice of penance, he preserved this purity during a long life, thirty years of which were spent in the world, and thirty-three in religion. Towards himself he was ever most severe and exacting; towards others, most benignant and charitable in his judgments; for himself he ever chose the lowest employments, the poorest of needful supplies: he shunned display, and shrank, in his humility, from well-merited praise, even that of his own Superiors. At the time of his blessed death he had labored for sixteen years in the missions of New France, with courage, devotedness, and profound humility. As observed before, his defective memory preventing him from mastering the Indian languages, he therefore devoted himself entirely to the service of those natives who could speak French, and of the other missionaries; never neglecting the French soldiers stationed near. At times the mission was greatly straitened for want of food: and the humble saint would then spend days searching in the forest for edible roots, and in fishing. He was very successful as a fisherman, and often supplied their table when they had little else to eat. He was a model of religious obedience. However important the affair he might have on hand, however difficult the task to which he was summoned, he was ever ready and eager to leave all, and obey the voice of his Superior. He did not pause to examine the nature of the duty, or his own ability to fulfil it—desiring only that the will of God might be done, and recognizing that will in the voice of his Superior. It was proposed, and even urged upon him that he should return to France, to spend his old age in peace and content among his own people. But he would not hear of it: "I know well," said he, "that I occupy the place of one who might be far more useful, yet I long to die on the field of battle. I know that many, more capable of doing good service, might fill my place, able, as I am not, to learn the Indian languages, yet I cannot relinquish the work I am doing to aid the poor savages who know our tongue, and to minister to the French soldiers here."

The grace he had so many times implored, to labor and suffer to the last, to make of his body a victim and a holocaust in behalf of his poor Indians and to the glory of God, was granted to Father de Noué, and the angels viewed the final sacrifice, while his poor Indian guides wept over it.

Great Men.

BY ETHEL TANE.

If he bid thee bow before
Crownèd mind and nothing more,
The great idol men adore;
Though his words seem true and wise,
He is a demon in disguise!
ADELAIDE PROCTER.

"NAME the most famous heroes the world has produced?" Does not this request smack somewhat of schooldays, of examinations that came round as relentlessly as the time for getting up in the morning? I hope it does; for I wish you to imagine yourself once more a youngster knowing history as yet but by "outlines" and catechism, and confronted with this query for the very first time. I am going to hazard a guess at the reply. "Alexander the Great, Julius Cæsar, Richard I, Cromwell, Napoleon the Great, Wellington, and —of course—"Washington." The list might be a little longer, and if my school-boy had Celtic blood in his veins, perhaps he would leave the Puritan out in the cold and give his place to Owen Roe O'Neil. This would not affect my main point. Both were men of the sword, and I am sure that with most children a hero simply means a famous soldier. As long as school histories give such minute accounts of all martial exploits, and crowd the great thinkers of the age into one concluding paragraph, so long must children think that there is no fame equal to that won on the battle-field.

It seems but natural that conquerors within the area of their exploits, should be deemed preeminently great, for they possess there the grandeur of an absolute and terrible power. Here is a man perhaps taller than any of his fellows, stern and grim of aspect; he is, we will say, a petty king; he has raised an army, trained it himself, and now leads it into the neighboring territory. In vain do forces commanded by commonplace leaders attempt to cope with his. Wherever he is, is victory. The country is ravaged with fire and sword, great spoils are taken, and then the conqueror goes on to other lands. No wonder this man is considered a hero. The meanest soldier and the poorest peasant believe in that genius whose brilliant and terrible achievements are spread before their very eyes. But the conqueror's influence is built on his fellow-creatures' fears, not in their love or gratitude. Is it very enviable?

And now we will glance at another class of heroes, conquerors too,—for all great men vanquish something. "To Castile and Leon, Columbus gave a new world." Such is the inscription on the tomb of one who will never be forgotten. It is an interesting story, that of this Genoese sailor, and possesses moreover a spiritual, allegorical meaning, so clear and simple that he who runs may read.

Columbus had never seen the New World,— that prize he dangled before the careless eyes of sovereign after sovereign,—but still he knew it must exist. He knew it, because study had given him a knowledge of the earth's shape beyond the common geography of his day, and he saw that another continent was needed to preserve the balance of the terraqueous globe. Of course, the sensible, cautious people thought him a dreamer; most folks do think those to be visionaries who believe in and preach what is yet unseen. Many delays, many disappointments were endured by Columbus; but the two great gifts of enterprise and perseverance were his, and he conquered in the end; with what results we know. The history of Columbus is a type of those of nearly all the great pioneers, whether discoverers, inventors or philosophers, who have opened the way into new spiritual or material regions. To gain the world's admiration at last, it seems almost necessary at first to bear its sneers.

But was the possession of that New World an unmixed blessing to Spain? Are reading and writing, printing, steam, or the sewing-machine unmixed blessings? How many lies are flashed around the world? How many souls owe their ruin to bad literature? We find curses mingled with all our temporal blessings, and the child of godless civilization may wisely bow before the great reformer.

It is unfortunate that this glorious title has sometimes been usurped by men altogether unworthy of it, for there is no benefactor like the true reformer. Well may we call the title glorious and even godlike, for who so well deserved it as He who came down to teach a doctrine which should change the whole lives of His sincere disciples. The Apostles, too, were reformers. They preached repentance—that is, reform—to the haughty Romans and the refined, effeminate Greeks; and then, when in later centuries the East and North sent forth their hordes of savages to overturn the classic civilization, the Church preached to them also, and at this hour it is still her special mission to reform the world.

We have admired the conqueror's genius, and stood in wonder at his career, grand and destructive as some volcanos' overflow; we have rendered a tribute of respect and gratitude to the heroes of human civilization, those to whom we owe so much, if we use and do not abuse the increase of power they have bequeathed us; but surely our deepest veneration and love must be kept for the Christian reformer, who, no matter where his place is, sees the evil within and around him, and strives against it ardently, yet wisely. It is a sad truth, but as long as life goes on, so long will the unpalpable dust of evil soil all the brightest and richest in God's creation. That which needs reform is everywhere. Moreover, "the harvest indeed is great, but the laborers few."

It may be that among those who read these words there are some who possess the divine gift of genius, the constituents of what the world deems a great man. Let such rejoice, and go forward to battle for the Truth.

But officers can do little if the rank and file are cowards, and it is the perfection of many slight details that makes perfect the work of art. We, of the common crowd form in the aggregate a mighty power. Though we shall never be deemed heroes, we may do heroic work. All of us, even the very least, can aid in the great labor of saving souls, and making the present world less full of shadowed places.

Jubilee of the Immaculate Conception at Lourdes.

IF it was proper that the Jubilee of the Immaculate Conception should everywhere be celebrated in the most magnificent manner, certainly at no place in the world was this duty more imperative than at Lourdes, and well indeed was the duty of gratitude and love accomplished. Every day during a preparatory novena, despite the rigors of the winter, large numbers made the crypt resound with their fervent prayers and lively chants of the Litany and the "Felicitation" to Mary Immaculate.

However, the winter became more and more severe. France and the greater part of the countries of Europe were covered with snow; the trains on many of the railroads were delayed, and it was still snowing at Lourdes on the eve of the festival. Hither and thither were tossed by the wind the numerous and beautiful streamers which decorated the façade of the Basilica, the large open space in front, and the Grotto. But all this glad decoration seemed to smile, like a confident prayer. The snow and the storm ceased before noon, and the weather became calm enough in the evening to permit the Procession of the Holy Rosary to go to the Grotto. This was the pious inauguration of the solemnity.

On the 8th, the day was magnificent. From noon, the brilliant heavens wore a hue of immaculate azure. Pilgrims had come during the preceding days, but arrivals were more numerous on the morning of the festival. Masses, as well as the distribution of Holy Communion to the faithful, began at 5 o'clock, a. m., and lasted till after 12 o'clock at noon. The Bishop of Tarbes celebrated Mass at 9, in the midst of exquisite chants recounting the grandeurs and the beauties of the Immaculate Virgin. The Bishop, having distributed the Bread of Angels for more than an hour and a half, was obliged to hand the third ciborium to a priest, who continued the distribution for some time longer. Solemn Mass was delayed on account of the immense number of Communions. The men of Lourdes, forming the Sodality of the Immaculate Conception, were obliged to wait a long time at the door, until place could be made for them in the Basilica. At last they entered with religious gravity, their banner at their head. More numerous than ever they filled the whole sanctuary and choir. Monseigneur Jourdan welcomed them with paternal bounty. He told them how happy he was to find them here again, as in preceding years, ever faithful to the Immaculate Virgin. She has visited and glorified their good village of Lourdes; they know how to be grateful, and they will ever be so; they will prove themselves worthy children of Mary, by imitating her virtues, and especially her invincible patience in the midst of the trials of life. The Mass, which was in the grave and solemn Gregorian Chant, was not finished till long after noon.

At 2 o'clock crowds besieged the door of the Basilica, only to find an immense throng already in possession. The sacred edifice presented an image of paradise, with its brilliant illumination and its chants, more harmonious and more entrancing than are heard at the grandest solemnities.

The Bishop of Tarbes drew his inspiration from the thoughts and sentiments suggested by this beautiful day. He proclaimed, with all the ardor of his heart and faith, the grandeurs of the Jubilee of the proclamation of the Immaculate Conception. This solemnity fills the whole Catholic world with great joy. We celebrate it even with a more lively joy in this blessed place where the Mother of God has appeared, and said, "I am the Immaculate Conception." This word of Mary was not the confirmation of the word of the Pope; it needed no confirmation; it was a continuation of this word—a new revelation. The whole world has heard it, and has been seized with joy, with hope, and with love. Mgr. Jourdan then displayed, by the light of the most profound doctrine, the grandeurs and the divine privileges of the Mother of God, immaculate in her conception. He concluded his beautiful discourse by clear and practical lessons which this mystery should impress upon the hearts of Christians, and especially of children of Mary. The afternoon service was indeed magnificent; but night had its incomparable charms.

At 7 o'clock the illumination was enchanting, the whole village of Lourdes was on fire. The valley of the Grotto looked like some fairy scene; the fine convents and the hotels, the private houses and the shops of the merchants, and even the thicket which crowns the hill directly opposite the Grotto, all seemed to vie with each other in colors the most lively, and most variegated, in chanting the glory of the Immaculate Virgin. The very stars in the beautiful heavens seemed to smile and leap for joy. In the centre of this marvellous panorama, the Basilica glows with incomparable splendor. The grand, architectural lines of the façade are marked by tracks of fire, as if by diamonds and precious stones. At the entrance rises a grand azure portico, under which appears a large, luminous statue of the Virgin. She appears to be leaving the Basilica in order to come out to her children, on her head glitters a golden crown. Higher up, Pius IX, in mosaic, smiles at the triumph of the Immaculate Virgin. Above this azure portico, from an immense aureola of dazzling whiteness, sparkle these grand words: "I am the Immaculate Conception." Still higher, towering in the air, entwined with the mystical rose, shines out a magnificent star. It is the morning star, clothed with the Sun which is this day risen upon the world. The large open space in front of the crowned Virgin is ornamented with vast circle of Venetian poles, on which, high in the air, float alternately pennants of the Pope and of the Immaculate Conception. These poles are supported in the air by pyramids decorated with green garlands and flags. They are joined together by green garlands, luminous cords, and Venetian lanterns, they form around the statue of the Virgin an immense crown, which seems to spread out towards the Gave, as if to embrace the valley, France, and the world, reminding one of the great festival of the coronation a few years ago.

The statue of Our Lady rests on a pedestal sparkling with sapphires, emeralds, and other precious stones, and on its head is a crown of a dozen brilliants. The sanctuary of the Grotto has had for the first time a decoration full of charm, of *éclat*, and of mystery.

In the interior of the sanctuary the cavity of the Grotto seems all on fire, and the Virgin's face appears to be more than ever radiant with smiles. Higher up, in the solitude of the rock, in the verdure of the sombre ivy, in the centre of beautiful foliage reflecting emerald and sapphire, beams the "*Ave Maria*" in the sweet and mysterious colors of the opal. How often, for now more than twenty years, has this mysterious "*Ave Maria*" been whispered at the feet of the Immaculate! How often has it there burst forth in all the transports of holy enthusiasm! But never was it pronounced with more lively feelings of love and joy than on this luminous night of the Jubilee. The large open space in front of the Grotto was filled by a compact crowd. There were many strangers, but more numerous were the inhabitants of Lourdes. In spite of the intense cold on the banks of the Gave, they were there of every age and condition—men, women, and children. The chanters of the Basilica having intoned the *Magnificat*, every voice, forming an immense choir, took it up with a kind of holy passion. When the grand canticle of Mary's joys is finished, the Superior of the Missionaries reminds the multitude of the grandeur of this place, of this moment, and of the holy function which is being accomplished. In presence of the Immaculate Conception of the Grotto, towards whom the whole Catholic world have their eyes turned at this moment, they are the representatives of the faith, of the love, of the gratitude, and of the confidence of all Catholic hearts towards the Immaculate Virgin on this Jubilee of her triumph. It is with all the grandeur of these divine sentiments that they are going to thank her for the benefits conferred upon the world by the promulgation of the dogma of the Immaculate Conception, and at the same time to beg of her to complete her work for the salvation of the world, the triumph of the Church, the glory of our country and the conversion of sinners. Then is begun a dialogue of Ave Marias, of sweet invocations and ardent acclamations to the Immaculate. Never did the Britons, the Vendeans or the Belgians mingle more enthusiasm in their acclamations and in their prayers, than was exhibited by these peaceable people of Lourdes, so familiar with these demonstrations, on that frosty night. But love is insensible to cold, and these people are worthy of their Mother.

The grand procession advances along the banks of the Gave. On every side is echoed the "*Ave Maria*" by a chorus of thousands, and the night is illumined by their thousands of torches. They proceed again to the Basilica and form in lines, and continue their admirable chants near the statue of the Virgin, already spoken of, erected in front of the church.

When they have placed themselves at her feet, like a lake of stars, the chants give way to the "*Ave Maria*," to sweet invocations, to the praises of her whom the Church crowned so gloriously in this place. These prayers, occasionally interrupted by sudden bursts of enthusiasm, are brought to a close by a loud cheer for the Immaculate Conception.

The cold was bitter in the open space before the church, as at the Grotto, but no one thought of leaving. The chanters are in fine spirits and they have resumed the popular canticle:

    Sur cette colline
    Marie apparut,
    An front qu'elle incline
    Rendons le salut.

Which may be freely rendered thus:

    On this hill
    Mary did appear.

Let us still
Salute her here.

The "*Ave Maria*" is again more than ever ardent on the lips of everyone, and the procession, reforming, begins to climb the holy hill. For the third time fervent prayer is the response to the exhortations of the missionary.

Finally, one last word, an epitome, as it were, of all the acts of holy fervor made throughout the Catholic world on this Jubilee—one last cry bursts forth and is heard far in the distance: "*Vive l'Immaculée Conception!*"

The Apparitions at Knock, Co. Mayo, Ireland.

WE have much pleasure in laying before our readers another account of the recent extraordinary events in Ireland, which has kindly been sent us by a well-known missionary priest of the Archdiocese of Tuam, who has visited the scene of the occurrence and heard the relation from persons who witnessed the Apparitions. The account is substantially the same as that published last week from the *Tuam News*, which we received through the courtesy of Very Rev. Canon Bourke.

GALWAY, IRELAND, January 12, 1880.

MY DEAR FATHER:—Many thanks for your most kind letter, and for sending THE AVE MARIA. I had not a moment till now to reply, as I have been away on missionary work till to-day. With great pleasure I send you the account of the Apparition of the Most Blessed Virgin at Knock, which I heard from the very persons who saw it, and at the place where it occurred.

On the evening of the 21st of August, 1879, the eve of the Octave of the Assumption of the most Blessed Virgin Mary, from a quarter past 8 till half-past 9 in the evening, during a fearful rain, there appeared to fourteen persons, of different ages, sexes and conditions in life, the following Apparitions, at the Catholic church of Knock, Co. Mayo, in the Archdiocese of Tuam. A good, sensible, pious girl, Mary Byrne (from whom, with others, I heard the whole account), was coming over to lock up the Church of Knock after the devotions of the evening, when to her great surprise she perceived the whole gable end of the outside lit up with a strange, supernatural light. On approaching nearer, she perceived distinctly, about the centre of the wall, an altar, surmounted by a cross, and on this altar was standing a living lamb, representing the "Lamb of God." At the right-hand side of this altar appeared St. John the Evangelist, bearing in his left hand a book, and his right raised towards heaven, in the attitude of preaching. At the right-hand side of St. John appeared the Most Blessed Virgin Mary, robed in white, with a crown on her head, and with her eyes and hands raised towards heaven, as if praying for the people. Immediately at her right appeared St. Joseph, in his bare head, with his gray hair falling carelessly about his face, which was bent in reverence towards the Blessed Virgin, his hands joined also in reverence towards the Mother of God. For about an hour and a half, in the downpour of rain (which did not appear to fall where the Apparition was), Mary Byrne, and those who had collected around her, fourteen in number, witnessed this wonderful Apparition.

The Archbishop of the diocese, Dr. McHale, appointed four ecclesiastics to inquire officially into the whole matter; and, after a searching inquiry and full deliberation, they have all given their written declaration that they can see no reason to doubt of the reality of the Apparition. Several well-authenticated miracles have since been wrought at the place of the Apparition, and especially by the mortar of the wall where the Blessed Virgin Mary made her appearance. . . . .

Very faithfully, yours in the Sacred Heart,

GALWAY, January 15.

MY DEAR FATHER:—I send you additional news about the Apparition at Knock, which I have just received from good authority—with an account of additional Apparitions and miracles which have occurred there.

The chapel, or Catholic church, of Knock, at which the Apparitions have occurred, is about five miles from Claremorris, and about the same distance from Ballyhaunis, County Mayo. In the gable end of this chapel, or rather of the sacristy, immediately behind it, there is a Gothic window, five feet by two; its lowest part being twelve feet from the ground. The remainder of the gable is plain, and covered with cement. It was on this gable end of the sacristy where the extraordinary lights were seen, in the midst of which appeared the Most Blessed Virgin Mary, accompanied by St. Joseph and St. John the Evangelist, and surrounded by brilliant stars, which changed the dusk of the dull, dreary evening into comparative brightness. In the centre, immediately under the Gothic window, appeared an altar, on which stood a lamb, surrounded by rays of light, and, immediately behind the lamb, a crucifix bearing the figure of our Lord. Through the brilliant, supernatural light that surrounded the altar, angels appeared to be moving. Immediately at the Gospel side of the altar appeared St. John the Evangelist, with a mitre on his head; and in his left hand, which he held over the edge of the altar, was the book of the Gospels, whilst his right hand was raised in the attitude of preaching or blessing the people, the first and middle fingers being extended and the others closed. At St. John's right stood the Blessed Virgin, having a large crown on her head, her eyes elevated towards heaven, and her hands raised as high as her shoulders, with the palms turned towards the people. Immediately to the right of the Blessed Virgin was St. Joseph, in his bare head, with his hands joined, and bending in veneration towards the Blessed Virgin. Until fully half-past nine, or near ten, the whole Apparition remained; and though it was pouring rain everywhere else, the place of the Apparition remained perfectly dry.

Last New Year's day, immediately after last Mass, as the people were returning in crowds from divine service, the Blessed Virgin again appeared, in the same place, and remained for an hour—from one till two o'clock. On Monday evening, the eve of the Epiphany, from eleven o'clock in the morning till two o'clock next morning, a bright supernatural light was again seen on the same spot by a large crowd of people, who remained on their knees during three hours, witnessing the wonderful Apparition. Already the place is covered with *ex-voto* offerings, such as crutches, walking-sticks, statues, etc., etc., sent by those who have been miraculously cured by the intercession of "Our Lady of Knock."

Within the last few days two very remarkable and well-authenticated miracles have been wrought by the same powerful intercession. Two girls have received their sight by the application of the cement from the spot where the Blessed Virgin stood. One of them, who, as declared by her own mother, was blind from her birth, miraculously received the use of her sight in the presence of several hundred people, at the very place where the Blessed Virgin appeared.

I remain, my dear Father, very faithfully yours in the Sacred Heart,

Devotion to the Souls in Purgatory.

The following interesting communication was lately sent to our valued contemporary the *Catholic Times* of Liverpool, England, by Rev. William J. Moser, of Peterboro':

A young servant who had been religiously brought up had adopted the pious practice of having a Mass said each month for the souls in Purgatory, making the customary alms from her very limited wages. Brought to Paris by her employers, she never failed to observe this work of charity, and she had always been accustomed to assist in person at the Divine Sacrifice which she had caused to be offered. Her intercession had for its more especial object the deliverance of the soul whose expiation had been nearly achieved. Soon God tried her by a long illness, which not only caused her to endure much bodily suffering, but also resulted in the loss of her situation, and she was reduced to her last resources. The day when she was able to leave the hospital, a single franc was all she possessed. She prayed to God with confidence for help, and went in quest of employment. She had been directed to a register office at the other end of the town, and proceeded there, but passing a church on the way she entered it. The sight of a priest at the altar reminded her that she had omitted this month her ordinary devotion, and this was precisely the day on which she had been accustomed to have Mass said for the souls in Purgatory. But then, if she applied her last franc to that purpose how, was she to provide herself with food? There was an inward conflict for a moment. "After all," she said to herself, "God knows that it is for Him, and therefore He will not forsake me." She entered the sacristy, made her offering and assisted at the Mass offered for her intention. Afterwards she proceeded on her journey, filled with anxiety it is easy to imagine. Absolutely destitute, how was she to satisfy her wants for that day? She had nowhere to go. Just, however, as she was turning a corner of a street, a young man, pale, of slight build and gentlemanly appearance, approached her and said: "Are you in search of a situation?"

"Yes, sir."

"Very well, go into such a street, and to such a number, to Madame ——; I believe that you will suit her, and that you will be happy there." He disappeared amongst the passengers without waiting to hear the thanks which the poor servant had commenced to address to him. She found the street, recognized the number, and ascended to the apartment of Madame ——. A servant was leaving the house, carrying a bundle under her arm, and muttering words of anger. "Can Madame receive me?" asked the new comer.

"Perhaps she can, perhaps she can't," replied the other: "What matter is it to me? Madame will tell you herself. I have nothing to do with her. Good-morning." And she descended with her bundle. Our heroine remained trembling where she was, when a sweet voice told her to advance, and she found herself in the presence of an aged lady of venerable appearance, who encouraged her to make known her errand. "Madame," said the servant, "I just learned a few moments ago that you required a housemaid, and I have come to offer myself to you. I was assured that you would receive me with kindness."

"My child, what you tell me is very extraordinary. It is only half an hour ago that I dismissed an insolent servant, and there is not another soul in the world beside myself who knows of it; who, then, has sent you?"

"He was a gentleman, quite young, whom I met in the street; he stopped me to tell me. I have thanked God for it, as it is necessary that I should find a situation to-day, for I am entirely without money."

The old lady could not understand who the person could be, and she became lost in conjectures, when the servant, raising her eyes to look about the room, perceived a portrait. "There, Madame," said she, "It is no longer a difficulty; there is exactly the face of the young man who spoke to me. It is at his instigation I have come." At these words the lady uttered a cry and nearly fainted away. She made the girl tell her all her history, of her devotion to the suffering souls, the Mass in the morning, and the meeting of the stranger. Then throwing herself on the neck of the young girl, she embraced her with tears, saying: "You shall not be my servant, but from this moment you are my daughter. It was my son, my only son, that you saw; my son, dead these two years, who owes his deliverance to you, and who has been permitted by God to send you here. Remain here, then, and be happy, and henceforth we will pray together for the suffering souls in Purgatory, that they may enter into a happy eternity."

Those who perform this charitable duty of assisting the holy souls in Purgatory are not forgotten, but they will be remembered in an especial manner and will themselves receive the benefit of such charitable aid, when they shall be in need of it—that is to say, that God will not permit a soul to be neglected in Purgatory who, in life, assisted the holy souls.

An Appeal for the Famine-Stricken Poor of Ireland.

Our readers are already aware that, on account of the continuous downpour of rain in Ireland, resulting in the destruction of fuel and field-crops, great want has existed for some time in that country. As some may not have heard of the extent of this want, we deem it our duty to make it known. It amounts now, in some places, to *actual starvation*. The Bishops and clergy of Ireland have been indefatigable in relieving the extreme destitution around them; but the little means at their command were soon exhausted, and they now call for help. Their appeal will not be unheeded. We contribute our own mite, and any money that may be sent us to feed the hungry and clothe the naked will be cheerfully forwarded.

To give some idea of the destitution in Ireland, we need only quote the following words of a correspondent of the London *Telegraph*: "The first cabin into which I went," he says, "was a place that an Englishman would think too bad for his pig. . . . . The man of the house—shoeless and coatless, pale and haggard sat idle upon a bag of Indian meal, beyond which his food resources did not go, and through the gloom around the hearth—there was no window to speak of—could be dimly discerned one or two crouching female figures. I never saw anything in the way of a home in a civilized country—and I have seen a good deal—more appalling than this. Yet here was the case of a man renting three acres of land, and usually getting what he would be content to call a living out of them. The half bag of Indian meal was all the family had, nothing more remaining on which, by sale or mortgage, money could be raised, and to the question, 'What will you do when the meal gives out?' came the despairing answer, 'The good Lord only knows.' Not far from this I was shown by my melancholy attendants into an equally wretched hovel where a widow, with seven young children, was fighting the bitter battle of life, and rapidly getting worsted in the struggle. She herself had gone out to gather what she could for dinner, consisting—oh, my brothers in comfortable English homes —of a single cabbage! But the poor little children half-clothed, thin and hollow-eyed, were there to plead with heart-rending eloquence for aid. Once more I heard the old story. The land had yielded nothing; no turf could be obtained for fuel short of a journey of eight miles, and the family had touched absolute destitution. Over the way, in an other apology for a dwelling place, I found three poor women trying to kindle a fire with damp beanstalks, their only crop."

Such destitution is enough to touch the most stony heart, but we blush to state that many of the Irish landlords seem little affected by it; others do what they can. Again, we say, anything sent to us, even a dime, will be cheerfully forwarded to the starving people. Let other less pressing calls of charity bide their time for a while. We have to deal now with absolute want.

Catholic Notes.

——The Holy Father has sent 10,000 francs ($2,000) for the relief of the destitute in Ireland.

——The death is announced of the venerable Canon Oakley, at the age of seventy-eight. R. I. P.

——Mr. George W. Childs, editor and proprietor of the Philadelphia *Ledger*, has given $1,000 to the Irish Relief Fund.

——The following sums have been sent us for the suffering poor in Ireland: Benj. Brueder, $1; F. and E., $2; Catharine McCormick, $5.

——Rt. Rev. Bishop Marty, O. S. B., the recently named Vicar-Apostolic of Dakota Territory, was consecrated at St. Meinrad's Abbey, Ind., of which he was formerly abbot, on the 2d inst, the Feast of the Purification of the Blessed Virgin. We hear that he will make Bismarck, Dakota, his residence for the present.

——A well-known correspondent writing from Rome under date of the 16th of January, says that the rumors current in this country concerning new dioceses and episcopal appointments are entirely without foundation. "The appointment of Rt. Rev. Bishop Elder to Cincinnati is the only one that has been made up to the present date, no matter what rumors prevail to the contrary."

——RESIGNATION OF BISHOP DUFAL.—We learn that Rt. Rev. Dr. Dufal, C. S. C., Bishop of Delcon, i. p. i., and Coadjutor to Rt. Rev. Bishop Dubuis of Galveston, has resigned his charge on account of continued ill health, etc. The Holy See has accepted the resignation. Bishop Dufal was formerly Superior-General of the Congregation of the Holy Cross, and Vicar-Apostolic of Eastern Bengal.

——DEATHS OF CLERGYMEN.—The Catholics of South Adams, Mass., are deeply grieved over the loss of their devoted pastor, Rev. Father McCort, whose death occurred last week. *The Catholic Universe* reports the death of Rev. John F. Koehn, of Sherman, Ohio. "The deceased was a most worthy clergyman, and enjoyed the respect and confidence of all who knew him." R. I. P.

——RELIGIOUS RECEPTION.—On the Feast of the Purification of the Blessed Virgin the following postulants received the habit of the Congregation of the Holy Cross at Notre Dame: Messrs. Marie Verdan, Daniel P. Toomey, Francis Bœres, James Ernsker, Patrick Mattimore; James Sweeney (Bro. Cleophas), and George Boone (Bro. Clement). The ceremony was performed by the Rev. Master of Novices in the chapel of the Novitiate.

——THE MARQUIS OF BUTE, desirous to promote Catholic education, and as far as possible to put within the reach of Scottish Catholics the benefits of university teaching of the first order, has generously subsidised St. Benedict's College, Fort Augustus, with £500 a year, to enable it to secure the assistance of two professors from national universities, who will assist the present staff in teaching classics and the different branches of science.

——Mr. Philip A. Kemper, of Dayton, Ohio, has for sale at the low price of $4, postpaid, a fine collection of religious pictures, three hundred in number, called the "Miniature Religious Art Gallery." The subjects are to a great extent new, and differ from the pictures to which the Catholics of this country have become accustomed. Thus, for instance, there will be found among them a number of very fine and correct representations of prominent places in the Holy Land, such as Jerusalem, Bethlehem, Nazareth, Calvary, and other celebrated points sanctified by the footsteps of our Divine Lord.

—A NEW CATHOLIC PAPER.—A Catholic paper is now published at Copenhagen, the capital of Denmark. It contains, besides leading articles on religious questions, ecclesiastical news, news of the world, etc., reports of sermons and religious services. This paper, as well as many other good works, is liberally supported by a wealthy Catholic merchant of Regensburg, Germany, who has established a branch of his house at Copenhagen. So great is the influence and respectability of this worthy gentleman, that when the king celebrated his silver wedding, several years ago, he received an invitation to the royal table in his capacity of church trustee of the Catholic congregation. The missionary district of Denmark belongs to the diocese of Osnabruck, in Germany.

—MR. HENRY LASSERRE, the well-known author, and M. de Freycinet, now chief of the French Ministry, have been devoted friends since their boyhood. During the year 1863, Mr. Lasserre suffered from inflammation of the eyes. Having made known this affliction to his Protestant friend, he received the following advice: " I have passed through Lourdes and visited its famous Grotto, where I saw the most wonderful things. I would earnestly advise you to give the famous water a trial. If I were a believing Catholic, and should happen to be sick, I would not hesitate a moment to do so. Besides, I have a personal interest in this trial." Mr. Lasserre postponed the trial for several months, until M. Freycinet at last succeeded in persuading him to go to Lourdes—writing an autograph letter in behalf of his suffering friend to the priest at Lourdes. A complete cure was the result, which had such an effect upon the mind of Mr. de Freycinet, that he resolved to begin the study of Catholic theology, and spent several months in conference with the illustrious Dom Gueranger at Solesmes. Why the illustrious statesman did not become a Catholic is best known to himself.

—OUR LADY OF LOURDES AND ST. FRANCIS XAVIER.—A correspondent of our valuable contemporary the *Indo-European Correspondence*, writing from Chanderragore on the Feast of St. Francis Xavier, says: " In the month of July last, my little girl was attacked with a serious complaint which puzzled even the doctors, and was daily losing her strength, and all who saw her were of opinion that she would never rise from her bed; but a mother's heart does not soon lose hope. One morning when I was particularly sad and anxious, the child being worse than before, a kind friend, quite unasked, sent me a Rosary that had touched St. Francis Xavier's body, and I with great faith and confidence placed it near my poor sick child; and from that day, nay, from that hour, she seemed to revive, and I never had the same anxiety on her account again. This occurred on the 27th of August, and in less than a fortnight my beloved child was able to walk a little, and was well in a month. I must mention that an operation under chloroform of a very serious nature was performed on the child on the 16th of August, she being just three years of age. Throughout her illness I had given her the water of Lourdes, also to my boy who was dangerously ill with a severe attack of typhoid fever, and in both cases I consider their recovery miraculous. I may add that I gave the Rosary to another desponding mother whose child was in a dying state, and that the little fellow is in a fair way of recovery. You are at liberty to give my name to all enquirers. All praise and thanks to our good Mother, the Immaculate Lady of Lourdes, and to the glorious St. Francis Xavier."

—1400TH ANNIVERSARY OF SAINT BENEDICT.— On the 21st of March the Benedictine Order will celebrate the 1400th anniversary of the birth of its great founder, St. Benedict. Extensive preparations, we hear, are being made everywhere throughout the world for the worthy celebration of this great occasion, particularly at Monte Cassino, the cradle of the Order. " To describe the influence exercised by the spirit of St. Benedict," says the learned Dom Gueranger, " we should have to transcribe the annals of all the nations of the Western Church, from the 7th century down to our own time. Benedict is the Father of Europe. By his Benedictines, numerous as the stars of heaven and as the sands of the sea-shore, he rescued the last remnants of Roman vigor from the total annihilation threatened by the invasion of the barbarians; he presided over the establishment of the public and private laws of those nations which grew out of the ruins of the Roman Empire; he carried the Gospel and civilization into England, Germany, and the Northern countries, including Sclavonia; he taught agriculture; he put an end to slavery; and, to conclude, he saved the precious deposit of the arts and sciences from the tempest which would have swept them from the world, and would have left mankind a prey to a gloomy and fatal ignorance. . . . . An incredible number of saints, both men and women, who look up to Benedict as their Father, purify and sanctify the world which had not yet emerged from the state of semi-barbarism. A long series of Popes, who had once been novices in the Benedictine cloister, preside over the destinies of this new world, and form for it a new legislation, which, being based exclusively on the moral law, is to avert the threatening prevalence of brutal despotism. Bishops innumerable, trained in the school of Benedict consolidate this moral legislation in the provinces and cities over which they are appointed. The apostles of twenty barbarous nations confront their fierce and savage tribes, and, with the Gospel in one hand, and the " Rule" of their holy Father in the other, lead them into the fold of Christ. For many centuries the learned men, the Doctors of the Church, and the instructors of youth, belong almost exclusively, to the Order of this great Patriarch, who, by the labors of his children, pours forth on the people the purest beauty of light and truth. This choir of heroes in every virtue, of Popes, of Bishops, of Apostles, of holy Doctors, proclaiming themselves his disciples, and join with the universal Church in glorifying God, whose holiness and power have shone forth so brilliantly in the life and actions of St. Benedict. What a crown, what an aureola of glory for one saint to enjoy!"

Confraternity of the Immaculate Conception
(Or of Our Lady of Lourdes).

" We fly to thy patronage, O Holy Mother of God !"

REPORT FOR THE WEEK ENDING JANUARY 27TH. The following petitions have been presented: Recovery of health for 120 persons and 4 families,—change of life for 64 persons and 10 families,—conversion to the Faith for 416 persons and 334 families,—special graces for 9 priests, 10 religious, 5 clerical, students and 6 persons aspiring to the religious state,—temporal favors for 58 persons and 13 families,—spiritual favors for 103 persons and 14 families,—the spiritual and temporal welfare of 11 communities, 6 congregations, 8 schools, 2 sodalities, and 2 orphan asylums,—also 31 particular intentions, and 11 thanksgivings for favors received.

Specified Intentions: Success of several Sunday-schools,—a number of little children,—recovery of large sums of money almost hopelessly lost,—deliverance from terrible temptations, and preservation from misfortune and accidents,—perseverance of many converts living among Protestants,—resignation to God's holy will for persons bodily afflicted,—peace and good feeling between married people,—deliverance from great temptations, and preservation from insanity,—a young priest aspiring to the religious state,—resources, employments, success in business, examinations, etc.,—recovery of health for a person suffering also an interior trial,—the conversion of some fallen priests, the case of one being very lamentable.

FAVORS OBTAINED.

The Superior of a convent informs us that a boy afflicted with epilepsy, who some time ago was recommended to the prayers of the Confraternity, has had no symptoms of them since he began to use the water of Lourdes. The mother of the child sends her grateful thanks. Thanks are also returned for the cure of a cancer, of many years' standing, by the application of the miraculous water. An old friend reports the restoration to health, and a happy return to his religious duties of a gentleman previously recommended to the prayers of the members. A zealous missionary writes: "Thanks to Mary Immaculate for many graces due to her intercession; among others, the conversion of three infidels, and the abjuration of a Protestant." ... A poor widow gratefully acknowledges that a near relative who had sued her unjustly has lost the suit. Another lady ascribes assistance unexpectedly obtained by her brother-in-law to the prayers of the Confraternity.

OBITUARY.

The following deceased persons are recommended to the prayers of the Confraternity: Mrs. CATHARINE ENRIGHT, of Altoona, Pa., who died January 12th. Mrs. O'HARA, of Lonesdale, R. I., whose death occurred last October. Miss THERESA O'DWYER, of McGillivray, Ont., who was relieved from a long and painful illness by a holy death on the 13th ult. MARY A. MARA, of Cambridge, Mass., who departed this life on the 20th of December last. MARY SHEA, of the same place, deceased January 2d. SISTER THERESA (Kelly), a member of the Society of the Holy Child Jesus at Sharon Hill, Pa., who was called to her heavenly reward on the 21st ult. Miss DELIA FERNEY, of Boston, Mass., who breathed her last on the 15th of January. Mr. DAVID O'BRIEN, of Marlboro, Mass., whose death took place some months ago. SISTER MARY ANNETTE (Matthews), of the Visitation Convent at Baltimore, who departed for heaven on the 24th ult. Mr. P. O'GRADY, of Creston, Iowa, lately deceased. Mr. PETER PEARL, of Baltimore, Md.; ANNA M. LEIENDECKER; EUGENE TUPZ and JOHN HAGAN, all of St. Louis, Mo.; EDWARD COGAN, of Washington, D. C.; JAMES and ELIZABETH ROACH; JAMES C. and URSULA ROACH; also Dr. HENRY MCDERMOTT, and Mrs. MARY BRADLEY, of Cannellsburg, Ind.; Mr. CHARLES MALLY, of Altoona, Pa ; JENNIE COLLINS, CATHARINE LANIGAN, MICHAEL H. GLEASON, Hon. T. FITZPATRICK, P. SINNOTT and T. LAPPIN, of South Boston, Mass.; J. BUHAN, of Cambridge, Mass.; all of whom died some time ago. And a number of others, whose names have not been given.

Requiescant in pace.

A. GRANGER, C. S. C., Director.

Youths' Department.

[For the "Ave Maria."]
Morning Thoughts.

BY LADY GEORGIANA FULLERTON.

WAKE up, my soul! thy first quick glance
Direct to God, and say:
"Thanks be to Thee, my God and King,
For Thy gift of this day."
In meek submissive love I kneel
And humbly kiss the ground,
Then to the nearest altar turn
With homage most profound
Upon my brow, and lips, and heart
The sacred Sign I make.
And the bright drops of cleansing dew
Blest by the Church, I take,
To Thine and Thy dear Mother's Heart
My worthless heart I give.
And in close union with them pray
Throughout the day to live.

[From the *Morning Star* and *Catholic Messenger*.]
An Episode of the Reign of Terror.

CHAPTER I.

DURING the *Reign of Terror* in France, the victims of the tribunals of the revolution were numbered by thousands. Those who were not put to death at the guillotine were condemned to an exile, where the intense suffering they were compelled to undergo ruined the most robust constitutions. With the advent of this new era of persecution, the majority of those who were condemned, exhibited all the heroic constancy of the early Christians, and thus rendered themselves worthy to suffer for their faith and for their king. While the blood of the martyrs was flowing in streams in the capital, many cities in the provinces endeavored to accumulate horrors sufficient to surpass in their intensity the massacres at the Abbaye. Lyons had its fusillades, and the drownings of the Loire have left a ghastly memory.

Among those condemned to deportation was the Abbé de Gervandun. This worthy priest was beloved by all, but more especially by the poor whom his charity had assisted. Knowing how highly he was esteemed, the tribunal of the infamous Carrier, at Nantes, did not dare to condemn him to death, fearing such action on their part would infuriate the populace and endanger their own lives. They therefore sentenced him to exile. On hearing the sentence, the good Father thanked God, and blessed his judges.

He was led back to prison and cast into a narrow cell; and being fatigued, notwithstanding his uncomfortable quarters he was soon enjoying a sweet sleep, a blessing always granted to those whose consciences are at rest. From this sleep he was suddenly awakened by loud and discordant sounds, accompanied by the most horrible curses and blasphemies.

Guards and jailors were running to and fro, the fear to which they were a prey being betrayed by their own voices. The Abbé Gervandun, uneasy as to the results of this nocturnal scene, knocked at the door of his cell.

"What is the cause of all this commotion?" asked the priest of his jailor, when he opened it.

The man, who was naturally of a kind disposition, shrugged his shoulders, and did not immediately reply. Fear had caused him to accept his present position, but while fulfilling its duties he treated kindly those under his charge.

"Rev. Father," he answered, respectfully—for his colleagues were too far off to hear his words, "it is nothing worthy of your attention."

"Still, you seem to be in great trouble?"

"It's but a portion of my business. We have here many who do not regard the guillotine in the same light as do you and the other priests. Two miserable wretches, who have stolen, pillaged, murdered, burned houses, and committed numerous other crimes, have been condemned to death. They are now no longer men, but wild beasts; they yell frightfully, and threaten to kill the first one among us that enters their cell; they will execute their threat, for despair has given them new strength; and they have broken their chains, and are now taking up the stones from the floor of their cell. The public executioner, who has just arrived, knows not how he will discharge his office. This time the condemned may kill the executioner.

"Unfortunate men!" muttered the priest.

He reflected a moment, then asked the jailor: "Do you think there is danger for the first one that enters their cell?"

"Yes, Rev. Father, there is danger of death."

"My friend," said the priest, "you have a family to support; the public executioners but obey the orders that are given them, but I am condemned to a slow death. If I fall, God will call me to Himself. Open for me the door of the dungeon that contains these men; I am sure I will succeed not only in calming them, but also in inducing them to accept their lot with entire resignation."

"You wish to attempt an impossibility, Rev. Father."

"Nothing is impossible in the name of the cross!"

"If those wretches were to murder you?"

"My duty is to endeavor to touch their obdurate hearts."

"I would consider myself responsible for what might befall you."

"If you refuse me you will be responsible for their damnation."

The jailor at these words took off his cap respectfully, and, making a low bow, said:

"Pass on, Rev. Father."

CHAPTER II.

Jomard, the jailor, was right in comparing the two condemned men to wild beasts. On the point of paying with their lives their debt to human society for the crimes they had committed, the love of life seized them with a brutal force. They could not bear the idea of thus suddenly ending their career, marked first by debauchery and then by crime.

Before falling into the hands of the executioner, they wished to revenge themselves on some one for the decree of the court, and, assisted by a prodigious strength, they turned everything they could lay their hands upon into weapons. Standing in a corner of their dungeon, with a mass of stones and other missiles heaped up before them, they stood ready to throw them at the head of any one that would approach them. The presence of any man whatever could not but exasperate these wretches; but the sight of a priest entering their cell excited an unspeakable wrath in their bosoms. When the priest entered the cell, they both advanced towards him with threatening gestures. The old priest waited for their approach with his arms crossed on his breast.

"What do you desire to do to me, my friends?" he asked kindly.

"What do we want to do?" replied the younger of the two, with a frightful oath; "we want to drive you out of this dungeon, where you have not been called."

"I do not come as a priest."

"For what reason, then?"

"I am condemned like you," he replied.

For the first time the murderers perceived that his hands were manacled; then the elder prisoner ran to the darkest corner of the cell, and returned with a file.

"We will now be three to defend ourselves," said he; "I will file away your handcuffs."

"It is not necessary," replied the priest; "I accept the decree of Providence with resignation. My life is in God's hands; He will do with me what He pleases."

"God!" replied Mark Angu, the younger prisoner; "He has long ceased troubling Himself about us. John Roulier, my partner, and myself, have committed so many crimes that we cannot hope for any mercy from His hands."

"You are mistaken," answered the priest; "whatever may be the conduct of men created after His image, however corrupted they may become by their passions, they can never wipe from their forehead the sign of children of Heaven; nor can they ever tear themselves entirely asunder from their Creator! Poor stray sheep, you thought yourselves stronger because you had become more impious! But now true courage consists in true repentance, in undergoing firmly the punishment you have but too well merited, and hoping for mercy from God's goodness."

Mark Angu let fall the file he held in his clenched fist.

"You come to tell us something terrible," he muttered, in a low voice; "we fear death. Think only of that awful machine which chops off a fellow in a moment, and makes of him but two bloody pieces!"

"Did not those you murdered also dread the death you inflicted upon them?"

The two men bowed their heads.

"Listen," said the priest, taking hold of the hand of Mark: "nothing can save you from paying the penalty of your crimes with your lives; guards and soldiers have been sent here to overpower you—more will be sent, if necessary, and you must yield at last. Bruised, wounded, half dead, you will be dragged to that horrid machine, the very name of which makes you shudder, and your terror will only increase your torments. What should you do before what is inevitable? Accept it. However, if there was a question only of your yielding to the representatives of the law that strikes you, I could comprehend your enraged struggle, your hopeless resistance; but your resistance will only serve to lose your souls beyond hope, without saving your lives. Listen to a friend, a father, to a prisoner condemned like yourselves, to a man who, having spent his whole life in relieving the distress of his fellow-men, is now placed on a level with those who have defiled their lives in the most atrocious manner. Death cannot terrify us thus, for death is for us a return to God, our Creator; the exchange of a miserable existence for a life of endless happiness. Had I spoken in this manner to you when you were free, and masters of your own lives, you would have repulsed me, but now the world you regret is powerless to free you; the threshold of this prison cannot be crossed by your friends, nor can your former accomplices assist you. You are alone in this dungeon, alone with me, that whole life love you, who am the last being that has any right to speak to you of hope when the executioner is waiting for you."

Angu hung his head, and sat down on the heap of ruins in the corner of the cell. Astonishment succeeded his anger; he regretted feeling troubled at the words of the priest, but he was no longer able to withdraw himself from their influence.

"Are you going to allow yourself to be moved?" rudely asked his companion. "A priest must tell us such things,—that's his trade; but people like ourselves understand the weight of words. When we yield to authority, the guillotine will only be the nearer. Old John Roulier will never let himself be caught by empty words."

"Were those merely empty words, those prayers you learned at the knees of your mother, when every night she made you address the Blessed Virgin Mary: *Pray for us sinners, now, and at the hour of our death?*"

"I was but a mere child then," muttered John Roulier.

"Man remains always the child of his heavenly Father, even if his mother is dead—that mother who taught him to pray and to believe."

"Say, shut up, there! Thunder and lightning, shut up!" cried Roulier, raising an enormous stone, as if to crush the skull of Abbé de Gervandun.

But as the priest did not move, Mark Angu jumped at his partner, and seized his wrist with such force that the stone fell heavily to the floor.

"What harm has this man done you?" demanded Mark.

"Why does he speak to me of my mother?"

"Our mothers," repeated Mark, "happily for them, they are dead. God alone knows how much mine loved me, and how shamefully I have repaid her affection!"

"You are sorry for it?" asked the priest.

"Yes," replied Mark. "She did not deserve so much sorrow."

"And you?" asked the priest, addressing Roulier.

"I have forbidden you to pronounce her name, under pain of death! Do you hear, under pain of death!"

The priest continued:

"I am condemned, and I accept my condemnation. For me, death has no bitterness. I wish I could get you to look upon it as the end of all suffering and the beginning of a new life, to which all those who repent of their faults can lay claim. You are moved at the remembrance of your mother. So much the better; you are already near to being moved at the name of God, your Father! He created you, He died for you: He, who was innocence itself, instead of fearing death went to meet it, and underwent the death of the cross to redeem your soul from damnation. He is waiting for you; He is calling you; He stretches out His arms to receive you, now, at this terrible and supreme hour! Do not thrust Him back, for He is a Father to you; do not put Him away from you, for He is the Divine Martyr expiating your crimes on the wood of the cross!"

The two men stood listening and motionless. Mark, his face hidden in his hands, felt his soul melting in repentance. John Roulier still resisted. The Abbé de Gervandun, drawing a crucifix from his bosom, came to kneel near Mark.

"Behold! your Master and your God," said he. "His arms, nailed to that infamous wood, cannot repel you. Cast yourself into His half-open Heart! You weep, you regret the wanderings of your life! One more effort, yes, only one more! Confess to me the crimes that have defiled your life. Your judges know them; I, your brother, know them not, but must hear them in order to pardon them."

Moved by the remembrance of his mother, reassured by the words of the priest, Mark commenced the terrible recital of his life. Then, in the midst of his sobs, as he heard the priest pronouncing over his head the words of absolution, a complete change took place in his whole being. He cast himself into the arms of the priest, and spoke to him of his repentance and gratitude with such a glee, that, conquered by this sight, John Roulier, mastering his rebellious nature, also cast himself into the arms of divine mercy with so great fervor that it drew tears from the eyes of the priest. An hour later, this dungeon, which had so lately resounded with blasphemies and threats, was filled with the voice of prayer from repentant sinners, imploring mercy from the divine goodness.

To encourage these unfortunate men, the priest recalled to their minds the parable of the prodigal son, and the history of the penitent thief. He assured them of God's forgiveness, caused heavenly hopes to revive in them, and instilled into their hearts some little earnest love for God, who was about to receive them into His mercy. At the hour appointed for the execution, the guards and soldiers approached the cell, dreading the bloody drama which they feared would follow the attempt to lead them out of their dungeon. The priest himself opened the door, and came out, supporting the two criminals, who, with calmness and submission, awaited the course of the law.

They permitted the executioner to bind them; implored for the last time the priest's blessing, and after having promised him to die as Christians, walked peacefully to the place where stood the dreaded guillotine.

The crowd of people, whose curiosity had been excited by the hope of witnessing a most desperate resistance, saw the two criminals kneeling on the highest step of the scaffold, repeating the words they had learned from their mothers; "*Holy Mary, Mother of God, pray for us sinners, now, and at the of our death. Amen.*"

St. Dorothy's Victory.

T. DOROTHY, the holy virgin of Cesarea in Cappadocia, was apprehended by Apricius, the governor of that province, on account of her professing the Faith of Christ. She was put under the care of her two sisters, Chrysta and Callista, who had apostatized from the Faith, that they might shake her constancy. But she brought them back to the Faith, for which they were afterwards burnt to death in a cauldron. The governor ordered Dorothy to be hoisted on the rack, and she said to him, as she lay upon it: "Never in my whole life have I felt such joy as I do to-day." Then the governor ordered the executioners to burn her sides with lighted lamps, and beat her for a long time on the face, and finally behead her.

Whilst she was being led to the place of execution, she said: "I give Thee thanks, O Thou, the lover of our souls, that Thou callest me to Thy Paradise!" Theophilus, one of the governor's officers, hearing her words, laughed, and said to her: "Hear me, bride of Christ! I'll ask thee to send me some apples and roses from this paradise of thy Spouse." Dorothy replied: "Well, and so I will." Before she was beheaded, she was allowed a moment for prayer, when lo! a beautiful child came to her, bringing with him in a napkin three apples and three roses. She said to him: "Take them, I pray thee, to Theophilus." Then the executioner struck off her head with his sword, and her soul fled to Christ.

Whilst Theophilus was jocosely telling his fellows the promise made him by Dorothy, he sees a boy bringing him, in a napkin, three fine apples and three most lovely roses, who, as he gave them, said: "Lo! the most holy virgin Dorothy sends thee, as she promised, these gifts from the Paradise of her Spouse." Theophilus was beside himself with surprise, for it was February; but, taking the gifts, he exclaimed: "Christ is truly God!" He openly professed the Christian Faith, and suffered a most painful martyrdom.

FREDERICK THE GREAT was very fond of arguing; but as he was known to end it sometimes by collaring his antagonist and kicking his shins, few of his guests were disposed to enter the arena with him. One day, when he was more than usually disposed for an argument, he asked one of his suite why he did not venture to give his opinion on some particular question.

"It is imprudent, your majesty," was the reply "to express an opinion before a sovereign who has such strong convictions, and who wears such thick boots."

THE AVE MARIA.

A Journal devoted to the Honor of the Blessed Virgin.

HENCEFORTH ALL GENERATIONS SHALL CALL ME BLESSED.—St. Luke, I, 48.

VOL. XVI.   NOTRE DAME, INDIANA, FEBRUARY 14, 1880.   No. 7.

[Copyright: Rev. D. E. Hudson, C. S. C.]

[For the "Ave Maria."]

St. Ignatius, Bishop and Martyr.

"DENY the Name of Christ," the tyrant said.
"That Name," the saintly Bishop made reply.
"My mouth is wholly powerless to deny."
Then came the threat: "They shall cut off thy head.
Thou canst not speak that Name if thou art dead."
"Yea," the brave answer rang exultingly,
"But it inscribed upon my heart doth lie.
I cannot cease to invoke that Name most dread."
Their threat fulfilled, they seek the martyr's heart;
  There, stamped as by a monarch's signet ring,
  In letters all of gold the Name they see.
O happy Saint! thy praise we gladly sing;
Well hast thou played the martyr's valiant part;
And Christ, thy Lord, thy Love, we praise in thee.

Shrine of Our Lady of Atocha, Madrid.

BY "E."

THE sanctuary containing the statue of the Virgin of Atocha is one of the most celebrated in Spain, ranking as third in order, being preceded only by those of Zaragossa and of Guadalupe. Besides the sonnets of Lope de Vega, Pereda, Marieta Quintana, Hurtado de Mendoza, and later, Father Villefanne, S. J., have written volumes upon it and upon the miracles wrought at the shrine. These various authors, whilst uniting in avowing the impossibility of fixing with certainty the epoch at which this devotion originated, agree in dating it from the remotest antiquity. Some conjecture it to have begun in 431, at the time of the celebrated Council of Ephesus, which condemned the impiety of Nestorius, Patriarch of Constantinople, who presumed to refuse to our Blessed Lady the title of Mother of God; the Spaniards of Madrid, eager to show their Catholicity, their tender devotion to Mary, and their obedience to the decrees of the Council, then carved this statue, graving on the wood whereof it was formed the Greek word *Theotokos*, which signifies "Mother of God"; whence, say the ancient manuscripts and monuments, this miraculous statue is styled *Virgo Theotoca*. However, the greater number of Spanish writers look on this statue as still more ancient, deeming it the work of St. Luke, or at least claiming that its coloring was originally due to the brush of that holy Evangelist, who, to excite the faithful to devotion towards the Mother of God, has left many pictures of the Blessed Virgin, which are still venerated in different lands. Others, again, hold that it was from St. Peter, the Apostle—who, according to some writers, visited Spain,—or from some of his disciples, that ancient Iberia received this precious gift. A small chapel was built to receive it in the quarter of Madrid * since known as *La Vega*, where it was held in popular veneration, and favored by Heaven with many striking miracles.

An ancient tradition, quoted by the Jesuit Guppemberg, in his *Atlante Mariano*, bases the devotion of the Spaniards towards the Sanctuary of Our Lady of Atocha upon the fact that the Moors, having dominated Spain, destroying entire cities, and threatening to extirpate, together with the Christians, even the very name of Christ, Ramiro I, King of Leon (843), was left with a few men-at-arms and two virgin daughters. Death seemed inevitable, and to save the honor of his daughters he led them to the Church of St. Mary of Atocha, where he persuaded them to suffer him to behead them rather than to remain exposed to the outrages of the enemy. The heads being severed, he placed them upon the altar, before the statue of the Virgin, and with his bloody sword in hand rushed furiously against

---

* Madrid occupies the site of the ancient Mantua Carpetanorum, called Majoritium in the Middle Ages. Its importance began only when made capital of Spain by Philip II (1563). Formerly it was a mere market-town, or straggling village, the property, in their own right, of the Archbishops of Toledo, primates of Spain.

the Moors, intending to sell his life dearly. But God ordained otherwise, and when, after a great slaughter and utter defeat of the Saracens, Ramiro re-entered the church to pray before the shrine, he perceived to his astonishment his daughters resuscitated, and the heads, thanks to the protection of our Blessed Lady, miraculously recollocated to the bodies.

St. Ildefonsus was such an illustrious client of the Mother of God that with her own hands, it is stated, she presented him with a robe of dazzling whiteness, in recompense of the zeal wherewith, when Archbishop of Toledo, in 657, he combatted the heresy which attacked her privilege of perpetual virginity, writing in defence thereof his famous work *De Virginitate Mariæ*, which, as the legend tells us, she held in her hand when she appeared to her faithful servant. This charming legend of the sacred *Casulla*, so popular in Toledo, and consecrated by the brush of Murillo, Rubens, and other celebrated artists, deserves a passing notice. St. Ildefonsus propagated most zealously the Feast of the Expectation of the Blessed Virgin, established for the 18th of December, by the Tenth Council of Toledo, held in 654, in the time of King Reicheswind and of St. Eugenius III, Bishop of that See.* Before Matines of that day, Ildefonsus rose at his usual hour to sing the praises of Mary, and proceeded to the Cathedral, followed by his clergy and attendants, bearing numerous waxen torches. Arrived before the door, the suite took to flight, terrified by the brilliant light issuing from the church. Ildefonsus entered, and advanced towards the altar, accompanied only by a deacon and subdeacon. As he prostrated himself, he perceived the Blessed Virgin Mary seated upon his ivory episcopal throne, surrounded by a troop of virgins singing songs of paradise, and holding in one hand his book, *De Virginitate Mariæ*, and in the other a beautiful white cassock, or chasuble, of heavenly tissue. She beckoned him to approach, and said: "You are my chaplain and faithful notary; receive this chasuble, which my Son sends you from His treasury." She then, with her own hands, adjusted the robe about him, ordering him to wear it only on the festivals celebrated in her honor. After the death of the Saint the ivory throne remained unoccupied, and the celestial garment unworn, until the advent of an unfortunate Archbishop named Lixisberto, who died in consequence of his timerity in seating himself on the former, and endeavoring to assume the latter. So true is this apparition that a Council of Toledo, held under Bishop Gilles, ordained that to perpetuate the memory thereof, a feast should be yearly celebrated, with office of double rite, which is still observed (Jan. 21) under the title of "Descent of the Blessed Virgin and her apparition to St. Ildefonsus"; and, remarkable to say, this same festival is solemnized in Egypt amongst the Copts.*

But to return. St. Ildefonsus had so tender a devotion towards Our Lady of Atocha that he frequently visited the shrine, offered wax and oil for the service of the sanctuary, and in a letter, still said to be preserved in the archives of Toledo, he invites a priest of Zaragossa to come to venerate the miraculous image. After his death, the faithful continued to honor the antique statue and to obtain numberless graces and favors at the shrine, until that fatal epoch when the Lord, irritated against the people of Spain, suffered them to fall under the domination of the Moors of Africa, who, crossing the Straits of Gibraltar under their renowned Generals Muza, Ben Nosiir and Taric Ben Zeyad, defeated and slew Roderich, the last of the Gothic kings of Spain, in the battle of Guadalete, July 26th, 711. This battle lasted three days, and is generally known as the battle of Xeres.† These barbarians, having rendered themselves masters of Toledo, advanced towards Madrid, which must, even then have been a stronghold, since it is stated that the inhabitants only yielded up the place under condition of retaining some churches wherein they could exercise full liberty of worship. These churches were, within Madrid, that of St. Martin; and without the city, the Chapels of the Holy Cross and of Our Lady of Atocha.

Amid the devotees of Our Lady of Atocha was a noble named Garcia Ramirez, who, fearless of the Moors, frequently quitted the city to pray before the statue; and in order to do so more freely, he, with his wife and two daughters, took up his abode in the village of Ribas, upon the banks of the Xarama, whence he could daily visit the beloved shrine, to weep over the miserable state of Spain and to pray for her deliverance. Four years had passed on in this way, when one day, on entering the sanctuary, he perceived that the statue was no

---

* St. Ildefonsus, successor to Eugenius, confirmed this decree, ordering this Feast to be styled the "Expectation of Our Lady," since it is celebrated eight days prior to Christmas. It has become very popular in all the churches of Spain, and has likewise received the title of "Our Lady of the O," because on that day, at First Vespers, begins the chant of the celebrated anthems known as the "O."

* This precious *Casulla* was carefully preserved for fifty-seven years in Toledo, and thence removed into the Asturias, to save it from the hands of the Moors. Upon the completion of the Church of San Salvador, at Oviedo, Alfonso the Chaste (802) had the *Santa Casulla* solemnly conveyed to that edifice, wherein it is kept to this day.

† This date has been much disputed, being frequently set down as November, 714; Mariana, Ferreras, and other historians, having been led into error by Don Rui Ximenes, Archbishop of Toledo, 1240, in his "History of the Arabs," the first intelligible account Europe received of that Eastern people. It is in Latin, and does not extend beyond the year of the Hegira 539, or A. D. 1140. This learned writer has not correctly computed the years of the Christian era as compared with the lunar years of the Arabian Calendar—hence the confusion, so oft verified.

longer in its niche. Unable to determine whether the Moors had lain sacrilegious hands upon the sacred image, or God, in His anger, had chosen to deprive the people of their Consolatrix, or if Mary herself had departed, to seek elsewhere more devout servants, Garcia began a most persevering search for the lost treasure, and after some time, suddenly discovered the statue in the midst of a thicket, upon one of those hills which overlook La Vega de Manzanares, towards the north, on the very spot where it is now publicly honored by the faithful. This translation was piously believed to have been miraculous.

Garcia, overjoyed, leaped from his horse, knelt to thank the Queen of Heaven, and, in obedience to an interior voice, resolved to build a chapel over the place wherein Mary so evidently desired to be venerated. His friends and fellow-Christians in the vicinity gladly entered into the project, and immediately began the foundation of a chapel, which their poverty and the unhappy state of the country alone hindered them from rendering truly magnificent. The suspicions of the Moors were, however, aroused on perceiving the Christians at work upon the new edifice or chapel, which was in their eyes but a pretext to cover the erection of a citadel to serve as a stronghold against their tyranny; they forthwith took up arms, resolved to disperse the workmen and to destroy every vestige of the supposed fortress. Garcia, full of confidence in God and in the Blessed Virgin, at the head of a handful of brave and resolute men rushed upon the surging crowd of Moslems who surrounded them, fought against them, overpowered, routed and completely annihilated them (720). Profiting by his victory, like a skilful captain, he advanced towards Madrid with his little troop, which was gradually increased by those whom the report of his triumph brought under his standard, took possession of that city, placed a garrison therein and enjoyed a conquest for several years. Finally, yielding to superior force, he agreed to cede Madrid to the Moors, under the promise that he and his companions should have free liberty to do public homage to Our Lady of Atocha in her sanctuary—a condition faithfully observed throughout the whole time of the Arab domination in Spain.

This devotion was kept up, like fire smouldering beneath the ashes, so long as the Moorish tyranny weighed over Spain, only bursting forth into full blaze when Alfonso VI, having conquered Toledo (1065), took and rebuilt Madrid and delivered the kingdom of Castile. A picture still to be seen in the Church of Our Lady of Atocha testifies to the devotion of this prince; it bears the inscription: "The Kings of Castile have ever been most devout to this holy image. Don Alfonso VI, who took Madrid from the Moors, to prove his piety paid homage to the Chapel of Our Lady of Atocha of the royal standard borne before him on the day of his victory, as also of that banner which he took from the enemy." These glorious trophies are still suspended in the chapel; the royal standard bears the image of Our Lady ornamented with castles and lions (Castile and Leon).

The Church of Our Lady of Atocha was long served by chaplains, who celebrated the Divine Office with due piety and edification, until Juan, third Archbishop of Toledo, after the expulsion of the Moors, eager to enhance the glory of Our Lady of Atocha, gave over that church and all its belongings to the Prior and Canons Regular of St. Leocadia de la Vega, of Toledo. The latter preserved it until 1523, when Hurtado de Mendoza, confessor to Charles V, founded the adjoining Convent of Atocha, which, with the church, he gave to the Dominicans, who still serve it. This Convent and Church of Our Lady of Atocha is a quarter of a mile from the city, joining the park of the Palace de Buen-Retiro. The church itself is in nowise remarkable, and Murray pronounces it in very bad taste. Above the massive altar are hung the banners of Spanish victories, and there lie buried Custaños, created Duke of Bailen, for his victory over the French at that place on the 18th of July, 1808; Palafox, who defended Zaragossa in the same year; Navaey; General Concha, Marquis del Duero, and General Prim, whose inlaid metal tomb is well worthy of attention. The ceilings were painted by Luca Giordano. The Chapel of the Blessed Virgin was formerly adorned with extraordinary magnificence. Somewhat sombre in structure, it was lighted by more than one hundred massive lamps of gold or silver, which burned day and night, and was constantly thronged with devout worshippers.

On the high altar of the church is the celebrated and much revered statue of Our Lady of Atocha, the Patroness of Madrid. It is carved in some incorruptible wood, the species whereof cannot be determined, as it is black and old; but notwithstanding its great antiquity, it has suffered no deterioration. It is about 3 ft. 3 in. in height, but when vested in long flowing garments which cover the pedestal of ivory and ebony upon which it rests, it appears still taller. Our Blessed Lady is seated on a throne carved from the same wood; her attitude breathes majesty and authority. She holds the Divine Infant somewhat to her left, and with her right hand offers Him a book and some fruit. Both Virgin and Child are of a dark brown tint, bordering upon black; time has despoiled them of their lustre and, to a certain extent, of their coloring. Skilful artists have vainly endeavored to reproduce this holy image upon canvas. The entire face, somewhat oblong, is pleasing and perfect as to proportions, with eyes large, full, serene, and modest, commanding at once love and respect; well arched eyebrows, aquiline nose, open forehead, small mouth, rosy cheeks, and features to correspond. The head, surrounded by an aureola with dazzling rays, wears a crown one inch high, of the same wood as the rest of the statue, and the feet rest upon a stool four inches in height, which is hidden beneath the mantle. Her vesture, of a dull red, is bordered with a sort of cord of precious stones; her mantle is apparently of gold tissue, powdered with *fleurs-de-lis*, some brilliant, some dingy, reflecting variegated tints of yellow and azure. The throne or armchair wherein the Virgin sits is covered with golden flowers; to the left side are certain ancient characters to which are given diverse interpretations, some deeming them to form the Greek word *Theotocos*—Mother of God,—whence is derived *Atocha*, which they view as a simple abbreviation of this glorious name bestowed upon Mary from the first centuries of Christianity. Other authors hold that their characters, though similar to Greek letters, do not clearly express the word supposed, and, avowing their ignorance as to the true sense of the inscription, think it more probable that the word "Atocha" is taken from the place where the statue was primarily honored, or at least where it was found by the pious Garcia, when it had been transported from its original sanctuary. This spot was thickly covered with furze or gorse —in Spanish, *atochar*—hence no doubt comes this popular appellation of the Virgin. Salazar de Mendoza supports this idea, citing in proof thereof a manuscript of the time of St. Ildefonsus, which he himself had read, wherein this statue is styled "the Virgin of the Atochar" (spot covered with gorse). Father Villafanne considers as better founded a third opinion, which declares "Atocha" to be merely an abbreviation of *Antiochia*, as if St. Peter, or some one of his disciples, had brought this statue from Antioch into Spain.

Before the era of political troubles which despoiled so many sanctuaries, the shrine of Our Lady of Atocha was possessed of immense wealth in gold, jewels, laces, and precious stuffs,—kings, princes and grandees of Spain having lavished upon it precious stones, jewels, and rich ornaments, as well to satisfy their devotion as to testify their gratitude for the countless favors obtained there. It had ladies in waiting, and a mistress of the robes, who is always one of the noblest and richest ladies of Madrid. Saint Simon speaks of the Duchess of Alba as filling that office in his time, adding that the position was eagerly sought after, notwithstanding the annual outlay attending it—over 50,000 livres being required to furnish laces, stuffs, etc. Neither trouble nor sacrifices are spared to adorn the statue in the most gorgeous style. It is frequently clad as a widow, but on great solemnities it is magnificently attired and covered with jewels as a queen.

So deeply rooted is this devotion towards Our Lady of Atocha in Madrid, as well as throughout Castile, that before this shrine are offered all prayers, vows, and public thanksgivings for all the necessities and prosperity of the kingdom, as well as on all occasions of illness or recovery of the king. She is the special Protectress of the royal family, and from time immemorial the sovereigns of Spain have never undertaken a journey without going previously to take leave of Our Lady of Atocha, and on their return never failed to visit that sanctuary to thank the Queen of Heaven for the protection accorded them, and to solicit the continuance of her favor. Alfonso VI, as we have seen, laid his banners at her feet; Charles V, Philip II, Philip III, Philip IV, Charles II, Philip V, Charles IV and Ferdinand VII were distinguished for their affection towards her. The latter when kidnapped by Sarary, Duke of Rovigo, in 1808, before starting for Bayonne, took from his breast the grand cordon of Charles III, from which was suspended a cross of large diamonds, which, together with his collar of the Golden Fleece, he hung upon her neck. During the war of independence the church and convent were destroyed, and the statue transferred to the Church of St. Thomas. Upon his restoration, Ferdinand VII ceded to the Dominicans whatever domains and indentures he possessed in Castile, and gave them all his jewels, and crosses adorned with precious stones, bidding them sell them, and with the proceeds rebuild the ruined church and monastery, which order was carried out with religious exactitude, under the direction of the architect Isidor Velasquez. Here the members of the royal family are married, as we have lately witnessed in the two successive nuptials of Alfonso XII; and when a queen is the bride, her wedding-dress is a perquisite of the shrine, as was observed in the case of Isabella II, mother of the reigning monarch. She was on her way to visit the shrine, February 6th, 1852, when she was stabbed by Martino Merino; and on the 18th of the same month, scarcely recovered from her wound, she again repaired thither to give thanks for her preservation, and to offer at the sanctuary the sumptuous robe she wore on the day of the attempt; the mantle with the dagger breach in it, and spotted with blood, together with the precious jewels and diadem of magnificent diamonds, was placed upon the head of the statue. Prince Amadeus of Savoy, when elected King of Spain, upon arriving in Madrid, January 2d, 1871, repaired first to the sanctuary of Our Lady of Atocha, and, an hour later, entered the royal palace whence the Revolution had exiled Queen Isabella II. Grave comments are made relative to the course pursued by Alfonso XII, who, after the late attempt upon his life by Otero Gonzales, went *first* to the theatre, and only the day following visited the shrine of Our Lady of Atocha to return thanks for his most providential escape from the ball of the assassin. This is declared the first instance of the kind to be met with in Spanish history.

The King of Spain goes in great state to attend the "*Salve*," or Benediction of the Blessed Sacrament, given in that church every Saturday at 4 p. m. This custom was observed as far back as 1700, and the Duke of Saint Simon devotes entire pages of his piquant "Memoirs" to descriptions of the pompous ceremonial observed by Philip V and his court in their weekly visit to Our Lady of Atocha, for the "*Salve*."

St. Isidore the Laborer, Patron of the city of Madrid, and of husbandmen, was, during his life, a most zealous devotee at this shrine, before which he was wont to pass long hours in fervent prayer. Wishing, in some measure, to mark his veneration for this sanctuary even after his death (May 15th, 1170,) he ordained that the Confraternity established by him in the parish of St. Andrew should go yearly in procession to do homage to Our Lady of Atocha, which pious custom was annually observed until the Moors were driven from Spain by Alfonso VIII, of Castile (1212). His wife, Maria Toriebia, later canonized under the title of *Santa Maria de la Cabeza*, shared his devotion and accompanied him in his daily visits to the Virgin of Atocha; this Saint is so styled because her head, placed in a separate reliquary, is frequently borne in procession to obtain from Heaven the blessing of rain, *cabeza* signifying head. Her remains were first interred in the little hermitage of Caraquiz, and in 1615, removed to Torrelaguna, where they were honored by all Spain with processions and pilgrimages; those of St. Isidore were buried in the Church of St. Andrew, and exposed to public veneration on May 10th. Actually, the relics of the holy husbandman and his *santa esposa* repose in the Church of St. Isidor el Real, in the Calle de Toledo, Madrid, built in 1651; his statue is by Perejra. He was canonized by Pope Gregory XV, March 22d, 1622, together with St. Ignatius of Loyola, St. Francis Xavier, St. Theresa and St. Philip Neri, at the special request of Philip III, of Spain, miraculously restored to health through contact with the body of the holy confessor, Nov. 16th, 1619.

NOTHING can be more necessary or more profitable than often to impress on souls the necessity of prayer.—*F. Mueller.*

THE title of Mother of God exalts the Blessed Virgin in dignity beyond the highest seraph in heaven, above any creature that God has created or ever will create.

'Beth's Promise.

BY MRS. ANNA HANSON DORSEY.

CHAPTER VII.
AUNT 'BETH.

THE "Cumberland" was at anchor in the harbor of Nice when the order came for her to return to the United States. Her cruise was over. The news was hailed with satisfaction by her officers, and with hearty cheers by the crew. That evening, when the band sent the tender strains of "Home! sweet home!" floating out upon the air, there were but few hearts on the old ship that did not turn with loving thoughts to the dear ones parted from so long ago. Nor is it strange that a regret on leaving those fair southern lands, now grown familiar in their beauty, in their treasures of art, of song, and of story, should have mingled with their joyous dreams of home and native land.

The wives of two of the officers of the "Cumberland" had joined them at Nice, soon after the arrival of the ship at that station, and had rented a furnished house in the city. Here Lieut. Morley and his wife, after leaving Naples, had taken delightful apartments, where they enjoyed the charms of a private establishment and the novelty of house-keeping combined. This was a pleasant arrangement for the ladies, especially while the ship was off on her summer cruise in the northern seas; and they formed a pleasant and friendly *coterie*, which, fortunately for their own comfort, remained unbroken until the moment of separation came. It was decided that they were to go home *via* Paris by the Havre steamer, and as Lieut. Morley was detached to take some official despatches, which Admiral Irwin—not knowing how his ship might be detained by storms or otherwise—wished to reach the Navy Department at Washington with as little delay as possible, the ladies were placed under his care until they should reach New York, where their friends would meet them. They had barely time to pack their trunks and be off in season to catch the steamer; fortunately for them—they had been in daily expectation of orders for several weeks—their collections of bric-a-brac and other purchases had been safely stowed in the hold of the "Cumberland" for some days, and their minds were relieved of all anxiety concerning them. At that time, officers of the navy were permitted to bring such matters home on the vessels to which they were attached, free of duty, which enabled them to procure many rich, useful, and beautiful things in foreign ports, at prices which there they could well afford, but the cost of which, at home, would have been simply ruinous.

On their arrival in New York, Lieut. Morley and his wife were to proceed without delay to

Washington, to transact some business which was the object of their journey, returning thence they were to go direct to "Ellerslie," to visit Aunt 'Beth, the young officer's only living relative, to whom he was very anxious to introduce his young wife, of whom he was very proud. Nor was it to be wondered at, for her beauty had not only matured into a rare loveliness, but her naturally amiable character had developed so many fine traits, that she was well worthy of the tender devotion he lavished upon her.

The party had travelled so rapidly that when they got to Paris they found to their great delight that they could spend two days there, sightseeing and resting, before going to join the homeward bound steamer at Havre.

The voyage was a tempestuous one, and Anne Morley was not only sea-sick, but awed and terrified beyond expression, although her husband was with her whenever he could spare a moment from the duties which, owing to the imminent peril the steamer was in, had devolved upon himself and others of the passengers. The ship was not well officered; the captain was not only inexperienced, and ignorant of his duties in such a terrible emergency as this, but in his desperation he took such frequent drinks of absinthe as would have incapacitated him for command had the sea been smooth as glass. He raved about like a madman; swearing, and giving orders which, if obeyed, would have sent the noble ship to the bottom in a short time. Finally, and fortunately for the safety of all on board, he fell to the deck in a fit. He was taken to his state-room, and the surgeon was summoned, who, having done what he could for him, locked him in, to recover at his leisure. In this emergency the officers surrounded Lieut. Morley and besought him to take command, at least while the storm lasted, acknowledging their incapacity to manage the ship. "It is an awful responsibility you wish to impose upon me, gentlemen," he answered; "but I have one here who is dearer than life itself, also friends who are under my protection, and for their safety and humanity's sake I accept it. Fortunately I speak your language; otherwise, what you ask would be next to impossible."

The storm seemed to increase in violence, and Anne thought she heard her husband's voice ringing out orders, quick and imperative, above the wild roar of wind and wave, and it gave her a feeling of safety. It was well that he had so fluent a command of French, for the seamen understood every word he uttered, and lost not a moment in obeying his orders, and by sunrise the steamer had worked her way out of the circle of storms that she had entered, and was in comparative safety, although the ocean was still lashing furiously, and appeared to threaten destruction. At the first moment that he felt he could be safely spared, Lieut. Morley went to see after his wife, almost fearing to find her half dead with fright.

"Oh, Arthur, my husband!" she exclaimed, clasping his neck as he stooped over to kiss her. "You shall never go to sea again. You must resign as soon as we get home."

"I don't think you'll ask that, my darling, when we get on dry land once more. Have you been frightened?"

"For you—yes; for myself, no," she answered. "I was more astonished, I believe, at the noise and din, and the pitching of the vessel, than anything else, until I'd think of you, then I'd feel as if I should die with terror. If I could have kept my feet I would have come to you."

"For what, my wife? Your presence in such a scene, distracting my attention even for a few moments, might have been fatal to all the efforts I was making to save the ship," he said, gravely and tenderly. "But see here! what's the meaning of these bandages around your wrist?"

"Oh, never mind that. It is nothing. I was only pitched out of my bed when the floor of the cabin was where the ceiling ought to have been. I didn't know where I was going, or what had become of me. I was tumbling about in such a heap, catching at things, until the surgeon happened to be going round and came in. He picked me up, and found out that my wrist was scratched, and sprained too, then he bound it up nicely, and fastened me in my berth by nailing these strips of canvas along the front here. He had hammer and nails, and bandages, and all sorts of things in his pockets. Then he made me drink some orange-water, which I detest, but it did me good. But what was best of all, he said you were all right, in such a torrent of French compliments that I began to think I had perhaps married one of Homer's Greek heroes. Don't look so grave; I assure you this is only a trifle,—and it was all very funny."

"Well, I'll laugh, then, my brave little wife. But I'm very sorry that you got hurt."

"It is nothing, Arthur. It has cured my seasickness, and, do you know, I'm so hungry I believe I could almost eat a piece of raw pork."

"That is good news! You shall have a royal dinner," he said, laughing, as he smoothed her bound-up hand very tenderly. "We shall be in smooth water by noon, I hope, and to-morrow we shall be sailing on a summer sea. But, no mistake! we've been in great danger. There was a time when I thought all further efforts to save the ship would be useless. If the brave fellows on board had not behaved so well—but never mind, it is over now, thank God!"

"I was saying my beads for you all the time, Arthur,—for all of us," she said, in gentle tones. "I believe our Blessed Lady has helped us through."

"You Catholics call her 'Star of the Sea,' do you not?" he answered. "Your religion is filled with poetry, my wife."

"And with something deeper than you know of, Arthur," she said. Then, to turn the conversation—for she never argued with him upon religious matters—she asked: "What became of the captain during the storm?"

"He was taken with a fit, and is quite ill," was all he said.

"I hope he is in no danger. He has been so very polite to us that I quite like him."

"The surgeon thinks him very ill, and no one is allowed to see him."

"I am so glad, Arthur, that we shall have a few days' calm weather, and time to rest a little before Aunt 'Beth sees me. I am such a fright, and look so ill, she might think you hadn't treated me well. Arthur Morley!" she suddenly exclaimed, running her hand over his clothes, "you are wringing wet! Do you mean to kill yourself? Go into the dressing-room this moment and put on dry clothes,"—they had taken two state-rooms, one of which was used for a dressing-room,—"and be sure to drink some French brandy." With thoughtful tenderness she thus hurried the careless fellow away, knowing that, stalwart and robust as he looked, he came of a weak-lunged race, and that every little cold he caught settled on his chest, giving him no end of trouble. And so be remembered, as without further delay he changed his dripping garments for others that were warm and dry.

The remainder of the voyage was very pleasant, and the ship arrived at New York in due time. After taking leave of her friends,—with whom her intercourse had been so pleasant for a year past,—and her husband had gone ashore with them to meet the relatives who awaited them on the pier, Anne Morley still lingered at the vessel's side, to catch a last glimpse of them and give a last wave of her handkerchief before they drove off. But throngs of people soon bid them from her, and she was about turning away to get in out of the wind when her attention was attracted towards a lady who had just alighted from a carriage. The latter had scrambled upon a pile of lumber, which elevated her a few feet above the heads of the jostling crowd, and she stood watching intently the passengers as they left the ship. She was small, and wrapped in a light travelling cloak, while the crisp wind sweeping in from the bay blew her pretty white curls so wildly over her face that Anne Morley could only catch glimpses now and then of a pair of keen blue eyes and cheeks as ruddy as a winter apple. She was irresistibly attracted to this stranger, on whom she had never laid her eyes before; her heart seemed to go out to her somehow, and she found herself almost wishing for such a mother, or such a friend, as she was sure she must be to those she loved. Then she wondered how, being so small and slight, she managed to keep her footing, with the wind blowing such a gale, until she noticed with what a determined air she braced herself against it, and how firmly her two small, nicely booted feet were planted upon her rough perch. Suddenly she caught sight of her husband, who, having placed the last lady under his care in a carriage, was making his way back to the ship through the crowd, when he heard, not far from him, a familiar voice shouting: "Arthur! Arthur Morley!" He looked around, saw the lady who was perched on the lumber, and in another moment his wife, who had seen and heard it all, saw him rush towards her, lift her down in his strong arms, never letting her feet touch the ground until he had hugged and kissed her two or three times to the amusement of those who, having nothing else to do at the moment, stood watching the scene.

"It is Aunt 'Beth—I know it!" said Anne, laughing. "Oh, I am so glad it is she! To think I was just wishing for her as my very own!" Then she hastened to the gangway, and before her husband could introduce her to his aunt she had thrown her arms around her and kissed her: "I've been watching her," she said, "ever since she got up on those boards, and I knew it was Aunt 'Beth as soon as she called you! Will you be my aunt too?—but oh, I forgot! I am Arthur's wife, you know!"

"Arthur's wife! My dearest, I think I should love you if you had never seen my boy; but now I shall love you for his sake and for your own too," said Miss Morley, embracing her warmly.

"I am glad you two have met, my dearest little auntie. I'm sure I didn't expect to see you here!"

"Did you suppose I'd let you bring your wife home to find no one to welcome you,—and you away three years! I've been in New York a week waiting for the steamer, and a precious two days' anxiety I've had since hearing of the frightful storms that it was feared she had encountered."

"Oh, yes! I forgot the storms. We did get into the edge of them, and had to run out of our course a few hundred miles to save ourselves; but here we are, all safe. But now, my dearest ones, I must hurry to catch the Washington train. Aunt 'Beth, take my wife home with you and get acquainted with her by the time I come to 'Ellerslie,' two days hence. You'll go, won't you, darling?" he said to his wife, whose eyes showed astonishment at this sudden change of plan.

"Willingly. Anywhere with Aunt 'Beth, if you promise me to be back in two days," she answered.

"What's the matter that you can't come with us, Arthur?"

"Nothing in the world but to report myself and deliver dispatches to the Department. I'll be back in two days, I hope," he said, laughing, as he kissed her.

Aunt 'Beth was sorry to hear this, but she only said: "One might as well live in Russia as to belong to such a despotic profession as yours."

But Miss Morley never fretted over things that were unavoidable; she only spoke her mind, and was done with it. She kissed him good-by, told him that his place at "Ellerslie" should be kept bright and warm for him, and to hurry home as quickly as possible. He embraced his wife, helped her and Aunt 'Beth into the carriage, and rushed off to give directions about the baggage, which was ordered to be sent to the Astor House; then he called a cab, and drove to the Fulton-street Ferry, crossed to Jersey City, and in less than half an hour was on his way to Washington.

"Now, my child," said Aunt 'Beth, as they were driving across the city towards the depot of the Hudson-River railroad, "don't *try* to love me, but love me if you can. My heart is open, and it will make me a very happy old woman if you'll walk in and take possession."

"There's no trying, Aunt 'Beth. I have loved you ever since I first knew you, and that has been from the time I was engaged to Arthur; he used to talk of you, and tell me so many delightful things about you and 'Ellerslie' that I could not help it. I used to feel afraid, though, sometimes; and once in a while a wee bit jealous; but now—now, Aunt 'Beth, I feel as if I should have loved my own mother as I love you. I have had good, kind friends. *Bonne Mère* Hamilton was kind, and generous, and very good to me—but it was different; I feel, somehow, as if I belonged to you. Only—only—but perhaps you do not know that I am a Catholic?"

"Yes: I knew all about it. It will make no difference to me, my child, if it is a religion that will help you to fulfil all the duties of life with a Christ-like spirit," said Miss Morley with grave tenderness. "You may trust me, Anne, my child; I don't know that you will love me on a closer acquaintance, but you may trust me, and I'll be true to you to the end."

Aunt 'Beth's heart was touched by the spontaneous affection expressed for her by her "boy's wife," about whom she had been having many misgivings lest she should win his love away from her in her old days. "For what," she often asked herself, "will a young, beautiful, fashionable woman care for such an old frump as I am?" But now all her fears had an end, and she took the young creature she had so much dreaded, without question or doubt, into her heart; nor did reason ever arise for either of them to repent it.

"Ellerslie" was a portion of certain old manor lands that had been in the Morley family for generations. The Morleys were of mingled Scotch and Dutch descent and had lived and died—aye, and been buried here on their own old acres, until Margaret von Plater—the last of her race—married Sir Arthur Morley, an English gentleman, who took her home to his own country, where she pined and grew so homesick that her physicians decided she must either go back or die. They returned to "Ellerslie," making it thereafter their home, except for two or three months of each year, when Sir Arthur visited England to look after his affairs. A son and a daughter—Lieut. Morley's father and Aunt 'Beth—were born of this marriage. They were not a long-lived race, the Morleys; and after some years, Aunt 'Beth found herself left alone at "Ellerslie" with her brother's only child—a boy,—who had been confided to her care by his dying father, his mother having died a few days after his birth. The old house at "Ellerslie" was a spacious two-story building, branching off into wings springing up into turrets, and rejoicing in other additions according to the fancy or convenience of successive owners—the quaintest, most incongruous, ivy-grown pile that was ever thrown together—but so filled with comfort, with elegance, and collections of everything old and rare, including books, that it was the most delightful home that can well be imagined. Surrounded by a spacious velvety lawn, shaded by groups of magnificent old trees, and decorated with flowers, fountains, and gray, pathetic-looking statues, placed there so long ago that lichens and mildew had leisurely worked their will upon them—it was not only picturesque, but devoid of that look of newness which tells one at a glance that there is no history or traditions to soften or charm the spot. It was even whispered that "Ellerslie" had a haunted room and a ghost-story, which of course invested it with an abiding interest.

But we cannot linger at "Ellerslie" now, however pleasant it would be to do so. Letters came from Lieut. Morley in a day or two, full of good news. He had received his promotion as Lieut.-Commander, and was ordered to the Portsmouth (Va.) navy yard on the 1st, which would give him three full free weeks at "Ellerslie"; and his wife and Aunt 'Beth had scarcely finished reading and talking over them with each other, exchanging their views on his promotion—which they both decided he deserved long ago,—and expatiating on his perfections generally, when he made his appearance, so jubilant and so happy to be "at home" once more, and with the two beings dearest of all the world to him, that they felt more than compensated for the pain of his short absence. United in affection, sympathy and culture, with a bright future before them, wandering through the old homestead, going over its far-off romances and its stirring traditions; driving through the lovely, picturesque scenery of the neighborhood, and exploring the wild nooks and wooded cliffs of the lake shore, Arthur Morley and his wife were, humanly speaking, as happy as one may ever hope to be on earth; and the time sped by only too swiftly. Not a day passed, however, when they all chanced to be together, that they did not urge Aunt 'Beth, by every persuasion they could invent, to accompany them to Virginia when they went to their new station. But she had many reasons to urge against it, some of which she kept to herself. In fact, Aunt 'Beth had, literally, taken root at "Ellerslie," and could not help feeling that it would go to pieces if she, the pivot on which it centred, should leave it. Who would keep affairs wound up regularly? who regulate them? what would become of her people, her poor? She could not see how it would be possible for her to go. But one night, after leaving Arthur to have his smoke out, on the veranda, Aunt 'Beth and the young wife went upstairs together to the room of the latter, where it had grown to be a habit with them to have a long good-night chat, before going to bed. Anne had been again urging her to go home with them, but she had not consented; she could not make it clear to herself how she could abandon all her active duties at "Ellerslie" unless there were higher duties elsewhere to demand her presence. "Young married people," she remarked, "are better left to themselves, to get used to each other."

"I want to tell you something, Aunt 'Beth," said Anne, leaning her head on Aunt 'Beth's shoulder as she sat on a low cushioned chair close by her, and spoke in gentle, tremulous tones of a time that was coming when she dreaded being alone with strangers—a time of all others in the life of a woman when she needs the tenderness and care of a mother's love. Aunt 'Beth understood now; she folded Anne to her breast, while womanly tears glistened in her eyes and dropped on the fair head, and, resting there, she yielded. "Not that I can go with you now, darling, but later, when everything is settled and in running order for the winter, I shall be sure to come; that is, if you think they won't hang and quarter me down there for being an abolitionist." A hearty laugh, close by, made them look up quickly to see Arthur Morley standing in the doorway where he had overheard the conclusion of Aunt 'Beth's speech, and knew that his wife had at last won her consent to go.

"That's just his old, boyish way!" said Aunt 'Beth, smiling, and looking up proudly at the tall, handsome man before her; in another moment he had lifted her up like a child and seated her upon his strong, broad shoulder, exclaiming: "There'll be no trouble on that score; we shall be shut up in the Navy Yard, my little Aunty, a mile from both cities, and shall see nothing of the peculiar institution. Hurrah! I'm so glad you are coming that I have half a mind to go out on the lawn and have a war-dance with you."

"If you do not put me down, Arthur, I will never come," said Aunt 'Beth, falling back upon a threat, knowing how perfectly helpless she would be to prevent it if he should undertake so wild a prank. He lowered her down very gently to her chair, and Anne, who had been looking on half amused, half frightened, took her hand and pressed it against her cheek, saying: "Arthur! how could you?" Aunt 'Beth laughed. "Did he ever tell you how, after fretting and fuming and tormenting me for two years to let him go into the Navy, he at last won my unwilling consent? I don't like the Navy, my dear, and never did; I always thought that landed proprietors should stay at home and plough their acres, instead of the salt seas, to say nothing of getting wrecked and drowned."

"What did he do, Aunt 'Beth? I'm sure, from the way he is looking, that it was something outrageous."

"It *was*, Anne, my love. We were in one of the rooms in the old Dutch part of the house, where the mantel-piece is half way up to the ceiling. He had just got a letter from the Senator from our State, an old friend of his father's and mine, offering him a midshipman's commission. I objected to his accepting it, and offered him anything, however costly, if he would only give it up. I urged, I entreated, and argued with him, and when I thought he was just about giving in, he picked me up and sat me upon the mantel-piece, declaring that he'd never take me down if I did not promise to let him go into the Navy. It was inglorious to yield, but I did; what else could I do? I should have broken my legs if I had jumped; and besides, a sudden dread struck me that if I opposed him any longer in the career he had set his heart upon, he might turn out good for nothing, and may be wicked, for you see, my dear, I knew his determined spirit."

"You were a wise, good fairy, and I now humbly beg pardon for putting you upon the mantel-piece, the choicest specimen of *virtu* that was ever set there. But I'm afraid I should repeat the experiment if it were to be done over again; for, notice, my wife, she admits that then and there she was convinced of her folly!" said the great handsome fellow kneeling down before them, folding them both in a tender embrace, and telling Aunt 'Beth how glad he was that she was coming to see them in their Southern home.

"And you're sure, on your honor now, Arthur, that I shall get into no trouble on the negro question?" she asked, quite seriously, as she got up to light her candle.

"Not unless you undertake to deliver a public abolition lecture," he answered, gravely. "In that case, I would not answer for your safety."

"Pshaw!" exclaimed Aunt 'Beth, then kissed them good-night, and went to her own room to think over things, feeling very happy, and very much surprised at herself.

"It certainly is the dearest old place I ever saw. No wonder Aunt 'Beth hates to leave it," said Anne Morley to her husband, the day they left "Ellerslie." The carriage was at a turn of the road which gave them the last glimpse of the place, and they both looked back regretfully at its gray turrets rising above the trees.

"That will be our home one of these days—when I retire from the service with the rank of Admiral," he said. "This would be a very pleasant thought, Anne, if another thought did not always come with it to sadden me. It is that, perhaps, when that time comes, Aunt 'Beth will be no longer there to welcome us."

"It would no longer be the 'Ellerslie' we love without her, and I won't think of it. There has been but one single drawback to my perfect content there—a thing which no one could help, and which I avoided referring to on that account," she said, speaking her inmost thoughts to her husband, as she always did.

"What was that, my darling?"

"Didn't you notice?" she asked, laughing. "But how should you, not being a Catholic?"

"Oh, now I understand! It is true you must have missed your church very much, just after a three years' residence in a Catholic country too! Why, my wife, you must feel like a heathen. I am very sorry."

"No, I don't feel like a heathen, Arthur; I knew that the only Catholic church about here was ten miles off, and that it was a mission chapel, only attended by a priest once a month. One of the Irish maids told me. So I read the Mass-prayers, and said the rosary in my room, on Sundays."

"One of these days we'll build a beautiful little Gothic chapel somewhere among the old trees at 'Ellerslie,'" he said, "if you'll promise not to spend all your time praying there."

"No fear of that. But what would Aunt 'Beth say?"

"I don't think she'd care at all, for herself; and she is so inedpendent of other people's opinions, that I don't think their prejudices would affect her in the least, especially if she thought it would make us happy."

"How kind you are to me, Arthur, about my religion!" she said gently. "I wish I were only devout enough to deserve it."

"Devout enough? Why, you're a real saint, woman! if you were to get much better, I should be afraid of you, and run off to sea," he replied, laughingly.

"I'm sorry to say that I fear I shall never be as pious as I would like to be," she said. Then, to change the subject, she directed his attention to a far-off view of Lake Seneca, over which were two or three small white-sailed pleasure boats gliding along with a pleasant breeze, giving life and movement to the scene.

(TO BE CONTINUED.)

Love's Work.

BY SUSAN L. EMERY.

"She never can forget what it cost her to become our Mother."

I.

"HEARKEN, Bernardo the robber!
In God's Name, hearken to me!"
"How now, thou hoary hermit;
What am I to thee?
Sin and shame and Satan's self—
They are my company.
I am lost forever," Bernardo saith,
His face like driven snow;
"No hope, no help, no pardoning grace,
A soul like mine may know."

"Nay," spake the hermit, steadily,
"My son, I tell thee nay,
While breath of life remains to thee,
Abide by this I say:
One day each week, harm man nor child,
In honor of Mary Queen;
In Mary's love, fast once a week,
Whatever be thy sin,
And she, our Mother, may gain for thee
To see in peace God's Face.
Awful as are thy many crimes,
Tremendous is His grace."

Assailed by pangs of sharp despair,
By sin made slave, laid low,
Henceforth the robber desperately
Doth keep one holy vow.
And lo! the soldiery of Trent
Meet him one fateful day.
What aileth Bernardo the robber,
That he doth not strive nor slay?
What aileth Bernardo the robber,
That he doth not wear his sword?
He is bound by a vow he will not break
To the Mother of the Lord,
He keeps it straight in the jaws of death.
Will she, too, keep her word?

II.

Within the judgment hall of Trent
Men look on his hoary head,
And pitying ask for clemency.
"'Tis an old, old man," they said.
And then a marvellous sight they saw,
And a marvellous answer heard,

For, in the face of endless death,
 Mary has kept her word.
This man who sinned with fearful sin,
 Repents right fearfully.
So sore his deep contrition was
 That all men wept to see,
Yet shuddered and shrank the while they wept
 As one shrinks from the leprosy.
" Death is my righteous doom," he saith.
 "Give me my doom," saith he.
" Let him die the death he hath earned," the judge
 Made answer solemnly.

Bury his body out of sight
 With little heed or care,
Ye citizens of Trent who tracked
 This lion to his lair!
Pray with white lips and trembling hope,
 " Have mercy on his soul!"
Can God Himself have grace enough
 To make such sinners whole?
Leave the polluted body
 In its dishonored grave,
An outlaw and an outcast
 Whom Heaven might scarcely save.

III.

What voice calls at thy gates, O Trent?
 What noble corpse is here,
Wrapped all in rich embroidered shroud
 Upon a stately bier?
Four holy virgins bear it,
 And Mary Mother is near.
" Say to the Bishop of this place,
 Ye guards of Trent!" she said,
" That with all proper state and pomp
 This corpse be buriëd.
It is my faithful servant's corpse,"
 Queen Mary Mother said.

Forth to the city's gate they throng,
 Bishop and knight and dame,
Burgher and serf and little child,
 With one accord they came,
" Needs must this be a saint," they cried;
 " Now what may be his name?"
They lift the face-cloth from the face,
 And then their cry rings loud
In wonder at the unlooked-for sight,
 For, 'neath that gorgeous shroud,
Bernardo the robber lies in state
 Before the amazëd crowd.

IV.

O men who scoff at Mary's power,
 Stand round this wondrous bier;
Cast at this tale of sin and grace
 Your cavil and your sneer!
God laughs your unbelief to scorn,
 For God's own dear Mother is here.

We who confess her name and power
Gather around a Cross,
To One thorn-crowned and bleeding there
 We tell our sin and loss,
And a voice replies with words that turn
 Mere earthly loves to dross:
" Behold thy Mother!" Then again,
 " Woman, behold thy son!"
We lift our eyes and lift our hearts,
 O God, Thy will be done!
Mother, through tears we plead with thee,
 Hearken unto thine own.

Thou never canst forget the pangs
 Endured beneath the Tree.
Thou never canst forget the souls
 Borne in those pangs by thee.
We challenge now and evermore
 Thy mother-love for men,
And to thy mother-heart commit
 Our utmost need and pain.
Through scorn and taunt we cling to thee,
 Pray for our souls. Amen.

The Companions of Monseigneur Ridel.[*]

THOSE who followed with so much interest the narrative of the sufferings and captivity of Mgr. Ridel, published in our previous volume, must have wondered what became, in the midst of the storm of persecution, of the missionaries sharing in the dangers and the apostolate of the venerable confessor of the Faith. Often, as we have seen, the illustrious Prelate, forgetful of himself, had all his thoughts directed to his fellow-laborers; and when, yielding to compulsion, he took the road of exile, he turned his eyes towards those mountains where the missionaries must have sought refuge. Then, shedding tears and raising his hands towards Heaven, he implored the Father of mercy to protect them in the midst of their perils, and to preserve them to their flocks.

Whilst the events of which we have published the account were taking place in the capital, the four missionaries who had succeeded in getting into Corea were denounced by name, and pursued for many months like wild beasts. God alone knows what they had to endure, without resources, or a shelter during a severe winter, suffering hunger and cold, every moment on the point of falling into the hands of the satellites, or becoming the prey of savage beasts, and weighed down with affliction and anxiety, their souls filled with bitterness at the thought of the evils which threatened their venerable Father and their dear neophytes. But God watched over them; they escaped every danger; and at present they are taking every advantage of the calm which has

---
[*] Abridged and adapted from the *Annals of the Propagation of the Faith.*

followed the tempest, to continue their labors amongst the Christians.

The sufferings and privations which these good missionaries underwent during the persecution, may be learned from the following letter written by Father Robert to his parents and friends in France. It is dated Corea, March 9th, 1878.

... I write these pages to you from my place of exile, uncertain whether they will ever reach you; for I have written three times already, and I doubt if the letters have ever come to hand. The courier sent by Mgr. Ridel to China was arrested, our letters were seized, and the persecution, up to that time somewhat mitigated, burst forth with greater fury than ever.

I go back now to Our Lady of the Snows (Manchuria) where I spent all the summer of 1877. At the end of August, Monseigneur Ridel having directed me to accompany him with my fellow-priest Father Doucet, I got ready immediately, and prepared myself by retreat and prayer for undertaking the perilous journey. Three days before starting, we began a *Triduum* in honor of Our Lady, patroness of Corea.

On the morning of the 10th of September, Mgr. Ridel gave his last blessing to the Christians who had collected to bid him good-by, and then we set out for Corea.

I shall not detail the small miseries of our journey. I had to serve an apprenticeship to that life of suffering to which I had aspired from my youth. Besides, we were soon compensated by the happiness we experienced in setting foot for the first time on the land of Corea, which so many martyrs have watered with their blood. Before entering on our mission, we had to disguise ourselves in the mourning suit worn by Corean nobles, and this was not accomplished without great difficulty. A small hole dug in the ground was where we effected the transformation. But what a dress it is! I could not help laughing when I saw Mgr. Ridel and Father Doucet thus accoutred. Fancy a pair of trousers with such large legs that you could easily put yourself into one of them, and a waistcoat after the same fashion; then socks so small and narrow that I could scarcely get my toes in. The whole suit was made of coarse hempen cloth. To complete the picture, add straw shoes, and hair raised on the top of the head in the shape of a tuft, and you will have an idea of our appearance.

When we arrived at Corea, Father Doucet and I had to separate from Monseigneur Ridel, who went to the capital, and take up our abode in a small Christian village, to study together the Corean language. On the way thither we said our rosary.

The Corean houses are most primitive, consisting of a few pieces of wood laid on top of each other and plastered with mud; an opening three feet high by two feet four wide, serves at the same time for a door and a window; a little straw on top to hinder the rain from getting into the apartment; a kind of stove outside, on which they cook rice, and two or three pipes under the house to carry off the smoke and warm the room. In winter you are frozen in them, in summer suffocated. The Coreans are generally low-sized, therefore it is that their houses are so low; Father Doucet and I could not stand straight in them. Besides, the Coreans are always lying down or seated on a mat, and we had to accustom ourselves to do as they did.

When we were installed in our apartment, the Christians of the village, delighted to have us amongst them, came to visit us. We were just as happy at finding ourselves among them. Our first thoughts were to give thanks to the Lord, who had so wonderfully protected us in our long and perilous journey. After a little collation, we took some rest. As for myself, I was so pestered by cockroaches I hardly slept at all. When I rose in the morning, my feet and hands were all swollen. The Corean houses are filled with vermin, the walls of our room were lined with them; it was a regular ants' nest. Early in the morning we raised an altar in the highest part of our chamber, and soon had the consolation of celebrating the Holy Sacrifice. Our first Mass was one of thanksgiving, to thank the Blessed Virgin for her protection.

On the next morning, the 22d of September, we set ourselves to study the language, but we had no Corean books, no dictionary, and the Coreans have no way of teaching. Our professor, although well versed in Chinese characters, did not know how to begin his lesson. We decided first to point with our fingers at all the things that surrounded us, in order to learn their names; but often he could not understand us, and recited endless histories of which we did not understand a word. More than once we were utterly discouraged; but having invoked Our Lady of Dolors, I felt courage again, and set myself once more to my task.

Six weeks had hardly elapsed when I received a letter from Mgr. Ridel. Considering the circumstances, and, above all, the danger there was in both of us living together, he ordered me to go to the province of X——, situated fifty miles farther on, in the middle of lofty mountains covered already with snow. When I arrived there I was to perform missionary duties in the place, attend the neighboring villages, and two Christian settlements far distant. Finally, I was to found a college, of which Mgr. Ridel named me the Superior.

Imagine my astonishment when I received the letter. I, so young and inexperienced, to separate myself from my brother priest, and to live in the midst of the mountains, hardly knowing the commonest words of the language. Besides I was to instruct young boys, when I myself had such need of a master to instruct and direct me. No wonder I was frightened, and filled with discouragement. But, on the other hand, had I come to the mission to do my own will? Far from that: to suffer and to die, had been my motto in leaving my parents and my country. To love God, to suffer for God, and to die for God: is not this the resolve which fills the heart of the missionary when he fixes his eyes on those far-off countries, where so many souls are lost for the want of priests to instruct and confirm them in the faith? Though destitute of all the qualities required for the duty which was imposed on me, I prepared to go to my new destination. I bade good-by to Father Doucet, whom I was not to see again for seven or eight months. When we parted I felt my heart ready to burst. Neither of us could speak; but our silence expressed the sadness of our souls.

I set out at three o'clock in the morning in great style, that is to say in a palankin, for I was now a Corean noble. Four Christians carried me in turn. Two others, leading the way, were loaded with part of my baggage, and discharged the duty of keeping off all intruders; in Corea, a nobleman in mourning should not be seen by anyone. Another Christian was at my side; he was my servant. He carried a long pipe, supposed to be mine. Finally, a neophyte brought up the rear, with orders to keep off travellers and followers of every description.

I was never in such a vehicle before; but never did I suffer so much. My legs were bent under me as I sat; and after a quarter of an hour in that posture I was very tired. I should have a thousand times preferred walking, but necessity compelled me to remain as I was for twelve long hours, without taking any food. That evening I slept in a pagan inn: I counterfeited the Corean noble so well that no suspicions were aroused. It was easy to act the character: all I had to do was to hide my face as carefully as possible with a sort of fan made of hemp. Next morning at three o'clock, after having partaken of a cup of rice, my Christians were ready to start. We had but twenty miles to go before reaching the mountains, but I felt them longer than the thirty of yesterday. At two o'clock, p. m., I got down from the palankin, to ascend the mountain on foot.

It was the 26th of November. The air was clear and cold. With a stick in my hand, straw shoes on my feet, and a straw hat on my head, I followed the track of my servant. I had hardly walked ten paces when my feet were soaked with snow-water up to the ankles. If I suffered in the palankin, it was nothing in comparison with what I had to endure ascending those almost perpendicular mountains, across rocks and through thickets, in the snow, sometimes in water. When we had to cross torrents we leaped from stone to stone. I rested frequently, sitting on the snow; then I strove to get on again. Finally, after three hours' walking, I arrived, more dead than alive, at the house which had been prepared for me. I made them bring warm water, and I bathed my feet, which refreshed me a little. I then met the Christians, who had all hastened to visit me. Great was their happiness to see me amongst them, and their joy made me soon forget all I had suffered. My altar requisites, which I had sent forward six days before, arrived almost at the same time as myself. As at that time of the year the satellites patrol the country everywhere, to hinder smuggling with the Chinese, I took the following precautions in transporting my altar requisites: I ripped up a bed cover, and placed in it my three chasubles, an alb, and some linen; I then had the cover sowed up again, so that no one could suspect that it contained any object of value. A Christian carried the altar-stone under his vest; another had placed my missal under his dress; finally, a third had placed, in a little bag suspended round his waist, my candlesticks, a bottle of wine for Mass, and my reading-desk. As for myself, I carried in the sleeves of my large mourning dress, along with my breviary and beads, a chalice and the box for the holy oils.

My Christians set about raising the altar at once. I then took my supper; but as I was very fatigued I had but little appetite. They brought me rice, meat, potatoes, chestnuts, pears, and red wine. They were sorry to see that I did not touch the food they had prepared. The Coreans cannot understand how the missionaries are able to live, eating so very little. In Corea they usually dress their food with castor-oil. They always eat rice, or potatoes and millet; this is not very strengthening food. They use also turnips and wild herbs. Such is the food, I do not say of all Corea, but of the country that I dwelt in. There are even provinces where they live on poorer diet, as I found out afterwards. After supper I said my rosary, then my night prayers, and lay down to rest. I slept on my mat better, perhaps, than if I had been in a good bed.

On the next day I again set to work to learn the language. This time the difficulties were less than at first. But the Corean language is not an easy one. The termination of the verbs vary infinitely; in a single verb you may find eight hundred of them. Moreover, the language changes its form according to the dignity of the person to whom you speak, or of whom you speak. But God always proportions His succor to the difficulties that we meet. Three months had hardly elapsed when I was able to begin the administration of my Christian settlement.

The administration of the Sacraments in Corea is done in the following manner:

The Christians come to the place of meeting, usually the house of the priest. Two of them are placed as sentinels at some distance from the village, to give notice if the pagans should approach. All the others are arranged in a circle. The catechist gives a list to the missionary, on which are inscribed the names and surnames, the age and condition, of the Christians who are to come to confession in the afternoon. Assisted by his servant and his catechist, the missionary interrogates them on the Sacraments of Baptism, Penance, the Eucharist, and Confirmation.

After the examination, which lasts ordinarily till eleven o'clock in the morning, the confessions begin. At half-past twelve the missionary takes his repast; then he continues to hear confessions up to four or five o'clock, in winter. He then reads his breviary and finishes his devotions, which last till supper. In the evening, if there be any baptisms to be administered, he collects the Christians together once more. At that time we run no danger from the pagans, for they never go out at night, for fear of the tigers, very numerous in Corea—above all, in the northern mountains, where every year a number of persons fall a prey to them. The next morning, before daybreak, the missionary celebrates Mass and gives Holy Communion; then the examination recommences as on the day before.

Whilst I was administering this small Christian settlement I derived the greatest consolation from the piety of my Coreans. Many of them travelled upwards of seventy-five miles, with snow half way up their legs, to receive the Sacraments. In France, I told them, there are 50,000 priests, and there are churches everywhere. "How happy the French must be!" they exclaimed. "With what fervor they must pray to God, and thank Him for being born in a country where it is so easy to save one's soul, where they can hear Mass every day and approach the Sacraments as often as they wish! We, poor unfortunates, pursued and hunted like wild beasts, do not know where to direct our steps. It is thirteen years since we have seen a Father; during all that time we have been deprived of the benefit of the Sacraments. At present, we have the happiness to be regenerated by Baptism and Penance; and when we have received the Bread of the strong, we are too happy; but will this happiness last long?"

I took up again the study of the Chinese language, the knowledge of which would be necessary for me as Superior of a college. Some days later, Mgr. Ridel sent me my two first pupils. They were named after the two Apostles Peter and Paul. I gave them lessons, and during the short time they spent with me I remarked their excellent dispositions. Pious, obedient, studious, and loving each other like two brothers, they followed all the advice I gave them.

On coming back from a walk, I learned that Monseigneur Ridel had been arrested on the 28th of January, with six Christians, and in the evening another courier brought me a letter which directed me to fly at once.

Up to the month of January, 1878, all had gone well. But at that time, couriers sent by Mgr. Ridel to the frontier to meet others despatched from China by Father Richard, were arrested on their return; they were searched, and the letters found on them were seized. When the satellites saw the European handwriting, they danced with joy and understood at once the importance of their capture. They brought the three Christians to the mandarin, who asked them from whom these letters had come, and to whom they were addressed. The Christians did not reply; unfortunately, a letter written in Corean characters and sent by a Corean, who was deputed to teach his language to our brothers in China, revealed all—the place where Father Doucet was concealed, the residence of Monseigneur Ridel, etc. Nothing more was wanted to rekindle persecution.

The mandarin sent off immediately to Seoul, to warn the king that strangers had come into his kingdom, and that their chief was at a certain person's house in Seoul. If there had been no Judas it would have been hard to find Mgr. Ridel, for many Corean names resemble each other; but in Corea, as everywhere else, Judases are always to be found, and soon one of them volunteered to conduct the satellites to the spot. On the 28th of January, Monseigneur Ridel was arrested. The Christians of Seoul took to flight at once, sending messengers to all the missionaries with a warning to conceal themselves.

I had then to prepare to fight, but first I concealed my things and dismissed my pupils. My Christians placed my books and my pious objects in large earthenware vases—I only reserved the strict necessaries to celebrate holy Mass—then they carried them to the mountain, where they were buried in pits dug for that purpose.

I confided one of my pupils to a Christian, to bring him to his brother, who, though a pagan, was a sympathizer with the Christians; the other pupil went away with the courier. At two o'clock the next morning I celebrated the Holy Sacrifice, at which all the Christians present were in tears. When I had received their adieus and partaken of some rice, I set out in the disguise of a servant, with a bundle on my back, my servant and two other Christians accompanying.

It was hardly two months since I had taken up my abode at K——, and I was now so attached to my little flock that I could not refrain from tears in leaving them. What was to become of these poor Christians? Nine years ago, flying from persecution, they found a refuge in these mountains, formerly uninhabited. They cut down the woods, cleared the lands and lived peaceably up to the present, faithfully practising all the duties of our holy religion. For food they contented themselves with potatoes and turnips; and they were happy in being able to praise and honor God, far from the tumult and superstitions of the pagans, notwithstanding their privations. I had a great weight on my heart; I would have put my flock in a place of security before my departure, but it was impossible. I could only pray for them, and I did it with all the fervor of which I was capable.

(TO BE CONTINUED.)

A Remarkable Incident.

THE *Semaine Religieuse* of Grenoble publishes the following remarkable incident, which was related by Father Lacordaire in one of his conferences, on the "Immortality of the Soul" at Sorrège:

A Polish Prince, De X——, an unbeliever and declared materialist, had written a work against the immortality of the soul, and was upon the point of having it published, when, while walking one day in his park, a woman bathed in tears suddenly threw herself at his feet and, in tones of deepest sorrow, said to him: "Good Prince, my husband is dead. At this very moment perhaps he may be in purgatory, may be suffering, and, ah, me! I am in such misery that I have nothing to offer to have a Mass said for the repose of his soul. Deign in your goodness to help me to relieve my husband." The gentleman, although he did not believe either in a future life or in purgatory, nevertheless had not the courage to refuse this earnest and tearful request. He took a gold piece in his hand and gave it to the woman, who went joyfully to the parish priest to have some Masses offered for her husband.

Five days afterwards, towards evening, as the Prince was shut up in his study revising his manuscript, he raised his eyes and saw standing before him a man dressed as a peasant of the country: "Prince," said this unknown person, "I come to thank you. I am the husband of that poor woman who asked assistance of you a few days ago that she might have some Masses said for the repose of her husband's soul. Your charity has been accepted by God, who has permitted me to come to thank you; your alms was the means of opening for me the gates of paradise." Having said this, the peasant disappeared like a shadow. The emotion of the Prince was indescribable, the effect upon his mind so irresistible that he immediately committed his manuscript to the flames, had recourse to the confessional, entirely changed his life, and persevered in the fervent practice of Christian Faith until his death.

A Couple of Questions.

Dr. Mahar in *The Catholic Universe*.

A correspondent asks us "to say in the next issue of *The Catholic Universe* whether or not we can pray and say Mass for the soul of one who died 'not a Catholic,' and to say also whether or not a person can belong to the soul of the Church without belonging to the body of the Church."

As to the first question, we have to say that the priest can offer up the Mass for any person or persons except those who are already damned, or excluded by some positive precept of the Church. There is nothing in the nature of the Sacrifice to exclude from benefit anybody except those who are already in eternal torments. Consequently to make it unlawful to say Mass for any persons not so condemned there should be a positive law. Such positive law does not exist, except with regard to *excommunicati vitandi*, of whom there are not probably more than twenty or thirty the world over, and among descendants of Protestants none. What is said of Mass can be said *a fortiori* of mere prayers, which can be said privately even for *excommunicati vitandi*—i. e., those so cut off by proper authority from the body of the faithful as to render it unlawful to have ordinarily any communication with them.

As to the second question, we have only to repeat in the first place the ordinary thesis of theology that all persons who are in the state of grace belong to the soul of the Church. As to the matter of fact, the number of such persons, baptized or unbaptized, among non-Catholics, we content ourselves with two citations. In the decrees of the Second Plenary Council of Baltimore, we read: "Since Christ clearly commanded all to obey His Church, and become members and obedient children of her, if they wish to be saved, not only did He never promise salvation to those out of the Church, but even threatened eternal damnation to those who depart from this life excluded by their own fault from the Church. But if they be in invincible error, and nothing be done by themselves to prevent a knowledge of the true Church, certainly God, who does not punish or damn any person except on account of his own fault, if they, although kept outside the body of the Church by this inculpable ignorance, notwithstanding, through the aid of God's grace, act in accordance with the Divine commandments, and those truths of the Christian faith which they acknowledge, will have mercy on them that they may not perish for eternity." (Tit. I. C. I., No. 5.)

To understand the special weight to be attached to these words it may be added that they are the precise statement substituted at Rome in place of some previous statement of the Fathers of the Council. This fact can be easily learned by consulting the "Instructio S. C. de Prop. Fide Generalis, De Decretis Concilii Corrigendis."

The other citation is from an Allocution of Pius IX (Dec. 9, 1754,) quoted in the Baltimore Decrees in the paragraph following the words cited above. "Who," says the Holy Father, "will arrogate so much to himself as to be able to designate the limits of this ignorance according to the condition and variety of peoples, r gions, minds, and so many other things? For, indeed, when we, freed from these corporal bonds, shall see God as He is, we shall certainly understand how closely and beautifully Divine justice and mercy are connected; but as long as we are on earth, with this mass that dulls the soul weighing heavily upon us, let us firmly hold from Catholic teaching that there is one God, one faith, one baptism; it is unlawful to go inquiringly further. We cannot in the translation do justice to the language of the Holy Father, but we have given the sense.

We know that the Catholic missionary is by Divine commission sent to labor incessantly to bring men into the true fold. He knows that there the grace of God can be found unfailingly. He knows nothing of, and must not look for, extraordinary dispensations of Divine mercy. At the same time, such dispensations may be made, and circumstances may sometimes indicate with probability a case in point, and justify a departure from the custom, generally observed and easily intelligible, of not asking the prayers of Catholics for those who die "outside the body of the Church."

Catholic Notes.

—Rev. Fathers Brady and Bourke, of Springfield, Ill., have our best thanks for numerous kind favors.

—The 6th Regiment of French Dragoons, in garrison at Chambery, Savoy, distributes twenty portions of soup every day to the poor children attending the free school of the Christian Brothers at that place.

—In answer to an inquiry of one of its correspondents, the Boston *Pilot* states that THE AVE MARIA is published by the faculty of Notre Dame. This is a mistake; it is not connected with the University, though emanating from Notre Dame.

—The twenty-fifth anniversary of the ordination of Rev. Father Maginn, of St. Francis' Church, Philadelphia, which occurred on the 23d ult., was celebrated with enthusiastic demonstrations of affection and esteem by his parishioners and friends.

—Of the thirty-four Cardinals and ninety-seven Bishops present at the proclamation of the dogma of the Immaculate Conception, in 1854, only five Cardinals—one of whom was Cardinal Pecci (Leo XIII)—and twenty-one Bishops and Archbishops remain.

—ORDINATION.—Rev. William Kroeger was ordained priest on the 26th ult., in the Cathedral at Fort Wayne, by Rt. Rev. Bishop Dwenger. Minor orders, subdeaconship, and deaconship were conferred on the three days preceding. The newly-ordained priest is a nephew of Rev. Father Kroeger, of Logansport.

—LENTEN REGULATIONS.—Right Rev. Bishop Dwenger announces that the Regulations for Lent in the Diocese of Fort Wayne will be the same as last year. As THE AVE MARIA has a general circulation in the United States and Canada, we refrain from publishing the regulations of any particular place, fearing to mislead our readers. The rules of some dioceses we have observed differ somewhat from those of others.

—*The Chimes* is the name of an interesting little paper for children, lately started in Baltimore. It is illustrated, and published weekly, as all such periodicals should be. The first number is quite attractive, both as regards illustrations and text. There is a pleasing variety of stories, poems, biographical sketches, etc., besides puzzles, parlor magic, and other miscellanea. The price is $1 a year. Address *The Chimes*, 53 Lexington St., Baltimore, Md.

—A NEED.—We need here in America an especial cultivation of good behavior, as a branch of rudimentary education in our district schools. The wear and tear of political liberty upon morals and manners is immense, and careful training in early years is necessary to avert the ruin with which it threatens our free institutions. The necessary training must be inculcated in our public schools, for the family, as the source of such instruction, has almost been swept out of existence.—*Boston Herald.*

—THE CROWN PRINCESS OF PRUSSIA.—It is reported that the Crown Princess of Germany, who spends the winter in Pegli, Italy, invited the Christian Brothers and the Sisters teaching the schools, together with their pupils, to be presented with a Christmas-tree at her residence, and that the invited guests returned overjoyed with the cordial reception given them by the Princess and her young family. They will certainly not forget to pray for the conversion of their benefactress and her children.

—PRELUDES, the elegant volume of poems lately published to aid in the rebuilding of the University of Notre Dame, by Mr. Maurice F. Egan, is highly praised by Mr. Longfellow.... "I have already read enough of it," he writes, "to see the elevated tone and spirit in which it is written. I feel sure I shall not be disappointed in the rest. I recognize in these sonnets a certain freshness in the thought and manner of expression which is very attractive. Might I ask you to congratulate the author for me on the promise and performance of his work?"

—Readers who are familiar with Father Sebastian Bowden's "Miniature Lives of the Saints," arranged for every day in the year, will be glad to hear that the same zealous Father of the Oratory is preparing for the press, on a somewhat similar plan, a "Life of Our Lady," divided into thirty-one short chapters—one for each day of the month. Among other features of the little volume will be one or two quotations from a rare old book about Our Lady, written by Father Cross, a Franciscan who lived in the reign of James II, and who was held in high esteem by that monarch and his queen.

—A MEMORIAL CHAPEL will shortly be raised in Paris as the most suitable monument of the grief of France over the untimely but heroic death of the Prince Imperial. The contributions to the fund for its erection already amount to two hundred thousand francs, a sum which is regarded as sufficient. Baron Haussman, in the meanwhile, has obtained the consent of the committee, of which he is president, to raise the proposed chapel on some suitable site between the Arc de Triomphe and the Invalides. The building, when completed, will stand in the midst of a garden.—*London Weekly Register.*

—A PROTESTANT TRIBUTE TO BISHOP ELDER.—"The Bishop has as yet received no official notification of his appointment as Coadjutor to Archbishop Purcell, so far as we know. By his lovely character, his energetic labors, his benevolence of heart, his assiduous care of his flock, and his charitable feeling, together with his remarkable talent, he has endeared himself to the whole community, and all will regret his removal, if he see fit to accept this new call. His administrative abilities in the conduct of the Diocese of Natchez have been of the highest order, and the people while they would part with him with tearful regrets, yet would consider that their loss was the gain of Cincinnati, and though they grieve, they would congratulate the Diocese of Cincinnati upon the acquisition of such distinguished business abilities as well as devoted piety as are summed up in the character of Bishop Elder."—*Mississippi Paper.*

—The Genuine Priesthood.—Describing the condition of the neglected poor inhabiting the courts and lanes off Weather Lane, one of the daily papers stated the other day, with so much truth, that no Protestant clergymen ever venture through those low and dark portals, but that hither come Catholic priests, "quiet, self-contained, ever thoughtful, ever useful men, doing good by stealth, without a thought of recognition beyond the inward sense of duty accomplished." Ah, yes; this is a Catholic priest, and no mistake. Such he was at the beginning, such he is, and such he will be to the end, like the Saviour of mankind from whom he originally got his authority and the grace and the power to exercise it. And it was such an authority and such a power as this that the so-called Reformation has sought to set aside. Thank God the people of England are nearly educated up to the mark of seeing through the fallacy.—*London Universe.*

—Munificent Prelates.—The Kolosca *Volksblatt* publishes a record of the alms donated by the Archbishop of the place, Cardinal Ludwig Haynald, for churches, schools, and charitable institutions, amounting to one million and a half of florins (more than $700,000). We know also from trustworthy sources that this noble prince of the Church has given a new missionary field to a large number of exiled German religious, whose services he lost no time in securing for his own portion of the Lord's vineyard. The Cardinal's magnanimous example has been followed by another Austrian Prelate, Bishop Roskovanny, of Neutra, who has on several occasions donated large sums, amounting to seven hundred thousands florins (about $300,000) for similar purposes, and pays for the board and education of six orphan children in the Neutra orphan asylum, conducted by German Sisters of Charity. With such prelates as these, there is hope that Catholic Austria will be able to fulfil her mission among the Sclavonian tribes of Eastern Europe, and perhaps recover her lost foothold in the Empire of Germany, the heritage of Rudolph of Hapsburg.

—Recent Conversions.—Rev. Patrick Toner, pastor of St. Vincent's Church, Plymouth, Pa., who, owing to a fall by which he sustained severe injuries, is detained in Europe by the advice of his physician, had the happiness, while visiting Biarritz, of receiving a distinguished convert—Major General Hicks—into the Church, on New Year's day. By permission of the Rt. Rev. Bishop of Bayonne, Rev. Father Toner received the General's abjuration of heresy, and gave him conditional baptism at his own—the General's—house, he being too unwell to go to the church. The General is now about 58 years old. His career in India was a brilliant and honorable one, but far greater honor and happiness is now his in becoming a member of the Holy, Catholic and Apostolic Church. . . . The Rev. W. H. Lyell, late rector of St. Dionysius's, Backchurch, in the city of London, is also a recent convert. . . . The London correspondent of the *Germania* in announcing that the Countess of Tankerville and her son, Lord Bennett, had returned to the bosom of the Catholic Church, says: "There is hardly a day in which the newspapers do not announce some conversion, and yet we must contest the view commonly held in Germany that England will soon be Catholic. Unfortunately, this view cannot be justified. Unquestionably, the Catholic Church in England has made great strides in the last fifty years, but still the ground has only been broken."

—Death of a Venerable American Missionary.—A cable dispatch from Laibach, Austria, to Rev. L. Buh, of Belle Prairie, announces the death of Rev. Father Pierz. He died on Saturday, the 24th inst., at the advanced age of ninety-five years. The name of Father Pierz is a household word among the Catholics of Northern Minnesota, and among the Indian tribes from Lakes Superior and Michigan to the Red River of the North. For almost forty-five years his life was devoted to missionary labor among those Indians. Sinking under the burden of age, and no longer able to undergo the toils and hardships of the missions, he obtained permission a few years ago to return to his native country, there to end his days. Father Pierz was a man of more than ordinary natural and acquired abilities, of singular purity of mind and simplicity of character; his whole soul was in the active duties of the ministry, and it was this that impelled him to seek in a foreign land and among a barbarous race a field for the exercise of his zeal. Weariness and privations were accounted as nothing; his sole object in life was the conversion and salvation of the poor Indians, and no cost nor sacrifice he thought worth considering which promised any measure of success. And he was successful. The wild prairies and trackless forests present, it is true, no monuments of the labors of the ardent missionary; these monuments are in the hearts of the Indian tribes, who, living, love and revere his memory, and in the hearts of the uncounted numbers of the departed who through his ministry were laved with the waters of life and are now in the enjoyment of the inheritance of the redeemed.—*Northwestern Chronicle.*

—Army Catholic Library Association.—With the laudable object of supplying Catholic soldiers with books and periodicals of their own faith, an Association under the above title has lately been formed of which Gen. John Newton, U. S. A., is President; Major Alex. Dallas, U. S. A., Vice-President; Captain V. Havard, Ass't Surgeon, U. S. A., Secretary and Treasurer. All these gentlemen are Catholics. "The importance and necessity of such an Association may be appreciated if we bear in mind that Catholics constitute at least one third of the army. It is well known that they labor under great disadvantages in regard to opportunities for self-amendment. Too remote from Catholic churches to attend divine worship, cut off from the influence of Catholic clergymen, who alone, as experience demonstrates, have any moral power over them, they often deteriorate in mind and character, and perhaps abandon themselves to vice. It is proposed by this Association to give them such guidance and assistance towards a higher moral life as may be found in carefully-selected books and periodicals of their faith. By affording them some of the means of becoming better men we render them also better soldiers, so that the efficiency of the service is increased at the same time that individuals are benefitted." It is sincerely hoped that this scheme, already organized, may meet with general approval and hearty co-operation. The work to be done is great, but if every one who reads these lines would send a donation, however small, its success would be ensured. We feel there are many readers of The Ave Maria who will be glad to aid in this good work. The good effect upon discipline resulting from the occasional visit of the priest at military posts has been frequently remarked; in a lesser degree, perhaps, this Association will do its share of good in the same direction. Address Captain V. Havard, U. S. A., P. O. Box 225, Wilmington, N. C.

—Lodge Surveillance in Belgium.—The Ger-

mania lately published the following: "At the present moment the chief interest of the public is occupied by the circumstances that occurred at the death of the Vicomte de Grinberg. That gentleman, who was a bachelor, belonged to a "Liberal" party and to the Lodge, and for a long time had been the Belgian Ambassador at Constantinople. He was possessed of a large property, the greater part of which he bequeathed to the Liberal University of Brussels. A long time before this, the Lodge had caused its members to declare before a notary and witnesses, that in case of death they would scorn to send for a priest, and that they would be buried with civil rites only. The "Gueux" hero, who had lately handed a considerable sum of money to the Minister van Humbeeck in order to injure the Catholic free schools as much as possible, had complied with this requisition. On the news of his illness two of his noble relatives hastened to his sick-bed. Lodge Brothers were keeping watch at the palace. As they were eavesdropping at the door of the sick-room, they heard some words of religious exhortation addressed by the Countess to the sick man; they sent for a police commissary, who forced himself into the sick-room, ordered the Countess to leave, and made the dying man sign a paper compelling his relatives to leave the palace. Meanwhile the Countess had re-entered at another door, but the commissary bade her depart instantly. As she did not obey, he put her out by force; she asked the sick man if it was his will; he said 'No,' very emphatically; but the Countess was forced to leave the premises. Up to this time the Brothers of the Lodge had not acted towards their dying associates in such a savage manner. With the "enlightened," however, who believe neither in God nor in an eternity, it is an axiom: "Neither at birth, nor at contracting marriages, nor at the hour of death, to come in contact with a priest." In wills made by Freemasons, we often find, in modern times, clauses to signify that any change of mind at the hour of death shall not be valid before the law, as this might be occasioned by imbecility. Manifestly in this case the Lodge Brothers were afraid that their friend would show some of this weakness, as they watched him day and night. The bounds of discretion are by such a proceeding overstepped. The "Liberal" papers sing hymns of praise about the unfortunate man, who died soon after the scene above described, "because he remained to the last moment faithful to the convictions of his life." Leopold I, who saw only the beginning of the "Liberal" evolutions which are now pushed to the utmost, declared that they would lead to barbarism. It is already reached. Such cases as the above must open everybody's eyes as to what "Liberalism" aims at, however much at times it may vaunt "its love to the religion of the Fathers."

Confraternity of the Immaculate Conception

(Or of Our Lady of Lourdes).

REPORT FOR THE WEEK ENDING FEBRUARY 4TH. The following petitions have been received: Recovery of health for 77 persons and 2 families,—change of life for 22 persons and 5 families,—special graces for 5 priests, 4 religious, 10 clerical students, and 5 persons aspiring to the religious state,—temporal favors for 22 persons and 7 families,—spiritual favors for 24 persons and 6 families,—the spiritual and temporal welfare of 8 communities, 3 congregations, 4 schools, and 1 orphan asylum,—also 15 particular intentions, and 4 thanksgivings for favors received.

Specified intentions: Several persons bodily and mentally afflicted,—a number of temporal favors are petitioned for, such as the favorable termination of lawsuits, resources, employment, etc.,—means for a religious community to increase its sphere of action, and resources for the same,—the conversion of a Catholic girl living with a Protestant family. She has neglected to practice her religion for many years, and is now very ill. Also all the particular intentions previously recommended.

FAVORS OBTAINED.

A lady returns thanks to God for the return of her husband after a long absence, and for his change for the better, manifested by his devout approach to the Sacraments. A mother writes: "My little boy had sore eyes for one year. I owe their wonderful cure to the water of Lourdes, which our pastor gave me. The child was nearly blind. I had to keep him in a dark room, and although only two years of age, he had to wear colored glasses. Now, thanks to God and our Blessed Lady, his eyes are perfectly well, and could not be better." . . . A husband returns thanks for the safe and happy delivery of his wife, recommended to the prayers of the Confraternity. "The water of Lourdes you sent us," says another correspondent, "I distributed to sick people, and it has always helped them. Within our family, from the oldest to the youngest, it seems a sure remedy in any kind of sickness." . . . Another grateful mother writes: "I wish to thank our Blessed Lady for favors obtained through the use of the Lourdes water. Last month, one of my children had a dangerous attack of membrane croup. The doctor thought she might choke at any moment, but almost immediately after taking a few drops of the blessed water she breathed freely, and in a few days was quite well. We also used the water on two other occasions with happy results."

OBITUARY.

The following deceased persons are recommended for prayers: Mr. MICHAEL J. KEAN, of Cumberland, Md., who met a sudden death on the 13th of January. Mr. JOHN L. TURNER, of Baltimore, Md., who departed this life on the 16th ult. Miss OLIVIA TURNER, sister of the above, who died while her brother's obsequies were being performed. Mr. DANIEL COYLE, of Altoona, Pa., whose death occurred on the 14th of January. Mr. PATRICK COMBER, who breathed his last at Philadelphia on the 24th of January, fortified by the Sacraments of the dying. Mr. —— CURTAIN, of Adair, Ont., who slept in the Lord on the 22d of January. His patience and resignation during his long illness were most edifying. Mr. JOHN HALTON, of Altoona, Pa., whose death is of recent occurrence. Mrs. SARAH DUNN, GEORGE and DANIEL DUNN, RICHARD and MARY MALONE; FRANCES O'NEILL, BYRLIANA MAYCOBE, ANN SCHOFIELD, all of England; MARY BEGLEY, a native of Ireland. WILLIAM CORCORAN, CHARLES and ELIZA CHRISTMAS, of Fall River, Mass., deceased some time ago. And several others, whose names have not been given.

Requiescant in pace.

A. GRANGER, C. S. C., Director.

Deaths of Clergymen.

At St. Vincent's Hospital, New York, on the 29th ult., Rev. Dr. Neligan. In the same city, on the 31st ult., Rev. Thomas Fitzpatrick. At Providence, R. I., on the same day, Rev. Peter Carlin. In Brooklyn, on the 2d inst., Rev. Robert Maguire, pastor of St. Paul's Church. On the 21st ult., at Cincinnati, Rev. James Bent, of Lexington, Ky. *Requiescant in pace.*

Youths' Department.

Hermann Joseph.

NEAR the Church of St. Mary, in Cologne, there once dwelt a poor but God-fearing couple, with an only child, named Hermann Joseph. The husband was a shoemaker, and he was assisted in his business by his wife. Little Hermann from his earliest years was a happy, gentle child. When old enough, his parents sent him to school, and daily, as he proceeded there, he was accustomed to enter the Church of St. Mary, and pray before a beautiful statue of the Blessed Virgin with the Divine Infant in her arms. There, too, did he resort on his play-days, till he became, as it were, familiar with these cherished figures, telling them all the little joys and troubles, the hopes and fears, of his simple heart; nor did he ever fail most devoutly to implore the blessing of the Holy Infant and the aid of His sweet Mother. At these times, we are told, the Divine Child would speak words of welcome to little Hermann, and the Virgin Mother would comfort him. Fain, too, would the boy have played with the beautiful Infant, but as he sat on His Mother's lap, raised by a pedestal, this was beyond young Hermann's reach. The Blessed Virgin consoled him however, and promised that his wish should be gratified when he grew taller.

At length this time came, and Hermann's hands could touch Our Lady's feet. This gave him great pleasure, for his piety had grown with his years, and he spent much time in praying before these loved friends, and even conversing with them. It chanced one day that the poor boy possessed a rare and fragrant apple, which he hastened to offer to the Infant Jesus. "My mother gave it to me," he said, "and I give it to you; do not refuse poor Hermann." The Holy Infant bent towards the boy, and received the apple from his hands, making his heart bound with delight that his little gift had not been despised. From that day the choicest part of Hermann's humble meal was thus offered, and, in like manner, graciously accepted. Time thus went on till the shoemaker was forced to withdraw his son from school, as he could no longer afford the cost of his education. Sorely did this grieve Hermann, for he truly loved learning. In his trouble he sought the accustomed spot, and there, with many tears, he knelt and told his grief. The Holy Virgin replied: "Be of good cheer, my son; he comforted; this shall not be"; while, to confirm her words, the Divine Infant smiled. Then she directed the youth to search in a particular part of the choir for a certain large stone: "Remove it," she continued, "and, beneath, you will find what you need."

Joyfully did Hermann obey; he found and removed the stone, and from under it took money sufficient to pay for his education and enable him to look forward to the career he longed for. Daily he continued his visits to his dear benefactors, but no more speech from them was vouchsafed him. When his education was completed he followed his early choice, and entered the monastery of Steinfeld, near Cologne. There, by day and by night, he labored incessantly in every study which could fit him to be a learned priest. But, alas, for human perfection! in his thirst for science he forgot the end which was beyond; nay, his cherished patroness no longer occupied his thoughts, unless recalled to mind by unavoidable duties. Then it was that he found himself most painfully changed; his mind was as a harp unstrung, his memory deserted his call. His strong clear intellect became utterly confused, and every effort to regain the mastery of his powers but plunged him deeper into helplessness. In this miserable condition, he once more thought of her who in his better days had so closely protected him, and obtained leave from his Superiors to revisit his early home. The next sunrise saw him at Cologne, in the Church of St. Mary, and kneeling in that corner which had witnessed his greatest happiness. There, as he meditated on the past and the present, and prayed earnestly tears flowed for his relief, while he cried, "Blessed Mother, forgive my heartless ingratitude, and intercede for me once more! Oh, sweet Jesus, have pity, and save me!" Night found Hermann still on his knees, and he was yet in his penitent posture when a deep sleep fell upon him, and with it came a heavenly vision. It appeared to him that he wandered into a garden of beauty, far surpassing the shores of his own Rhine, where flowers of celestial bloom and fruit of most exquisite flavor shone amidst undying foliage, and the air was fragrant with the sweetest odors. Birds of bright plumage sang among the branches, and water of crystal flowed around. He saw no sun there, yet all was radiant. He felt at once that this glorious place must be the paradise of an eternal world, and as he pondered thus, he beheld the holy group of St. Mary's in Cologne. At once joy returned to his heart; the Blessed Mother advanced to greet him, while the Infant Saviour clapped His little hands; a loud hosanna was heard around, and the birds more joyously carolled their praise. "Hermann Joseph," said the Blessed Virgin Mary, "enter, my son, and be welcome." He entered, and saw a feast of heavenly magnificence. Around the table stood the degrees of celestial powers, the angelic host, the martyrs, confessors and virgins, while bright wings harmoniously waved their welcome of the Infant King, His Maiden Mother, and the returned wanderer. Joyously their song of thanksgiving proclaimed that the lost sheep was found, while Hermann, all amazed, looked upon the festal board, for there stood every humble gift which, in his youth, he had offered to the Holy Child in Cologne, and nothing more. Then the Virgin Mother placed him by her side, and from her lap the Infant Jesus reached forth the fair apple which had been Hermann's first tribute to his Lord, and bade him "Welcome." At the word, Hermann awoke; around him, in the church, was the darkness of night, save the distant twinkle of the lamp of the Blessed Sacrament. But while he yet knelt, the holy figures before him became radiant with light, and he felt that, in truth, he that had left his Father's house, had now indeed returned, and been forgiven. He arose full of humble thankfulness, took leave of his family, and proceeded to his convent, where each year found him steadily increasing in wisdom, and in the spiritual life, till, full of years, he departed in the odor of sanctity.

In the Church of St. Mary, in Cologne, which is itself of great antiquity, is yet to be seen the marble group commemorative of Hermann Joseph's first offering. He is kneeling, and holding up the apple, while the Infant Jesus bends from His Mother's knee to receive it.

Gluck and his Rosary.

ONE of the greatest artists of the last century, one of the most learned composers that has ever existed—the illustrious Gluck, preceptor in vocal culture to Marie Antoinette, was distinguished by his fidelity to the recitation of the rosary. This devotion preserved him from the philosophical and irreligious spirit that pervaded the society in which he was constantly obliged to move during his long and brilliant career. Like the greater number of famous artists, the celebrated composer learned the first elements of his art beneath the roof of an ancient cathedral. One day, says his biographer, a poor couple brought before the provost of the Cathedral of Vienna a pale, delicate-looking child, to obtain his admission among the number of children who sang the praises of the Lord of Heaven. The child was as happily gifted in heart as in mind. His voice was so wonderfully rich, its expression so pure, that whenever he sang the Cathedral was filled with an immense crowd listening in admiration. Thus passed Gluck's early years, advancing in art as well as in piety. Often, during the religious ceremonies, when the organ filled the vault with its sacred melody, the child was moved to tears. Often, too, when his youthful comrades were engaged in their innocent games, he was discovered alone praying in the deserted church. At evening when the rays of the setting sun scattered over the stalls of the sanctuary the varied hues of the stained-glass windows, Gluck, prostrate at the foot of the tabernacle, meditated and prayed. On one occasion, after he had sung better than usual an anthem of our Lady, as he was about to leave the church he was met by a venerable religious. "My son," said the man of God, "you have caused me to shed tears of joy to-day. I regret exceedingly that I cannot give you something as a testimonial of my gratitude and delight; but take this rosary, and keep it in memory of Brother Anselm. If you cannot recite it entire every day, at least, say a part; and if you are faithful to this practice, I assure you that you will be as dear to God as you will certainly one day be great among men."

Gluck faithfully recited his rosary. His family was so poor that they could not furnish him with means to continue his studies; but the young man was not discouraged, and continued his pious practice. One evening, a knock was heard at the door of the poor dwelling. It was the celebrated chapel-master, who, having been charged with the task of collecting the works of Palestrina in Italy, came to take Gluck with him and have him continue the studies so happily begun. From that time he advanced rapidly; but never did he cease to be faithful to the counsels of religion and the practices of piety. At the court of Vienna—that court then so irreligious—amid gayety, amusement and pleasures of all kinds, the illustrious composer might be seen at evening separating himself, and, as a priest would do in order to read his breviary, seek some secluded spot to recite piously his rosary. And when, after a long and glorious life, death came to claim him, he was found ready. He still held the poor and precious rosary of Brother Anselm; it had never left him, and he continued to recite it up to the time of his death.

WHEN St. Andrew first caught sight of the gibbet on which he was to die, he greeted the precious wood with joy. "O good cross," he cried, "made beautiful by the limbs of Christ, so long desired, now so happily found! Receive me into thy arms, and present me to my Master, that He who redeemed me through thee may now accept me from thee." Two whole days the martyr remained hanging on this cross alive, preaching to all who came near, and entreating them not to hinder his passion.

THE AVE MARIA.

A Journal devoted to the Honor of the Blessed Virgin.

HENCEFORTH ALL GENERATIONS SHALL CALL ME BLESSED.—*St. Luke, i, 48.*

VOL. XVI.   NOTRE DAME, INDIANA, FEBRUARY 21, 1880.   No. 8.

[Copyright: Rev. D. E. Hudson, C. S. C.]

[For the "Ave Maria."]
The Close of the Carnival.

BY ELEANOR C. DONNELLY.

THE torches dance along the dusky street,
  And, in their glow, the wide piazza swarms
With brilliant shapes, grotesque and motley forms,
Mummers and masques, who chant a chorus sweet.
From marble balconies fair ladies lean,
And jewelled fingers rain upon the scene
Gilded confections, fresh and fragrant flowers,
And perfum'd waters in rare, radiant showers.
But lo! above the laughter and the song
Tolleth the midnight bell! Lights disappear,
  In sudden darkness melts the silent throng,—
The ashes and the gloom of Lent are here.
Ah! even so, my soul, Life's Carnival, one day,
Shall fade into the gloom and ashes of decay!

The World Converted by a Crucified Jew.

JESUS CHRIST was a crucified Jew. All Christian writers from the days of the Apostles up to the present time are a unit in proclaiming this fact. The Jews assert it in their Talmud; their historian, Josephus, says that Jesus, better known by the name of Christ, was a Jew of Galilee, and was punished by the death of the cross. The pagans testify in like manner as the Christians and Jews. Tacitus affirms that Christ, the Author of the Christians, was suspended on a cross by Pontius Pilate, Governor of Judea, during the reign of Tiberius. Celsus, the philosopher, says that the Master of the Christians was nailed to a cross. The Emperor Julian reproached the people for quitting the eternal gods, to adore the wood of a cross, and a Jew who died thereon. It is irrefutable that Jesus Christ was a crucified Jew. This is the first fact.

The second fact, that which everyone sees with his eyes, is that the world is Christian; that the world adores this same crucified Jew as its God. This second fact is no less incontrovertible than the first; it is its natural and unavoidable consequence. How could such a cause produce such an effect? How has the world been made to adore a crucified Jew, and, adoring Him, become what it has—Christian? What is there in the explanation, a Christian universe? To properly appreciate it, we must first understand what the pagan world was, and how much it produced of greatness, of perfection, and of sublimity in religion and morals for the advancement and elevation of society, and then compare this result with what is common and of daily occurrence in the Christian world. Of all pagan nations, the most learned and intelligent were the Greeks; of all the people of Greece, the wittiest and most intellectual were the Athenians; and of all the citizens of Athens, the most spiritual were Socrates and Plato, master and disciple: hence, Socrates and Plato are pagan intellect and reason raised to its highest power.

Plato, seeking to establish the first and most important truth, viz., the existence and nature of a Supreme Being, said: "As to the Creator and the Father of this universe, it is difficult to find Him, and when He is found, it is impossible to make Him known to the public." And his master, Socrates, in the most solemn moment of his life, when interrogated by the magistrates of the city, feared to explain himself clearly on this subject; and behold now, everywhere, Christian people chant publicly at Mass, *Credo in unum Deum, Patrem omnipotentem, factorem cœli et terra, visibilium omnium et invisibilium—*"I believe in one God, the Father Almighty, Maker of heaven and earth, and of all things visible and invisible." This is what the child sings with the people; he hears it explained at Catechism—a manner of instruction which appears to us the most simple, but which by its clearness, and by its religious and moral unity, would have filled Socrates and Plato with admiration; and we fear not to say that had the simplest of our Catechisms fallen into the hands of those great geniuses it would have satisfactorily proved to them that, somewhere in the world, Heaven had revealed Itself to earth.

Finally, what neither Socrates nor Plato dared to condemn openly, "*the vanity of idols*," women and children proclaim in chanting Vespers: "Our God is in heaven, He hath done whatsoever He would. The idols of gentiles are silver and gold, the work of the hands of men; they have mouths and they shall not speak, they have eyes, and they shall not see...... let those who make them become like unto them; and all such as put their trust in them."

This is what Socrates and Plato inwardly acknowledged, but dared not openly avow. Interrogated by Dionysius, King of Syracuse, on the nature of the *First* Being, Plato speaks of a *second* personage in God, but in enigmatical terms, fearing lest his reply, falling into other hands, might be understood. Far from fearing to speak the truth, behold! everywhere at the present day, the Christian world proclaiming this great mystery as it chants the Symbol, *Et in unum Dominum Jesum Christum*—"I believe also in one Lord, Jesus Christ, the only-begotten Son of God, born of the Father before all ages. God of God; Light of light; true God of true God; ...." In the same letter to King Dionysius, Plato speaks of a *third* Person in God; but with the same obscurity, with the same fear of being understood; and throughout the world a Christian people raise aloud their voice and sing, *Et in Spiritum Sanctum*..... "and I believe in the Holy Ghost, the Lord and Lifegiver, who proceedeth from the Father and the Son: who together with the Father and the Son is adored and glorified: who spoke by the prophets."

While considering the imperfections of society and human laws, Confucius, Plato and Cicero conceived a perfect society, wherein God would be the Supreme Ruler, and His word the supreme law, and all human laws would be subservient and assimilated to this divine law and supreme sovereignty. Confucius looked for the coming of the Holy. Socrates hoped for it, but as possible only through a special favor of the Divinity. Cicero, who lived only forty years before the birth of Christ, spoke of it as a fact which was to be realized in a short time. To-day, throughout the entire universe, in the land of Cicero, of Plato and of Confucius, the people sing this divine mergence of mankind: *Et unam Sanctam Catholicam et Apostolicam Ecclesiam*,—"And one Holy Catholic and Apostolic Church"; *One*, in its faith and government; *Holy*, in its doctrine, its worship, and in a great number of its members; *Catholic* or universal, reaching all times and all places; *Apostolic*, descending from the Apostles by the uninterrupted succession of its pastors; *Church*, society of God with the angels and with men who adore and serve Him; a society, whose fountain head is Jesus Christ, whose law is no other than the divine reason and eternal wisdom which created and governs the universe.

Unific society! holy, perpetual, and time enduring, under the all-powerful leadership of its omnipotent Founder, God. All this we see with our own eyes; all this, so marvellous that the Platos and Ciceros in their ideal society never imagined anything so beautiful. But what is most extraordinary is our failure to properly appreciate and admire it—due, doubtless, to our great familiarity therewith—so much are the most common ideas of Christianity elevated above the most lofty ones of paganism and pagan philosophers. And all this is the work of a crucified Jew! Now, what is a Jew? From time immemorial, whenever one wishes to paint at a single stroke a usurer, a cheat, etc., he says he is a Jew. This word has become so synonymous of cupidity, of cowardice, of an incorrigibly corpuscated individual, that it is almost an injury to say to any one, "You are a Jew!" And neither time nor efforts have been able to purge the Jew from this state of feeling. Yes, the Jew himself blushes at the name, so much is it abased; and in its stead he affects that of Israelite, because it is more unusual and less opprobrious.

But what is a crucified Jew? Among the Romans and Jews it was something more ignominious than even hanging is with us. They condemned to the cross only slaves and the vilest of scoundrels; therefore, according to human ideas, a crucified Jew represents the last degree of degradation and ignominy. And yet it is a crucified Jew who has operated and perfected, even after His death, this marvellous regeneration of the universe, which to-day we behold with our own eyes, and which we call Christian society in the person of the Catholic Church! How explain this? This problem is still more curious, from the fact that this posthumous work is invincible to all attacks.

Sixty years ago,* some men annoyed by the fact that twelve fishermen from Galilee had established Christianity in the world, wagered to destroy it; wit, and talent of speech, a sarcastic spirit and winning address, science, fine arts, literature were added, and all were brought into requisition to accomplish this unholy end.

The world, which had perverted these men—and which they in turn had perverted a great deal more—applauded their efforts. Princes, nobles, and even churchmen became their dupes; one of the leaders exclaimed, "If I had a hundred thousand men, I know what I would do!" He *obtained more* than he asked for; the whole of France was abandoned to his disciples, together with a million of soldiers to regenerate Europe. At once

---
* This has reference to Voltaire and the Encyclopediac attacks, and from it the date of this writing can be inferred. It is a translation from an old French MS., learned and curious.

religion is proscribed, her temples profaned, her ceremonies scoffed at, her ministers banished or put to death, her Pontiff dragged from the Chair of Peter to a dungeon and dying in chains, and with what result? The successors of these men of destruction recognize that the attempt has not succeeded; they even feel that it has recoiled upon themselves. They find themselves reduced to trouble for the possession of their lands, their treasures, and their very homes! for from the principles which they inculcated and evolved against the Church have come forth doctrines and societies which now ask, and perhaps one day will compel by revolution, equal partition of property. The princes and nobles, despoiled of their privileges, and exposed at any instant to exchange their palaces for a dungeon, for exile, and perhaps for the scaffold, seek consolation for their downfall in this same religion.

Religion alone has survived the contest, unshaken and unchanged, freed from scandals and unworthy ministers, who by their lives and presence cursed the world. Ages and kingdoms, and nations the most powerful, have gone down the tide of time, and been numbered with the things that were; religion alone survives in all the strength and beauty of her eternal youth. Still sits her Sovereign Pontiff in the Chair of Peter, instructing both subjects and rulers, whilst the most powerful monarch the world ever saw could not succeed to himself. In previous times a still more desperate struggle had taken place. The world had been vanquished by the Roman Empire; the Roman Empire in all its strength attacked Christianity at its very birth, in all its weakness; assailed it by intimidations, by violence, by seductions, and by means which appear altogether disproportionate. The Christians did not repel force by force. A few among them, at sight of the tortures, renounced Christ; a far greater number expired confessing Him to be God. The Roman Empire after having thus slain them during three centuries, declares itself vanquished, lowers its eagles and fasces before the unconquerable truth of the Crucified One, and with the Christians—now become more numerous than ever—adore Him as God; and the army of the Cross, issuing victoriously from the struggle, perpetuates more gloriously and faithfully than ever the doctines and teachings of its Divine Leader. Hence the problem reduced to its simplest form, "A crucified Jew established after his death a religious society, which, from its humble point of departure, has spread over the entire world."

In the success of Mahomet, we see a conqueror, we behold armies, we feel the power of the sword! In his religion we see a mingling of Christianity, of Judaism and of Paganism; we behold a morality and a paradise of Epicureans purchased at a trifling cost, and we understand *why* men embraced such a religion, preached in such a manner. Since the enthusiasm of the sword died out of it, however, Mahometanism is in its decay; it is even necessary that Christian kings sustain it in its agony, through fear of being entangled in its carcass. But between a crucified Jew and Christian society, are there such like proportions? A Jew, crucified by the Romans, crucified by request of the Jews, and consequently an object of aversion to Jews and Romans alike, converts the Romans by the Jews, and makes Rome the seat of an empire bounded not even by the rising or the setting sun, but reaching round about the earth; and from its uttermost limits up to and even through the bright spangled archway of the heavenly vault to the very throne of God, where rests "the Lamb without spot on Calvary slain." This is the spectacle given to the universe. Do we reflect enough on this? Is this natural? Is it according to human power?

Let us now see what men have thought on this subject who are not to be suspected of partiality either to Christ or Christianity. One, like Gibbon, the historian; another like Bayle, who having become a Catholic, then an apostate, and finally a leader of modern incredulity, has said "that the Gospel preached by men without name, without education, and without eloquence, cruelly persecuted and destitute of all support, was in a short time firmly established on earth, is a fact which no one can deny, and which proves it to be the work of God." Rousseau of Geneva, who from a Catholic became an apostate, and finally uncertain as to what he was or would be, was no less struck by this marvellous fact; he says: "After the death of Jesus Christ, twelve poor fishermen and artisans by the order of their Master undertake to instruct and to convert the world; their method was simple: they preached without art but with a convinced heart; and of all the miracles with which God honored their faith, the most striking was the sanctity of their lives. Their disciples followed their example, and their success was marvellous. Pagan priests in alarm warned the princes that the state was in danger because of the fewness of the offerings to the heathen gods. Persecutions followed, but they only tended to hasten the establishment of the religion they endeavored to smother. All the Christians aspired to martyrdom, all nations came to Baptism; the history of these first ages is a continuous prodigy."

Here are three men who have endeavored all their lives to explain the establishment of Christianity by natural and human causes, and yet they finally explain it only by supernatural and divine ones. One recognizes it as the work of God, another views it as the effect of a miraculous power, the third speaks of it as a continual prodigy!

(CONCLUSION NEXT WEEK.)

The Two Kings.—An Incident in Rhyme.

A. J. D. in "The Illustrated Catholic American."

THE FIRST KING.

WHAT splendid array sweeps suddenly by,
  Outrider impetuous with steed reined back;
His bright tassel'd trumpet winding a cry,
And the sun on his mantle of yellow and black?

The sound is familiar to many who hear:
  See the people retreat, like a moon-smitten tide;
With uncovered heads, they stand ready to cheer
For King Don Alfonso and his Austrian bride.

One glance at the pair, and the cavalcade passes,
  And the notes of the trumpet are heard from afar,
The crowded street fills with the resurging masses,
The cortege has vanished like the flash of a star.

THE SECOND KING.

Another procession saw Madrid that day,
  There was no call of trumpet, no shouting for joy;
The broken light play'd on no brilliant display:
  It was only a priest, and a sombre-frock'd boy

Tho' absent the clarion, there tinkled a bell,
  And the people uncovered, and knelt on the ground,
Thro' all the long avenue a deep quiet fell,
For Jesu, the King, was passing, discrowned.

A very short pause, a softly-breathed prayer,
  As He slowly moved by and was lost to the gaze.
The little bell's tone ceased to vibrate the air,
And the people uprose and passed on their ways.

THE MEETING.

Yet a call from the trumpet is heard faint and sweet,
  Then all of a sudden it is lost to the ear;
The two Kings are meeting at the turn of the street,
And again a deep silence is felt far and near.

But one moment of waiting, when out from his coach
  Forth steps Don Alfonso and his Catholic bride,
The humble priest standing, as they quickly approach,
And adoring, they kneel on the pave, side by side.

"Of all Spain I am King, and my majesty great,
  But I bow to the greater of Jesu, my Lord.
Pray ascend to my place in this carriage of state,
  'Tis not fit that I ride when my God walks abroad."

UNITED.

So the priest passes on, with our Lord in His place,
  And the people they follow with reverent mien,
Adoring the dead Christ, who has given this grace
  To King Don Alfonso and his Austrian Queen.

And the little bell tinkles, but no trumpets blare,
  And the movement is sober as befits the great rite,
The crowd it has vanished, the Prado is bare,
  The cortege with Jesu has passed out of sight.

. . . .

O thrice happy Spain! how great is the blessing
  In the Faith that you cherish, and cherished of yore,
When your King thus remembers, in public confessing,
  The love that he bears for the God you adore.

'Beth's Promise.

BY MRS. ANNA HANSON DORSEY.

CHAPTER VIII.

"ALL'S WELL."

THE old trees at "Ellerslie" began to put on their rich attire of crimson and gold, warning Aunt 'Beth that the time drew near for her to go South. In her regular, methodical way, she set about making the necessary preparations for the journey, nor did she let the urgent weekly letter that she received regularly from the Morleys fluster or hurry her in the least. Certain things had to be done, and the right sort of a person left in charge—some one who would faithfully carry out her directions, and see after her poor neighbors, who would otherwise suffer during the winter—or she could not leave "Ellerslie."

At last she found what she sought—a widow of middle age—an upright, good, sensible woman, whose very limited means made the situation offered not only acceptable, but providential. A week spent at "Ellerslie" with its mistress, going over everything with her, receiving her instructions, and seeing her method of managing, made the Widow Trott feel that she might safely assume the responsibility of affairs left under her charge. Notwithstanding that everything which human foresight could suggest was provided for, Aunt 'Beth left home with many serious misgivings; not that she distrusted Mrs. Trott's good intentions, but her executive ability might fall short of her intentions; "then," thought she, "there's no telling what will be the result"; there was, also, the Southern "institution" she so much dreaded and disliked, awaiting her at the end of the journey; in short, the little woman was nearer being in a state of mind best known and understood as a "stew" than she had ever been in all her life. But the pleasant excitement, and the very motion of travel, with all its varied panorama, diverted her thoughts from her cares and the possibilities associated with them; and at last her heart grew full of the happiness that awaited her in the society of the dear ones she was so anxious to see, even to the exclusion of the haunting shadow of negro slavery that had so much and so often, like a very nightmare, disturbed the pleasant anticipations of her visit. On the beautiful bay, with a bright sky overhead, and the crisp salt breeze fanning her cheek, the fine steamer bore her swiftly towards them with just motion enough to exhilarate and not sicken. The broad stretch of sky bending down in the distance, like a sapphire wall, behind the white-crested waves—the passing sails—the snowy sea-gulls flying by—the distant, dreamy-looking shore, charmed Aunt 'Beth into admitting to herself that she was really glad she had come—that there was, after all, a charm about the sea; and she no longer wondered at Arthur's infatuation for it. The sunset, far landward, was glorious; the starlit night more splendid than any she had ever seen, so large and bright shone every gem that studded the azure heavens; while the frothing waves around and in the boat's wake were golden with phosphorescent radiance. At last—wearied, yet reluctant to close her eyes on all this wondrous beauty, so new to her, and so vast that a sense of awe mingled with her enjoyment—Aunt 'Beth went to bed, where, "rocked on the cradle of the deep," she slept through the livelong night, and, until a gleam of sunlight flashed through the window into her face, as soundly as if she had been reposing on her own down pillows at "Ellerslie." She opened her eyes, glanced round, and wondered where on earth she was; then she heard voices, and a low, rippling laugh at her door—finally, a light tap; in another moment she had sprung up, opened the door, and was in Anne Morley's arms, with Arthur bending over to kiss and welcome her. "But how did you get here, my dear ones?" asked the insular little woman. "Did the boat stop and take you up somewhere?"

"The boat is in the Norfolk dock, Aunt 'Beth," said her nephew, laughing, and kissing her again. "She got in half an hour ago, and we came over in the steam-tug to take you and your trunks home."

"But I must dress myself, Arthur! Do you think they'll wait? I can't go this way, you know?" said Aunt 'Beth, quite in a fluster.

"Of course not," he answered, gravely, while his eyes twinkled merrily; "but you can take your time, Aunt 'Beth, about dressing: the boat won't stir again until this evening. Meanwhile give me your checks; I'll go and have your baggage put on the tug—it will save time. Don't you think the South agrees with us?"

"Yes," said Aunt 'Beth, giving him the checks; "you both look radiant. Now, Anne, my dear, help me a little, for I really believe I am in a tremor."

Soon they were steaming across the channel and up towards the Navy Yard, leaving the dingy, lifeless-looking old city of Norfolk, and the straggling town of Portsmouth, on the opposite shore, behind them. Having landed at the dock of the Navy Yard, delighted and exulting at having her there at last, the Morleys with glad words of welcome led her by paths that wound through plantations of pomegranate trees, past great fig-trees, clustering roses, and trailing jasmine, to their own pleasant home, where the wide-latticed veranda, and the open windows shaded by oleanders in full bloom, and crape myrtles loaded with their delicate pink blooms, seemed waiting to receive the expected and long-hoped-for guest. A delicious breakfast awaited them in the coziest of dining-rooms—where, although the weather was balmy, a bright little wood fire was blazing on the hearth, scarcely brighter than the highly-polished brass andirons that supported it. All that ample means and refined taste could accomplish had been brought into requisition to make this home attractive and delightful; and Arthur Morley and his wife found there, in each other's society, happiness rarely vouchsafed to human hearts. It was a busy day: so much to talk over, so many questions to ask and answer; then the unpacking and arranging Aunt 'Beth's drawers, wardrobe, etc. It was a happy as well as a busy day; and when it was over, and Aunt 'Beth went to bed, she thought she had never been so happy in all her life. As she lay thinking—as she always loved to do before falling asleep—she heard a distant but clear tap of bells, followed by a cry of "All's well!" which was repeated from one point to another, in varying tones, until at last it faintly sounded far off; then all was silent. She did not know what it meant, but it rested her, and somehow touched her. It was the cry of the sentinels on the various United States vessels lying in the river around the Navy Yard, waiting for repairs or supplies—some of them there to go out of commission, others to be fitted up for sea, and whenever their bells tapped the hour, "All's well!" sounded like a message of peace and safety from the sentinels who guarded them. The happiness of her nephew and his wife, their perfect and entire trust in each other, filled Aunt 'Beth with a satisfaction of mind not easily described. Their oneness of purpose, their sympathies, tastes and aims were in such accord that it came nearer to her ideal of a perfect union than any she had ever seen; and yet—but she did not recognize the fact —there was one thing needed to make it so, *a oneness in Faith*, without which no marriage is sacramental and perfect.

As yet, Aunt 'Beth had seen nothing of "the

peculiar institution," to disturb her; she might as well have been at "Elleralie," so far as that was concerned. The household servants were a sleek, contented set, well-mannered, neat in their dress, obedient without servility, cheerful without familiarity, and full of pride in all that concerned the position and surroundings as well as the family consequence of their temporary master and mistress, and, withal, very children in their affection and docility towards them. She would not believe that they were slaves until seriously assured of the fact, and she felt honestly glad that the "institution" had some bright spots, especially when she learned that these represented a class to be found all over the South. It gave her something new to think about, and lulled some of her prejudices to rest; for, as she reasoned in her terse way, "seeing is believing."

Sunday came. The air was as full of sunshine, of the warbling of birds, of the fragrance of roses, as in June. The great oleander blossoms nodded in the sweet salt breeze, and gay butterflies, like winged jewels, flashed and circled around them, and there was a drowsy humming of bees among the spicy carnations lower down that made the harmony of the scene complete. Aunt 'Beth stood on the veranda drinking it all in, and wondering if it could indeed be near the last of October.

"I've been up to your room looking for you, Aunt 'Beth, to ask if you would like to go to church. Arthur will go with you; he has a pew in the Episcopal Church. I will leave you both there, and go on to my own church," said Anne Morley, as she pinned a cluster of white jasmine on the ribbon bow which fastened Aunt 'Beth's fine lace collar.

"How far off is your church, dear? Within easy distance I hope; for you should not take long walks, you know?"

"Oh no," she answered, with a bright smile: " I don't. Both churches are over a mile away; and Arthur—I didn't tell you—bought me a light pretty carriage and a strong, gentle horse, that I might have no trouble about getting to Mass. He goes with me sometimes, and has been only once to his own church. Indeed, Aunt 'Beth, you'll have to talk to him about it; don't you think he ought to go?"

"My dear, if Arthur was a member of that church, he'd go—depend upon it,—for he never shirks a duty, let it be what it may—he never did. I never meddle in such matters. People must fight out their own battles with conscience. I'm clear for everyone's doing just what he thinks right and best in the service that he owes his Creator. That is my creed," answered Aunt 'Beth, in her calm, incisive way.

"But you know, dear Aunty, he told me that he was going to take you to church to-day," said Anne.

"I am not going, my child. I'd rather sit here in this quiet and beautiful spot, and read my Bible; it will do me more good than being in a crowded church, where most of the people are thinking about what other people have on, and the sermon is full of everything except 'Christ, and Him crucified.'"

"Oh, Aunt 'Beth, that is very severe!" said Anne, gently.

"It's the truth, according to my view; but don't mind my opinion."

"Perhaps—would you come with me, then, Aunt 'Beth?"

"No, my dear; I have my Bible in my native tongue, and I can understand all that I read in it. Services conducted in Latin would be worse than 'sounding brass and tinkling cymbal' to me. I mean no offence, my love; but it is a fact."

"Be happy in your own way, Aunty 'Beth. I must run away now to get ready; it is nearly time to start," said Anne Morley, kissing her as she went away to dress.

And Aunt 'Beth was left to her own devices after this, so far as going to church was concerned; and she continued to enjoy her inalienable right as an American in the exercise of a liberty of conscience that was without guide or compass, and as near the confines of infidelity as it could be without crossing the line that divided it from Christianity. But, humanly and morally speaking, Aunt 'Beth was a good, exemplary, sensible woman; her principles were high and noble, and every quality of her mind and heart, true, generous, and intolerant of all meanness. She gave of her substance with a liberal hand to the poor; aye, for a principle she "would have given her body to be burned"; but what was it all without faith—without that vivifying element which would have transformed and consecrated her natural gifts into fruits meet for heaven?

Time sped swiftly and happily on. In the daily intercourse with her "children," as she called the Morleys, nothing seemed wanting to Aunt 'Beth's happiness, while the novel surroundings gave ample occupation to her active and observing mind. The immense work-shops were full of interest—the great ship-house, where a large ship-of-the-line was being built—the hundreds of busy and skilled workmen coming and going at regular hours—the dry-dock, the ships, the flowers, the late figs, purple and luscious; delightful little trips in the tug outside the harbor—sometimes a row on the river, with her dear ones always near her—and, last of all, the "All's well!" of the sentinels through the night, which fell upon her ear like a blessing, filled every hour with strange enjoyment. But after it had all grown familiar, this *dolce far niente* style of living, and the sweet, dreamy air, together infected Aunt 'Beth with a certain degree of languor and made her fear that she was getting too well satisfied at having nothing to do—no cares, no plans to carry out through difficulties, nobody to manage, to advise, to help, or to scold. So, one day, after thinking it over and giving herself, morally, quite a shaking up, she went down to Anne and told her that if she did not let her help in some way about something—she didn't care what—she'd pack up her trunks and go back to "Ellerslie," where there was no end of things waiting to be done. "Indeed, my child, I am quite demoralized by this soft Southern way of living; the air is not good for me; my energy seems to be oozing away with my breath," she said, dropping into a chair and folding her small hands helplessly together.

And Anne, after laughing at her explosion, told her that she could think of nothing except some shopping that had to be done, which she had put off from day to day, dreading the fatigue.

"Nothing fatigues me so much as idleness—but you are not idle, my dear; you are always doing something or other—not work, it is true, but you are occupied. Of course it would tire you to go about shopping, and I'll be your factor most gladly while I am here." Then followed a talk over what was to be got—lace edgings, embroidery, silk, and linen cambric, to complete some dainty little garments that were kept in a covered workbasket, with rose-leaves sprinkled plentifully between them.

"Arthur has to go over to Norfolk to-day, Aunt 'Beth, to see about supplies or something, and he'll show you the main street, where all the stores are. The steam-tug goes and comes every hour, and it will be a nice little jaunt for you."

"Anne, my love, if I were to stay here much longer you'd get a rattle and bells for me, I expect —you seem to think amusement so necessary for me," said Aunt 'Beth, in her quaint, quiet way. "I don't want to be amused: I want to feel as if I had some purpose in life, and to be of use to somebody."

Aunt 'Beth went, and was so successful that she afterwards made many trips to the old borough to make family purchases, serene in the consciousness that she was of some use, not only in selecting with judgment, but in saving these poor inexperienced children from being cheated right and left.

But one fatal day—fatal in its results to Aunt 'Beth's peace of mind—there was an urgent demand for certain articles that could only be procured on the other side of the river. The steam-tug was out of order, and in the dock for repairs; the executive officer of the Yard and Lieut.-Commander Morley had gone to inspect some ships that were to be put into commission; the Commodore was in Washington, on business for the Department, and it was impossible to get either gig or barge for want of somebody who had authority to give the order for one. But Aunt 'Beth had the faculty of making one thing do when another failed, and, being determined to attend to the matter in hand, proposed driving into town and going across on the ferry-boat.

"It's the most direct route, and much nearer the stores," said Anne, "but not always pleasant, owing to various reasons—sometimes they take over cattle, sometimes horses, or mules, to the Norfolk markets. I'm afraid to have you go."

"I'm not afraid. Tell them to get the carriage round, my dear, while I run up and get my things on," said the alert little woman.

The ferry-boat was not crowded, and there were no cattle or horses on the deck. Aunt 'Beth was pleasantly seated by a chatty old woman with a sunbonnet on, where she had a wide view of the beautiful river up and down. Very soon her attention was attracted to a novel spectacle. It was a large brig, lying low in the water, her deck unobstructed from bow to stern, and crowded with a motley assemblage of negroes, men, women and youths of both sexes—all gaily attired, some dancing to the music of violins and banjos, while others lounged in the sun, smoking, or seated in groups, were laughing and talking, and mending old or fashioning new garments. It was a New Orleans slave-brig waiting to complete her cargo of negroes for the sugar-plantations, the cotton-fields, and the rice-swamps of the far South, where this sort of "chattel" brought good prices at all times.* Aunt 'Beth, not knowing what it meant, looked approvingly on the festive scene, and wondered what happy occasion had brought so many of this dusky race together.

"Them's mighty merry, considerin'," said the old woman in the sunbonnet.

"Very. Perhaps they have been set free, and are going North!"

"Free! laws!" exclaimed the woman, pushing back her sunbonnet and laughing at Aunt Beth's verdant simplicity. Why, that's the New Orleans brig, and she's waitin' to git loaded up with niggers to sell South. They lets 'em have a good time, as you see, so's not to git discouraged and spile their good looks; but thar's men thar with guns keepin' guard, so's none of 'em 'll git off."

Aunt 'Beth turned away suddenly, heart-sick, and tingling all over. She had run against it at last, this thing that she had always hated with such righteous indignation, but she wisely held her tongue—not knowing how far she might go if she should speak—and walked back to the other end of the boat, out of sight of the slave ship. She thought, as she stood leaning over the railing,

---

* This is not introduced with any desire of rekindling old issues, but simply as a true and common incident peculiar to that region, and to times now happily belonging to the past; also to show the effects of the "system" upon one of the living characters of the story, opposed by lifelong prejudices to it. A. H. D.

while swift tears dripped over her old cheeks into the blue, sunny waves, that she would go straight back to "Ellerslie." But no! she could not leave Anne now until all was well with her.

The ferry-boat was at her wharf, and Aunt 'Beth landed with the other passengers and proceeded to attend to the business which had brought her over. She dreaded going back by the ferry; she would have avoided doing so at any cost, but she knew of no other way to get home, and the carriage would be waiting for her. Fortunately, she met one of the junior officers of the Navy Yard and his wife, who stopped to speak, and told her they had hired a nice row-boat to take them home, inviting her to go with them. She would have accepted gladly, but there was the carriage! She mentioned her difficulty, thanking them at the same time; but Ensign Moore told her if she preferred crossing with his wife he would go by the ferry, and he be only too glad of a ride in Mrs. Morley's nice turn-out. "The fellows who are to row you over," he said, "are steady and reliable, and you'll be perfectly safe."

Aunt 'Beth, who would have been willing to start in a cockle-shell, so great was her horror of passing anywhere near the New Orleans brig, was glad to accede to the young officer's plan. Having finished all that she had to do, went down with them to the pier, and, to her great relief, they were soon on their way home, leaving the black plague-spot of the river farther and farther away with every pull of the oars. Ensign Moore got home in advance of the two ladies, and sent in word that Miss Morley had preferred coming over in the row-boat with his wife which, at once quieted the sudden uneasiness Anne felt when she heard that the carriage had arrived without her. A little later, Aunt 'Beth walked in with her arm full of dainty bundles, pleasant and serene as usual, keeping back all that was disagreeable, and seemingly intent on showing what she had brought; well pleased that every article was "just the thing," and pronounced "lovely," she went to her room to lie down and rest. That evening, after dinner, Anne excused herself and went into the library to write letters to her brothers, one of whom was on the coast of Africa, the other at a post on the Pacific slope; and to *Bonne Mère* Hamilton, who, with her party, was spending the winter in Rome. Aunt 'Beth took the opportunity—after the servants had cleared off the table, and gone—to tell her nephew what she had seen on the river that day, and give expression to her pent-up feelings on the subject of slavery. He could not agree with her extreme views, nor argue against principles which were fine in theory, but, as he viewed the subject, impracticable; and when he finally declared his firm belief that the negroes were better off in their present condition than they would be if free, she thought it useless to continue the discussion. She stood a moment, her countenance wearing a troubled expression, and passed her small hand several times over his hair, then kissed his forehead, and was turning to leave the room when he threw his arm about her and said: "That means, 'He is joined to his idols; let him alone'; doesn't it, Aunt 'Beth?"

"Yes. If you had lived at 'Ellerslie,' on your own acres, instead of going into the Navy, you would have escaped this moral contagion. Do not speak to Anne of my adventure to-day; it would only worry her. Now I must go, Arthur; I am really very tired." He lighted her candle for her, kissed her good-night, and offered to carry her upstairs, and would have done it had she not been a little too quick in escaping from the room.

One day there was great joy in the Morleys' home—a deep, quiet, thankful joy—a "man-child was born to them"—a fair, healthy, perfect babe, whose presence awakened strangely mingled emotions in their hearts, lifting them nearer to Him who had confided this spotless soul to their keeping; and with the mysterious tenderness which the first wail of its new life unsealed, a sense of responsibility stole upon them, which tempered their joy into an almost silent thoughtfulness.

The day that the little stranger was four weeks old, it was arranged that he should be taken over to the church in Portsmouth to be baptized. Half hidden in clouds of rare lace that ornamented his swaddling clothes, and wrapped in a white, satin-lined cloak of richly-embroidered cashmere, the babe lay sleeping in his proud young mother's arms, as fair a picture as one of Fra Angelico's ideals, while Arthur Morley and Aunt 'Beth looked on, worshipping, not as did the shepherds or the wise men of old, who offered gifts to the Divine Babe, but with all the simple, natural human love their hearts were capable of.

The good clergyman met them in the church, and conducted them to the baptismal font, and when everything was ready for the ceremony to begin, he asked who were going to stand as sponsors for the child. They had not thought of this. Morley did not understand; Aunt 'Beth had heard of godfathers and godmothers, but had not the slightest idea of their spiritual significance in a ceremony like this, and whispered to Anne that *she* would stand for the child.

"The godmother must be a Catholic, I believe," returned Anne, also in a whisper.

"The fact is, Father," said Arthur Morley, "my wife is the only Catholic of the family Is it absolutely necessary to have sponsors?"

"Yes, when possible. But I think I can arrange it, if you will not object," said Father O'Meara.

"We leave it entirely to you, Father; only make

the boy a good Christian, however it's to be done."

"There is a lady here, madam, in the sacristy who is the President of our Sanctuary Society," said the good clergyman, addressing the young mother, "who will, I am sure, willingly stand as the child's godmother, and I will be his godfather."

"A perfect stranger, Anne," whispered Aunt 'Beth; "I wouldn't have her."

"Never mind; it is only a form, you know," said Arthur, who overheard her—which showed how much he knew about the matter.

Anne herself, owing to her defective religious education, knew very little about it either, beyond the fact that Baptism was the first necessary step to be taken to make her child a Catholic. The lady consented, and came back with the priest, who introduced her to the party as Mrs. Grantly. Taking the babe from his mother's arms, she held it tenderly in her own, the ceremony proceeded, and the child became one of the fold of Christ, marked with His sign, anointed with chrism, and liberated in the Name of the Most Holy Trinity from the thraldom and stain of original sin. Anne had scanned the face of her child's godmother jealously at first, but when she noted its patient, saintly expression, the tender, motherly light in her eyes, her heart went out to her, and she felt perfectly reconciled to the new relation so unexpectedly established between them, complete strangers as they were to each other. When the ceremony was ended, and her babe was returned to its mother, she thanked Mrs. Grantly in her own winning way, and told her that, her boy now having a claim upon her, she hoped that she would be kind enough to come often to see them, which the good lady promised to do. Arthur also thanked her and the good priest; while Aunt 'Beth, feeling that there was nothing for her to say, behaved only as a well-bred lady should to strangers with whom she was accidentally made acquainted. But there was a little aside which Arthur Morley had with Father O'Meara which none of them noticed. He drew him apart, and told him he believed that there was a large number of his congregation employed at the Navy Yard, and if any occasion arose in which he could be of use, to call upon him: then bade him good-day, leaving a well-filled purse in the hand he had just grasped, saying: "For your poor"; and jumping into the carriage, they drove off. It was a blessed day for Father O'Meara; he was that morning without a penny, and wondered whence and how help could come. He had implored the assistance of Our Blessed Lady of Perpetual Succor, who had heard his petitions and pitied the necessities of her poor flock by sending him a far larger sum than his present need required, and also a friend who had promised his influence in case any difficulties should arise between the chief workmen at the Yard and themselves.

Aunt 'Beth had thought the Baptism of little Arthur a species of jugglery, but she said nothing about it, seeing that he flourished and waxed fat and strong; and, being a generous soul, she soon began to tolerate, and then to like, his godmother, Mrs. Grantly, who was again invited, and came quite frequently to see him. She felt now that, with so safe and kind a friend to leave with Anne and the boy, she might think of going back to "Ellerslie." But Arthur and his wife entreated her to remain until spring, telling her that the winter up there, after this pleasant, mild climate, would kill her; but she didn't think so, as she had been accustomed to severe winters all her life; on the contrary, she thought if she remained South any longer her health would break down. But they would hear of no such "nonsense," and promised her, if she would stay, that they would come the following summer, and bring the baby to "Ellerslie"—"won't we, Arthur?" pleaded Anne.

"Yes, of course we shall! Nothing would please me so well as to get away from the salt water a little while," he answered.

"Very well, I'll consider it; you must give me two weeks to think it over, and to hear from my agent and Mrs. Trott, for I'm so sure that things have been going heels over head since I came away, that it will take a regiment of horses to bring my affairs back to order."

"I don't believe a word of it, Aunt 'Beth; you don't either," said Anne, laughing.

"But I do, and that makes a difference, you see. I've been playing Lady High Horse long enough, and I want to be doing something useful."

"As if you were not always doing something useful!" said Arthur Morley, stretching out his arm to scoop her up, perhaps to his shoulder, but she was too quick for him, and placed a chair between them before he got near enough. He never ventured to tussle with Aunt 'Beth, not thinking it respectful, so he stood leaning against the mantel-piece, looking innocent of all mischief.

"Useful, do you think? If fiddling around the house, and hunting up fid-fads in the shops for Anne and the Grand Llama can be called useful occupations, then I admit that my time has been well spent," returned Aunt 'Beth, laughing.

Several friends dropped in, one after another, and the conversation was discontinued, but the Morleys felt sure that she would not leave them until spring.

(TO BE CONTINUED.)

ANY one who is curious to know how the world could get on without him can find out by sticking his finger into a tub of water, then withdrawing it and looking at the hole.

The Companions of Monseigneur Ridel.

(CONTINUED.)

WHEN I left these unfortunate people, I had to climb mountains up to my knees in snow, with the thermometer at 31 degrees below freezing point. I had hardly arrived at the top of the first mountain when I was compelled to rest, through sheer exhaustion. Thus far we had followed the tracks of the tigers, which abound here, but my people were not very courageous, and if they had not been with a missionary they never would have dared to travel by night. They imagine that his presence is enough to frighten and put to flight those terrible animals.

After a short halt, I started again; this time we had to descend, but soon again to climb up, and so on. At three o'clock, p. m., exhausted with hunger and fatigue, I sat down under a fir-tree. My servant went into a village and bought a pennyworth of rice—all that he could get there—and brought it to me. We shared this small allowance of food, and continued our journey, resting from time to time. In the evening I had to put up at an inn, and to do this I was obliged to feign sickness. I was indeed ill, from suffering so much in my feet and legs, and in my whole body. They asked us whence we came, and where we were going in such dreadful weather. My servant, who is never at a loss as to what to say, replied in a way to avert suspicion, and passed me off as his relative. The next morning at daybreak, we recommenced our journey, ascending and descending by paths impossible to describe. We had taken care to put a little rice in our handkerchiefs, and this we ate at mid-day, though the rice was frozen.

In the evening we arrived at the Christian settlement of K——, where everyone was surprised to see us in such a state. My feet were bruised and my hands covered with blood, in consequence of falls on the ice. I kept up the courage of the Christians as well as I could, and admonished them to prepare themselves promptly to receive the Sacraments. In the morning I set about confessing, baptizing, and fulfilling the other functions of my ministry. Meanwhile I sent a courier to K——, to keep myself informed of all that went on. Another set out to buy me a house in the most deserted mountains of Corea, where I could retire with a few Christians if it became dangerous to stop at K——. Some days after, the first courier returned, bringing the news that all the Christians of K—— had taken to flight, and that my house and that of my servant had been burnt. All the stores which I had laid up were lost. My second courier came afterwards; he had bought and paid for in cash two houses, one for myself, the other for the Christians who should accompany me. They were twenty-five miles off, in the midst of the wildest mountains, where the only nourishment was potatoes. I gave up these houses because they were in the neighborhood of many pagan habitations.

Having finished the administration of the Christian settlement of K—— I sent a messenger to P——, to summon the Christians there to prepare themselves to receive the Sacraments. Think of the joy of those Christians! the greater number of them had not seen a missionary for thirteen years. They hastened to make preparations to receive me, but on the eve of my departure, after having baptized a pagan thirty-five years old, to whom I gave the name of Augustin, a courier from Seoul came to me with information that the king had sent satellites through all his dominions to arrest the missionaries; that they had already come to the town of K——, and to P——, where they had burned the house which was used as a residence by Father Doucet and myself when we came into Corea; and that they had arrested many pagans having the same names as the Christians of the village; and finally, that I ought to fly immediately.

On hearing this intelligence, I had to take to flight once more. But where to seek refuge? Some advised me to go to P——. "But," I replied, "if the satellites have come to P——, where there are only five Christian houses, will they not go to P——, where there are twenty? And besides, would it not be more suitable that the Christians should be ignorant of my place of concealment?" I therefore gave directions to my people to prepare to start for the province of H——, in which there were only three Christian houses. In the evening I heard the confessions of two persons ill of the plague, and some others. At three o'clock in the morning, I celebrated Holy Mass, and was ready to start. As at K——, there was extreme grief felt; they wept, they wailed, and I could not help mingling my tears with those of my poor Christians.

The new journey lasted two days. I suffered from fatigue, hunger, and cold. Being asked at an inn why I took such a journey in the mountains, where the tigers were so numerous and nothing but snow during seven months of the year, my servant replied that he was seeking a wife for his son. They asked me no more questions.

I arrived on the 19th of February, at K——, where lived the Christians among whom I had come to seek hospitality. I was half dead with fatigue, having travelled on that day 100 lys (ten leagues), which, on account of the difficulty of the roads, is equal to at least twenty French leagues. Thus, during the not quite four months that I had passed in Corea, I had crossed the entire breadth of the kingdom (65 leagues), not for the purpose of preaching and teaching, but in order to escape the satellites.

Next morning the Christians of K—— wished to receive the Sacraments. I heard their confessions, baptized six adults, administered the same Sacrament to three others, and confirmed eight neophytes. I could not give them Communion, as I had not my altar requisites. They edified me greatly by their piety and fervor. Last year, a woman of the village—though in the seventh month of her pregnancy—travelled eight leagues of the road in wintry weather, up to her ankles in snow, for the purpose of being baptized; but, not arriving until after Father B——'s departure, she was obliged to return without receiving the Sacrament. God, however, was pleased with her faith; and now, flying before the persecutors, I was led to take refuge in the very house of this courageous catechumen. You may guess what a happiness this was for us both.

Whilst at K——, I witnessed a similar fact. In the month of February, a woman sixty years of age came a distance of 20 leagues to be baptized. At that season the snow is sometimes two feet deep in the mountains. I found her too ignorant of the Faith, and she was obliged to return without baptism. Greatly afflicted by my refusal, she said to me: "Let the Father impose on me a long and difficult penance and as many pains and prayers as he likes, if he will only baptize me." I consoled her by explaining to her that if I baptized her then, when she was so badly instructed, I would commit a sin myself, and she would receive less spiritual benefit from the rite.

"But," added she, "if the Father is seized by the satellites, what will become of me?"

"Never fear," I said to her; "I shall not be taken this time; and next year I will baptize you, and give you the name of Magdalene. A great sinner was Magdalene, but by her tears and penitence she became a great saint."

"Oh," said the poor woman, "I will begin from this very day to pray to St. Magdalene to watch over the Father and protect him; and I will learn my catechism so well, that next year you cannot refuse me the grace of baptism, of which undoubtedly I am not worthy at present."

Examples of such lively faith are by no means rare in Corea. If they had only a little liberty, all anxiety as they are to learn the truth, the Coreans would be converted in great numbers; but they are fettered by apprehension and the fear of death. In Corea a Christian is regarded as the declared enemy of the kingdom, and if discovered, he is sure to be sent to heaven with all expedition: death is his portion.

I might remark in passing that the Coreans are very unfortunate. They are overwhelmed with taxes, pillaged by the satellites, plundered by the numerous brigands of the country; all, from the emperor to the lowest official in the empire, conspiring to oppress the lower classes; the only question being, which shall levy the greatest exactions, and show the most cleverness, and thus arrive at the highest dignities. The people, not daring to raise their voices in complaint, lest they should lose their lives, try to imitate their rulers and indemnify themselves as best they can.

The Christians, in spite of the persecution, wished to entertain me in their own fashion. As it was the eve of the Carnival, the reason was all the greater for allowing themselves the luxury of a little meat, for they are not in the habit of taking any during the entire Lent. They therefore purchased two fat dogs for two francs, and served them up with sauce. The Coreans prefer dog-flesh to pheasant, and consider it superior to every other. At great feasts, if they had all the *ragouts* of the royal palace on the table, they would think they were ill provided unless they had a dish of dog. They brought me two porringers of this delicacy, thinking they were giving me the greatest treat. But no sooner did I inhale the odor of the repast than my appetite vanished. I sent away the dish in all haste, to the great astonishment of my attendants, who asked me with anxiety whether I was ill. "No," I replied; "it is only a slight indisposition, caused by the smell of the food you have brought me, for in my country dog-flesh is not eaten."

"Is it possible," cried they, "that the French do not eat dogs! They must be very delicate indeed, for we consider this food a great luxury!"

While waiting for the persecution to cease, for I thought it must be nearly coming to an end, I began to study the Chinese characters. Alone in a dark little room, out of which I could not venture, seeing that the pagans were continually passing before the house, I was often weary enough. But the will of God before all! My position was easier than that of my Vicar-Apostolic, who was languishing in chains. On the 5th of March, three robbers passed the night in the house which served me as a hiding-place. You may imagine that neither the Christians nor I closed our eyes for an instant. However, we got off with the fright. They were regaled with potatoes, the only food of the country, and dismissed very politely.

To-day, the 9th of March, the weather is magnificent, at least as far as I can judge, looking through my paper window. The sky is clear, and the sun is shining on the peaks visible from my cabin. Their summits are covered with snow, and, reflecting the light, display a dazzling spectacle. How I long to be able to go out! But it is not possible; I am not allowed to contemplate the beauties of nature. I willingly make the sacrifice, and offer it with all my heart to my Divine Master. Another thought troubles me: where are my brother priests? Doubtless like myself, in some poor little hut in the recesses of the mountains. And my Vicar-Apostolic, how fares it with him in his prison at Seoul? Ah, perhaps he is more fortunate than his missionaries, for I have been told that he has won the palm of martyrdom. I hope and fear it at the same time. If it be so, what joy for heaven! but what a sorrow for the Church of Corea, deprived of the best of fathers! I also desire to follow in his footsteps and to shed my blood for Him who has poured out the last drop of His to deliver us from death and to give us eternal life. But am I worthy to die for my God? No: I dare not hope for so great a happiness. At least, do Thou, my Divine Saviour, strengthen me to support with patience and resignation the pains and miseries of this mortal life, so that I may merit to enjoy the crown of immortality which Thou hast promised to those who shall persevere to the end in Thy holy service. Always and everywhere I shall strive to conform myself to the impenetrable designs of Thy Divine Providence. And how great will be my happiness if, after having worthily and fruitfully fulfilled my apostolic career, I can repeat those beautiful words: *Bonum certamen certavi, cursum consummavi, fidem servavi!* "I have fought the good fight; I have finished my course; I have kept the faith."

MARCH 12.

I learn that Mgr. Ridel has not been put to death, and that the eighteen Christians imprisoned with him receive no food except what is absolutely necessary to keep them from dying of starvation. Two of the number have been put to the torture. The first servant of Mgr. Ridel was interrogated by the ministers of the king. He was asked the name of the place where the missionary was staying who had been seen two months before with the Vicar-Apostolic. "In Corea, where persecution is always raging," he replied, "two missionaries cannot reside together; and if one has been seen with the Bishop, he was only there for the moment, and must have gone away immediately to attend to his duties. I do not know to what part of the country he has gone." The second servant was not more than seventeen years old, and it was feared on account of his youth, the violence of the tortures might exhort from him some compromising expressions; but when summoned to apostatize and reveal the retreat of the missionaries, he replied with firmness: "The Catholic religion forbids us to apostatize, or to denounce those who expose themselves to death in coming to instruct us."

The same courier tells me that most of the Christians of K—— have sought refuge in the mountains, and that my effects, which were hidden for more than a month, have been carried by four neophytes to another Christian settlement, where they buried them once more. No news of Father Doucet, nor of my other fellow-priests; all I know is that they have not yet been arrested.

My Christians tell me that it is impossible for me to remain any longer with them, for if the satellites re-enter K——, I shall inevitably be discovered and taken. I am sending two Christians to prepare a new hiding-place in the mountains of the north, where snow remains up to the month of August, and tigers abound. I have ordered them to purchase two houses; one in the least inhabited part of the mountain, for myself and my servant and his family; the other at some distance from the first, for a family of Christians, who, in case of pagans coming to these parts, will prevent their ascending higher. In the midst of these mountains no food can be had. "What will become of the Father?" said the Christians to me. "Never fear: I can live like yourselves on potatoes and oats. Here I have a little rice, some potatocakes and barley meal, with garlic and wild onions for a dessert. If I have no rice down there, I shall not die for want of it, for there are plenty of potatoes, they say."

My Christians set out, and fifteen days later they returned beaming with joy. They had purchased two houses: one, with two fields of potatoes, cost seven francs; the other, smaller and surrounded by two acres and a half of arable land, cost four francs. These two houses, situated on the slope of the highest mountain of the province, the wood on which has never been cut down, were abandoned by the pagans on account of the tigers, which had devoured several of their children. Every night the howling of these animals is to be heard. The inhabitants of the neighborhood take the precaution of making fast their doors and windows by means of enormous trunks of trees, which they roll forward as soon as the sun sets, and do not remove until sunrise next morning. Several times the tigers came in broad day-light and carried off their pigs before their eyes. This was the place in which I was going to spend the summer.

For prudence sake I procured, for eleven francs, an old Corean gun, and gave it to my servant. The Corean guns are very heavy, and when you want to use them you have to fire them off with a lighted coal, thereby running a great risk of wounding yourself.

Before repairing to my new residence, a courier from Seoul informed me among other things that the satellites in over-running the environs of K—— had done a great deal of damage, but at the expense of the pagans. The latter, having taken possession of the effects of the Christians who had taken flight, were treated as robbers by the king's envoys, and beaten with the ratan; in their turn they were now obliged to fly. There is much talk of an approaching war with Japan; but nothing can be known for certain. The king of Corea in speaking to his ministers said to them: "Up to this, the law of the kingdom punishes with death every stranger who dares to come into our country. If this law were abolished, and the Bishop sent back to his own country, what would you think of it?" One of the ministers replied: "The language of the king appears to me very strange; it is the first time I have heard such words. How could we send back to his own country a man who, in spite of the laws of our land, has introduced himself secretly into Corea to teach our people a perverse doctrine? If the king send away the Bishop, will the satellites who have been sent to search for the four other Europeans, take much trouble to hunt them up?" On hearing these words, the king merely gave orders that the Bishop should not be maltreated. Finally, three satellites commissioned to discover the missionaries having been killed by robbers, the persecution raged with greater violence than ever in the southern part of Corea.

On the 13th of April, after having administered the sacrament of penance to all the poor Christians whom I was about to leave, perhaps forever, I set out, accompanied by my servant and two other Christians. It was not very cold, but the wind blew violently. There had been rain the previous evening; the roads were heavy, and sometimes we were ankle-deep in water. In turning our steps to the north we soon struck the snow.

This day's journey cost me more than all the others together. During those two months of exile I had lost a great deal of my strength, owing to the bad food of the country. Towards noon, being quite overcome with fatigue, I sat down at the foot of a mountain to partake of such refreshment as we had with us. My good Christians, seeing my feet sore and swollen, said to me: "Father, it must be confessed that the road to heaven is not an easy one."

"Yes," I replied; "but think of what recompense after a life so short compared with eternity, and of the terrible torments prepared for those who die in a state of mortal sin!" I set out again, but only to sit down once more after a few minutes; and so it went on until I arrived, more dead than alive, at my abode in the evening. But I was at last at home, and fully resolved not to leave it as long as the persecution lasted.

The day after my arrival (4th of April) I examined the topographical position of the place, and after many researches and inquiries I was able to understand where I was. This mountain is the highest of all the surrounding mountains, and belongs to the chain which crosses Corea in its entire length. It has plenty of trees: firs, birches, cedars, etc., but no oaks or beeches. In the parts that are not wooded, enormous pointed rocks rise into the clouds, and serve as hiding-places for the tigers. The evening before my arrival, the roaring of these animals was louder and more prolonged than usual. "No doubt," said my people, "they are roaring for the last time; for, as soon as the Father arrives they will quit the neighborhood." The thing may seem incredible, but nevertheless, since I came here, a month and a half ago, they have not been heard even once. The pagans living at the foot of the mountains have seen their pigs and dogs carried off in broad daylight, and under their very eyes, whilst neither my Christians nor myself have seen or heard anything of them. How can we help recognizing in this an effect of the protection of Divine Providence?

By another courier I heard on the 15th of April that none of our priests had been arrested, but that more than fifty Christians of the south of Corea were confined in the prison of Seoul, and that several had died in it of starvation. The massacre of the three satellites by the robbers has greatly aggravated the persecution in the south of the kingdom. The Christians are flying in every direction, abandoning their houses, their fields, and their cattle, to save their miserable existence. Bands of robbers are overrunning the country. The plague has also made its appearance, and victimized a considerable number. In a Christian village, consisting of only twelve families, nine persons have died. Lastly, the tigers are making great ravages. In a single village near the capital, fifty persons have been devoured in a few weeks. The weather is bad, snow still falling, and it is greatly to be feared that this will also prove a famine year.

Impenetrable indeed are the designs of God. What is there in store for this kingdom of Corea, where so many generous martyrs have confessed the faith by the effusion of their blood? In seeing so many scourges desolating their country, will not the pagans at last open their hearts to the voice of the Gospel! I do not think it necessary to go far in search of the cause of these calamities: it is, in my opinion, to be found in the obstinacy of the king and mandarins in shedding the innocent blood of the Christians. Liberty is given to robbers and assassins; but the Christians are slaughtered without mercy. The people themselves, horrified at seeing human blood shed under such pretexts, ask themselves what crime has been committed by these people, who seem to be the best in the whole country. Let us beg of God to vouchsafe in His mercy to pardon our persecutors, for, like the Jews who crucified our Lord Jesus Christ, they know not what they do.

For more than a month I have had no news. In the hollow of this desert mountain, I am, as it were, forsaken, having no other food than a little rice—which has to be procured from a distance of eight leagues,—some frost-bitten potatoes, and wild herbs by way of vegetables, such as ferns, nettles, brambles, etc., without oil or any seasoning. The eight Christians who accompany me are likely to die of hunger, for there is nothing to be bought. I have still fifteen double measures of oats; but when that is exhausted what shall we do for food? God will provide; may His Name be blessed! I await with impatience the end of this persecution. For want of substantial food, my strength has completely failed. And yet I am full of confidence all the time. I have not come on the mission to take my ease, but to conform myself to the holy will of God. I give myself entirely to Thee, O my God! and I accept from my heart the afflictions and miseries of this life, in expiation of my faults, happy in being able to suffer something for Him who has not disdained to shed the last drop of His Blood for the salvation of men.

(TO BE CONTINUED.)

Letter from Rome.

ROME, January 20, 1880.

DEAR "AVE MARIA":—Callous, in good sooth, must be that Catholic who, having the good fortune of living in Rome, feels not, at least, a transient sentiment of religious enthusiasm on witnessing the universality of his Church as evidenced in the sacred Octavarium of Epiphany which is celebrated yearly in the Church of Sant' Andrea della Valle. To see Masses celebrated in the Syro-Maronitic, in the Greco-Melchitic, in the Chaldean, in the Greek and Armenian rites, and to know that each individual celebrant believes and represents hundreds of thousands of believers in the formula *ubi Leo, ibi Petrus—ibique Ecclesia;* to hear successively in German, in Spanish, in English, in French, in Polish, and in Bohemian, men preach Jesus Christ and Him just born under the ægis of the same principle; to witness in the evening of each day the majestic old ritual of the Latin Church executed by young seminarians of every land and clime, and to know that all these are animated with immovable faith in that very same principle, is, indeed, something to grow enthusiastic over, and presents a grand contrast against the Babelic confusion and disheartening inefficiency of the many interconfounding sects of the nineteenth century. The exercises of the Octave of the Epiphany were instituted in the year 1836 by the venerable servant of God, Vincenzo Pallotti, the founder of the Pious Society of the Missions. Each day of the Octave is thus divided: The church is opened at 5 o'clock, a. m.; at half-past five, a Low Mass, the rosary and prayers; at 6 o'clock, an Italian sermon, followed by Benediction. At 9 o'clock, High Mass in the Latin rite. At 10 o'clock, Solemn High Mass in some of the Oriental rites. At 11 o'clock, a sermon in some foreign language. At 3 o'clock, p. m., spiritual reading, rosary and prayers. At half-past three, an Italian sermon, then Exposition of the Blessed Sacrament. At half-past five, reading again, the third part of the rosary and prayers. At 6 p. m., a third sermon in Italian, followed by Benediction. During the Octave a magnificent crib is exposed to view behind the high altar, representing the adoration of the Wise Men. The figures are life-size, and the crib itself very large, and beautifully illuminated by a great golden star above. The whole is the gift of Prince Torlonia.

It is needless to say that these ceremonies attracted the native Romans and foreigners in shoals. The magnificent robes and crowns worn by the Oriental Prelates during the celebration of Mass were objects of great admiration; and contrasted with the strange monodies sung by the assistants and the mystic ceremonies of the Eastern rites, stood the grand and imposing simplicity, not devoid of mystic significance, of the Latin rite. Yet under the diversities of form every soul present saw unity of substance—to wit, one faith.

I would fain turn back to Twelfth-Night as celebrated in the American College. A time-honored custom of the institution assembles the Superiors and students in the spacious old parlor after supper. A bright fire burns on the hearth. The big chandelier is lit up, giving a pleasant, cozy glow to the room, and revealing in tempting relief on the table in the corner the enormous Twelfth-Night cake charged with the traditional bean, and flanked by sturdy decanters of honest wine. For a few hours there is a communion of innocent mirth and good spirits varied with music. The old-time songs of the home beyond the seas are sung, and the last pieces on the programme are, and always have been, those two beautiful effusions of our national muse, "The Old Folks at Home" and "My Old Kentucky Home, Good-Night!" This year a distinguished guest assisted at the entertainment in the person of the Right Rev. Joseph P. Machebœuf, Vicar-Apostolic of Colorado; in fact, the principle feature in the evening's entertainment was the presentation to him of a beautiful address of congratulation on the part of the students. It was couched in the following lines, composed for the occasion by Mr. Austin O'Malley, a student of the College:

'Mongst men are those to whom when snows
Which we are wont to call "the years,"
Are sleeping on their rev'rend heads,
The consciousness of days well spent
Is sweeter far than fortune's smile:
And though old Time be harsh, his hand
Brings out the wondrous beauty of
Their sinless youth, their manhood true,
And holy eld, as crushing feet
Set free the fragrance of the flow'r.
———— For that *you* have this consciousness
We thank our God.
    The Father sends
Adown your prairies th' Springtide wind,
And leading back the youthful sun
To frozen hills, it driveth out
The Winter's flock of dusky clouds,
And wakes to life the blossoms that
Have slept: and never weary grows the wind,
But after many days it dies
At Summer's feet. 'Tis thus with you.
The Father gave to you to lead
His Infant Christ down into th' West,
To drive the clouds of sin and death
Back to their gloomsome hell, to wake
To life and love the souls that slept.
And never weary have you grown,
And after many days to rest
You'll sink at Mary's feet. Again,

For that you have this consciousness
We thank our God.
    And this we ask
From thee:—when snow of years shall fall
Beyond thy locks and e'enmost close
The eyelids of thy memory,
At each recurrence of this Feast
As with the holy Kings you praise
Our Baby Christ, the beams of thought
May kiss away the Snows, and you
Will look upon us, praying for
    Our souls.

The good Prelate was deeply moved by the recital of these lines, and expressed as much in the few remarks he made in reply. There was considerable amusement when the cake was cut and divided. The lucky owner of the bean received as a present a copy of the *Rituale Romanum*.

The Cause for the beatification and canonization of the Venerable Père Claude Columbière, the Apostle of the Sacred Heart of Jesus, is at last before the Sacred Congregation of Rites. The Holy Father was pleased to ratify, on the 8th inst., the Sentence of the Congregation of Rites of the 18th of December, which admitted the signing of a Commission for the introduction of the Cause. The Pope signed the Commission with his own hand. He has also established a commission to deliberate on the publication of the various Catalogues of the Vatican Library; it is composed of his Eminence Cardinal Pitra, Librarian of the Holy Roman Church; of Mgr. Capecelatro, Vice-Librarian; of Mgr. Martinucci, First Custodian; of Rev. Father Bollig, S. J., Second Custodian, and of the Comm. Gio. Battista De Rossi. His love of studies and his great desire to encourage them have prompted him to provide also for the convenience of all who wish to consult documents in the Vatican archives. He has given orders that a large hall be fitted up in the archives and furnished handsomely with desks, chairs, stationery, etc.

Mgr. Tripepi, who organized last year that splendid demonstration of Catholic journalists, has, in view of the universal enthusiasm aroused by the Encyclical *Æterni Patris*, conceived the notion of inviting to Rome the representatives of all the sciences, in order to offer a splendid demonstration of homage to Pope Leo XIII, the restorer of Christian Philosophy. The Pope has approved the idea. The day chosen for the audience is the 7th of March, 1880, feast of the Angelic Doctor, and also the fiftieth anniversary of the public scientific dispute sustained in the Roman College by young Gioacchino Pecci, now Pope Leo XIII. The representatives of the Catholic universities, academies, scientific associations, institutes, seminaries and colleges throughout the world are invited to attend. On the 6th of March there will be a general preparatory assembly of the scientific men, in which discourses befitting the occasion will be pronounced. On the morning of the 7th all will hear Mass at the altar of St. Thomas Aquinas in St. Peter's. The audience will take place at noon. In the evening, the Arcadians will give an extraordinary tournament in honor of the Angelic Doctor, and of his vindicator Leo XIII. Those who intend to participate in the demonstration are requested to write to Mgr. Tripepi, *Direttore del Papato*.

Speaking of demonstrations in honor of the Papacy brings to my mind a subject upon which it had often been my intention to descant at large. I mean the devotion of the Italians to the Pope. It sounds queer to American ears—that phrase, "Devotion of the Italians." Americans are accustomed to associate the Italians with most, if not all, of the bitterness of the present condition of the Papacy. Yet I take it upon myself to affirm that a great, a sterling, and a universal devotion exists among the Italians for the Papacy and for its incumbent. I deduce my conclusion from figures—from the enormous sums of money contributed by the Italians towards the support of the Holy Father—and I quote from the statistics of the *Unità Cattolica*. That excellent journal alone has laid at the feet of the Holy Father the enormous sum of 5,201,493 francs, all the result of subscriptions among its Italian readers. Up to Jan. 1877, it had collected the sum of 4,882,886 frs. In 1877 it collected 146,437 frs.; in 1878, 73,000 frs.; in 1879, 99,170: Total as above. This magnificent sum does not include the presents in gold and objects of art, which exceed in worth a million francs; nor the other legacy of one million francs left to the Holy Father through the columns of the *Unità Cattolica* by the munificent Duchess of Galliera. These figures are eloquent—so much the more so because they represent but a part of the devotion of the Italians to the Pope—that part, to wit, which reads the *Unità Cattolica*. When we remember that every Catholic journal in the Peninsula also receives subscriptions of Peter's Pence, and presents at different periods conspicuous sums to the Pope, we will refrain from asserting that the Pope is supported entirely by foreign contributions, and that the devotion of his own countrymen is merely nominal.

ARTHUR.

Catholic Notes.

——The latest clerical convert to Catholicism is the Rev. William H. Lyall, Rector of St. Dionis, Backchurch, London. Mr. Lyall's wife has been a Catholic for some time.

——We hear from Paderborn that among the manuscripts of the late Bishop Conrad Martin an excellent essay was found, and is now in press. Its title is "*Die Evangelischen Parabeln Theologisch Erklärt*" (The Parables of the Gospel Theologically Explained).

——The Cork *Examiner* says that all the leaders and members of that Ritualistic Institution, St. Peter's Retreat, at Dalwich Common, South London, have been converted to the Catholic Faith, and that the superior has explained and justified this step in a public letter.

——END OF THE KUPELIAN SCHISM.—Monsignor Hassan sent a dispatch to Rome on the 12th ult. stating that the two last of the Armenian Bishops who adhered to the new schism of Kupelian had tendered their submission. Thus the schism is virtually at an end. It will be remembered that Mgr. Kupelian himself submitted some time ago.

——That distinguished missionary Rev. Father Henneberry, who for the past two years has been giving missions in the Australian colonies, promises to become a second Father Mathew in the cause of temperance. He has given the pledge to over 34,000 persons during the last two years, and, as a rule, it has been faithfully kept. May the good missionary be long spared to his labors, and may they be blessed a thousandfold!

——A few days ago a young Protestant mother called upon a Catholic lady, and told her that her baby had been christened the day after Christmas. "Well, did the child cry at the touch of the water?" "Oh, no," the mamma replied; "the minister only put the water on the frock." "What!" exclaimed the Catholic lady, "did he not pour the water on the head or face?" "No," she replied, "*only on the frock;* it was so kind and thoughtful of him!" (mentioning the parson's name).—*Catholic Times.*

—VERY REV. FATHER PROULX.—His Holiness Leo XIII has conferred upon this venerable ecclesiastic the dignity of Domestic Prelate. The Toronto *Globe* says of him: "Monseigneur Proulx was ordained priest in 1833, and is the scion of a noble family in the province of Quebec who were obliged to flee to New France in order to escape the horrors of the first French Revolution. He civilized and converted the Indians of Manitoulin Island. He baptized 1,200—mostly adults—in two years, and his labors in this city during the ravages of the terrible plague of '47 and '48, in which his fellow-laborer, Bishop Power, and other priests, were stricken down, are well-known to all classes of the community."

—THE DEDICATION OF ST. IGNATIUS'S CHURCH, SAN FRANCISCO, CALIFORNIA, took place on Sunday, February 1st, Most Rev. Archbishop Alemany performing the august ceremonies, which were witnessed by an immense concourse of people. The procession was marshalled by the gentlemen of the Sodality of the Blessed Virgin Mary, who also acted as ushers and escorts. They were subdivided, into ten divisions, each under a director, and all under the supervision of Prefect James R. Kelly. Pontifical High Mass was sung by Most Rev. Archbishop Alemany, assisted by Rev. Fathers Tornielli and Calzia as deacon and subdeacon. The dedicatory sermon was preached by Right Rev. Bishop Healy, of Portland, Maine. At half-past seven in the evening, Pontifical Vespers were sung, Right Rev. Bishop Healy officiating, and an eloquent sermon was preached by Very Rev. Father Prendergast, Vicar-General of the Archdiocese. St. Ignatius's Church is under the zealous and devoted pastoral care of Fathers of the Society of Jesus. The 1st of February was a great day for the members of St. Ignatius's parish.

—AN INDIAN'S VISION.—In a recent lecture on the Church in Montana, Rev. L. B. Palladino, S. J., related the following incident: "While I was staying at St. Ignatius's, an old Indian, by name Quiqulitzo, a man intensely pious, and who would give you the distance between two places by the number of rosaries he was in the habit of saying in going from one to another, was fishing one day at Flathead Lake, when, of a sudden, he saw something that seemed, as he said, to take his breath from him. He dropped his line, and away he started for the mission. On entering my room, he said abruptly to me: 'I saw Sinze Chitaky!' This was the Indian name of good Brother Vincent Magri, a favorite with the Indians at St. Ignatius's, where he had lived a number of years, but who was then stationed among the Cœur d'Alene Indians in Idaho. 'I saw him,' continued the Indian, raising his eyes to the sky, 'riding in a most beautiful thing.' The only description he could give was that it resembled a chariot, and that he had never seen anything like it. Several days after, we received letters with the news of the demise of the Brother, which had occurred some four hundred miles from St. Ignatius's."

—A RECONCILIATION.—The reconciliation of Mr. William Grant, of Peckham, which took place on Monday, at the Church of St. Mary of the Angels, Bayswater, is one of the instances of God's long-suffering towards those who have been so unfortunate as to make shipwreck of their faith. Mr. Grant commenced life as an ordinary Church of England Protestant; was received into the Church in 1857; by a process happily unique left the Catholic Church, eleven years later, for Irvingism; abandoned that body after a five years' experience; and has since been an attractive adherent of Ritualism, and an office-bearer in the recently formed "Order of Corporate Reunion." His spiritual life for the past twelve years has been a series of disappointed hopes and aims; and he returns to his allegiance a wiser, if a sadder, man. Fortunately for himself, he seems to have carried with him in his wanderings a precious talisman in the shape of an intense devotion to the Immaculate Mother—in whose honor, indeed, he has broken a lance both with the Irvingites and with that section of the Ritualists which discredits devotion to our Blessed Lady; and Mary has not forgotten him in his need.—*Catholic Times.*

—THE AUSTRIAN EMPIRE AND THE HOLY SEE.—The Austrian Prime Minister, Von Haymerle, in a speech delivered in the Reichstag (National Assembly) earnestly urged the necessity of maintaining the representatives at Constantinople and at the Holy See as "Botschafters"—that is, embassadors of the first rank. By the course of events, the Austrian interests in Turkey have become the most important of all foreign relations; and the fact that the embassy at Rome is placed on the same footing with that at Constantinople gives ample proof of the sagacity of the Austrian Chancellor. More remarkable still are the words spoken on the same occasion on the relations to the Holy See. "There could not be any reason," said he, "that the present Pope, who enjoys the sympathies of all Europe on account of his great learning and virtue, should be treated with less consideration than his predecessor. The right of sovereignty has always and by everybody been conceded to the Holy See. Its jurisdiction and power could not be limited upon the extent of a certain territory, but the Papal sovereignty does actually represent a great and most influential power, of which the efficacy upon individual states is beyond all question."

—THE CHURCH A GREAT POWER.—A German Protestant professor of philosophy recently uttered words so significant that they have made a profound sensation alike among Catholics and Protestants: "Let us throw a glance at the recent past. The youngest and one of the most powerful empires of the world saw fit to declare war against the Church; and to-day we see her desiring to make peace with the Church. This empire came out of all its battles crowned with victory; against it is arrayed only the Catholic Church, shining more glorious than ever. The armies of false science have often been brought to bear against the Papacy; she has each time come off the victor, radiant and stronger than ever. The armies of politics have been tried against her; only the temporal power of the Pope has fallen. The spiritual throne has been strengthened; it is firmer, more solid than ever. The Catholic Church can say of herself with pride—with just pride—'When I am persecuted, I triumph.' How does this come? I am about to tell you that in these conferences. I will give you at once a brief answer: The Catholic Church has behind her a career of 1,800 years; she has become a power strongly anchored in human hearts, and we are not evil enough to wish to destroy a power which has struck such deep root into the hearts of men."

—REV. FATHER ROBERT FULTON, S. J., late President of Boston College, and Founder and President of the Young Men's Catholic Association, was tendered a farewell ovation on Thursday evening, Feb. 5th, by the young gentlemen of the Association, and one which, judging by the reports in the daily papers, was in the best of taste and will prove a memorable affair to all who witnessed it. The hall of the college was beautifully decorated with evergreen and ivy, and the audience embraced the Catholic *élite* of Boston. Among the guests were His Excellency Gov. Long, Hon. Mayor Prince, Aldermen O'Brien and Flynn, with their ladies; Mr. John Boyle O'Reilly, editor of the *Pilot*; Rev. Edward Everett Hale, and many of the principal citizens of Boston, with a large company of ladies. An address to Father Fulton was delivered by Mr. James R. Murphy, Vice-President of the Young Men's Catholic Association; and the poet-editor, Mr. John Boyle O'Reilly, read a beautiful and appropriate ode entitled "The Empty Niche." An address was also delivered by Rev. Father O'Connor, President of the College and successor to Father Fulton, and some feeling and appreciative remarks were made by Gov. Long and Mayor Prince. An excellent collation and music were subsequent features of the entertainment. It was a sad leave-taking for those present, who have become affectionately attached to Rev. Father Fulton during the seventeen years he has spent among them.

Obituary.

Died, at the Convent of the Society of the Holy Child Jesus, Sharon Hill, Delaware Co., Penn., on the evening of the 21st of January, 1880, SISTER THERESA KELLY, in the forty-third year of her age, and the sixteenth of her religious life.

Devoted in a special way, even by the exercises of her holy rule, to the contemplation of the mysteries of the Holy Childhood, there seemed a special fitness in the death of Sister Theresa during Christmas-tide, when our Lord, in His beautiful and most winning Childhood, is drawing all Christians to His crib, and attracting innocent souls to the contemplation of His Incarnation. It was as if she were indeed to continue in heaven the meditations which she had loved most on earth. Although Sister Theresa had been indisposed for a week, not the slightest fear had been entertained for her recovery. An hour before her death she was walking about her room and speaking cheerfully with the infirmarian, and through the whole day had been as lively and bright as usual. At five o'clock in the evening she was seized with convulsions, and in half an hour she had gone to her Lord, whom she had served so faithfully and so generously. But though sudden, her death was not an "unprovided" one. In a very distinct manner, Sister Theresa had kept herself always prepared for death, and her whole religious life had been a preparation for this sudden slipping off of the coil of mortality. To be a good and holy religious, as Sister Theresa was, is to rob death, let it be ever so sudden, of its terrors; and is, also, to impart the most abundant consolation to those friends, and those near of kin to her, who survive to mourn her loss. But we must still feel bound to offer suffrages for her dear soul's repose, and this is what we desire to ask for her in this brief notice. It is in death that we see the good religious reaping the fruit of years of self-denial: for to whom are suffrages given with such fidelity as to companions in religion? *Requiescat in pace.*   E. A. S.

Confraternity of the Immaculate Conception
(Or of Our Lady of Lourdes).

"We fly to thy patronage, O Holy Mother of God!"
REPORT FOR THE WEEK ENDING FEBRUARY 11TH.

The following petitions have been received: Recovery of health for 58 persons and 2 families,—change of life for 32 persons and 3 families,—conversion to the Faith for 39 persons and 9 families,—special graces for 12 priests, 6 religious, 2 clerical students, and 2 persons aspiring to the religious state,—temporal favors for 43 persons and 10 families.—spiritual favors for 52 persons and 9 families,—the spiritual and temporal welfare of 8 communities, 5 congregations, 6 schools, and 2 hospitals,—also 30 particular intentions, and 11 thanksgivings for favors received.

Specified intentions: The acquittal of two men accused of a crime, and the removal of the scandal caused thereby,—preservation of a district from epidemic diseases,—courage for some persons to attend their religious duties,—perseverance in the faith for children obliged by force of circumstances to frequent non-Catholic schools,—several suffering people in Ireland,—a family of children dangerously ill with scarlet-fever, —several influential and wealthy men addicted to intemperance,—a father much in danger of losing his mind through intemperance, and happiness for his family suffering from his bad temper,—several widows and orphans much distressed,—several persons threatened with insanity, and 4 other special intentions.

FAVORS OBTAINED.

"I return my thanks to the members of the Confraternity. My daughter, who was about to marry a Protestant, has parted his company, and now attends to her religious exercises very regularly." . . . Another parent states that her daughter who had absented herself from home has since returned and has approached the Sacraments. A gentleman much afflicted with nervous debility and sleeplessness gratefully acknowledges the benefit he has received from the water of Lourdes, feeling now as well as ever. We have received the following letter from a grateful friend: "I wrote to you some three years ago, recommending the conversion of my sister, who, I was afraid, was forsaking her religion. Now, thanks be to God, she is entirely changed; she has been invested with the Scapular, and has frequently approached the Sacraments. I also return thanks for the restoration of my husband's health, effected by the Lourdes water."

OBITUARY.

Of your charity pray for the following deceased persons: Mrs. ELLEN FOWLER, of Altoona, Pa., who was relieved of her sufferings by a holy death on the 2d inst. Mr. JOHN E. CREADY, whose death occurred at South Pittsburgh, Pa., last December. Mrs. KOLKER, of Mount Carmel, Iowa, who breathed her last on the 31st ult. Mrs. LUCY WILCOX, of Philadelphia, Pa., who died suddenly on the 22d of January, aged 79 years. Mr. JAMES MOORE, of Cascade, Iowa, who departed this life on the 5th ult. Mr. CORNELIUS Z. GOUNOUD, deceased at Napa, Cal., the 30th of January. Mr. J. KELLY, who slept in the Lord at Columbus, Wis., on the 7th ult. Miss M. GRIFFITH, whose death took place at Summit, Wis., on the 31st of last month. Mrs. E. SEERY, of Ware, Mass.; VERY REV. CHARLES CARTER; MOTHERS HELEN and GERTRUDE, of the Society of the Holy Child Jesus, recently deceased. And several others, whose names have not been given. *Requiescant in pace.*

A. GRANGER, C. S. C., Director.

Youth's Department.

Ave Maria!

AVE MARIA! hear the prayer
Of thy poor, helpless child;
Beneath thy sweet maternal care
Preserve me undefiled.

Ave Maria! for to thee,
Whom God has pleased to choose
The mother of His Son to be,
No prayer will He refuse.

Ave Maria! then implore
This only grace for me,
My heart to give for evermore
To God alone, through thee.

The Telescope.

A FAVORITE resort of the French kings used to be St. Germain Louis XIII built an observatory there, and placed a fine telescope in it. One day the king, as though by inspiration, turned the instrument towards a remote spot, where the Seine, forming an elbow, embraces the extremity of the wood of Chalon. He saw in the current of the river two bathers who were apparently engaged in teaching the art of swimming to a third, much younger. The latter, a youth of fourteen or fifteen years, escaped from their hands, and ran off on the bank to take his clothes and dress. They recalled him, jesting and laughing the while, but one could see that he did not care for any further lessons from them. Then the two bathers threw themselves upon him, and dragged him by force into the river, where they drowned him.

Having sunk their victim, they looked anxiously about on both sides of the shore, then, reassured at seeing no one, they took up their garments and walked along the river bank in the direction of the castle. The king, flinging himself on horseback, ordered five or six musketeers to accompany him, and rode off at their head. He was not long in overtaking the murderers. "Gentlemen," said he to them, "you were seen to go out three; what have you done with your companion?"

This question, asked in a decided way, dismayed them somewhat, but soon they replied that their comrade, having wished to practice swimming, they had left him in the river by the angle of the forest, near where his clothing was to be seen on the grass.

At this reply the king ordered their hands to be tied; and the musketeers having moreover bound them to one another, led them to the old castle, where they were separately incarcerated. His majesty, whose indignation was at its height, commanded the immediate appearance of the grand provost, and having related the facts to him as they had transpired under his very eye, ordered justice to be immediately enforced. The grand provost implored the king to consider that at so great a distance, and through a telescope, things might have appeared differently from what they really were: that instead of holding their friend under the water, the two bathers might have been occupied only in supporting him.

"No, monsieur; no," replied his majesty; "they drew him into the water in spite of himself, and I saw their struggles, and his too, when they sunk him."

"But, sire," replied the scrupulous magistrate, "our criminal laws require two witnesses; and your majesty, powerful as you are, supplies but one."

"Monsieur," replied the king, gently, "I authorize you to state in your sentence that you have heard as witnesses the King of Navarre and the King of France."

Seeing that the judge still hesitated, his majesty became impatient, and said, "The King Louis IX, my grandfather, often executed the law in the forest of Vincennes; I will, to-day, do the like at St. Germain."

The throne-room was immediately prepared. At his request, twenty of the leading *bourgeois* were called from the town to the castle; the lords and ladies of the court shared the benches with them. The king, decorated with his orders, mounted the throne, and the murderers were brought in. By their contradictions and their ever-increasing embarrassment, the audience easily recognized their guilt. The unfortunate young man was their half-brother, who had just inherited a fortune from their mother, who had married twice. These monsters had put him to death out of vengeance and cupidity. The king condemned them to be bound and thrown into the river just at the spot where they drowned their young brother.

When they saw the king descend from the throne, they threw themselves at his feet, and, while confessing their crime, implored his mercy. The king thanked God for the confession which had just escaped them, but confirmed the sentence, which was put into execution before the setting of the sun which had shone upon their foul deed. The following day the three bodies were found together, two leagues off, under the willows which border the meadow beyond Poissy. Orders were sent to bury them separately. The body of the poor youth was brought to St. Germain, where, at his majesty's wish, obsequies befitting his innocence and his misfortune were performed.

Four Saintly Stories.

TRANSLATED FROM THE FRENCH BY SUSAN EMERY.

I.

SAINT CLARA was so much esteemed for her holiness, that not only the Bishops and Cardinals, but even the Pope himself desired to converse with her. Once the Holy Father came to the convent where she was, to hear her speak of heavenly things. And as they were together, speaking of various matters, St. Clara had the table laid and bread set upon it, that the Holy Father might bless it. Then, the spiritual conversation being ended, St. Clara knelt with great respect and begged the Pope to bless the bread placed upon the table.

The Holy Father replied: "Very faithful Sister Clara, I desire you to bless this bread, and to make upon it the sign of the holy Cross of Christ, to whom you have given yourself entirely."

Saint Clara said to him: "Most Holy Father, excuse me; I should deserve to be greatly blamed if, in the presence of the Vicar of Christ, I, who am a lowly and miserable woman, should be so bold as to give this blessing."

The Pope replied: "In order that this may not be laid to presumption on your part, but that you may have the merit of obedience, I command you to make over this bread the sign of the Cross and to bless it in the name of God."

Then Saint Clara, like a true daughter of obedience, devoutly blessed the bread.

Wonderful thing! immediately the sign of the Cross appeared perfectly traced upon each piece of bread.

Then a part of these pieces was eaten, and the rest kept on account of the miracle. The Holy Father, who had seen the miracle, took one of these pieces, and, giving thanks to God, he departed, leaving his benediction with Saint Clara.

At that time, both Sister Ortulane, mother of St. Clara, and Agnes, her sister, were living in the same convent. With them lived many other holy religious, to whom St. Francis sent a great number of sick people; and they, by their prayers and by the sign of the Cross, restored them all to health.

II.

St. Louis, King of France, went from place to place on pilgrimages, to visit the most famous sanctuaries. Having heard Brother Giles's great holiness praised, he resolved to visit him. Therefore he went to Perouse, where Brother Giles was dwelling. He came to the convent door like some poor, unknown pilgrim, with a few companions, and asked urgently for Brother Giles, but did not tell the porter who he himself was. The porter went to Brother Gilles and told him that there was a pilgrim at the door, asking for him; and God revealed to him that it was the King of France.

With great fervor the holy man left his cell and hurried to the door. Without any questions, and never having seen each other before, they fell upon their knees, embraced each other with great familiarity, as if for a long time they had been very dear friends.

They remained together for a long while, but neither spoke a word. When they separated, St. Louis proceeded on his travels, and Brother Giles returned to his cell.

The king being gone, a Brother asked one of his companions who it was that had embraced Brother Giles so ardently; and he replied that it was Louis, King of France, who had come to see the holy man. The Brother told the others, and they were much chagrined because Brother Giles had not spoken; and, greatly afflicted, they said to him: "Oh! Brother Gilles, how could you show so little courtesy! That holy king came from France to see you and to hear you speak some good word, and you said nothing to him!"

Brother Giles answered: "My very dear Brothers, do not be surprised that neither he nor I could say a word. As soon as we embraced, the divine light revealed and manifested his heart to me, and mine to him. So, by God's help, we looked into our hearts, and knew much better what we wished to say to each other than if we had used words. Such is the powerlessness of human speech to express clearly the secret mysteries of God, that words would have been a trouble to us rather than a consolation. Therefore, understand that the king has gone away perfectly content, and his soul thoroughly comforted."

III.

After St. Francis' death, two brothers lived under his rule in the province of the Marche. One was named Brother Humilis and the other Brother Pacificus, and both were men of great sanctity. The one, Brother Humilis, dwelt in the monastery of Soffiano, where he died; and the other dwelt in another monastery very far distant. It pleased God that Brother Pacificus, being in prayer one day in a solitary place, was rapt in ecstasy, and saw the soul of Brother Humilis mounting straight to heaven without delay and without hindrance.

It came to pass that after many years this

Brother Pacificus was sent to the monastery of Soffiano, where his brother had died. At that time the brothers were moving from one monastery to another the remains of the religious who had died. When they came to the burial-place of Brother Humilis, Brother Pacificus took the bones, washed them with costly wine, and then wrapped them in a white cloth.

The other brothers were astonished, and it did not seem to them that this was a good example; since, for a man of so great holiness, Brother Pacificus appeared to show more respect to the remains of his friend than to those of the others, who had not been less holy.

Brother Pacificus, humbly desiring to satisfy them, said: "My dear Brothers, be not astonished that I have done for the bones of my friend what I have not done for the others. Blessed be God! for it is not, as you think, poor earthly love which influences me, but I have acted thus because at the moment when my brother quitted this life, while I was praying in a solitary place and far from him, I saw his soul mount straight to heaven; I am certain, then, that his bones are holy, and that they will one day be in paradise. If God had given me the same certainty in regard to the other Brothers, I would have paid the same respect to their remains."

And the Brothers, seeing by this narration how holy and devout were the prayers of Brother Pacificus, were greatly edified, and began to praise God.

IV.

Brother James of Fallerone, a man of great holiness, was once very ill in the monastery of Moliano. Brother John of Alverno, who was living at Massa, learned of his illness, and, because he loved him as his tender father, began to pray for him, asking God to give Brother James health of body if that were best for his soul. As he was devoutly praying, he was rapt in ecstasy, and saw in the air a great host of angels and saints above his cell, which was in a wood; and this apparition shed abroad such splendor that all the country around about was illumined. Among these angels he saw the sick Brother James, for whom he was praying; he saw him standing, clothed in white and all resplendent. He saw, moreover, in the midst of the heavenly host, St. Francis, adorned with the sacred stigmata of Christ, and covered with glory; he saw also, and recognized, the holy Brother Lucido and the old Brother Matthew of Monte Rubbiano, and several other Brothers whom he had never seen or known in this life. Brother John felt so great joy at this revelation, on account of the salvation of his friend's soul, that he felt no trouble about the death of his body; but with great tenderness of heart he called to him, saying inwardly: "Brother James, my sweet father; Brother James, my sweet brother; Brother James, most faithful servant and friend of God; Brother James, companion of angels and saints!"

With this certainty and joy, Brother John came to himself again, and immediately he departed to visit Brother James at Moliano. He found him so dull that he could hardly speak; he announced to him the death of his body and the salvation of his soul, according to the assurance which he had by means of the divine revelation. Thereupon Brother James was greatly rejoiced; and he received his friend with a gracious smile, thanking him for the good news which he brought him, and recommending himself to his prayers.

Then Brother John begged him tenderly to return to him after his death and reveal his state. He promised to do so, if it pleased God; and feeling the hour of his departure draw near, he began devoutly to repeat this verse of the psalm: "I will fall asleep in peace for the eternal life, and I will rest."

After he was buried, Brother John returned to the monastery of Massa, where he awaited the fulfilment of the dead Brother's promise. That day, as he was praying, Christ appeared to him with a great company of angels and saints, but Brother James was not among them; whereat Brother John marvelled much, and he recommended him devoutly to Christ.

The next day, as Brother John was praying in the forest, Brother James appeared to him, all joyful, and accompanied by angels. Brother John said to him: "O very dear father! why did you not come to me before?"

Brother James replied: "Because I still had need of some purification; but at the same hour that Christ appeared to you, and you recommended me to Him, He delivered me from all pain." At these words Brother James disappeared, and went away to heaven with the blessed company of angels, and Brother John remained greatly consoled.

Brother James of Fallerone died on the vigil of St. James the Apostle, in the month of July, in the monastery of Moliano, where, through his merits, many miracles were worked.

COLUMBUS, the discoverer of America, was one of the noblest benefactors of the human race. Unlike other great men, whose genius promoted the interests of their own particular country, Columbus by his achievements influenced the destinies of the entire world. His character combined all the elements of true greatness. After repeated disappointments, that wasted the best years of his life, he finally triumphed over the prejudices and ignorance of those who regarded him as a wild visionary, and discovered a New World.

THE AVE MARIA.

A Journal devoted to the Honor of the Blessed Virgin.

HENCEFORTH ALL GENERATIONS SHALL CALL ME BLESSED.—St. Luke, i, 48.

VOL. XVI.   NOTRE DAME, INDIANA, FEBRUARY 28, 1880.   No. 9.

[Copyright: Rev. D. E. Hudson, C. S. C.]

[For the Ave Maria.]
Christus Consolator.

BY M. J. C.

FROM this unsounded sea of mortal grief,
'Mid these wild storms that rack my wounded breast,
To Thee alone I turn me for relief:
    Thou art my rest.

In doubt and darkness, still those eyes divine
Meet my sad glances, full of heavenly light,
And bid the day-star o'er my pathway shine,
    In sorrow's night.

Shall I not trust in Thee? Ah, Death may chill
With his benumbing touch this mortal frame,
And bid this fluttering heart's wild pulse be still;
    But Thy loved Name

Shall be the last breath of these murmuring lips,
Thy matchless love Life's last sweet memory,
Until these eyes, unveiled from Death's eclipse,
    In heaven shall gaze on Thee.

Hath He not loved me? Through the 'wildering track
Of many centuries that since have rolled,
To that last night of grief and fear look back,
    My shrinking soul.

To that dim garden scene, when friendly night
Mantled the earth with its o'ershadowing veil:
Is that sad, prostrate Form the Lord of light,
    Discrowned and pale?

'Tis He! my God! my Saviour! Master! Friend!
And sorrowing angels view Him from above;
'Tis He! and Life and Time itself must end
    Ere I forget His love.

These tears of mine were also shed by Him,
Nay, more: His bloody sweat bedewed the ground:
While at His anguish awe-struck cherubim
    Watched wondering round.

And shall I fear to taste the bitter cup
Which He, my Master, drained? and passing o'er
The heavy cross, refuse to take it up,
    Which Jesus bore?

No! no! my part is chosen; I will tread
Unshrinkingly, the path that Thou didst go,
Though waves of bitterness o'erwhelm my head,
    My Guide I know.

'Mid all life's sorrows still in Thee I trust,
Thou art my Master, and my heart's sole Lord;
And when my mortal part is dust to dust,
    Thou wilt be my reward.

The World Converted by a Crucified Jew.

(CONCLUSION.)

IT is a fact that since the creation of the world all the nations of the earth awaited the coming of a Holy One, who should be a Mediator and a Reparator of all things; they even expected Him to appear in Judea; respecting this fact we have the testimony of Suetonius and Tacitus among the ancients; and of Boulanger, Voltaire, and Volney, unbelievers of more recent times.

Thus for four thousand years all nations awaited the coming Mediator with daily increasing hope, until eighteen centuries ago, when Jesus Christ came to make Himself known as the long-expected Saviour, and from that time forth the nations no longer await him. For eighteen centuries, all peoples have agreed in proclaiming that the Mediator came, and is Jesus Christ; or that mankind has duped itself in awaiting this Mediator for four thousand years, or in ceasing to await him since Jesus Christ has appeared on earth!

With what faith, what love, and respect, then, will we not henceforth read the Gospel; that Gospel of which it has been said by one who cannot be suspected of partiality, * "This Divine

* Rousseau's "Emile." 2d Correspondence with the King of Poland.

book, the only one necessary to a Christian, and most useful to all, has only to be meditated to instil into the soul love for the Author, and a firm purpose of obeying His precepts. Never has virtue spoken with so mild a tongue; never has the most profound wisdom spoken with such energy and simplicity; and laying it aside, one feels improved by it." If the impious man speaks thus of the Gospel, what then must the Christian say? But let us continue citing from this same author in his "Emile": "I avow that the majesty of the Scripture astonishes me, the sanctity of the Gospel speaks to my heart; compare the writings of the philosophers with all their pomp, and how insignificant do they appear! can it be that a book, at the same time so sublime and so simple, is the work of men? Can it be that He of whom it speaks is but a man Himself? Is this the tone of an enthusiast, of an ambitious sectary? What touching grace in His instructions! what sweetness, what purity in His ways! what elevation in His maxims! what profound wisdom in his discourses! what presence of mind, what fitness in His answers! what empire over his passions! where is the man, where is the sage, who knows how to suffer and die thus, without weakness, without ostentation?

"When Plato depicted his imaginary just man, covered with all the opprobrium of crime, and worthy of all the price of virtue, he pictures Jesus Christ; indeed the likeness is so striking that all the fathers have felt it, and it is not possible to mistake it. What prejudices, what blindness must possess us, to dare to compare the son of Sophronicus with the Son of Mary! what distance between the one and the other! Socrates dying without pain, and without ignominy, sustains easily to the end his personality; and if this easy death had not come to honor his life, one would doubt whether, after all, Socrates with all his intellect was but a sophist. The death of Socrates philosophizing tranquilly with his friend, is the sweetest that one can desire; that of Jesus expiring in torture, insulted, derided and cursed by a people, is the most apalling that one can imagine. Socrates taking the poisoned cup, blesses the weeping one who presents it to him; Jesus in the midst of His agony prays for His executioners who rage around Him. Yes! if the life and death of Socrates are those of a sage, the life and death of Jesus Christ are those of a God."

After these irrefutable testimonies we will cite one other; that of one of those very rare men whom Providence raises up from time to time to chastise and reform peoples and rulers, in order to change the face of the universe; a man who in history takes rank by the side of Nebuchodonosor, of Cyrus, of Alexander, of Cæsar, and of Charlemagne. This man is Napoleon. After having served as a rod in the hands of God to chastise unruly nations; deposing and elevating kings and giving thrones, he dared to place his hand on the Church of God; but he soon saw himself dethroned, and cast on a barren isle in the midst of the lonely ocean. There, meditating at leisure upon all the events which had passed before his eyes; considering the difference between the works of men and those of God, he invincibly concluded therefrom the Divinity of Jesus Christ. "I know mankind, and I am a judge of men," said he, "and I tell you that Jesus Christ is not a man." Then, having developed his conviction, he said one day to one of his companions in arms: "You do not see that Jesus Christ is God? Well, sir! I have made an error in creating you a general!" Again, at St. Helena, he said that several times approaches had been made to him, pressing him to declare himself the head of a religion by putting aside the Pope. "They did not even stop there! they wanted me to create a religion to my taste, assuring me that in France and the rest of the world I was sure of finding partisans and devout followers of the new creed. One day, however, when I was urged more strongly than usual on this subject, by a personage who saw under this idea a great political blossom, I stopped him abruptly, 'Enough, sir, enough; do you intend also that I too should be crucified!' and as he looked at me in a bewildered manner, replied: 'It is neither thought nor wish of mine.' 'Well, sir, it is this which is necessary for a true religion! and after that one I neither know nor wish to know any other!'"

Although the time when Napoleon thus spoke is comparatively recent, the enemies of Christ pretend that they have made progress since then, and that the world has gathered light. But it remains proven to all those who do not shut their eyes in order not to see, that so long as the endeavor to explain the phenomena of the crucified Jew and of Christian society shall be made through human reason alone, we shall invariably fall into an abyss of obscurity and contradiction. If, on the contrary, this crucified Jew is the Messiah announced by the prophets; if this Son of man is at the same time the Son of God; if He has said that He was so, and has proved it by His miracles; if He has predicted that He would die on the cross, that He would rise again from the dead, that He would send the Holy Ghost, and that He has kept His word, then, and only then, all explains itself; then we conceive that the Apostles believed in Him; then we conceive that they have preached His resurrection and His Divinity all over the world, and that they have rejoiced to suffer for Him all sorts of outrages and torments, and even death; then we understand the martyrs and the Christian universe.

We may appropriately conclude with Lacordaire's sublime apostrophe to Jesus Christ: "There is a Man over whose tomb love still keeps guard; there is a Man whose sepulchre is not only glorious, as was predicted by the prophet, but even beloved. There *is* a Man whose ashes, after eighteen centuries, have not yet grown cold, who is every day born anew in the memory of countless multitudes, who is visited in His tomb by shepherds and by kings, who vie one with another in offering Him their homage. There *is* a Man whose steps are continually being tracked, and who, withdrawn as He is from our bodily eyes, is still discerned by those who unweariedly haunt the spots where once He sojourned, and who seek Him on His Mother's knees, by the borders of the lake, on the mountain-top, in the secret paths among the valleys, under the shadow of the olive trees, or in the silence of the desert. There *is* a Man who has died and been buried, but whose sleeping and waking is still watched by us; whose every word still vibrates in our hearts, producing there something more than love, for it gives life to those virtues of which love is the mother. There *is* a Man who long ages ago was fastened to a gibbet, and that Man is every day taken down from the throne of His Passion by thousands of adorers, who prostrate themselves on the earth before Him, and kiss His bleeding Feet with unspeakable emotion. There *is* a Man who was once scourged, slain, and crucified, but whom an ineffable passion has raised from death and infamy, and made the object of unfailing love, which finds all in Him, peace, honor, joy—nay, ecstasy. There *is* a Man, who, pursued to death in His own time with inextinguishable hate, has demanded apostles and martyrs from each successive generation, and has never failed to find them. There is *one Man*, and one alone, who has established His love on earth, and it is Thou, O my Jesus! Thou who hast been pleased to anoint, to consecrate me in Thy love, and whose very Name at this moment suffices to move my whole being, and to tear from me these words in spite of myself."

JESUS CHRIST yesterday, and to-day, and the same forever! These words of the Apostle express at once the noblest and the most delightful occupation of our lives. To think, to speak, to write, perpetually of the grandeur of Jesus—what joy on earth is like it, when we think of what we owe Him and of the relation in which we stand to Him? To know God and to understand His ways is the great end of life, and to walk His presence is all sanctity. We are God's own creatures, and God is our own God. All else will fail us, God never will. The death of Jesus is the life of every one of us. We live because He died.—*Faber.*

'Beth's Promise.

BY MRS. ANNA HANSON DORSEY.

CHAPTER IX.
THE YEARS ROLL ON.

AUNT 'BETH was half inclined to yield to the wish of Arthur Morley and his wife to remain with them until the spring. She was scarcely conscious of the strong hold that "the boy," as everyone called the baby, was gaining upon her. She thought she had very commonsense views about bringing up children, and was full of wise saws as to how he should be managed, and insisted that, his will and temper should be brought into subjection from the start. She looked on calmly, and never fondled him as the others did; but notwithstanding all her efforts to conceal it, she showed by a thousand little attentions, and in various ways, that "the boy" had entered into her heart and reigned king. The Morleys had many a quiet laugh over it all, but they were well satisfied.

Within a few days of the expiration of the two weeks she had taken to decide the question of staying where she was, or going back to "Ellerslie"—and had almost decided to remain—she drove into town one morning, at the request of her nephew, to buy a lot of provisions and other necessaries for the family of one of the workmen, who had fallen from a high scaffolding and lost his life, leaving a wife and little ones entirely destitute. Aunt 'Beth was in her true element on such a mission of charity as this, and entered upon it with zeal. Having completed her purchases, and directed that everything should be sent as soon as possible to the address she had given, she stepped out of the store to enter the carriage and visit the afflicted family, to ascertain if she could be of any further use. The carriage was on the other side of the street, under the trees, and while waiting an instant to catch the eye of the coachman, her attention was attracted by groups of silent men and women here and there on the sidewalks; then by a chorus of voices which rose and fell in a wild, pathetic chant, and seemed to come from a cloud of dust that was moving slowly down the street, towards her. She thought it was a procession of laborers on their way to a funeral; but now they were passing quite near, and to her horror she saw that it was a large band of negroes, the men handcuffed together in couples, also the women and young girls, among them some beautiful quadroons; most of them were barefooted; some looked surly, others defiant, some indifferent—all of them marching under guard of the slave-drivers—who were mounted, and rode up and down the line—keeping step to the old plantation ditty they were singing.

"Where are they going?" asked Aunt 'Beth of a negro man standing near her. She spoke under her breath, with suppressed indignation, while a great throb of pain in her heart nearly choked her.

"To the brig, missis," answered the man, in a low tone.

"What have they got them chained for? My God! look at those mothers, those beautiful young girls!" she exclaimed, forgetting all caution.

"They have to do it, missis, to keep' em from runnin' off, or killin' themselves. Sometimes they does that," said the man, in the same quiet tones.

"And no wonder! It is an outrage against humanity! Oh, my God! how long will such things be! Here, my man, here's a quarter; run over to that carriage on the other side of the street and tell the coachman to come here immediately." She felt that she would not be able to hold her peace if she remained, and would have to cry out aloud "in the market place" against this terrible outrage on nature and humanity.

"Who is that crazy woman?" asked a rough-looking man of another, both of them having overheard the conversation.

"Abolitionist sure!" returned the other, with a loud, coarse laugh. "Hurry up, old gal, and git out quick."

No need to hurry her. The carriage had driven round in the rear of the procession, and she had gone swiftly to meet it. Cat-calls and shouts followed, and a crowd of roughs were rushing towards her, but not in time to harm her, for she had sprung into the carriage, snapped to the door and ordered the coachman to drive off immediately, which he, frightened half to death, did at full speed, Aunt 'Beth leaning, white, against the cushions, her heart full of the great injustice she had looked upon.

"It is no use to make a scene," she argued with herself as she got in sight of home; "if I say all there is in me to say against this nefarious, criminal traffic, it will only make Arthur and his wife uncomfortable, for they have no lot or part in it. All that's left for me to do is to get out of it; and I'll go right up to my room the moment I get home and begin to pack, so that I can get off by the boat to-morrow night." To say was to do, with Aunt 'Beth. She told the Morleys that night that she was going home, then quietly related what had happened, as she found that the coachman had already given his master a garbled and exaggerated statement of the affair. No persuasions or pleadings could change her purpose. "I have been very happy with you, my dears,—with you and 'the boy,'" she said, her lip and chin trembling; "but it is only wasting breath to say another word. I should stifle here, after what I have seen, or be mobbed, as I was near being to-day. It is best for us all that I should go now. I can do nothing against existing evils, the thought of which harrows my very soul. Next summer you will all come to me at 'Ellerslie.'" Tears were shed, farewells spoken, some charitable commissions and a generous sum of money placed in Anne's hand, for Father O'Meara to distribute among the needy of his flock, then Aunt 'Beth shook the dust of slavery from her feet, and turned her face homeward. On arriving she found, contrary to her forebodings, that during her absence everything had gone on with the regularity of clock-work, in the house department and upon the farm; there was no speck or flaw to hang a complaint on, which afforded her such satisfaction that she persuaded the Widow Trott to remain with her so long as she could feel satisfied at "Ellerslie," and gave her manager permission to have an addition built to his house, a favor that he had been persuading her for the last year or two to grant.

Years passed on—years of mingled joy and grief to the Morleys. Their darling boy gladdened their lives for three blissful years, then died of some sudden disease—passed from them as if some great angel of God had swooped down out of the heavens, darkening the sunshine with its mighty wings, and snatched him from their arms, bearing him far out of sight, beyond that thin but impenetrable veil which no mortal eye can pierce. Grieving for her first-born, it was many, many long, weary days before Anne Morley could be comforted; she rebelled against the will of God in removing her child, and in her soul called it a cruel decree; she fed upon her grief, and lived only with the memories of her dead, seeking no consolation in religion, and closing her eyes to the solace that faith would have revealed. It was a selfish sorrow, that took no heed of one as deep that was being borne with silent endurance by her husband, for her sake, until his pale countenance and heavy eyes betrayed many a sleepless vigil, and the heaviness of his heart; then she felt how cruel she had been not to share his sorrow, and give to him at least the tender cares which would have gone far towards filling up the empty place in his heart.

Two or three years, with their flowers, and bird-songs, their snows and stormy winds, rolled over the little grave, and the beautiful boy now lived as a fair dream in the memory of Anne Morley and her husband, a vision just hovering on the border-land of reality, as sad as it was fair. It is true that "troubles never come alone," and the young mother was just getting over her grief, and beginning to renew her interest in life, and feel that there was yet happiness on earth for her, when news came one day that Frank Hamilton, her brave, handsome brother, had been killed in a skirmish with hostile Indians, while out on a scouting expedition. A few months later, a morning paper announced the loss of the United States sloop of war "Shark," commanded by Captain Henry Hamilton. Officers and crew perished. The last seen of her, she was reported as scudding under bare poles in the neighborhood of the Bahama banks. Soon after, the hurricane must have struck her. That was all: no vestige of her was afterwards seen, not one of her brave crew ever returned to tell the tale; no line from the deep ever drifted ashore to relieve the aching, weary hearts that for weeks and months expected their return, in the vain hope that they had in some way been saved. Vain indeed! for it was said that the "Shark," with her heavy cannon and closed hatches, had gone to the bottom, where an eternal calm holds all that reaches it, until "the sea shall give up its dead." How had they lived, these two spirited, brave young fellows who had been educated without proper religious training? They were known as Catholics, and good fellows; their classmates, and friends wherever made, loved them; but how had they died? The doom of both was sudden; had they time to utter that one fervent, true, and saving prayer of contrition, which Infinite Mercy may accept at the very last? Who could tell? After the first shock of grief had passed, Anne had Masses said for their repose, and offered more than one Communion to the same end. Throughout their married life, Commander Morley—he had gone up another grade in the service—had been true to all the promises he had made his wife about her religion; he never knowingly laid a straw in the way of her observance of its practices, and invariably showed a degree of respect for it, which was mistaken by some for a leaning towards it which would one day bring him into the Church. But nothing was further from his thoughts; in fact, the subject was one of utter indifference to him, only insamuch as his wife was a Catholic he felt in honor bound, and for her sake, to tolerate her belief with every outward show of respect. So far, this was well enough; but she—not too strongly grounded in the vital principles of her faith—needed peculiarly all the helps that a oneness of belief between them would have given her. There were a thousand influences pervading her daily life which tended to enervate and weaken that firm cleaving to the practices of her religion so essential to one under such circumstances. Her husband was true, honorable, and altogether perfect in her eyes; "how, then," she sometimes asked herself, "could his becoming a Catholic make him better? Was he not a man of clean life, good to the poor, and tolerant of the errors of others, and altogether *sans peur, sans reproche*? Why, then, when he was so liberal in sentiment, and so kind to her, so considerate in everything relating to her belief and practice, should she make him uncomfortable by discussions which would make him think that a difference in faith was making her unhappy? No: it would neither be fair nor generous of her, and she would let him see that although a Catholic, she could be as liberal as he was. Anne Morley's highest earthly happiness was in her husband's companionship, and occasionally, instead of going to Mass on Sundays, she remained at home to hear him read from some book in which he was deeply interested, to enjoy a long walk with him, or sit with him in the library listening to his delightful talks about things and places he had seen abroad; or, best of all, hearing his plans for their future, when, having retired from the service, he would take her home to dear old "Ellerslie" to live. In the circles which the Morleys frequented there were few, if any, Catholics, so that she was quite cut off from those associations which, by the force of example, would at least have kept her in mind of her religious obligations. They were all refined and cultured people, her husband's old friends, who had known him ever since when, as a young ensign, he was on the staff of the Admiral's flag-ship, which had wintered near their beautiful city. Time and again they had received her with the most flattering courtesies, and admired and made much of her. In the midst of surroundings all pleasant and delightful to the egotism and latent vanity of human nature, is it strange that she should have forgotten holydays of obligation, feasts, fasts, and festivals? Now and then, the memory of her baby and of her brothers took possession of her, when,

"....Impetuous with emotion
And anguish long suppressed,
Her swelling heart heaved, moaning like the ocean,
That cannot rest";

and she sought the Sacraments, as one flying to a city of refuge, for help and solace; then the storm having passed, she would again lapse into delusive calm, satisfied with what she had done. But conscience was not silent; when is this inexorable angel of the soul ever silent? But she knew how to temporize and answer its whisperings in a way that quieted her scruples. "It is my duty," she would say, "to make my husband's life happy; and when is he so happy as when I am with him? How can I, after all his kindness about my religion, be running off to church, leaving him alone at the very time he most wants me? I shall not do it! but by and by, when he goes off to sea, I mean to be very good, and attend regularly to my duties." But while she thought that she was sacrificing herself to her mistaken ideas of duty, she was only obeying her own secret inclinations.

At last a day came when, his term of shore duty having expired, Arthur Morley was ordered to sea in command of the ship that took him out to join the Asiatic squadron. It can be imagined how bitter the separation was between hearts so united and so blindly devoted to one another as were these two, and it is therefore useless to dwell upon it. Anne was very heart-sore and despondent. She had hung a medal of our Blessed Lady around his neck the day he left her, and the next morning received Holy Communion, which she offered fervently for his safety, not discerning how entirely human her motive was. But her grief made her restless; friends thronged around, but failed to cheer her; everything reminded her too much of her husband. Sometimes she almost fancied she heard his footsteps, and turned her head towards the door, only to remember how many thousand miles of water were between them; then she would drop her face in her hands and have a good cry. She could not stand it, and determined to have all her furniture and household goods stored, give up her house, and go to "Ellerslie," where she would have a willing listener whenever she wanted to talk of her absent one, in Aunt 'Beth, who was so near and dear to him, and who, in turn, would tell her a thousand interesting things about him, of which she had a store. Did Anne Morley forget that there was no Catholic church within ten miles of "Ellerslie" —most of the people who inhabited that region being Lutherans and Presbyterians—and how almost impossible it would be to "attend regularly to her duties," as she had promised herself to do when her husband went on his next cruise?

Aunt 'Beth received her with open arms, and warm, welcoming words, but was pained to see that the roses had faded out of her cheeks and the light out of her beautiful eyes,—that her step was languid, and that the only interest she showed in life was when she was talking or hearing of her husband. "This will never do!" thought Aunt 'Beth; "brooding over a thing that can't be helped! It is not a healthy condition of mind for any human being to indulge in." Then this indefatigable midget of a woman began to tax her ingenuity to invent little occupations for her guest, and awakened in her a certain interest in them, by declaring that it would be the greatest help in the world to her if she would only take them in hand, which she did, languidly at first, but found, in a day or two, greatly to her own surprise, that they interested and diverted her mind from her despondency. After awhile, long and loving letters began to come from over the seas, at regular intervals, which cheered and comforted her; and as her health improved in the pure, bracing air of "Ellerslie," she began to measure the time as it passed, and to look forward with bright anticipations towards the end of the cruise, when her husband would be restored to her. But sometimes there would be a delay in getting her letters; then, sad and silent, she would imagine all sorts of dreadful things—cyclones, wreck, disaster, or perhaps sickness and death. On one of these occasions, Aunt 'Beth felt herself called upon to reason with her in her terse, wholesome way about the folly of "borrowing trouble."

"But I have had so much trouble, Aunt 'Beth, for one so young!—how can I help it?" she answered, in despondent tones. "First of all, my baby died; then my brother; and now, separated from Arthur, oh, Aunt Beth! why shouldn't I feel afraid?"

"It's tempting Providence to be making moans over the living. You didn't expect Arthur was going to sail ships over dry land when you married him, and although I hate his being a sailor I wouldn't have him resign until he gets to the top of his profession. All trials are disagreeable; but I tell you, my child, when they belong to the past they are gone from us, and it is as senseless to be moaning over them as it is in a child to cry for a star. So cheer up, Anne; you have Arthur and your old Aunt 'Beth, and no end of time to do good in. Look forward towards the happy future awaiting you, and stop fretting."

"It is all true what you say, Aunt 'Beth; but I can't help it; it is my nature, I suppose," she said, almost in tears.

"If it's your nature, then the sooner you begin to fight your nature the better for your happiness," burst out Aunt 'Beth; "a rational creature has no right to let nature hold her in leading-strings. Come now, Anne; let's see what trying to do a little good for other people will do for you."

"How can I do good, Aunt 'Beth?" she asked, sadly.

"In ten thousand ways! there is good to be done to somebody, in some way; for something or other is always lying around loose for some hand to take up and put through. You can begin now by sewing up the seams of this skirt for old Mrs. Pentz, down by the mill."

"Give it to me, Aunt 'Beth," said Anne, an involuntary smile dimpling her cheeks. "I'll sew up all the seams you'll give me."

"There are other things to do besides sewing up seams. There's that ignorant little Arab that I found, half starved and astray, on the roadside, the other day. I scooped her up and brought her home, but I have not had time yet to see anything more about her than to have her washed and put into warm clothes. In fact, I think she does nothing but eat, and play with the dogs. Take her in hand, and try to civilize her by teaching her something; you could not find better work," said Aunt 'Beth.

"I'm afraid it will be like the task of Hercules; but I'll try," replied Anne, amused and interested in spite of herself.

It had occasionally occurred to Aunt 'Beth as something rather strange that Anne had expressed no desire since she had come to "Ellerslie" to go to church—her own church—which, it was true, was ten miles off; but what of that, when there were a carriage and pair of fast-trotting horses to take her to it? She knew Anne was a Catholic; at least she supposed she was still one, having heard of no change; and, if so, she wondered why she didn't get more comfort and courage out of her religion! But perhaps she herself had been remiss in not offering the carriage to her, and even accompanying her; but, not being religious herself, she always felt a delicacy about making suggestions to other people. However, she determined that she would on the following Sunday make the attempt; and if it failed, then she would feel no reproaches of conscience about it.

The day after the conversation related above, Anne's letters came—bright, fond letters from Arthur, filled with all the tenderness that her heart craved, and a great deal more relating to the strange world he was visiting, its old, wonderful civilization, and the customs of its remarkable people, which interested her greatly. She and Aunt 'Beth read them again and again, talked and pored over them, rejoicing that all was well with the writer; that there had been no cyclone, no wreck, disaster, nor sickness. On the contrary, the voyage so far had been uninterruptedly pleasant, which gave the writer an opportunity for a few remarks about the "folly of fretting when there was nothing to fret about"; all this was taken very amiably, for the young wife's heart was relieved of its anxiety and dread, and she could afford to take Aunt 'Beth's affectionate chafing with a smile. Then two happy days were spent in answering the letters, writing steadily from morning until night—taking care to write cheerfully, which she knew would please him,—and thinking nothing concerning Aunt 'Beth and herself, and all that was going on at "Ellerslie," too insignificant to relate—a letter laden with love and devotion, which was at last finished and sent away to Hong-Kong. She had forgotten all about Aunt 'Beth's Arab, and it was Sunday. The drive to church was proposed—as planned by Miss Morley,—and as it was a lovely, crisp, frosty day, Anne seemed only too glad to go, and they started immediately after breakfast. But, oh, the roads! corduroy roads up hill and down dale, that jolted and racked Anne Morley's tenderly nurtured, sensitive frame until she cried out, hurt and bruised, at every step of the way. Aunt 'Beth was so light and small that she only bounced, not seeming to mind it in the least, except once when she began to say something, and a more vigorous jolt than any they had yet endured snapped her teeth together on the end of her tongue, which not only pained severely, but bled freely. When they got to the poor, miserable little chapel erected near the iron works, it was crowded with laborers and their wives; the benches were all occupied; Mass had begun, and Aunt 'Beth and Anne had to kneel on the bare floor, among a number of men and women poorly clad, who seemed devoutly intent on the Divine Mystery of the altar, whispering their prayers, some telling their beads, with simple faith, and fervor,—as if, having got into their Father's house once more, they meant to tell Him all that was in their hearts. After Mass, the clergyman who officiated turned to address a few words of mingled encouragement, rebuke, and cheer to his people; his face showed lines of care and toil; his words were simple and strong; and he spoke with a brogue which to Aunt 'Beth sounded barbarous. But there was unction and divine truth in all he said; his apostolate among the rude flocks spread here and there through his mission had been full of hardship, privation, and conflict, but he knew he had won their hearts; and they knew him, they heard him as a father, and sought with simple mind to obey him in all that pertained to the good of their souls. Even the turbulent ones among them yielded in a degree to his sway; they knew that he had the courage of a lion, and respected him for it; and while they did not give up all their evil habits, they were more peaceful towards their families and neighbors. It was an humble, but heroic life he led, braving dangers of sea and land, under the burning suns of summer, and through the bitter and frequently almost impassable snows of winter, sometimes really in want of the commonest necessaries of life, and often sorely spent with fatigue; a life as precious in the sight of God as if he had been lapped in luxury, clothed in jewelled dalmatics, and daily pouring forth the burning eloquence of exalted genius to listening thousands of the great, the wise, and the noble of the earth. But Anne was half dead with fatigue; she could only whisper a few *Aves*, with an effort to do so devoutly; and Aunt 'Beth, almost as tired, heartily wished it was over and they on their way home. At last the congregation was dismissed, and, being near the door, they escaped without being jostled and crowded, pausing only long enough to drop a generous contribution into the poor-box. They hurried away to the carriage, thankful to escape and turn their faces homeward. Aunt 'Beth did not complain, but she was very tired and very grim. The whole thing had been Greek to her; but to Anne, it was the one same Sacrifice she used to assist at with so much fervor and emotion in the grand cathedrals abroad, only here it was the loneliness of Christ in His poverty, while there, He was throned in royal splendors; did she indeed realize that it was one and the same adorable Divine Mystery? The fatigue and jolting made her feverish, and she was not well enough to leave her bed for a day or two. After this, nothing more was said about going to the little church ten miles away. When quite recovered, Anne, true to her promise, took in hand the young gypsy Aunt 'Beth had spoken of, and found her, with her quaint, wild ways, as amusing as she was perplexing; but little by little, with coaxing, presents, and indulgence, she got a certain control over her which made her task more easy.

(TO BE CONTINUED.)

The Priest's Leap.

A LEGEND OF THE PENAL TIMES.

T. D. Sullivan in "The Dublin Nation."

THE priest is out upon the hill before the dawn of day;
Through shadows deep, o'er rugged ground, he treads his painful way.
A peasant's homely garb he wears, that none but friendly eyes
May know who dares to walk abroad beneath that rough disguise.
Inside his coat and near his heart lies what he treasures most,
For there a tiny silver shrine contains the Sacred Host.
Adoring as he goes, he seeks a cabin low and rude,
To nourish there a fainting soul with God's appointed food;
For so it is within the land whose brave and faithful race
In other days made all the isle a bright and holy place.
Its temples are in ruins now, its altars overthrown;
Its hermits' cells in cliff and cave are tenantless and lone;
The ancient race are broken down, their power is passed away,
Poor helots, plundered and despised, they tread the soil to-day.
But yet, though fallen their fortunes be, through want, and woe, and ill,
Close hid, and fondly loved, they keep their priests amongst them still—
Their faithful priests, who, though by law condemned, denounced, and banned,
Will not forsake their suffering flocks, or quit the stricken land.
The morning brightens as he goes, the little hut is near,
When runs a peasant to his side, and speaks into his ear:
"Fly, Father, fly; the spies are out; they've watched you on your way;
They've brought the soldiers on your track, to seize you or to slay!
Quick, Father, dear! here stands your horse; no whip or spur he'll need;
Mount you at once upon his back, and put him to his speed.
And then what course you'd better take, 'tis God alone that knows—
Before you spreads a stormy sea, behind you come your foes;
But mount at once and dash away; take chance for field or flood,
And may God raise His hand to-day to foil those men of blood!"

Up sprang the priest; away he rode; but ere a mile was run,
Right in his path he saw the flash of bayonets in the sun;
He turned his horse's head, and sped along the way he came,
But oh! there too his hunters were, fast closing on their game!
Straight forward, then, he faced his steed, and urged him with his hand,
To where the cliff stood high and sheer above the sea-beat strand.
Then from the soldiers and the spies arose a joyful cheer,
Their toilsome chase was well-nigh o'er, the wished-for end was near;
They stretched their eager hands to pluck the rider from his seat—
A few more lusty strides and they might swing him to their feet;
For now betwixt him and the verge are scarce ten feet of ground—
But stay!—good God!—out o'er the cliff the horse is seen to bound!
The soldiers hasten to the spot, they gaze around, below,
No splash disturbs the waves that keep their smooth and even flow;
From their green depths no form of man or horse is seen to rise,
Far down upon the stony strand no mangled body lies;
"Look up! look up!" a soldier shouts; "oh! what a sight is there!
Behold, the priest on horseback still, is speeding through the air!"
They looked, and lo! the words were true, and, trembling with affright,
They saw the vision pierce the blue and vanish from their sight.

Three miles away, across the bay, a group with wondering eyes
Saw some strange speck come rushing fast towards them from the skies.
A bird they deemed it first to be; they watched its course, and soon

They deemed it some black burning mass flung
from the sun or moon.
It neared the earth—their hearts beat fast—they
held their breaths with awe,
As clear, and clearer still—the horse—and then—
the man—they saw!
They shut their eyes, they stopped their ears, to
spare their hearts the shock
As steed and rider both came down and struck
the solid rock!
Ay, on the solid rock they struck, but never made
a sound;
No horrid mass of flesh and blood was scattered
all around;
For when the horse fell on his knees, and when
the priest was thrown
A little forward, and his hands came down upon
the stone,
That instant, by God's potent will, the flinty rock
became
Like moistened clay or wax that yields before a
glowing flame.
Unhurt, unharmed, the priest arose, and with a
joyful start
He pressed his hand upon his breast—the Host
was near his heart.

Long years have passed away since then, in sun
and wind and rain,
But still of that terrific leap the wondrous marks
remain.
On the high cliff from which he sprang, now
deemed a sacred place,
The prints left by the horse's hoofs are plain for
all to trace;
And still the stone where he alit whoever likes
may view,
And see the signs and tokens there that prove the
story true;
May feel and count each notch and line, may measure if he please,
The dint made by the horse's head, the grooves
sunk by his knees,
And place his fingers in the holes—for there they
are to-day—
Made by the fingers of the priest who leaped
across the bay.

SCIENTIFIC truth cannot contradict religious truth, but scientific error can; and the path of science ever lies, through error, more or less partial to truth.—*Aubrey de Vere.*

"O MY EUSTOCHIUM, my daughter and my sister—for my age and my charity allow me to give you these names—if by birth you are the first among Roman virgins, strive all the more to accomplish your work to the end, and do not lose, through the folly of a half sacrifice, present and future joys."—*St. Jerome to Eustochium.*

The Companions of Monseigneur Ridel.

(CONCLUSION.)

SUMMER has begun: and now five months have elapsed since the persecution was inaugurated by the arrest of Mgr. Ridel; and our Vicar-Apostolic is still in prison. The satellites sent in search of us have returned to Seoul without capturing a single missionary. The excuse they have given the king is, that in the south of Corea the Christians are too numerous, and that if they were taken the rice culture would become impossible. Are we to give credence to this report, which was brought to me from Seoul last week? I hesitate to believe it, and yet it would appear that the arrests have ceased.

I have despatched a courier in search of my two pupils, that I may continue their instruction here, where I am in comparative safety. I must, however, use every precaution so as not to arouse the suspicion of the pagans. During the last few days I was very nearly discovered; it happened in this way. Having no food for myself or my people, I sent two Christians to buy five bushels of rice and thirty of millet. They went to a place situated six leagues from my residence, bought the provisions, and hired three bullocks to carry the load. The pagans of the neighborhood, who live entirely on potatoes, oats, and turnips, seeing all these provisions taking the road to that part of the mountain where I was living, were soon in a state of commotion; they assembled together, held a consultation, and came to the conclusion that a rich family must have settled among them. "Perhaps they are nobles," said they, "and, if so, what will become of us? Being of a better condition than ourselves, they will look down upon us, and may be oppress us in the end." In Corea it is the privilege of the nobles and the wealthy classes to oppress all that are beneath them in position. They deliberated therefore for several days as to what they ought to do, and even invited the neighboring villages to take part in the councils. My servant, having gone to pay for the provisions among the pagans of the vicinity, heard of what was going on, and reported the news to me. I immediately despatched two Christians to ease the minds of the pagans, without at the same time compromising ourselves, a thing not easily done on account of the superstitious rites which take place at certain seasons of the year, and to which all the people of the same village must give some pecuniary contribution.

My messengers set out, and after a day's deliberation they succeeded in satisfying everyone. It was arranged that they should pay every year twelve ligatures in taxes. As for the money for superstitious observances, they refused it point blank, observing that on account of their distance from the village, they preferred to live alone, and do all that their feelings should suggest to follow in the footsteps of their ancestors. One of the pagans insisted strongly, saying that it would be better for all, with common accord, to sacrifice to their deceased relatives, and to the genius of the mountain. But our Christians persisting in their refusal, a worthy pagan remarked that in material things people might be compelled to act in concert, but when it was a question of worshipping one's ancestors, or the god of the mountain, no one should be constrained, and each should be free to do whatever he was inspired to do by a filial piety and a love for the divinity. "Thus," concluded he, "these men who have become our neighbors, consenting to pay taxes like ourselves to the mandarin and to our village, should be perfectly free to act as they think proper; in other matters, therefore, let them not be annoyed."

Next day, two other pagans, hearing that a rich family had come to settle among them, arrived at daybreak, and came to my house while I was in the act of celebrating the Holy Sacrifice; were it not for my dog I should have been discovered. My servant went out immediately to receive the inopportune guests, invited them into a hut which I had caused to be built near at hand in case of accident, and succeeded by the charm of his conversation in delaying them until I had finished the Mass, after which the Christians retired quietly, closing my door and taking their way as if they were gathering vegetables. The two pagans came asking to borrow money. My servant answered that he had brought with him all his fortune, consisting of a hundred ligatures; but that having been obliged to purchase provisions and seed-potatoes, very little remained to him. "I am going," he added, "to order you a cup of millet each, and after you have breakfasted with us, you can take the road home again, and leave us in peace for the future. This little incident occurred to distract our attention just at a moment when I was regretting not having news of my fellow-priests and the Christians.

The courier whom I had sent to look for Father Doucet at length brought me a letter from him, the first since the beginning of the persecution. Obliged to hide after he had administered the Christian settlement of K——, Father Doucet retired to a hut at some distance from that place, on the slope of a mountain, where he had to suffer a great deal of privation. He was even obliged to pass a night in the middle of February in a cavern. As he was very much exposed in that place, and there was no refuge for him except among the Christians of P—— or K——, about 500 lys from the place where he was, I invited him to meet me in one of these two settlements, so that we might confess to one another. He replied that, notwithstanding the earnest desire he had to go to confession, it would be utterly impossible for him to make the journey of 500 lys through a pagan country. I had therefore to resign myself to the will of God, and offer Him this sacrifice, the most painful of all, for circumstances obliged me to infringe the rule of our Congregation, which makes it a duty for the missionaries to confess every fortnight, or at least every month. Father Doucet, who had received the courier from China, informed me that Russia had conquered Turkey, that the king of Italy had died after receiving the Sacraments, and that God had called to Himself the well-beloved Pius IX. This was the sum total of the news I received from Europe during a year. What of my parents, my poor father, who so generously offered to God the son he loved so tenderly? And my good mother! No doubt, she weeps, thinking of the child whom she believes she has lost forever, while he all the time is full of life and health. But, dearest mother, what use in weeping for him who during so long a period has been an object of anxiety to you? Would it not be far better to pray for one who has such great need of prayers? Many a time already have I mingled my tears with yours, regretting, not that I had left you, but that I had so little loved you while still with you.

On the return of the courier whom I had despatched to Father Doucet, I sent my servant to look for my two pupils; one was in the environs of Seoul, and the other at P——, with his brother. He found neither the one nor the other. The pupil belonging to P—— had left with one of his relatives, to settle at a place 800 lys farther on, in the province of K——. Not wishing that the boy should pass the summer with pagans, I sent my servant with orders not to return without him. Meanwhile I received a courier from Father B——, the first that came to me since the persecution. Father B—— desired me to get near Father Doucet, so that we might have an opportunity to make our confession. Three Christians, therefore, set out to look for my fellow-priest, for whom I had a house prepared in one of my settlements, at only 100 lys distance from my habitation. I sent to Father B——, at his request, my breviary, a box of altar-breads and two bottles of Mass wine, for he had lost all since the arrest of Mgr. Ridel. Finally, Father B—— mentioned some prayers which he wished my Christians and me to say, asking of God the deliverance of our Vicar-Apostolic, and the cessation of the persecution.

During these six months I have not lost my time. Besides administering the two settlements, I had learned a little of the Corean language, some of the Chinese characters, and especially the way in which the Christians and papans live. Young and inexperienced at the breaking out of the persecution, I was obliged to depend on the advice of catechists and my servant, and very often things turned out much to my discomfort. Taking advantage of my ignorance of Corean customs, my people paid no attention to my wishes. On receiving news of the arrest of Mgr. Ridel, I wished to remain at my residence in K——, where, as it has turned out, the satellites did not make their appearance; but the Christians told me no end of stories to prove to me that my position was not tenable. I must tell you in passing that the Coreans are very timorous. When they hear the word persecution, they keep repeating it, and prepare to fly on the first alarm. Now I know them better, and if persecution should break out again, I am determined not to fly until I shall be actually in danger. I am expecting Father Doucet; as soon as he arrives at K——, I shall set out for that settlement.

JULY 10.

Monseigneur Ridel set out on the 11th of June for China. What joy! This is the first time that such a thing has been done in Corea; for the law enacts that every stranger discovered in the kingdom shall be put to death. It was on a formal order from the Emperor of China that our Vicar-Apostolic was sent out of the country Formerly they took little heed of China when the missionaries were put to death. Let us hope, therefore, that God will deign at last to turn the eyes of His mercy on this land of Corea, watered with the blood of so many martyrs. Now that our Bishop and our Father has been set at liberty, nothing remains for us, his children, but to thank God for so great a benefit, and to beseech Him to touch the heart of the King of Corea, so that before long the light of Christianity may shine in all its splendor in this country.

I set out on the 29th of June for K——, which is 100 lys from my residence. The heat was intense, and I came near dying while crossing the high peaks of H——. I was overtaken by a violent storm when within a quarter of an hour's walk of the Christian settlement of M——, where I arrived drenched to the skin. It was just an occasion for saying:

"The team was sweating, puffing, quite worn out,"

for La Fontaine's fly was all I wanted to excite me, and aid me to scale the mountains.

At K—— I met Father Doucet, whom I had not seen for six months. I threw myself into his arms and speedily forgot all the sufferings of the journey. During five days we mutually encouraged each other to bear bravely whatever difficulties we should meet with in the administration of the settlements. Our first thought had been to make a retreat; but, having so many things to regulate, we put off the exercise for a month and a half later, when Father Doucet will come to me in the heart of the mountains of H——. There we can recollect ourselves more easily, for I live in a real solitude, having no distraction but the cawing of the rooks and the cry of the stags. Fortified by the grace of the Sacrament of Penance, and by the exhortations of my fellow-priest, I joyfully retraced my steps to my abode, where I arrived on Sunday evening, the 6th of July, in order to celebrate Mass next day.

SEPTEMBER 30, 1878.

On the 14th of July, my two pupils arrived, and thenceforth I occupied myself teaching them the elements of the Latin tongue. It was difficult both for the master and the scholars, for we had no books of any kind. I set about writing a little Corean grammar, very incomplete indeed, yet sufficient for teaching them the declensions and the verbs. I have forgotten the order and the connection of the rules, so that I shall be obliged to stop there, if next year new missionaries do not come into Corea.

After teaching class from the 15th of July to the 25th of September, I received orders from Fr. B—— to establish myself at two days' journey from Seoul. I set out with all my people for the settlement of K——, while waiting to have a house prepared for me at S——, about 200 lys (20 leagues) from the capital, a house in which I shall take up my abode at the tenth moon. . . . . .

I have been administering the settlement of K—— during the last few days, and have been much edified by the fervor of my Christians. Next week I shall set out to administer the other two places, where I hope to meet with the same consolations. During this interval I shall confide my pupils, three in number, to the care of a Chinese master, who will teach them the Corean characters and handwriting.

My fellow-priests are occupied in the ministry, and this work is productive of fruits of salvation. May God be thanked for this! The Christians are coming back by degrees to the fold. Let us hope that God will be at length touched by the prayers of all the fervent souls interested in our mission, and will open the eyes of these unfortunate Coreans to the light of the Gospel.

The persecution, if not extinct, is, at any rate, lulled. For some months there have been no arrests, or even annoyances from the satellites. All is now quiet. The satellites are on the search for robbers, very numerous at this period. Of the poor Christians arrested at the same time as Mgr. Ridel, there are now only fifteen in the prisons of Seoul. Receiving no other food than two spoonfuls of rice a day, most of them died of famine, others died of sickness, and some, it is said, were killed.

Here I bring to a conclusion a journal written

in a little cell in the depth of my solitude, with no table but my knees. You will find it, no doubt, very difficult to read. Pray for me, dear parents, for you know well that I stand greatly in need of your prayers, to support me in the midst of the pains and privations of the apostolic life.

What the Room of a Christian Ought to be.

A PAGE FROM THE LIFE OF M. DUPONT, THE HOLY MAN OF TOURS.

DURING the last years of his life, when infirmities and cruel sufferings made him a prisoner in his room, it was edifying to see with what resignation M. Dupont submitted to this forced retirement. We learn it from the charming little description he has left us in his own handwriting under the following heading: "What the room of a Christian should be."

Do you wish to know what your room is?

It is, even in the middle of the city, a little hermitage, of which you are the recluse; there it is that one practises unobserved and securely any devotion of predilection; you kiss the floor, you prostrate yourself, you strike your breast, you press your lips on the sacred wounds of the loving Saviour; in a word, you do all that a hermit does in his wilderness.

Do you wish to know what your room is?

It is a little sanctuary, of which you are the priest. Your oratory is the altar. The crucifix, the image of the Blessed Virgin, the holy water, produce holy affections in the soul; your heart is the lamp which consumes itself before the Lord; your prayers are the incense and the perfume. Oh, how sweetly the Blessed Virgin, retired and alone in her cell at Nazareth, drew down upon herself the eyes of the Blessed Trinity!

Do you wish, finally, to know what your room is?

It is a little heaven, St. Bernard tells us. What, indeed, do they do in heaven that cannot be done in a cell? There, God is honored and loved and served in full freedom: among the angels and the saints, entertainments are unspeakable delights; here, one lovingly sighs after the Divine Lover, relates to Him what He loves to hear, speaks to Him of His chaste affections, and enjoys His favors. And now, to close and resume, whatever your solitude may be, bear in mind that there are in it continually five persons: God the Father, God the Son, God the Holy Ghost, your Guardian Angel, and yourself; but remember also the beautiful words of Saint Gregory the Great: "What can an exterior solitude avail, if the solitude of the heart is neglected?"

Ah! this precious solitude of the heart was during a long period well kept by the holy man of Tours. There it was that he had learned how to appreciate the solitude of his room. This little room, on the first floor, was to be the scene of the last trials of the "Christian," and then his mortuary room, soon afterwards to be changed by the ecclesiastical authority into a sanctuary—and, by God's own mercy, into a miraculous one.

Wealthy as was its occupant, any common observer could at once notice that Mr. Dupont's ambition was not displayed on the walls or on the carpets of his room; it soared higher. It stood in keeping with his modest habits, and fairly compares with all the rooms we have had the good fortune to visit among those once inhabited by saints, and in which the chief ornament is invariably the sign of our salvation. What a difference between those humble abodes of virtue and the luxurious, palatial suits of room, in which the votari-s of the world sought comfort, pleasure and enjoyment! But even these sumptuous residences did not render their owners immortal; they too passed away, like the poorest among their fellow-beings, who never possessed nor cared for any of these enjoyments of a day. What do they think now of those deceitful, costly contrivances in which they forgot their eternal interests? They *now* pay the penalty of their folly, while our saints enjoy the reward of their mortified life. The warning is severe, but clear. It begins at Bethlehem, continues at Nazareth, and closes at Calvary. The saints understood it and acted upon it, and found in it a secret virtue; namely, that of despising the fleeting gratifications of this life, and of raising their hearts to the possession of heaven.

"Show me the books you read," said once an experienced judge, "and I will tell you what sort of man you are." The same applies to the room in which we live. An observing visitor will soon find out what sort of an occupant lives in it.

It will not avail to say that circumstances and social position impose obligations to which we must submit, unless we pretend that the requirements of society dispense us from those of the Gospel. The higher a Christian stands in society, the more is, often, expected from him; at least, the greater is his obligation to guard against danger. Heroic souls have been seen moving in the highest ranks, unimpaired; witness, among thousands, the illustrious Roman lady St. Cecilia; through the golden fringes of the robe in which she fell a martyr, can be seen, even now, after 1600 years, the hair-cloth she wore under the costly dress suited to her rank: she moved in the noblest circles of the world, but she was not of the world. *Spiritus Dei ubi vult spirat.* Mr. Dupont never was a monk; he, too, lived in the world for seventy-nine years; and yet he never belonged to the world, but to God.

A poor man's prayer may be more valuable than a rich man's gold.—*St. Liguori.*

[From the London Universe.]

The Art of Printing and the Catholic Church.

The Elizabethan tradition against the Catholic Church still, in some respects, survives in England. In no point is it more marked than in the calumnious charge that Bishops and priests and monks opposed, tooth and nail, the art of printing, out of fear lest the spread of knowledge might shake the faith among the people. The exact reverse of this narrow-minded jealousy is the truth, for Bishops and clergy took a most active part on its first invention in promoting the art of printing. Many Catholics even, by dint of hearing the charge repeated by Protestants at home and abroad have been led to fancy that the Catholic Church frowned upon Guttenberg's glorious invention.

In proof of the zeal with which Cardinals and Bishops, priests and monks labored to promote the art of printing, we will record a few facts for the information of our Protestant readers, and to remind Catholics of the debt of gratitude they owe to the foresight and wisdom of their clergy. It was welcomed in the first instance by Bishops and priests in Italy, Germany and France as a "divine," a "holy" art, as a "divine gift." It was not by mere accident that the first attempts at printing were made in episcopal cities like Mayence and Strasburg under the protection of an enlightened and, at the same time, well-endowed clergy. But it was not merely with good words or money that the new art was promoted; many of the secular and regular clergy took an active and personal part in the work as practical printers. They became apprentices in the new art, and, when they had attained sufficient skill in the work, they set up as master printers in order that, while some preached the Gospel direct to the people, others might be enabled, by the printed word, to convey the tidings of Divine truth beyond the walls of churches and schools.

We have before us in a recently-published catalogue, a list of secular priests—some of them canons—to the number of twenty-five, chiefly in Italy and Germany, who worked regularly as printers, and signed their names on the proof thus: M., or N., priest or canon of Rome, of Milan, of Regensburg, or of Chartres, as the case might be. The work of printing, however, by ecclesiastics was chiefly carried on in the monasteries. The monastic printing-offices were partly such as were worked by the monks themselves as compositors; and others where foreign printers were allowed to work inside the monasteries, either for the benefit of the monks or on their own account. One brotherhood in Germany was pre-eminently distinguished; they were called *Fratres vitæ Communis*, founded by G. Grote. No community and no order showed such active energy in the work of popular education and instruction as the brothers of this community, who might be fitly called "The School and Printing Order of the Middle Ages." Preaching, writing and printing went hand-in-hand in those times, as is shown by one of these brothers, who was a printer at Rostock, in Germany. At the conclusion of a work which he had himself composed and printed he writes thus:

"We, the brothers, priests and clerics who preach not by word of mouth, but by writing and printing," etc.

The catalogue to which we have already referred contains a list of monastic printing-offices divided into two classes: the first, those where the monks themselves were the printers; the second, where printers who were not monks worked. The number of the first class is as follows: in Italy, 4; in Germany, 11; and at Cettinge in Montenegro, 1.

The second class is still more numerous; in Italy, 7, including one in Rome and one in Sublaco; in Germany, 5; in Spain, 4; in France, 1; at the Benedictine Monastery of Cluny, in England, 2; one at the Benedictine Abbey of St. Albans, called the Schoolmaster of St. Albans, and the other at Westminster Abbey, where William Caxton and his men worked under the patronage of the Benedictines; and finally in Sweden, 1.

The duty of correcting the press was, as a rule, in the hands of the clergy, but the correctors of the press at that time did not merely revise the text, but acted as editors. Bishops even acted in the capacity of correctors of the press, as, for instance, in the printing-press at Rome the Bishop of Aleria, who worked day and night. Cardinals and Bishops invited printers from Germany to come to Rome and to their episcopal cities in Italy, and supported them and promoted their work in every way. Especially active in this respect were Cardinals Turrecremata, Caraffa and Nicholas of Cusa; the Bishop of Aleria, who was the special patron of the printer Pannarty and his companions, paid the following just tribute to the College of Cardinals:

"We have not found one in the Sacred College of Cardinals who has not shown us his good will and his favor in such a way as to show that the higher their dignity the greater is their love of learning and knowledge. Would that we printers could say the same of other ranks in life."

Had we space at our command, we might give a striking list of Bishops who in every country promoted the art of printing; we cannot, however, refrain from reciting the names of Cardinal Ximenes, the Archbishop of Toledo; of Fray Fernando, Archbishop of Granada, and of Bishop John VI, of Salhausen, who invited a printer from Leipsic to set up a printing-press in his episcopal palace.

We have brought forward evidences more than enough to convince every impartial mind of the lively interest and active part which the Catholic Church throughout Europe took in promoting Guttenberg's noble invention. We may safely say that no friendly relation can be conceived between the clergy and the promoters of the art of printing which was not found to have existed in days when, without such cordial co-operation, this great means of spreading knowledge and happiness might have been, if not jeopardized, at any rate retarded.

Right Rev. Bishop Marty, O. S. B.

Condensed from "The Louisville Courier-Journal."

The Rt. Rev. Martin Marty, Bishop of Dakota, was born in Switzerland, and is about 42 years of age. In his youth he studied in Switzerland and Austria, having first devoted himself to medicine. When he had about completed his education for this pursuit, a change took place in his mind, and he resolved to devote himself to the Church. With this determination he entered the monastery of Maria-Einsedln, in Switzerland, celebrated as a place of pilgrimage, and as an educational institution of profound influence. Napoleon here made his First Communion, and afterward presented to the community a magnificent solid gold chandelier of great size, which is suspended in the chapel, and which is regarded as a masterpiece of art. Having his former studies completed, the young aspirant soon finished the theological course, and was raised to the priesthood shortly after attaining his majority. He remained in the monastery, however, and assisted in teaching and in ministering spiritually to the pilgrims, who resorted to the spot. Recognizing his eminent ability, the Superior of the Benedictine Order selected him to come to America and assist in the establishment of a new abbey and college. Arriving here, he discovered that Bishop de St. Palais, of the diocese of Vincennes, was in need of German priests, and, with his two companions, proceeded to Vincennes. Here they were received with open hands, and their plans warmly encouraged. After consultation, Father Marty purchased a tract of seven thousand acres of land in Spencer County, where the foundation of an establishment of Benedictines had begun in 1852. Portions of land were sold to emigrants who were invited from Germany and Switzerland, and in that way in a few years the first Catholic congregation of St. Meinrad's was formed. From St. Meinrad's the priests attended the other towns and villages that sprang up along the river and interior.

Spencer and Dubois Counties in Indiana have, through the efforts of these priests, become almost entirely Catholic, and there are probably few more thrifty and apparently contented and happy communities in the country. The people in the interior preserve many of the customs of Europe, and much of the simplicity of the foreign peasantry. The farmers wear wooden shoes, as do the women; and in Dubois County an idle man is regarded pretty much as a thief would be in other places. Everybody is occupied, and the song of industry steals like the hum of bees along every hill and dale, and rises from every hamlet in the county. Most of the people speak the German language, and in fact, one might ride for miles without hearing an English word spoken or seeing anything which looked American. The houses are all modest, but substantial and comfortable, and the barns are every year filled with the products of the fruitful soil.

There are churches scattered throughout both counties, at Fulda, Ferdinand, Jasper, Troy, Tell City, Huntingburgh, Rockport, Cannelton, Marie Hill, St. Anthony, and other places, all under the supervision and influence of the Abbey of St. Meinrad's. At Jasper which is the county seat of Dubois, there is a stone church, which has been in course of construction for ten years, and has cost $100,000, having just reached the cornice.

When the land was sold to emigrants a large portion of it was retained, and upon it was erected a large, commodious, substantial building of hewn stone. This is the monastery and college of St. Meinrad's, where twelve professors are employed and about forty theological students are annually instructed, besides many more in other branches of education. The theological students mainly pertain to the diocese of Vincennes, although the high standard of scholarship has invited students from all parts of America and from the most distant dioceses.

It may be said that all this is the work of "Father" Marty, as he was affectionately termed by all. His energy moved, his wisdom decided, and his foresight conceived everything. Recognizing this, Pope Pius IX, on the 21st of May, 1871, appointed him first mitred Abbot of St. Meinrad's, and shortly afterward he was solemnly installed by Bishop de St. Palais. An enormous assemblage of people gathered on the occasion, and the ceremony was performed in the open air in order that all might see.

Father Marty was thus placed at the head of this important establishment at the age of 33. In a few years the college was so established, and the community so inspired by his energy and ideas, that his presence was not essential. He was then called upon to go among the Indians of the West as a missionary, and this difficult and severe task he accepted with cheerfulness. He first went to Dakota, some three or four years ago, and devoted himself to the study of the Indian languages, that of the Sioux nation in particular. Being a thorough linguist, he was not only able to acquire the language for speaking, but arrived at the roots, and returning to St. Meinrad's Abbey, he shut himself up for six months and wrote a grammar and a dictionary. With these instruments he taught twelve priests and twelve Sisters of Charity to speak the language of the Sioux, and, taking them with him, returned to Dakota. At Bismarck a school for the Indians was established by the Sisters, who have since been busily engaged in instructing and civilizing them. Among these rude savages Father Marty's name was a reverential word. Alone and unprotected, with his missal and his cross, he wandered at will into the most inaccessible fastnesses and among the most hostile groups; everywhere he was received as a friend and protected from all exterior dangers. So well known was he among them, and so well trusted, that twice he went into the hostile camp of Sitting Bull, even when that warrior had sworn death to every white man, and ultimately did all that was done toward protecting the lives of the white settlers and taking the edge off Sitting Bull's anger. In these acts he was authorized by the Government, and his work was received with all the honors that the state could bestow upon the churchman.

Catholic Notes.

——CONTRIBUTIONS FOR IRELAND.—Bridget Moran, 25 cents; "One of the Macs," $5; L. Divan, 50 cents; Thomas Coady, $5; Mrs. Margaret Davlin, $5; Charles Davlin, $5; Mrs. Julia Davlin, $2; others, $1.50.

——We regret to hear that *The Angelus*, an excellent little Catholic magazine published by R. Washbourne, of London, England, has suspended publication.

——MR. P. A. KEELY, the well-known architect of Brooklyn, L. I., has drawn plans for, and superintended the erection of, more than 3,000 churches in the United States and Canada during the past thirty years.

——THE ABBÉ NOIROT, one of the most widely-known priests in France, has just died at the venerable age of 86. He was the preceptor of Frederick Ozanam and other famous men, and the esteemed friend of Lacordaire, Montalembert, and Lamennais.

——The Spanish population of San Francisco has erected a beautiful church in their city at a cost of $52,000. It is under the patronage of Our Lady of Guadaloupe. *The Monitor* states that it will be ready for dedication by Palm Sunday, and that it is entirely free from debt.

——MISS HELEN GLADSTONE, who died recently, was the famous Ex-Premier's favorite sister. Her conversion was such a shock to him that it is supposed to have been the cause of his writing his pamphlet on the Vatican Decrees and his estrangement from the friend of his youth, Cardinal Manning. It is rumored that since his sister's death, the Right Honorable gentleman has made some friendly overtures to the Cardinal with a view of closing the breach that has for some time existed between them.

——ORDINATION AT NOTRE DAME.—On the 18th inst. Rt. Rev. Bishop Dwenger conferred the order of subdeacon on Messrs. Dennis Hagerty, Alexander

Kirsch, Paul Kollop, James Rogers and Joseph Sherer. Messrs. Patrick Moran and Peter Rosen received tonsure. Rev. Messrs. Hagerty and Kirsch were elevated to the diaconate on the following day. All are professed members of the Congregation of the Holy Cross. The beautiful and impressive ceremonies were performed in the Church of Our Lady of the Sacred Heart.

——LIKE BARON DE GÉRAMB, who after shining as one of the first dandies of his day became a silent and prayerful Trappist, the engineer Pievani of Milan, one of the heroes of the Revolution, became a Capuchin. Fired with enthusiasm, he became one of the celebrated *Mille* of Garibaldi, and disembarked at Marsala in 1860 to assist in driving the legitimate sovereign from his throne and in establishing the anarchy which still subsists in Sicily. Pievani died a few days ago, a Capuchin friar, in the Capuchin Hospice of San Maurizio, in Lovere. He had assumed the habit of the Order a short time ago, and had the happiness of dying in his converted state, piously assisted by his brethren of the Hospice. Even General Carini had the grace given him to repent.—*London Register.*

——DEVOTION TO THE BLESSED VIRGIN IN GERMANY.—Very Rev. Father Hoffman, curate and Archpriest at Rohrbach, in Alsace, author of a series of articles treating of the devotion to Our Blessed Lady in Catholic Germany, begins the introduction with the remark that in judging any nation we must always consider its various features; and to be impartial, we must take both the divine and the human elements—the good and the evil—into consideration, since without this our views would be necessarily incomplete, if not unjust. Thus, when treating of Germany, we must make a distinction between the Catholic and the Protestant nation, two elements widely differing in themselves, and strictly opposed to each other, forming in reality two societies—the children of the Church and those of sectarianism. Hence we see devoted servants of the Blessed Virgin and fierce enemies. Here, as everywhere, the former are convinced that those who have not Mary for their Mother have not God for their Father. To-day, when the Catholic Church in Germany offers to the world the sublime example of patient resistance and practical faith, it is well to search at the bottom of these things for the secret of a power like this: which is evidently nothing else than a special protection of her who has been chosen by God Himself to crush the infernal serpent's head."

——THE LATE VERY REV. FREDERICK OAKELEY was the youngest son of Sir Charles Oakeley, Bart., formerly Governor of Madras. He was born at Shrewsbury, Sept. 5th, 1802. Before going to the University he was a pupil of the late Bishop Sumner, then curate of Highclere, Hampshire, in whose house he resided from 1817 to 1820. On proceeding to Oxford he became a member of Christ Church, but he was elected a Fellow of Balliol College in 1827. His academical career was a brilliant one. He graduated B. A. (second class in classics) in 1824; gained the Chancellor's prize for the Latin essay in 1825, and carried off the Ellerton Theological Prize in the same year. He was appointed Prebendary of Litchfield by Bishop Ryder in 1832, and in the same year was nominated Select Preacher of the University. He also filled the office of Public Examiner at Oxford at a somewhat later period. In 1837 he received the appointment of Whitehall Preacher for Oxford from Bishop Bloomfield, who in that year amalgamated into a single preachership for each of the two Universities the twelve which had previously existed, and selected Mr. Oakeley as preacher for Oxford and the present Bishop of Worcester for Cambridge. In 1839 Mr. Oakeley became minister of Margaret Chapel, Margaret Street, London, where he introduced the more reverent form of external worship which now goes by the name of Ritualism.

——THE BENEFIT OF PERSECUTION.—We clip the following from a serial published in the *Katholische Volkszeitung* of Baltimore: "It is of immense profit to the Catholic Church in Prussia that the persecution now raging teaches her how to stand on her feet again. The large material losses are more than compensated by the spirit of generous self-sacrifice developed among her faithful children. How glorious are not the Irish in this respect, who, although downtrodden for many centuries, and in spite of their great poverty, give their last penny for their Faith and their Church! What a glorious spectacle is presented by the English Catholics, who never tire in collecting their alms for the erection and improvement of their churches and the foundation of schools for children! And France, and Belgium! how marvellous the sums contributed by the Catholics of both these countries for ecclesiastical institutions, and especially for the Catholic universities! And since the youthful Church in the United States has become already so strong and influential that it has stirred up the envy of all sectarian denominations, do we not know that her power and influence rest in her independence and in the generosity of her children? The German Catholics will no longer be outdone by their Catholic brethren in other countries; the days of tribulation will make them worthy to rival their brethren in offering charity to the chosen Bride of the Lord."

——THE APPARITIONS IN IRELAND.—We have been favored with a copy of the *Dublin Nation* containing a long account of the recent apparitions at Knock, together with a wood-cut of the chapel, to which pilgrims are flocking from all parts of the country. "At present," says the report, "the wall, as high as the hand can reach, is denuded of its coating of cement, and even the mortar from between the stones has been scraped out by visitors to the scene, who wish to carry away with them some relic of that portion of the building. A number of sharp stones which had been used by the people in hammering off the mortar and cement were lying about the ground. Against that part of the wall on which the vision of the Virgin was seen, a little wooden tablet has been set up, and a small shelf, on which are placed two candles in candlesticks, and two small statues; under these is a box with a slit for offerings, and around it a rough wooden paling, within which are placed the crutches and sticks of persons who have been cured of their ailments. On the tablet the following inscription is painted: 'It is important that any miraculous cures wrought here should be made known to the parish priest.' When I visited the place, ten or twelve, including some well-dressed women, were outside praying before the scene of the apparition; two or three, bareheaded in the cold winter wind, were walking round the church praying, some one having told them that three 'rounds' of this sort ought to be performed; and one poor cripple performing those penitential circuits toiled his way painfully along on hands and knees."

——AID FOR IRELAND FROM THE DIOCESE OF FORT WAYNE.—From the following list of collections in the Diocese of Fort Wayne, and the prompt remittances made to the Bishops of the most needy places, it will be seen that Mgr. Dwenger's sympathy with the starving poor of that country has assumed the practical form in which alone true sympathy consists. We know of no surer or more prompt way of transmitting succor than through the hands of our Bishops, who will lose no time in sending the money direct to the points at which it is most needed. In a letter published recently by a clergyman in the Diocese of Clonfert it is stated that unless relief is soon received many will have become prostrated, or have died of starvation. The following are Bishop Dwenger's collections and remittances up to Feb. 14: Cathedral, $357; Irish Benevolent Society, Cath'l., $105; St. Joseph's Benevolent Society, Cath'l., $50; Sodality, $50; Two young ladies, $12; Total Abstinence Society, $50; St. Mary's Church, Fort Wayne, $75; St. Paul's Church, Fort Wayne, $42; St. Mary's Church, Lafayette, $254; St. Boniface, Lafayette, $50; Logansport, St. Vincent's Church, $111.75; Logansport, St. Bridget's Church, $33.25; Logansport, St. Joseph's, $23.60; Peru collection, $178.87; South Bend, St. Patrick's Church, $68; South Bend, St. Joseph's Church, $18; Notre Dame, $44; Crawfordsville, $103; Lagro, $97; Tipton, $50; Anderson, $37.50; Decatur, $40; Arcola, $28; Hobart and Turkey Creek, $27.60; Winnamac, $15; Lebanon, $21; Warsaw, $21; Laporte, St. Joseph's Church, $13; Rensselaer, $11; Chesterton, $8.44; New Haven, $36; John J. Brooks, $10; Kensington, $14.35; Michigan City, $59; Marion, $35; Union City, $41; Muncie, $33.50; Columbia City, $22.75; Colfax, $20.55; Goshen, $20.50; Girardot, $10.80; Mrs. Murphy, $5. The following amounts have been sent to Ireland: January 19th, to the Bishop of Galway, £50, and to the Bishop of Kerry £50; on the 23d, to the Bishop of Sligo, £50; on the 24th, to the Bishop of Raphoe, £30; February 3d, to the Bishop of Clonfert, £50, and to the Bishop of Killala, £50; on the 4th, to the Bishop of Achonry, £50; on the 6th, to the Bishop of Galway, £30; on the 10th to the Bishop of Elphin, Sligo, £50. Total, £430. We learn that $175.44 have since been added to this amount.

—— BLESSING OF A BELL AT MACON, GA.—On Sunday evening, Feb. 8, the new bell recently purchased for St. Joseph's Church, of which Rev. Father Louis Bazin is the beloved pastor, was presented at the close of a banquet spread in honor of the occasion. The new bell is the gift of the Hibernian Society, of Macon, and the presentation was made in its behalf by the President, Mr. Patrick Peyton. In the evening, a very large audience had assembled in the church to witness the blessing of the bell, many Protestants being among the number. Rev. Bishop Gross performed the ceremony, assisted by Rev. Dr. Semmes, Rev. Father Bazin, and Rev. Father O'Brien of Atlanta. After the ceremony, the Bishop delivered a very impressive discourse, judging from an extract in one of the daily papers. The principal uses of the bell were admirably recalled to the mind of the audience: first, its ringing out the glad tidings of baptism, when all the world could know that another human being had been regenerated, and made a child of God; when sorrow, or passion, or misfortune embittered life, the musical sound of the bell called up the remembrance that there, in the house of God, the balm of Gilead was to be found. It was also one of the strong influences to check infidelity and call back those who had gone astray, to be again arrayed in the robe of sweet innocence and trust in God. Then, too, when the last bell tolls, as it will for all, it tells of another soul that has gone where there is no more grief. The Bishop's discourse evidently made a great impression on the audience. The service was closed with solemn Benediction of the Blessed Sacrament. The bell is a handsome one, 2,100 pounds in weight. On one side is the legend, " By the generosity of the following members of the Hibernian Society of Macon, Ga., and as a mark of esteem for the Rev. L. Bazin, pastor of St. Joseph's Church, was I cast." The names are as follows: P. Peyton, President; L. Vannucki, Vice President; P. Crown, Treasurer; D. D. Tracey, Secretary; C. C. Craig, A. Gorman, Thomas Pierce, Thomas Battle, P. Henry. Below are the words: " When the donors will be smouldering in the grave, and their names forgotten, I will still ring to their memory and call the living to the house of God." On the other side, in Roman letters, are the words: "Twenty-fifth anniversary of the definition of the dogma of the Immaculate Conception of B. V. M., 8th of December, 1879. *Mariâ sine labe originali concepta, ora pro nobis.*" The sponsors of the bell were Mr. Patrick Crown and Mrs. Mary Howland.

New Publications.

STUMBLING-BLOCKS MADE STEPPING-STONES ON THE ROAD TO THE CATHOLIC FAITH. By Rev. James J. Moriarty, A. M., Pastor of St. Patrick's Church, Chatham Village, New York. New York: Catholic Publication Society Co., 9 Barclay Street.

Coming in a peculiar Quaker suit of mild dove-color, this little work is a simple and admirable exposition of those truths of Catholic doctrine which present the greatest difficulty to those of our fellow-citizens who believe already in the Christian religion, for to such only is it addressed. "The Sacrifice of the Mass and its Ceremonies," "The Confessional," "The Invocation of Saints," "Devotion to the Blessed Virgin Mary," "Purgatory," and "Infallibility," the headings of the various parts into which the work is divided, sufficiently indicate the dogmata with which the pious and learned author deals. It is needless to say that he supports them by evidences from the Holy Scriptures, from the Fathers of the Church, from other historical sources, from the necessities of the case, and from the needs and instincts of humanity. An able work, and one which it is undoubtedly good to disseminate among those who are still seeking the light.

THE HOVELS OF IRELAND. By Fanny Parnell. New York: Thomas Kelly, 17 Barclay Street. Published for the Benefit of the Irish Land League.

This little pamphlet proves satisfactorily that there are poor people in Ireland, and intimates that the cause of poverty is the want of home rule. The talented authoress exhibits the usual sympathy with suffering indignation against the real or assumed oppressor, and devotion to "the cause," which we expect to find in works of this sort. The style of argument may be instanced by the following excerpt: "It is an unhappy fact in human nature, that if any individual or people, who by a combination of certain qualities of hardness, toughness, selfishness and thorough unscrupulousness, has achieved showy material successes, only insists positively enough and blatantly enough that the sky is black and not blue, and that the sun is the source of darkness and not of light, presently, one by one, every other individual or people begins to think that there must be something in it, or such a successful, and consequently superior, individual or people would not proclaim it so incessantly." Yes; "if!" If the half of eight were three, what would the sixth of twenty be? If an individual or people, laboring under so distressingly abnormal a condition of the perceptive organs as hypothesized, were to achieve "showy material successes," then human nature would be so different a thing from what we know it to be, that we could be no longer sure of any unhappy or happy "facts" connected with it.

—MISSA IN HON. S. GALLI, by Prof. J. Singenberger; also a collection containing an *Asperges me, Vidi aquam*, and *Ecce Sacerdos*, all arranged for two voices, with an organ accompaniment. The Mass has also a bass part ad *libitum*.

Prof. Singenberger is indefatigable in composing easy church-music to facilitate the work of reform and gradually expel the profane and ridiculous miscalled "church-music" to which so many of our choirs still cling so tenaciously. In this country, where music is still so backward, the works of the older masters are too difficult, and to some extent those also of the present Cæcilian school. Prof. Singenberger is the author of a number of Masses and shorter pieces admirably suited to supply the existing want, and which are in great demand among choirs who have not yet made much progress. To such we recommend the above publications as uniting the greatest simplicity with a due regard to piety and devotion.

PICTURESQUE IRELAND. Edited by John Savage, LL. D. Part 7. Price, 50 cts. New York; Published by Thomas Kelly.

The present part of this excellent work is as elegant and attractive as any which have preceded it. The illustrations are, like those of the other parts, numerous and of a high order of execution. There is also a very good colored map of Mayo, full page. The text is readable throughout and evinces a thorough knowledge of the scenes described. "Picturesque Ireland" is creditable alike to its editor and publisher, and deserves a wide sale.

—"THE STATIONS, or HOLY WAY OF THE CROSS, containing the shorter form taken from the *Raccolta*, and the form of Blessed Leonard of Port Maurice as used in the Coliseum at Rome," is the title of a convenient little manual of devotion just issued by P. O'Shea, 37 Barclay street, New York. The book is neatly gotten up in stiff paper cover, and contains, besides the devotions for the Way of the Cross, Prayers to Our Lady of Sorrows, to the Most Holy Wounds of our Lord, to Jesus Crucified, and the Prayer of St. Gertrude to the Sacred Heart. The principal parts of the devotions are printed from large, clear type, and the Way of the Cross is illustrated with fourteen excellent woodcuts. The price of the book is five cents, which may be sent in stamps.

Confraternity of the Immaculate Conception
(Or of Our Lady of Lourdes).

"We fly to thy patronage, O Holy Mother of God!"

REPORT FOR THE WEEK ENDING FEBRUARY 18TH.

The following petitions have been received: Recovery of health for 96 persons and 6 families,—change of life for 37 persons and 8 families,—conversion to the Faith for 50 persons and 7 families,—special graces for 10 priests, 5 religious, 3 clerical students, and 2 persons aspiring to the religious state,—temporal favors for 37 persons and 13 families,—spiritual favors for 72 persons and 18 families,—the spiritual and temporal welfare of 7 communities, 5 congregations, 8 schools, 2 orphan asylums, 1 hospital, and 1 sodality,—also 99 particular intentions, and 5 thanksgivings for favors received.

Specified intentions: Several priests and religious in ill health, among whom are some engaged in teaching,—recovery of just debts, and other favors in the temporal order, previously mentioned,—information of a vessel and its crew supposed to be foundered; the families of these seamen,—several children, baptized Catholics in their infancy, but brought up Protestants,—success of several missions,—conversion and return to the Faith of a truly charitable person,—peace and harmony within and between several families,—a young man, the only son of a widow, imprisoned for life,—speedy return to their families of some absent persons,—success of the Afghanistan missions,—reconciliation of two persons at variance.

FAVORS OBTAINED.

A pious lady writes: "The colored woman spoken of in my last letter I may say has been miraculously cured. Some days after writing you, I gave her a few drops of the water of Lourdes. Next day the cough left her, and the swelling commenced to subside. Her lower limbs were frightfully swollen and entirely powerless; for over four months she had to be lifted in and out of bed to the arm-chair she occupied through the day. The night of her cure, having said the final prayer, she felt impelled to see if she could not use her feet, as she felt so much better. So, without waking her sister who nursed her, she raised herself from the bed and walked across the floor. Her sister, happening to awake, was horrified, thinking her strength had returned momentarily before death, as often happens; so she tried to grasp her to bring her to her bed, but she cried: 'Let me alone, sister; I tell you I am cured.' Two or three days afterwards the sick woman walked alone half a square to a friend's house, and she expects soon to be at her usual employment. I gave her a miraculous medal, and a catechism which she promises to study."

OBITUARY.

The following deceased persons are recommended to the prayers of the Confraternity: Mr. PATRICK MURPHY, of Washington. D. C., who was killed by the cars on the 6th inst. Mr. BRYAN HART, who died on the 24th of January, at Waterford, N. Y. ROSE O'NEILL, whose death occurred on the 10th inst. BENARD BRADLEY, who departed for heaven on the 13th of this month. Mr. JAMES QUINN, of Hammond, Wis., and Mr. EUGENE FUSZ, of St. Louis, Mo., recently deceased. Mrs. EUGENIA DOLL, Mrs. E. BONARD, and Mr. JAMES L. MOORE, of Cascade, Iowa, who died some time ago. And several others, whose names have not been given.

Requiescant in pace.

A. GRANGER, C. S. C., Director.

For the Rebuilding of Notre Dame.

The following contributions are from the parishioners of Rev. Father Ward, Clyman, Wis.: F. Chapman, $2; James Brennan, $3; Frank Chapman, Jr., $1; James Moran, $1; Christopher Luard, $5; Edward Corey, $2; John Dempsey, $2; Daniel Collins, Jr., $1; G. Meyer, $1; J. Holstein, 25 cts.; J. Metzger, Sr., $5; F. Kieffer, $1; J. Wenhr, $1; Jos. Metzger, Jr., $1; S. Müller, 50 cts.; J. Wenhr, 35 cts.; A. Galmann, $1; F. Galmann, 25 cts.; J. Metzger, $1; L. Kasper, 50 cts.,; B. Spigilhof, 50 cts.; P. Nels, $2; J. Engelhardt, 50 cts.; F. Coler, $5; P. Kennedy, 50 cts.; Owen Farmer, $1; Patrick Curley, $1; Edward O'Connor, 50 cts.; Patrick Burke, 50 cts.; John Burke, 50 cts.; Mary Reilly, $1; Mrs. Ryan, $1; Edward O'Keefe, $1; James Darcy, $2; Dennis Darcey, $2; Edward Collins, $1; Thomas Darcey, $1; William Dowling, $2; J. T. Walsh, $2; Patrick Stanton, $1.

Youth's Department.

The Story Pearlie Liked Best.

BY M. J. C.

"DEAR AUNT RITA," said little Pearlie, "people ought to be very kind to good little girls; don't you think so?"

"'Yes, darling,' said I; "what do you think any good girls just now wish for most?'"

Pearlie, one of the best and dearest of little girls, looked very thoughtfully at the auntie whose namesake and darling she was.

"Auntie, you can tell nice stories—fairy stories sometimes, very nice indeed—but oh, auntie!" in a beseeching tone, clasping my hand in her two tiny ones, "once in a while such pretty stories; 'Catholic Legends,' I've heard you call them. I've only heard such a few little ones, but I loved them better than all the fairy tales; and I've heard mamma say that when she was quite a small girl, and you almost a big one, you used to tell her so many, such lovely stories of this kind. Tell me one now, auntie, if you please. Do you remember one you used to tell mamma, about 'Blind Agnese'?"

Sad indeed were the memories that rushed over me as the child talked on. The days when I, so young myself, yet a fervent Catholic, had hoped to lead my dear child-sister into the same safe Fold; the sad events that parted us for years, and her long forgetfulness, natural enough at her age; all—with my own griefs—rushed over me, and made speech impossible for a while. The dear, sympathetic little soul divined the meaning of my bended head, sorrowful glance, and silenced tongue.

"Don't cry, auntie dear," she whispered; "I mean to be a Catholic, even if poor mamma wasn't; and now please tell me one of the nicest, darlingest legends you know. Wait a minute, auntie; I want the story to be 'way back in what *you* call the 'Ages of Faith,' but mean, ignorant people" (in a very contemptuous tone) "call the 'Dark Ages.' 'Dark Ages' indeed! when angels kept coming down to earth. Go on, auntie dear! Something real nice now."

I reflected. The child's mind was peculiar, and as it had been a long while since I had told her a legend of this kind, I wished to impress her deeply. I had many in my mind. Finally, knowing her poetic temperament, I decided on what I would tell her.

"Pearlie," said I, "you have often listened while your mamma and I were talking of great poets of different lands. How many names can you remember of great poets, of any and every land?"

Pearlie, nine years old, very bright, and thoughtful, mused for a moment, then murmured, dreamily: "Shakespeare";—after a pause—"let me see, who wrote that book you love so, about the fairy queen? you know, oh, you know, auntie! and somebody who wrote about Heaven and Purgatory and Hell; that is all I remember you two talking about, and I only remember the names of those, and a few pretty stories you have told me out of them."

"Dear Pearlie, the literature, and especially the sacred poetry of Christendom, is full of exquisite stories and legends, illustrating the glories and the triumphs of the Faith, and one of these I will tell you now. It was told first in beautiful poetry by a Spanish poet, named Calderon. He lived and wrote in what we call the seventeenth century—that is, between 1600 and 1700, A. D. He wrote many fine works, mostly in a dramatic form—that is, like a play, to be acted,—some patriotic, some comical, but many of the best what we may call sacred dramas; that is, dramas intending to honor God and His Church. Among these, one of the most beautiful was entitled 'The Virgin of the Shrine,'* illustrating the nature of the miracles and sacred legends that grew up from the incidents of the wars between the Moors and the Spaniards in Andalusia, in the south of Spain. The Spaniards were of course faithful, devoted Catholics—as they have ever been; the Moors were even worse than heretics, as they renounced our Blessed Saviour Jesus Christ altogether as a Saviour and Redeemer, and ignored completely the mediatorial office of our Blessed Lady. These Moors—so named from Morocco, a country on the northern coast of Africa—which, as you can see by your map, is just opposite to the southern coasts of Europe, such as Naples and Sicily in Italy, and Andalusia in Spain—had by force of arms completely overrun some of those countries, and had it not been for two great battles by sea and by land, of which I may tell you some other time—as their memories are, and ought to be, most dear to every Christian heart, whether Catholic or Protestant,—the Mohammedans might have overrun Europe and extinguished Christianity.

"But you do not understand all this yet awhile, my darling, and we will return to the play of the poet Calderon. He had written several other plays before this one, but this was greatly admired, though somewhat faulty in construction. Its action begins in the great Cathedral of Toledo (a city in Southern Spain), in which cathedral is

---

* Or "Sanctuary."

a miraculous image of our Blessed Lady, greatly revered by all the people. This image of the Blessed Virgin is the link which holds all the acts of the play together, as many years elapse between each act."

"Aunty," said Pearlie, "did they worship that image of the Blessed Virgin as everybody worships God? I know they must have loved the dear Mother of Jesus, but I don't believe *that* story."

"No, my dearest, no! We love, we honor, and venerate the precious Mother of our Saviour Jesus; but He is God; she is not: yet, never forget, she is the *Mother of God*, and we should pay her all but infinite homage."

"I always will love her, aunty. She is my mamma in heaven, isn't she?"

"Yes, my child, indeed she is. But we will go back to our legend. When it begins, the old city of Toledo is under the sway of the Christian Gothic kings,—you will soon learn what those terms mean,—and all is joy and pious hope in the city, confiding trustfully in the protection of the Blessed Virgin, represented by the lovely image of her in the Cathedral. But somehow a sinister prophecy gets out among the people that the enemy is to capture the Christian city; the venerated statue, thank God! is not to be captured, but mysteriously hidden; during the time the Moors are to rule the city.

"Of course in this little story I cannot mention all the scenes, or each of the characters; it is enough to say that at last the heathen Moors invest, and finally take the great city. On the eve of the day when the Moors are to enter the Christian city in triumph, a sad, sad, procession is seen leaving the doomed place. The Archbishop of Toledo heads the procession, walking barefoot, and he bears hidden under his garments as many of the precious relics belonging to the different churches of the city as he could carry. He is followed in the mournful procession by many holy abbots, priors and priests, bearing other sacred relics, comprising all which they specially value in the city. Why, then, do they all look so very sorrowful? Can you not guess the reason, my dear Pearlie, from what I have told you?"

"Why yes, dear aunty, of course I can. They had only a lot of relics with them, and what had had become of that blessed statue of the holy Virgin of Toledo?"

"Clever child! you are right. Surely you will become a good Catholic some day. You have all the instincts of one. Yes; you discern the very reason why their march was so mournful, and why, remembering the prophecy, the events would sadden them so much. I will tell you why it was. On the eve of their exit from the city, the first thing the Archbishop, together with all good Toledans, thought of was the statue. That, before all, was to be saved from the profaning touch, or even look, of the Moor. Not a citizen present who would not gladly have laid down his very life for her. Yet, how to give her up! How to part from her; to let her go out of the city! What calamities, of any and all kinds, might not befal them in her absence."

"Why, Aunt Rita! you don't mean to say that the people really thought that the real, sure, true, Blessed Virgin in heaven would never hear them any more, because that one special statue was carried away, do you?"

"No, my child; the dear Mother of God always hears the voice of supplication; yet if ever you do become a Catholic—which may God grant!—you will learn the peculiarly Catholic belief, and imbibe the Catholic feeling that God chooses for His own wise ends, and in His own wise ways, to put a special blessing upon certain things and certain places. We seek some special blessing of Him. He chooses that we shall seek it by special channels. And above all, He chooses that the Blessed Mother of His only Son shall be always and ever honored, in every possible way, and never fails to bless every one who proffers his petition through her. These poor Toledans, so long accustomed to associate their granted petitions with that special statue of their heavenly patroness, might be excused anyway; but if the old legend I am about to tell you was really true—and in these days of far greater miracles we may easily believe it—it was indeed a miraculous statue."

"Oh, yes, aunty! only think of what you told me about the family that went to Lourdes, and the boy cured there. Oh!"—and a sudden shadow darkened the young, happy face—"oh, aunty, if poor cousin Hatty could go to Lourdes—but perhaps the Blessed Virgin—"

"Say 'Our Lady,' my dear, or 'Our Blessed Mother.' I love to have you call her Mother." And well I might love the sound from the lips of the dear child who might so soon be otherwise wholly motherless.

"Our Lady, then! perhaps she wouldn't cure poor Hattie because they are such Protestants. But I wish she would."

"Pearlie, dear, we will talk another time about Lourdes. Now, only this: did you ever read the upper one of the two little prayers over my writing-table?"

"Oh! the one you call '*Memorare!*' Let me read it now." And the young, sweet voice murmured the dear words—the blessed words which have whispered hope to so many sinking, despairing hearts—faith, trust, joy to so many dying souls: "Remember, O most compassionate Virgin Mary! that it was never known that any one who fled to thy protection, implored thy help, and sought thy intercession, was left unaided by thee!" Here the child paused, her eyes full of thought, and looked at me.

"Is that true, aunty—really, surely true?" she asked, earnestly, almost solemnly.

"I have always found it true, Pearlie, since I was young as you; and among the millions who have joyfully testified to the truth of these words, no one was ever found who cried, 'I trusted in her and she helped me not.' Never fear to go to her for help, if only you go loving her, trusting her. But how you keep on making me run away from our legend!"

"Why, aunty, the legend is all the nicer for all this nice talk with it. Lots of big people—real good people too—don't at all know how to talk to little people. They make us so tired!" said the child, complainingly.

"Well, dear, at last the Toledans consented. Much as they thought of their own needs, they cared much more for the dear image of their Mother in heaven. But as those employed by the Archbishop try to remove the statue, they find, to their wonder, that it is immovable; no force applied to it has any effect. News of this wonder spread fast; the people one and all hastened to the Cathedral, and, recognizing the miracle, rent the air with their cries of joy and thankfulness. 'She will not go! Our Mother will not abandon us! What mother abandons her children to the wolf?'

"'Yes, my children,' said the venerable Archbishop, 'we thought it needful to protect her; she will guard herself and us. But though our Lady wills her image to stay with you, she evidently does not intend it to remain there, thus exposed to insult or outrage. She will teach us what to do.'

"So when the Moors are at the very gates at midnight hour, the Bishop, the governor and others entering the Cathedral in haste, found that the statue now moved easily, and though they upheld it, it guided itself and them to a certain place, and stopped once more immovable.

"They raised the marble slabs of the pavement in that spot, and lo! far down, a secret, dark crypt, no one of them had ever heard of, and stairs leading to it. Carefully they placed their treasure in the niche prepared; replaced the Cathedral pavement, and went away. But before they went, they prayed fervently that the desolation of their temple, and the exile of their best treasure from its high place might one day end. In the course of the poem long years are supposed to elapse, reigns to succeed each other, and the Moors still hold Toledo, still profane the Christian Cathedral by using it as a mosque. But at last the infidel emblem is lowered, and the cross once more adorns a victorious banner. Under King Alphonso the Christians once more possess Toledo. But by this time generations had perished since the sacred and dear image of Mary had been hidden away. None knew now the secret of its retreat, yet fond memory of it still lingers in the people's hearts. But God had willed it to be recovered, and returned to its high place of old."

"And how was it recovered, aunty? by a miracle I am sure, since no one now knew where it was hidden?"

"Yes, my child; by a glorious miracle. Alphonso—though Catholic, of course—was so poor a Christian that he even left the Cathedral still in the hands of the Moors. The Archbishop sternly remonstrates; the people are ready to rebel; but the king pays no heed to them. Constance, his pious queen, grieved at such impiety, seizes it during an absence of the king, despoils the Moors, and gives up the church to the Archbishop. Of course Alphonso became very angry on hearing of this action; he hastened to Toledo, and, entering the Cathedral, found Queen Constance standing before the altar, her crucifix in one hand and a dagger in the other. Kneeling before her husband, she offered him the knife and besought him to kill her at once rather than give back to the infidel the Christian church."

"And was he wicked and cruel enough to do either?" cried Pearlie, indignantly.

"The legend says that at that moment a strain of seraphic music swells upon the air, and rays of bright light issue from the marble pavement at a certain spot. The floor opens, and all are amazed, enraptured as they behold that glorious form, radiating the light of heaven. Of its own accord the statue rises and stands beside them, gazing on the Moorish chief, who had followed the king to take possession of the church. The unhappy man cast himself at its feet and abjured his errors, adopting the Christian Faith, as did soon after many other Moors and many Jews.

"Even a little girl like you can easily imagine the joy of all the people of the city; the immense procession, the music and shouts of joy amid which the 'Blessed Lady of Toledo' was borne back to its niche in the long desecrated Cathedral."

"That's a nice legend, aunty."

———

A marquis who was admitted to an audience with the late Pontiff Pius IX, complained of the great corruption of society, and seemed to think there was no way of correcting it.

"Pardon," exclaimed Pius IX, "I know an excellent remedy for this great evil."

"What is it, Holy Father?"

"It is this: that in the application of the remedy each one should begin by reforming himself."

Any one who reforms his own conduct does a great deal towards reforming others.

THE AVE MARIA.

A Journal devoted to the Honor of the Blessed Virgin.

HENCEFORTH ALL GENERATIONS SHALL CALL ME BLESSED.—St. Luke, I, 48.

VOL. XVI.   NOTRE DAME, INDIANA, MARCH 6, 1880.   NO. 10.

(Copyright: Rev. D. E. Hudson, C. S. C.)

[For the "Ave Maria."]

Sponsa Dilecta Christi.

BY J. W. S. N.

LIKE Mary in the Temple, dwell, dear child,
  Blooming in cloister shades a lily-flower;
  Sweet innocence thy priceless, peerless dower
As zeal placed on thy heart that, undefiled,
From thoughts of God and heaven is ne'er be-
    guiled.
  Veiled from thy happy, radiant, bridal hour;
  E'er mindful of thy Hidden Spouse's power,
—The promise of His Sacred Heart so mild.

Flower of the lily! on thee heaven's dews drop
    down,
  Treasure the sweetness of the Hidden Life;
  Thy Nazareth is Mary's Paradise.
Jesus is thine; thy Spouse; thy Virgin crown,
  Mary and Joseph guard thee from all strife,
    And hedge thee 'round with grace from
      worldly eyes.

The Cult of Mary in its Relations with the Dogma of the Mediation of Jesus Christ.

PROTESTANT theologians exonerate the Church from the stupid calumny of making a goddess of Mary; but none the less they make it a reproach to the Church "that the intercessory power attributed to Mary is a power altogether outside Christian dogma; a power which has no warrant from Scripture; a power which is injurious to the dogma of the Mediation of Jesus Christ, sole Mediator between God and man." Every word of his objection is false. The contrary is the pure truth.

The Church in her prayers addresses the Lord: "Grant, we beseech Thee, that we may be sensible of the benefits of her intercession, by whom we have received the Author of Life, our Lord Jesus Christ, Thy Son": *Tribue, quæsumus, ut ipsam pro nobis intercedere sentiamus, per quam meruimus auctorem vitæ suscipere, Dominum nostrum Jesum Christum filium tuum.*

Again, the Church prays in these words: "O God! who didst wish Thy Word, by the message of an angel, to be clothed with flesh in the womb of the Blessed Virgin Mary; grant us, Thy suppliants, that believing her to be truly the Mother of God we may be aided by her intercession": *Deus, qui de Beatæ Mariæ Virginis utero Verbum tuum, angelo nuntiante, carnem suscipere voluisti; præsta, supplicibus tuis, ut qui vere eam genitricem Dei credimus, ejus apud te intercessionibus adjuvemur.*

We see, therefore, that it is on account of the share Mary took in the accomplishment of the great mysteries of the Redemption, and because she is really the Mother of God, that the Church confides in the efficacy of her intercession and her prayers, to make us feel the effects of the Redemption. Nothing is more just, or more reasonable, and at the same time more magnificent or more sublime than this philosophy of the Church.

To countenance itself in its mendacious grimaces of interest for the dignity of Jesus Christ, heresy relies on those passages of the Bible which attribute to the Author of grace alone the gift of all graces, and which do not urge the necessity of intercession and mediation with the Mediator. But does not the Bible show us Jesus Christ accomplishing the three ineffable Mysteries which contain the whole economy of His redeeming action, in the presence and with the concurrence of Mary? Whilst yet an infant, He *revealed* Himself for the first time to the world in the persons of the Magi. The Bible tells us that this magnificent Epiphany took place only in the presence of Mary, His Mother, and that in her arms He received the first adoration of the representatives of our humanity: *Invenerunt puerum cum Maria Mater ejus, et procedentes adoraverunt eum.* The Bible also tells us that the Divine Redeemer consummated His bloody sacrifice under the eyes of His Mother, and that to her bosom, while expiring, He confided the secret of His love, and the riches of His goodness: *Stabat juxta crucem Jesu mater ejus.*

Finally, it is the Bible which tells us that the Man-God returned to heaven and sent the Holy Ghost upon earth, to effect a new creation, to change the face of the earth, and to establish the Church in the midst of His disciples assembled in the Cenacle, in prayer, with Mary His august Mother: *Erant perseverantes unanimiter in orationes cum Maria, matre ejus.*

Has not the Church, then, good reason to conclude from these magnificent manifestations of the Divine thought, that God, who did not choose to accomplish these great mysteries without the concurrence of Mary, is pleased to communicate their effects through her intercession and mediation?

The royal prophet said to the Lord: "Thou hast honored Thy friends exceedingly, O God! Thou hast exceedingly strengthened their power": *Nimis honorati sunt amici tui, Deus; nimis confortatus est principatus eorum.* Now, can we believe that God who thus favored His friends and servants, has not chosen to lavish honors and confer an empire upon her who gave Him birth? Can we suppose that, having made the apostles and saints princes, He has not made His Mother a queen? And how could He make her queen of heaven and earth, of which He is king, unless He granted her the power to obtain for those who claim her aid, all kinds of graces by her prayers and intercession? It is said of Solomon that on having attained supreme authority his first thought was to place his mother on a throne at his right hand. Can we believe that the true King of Wisdom would be less generous and less mindful of her who gave Him His humanity?

There is, therefore, no exaggeration in that expression of St. Bernard: "Jesus Christ, who came to us through Mary, has wished that all graces should come to us through Mary only": *Omnia nos habere voluit per Mariam.* Jesus Christ is truly the real and only Mediator between God and man; but why should He not have constituted a Mediatrix, in the person of His Mother, between man and Himself? Why, though reserving the exercise of His justice, should He not grant His Mother a share in the exercise of His mercies?

The reality of this mediation of Mary between her Divine Son and men is most clearly manifested in the Gospel itself. We will not dwell upon that memorable event related by St. John, that Jesus Christ at the solicitation of his Mother came to the rescue of the couple at Cana, and although He declared His hour had not yet come He did not hesitate to grant Mary's petition, thus evidently wishing to teach us that He would honor the pious prayers of His Divine Mother in our favor, and that the series of the works of His mercy and goodness in our regard would ever continue to flow through the same channel. We will call the reader's attention to those touching words with which the Son of God, at the moment of consummating His mediation between heaven and earth, proclaimed Mary the Mother of the faithful, represented by St. John: *Mulier, ecce filius tuus—Ecce mater tua.*

Now, either these words of the dying Saviour have no meaning, or they mean only this: that by the desire and command of Jesus Christ, Mary should care for all the faithful as if they were her own children, or Jesus Christ Himself; and that the faithful should have recourse to her, place their confidence in her, and honor her as their Mother. But as this article, as well as the other articles of the precious testament of the Redeemer, was not a temporary disposition, having its validity only during the lifetime of Mary and St. John; as it was a law, and an institution, which the Son of God established to last during the existence of the Church; in what, and how, could Mary in her glory take any interest in the affairs of the faithful, unless by praying for them and interceding for them with her Divine Son? And why should the faithful address Mary, as children would a Mother, unless she is willing to be their Mediatrix with the Mediator Himself? Unless, therefore, we wish to do violence to the sacred texts and give a false meaning to the words of the Redeemer of the World, we cannot help seeing in these His last wishes, the loving thoughts of having, by the efficacy of His words, created Mary a true and special mediatrix between Him and His disciples, as He is the universal Mediator between God and men.

The prophet Isaias had said: "A stock shall arise from the root of Jesse; and a flower shall blossom from his root; and the spirit of the Lord shall rest upon him": *Egredietur virga de radice Jesse; et flos de radice ejus ascendet; et requiescet super eum spiritus Domini.*

There is no doubt but that this prophetic stock was a figure of Mary, and this miraculous flower a symbol of Jesus Christ. St. Bonaventure in commenting upon this graceful prophecy, says, that as he who wishes to possess the spirit of the Lord must seek it in the flower of Nazareth, in Jesus Christ in whom it dwells, so he who wishes to find Jesus Christ must go to the stock of Jesse, to Mary, from whom He is never separated: *Qui spiritum Domini adipisci desiderat, florem in virgâ quærat.*

This is the beautiful thought which the first Christians expressed in colors and in stone, in those frescoes and bass-reliefs which are found in great numbers in the ancient catacombs of the martyrs in Rome, and in which the Divine Jesus is always pictured in the arms of Mary, as if He were unwilling to receive the worship and love of men except at Mary's hands. This is a beautiful commentary on those words of the Gospel: "They found the Child with Mary His Mother: *Invenerunt puerum cum Mariâ Matre ejus.* Words could not be more eloquent than these signs. They teach us that the mystery of the mediation of Mary, begun in the stable at Bethlehem, in favor of the Magi, continues always in favor of all the faithful; that we cannot find Jesus except with Mary and through Mary; and that no one, as Richard of St. Laurence says, goes to Him unless the charms of His Mother and the grace of His Father draw him.

In what, then, does the belief of the Church in the mediation of the charity of Mary with her Divine Son—in what, then, does this belief, based upon the economy of Christian dogma, upon the testimony of the word of God, upon the ancient and constant practices of the faithful and upon the happy influence it has exercised over the dispositions of the nations, detract from the dignity and efficacy of the grace of the divine Mediator?

"Ask what thou wilt, my mother," said Solomon to the woman who bore him into this world; "I stand ready to grant all thy desires, as becomes my duty to thee." *Pete a me, mater mea, neque enim fas est ut avertam faciem meam a te.* How could the Son of God allow the son of a man to surpass Him in the respect every son owes his mother? Why should the children of the Church slight the divine power of the Redeemer, in believing that He will always graciously hear the petitions of His Mother, as the son of David heard Bethsheba's? Why should it be absurd to suppose that Jesus Christ, who anticipated His hour and effected His first miracle at the request of Mary, should refuse, were it necessary, to perform new miracles at the instance of His Mother in favor of those who trust in the mediation of her maternity and her tenderness? Why should we be stretching our faith too far in believing that the King of Heaven will ever find it good that we should send our petitions to Him through His Mother, as the kings of earth find it good when their subjects claim favors from them through their courtiers? Does the child who runs to its mother to obtain from its father that which the feeling of timidity inspired by the paternal authority prevents it from asking directly, disregard in the least, on that account, the rights of the author of its days? And if this child, conscious of having provoked the anger of its father, engages by its entreaties its good mother to appease him—if it hopes to obtain through her a pardon, which it fears may be refused, does it in the least show a disregard; or does it not, on the contrary, render homage to the dignity, the superiority, and authority of its father? How then would the Christian soul disregard the power of the mediation of Jesus Christ and the riches of His grace in seeking them through the intercession of Mary? And how should the sinner, trembling at the enormity and number of his crimes, and terror-stricken at the thought of having Christ for his Judge—how should he be wanting in reverence to the sole Mediator, in hoping to be more favorably heard through the pleading of that advocate, whom in dying Jesus left to all Christians to be to them a Mother?

'Beth's Promise.

BY MRS. ANNA HANSON DORSEY.

CHAPTER IX—(Continued).

WE should be glad to linger longer at "Ellerslie," the sweet, peaceful home of a race whose record showed no stain, but our limits forbid it. Anne Morley remained with Aunt 'Beth until her husband's return, soon after which they removed to Boston. They established their home in the fairest part of the city, and were soon surrounded by the best of social and cultured associations. Rarely indeed do human beings enjoy such felicity as these two found in each other's society after their long separation. In the sweet quiet, and pure air of "Ellerslie," Anne had grown strong, and with perfect health had ripened into wonderful loveliness. Proud of the admiration she excited, Captain Morley urged her to go into society more than she had previously done—to visit the opera and theatrical entertainments, and whatever amusement promised enjoyment. It was all novel and delightful, this new phase of her existence; she gave her past, with its sorrows, no more tears; only now and then a transient sadness swept, like the shadow of a cloud, over her, when memories of her lost and loved rose, phantom-like, in her thoughts or dreams. She arrayed herself in rich attire and jewels, always in good taste, but very elegant, taking a strange delight in her own beauty and in the effects produced by her rare *toilettes.* "It makes my husband proud of me—it pleases him to see me adorn myself in this way, and go into society with him," she whispered now and then to her conscience; "he enjoys such things, and I have no right to deprive him of them by remaining at home." It was true, he was glad to see her beautiful—richly dressed, and admired, but had he imagined for an instant that she was indifferent to it all, he would have been satisfied to have lived more quietly at home with her and his books, and in the society of a few chosen friends; but he believed sincerely that she was heartily enjoying herself, as in fact she was. Anne gave but little thought to religious matters nowadays, consequently there was nothing to restrain her; she was by nature one of those whose heart readily and willingly exulted in the glories of Tabor, but shrunk and fled away from the gloom of Calvary; her æsthetic tastes enjoyed, and were gratified beyond expression, by the splendid solemnities of her faith, the magnificent music, superb altars, the rich vestments, and clouds of incense, as she had seen them abroad in great cathedrals of carven marble; in fact, there had always been a great deal of shallow poetic sentimentality in her religious ideas and impressions, instead of that deep, vital principle that is the outgrowth of a religious education, which Anne Morley never had. She was too young when her mother died to remember the pious lessons she had taught her, her education had been a godless one, and her lot had been cast among those who professed a variety of creeds, or no creed at all; indeed, religion would have gradually become a myth to her, had she not been obliged while at boarding-school to attend a fashionable church with the others, having it impressed upon her mind that it was as necessary a part of her education as music or dancing, to learn how to walk up the aisle with grace, and behave decorously in her pew; it was the proper thing, her teacher informed her, and one which society would expect of her. Is it any wonder that so grave results should have followed, that her faith was not to her a firm, deeply rooted principle, or that she wore it so lightly as to put it off and on, according to the caprice of circumstances? Rather, is it not strange that, with all the disadvantages under which her life had been passed, even a spark of faith had been left to her? And yet she always called herself a Catholic, and in her inmost heart retained a tender devotion to the Blessed Virgin, whom she had learned to love far away in the past, with her head nestling against her mother's breast.

One day, soon after the Morleys settled in Boston, they were at a reception, at which the *élite* of fashion and intellect were present. A lady asked Mrs. Morley what church she would attend, excusing the question by observing, "if she had not quite made up her mind she wished to offer Captain Morley and herself seats in her pew at Trinity."

"I intend going to the Catholic Church—I am a Catholic, you know—but thank you very much, all the same," she answered, pleasantly. The looks of astonishment and the silence that followed surprised her—also glances that swiftly passed between several ladies standing around her; she did not know what it meant then, but she understood it perfectly when she went to Mass on Sunday. The church was old, dingy and small, its four square walls, and eight glaring windows, unrelieved by pictures of saints and martyrs, unstained by richly-hued delineations of sacred things. There was the altar, with lights, and bouquets of tawdry muslin flowers; there was the crucifix, and a poor painting of the *Mater Dolorosa* behind and above it, but everything betokened poverty; and this was then the Cathedral, sounding grandly, and giving one visions of space and splendor, its title derived from the Bishop's chair which stood on the right of the altar, worn and shabby, like all around it. The congregation was composed of plain, rough-looking people, very devout, but not a fashionable person among them. Servant girls, warm and glowing with the faith they had imbibed with their mother's milk in the old Island of Saints beyond the wide seas, knelt there in numbers, arrayed in their gay and somewhat "loud" holiday finery; strange-looking old women, wrapped in great plaid woolen shawls, although the weather was melting, their honest, wrinkled faces showing the wear and tear of toilsome, weary years, their labor-hardened hands, ungloved; men in the coarse habiliments of poverty, and others whose sleek garments, which set uneasily upon them, indicated prosperity; and scrubby-looking boys, not over clean in their persons, filled the pews:—the advance army of the Lord who planted the Faith in "Boston-town," and erected the banner of the Cross above the graves of the Puritans. Anne Morley was disgusted at finding herself in a crowd of "low, ignorant people"; the plain, simple sermon fell upon "ears that heard not"; she followed the Mass without devotion, said a few languid *Aves*, and made up her mind to come no more. She told her annoyance to her husband, whom she found waiting at the door for her when she went out. He laughed at her, and promised to make some inquiries about the other Catholic churches in Boston, and hoped to be able to find one that it would be more agreeable to attend. But his quest was in vain. The same class of people formed the congregations of the other two, which were situated in outlying parts of the city, and a friend to whom he confided his difficulties told him that to attend any one of them would be to lose caste in the best Boston circles.[*] Captain Morley with all his fine, noble traits, was but human, and here his one weakness cropped out. He hated to do anything that appeared odd or conspicuous, and was far more sensitive about his wife being placed in such a position than himself. He reported to her what he had heard, remarking: "If you have no objections, darling, I shall be much pleased if you will refrain from attending those churches while we are in Boston; in fact," he added, "I ask it as a favor to myself that you either remain at home with me, or that we go to 'Trinity' together. I have been going with you ever since we were married, and I really fail to

---

[*] A real experience of many years ago.

see why one Christian church won't do as well as another; they have a famous preacher at 'Trinity,' and the most magnificent music I have ever heard out of Italy; then, we know most of the people who go there. I don't really think, Anne, that you will see or hear anything there to harm you; still, I won't insist upon it; you must do just exactly as you please."

"No: I suppose not," she answered, slowly; "but, Arthur, you know I cannot give up my religion?"

"Don't! I wouldn't have you do such a thing for the world! I don't ask it; your faith will keep, and I shall be ordered somewhere else in about six months, where things will be different. You know I am here on temporary duty only," he said, smoothing her beautiful hair with tender, caressing hand.

"I'll think over the matter," she said, and the subject was changed. And the more she thought of it the more she felt disposed to yield. "My husband," she argued, "always so kind and liberal—almost a Catholic himself—who has never opposed, but rather encouraged, me in the practice of my religion, would never have advised me as he has done if it were wrong"; and she ended by consenting to his wishes, thus relinquishing for worldly motives and human love that which was worth the sacrifice of all that earth could give, even life itself.

But Captain Morley was not ordered away so soon as he had expected to be; they were there two years, and during that time Anne had lulled to rest her scruples about attending her own church. It is true that she went but seldom to "Trinity," and when she did, it was only to hear the superb music, as she would have gone to the opera, and listen to the flowing eloquence of the fashionable preacher. How could she feel devout, or even breathe a prayer where all was shadow without the substance, where forms and words were without significance? But far astray as she was, a day never passed that one or more "Hail Marys" were not whispered to her who is the "Help of the weak," and "Refuge of sinners." It seemed somehow to comfort her, and make her feel that she was not quite an outcast from her Faith. She still called herself a Catholic, and her friends complimented her on being a *liberal one;* she did not conceal her reasons for not attending her own church, and they commended her courage in not mixing herself up with what they were pleased to call "a disagreeable rabble"; she was courted and admired, and the low, inexorable whispers of conscience were silenced by specious reasoning.

About this time her little daughter, the 'Beth of our story, was born. Anne had many tender thoughts of her mother and of her little boy in heaven as she held her babe close to her bosom; the best and holiest feelings of her nature were stirred while she gazed down on the innocent face slumbering upon it, and in the quiet of the darkened room, a "still, small voice" whispered: "Faithless one! deprive not that soul, committed to thy care, of the waters of life!" Again and again came the low, stern whisper, giving her no rest by its importunities. One evening, holding the little creature towards her husband, who had been watching it with infinite tenderness, mingled with a species of wonder at its helplessness, its infantile beauty, and the mystery of its life—so like the bud that enfolds the future flower—she said: "Arthur, my baby must be baptized by a Catholic priest, you know?"

"Of course, darling; I have been waiting for you to speak, and thought perhaps it was too soon," he replied, as he kissed her forehead, and smoothed with lightest touches the silky head of his little daughter, not daring to take her in his arms, she was so dainty and small, lest he should let her fall, or break her, like a fine piece of porcelain. "The midget is three weeks old—is she not? She can be bundled up, you know, and the nurse can take her to the Cathedral in a carriage."

"And you, Arthur?"

"Oh, I shall go along, of course. I am glad of this bright summer weather," he said, in his pleasant, cheerful way. "But would you not rather wait until you are strong enough to go too?"

"No," she answered, in a low tone; "something might happen. I wish it done at once.".

"I'll go to the Bishop, and have it all arranged the first thing to-morrow morning. Want the Bishop to baptize her?" he said.

"Yes, I would like it very much; but, Arthur, what shall we do for a godmother?"

"I don't know," he said, musingly, remembering a former difficulty. "Ah, now I think of it: I saw your respectable nurse with a rosary in her fingers the other evening; maybe she's a Catholic: if she is, she'll do very well,—for it's not likely we shall ever see her again after we leave Boston —and the ceremony will be private, so what odds?"

"Yes: that would do. I'll ask her if she's a Catholic, and if she'll 'stand,'" replied Anne.

The nurse—Mrs. Kilmurray—was a Catholic, a devout Irish Catholic, who had given her infant charge many a sprinkle of holy water since its birth, and made the Sign of the Cross with its tiny hand upon its forehead and breast morning and night, commending it to the tender care of the Immaculate Virgin Mother; and no words can express the delight she felt on learning that the little creature was to receive Christian Baptism. She readily consented to "stand" for the child, who was baptized by the Bishop, at the Cathedral altar, he also being sponsor for the innocent soul just cleansed of its stain. Captain Morley told the Bishop that his wife was a Catholic, but not yet able to venture out, and he had asked no further questions, satisfied that she—the Catholic mother—would watch over and help the child to "carry its baptismal robe unspotted to the judgment seat of Christ." Oh, awful charge, which makes the very soul of such as receive it tremble! Anne Morley thought she had performed her duty, and all that was required of her, in having the little one baptized a Catholic, and rested satisfied; "for by the time she will be old enough," she reasoned, "we shall be living somewhere else, and I shall be able to bring her up in her Faith." She called her daughter 'Beth (Elizabeth), after Aunt 'Beth, and was happy; the desolate spot in her heart, left empty by the death of her first-born, was once more blossoming and filled with an earnest, living love. There was nothing to cloud her temporal happiness; and to crown it with greater joy, they had a short visit from Aunt 'Beth, whose chief delight lay in the fact that the babe had been born on free soil, and who, with her quaint sayings and loving ways, filled their pretty home with the sunshine of her true, affectionate heart, leaving behind her, when she went, pleasant memories, which prevented its growing dull.

Following close upon these events came the War of the Rebellion (we all remember it) with its anguish and fury and bloody carnage, when it seemed that the final *Dies Iræ* could hardly be worse, or more terrible when it came. Captain Morley was ordered to a ship in Southern waters, and from that time until the forces of the Government overwhelmed and crushed out the disloyal power, opposing it on land and sea, he was separated from his family, winning laurels, doing brave, constant, and important service, wounded once, and taking part in the most perilous movements that were made. Aunt 'Beth besought Anne to come to "Ellerslie" with her child, but she thought she would be nearer to her husband in Washington, where she would be sure to hear at once all the official reports, and get news of him from the Department when letters failed her. She took a house, and soon had it looking like home—just as he used to love to see it—with the old familiar adornments of pictures and costly ornaments they had collected abroad, and all those little elegancies which impart an air of refinement to a dwelling which no upholstering, however rich, can give. Secluding herself from society, finding her only happiness in the companionship of her winsome little girl, now two years old, and living in a constant fever of waiting, through four long years that were fraught with dread, that often made her heart stand still—each day that dawned, presenting the possibility that before night tidings might come that Arthur was killed—time dragged on sadly and wearily. She found no solace in religion, for she had never resumed the practice of her Faith; and when she did go to church it was to a Protestant one, to pray for her husband's safety; "for was it not most proper," she asked herself, "that she should go to his own church to pray for him?"

How proudly her heart swelled when news came of the victories in which he had taken part, when she saw his name mentioned for bravery, and heard him spoken of as one of the deliverers of his country! In the bright galaxy of names that were being recorded in history as the heroic defenders of the Government, none stood with greater lustre than his. Then came a day, of triumph and rejoicing; the war was at an end, her hero came home covered with laurels, and in the embraces of wife and child felt more than rewarded for all that he had endured. Aunt 'Beth rushed down from "Ellerslie" to welcome him, and hugged, and kissed, and cried over him, until they had to threaten her with *sal volatile* before she would compose herself, which made her so heartily ashamed that she adored him in silence for the next few days. *Fêtes*, dinners, entertainments civic and social, welcomed the heroes of the war, and never was there a prouder woman than Anne Morley—prouder of him in his battle-worn, sun-faded, smoke-stained uniform, than in the resplendent one with a magnificent sword that Aunt 'Beth, without asking any one's consent, had given him. She wanted to have a gold medal struck off at Tiffany's with the names and dates of the victories he had taken part in, the names of the rebel ships and forts he had captured, but she convinced her at last that such a medal as that could only be received from Congress, and as he was only one of many who deserved such honors, and some more than he did, he did not suppose that the Government, in the present crippled state of its finances, would be able to make so costly an outlay for mere decorations. Aunt 'Beth thought it would be nobody's business if she chose to present such a medal to her own nephew, to keep in his family as an heirloom, especially when he so richly deserved it; but he was firm, and finally talked her out of it, not that she was convinced of his being right, but because he had made her understand that to do such a thing would not only make him ridiculous, but also displease him. Then she presented him with his new uniform, epaulettes and sword, which he accepted gratefully, but declared they were much too fine for him.

Several happy years succeeded, marked by the usual changes incident to naval life; 'Beth, just growing out of her girlhood, was very lovely, a softened, feminine likeness of her father, and a character in which there were many traits more resembling his than her mother's. She had lived in ignorance of her Faith; she had never heard that her mother was once a Catholic, or that she herself was one by baptism. Captain Morley had observed from time to time that his wife seemed to have given up her old belief, but as she was all the same to him, and was apparently happy, he gave himself no concern about it. They had a family pew at St. Mark's—the fashionable Episcopal Church—when they lived in Washington, and 'Beth was to all intents and purposes a Protestant.

A large package, stamped with foreign postmarks, and directed to Captain Morley, arrived one day. He was at his office in the Navy Yard, and the curiosity of 'Beth and her mother was highly excited. The seal was large, and bore the most imposing heraldic devices; it was postmarked Rome. It contained a surprise to them all, which at first made them speechless, and then made them laugh. It was from *Bonne Mère*—no longer Hamilton—but Madame le Princess Piccolomini il Sforza. She was married, and lived in a palace hundreds of years old, which, owing to the poverty of its patrician owner, had been rented out in "flats" and shops ever since he had come into possession, the only ancient splendors of his race left in it being some ragged tapestry, a picture by Cimabue, a Raphael, and one or two others equally valuable, which hung in his own apartments at the top of the house, and which he would not have sold had he starved. We can't dwell on this episode, and will only say that Prince Piccolomini il Sforza's rich American spouse renovated and restored the splendors of that old palace, and bore her grandeur with becoming dignity. She had also become a Catholic, but how much expediency had to do with her conversion we cannot say. Last of all, she wrote that she had settled fifteen thousand dollars upon Anne Morley, being the most that she could ever do, and had instructed her lawyer in Boston to pay it to her order whenever she chose to draw it. It was an affectionate, loving letter, filled and bursting out all through with a delightful sense of her rank and dignities, and ending with the hope that they would soon revisit Europe and pay her a visit. She did not tell them, however, that her princely husband was nearly eighty years old, slightly paralyzed, and had to be lifted about by his servants, or that he had a temper like Vesuvius, which she did not mind in the least, being always able to escape it by going out to drive or visit, until once, being more violent than usual, she threatened to cut off his supplies of money and go back to the United States, which had the most soothing effect, and he gave the reins into her own hands ever after. And so we leave the illustrious pair.

Another cruise of two years, and Captain Morley was assigned to the command of the Naval Academy, where, he was assured by "the powers that be," he should remain for four years, "a compliment due," they said, "to his distinguished services." How much the Morleys enjoyed their new home, with its exquisite surroundings, its congenial society, its order, its music, its pleasant gaieties, and its perfect water view, need not be described; they lived there, however, but two years: through intrigue and favoritism, Captain Morley was superseded by a personal friend of the appointing power, whose record was without distinction or extraordinary merit, and was placed in command of the "Portland," a splendid new steamship, considered the finest in the Navy. He was too proud, and felt too deeply stung by the injustice done him, to ask a question or utter a remonstrance: he simply obeyed orders. His family went back to their home in Washington, and he sailed away, never to return to them again—dying, as we have related, after saving his ship—whose timbers, had they been of gold—whose masts, had they been studded with precious stones—and even had she held an array of the greatest treasures upon earth—had not been worth the sacrifice of a life like his. It is at this period of Anne Morley's life that our story opens, that she found herself without support from that source whence alone it comes. With her idol shattered, and human love—the staff upon which she had so long leaned—broken and fallen from her grasp, is it any wonder that her anguish was two-edged, like a sword; that conscience stung her by whispering, "Thy sin has found thee out"; that her pastor's well-meant offices could not touch or help her grief?

(TO BE CONTINUED.)

"Refuge of Sinners."

BY A. M. G.

MOTHER most pure, on thy wandering child
Look down with compassionate glance;
Afar to the desert of sorrow beguiled,
No more let my footsteps advance.

Wild rages the tempest; tenebrious clouds
Exclude every ray from my sight;
Sin's fearful sirocco my pathway enshrouds,
I am bowed to the earth by its might.

But the rays of thy love, dearest Mother, I know
Can pierce through the gloomiest cells;
From that love nothing human hath fallen too low
Where the breath of the Deity dwells.

Then aid me, O "Refuge of Sinners," to flee
From the wrath and the judgment to come,

Ere time's rapid wheel shall be broken for me,
And my lips in death's silence grow dumb.
CROMPTON, Feb. 26.

How an Act of Devotion to Our Lady was Rewarded.

IT was a cold night in the month of December; the snow with its white mantle covered the earth, and all nature seemed as though life had fled and left no trace of animation behind. Not a sound was heard, save that of the lonely watchman making his usual rounds. The moon shone brightly, casting a splendor over the whitened streets, whilst the countless stars seemed to vie with each other in adding brilliancy to the scene. The city of P——, long remarkable for its spacious streets and fine buildings, was on this particular evening a spectacle well worthy of contemplation. On one of its private avenues, before a large brown-stone house, stood a carriage, awaiting the return of its owner—a physician—who was attending a dying patient. The State House clock struck two, when the door opened and the doctor made his appearance, wearing a sad and disappointed look on his face. On reaching the carriage his first words to the coachman were: "John, Mrs. R—— is dead; she breathed her last about half an hour ago."

John was heard to say in a half-audible tone, "The Lord have mercy—but, sir, had she a priest?" John being a Catholic, his first thoughts were turned to the *soul* of the departed.

But let us return to the chamber of death, and contemplate the sad scene there presented to us. Mr. R—— stood by the bedside of her whom he loved most dearly on earth, and on whom he had lavished his abundant wealth in every way that this world's vanity could desire. His heart upheaved with anguish as he gazed upon the cold, inanimate form whose eyes had forever closed to this world and all its pleasures. Never again would she look on the beautiful balls with their rich appointments or the costly furniture of the spacious parlors; never more would she join in the gaieties of the opera and the ball-room, whither she was wont so often to resort; never again would those cold lips utter words of praise or flattery on the vain things of earth, nor words of scorn and contempt on that which was good and holy. No longer could those ears drink in the words of kindness uttered by a devoted and loving husband, or the innocent prattle of dear and loving children. Yes: death, with his icy hand, had touched a shining mark, and that mansion which once rang with song, and music, and joyous mirth, is now hushed with the silence of the grave.

After the interment of his wife, Mr. R——'s great anxiety was as to whom he should confide the care and education of his two daughters. Happily for all concerned, he thought he could place them in no better keeping than that of the Sisters of Charity, who conducted an academy for young ladies near the city of P——. Mr. R—— was not mistaken in his choice, and in a short time the good seed sown in virgin soil brought forth fruit in abundance. The month of May being near at hand, the good Sisters were preparing to decorate the altar of our Blessed Mother in the chapel attached to the academy, that they might carry out the devotion of the month in a holy and becoming manner. The two young Misses R—— looked with amazement at what was going on, but could not understand its meaning. They surmised in their young hearts that the good Sisters were doing all for a worthy purpose, and resolved to help them in some way. Divine Providence had something in store for them, which, in His own good time, He bequeathed in the precious legacy of faith.

The young ladies informed their father of what the Sisters were doing, stating that all the pupils of the academy were making donations for the purpose of decorating the altar of the Blessed Virgin; they did not ask anything directly for that purpose, but the keen perception of the parent, aided by the inward admonitions of a good and liberal heart, moved him. He was not unmindful of his daughters' honor, and did not wish them to be counted illiberal amongst the pupils. After reading their letter, he decided to take some action in the matter. He therefore wended his way to a florist's, and at a great expense purchased a number of beautiful lilies, which he sent to the Sisters for the adornment of our Blessed Mother's altar. These flowers were among the most beautiful decorations on the altar. May we not ask, what must have been the feeling of the two girls when they beheld the kindness, and considered the thoughtfulness of their dear parent, in forwarding such an appropriate offering to the altar of her who is styled the "Lily of Israel"? They asked, in the simplicity of their young hearts, "What inspired father to make such an appropriate selection?" Ah, dear young creatures you did not understand his motives nor the prompting of his heart, moved, perhaps by the invisible spirit of grace, and the loving intercession of the Blessed Virgin!

Shortly after, as Mr. R —— was one day walking down Chestnut street, curiosity prompted him to enter a picture-gallery; this gallery contained a large number of paintings, some of which were executed in a manner that would shock the sense of delicacy to look upon them. A great many paintings of the heathen gods and goddesses were there, and amongst them hung the likeness of the Queen of Heaven. Mr. R—— looked on with astonishment, wondering in his heart how man could be so depraved or have so little respect for the Mother of his God and Redeemer. The protracted stay of Mr. R—— drew the attention of the proprietor, who accosted him, when the following conversation took place:

"I think," said Mr. R——, "that it is not proper to have a painting of the Blessed Virgin hung between such nude paintings as these."

"I perfectly agree with you," replied the proprietor; "but this is a very costly and original painting, and as very few Catholics visit our gallery, we are obliged to keep it in a conspicuous place to attract the notice of buyers."

"That is all very well," remarked Mr. R——; "still, though I am not a Catholic, I feel that there should be more respect shown to the Mother of God."

"I have simply given you my reasons," returned the proprietor.

Mr. R—— asked the price of the painting, which was seven hundred dollars, for which amount he filled a check before he left the store, giving orders to have the painting of the Madonna carefully packed and forwarded to the Sisters.

After the elapse of a few days, the box, with its valuable contents, was received in good order, and the likeness of "Mary Immaculate" found an appropriate place in the chapel of the good Sisters. Only a few days had passed after the reception of the precious gift, when Mr. R—— received a letter from his daughters, apprising him of their determination to become Catholics. He replied immediately, informing them that in a few days he would see and talk with them on the all-important subject of their salvation. But Providence in His goodness and mercy ordained it otherwise; Mr. R—— was absent from home for three weeks, which fact prevented him from fulfilling the promise made in the letter to his daughters. On his return home, he lost no time in paying the promised visit. It happened that a few days previously the good Father Smarius had arrived to conduct a retreat for the Sisters. It was mooted about by the young Protestant ladies that the two Misses R—— were going to become Papists (as they were pleased to call them). The young ladies laughed and joked, and said it was only a whim or fancy of the young R——s, and that they would not remain Catholics long. Father Smarius was informed of the desire of the two young ladies to become Catholics, but he prudently remarked that they should obtain the consent of their father before taking such an important step. Mr R—— on being presented to the good missionary, lost no time in introducing the all-important subject that occupied his mind. The good Father listened attentively to all Mr. R—— had to say in regard to the matter, and then replied with all the feeling and joyfulness of a glad heart: "Mr. R——, it gives me inexpressible joy to learn that your daughters have come to such a worthy and generous determination, and that you make no objection to it."

Mr. R——, after listening to the kind words which fell from the lips of the good priest, said, with all the simplicity of a child stating its wants to a parent: "I cannot see, dear Father, why I should not receive Baptism along with my two children."

Mr. R——, having been carefully instructed, was baptized with his daughters the following day.

Dear reader, kneel in spirit before that altar in the academy, adorned with sweet-sented flowers, sending up the sweet fragrance of their odor to the throne of heaven, where is seated the Blessed Mother of our Redeemer! Behold that painting of the Immaculate Virgin looking down, as it were, on that group receiving with reverent mien the water of regeneration. Imagine the heart of the good priest throbbing with joy, as he pointed out to the assembled worshippers, the causes of such unlooked-for conversions. Observe the finger of God's anointed, pointed at the likeness of "Mary Immaculate," while these sweet words fall from his lips, "She it is that you may look up to and thank for all the graces that has been showered upon yourself and your children! Pray to her, and never forget to beg her intercession in your behalf, that you may have the grace to persevere, and walk upright in the paths of virtue." Cast your eyes over that assemblage, and examine the faces present. There you can perceive the mild and joyful countenances of the good Sisters beaming with delight, their hearts leaping with joy at the blest harvest they were reaping from the seed sown in good and worthy soil. There also, you can see the eyes of seven young women, that but a few days before were cast in derision on these two innocent lambs, melted to tears on beholding the father standing with his daughters and receiving the outward sign and inward grace of the Sacrament of Baptism. There you can hear the low whisper repeated from one to the other, "We thought it was all a whim of the two young R——s, but look at their father! he is an old man, and educated, and knows what he is doing." Let us conclude by praying that we may all have constant recourse to that inexhaustible mine of imperishable riches, the ever glorious and Immaculate Virgin Mary. She is an everlasting flame of love, that receives its heat from her Son, Jesus, to warm the cold, and melt the most obdurate hearts of sinners who approach her; she is a beacon light that guides the footsteps of the wayward, wandering traveller, who journeys in far-off lands. Yes: Mary is the Star that never sets, but forever shines, pointing out the dangers that beset the pathway of her children, guiding them safely through the tempest of sin and death to their eternal and heavenly home. She is the garden whence the most fragrant flowers of piety can be culled and the purest lilies of virtue and holiness can be gathered, with which to adorn the soul and honor her Divine Son.

The Tomb of St. Peter of Alcantara.

ST. PETER OF ALCANTARA, was the reformer of the Strict Observance of the Franciscan Order. His tomb is still preserved in a village called Arenas in Spain. From Madrid to Talavera, nothing worth attention can be seen. The landscape is dreary and unattractive; only a few shrubby trees here and there break the monotony of these arid fields. Near the station of Talavera can be seen the ancient "Ebora Carpathian," now almost a heap of ruins, preserving no vestige of its past splendor. The streets are rough and dirty, the public walks abandoned or destroyed, and the convents and sacred temples turned into storehouses,—the whole filling the heart of the visitor with sadness.

There is, however, in this town, something worth visiting. It is the grand old hermitage of Our Lady "del Prado," built by Luida II over the ruins of a pagan temple dedicated to the goddess Ceres. It is also worth while to recall the church of the monastery which once belonged to the Jeromites. Coming out of Talavera by the gate called in ancient times "Cuartes," you notice a white house close at hand, where, according to tradition, the historian Mariana was born. Reaching the summit of a steep hill, the appearance of the country around suddenly changes, as if by magic, and you imagine yourself transported into paradise. A great variety of trees appear, principally the chestnut and oak, but the lemon and the orange are not wanting; on every side you see brooks and springs, and hear the murmur of falling waters. The air is balmy, and lofty pines, covering the far-off hills, seem almost to touch a sky of transparent color. The country around which Arenas is situated is the most poetic of Galicia. You imagine you see Suris transferred into Spain. If Arenas of San Pedro were situated near the Mediterranean, and not in Spain, it would undoubtedly be visited by every tourist. The parish church is of the Gothic style, and well furnished with pictures; you can see the ruins of a castle of the Middle Ages, that in its day must have been of grand style; there also is to be seen a fine palace where the infant Don Luis was exiled. A beautiful walk brings the pilgrim from the town to the convent, which is surrounded by majestic old oaks, and at one side of the road you hear the pleasant murmur of a running stream.

The Franciscans of Strict Observance have once more been permitted to occupy their convent. The first place that pilgrims generally visit is the chapel of the Saint, where, after a life of astonishing penance, his sacred remains now rest. How easy and pleasant it is to pray there! within, you listen to the strains of the organ; without, you hear the sweet songs of the birds, and the very air itself seems filled with a perfume of holiness. The chapel of the Saint is round, and the architecture is Greco-Roman, similar to that of the royal chapel at Madrid. It bestows fame on the name of the lay-brother who designed it. The convent has nothing singular, excepting its cells, which are very small, as the holy founder prescribed they should be. Close to the convent is an orchard belonging to the Marquis of Miravel, who has kindly given the use of it to the religious. It was in this convent and orchard that St. Peter did such penance, that, dying, he asked forgiveness of his body for having treated it so harshly. There you can see his cell, so low and small that he could neither stand erect nor lie down in it. There also is the pond of water into which, in winter, he would plunge himself; there, too, is the prickly shrub on which he used to roll himself, and come out bleeding. This shrub has since lost its thorns, while the others around are full of them. It seems a contradiction to have a brier without thorns, but such is the fact.

The Feast of the Saint, which falls on the 19th of October, is celebrated every year with great pomp at Arenas; the villagers from the surrounding country flock there by thousands. There is a procession in the afternoon, in which an image of the Saint is carried in great pomp through the streets. During the procession the devout pilgrims lay their offerings at the feet of the Saint. Faith still lives amongst the Spanish people, and, in spite of the cold wind of incredulity that blows from every quarter, it is impossible to visit the tomb of St. Peter of Alcantara, without feeling an increase of devotion and less repugnance to embrace Christian penance.

YOU will catch more flies with a spoonful of honey than with a hundred barrels of vinegar.

WERE there anything better or fairer on earth than gentleness, Jesus Christ would have taught it to us; and yet He has given us only two lessons to learn of Him—meekness and humility of heart.—*St. Francis of Sales.*

A Beautiful Example of Moral Heroism.

ON reading the following letters, which were published by the *Catholic Telegraph* some years ago, and which now come to us through the columns of the *Catholic Standard*, we could not repress a glow of enthusiasm at the noble spirit of moral heroism manifested by the young lady. Such examples are rare in our days. We trust the present one will not be lost on our readers. If young Catholics would read Rev. Father Lambing's excellent *brochure* on "Mixed Marriages—their Origin and Results," there would not be so many unfortunate marriages and so many defections from the faith. Few persons have any idea how many renegade Catholics there are in the United States.

———, Dec. 1, 1854.

DEAREST ———: The mutual regard which I am so happy to know exists between us, and the exchange of sacred vows which I ardently expect will be the result before long, give me courage to consult with you on a subject which is of the first importance, and one which my relatives are pressing on my attention. Amongst the obstacles to happiness, there are none so likely to produce discontent as a want of union in religious sentiment. If we offer our devotions at the same altar in religion, as well as love, you must be aware, dear ———, that it will cement in a wonderful degree our hearts. Do you think, then, that you could worship with me in the Presbyterian or any Protestant Church? In our happy country all religions are alike, and your good sense must assure you that forms of faith are of small importance, provided our lives be virtuous. Moreover, dearest, in marriage we must not overlook those less sentimental but more solid considerations which have reference to the prosperous condition of worldly comfort and respectability. There is, as you are aware, a very deep-rooted antipathy to the faith in which, without any fault of yours, you have been educated, and it would seriously interfere with my successful pursuit of business were I to contract so close an intimacy with a person professing Roman Catholicism.

Should you resolve, however, as I have no doubt you will, to worship the *same* God only in another Church, we will both acquire a sympathy and regard, the consequences of which will be truly desirable and most propitious to our welfare. I know that, in a matter like this, you will wish to consult your friends, though their consent, you know, is not at all imperative; yet, in order that you may do so with freedom, I give you my full consent to make known my sentiments privately or publicly, as you may think proper. Though you may call this a business letter—it is so different from our usual correspondence—and laugh at my seriousness, yet I shall expect your answer with great anxiety. In the mean time my heart is ever yours, and your image is daguerreotyped upon it indelibly by love's own warm impress, and with his fidelity to the original.

Believe me, dearest ———, to be ever yours, in life and death.

———, Dec. 3, 1854.

DEAR ———: I received your letter just ten minutes since, and my judgment tells me to answer at once, without any consultation, because none is needed. When you asked me to give you my heart and its affections I consented, because I admired and respected and loved; but I did not at the same time agree to surrender to you my soul and its eternal hopes. Had you asked me to make such a sacrifice as that, I would have refused not only you but an Archangel, could any such bright spirit propound a like question to me. Remember, dear ———, that religion with us Catholics is not an opinion at all—it is far more, even, than a logical conviction—it is Faith, which is grand and powerful in proportion to the divinity in which it trusts. Such is my idea of Faith, but I do not pretend to be a theologian. Now, dearest ———, I could not, without a horrible contempt for myself, surrender God to win a husband even as accomplished as you, and the only one to whom I have plighted vows of love. I would be guilty of an enormous crime if I were even to pretend to a conversion in which my understanding and heart had no part. Every idea of honor which I have learned forbids such a prostration of my character. You could not even respect me yourself could I be so easily induced to desert my hopes of heaven. Could I be faithless to God and faithful to man? I knew, dear ———, that you did not agree with me in my religious sentiments, but I never thought of requiring from you such a heavy obligation as you would impose upon me.

But I must argue the question with you: for though you are a lawyer, I am not afraid of entering into a little controversy with you; so now look grave, for I am going to lecture you. You say, dear ———, that "in our happy country all religions are alike." Well, granted; why, then, can't you relinquish yours and join mine? Wouldn't that be as reasonable as for me to relinquish mine and profess yours? But you place it on the ground of expediency—on the unpopularity of our Church. Well, you need not change yours; you would do wrong to abandon your creed and unite with mine, unless you firmly believe in it. As for the smiles of worldly prosperity, though I would not uselessly disregard them, yet a true-born American, with a proper estimate of her honor, would prefer the rags of poverty, sooner than clothe with silks a dishonored and violated conscience. Your own good sense and enlightened mind will convince you, dear ———, that I am right; and I am confident that your reply, which I will expect with anxiety, as you do this, will remove this thin mist from the bright eyes of love, whose light I hope will ever beam gracious in our lives.

Yours truly,

———, Dec. 9, 1854.

DEAR MISS ———: I most candidly acknowledge that your letter has greatly disappointed me. I thought that your superior intelligence had risen above all those antique and musty opinions, whose proper period was the middle ages, and their proper locality in Spain. I have now and then observed among Catholics, educated like yourself, a strange fashion of ascending above the realities of life on the airy pinions of what you call faith. But such theories do not advance a professional man—do not roof a house, or supply the necessities, much less the elegancies of a home. I thought on this account you would readily enter into my views, but you refuse to do so. Well, I will abandon my request. I am too much devoted to you to allow even a difference like this, serious and most important as it is, to weaken the love which unites our hearts. You ladies, and you are the very first amongst them all, dear ———, contrive occasionally to introduce such exalted notions into your beautiful heads, that to remove them would be as easy as to attempt to chain the zephyrs, or to rob the violet of its perfume. Well, then, in conclusion I must inform you that I have read your letter to the family. It would be improper to deceive you on the subject of my parents' opinions. Their attachment to the Presbyterian faith is great; and the idea of union with a Catholic, even with you, whom they know so well, and highly respect, darkens their countenances, and distresses me very much. They have, however, renewed their consent, but they require us to be married by a Presbyterian clergyman. This, dear ———, I agree with them in asking as a right, because it is a duty I owe them not to distress their hearts nor do violence to their religious principles by permitting the ministry of a Catholic clergyman. As your Church, dear ———, does not consider such marriages invalid, you can have no objection to this arrangement, which will unite us never again to part in life. Understand, dearest, that I am compelled to consider the ministry of a Protestant clergyman *only* indispensable to our union.

Your devoted ———,

———, Esq.: Dec. 12, 1854.

DEAR SIR: I shall not ask you to "do any violence to the religious principles of your parents," nor will I consent to have any offered to mine. When I consented to marry you, I was not aware that your father and mother, with "their religious principles," were included in the agreement. The care which you have not to offend your parents cannot be greater than that which I must observe not to offend God

The tone of your letter betrays the spirit of your love. It is not a rosy spirit, as poets and lovers have described it, but a spirit hedged round with thorns. I think, sir, as I am still free, I had better remain so. You will find some one who will readily consent not to "do violence to the religious principles of your parents." If I consented, sir, to be a slave before marriage, by surrendering my rights of conscience, I feel quite satisfied that I would deserve to be something worse than a slave after marriage. I had little thought that this would be the *finale* of so many pleasant days, words and letters. If you should feel it as much as I do (for I care not to conceal my emotions), you can have recourse to that world which you fear so much, for consolation. As for me, I will try to forget a love which was so unworthy that it refused to be appeased except by the sacrifice of honor and conscience. No more from

Yours, etc., ———.

Catholic Notes.

—ADDITIONAL SUMS FOR IRELAND.—A widow's mite, 25 cents; John Ledwige, $1.

—We are under many obligations to Rev. Fathers Ward and Hughes, S. J., of St. Louis, Mo., for a considerable addition to our subscription list, and for kind favors to our travelling agent.

—A ROYAL CLERIC.—Count Alexander Ilinski, formerly page and *aide-de-camp* of the Czar, lately received clerical tonsure and the four minor orders at the hands of Mgr. de Langalerie, Archbishop of Auch, in the cathedral of the same city.

—An infidel paper published in Bologna, Italy, praises the Capuchin Fathers of that city for their charity in dispensing daily from 1,200 to 1,300 rations of soup to as many poor people, and distributing at the same time 1,800 large loaves of bread.

—Mgr. Besson, Bishop of Nimes, has entrusted to the celebrated sculptor Cabuchet a statue of Père Bri- daino. This eminent Catholic artist is the one who executed the famous statue of Our Lady of Lourdes in white marble which stands over the grand altar in the Basilica of Lourdes.

—"MISSIONES CATOLICAS."—Since the first of January, a Spanish edition of *Les Missions Catholiques*, under the patronage of Mgr. d'Urquinanona, Bishop of Barcelona, Spain, has been published semi-monthly in that city. The new *Missiones Catolicas* already enjoys an extensive circulation among Catholics at home and abroad.

—A TRULY GENEROUS WORK.—The good effected by St. Raphael's Association for the assistance of emigrants becomes daily more apparent. Thus a little girl, ten years old, was enabled through the charitable aid of the agents of this society, to travel from Hamburg, Germany, to Columbus, O. There are agents at Hamburg, Bremen, New York, Baltimore, and other cities.

—ORDINATION AT THREE RIVERS, QUEBEC.—Rev. John W. Considine, who had received the other sacred orders at Christmas, was elevated to the dignity of the priesthood on the 21st ult. On the same day Mr. Wm. O'Connor received minor orders. The former is attached to the Vicariate of Northern Minnesota, the latter to the Diocese of Portland. Rt. Rev. Bishop Laflèche officiated.

—SIT NOMEN DOMINI BENEDICTUM.—According to a pious custom, two hundred devout men of all classes of society in Paris spent the night of the 31st of December before the Blessed Sacrament, in the Church of Our Lady of Victories. At the first stroke of the bell, announcing the solemn hour of midnight, all prostrated themselves for a few moments, and after rising, repeated three times the words, "*Sit nomen Domini Benedictum*." Prayers were then offered in common for the welfare of the entire world. At the conclusion of the prayers, some repaired to the sacristy to take a little rest on mattresses placed on the floor, each taking his turn of repose and adoration.

—A SCENE AT THE BATTLE OF GETTYSBURG.—Major General St. C. Mulholland has contributed to *The Philadelphia Times* the following interesting reminiscence of the battle of Gettysburg. The scene described must have been very impressive, and it is not surprising that it is still remembered with so much vividness by those who witnessed it. "When the third Federal Army Corps is forced to retire before the Confederates, help is called for. General Hancock tells Caldwell to have his division ready. "Fall in!" and the men run to their places. "Take arms!" and the four brigades of Zook, Cross, Brook and Kelly are ready for the fray. There is yet a few minutes to spare before starting, and the time is occupied in one of the most impressive religious ceremonies I have ever witnessed. The Irish Brigade, which had been commanded formerly by General Thomas Francis Meagher, and whose green flag had been unfurled in every battle in which the Army of the Potomac had been engaged, from the first Bull Run to Appomattox, and was now commanded by Colonel Patrick Kelly, of the eighty-eighth New York, formed a part of this division. The brigade stood in column of regiments, closed in mass. As the large majority of its members were Catholics, the chaplain of the brigade, Rev. William Corby, C. S. C., proposed to give a general absolution to all the men before going into the fight. While this is customary in the armies of Catholic countries of Europe, it was perhaps the first time it was ever witnessed on this continent, unless, indeed, the grim old warrior, Ponce de Leon, as he tramped through the everglades of Florida, or De Soto on his march to the Mississippi, indulged in this act of devotion. Father Corby stood upon a large rock in front of the brigade; addressing the men, he explained what he was about to do, saying that each one could receive the benefit of the absolution by making a sincere Act of Contrition and firmly resolving to embrace the first opportunity of confessing his sins, urging them to do their duty well, and reminding them of the high and sacred nature of their trust as soldiers and the noble object for which they fought. The brigade was standing at "Order arms." As he closed his address every man fell on his knees, with head bowed down. Then stretching his right hand towards the brigade, Father Corby pronounced the words of the absolution. The scene was more than impressive, it was awe-inspiring. Near by stood Gen. Hancock, surrounded by a brilliant throng of officers who had gathered to witness this very unusual occurrence, and while there was profound silence in the ranks of the Second Corps, yet over to the left, out by the peach orchard and Little Round Top, where Weed and Vincent and Haslett were dying, the roar of the battle rose and swelled and re-echoed through the woods. The act seemed to be in harmony with all the surroundings. I do not think there was a man in the brigade who did not offer up a heartfelt prayer. For some it was their last; they knelt there in their graveclothes,—in less than half an hour many of them were numbered with the dead of July 2."

——TITIAN.—Several magnificent religious pictures entitle Titian to a first rank among Christian painters. This supreme master of color belonged to the school of Venice. His master was Bellini, chief founder of the school; his fellow-pupil, Giorgione, second only to Titian. His birth happened in 1477; his death in 1576. Light and splendor and joy distinguish the creations of his brush. His long life was entirely devoted to his art. He painted in every style of subject—mythological, historical, ecclesiastical. Popes, emperors, and kings sat to him for their portraits, as did most of the great men and many of the beauties of his day. Strange to say, many of these portraits now derive their only distinction from the hand that painted them; their names have perished. The national collection at Madrid is rich in his works—richer than any other in the world except Venice. The sacred picture by which Titian is perhaps best known is the "Assumption of the Madonna," painted in 1576, for the Church of Sta. Maria Gloriosa de' Frari, and now in the Academy, Venice —one of the most glorious pictures in the world. Its dimensions are very large, the figures exceeding the size of life. The Duomo at Verona possesses another of the same subject, less important and less famous. An "Entombment" of Christ in the Louvre, Paris, is a work of the truest and deepest pathos, heightened by the solemn light of evening that pervades it. The contrast between the character of the Mother's sorrow and that of the Magdalene, who supports her, is one of the finest conceptions in religious art. The Venice Academy now possesses a beautiful painting of the "Presentation" of the blessed child Mary in the Temple. Amidst a wondering and admiring crowd, the young bride of Heaven mounts the steps to the Temple gate, where the high-priest awaits her to bless her act of early consecration. In the Church of St. Nazzaro, Brescia, a remarkable picture of the "Resurrection" in three compartments, flanked by the "Annunciation" in two, adorns the high altar. The noble donor, of the Averoldo family, is accompanied by St. Sebastian and St. George. The twilight landscape in the central scene is especially noteworthy.

More famous is the "Martyrdom of St. Lawrence" at Madrid—of which a copy also exists in the Jesuits' Church at Venice—exhibiting the supernatural courage of the martyr in contrast with his fiery trial, and, incidentally, the antagonistic effect of the beam of glory falling from above upon the Saint in its struggle with the reflection of two vessels of burning pitch below, which light the scene. In the Vatican collection a well-known picture represents a group, or "Santa Conversazione," as it is called, of saints; in the upper portion heaven is opened, and reveals the Madonna and Holy Child seated on clouds, attended by cherubs, and bending downwards to the august company below, consisting of St. Nicholas, in his vestments as a Bishop; on his right hand St. Peter, and on his left St. Catharine. St. Antony of Padua and St. Francis stand together, next to Peter, and, on the outside, St. Sebastian. Above all, in a serene and cloudless light, broods the Mystic Dove.—"*Catholic World*" *for March*.

——MISSIONARY NOTES FROM AFGHANISTAN.— From a letter of a priest of the Congregation of St. Joseph, we glean some interesting facts regarding the missions in Afghanistan. The zealous missionary states that until the time of his writing he and his two assistants were the only Catholic priests in all Afghanistan, but that lately they have been reinforced by four others from the mother-house at Mill Hill, near London. Two of these are to remain with him at Cabul, whilst of his first two companions, one is already installed at Lundi Katal, the other at Candahar, each distant about three hundred miles from Cabul. After a description of the soil, its productions, and the climate, the writer says that although the inhabitants profess the Mohammedan religion, most of them know the Koran only by name. Their fierceness, vindictiveness and treachery know no bounds. For the present, the new missionaries are employed as field-chaplains with the British forces, 5,000 of whom are stationed near Cabul, under the command of General Roberts. Of these 5,000 men, 2,000 are Europeans, and 600 of them Catholics. A graphic description is given of the campaign, and the dangers and difficulties the little army had to overcome. God had until then watched over the Catholic soldiers, none of whom were killed or fatally wounded in the battles preceding the assault upon Cabul and the subsequent explosions at Bala Hissar. On returning from a visit to Cabul, the missionary found on his return to Bala Hissar several Armenian Catholics, who were overjoyed at meeting him, as they had not seen a Catholic priest for many years. As evening was fast setting in, he was obliged to appoint another day for a regular visit. On his arrival, at the time appointed, he met with a most respectful and hearty reception, men, women and children joining in it. Their chief and spokesman, who was able to converse in tolerably good English, said that he was the confidential servant of Amadullah Khan, the only son of a deceased elder brother of Yakoob Khan, and heir presumptive to the crown. He further stated that their ancestors had been transported two hundred years ago by Nadir Shah from Persia to Cabul, but that, excepting a few occasions when the Mussulman populace were over-excited by fanaticism, they had not much reason to complain. One of these occasions was the late massacre of Major Cavagnari and his escort. This unforeseen event obliged the Armenians to hide themselves for a few days, but after that they were left unmolested. They felt much distressed over the destruction of their dwellings and little chapel. The missionary requested an interview with General Roberts, who received him with great kindness, regretting, however, that the total destruction of the suburb of Bala Hissar and the expulsion of all its inhabitants had become a strategic necessity. But he promised to provide suitable lodgings and a new chapel at Cabul for the Armenians, who were much consoled by this gratifying news. They asserted that day and night they were praying for the conversion of the Afghans, thirty of whom, dwelling in Cabul, were already Christians at heart, but restrained by fear from an open confession of the faith. They also pointed out the tomb of a young Armenian who had suffered martyrdom at the hands of the Mussulmans. A very interesting feature of the report is an account of a visit paid by Amadullah Khan, the heir presumptive, to the tent of the missionary. He is a young man of twenty-one years, well disposed, and not the least prejudiced against the Christians. The visitor parted from his host on the most friendly terms, and the latter expects much benefit for the mission should Amadullah ever ascend the throne. For the present, however, there is no probability of such an event.

—ANOTHER PROTESTANT ADVOCATE OF RELIGIOUS AND MORAL TRAINING IN THE SCHOOL.—The daily papers give an account of a lecture delivered at the First Baptist Church in Philadelphia, Feb. 25th, before a large and intelligent audience, by the Rev Geo. Dana Boardman, D. D., on "The Respective Relations of Church and State to Education," which it is said will "raise a breeze." The preacher is pastor of the church in which the lecture was delivered, has a high-toned congregation, and enjoys a wide-spread reputation as a Biblical lecturer. In the course of his lecture he spoke of Christ as the centre and source of all true education, and maintained that unless religious instruction be combined with secular education in the schools, the population must eventually be made up largely of moral monsters. In the first place, he said, the spirit of the Constitution was disregarded by the reading of the Bible in the public schools. On the other hand, those schools were not calculated for the bringing up of children in the Christian faith, or with any other religious conviction. The lecturer then spoke strongly in advocacy of the establishment *of parochial schools everywhere, by all religious denominations*. And this is just what is wanted in these United States at the present time. The present system of public instruction has been in use only for a little more than a quarter of a century—not half the ordinary span of a lifetime, and the evil results are already so many and so glaring that sensible people, even among its most ardent advocates, begin to see the necessity of a reformation in the school system. Catholics saw this from the first, but they were decried as enemies of education and would not be listened to. When the present godless educational system was introduced, a man could place a reasonable share of dependence on other men; but now a person knows not whom to trust, for dishonesty has become a common trait; from the travelling agent up to the bank president, and from the simple clerk up to the highest government position, trickery and defalcations are common. Catholics do not want to do away with even one of the public schools; they are all wanted, and more too. But let each denomination be given so much *per capita* for all children attending school, and we dare to say that in twenty years the number of schools will be doubled, the education will be better, and a foundation will be laid for that moral and religious element in our population which alone can preserve free institutions. We are Catholics; but for those outside the visible pale of the Church we know that religious instruction of any kind is better than infidelity. Godless teaching threatens the very foundations of society. We learn that in the State of Massachusetts, which, according to last year's census, has a population of 1,652,000, no less than 7,223 divorces were granted from 1860 to 1878—an average of 400 a year. The same state contains 475,000 Catholics, among whom there were no divorces. Here is food for reflection.

New Publications.

SHORT MEDITATIONS FOR EVERY DAY IN THE YEAR; Intended Chiefly for the Use of Religious. By an Anonymous Italian Author. Translated by Dom Edmund J. Luck, O. S. B., Priest of the Cassinese Congregation of the Primitive Observance ; Prefaced by a Recommendation from His Eminence Cardinal Manning. 1879. New York and Cincinnati : F. Pustet. Two Vols. 16mo. Price, $3.50.

We cannot do better than use the words of Cardinal Manning in his Preface to this work to make known the merits of this new book of Meditations. "*The Annus Liturgicus* of Dom Gueranger has beautifully illustrated the wisdom of the Church in its yearly round of Sacred Lessons, and in the unvarying sweetness and significance of its Solemnities and Feasts. In every year the whole Revelation of Faith returns, mystery by mystery, dogma by dogma, precept by precept, upon our intelligence and upon our hearts. The *Sex credendi* is the *Sex orandi*, and the worship of the Church preaches to the world without, and to the faithful within the sanctuary. To those that are without, it is a visible and audible witness for the kingdom of God; to those that are within, it is a foresight and a foretaste of the beauty and the sweetness of the worship of eternity.

If preachers will follow the Church as it moves year by year in the cycle of eternal truths, and will explain pastorally in simple and manly words the Epistles and Gospels by which the Church, or rather the Holy Ghost, teaches us the meaning of Feast and Fast as they come and go, they will year by year declare to their flocks the whole counsel of God, and keep back nothing which is for their perfection. Not so when texts are chosen at random and sermons are preached without continuity or relation to the fulness and unity of faith.

What is true of sermons is true likewise of meditations. The best Manuals of Meditation for general use are those that attach themselves to the Church as it moves through the liturgical year, and follow in its course. Such manuals enable preachers to expound the mind of the Church in all its festivals, and prepare the faithful to receive their teaching with a readier and more complete understanding.

The present manual is one of this kind: full of a simple and homely exposition of the eternal truths in which and by which we must live and persevere to a holy death. Every one, in every state in the world, in the priesthood, in the cloister, will find in it what is enough for Christian perfection: for perfection consists in the love of God and our neighbor. In charity is all perfection: out of it, none: for "God is charity, and he that abideth in charity abideth in God, and God in him, now and in eternity." The oft-quoted words of St. Augustine may be taken as a standing apology for the multiplication of books treating the same subjects. The style and manner of one author will please this one, the style and manner of another will please that one. Some souls are reached more readily through the intellect; other souls are touched at once by an appeal to their affections. Thus the variety of books of devotion as meditation conduces to satisfy the needs of every variety of souls. We have no doubt that this manual will satisfy many who, perhaps, have not yet met a book whose mode of treating the solemn truths of religion harmonized with their dispositions and temperament.

THE SACRED HEARTS OF JESUS AND MARY Venerated in the Spirit of the Church and of her Saints. A Manual of Devotion Intended for the Members of the Apostleship of Prayer. Compiled from the German Publications of the Rev. Jos. Aloysius Krebs, of the Congregation of the Most Holy Redeemer. New York and Cincinnati: F. Pustet & Co. 495 pages. Price, in neat cloth, $1.

This is not a prayer-book, such as prayer-books ordinarily are, and such as one expects a general prayer-book to be, and yet it contains all that is actually necessary in a prayer-book—namely, devotions for morning and evening; prayers before and after Holy Communion; the Litany of the Blessed Virgin, of the Saints, of the Holy Name of Jesus; devotions for Mass, Vesper Psalms, Benediction Service, etc. But it is chiefly a book of devotions to the most Sacred Heart of Jesus and the Immaculate Heart of Mary, as the title indicates, and in this sense it is one of the most complete devotional works we have met with. It seems to us a mistake on the part of the publishers, or compiler, to state in the title-page that the manual is intended for the members of the Apostleship of Prayer; this may be taken to imply that it does not suit other special devotions as well, as that to Our Lady of the Sacred Heart, etc., or general devotion, while the contrary is the case. This Manual is a compilation from three German publications of the Rev. Jos. Aloysius Krebs, C. SS. R., which in nine years had gone through twenty-seven editions (85,000 copies), and contains within the compass of one book many of the devotions in honor of the Most Sacred Heart of Jesus and the Immaculate Heart of Mary recommended by Holy Church, with fragrant devotional flowers culled from the gardens of the Saints and other servants of God. This little book will be welcomed by all devout souls,—but more particularly, of course, by those for whom it was chiefly intended. The English edition bears the *imprimatur* of the Bishop of Southwark.

—"THE INTRODUCTION OF CATHOLICITY INTO NEW ENGLAND,"—a lecture delivered by the Rev. James Fitton, rector of the Church of the Most Holy Redeemer, Boston, and published at the request of the Catholic Union, forms a neat octavo pamphlet of 21 pages, printed at *The Advocate* office, East Boston. This lecture of Father Fitton's contains many interesting incidents in the early history of the Church in the Archdiocese of Boston, and, coming from such a pioneer priest as Father Fitton, will no doubt be eagerly sought for by many. Rev. Father Fitton was a pupil in the first school erected by the great and good Father Matignon, D. D., and the saintly Bishop Cheverus, in Boston, and it was a happy thought to the members of the Catholic Union to obtain some of his reminiscences in the form of a lecture.

—We have received from the publisher, John F. Weishampel, Jr., bookseller and stationer, No. 8, under the Eutaw House, Baltimore, Md., an excellent New and Enlarged Map of Baltimore City, including Waverly, Hampden, Canton, and all the Parks, prepared from the latest surveys. Among the places of note on this map are the earthworks at Patterson Park, in the eastern suburb of the city, thrown up by the Americans on the approach of Gen. Ross's army; and Fort McHenry, at the entrance of the harbor, bombarded by the British fleet, and before which, on a British vessel, was composed the national song, "The Star-spangled Banner," by F. S. Key.

Obituary.

Departed this life, at St. Mary's Convent, Nauvoo, Ill., on the 21st inst., SISTER JOSEPHINE (Miss Margaret Radell), aged 23 years. Her beautiful and edifying death was truly the echo of a holy and innocent life. Having made her religious profession with more than ordinary fervor only a few weeks previous, she confidently, and with truly heroic fortitude, supported an agony of fourteen hours, when it pleased God to take her pure soul to Himself.

Those who witnessed the fearful struggle so patiently and sweetly endured, have learned a lesson that shall ever be remembered: "Precious in the sight of God is the death of His Saints." M. A. H.

Confraternity of the Immaculate Conception
(Or of Our Lady of Lourdes).

REPORT FOR THE WEEK ENDING FEBRUARY 25TH. The following petitions have been received. Recovery of health for 96 persons and 4 families,—change of life for 29 persons and 3 families,—conversion to the Faith for 46 persons and 5 families,—special graces for 2 Bishops, 11 priests, 26 religious, 5 clerical students, and 3 persons aspiring to the religious state,—temporal favors for 43 persons and 7 families,—spiritual favors for 62 persons and 5 families,—the spiritual and temporal welfare of 7 communities, 5 congregations, 8 schools and 1 seminary,—also 68 particular intentions, and 6 thanksgivings for favors received.

Specified intentions. Protection of 3 absent sons of a devout Catholic family,—means to meet pressing obligations,—the removal of what may prove the occasion of scandal,—happy death for several religious who are in consumption,—a good pastor for a congregation,—several persons deprived of sight, and others with impaired hearing,—God's blessing on the choice of a state of life,—the recovery of some debts,—success of several missions—the prevention of a mixed marriage,—means to build a new church for a poor country mission.

FAVORS OBTAINED.

Several recent conversions are attributed to the prayers of the Confraternity, among which are some persons addicted to intemperance, the reconciliation of a husband and wife who had been separated for a considerable time, but are now living together in peace. A friend writes: "Sincere thanks are returned for the favorable decision of 5 law-suits, the recovery of 2 persons' health, and the happy death of a mother and daughter." .... A poor woman, a convert, returns thanks for the conversion of her children to the true Faith. The following cures by means of the water of Lourdes are reported: A young person, who had been almost blind since her birth, had her sight restored after using some of the miraculous water. Her eyes, which previously were in an inflamed and unhealthy condition, are now as clear and bright as could be wished. The cure was effected after the expiration of a novena. An aged man had lost the sight of one eye by an explosion last June; soon after the other eye became so much affected that the doctors thought of removing the injured one, to save the sight of the other, but the members of his family applied the water of Lourdes and made a novena, and before its close perfect sight was restored to both eyes. Another gentleman suffering from a sore on his face, which was pronounced to be a cancer, was also cured by applying the miraculous water. A pious correspondent informs us that her brother, who was dangerously ill, has been cured by the prayers of the Confraternity and the offering of a Mass. A grateful mother returns thanks for the cure of her son, who had been sorely afflicted with St. Anthony's dance, but who is now as well as ever, and able to go to school.

OBITUARY.

We recommend the following deceased persons to the prayers of the Confraternity: SISTER M. OF ST. ANYSIA, who died peacefully at St. Mary's, Notre Dame, Ind., on the 22d ult. MOTHER MARY WARDE, of the Sisters of Mercy, whose holy life was crowned with a precious death at Cork, Ireland, on the 15th of December last. She was in the seventy-third year of her age and the forty-ninth of her religious life. Mr. FRANCIS VIENRA, of Louisville, Ohio, who slept in the Lord on the 2d of January, at the age of seventy-nine. Mr. JOHN J. DENNEHY, whose death occurred after a short illness at New Orleans, La., on the 31st of December. Mrs. MATILDA LANGE, deceased last November at Wilmington, Del. Mr. HOWARD ADAMS, who breathed his last on the 12th inst., at San Francisco, Cal. Mrs. JOHANNA MCATEER, of Oil City, Pa., who rested in peace on the 11th of January. Mr. D. J. VAN SPANEDONK, of New York city, whose death took place on the 22d ult. Messrs. DOUGHERTY and CASSIDY, who were burned to death on the 20th of February. Mrs. ROSE CONWAY, of New York city; Mrs. ANNE WALSH, of San Francisco, Cal.; Miss ELLA HEANY, of the same city; Miss CATHARINE BRADLEY, of Denver, Colorado; Mrs. ANNE SMITH, of Hancock, Minn., recently deceased. Mr. BERNARD MOONEY, Bardstown, Ky.; Mr. J. MCHUGH; Mr. P. BRADY; Mrs. ELLEN DUGAN, H. DUGAN; VERY REV. THOMAS MEADE, deceased some time ago. And several others, whose names have not been given.

Requiescant in pace.

A. GRANGER, C. S. C., Director.

For the Rebuilding of Notre Dame.

Mr. and Mrs. James Killion, $2; Mrs. Ahearn, $1; Edward O'Donnell, $2; Mr. Henry Grine, $1; Mrs. Catharine Kalmes, $1; Mr. John Magnet, $1; Mrs. Catharine Claus, $2; Mr. Michael Moriarty, $5; Mrs. Edward Walsh, $5; Mr. John O'Cleary. $2; W. L. S. Gray, $1; Miss Hanora Kane, $1; Mrs. Anne Weldon, $1; Mrs. M. Cavanaugh, $1; Miss Catharine Geer, $1; Henry Freidhoff, $1; Christiana Freidhoff, $1; Matthew Dunn, $1; Mrs. Catharine Gallagher, $1; Mrs. Mary Manning, $1; Jennie Manning, $1; Michael F. Manning, $1; John Gleeson, $1; Miss E. C. Spain, $1; Mrs. Sarah A. Harden, $1; D. J. Miller, $1; Miss Annie McCallion, $1; Mrs. J. Delaxy, $2.50; Mrs. Dick, $1; A Friend, $5; Miss Ann McElbaney, $1; P. J. Dunphy, 50 cts.; Mrs. W. J. Campbell, $1; Mr. John Reddin, $5; A Sympathiser, $2; Miss Annie McCoy, $5; Mrs. Johanna Connor, $5; Miss Ellen Moriarty, $1; A Friend, 50 cts.; A Friend, $5; Mrs. W. Bacome, $2.50; A Friend, $5; Miss M. Lynn, $1; James McGarrity, $2; A Friend, $2; Mrs. W. J. Thompson, $1; Mrs. J. Tracy, $2.50.; Mrs. Margaret Hauschattes, 50 cts.; Mrs. M. Scarret, $1; Miss Margaret Davlin, 18; Charles Davlin, $1; Mrs. Julia Davlin, $1; Mrs. John Sullivan, $1.50; For Mary Prior, $1.

Youth's Department.

The Palm Branch.

BY N. J. O'CONNELL FFRENCH.

(Founded on Fact.)

IT was Christmas night. There were but few pedestrians on the streets of Boston, which, covered deep with frozen snow, offered an insecure and even dangerous footing to the belated traveller. People evidently considered that home was the most comfortable place on that bitter cold winter's night, and wisely basked in the "bonny bright blink of their ain firesides."

Being but a comparative stranger in the great literary capital of America, and without home ties of my own, I was celebrating my Christmas with a family of French descent, with whom I was acquainted, and in whose refined and agreeable society I had often passed pleasant hours. My hosts, the G—— family, were represented on that occasion by three generations; the grandfather and grandmother, with their two sons, accompanied by their wives and children. None but the old couple themselves had ever seen the shores of sunny France, the other members of the family having been born under the Stars and Stripes.

A very merry group we were, I assure you; and the young folk, who were in great force, entered with a full zest into the spirit of the occasion. The joyous observance of the sacred festival of Christmas is becoming every year more general throughout America, especially in the great Eastern cities, and this family had also adopted the good old custom.

One group of children were engaged in the absorbing game of "What's my thought like?" while another, somewhat more advanced in years, were earnestly discussing the relative merits of the various Cribs they had visited during the day. You see the hour had not yet arrived for a revelation of the resplendent and crowning glory of the evening, the long-looked for Christmas tree; so there was "a pause in the day's occupation," a lull of expectancy which had to be filled up somehow. The elder portion of the company had gathered around the fire, conversing sociably and enjoying the pleasant domestic associations, when all at once the children seemed to weary of their games; their mirth was hushed; and their impatience for the arrival of Santa

Claus revealed itself by a deep silence. "Oh, dear," at length said one little fellow, boldly, "I do wish he would come down the chimney quick! He must have an awful lot of places to go to before he comes to us, or he'd have been here long ago. Hurry up, Santa Claus; hurry up!"

"I tink," cried one sturdy mite of an urchin, named Hypolite, "I tink he must hab a vevy, vevy old horse, like Uncle Geordie's, and dat he go, oh, vevy slow!"

There was a general laugh at this explanation. "Grandpapa," said Louise, the eldest of the girls, a lass of some twelve summers, "you know you promised last week that you would tell us the story of the palm branch, on Christmas day. Will you tell us now, grandpapa, whilst we are waiting?"

Happy suggestion! There was a chorus of irresistible childish pleadings, to which a sterner heart than grandpapa's must have yielded.

"Well, my children, I will relate that true story to you. But first bring me the glass case with the holy branch."

Soon there was placed in his hands a small case made of walnut-wood and glass, which enclosed a withered palm branch.

How vividly do I recall that venerable figure, as he sat with the little case on his knees, the ruddy firelight playing on his silver locks, and lighting up the comeliness of a serene old age which beautified his countenance! Ah, my dear old friend, many, many years have passed since I heard you narrate that simple story of your life, and you have long since gone to your eternal reward; but I fancy I can see and hear you now, as I did on that Christmas night so long ago. My memory does not fail me in one particular, either of matter or manner. The earnest, solemn tones, the eloquent gestures, even the quaint French phrases, which I thought lent an additional charm to the recital—all, all are present to me even at this very moment. But while I relate your touching experiences as nearly as I can in your own reverent spirit, I will omit those foreign peculiarities of expression, which in you were natural and proper, but which rehearsed by me; might seem trivial.

"It is true, my little ones, that I promised to tell you the story of this withered palm branch, and to explain to you why I have so carefully preserved it in this case. The history of this palm is the history of the most important event in my life; and I want you to listen to it attentively, and to remember it always, so that in after years you may profit by the lesson that it teaches—a lesson which I learned through a bitter experience. Were it not for this little branch, small and trifling as it appears, I should not see around me to-night my children and my children's children; Heaven bless you all!—and worse still, I should have been denied the prospect of seeing, as I now hope to do before many Christmas days have passed, the good God face to face.

"I was born, as you know, dear children, in that sunny land across the waves—our beautiful France. Marseilles was the place of my birth. I was an only child, and lived with my widowed mother. My father I do not remember ever to have seen—he died in my infancy; but from all my revered mother told me, he must have been a perfect model of a Christian man. She cherished his memory most tenderly, and her constant prayer, her highest ambition was, that I might tread in his footsteps. Alas, how sadly was she to be disappointed! The greatest anguish of my life is the remembrance of the sorrows I caused to her loving heart! this, even now, is a subject of remorse and penitence.

"My early years up to the age of fifteen or sixteen were the best and brightest of my life. Marseilles is a beautiful city. Many of the streets, or *cours*, as they call them, are shaded by rows of immense trees, and the buildings are very grand, especially the churches. Ah, they were my delight, those beautiful churches! How grand they looked on the evening of a *fête* day!—the altars a blaze of light even up to the lofty ceiling—the exquisite flowers, with their rare and delicate odor—and the sacred music swelling through the nave and aisles! I used to serve on the altar then; it was my dearest privilege, my choicest pleasure; and when, amidst the breathless hush of the congregation, the Heavenly Benediction was given, the prayers of my innocent heart went up like the sweet-smelling incense to God, and I felt there was even a heaven on earth! Such pure, transporting joys, are found only in religion.

"My days were spent in the class-rooms of the *Frères des Écoles Chrétiennes* (Christian Brothers we call them here). I soon learned to love the good Brothers, and became one of their favorite pupils. Happy, happy days! too soon to pass away. I have said that Marseilles is a beautiful city, and I have said truly; but as in all large cities, there are many wicked people to be found there. People of all nations came to Marseilles. Italians, Greeks, Spaniards, Turks, Egyptians, and traders from the many islands of the Mediterranean. Such people too often lead a wicked, dissipated life; but there is a flavor of romance about their dashing, reckless manners that has a strong attraction for most boys. The beautiful ships, and the careless, free-and-easy life of the sailors, fascinated me, I know. Enticed by some companions, I absented myself from school a couple of times, and the hours that I should have spent at my books I spent down by the wharves, amongst the shipping. At first I was merely reprimanded, but mere talking had no effect; the fascination was so strong upon me that my books grew distasteful; my once loved teachers were looked upon as tyrants, and day after day I sought my former haunts. The conversation of the sailors, garnished as it was with oaths and curses, and too often by even worse language, at first shocked me. By degrees, however, this feeling began to wear off, and at length I could not only listen to this unchristian and indecent language, but even laugh at it.

"My poor mother, who had never chastised me in her life, hesitated now to inflict corporal punishment. She did all she could by entreaties and by threats to wean me from my evil companions, but it was all to no purpose. I openly disobeyed and defied her, and I had even the meanness to endeavor to hide my delinquencies by lying. At length, despairing of controlling me in any other way, she reluctantly requested her brother to chastise me. Now, my uncle George, had, of late, frequently discovered and brought me back from the wharves, and had, by so doing, I thought, merited my hatred. I did not then believe, as I now do, that he was my true friend. Punishment from his hand was particularly hard to endure. I resisted stoutly; but what was I, a mere boy, in the hands of a strong man? The night I was whipped I ran away from the happy home of my boyhood—from my tenderly loving and nearly broken-hearted mother—the next day I was on the high seas. I had shipped on board an Italian trader that was to touch at several of the principal Mediterranean ports.

"The remorse, which for the first few weeks gnawed at my heart, gradually lessened, and after a couple of months scarcely troubled me at all. Though I had hardships to endure, I really liked the sea, and enjoyed visiting distant lands and seeing strange people. I was three years on that voyage—three long years before I saw again the well-known harbor of Marseilles. I was paid off, and with my pocket heavy with coin, my heart light at the prospects of meeting my beloved mother once again (for I loved her still, in my selfish way), I hurried towards my old home. During my absence I had never written to my mother. False shame prevented me, and I had the idea that I would return unexpectedly with a purse full of money, pour it into her lap and beg her forgiveness for the past. I almost flew along the street. At length I was at the door I had so often entered as a joyous, innocent boy—the place looked the same as ever. The door was fastened. I knocked. O my children! I pray you may never suffer what I suffered when that door was opened. *A strange face was before me.* My mother had been dead more than two years. Then, indeed, I felt the curse of disobedience, a curse that pursued me through many years of my life, that deprived me of my mother's dying blessing, that now condemns me to die an exile from my native land."

The old man bent his grey head and covered his face with his hands, while through his fingers great tear-drops trickled slowly down. The silence was for a long time unbroken save by the stifled sobs of those around. At length, but with quivering voice and trembling lips, Monsieur G—— resumed his narrative.

"Before a week had passed I was again upon the sea. Eager for adventure and excitement, and anxious to obliterate all recollection of the past from my memory, by a complete change of scene and associations, I made a voyage to the west coast of France. This completed, I visited successively England, Holland, Belgium, several ports in the Baltic Sea and in the Gulf of Finland. Six years of my life were thus spent. I had become a thorough sailor, and if I acquired some of the good qualities of a seafaring man, such as hardihood, generosity and frankness, I most assuredly did not escape his failings. Dissipation, improvidence, disregard of religion are the sailors' vices and these, alas! were also mine. yet at times the 'still, small voice of conscience' would disturb and disquiet me. Ah, my little ones, we cannot completely silence that reproachful voice even in such a life as I led, and often in the quiet watches of the night when I paced the deck and gazed over the waste of waters upon which our good ship seemed but a speck, or when I looked up to the firmament, whose vast arch was spangled with those ever-burning lamps, the stars—that inward monitor would speak to my soul. Would to God I had listened to the reproaches and warnings of that heavenly monitor. But it was not to be—at least not yet; not before my proud spirit had been chastened and humbled in the crucible of affliction. When approaching the twenty-sixth year of my age, I joined in London the crew of a merchantman bound for Valparaiso, in Chili. We had a splendid voyage, experiencing some rough weather off Cape Horn, but nothing to speak of. We were now nearing the end of our journey, when, one evening about 'eight bells,' as we sailors say, or four o'clock in the afternoon as you would call it, we noticed a black cloud rising on the western horizon. At first it was scarcely perceptible, but it rapidly increased in size until soon the whole heavens were darkened. The wind rose and began to blow a gale. All hands were piped on deck and orders given to take in every spare stitch of canvas. Then all was hurry and bustle on board. The precaution was not taken a moment too soon, for scarcely had we completed our task, when the storm, with the suddenness peculiar to those tropical regions, burst upon us in all its terrible fury. Never shall I forget that night of terror. The billows rose mountain high, and as our good ship plunged through the black and seething waters we thought every moment that our last hour had come. Many prayed that night to whom the accents of prayer had become as a strange language learned in childhood and half forgotten. Then, then, O my children, did I recall in the bitterness of my soul, all the follies and impieties of my wild and wilful life—then did I earnestly beseech for mercy and forgiveness, and resolve over and over again to amend my conduct, if, through God's exceeding goodness, I should have the opportunity. Alas, such resolutions are too often prompted by mere selfish fear, rather than by a sincere and heartfelt feeling of repentance.

"At last, just as morning was breaking and the fury of the storm was beginning to abate, the carpenter announced that our vessel had sprung a leak which it was impossible to stop. The pumps were quickly at work, and for two long hours did we strive for dear life, all the more eagerly that at daybreak we had sighted land, about twelve or fifteen miles distant. Our efforts were useless: the ship had to be abandoned. The boats were manned. One stove, and sank when scarce three oars' length from the vessel's side, and all her crew perished. The other, in which I providentially found myself, reached the shore in safety, after incredible escapes. We landed at Conception, a large town in Chili, and the hospitable inhabitants vied with each other in ministering to our wants. Cordials and other restoratives, also dry clothing, were quickly provided, and we soon felt refreshed and invigorated. With a heart full of gratitude for my escape from a watery grave, and perhaps from a spiritual death, more terrible still to contemplate, I hastened to the nearest church to pour out my soul in thanksgiving. It was Palm Sunday; the church looked like a forest temple of waving boughs; it seemed as if inanimate nature had come to join man in the worship of the common Creator.

"I entered and prostrated myself in prayer, and then and there solemnly pledged myself to change my life, promising especially never to miss hearing Mass on Palm Sunday when it was in any way possible. Of all my good resolutions, this, I confess with shame, was the only one I kept. On retiring from the church I carried with me a branch of the blessed palm, the same which you now see.

"Well, my children, not to weary you with minute details—I continued for three years longer to follow the sea for a living, and, I regret to say, to pursue the same godless course of life that had now become a second nature to me. True, I was not quite so reckless and improvident; I began to save money, but in other respects I was unchanged. Three years had thus passed, when I found myself in Boston, whither I had come on some business. My affairs arranged, I was about to return to my ship, when I was suddenly prostrated by illness, and for two weeks I lay helpless, and almost unconscious. In the house in which I boarded were a French lady and her daughter; who, commiserating my position. and knowing that I was a countryman of theirs, nursed and tended me as though I were their own son and brother. Observing the palm branch which I always carried with me and fastened above my bed, they imagined I was a practical Catholic.

"One day when my sufferings were more severe than usual, the elder lady said to me: 'My friend, it is always well to be prepared for the worst; none of us, even the youngest and strongest, know when we may be called upon to appear before our eternal Judge.'

"'My God!' I exclaimed, in a frenzy of despair, 'am I about to die? Speak the truth, madame: does the doctor say I shall die?'

"'Calm yourself, my friend,' she replied; 'the doctor has not said that you are in immediate danger; but he fears that if your disease does not soon take a favorable turn, your chances of recovery are but slight. Now, would it not be well to anticipate the worst, and to prepare for death as a Catholic should?'

"She spoke so gently and sweetly, with such simple faith and devotion, that I almost thought my dear departed mother had returned to earth again. The priest came, the confession of many sinful years was made, the Holy Communion given, and there was, I trust, 'joy in heaven over one sinner that had truly repented.' Next day the crisis of my sickness was safely past, and after that my recovery was speedy. I arose from my sick-bed a new man in body and soul, and thenceforth all my affairs seemed to prosper, and I led a good life.

"I have told you that the good French lady had a daughter; well, she became my wife. Such a pretty little body as she was then, with her dark silky hair and bright black eyes! Would you ever think, Hypolite, that such hair could become gray and such eyes dim? would you ever think——"

"Oh, he means g'anma!" cried Hypolite; "dear ole g'anma!"

"Yes," replied the old gentleman, rising from his chair and gallantly saluting his venerable wife with a cordial embrace, "yes, child, I mean grandmamma. Remember, my children, that when age dims the eye and silvers the hair, no sweeter consolation can you cherish than the knowledge that you were always obedient, loving, and respectful to your parents. Remember, too, that all good and solemn resolutions or promises to God should be religiously observed. Such acts are sure to merit a reward. If you but learn these two lessons from what I have told you, it will not be in vain that I have related the story of this little palm branch."

"Oh, you dear, dood ole g'anpa!" cried Hypolite, with boisterous affection, climbing on his grandfather's knee; "if you was a naughty boy once, now you are a darling, dood ole g'anpa!"

At the conclusion of this exclamation of Hypolite's, the door was opened and the arrival of the tardy, but almost forgotten, *Santa Claus* announced.

The Rain-Drops in Council.

THERE was once a farmer who had a large field of corn; he plowed and planted the corn, and harrowed it, and weeded it with great care, and on this field he depended for the support of his family. But after he had worked so hard, he saw the corn begin to drop and wither for want of rain; he thought he would lose his crop. He felt very sad, and went every day to look at his crop, and see if there was any sign of rain.

One day as he stood looking at the sky—and almost in despair—two little rain-drops up in the clouds, over his head, saw him, and one said to the other: "Look at the poor farmer! I feel very sorry for him; he has taken such pains with his field of corn, and now it is all drying up for want of rain; I wish I could do something to relieve him."

"Yes," said the other, "but you are only a little rain-drop; what can you do? You can't wet even one billock."

"Well," said the first, "to be sure I can't do much; but I can cheer the farmer a little, at any rate, and I am resolved to do my best: 'I'll try, I'll go to the field to show my good will, if I can do no more; so here I go.'" And down went the rain-drop, and came pat on the farmer's nose, and fell on a stock of corn.

"Dear me!" said the farmer, putting his fingers to his nose, "what's that? A rain-drop! Where did it come from! I believe we shall have a shower."

The first rain-drop had no sooner started for the field, than the second said: "Well, if you go, I believe I will go too," so down went the second rain-drop on another stock.

A great many other rain-drops having come together to hear what their companions were talking about, one of them said:

"If you're going on such a good errand, I'll go too"; and down he went. "And I," said another; "And I," "And I," "And I," and so on till the whole shower of them came, and the corn was all watered, and it grew and ripened, all because the first little rain-drop determined to do *what* it could.

Never be discouraged, dear children, because you can t do much. Do what you can. Angels can do no more.

A Good Rule.

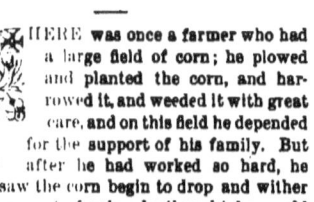

A CERTAIN khan of Tartary, travelling with his nobles, was met by a dervish, who cried with a loud voice: "Whoever will give me a hundred pieces of gold, I will give him a piece of advice."

The khan ordered the sum to be given him, upon which the dervish said: "Begin nothing of which thou hast not well considered the end."

The courtiers, hearing this plain sentence, smiled, and said with a sneer: "The dervish is well paid for his maxim."

But the khan was so well pleased with the answer that he ordered it to be written in gold letters in several parts of his palace, and engraved on all his plate.

Not long after, the khan's surgeon was bribed to kill him with a poisoned lancet, at the time he bled him. One day, when the khan's arm was bound, and the fatal lancet in the hand of the surgeon, the latter read on the basin:

"Begin nothing of which thou hast not well considered the end."

The khan, observing his confusion, inquired the reason; the surgeon fell prostrate, confessed the whole affair, and was pardoned, but the conspirators were put to death.

The khan, turning to his courtiers, who had heard the advice with disdain, told them that the counsel could not be too highly valued which had saved a khan's life.

A sportsman one day set his dog after a hare. "Seize him! seize him!" cried the sportsman.

The dog sprang forward with all his might, caught him at last, and held him fast with his teeth.

The sportsman then took the hare by the ears, and said to the dog: "Let go! let go!"

The dog immediately let it go; and the sportsman put the hare into his game-bag.

A party of villagers had been looking on; and an old peasant, who was of the number, said: "The miser is just like this dog. Avarice calls out to the miser: 'Seize it! seize it!' and he obeys, and pursues, with all his power, the riches of this world. At last Death comes, and says: 'Let go! let go!' and the wretched man is obliged to give up, without the riches which he obtained with so much labor.

THE AVE MARIA.

A Journal devoted to the Honor of the Blessed Virgin.

HENCEFORTH ALL GENERATIONS SHALL CALL ME BLESSED.—St. Luke, i, 48.

God the Beginning and End of True Science.

AN idea seems to prevail among many non-Catholics—and some Catholics, even, are affected by the atmosphere of unbelief around them—that Science and Theology conflict, and that the deductions of science have proven some of the collateral issues of Theology to be false. A great mistake, and a most unphilosophical one. Everything in creation clearly marks its coming from and existence by the power of God, just as clearly as everything conceived by the mind or made by the hand of man denotes its origin, or rather the medium that brings it forth. Without speaking of the trinity in nature, that would seem to reflect the Trinity of Persons in the Godhead—namely the animal, vegetable, and mineral kingdoms,—the three cardinal colors, and the three rays into which white can be divided,—the three operations or processes of reasoning in the human mind—we shall find in the movements or functions of nature a degree of perfection, of order, so far transcending those of the works of man, and independent of him, that instead of believing, on the one hand, the ridiculous idea of Cousin and the French philosophers that man is himself a deity, and not, as the Scripture has it, a little less than the Deity,—or on the other, with Haeckel, Buchner, and others, that nature possesses in itself all the essential elements of its being, of its movement, and of its prolongation,—we find it infinitely more easy to trace the existence and government of all created things to one Supreme Being—God—than to attempt to explain them in any other way. From the thousands, nay, millions, of great orbs rolling in space, and which never come in contact, to the most minute atom of existence, everything gives testimony to the Hand of an Allwise Being. So precise are the movements of the heavenly bodies that an astronomer can with absolute certainty estimate their position and movements many years in advance. "At this moment," says the learned Father Rawes,* "this planet on which we are, is at a certain point of space ninety-one millions of miles away from the sun. In six month's time it will be ninety-one millions of miles at the other side of the sun. In six months more it will be back here. Now suppose that you were able to hang in space a great ring eight thousand miles in diameter, and let the earth pass through it at this moment. Then the earth would go on its yearly course, and traverse its six hundred millions of miles. Astronomers could calculate to the breadth of a hair the place in which that ring must be hung, so that the earth might pass through it when it finished its revolution, though the line of its apsides, that is the major axis of the ellipse in which it moves, only makes a complete revolution in twenty-one thousand years. What are this precision of movement in the earth, and this wondrous power in the human mind, but the Hand of God, manifested in created things? Go back as far as you can in the life that has been on this globe," he continues, "and you never find anything imperfect,—anything that looks as if it were a trial, to be afterwards improved. *No one has ever found a creature that is not perfect of its kind.* The corals, graptolites, and other forms of life in the Silurian seas, were—so we can tell by their fossils—as perfect and as complex as the creatures that are around us now. All things that God has ever made were perfect when He made them. Then go down as far as you can in vegetable life, and you come to those marvellous diatoms that no one can look at without wonder and awe. You get a white speck of dust that you can hardly see; you put it under the microscope, and then you find that it is a little shell most exquisitely chased and carved. A great naturalist showed that there were forty-one thousand millions of these shells in a cubic inch of chalk, which was formed of them entirely, and that consequently a hundred and eighty-seven millions of them only weighed a grain. It is im-

* GOD IN HIS WORKS. By the Rev. Father Rawes, O.S.C. London: Burns, Oates, & Co.

possible to look at them without saying over and over again in one's heart those words of St Augustine, '*Deus maximus in minimis*'; for anything more wonderful in creation no intellect can imagine." And these infinitesimal creatures are perfect of their kind; they follow an order, a regular system, no less remarkable in its way than that observed in the larger species of creation and in the movements of the heavenly bodies.

The boundless power of God is so clearly manifested in every particle of creation that no reasonable human being should mistake it. It is seen in even such trifles as a blade of grass or a drop of water. A blade of grass being once destroyed, all the power of man cannot restore it to life; and without the germs, or productive powers stored up in nature, all the scientists in the world could not create or produce a simple leaf of clover. Whence, then, come these germs, these wonderful powers, but from a higher power—the omnipotent power of God? And as a man cannot give anything to creation, so neither can he take anything from it. It may seem that a thing is destroyed—that wood, for instance, is destroyed by fire—but it is not; it only takes other forms; nothing is entirely lost, nothing destroyed. What is lost in one form is given to other forms. So also with power. Man cannot *create* the smallest possible amount of power or force. Whether he uses steam, or levers ever so many times compounded, or anything else of the kind, the result will not *create* an ounce of force or power. Levers do not create power—they simply concentrate or transfer that which already exists; steam itself is a product from other things, and the power evolved from it is the product of the water and fuel. With levers, what is gained in power is lost from time, and *vice versa*. So that man creates nothing—destroys nothing. Notwithstanding his great power and ingenuity, he has no power to *create*. Whence, then, comes this wonderful thing, creation, in its varied forms? It does not come from man—it cannot exist of itself—therefore it exists and moves by a far greater power than that of man, the Power of God. Nothing can exist of itself—nothing move of itself. Some silly men, assuming the title of philosophers or scientists, have asserted the contrary, but their assertions are manifestly foolish. As well might they assert that factories and workshops, with their complicated machinery, could run, or go on working, without the aid of man. And yet, where is the factory, the workshop, which is a millionth part as complicated in its mechanism as this wonderful universe that we behold around us—with its myriad organisms, from the millions of worlds whirling in space with awful velocity in a kind of mazy dance, as it were, and yet never coming in conflict, to the tiniest animalcule, invisible to the naked eye, which forms part of a world that we cannot see, but which has its genera, and species, and economy in the plans of creation. What more nicely balanced, for instance, than the power of gravitation as opposed to the centrifugal force of this revolving earth which we inhabit? Suppose one of those so-called scientists that would have the universe exist and act of its own accord should take us into a machine shop or factory, in which hundreds of pulleys and gear wheels and various kinds of machinery are driving with great speed, and tell us that all this machinery existed there from all eternity, and would run on thus for all eternity without the aid of man, we should assuredly take him for a lunatic. And so also should we regard those as lunatics who assert that the world, or Nature, as they term it, exists of itself, evolves from itself, and needs not the power of God.

Father Hecker tells us in his "Aspirations of Nature"* an interesting anecdote of a celebrated scientist who was led into the Catholic Church by the study of nature. This man,—Prof. H. he calls him—we think we know whom he means, but we are not sure—was so distinguished for his researches and discoveries in natural history that his writings merited translation and publication in France. One of his discoveries was that of a family of *animalcula*. One day, observing these by the aid of a microscope and with more than usual attention, he perceived that they had a perfect system of an organized government. There was a chief, with subordinate officers, each having his own duties to perform, and acting in unison and perfect order. This unexpected discovery surprised the Professor, and led him to turn his observations abroad upon the wide field of nature. Everywhere, to his satisfaction, he found the same unity, the same laws, the same harmony, the same form of government, from the meanest floweret or insect to the vast planetary system of worlds. A thought occurred to him at this moment, as to whether this universal form of government, found in all nature, was not a stamp and similitude of nature's Author; and whether, if God had made known His will to His rational creatures, He would not display the same laws, the same government, but only in a higher and more perfect form. The Professor had been bred a Protestant, but on arriving at the age when men are accustomed to do their own thinking, he found that his religion neither answered his reason nor satisfied his conscience. He therefore abandoned the religion of the 16th century, began to read the works of French philosophers, gave up all ideas of Christianity, and ended in becoming a Deist. After discovering the law above mentioned, that ran through all nature, his curiosity was excited to see whether he could find it

---

* ASPIRATIONS OF NATURE. By I. T. Hecker, Author of "Questions of the Soul." N. Y.: Catholic Publication Society.

in any one of the prevailing systems of religious belief. Of the dissensions and degrading doctrines of Protestantism, he knew sufficient from his own experience. There was no way left but to examine Catholicity His acquaintance with the Catholic Church was very slight; no priest resided in his village, but on inquiry he found a Catholic in the place who was prepared to give him the information he desired. The Professor was gratified to find in the Catholic Church the same organization, the same laws, the same form of government which he had found in all nature. His conclusion therefore was that the Catholic religion had for its author the great Author of all nature and of the vast universe. Too sincere not to acknowlege the truth when known, too earnest not to be faithful to the light he had received, and to his convictions, the Professor started for the metropolis to have an interview with the Catholic Bishop. He introduced himself to the Bishop as Mr. H. On taking a chair, it occurred to the mind of the Bishop that the gentleman's name was the same as that of a celebrated Professor of Natural History. Asking his visitor about it, the latter modestly replied that people sometimes called him by that title. On learning the purpose of his visit, the Bishop asked him what it was that first directed his thoughts to Catholicity, and the Professor replied, quickly, and with animation,

"BUGS! BUGS! BUGS!"

"Bugs!" repeated the astonished Prelate. "What have these to do with the truth of the Catholic religion?" Whereupon the Professor related the facts mentioned above, and the Bishop found them satisfactory as well as amusing. In due time, adds Father Hecker, the Professor became a member of that Church whose doctrines are consonant with the dictates of Reason."

THE first ship ever built in California was the work of Father Ugarte, a Jesuit missionary, in 1719. It was also under his direction that the first fields were planted, the first orchards set out, the first vines grown, the first grapes pressed, and the first spinning wheels and looms employed.

OUR brains are seventy-year clocks. The Angel of life winds them up once for all, then closes the case and gives the key into the hands of the Angel of Resurrection. Tic-tac! tic-tac! go the wheels of thought; our will cannot stop them: they cannot stop themselves; sleep cannot stop them; madness only makes them go faster; death alone can break into the case, and, seizing this ever-swinging pendulum, which we call the heart, silence at last the clicking of the terrible escapement we have carried so long beneath our wrinkled foreheads.—*O. W. Holmes.*

Two Saints.

BY ELIZA ALLEN STARR.

BEYOND the Roman walls,
   Where Roman sunlight falls
     On San Lorenzo's front, in pictured gold,
       And campanile old;
Where San Lorenzo on his pillar stands,
The martyr's gridiron in a deacon's hands,
While from his crypt beneath the pilgrim's feet,
His bones exhale a virgin odor sweet;
   Where cypress unto cypress waves,
And cypress avenues long shadows throw
   Upon the turf below—
More solemn for the sunshine overhead—
     The Romans make their graves;
   Here bring their dead;
Beggar and prince and stranger share
   The rapture of the sacred air;
Share, too, the "Rest in peace," which, under breath,
The pilgrim sighs along this field of death.

But not alone
Does San Lorenzo light each old mile-stone
   On the Tiburtan Way.
Tradition tells how on a station-day,
From *Ave* unto *Ave*, stood a dame,
One of Rome's noblest, with the poor and lame
And wretched of all sorts, who huddled there
   Urging the beggars' prayer;
     Held forth, as they,
A suppliant palm to every passer-by,
Heedless of sneering lip or scornful eye;
Craving, with many a piteous look and sigh,
Alms for the poor within her palace gate,
   Left desolate
By wars and famine; tended by her care,
   Cheered by her smile, who bore
Her share of these disasters but to make
Her pity one more flight, celestial, take.
   Nor before
Ave Maria! from the belfry's height
   Flooded the long twilight
   With melody, did that thin face
   Bow, for a moment's space,
   Upon the altar step; then turn
   Toward the city portals stern;
Up the steep Esquiline, then down its street
   Passing with footstep fleet;
Threading the very heart of ancient Rome;
Crossing the Tiber to Trastevere;
Where, her soul still rapt in blissful revery,
   The lady finds her pillaged home;
No longer rich, save in the sick and poor
   Crowded within its door.
Frances of Rome, the Romans proudly call
The beggar of that day outside the wall;
And with her martyred Deacon's cherished fame
Entwines Francesca's virtues and her name.

What wonder beggars gaily congregate
   At San Lorenzo's Gate,
Or in the shadow of the portico
Of his Basilica! Ages ago
Rome's poor were counted by him as the gold
And silver of the Lord; the wealth untold
   Of Christians; priceless hoard
Beyond the clutch of thieves forever stored.

Or, say: what wonder if these beggars crowd,
  With looks complacent and half proud,
Along the steps which lead us to the shrine,
O'erlooking the razed Forum and the line
Of Cæsar's palaces, of her whose palms
Had been stretched forth, like theirs, for Christian
    alms?

Rome's best patricians, all in fair array,
Come forth upon Francesca's festal day
To honor their loved patroness, as due,
At her own shrine; and beggars flock to claim
With an arch smile, all in Francesca's name,
The alms for which, on other days, they sue.

Pause, stranger, pause; and, pilgrim, heed thou well
What Rome, to-day, exultingly will tell
E'en through her beggars. Who could here withhold,
From a Francesca's hand, Lorenzo's gold?

NOTE.—In the Golden Chapel of the Vatican are still to be seen Fra Angelico's frescoes, representing Saint Laurence distributing alms to the poor, according to the Introit of the Office used on the vigil of his Feast; "*He hath distributed, he hath given to the poor.*" Ps. 112-9.

"SPRING PARK," Octave of Saint Laurence, 1877.

'Beth's Promise.

BY MRS. ANNA HANSON DORSEY.

CHAPTER X.
"SURSUM CORDA."

AUNT 'BETH, her heart heavy with her own grief, which she had so generously concealed, went home to "Ellerslie," wisely judging that it would be better for Mrs. Morley to be thrown upon her own resources, and compelled, in a way, to occupy her mind with the necessary, everyday affairs of life. But it was with benumbed faculties, and as one in a dream, that Anne began once more to look after the affairs of her household. Every object was so closely associated with her lost happiness that she was frequently overcome, and thought she must give up all effort; but her lawyer came to her rescue, with business affairs important to her interests, which she was obliged to listen to, and go over with him, time after time; a task both tedious and perplexing, but which drew her out of herself, and acted as a moral tonic, without her being in the least conscious of it. Gradually she found strength to choke back her grief, and resume the broken thread of her duties; she even had courage to see some of her husband's old friends. Captain and Mrs. Brandt were daily visitors; also the Rev. Mr. Haller and his amiable wife, and all were unremitting in their efforts to help her bear the burden of her great grief; but how futile their well-meant intentions proved, it is needless to say. Unconsciously, she let 'Beth steal back to her heart, and hover around her with her childish, winsome ways; she accepted all her sweet, tender services with a vain attempt to smile as she used to, which was even more painful to see than the habitual sadness that had settled in deep lines upon her countenance. Nevertheless there was a look of love and fondness in her eyes as they rested upon her face, or followed her here and there, which satisfied the girl—who had not been slow to notice these signs of return to a more natural condition of mind—that she was more and more necessary to her. Nor was she mistaken. Mrs. Morley felt conscious of this growing dependence upon 'Beth; she was restless and uneasy in her absence, and realized a glow of relief in her presence when she returned. With 'Beth near her, moving about her, or sitting at her knee, talking of all the pleasant things she could think of, she had a sense as of something yet left upon earth for her to love and cling to. Not that she could ever be solaced, she thought, in the bitter loss that she had sustained; not that any living being could satisfy her desolate heart, nor any companionship, however dear, take the place of the one gone from her; but she loved her child none the less, and she would try to live for her sake. It was only at night—after 'Beth had done all that she could to comfort and cheer her; had watched her like a young mother-bird while she tried to eat the tempting morsels which, with her nurse's help, she had prepared for her, and sat chatting with her through the long evenings on topics she formerly liked,—listening attentively, with face white and passionless, sometimes asking a question, while her long, fair hands lay idly folded on her lap, or held close in 'Beth's loving clasp; it was after the last "good night," when sweet parting words had been whispered, and she was left alone, that she allowed her pent-up feelings to hold sway. Sometimes the dawn found her prostrate upon the floor, almost fainting with anguish; and many a night she lay upon her pillow staring into the dark, thinking, thinking, until her brain fairly reeled with the visions she conjured up, and nature was ready to break down for want of sleep. "Why should I want to be comforted," she asked herself, " when I only ask to die?"

"To die!—and then—what!" echoed her soul, in the hushed darkness.

"Then—what, indeed!" she whispered. "For me, to die means despair! I have spurned Heaven! I have forfeited Its help by my faithlessness, and now that there is nothing human that can bring peace, what claim have I upon It! Oh, no: I have no right to the mercy of Him who has chastised me in His wrath, and who alone can heal!"

What a stranger had she made herself to Him, that she should now doubt His compassion and His readiness to receive—aye, to seek her in the very wilderness into which she had wandered, so far from His fold, to release her from the thorns which pierced and held her back, and lead her by His own right hand to safety and peace! But, blinded by her grief, and overcome by her culpable neglect of her own best interests, is it strange that she could not realize in the crucial trial that had suddenly come upon her, that He whom she most needed stood patiently waiting, waiting at the door of her heart, waiting for her to open unto Him and invite Him to enter? In such a struggle as this, human endurance must give way, unless the hand of infinite Mercy is stretched out to save, and bring light and comfort to the despairing soul.

Friends had whispered to 'Beth that she must persuade her mother to go out into the sunshine and air. She accordingly hinted her wish in this matter several times, but her mother had taken no notice, except once, and then only to remark: "I do not wish to go out, my child; I am better here."

"She'll never go unless I propose a visit to papa's grave," 'Beth said one day to Captain Brandt, who was again urging the question.

"Go there then, my dear; there's plenty of sunshine and air between here and the cemetery, and where is there more of it to be found than just there? She'll breathe it in, and bask in it without knowing it; a change of any kind will break up her gloomy habits. If I had my way, I'd take her across the plains on a mule!" exclaimed Captain Brandt, biting off a piece of tobacco with a savage jerk.

"Oh, Captain Brandt, don't speak so of poor mamma!" said 'Beth, with quivering lips.

"It would give her new life; I tell you, 'Beth, her blood has got soured with grief, and is drying up in her veins, and nothing but fresh air will save her. Out on the plains, she'd have to live in it, and keep on moving, for 'twixt the Indians and buffaloes, there's no time to halt or mope there. But I don't suppose she'd ever consent to go. Anyhow, Beth, get her out of the house," said the old sailor, as he went out. And the more 'Beth thought of it, the more necessary it seemed to her to follow his advice.

"Mamma darling," she said, one lovely, balmy morning in May, when the air was laden with the sweet odor of newly-blossomed trees, of early flowers and fresh-springing grass, "I have some beautiful flowers, and I want to go—you and I—and lay them upon papa's grave. Oh, mamma, he loved flowers; and I think, somehow, he'd be glad to have us go." Anne had ceased visiting the cemetery for some time, for the utter silence of that grave which held all she had most loved, seemed to chill and mock her grief, until she began to feel that he was not there, but nearer to her in their old home, living in the fond memories that clung to each familiar object.

"I'll go with you, darling," she answered, after a little while; but you must help me; these new things are awkward to me." And 'Beth arrayed her in her widow's bonnet, with its black veil, dropping to her feet, laid the crape-bordered mantle about her shoulders, then got her basket of flowers, and led the way to the *coupé*, which she had ordered to be in readiness, lest her mother— if there was any delay—should lose courage and not go. In the beautiful solitude of the "City of the dead," with only the sweet sounds of nature to break the silence, a feeling of calm stole into her poor stricken heart, and, kneeling by the grave, she realized that it was indeed her loved one's last resting place; that he was sleeping there within reach of her hand, but she could not touch him; within sound of her voice, but he could neither hear nor respond to it, "so near and yet so far apart were they." A wild impatience surged through her heart, and, bowing her face upon the grass, all starred with violets, that roofed his dark dwelling, she prayed to die. 'Beth had strewn her beautiful flowers with tender, dainty care, and stolen away, thinking her mother would prefer being there alone, and that her emotions were too sacred even for her eyes to look upon. The sun was setting behind the grand old oaks that shaded the cemetery, lighting up the picturesque heights beyond, and making the white carven angels upon the tombs seem tremulous with life. The golden beams flickered through the leaves, gently stirred by the soft south wind; the birds were trilling their last song, while the river below, sweeping over its rock-strewn bed, added its low murmuring music to the harmony of the scene. 'Beth was sitting on the steps of the ivy-covered chapel, watching the shifting splendors of the west, too absorbed to observe one of the guards, who, not seeing her, approached her mother and, touching his cap, told her the hour had come for closing the gates, and passed on. Mrs. Morley pressed her lips to the grave, and standing a moment, looked around for 'Beth, then called her, and leaning upon her strong young arm, they started homeward.

The visit to her husband's grave, so far from having a soothing effect on Mrs. Morley, gave a new and unexpected phase to her grief; she inwardly and ceaselessly reproached herself for staying away so long, called herself cruel and selfish, and now went every day, through fair and foul weather. Sometimes she went alone, and remained from morning until evening; it seemed to be a renewal of her sorrow in another and more hopeless form. Captain Brandt began to fear that her mental forces were becoming weakened by such morbid and persistent indulgence, but assured 'Beth all through—without referring to his own uneasiness—that "being so much in the air would do her mother good, no matter where she went," and she would have been comforted, had not old Andrew told her once or twice—in a very cautious sort of a way, as if he were keeping something back which she ought to know, but dreaded to tell her—that he "didn't think it was safe for Missis to go out by herself so often; not jest yet, anyhow, 'cause she was so bowed down." And 'Beth, filled with a vague uneasiness, grew pale, and watched for her mother's return whenever she went alone to the cemetery, with an anxiety so intense, that her relief on seeing her when she did get back would almost overcome her. She did not know what she dreaded; sometimes she felt that she was being put aside from her mother's love again, although she was very tender and kind to her, only there was a far-away look in her countenance, and she was even more quiet than heretofore, scarcely ever volunteering a remark, and answering only when she was spoken to. Then the poor girl remembered having heard of persons who had died of grief; suppose some day she should be found lying dead on her father's grave! Altogether, 'Beth was very miserable.

One evening, on her way home from the cemetery where she had been since noon, Mrs. Morley, feeling oppressed, directed the driver to stop the *coupé*, and, getting out, told him to drive home, as she intended to walk the rest of the way. It was a strange impulse, at that hour—twilight—but she felt that she must have air, and that perhaps walking would counteract the peculiar restlessness that had for several days distressed her, a restlessness that tingled through her frame at times like an electric shock, and seemed to expand itself in her brain, until it throbbed with a violence almost unbearable. Clouds were indeed darkening around her; a crisis was approaching; the crystal vase of reason was already trembling; sooner or later, if no help came, it would fall in shattered ruin, a prey to an unsanctified sorrow.

As she walked slowly on, she heard soft strains of music drifting through the shadows; the sweet, solemn tones floated nearer and nearer; the harmony grew more distinct and familiar; she stopped, and, looking around her to see if she might learn whence came the sounds, saw dimly, through the twilight, that she was near a Catholic church, the doors of which were open, and the interior lighted. It was an old church standing back from and above the street; almost involuntarily, she ascended the stone steps leading up to it, and went towards the door, meaning only to look in, and come away. Far back she saw the altar, radiant and rich with its lights and flowers; she saw clouds of incense floating upward from a censer in the hand of the officiating priest, whose gold-broidered vestments glittered with every motion, the fragrant mist spreading like a veil around the holy place; while faintly through it she saw the image of our Crucified Lord, His thorn-crowned Head inclined towards her. Between the sanctuary and the door knelt an adoring multitude; the mellow tones of the organ, and sweet, prayerful voices chanting the *Tantum ergo*, over all. Suddenly as she gazed, she longed to enter and lay her burden before that Divine PRESENCE whence help comes to the weary. If she could only get in unseen, to hide behind a pillar, and wait if haply some touch of divine pity might not reach her; if she could only kneel and touch the "hem of His garment!" "Am I awake?" she asked herself as these thoughts swept through her mind; "have I indeed been slumbering in the valley of the shadow of death?" There was no human motive now to draw her there, as in the flush and pride of other days; she was stripped of all life's illusions, her idols were shattered, and she was thrown helpless and humble, and almost dispairing, at the Feet of Him to whom she had been so faithless, and whose anger she felt was kindled against her. Still the desire to enter the church possessed her. She crossed the vestibule, but having reached the inner door—like Mary of Egypt—something withheld her; perhaps her courage failed; and she knelt, for the solemn strains of the *Tantum ergo* had ceased, and she saw, through the curling mist of incense, the priest, elevating in his veiled hands the Sacred Host, in its aureola of gold and gems. With head bent low, she knelt, until the adoring silence was broken by the joyous *Laudate Dominum*, and rising, she quickly left the church, for the *Laudate* smote her heart as though mocking its desolation.

When she reached home she found 'Beth waiting, and uneasy beyond expression at her long absence. She threw herself on her mother's breast, and burst into tears. Mrs. Morley kissed her tenderly, smoothing back the golden hair from her broad white forehead, while she gazed with a strange, newly-awakened pity, into the pale, sorrowful face pillowed upon her bosom.

"'Beth, darling, don't cry; I am safe and well, you see," she said, feeling for the first time how selfish her grief had made her towards this tender, loving heart, which had so willingly devoted itself to her, offering the precious pearl of her young life to be dissolved in the bitter cup of her grief, if so it might comfort her.

"Oh, mamma! I was so afraid something would happen to you when the *coupé* came back without you. Don't go without me again; don't, dearest!" she pleaded.

"Not to stay so long, darling; sometimes we will go together. Won't you give me a cup of hot tea? and I think I could eat something nice, if you'll prepare it."

'Beth sprang up, saying that she would have everything ready in five minutes; when had her mother asked for anything to eat before? The air was doing her good after all, and Captain Brandt was right! She watched her mother as she took her tea with an evident relish, and spent the evening, leaning upon her knee, chatting as she used to do, until bed-time. Had she seen her, later on, draw a medal from her bosom, and with a whispered prayer, press it to her lips, and in pleading accents say: "Oh, Refuge of Sinners, is there mercy for one like me!" 'Beth would have wondered, and would have feared that the fresh air had not, after all, done her mother so much good as she hoped it had. The long visits to the cemetery were discontinued, and whenever she went now 'Beth accompanied her. Very often Mrs. Morley went out alone, never staying over an hour, and although 'Beth would have liked to go with her, she did not urge it, being satisfied that she went only for air and exercise. "But where can she go?" thought 'Beth; "she does not go to the cemetery: it is too far"; but she checked all further conjecture about her mother's movements, feeling that it was neither delicate nor proper, even to wish to know that which, for some reason or other, she refrained from confiding to her. She imagined that these walks did her mother good; she certainly appeared stronger, and there had come into her grief-worn face a something—'Beth could not tell what—that gave her a more peaceful look.

Mrs. Morley's pastor often called to see her; she was always polite and friendly towards him, but he had to acknowledge that all his attempts to minister to her spiritual needs were fruitless: she liked him as a friend, and as a friend received him; and so long as his conversation was confined to an interchange of opinions, or to topics of general interest, her manner was unchanged; but whenever he—good, well-meaning man that he was—began to speak of the consolations of the religion which he thought she professed, and urge them upon her, she withdrew, as it were, into herself, became very quiet, and often leaned back with an expression of pain and weariness that both mystified and hurt him. He would then rise, and after a few friendly words of admonition, take leave, wondering if perhaps her mind were not disordered by the great shock it had sustained. Old Andrew's time was taken up attending the door-bell, receiving the cards, and answering the inquiries of those who called to ask after Mrs. and Miss Morley, for it was understood that visitors were not admitted; even the few who had at first been received had since been so often denied, as to cease expecting to see the invalid. Nevertheless, flowers the rarest and fairest, made up into beautiful forms, and many kindly messages with them, were left all the same, with the cards, touching her poor heart deeply; but the flowers all found their way to the one loved spot where her earthly hopes were buried, where she and 'Beth used to go together and arrange them.

One evening 'Beth was returning from a walk she had taken with an old schoolmate, whom she had just parted with at her own door, and, finding it later than she supposed, quickened her steps almost to a run, fearing her mother had returned before her, and would miss her. Approaching a church that stood many feet above the level of the street—a quaint, ancient edifice, which she had once or twice observed in passing, because it was so unlike the newness of the city that had grown up around it—a bell suddenly rang out above her head; she started, and involuntarily looked up and around her, when, to her surprise, she saw her mother come out of the church and descend the steps to the sidewalk. Here was a revelation: her mother in a Roman Catholic church! What did it mean? She did not stop to think, for there was no thread of a clue to lead her out of the confused labyrinth of ideas into which the sight all at once plunged her. She only stood waiting until she got near enough; then saying, in her sweet, tender way, "Mother," put her hand through her arm and told her how she was just hurrying home, afraid she would get there before her, when the bell sounding right over her head startled her, and made her stop and look round; "then I saw you, mamma, and I am so glad we met!"

"Yes, darling, so am I, for I was just thinking of you."

"Are there any old paintings in there, mamma?" asked 'Beth, pressing her mother's arm close to her loving heart; "I suppose in Europe, people are always going into the churches to look at the fine, famous pictures?"

"Yes: the great churches of Europe are rarely empty of sight-seekers," she answered, quietly, "It was one of my chief pleasures, when abroad, to spend much time in them. But where have you been, my child?"

"Ella Moore called for me to take a walk, dear mamma; and we went to the Capitol, and watched the sun go down from the portico. Oh, it was so lovely! and I wished all the time for you, for the brightness, mamma, went so far back, that it looked as though we might see into the very heavens! Just look! the bronze-red clouds, all edged with gold, are still banked up there, and the pale green that we see between them, looks like a bright, calm sea."

"It is very beautiful, 'Beth; I am glad that you love nature," said Mrs. Morley, sadly.

"Do I love nature, mamma?" asked 'Beth, with a little laugh.

"How could you take pleasure in it else?"

"Then I shall go on loving everything on earth, in air and sky, that is beautiful!" exclaimed 'Beth. "But it seems to me, there's something with a deeper meaning in nature than the simple beauty that attracts and dazzles us, for while I looked this evening at the splendors that lit up the clouds, and the hills, and the beautiful river, I thought of everyone I ever loved, and somehow it seemed different from my thoughts of them at other times: it made me happier."

Mrs. Morley did not speak; her heart was too full of bitter thoughts of *what might have been* but for her faithlessness. Had she but paid less regard to human respect in those days long ago, when, through fear of the sneers and neglect of fashionable friends, she shrank from contact with the poor and lowly, and but too willingly took the first false step that led her farther and farther away from her Faith; had she but shown a little courage and constancy, how could she tell what effect it might have had upon the mind of her husband, who was always so firm in acting out his principles, who ever respected one all the more for being consistent and true to his standard of right, and would have suffered death rather than have been derelict in duty? Oh, had she only been faithful, as he would have been in her place, he might have been won at last, by her prayers and example, to become a Catholic! then—then—how different all would have been when the blow fell! when, united in faith, she could have followed and aided him by her prayers; and, through the blest communion of saints, found peace and hope for her sorely-stricken heart! In that oneness of Faith, she could have thought of him indeed in that same spiritual way that 'Beth, looking heavenward, had thought of the friends she loved; looking with the eyes of her soul far beyond the veil, she could have beheld him reposing in the ineffable peace, the unspeakable brightness of the Land of the Living, and grown happy in the hope of a blest reunion with him, even while suffering the burden of her cross. But now, what consolation could she lay hold upon? Outcast from her Faith by her own act, in having yielded all to human-love, and an undue regard for worldly opinion; stung by remorse, and almost despairing, she yet yearned for the Sacraments she had so long neglected; but who could help her, what hand would be outstretched in the darkness to lead her back to the heritage she had forfeited?

'Beth did not interrupt her mother's silence; she was too well satisfied to know she was by her side, to feel the gentle pressure of her hand upon her arm, and be sure that the broken fibres of her sorrow-stricken heart were twining themselves about hers with the old love.

After this, 'Beth knew the secret—yet not all—of her mother's lonely walks, and although wishing and hoping for some intimation, even the slightest, of a desire that she should accompany her (and even waited for it), it did not come, and she had too much delicacy and tender respect for her to obtrude on her devotions. "It is strange," thought 'Beth, "that my darling should go to the Roman Catholic Church instead of her own; but if she finds comfort there, I'm glad she goes." 'Beth little knew that she herself was a "Roman Catholic" by baptism.

"May I come for you, mamma?" she said one afternoon, as she saw her mother preparing to go out. "It is a lovely evening, and I am going to take a walk."

"Yes, dear, if you wish to; you will find me at the old church," said Mrs. Morley.

"Wish to! oh, you darling mamma, I'd wish never to be out of your sight, but to be fastened to your very apron strings, so that you couldn't get away from me!" said 'Beth, her arm around her mother, her cheek pressed against her wan face. "I'll be sure to meet you."

Mrs. Morley visited the old church every evening. Kneeling out of sight, hidden by one of the great pillars, it could scarcely be said that she prayed. It was the Octave of Corpus Christi, and Benediction was given every evening; but with bowed head she did not lift her eyes towards the solemn splendors of the altar, which in former times used to excite her emotions, and exalt her mind and imagination to a very devout frame, due, however, more to her poetic temperament and a love for the beautiful, than to a genuine, well-grounded religious sentiment; nor can it be said that she prayed with her lips, or even framed the cry of her burdened soul into words; and yet what more eloquent appeal for divine mercy could there be, than the blended anguish and remorse that wrung her heart, the humility that kept her afar-off, feeling that she was unworthy to "touch the hem of His garment," or look upon the glory of the countenance of Him in whose presence she waited? This place was to her as a "city of refuge," where she was learning by slow degrees the meaning of true repentance, and the uses of sorrow. Her religion had in past times been the shallow sentiment of an ill-regulated mind, which she had weakly abandoned when it was stripped of the splendors she loved, and she had found herself placed in contact with poverty and humility. All the grand privileges of her Faith had been hers—the graces, the merits, and the divine helps of the Sacraments, with their consolations and their crowning satisfactions; but in an evil hour she had cast all aside as worthless, leaving herself without shelter or support wherewith to brave the storms and tempests now making such wreck of the fair edifice of her earthly happiness. Thoughts like these were not wanting to her; her conscience, like an accusing angel, reminded her of her faithlessness, of her loss, of the waste of years, and the prodigal casting away of graces, until there, kneeling away out of sight in the shadowy and solemn silence of the old church, she would involuntarily cry out: "Mary, conceived without sin, pray for me a sinner who hath recourse to thee!" for she remembered that Mary was human and had suffered beyond all creatures, and that she would pity and intercede for her, when, through her own unworthiness, she dared not address HER DIVINE SON.

(TO BE CONTINUED.)

Rev. Father Ennemond Masse, S. J.

FATHER ENNEMOND MASSE was born in Lyons, France, in the year 1574. From his earliest youth his fervent piety was observed by all; but as we have chiefly to consider his missionary labors, we need only state that from the hour when he first heard of the glorious triumphs for the faith of the great St. Francis Xavier in the East Indies, one sole thought occupied his mind: how he could shed his blood, or at least, spend his whole life for the salvation of souls. This thought gradually became a strong desire; this desire, a resolution; this resolution, increasing with his age, led him to ask admittance into the Company of Jesus, the grand missionary Order of the age. He was twenty years old when admitted, and though the Superiors deeply appreciated his fervent and heroic spirit, a weakness of the eyes, from which he suffered, made them incline at first to send him for a time to one of the houses of probation.

This intention distressed him, and being—as every fervent Catholic missionary has ever been—a devout client of the Blessed Virgin, he had recourse to her, and with the simplicity of a child he implored her by some special sign to indicate her will, and to assure him that he could and should be enabled to persevere in the Institute. Having prayed with ardor, he seized a book, opened it, and, not at all to his surprise—so great was his faith—read the very finest print without the least difficulty. After this evident proof of his vocation, his Superiors made no further objection to his immediate reception as a member of the Order.

At the same time that our good and fervent novice received this blessing of strengthened eyesight, he also received through the intercession of his Virgin protectress a far more precious and rare gift; namely, the gift of perfect purity through life. Those of the Fathers who knew him most intimately, often declared that he never experienced anything like a rebellion of nature.

It is true that those who are thus tempted, and who, like St. Paul and many other holy saints, bravely resist and crush such temptations by the practice of penance, gain perhaps a higher merit in that respect by their valiant warfare; yet it cannot be denied that the gift of perfect purity, and a perfect indifference to such attacks, is a great grace. This blessing followed Father Masse throughout his entire life. Whatever other trials and temptations he had to endure, he never had to suffer from this one. Soon after his profession he received ordination, and was appointed assistant to the Rev. Father Pierre Coton, at that time confessor and preacher to Henry the Fourth.

Although he endeavored here, as everywhere, to do his duty faithfully, the atmosphere of a brilliant court by no means agreed with the spirit of the young priest. His soul was on fire with zeal for the foreign missions, so ably opened by the saintly pioneers whom the Church had sent forth, both to the East and to the West: to the rich, thickly-peopled cities, and ancient civilizations of Japan and China, on the one side; and on the other, to the dense wildernesses of North America, with their savage and cruel inhabitants. So fervent was the flame of Father Masse's zeal for missions, that it soon communicated its fire to other hearts; his Superiors at last approved of his evident vocation, and he went forth with their consent and blessings as an assistant to Father Pierre Biard, for the mission of Acadia, one of the stations of New France.*

Father Masse embarked at Dieppe in 1611, and with his associate, Father Biard, represented one of the two religious Orders who first of all occupied the territory called New France, and commenced missionary labors there. The sufferings, the hardships, and the privations which these two worthy men underwent after their arrival in the New World, can scarcely be described, and would hardly be believed if they were faithfully painted. Indescribable was the joy with which the fervent missionaries accepted all the privations, and embraced all the humiliations, to which they were exposed. Having for months at a time only acorns for food; overwhelmed with injuries by the very people they had come to benefit and bless; calumniated, and even imprisoned, by those of their own race to whom they had rendered all the charitable services that religion inspires; the two devoted missionaries lost neither courage nor faith, nor even shrank from the rudest and hardest toil that their high ideal of Christian duty en-

---

* Acadia, now called Nova Scotia, was one of the sea-coast provinces of the country then termed New France, and now Canada. It has been immortalized in literature by Longfellow's beautiful poem of "Evangeline"; in which, for a Protestant poet, he has done full justice to the radiance cast by the old Faith on village life and individual character, as he has also justly portrayed the cruel policy of the English in regard to the poor Acadians.

joined. One of these very Frenchmen who had thus ill-treated the saintly missionaries, dying, not long after, deprived of the aid of a priest and the Sacraments of the Church, confessed with sorrow and penitence that he was justly punished for the cruel treatment he had given the good Fathers.

About this time (1613) the piratical expedition commanded by Captain Argall, of the English settlement of Virginia, made a descent upon the coast of Maine, landing at the site of the little colony of Pentagoet,* which village they utterly destroyed, taking all its inhabitants prisoners. Among others, they seized our missionaries—then absent from their own special home, if any place might be called home to them in this wild country; they seized them, pillaged them of the little they had, and took them as prisoners on board their ship, which was headed for England. But a storm rising, drove these mariners far out of their way, and they soon found themselves near the harbor of Fayal, of the Azores' Islands.

Full of dread at the idea of entering a Catholic port after a piratical descent upon a Catholic settlement, and with two priests as prisoners on board, their first idea was to murder their prisoners. Most happily for themselves, as well as for others, the providence of God did not permit the accomplishment of this deed. A most fortunate thing it proved afterwards for these barbarous English privateers that they did spare the lives of their innocent prisoners; for on their arrival in England, the captain and crew were arraigned before the Admiralty Court for certain crimes which it chanced that—guilty as they were in other respects—they had not committed, and the testimony of their prisoners, who gladly swore to the truth—saying nothing of the cruel treatment they had personally received—sufficed to acquit them.

Fathers Masse and Biard at last regained the soil of France, worn and weary, with emaciated bodies and ragged garments, but with hearts burning with the same fire of zeal for the missions with which they had first started from their native land, and which had animated and inspired them to labor and suffer ever since.

Although he had experienced only constant sufferings in the mission of New France, Father Masse's only thought and desire was to return there at once. He found little sympathy in France, even amid his brethren in religion; they were shocked—not so much by the sufferings of the worthy priests, as by the apparent uselessness of their efforts and endurance; and they seemed to think that so much zeal and fervor might be better employed in other fields. But good Father Masse's heart was wedded to his American mission. Finding earthly ears closed to him, he assailed Heaven with his prayers. His mission in the New World, which he so ardently loved, he called his "Rachel," and declared that to be restored to it once more he would serve as long and as faithfully as Jacob of yore served Laban; so earnest was his zeal that he wrote out his resolutions, as follows:*

If Jacob served fourteen years to obtain his Rachel, how much more should I be willing to serve that length of time for the sake of my mission in Canada, my dear mission, adorned with so many kinds of crosses, each so precious, so adorable. An employment so grand! A vocation so sublime for a child of God! In a word, it is the Cross itself, and the holy dispositions necessary to one who daily bears the cross, that I entreat for. Therefore I make, and record, the following resolutions:

1st. To sleep upon the floor, without mattress, pillow, or sheets; yet to have my cell so furnished that this penance will be noticed by no one.

2d. To wear no linen, except a collar.

3d. To wear a hair-shirt whenever I say Mass; for this penitential garment is a memorial of the Passion of my Master, who is offered up in this great Sacrifice.

4th. To discipline myself every day.

5th. Whatever may have been the number and pressure of my engagements, if I allow myself to dine before making my examen of conscience, to eat only as on a fast day.

6th. Never to gratify any temptation of the senses, however innocent it may seem to be.

7th. To fast strictly three times a week, without allowing any one to see that I do so; and to eat usually at the second table, in order that no one may observe it.

8th. Whenever I utter a word even in the least degree contrary to charity, to put something bitter or disgusting into my mouth.

These holy resolves were to Father Masse what the sheep of Laban were to Jacob: an earnest of the possession of the beloved Rachel; these were the means by which he sought to purchase his heart's desire, the painful, yet dear, mission of New France.

Heaven could not resist such intense desires, such fervent offerings; his perseverance was rewarded, and in the year 1625 he was again sent to the mission he so much loved. Here he found his Rachel, that is, the cross, in abundance. For at this time the vessels from France failed to arrive for some months, and Father Masse, with Father Noué† as assistant, labored in the most menial ways to sustain life amid the French garrison and the missionaries in Canada. They fished, they dug edible roots, they cultivated the

---

* Now the mouth of the Penobscot.

* These are still preserved in the Annals of the Society of Jesus. This is translated *word for word* from Fr. Masse's MS.
† The same of whom a sketch has been given in No. 6.

gardens, and made themselves the servants of all, that they might win souls to Christ.

But, alas! the end of this cross was but the beginning of another. Circumstances forced the poor missionary again to return to France, greatly to his regret. All these contradictions only increased his love and zeal for the mission —the *Rachel*, as he loved to call it—to his eyes so fair; to all others, so hideous and frightful.

Though in his native land, Father Massé considered himself as an exile, and offered up innumerable vows to God if He would once more permit him to return to the mission of New France. God could not resist the persevering prayers of such a soul; so we find Father Massé entering again on his missionary field in the year 1633, where for thirteen years more he labored faithfully and well. He had longed for the grace of martyrdom, but God was not pleased to grant to His humble servant this petition. He died in his rude penitential bed at the mission of Sillery, near Quebec, in the year 1646, full of days and of merits, and in the midst of the savages for whose salvation he had labored so diligently. He received the Sacraments of the Church, and up to his last moment gave proof of the fervent love he cherished for our Blessed Mother. Long after he was too feeble to speak, to move, or even to indicate by a look the emotions of his heart, he would still, whenever the Blessed Virgin, or her holy spouse St. Joseph, was mentioned, make some movement of his body or his hand to indicate how dear was the subject to him.

After Father Massé's death a paper was found, among his letters and other *memoranda*, recounting, one by one, every grace and blessing he had received from childhood to death through the intercession of the most holy Virgin and her chaste spouse St. Joseph, especially when their aid was invoked during the holy Sacrifice of the Mass.

Great as was the purity of his soul, his fervent charity was equally great; he would abase himself to any service, for even the least of his brethren or his Indian converts. He taught himself to be at once a woodsman, cutting down the great forest trees; a boat-builder; and with his companion, Father Biard, he rendered all sorts of service to the mission. But many and diversified as were the talents which in this wilderness our good Father manifested for the physical good of the mission, they were naught compared with the zeal he showed in gaining souls for heaven.

Father Massé was doubly an exile, doubly a martyr in soul. He was first, in youth, an exile from his home—*la belle France*—so justly dear to all her sons, exiled by his own high sense of duty; then, some years later, after having learned to love so dearly his mission-field, and to appreciate its wondrous possibilities, we see him banished to France. Yet this apparently cruel blow only intensified his fervor and zeal, and therefore rendered him a more useful missionary. "God's ways are not always as our ways," and His true servants, bowing humbly to His appointments, are always blessed in the end by so doing. Father Massé was a faithful servant of God, and though not rewarded with the crown of martyrdom, yet his memory is blessed, and his name is fragrant in the annals of the Church's missions in North America.

As we have said, Father Massé was interred where he died, at Sillery, near Quebec. He was buried in the Chapel of St. Michael, mourned by hundreds of his Indian converts. In the year 1869, a noble monument of marble was erected in honor of the devoted missionary, amidst a throng of people, gathered from every quarter, to honor his memory.

The Apparitions at Knock.

PERSONAL SKETCHES OF THE WITNESSES. AN INTERVIEW WITH THE PARISH PRIEST. NOTICES OF CURES.

From the "Dublin Weekly News" of Feb. 14.

I promised, in my last letter, to lay before your readers particulars of the evidences, as to the several apparitions, which I collected directly on the spot. Be it observed, at the outset, that I took nothing at all upon hearsay. Such testimony, if gathered, would fill a volume, for everybody I met was full of what he had heard respecting the wonderful sights beheld at various times within the past six months on the gable of the now famous village church. The persons examined by me, and referred to in the narrative, are only such as declared that they saw with their own eyes what they described. Feeling the grave responsibility of the duty imposed on me—the duty of acting, in this extraordinary case, as the medium of communication between the people at Knock and the general public of this and other countries—I governed my course by two principal rules of action: the first of them being to take none but direct evidence; and the second, to test both the credibility and memory of the witnesses by carefully noting their manner while I conversed with them, and by putting such questions as enabled me to judge how far the narrative given by each one was consistent with itself, and with the accounts recived by me from others.

The Apparitions to be dealt with in these letters are three in number—namely, that of the 21st of August, 1879, the eve of the Octave of the Assumption; that of the 2d of January, in the present year; and that of the 5th of January, the eve of the Epiphany.

For the convenience of the reader, I propose to arrange the evidence so as to retain those dates in their proper order.

On presenting myself at the house of Mrs. Byrne— which stands a couple of fields distant from the high road, and in the immediate neighborhood of the church —I found the family occupied in extending hospitality to quite a number of visitors. Some were neighbors, who had happened to drop in for a chat on their homeward way from the village; others, travellers from a distance, were anxious, like myself, to hear from the lips of the eye-witnesses a full and particular account of the wonderful Apparition of last August. Seated beside the kitchen fire, Margaret Byrne, the younger sister, conversed with a group of women and girls, while Mrs. Byrne entertained the rest of the visitors in the parlor, and Mary, the eldest sister, went busily to and fro, providing some little refreshment for the guests. As I waited, I glanced around, and saw that the inside of the dwelling was comfortable, and neat in its appearance. The "dresser"—familiar to all who visit Irish rural homesteads—stood laden with its rows of plates and dishes. The furniture of the apartment was suitably substantial, and various articles of home and farm use were carefully arranged about the place. There was no disorder visible; no trace of the want of a woman's hand. On the side of the kitchen next the entrance door there is another room, and on the side next the open fireplace a narrow passage leads, past the side wall of the chimney, to the parlor. Mary Byrne kindly promised that as soon as she had discharged her household duties she would tell me of her experience on the 21st of August, but I excused myself for troubling her at a time when she was so busily engaged, and arranged to come back again in the course of the day. On my return, she ushered me at once into the parlor—a room betokening, not alone neatness, but good taste—and after an offer of hospitality, made with a grace and cordiality often missing from the homes of wealth and rank, we proceeded to deal with the object of my visit. Before I report the interview, let me say a few words in description of Mary Byrne. She is tall—very tall for a woman—erect in carriage, thin, black-haired, has an oval face, with a tint of brown approaching almost to olive; regular features, and eyes, not very large, but dark and brilliant. She looks a questioner in the face when about to give an answer; her voice is agreeable; and she never delayed to reply except when my question was such a one as called for a special effort of memory. Our conversation was as follows:

I understand, Miss Byrne, that you witnessed an extraordinary phenomenon here, at the Chapel of Knock?
Yes, sir; I did.
When did you see it?
On the 21st of August.
At what hour.
About eight o'clock in the evening.
There was daylight at the time?
There was; good light.
Where were you?
I was going from the house to the chapel.
Were you alone?
No: Mary McLaughlin, Father Cavanagh's housekeeper, was with me.
Why were you going to the chapel at eight o'clock in the evening?
I was going to lock it.
Well?
When we got to the wall by the schoolhouse, I looked up to the chapel, and I saw the three statues.
Did the figures look like statues?
Yes: they looked so like statues that I thought Father Cavanagh was after sending for them, and I wondered he never told us about them.
What size were they?
About the same size as living people.
And what color?
White.
Now describe the figure that appeared to be next the road.

St. Joseph was at that end of the gable. There was a stoop in him, and he was facing towards the Blessed Virgin. I remarked his venerable grey hair and beard. The side of his face was turned to us.
What was the next figure?
The Blessed Virgin Mary. Her full face was turned out. Her two hands were raised up. Her eyes were also raised up, in the form of praying.
Was every part of the figure the same color as all the rest of it?
No: she wore a beautiful crown; it looked like gold; and the face appeared to be a yellower white than the body of the cloak.
How was the figure robed?
There was one large cloak pinned to the neck, and falling loose over the arms, and there was another garment inside; it was tighter to the figure, and there was something like "puffing" up the front of it.
What was the third figure?
St. John. He was to the left of the Blessed Virgin. He appeared wearing a mitre and a long robe. He was partly turned away from the other figures, facing a plain altar, like marble, with a lamb on the altar, and a cross on the lamb's shoulder. There was a large book, like a missal, open on his left hand, and his right hand was raised up, with the two fingers next us bent.
Did the figures appear to touch the ground?
No: they were about a foot from it; there was uncut meadow that time in the chapel yard; it was about a foot high, and the figures seemed to be just touching the top of it.
When you saw them first, did they seem to be up against the gable?
When we saw them first (that was from the wall of the schoolhouse), we thought they were a couple of feet out from the gable, and then, when we went on, they seemed to go back into the gable, and when we came close up they looked as if they were standing against the wall. I put out my hand, and thought to touch them, they looked so solid, and I found nothing. An old woman tried to kiss the Blessed Virgin's feet.
That evening, was the weather wet or dry?
There was heavy rain coming up from the south against the gable, but no rain fell on the ground within two or three feet of the wall.
Was there any wind?
No.
How long did you stay looking at the figures?
From about eight o'clock till about half-past nine, or a quarter to ten.
Was there any change in the Apparition while you were looking at it?
It was just the same all the time.
Was it still there when you left?
It was.
Why did you leave?
We heard that a woman in the village, Mrs. Campbell, was just dying, and we all went off to see her.
How soon did you go back to the gable of the church?
In about ten minutes. The place was quite dark then. The rain was pouring still.
Was the space about the gable still dry, as before?
No: it was wet when we went back.
How many people saw the appearance, to your knowledge?
I think there were about twelve.
Why were there so few people to see such a wonderful sight?
There would be a great many, but we were so rapt up in it that we did not think of calling anyone. Father Cavanagh's housekeeper forgot to call him out to

see it. When at last she did tell him that she had just seen the Blessed Virgin at the chapel, he thought that what she saw was the reflection of the stained-glass window of the Immaculate Conception. [This window is in the western transept.]

Did you ever see any strange appearance at the gable since?

Yes, three or four times since, at night. I saw lights, like stars, coming out through the gable in a blaze, and then disappearing, and I saw a beautiful light like a moon shining, although the night was dark.

On the 21st of August, as soon as you saw the figures, I believe you came back for your brother Dominick?

Yes; I ran back straight to the house; Dominick was tired after mowing all day, and he was lying on the bed. I asked him to come out to see the Blessed Virgin. First he didn't give heed to me, but when I asked him the second time and ran away out again, he ran out after me and up to the school-house.

Did your mother and your sister Margaret come up at the same time?

No: they came a few minutes after. I sent down a little girl, Catharine Murray, for them, and they came up with her.

Such is the story of Mary Byrne as I had it from her own lips. The reader will observe that this account is fuller than any of the others, and enters into several novel particulars. The reason of this is simply that, as I found her prompt to answer, and anxious to clear up every point that seemed to me to suggest examination, I availed myself in a special degree of her sympathy and intelligence. Her manner during the interview was serious and collected: her self-possession was perfect; and, as I have before observed, she never delayed to answer except when an inquiry was made which called for an active effort of memory.

Margaret Byrne, the younger sister, was next called in. She was wrapped in a heavy shawl, and appeared to be in very delicate health. She is tall, like her elder sister, but otherwise there is little resemblance between them; for whilst Mary is dark-eyed, brown-complexioned, and quick of thought and speech, Margaret is very pale, with eyes of a bluish tint; she takes some time to reflect, and her manner of speech is slow, but this heaviness, no doubt, springs from the languor induced by long indisposition.

I asked her: Did you witness the Apparition of the 21st of August?

I did.

How was your attention called to it?

My sister Mary sent Catharine Murray back to the house to call me. I went with her to the wall of the school-house, where Mary and my brother Dominick, and Mary McLaughlin, the priest's housekeeper, were together.

The witness then went on to describe the appearance on the gable, and the occurrences of the evening until the family returned to their home. In all that she said to me, her sister's evidence was confirmed. She related nothing new.

The mother, Mrs. Byrne, next came in. She is a woman well on in years, and must have been tall and stately in her youth. Now she is very much bent and wasted. Her dress is that usually worn by the elder women in the country—white cap, crossed shawl, dark gown, and apron. She impressed me as a person of considerable intelligence, and her readiness to answer was quite evident.

How did you come to know, Mrs. Byrne, I asked, of the appearance on the 21st of August?

Catharine Murray, the little girl, came running into the house, and she said, "Come on, till you see the Blessed Virgin at the chapel!"

What time was that?

I think it was eight o'clock, or a little after.

Did you go out at the same time as your daughter Margaret?

I did. We went up to the wall of the school-house, where Mary and Dominick and Mary McLaughlin were before us.

Mrs. Byrne then gave an account which was practically a repetition of that already given above.

I asked to see the little girl, Catharine Murray, and she was brought in at once. She is not more than about nine years old. I found her very shy and timid, but I gathered from her that she also had seen the three figures on the gable as described, that she had been sent from the school-house wall to call Mrs. Byrne and Maggie, and that she had gone back again with them. While I talked to the little girl she kept fast hold of Mary Byrne's dress, and when I asked her what size the figures on the gable were, she answered, with an upward glance at her protectress, "They were as big as Mary!"

I took my leave of the Byrne family with a decidedly strong impression in their favor. Everything I saw of them—their appearance, their home, their manners—and everything I heard of them from neighbors who have known them all their lives, led me to judge of them as honest, industrious, and respectable people whose word upon any matter to which they solemnly pledge it ought to be treated with attention and respect.

My next interview was with Mary McLaughlin, Archdeacon Cavanagh's housekeeper, whose name has been so often mentioned during the course of this inquiry. She is a person of middle age, robust and florid, with a loud voice, a steady flow of good spirits, and a very hearty and cordial style of address. I found there was no occasion to ask her any questions. She told me what she had to tell without them.

On the 21st of August, she said—it was a Thursday evening—I wanted to go over to Mrs. Byrne's. (The two houses are distant scarcely a ten minutes' walk.) About half past-seven o'clock I went to Father Cavanagh (pointing to the sitting-room usually occupied by his reverence). He was reading his Office at the time. I asked him for leave to go to Mrs. Byrne's. When he is reading his Office he never speaks to anyone, but he made a motion with his hand that gave me leave to go, and I went away at once. I only stopped at Mrs. Byrne's a few minutes, and when I was coming out of it, Mary Byrne came with me to lock up the chapel. Our way was alongside the wall by the school-house. She then described the Apparition of the three figures and the altar on the southern gable. I need not set down her words, nor do any more than state that they expressed the same experience as that of the other witnesses whose evidence is already before your readers. Mary McLaughlin concluded: For a long time I didn't think of calling Father Cavanagh, but when I came back I told him we were after seeing the Blessed Virgin at the chapel.

The Archdeacon's residence stands about five minutes' walk from the village and the church. It is not on the high road, but a few yards up a narrow by-way. No pastor in the land occupies a more modest dwelling. The low thatched roof, the rude whitewashed walls, the few diminutive windows, all might lead the passer-by to look on it as the home of a small farmer, save for the low wall in front, the neat little wooden gate, and the narrow strip of grass separating the dwelling from the road. Here is the abode of a devoted ecclesiastic whose reputation for sanctity has spread far beyond the sphere of his ministrations. The care of a large and mountainous parish makes exacting demands on the energies of body as well as mind, and hence it is that Archdeacon Cavanagh has but little time to spare from the calls of his spiritual stewardship; but of the time he can call his own, the greater part is spent before the altar of that church now linked with what may be perpetual fame.

I found the Archdeacon in his kitchen—the central apartment of his three-roomed dwelling—with its floor of clay, its open hearth, and huge projecting chimney. He was conversing with two or three of his brother clergy, and was surrounded by a small crowd of men and women of his flock, almost every one of whom had evidence to give of bodily ailments lessened or entirely cured by visits to the church of the Apparition. The Archdeacon came forward courteously to greet me. I was impressed, at the same moment, by the sweetness of his manner and his commanding aspect. Though still in the prime of life, he is somewhat stooped, but so liberal is his stature that, even with the stoop, he towers over men of average height, and has to look a good way down in conversing with the general run of people. I must try in a few words to give an idea of his countenance and manner. His forehead is lofty, his face long, and full of healthy color, his features regular and firm, his eyes blue, full, and expressive; his whole air denoting gentleness and benevolence. He speaks with an easy fluency; his manner in conversing upon interesting themes becomes thoroughly energetic, and he occasionally uses gesture with very telling effect to add to the expressiveness of his language. What charmed me most of all in him was his fatherly tenderness in speaking to his own poor people.

In the course of our interview, Archdeacon Cavanagh told me of the eagerness of the people, who came in multitudes from far and near, to possess themselves of cement or mortar from the wall of the southern gable. When the cement that was near at hand had been entirely picked away, the mortar was rooted out from between the stones, then the stones themselves were detached, and in a few days a large hole appeared in the wall; a second hole was soon after made. The sheathing of planks had to be put up, or the wall would have rapidly disappeared. The Archdeacon went on to speak of several cases in which persons undergoing some bodily suffering, who applied to the parts affected water in which some of the cement had been dissolved, or had drunk water collected from the ground in front of the gable, were cured, or, at least, afforded much relief. Referring to the Apparition of the 21st of August, he said: "When my housekeeper returned home that night, she said that she had seen the Blessed Virgin at the chapel. At first I gave no serious attention to her words; and afterwards, when I began to think that a wonder might really have been witnessed, I concluded that the people did not leave the church until the Apparition was no longer visible, so I remained at home that night. Ever since, this has been to me a cause of the deepest mortification. I console myself, however, with the reflection that it was the will of God. It was the will of God that the vision should be shown to the people, not to the priest. If I had seen it, and if I had been the first to speak of it, many things would have been said that cannot now be advanced with any fair show of reason or probability on their side."

The strong emotion of the good pastor was so apparent as he spoke that I deemed it my duty to be silent. After an interval in which nothing was said, I ventured to ask: Have you not lately seen an appearance at the church?

Yes. On the 2d of January, between eleven and twelve o'clock in the day, as I was going up towards the church, I saw lights upon the gable, and on the outer side of it a pillar—pedestal, column, cap, and all parts, perfect. The pillar supported a figure. What the figure represented I was not able to distinguish. Other pillars, decreasing in size, stood along towards the centre of the gable. The smallest was next the centre. On the inner side of the gable wall I saw exquisite luminous scrolls extended.

Did any other persons witness this?

Yes: several others saw it.

Before I said good-by to Archdeacon Cavanagh, he informed me that he had in his hands the depositions of sixteen persons, with reference to the visions at the church. They had been taken by a tribunal duly appointed for the purpose, and would be submitted in due course to the judgment of ecclesiastical authority.

One of the clergy whom I met in Archdeacon Cavanagh's house was Father Loftus, the pastor of the neighboring parish of Castletown. He gave evidence of two remarkable cures. A girl in his parish had been afflicted with a running sore in her leg, which caused her terrible agony, and occasioned continual trouble to all about her. For a long time she was unable to quit her home, or to make any use of the diseased limb. Her relatives brought her to Knock. She prayed there, and was taken home again, and now she is going to school as well as ever. In the other case, of which Father Loftus has also personal knowledge, a little girl named Gallagher had been suffering for years from a dreadful disease of the eyes. The keen pain she was enduring compelled her to keep them tightly shut. There was a constant flow of fluid, in such quantity as to saturate her pinafore. It took the efforts of two people to force the lids asunder, and when this was done, the matter collected between the eyeball and the lids would sometimes run out as if driven from a tube by force. This poor child was taken to Knock. Up to the period of that visit, her stepmother, though living in the same house with her, had never seen her eyes, so fast had they been closed by dint of pain. Now, as Father Loftus assures, the eyes are open in the natural way. They look quite bright and clear, and the girl's sight is so fast improving that in small pictures placed before her she can distinguish the dress and appearance of the figures.

I close here for the present, reserving until next week the evidence of four witnesses who saw the Apparition, of the 5th of January. My forthcoming letter will also contain particulars of another visit to Knock by me, as accounts have reached me within the past few days of numerous miraculous cures effected lately at the church, and I intend to proceed immediately to the spot, with a view to direct investigation.

THERE is no solace for grief like that of solacing the sorrows of others; and no happiness like that of adding to their happiness.

ONE of the greatest evils known in the family circle is the disrespect so frequently shown between members, one to another, in speech, action, and dress. The gruff "Yes" or "No" in answer to a pleasant query, leads to unpleasant consequences, and begets a cold style of address on either side, which sooner or later is adopted by the younger members, and the love and affection which should dwell within is dispelled like dew before the morning sun.

Catholic Notes.

——VERY REV. DOM FINTAN MUNDWILER, formerly prior of St. Meinrad's Benedictine Abbey, Spencer Co., Ind., has been elected abbot, vice Rt. Rev. P. Martin Marty. He is a native of Switzerland, and a priest of great zeal and learning.

——DEATHS OF CLERGYMEN.—Rev. Father James Phelan, of the Church of Our Lady of Mt. Carmel, Astoria, N. Y., died on the 2d inst. The demise of Rev. Victor D'Hémécourt, the assistant pastor of St. Patrick's Church, New Orleans, La., is also of recent occurrence. R. I. P.

——MADAME BOUDREAUX.—Information has been received of the death of Madame Boudreaux, of the nuns of the Sacred Heart, who left this country a few weeks ago, with a number of other religious, to establish a convent in New Zealand. She had only been in that country a few days when she died, after a brief illness. R. I. P.

——THE DEATH OF VERY REV. CHARLES W. RUSSELL, D. D., for many years the respected President of St. Patrick's College, Maynooth, Ireland, was announced by cable last week. He had the reputation of being one of the most learned priests in Ireland, and was a prolific writer on theological and philosophical subjects. R. I. P.

——AID FOR THE CATHOLIC INDIAN MISSIONS.—The St. Ludwigs Missionary Society, at Munich, has given $189.75 to the Bureau of Catholic Indian Missions at Washington, D. C. St. Leopold's Verein, at Vienna, Austria, has also given $205, for the same object. These donations, and we suppose many more, are the result of the recent visit of Very Rev. Fr. Brouillet, the head of the Bureau, to Europe. May the example of our German brethren find imitation in this country!

——THE WORKS OF ST. THOMAS are to be republished at Rome in an entirely new edition, the printing of which will be done at the office of the Propaganda. Cardinals de Luca, Simeoni and Zigliara have been appointed supervisors of the work, and to the *Summa* is to be added the Commentary of Cardinal Cajetan, whilst the *Summa contra Gentiles* will have that of Francisco de Sylvestri's, of Ferrara. Special care is to be taken for the best possible typographical execution. The Holy Father himself has set aside a considerable sum for the expenses of the edition. All the profit arising from the sale is to be devoted to the editing of the writings of the most famous commentators of St. Thomas, the above-named three Cardinals selecting the authors.

——MISSION WORK AT THE CAPE OF GOOD HOPE.—Two Trappist monasteries are to be established at the Cape of Good Hope, for which end twenty-five members of this austere order will shortly take their departure to Africa. Mgr. Ricards, V. A. of the district, is desirous to unite the Trappist colony with that of the Jesuits, already established in his missionary district. The scholastics of both communities will make their course of theology together. The Trappists will be employed in teaching agriculture and trades to the converted natives, and in administering to their spiritual wants; while the Jesuits will be engaged in distant missions. The colonial Government takes a lively interest in this project, and has promised abundant assistance.

——"THE IMITATION OF CHRIST."—A lithographed fac-simile of the original M. S. of the *De Imitatione Christi*, preserved in the Royal Library at Brussels, has just been published in London by Elliot Stock. It has an introduction by Mr. Charles Ruelens, curator of the department of manuscripts, in which he says "that no book, save the Holy Bible, has been so frequently reproduced as the Imitation of Christ." The monks were always transcribing it in the Middle Ages, and thousands of editions have appeared in different lands and tongues. The manuscript is a small volume, composed of 192 leaves of paper, intermixed at irregular intervals with leaves of vellum. That it was from the very hand of Thomas himself is attested by a subscription. The care displayed is evidenced in the table of the treatises placed at the beginning of the volume by the author's hand.

——THE KING OF PORTUGAL is possessed not only of a good literary taste, but also of considerable ability. He has already translated into Portuguese several of Shakspere's best productions, among them "Hamlet" and "Macbeth." What is more to his credit, however, is the fact that of late, as we learn from that excellent Portuguese paper the *Jornal de Noticias*, of Erie, Pa., the king has given the copyright of one of his plays—"Macbeth," if we recollect aright—to an association in Lisbon for the support of an infant asylum. This is the way the good Catholic kings of old ruled, like Charlemagne of France, Alfred of England, Isabella of Castile, and St. Loius of France. Monarchy has now become a synonym for tyranny and oppression, but there are still a few among the crowned heads, and they are Catholics, like the King of Portugal and Francis Joseph of Austria, who have a care for the welfare and happiness of their subjects.

——ST. CATHARINE OF SIENNA.—The Father-General of the Dominicans has addressed to all the houses of the Order a circular letter inviting a fervent celebration—with all due pomp and circumstance—of the fifth centenary of the death of the holy St. Catharine of Sienna. The Church observes the festival on the 30th of April, and consequently that date, in the current year, will be marked by the grand series of devotions the Father-General calls for. St. Catharine of Sienna died at Rome at the early age of forty-two, after a life spent wholly in the service of the Church and in conferring blessings on those about her. Her remains repose beneath the high altar of the Church of St. Mary *Sopra Minerva*, belonging to the Congregation of Friars Preachers. The late beloved Pontiff, who had a special devotion to St. Catharine, placed her in the rank of patrons of the city of Rome. We need hardly say that the great Dominican Order will worthily honor the message of their chief. They have never, throughout their sublime history, been lukewarm in responding to the claims of duty, and as St. Catharine was, is, and ever will be, one of their glories, their observance of her fifth centenary will be a red-letter day.—*Liverpool Catholic Times.*

——REV. FATHER F. E. BOYLE.—From a letter of "Mignon," a non-Catholic, and the special Washington correspondent of the New Orleans *Picayune*, we clip the following in regard to the zealous pastor of St. Matthew's Church, Washington, D. C.: "For five consecutive Sundays it has been my pleasure to visit various 'folds' on a tour of inspection. The result is most favorable. Let me say here the church edifices do not compare with the majority of sister cities—but the congregations are another matter; they are rich in material and great in renown. The first Sunday upon inspection duty found me at St. Matthew's Church, an old time-honored edifice, not particularly attractive, corner of Fifteenth street and G. Father Boyle, the pastor, is an honor to the Church, and the pride of his people, a magnet that draws, judging from the congregation. Father Boyle is an orator and finished writer—in fact a comprehensive man, and therefore ranks high in the calendar of eminent divines. The congregation at High Mass is most *distingué*. The Foreign Legations are largely represented; also the executive, judicial and legislative branches. The music is excellent. At St. Matthew's the Diplomatic Corps are found in large numbers. Foreign Ministers, as a rule, with the *attachés*, are in attendance; Senator Kernan and family, Admiral Sands and family, Col. and Mrs. Goodfellow, Mrs. Gen. Sherman, Mrs. Admiral Dahlgren, and many others of equal prominence. Upon the whole, the general appearance is favorable with any church in America for distinguished attendance, indicating the largest percentage of native Americans of any Catholic church I have ever visited."

Obituary.

COL. JAMES EDWARD M'GEE.

The prayers of the readers of THE AVE MARIA are requested for the repose of the soul of Col. James E. M'Gee, whose precious death occurred in New York on the 21st ult. The deceased, like his brother, Thomas D'Arcy M'Gee, was a man of distinguished ability and varied accomplishments. He was a writer for the *Catholic World*, and for some time edited *M'Gee's Illustrated Weekly*. At the outbreak of the late civil war, Col. M'Gee recruited a company for the 69th N. Y. Volunteers, and went forward as its captain, remaining at the front till the close of the war. He received a slight wound before Norfolk, and for gallant services was advanced to a Lieut.-Colonelcy. Always a fervent Catholic, his life throughout was most exemplary. No one ever heard a profane or vulgar word fall from his lips and for this he was admired by his associates everywhere. Col. M'Gee was a native of Carlingford, Ireland, and was about forty-six years of age. He leaves a wife and two children to mourn his loss. May he rest in peace.

Confraternity of the Immaculate Conception
(Or of Our Lady of Lourdes).

"We fly to thy patronage, O Holy Mother of God!"
REPORT FOR THE WEEK ENDING MARCH 3RD.

The following petitions have been received: Recovery of health for 89 persons and 3 families,—change of life for 22 persons and 2 families,—conversion to the faith for 36 persons and 6 families,—special graces for 5 priests, 4 religious, 2 clerical students, and 3 persons aspiring to the religious state,—temporal favors for 25 persons and 3 families,—spiritual favors for 31 persons and 2 families,—the spiritual and temporal welfare of 6 communities, 5 congregations, 6 schools, 1 seminary, and 5 sodalities,—also 31 particular intentions, and 4 thanksgivings for favors received.

Specified Intentions: The acquittal of one accused of a crime,—conversion and preservation of morals of the non-Catholic children attending a public school,—return to the Faith of a young convert who has fallen away, and of another who has ceased to practice his religion,—an honest man in great affliction on account of considerable losses,—help for several parents to control their children,—the cessation of an epidemic among the children of a school,—several disobedient and wayward children—and all the other intentions specified in previous reports.

FAVORS OBTAINED.

A missionary priest writes to us: "Many of my people are suffering from various ailments, which, it seems, nothing will cure but the Lourdes water. Only the other day a woman asked me to thank the Sacred Heart, through the *Messenger*, for the seemingly miraculous cure of her son. I saw the man twice, and must say I had not the slightest hope of his recovery. The disease had reached its height, when his mother, a pious woman, gave him a few drops of the miraculous water, and almost instantaneously there was a change. The sick man began slowly to improve, and now he is well again, thanks to the Sacred Heart and the Blessed and ever glorious Virgin Mary. I should not have omitted to say that the man suffered from three different diseases at the same time." ... A worthy and pious lady states that after making two novenas and by repeated application of the water of Lourdes, she became gradually relieved from a very painful rheumatic disease, and is now perfectly well. . . . "A young man who had been suffering for a long time from a sore on his face, pronounced to be a cancer, was entirely cured after using the water of Lourdes." We have been requested to say a Mass of thanksgiving for the cure of a certain person, effected after a novena. We omit several other favors for want of space.

OBITUARY.

Of your charity pray for the repose of the souls of the following deceased persons: REV. BERNARD MACKIN, a missionary in Dakota, who went to receive the reward of his labors on the 21st ult. MR. W. P. PADGET, of Grahamstown, Ky., who breathed his last on the 12th ult., after receiving the last rites of the Church. MR. JAMES HOOPER, of Baltimore, Md., who departed this life on the 22d of February, fortified by the consolations of our holy religion. MR. CHARLES LANGUEMARE, whose death occurred at St. Louis, on the 24th ult. MARY L. SINANA, a pious young Indian girl of Devil's Lake Agency, Dakota, who departed for heaven on the 6th ult. MRS. MARGARET WOOD, of Milwood, Mo., who slept in the Lord on Feb. 17. MR. JOHN A. CHRISTY; MRS. LOUISA O'RIELLY; MR. N. CUMMINGS, Mt. Carbon, Pa. MATTHEW VOWELS and DAVID RICKET, of Lebanon, Ky., whose deaths are of recent occurrence. MISS SABINA MCCULLOUGH, MARY DALY; MRS. M. PIDGEON; E. CHAPEZE; BENJAMIN, CHARLOTTE and HENRY CHAPEZE; MRS. NORA HAYES. MRS. P. TURNER, MISS MARY A. WOODS, MISS CATHARINE MCCARTHY, and MR. J. M. NICHOLS, all of Philadelphia, Pa. DR. BENJAMIN WATHEN, MRS. ELIZABETH WATHEN, WILLIAM FEAMAN, MISS ALICE A. BROWN, MRS. ANNE SMITH, of Hancock, Minn. MRS. HENRY KEEGAN, of Dorchester, Iowa. MR. JAMES W. BARBET, MR. DANIEL J. MCELHOY, of Louisville, Ky. MISS MARY MACKIN, of Baltimore, Md. MISS NANNIE MACKIN; MR. GEORGE FULWILER, of Dayton, Ohio, all of whom died some time ago. And several others, whose names have not been given.

Requiescant in pace.

A. GRANGER, C. S. C., Director.

GOD converses familiarly with man in prayer, and often reveals to him many things between an "Our Father" and a "Hail Mary."—*Father Olivaint, S. J.*

Youth's Department.

The Children in the Wood.

NOW ponder well, you parents dear,
   These words which I shall write;
A doleful story you shall hear,
   In time brought forth to light.
A gentleman of good account
   In Norfolk dwelt of late,
Who did in honor far surmount
   Most men of his estate.

Sore sick he was, and like to die,
   No help his life could save;
His wife also as sick did lie,
   And both possessed one grave.
No love between these two was lost,
   Each was to other kind;
In love they lived, in love they died,
   And left two babes behind.

The one, a fine and pretty boy,
   Not passing three years old;
The other, a girl more young than he,
   And framed in beauty's mould.
The father left his little son,
   As plainly doth appear,
When he to perfect age should come,
   Three hundred pounds a year.

And to his little daughter Jane,
   Five hundred pounds in gold,
To be paid down on her marriage-day,
   Which might not be controll'd:
But if the children chanced to die,
   Ere they to age should come,
Their uncle should possess their wealth;
   For so the will did run.

"Now, brother," said the dying man,
   "Look to my children dear;
Be good unto my boy and girl,
   No friends else have they here:
To God and you I recommend
   My children dear this day;
But little while be sure we have
   Within this world to stay.

"You must be father and mother both,
   And uncle all in one;
God knows what will become of them,
   When I am dead and gone."
With that bespake their mother dear,
   "O, brother kind," quoth she,
"You are the man must bring our babes
   To wealth or misery.

"And if you keep them carefully,
   Then God will you reward;
But if you otherwise should deal,
   God will your deeds regard."
With lips as cold as any stone,
   They kissed their children small:
"God bless you both, my children dear";
   With that their tears did fall.

These speeches then their brother spake
   To this sick couple there:
"The keeping of your little ones,
   Sweet sister, do not fear.
God never prosper me nor mine,
   Nor aught else that I have,
If I do wrong your children dear
   When you are laid in grave."

The parents being dead and gone,
   The children home he takes,
And brings them straight unto his house,
   Where much of them he makes.
He had not kept these pretty babes
   A twelvemonth and a day,
But, for their wealth, he did devise
   To make them both away.

He bargain'd with two ruffians strong
   Which were of furious mood,
That they should take these children young
   And slay them in a wood.
He told his wife an artful tale:
   He would the children send
To be brought up in fair London,
   With one that was his friend.

Away then went those pretty babes,
   Rejoicing at that tide,
Rejoicing with a merry mind,
   They should on cock-horse ride.
They prate and prattle pleasantly,
   As they rode on the way,
To those that should their butchers be,
   And work their lives' decay.

So that the pretty speech they had,
   Made murderer's heart relent:
And they that undertook the deed,
   Full sore did now repent.
Yet one of them, more hard of heart,
   Did vow to do his charge,
Because the wretch that hired him,
   Had paid him very large.

The other won't agree thereto,
   So here they fall to strife;
With one another they did fight
   About the children's life:
And he that was of mildest mood,
   Did slay the other there,
Within an unfrequented wood;
   The babes did quake for fear!

He took the children by the hand,
   Tears standing in their eye,
And bade them straightway follow him,
   And look they did not cry;
And two long miles he led them on,
   While they for food complain:
"Stay here," quoth he, "I'll bring you bread,
   When I come back again."

These pretty babes, with hand in hand,
   Went wandering up and down;
But never more could see the man
   Approaching from the town:
Their pretty lips with blackberries
   Were all besmear'd and dyed,
And when they saw the darksome night,
   They sat them down and cried.

Thus wandered these poor innocents
Till death did end their grief,
In one another's arms they died,
As wanting due relief:
No burial this pretty pair
Of any man receives,
Till Robin Redbreast piously
Did cover them with leaves.

And now the heavy wrath of God
Upon their uncle fell;
Yes, fearful fiends did haunt his house,
His conscience felt an hell:
His barns were fired, his goods consumed,
His lands were barren made,
His cattle died within the field,
And nothing with him stayed.

And in the voyage to Portugal
Two of his sons did die;
And to conclude, himself was brought
To want and misery.
He pawn'd and mortgaged all his land
Ere seven years came about,
And now at length this wicked act
Did by this means come out.

The fellow that did take in hand
These children for to kill,
Was for a robbery judged to die,
Such was God's blessed will.
Who did confess the very truth,
As here hath been display'd:
Their uncle having died in jail,
Where he for debt was laid.

You that executors be made,
And overseers eke
Of children that be fatherless,
And infants mild and meek;
Take you example by this thing,
And yield to each his right,
Lest God with such like misery
Your wicked minds requite.
—*Old Ballad.*

St. Frances of Rome.

BY M. F. S.

WAR was raging throughout Europe, and the holy city of Rome was full of trouble; its churches burned and destroyed by heretics, and its streets the scene of terrible and bloody contests, when St. Frances, the child of Paul Bussa, was born there in the year 1334.

On the day of her birth she was carried to the Church of St. Agnes, and baptized in the presence of many devout persons who were praying for the blessing of God to descend upon their city; but they did not know that their entreaties were to be heard, and the benediction bestowed, by means of that little babe of a few hours old, who was to be so powerful in God's hands to raise the piety of the people, and bring back peace among them.

We hear that the little Frances was from her infancy unlike other children; such a heavenly light shone in her eyes, and such an unusual sweetness rested upon her features, that her mother always felt as if she had one of God's angels in her home.

At two years of age she loved to go by herself into quiet corners, and putting her little hands together, pray to God, or recite hymns to the Blessed Virgin. When she was six years old she received the Sacrament of Confirmation in the Church of St. Agnes, where she had been baptized. In imitation of some of the saints of whom her mother had taught her, Frances began to give up eating eggs, and meats of every kind, living on boiled vegetables and bread, and drinking only pure water from that time. She obeyed her confessor in everything, and often begged his permission to practice penances. Sometimes the priest yielded to her desire, but more often he refused his leave, and she submitted quite cheerfully, without a word of regret, or a shade of disappointment on her face.

Thus the life of the little Frances was as perfect as a child's life could be; no untrue words were heard upon her lips, no passion disturbed her pure heart; every little action was done to please God, and the least fault caused her to shed most bitter tears of sorrow. Wonderful as all this may seem, we must remember that God chooses His saints to come to Him in different ways; some by their great contrition for early sin, some by terrible penances, some by easier ways of love, some by innocent holiness, even from their birth, like St. Frances of Rome, in preparation for the favors He intended to give her in after years; but each one has been faithful to the special grace given him—all have walked steadily along the path our Lord pointed out, and thus reached that perfection which was to lead them to the high places they hold in heaven.

All who love Jesus Christ love the poor who were so very dear to Him; and thus, as Frances grew in devotion, her works of mercy increased, and to many a sad, troubled heart, her face, and smile, and sweet voice, brought comfort and hope. From a very early age, our Saint had proposed some day to enter a convent, and give all her life to God as a religious; but she never talked freely and lightly of this great desire, believing it too sacred to be known to any but God and her confessor. Her parents began to notice what an unusual life she led, and finding in reply to their questions how great was her wish to be a nun, they smilingly told her it was a girlish fancy, and that she had already been promised as the wife of Lorenzo Ponziano, a youth of noble family, and possessed of a large fortune.

Frances sank on her knees, and begged her father to alter his plans, and allow her to do what she believed was God's will, but in vain; he declared that he had made the promise and nothing should persuade him to break it, and that she, as a dutiful child, must yield her desire to his. Rising from her knees, the Saint went to her own room, and there, prostrate before her crucifix, she implored God's blessing, and begged Him to prevent her being married, if it was His will for her to become a religious. She then went to her confessor and told him what had happened, and he promised to pray for her, and ask light from God about her future life. "If your parents continue to insist on your being married," he said, "believe that God asks you to offer Him this sacrifice. Have only one thought—the sweet will of God. Lay down your own wishes at His feet, and if He refuses you the life you desire, accept the one He offers you, and be His faithful servant."

The marriage soon took place amidst the rejoicings of the family of Ponziano, and Frances went to her new home, where she led the same holy life to which she had been accustomed; but she managed to act with such discretion that her piety offended no one, whilst her sweet temper and kind manners charmed them all. Still, though she was forced to take some share in public amusements, she always abstained from dancing and card-playing, and every moment which she could call her own was spent in prayer, either in one of the churches of Rome, or in her own room.

Of course there were many persons who laughed at her, and called her piety absurd in one so young: others would have persuaded her husband to interfere, but he looked upon her with too much love and respect to prevent her following where God led her, whilst his father and mother said she was an angel of peace to their house and, indeed, her gentle influence seemed drawing them all nearer to heaven. But soon a severe illness came upon her, to the great distress of her friends. Frances alone was quite calm, willing to live or die according to God's pleasure. The worst night of her sufferings came, she was exhausted and motionless with pain, when suddenly a light broke in upon the darkened room, in the midst of which stood a majestic figure wearing the robe of a pilgrim, but shining like brightest gold. "I am Alexis," he said; "I am sent from heaven to ask if thou choosest to be healed."

The Saint murmured, faintly: "I have no choice but the will of God. I accept life or death as He pleases."

"Life then it shall be," said Alexis; "for God's will is that you should remain on earth to glorify Him"; and spreading his mantle over Frances, the vision disappeared, leaving her free from pain, and perfectly well.

Astonished at God's great mercy, she rose softly, and, kneeling on the floor, gave thanks to Him, and then she hurried to the bedside of her sister-in-law, who was also very holy, and her best beloved companion.

"Vannozza, dear Vannozza!" Frances exclaimed, waking the sleeper so suddenly that she cried out: "Who are you? It sounds like the voice of my sister."

"It is I—your sister," replied Frances, and then relating what had happened, she bade Vannozza praise God for His favor to her, and as soon as morning broke they hurried together to the Church of St. Alexis, to venerate his relics and give him thanks.

Her restored health was the source of great joy to her husband and family, who received her as given back to them by God from the arms of death. After this illness and miraculous recovery, Frances gave her life more and more to prayer and penance, feeling that God asked it from her in return for His mercy. All the time which she had at her disposal was given to religious practices, or to visiting the hospitals and bestowing alms upon the poor. But God allowed the Saint in many great temptations and sufferings even to see visibly the evil spirit, although he was not permitted to do her harm. This was to teach her great humility, so that she might depend only on divine help and grace.

A terrible famine broke out in Rome, and the Poziani, being rich, did great acts of kindness to the sufferers, giving them presents of corn, wine, and clothing, while Frances and her sister, Vannozza, visited the hospitals and the most miserable parts of the city. But at last even their stores failed, and these two noble women went about begging for the poor they loved so much, asking with tears for help for the starving, dying people who were lying in crowds at the corners of the streets.

One day St. Frances took her sister and a pious servant to the corn-loft, to see if a few grains might not still be left, and after a long, patient search, they collected about a measure, which they were joyfully carrying off when Lorenzo entered the granary, and, looking round, beheld with surprise about forty measures of shining, yellow corn wich had been supplied miraculously by angels.

But not only thus did God help His servant—not corn alone, but wine was needed by her sick poor, and she had drained the casks to the last drop for them. Her brothers, and even her husband, reproached her for giving all they had, which she bore in gentle silence, and then, lifting up her heart in faith and prayer to heaven, she replied: "Do not be angry. Come to the cellar.

It may be that through God's mercy there is now wine in the cask"; and following her, unwillingly, they found a supply of richer wine than had ever been known before.

It would take too long to tell all the wonderful things which happened in the life of Frances—great troubles amongst her relatives, the loss of her children, the strange visions which God sent to cheer and console her, and the miracles He worked through and for her—we must pass on to the strange, unusual grace which was bestowed upon her in having the power to see her angel guardian always at her side. We know by faith that each one of us has a heavenly companion ever near us in danger or temptation, but St. Frances could see this angel form distinctly, although it was not visible to other people, and at night she could easily write by the light of the dazzling brilliancy shed around her. It was a wonderful grace, and Frances renewed her efforts to lead a life of perfect holiness with this guide always by her. When she committed the slightest fault, the angel seemed to disappear, and it was only after examining her conscience and confessing her failing, that he returned. Frances divided her own money into two parts—one half was given to buying food for the poor, the other for clothing and medicine for the sick; her own dress was only of a coarse, dark-green material, patched with any bits of cloth which came in her way.

There were many devout women in Rome who had been imitating the life of St. Frances, and they desired to be together, keeping certain rules, looking to the Saint to give them advice and act towards them as a mother. St. Frances prayed much to know God's will, and that she might more certainly obtain His guidance, she undertook a pilgrimage in the company of Vannozza and another woman of piety, to "St. Mary of the Angels," in honor of the Blessed Virgin and the Saint of Assisi. They went on foot, without money or provisions, out of the city and along their way under the burning August sun, parched with thirst and weary from the heat, and as their pilgrimage was nearly ended a stranger met them, dressed in the habit of St. Francis, who spoke with them of the sufferings of Jesus and the love of Mary. It was the Saint of Assisi, who blessed the little company, and touching a wild pear-tree by the wayside, brought down from it fruit to quench their thirst and send them refreshed upon their way. That day they reached the church to which their pilgrimage was made, and next morning received holy Communion. There and then Frances had a vision, encouraging her to carry out the plan she had thought of.

A great trouble came to our Saint on her return to Rome. Her confessor, who had been her early friend and guide, had died during her absence, and it seemed as if she needed him more just then to advise her how to arrange for beginning the religious house she intended. But God watched over her, and directed her to seek help from another holy priest, and after a great many difficulties her scheme was carried out. Ten devout women of noble family gave themselves entirely to God under the name of "Oblates," to live for His glory in religion.

Lorenzo died in the grace of God, breathing blessings upon his holy wife; and then, bidding her only remaining son farewell, Frances went to spend the last years of her life alone with her Lord. Wonderfully her days passed now; more and more supernatural favors were poured out upon her; but the end was very near, and when a violent fever came on, her body, already worn out with labor and fasting, had not strength to recover it. The news of her illness spread through Rome, causing the greatest distress among rich and poor, and crowds surrounded the convent, trying to get to her dying bed. As many as she could receive were taken into her presence, and she had a loving word for each. Glorious visions passed before her. The evil one, who had been permitted to try her so often, was powerless now, and God's peace was all around her. For the last time she received the Holy Communion, whilst angels seemed to make soft, sweet music in her ear. The nuns, her Oblates, wept bitterly as they knelt round her bed, and begged her to implore God to spare her to them longer. "His will is my will," she murmured. "I am ready to remain, if it is His pleasure."

But after that she grew worse. There were last words with her son, Baptista, last instructions to the sorrowing nuns, and then a sublime beauty beamed upon her face, her eyes closed, and her spirit returned to God.

Even as she lay in death, it pleased the Almighty to display His power in healing sickness by the touch of her holy body, and every one declared that "Frances was a saint." That was the feeling of loving, grateful hearts, but the Church echoed it, and the 9th of March was the day appointed for her festival, and nobles and beggars alike rejoiced, and the grand old city was illuminated upon the night when it was proclaimed that their own loving, humble Frances, who had knelt before their altars, and begged in their streets, who had shared in their sufferings, and brought down heavenly blessings by her prayers, should be forever the Saint of Rome.

NEVER allow yourself to be overcome by trifles. If a spider breaks his web fifty times, fifty times will he mend it. Nothing is worth having which it didn't cost something to obtain.

THE AVE MARIA.

A Journal devoted to the Honor of the Blessed Virgin.

HENCEFORTH ALL GENERATIONS SHALL CALL ME BLESSED.—St. Luke, 1, 48.

VOL. XVI.   NOTRE DAME, INDIANA, MARCH 20, 1880.   No. 12.

Feast of St. Joseph.

"I predict good for the time to come. St. Joseph is better known, more loved, more honored: he will save us."—*Pius IX.*

"THE Holy Ghost," says an eminent French Prelate, "wishing to give us an abridgement of the glories of St. Joseph, has comprised all in these two words, *Virum Mariæ*—the husband of Mary." The devout child of the Church, who understands and loves the idea that Infinite Wisdom and Infinite Holiness prepared in Mary an immaculate abode for the Eternal Word, eagerly grasps the thoughts with which these two words fill the mind. The husband of Mary! with what perfection of virtue must not his life have been adorned! where shall we begin to contemplate it, and what point shall we select? If the study of the perfections of the Virgin Mother be as vast a theme as the study of the universe, surely the perfections of her virgin Consort must present all the varied attractions of the scenery of a whole world.

Let us place ourselves in some sequestered Alpine valley; high above us in the blue heaven rolls the sun, turning to gold and silver the snows and glaciers of that lofty mountain-peak that towers above the others of the range. High as it rises, it only serves to give us a more definite idea of the vastness of the upper depths into which its summit plunges. Between us and the fir forest, beneath whose dark green boughs the snow-drifts are lost to view, green hillocks rise wave-like one above the other, until the highest one rests at the foot of the beautiful green Voralp, in which the majesty of the mountain mingles with the gentle picturesque beauty of the hill country. The heights of the mountain-peak may be inaccessible to our steps; its snows and its glaciers may dazzle our eyes; but the Voralp we can, at least, partially explore. Unaccustomed feet will weary in traversing its slopes, for they are higher and steeper than its unassuming beauty would lead us to suppose. We will often pause, weary and breathless; but we are coming nearer to the mountain, learning more about its abysses and grandeur, and we are gaining a wider view of the valley.

Meditation will unfold to us a parallel scene in the world of spiritual beauty and sublimity, when we choose for our theme the Holy Family. There stands St. Joseph between us and its other members; and while we contemplate them, he appears to our feeble spiritual vision, merely an adjunct; and we are, perhaps, scarcely willing to credit that which we are told of the wonderful sweetness of his holiness. Like the garment of beautiful verdure nourished by the moisture from the mountain, and vivified by the life-giving rays of the sun, St. Joseph's soul was adorned with a thousand virtues resulting from the companionship of Jesus and Mary. Studying him closely, will bring to our view bewildering heights of sanctity for which we were wholly unprepared, and the marvels of Our Lady's purity appear before us in a new light.

Which one of the many rare flowers of holiness shall we choose for contemplation? Where shall we take our stand to widen our outlook, to gain a better insight into the life of the "Husband of Mary"? The Scripture speaks but briefly of him, yet, each sentence concerning St. Joseph is fraught with the deepest meaning. Son of David; husband of Mary; a just man: these are the epithets bestowed upon him by the Holy Ghost.

The just man is one of the most beautiful of Scriptural characters—one whose life is blameless, and full of gentleness and kindness; blameless not only before man, but before God; gentle and kind, not from amiable indolence, but from the knowledge that whatsoever kindliness is shown to the least of God's creatures, God will accept for Himself. Hence we find Holy Writ magnifying his virtues. Moses, David, the wise man, and all the prophets combine to sing his praises. According to them, the just man walks with God; he heeds not the evil hearing, for his heart is anchored in holy hope; he shall flourish forever before the Lord, like the palm-tree, like the lily, and like the Cedar of Libanus.

This is what St. Matthew tells us of St. Joseph when he calls the "Husband of Mary" a just man —leaving us at liberty to infer therefrom that his life was full of the virtues to be expected from the Son of David. But if the Scripture epitomizes, tradition amplifies, and from it we obtain more detailed information of the glories of this hidden life.

When we begin to distrust tradition, it is when our faith is growing weak, or when we have been accepting as true, standards other than Catholic. Perhaps, however, the majority of those who recoil from tradition, do so because they do not rightly understand what it is; they class its records with wild improbable legends, or else look upon them as pious gossip, certainly showing a more Christian disposition than malicious gossip; but nevertheless just as unfounded, just as unreliable. Catholic tradition has claims superior, vastly superior, to tales founded on mere hearsay. We are not now dwelling on the poetic fancies which embellish the folk-lore of Catholic bards, but on real tradition which is nothing else than religious history—a history far more reliable than secular narratives, whose *dictum* no one disputes. In the early ages of Christianity, tradition lived, not only in the mouth of the faithful, but in documents and chronicles which attained a venerable old age, before yielding up their great treasure to a Jerome, an Ambrose or an Augustine; they passed into oblivion, returning to dust, but the spirit, the soul of their being lives on forever in the writings and teachings of the Doctors of the Church.

It is to such traditions that the pilgrim to the shrines of Bethlehem is referred, when he stands amid the ruins of the ancestral home of St. Joseph. All the more sacred spots have been visited; and while pilgrims wend their way out of the village down into the plain to seek the fields where, while keeping the night watches over their flocks, the shepherds heard the glad tidings from the angelic choirs, the guide bids the traveller pause amid what is now a mere heap of hewn stone, but which was evidently once a spacious house. Standing beside one portion of the ruins, where evidences of ecclesiastical architecture are readily traced, the brown habited, sandalled guide, a Franciscan lay-brother, tells the pilgrims the traditions of the spot, traditions which though not inspired, are nevertheless authentic. This was St. Joseph's inheritance; inherited, it is thought by some, after the return of the Holy Family from Egypt; but by others it is called the house of Jesse, and the house of St. Joseph's youth. In the early ages of Christianity, and in the days of the crusades, chapels were erected to honor and perpetuate this tradtion, but their ruins now mingle with the relics of the house out of which they arose. Only the stones remain, on which the hand of time is busy obliterating the marks of the chisel, yet they are preaching a powerful sermon from these texts, "I have chosen to be an abject in the house of the Lord rather than to dwell in the tabernacle of sinners." (Ps. lxxxiii, 1.) "And everyone that hath left house or brethren or sisters, or father, or mother or wife or children or lands—for My name's sake shall receive an hundredfold and shall possess life everlasting." (Matt. xix, 29.) This was what St. Joseph forsook when, rather than dwell with those whose whole life was spent in sin, he chose to be the humble carpenter of Nazareth. He loved truth and holiness rather than honor and riches—and on earth he was the companion of Jesus and Mary, and while that which he relinquished has crumbled into nothing, he dwells on high in unending glory.

There is a little chapel in Nazareth whose white stone walls rise above the dwellings in the Mussulman quarter of the village. It is always closed, save when Mass is celebrated there, or when it is visited by pilgrims. It is small and unpretentious; the seal of the Holy Land is marked in rosso-antico on its marble altar, and a stone ballet on the wall records that this chapel was erected by the piety of the citizens of Milan to honor the spot on which once stood the workshop of St. Joseph. There is something striking— nay, touching—about those closed doors, closed because those who surround the spot comprehend so little the marvels which once occurred there. Yet, are not the doors of that workshop closed to the world at large? It is not valued or understood by the world in general any more than it was by the people of Nazareth; even those who speak of it the most frequently are often those who least comprehend its wonderful lessons of self-abnegation.

That true art which has its foundation in solid piety, that is the fruit of well ordered meditations, brings to our view many of the beautiful secrets of the hidden life led in this workshop by our Lord and St. Joseph. Now it is the true man, now the true God, that the artist seeks to portray; now it is one incident of the Holy Infancy, now it is another; and through it all appears that wonderful subjection to St. Joseph which is in itself a never-ending source of meditation. Now our Lord is planing a board under St. Joseph's supervision; then assisting His Mother by filling her basket with scraps and shavings. Now He has taken the compass and rule from St. Joseph's hand and is showing him an easy method of solving a difficult problem of measurement. Then in the intervals of labor, St. Joseph is teaching the Divine Child to read, and Infinite Wisdom condescends to be taught by a creature.

While we gaze on such creations of the brush, we learn more and more of the unique vocation of St. Joseph; and while we admire the perfection of his fulfilment of its duties, we gain courage to call upon him for assistance in the performance of the obligations of our own station. Truly St. Joseph is the Patron of the Universal Church, for to him was subject its Founder; and he is an appropriate patron for each and every one of us, whatever our rank in life may be; prince and peasant may alike claim him for their own. The rich, he teaches not to value the transient goods of the world beyond salvation; to the poor, he furnishes an example of industry and contentment; and to the religious, he shows the peculiar excellence of the virtue of voluntary poverty.

Let us seek to know more and more of St. Joseph, let us love him more and more, and when in the moment of trial and temptation we call upon him, he will hear us, he will assist us.

Lenten Thoughts.

BY MARY E. MANNIX.

NOT by penitential fastings lowly—
Chastenings of the body—may we merit
Gifts of grace; abasement is unholy,
Worthless all, without the contrite spirit.

Pallid visage, sombre robes, and ashes,
Vanity and pride of life may cover;
Under downcast eyes what subtle flashes,
What emotions, unsubdued, may hover!

So the Pharisees of old proclaimed them;
Sackcloth garments, loud and ceaseless praying;
Hypocrites and liars Jesus named them,
Turned their boasting to their own gainsaying.

Come we not as they, with bold confession,
False acknowledgment of false desires;
Weep we not aloud each poor transgression,
Lest we, too, be hypocrites and liars.

Not, like them, regardless of the spirit,
Reading but the letter of salvation;
Haply in our blindness to inherit
Judgment from God's holy ordination.

Sin we not as they—whom no man showeth
Of his penitential deeds and prayers,
Of whose works and watchings no man knoweth,
Unto heaven a worthy record bears.

Let us seek to draw our footsteps nearer
One whose hidden fast was long and lonely,
That our chastened eyes behold the clearer
Penitence in humble vigils only.

'Beth's Promise.

BY MRS. ANNA HANSON DORSEY.

CHAPTER XI.

"Dear Lord! admit me to Thy sanctuary,
The light shines through Thy door;
And oh! the night has been so wild and dreary,
Say, shall I wander more?
—Look on the face of thy fair Mother, Mary,
Ne'er shadowed by a sin,
Whilst angels ope Thy longed-for sanctuary
To take Thy suppliant in."

A plain room with a low ceiling, half library half dining-room, with old-fashioned furniture, windows that open over a small flower-garden, and let in the south-west breeze laden with the sweet breath of lilies and tea-roses that flourish so profusely below. A breakfast-table stands in the centre of the room, at which two Catholic clergymen sit at their morning meal. The elder of the two, Rev. Father Gibson—more familiarly known among his people as "Father Thomas,"—is pastor of the old church near by; his pleasant, kindly face, is surmounted by a rim of short, curling white hair, upon which his *bonnet-carre* has been dropped onesidedly, giving emphasis to a pair of dark, twinkling eyes, at the corners of which the lines of mirth are plainly discernable; mirth, which never failing into levity, helps to keep his digestion good, and himself from despondency, when the woes, and sins, and distresses, in the confessional and out of it, are poured into his ears, with his church debts added as the "last feather that threatens to break the camel's back." He thinks sometimes, when tried to the very verge of endurance, that he'd like to go and hide himself in a desert and become a saint, until a Mass, or his rosary,—or some good act that helps a fainting heart,—disperses the cloud, and makes him sure that the idea of a desert is a temptation, and that his right place is here instead of there.

The other ecclesiastic, is a young man just home from the American College at Rome, where he studied and was ordained; he possesses a grave, intellectual countenance, upon which the responsibilities of his sacred calling weigh heavily. He had been out ever since his Mass at five o'clock, taking the Blessed Sacrament to two sick penitents, who lived on the confines of the city, and administering it as Viaticum to another who was dying. He is quite ready after his long tramp, for a cup of coffee and a chop. The pain his sensitive nature has endured in seeing human sufferings which he has no power to alleviate, in witnessing the death pangs of one passing away into the great hereafter, where he could only follow him with his prayers, makes refreshment not only welcome but necessary. There is a sad, heavy, look on the young clergyman's face, which even the air and sunshine, and the plain good fare before him, together with Father Thomas's cheerful words, do not suffice to drive away. He is the Rev. John Allan, the pastor's assistant, and, in all things pertaining to his vocation, is a man after his own heart, except that he is too much given to down-heartedness over ills for which there is no remedy. Father Thomas does not approve of sadness: he thinks it enervating to soul as well as body, and sets himself to work whenever an opportunity offers, to show him how to bear his yoke more cheerfully; not by reproofs, or theological counsels, or grave discourses, but by trying to infuse a little of the sunshine of his own nature into him, and by showing him that it is better to look up than down.

Father Thomas observes how silent and dejected his companion is, and begins to talk.

"John," said he familiarly, with a twinkle in his eye, "how did you find my old friend, Mrs. Grupp this morning?"

"She told me she had been very ill—in fact looked so—until she received the Blessed Sacrament, then she gave a great sigh of relief, and seemed to revive."

"And how then?"

"I don't know really; I had to come away immediately to go to the other end of the city," he replied, looking up with inquiry in his eyes.

"It is well for you, then. She used to scold me up hill and down dale everytime I went to see her, and also the ladies who supported her. She didn't mean a bit of harm, it was a way she had of showing her gratitude; but I usually got the benefit of it all. Sometimes the tea a lady brought her wasn't fit to drink; or 'Miss Harriet had skimped her in sugar,' or the 'young chit they sent to read to her, didn't understand the King's English,' or 'Father Thomas was always in such a hurry and "puffed" about the room at such a rate that he took her breath away'; then when I tried to be very quiet and amiable with her, and took no notice of her sharp speeches, she declared I was laughing at her, and told me I needn't come any more."

"I see she's quite a character, but she's very devout. Did you go again?" asked Father Allan, quite amused.

"I'll tell you presently, for I want to say something about 'Miss Harriet,'* who is very near being—if not one already—a saint. She has won a title to all the beatitudes, by a constant and unobtrusive practice of every Christian virtue. In season and out of season, through cold and heat, rain and snow, slush and mud, she trots about among the poor and destitute, relieving their wants, and never resting, although a luxurious home invites her to a life of ease. She went to her confessor one day and told him she was in trouble. Of course he expressed sympathy, and a readiness to help her if possible. Well, the trouble was that 'Miss Harriet's' poor were all so grateful, and received her gratuities of every description with so many blessings, and warm, gushing thanks, that she began to feel uneasy lest her self-love was being too much pampered, and that instead of serving the poor for the love of God, she was doing it for her own gratification; and she begged him, if he knew of any very needy persons, who would never thank her for anything, but find fault, and rail at her, that he would please entrust them to her attention and care. Good Father D—— saw she was in earnest, and although he didn't think 'Miss Harriet' needed any such discipline, he yielded to her entreaties, and sent her to Mrs. Grupp. She has attended her faithfully, and gets all, if not more than she bargained for. Still she never utters a complaint, but I've heard of some of her experiences with her client, and sometimes I have met her coming out as I was going in, and noticed that her bonnet was bent and awry on her head, and her shawl hanging loose, while her face was flushed and careworn, by which signs I knew she had been in a sort of hurricane upstairs. And so it will go on to the end, for she'll never give up anything she undertakes for the love of God. She's one of that noble army of "old maids" that our holy religion exalts and dignifies by the good they do, and the life of self-sacrifice they lead. But I can't help having a quiet little laugh at 'Miss Harriet' when she comes in with crumpled bonnet and worried look, on some of her errands for her poor, for I know that she has been to see Mrs. Grupp, who does not exactly beat her but puts her into a flurry that just brings her to the verge of impatience, and humiliation."

"Some one ought to take Mrs. Grupp in hand," said the young priest.

"God bless you, Father John, what's the use! You never smashed a chestnut when you were a boy, because the burs pricked your fingers—not you! you handled it very patiently and found a

---

* "Miss Harriet" and Mrs. Grupp are characters drawn from life, and what is here related of them really occurred. "Miss Harriet" was patient with her poor client to the end, received her last breath and her dying blessing, and gave her a grave in her own burial lot.

ripe delicious nut inside. That poor old creature is diseased, and never knows a moment's rest; nerves and muscles, rack her with pains and aches, which crop out in scolding and fault-finding, but under all that, she's a patient, long-suffering soul, for she *never murmurs against the will of God* in afflicting her with disease and poverty."

"The world is filled with strange contradictions," remarked Father Allan; "and I see what a special grace it needs to deal with souls, lest in trying to weed out the cockle, we destroy the wheat."

"Just so," said Father Thomas; "now I'll tell you about my last visit to Mrs. Grupp after she had told me not to come any more. She sent for me, and I was so grave, being determined if I could help myself, not to offend her—that she cried and went on like everything, said I was angry with her, and that it was cruel to be offended at a poor old woman, old enough to be my mother. I pacified her as well as I could, and promised to bring the Blessed Sacrament to her the next morning, which I did. Nature has given me a keen sense of the ridiculous; it is my besetting weakness, and it occasionally happens that at the most unfitting time, something or other will obtrude itself on my attention in such an absurd way that, notwithstanding all my efforts to repress it, I am fairly choked with laughter. I would give the world to strangle this natural depravity, and I can only hope our good Lord will be merciful to me. Well, I went that morning to give Holy Communion to Mrs. Grupp, who—poor old soul!—was in a most serene state of mind, laying back on her pillows, with a clean, wide-ruffled cap on, her hands folded upon her breast, and everything spick and span clean around her. 'Miss Harriet' had been there, and had arranged everything before I arrived, and there was promise that all would go well. After laying the Sacred Host upon her tongue, I turned towards the table to gather up my book and stole, when she burst out with: 'Ah-h-h! Thanks be to God! I feel as strong as a horse!' It took me so by surprise that I could scarcely control myself, and was fairly convulsed with laughter when I left the room. It was after that I turned her over to your care."

Father Allan laughed. "A laughing devil," he said, "is pretty hard to subdue; he's forever springing a mine under one at the most unexpected times, and just when you think you've conquered him."

"That's so; but there's another devil worse yet, John; a lachrymose devil, that makes one look through smoked glass all the time, until one thinks the very sun has been shorn of his beams," said Father Thomas. "Let us guard against both. But now, to change the subject. Have you observed a lady in deep mourning who has been visiting the church every evening, since early in May? She seems to be deeply afflicted, and I am sure she is not a Catholic."

"Yes, I have indeed; and I have been tempted to speak to her several times when I found her kneeling all alone, for I thought, perhaps, she was waiting, hoping for help. I also think that she is not a Catholic, because I have not observed her at any of the early Masses."

"I'll tell you what happened yesterday. It was quite dusk when I left the confessional, and as I went towards the sanctuary, to go through to the sacristy, I saw this lady almost prostrate, her head bowed upon the step outside the railing, so motionless that I thought she had fallen asleep, or might be—God help her!—dead. I touched her shoulder lightly, she raised herself up, and turned towards me with such a woebegone look in her white face that, accustomed as I am to all phases of human grief, it startled me. The light from the sanctuary lamp shone full upon her, or it is possible I should have passed without observing her. 'Pardon me for disturbing you, my child,' I said; 'it is late, and we are about closing the church door, or I should not have done so.'"

"'Thank you, sir,' she said, drawing the long black veil she wore over her face; 'I have no right to ask it, but may I come again?'"

"'Certainly, my child; here in the sanctuary of God all may come, especially is it open to those who are burdened with sin and grief.' She bowed her head and left me. I really wish we could help her if she needs our help, or lead her back to the Good Shepherd of souls if she has gone astray."

"It seems to me, Father Thomas, that you might speak to her again, having spoken once, and as a priest and servant of God, ask her if you can help her, knowing as a priest, what a great relief it is to the unfortunate to pour out their sorrows under the seal of confession. I don't think it would be amiss to speak to her on that subject; you might ask her if she is a Catholic, or if she wishes to become one."

"I was thinking the same thing, John," said Father Thomas, thoughtfully, "and I'll do it, that is if she comes any more."

By this time breakfast was over, and message after message was brought in, first to Father Thomas, then to Father Allan, from persons waiting to see them; some on business, some for alms, some with tales of real distress requiring immediate relief; indeed the day promised no end of variety and perplexity, in affairs which required the "wisdom of the serpent and the gentleness of the dove" to get through with. Now and then Father Thomas's hearty laugh was heard, when after having had all his sympathies aroused by tears, and sobs, and broken words, which it seemed to him must preface some sad human tragedy, "the mountain at last brought forth a mouse," proving to be nothing more than morbid imaginations, or hysterical chimeras, which the application of a little strong common sense, seasoned with good-natured sarcasm, and plain wholesome advise, succeeded in relieving. Then there were tough cases, who fought it out with one or the other of the pastors; ignorant, hard-headed men, whose ideas went round and round in a narrow circle, always coming back to where they started, who had come for advice, and ended by laying down the law themselves; between whiles, devout persons who "just stepped in" for this or for that trifling excuse, and prolonged their call to a visitation, forgetful that the time they were encroaching upon belonged to higher and more weighty duties than their entertainment. Sick calls, and all the incidental interruptions that wait upon the daily life of a Catholic priest, leaving him no time until near midnight to read his Office, were not wanting here; the putting aside of self was the rule of life, and fulfiling the duties of their holy vocation, their only reward. On this particular day, when twilight had brought a slight cessation of wearisome duties, Father Thomas went into the church to spend a half hour before the Blessed Sacrament, knowing that there he would be sure to find the help that his disturbed mind so much needed. He had quite forgotten the lady of whom he had spoken that morning at breakfast; but as he entered the sanctuary, he saw a dark figure kneeling on the side near the shrine of Mary Immaculate, half concealed by a pillar, her head bowed upon her folded arms. Forgetting his own weariness of mind and body, his great, kind heart, full of human sympathy and a divine wish to lead the strange mourner to the source of all consolation, Father Thomas invoked the aid of her who is indeed the "Gate of Heaven," the "Comfortress of the afflicted," and approaching her sat down on one of the sanctuary chairs near by, and laid his hand for an instant upon her arm to attract her attention.

"My child," he said, as she lifted her head, showing the same white sorrowful face that had before so moved his pity; "pardon me: I seek only your own good in speaking to you. May I ask if you are a Catholic?"

"I was once," she answered, in almost inaudible tones; "but I have forfeited all right to the name." What moved her to tell him—a stranger —this without reserve? Was this the opportunity her poor soul had been waiting for? Was this the supreme moment in which, by her own will, all might be saved or lost, other and higher graces be given, or forever withdrawn?

"Not so, my child, so long as repentance is left for us," answered Father Thomas, quickly. "Do you repent?"

"Yes, I repent, but too late, too late! Oh, leave me sir, leave me to my hopeless misery, for you can do me no good," she said, wringing her hands.

"I came not to call the just, but sinners to repentance," said the good priest. "These are the words of Jesus Christ Himself. Despair of mercy no longer, my child; there in the tribunal of penance, come and be reconciled with Him, who only waits to forgive you, and heal your wounds. I know nothing of your life, but I tell you in the name of God, whose minister I am, that if you will enter there with a penitent heart, your sins, though they be as scarlet, shall be made whiter than snow. Come!"

"Oh, I dare not! I dare not!" she said, irresolute, yet half rising.

"Follow me, my poor child," said Father Thomas rising to go to his confessional.

Obeying some interior impulse, and as if driven by desperation, she followed him, and, entering the confessional, she sank, almost fainting, at the little window through which penitents whispered their sins to the priest on the other side. The first step taken, it only required a few encouraging words to unseal her lips, and she poured forth without reserve the sins and sorrows of her life into his patient ear. The conference was long, and with the help of her confessor, her conscience was "searched as with lamps," and winnowed of its long arrears of sin, above which the dust of years of neglect had accumulated. Before she rose to go, she received absolution, and was on the morrow to receive Holy Communion. Not only that great boon, but the good priest told her that he would remember her husband in the Holy Sacrifice, and that she also, trusting in the infinite mercy of God, could pray for him, and offer future Communions for his repose: "for only our Divine Lord knows what saving prayers went up from his heart in that raging storm; we cannot tell that his last acts of contrition were not as perfect as those of a saint. Under those suppositions, and knowing that God judges not as man, but by the intentions of the heart whose every secret is laid bare to His Allseeing Eye, I will pray—yes—offer the Divine Sacrifice for his eternal rest."

'Beth had come, and waited outside for her mother; but as she did not appear, she ventured into the church; the light being dim, she went up and down the aisles thinking to find her in one of the pews; not seeing her—she was then in the confessional—she fancied she had gone home, and hurried away.

Solaced and comforted, Mrs. Morley could scarcely realize that the softened, almost joyous heart she bore home with her, was the same cold, heavy, despairing one that she had been bearing these many days. She walked on under the starlit heavens, scarcely conscious of the ground under her feet, the glad whisper of "saved! saved! saved!" upon her lips. She had indeed found the Physician of souls, who poured divine balms into her wounds, healing them, and making her whole, as He had once healed the lepers by the wayside. Father Thomas had done wisely in not requiring a stern probation to test her sincerity; her heart he saw had been sufficiently bruised, and the temporal punishment of her guilt bitter and severe enough; "a little more of it," he thought, "and God only knows how it would have ended." And kneeling there, before the Divine Presence, his heart lifted up above all distractions, he gave thanks for the good work he had been led by the grace of God to do. He felt refreshed as with new wine, and went back to his house with a cheerful mind, ready and willing to shoulder his crosses and burdens as they came.

(TO BE CONTINUED.)

St. Patrick's Day.

BY F. W. FABER, D. D.

I.

ALL praise to Saint Patrick who brought to our mountains
The gift of God's faith, the sweet light of His love!
All praise to the shepherd who showed us the fountains
That rise in the Heart of the Saviour above!
 For hundreds of years,
 In smiles and in tears,
Our Saint hath been with us, our shield and our stay;
 All else may have gone,
 Saint Patrick alone,
He hath been to us light when earth's lights were all set,
For the glories of faith they can never decay;
And the best of our glories is bright with us yet,
In the faith and the feast of St. Patrick's Day.

II.

There is not a saint in the bright courts of heaven
More faithful than he to the land of his choice;
Oh, well may the nation to whom he was given,
In the feast of their sire and apostle rejoice!
 In glory above,
 True to his love,
He keeps the false faith from his children away:
 The dark false faith,
 That is worse than death,
Oh he drives it far off from the green sunny shore,
Like the reptiles which fled from his curse in dismay;
And Erin, when error's proud triumph is o'er,
Will still be found keeping St. Patrick's Day.

III.

Then what shall we do for thee, heaven-sent Father?
What shall the proof of our loyalty be?
By all that is dear to our hearts, we would rather
Be martyred, sweet Saint! than bring shame upon thee!
 But oh! he will take
 The promise we make,
So to live that our lives by God's help may display
 The light that he bore
 To Erin's shore:
Yes! Father of Ireland! no child wilt thou own,
Whose life is not lighted by grace on its way;
For they are true Irish, Oh yes! they alone,
Whose hearts are all true on St. Patrick's Day.

Palm-Sunday.

"The multitude goeth out to meet the Redeemer with flowers and palms, and payeth the homage due to a triumphant conqueror.... The Hebrew children, bearing branches of olives, went forth to meet the Lord.... The Hebrew children declaring the Resurrection of Life with palm-branches, cried out, Hosanna in the highest."—*Anthem for the Procession (Roman Office of Palm Sunday).*

"And when He was coming near the descent of Mt. Olivet, the whole multitude of His disciples began with joy to praise God with a loud voice for all the mighty works they had seen, saying, Blessed be the King who cometh in the name of the Lord: peace in heaven and glory on high." (Luke, xix, 37, 38).
—*Anthem for the Procession (Missal of Lyons).*

TO the human mind, there seems almost an incongruity in the burst of joy with which the sad mysteries of Holy Week are ushered in; yet in so doing, the Church is but following the precedent established by her Divine Master. That incongruity is true only as to appearance, for the jubilant welcome accorded to our Lord was a fitting expression of the joy felt by all creation at the prospect of a speedy reconciliation with its Creator. There was a new accession of peace and glory among the angelic choirs, and it found vent in inspiring the multitude with anthems of praise, whose echoes will continue forever.

There is hardly another fact of either sacred or profane history to which more frequent allusion is made in literature, than this triumphal entry of our Lord into Jerusalem, and it is cited as the most remarkable example of the fickleness of popular opinion. Yet though many who sang Hosanna, were found not a week later among those who shouted, "Crucify Him!" there was a double current of feeling in Jerusalem on this day. Like the waters of two mighty rivers meeting, each struggled throughout that Paschal week for the mastery; the more turbid and rapid conquering and hiding the clearer stream, while the last drop of limpid water welled up in the tearful entreaty of Pilate's wife, "Have nothing to do with this Just Man."

In that portion of the office for Palm Sunday which relates to the blessing and procession of the palms, although the Roman Missal places distinctly before us the fact that when the triumphal demonstration was most jubilant, then were the scribes and pharisees the busiest with their evil conspiracy; yet it does not dwell on this particular point in so striking a manner as the Missal of Lyons. In the selection of Scriptural quotations to be chanted during the procession of palms, we find the liturgy of Lyons mingling, in apparent confusion, the shouts of welcome with narratives of the sittings of the council of chief priests, and concluding the whole with an anthem; the first part complaining of the tongue of the wicked and of evil words, while the second part reiterates the Hosanna ine xcelsis.

The years have been gathered into centuries, but these shouts of triumph have never died away. As the multitudes rushed from the many gates of Jerusalem they began a procession that was to last until the end of time; for each year the children of the Church, bearing green boughs and chanting anthems of praise and welcome, go forth to meet their Saviour.

Was this triumphal entry a spontaneous demonstration on the part of those followers of our Lord whom the Pasch had assembled in Jerusalem from the different parts of Judea and Galilee, or was it simply the result of a special agreement among themselves? On this point the Evangelists are silent, but we may judge from their descriptions that it had the characteristics of an unpremediated burst of exultation, where each one gave vent, as seemed best to him, to his joy and reverence. In the latitude allowed by the Church in the celebration of Palm Sunday, she imitates these characteristics; for though the ceremonies she prescribes for her ministers suffer no change save that of rite, the laity in each nation or province participate in the ceremony according to the method which is there found to be the most practicable.

The perusal of the anthems of these ceremonies, according to the Roman rite, presents to the eye of meditation different groups among the exultant throng; some are marching decorously, carrying the reward of victory—palm-branches—with which to salute the Conqueror even before His predestined victory; others are bringing flowers, others olive branches—the symbol of peace as palms are of glory; others are busy breaking the green boughs from the trees to strew them over the garments which have been spread on the way; and in advance of all, are bands of children carrying palms, olive boughs, and green branches, while they sing in prophetic strains.

To one or the other of these groups, each Catholic nation joins itself, imitating by the peculiar customs of each province, here one and there another, of the actions of the multitude. No one narrative of the Evangelists furnishes us with nearly so accurate an idea of this demonstration as does that portion of the Catholic liturgy to which reference has been made. St. Matthew and St. Mark speak of the garments spread in the way, of the green boughs cut from the trees by the road side, and of portions of the glad canticles. St. Luke, after giving us, as it were, another verse of the hymns of praise, passes without mention of the green branches to a narration of the displeasure of the pharisees; while St. John tells of that procession which went forth bearing palm-branches, and saluting Christ as king of Israel.

This last is the procession to which the city of Rome joins herself; here we meet the clergy of the grand cathedrals of the Old World; it is they who each year bear the palm-branches among the multitude of nations and tribes composing the Catholic Church. The inhabitants of cooler climes, where the palm-tree cannot live, content themselves with emulating those who cut down green boughs from the trees by the wayside, and they make their churches green on this day with branches of box-wood or sprigs of myrtle; while, perhaps in memory of those who went forth bearing flowers, the inhabitants of Southern Germany select for their palms the catkin blossoms of the willows and poplars, thus offering to God the very first evidences of the reanimation of nature. Even those races to whom Easter-tide comes before winter has abdicated its throne, find a beautiful symbol of joy in the branches of those trees whose mantle of perpetual green is to such nations a compensation for the ever-blooming forests of the tropics.

One beautiful feature of Palm-Sunday in Catholic Europe arises from the fact, that there, custom and discipline limit the distribution of palms to the clergy, and to those confraternities whose members are permitted to have places in the sanctuary. The laity must provide themselves with their own palms, which they have ample opportunities of purchasing, not only from the peasantry, but from the beggars congregated on the church steps. Thus the streets of a Catholic city on Palm-Sunday morning, are green with the branches held by those who are hastening churchward. No one crosses the sacred threshold without his green bough, which will be hallowed by being held aloft during the blessing.

Among other peculiar customs relating to Palm-Sunday may be cited those of Venice and Genoa. In the former city, palms are distributed only among the clergy and the men who belong to confraternities; but in the afternoon, an acolyte visits each house in the parish and leaves there as many branches of box, myrtle or olive, as there are members of the family. In Genoa, palm-branches are borne by the clergy and by the little children, but not by adults; this is in memory of the Hebrew children having carried palms and olives to greet the Lord. Infants whose chubby hands have scarcely learned to grasp, are held up by mothers and nurses to receive the blessing given to the branches held by the children. School girls and school boys step reverently forward to the railing, to present their branches of palm and olives to the holy water and the incense, which will make them emblems of peace and joy, to be delivered by these young hands to the older members of their families.

Nor is it wholly without profit to the soul to dwell upon these externals, for it is by visible things that we are carried forward to the love of those that are invisible. Any form of decoration, any series of reflections that help to make the events of our Lord's life more of realities to us, prepare the soil of our hearts to receive the good seed of the Gospel. Neither do we fail to reap benefit from learning the various methods by which different portions of the Church honor the same mystery. It is well, even while we are most intent upon following the rubric and ritual of that portion to which we belong, to let our minds pause for a moment to recollect the variety of praise that the Church is uttering, so that we may the more perfectly unite our intentions with those of the faithful throughout the world; and when we realize all that the Church is doing to glorify God, our minds are carried forward insensibly to contemplate the magnitude of God's glory, that boundless ocean of light, one ray from which will so illumine our souls, that we may be always able to perceive the path of duty.

In whatever manner we assist at these beautiful ceremonies, whether we choose to follow attentively the prayer of blessing and the anthems of the procession, or whether we wish to join ourselves in spirit to the original celebration by meditation, either by accompanying our Lord from Bethphage, or by going out from Jerusalem to meet Him at the foot of Mount Olivet, we are preparing our minds in the best manner to dwell upon the mysteries of the great victory of Life over death. Therefore, "let the faithful join with the angels and children singing to the Conqueror of death Hosanna in the highest."—*Anthem of the Procession of Palms (Roman Missal).*

A Famous Picture.

FROM one of an admirable series of articles in the *Catholic World* on Christian Art, we extract the following account of Leonardo Da Vinci's *Last Supper*. The *Catholic World*, by the way, like good wine, seems to improve with age. It is a publication of which every American Catholic has reason to be proud.

.... Sixteen years of his life were passed at Milan; and when his patron [Ludovico Sforza, afterwards Duke of Milan] fled in 1499 before the victorious arms of Louis XII of France, Leonardo returned to Florence. Three years before, however, he was commissioned to paint a picture for the refectory in the Dominican convent of Sta. Maria delle Grazie—a work which at once placed him at the head of Italian art up to that date (1400-7). The subject he selected was the "Cenacolo," or the Last Supper, of the Redeemer; and the moment of representation is that immediately succeeding the announcement, "*Unus vestrum me traditurus est.*" The scene depicted in fact is that recorded in the next verse of the Gospel: "*Contristati valde, cœperunt singuli dicere: Numquid ego sum, Domine?*" (Matt., xxvi, 22). No picture in the world, perhaps, is more universally known, in outline at least; the subject is of a kind that makes it admissible into hundreds of collections, which would be closed against a print or engraving of many other incidents in Catholic history. The amount of concentrated thought in it, also, commends it to the attention of persons for whom the emotional has but little attraction. The Redeemer and His twelve Apostles are seated on one side of a long table, as in a religious house—the space actually covered by the original being twenty-eight feet in length, and the figures larger than life, so that when looked at in their places, above the prior's table in the refectory they should appear of the same size as the friars seated below them. The Master's meek reproach has fallen among them like a thunderbolt from a clear sky. The quiet company is instantly broken up into groups, protesting, consulting, sympathizing with the mighty sorrow just revealed to them. On the right of the Redeemer's Person, in the centre, St. John has just risen from his recumbent position on the Sacred Heart, at the appeal of St. Peter, to repeat his query, "Is it I?" St. Peter, in stretching over him, has displaced Judas, who, in drawing back, upsets the salt—a popular token to this day, of evil or sinister fortune. Behind St. Peter, his brother, Andrew starts back and elevates his hands in horror. St. James the Less, stretches over Andrew to touch Peter's shoulder, and inquire the meaning of it all. At the end of the table, on the spectator's left, St. Bartholomew springs to his feet, and leans forward as if to hear more. On the Redeemer's left hand, St. James the Greater falls back with extended arms, in grief and amazement. Over His right shoulder, St. Thomas holds up a finger, menacing the traitor, whoever he may be; and over St. James' left, St. Philip, standing erect, appeals to Him who knows all, if it is he. Next to him, St. Matthew with outstretched arms, repeats the Master's word to his nearest neighbors at the end of the table, St. Jude and St. Simon. The variety and individual beauty of the several heads, are equalled by the expressive management of all those hands, which are as eloquent in their different ways, as so many tongues. The traditional relationship between Christ, the Jameses, and Jude, is indicated by a family resemblance among them all.

But how shall we describe the majesty of the central Figure, the "deep inner lakes of sorrow" reflected in His speaking countenance? "Nonne ego vos duodecim elegi, et ex vobis unus diabolus est?" (John, vi, 71). The hands are as eloquent as the face. One of them (the right) is placed palm downwards on the table, the other in the reverse position—a difference in which some critics read the alternative of welcome and of warning, of the Redeemer and of the Judge. Thus, by a marvellous combination of imaginative and intellectual power, to which the artist's unerring skill lent itself in willing service, the momentary passage of a wave of intense feeling, is revealed in every member of the company, and in responsive harmony with the Master's mighty grief. One figure alone—that of Judas—is excepted; but he too, has his simultaneous emotions, of brazen defiance and grasping avarice. He clutches the money-bag in one hand, while the other is ready to receive the Sacrament from the hand of Christ. Thus, Dante, whom few things escaped, describes the avaricious as rising to judgment with closed fist. The subsequent history of this great picture is a sad one. It was painted, not in fresco but in oil-colors, on a wall liable to damp owing to the low situation of the convent; in consequence of which the colors had faded within fifty years after it was finished. Then came the restorer with his officious brush, effacing nearly every line of the master; so that at present hardly anything can be made out as certainly his. To make up for this, however, many cartoons and studies of heads, preserved in art-collections, attest his consummate skill. Several complete copies, also, of the work were executed by Da Vinci's pupils during his life, and soon after his death, one of which, formerly belonging to the Carthusian convent at Pavia, is now possessed by the Royal Academy of Arts in London. . . . Before passing on to the next master on our list, let us take one parting glance at Leonardo's great picture. We never look at it, but we are reminded of an anecdote related by a traveller in Spain, in the days before the dissolution of the convents. An aged lay-brother was showing him over his monastery; they came to the refectory, which was inspected, and as they were leaving it, the old friar pointed to a picture of the "Last Supper" over the cross-table, and thus addressed the stranger: "It is nearly fifty years since I first entered this house as a youth. The seniors of that time are long since dead; many more have come and gone since then; but, year after year, those solemn figures look down upon me from the wall like friends of my youth. So that, at times, I am almost disposed to think that, in this world of change, they are the realities and we the shadows."

The Apparitions at Knock.

(CONTINUED.)

From "The Dublin Weekly News" of Feb. 21.

I visited Knock again since the date of my last letter, and learned there a great deal that deeply interested me, and that will, I think, prove of interest to your readers. From the lips of the parish priest himself, I obtained the full particulars of another appearance over the altar of the church, seen by himself and several other persons on the nights of Wednesday and Thursday, the 11th and 12th of the present month. I have also collected numerous proofs, both by letters and by word of mouth, of wonderful cures experienced on the spot. All these it will be my duty to communicate to the public, but before I proceed to do so, allow me to continue the narrative presented in your last issue by reporting my conversations with Miss Anderson and Miss Kennedy, of the Knock Female National School, respecting the appearance seen on the gable of the church towards midnight on the eve of the Epiphany.

It was about the hour of noon as, quitting the high road, I passed along by a path, having on one side the schoolhouse wall so often referred to, and on the other, the open space of the church ground, now filled with people, mostly praying. At the inner end of the path is the girls' school. It is a low, slate-roofed cottage of one small room, with a very [modest window on either side of the door, the latch of which is lifted by a piece of string hanging on the outside. As I approached, no sound came to my ears—none of that buzz of many voices which usually challenges one's ears wherever the young idea is being instructed. The place indeed was so still that I began to wonder if the young people were enjoying a holiday; but not feeling myself at liberty to end the doubt by pulling the string, I knocked. A little girl immediately opened the door. Then I saw a class seated hard at work, not more than a couple of feet away from me, and the school, or at least as much of it as I could see from my post of observation, was crowded with little girls, to all appearance very studious, and to a certainty very quiet and docile pupils. In answer to my inquiry, "Can I see Miss Anderson?" Miss Anderson herself, the mistress of this busy and noiseless hive, came forward. She is a very young lady, of medium stature, pale, with a faint tinge of color, fair-haired, blue-eyed, and of a remarkably gentle and engaging manner. Her face is frank and wistful in its expression. As she speaks, her earnest eyes commend her words to the listener's belief. I doubt if I have ever met any one on whose candor I at once felt disposed to place more reliance. My first impression, in this regard, was decidedly favorable, and I found no reason afterwards to change it. Inquiring when she would be at liberty to afford me a short interview, I learned that in about half an hour the girls would be out for recreation. Returning accordingly, I found Miss Anderson conversing with a few friends. She conducted me to a desk at the farther end of the school, where the following conversation passed between us:

I believe, Miss Anderson, you are the head teacher of this school?

I am.

May I ask if you are a native of this locality?

No: I come from Castlebar.

How long have you been mistress here?

Five years—three as assistant, and the last two as principal.

Have you seen a strange appearance on the gable of the church?

I have.

On what date?

On the 5th of January.

At what time, day or night?

About eleven o'clock at night.

How did you happen to be in sight of the gable at that hour? Do you live here at the school?

No: I live at the post-office, down at the cross-roads; but on the night of the 5th of January, about half-past ten o'clock, I came up to the chapel, in company with Miss Kennedy, my assistant, who lives in the same house with me.

Why did you come to the chapel at so late an hour?

Because it was the eve of the festival—the eve of the Epiphany, and we were in hope of seeing something.

Was there any one except Miss Kennedy in your company?

Yes: Anne Mullen, a servant in the house where we reside.

How old is she?

About 15.

Well, did you see anything as soon as you came up?

No: not at first. We came down to the gable of the school, and we knelt outside it, and said the rosary.

At which of the school gables did you kneel?

The gable facing the chapel.

[It will be borne in mind that the schoolhouse stands within the church enclosure, in a corner at the southern end.]

Well, how did you come to notice the appearance?

Mrs. Killeen, a woman of the village, called our attention to the gable of the church. Then I saw, on the side of the gable towards the road, a row of lights along the wall, from the edge of it to the direction of the window.

Were they bright?

No, not very bright.

Were they equally distant from each other?

They were, as well as I remember.

Were they large? Were they as large as the crown of my hat? [I pointed to my hat—an ordinary round one—which lay on the desk beside me].

Not quite, as large, but nearly so.

What shape were they?

Not entirely round, but more of a round shape than any other.

Did you see any lights except those in the row?

Yes; scattered up and down the gable in several directions, there were numerous other lights the same as those in the row.

Now, did any changes occur in the appearance of the lights while you were looking at them?

Yes, there were frequent changes. The lights would fade slowly, until they got very dim, and then of a sudden brighten out again, but they never got very bright.

Did the lights decrease in number while you were there? I mean, did some of them vanish before others?

No.

Did you notice anything else?

Yes; after a time I saw other lights like stars; they appeared as if coming out at different parts of the wall; they were sparkling and twinkling like stars. This continued for a length of time.

Were the stars much brighter than the large roundish lights?

Very much brighter; quite different in appearance.

Did you notice anything else?

I did: after seeing the lights and the stars, I saw, lower down near the ground, a small figure, about a foot and a half in height. From the appearance of the head and shoulders, I took it to be a figure of the Blessed Virgin.

At what hour did you go home?

About two o'clock.

Had the figure then disappeared?

I think it had.

Had the large lights and the stars disappeared?

The large lights had disappeared, but a few of the stars had not.

Were there others, besides your party, about the gable at any time while you were there?

There were about 16 or 18 persons.

Name some of them.

Pat Byrne and his daughter and son, Judy Campbell, Bridget Mullany, Pat Killeen and Mrs. Killeen, and their two sons; two of the police, Mr. Collins and Mr. Fraher, and some people I did not know.

You say the figure was low down on the gable, and that the row of lights was under the window. Can you tell me whether any of the appearances were higher up on the wall than, suppose, the arm of a tall man would reach?

Oh yes, certainly; some of the appearances were quite close to the top of the gable.

What sort of a night was it?

Extremely dark, and misting.

What color did the gable look?

It looked very dark—almost black.

I wish to know, Miss Anderson, whether the church continues to be much visited.

It is thronged almost every day. On Mondays and Thursdays immense crowds come to the place, and priests and nuns pay visits here from every part of the country. Several persons who have been cured have made offerings, such as candlesticks, vases, and statuettes, for the church.

From Miss Anderson I learned some additional particulars of the case of the little girl, Gallagher, of Castletown, whose case I recorded last week, on the direct authority of the parish priest of Castletown, Father Loftus. The girl is now about ten years old. She had been blind for at least two years, and had been treated by Dublin doctors without any improvement resulting in her condition. Her father at last brought her to Knock. She knelt and prayed for awhile before the gable. Then her father lifted some of the clay and threw it against her eyes. She saw, and cried out, "I am cured!"

Another case mentioned by Miss Anderson was that of Fergus Fallon, of Mace, County Mayo. He had been for fifteen years unable to walk. The sinews of one of his legs were very much contracted; he had been to several institutions, and had been told by eminent doctors that his case was beyond the reach of skill. He visited Knock and prayed there, and numbers of people, who had noticed him move painfully up to the gable with the aid of a pair of crutches, were amazed to see him suddenly get up and walk about, leaving both the crutches behind him in testimony and in memory of the cure.

During my interview with Miss Anderson, Miss Kennedy, the assistant teacher, was also present in the school. She is about the same age as Miss Anderson— not more, I should imagine, than twenty-three. Her face is round and fresh-colored, and I think a physiognomist would set down truthfulness and good humor as among the leading traits of her disposition. She confirmed in all essential points Miss Anderson's narrative, as given to me, and as I have reported it above. She also told me that her father, who is about fifty years of age, and lives at a place called Glenn Tavrene, near Kilkelly, County Mayo, had been cured of deafness and pain in the ears—an ailment of long standing with him. He put some cement from the gable under his head at night, and in the morning he was well, and has been quite well since.

Next week I shall complete the narrative concerning the 5th of January by presenting the evidence of sub-constables Fraher and Collins, of the Knock police station.

On my last visit to Knock, I called on Miss Anderson and Miss Kennedy at their private residence. In the presence of Miss Kennedy, Miss Anderson handed me this written statement:—"On Monday, 2d of February, about ten o'clock at night, Miss Kennedy and I were startled by hearing the chapel bell ring. [There had been an arrangement made that the chapel bell should be rung in case of any strange appearance.] We went up towards the chapel, and on coming to the gable, saw about fifty or sixty persons there. The part which is boarded over was covered with a cloud of light, and we saw sparks flashing from the part near the ground, where we saw the small figure on the night of the 5th of January. We remained for a long time watching it, until it had almost vanished."

Proceeding from Miss Anderson's to the house of the parish priest, I went into the church on my way. Night was closing round at the time. Sheets of rain were pouring down from a sky all densely piled with massive clouds. Fierce gusts of wind rendered it hard to keep one's footing, and all but impossible to move in any direction. There was nobody visible on the road or about the village. I expected to find the church almost deserted. But the church of Knock is never deserted now. In any sort of weather, at any hour of the day or night, there are worshippers to be seen in that humble temple. I found a row of silent figures along the entire length of the sanctuary; one solitary suppliant here and there in a dim corner, scarcely visible by the fading light of day, and groups before the pictures of the stations. The intense stillness was only broken, now and then, by a deep ejaculation.

Passing out by the doorway opposite the altar, I bent my way against the storm to the southern gable, my purpose being to see if any crutches or sticks had been left since my previous visit. I found the receptacle quite filled with sticks and crutches; of the latter, as well as I could make out, there were a dozen or so; of the former, there cannot have been less than about sixty. Standing upright in the midst of the mass of tangled wood I saw a fashionable umbrella of green silk, now somewhat stained by exposure to rough weather. This, I learned, had been left by Miss Margaret O'Neill, of Dublin, who had suffered for years from hip disease, which caused a considerable shortness of one leg, obliging her to make use of the umbrella I saw, to assist her in the act of walking. She came to Knock with her mother on the 6th of the present month, stayed up all night praying in the church, and was able to walk next day without the help of the umbrella, which she left behind in token of her recovery.

I found Archdeacon Cavanagh in his study, seated at a large and massive table, on which there were so many letters awaiting attention that I concluded the correspondence of the pastor of Knock must be more extensive at present than that of a prime minister or an editor of a popular paper. After a little conversation, I remarked to the Archdeacon that I had heard, in the village, of other wonderful appearances, recently witnessed, both at the gable and inside the church.

Yes, he said, last night [Thursday, the 12th inst], about half-past nine o'clock, I and several others, saw a most brilliant star outside the gable. It lit up the whole place. It came and struck against the spot where the Apparition of the Blessed Virgin was seen, and flashed with the quickness of lightning. I have frequently of late, about eight or nine at night, seen a golden light floating about the gable, with stars and brilliant lights flashing through it, but I never saw anything so dazzling as that one star last night.

And also inside the church, have appearances been seen?

They have. I have seen them myself: both last night and the night before, I saw stars above the altar, on both sides of the little stained-glass window representing the crucifixion of our Lord. Three of them were very plainly visible, one large, on the right-hand side of the window, and two of a smaller size, on the left. I thought I also saw a number of small stars shining much more faintly than those three principal ones, scattered about the space on either side of the window.

How was the church lighted at the time when you saw the stars?

The altar lamp was lighting, and also a small lamp before the Blessed Virgin's altar, and there were a few candles lighting through the church.

How many others saw the stars?

All the people in the church.

Our conversation went on for a considerable time, but at present I shall confine myself to recording what occurred with reference to the case of Miss O'Neill. I mentioned that I had seen a silk umbrella outside the gable, and had heard that it belonged to a young lady from Dublin, lately cured of hip disease, after spending a night at prayer in the church.

That is the truth, the Archdeacon answered. She was cured on her first visit. Read this letter from her mother, a most pious and exemplary woman. He handed me the letter, which, by permission, I lay before your readers:

DUBLIN, February 8, 1880.

VERY REV. ARCHDEACON—It is with no ordinary amount of pleasure I write, to express the happiness it affords me to say my daughter is still improving every hour since we had the great blessing of visiting Knock. We are wishing for the time to come to renew our visit to that holy place. There is not a shadow of doubt but Knock is specially blessed, for whilst I was there I felt intensely the influence of religion; God be praised forever! Now, at your own convenience, I would like you to let me know what you would like for the large altar, or if you have a good harmonium, or for some useful present for the church, as I wish to make an offering to God for His greater glory and honor. Margaret will write to you in a few days herself, as I think it is better to wait for a little while, and, please God, she will be perfectly restored with God's help. If it would not be too much, I would ask you to say one Hail Mary for me before the place where the Blessed Virgin appeared. I will not trespass on your time with a longer letter, but will conclude, hoping with the help of God soon to be able to visit Knock again. I enclose you the names of people that I had the happiness of seeing miraculously cured.

I have the honor to remain, yours most respectfully,
MARY JOSEPH O'NEILL.

I do not envy the person who can read this affecting letter without a thrill of responsive feeling, and a reflection that there is nothing in this world more contemptible or more pitiful than the mockery of the stolid unbeliever. Before taking my leave of the pastor, I asked him—Have you read the detailed accounts, relating to the Apparitions, which have been given in the *Nation* and *Weekly News?*

I have read them, he replied, with much satisfaction, for I have found them substantially correct.

He then confided to me a diary, which he had written throughout with his own hand, containing brief notes of all the miraculous cures at Knock from the date of the appearance of the first Apparition, down to the date on which he handed me the record. This document, emanating from the parish priest himself, is one of extraordinary authority, and of an interest not to be surpassed, and permission is given to me to draw upon it in my further letters on the subject.

I am also enabled to furnish you to-day with a full and perfect copy, of the text of the depositions made before the tribunal of clergymen appointed by his Grace the Archbishop of Tuam, as the Prelate having episcopal jurisdiction over Knock, to investigate the facts regarding the Apparition of last August. The commissioners were Archdeacon Cavanagh; Canon Waldron, parish priest of Ballyhaunis; and Canon Burke, parish priest of Claremorris. By request of the Archdeacon, the following clergymen also attended, and assisted the commission in its proceedings:—Rev. James Corbett, C. C., Claremorris; Rev. Michael O'Donoghue, C. C., Ballyhaunis; Rev. Michael Heany, C. C., Auglismore; Rev. Michael Curran, C. C., Claremorris; Rev. James Killeen, C. C., Crossboyne; and Rev. Father M'Alpine, C. C., Ballindine. The commission sat for one day only, in the sacristy of the church of Knock, and personally examined every witness. Archdeacon Cavanagh than reported to the Archbishop that his decree had been duly executed. With his Grace now rests the question whether he shall make a report to the Holy See.

In my letter of next week, I mean to give a fuller account of my last visit to Knock, and to publish some most interesting letters from persons cured by visits to the church. I shall also report at length my interview with the Archdeacon, and furnish extracts from his diary—the most wonderful record, I certainly say, that has ever come under my observation.

DEPOSITIONS

Taken at the Catholic church of Knock, on the 8th of October, 1879, by the Very Rev. Bernard Cavanagh, Archdeacon, parish priest of Knock; the Very Rev. James Canon Waldron, P. P., Ballyhaunis; and the Very Rev. Ulick J. Canon Bourke, P. P., Claremorris—the commissioners appointed by his Grace the Archbishop of Tuam to hold an investigation respecting the Apparition reported to have been seen at the Catholic church of Knock on the 21st of August, 1879, the Eve of the Octave of the Assumption:—

I, Mary M'Laughlin, live in Knock; I am housekeeper to the Rev. Archdeacon Cavanagh; I remember the evening of the 21st of August; I just passed at the hour of seven and a-half o'clock; I passed from Father Cavanagh's house, on by the chapel, towards the house of Mrs. Byrne (widow); on passing by the chapel I saw a vision, in which there appeared to be three figures—one that of the Blessed Virgin Mary, one of St. Joseph, and a third which I recognized as that of St. John the Evangelist; the figures were, as appeared to me, nearly life-size, but presenting in their mute and silent aspect, the appearance of statues; they were all radiant with a silvery whiteness, which reflected a bright light, that attracted my attention; the pose of the Blessed Virgin Mary was that of a woman standing quite erect, in the attitude of prayer, her eyes turned towards heaven, her hands, raised, like those of a priest at Mass in saying the collects, with the palms open and slightly upturned; this image like the rest, was of a silvery brightness, and elevated one foot from the ground where they appeared; the image of St. Joseph appeared to the right of the Blessed Virgin Mary, having his head slightly turned towards that of our Blessed Lady; the image of St. John appeared on the left of the Blessed Virgin Mary, radiant with light, and holding a Mass-book or book of Gospels in his left hand, the right raised in the attitude of one who was preaching, the index finger and the middle finger, the two only, raised, with the thumb leaning on them, and the other two fingers compressed, as if he were forcibly explaining some point of doctrine; he wore a mitre, and turned a little from the Blessed Virgin Mary towards the altar; these three figures appeared to be standing at the south gable of the chapel; when I passed, I saw these figures for fully five minutes; I then went on to the house of Mrs. (widow) Byrne; I stayed there fully half an hour; I returned then with Miss Mary Byrne, and she and I beheld the same as that which I now describe, but much more fully and more brightly; I was so taken with the sight that I could not help asking Miss Byrne to go for her mother, Widow Byrne, and her brother, her sister, and her niece, who were in the House which she and I had left; I remained until they came to the spot where I was looking on observing the vision; I was outside the ditch at the time, and leaned across it in order to see fully and leisurely the whole scene; the ditch or wall is in front of the gable, and fully thirty yards from the figures which I beheld; I remained fully a quarter of an hour; I told her then to go for her uncle, Bryan Byrne, and her aunt, Mrs. Bryan Byrne, and any others of the neighbors she could see, in order that they might witness the sight we were then beholding; at that time it was a quarter past or half-past eight o'clock; it was quite dark, and the sun had set that evening at a quarter past seven o'clock, but as a fact the sun had not been seen that day, or at least from mid-day; it was pouring rain at the time, and the rain had continued the whole evening; on this occasion I not only beheld the figures I have just now described, but also an altar, further on to the left of the statue or image of our Blessed Lady, and above the altar, a lamb, about the size of a newly yeaned lamb, say a fortnight or three weeks old; behind the lamb appeared the cross, lying, not elevated, and the body of the lamb a little removed in front of it, and not resting on the wood of the cross;

around the lamb a number of gold-like stars in the form of a nimbus or halo; this altar was placed right under the window outside, which is the middle of the back of the church at Knock, and more to the east of the figures; at about half-past eight o'clock, I went to the priest's house, and told the Rev. Archdeacon Cavanagh of the scene I had witnessed: and asked him to go to witness it; he appeared to make nothing of it, and did not go: it was raining, as I have stated, and the wall on which the figures appeared had a bright dry appearance, while the rest of the wall appeared to be dark; I did not return to behold the vision after that, remaining for the night in my house; on the following day, the Rev. B. Cavanagh heard all about the vision from the others who had seen it, and then recollected that I had told him about going to see it the previous evening.

her
MARY ⋈ M'LAUGHLIN.
mark.

Witnessed by U. J. Canon Bourke and James Canon Waldron.

Testimony of Mary Byrne (aged about 26 years):—

I came with Mary M'Laughlin (whose testimony has just been given) on the evening of the 21st of August at the hour of a quarter past 8 o'clock; I had never heard a word of the vision seen just before that by Miss M'Laughlin; the first I learned of it was on coming from mother's house in company with Miss Mary M'Laughlin, and at the distance of 300 yards or farther from the gable of the chapel, and at the hour just named—8¼ o'clock—I beheld three figures standing out from the gable, rather to the west side of it, and a little out from the wall, and at the height of about 1½ or 2 feet from the ground; the figure of the Blessed Virgin appeared to be larger than that of St. Joseph, or of the episcopal figure having the mitre on his head and the book of Gospels in his left hand; the Virgin stood erect, above the ground, as just described, her hands, raised, as stated above, and her eyes looking towards heaven; she wore a large cloak, of a white color, hanging loosely, around her shoulders, and fastened at the neck; she wore a crown on her head, a rather large crown, and, as it appeared to me, somewhat brighter than the dress or robes worn by the Blessed Virgin Mary; in the statue of St. Joseph the head was slightly bent, and inclined, so to speak, towards the Virgin; it represented the Saint as somewhat aged, with greyish beard and hair; the third figure appeared to me to be that of St. John the Evangelist: I do not know why I thought so, except the fact that at one time I saw a statue at the chapel of Lekanvey, near Westport, very like the figure I saw on the present occasion holding the Gospel book and looking towards the altar; I remark that the statue I saw at Lekanvey chapel must had no mitre on, while the figure I saw in the vision had one; the statue at Lekanvey had the book in the left hand and the fingers raised, and it was this similarity of the figure and pose that made me surmise that the third figure was the likeness of Saint John, the beloved disciple of our Lord; I am not sure what saint particularly or especially this third figure symbolised; all I know is, it appeared to me to be like that of Saint John the Evangelist; the Saint appeared to me to look towards the altar, which stood to the east side from him, towards the centre of the gable, and under the window; the altar appeared to me to be a large full-sized altar, such as is usually seen in Catholic churches; it had no candles or linens, nor any ornamentation of a special kind, but above the altar, and resting on it, was a lamb with its face towards Saint John, thus fronting the western sky, its front feet slightly bent, as is usual with a lamb in a reclined position; the hind feet were rather stretched out, or stretched back, so to speak; I saw no cross on the body of the lamb; I saw golden stars, or small brilliant lights, glittering like jets, or like glass balls reflecting the light of some luminous body; I remained from half-past eigth o'clock till after half-past nine; it was raining at the time, and dark also; there were about ten of us present; we were not on our knees at the time, but reclining on the wall or ditch fronting the vision; I went away at half-past nine o'clock to see Mrs. Campbell, who was ailing, and whose death was expected; after twenty minutes or so I returned, and came by the chapel gable, the vision had by this time vanished and the place was quite dark; the gable appeared dry although it was raining heavily; also while the vision lasted, the night was dark; the place where the vision appeared was quite dry.

Signed by MARY RYAN.

Witnessed by all the priests who are deputed to see to the truth of this matter.

The testimony of Dominick Byrne, jr., brother to Mary Byrne (aged 20 years):—

I left my father's house on the evening of the 21st of August, at about 8 o'clock, or a few minutes later. When on coming in, my sister exclaimed, "Come, Dominick, and see the Blessed Virgin Mary as she appears to us down at the chapel!" I said, "What image?" and then she told me what she had seen, as just now described by her; I went with her then, and by this time some ten or twelve people had been collected around the wall fronting the gable of the chapel where the vision was being seen; I beheld the three statues or likenesses as now described—that of the Blessed Virgin Mary, of St. Joseph, and that which I thought, or heard from my sister, was the likeness of St. John the Evangelist; I saw the altar and lamb too, but not the cross; I saw them just as they are described in the testimony of my sister; I was filled with admiration at the sight I saw; I was so affected that I shed tears on the occasion; I continued there, looking on, for fully an hour; I then went away with my sister; when we returned the vision had disappeared.

DOMINICK J. BYRNE.

Witnessed as the rest, by the priests present.

Catholic Notes.

—The death is announced of Colonel Sir Peter Fllose, a distinguished Catholic officer of his Highness Maharajah Scindia.—*Indo-European Correspondence.*

—MGR. DE LA BOUILLERIE, Coadjutor Archbishop of Bordeaux, has just published a work on "Man: his Nature, his Faculties, and his Final End, according to the Philosophy of St. Thomas Aquinas." This anthropological treatise will appear shortly in English, with notes by Monsignor Capel.

—An Italian priest and philologist, Rev. Bernardino Peyron, has discovered in the binding of a Greek manuscript from the ancient Library of St. Ambrose, on Mount Athos, two fragments of St. Paul's Epistles in the Greek text. Similar fragments at Paris have long been highly valued.—*Catholic Times.*

—CARDINAL MANNING.—Edward Yates says of

him: "In the case of Cardinal Manning, exemplary blamelessness of life is united with indefatigable public activity. That impressive and ascetic presence, with the face whose sharp outline takes us back into the Middle Ages, is well known on every platform on which social improvements are advocated, and is a power with the English public."

—DEVOTION TO THE POPE.—A Mr. O'Gorman, a gentleman of Irish descent but of French birth, lately became naturalized as a Swiss in order to enjoy the privilege of serving in the Swiss Guard. When he entered upon the office, as a mark of gratitude for the honor he had obtained, he presented, it is said, $60,000 to the Peter's Pence fund. The father of this gentleman is also a chamberlain of the Pope.

—DEATHS OF CLERGYMEN.—We deeply regret to announce the death of several other clergymen, viz.: Rev. Michael Driscoll, S. J., who died at St. John's College, Fordham, New York, on the 4th inst.; Rev. William Costigan, on the 2d inst., in New York city, where he was assistant pastor of the Church of the Holy Cross; Rev. John Keller, of Mobile, on the 28th ult.; and Rev. A. H. Cecl, at Hoboken, N. J., on the 7th inst. R. I. P.

—BACK NUMBERS OF THE AVE MARIA.—Those of our subscribers who are in need of back numbers of THE AVE MARIA for the completion of sets or volumes, should apply for them at once, as we intend to send to the paper mill soon our entire stock of back numbers, except, of course, those of the current volume. Our supply of many of the old numbers being now entirely exhausted, we have decided not to preserve the rest any longer than is necessary for the accommodation of those who may need certain numbers of them for the completion of files.

—A NEW CATHEDRAL AT LONDON, CANADA.— We are happy to learn that subscriptions are rapidly flowing in towards the fund for a new cathedral at London, which his Lordship, the Right Rev. Bishop Walsh, recently announced his intention to build. The work will be commenced this spring, and it is estimated that the entire cost will be not less than $100,000. For this amount a magnificent edifice can be constructed at the present time, one which will be an adornment to the Forest City and a monument to the pious zeal of its Catholic citizens.—*The Tribune* (Toronto, Can.)

—FURTHER AID FOR IRELAND FROM THE DIOCESE OF FORT WAYNE.—The following additional collections have been made since the publication of a former list: Holy Trinity, Benton Co., $140; Kentland, $118.50; Laporte, St. Peter's, $75; Laporte, St. Joseph's (2d collection), $12; Delphi, $55.25; Mishawaka, $55; St. John's, Lake Co., $47.18; Fowler and St. Bridget's, $45; Earl Park, $44.05; Elkhart, $39.05; Otys, $30; St. Anthony's, Benton Co., $24; Crown Point, $23; Tipton (2d collection), $20; Leo, $13.24; Ladoga, $11.80; Mary's Home, $12.50; Valparaiso, $448.26; Wabash, $41.25; Clarke's Hill, $0.08; Francisville, $8.50; Andersonville (2d collection), $3; Crawfordsville (2d collection), $3; St. Michael, Allen County, $30.70; Frank Viviat, $10. The remittances to Ireland now amount to £700.

—MR. COVENTRY PATMORE has presented to the Library of the British Museum a copy, printed on vellum, of the entire works of St. Thomas Aquinas, published at Rome, "apud heredes Ant. Bladi," seventeen vols. fol., 1570-71. This work is, according to Brunet, probably the most extensive work, so far as regards the number of volumes, ever printed on vellum. The copy presented by Mr. Patmore formerly belonged to Pope Pius V, who is said to have presented it to King Philip II of Spain, by whom it was lodged in the Escorial, and there kept until the invasion of Spain under Napoleon, when it disappeared. It afterwards came into the possession of Sir Marmaduke M. Sykes, from whom it was purchased by the late Rev. Theodore Williams, Vicar of Hendon, who had it bound in twenty-one volumes, in a magnificent purple morocco. No other copy of this magnificent work printed on vellum is known, except that in the National Library at Paris.—*The Athenæum.*

—TYPOGRAPHICAL ERRORS.—Our attention has been called to a number of typographical blunders which have crept into recent issues of THE AVE MARIA, and the indicator expresses the hope that they will not be so frequent in future. We hope so too, but can offer no guarantee. Those who know anything about printing must know what a fatal facility there is about it for making mistakes. The wonder is that they are not much more frequent, especially in daily and weekly publications, which are invariably made up in a hurry. As for quotations from foreign languages, on which our good correspondent lays particular stress, we have only to say that printers seem to imagine that it detracts from their interest to have them any way correct: and perhaps it does, somewhat. Typographical errors are almost inevitable, no matter what amount of care may be used, and it is more precise than wise to pay much heed to them in publications which appear daily or weekly.

—THE ABBÉ DEBAIZE.—The papers have announced, in a few lines, the death of the Abbé Debaize, a French priest, devoted to geographical exploration. But his demise demands more prominent remark. He was one of those heroic sons of the Church whose aim is always to be in the van of progress, and who studied science as he had studied religion—solidly, profoundly, and laboriously. The French Government, recognizing in him a man of singular aptitude for African exploration, granted £4,000 to assist him, and he left Paris for Zanzibar in March, 1878. He reached Ujiji in about a year, making valuable discoveries by the way, and some of our readers may remember that, upon his authority, we exploded some of Stanley's romances. Providence did not spare him to finish his work. He succeeded in getting a considerable distance, and intended establishing stations at the north end of Tanganyika, and then exploring the western slopes of the Blue Mountains and the countries between the southern end of Albert Nyanza and Lake Tanganyika. We do not know as yet what jottings he has left, or their completeness as a record; but from the extreme keenness of his powers of observation, his remarkable grasp of geographical matters, and his capacity for work, we have good reason to hope that the world will gain much from his labors. May he rest in peace in his distant tomb!—*Liverpool Catholic Times.*

—THE GOLDEN GATE.—As one stands upon Mt. Olivet and gazes up the city of Jerusalem, the eye rests upon one portion of the wall where there are two highly-ornamented arches protruding from the heavy masonry. Many of the paths intersecting the valley of Josaphat converge at this point, but there is no means of entering the city, although the arches would seem to indicate the former existence of a gateway. To the left lie the structures built upon the site of the Temple, and the stranger naturally surmises that these arches must have once formed a part of "the gate called the Beautiful." Such is the appearance presented at this day by the gate through which our Lord made His triumphal entry into Jerusalem. Here too, it was, that the Emperor Heraclius received the true Cross from the Persians, and placing it on his shoulders he carried it hence in triumph to Mt. Calvary. In honor of these two events, the Crusaders permitted this gate to be opened but twice a year: on Palm-Sunday, and on the Feast of the Exaltation of the Holy Cross. This is one of the many places in Jerusalem where the pilgrim may gain a Plenary Indulgence by simply reciting a *Pater* and an *Ave*, a privilege granted by the Bull *Unigeniti Alti Dei* in 1688, and confirmed by Pius IX February 22, 1849. Believing in a spurious prophecy, that on a Friday the Catholic powers will enter Jerusalem through this gate to make themselves masters of Palestine, the Mussulmans have walled up the entrance, but they are not aware that by so doing they fulfil a true prophecy, "And He (the Lord) brought me back to the way of the gate of the outward sanctuary which looked towards the east, and it was shut. And the Lord said to me: This gate shall be shut, it shall not be opened, and no man shall pass through it, because the Lord God of Israel hath entered by it, and it shall be shut." Ezechiel, xliv, 1, 2.

New Publications.

THE CHRISTIAN MOTHER: THE EDUCATION OF HER CHILDREN, AND HER PRAYER. From the German of Rev. W. Cramer; Translated by a Father of the Society of Jesus, with the Permission of Superiors. New York, Cincinnati, and St. Louis: Benziger Brothers.

This little book will remind many mothers of their duty towards their children; for children are but too often neglected in our day. There are many mothers who are satisfied to turn their little ones over to the care of another; and many more who never think of giving the initial direction of the affections towards spiritual things. There are too many who are culpably ignorant of their duties; and too many who slight their holy duties at home for the frivolous amusements of fashionable society. Though imperfect in many ways, this treatise will prove very useful. It is made up of instructions and prayers, suitable for the use of mothers and wives. It has the approbation of Cardinal McCloskey, and the Archbishop of Baltimore.

—We are glad to learn that *The Illustrated Catholic American*, which was started in New York by Messrs. Hickey & Co., at the beginning of the year, is meeting with much success. Nine numbers have now been issued, each one replete with good illustrations and excellent reading matter, so varied as to suit all tastes. It is the intention of the proprietors to add new features of interest, and make notable improvements in the departments already existing, as soon as the circulation of the journal is sufficient to warrant the expenditure. There is a tendency, we know, to disfavor the increase of Catholic papers, particularly as those already existing are not more generally patronized. But this is a mistake. New papers affect the old ones in two ways—both beneficial: they either improve or gradually replace them. It would certainly be to the advantage of Catholic literature in general, if certain papers claiming to be Catholic should cease to exist. We rejoice to see Catholic periodicals increasing on all sides, for they work up fallow fields, and obtain scores of new patrons for Catholic literature, in places where their predecessors have not penetrated. In the end only the best will survive, and there will be ample room for them, no matter how numerous they may be. *The Illustrated Catholic American* is a handsome 16-page paper, similar in form and "make-up" to the other illustrated papers of the country. We wish it abundant success, and trust that its circulation will continue to increase in proportion to the efforts that will be directed to make it worthy of its high title: "An Illustrated Journal of Information and Recreation for the People."

—Since January, when it began the Second Volume of its Third Series, in its present handsome form, it has been our desire again to call attention to our excellent contemporary, *The Messenger of the Sacred Heart of Jesus*, published by the Jesuit Fathers at Woodstock College, Howard Co., Maryland. Besides articles of a devotional character, poetry, sketches, etc., *The Messenger of the Sacred Heart* is also the principal medium in this country for spreading the beautiful devotion of the Apostleship of Prayer, Rev. Father Sestini, S. J., editor of the *Messenger*, is also the Director of the Apostleship of Prayer in the United States. Like the Association of Our Lady of the Sacred Heart, the Confraternity of the Immaculate Conception, or of Our Lady of Lourdes, etc., the Apostleship of Prayer is doing wonders both in the spiritual and temporal order and the monthly visit of the *Messenger* is no doubt a welcome one to thousands of its members. Each number contains a handsome illustration. The price of subscription for this excellent monthly is $2, a year.

—We have received Nos. 11 and 12 of the *Periodische Blaetter* edited by Dr. Sheeben and published by F. Pustet. This publication hardly needs any further recommendation, as its worth and merit are both well known and acknowledged in German literary circles. To those who are not yet acquainted with the *Periodische Blaetter* we would say that its object is to review the great questions of the day, and the position they assume with regard to religion. The contents of the present numbers are up to the usual high standard. The article on the Christian Idea of State, is by far the best exposition of that subject we have met with, while that on The True and Practical Position of Catholics towards Modern Liberty is a masterpiece. We can heartily recommend the *Periodische Blaetter* to all who are conversant with the German language.

Confraternity of the Immaculate Conception
(Or of Our Lady of Lourdes).

"We fly to thy patronage, O Holy Mother of God!"

REPORT FOR THE WEEK ENDING MARCH 10TH.

The following intentions have been recommended: Recovery of health for 94 persons and 3 families,—change of life for 28 persons and 3 families,—conversion to the Faith for 32 persons and 5 families,—special graces for 3 priests, 8 religious, 2 clerical students and 3 persons aspiring to the religious state,—temporal favors for 29 persons and 4 families,—spiritual favors for 41 persons and 3 families,—the spiritual and temporal welfare of 7 communities, 2 congregations, 4 schools, 2 hospitals and 3 orphan asylums,—also 47 particular intentions and 6 thanksgivings for favors received.

Specified Intentions: The particular intentions of several religious,—success in an undertaking for the support of a family, and other temporal favors,—a number of insane persons,—permanent employment for a young man to support his widowed mother,—an aged widow, who is in danger of loosing her property by the failure of a prominent business man,—termination of a misunderstanding between three persons,—means for a religious community to rebuild a home for destitute orphan girls,—a worthy family much afflicted by the loss of property,—several persons suffering from a complication of diseases,—a lady in mortal illness who despairs of her salvation, and refuses to see a priest,—a husband inconsolable over the death of his wife,—a young lady afflicted with temporary blindness.

FAVORS OBTAINED.

"It is with sentiments of the deepest gratitude to our Blessed Lord and His holy Mother," says a pious correspondent, "that I write the following lines. In July 1878 a tumor appeared in my right ear. It seemed to have grown instantaneously, for I had not felt any pain previous to the appearance. It filled the entire cavity of the ear, and at times blood oozed freely from it. I was advised to use a relic of St. Edward, and meanwhile several novenas were recited by some fervent souls. The tumor decreased greatly in size and there was little inflammation; still it did not entirely disappear. I then had recourse for the first time to medical aid. The physician stated that it was one of the worst cases he had ever seen, the only remedy being to cut it out, and even then it might grow again. In my distress I had recourse to Our Lady of Lourdes. On the 13th of January the tumor became black and projected almost to the cheek, causing intense pain. It continued this way for three days, when, wonderful to relate, after bathing it with the water of Lourdes, it came out entirely, leaving no trace whatever."

OBITUARY.

Of your charity pray for the repose of the souls of the following deceased persons: Mr. JOSEPH J. BOLSIUS, who departed this life at Leiden, Holland, on the 19th day of January. Mrs. MARGARET KENNEDY, and MRS. MARGARET GAFFNEY, who fell asleep in the Lord on the 20th ult. at Thompsonville, Ct. Mr. MICHAEL LENNEY, of Chester, Pa., a devoted client of Our Lady, who died an edifying death on the 26th ult. Mr. MANNIN, who met death by poisoning on the 22d ult. Mrs. M. McNORTON, of Marengo, Iowa, who passed out of this life on the 27th of February. Miss MARY ANN MULLIN, of New York, who departed for heaven on the 28th ult. Miss FANNY MYERS, of Loretto, Pa., who breathed her last the 8th inst., fortified by all the consolations of our holy religion. MOTHER MARY STANISLAUS and SISTER MARY IGNATIUS, members of the Community of the Sisters of the Holy Child Jesus, recently deceased in England. SISTER MARY JOSEPH, of the Order of Mercy. MRS. ELIZABETH LYONS, of Chicago, Ill. MESSRS. JOHN BRENNAN, JOSEPH KEEFE and PATRICK DONOVAN, of Austin, Minn. MR. JAMES D. CUNNINGHAM, of East Boston, Mass., and MISS ELLEN COLLINS, of Brighton, Mass., whose deaths are of recent occurrence. MISS MARY CUMMINGS, of Somerville, Mass.; MRS. MARY A. SLEVIN, of Philadelphia, Pa.; MR. EDWARD COGAN and MRS. MARGARET HAYDEN, of Washington, D. C., MR. WILLIAM P. LOLOR, of St. Louis, Mo.; MRS. E. FLOURNEY, of Richmond, Va.; MR. JOHN GILL, MR. BEACHNER, all of whom died some time ago. And several others whose names have not been given.

Requiescant in pace.

A. GRANGER, C. S. C., Director.

Youth's Department.

Santa Maria del Mar of Barcelona.

OVER the portals of one of the grandest as well as the most ancient churches of Barcelona, "Santa Maria del Mar," can be seen a statue of Our Lady, made of stone, representing her Immaculate Conception. Its face inclines slightly to the left; its eyes express deep tenderness and compassion.

There is a remarkable incident connected with this statue. About three centuries ago, near the Convent of St. Augustine—since destroyed—lived a mother and her only son; the son was a weaver by trade, and the mother used to spin a fine silk thread.

It was on one of the last days of November, about seven o'clock in the evening, and quite dark; no sound was heard save that of the loom and the spinning wheel. It seems that the son and the mother were endeavoring to finish their day's work before the "Queda," which was rung at 8 o'clock, at which hour all the lights and fires were extinguished, and everyone had to retire till the next day.

A small lamp was throwing light upon the scene; the mother would occasionally cast a furtive glance at her son, as he every now and then cut with the fine scissors of Toledo the threads that broke. Barcelona, always celebrated for its industry, was at that time a rival of Milan, for silk webs were appreciated not only in Spain but even in foreign countries.

The boy suddenly stopped his work and said, "Mother, did you hear a cry?"

The mother ceased spinning, and a voice at a distance was heard crying out, "Help, help! murder, murder!"

"May God help us," said she "it is the voice of our neighbor, the usurer Lucas."

The young man left his loom and went to the door.

"Where are you going, Severo?" said the mother, alarmed.

"To help our neighbor," answered the generous-hearted youth.

"Have nothing to do with him," replied the mother; "you know our neighbor is a usurer, and he may be disputing with some one of his creditors, trying to extort his very soul. It is not worth while that a quiet man like you should trouble yourself about him."

"Excuse me, mother," said the son, putting her gently aside; "he is our neighbor, and charity obliges me to aid him."

Next a cry of anguish was heard, and a scream from the belfry of St. Catharine. The youth freed himself from the grasp of his mother, and went out. The streets were dark, save the dim glimmer of a lamp, burning before a stone image of St. Austin, close by the convent. By means of the light of that lamp the poor woman saw her son enter the house on the other side of the street.

Soon after the young man returned, pale and trembling, and shut the door. He sat down near his mother, hardly able to breathe. "What has happened?" asked the mother; "what is the matter with you, my son?"

"Our neighbor has been murdered," answered Levero; "and I arrived only in time to see him gasping his last."

At that instant the great bell of the cathedral sounded the "Queda," to which the bells of the parish church and convent responded. The mother and the son were dumb with terror. Steps were heard in the street. It was the night patrol.

"It is the night patrol," said the mother, trembling. "He stops in front of the neighbor's house."

"Mother," said Severo, "the door of the house of Luca is open, the patrol will see all. God grant that the assassin may be discovered!"

Presently knocks were heard at their door. The mother and son tremble.

"Who's there?" asked the mother.

"Open to the law officer of Alianor," answered the person outside.

"The officer of the law may come in," replied the woman, opening the door.

"You shall have to pay a fine," said the officer; 'the bell sounded, and you have your light still burning."

"The last stroke of the bell did not sound yet," said the woman.

"Let it go for this time; but tell me did you hear any noise from the house in front?"

"No," answered the mother and the son, both becoming pale.

Then the officer presented a pair of scissors, and asked the young man: "Do you know these scissors?"

The youth became livid, clasped his hands in despair, and said: "I am innocent, I can swear it before my God."

"Nobody said you were guilty, young man. These scissors were found lying at the side of a man who has been murdered, and belong to some person of your trade, to a weaver of silk. Come with me, and you shall answer before the judge.

In vain poor Alioner asked for mercy; in vain did she declare her son innocent before the officer of the law."

"I cannot help it," said he; "you say that you do not know, but the scissors found near the corpse of Lucas are those of your son."

He took with him the youth, almost senseless, and the poor mother fell to the ground half dead, saying: "Virgin Mary, have pity on me, and save my poor boy!"

At that moment all the bells of Barcelone repeated the last sound of "la Queda." "The Queda," or put out your light, was rung in olden times at 8 o'clock, as at present the bell for the dead is in Catholic countries. Then it was prohibited under fine, to go out of the house after the last sound, except for some very urgent necessity, on account of the streets being perfectly dark, which gave occasion for many crimes.

How sadly the hours pass by when misfortune has alighted at our door! At such times, it seems as though God Himself had forgotten us. Three months after Lucas was murdered, if we look into Santa Maria del Mar we shall see a poor woman kneeling before a picture of Our Lady. She was dressed in the Franciscan habit, which she had put on to appease Divine justice, and to obtain the grace for which she was asking. Three months of continual grief, had changed her once handsome face almost beyond recognition. She loved her truly deserving son with all the tenderness of an affectionate mother; it will not be difficult, therefore, to imagine her anguish when she learned that he was sentenced to an ignominious death in punishment for his supposed crime. Circumstantial evidence was strongly against Severo, and justified the law in condemning him. The judges only smiled at the loud protestations of the mother in declaring his innocence, deeming it but natural for a mother to defend the life of her son, even by perjury.

The fatal day of the execution had arrived; near the market, at a place called "Born," where the Church of Santa Maria has a rear entrance, a scaffold had been erected. The great bell of "Santa Maria del Pino" was calling for the prayers of the faithful in behalf of the doomed man, a pious custom that has been retained to this day. A procession was slowly moving on in one of the streets close by, in the midst of which, surrounded by priests, could be seen a poor youth, pale as death, his hands tied, and a rope around his neck, proceeding with feeble step to the place of execution. On arriving, he requested to be allowed to pray for the last time before a venerated image of the Mother of God above the portal of the church. His request was granted. The poor youth, raising his eyes to heaven, prayed: "Oh, my Mother! thou knowest that I am innocent, that I have never shed human blood; but since I cannot escape the scaffold, watch over my poor earthly mother. I beseech you; be her protectress, since I am doomed to die." As soon as he had finished, the image, which had its head erect and looked towards heaven, bowed down, and looked pitifully at the condemned man; then a voice, like the roaring of the sea, was heard throughout the whole place— the crowd cried out: "He is innocent! the Mother of God has proved it." A great tumult followed, the crowd forcibly rescued the supposed criminal from the hands of the soldiers; then a woman was seen coming quickly out of the church; seizing the young man, she brought him into the church, crying out: "My son! my son!"

The doors of the church were closed; the crowd, full of enthusiasm, shouted: "Bravo, Alioner! you have saved your son! He is in a sacred place, and let no one dare to take him out."

A great controversy between the ecclesiastical and civil authorities ensued, but the changed attitude of the image, which remains to this day, so convinced the Government officers that the youth was set free. Thus it was that the parish church of Santa Maria amongst other privileges had this one: if any culprit could escape and obtain refuge within it, the civil power could not take him by force. This privilege was retained till the beginning of the present century.

Some time after the above mentioned incident, two famous robbers were caught and sentenced to death, and at the foot of the scaffold they confessed that they had murdered the usurer, Lucas, in order to obtain his money.

Every evening towards dark, a woman, accompanied by a robust young man, bearing a can of oil in his hand, might be seen entering the Church of Santa Maria del Mar, to pray, and to fill and trim a lamp which hung before the image of the Immaculate Virgin. Years passed, and the same touching scene was repeated. One day, however, the young man with his eyes moistened with tears, and dressed in mourning, came alone to fill the lamp. His mother had gone to her reward. Some time after he married, and then, accompanied by his wife, as previously by his mother, he continued the beautiful devotion, and in gratitude for his miraculous deliverance from the gallows, he never failed during his whole life in the performance of this act of piety.

WHOEVER does not pray for his parents is an undutiful child; whoever does not pray for the Pope is an indifferent Catholic. Let us always be faithful to these duties.

Why St. Joseph is so Busy.

FROM THE FRENCH, BY THE AUTHOR OF "TYBORNE."

A Legend for his Feast.

A PIOUS mother once asked St. Joseph to act as godfather to her new-born babe. The Saint consented, and brought to the baptism, as his present, a white robe. It was light as air and sparkled as though set with diamonds.

"He looks like an angel!" exclaimed the delighted mother, when the little Joseph was clothed in his godfather's handsome gift.

"He is one," replied St. Joseph; "and he will continue to be such while that robe remains pure and sparkling as it is at present."

"Alas," said the poor mother, "how can that ever be? a little child never keeps its things clean even for an hour!"

"Fear not," said the Saint; "this is a heavenly robe, and the angels will take care of it until the child is old enough to do so himself."

"But how can he wear a little robe like that when he grows tall?" asked the mother.

The Saint smiled and said: "The gifts of Heaven are large enough even for giants. The robe will grow with his growth. It will never leave him, he must bring it with him to judgment. It is his passport for the next world; and by this robe, God will recognize him as His child when he presents himself at the gate of Paradise. So you who have charge of him must bear in mind that it is not exterior things which can soil this robe, but only interior ones. As long as his will is firm and his heart pure, the robe will remain spotless as it now is, and no one can deface it; nothing but his own will can tarnish it. But every sin will stain it."

"Alas, good St. Joseph," said the mother, "you know how weak are mortals; how can he help staining his robe when it is so hard to avoid sin?"

"You speak the truth," returned the Saint. "But has not the Divine Redeemer placed the antidote by the side of the evil? When the robe is stained, the waters of heaven can always cleanse it. Even though it were to become as black as ink, never let your child hide it under his other garments, for the waters of heaven are the tears of the saints, and I have often seen them fall upon the stained robe of those who had not courage to seek for their own cleansing. But now I must bid you farewell; I have no more time to spare. Last night, the devil injured several rounds of the ladder which souls have to climb before they reach heaven; and besides that, Our Blessed Lady says that some of the steps are rather high for small persons, and it is my business to see to that." So giving his benediction, St. Joseph disappeared, to the great regret of the mother, who wanted him to stay and partake of the christening feast.

The Palm-Trees of San Remo.

NOT far from Nice, just at that point of the celebrated highway of the "Riviera"—that route in which are blended the beauties of every variety of scenery—at that point where the Apennines are lost in the Alps, stands the quaint old town of San Remo clambering down the rugged slopes amid terraced gardens and groves of vines, cypresses and palms to reach the golden sands washed by the blue waves of the Mediterranean. Vineyards and orange orchards are nestled in the sunny nooks and beautify the fertile valleys. Here the invalid comes in search of health, and the artist to seek from nature inspiration for his pencil. The palm-trees lean gracefully seaward to catch the warm breezes wafted over the sea from the Egyptian shores, and if they are less majestic than the lofty date palms of Cairo and Alexandria, their story, so full of beautiful associations is a rare compensation.

There stands in front of the great Vatican Basilica, St. Peter's at Rome—a mute witness of the vicissitudes of time, the huge obelisk which Caligula brought to Rome and placed in the Vatican circus. In 1586 Domenico Fontana, at the order of Pope Sixtus V, undertook the difficult task of removing it to its present location. This involved the most complicated problems of mechanics, and so much danger attended the transportation, that it was to be performed in complete silence. Anyone of either the workmen or of the by-standers who would utter a single word was to be punished with death. Among the many calculations which this work necessitated, Fontana had forgotten to allow for the effect produced by the great strain on the ropes, and there came a moment when the cordage of the pulleys appeared to be about to snap asunder. At this moment one of the workmen, a sailor from San Remo by the name of Bresca, risking his life to save that of others, shouted aloud: "Water on the ropes." His voice rang like a trumpet through the Vatican Piazza, for it was one accustomed to be heard above the raging tempest. It produced the effect of mechanical obedience on the part of those who heard him, and their speedy execution of his command secured the success of that truly herculean task.

When Bresca was brought before the Pope, Sixtus V spoke to him of reward, and not of punishment. When pressed to state what he desired as a testimonial of his presence of mind and spirit of self-sacrifice, he told the Pope with sailor-like simplicity that he had observed that the palms used at St. Peter's on Palm-Sunday were by no means as beautiful as they should be for so grand a church, and that he would like to secure to his family the privilege of supplying the palms for St. Peter's, until the end of time from the fine palm-trees on their plantation near San Remo. This request was granted, but the Chapter of St. Peter's did not place much faith in Bresca's fulfilment of his part of the engagement, so it was greatly to their surprise, that during the Passion Week of the next year, a barge laden with beautiful palm-boughs was seen slowly moving up the Tiber with Bresca in command. This was the first cargo from San Remo, and through the centuries which have elapsed since Domenico Fontana's great task was accomplished with the aid of the sailor from the Riviera, the palms borne by the greatest dignitaries of the Catholic hierarchy have always been brought from the date orchard of the Brescas of San Remo.

VENERABLE FATHER HOFBAUER could do a little pleasant teasing sometimes, but never in such a manner as to pain or offend. Once, as he was in the garden of a Hungarian noble, his companion, a student, exclaimed, as they walked through a shaded avenue, through the trees of which the clouds assumed the most fantastic shapes: "Oh! what beautiful clouds one sees in these gardens." The Father never afterwards met the youth without making some allusions to the "beautiful clouds in the garden."

One may easily infer how amiable was the piety of this saintly priest. To the day of his death, he ate, drank, and was clad like the poor; yet he obtained an influence over the noble and the learned which was truly wonderful. His old blue cloak was as well known in Vienna as Louis Philippe's umbrella in Paris a little later; Compared with the men by whom he was surrounded, he was a child; he valued things only inasmuch as they led souls to God. He despised them in proportion as they drew souls from Him.

THE AVE MARIA.

A Journal devoted to the Honor of the Blessed Virgin.

HENCEFORTH ALL GENERATIONS SHALL CALL ME BLESSED.—St. Luke, i, 48.

VOL. XVI.   NOTRE DAME, INDIANA, MARCH 27, 1880.   NO. 13.

The Resurrection of Our Lord Jesus Christ.

WITH unceasing voices, the angels, the heavens, all the heavenly powers the cherubim and seraphim, are proclaiming the wonders of God's mercy, majesty and might; and more than once have the heavens opened, so that earth might hear and learn the canticles of paradise. It was the shepherds that first heard the *Gloria in excelsis*. The Church tells us that when the multitude saluted our Lord with "Hosanna to the Son of David," unseen angels blended their voices with those of the children, thus inspiring this hymn. St. John during his sojourn on the Isle of Patmos, heard the sublime praises of the Eternal Father, and of the Lamb without spot; but on Mary's ears alone fell the glad strains that proclaimed the glories of the Resurrection. Earth listened in vain for the echo; the Gospels were silent; even St. Luke, who has preserved for us so many of the grand poems of the Incarnation, omits this one, leaving it to be one of the many revelations of younger centuries—revelations which continually prove the truth and sanctity of the Catholic Church. Nearly six centuries later, the angels sang it again: this time it was penitent and suppliant Rome that received it as a gauge of mercy and pardon; and this canticle took a place in Catholic liturgy, equal in rank to the *Ave Maria*, the *Gloria in excelsis*, and the *Hosanna Filio David;* and this day, the glorious tidings which it contains have already gone abroad even to the uttermost parts of the earth.

O Queen of Heaven, rejoice: Alleluia. For He whom thou didst deserve to bear: Alleluia. Is risen again as He said: Alleluia. Thrice the angelic messengers paused in their message; thrice they paused to praise God; and with them we also pause to say, God be praised, that at last thou canst rejoice, O Mary! God be praised, thou didst merit to be the Mother of the Redeemer! God be praised! thy Divine Son is risen again as He said.

Where was this salutation uttered? St. Luke tells us that Gabriel was sent to a city of Galilee called Nazareth, and that there the words "Hail, full of grace!" were first spoken; there was the Incarnation announced. Is it known where the angels declared to Our Lady that the Resurrection was now no longer a prophecy but a fact? The holy Scripture leaves the Blessed Virgin at the foot of the Cross; the *Via Crucis* presents her to us as receiving the dead Body of her Son in her arms, and as accompanying It to the tomb; the traditions of Palestine follow her further. The pilgrim to Jerusalem, on entering the Holy City, first turns his steps towards the Church of the Holy Sepulchre, that wonderful basilica beneath whose roof are collected so many of the precious memorials of the Passion and Resurrection of our Lord. Truly wonderful is this structure, both in association and in story; erected, destroyed, re-erected, in decay, repaired, owned by Christians, pillaged by pagans, decorated by empires; composed first of separate edifices, afterwards united into one; built by an empress, rebuilt by a monk; repaired by different princes; converted into one by the Crusaders—so the centuries write its history. The pilgrim winds through the mazes of this unique building, ascending and descending stairways, for the pavement follows the natural configuration of the ground; at each step he receives new impressions as he listens to his Franciscan guide.

Calvary and the Holy Sepulchre have been visited; and the pilgrim, still under the guidance of a monk, passes across the aisle north of the chapel inclosing the Holy Sepulchre, until he reaches the Chapel of the Apparition of Our Lord to the Blessed Virgin. This is a rectangular apartment, having three altars, and furnished with stalls like a cathedral choir. Here the

Franciscans, who have their convent attached to the northeast corner of the Basilica, recite by night and by day the Hours of the Divine Office.

The traditions of the Holy Places were never lost to the Christians of Jerusalem, even when the Romans buried these shrines beneath rubbish, and erected thereon temples to Jupiter and Venus. Even when they forbade the Christians to visit them, descriptions of each place of note were carefully preserved by the faithful, so that when St. Helena began her holy task, she had only to order this rubbish to be removed, to be able to trace out the locality of each event. She knew that St. Joseph of Arimathea owned a cottage in that same garden, where lay the sepulchre which he relinquished to our Lord; she knew that he had placed this house at the disposal of the Blessed Virgin as long as she desired to be near the tomb of her Son. Knowing precisely the direction in which this lay from the Holy Sepulchre itself, St. Helena had no difficulty in determining the spot on which to erect the oratory commemorative of the meeting of our Lord and His Blessed Mother after the Resurrection. We can well believe that it was impossible to tear our Lady away from the spot where her Divine Son was lying lifeless; others might go to their homes, but not she; others might prepare their fragrant spices, but she better understood the prophecies; she knew that the Resurrection was at hand. She might consent, as a matter of form, to accept the hospitality of St. Joseph of Arimathea, but we can believe that at the first opportunity she left its shelter to approach as near as the guards permitted to the thrice Holy Tomb.*

Nor is it so strange that the Gospels omit to describe this joyful meeting, which filled our Lady with an ecstasy of heavenly delight. The concluding chapters of each of the four Gospels are a collection of the most important proofs of the truth of the Resurrection and the Ascension. The preceding chapters were merely narrations of well-known facts; but after the Resurrection, the Gospels assume the character of a *proces-verbal*, and only such witnesses are summoned as would have their testimony considered admissible in a court of law. It is evident that even Mary Magdalen was slow to understand, though eager to believe and to love; for so little prepared was she to find her Lord arisen, that she wept because His Body had been taken away, and her tearful eyes failed to recognize Him when He stood before her. There is something touchingly fitting in Mary Magdalen's having been chosen to announce to the Church this crowning mystery of the Divine Humanity. It is to our Blessed Lady that we owe all our knowledge of the manner in which the mystery of the Incarnation was accomplished; but to tell a sinful world that its Redemption was finished and proven, was the task of her who had been forgiven many sins, teaching us the high esteem in which repentance and penance are held by God. She who was Immaculate tells us, He was the Son of the Most High made Man by the power of the Holy Ghost; but it is she, whose soul was cleansed through bitter tears, through much penance, who declares to us that as He was free among the living, so was He also "free among the dead." "He has risen again as He said." And if we desire more proof of the Resurrection than we derive from the testimony of the prophets, of Mary Magdalen, of the Apostles, of the incredulous pair at Emmaus, and of the still more incredulous Thomas, we have it in the truth of the words of the collect, "by the Resurrection of our Lord Jesus Christ Thou hast been pleased to fill the world with joy." There is no other joy like it, for it intensifies all our happiness, it chastens all our grief. The very thought of this mystery ages before its accomplishment, brought forth from the heart of Job, when he was at the lowest depth of misery and desolation, one of the most joyous canticles recorded in Holy Writ. Nor is his and our joy without reason, for the Resurrection of our Lord is a pledge of our own immortality, a proof of His Divinity—" We know that our Redeemer liveth, and that in the last day He will raise us up, and in our flesh we will see Him who is risen again as He said."

HAPPY the man whose life is one long *Te Deum!* He will save his soul; but he will not save it alone, but many others also. Joy is not a solitary thing, and he will come at last to His Master's feet, bringing many others rejoicing with him, the resplendent trophies of his grateful love.—*Faber.*

---

* From the unique and interesting guide-books of Palestine, published with the permission of Superiors, by Brother Lavinus (Frère Liévin), the Franciscan monk, for many years the guide of Latin pilgrims to the Holy Places, the following account of the tradition of the chapel of the Apparition of our Lord to the Blessed Virgin is copied : " Malgré les pressantes sollicitations de ses amis, la Mère de Jésus, nous dit la tradition, ne consentit pas à s'éloigner du Tombeau dans lequel on venait d'enfermer le corps de son Adorable Fils car elle savait que le jour de sa resurrection était proche, Joseph d'Arimathie mit a sa disposition la maison de campagne qu'il possédait dans le jardin même où se trouvait le Tombeau. Marie l'acceptait mais sans presque en user ; car elle passait la plus grande partie du temps à une très petite distance du sépulchre aussi près que les soldats qui y faisaient la garde le lui permettaient. N.-S., pour récompenser sa Mère de tout ce qu'elle avait souffert durant sa Passion, et aussi pour l'honorer et lui témoigner son amour s'empressa de lui apparaître en ce lieu, afin que la joie de son triomphe tarit la source de sa tristesse et de ses larmes. . . . . La chapelle de l'Apparition de N.-S. à sa très Ste Mère a trois autels. . . . celui du milieu. . . . a été consacré à la Ste. Vierge pour perpétuer la mémoire du miracle de l'Apparition de N.-S. à sa Ste. Mère."

The First Good Friday Night.

BY ELEANOR C. DONNELLY.

"Weeping, she hath wept in the night; and her tears are on her cheeks; there is none to comfort her of all them that were dear to her."

I.

A LOW, wide room, dim with the shades of night,
And silent as the chamber of the dead;
A single lamp, its melancholy light,
  Sheds in the midst: and there, with muffled head,
  With drooping form, and tightly-folded hands,
  Our Lady at the little table stands.

II.

The strongest rays upon her face are thrown:
Within her mantle's azure depths enshrined,
The profile, pure and cold as carven stone,
  Against the dark, blue, back-ground is defined;
  The ashen lips, half-open, as to speak;
  A great tear trembling on the oval cheek.

III.

For, lo! the while she stands and mutely mourns,
Before her, on the little table lie
The scourge, the nails, the sponge, the crown of thorns,
  On which the crimson Blood is scarcely dry;
  The Precious Blood, that, but some hours ago,
  Welled from the bruised Heart of the Man of Woe.

IV.

Once more, before the Mother's vision surge
The dreadful scenes: once more, upon the air,
She hears the fierce sound of the cruel scourge,—
  She sees the mangled Flesh,—the Bones laid bare;
  The helpless Victim to the pillar bound,
  Bearing the lash with patience most profound.

V.

Mark how she shudders! Shouts of fiendish sport
Break on her ear. Her heart throbs strong and fast.
—The soldiers gathered in the outer court,
  A scarlet cloak about her Son have cast:
  And on His head have press'd so sharp a crown,
  That blood and tears His sacred Face run down.

VI.

And forth they go, and forth the Lamb divine
Goes with them, bearing on His wounded back
The heavy cross; but where the blood-drops shine
  Like rubies, in the gentle Suff'rer's track,—
  The Mother follows, painfully and slow,
  Wrapp'd in the mantle of her mighty woe.

VII.

One look He gives her,—shaking back the veil
Of tangled hair that 'thwart His vision lies,
He gazes in her visage, pure and pale.
  With tend'rest love out-leaping from His eyes:
  One glance of mute, of sweet farewell,—and then,
  The blood-stained tresses hide His face again.

VIII.

And when she next beholds It, It is drench'd
  With sweat of agony. O pitying heaven!
The blessed Bones are from their sockets wrench'd,
  And, thro' His hands and feet, the nails are driven;
  And, high above her (like a dove's sad note),
  His dying moans adown the darkness float.

IX.

Ah! if her loving hand could reach His head,
  How sweet 'twould be to wipe that bleeding Face;
To lift the dear Limbs from their bloody bed,
  And fold them fondly in her close embrace;
  Each open wound to touch, and bathing, bless,
  With all a mother's tears of tenderness!

X.

Hark! 'tis His voice: "*I thirst!*" On such sweet lips
  The purest dews of heav'n should, cooling, fall!
Alas! alas! amid the dark eclipse,
  His mouth is drench'd with vinegar and gall.
  —Earth's countless fountains cannot here afford
  One draught of water for their dying Lord!

XI.

The red Wounds widen; quicker comes His breath—
Slower and slower throbs the breaking Heart:
The thorn-crown'd Head droops lower still in death;
  The dim Eyes close,—the white Lips fall apart;
  One piercing cry the mournful Mother hears,
  And lo ! it wakes her from her trance of tears!

XII.

The scourge, the nails, the sponge, the thorny crown,
Upon the table lie,—O bitter sight!
But close beside her kneels the dear Saint John,
  Sharing the vigils of that solemn night;
  And fair-haired Magdalen, her kisses sweet,
  Doth, pitying, rain upon our Mother's feet.

MY experience is, that Christianity dispels more mystery than it involves. With Christianity, it is twilight in the world; without it, night. Christianity does not finish the statue—that is heaven's work; but it "rough-hews" all things,—truth, the mind, the soul.—*Madame Swetchine.*

'Beth's Promise.

BY MRS. ANNA HANSON DORSEY.

CHAPTER XI—(Continued).

"OH, darling!" cried 'Beth, who had heard the hall door open, and ran down hoping that it might be her mother coming in, "*where* have you been so long?" and before her mother could reply, folded her in her arms, and kissed her, as if it were enough just to have her back.

"I will tell you, 'Beth," answered Mrs. Morley, returning her caress, "after dinner, and when we are quite alone." And 'Beth saw in the pale, still beautiful face, and heard in the calm, sweet voice, a something which she could not define, for it was something that expressed peace, humility, and yet exaltation; but whatever it might be, the change in the dear face was so apparent that it made her happy without knowing why. She busied herself taking off her mother's bonnet and wraps, and smoothing her fair, waving hair —which now showed many a thread of white —with gentle touches, and rested her cheek carelessly upon it for a moment.

At dinner, 'Beth talked and chatted about all the pleasant things she could think of, more than satisfied with the fond smile and loving look turned towards her, and, above all, with that indefinable change that had so transfigured her mother's countenance. Her spirits rose almost to merriment, and her sweet laugh, so long hushed, rippled out now and then, as it used to do, to old Andrew's great satisfaction, as with a smile on his brown face, he moved round the table. After dinner, Mrs. Morley and 'Beth went up stairs to their cosy sitting-room, where, having drawn her mother's chair out of the draught of the window, and lit the shaded Argand lamp, she closed the door and cuddled herself on a low cushion at her feet, resting her folded arms upon her knees, her face lifted up to hers full of expectation.

"Now, mamma, tell me all about your adventures in that old church? Where were you when I was looking for you?" she said.

"I was in the confessional my darling," she answered gravely, holding 'Beth's hands folded between her own.

"In the confessional!" cried 'Beth with wide-open, wondering eyes, as she straightened herself up; "dear mamma! why did you go into that terrible place? Oh, I should have been so afraid!"

"I went to confess my sins, my long faithlessness, my neglect of the highest and most sacred duties; for know, my child, that I was born a Catholic, and was one—until shortly before you were born—for many years."

"Oh, mamma! *You! you!* How *could* you be a Roman Catholic!" exclaimed 'Beth, almost overcome by this revelation. "And I, what am I?"

"You are a Catholic by baptism! Oh, my child, forgive me!" cried Mrs. Morley, bowing her head on 'Beth's shoulder, and folding her to her breast; "forgive me for having by my faithlessness made you a stranger to the one divine Faith, an outcast from your true heritage."

"Mamma! don't grieve. I am nothing. you know? and I don't think I could ever have been a Roman Catholic. But if it makes you happier to go back to that church, I would not for all the world you should not do so; for oh, dear mamma! I have one only wish on earth, and that is to see you happy."

"I believe you, my child, but won't you try and help me to expiate my sin by coming with me? Won't you console me by the assurance that you will make yourself acquainted with the Catholic Faith, and mayhaps repair my great fault towards you, by becoming one?"

"Yes, mamma," said 'Beth, after a thoughtful pause, during which she weighed the decision she should make; "I can promise that, if *you* will teach me, and not want me to go to one of the priests in a confessional. It seems so mysterious to be shut up in a box telling your sins to a mortal man!" 'Beth spoke as she believed, simply and truly; she was as ignorant of the Catholic religion and its practices as any native of pagan lands could be; she had only heard the people they knew and associated with, saying strange things about it, and had read sentimental Protestant books, from which she had summed up an ideal that was as far from the truth as the East is from the West. Therefore it was not singular that she felt both shocked and astonished when she learned from her mother's own lips that she, in whose character she believed every perfection met, was a Roman Catholic.

"The confessional, my child, is unlike what you think; it is the gate of heaven; and had I not found my way back to it, do you know what would have happened?"

"I cannot think, mamma. What?"

"I should have lost my reason—I should have gone mad. I was very near it, my child. What with the sorrow that has crushed and left me desolate on earth, without solace, or any Divine support—having forfeited all by weakly abandoning my Faith—a cold despair was freezing me; every day I grew more hopeless, and only longed for death, until one evening—that evening I sent the carriage home without me—attracted by the sounds of an organ, and the old familiar strains of the *Tantum ergo*, I discovered that I was in the neighborhood of a Catholic church. A strong impulse seized me to approach, and enter; but I got no farther than the door, when I knelt, and then, by the grace of God, the depths of my soul were stirred, and I felt that there might even yet be hope for me."

"Oh, mamma!" sobbed 'Beth, burying her face on her mother's bosom, "and you bore it all by yourself. I would have tried to comfort you."

"There was no earthly healing for remorse, for sorrow like mine. It is only in the Divine Sacraments of the Catholic Church, where from the cradle to the grave, the faithful soul finds help and consolation, that it is to be found—aye—and beyond the grave, help for our departed," said Mrs. Morley, closing her eyes, while her lips moved with a whispered prayer for her husband's repose.

"It all sounds strange to me, mamma; of course I cannot understand it yet," said 'Beth gently, her words giving renewed pain to her through whose fault she had grown up in such ignorance, but she vowed in her inmost heart, that if penance and prayer would avail, her child should be brought back to the Fold from which by her culpable negligence, she was so far astray.

"To-morrow morning at early Mass—all unworthy as I am—I am to receive Holy Communion. And this is all, my child, that I have to tell you now. I shall carry the grief of my great loss to the grave with me, but my cross is lightened by hope, for He who died upon the Cross, will help me to bear mine to the end," said Mrs. Morley, in low, firm tones.

"May I go to church with you, mamma—I mean to-morrow?"

"Yes, dear child."

"But, mamma—but—" began 'Beth, after a silence of some minutes, and hesitating, as if not quite sure whether she was right or wrong in saying what was in her heart; "I mean, mamma, what will they all say when they hear this?"

"Who, my 'Beth?"

"The pastor and all the people we know."

"They'll probably say that I have lost my mind, not knowing that I have just recovered it. But that is a small matter, my child; human respect and I have shaken hands I hope forever."

It was exactly what everyone did say when it was known that Mrs. Morley had become a Catholic. "Poor thing!" they said, after telling the news to one another: "the shock of the Captain's death quite unsettled her mind, and you know she was not a communicant in our Church; she only came now and then, when she had something new and elegant to parade!" Others who knew that she had formerly been a Catholic, but had fallen off from the practice of her religion for some reason or other, declared that in permitting it to be understood she was a Protestant all that time, she not only showed great weakness of character, but hypocrisy! Then they pitied 'Beth, "a sweet, lovely girl," they said; "so devoted to her mother that there was no hope but that she would be perverted by her example—and just as she was going to be confirmed too!" The pastor, hearing the rumor, thought, "if it were true, it explains a great many things which had been inexplicable to him," and he hastened to pay Mrs. Morley a visit, to learn the facts of the case from her own lips. She received him with her usual courtesy, but when he questioned her, she declared her Faith in tones so firm and decided, yet tempered with humility, that he felt it would be in the last degree useless to discuss the question any further. In fact, although he was grieved, he behaved remarkably well, and expressed a hope that she would find all the spiritual comfort and succor she needed in the Faith she once found wanting, but to which she had returned.

"Not my Faith that was wanting, but me," she answered, quickly. He bowed, and said:

"But your daughter, Mrs. Morley? she has been brought up in our church, instructed in our belief, and is ready for confirmation; I hope most earnestly that you will lay no obstacles in her way, that you will not seek to drag her into the errors of Romanism!"

"My daughter is a Catholic by baptism, and as through my most culpable negligence she has become a stranger to her holy Faith, I shall spare neither prayers, nor tears, nor influence, to repair my great fault towards her, until, by the grace of God, she is restored to the Church. And now my dear sir, that you have discharged what seemed to you a duty, in coming to speak with me, and as it would be useless to continue the interview, would it not be well to make an end? Permit me, however to thank you most gratefully—you and your good wife—for your sympathy, and your well-meant efforts to comfort me, by all the helps your belief afforded, in my severe affliction. But you see now that, longing only for the divine aid of my own forsaken Faith, how impossible it was." She held out her hand to the Rev. gentleman, who took it instantly in his own, bowed, and taking up his hat, withdrew. Not that he felt he had nothing to say, by any means; he could have piled up arguments, and opinions, and perverted theological doctrines from saintly Fathers, and great councils, enough to have overwhelmed any ordinary person; but in the face of such a firm, positive avowal of faith, he saw that it would be simply a waste of time to attempt it. "And, after all," he thought, "she has—like the sow—only returned to the mire of the corruptions of the Romish Church; she has never in truth been one of us, 'she is joined to her idols,' and there's nothing to do but to 'leave her alone.'"

Captain Brandt was furious with everybody, and swore roundly. "Hadn't every ship a right to tack round to catch the wind, why shouldn't Mrs. Morley if she had a mind to? Whose business was it? Was she an American, or a Russian; had she freedom of conscience or had she not? And he ended by telling his wife that if he heard another word of it under his own roof, he'd go straight over to Catholicity himself." Then he marched off to pay Mrs. Morley and 'Beth a visit, just as if nothing had happened, determined that they should not know from him that he had heard a word. But he told Mrs. Brandt when he went home that Mrs. Morley was looking more like herself than he had seen her since poor Arthur died, not that the sorrow had gone out of her face, but there was something, he could not tell what, "that seemed somehow to brighten it—you know, wife—like light on the edge of a cloud. I've seen it a thousand of times at sea, when I've been looking out for squalls. Well, *that* was in her face along with the cloud, and she was going over 'Beth's French lesson with her, and told me that 'Beth's teacher came now on regular days to give her music lessons. So if turning Catholic is any sign of derangement, she takes a mighty sensible way of showing it." It was a nine day's wonder—Mrs. Morleys perversion, as they called it—then something else, more racy and satisfying to gossipping, scandal-loving human nature, arose on the social horizon, which cast it quite in the shade. People still called and left cards; the position of the Morley's could not be ignored by society; it was only a few sanctimonious members of Mr. Haller's congregation, who were formerly most assiduous in their attentions, who now pursed up their lips, and with uprolled eyes, announced that they could have nothing more to do with them. But Mrs. Morley, pursuing the even tenor of her way, her sorrow consecrated by penitence, gave no thought to what might or might not be the opinion of former friends and acquaintances—not from pride or arrogance on her part, but because she now had aims and hopes, in contrast to which all else was as nothingness.

CHAPTER XII.

WHAT 'BETH PROMISED.

'Beth did not go to Mass with her mother, as she had asked permission to do, on the morning that Mrs. Morley received Holy Communion. She shrank from it somehow, dreading, she knew not what; and when her mother awakened her very early to get ready, she said: "I think I won't go, mamma, unless you wish it very much."

"Very well, my 'Beth, I'll take you in my heart this morning; by-and-by, you'll come with me, wont you?"

"Oh yes indeed, mamma!" answered 'Beth, already repenting her determination, and half inclined even then to spring up and go, but Mrs. Morley was already down stairs, and hearing the hall door close, she knew it was too late. Then she buried her face in the pillow, and had a soft little cry to herself, fearing that her mother might take her action as not altogether kind, and feel that she was setting herself up against her being a Catholic. "No, no! she must never think that," she murmured; "for I, of all creatures, would be the last to deprive her of the slightest comfort."

After breakfast, when Andrew had arranged the room, and taken himself to the kitchen to enjoy his own comfortable meal, 'Beth went, and leaning over her mother's shoulder, whispered: "You are not displeased with me I hope, dear mamma!"

"No, no, my darling," said Mrs. Morley, who had remained almost silent during breakfast; "I believe I have been very quiet, but what I have done this morning has made me so, for the Holy Communion, as Catholics receive it, is not a symbol, as in other churches."

"What is it then, dear mamma?" asked 'Beth, and drawing a chair to her mother's side with a look of inquiry in her eyes—so like her father's— she waited the answer.

"It is really and substantially the Body and Blood, Soul and Divinity of our Lord Jesus Christ Himself, which He gives us, becoming at once our food and guest; a Sacrament which cannot be lightly received, lest we receive Him unworthily and to our own condemnation."

"How strange!" said 'Beth, "I do not understand it, mamma; it seems such a tremendous thing to believe! But let me go with you the next time?"

"Certainly, my child. To-day week—Friday— you shall accompany me," answered Mrs. Morley. She did not urge 'Beth to further inquiry by pursuing the subject, for in the deep humility of her spirit, she felt herself unworthy of teaching those divine truths which she had so long cast aside as not of any worth. She could only pray in deep penitence of heart for her child, and offer her very life a willing sacrifice, if so Almighty God would accept it, for her return to the one and only true Fold, from which, through no fault of her own, she had so blindly wandered.

'Beth was up and dressed, and waiting for her mother, on the Friday morning that they were to go to Mass together. When she opened the door and found her ready, she smiled, and embracing her, they started at once. The silence, and the beautiful tints of the morning, the twittering of birds, and the sweet fragrance of new blooming flowers in the park, and the calm quiet—for the city was not yet astir—tended to tranquillize the mind, and dispel its distractions, leaving it more disposed for devotion, and a participation in those divine mysteries which awaited the faithful, who at this hour were crowding the Catholic churches of the metropolis. 'Beth thought it was the loveliest morning that had ever dawned upon earth, and wondered if the roses over her father's grave were not all a-bloom and sparkling with dew. The thought of him was also in her mother's heart, though in a different light, which, at present, 'Beth could not realize, but by-and-by would not only come to understand, but also to share. Everything about the church seemed strange to her. Soon after they were seated, the acolytes and priest approached the altar, and the Holy Sacrifice began. She understood nothing that was done; she watched every movement of the officiating priest, and his white-robed attendants; she wondered why he held up the golden chalice so that all could see it, and what meant the bowing and the genuflections, and changing of the great book from the right to the left side of the altar. It was all a mystery to her, but she was moved by a something—she could not tell what—and felt more deeply impressed than ever before in her life. This is the experience of hundreds of Protestants, even the most careless, who say frankly: "I feel nowhere else such a strange awe as I do in a Catholic church, even when there's nothing going on. It always surprises me, and I wonder what it can be." It is useless to tell them that it is the abiding and Real Presence of Jesus Christ, there throned upon the altar, flowing out and making holy the very air they breathe, that so impresses them; they only smile incredulously, having no faith in the divine Mystery, and believing only such portion of the words which He uttered when giving it to the world, as they *think* they understand; while they "trample under foot" those others, which are indeed the spirit and the life.

When Mrs. Morley left the pew to approach the sanctuary railing, where all kneel to receive, nothing could equal 'Beth's surprise when she saw the throng that also went—their silent, devout aspect, the gravity and the serenity of each face, and the singular order of their going; rich and poor, negro and white, high and low together—there was no distinction there at the Table of the Lord, as she had seen elsewhere; and she thought that everyone must indeed believe what her mother had told her of this mysterious Sacrament. It made a strong impression on the girl's mind, and when her mother—having received—returned to her seat, she noted how almost transfigured her countenance appeared, in the humility and peace of its expression; tears filled her eyes, and she thanked God in her inmost soul that there was a faith in which her broken heart had found solace and peace. It did not matter to her in the least whether it was a true faith or not, it was enough for her to know that her mother believed it to be true, and had found comfort in it.

Something like resignation began to settle on Mrs. Morley's sorely-tried heart after this, and if at times, her loss stirred nature into occasional periods of grief, she was no longer comfortless, and knew whence to fly for solace, where, as in a place of refuge, grace and strength ever abounds.

(TO BE CONTINUED.)

Hymn "Vexilla Regis Prodeunt."

ORIGINAL, BY ST. VENANTIUS FORTUNATUS (530-609), BISHOP OF POICTIERS.

VEXILLA Regis prodeunt:
Fulget crucis mysterium.
Qua vita mortem pertulit,
Et morte vitam protulit,
Quae vulnerata lanceae
Mucrone diro, criminum
Ut nos lavaret sordibus,
Manavit unda et sanguine.
Impleta sunt, quae concinit
David fideli carmine,
Dicendo nationibus:
Regnavit a ligno Deus.
  Arbor decora et fulgida,
Ornata Regis purpura,
Electa digno stipite
Tam sancta membra tangere.
  Beata, cujus brachiis
Pretium pependit saeculi,
Statera facta corporis,
Tulitque praedam tartari.
  O Crux, ave, spes unica! *
Hoc Passionis tempore,
Piis adauge gratiam,
Reisque dele crimina.
  Te, fons salutis, Trinitas,
Collaudet omnis spiritus;
Quibus Crucis victoriam
Largiris, adde praemium. Amen.

TRANSLATION, BY DR. NEALE.

The royal banners forward go,
The cross shines forth with mystic glow;
Where He in flesh, our flesh He made,
Our sentence bore, our ransom paid.
  Where deep for us the spear was dyed,
Life's torrent rushing from His side;

---

* The last two stanzas are not by Fortunatus: they are of later date.

To wash us in the precious flood,
Where mingled water flowed and blood.
   Fulfilled is all that David told
In true prophetic song of old;
Amidst the nations, God, saith he,
Hath reigned and triumphed from the tree.

O tree of beauty, tree of light;
O tree with royal purple dight!
   Elect upon whose faithful breast
Those holy limbs should find their rest.

On whose dear arms so widely flung,
The weight of this world's ransom hung,
   The price of human kind to pay,
And spoil the spoiler of his prey!

O Cross, our one reliance, hail!
This holy Passiontide avail
   To give fresh merit to the saint,
And pardon to the penitent.

To Thee, eternal Three in One,
Let homage meet by all be done.
   Whom by the Cross Thou dost restore,
Preserve and govern evermore. Amen.

A Martyr to the Secret of Confession.

A Catholic paper published at Lemberg, Austrian Poland, relates the following remarkable fact: In the year 1853, Rt. Rev. Bishop Borowski, performed in the Catholic Cathedral at Shitomir, in Russian Wolhynin, the mournful ceremony of ecclesiastical degradation. All present, even the Bishop himself, were moved to tears. The unfortunate priest who was subjected to this awful humiliation, had always been known as one of the best of men, and was highly esteemed by all for his many virtues and his holiness of life. His name was Kobilowicz, and was curate of Oratow, in the Ukraine. He had been charged with the murder of a certain Government official. A shot-gun was found behind the main altar of the church, which, showing that it had been recently discharged, and belonging to the curate, served as convincing evidence against him. The unfortunate man, in spite of his protestations of innocence, was found guilty, and sentenced to servitude for life in the mines of Siberia, where he remained for twenty years. At the expiration of this time, the organist of the Oratow parish declared upon his death-bed, in presence of a deputy judge and a large number of inhabitants, that the priest was innocent, and that he himself was the murderer of the Government steward, whose widow he desired to marry. He said that he had taken the priest's shot-gun, and hid it behind the altar, showing it afterwards to the prosecuting attorney, before whom he denounced the priest as the assassin; yet seeing the worthy man arrested, he visited him in his dungeon and confessed his crime. Thus whilst the lips of the priest were sealed even as in death, by virtue of the Sacrament, the unfortunate culprit had not the courage to man open avowal of his crime. The priest, by a single word, might have delivered himself from this grave accusation, but he preferred to suffer a punishment even worse than death itself rather than betray the secret confided to him in the holy tribunal of penance. All he would do, was simply to avow his innocence.

In consequence of the organist's revelation, orders were immediately sent to Siberia for the release of the courageous priest. But the holy martyr had already passed to his eternal reward, having faithfully preserved his secret until the hour of his death, when he delivered it inviolate into the hands of his Supreme Judge. Well may be said of him what the Church sings in her office on the feasts of holy martyrs: Beatus vir qui suffert tentationem, quoniam cum probatus fuerit, accipiet coronam vitæ, quam repromisit Deus diligentibus se. (James, 1–12.)

Why did Our Saviour Prefer the Death of the Cross?

SEVERAL reasons are assigned by the Fathers of the Church as to why our Saviour chose the death of the Cross: 1st; To take away all fear of death from Christians. Many do not fear death in general, yet nature invariably shrinks from particular kinds of death. Now, as the death of the cross was the most painful and humiliating that could be borne, our Lord did not hesitate to adopt it as an example of most sublime heroism. 2d; To show the peculiar type of original sin. Adam violated the direct command of God in eating the fruit of the forbidden tree. In atonement for this disobedience, and for all the sins of the world, we behold the second Adam, the blessed Fruit of the Immaculate Virgin, a spectacle for men and agels, hanging on the tree of shame. 3d; To signify the entirety of Redemption. The four corners of the cross are a type of the four quarters of the heavens. 4th; To manifest our reconciliation with Heaven: the Mediator 'twixt God and man being suspended between Heaven and earth. 5th; To purify all creation. The earth, stained by sin, has been sprinkled with the blood of a God made man; the air received his hallowed breath and His ardent sighs of prayer. 6th. To prove the truth of the words spoken by our Lord: "And I, if I be lifted up from the earth, will draw all things to Myself." (John xii. 32.)

The Apparitions at Knock.

(CONTINUED.)

EVIDENCE OF THE POLICE. ANOTHER INTERVIEW WITH THE PARISH PRIEST. THE PILGRIMS.

From "The Dublin Weekly News" of Feb. 28.

After leaving the Knock Female National School on the day of my first interview with Miss Anderson and Miss Kennedy, the teachers, I proceeded to the police-barracks, which stands on the right-hand side of the Claremorris road, about a furlong distant from the village. I entered the barrack and inquired for Mr. Fraher and Mr. Collins. Both happened to be in at the time. They received me very politely, and, as soon as they learned the purpose of my visit, declared themselves ready to tell me all they knew. I seated myself on a form at the table in the centre of the dayroom, while the sergeant of the station and several of the sub-constables stood around. I first addressed my questions to Sub-Constable Edmund Fraher, a young man of about five or six and twenty, of middle stature, pale, good-looking, without a beard, but wearing a small moustache. The expression of his countenance is resolute and calm, and his manner is deliberate and quiet.

I am informed, Mr. Fraher, that you saw strange appearances on the gable of the chapel of Knock on the night of the 5th of January.

I did; on the night of the 5th, or morning of the 6th. Past midnight?

Yes.

How did you come to be at the chapel so late that night?

Sub-Constable Collins and I were out together on duty. It was just about twelve o'clock when we reached the chapel. As we passed it by on the road, we heard the voices of people praying aloud, not in the chapel, but outside it, near the gable. We went in to find the cause of the people being there. At first we saw nothing particular. After five or ten minutes I observed a row of lights extending across the wall of the gable.

Were they bright?

No: they were dim, and of a whitish color.

What shape were they?

They were shaped like a sort of circle.

Now, as to the size: were they as large, say, as the crown of this hat? [The hat was the same I had pointed out to Miss Anderson.]

No: they were about half as large.

Did these lights move?

No.

Did you observe anything else?

I saw other and brighter lights appear suddenly on different parts of the wall. One of them would shine out, dash along the wall, and disappear. Then, after two or three minutes, another would come in a different part of the wall, and it would disappear in like manner.

Did you see any appearances like stars?

No.

Or anything like a statue or human figure?

No.

How long did you remain near the chapel?

About an hour.

That is, you arrived there about twelve o'clock, and left the place about one?

Yes.

Now, did the lights you saw—the roundish dim lights and the brighter flashing ones—seem to you as if they were cast upon the wall by any contrivance—say by a person operating from behind a wall or hedge?

They did not look at all like anything of that kind.

Can you suggest or imagine any natural cause to account for the appearances you have described?

I cannot.

How many persons were present outside the gable when you were?

About fourteen.

I next addressed myself to Sub-Constable Bernard Collins, a bearded, brown-complexioned, soldierly-looking man of about thirty, and he proceeded at once to tell his story:

Sub-Constable Fraher and I were passing by the chapel on the night of the 5th of January, and we went into the chapel yard, as he has told you. The time was then about three minutes to twelve. At first I saw nothing of an extraordinary nature, but after a few minutes I noticed a row of lights of a round appearance, across the whole breadth of the the gable nearly, about a yard under the window.

About what size were they?

About as large as the bull's eyes that are painted on targets. [This answer was given after a little reflection.] These lights used to fade out almost entirely, and then slowly brighten again, and this happened a number of times. I also saw bright flashing lights at each side of the gable window. These used to come and go like flashes, and they were almost continual.

Did you see anything else?

Yes; I saw one star, at the east upper corner of the gable. It remained some time, and then it vanished suddenly. It was small and very brilliant—dazzling.

Was this star much brighter than the flashes you describe?

It was.

And the flashes—were they brighter than the row of lights that used to fade and appear again without any change of position?

Yes, they were.

Then, as I understand you, there were in the whole appearance three different sorts of light—three quite distinct degrees of brightness?

Yes.

Were any of the appearances that you saw lower down upon the gable than the level of the people's heads?

No: they were all above that level.

What sort of a night was it?

It was very dark and wet; there was thick, heavy cutting rain.

How does the gable look in rainy weather?

It looks very dark; I may say it looks black in rainy weather, at night.

Do you imagine that the appearances you saw could have been produced with a magic lantern, or any instrument of the sort, used by a person hidden somewhere about the place?

No, I do not imagine so. The lights were not like any light produced by such a means. Besides, I searched behind the schoolhouse wall, and behind the other walls and through the fields about. I searched the whole place as closely as if I was looking for a thief, and there was none to be found.

Did you come away about one o'clock with your comrade?

I did.

Now, can you compare the lights you saw with any lights familiar to our experience?

No: I could not compare them with any other lights I have ever seen. I cannot describe the difference.

In fact, they were indescribable?

They were.

Do you know of any remarkable cure that has been effected at Knock?

Yes: I know a man named Fergus Fallon. He had a pair of crutches, and he was unable to walk for sixteen years. He came here, and prayed at the chapel, and he was cured, and left the crutches after him.

And did he walk away?

He ran away!

I shall have occasion again to refer to the case of Fergus Fallon. I now submit to the public judgment the evidence placed on record respecting the Apparition on the night of the 5th of January. It will be needful to bear in mind that Miss Anderson and Miss Kennedy state they were about three hours before the gable, while the period covered by the visit of the subconstables of police is fixed by themselves as extending only from twelve to one o'clock.

I promised in my last letter to give some further details of my recent interview with the Archdeacon. Referring to the appearance of a dazzlingly brilliant star outside the gable of the church on the night of Thursday, the 12th of the present month, he informed me that among the persons who, together with himself, beheld it, were two nuns who had come to pay a visit to the church from their convent many miles away. The Archdeacon also told me that a few nights previously a star and an appearnce as if of a small statue had been seen at different times in two of the windows of the church. I may here explain that the windows in both the transepts are stained-glass, and there is a very small oval stained-glass window directly over the high altar. Within the sanctuary, on each side of the high altar, there is a red glass window, and all the remaining windows of the church are plain. I asked if the appearance just described had been seen in the windows of stained or colored glass, or in those that are of ordinary material. The Archdeacon replied that the statue and the star had appeared in two of the plain windows, and had been clearly visible to the people who were then inside the church. He further informed me that on one occasion, people praying outside the church at night, had seen a figure in one of the windows. It appeared as if coming up from the inside. Two ladies who were present at the time of the Apparition, described the figure as being crowned, and enveloped in a large loose cloak. Often, of late, in the course of the evenings, about eight or nine o'clock, a cloud of golden light had been seen upon the gable—both by the Archdeacon himself, and by many of the parishioners and visitors—and flashes, and stars of singular brilliancy, had sparkled and darted through the cloud. I observe that, as time goes on, and as the attention of numbers of people is more continually directed to the Church of Knock, and especially the gable identified with the 21st of August, the more do we hear of appearances that cannot be accounted for, except by recourse to the thought of the supernatural. The persons who tell of these appearances, and who solemnly declare that they saw with their own eyes what they describe, are numerous, respectable, and respected among their neighbors. They do not shirk any question from the most critical inquirer. They can be easily found any day by whoever desires to see them. Their answers are frank and civil, equally free from any trace of hesitation or of audacity; and the body of evidence represented by their united testimonies is such as no thoughtful man can disregard.

After the Archdeacon had described the appearances which I have just now recorded, I asked: Are there any cases of remarkable cures that you can call to mind at the present moment?

Yes, many of them; I shall mention one or two. A Cork girl, Bridget Mary Galvin, lately paid a visit here, and prayed to be restored to health. She was suffering from hip disease and weakness of the spine. She had been seven months a patient in a Dublin hospital, and five weeks in a hospital at Cork. Her family spent about £20 in feeing doctors. But all was of no avail. The disease was so acute, that she could not move at all without the help of a strait jacket. She came and prayed here as a last resource, and now she is quite recovered. There was also a very remarkable case of a little girl named Kate Cassidy, who was born here at Knock. She is about five years old. The child was about to take off her boots one night, and not being able to untie the knot on the string of one of them with her fingers, she endeavored to do so with a fork. While she was pulling at the fork, it came suddenly out of the knot with force, and the point penetrated her eye, rendering it quite useless, and the poor child suffered intensely. Her father got a letter from Mr. Strickland, of Loughlynn, to procure her admission as a patient to St. Mark's Ophthalmic Hospital in Dublin. I met him one day on his way to Knock with the child. He had Mr. Strickland's letter with him, and had not yet made use of it. He consulted me as to what he ought to do. I said to him, "As you did bring her here, continue your prayers for her; persevere for a little time, and see what the Mother of God will do." He acted on my advice. The child is now quite well. This happened about five weeks ago. You will find many other fully verified cases in my diary.

My next inquiry was directed to a matter which had often been in my thoughts since the day of my first visit to the place.

How do the people who come here from distant parts, in such large numbers, procure accommodation during their stay?

Some of them manage to get food and lodging in the houses in the village, or at some little distance. But, as you can see for yourself, there are few houses here, and as yet, no regular means of accommodation have been provided. I hope, indeed I expect, that this want will be very soon supplied. In the meantime I am obliged to keep open the church all night, owing to the great number of strangers who cannot procure any accommodation. They remain the whole night through, about the gable, or in the church, engaged in prayer. They join in the Rosary of the Blessed Virgin, and prepare themselves for Holy Communion. The devotion of the people is extraordinary. Their piety and fervor are such as I could not imagine to be exceeded. I hear confessions every evening, often remaining in the confessional till nine or ten o'clock.

At nine o'clock every morning we have Mass, and large numbers receive Holy Communion.

I presume you have a curate living at Knock?

No: the parish is very large. and Father Heany, my only curate, lives several miles away, at Aughamore.

Then I conclude that you perform the usual parochial work of this portion of your parish, as well as the special labors now laid upon you by the religious fame of Knock and the constant stream of visitors to the place?

Yes: besides the duty in the church, and meeting strangers who call upon me from day to day, I attend to sick calls, and the general spiritual wants of my own flock.

Then how is it possible for you to manage your correspondence? I can see by a glance at your table how extensive it has become.

It has become quite unmanageable. For a while I tried to answer every letter I received, but I have had to abandon the attempt. Letters come daily, from all parts, in such overwhelming numbers, that I can scarcely find time to glance at them, much less to give each one a reply. I have been obliged to write to the press, in order that the public may be made aware of this.

I shall publish what you say upon this subject as soon as I can; and when the public know of the extraordinary pressure on your time, I hope no one will be so unreasonable as to trouble you with a letter, unless upon urgent cause, or, at any rate, for very sufficient reason. I have heard that your church was wrecked by a storm some time ago.

Indeed it was. That happened about two years since, at the time of a violent storm. The slates and tiles were torn off and the windows were shattered; the altar, candlesticks and the pictures of the Stations of the Cross were destroyed, and the only statues in the church, those of the Blessed Virgin, St. Joseph, and St. Aloysius, were broken to pieces. To add to our misfortune, two statues that I ordered, were broken in transit to Knock. At last I got two statues safe from Lourdes. One of them is Our Blessed Lady; you have seen it on the left of the altar.

Before leaving the village, I went once more to visit the church. It was now a long time after dark. The thickness of the gloom rendered it no easy task to make one's way. The wind moaned and whistled dismally around the lonely church. Rain fell in torrents from a scarcely visible sky. Through the windows of the church there shone a light so faint that I doubt if it would be noticed except by an eye of keen inquiry. The doors stood open. I entered, and looked around. Motionless forms were to be seen on every side; some were seated on rows of benches on either side of the altar, immediately outside the sanctuary-railing. Others were kneeling in front of the altar. Others, apart, were almost prostrate; and little groups were praying together before the pictures of the Stations of the Cross. A solemn silence pervaded the dim interior. For a few moments I did not remember the special object of my visit. It was to obtain a view by night, of the spot above the altar, described by Archdeacon Cavanagh as that upon which he and others had seen three stars on the night of the 12th of the present month. This spot is a narrow strip of wall, extending across the sanctuary, between the top of the altar structure and the roof. In the centre is a very small stained-glass window. I now saw that the lights in the church at night-time were precisely such as had been stated to me by the Archdeacon in describing the appearance of the 12th; a dim red light from the sanctuary lamp; a faint white light from the lamp on the Blessed Virgin's altar; one candle within the sanctuary; and two or three others at points in the church where one person was reading a rosary or a litany, whilst a group around him joined in the responses. It may be said that these lamps and candles, faint and few, only made the darkness visible. The strip of wall above the altar is painted over, and by day it looks dark-green, but now it appeared as black as ink. I scrutinized it carefully for several minutes together, and had to conclude that the appearance of stars, described to me, can be just as little accounted for by any natural causes of which I have the least idea, as the previous Apparitions of the 21st of August and the 2d and 5th of January.

My next letter will be devoted to laying before your readers, a record of the names and addresses of persons cured at Knock, together with some particulars of the more remarkable cases, all supplied and certified by the parish priest.

DEPOSITIONS

Taken at the Catholic church of Knock, on the 8th of October, 1879, by the Very Rev. Bernard Cavanagh, Archdeacon, parish priest of Knock; the Very Rev. James Canon Waldron, P. P., Ballyhaunis; and the Very Rev. Ulick J. Canon Bourke, P. P., Claremorris—the commissioners appointed by his Grace the Archbishop of Tuam to hold an Investigation respecting the Apparition reported to have been seen at the Catholic church of Knock on the 21st of August, 1879, the Eve of the Octave of the Assumption:—

[CONCLUDED.]

Testimony of Mrs. Margaret Byrne:—

I, Margaret Byrne, wife of Dominick Byrne, of Knock, live near the chapel; I remember the evening of the 21st of August; I was called, at about half-past eight o'clock by my daughter Margaret, to see the vision of the Blessed Virgin Mary, and other saints, who appeared just then at the gable of the chapel at Knock; it was just dark; it was raining; I came with others to the wall opposite the gable; I saw distinctly the three images or likenesses of the Blessed Virgin Mary, of St. Joseph, and, as I thought or heard, of St. John the Evangelist; I saw an altar too, and a lamb somewhat whiter than the altar, but I did not see the cross; the Virgin Mary appeared in the attitude of prayer, with her eyes raised to heaven, a crown on her head; the image of St. Joseph appeared as just described by the others who have given testimony; [Witness did not hear the testimony, but she repeated it, and it coincides with all that already given]; I remained looking on for fifteen or twenty minutes, and then returned home.
her
MARGARET ✠ BYRNE.
mark

Testimony of Brigid Trench:—

My name is Brigid Trench; I live near the chapel of Knock; about seven o'clock on the night of the 21st of August I was in the house of Mrs. Campbell, which is quite near the chapel; while there, Mary Byrne came in and said there was a light to be seen at the chapel such as we never beheld, and told us to come to see it; I asked her what it was, and she said the Blessed Virgin, St. Joseph, and St. John were to be seen there; I went out immediately, and came to the spot indicated; when I arrived there, I saw distinctly the three figures, and threw myself on my knees and exclaimed, "A thousand thanks to God and the glorious Virgin, who have given us this manifestation!" I went immediately to kiss, as I thought, the feet of the Blessed Virgin; I felt nothing but the wall, and wondered why I could not feel with my hands the figures I had seen so plainly and distinctly; the three figures appeared like statues; they were standing against the southern gable of the chapel, about two feet from the ground; the figure of the Blessed Virgin was in the centre, clothed in white, and covered apparently with a white garment; her hands were raised in the position in which the priest is in the habit of holding his when celebrating Mass; I remarked distinctly the lower portions of her feet, and kissed them three times; she had something on her head resembling a crown, and her eyes were turned up to heaven; I was so taken with the Blessed Virgin I did not pay much attention to anything else, but I also saw the two other figures—St. Joseph standing to the right of the Blessed Virgin, with his head bent towards her and his hands joined, and the figure I took to be St. John was standing at her left; I heard those around me saying it was St. John; it was raining very heavily at the time, but no rain fell where the figures were; I felt the ground carefully with my hand, and it was perfectly dry; the wind was blowing from the south at the time, right against the gable of the chapel, but no rain fell on that portion of the chapel on which the figures were; there was no sign of life about the figures, and I could not say if they were alive or not; but they appeared to me so full and life-size, that I could not understand why I could not feel them with my hand; there was an extraordinary brightness about the whole gable-end of the chapel, and it was remarked by several who were passing on the road at the time; I remained there for about an hour, and when I came there first I thought I would never leave it, and would not have gone so soon but I thought the figures would remain there always; I was saying my beads while there, as I felt great delight and pleasure in looking at the Blessed Virgin; I could think of nothing else while there but giving thanks to God, and saying my prayers.

her
BRIGID ⋈ TRENCH.
mark.

Testimony of Patrick Byrne:—

I live quite near the chapel; I am sixteen years old; I remember the evening of the 21st of August, Thursday, the evening before the octave; Dominick Byrne, Junior, came to my house and said that he had seen the biggest sight he had ever witnessed; it was half-past eight o'clock; it was raining; I went with him to the gable of the chapel of Knock.

[This witness came in from the road to the west of the gable; and from it, as he was coming in to the area, he saw the figures as just described, distinctly and clearly, and has given testimony just in accordance with the other witnesses. He remained only ten minutes and went away. All occurred between half-past eight and nine o'clock.]

Testimony of Patrick Walsh, aged 65 years:—

My name is Patrick Walsh; I live in Balindurls, an English mile from the chapel of Knock; I remember the 21st of August, 1879; it was a very dark night and raining very heavily; about nine o'clock I was going on some business through my land, and about a half a mile from the chapel I saw a very bright light on the southern gable-end of the chapel; it appeared to be a large globe of most brilliant light; I never saw so brilliant a light before; it appeared high up, and was circular in its appearance; it remained quite stationary, and retained the same brilliancy; all through the following day I made inquiries to know if there was any bright light in the place that night, and it was then I heard of the vision.

Testimony of Catharine Murray, granddaughter of Mrs. Berin, aged eight years and six months:—

I saw the Blessed Virgin Mary and St. Joseph and St. John, or what was told me was the likeness of St. John; I saw the altar; saw this for fully twenty minutes.

Testimony of John Curry, a young boy between five and six years old. He testifies to the same as the others.

Testimony of Judy Campbell:—

Mary Byrne called at my house after eight o'clock, p. m., and asked me to come and see the great sight at the chapel. I ran up and saw the three figures, representing St. Joseph, St. John, and the Blessed Virgin, and also an altar and the figure of a lamb, with a cross reclining on his back. I saw the most beautiful crown on the Blessed Virgin. The Blessed Virgin was in the centre, St. Joseph on the right hand of the Blessed Virgin; what I thought was the statue of St. John to the left, a book in his left hand, and his right hand raised with the first and second fingers closed, and as if he was preaching. The night was very wet and dark. There was a beautiful light shining around the statues. I went within a foot of them. None of us spoke to them. The reason why we believed that it was St. Joseph and St. John was that there were some years ago statues in the chapel representing St. Joseph and St. John. I beheld it half an hour. There were about twelve persons present who saw it. All the statues appeared dressed in white. St. John wore a mitre. The night was rainy, but where the statues were was quite dry. JUDY CAMPBELL.

Testimony of Margaret Byrne:—

I went to close the chapel door about 7.30 o'clock p. m.; on my return I saw something white at the south gable, but passed no notice at the time; my niece, Catharine Murray, about eight o'clock called me to see the Blessed Virgin and other saints that were standing at the gable of the chapel; I went up, and there beheld the Blessed Virgin, with a bright crown on her head; St. Joseph on her right hand, his head inclined towards her; and St. John on her left, with a book in his left hand, and his right raised, as if preaching or reading out of the book; the Virgin appeared with uplifted hands, as if in prayer, and her eyes raised up towards heaven; I saw there an altar; it was surrounded by a bright light, as well as were all the statues; it was pitch dark and raining heavily, and still there was not one drop of rain near the images; there was a mitre on St. John like what the Bishops wear; I was only there a quarter of an hour or so; there were five others present at the time I saw it; I remarked a beard of a greyish color on St. Joseph; all the figures seemed dressed in white; the Blessed Virgin had a white cloak on; the reason I knew St. John was, I saw a statue of him at Lecanvey chapel. MARGARET BYRNE.

Witnessed as the others.

Testimony of Dominick Byrne:—

My cousin, Dominick Byrne, came here about eight o'clock p. m., and called me to see the vision of the Blessed Virgin and other saints at the south-gable of the chapel; I went with him, and when we came to the the chapel we saw the image of the Blessed Virgin, with her hands uplifted, and her eyes turned up to heaven, as if in prayer, and dressed in a white cloak; to her right I saw St. Joseph, and to her left St. John, as the others told me; I also saw an altar there, and figures representing saints and angels traced or carved on the lower part of the altar; the night was dark and raining very hard, yet these images appeared as plain as the noonday sun. DOMINICK BYRNE.

All the depositions were duly witnessed by the clergymen conducting the inquiry.

Catholic Notes.

——ADDITIONAL SUMS FOR IRELAND.—T. F., $2; Stephen Buckley, $5.

——The death is reported of the venerable Father Gil, S. J., assistant of the Superior-General of the Society of Jesus. R. I. P.

——OUR LADY OF LOURDES.—The twenty-second anniversary of the Apparition at Lourdes was solemnly observed from the 14th of February to the 4th of March, the ceremonies terminating every evening with a sermon, followed by Benediction.

——NEW APPOINTMENTS.—A cable dispatch from Rome to the *New York Freeman's Journal* announces that the Holy Father has approved and named Rt. Rev. Bishop Heiss, of La Crosse, Wis., as coadjutor, with the right of succeeding, to the Archbishop of Milwaukee; and Very Rev. John A. Waterson, President of Mount St. Mary's College, Emmittsburg, Md., to be Bishop of Columbus, Ohio.

——NEW CONVENT AND SCHOOL AT JOHNSTOWN, PA.—The spacious and elegant convent and school buildings begun last summer by Rev. Father Gallagher, of Johnstown, Pa., are now completed and nicely fitted up. The whole structure is entirely free from debt, affording another instance of how much may be accomplished in a short time with limited means, when the zealous efforts of a pastor are seconded by a united and self-sacrificing flock.

——A GENEROUS OFFERING.—In response to an order of the French Episcopate for a collection to be taken up in the churches of their dioceses for the suffering poor of Ireland, Brother Irlide, Superior-General of the Christian Brothers, sent the sum of 2'000 francs to his Eminence Cardinal Guibert. This sum, hitherto kept on deposit, was a present of the city of Boston, in testimonial of the devotion manifested by the Brothers of the Christian Schools during the siege of Paris.

——THE ARCHBISHOP OF PARIS speaks as follows in his Lenten Pastoral on the question of education: "The education of children belongs by right to their parents, who are also allowed to confide this duty to others, and hence may select such teachers as share their own religious convictions. The Church does not condemn lay-teachers by any means, but looks upon religious teachers, exclusively living up to their calling, as giving a better guarantee." The Archbishop, in conclusion, calls upon the rulers of the state to respect the rights of parents over their children, and expresses the hope, that France will not allow herself to be deprived of her Christian liberty and faith.

——PARDON US AND SHOW THYSELF A MOTHER. —A French Capuchin Father has just published an excellent work entitled "Our Lady of Lourdes and the Immaculate Conception," in which he relates that in 1876, an image of Our Lady of Lourdes was fiendishly profaned at a public masquerade, held in Rio Janeiro the capital of Brazil. Monsignor de Lacerdo, Archbishop of that city, protested against this sacrilege in a pastoral letter, calling upon his flock at the same time to offer a golden chalice to the sanctuary of Lourdes, in reparation for the deed. On the 8th of December last, this chalice was taken to Lourdes by a Lazarist Father, and presented to the sanctuary. The foot of the chalice bears the following inscription: *Refugium peccatorum, da veniam nobis, et monstra te esse matrem.* "Refuge of Sinners, pardon us and show thyself a Mother."

——WORSE THAN AMERICAN POOR HOUSES.—The following advertisement was issued not long since from the mayor's office in a village of Rhenish Prussia. "*Eine arme Mannsperson*" (although meaning a *male pauper*, the expression, by a singular freak of German grammar, is put in the feminine gender) able to do some light work, will be given for board to the lowest bidder offering to *keep her*. Recompense to be paid from the '*Armenkasse*' (poor funds)" The *auction* was to have taken place on the 22d inst., at the mayor's office. Before being exiled from Germany, the little Sisters of the Poor took care of helpless paupers. Other now exiled female congregations took care of the orphans. Since the departure of these good religious from the fatherland, auctions of paupers and orphans for "their keep" have became of frequent occurrence.

——A NEEDY MISSION.—A zealous priest at the West requests us to make known to the charitable readers of THE AVE MARIA the great needs of a mission to which he has lately been appointed. He ministers to two others, but they are equally poor, and he is often in want of the common necessaries of life. The new mission, which covers an area of 1,000 square miles, contains only 20 Catholic families, but there are numerous apostates. He finds boys and girls from fifteen to nineteen years of age who have never been taught a word of the catechism. The little church is in a wretched condition; there is no bell to summon the people, no ciborium, no religious picture or statue, and only one old set of vestments. The chalice is unfit for use. Any contributions for this needy mission, however small, that may be sent in our care, will be promptly forwarded to the priest in charge.

——THE LATE MONSIG. RUSSELL.—The following passage in Cardinal Newman's *Apologia* derives a fresh and a sad interest at this moment, when the grave is hardly closed over the zealous ecclesiastic to whom it refers. "Dr. Russell," says his Eminence, "called upon me in passing through Oxford, in the summer of 1841, and I think I took him over some of the buildings of the University. He called again another summer on his way from Dublin to London. I do not remember that he said a word on the subject of religion on either occasion. He sent me at different times several letters. He was always gentle, mild, unobtrusive, uncontroversial. He let me alone." In a word, Monsignor Russell understoood the sensitive minds he had to deal with at Oxford, and did not drive them. He knew that a silent witness to truth is often ten times more telling than any amount of argument or invective. And the manner in which his hopes were realized ought to encourage all who are laboring for similar results in the same quiet but effectual way.

——A PETITION OF THE BOHEMIAN BISHOPS.— The Bohemian Bishops have drawn up a petition to the Austrian Minister of Public Instruction, protesting against the maintenance of the public-school laws, issued during the so-called progressive and liberal era, and asking for a re-establishment of denominational schools. Should their just demands remain unheeded by the Government, the Bishops of Bohemia and their brethren in the realm, will consider it their duty to refuse any assistance in the carrying out of these laws, and will call upon their people to send their children only to those schools where sound religious and moral instruction can be warranted. The time for such a petition has been most happily chosen. All men of positively religious principles, irrespective of nationality or creed, have become perfectly disgusted with a public-school system, which ten years of practical experience have proved to be a signal failure. There is now a conservative majority in both branches of the Austrian legislature; the liberal Minister von Streymeyer, who for years has kept up a silent and annoying *culturkampf*, has resigned and given place to the conservative Baron von Kriegsau, who some years ago was pensioned off by the progressive, or rather infidel, ministry. It is reported that the conservative legislators of all shades have resolved in their clubs to support the petition of the Bohemian Bishops.

—QUEEN MARGARITA.—Several Italian journals positively assert that Margarita, the young Queen of Italy, whose physical health has become much impaired since the attempt on King Humbert's life at Naples, is now in great danger of losing her reason. Like Charlotte, the unfortunate wife of Maximilian of Mexico, she imagines her life threatened even by her nearest friends and relatives. Moments of mental aberration are of frequent occurrence. Thus on one occasion, she wanted to drive to the senate and deliver a speech on the taxes of bread-stuffs. Not long since, the unfortunate Queen returning from a drive, and entering the city through the Porta Pia, ordered her coachman to halt, then alighted, and before any one of her attendants could prevent it, started on a run to the Quirinal Palace, scattering at the same time all the money she had in her possession on the pavement. Arrived at the palace, she is said to have run through the garden to the chapel, built at its farthest end, where she remained for a long time, until persuaded with the greatest difficulty to repair to her apartments. The King has called upon three of the most expert physicians for a consultation. The official papers at first endeavored to deny the report of the Queen's derangement, but its veracity is now established beyond doubt. If a virtuous and charitable princess, whose only crime was to have been betrothed for political motives to her first cousin is thus afflicted, what punishment may not the real perpetrators of the spoliation of St. Peter's patrimony expect?

—THE DISTRESS IN IRELAND.—In a recent letter to Rt. Rev. Bishop Dwenger, of Fort Wayne, acknowledging contributions for the relief of the suffering poor in Ireland, the Bishop of Kiliala says: "The town of Ballina, situated on the confines of the counties of Mayo and Sligo, contains a population of nearly 6,000 inhabitants. Of those, over 2,000 are at present in absolute destitution, without employment, without credit, and without any means of support besides what they can procure from the benevolence of others. This benevolence being of a local nature, and for some time overtaxed, is beginning to fail, and the destitution of those who were dependant on it has now become extreme. Most of the tenant-farmers, who live within four or five miles of the town, are very poor. They hold but small portions of inferior land, and hence, in the best times, they were on the brink of poverty. This year, the remnant of their potato crop—which was their principal support—is already consumed, and numbers of them now swell the mass of poverty that inundates the town."

The Bishop of Donegal writes: "I beg to acknowledge, with most sincere gratitude, the receipt of your lordship's kind letter, inclosing £50 for the relief of the destitute people of this diocese. Great as is their distress at present, it would have been much greater had not the kind-hearted people of America come so generously to their aid. We are daily receiving the strongest proof of their sympathy and munificent charity, for which I trust the God of charity will reward them a hundredfold. The poor sufferers are praying fervently for their generous benefactors. In order to keep this sacred duty continually before their mind, I have ordered public prayers every Sunday, in all the churches of the diocese, for the spiritual and temporal welfare of all who aid us in our present straits; and there could not be a stronger proof of the gratitude of the poor people than the fervor with which they offer these prayers...."

New Publications.

THE BROWN SCAPULAR OF MOUNT CARMEL: A Manual for the Use of the Members of the Confraternity of the Scapular and the Third Order of Our Lady of Mount Carmel. By the Rev. Father Pius, O. C. C., Prior of the Carmelite Monastery at Niagara Falls, Canada. 277 pp., 16mo, Price, in cloth, 50 cents. Sold by Fr. Pustet and Catholic booksellers generally.

This neat manual, we feel sure, will everywhere meet with a most cordial welcome, which it certainly deserves. A book specially devoted to the Confraternity of the Scapular, it will find the clients of our Blessed Lady in every hamlet—nay, in almost every Catholic household. The book itself is admirably arranged; everything referring to the Scapular of Mt. Carmel is given in a condensed form, so that the Rev. clergy, and lay members of the Confraternity, have in it a handy medium of reference for the reception and instruction of members, the Indulgences to be gained by them, and the special devotions of the Confraternity. The manual contains a Calendar or Directory of the Saints of the Order for every day in the year; an excellent History of the Order, compiled from the most approved sources; the Rules of the Third Order; the Little Office of the Blessed Virgin, According to the Rite of the Order of Mt. Carmel (the same as the Little Office in common use), and Prayers for Mass. We hope that before the second edition of this excellent little work is published, the learned compiler will have it revised by some one familiar with our peculiar English idioms.

THE CHURCH OF THE PARABLES AND TRUE SPOUSE OF THE SUFFERING SAVIOUR. By Joseph Prachensky, Priest of the Society of Jesus. New York: The Catholic Publication Society Co., No 9 Barclay St.

Taking the several parables of the Good Samaritan, the Good Seed and the Cockle, the Mustard Seed, the Leaven, the Treasure in the Field, the Pearls, the Net, the Scribe, the Pharisee and the Publican, the Prodigal Son, and the Marriage Feast—the author proceeds to show that the Catholic Church is the Church of the Bible. These parables constitute the first part of the work. The second part consists of two chapters on the Church, the True Spouse of Christ. With respect to style and language, the author says in the introduction, that he has endeavored to write so plainly and simply that even the illiterate may understand.

LAST JOURNEY AND MEMORIALS OF THE REDEEMER; or, Via Crucis as it is in Jerusalem. With Topographical, Archæological, Historical, Traditional, and Scriptural Notes. By Rev. J. J. Begel, Pilgrim to the Holy Places. With Numerous Engravings. The Catholic Publication Society Co., No. 9 Barclay St. New York:

This work contains much that will satisfy the pious curiosity of the devout reader, in regard to the locality and instruments of the Passion of our Lord. It was evidently a labor of love for the Rev. author, to attempt a reproduction of his impressions in the Holy Places for the benefit of others.

—— *The Catholic Children's Magazine* is the title of an attractive little periodical for the amusement and instruction of little folks, published by Messrs. Duffy & Co., of Dublin. It contains thirteen pages, and is issued monthly. The price is extremely low, considering the excellent dress, being only a penny a number. The illustrations, of which there are several in each issue, are very fair, and the reading matter is both interesting and varied. The editor seems to know just what will be likely to please children, and always keeps to their level. The number for March, which has just come to hand, contains a hymn to St. Joseph, set to music, and other seasonable pieces. We hope that this little magazine will obtain a wide circulation.

RECEIVED:—The Life of Our Lord and Saviour Jesus Christ, and of His Blessed Mother. From the Original of Rev. L. C. Businger, by Rev. Richard Brennan, LL. D.; etc., etc.

Mixed Marriages.

[CORRESPONDENCE.]

EDITOR OF "THE AVE MARIA":—I have noticed with great pleasure the efforts you have made, from time to time, to discourage the evil of mixed marriages among Catholics. It seems to me there is great apathy on this subject among our people generally, and it has occurred to me that it would be an excellent plan for you to gather facts and statistics calculated to throw light on the question of the effect of mixed marriages as illustrated in practice. Nothing tells like facts. With this view, I have taken pains to gather the statistics, on that subject, in the New England village where I live. I knew there were a number of leading families among us, in which the husband or wife was once a Catholic, but until I commenced my inquiries, I had no conception of the real facts of the case. I confess I have been astounded by the result. The population of our village is estimated at about 4,000, of whom 1,000 are Catholics, mostly Irish, but a few French. I have counted nineteen families in which the husband or wife was once a Catholic, but by marrying Protestants have, in every case except one, fallen away both from the profession and the practice of their religion. Of these, four are husbands, the rest wives. Of the husbands, two are French, one German, and one Irish. Of the wives, one is French, all the others Irish. In one case the mother has fallen with the daughters. These families are of various states and conditions in life, from the reputed millionaire to the laborer; but fully one-half are of what is called the more respectable class. Some of them go to the Protestant church, and send their children to Protestant Sunday-schools, whilst others, I believe, never darken a church door of any kind, and, as far as religion is concerned, are little better than pagans. *In not one single instance do I find the Catholic converting the Protestant;* and though, in some cases, there seems to have been a conversion of the Catholic to some phase of Protestantism, yet I have good reason to believe that in most, if not all, cases there has been no real change of faith, but simply an external conformity, through a weak compliance with the wishes of the Protestant partner. They have sold their birthright for a mess of pottage.

I would fain persuade myself our case is an exceptional one; but I fear a similar investigation in other places, especially in our large cities, would reveal a state of facts even more deplorable than those here made public. I am aware that the Protestant partner is sometimes converted by the faithful Catholic; but such cases are certainly the exception. It is hardly too much to say that mixed marriages are an unmixed evil. It is dangerous ground to tread upon. The Catholic who values his salvation above every other consideration, will be very slow to enter upon it.

FIDELIS.

Obituary.

THE LATE FATHER CHAMPEAU, C. S. C.

Neuilly-sur-Seine has lately experienced a great affliction. Its Christian families had the sorrowful duty yesterday of consigning to their last resting place the earthly remains of Rev. Father Louis Dominic Champeau, First Assistant General of the Congregation of Holy Cross, and President of the College of Our Lady of Holy Cross at Neuilly, who fell asleep in the peace of the Lord on Saturday last, at the age of sixty-two years. It may also be said that this good priest sleeps surrounded with the affectionate regret of his religious brethren, of his dear pupils, and of all the families who had entrusted to his ripe wisdom and great knowledge the education of their children.

Rev. Father Champeau was successively a college President at Mans, Nevers, and Orleans. Afterwards he came to Paris to establish in the *Quartier des Ternes* the noble Institution of Holy Cross, which he afterwards transformed into a college, and removed to Neuilly-sur-Seine, a situation most delightful in every respect. In the difficult position which he occupied, he invariably displayed the dignity of the priest, the consummate prudence of the skilful administrator, and the ripe wisdom of the Christian teacher. In him, zeal and prudence were harmoniously blended, and this union gave his authority a charm which words cannot describe.

All Christian hearts will be the more inclined to share the grief of the religious families of Neuilly-sur-Seine, of which we are but the feeble echo, when they learn that the last great act of Father Champeau's life, was to receive into his college the Christian Brothers, who had been expelled by the radical administration, which reigns at Neuilly as well as at Paris. And while the three hundred students continued their studies without interruption, Rev. Father Champeau managed to make sufficient room in his establishment to allow the Brothers to give instructions daily to more than three hundred children, until the generosity of the friends of religious education can open for them the admirable free school of which they have been put in charge.

After a life such devotedness, God will certainly receive into His bosom a just man, who, like Rev. Father Champeau, lived only for the glory of His name. *Requiescant in pace.—Louis Leclerc in L' Universe.*

Confraternity of the Immaculate Conception
(Or of Our Lady of Lourdes).

"We fly to thy patronage, O Holy Mother of God!"

REPORT FOR THE WEEK ENDING MARCH 17TH.

The following petitions have been received: Recovery of health for 115 persons and 3 families,—change of life for 53 persons and 4 families,—conversion to the Faith for 55 persons and 5 families,—special graces for 10 priests, 6 religious, 3 clerical students, and 7 persons aspiring to the religious state,—temporal favors for 29 persons and 6 families,—spiritual favors for 77 persons and 8 families,—the spiritual and temporal welfare of 9 communities, 7 congregations, 6 schools, 1 hospital, and 3 orphan asylums,—also, 37 particular intentions, and five thanksgivings for favors received.

Specified intentions: Opportunity for several Catholic parents to live near a church, and for their children to receive a Catholic education,—grace for several young persons of both sexes to know their vocation,—peace and harmony in several families,—removal of obstacles to a religious vocation,—a poor man afflicted with epilepsy,—several persons who are ruining themselves by intemperance,—a priest for a certain mission in the South,—some children baptized in the Church, but now separated from it,—the conversion of a young lady dying of consumption,—the conversion of a worthy Protestant gentleman,—the needs of a very poor mother.

FAVORS OBTAINED.

A Christian mother writes: "My son who was so disobedient, has shown himself very submissive and amiable since he was recommended to the prayers of the Confraternity, and I have been entirely relieved of my nervous prostration." Another lady says: "The water of Lourdes has cured me of a sick headache, which had troubled me for years, so much so, that I often feared I would become entirely deranged. My husband gave me three drops of the miraculous water, and in less than five miuntes I was as well as ever. It has also cured my child of a a severe earache of long standing. Some of the water was given to a friend for his sister, who was deranged; a novena was said, and a complete cure was effected. A Mass of thanksgiving has been said in our little church. "Another remarkable case has been reported of a young man, eighteen years old, about to have his leg amputated, made use of the water; and before the close of a novena was as well as ever.

OBITUARY.

The following deceased persons are recommended to the prayers of the Confraternity: SISTER MARY ALOYSIA, a devoted member of the Community of the Sisters of Notre Dame, at San José, Cal., who slept in the Lord on the 31st of January, in the sixty-second year of her age and the forty-second of her religious profession.

SISTER MARY AGNES (Donnelly), who went to her reward on the 10th of Febuary, and SISTER MARY BORGIA (Dent), who departed for heaven on the 11th inst. Both were devoted members of the Community of the Visitation at Frederick, Md. Mrs. MARGARITA BREDEL, whose death took place on the 7th ult, in Germany. Mr. DEAN PIERRE, of Milton, Mass., a convert on his death-bed, who departed this life on the 13th of January. Mr. JOHN A CHRISTY, deceased at Oil City, Pa., on the 13th ult. Mrs. L. C. O'REILLY, whose exemplary life was crowned by a holy death on the 15th of February, at Pittsburg, Pa. Miss MARY O'HALLERON, of Oakland, Cal., an estimable young lady, who died a precious death on the 6th inst. Dr. L. TRIGANT DE BEAUMONT, who breathed his last on the 20th ult. Mrs. E. DRYDEN, of Martinez, Cal, who was killed by an accident on the 1st of February. Miss LIZZIE ROACH, aged 19 years, whose death occurred on the 16th of Feb. Mr. JOHN B. MCCONNELL, of Philadelphia, Pa.; Miss RACHAEL TOMLINSON, of Loretto, Pa.; Mrs. MARGARET DOYLE, of Bellewood, Minn.; Miss JANE AGNES HYATT, of Washington, Ind.; Mr. CHARLES MCINTYRE, of New York city, and Mr. MICHAEL CASEY, of Boston, Mass., who died recently. Mr. P. H. O'CONNOR, of Sonoma, Cal.; Mrs. B. HAYDEN, of Bardstown, Ky.; Miss ROSE ANN and Mr. MICHAEL HARKINS, of Stockton, Cal.; JOHN MARR, JOHANNA MARR, MARY SULLIVAN, MARY FEENEY, CATHARINE DWYER, PETER KEATING, JOHN FRITZ, PATRICK and JAMES FARRELL, THOMAS FLANIGAN, MICHAEL FITZPATRICK, and Mr. JOHN COFFEY, Mrs. BUTTERLY, and MR. MACHIEL, who died some time ago. And several others, whose names have not been given.

Requiescant in pace.

A. GRANGER, C. S. C., Director.

For the Rebuilding of Notre Dame.

Miss E. Lamb, $1; Mrs. James Foley, 50 cts.; Jane O'Neill, $1.50; William Hughes, $5; Mr. James Devlin, $2; Mrs. D. Sheerin, $1.50; Rev. Father Strub, C. SS. P., $2; Mary Murphy, $1; Mrs. Mary Mudd, 45 cts.; Miss Mary Brunk, 50 cts.; Nellie Jarboe, 50 cts.; Miss E. Doyle, $1; Mrs. A. Fitzgerald, $1; G. A. Tobin, $1; Mrs. Rosanna McNamee, $1; Mrs. E. C. McCallion, $1; Miss Ellie McCallion, $1; Miss Annie Devenny, $2; Mrs. Ellen Reynolds, $1; Mr. Richard McCallion, $1; Mrs. Richard McCallion, $1; Mrs. Catharine Hookey, $1; Mrs. Mary Cleary, $2; Miss K. Slint, 50 cts.; Bet. Lennon, $1; Mrs. Anna Fortime, $1; Miss Annie McEnbill, 50 cts.; John Widden, $1; John, Mary, James, William, John jr., and Mary Cleary, $4; James and Catharine Fitzgerald, $4; Margaret Lawlor, $5; Michael Delany, $1; Charles Delany, $1; John Wheelan, $1; Ellie Prendergast, $1; Rosanna Adlaid, $1; Mrs. A. G. May, $2; Mr. Z. Ruffis and family, $1; Mrs. Deveaux, $2; Through Mrs. Ellen Mass, $15; Amelia Clark, 50 cts.; Bridget Donaghue, $1; Mr. John Hanley, $2.

BY prayer alone is to be obtained courage, protection, fortitude, magnanimity, and endurance in suffering and adversities.—*Rev. Fr. Müller, C. SS. R.*

Youth's Department.

The Foot of the Cross.

BY EVA.

"Now there stood by the Cross of Jesus His Mother."

HE stood: beneath His Sacred Cross
When all was wrapt in gloom,
While earthquakes rent the hardest rocks
And woke the silent tomb.

She stood: as mother never stood,
To see her first-born die,
Her tears were mingled with His Blood,
While hours three went by.

She stood: while from His Sacred Wounds
The purple life-Blood flows;
No passing fit of fainting gives
The Mother's heart repose.

She stood: though anguish rent her soul,
When all she loved most dear
Was given gall to quench His thirst:
No moan escaped her here.

But yet she stood:—with heart transfixed—
A soldier drawing near,
With trembling hand pierced through the Heart
Of Him she loved most dear.

She stood: with meek majestic mien,
While scoffing Jews deride;
A model for those faithful souls
Who love the Crucified.

THE FIRST PRINTED BOOK.—The first printed book known is the celebrated Mazarin Bible in two folio volumes. It was so called from the discovery of a copy in the library of Cardinal Mazarin, at Paris, about the middle of the last century, since which time seventeen other copies have been found in various parts of Europe; of these, nine are in public, and nine in private libraries. It has no date, but at the end of each volume of the copy in the Royal Library at Paris, is an inscription in red ink. That in the second volume is as follow: "This book, illuminated and bound by Henry Cremer, Vicar of the Collegiate Church of St. Stephen at Mentz, was completed on the Feast of the Assumption, A. D. 1456. Thanks be to God. Halleluiah."

The History of a Conversion.

HERE resided, some years ago, at W——, England, a naval captain with his family, whom we shall introduce to our readers under the name of Hopkins. He had an only child, a daughter, about seventeen or eighteen years old. Having heard a great deal about "Romanism," Selina determined on seeing for herself, and was led one Sunday to enter a small Catholic church at R——, dedicated to St. Augustine. She went there merely for the purpose of seeing and mocking; but as she afterwards remarked, she observed such apparent devotion in the worshippers, especially at the solemn and awful moment of the elevation, that she was completely awe-stricken. She went again and again, and at last called on the aged missionary who had charge of the congregation.

After two or three interviews with the Benedictine Father, she placed herself under instruction, and was about to become a member of Holy Church, when it pleased God to afflict his penitent child with a severe illness. Her life was despaired of. Father D——, on hearing this, called at her father's residence, and was thus accosted by the Captain: "No popish priest shall enter my door. My poor Selina is now dying in consequence of your cursed humbug, so, leave my house immediately; and I give you this notice, that I will shoot you, or any of your crew, that ever dares to cross the threshold of my door. No child of mine, living or dying, shall ever become a Papist. For that purpose I have purchased this brace of pistols, which I have loaded with the intention of shooting any priest that may come in my way. Leave my house immediately, or I will put you out!"

Poor Father D——, affrighted at this rude reception, left Captain Hopkins' house, praying for him and his dying child; and when he offered the Holy Sacrifice of the Mass he besought our gracious Redeemer to bring about the conversion of the family.

Three weeks had elapsed since his last attempt to see his neophyte, and fortify her with the sacraments, when he was informed by her medical attendant that she could not survive the night. What was he to do? Was he to allow a poor sinner to appear before her Judge unbaptized and unabsolved? In his perplexity, he turned towards her who is indeed the "Refuge of Sinners," and in the hour of need the "Consoler of the Afflicted." He knew that Jesus never refused a petition presented by His Mother, and to her he now turned for aid, and aid he found at the very last moment, when all was apparently lost.

It was the Feast of Our Lady of Snow (Aug. 5). He had said his Little Hours and was waiting for his humble repast, heart-sick at the thought of his young convert dying without the Sacraments, when a ring at the bell announced a visitor, and the card of a priest of a neighboring city, whom we shall call Father Henry, was handed to him. How warm would Father Henry's reception have been had Father Dunstan known that this good priest was to be the instrument selected by Providence to lead poor Selina into the Fold!

The stranger informed his venerable host that he had been sent by his superior to aid him in a mission.

Father Henry noticed, during their meal, that Father Dunstan seemed troubled, and on inquiring the reason, had the case of Miss Hopkins stated to him. "Will you," said he to Father Dunstan, "allow me to call on her?"

. "You would go to certain death, Father Henry. Captain Hopkins would certainly murder you."

"What matters it? I can die but once; and what cause more glorious to die for, than that of reconciling a dying penitent to her Saviour? Let me go, and in an hour from this Miss Hopkins will be a Catholic."

Father Henry changed his dress and proceeded to the house of Mr. Hopkins. On arriving, he inquired of the servant if Miss Hopkins were still living. Being answered in the affirmative, he requested permission to see her, and desired the footman to tell his master that he was a physician, and that having heard of Miss Hopkins' case, he had called to see her, fully believing that he could do her some good.*

He was admitted into the drawing-room, and soon was joined by her disconsolate parents. He expressed a wish to see the sick girl. "Oh, sir," said Mrs. Hopkins, "if you can be of any service to my poor, sick child, all we have shall be yours; her sufferings are extreme."

"Yes," interrupted her father: "Popery has caused it all; I am sorry I did not shoot that old hypocrite,—Father Dunstan, as they call him, when he came here the other day; but I have my pistols ready for him if he dares to come again. But he won't do that. It is all very well to talk of heaven and hell when there is no danger; but I am too well known, sir, in W——, for any man to dare oppose me."

"Let us not talk about religion, Captain; I wish

---
* Father Henry had practised as a doctor before becoming a priest.

to see your daughter and feel assured that I can relieve her." Father Henry, bearing in his bosom the true Physician of souls, was conducted to the dying girl's room, who seemed agitated on seeing a stranger, but was immediately calmed on his whispering, as he approached to feel her pulse, "I am a priest." Shortly after, on some slight pretext, he induced Mrs. Hopkins to leave the room. Being alone with his patient, he said: "Now, my child, there is no time to be lost, I will baptize you at once."

While Father Henry was administering the Sacrament of reconciliation to the dying girl, the door opened, and the curate of St. Mary's entered the room; but on perceiving the stoled priest standing by the bed, he instantly ran out, exclaiming: "A Popish priest is in the house, Captain Hopkins; come up stairs immediately!" The priest being thus interrupted, locked the door, and quietly proceeded to administer the last Sacraments. As he was about to give her the Holy Viaticum, the Captain came to the door, demanding admittance. "As soon," replied the priest, "as I have done my duty, sir, I will admit you." He then conferred on the dying girl the Sacrament of Extreme Unction.

After uttering the last words of the prayers appointed by the Church, he opened the door and stood prepared to receive the fatal bullet; for Captain Hopkins, followed by the Anglican curate, entered the room holding in his hands a brace of pistols, and exclaimed: "Sir, you are a Popish priest, and I have sworn to shoot the first priest that would dare to cross the threshold of my door."

"Are you aware, Captain, that I am quite prepared for death? But remember the probable consequences of your violence. It will assuredly hasten the death of your daughter, and you will then appear before your God guilty of a two-fold murder,—that of your own child, and of a stranger, who merely came to discharge a sacred duty. Fire if you will!"

But the arm of the infuriated man seemed paralyzed, and bursting into tears, he fell at the missionary's feet, and cried out: "I am now convinced that your religion is true, and I will, please God, become a Papist as soon as you think proper. I am certain that no person would have dared to act as you have done." Then, turning to the curate, "you may leave my house, for I am now resolved to become a Roman Catholic, when I shall have been instructed by this brave young clergyman. But stop; let me show you both that I was serious in my intention to kill. I now, Rev. Father, present you with these loaded pistols. Keep them as a memento of your triumph over one who, till to day, was a bitter enemy to your religion. Let people say what they may, I am now convinced that the Roman Church is the true one;

for no sect could have induced her ministers to act as you have done this day."

Miss Hopkins had the happiness, before her death, of seeing her parents received into the bosom of the Holy Catholic Church.

Death of a Devout Client of Mary among the Sioux Indians.

MARY LAURA SINANA, an Indian girl of the Sioux tribe, was born in the year 1866, on the northern prairie, in the vicinity of Turtle Mountain, Northern Dakota. When she was four years of age, lightning struck the tent in which the family were living, killing the mother instantly. When five years of age, her sister, in a fit of anger, threw the innocent little child to the ground with such violence, as to seriously injure her spine; thus it happened that her life was twice miraculously preserved by Divine Providence. She received, however, but little medical attendance, and remained a cripple up to the hour of her death. Sinana, her father, belongs to Devil's Lake Agency, which he makes his home when he is not farther north, hunting, in the vicinity of Turtle Mountain. In the fall of 1874, the Sisters of Charity—Gray Nuns from Montreal, Canada—arrived here and opened a boarding-school for the Indian children of both sexes; they succeeded in getting from Sinana his little girl, still a heathen. In the spring of 1875 he came to take her to his camp for a week, as he pretended; but before the expiration of that time, he decamped for his beloved hunting-grounds around Turtle Mountain, taking the child with him. After six months' absence, he returned, and the good Sisters again urged him to send the child to school. She was of a very amiable and innocent disposition, possessing none of the wild, rough ways of the other children of the tribe; she therefore hesitated to return to school, as she had not proper or sufficient clothing in which to present herself; however, she notified the Sisters by one of her aunts, that she would attend school with the greatest pleasure, provided they would call at her father's tent and furnish her with a suitable dress. Ever after she remained at the school; even during the vacation, she preferred to remain with the Sisters rather than spend the time with her relatives in the tribe.

Her father started for the hunting-ground in 1877, and has not since returned, though he is heard from occasionally. Besides her father, she has one brother, about sixteen years old, and two sisters; the younger one is about eighteen years of age and has been attending the mission school at the Agency for more than a year. She is very intelligent and religiously disposed, and received the Sacrament of Baptism on the 18th of April last year. The father, the brother, and the oldest sister are, unhappily, still heathens.

Mary Laura Sinana applied herself with a rare zeal to the practices of our holy religion, and to her great delight, was deemed worthy to receive the Sacrament of Baptism at the hands of Rev. Father Louis Bonin, on the 2d of April, 1866, being then in her 10th year. Major James McLaughlin, United States Indian Agent, and Mrs. McLaughlin acted as sponsors. So well did she correspond with the grace received, that she excelled all the children at school in virtue and piety. From the day of her baptism, she looked forward to that of her First Communion with an ardent desire; this happiness, however, was not granted to her till after long and severe trials. She, together with eight of her Indian schoolmates, made her First Communion on the Feast of St. Joseph, 1879, at the age of thirteen. How great her happiness was on that memorable day cannot be described. For months previous, but more particularly from that time till her death, she would not allow a single day to pass without saying her rosary. She cherished a most earnest and tender love towards the Mother of God, and on her feasts would always receive Holy Communion. While she was able to walk, she continued to visit the statue of the Blessed Virgin in the chapel, and recite her rosary there. On the three days previous to her death, she kept repeating, "Our Lady of the Sacred Heart, pray for me"; "Our Lady of Seven Dolors, pray for me."

Her love and faith towards Jesus in the Blessed Eucharist were truly edifying. She visited the Blessed Sacrament daily, and often more than once a day. During the past eight months, being unable to walk, she was carried on a chair, at a convenient hour of the day, and placed before the Blessed Sacrament. It was touching indeed to see her, her innocent eyes fixed on the tabernacle with looks of longing and adoration. In like manner would she gaze on the statue of the Blessed Virgin, and on the picture of Our Lady of Seven Dolors. Her greatest delight, however, was to visit our Lord in the Blessed Sacrament, and to receive Him into her spotless and innocent heart. The two months following her First Communion—April and May—she received the Holy Eucharist once a month; from June last year to February this year, she was permitted to receive every fortnight; andd uring the first week of last month—which was her last on earth—she received the Sacred Host three times, making a total of twenty-two Communions in less than eleven months. Truly, every one of her Communions was received with the same earnest feelings and worthy dispositions as her first one; which is, alas! but too seldom the case nowadays.

On Septuagesima Sunday, the 25th of January last, she attended high Mass for the last time, seated as usual in her chair. From that time her strength failed very rapidly. On February the 1st she made her confession, and on the day following, it being the Feast of the Purification, she received Holy Communion, as she was wont to on the feasts of the Blessed Virgin. During her long illness she always insisted on being carried to the chapel to make her confession and thanksgiving, and she likewise received in the chapel, seated on her chair. On the 2d inst., the Feast of the Purification, she received Holy Communion in her room—not as viaticum, however. She was so low that it was then deemed advisable to administer the Sacrament of Extreme Unction, which was accordingly done by the good missionary in presence of the Sisters and all the school-children. The sick child accompanied the ceremonies with fervent prayer. On the night of the 4th ult., the priest was called to her bedside at 11 o'clock, heard her confession and administered Holy Communion After these ceremonies, and the thanksgivings were completed, the good child expressed in a loud tone of voice how happy she felt, although she had not been able to utter a single loud word for many days previous. At five o'clock on the morning of the 6th, the day of her happy death, the good missionary again administered Holy Communion, which she received with an ardent desire and great piety, saying: "This will be my last Communion, Father!" and so it was; she expired at half-past three p. m., the priest, the Sisters, and the school-children, being present. She died at the moment these solemn words from the Litany of the Dying were pronounced, "Depart, Christian soul, out of this world!" On the following day a *Requiem* High Mass was sung for the repose of the departed. The funeral service took place at two o'clock p. m. Major and Mrs. McLaughlin together with the Agency employes, the Sisters, the school-children, and a large number of Indians were present. All had looked upon Mary Laura as almost a saint. May our lives be as pure, and death as consoling as hers! May the soul of the little Indian maiden rest in peace.

DEVIL'S LAKE AGENCY. M.

An Anecdote of Marshal Soult.

ON a certain day in the year 1830, a diligence, left the city of Paris for Marseilles, with three passengers—a priest, a young officer, and an old man with a gray beard. The priest soon occupied himself with the recitation of his breviary; the young officer passed the time in humming, and the old man was immersed in profound meditation. Finally, the young officer, tired of humming, and disposed to enjoy himself at the expense of the priest, began to assail him with sarcastic remarks on prayer, the Blessed Virgin, and similar subjects. The priest, at first, answered in a calm and dignified manner, but observing that the discussion was becoming heated, and fearing it might end in a breach of charity, he politely requested the officer to permit him to continue his devotions. His tormentor then began to sing an impious revolutionary song, but failing to disturb the good priest, he became even more insulting and abusive than before. The old man who had listened attentively, now broke silence, and reproving the officer, entreated him to have more regard for the glorious uniform he wore, and not disgrace it by such shameful and unbecoming conduct. The young officer received this reproof with scorn, and mockingly replied: "If you were not so old I would ask for your address, and seek satisfaction for your impudence at the point of the sword." The old man calmly handed him his card, upon which the astonished officer read, the honored and illustrious name of "Marshal Soult." Changing color and trembling with fear, he humbly sought pardon both from the marshal and the priest, which was generously accorded him. He had received a lesson, however, which he never forgot, and he always kept in mind the words which Marshal Soult addressed to him: "In my long career, which has not been without glory, I never repented having protected, defended, and respected the priest, the aged and the weak."

Eighteen years afterwards, in the sad and infamous days of 1848, in the suburb of St. Anthony, two victims gloriously gave up their lives: General Duvivier and Mons. Affre.—or the officer and the priest of the diligence of 1830—the one a martyr of duty, the other, of charity.

Kind words produce their own image on men's souls; and a beautiful image it is. They soothe, and quiet, and comfort the hearer.—*Pascal.*

THE

AVE MARIA.

A Journal devoted to the Honor of the Blessed Virgin.

HENCEFORTH ALL GENERATIONS SHALL CALL ME BLESSED.—St. Luke, i, 48.

VOL. XVI.   NOTRE DAME, INDIANA, APRIL 3, 1880.   NO. 14.

[For the "Ave Maria."]

Regina Cœli Lætare.

BY CHARLES KENT.

GREAT Queen of Heaven, rejoice,
Lo! He whom thou didst bear
Hath risen! Raise, then, thy voice
To God for us in prayer.

The Feast of the Annunciation of the Blessed Virgin Mary.

THE heat of the summer sun had scorched and parched the stony soil of the valleys and plains of Judea; naught of verdure was seen save on the feathery boughs of the palm-trees, or on the sombre foliage of the fig and the olive, or along the course of streamlets fed by unfailing springs; everywhere, over the yellow landscape, rested the cream-colored tints of the Syrian atmosphere. It was the hour of incense; and amid the throng of buyers and sellers—of the thoughtless ones, already weaned from the practices of religion—were groups of the piously-disposed hastening to the Temple to assist at the Sacred Offices. In the inner court of the Temple, Zachary, the priest, stood before the golden altar to offer to the Lord the sweet savor of the everlasting incense.* As the fragrant cloud rose heavenward, he beheld the radiant form of the Archangel Gabriel standing beside the altar. Overwhelmed with fear and doubt, Zachary listens to the message of heaven; and to his questioning reply, the angel gives an answer of rebuke, in which he pronounces a sentence of punishment. Zachary stood high in the sacerdotal order: higher authority than his did not exist among the children of Israel; but to him the angel appeared as a superior, and spoke as if speaking to a subaltern.

Six months later, the hills, the mountains, the valleys and the plains were again rejoiced in their garments of spring verdure; flowers were blooming by the brookside, and Cedron was again rushing through the valley of Josephat. This was the time of which the Scripture had spoken: "The winter is past, the rain is over and gone, the flowers have appeared, the voice of the turtle is heard in our land. Arise, my love, my beautiful one, and come." The midnight stars were looking down upon the little town of Nazareth, nestled on one of the hilly slopes of Galilee, when the voice of this invitation sounded in the ears of Mary: "Arise, my love, my dove, my beautiful one." And Mary arose, to pray until "the day should break and the shadows retire."* Thus the angel found her, sending up from her pure heart the sweet savor, the everlasting incense of fervent prayer. Gabriel was in the presence of Mary, the subject before his future Queen; he kneels, we may well believe. Thus many a Christian artist depicts him; and we, who learned to repeat his words beside our mother's knee, can never think of them as being first spoken in any but a most reverent posture. Though momentous was his embassy, Gabriel did not disclose it immediately as he did his message to Zachary, but he prefaced it with a most worshipful salutation, "Hail, full of grace! the Lord is with thee: blessed art thou among women."

Mary was troubled at these words; what might they mean? But hers was a fear springing from humility, not from want of confidence in God. Seeing her confusion, the angel replied to it in the words with which he first addressed Zachary. "Fear not"; and then he declared to her that, having found favor before God, she had been chosen to

---

* Exodus, xxx, 7, 8.

* Canticles ii.

be the Mother of the Redeemer. Like Zachary, she inquired how this might be; and for her the angel had no stern rebuke; he acknowledged her right to understand the manner in which the Mystery of the Incarnation was to be accomplished, and thus, Mary was the first of the human race to receive a theological definition concerning the Incarnation. As she finished the beautiful formula in which she expressed her consent, then was fulfilled the prophecy contained in these words of Wisdom: "When all things were in quiet silence, and the night was in the midst of her course, Thy almighty Word leaped down from heaven, from Thy royal throne."*

No other theme has furnished so many inspirations to Christian intellect as the scenes of the Annunciation. In Catholic countries, its mystery is made the keynote of every new undertaking, or study; the first words uttered in a foreign language are those of the Hail Mary. When the wearisome exercises of vocalization have trained the throat *fa* long, an *Ave Maria* is the first composition on which the voice tries its powers; and the Catholic artist paints, for his first finished work of art, his meditation on the Annunciation. Thus, in the pious, prayerful days of his youth, before he defiled his pencil with his daring emulations of the degradation of pagan art, Titian painted a most touching picture of the Annunciation. There is a tenderness and devotion in the conception and execution of this painting which make it appeal to the Christian heart far more powerfully than his later religious works, which though they exceed it in technical perfection, are so deficient in true Catholic inspiration. Perhaps it was the very devotion that prompted this lovely painting, which procured for Titian the immense grace of an old age in which to repent.

It would seem at first thought that there was only one scene in the Annunciation, but the meditations of Catholic artists unfold to us many, the exceeding probability of each one vouching for its truthfulness. Guido Reni carries us into heaven itself, and bids us contemplate Gabriel receiving his message from the Eternal Father, and from the expression of endless wonder on the countenance of the Archangel, we gather a new idea of the immensity of this mystery. To Perugini's mind came another revelation—a twofold one: the unconscious piety of the Blessed Virgin, and the joyful haste of Gabriel to announce that the work of man's Redemption was about to begin. All his paintings on this subject illustrate this phase of the Annunciation; whether descending from heaven, or passing through the doorway, or actually in the presence of Our Lady, his Gabriel is always in the attitude of exuberant, exultant haste.

* Wisdom, xviii, 14, 15.

Guilio Romana's Annunciation is like a page from some rare volume of mystic theology. Our Lady is kneeling, but her knees scarcely touch the ground; her form is rigid with ecstasy, and her fixed, pallid features, glow with an ethereal light. Gabriel also kneels, for he has just begun the words of his salutation. The moment of the salutation has been a favorite point with German artists in every age. The closed doors of that wonderful triptych, the Dombild of Cologne, first rare gem of the art of the Middle Ages, which depends not on the renown of its artist for its fame, give us a most beautiful representation of this moment, when Gabriel bent his knee to the Virgin of the House of David, the spouse of the Holy Ghost. That gifted son of St. Benedict, Obwexer—who, because his art sprang out of his vocation, and not his vocation out of his art, succeeded where Overbeck failed—clothes this idea with all the beautiful perfection of modern art. Full of sweetness and dignity, Our Lady rises to greet the honored guest; and, as if awestruck by her exceeding holiness and purity, and by her exalted mission, Gabriel bows and bends his knee. It is the amen, uttered by Christian art of the nineteenth century to the grand *Credo* of mediæval painting and sculpture.

The Annunciation may be viewed in a practical light, as well as poetically, artistically, or theologically; and as we meditate on it, we can each time draw some new lesson therefrom for our daily guidance, for it is an unfailing storehouse of rare spiritual treasure. Among all the points worthy of imitation in the conduct of Our Lady on this occasion, is her readiness to accept a new and unexpected duty, when it was shown that such was the will of God. It has often been remarked that Mary never sought fame; but we must observe, neither did she refuse it when it was involved in her duty. And it was no common renown that she accepted when she said, "Be it done unto me according to thy word." It had begun to assume a definite form more than a century before, when Isaias foretold that a Virgin should bring forth a Son (Isaias, vii, 14); and it had reached to the ends of the earth. In the forests of Chartres in distant France, and in the wooded solitudes of Carmel,* were found the altars and the votaries of the Virgin Mother. With the clear gaze of prophecy, Mary saw that this fame would be unending—"All generations shall call me blessed"—and she bowed her head, and said: "Behold the handmaid of the Lord!" This should teach us to accept all the duties which God sends us, no matter what conditions may be

* "La tradition nous apprend que, l'an 83 de notre ère les Eremites de Mont Carmel transformèrent en église un oratoire déjà élevé même avant le christianisme, en l'honneur de la Vierge qui devait enfanter, *Virgini parituræ.*"—*Franciscan Guide-Book of the Holy Land.*

inseparable from them. If tasks apparently contradicting our vocations are presented to us, let us examine the matter carefully, as Mary did, before deciding what course to adopt, and let neither publicity or fame appall our humility; there is nothing to fear, God balances all things; before all generations could call our Lady blessed, this other older prophecy had to be accomplished: "Oh, all ye who stand by the wayside, attend and see if there be any sorrow like to my sorrow!"

Let us resolve, then, to endeavor to imitate Our Lady as closely as possible in her true humility, her true obedience, and whatever God may require of us; let us be always ready to say, behold the servant of the Lord!

'Beth's Promise.

BY MRS. ANNA HANSON DORSEY.

CHAPTER XII—(Continued).

'BETH had many questions asked her, of course, by friends when they met—questions as to *her* intentions, etc., which she answered with quiet dignity, without giving anyone very decided satisfaction. "No!" she said to one, "I am not a Roman Catholic; I may never be: but if I am ever convinced that I ought to be one, nothing will prevent me." "Oh yes," she answered another, "I go to church with mamma; I could not let her go alone." "Sorry mamma's a Roman Catholic!" she replied to one who was trying as to what sympathy would do; "Oh no! I am glad beyond words, for her religion is a great comfort to her."

Mrs. Morley's strength gradually returned, and she found constant occupation; helping 'Beth with her French and music, guiding her taste in reading, and initiating her into the mysteries of domestic economy, filled up much of her time, leaving her yet some hours to visit several poor and destitute persons whom she assisted; to spend a half hour each day before the Blessed Sacrament, and to drive over to the cemetery two or three times a week to kneel at her husband's grave, and pray for his repose. 'Beth, now ripening into a beautiful womanhood, learned many lessons from her mother's daily life, which helped to prepare her mind for the reception of the truth, lessons which were "preparing the ways of the Lord and making His paths straight" through the erroneous ideas that still clouded it. Intelligent and of quick perception, she discerned the *motif* from which sprung so much good fruit; she read books explanatory of the Catholic Faith, as she had promised, and did not even shrink from, or avoid Father Thomas when he came to visit her mother. Indeed they became such friends, that in her frank, direct way, she used to ask questions, and state objections to this and that, concerning the belief of Catholics, with an amiable, pleasant audacity, that amused him, and which, after chafing her a little, he would explain in such a way, with such sweet gravity and clearness, that she would end by declaring herself "convinced, but not believing."

"In short, my dear child, your mind is in the centre of a right-angled triangle, groping about for the longest side," he said, laughing.

"A what?" she asked, with wide open eyes.

"A hypothenuse."

"Good evening, Rev. Father," she answered, laughing, and courtseying; "if it were anybody but you, I should think that was swearing. I'll take a run in the air to get it blown off."

"Blessings follow you, child," said Father Thomas, in his cheerful way, as 'Beth flitted out of the room. He was very fond of the bright, pure-minded, young creature, whose fine qualities had won his respect, and for whose conversion he prayed daily.

'Beth had been surprised at one thing which, motives of delicacy prevented her talking over with her mother. She had gone to church several times towards evening to walk home with her when she had gone to confession. Sometimes she waited in their own pew for her, knowing where she was; sometimes outside in the air. But one sultry evening—it was now July—a storm was threatening, and she went in, entering one of the lower pews near the bottom of the church, where a breath of air now and then drifted in through the open door, to watch for her mother; when her attention was attracted by quite a number of persons kneeling around a confessional, whose appearance betokened them as belonging to that class which Christ had declared His Church should always have with it—a class, which ever since the words were spoken, has been one of its distinctive marks, and is seen there as nowhere else upon earth. Their garments were faded and worn; some of them looked squalid and soiled; there were faces hardened in every line by care and privations; eyes restless and sad, countenances troubled yet patient. There were negro slaves kneeling among them—never hustled out of the way here in their Father's house—some of them clean and tidy, others ragged, and stained with daily toil; and there in the midst 'Beth saw her mother kneeling—her mother, once so fastidious that contact with such persons would have sickened and disgusted her. But there she knelt, next to the door of the confessional, unconscious—'Beth thought—in the intentness of her devotion, of her surroundings, until she saw her rise and go towards a feeble, poverty-stricken woman, who was evidently suffering from disease, put her arm about her, and support her to her own place which was next in the order of entering the tribunal of penance; then leaving her, she went and knelt below all the rest. It was so quietly done as to be scarcely noticed, and in a few moments she saw the feeble, tottering creature go in to lay the burden that oppressed her at the feet of one, who, divinely commissioned, was vested with power to loosen and remit the bonds of iniquity. Cannot we see in this little act how changed this woman was from the proud, sensuous, frivolous one of long ago, who abandoned the practices of her religion through human respect and self-love? It impressed 'Beth strangely; she thought that a religion which could overcome nature in such a way as that, came very near the spirit of the "Sermon on the Mount," and other things she had read of, in the New Testament—read of as things that had happened in the far past, to be admired, but which could not possibly be imitated now. The storm that had been brewing when 'Beth came in, had spent a heavy shower, then rolled southward with its deep thunders and vivid lightnings, cooling the air, and mother and daughter walked home through the pleasant dusk, arm in arm, saying little, but happy in each other's presence, their hearts occupied with thoughts and questions concerning that "Kingdom which is not of this world."

One morning Andrew brought Mrs. Morley a letter while she and 'Beth were at breakfast. It was from Aunt 'Beth, urging them to visit her. She was not well, she wrote, and wanted them both. "I got your letter telling me that you had gone back to the Catholic Church; I always thought, my dear Anne, that you'd take up your old creed again; and as you were brought up in it, it was the right thing for you to do; and above all, I am particularly glad that it has been such a comfort to you in your time of trouble, for there are troubles on earth that only God can reach, and yours was one of them. I believe—unwilling enough—that I am getting very old. My years ought to have convinced me of that long ago, but the symptoms are new to me, never having lived with old people to become acquainted with their infirmities, or felt anything like this before; I don't know what to make of it; at any rate come and see if you can find out for me. Things are lovely at old "Ellerslie," the hops are nearly ripe, the lake is a picture, and 'Beth will revel in it all—hops, roses, boating and everything—so don't fail me. Oh! I forgot to tell you! there's a nice little Roman Catholic chapel quite near us, built on the grounds adjoining "Ellerslie," by a rich New Yorker, who bought the old Tracy House two years ago, and spends the summers here with his family. They are very nice people, I understand, but as I never go from home these days, I do not know them. So, my dear Anne, you won't have to jolt over ten miles of rough road, as you did once, to get to your church. Our new neighbor's name is Dulaney. Don't fail to come to your loving aunt,
ELIZABETH MORLEY."

'Beth was wild to go, but Mrs. Morley could not decide at once. They talked long over it, and read Aunt 'Beth's letter again and again, and each time it seemed to have a more pathetic meaning. "I am not well, and want you both," and "I am getting very old, I fear"; were strange words to come from that energetic little woman, who never had headache, toothache, backache, or any other ache or pain in all her life, and who always looked on most of other people's ailments as the results of indolence, selfishness, or what she called "megrims." It was a thing to be thought over, their going; "For," said Mrs. Morley, "it is clear that she needs us; I never knew her to complain before; and if I can so arrange it, we must go. I'm afraid dear Aunt 'Beth is breaking up."

"I hope not, mamma," said 'Beth, her eyes full of tears. "I had a kind of fancy that Aunt 'Beth was immortal, she was always so full of life and energy. I'll cheer her up, and you'll do her good, and oh, mamma! won't I revel among the hops, and on the lake!"

"Yes: you will enjoy a change, my darling. I must see Mr. Harris about that business he told me of yesterday, then there are some other things to do—yes—I think I may have matters arranged," said Mrs. Morley.

"Having faith that you will, my mamma, I'm going straight down town to buy the widest brimmed straw hat that I can find, for I intend to live out of doors if we go to 'Ellerslie.' Shall I stop and tell Father Thomas that we think of going?"

"No need, my dear, I shall see him at church this evening."

"Yes," thought 'Beth, as she left the room, "go there and kneel among those distressed and not over-clean people around the confessional. It is not their poverty—oh, no! I would do anything to help them, poor souls! but what good does it do mamma to be crowded in with them, and pushed out of her place, and be made to wait to the very last sometimes?" 'Beth did not know that this was one of the ways taken by her mother to expiate her former sins of pride, and over fastidiousness; hence, whenever she thought of it, she quite raged in her heart, against what she considered a most unnecessary exposure of her health to contact with unknown ills.

"Any one who did not know her as I do," 'Beth went on thinking, while she put on her things to go in quest of the wide-brimmed hat—"would suppose that my mother was the greatest sinner living from her going to confession so often. I do wonder what she can have to tell, she who never commits even a slight wrong. Heigh-ho! I wish, I wish I could believe all that she does!"

It was decided that they were to go to "Ellerslie." Their preparations were all made, and they were to start on Thursday. Mrs. Morley received Holy Communion on Wednesday morning; in the afternoon she and 'Beth drove to the cemetery, and spread fresh flowers over the grave so dear to their hearts. Andrew was made happy by being left in charge of it during their absence, with an order for flowers whenever he called for them to lay there. Mrs. Morley had arranged with Mr. Harris what was to be done in regard to a certain disputed title to some city lots, signed some papers, and then went to call on Father Thomas, and leave a sum of money for some of her pensioners, whom he promised to see after himself; and having attended to a few other matters, hastened home to rest an hour before packing. Everything was at last completed, Andrew had strapped the trunks, and had them taken down to the hall, after which he went to the railroad-office to buy two through tickets to New York. At bed-time Mrs. Morley and 'Beth sat together, as was their way, talking over matters of interest, and of their journey—'Beth describing the hunt she had after the hat, which she at last found in a little shop kept by a German at the very extremity of Seventh street, Mrs. Morley listening with patient love. But she was more quiet than usual tonight; there was an expression of deep sadness on her face, and an abstracted look in her eyes which 'Beth was not slow to note, and renew her efforts to dispel.

"You are tired, darling," she said at last, "and I should not have gone on chattering so long. Go to bed now, and I'll be just as still as a little mouse."

"Presently—after I have said something, my 'Beth, which I have been wishing to say for some time past," said Mrs. Morley, smoothing the bright hair away from 'Beth's forehead.

"Yes, mamma," she answered, somewhat startled, lifting her beautiful eyes to her mother's, with a frank, expectant look.

"My darling! how much I wish that I could save you from the rough places of life, its passion, its pain! But this being impossible, as trial is one of the conditions of existence—nor do I know that it would be well for it to be otherwise—I will do what I can, with your consent, to avert some of those bitter sorrows which have so desolated my own life. You have heard, my 'Beth, how, and under what circumstances I lost my brave, noble father, an officer of the army, and how my mother, dying of a broken heart shortly after, left me—a little child—and my two brothers to the care of a stranger—our stepmother. You have heard how my brothers—so handsome and brave, and I so proud of them—one in the army, the other in the navy—perished each at his post of duty. 'Glorious deaths!' people said; but ah! what a mockery such glory is to the bereaved heart! But the last blow, the bitterest and most crushing of all, you know of my child, but you can never, never measure its pain. And it is to avert the anguish of my lot from you, that I feel not only justified, but think it a duty as your mother, in asking you to make me a promise."

"Mamma, I will promise anything you may ask, because I know you love me too well, and are too good to want me to promise a thing that will not be best for me. What is it?" said 'Beth, with loving trust beaming in her countenance.

"Promise me, as if it were my dying request, never to marry into the Army, or the Navy, or in any branch of the service, the pursuit of which exposes one to peril and violent death. Had my loved and lost ones been civilians, they would have lived, and you and I had not been left orphaned and widowed. Glory! ah! I hate the word, when I think of all that it means to me! Can you promise what I wish, 'Beth?'"

"Certainly I can, mamma, darling. I'll do more. I'll promise never to marry at all; wouldn't that be best? then, you know, I could be like Aunt 'Beth; and we would never separate," said the girl, with a bright smile.

"No! no! not that. A woman is happier for marrying, unless she have a vocation for a higher and holier state of life; otherwise it is her destiny and her duty. A happy marriage seems to me, and is, no doubt, one of the most perfect conditions of human life. But promise me, oh 'Beth, promise me most solemnly, that which I ask of you!"

"I do, I do, mamma, and I call God to witness my promise, which I would die rather than break," said 'Beth, leaning her head upon her mother's breast, who embraced her fondly, thinking she had done the best thing she could for the safety of her future peace and happiness.

"The sweet Virgin Mother be your help, my 'Beth. To her holy care I confided you when you were born; knowing how unworthy I was, I prayed her to be a Mother to you."

"I am glad to know that, mamma, for I have always had a strange sort of veneration for her." Then after a little more talk, they separated for the night.

And this was 'Beth's Promise. Could either of them have looked into the future, would it have been asked, or given?

(TO BE CONTINUED.)

Our Lady's Sennight in the Household of Faith.

INTRODUCTION: TWILIGHT.

C. I.

"'AVE MARIA!' o'er the earth and sea
That heavenliest hour of heaven is worthiest thee!

C. II.

"'Ave Maria!' blessed be the hour!
The time, the clime, the spot where I so oft
Have felt that moment in its fullest power,
Sink o'er the earth so beautiful and soft,
While swung the deep bell in the distant tower,
Or the faint, dying day-hymn stole aloft,
And not a breath crept through the rosy air,
And yet the forest leaves seemed stirr'd with prayer.

C. III.

"'Ave Maria!' 'tis the hour of prayer!
'Ave Maria!' may our spirits dare
Look up to thine and to thy Son's above!
Ave Maria!' oh! that face so fair!
Those downcast eyes beneath th' Almighty Dove—
What though 'tis but a pictured image strike—
That painting is no idol—'tis too like."

She who said, "I am black but beautiful. Do not consider that I am brown,"* has made sacred the choice of her children—the aurora of morning and the dusk of evening—by accepting the twilight as her peculiar hour for the homage they give—for the love she returns! Should not we breathe an evening Ave after the *Veni Sancte Spiritus* of invocation to her Bridegroom, for the knowledge of Mary and the love of Mary, as we enter upon this Seven Nights' Entertainment of our dear Queen by her favored children, the pious Catholic poets? But the less we say about piety just at this stage of our performance, the better for our reputation for "discernment of the spirits." Whose *Ave Maria* is this just cited? whose thoughts, as the night-shades fall, and, evening closing, warns busy eyes to shut awhile the outer gates and look within? *Ave Maria*, varied often—intoned by any mouth, it is always the cry of the soul congratulating the approach of one of our weakling kind—though sinless—so awfully near the inaccessible that it takes the breath of the reverent to think it: leaving but a "Hail" to express what an Archangel could only say in faltering phrases. Even the scoffer must swallow his own venom, and in pronouncing *Ave Maria!* involuntarily witness to her Queenliness, as once did he who mocked her Son with "*Ave Rex!*" give testimony to the royalty proclaimed at the head of the Tree: "Jesus of Nazareth, King of the Jews."* The double *Ave*, like the double *Fiat*, shall ever exert an omnipotence of love over the human spirit that human love shall never rival, and human hate, though inspired of hell, shall never extinguish.

Byron can no more tarnish the Catholic world's *Ave*—caught from heaven—by its being incorporated in the mire of his Don Juan (Canto III) than by his immediately succeeding sneer at mock-devotion.

Say an earnest *Ave* of reparation, forgiving reader, as you hear:

"Some kind casuists are pleased to say
 . . . . I have no devotion;
But set these persons down with me to pray
And you shall see who has the properest notion
Of getting into heaven the shortest way. . . ."

But some one calls a "Halt!" Have we set out to abuse poor ill-fated Byron, on our journey through pleasant meadows strewn with Catholic flowers for the triumphal entry of the Queen of the broad earth into her own household of Faith? No! peace to his dust, if peace there be; and more! rest through merciful Mary to his restless spirit. On the contrary, we would contrast his grudging generosity with the miserliness of the great Catholic poets in slighting a theme, the source of the inspiration of the highest flights, of the most spiritual arts, in their efforts to lift man above the clouds and give him a glimpse of the glory streaming from the gates of heaven ajar. Excepting Chaucer—Catholic, though possibly tainted with some of the liberalism of Wickliffe—with, perhaps, John Gower, and the too little known poet-priest Robert Southwell, Jesuit martyr of England, to whom shall we cry for a note of praise to Mary in her ancient "Lady's Dowry"? Call the roll!—Alexander Pope, who confessed it a good day's work to spin a single thread of the gaudy tinsel of the "Rape of the Lock"; Pope, whose Dunciadic pronouncements consigned more unworthies to present hell and future ignominy, than would rival Dante's vocabulary in his "Inferno"! "Eh! sirs, I lived in times when Catholicity was only honored in effigy by the enlightened British public." No worse recommendation to English fame. Hence, forgive this trifle (Messiah):

"Rapt into future times, the bard began:
A Virgin shall conceive, a Virgin bear a Son!
From Jesse's root behold a branch arise,
Whose sacred flower with fragrance fills the skies.
The ethereal spirit o'er its leaves shall move,
And on its top descend the mystic Dove. . . ."

And, well!—in "January and May," none too de-

---

* Canticle I, 4, 5.

* John, xix, 21, 22,.... The reader, unfamiliar with the sacred text, will remark that when "the chief priests of the Jews said to Pilate: Write not the king of the Jews, but that He said, I am the king of the Jews," Pilate's laconic answer was: "What I have written, I have written."

cent a place for the pure Queen, I substitute for Chaucer's
—" A Sainte Marie, benedicite!"
this more congenial paganism:
"Ah! gentle deities!"—
—*Exit Pope.*

John Milton!—(who, as is related by his own brother's testimony, died a Catholic—" Papist ") —" Gracious 'Virgin Blest,' as I have called thee, yet a Protestant, in my 'Ode on Christ's Nativity '—too late did I know thee, too late did I love. Forgive my ignorance and miseducation!" John Dryden!—convert, confessor to the Catholic Faith at the Revolution—pay thy respects to thy Lady-Queen. "Lady of the broad earth, Heaven's Queen, enthroned! I regret time nor occasion did serve for thy praise, and hold thy poor servant excused." Tom Moore!—no convert, but Catholic of Catholic sires—proud son of song! matchless musician! one of the world's few national bards—where thy chant to Mary? where thy spirit-thrilling chords? where the rapt poetic eloquence that fired the world? Where thy praise of her who, perhaps, alone of human kind, could transcend the flight of thy brilliant fancy, and tax thy flowing numbers for more melody, rhythm—the angelic? Echo only answers: "Where?" Shakespeare!—name—but none is like thee! Thou wert a Catholic; thy works pander to no heresy! What has thy silver tongue in metric song to sing for Blessed Mary?

Pucelle. . . . " Heaven and our gracious Lady hath it pleased
To shine on my contemptible estate;
Lo! whilst I waited on my tender lambs,
And to sun's parching heat display'd my cheeks,
God's Mother deigned to appear to me,
And, in a vision full of majesty,
Willéd me to leave my base vocation,
And free my country from calamity;
Her aid she promised and assured success;
In complete glory she revealed herself;
And, whereas I was black and swart before,
With those clear rays which she infused on me,
That beauty I am bless'd with which you see."
—*Henry VI, Part I.*
And,
"Christ's Mother helps me, else I were too weak."

Alas! that the comparison one would commence to institute between the greatest English and the greatest German poet—Schiller—on the same theme—should be checked on one's lips in mid utterance; and that English prejudice should warp the mind of the greatest of mere secular geniuses so far as to transform the little less than angelic Maid of Protestant Schiller into the nameless female of Catholic Shakespeare!

"More, more!" cry the Queen's courtiers. "Resume her praises, greatest of bards of all the lands!"

RICHARD. "Shall we go throw away our coats of steel,
And wrap our bodies in black mourning gowns,
Numbering our "*Ave Marias*" with our beads?"
—*Henry VI, Part III.*
Gloucester—the wicked—of Queen Margaret:
" I cannot blame her by God's holy Mother!"
—*Richard III.*

And for the rest, great Shakespeare's more than one thousand pages of *nonpareil* are deaf and dumb. *Exeunt omnes.*

NIGHT I.

CONCEIVED IMMACULATE.

Many days and nights are given to the feasts of the Blessed Virgin by Holy Church—a whole month at one time, a week of an octave at another. But it is remarkable that many of her festivals commemorate events happening principally in the night. Our Lord's Nativity, and her own; His Resurrection and Her Assumption; Epiphany—for the star was seen to stand over the stable of Bethlehem; Feast of the Seven Dolors—for the Passion and Burial, occurred in darkened day and night; Feasts of Mount Carmel and Our Lady of the Snow, both originating like Our Lady of Mercy—*de Mercede*—in visions at night; as well as Most Holy Rosary, are manifest proofs. And do we not love to think that it was in the "religious twilight" of the failing day and falling night of the divine twenty-fifth of March, that the glorious one of the Seven "who burn like lamps before the throne" floated in upon her astonished vision, bent the archangelic knee, and delivered the secret of the Great King? It might well have been. The night is more hers, because then she can take her accustomed throne in mid heavens, rest her feet on the bright crescent moon that yields itself her ready footstool, and the stars that bend about their radiance in gleaming rows to bind her pure brow as with a coronet, while the gracious Queen doffs her too dazzling mantle—the sun—lest timid children of men might fear to approach her. At such an hour we attempt these entertainments, which at the same time may afford some justification for a former assertion, that our day was destined to see a revival of Catholic poetry, especially in the English tongue; indeed we were in the midst of a poetic *renaissance*. As in our former articles, we leave our elders of English poetry in the Protestant shade they loved too well, and hasten on to the incoming light of the nineteenth century, where, amidst the glare and flare of modern Bengal lights, arises a steady white flame of Catholic poesy—not brilliant, nor ascending high, but distinct withal—a growing splendor, a sun being born from the womb of night, a brighter earnest of what there is to be.

The sovereign Lady, holding her court in the

midst of her own, turns aside her gracious face with a shade of pitying sorrow, as the older poets make their excuses for their passionless devoir. Shall we please her better, and succeed in bringing back the smile so habitual to her, by introducing more modern troubadours? Let us essay, that she may not have cause to retain the serious air which seems now to preoccupy her majesty. "*Dignare me laudare te Virgo sacrata!*"* exclaims a holy priest, who labored well and truly in life for her and her Son's glory. Sweet-souled Father William Frederick Faber's hymns to the glorification of his Queen's Immaculate Conception are so well known, that we would scarcely dare to repeat them in this holy presence, were it not for the word of—was it Lacordaire? "Love," said he, speaking of the beads, "love has but one word, and in saying it forever, it never repeats."

However, let us hear the one less familiar to all: 'tis simple, childlike, if you will:

"O Mother! I could weep for mirth,
Joy fills my soul so fast;
My soul to-day is heaven on earth,
O could the transport last!
I think of thee, of what thou art,
Thy majesty, thy state:
And I keep singing in my heart—
Immaculate! Immaculate!
When Jesus looks upon thy face
His Heart with rapture glows,
And in the Church, by thy sweet grace,
Thy blessed worship grows.

"The angels answer with their songs;
Bright choirs in gleaming rows,
And saints flock round thy feet in throngs,
And heaven with bliss o'erflows."

If one asked the favored priest what riveted so his eye upon the holy mountain, he would answer in rapture:

"Immaculate Conception! far
Above all graces blest,
Thou shinest like a royal star
On God's eternal breast!"

The author of the serious and theological "*Lyra Catholica*," who proves to be no other than Cannon Oakley, the writer to whom priests and laity are indebted, himself a convert, shall follow the flower of Pusey's and Newman's flock.

"'Tis from the mystery we hail this day
Her glory issues as her merits date;
We sum her panegyric when we say,
Mother of God, conceived Immaculate!

"What truths are lock'd within that ample phrase,
What fonds of virtue and what depths of power!
A life of peaceful love and ceaseless praise,
And years of merit centred in each hour.

---
* Deign to permit me to praise thee, Holy Virgin.

"No stain of earth her sacrifice to mar,
No fault or flaw its beauty to impair:
The Spirit's life without the Flesh's war,
Each word an oracle, each thought a prayer.

"Bend, O ye angels, o'er the gracious sight,
Return abash'd, ye sinners, from the view,
Humbled, yet thankful, that a Queen so bright
Should yearn with all a Mother's love o'er you."

There is a poet, as we take it, among the sweetest and deepest our day has produced—as veritable a knight of Our Lady as ever the glorious St. Bernard was her privileged secretary.

Under the banner of St. Philip Neri, on whose folds flashes the legend: "The Madonna should be our Love," he buckles on his warrior-priest's armor, sets his lance in rest, and with open visor charges boldly into the arena of the American public, while there gleams on his breastplate, challenging every foe:

BEATÆ:
SEMPER VIRGINI;
DEI GENITRICI;
MARIÆ:*

"A man who has given his heart to the Immaculate—taking her for the only Lady of his love, serving her and doing battle as her 'True Knight.'" Fr. Benj. Dionysius Hill—an adult convert—revels in the new light spread about him, dazing his eyes to things external, and illumining them to feast on the beauty of the glory of God's House—its sun, the Lamb; its fair moon, Queen Mary.

Let him join his brother-priests in their lauds of the 'Ideal Womanhood' they need not fear to worship or serve to entirely, as their Queen."

TOTA PULCHRA.†

"Can God so woo us, nor, of all our race,
Have formed one creature for His perfect rest?
Must the Dove moan for an inviolate nest,
Nor find it e'en in thee, O 'full of grace'—
In thee, His Spouse? Or could the Word debase
His Godhead's pureness when He fill'd thy breast,
Tho' Moses treasured up, at His behest
The typical manna in a golden ‡ vase?
Who teach that sin had ever aught in thee,
Utter a thought the demons may not share—
Not tho' they prompt it in their fell despair:
For these, while sullenly hating the decree
That shaped thee forth Immaculate, 'All Fair,'
Adore it still—and must eternally!"‖

"And whoso gainsays it," challenges the chevalier, "let him be anathema; for my Fair One's honor I will combat to the death."

Both sexes, as both continents, must join to praise the One above all praise. For here also can it be truly sung with St. Thomas:

"Quantum potes, tantum aude,
Nec laudare sufficis!"

---
* "To the Ever-Blessed Virgin, Mother of God, Mary."
† Cant., iv, 7.   ‡ Ex., xvi, 33 : Heb., ix, 4.
‖ *Cath. World*, Dec., '77.

Harriet M. Skidmore, under a name most fitting —"Marie"—shall intone thy hymn to

OUR PATRONESS.

The royal Maiden, full of grace,
  In robes of dazzling white:
Fair daughter of our fallen race,
The beauty of whose queenly face
  No blemish dared to blight,—

. . . .

She is the guardian of our land
  Our starbeam, bright and blest:
Our Patroness, whose bounty rare
Sheds benisons and graces fair
  O'er all the favored West.

. . . .

Lo! framed in drear December skies,
  Apocalyptic dream!
While far the shadowy monster flies,
We see the star-crowned figure rise,
  Enthroned on crescent beam.
Sancta Regina! at thy feet,
  In homage fond we bow—
Thy subjects pay thee tribute meet,
And own the diadem complete
  That decks thy queenly brow.

Immaculate! O title fair!
  Crown-jewel, all thine own!
Ah, well may earthly echoes ring
The joy the seraph courtiers sing
  Around thy dazzling throne!" *

. . . .

Therefore, as of our Patroness, we beg another boon with her valiant, though Catholic knight on Dies VIII. Dec. MDCCCLXIX.†

. . . .

This day we hail thy victory, and claim
  Thy prayer omnipotent. Nor let it rise
For us alone that boast to love thy name:
  But those, unhappy, that have dar'd despise,
Who came for them, not less by *thee* He came!
  Thro' *thee* must break unclouded to their eyes.
Ah, Mother's Heart! how long, then, wilt thou wait
  Till *all* thy children sing 'IMMACULATE?'"

* Beside the Western Sea. P. 228.   † Vatican Council.

(TO BE CONTINUED.)

THE Gospel does not make mention of any appearance of Jesus to Mary, because it records, in a special manner, only those that were intended to convince the disciples, and, through them, the entire Church; and besides, Mary was as much convinced by her faith alone, as the disciples were by the vision of their divine Master conversing and eating with them. But a pious tradition, the general opinion of the saints, and special revelations, particularly those made to St. Bridget, do not permit us to doubt that our Lord, after His resurrection, appeared to her to reward her for her faith, her love and compassion, and to make her joy equal to all her past sorrows.

Reparation by Religious Orders.

From "The Messenger of the Sacred Heart of Jesus."

THERE is at the present hour one thought preoccupying the best minds; one sentiment which has irresistibly taken possession of those hearts most devoted to Jesus Christ and to His Church; one duty which seems to impose itself more and more imperiously upon the servants of God; the thought, the sentiment, the duty of reparation.

Outraged as He has never been before, boldly attacked by a conspiracy which tends to openly deprive Him of the empire of humanity, the Divine Majesty must be avenged by an expiation in proportion to the crime. God has not ceased to use mercy in our regard; He is still disposed to shed upon us, as He has promised, all the blessings of which the Heart of Jesus is the source; but before He glorifies His goodness in us, He wishes us to secure the rights of His justice. We cannot obtain an extraordinary effusion of saving graces, except in so far as we participate in a more than ordinary measure in the expiations by which they were merited for us. Becoming our Redeemer by making Himself our ransom, the God-Man calls upon His most devoted servants to accomplish with Him this twofold condition of our deliverance; He offers to make us saviours with Him, provided we consent to become victims with Him.

But among all the different classes of Christian society, there is one upon which this duty common to all the true friends of Jesus Christ imposes itself as a special privilege, and as an obligation of their calling, and this is the Religious.

The religious is a voluntary victim. Little satisfied with strictly obligatory sacrifices, figured by the victims which the people of old immolated at the entrance of the Temple, the religious advances further into the sanctuary; he ascends the altar of holocaust, and by his three vows immolates himself unreservedly to the Divine Majesty. These vows have often been compared to the three nails which attached our Divine Saviour to the cross. In truth, all the glory of the cross of the Saviour results from the victory of which it has been the instrument over the three murderous appetites which instigated man to revolt against his Creator—pride, sensuality, and cupidity. The Divine Lamb expiates these crimes, and delivers us from them by His death upon the cross, stripped of everything, surfeited with ignominy, and bowed down with sorrow. By his triple vow of poverty, chastity, and obedience, the religious in turn makes himself a victim for these three kinds of prevarication; he reproduces in himself the Sacrifice of Calvary, and it suffices for him to be consistent with himself not to render himself guilty, through the whole course of his religious life, of any robbing of the holocaust which he has voluntarily offered; by him, the first and essential condition of the salvation of the world will be perfectly fulfilled; the sins of men will have as many repairers as there are religious.

Being thus perpetually indemnified by this holocaust, so continually renewed in all parts of the world, for the outrages constantly heaped upon Him every where, Divine Justice cannot fail to withhold the thunders of its anger, and allow free scope to Divine Mercy.

Why is this not so? Why does God find Himself constrained to defer the blessings so often promised, and still strike us with the scourges of His wrath? Are there not enough voluntary victims to satisfy all the requirements of His holiness? Those chosen souls, who, by the vows of religion have wished to die to the world, to live only for Christ, may be counted by hundreds, nay, even by thousands in Catholic countries. How then can God, who was willing to save Sodom if but ten just could be found, hesitate to pardon our sins, however great they may be, when, for their expiation, thousands of victims are constantly uniting their immolation to that of the Divine Lamb?

To this question our Lord has replied through a chosen soul who died not long ago in Italy, in the odor of sanctity, and whose life has just been written by her director, a venerable religious of the Order of St. Francis. This admirable life, composed of heroic acts and miraculous signs, is alone sufficient to accredit the mission of the servant of God. We have, besides, been able to inform ourselves at Rome, from the best authorities; and the statements which we have received leave not the slightest doubt, either as to the veracity of the historian, or the holiness and divine mission of his heroine.

What was the object of this mission? To announce as far back as 1842, the disasters which, since that time have fallen upon Italy, and upon all Christian society; to predict at the same time the happy issue of this terrible crisis, the complete triumph of the Church and the regeneration of society; but especially to impose in God's name, as the condition for the prompt accomplishment of these promises, the reformation of religious communities.

In the mouth of Mother Agnes, Clare Steiner, as well as in the thoughts of God who inspired her, the word reform does not signify the cessation of grave abuses or the re-establishment of regularity. The communities to which that servant of God belonged, and in whose respect she was able to accomplish her mission, were not at all relaxed in the ordinary sense of the word. In the eyes of the world they were irreproachable, and yet, they did not satisfy the requirements of the Heart of the God, who expects from these privileged souls a generosity proportioned to the favors with which He loads them. He wished them to aid Him more efficaciously to expiate the crimes of sinners and to save the world. The reform which He asked of them did not consist in the rigor of bodily mortifications; Mother Agnes, on the contrary, at the same time that she led the communities of her Order back to primitive observance, mitigated the rule of St. Clare in this respect, so that to keep it perfectly, might be possible to all constitutions. What God commanded her to ask in His name of the daughters of St. Francis and of all religious; the essential condition, upon which He made the turning away of the scourges of His justice, and the pouring out of the blessings of His mercy to depend, was perfect detachment, and unreserved devotion, in souls especially consecrated to Him. Such was the reform which He desired, and which He still desires to see introduced into all religious communities. What the Divine Redeemer said to Mother Agnes with regard to the religious men and women of her Order, who were the immediate object of her mission, those of all other Orders can and should apply to themselves; for assuredly the Saraphic Order is not the only one capable of this salutary reform. Let us listen to the words which our Saviour addressed to His servant, March 25th, 1844, in order to determine her to overcome the resistance which her humility had hitherto opposed to the accomplishment of her mission:

"While I was meditating upon the Passion, our Lord said to me: 'How much longer will you refuse to manifest the designs which I have formed for the welfare of the Holy Church?' Several months have already passed, and you have not opened your mouth.' He then repeated to me three different times that what He wanted was reform. And as I experienced great difficulty in believing what I heard, 'I wish,' said He, 'that monasteries, professing the rule of St. Clare, should be renewed in spirit.' I answered: Lord, there would be few to understand the necessity of this renovation, even if the proper authorization to effect it could be obtained. 'What matter is that?' replied our Lord; 'I ask but for three, and you will find them. I wish the religious to rise at night to repair the outrages of a blinded world by their fervent praises. I wish to see them clothed with the livery of their mother. I wish My spouses to lead the life of which I gave them an example during thirty-three years; My grace will suffice for that. They must seek to please Me by love of poverty. But how many are there who bind My hands and prevent Me from shedding upon them more light and more graces, by secret bonds which they do not break. This is what prevents Me from holding back My hand, and from stopping the scourges which My people have drawn upon themselves by the increase of their crimes. While Christians are persecuting Me more cruelly than infidels, even in houses which are consecrated to Me, I find many souls who treat Me coldly.' But, Lord, said I, what can I do, who am the first to be guilty of this ingratitude? I can do nothing. Enlighten the Superiors that they may take this work in hand. Have mercy, O my God! He answered: 'Pray to Me by My Heart, that thus you may obtain mercy from My Father! It is for this reason that I have made you share My sufferings. I have shown you the wars, the agitations, the miseries which I am preparing to send. Delay, therefore, no longer to accomplish My will and to make known My requirements.'"

One year later, Mother Agnes wrote:—"God has shown me that the chastisement of the sins of the world could be no longer delayed, because of the relaxing of fervor in the bosom of religious orders and among the clergy in general. There doubtless will be men who, to conform to the requirements of Divine Justice, will take reform in hand, but they will render it useless, because they do not animate it with the true spirit."

However, the humble religious still hesitated to believe herself invested with so great and difficult a mission to the holy tribe, and she confined herself to doing penance on her own account, to weeping and praying for the salvation of the world. Our Lord then said to her more expressly: "I wish you to address yourself to the Holy See, and make known My will with regard to the reform of the religious state, and of the punishments which will not fail to be let loose, if haste is not made to prevent them. You will be held to account for it if you delay longer to manifest what I have so often repeated to you. If you are not believed, you need not trouble yourself about it; the important part is, that you should no longer defer to announce the coming chastisements, for they are coming."

Mother Agnes finally obeyed. She spoke to the Holy Father, giving him manifest evidences of her celestial mission. We must say, however, that this mission, although recognized and favored by the Vicar of Christ, obtained but a very incomplete result, and had, to prevent its success, made much more advantageous use of the illusions of the good than of the open opposition of the wicked. What we now desire to make prominent, is the thought of the Divine Saviour in regard to Religious Orders, and the kind of co-operation which He asks of them, to hasten the triumph of the Church and the salvation of society. This thought evidently has not changed. If Italy, and the whole of Catholicity, might have been preserved from the afflictions which desolate them by the fulfilment of the condition of Mother Agnes, it is only by accomplishing it to day that we can hope to obtain a prompt cessation of those evils. What condition is this? We have already seen. There is no question for Religious communities of putting an end to grave disorders which, thanks to God! do not exist. There is no question of restoring to the rule a vigor which it has never entirely lost; there is no question of heroic mortifications, or of rivalling the macerations of the old penitents. The heroism which the Divine Saviour desires to find in souls especially devoted to Him, is that of love, of interior renouncement, of zeal for His interests. At the moment when the hatred of His enemies passes all bounds, and finds a powerful auxiliary in the afflicting indifference of the greater number of Christians, the Heart of Jesus seeks hearts to love Him without measure, and He expects to find such especially in Religious communities.

We surely do not need a special revelation to know the desires of the Heart of Jesus upon this subject, or to admit their evident justice. It is not, necessary, therefore to insist further in order to lead the associates of the Apostleship to propose to themselves this special intention during the coming month, and to place it foremost among those which they make each day, for it certainly occupies a first place in the intentions of the Divine Heart. While imposed upon religious by the love which they owe to themselves, and upon other Christians by fraternal charity, this intention is recommended equally to all, by zeal for the interests of the Church and of society. Independently of the divine promises, is it not clear that if the Orders recover their primitive fervor, nothing more would be wanting to effect a real transformation of the world? Each Order has had its heroic age, during which its action upon society was as beneficial as powerful. If they could all revive the virtues of that age, should we not also see a return of its wonders? This is, indeed, an ideal which human nature would find it difficult to realize. Very few streams preserve, during the whole of their course through the plain, the purity of the source; and, in the supernatural as well as the natural order, God does not always grant the sons of heroes the extraordinary gifts of their fathers. But without the presumption of completely realizing the ideal, we should still tend towards it, and consider ourselves happy, to have all our brethren aid us to reascend the slope down which human weakness has made us slide. May we not believe that, in the designs of Providence, the attacks of anti-Christian revolution are intended to render us this service? Surely there can be nothing more unjust than the accusations brought against Religious Orders, nothing more iniquitous than the persecutions and spoliations of which they have been the victims for the last century. But ought we not to attribute to ourselves, in a certain measure, the facility with which these accusations find credence, and the power which God permits our persecutors to exercise? Calumny could not so easily be fastened upon us if our entire lives constantly refuted it by the practice of virtues as heroic as those of our ancestors, if persecution was for them a meritorious trial, is it not for us a necessary stimulant? If the world is unjust in imputing to us vices of which we are not guilty, is not God right in preventing us from contenting ourselves with a mediocrity contrary to the perfection of our state? Social tempests as well as atmospheric agitations, have their causes in the designs of God; they purify the granary of the Lord, and, by disturbing the wheat, carry away the useless chaff. If we wish the tempest to be soon calmed, let us hasten the purification which it is intended to effect.

This is what all the members of our holy league are going to ask for religious during this month, and what the religious who belong to it will ask for each other; that each one of these chosen battalions of the army of Christ may fully respond to the designs of the Divine Chief, and take, in the line of action, the special part which belongs to it. Nothing more is required to assure victory; For each Order has a special mission, which consists in reproducing some aspect of the life of the God-Man, and of exercising in the Church and in society a part of its action. If all these parts were perfectly fulfilled from their combined action, there would result to the eyes of the world so splendid a revelation of the beauty of Jesus, and so powerful a radiation of His love, that nothing would be able to resist it. How then, doubt that the Heart of God will be even more sensible than the souls of men to this reproduction of the beauty of His only Son, and of His immolation upon Calvary? If each religious is a victim, whose sacrifice should reproduce that of the Saviour, how can Divine Justice fail to be satisfied, when, in thousands of victims, it finds, in all its integrity, the holocaust of the Divine Lamb? No, truly, whatever may be the crimes of men, its thunders will be turned aside; or if they are hurled upon the earth, it will only be to strike obstinate sinners.

To spare Italy the scourges which have afflicted it for the last twenty years, our Saviour asked only three religious communities perfectly restored according to the reform of Mother Agnes; how much greater miracles will He not perform in favor of society, if He finds everywhere communities equally fervent to appease His anger?

This is what we will ask of Him, and what we will endeavor to accomplish within the measure of our power; for there is no religious who cannot labor for the perfect reform of his Order by perfectly reforming himself. While we pray that the crimes of sinners may be repaired by the immolation of generous souls, let us begin by accomplishing this reparation in ourselves; let us make ourselves victims by completing to its fullest extent the sacrifice of each day and each moment imposed upon us by our vows and our rules. This is the first immolation which God asks of us—regularity. Let us join to it the immolation of patience, by accepting with love and thanksgiving the crosses of every nature which Providence is pleased to place upon our shoulders. Finally, let us complete the offering by giving our hearts up to the flames of charity and zeal, and by animating all our works with an ardent desire for the glory of God and the salvation of our brethren. By this triple immolation, even when our strength will not permit us the extraordinary macerations of the holy penitents, we can contribute our part to the grand work of reparation, and hasten in some manner the triumph of the Church.

The Fisherman's Prayer.

BY T. D. SULLIVAN.

THE sun is setting angrily,
  In threat'ning gusts the wind is blowing—
Holy Mary! Star of the Sea!
Speed our small bark fast and free
  O'er the homeward way we're going!

We left the land as the morning bright
  Purpled the smooth sea all before us;
We prayed to God, and our hearts were light,
We placed our bark in thy saving sight,
  And knew thou wouldst well watch o'er us.

But now the sun sets angrily,
  From black wild clouds the wind is blowing;
Holy Mary! Star of the Sea!
Send our small boat fast and free
  O'er the darkling way we're going!

We fished the deep the live-long day,
  The waves were rich, through God's good pleasure;
We ventured far from our own bright bay,

And lingered late; we fain would stay
Till filled with the shining treasure.

But now the night falls threat'ningly,
The sea was high, with the fierce wind blowing,
Holy Mary! Star of the Sea!
Our light, our guide, our safety be,
O'er the stormy way we're going!

We pass the point where the tempest's strain
Is lightened off by the land's high cover;
Our village lights shine out again—
I know my own in my window-pane,
And the tall church towering over.

Holy Mary! Star of the Sea!
With grateful love our hearts are glowing;
Behold we bless thy Son and thee!
Oh, still our light and safety be,
O'er the last dread course we'er going!

The Apparitions at Knock.

(CONTINUED.)

ARCHDEACON CAVANAGH'S DIARY. THE CURES EFFECTED SINCE AUGUST LAST. DECLARATION AND LETTER OF PATRICK SCOTT, ETC.

From "The Dublin Weekly News" of March 6.

I now proceed to submit to your readers the substance of the diary kept by the parish priest of Knock. He began the record on the 31st of October, 1879. The date of the earliest Apparition was the 21st of August. A cure of deafness and pain in the ear was reported twelve days later, and several others in the course of the subsequent weeks, but Archdeacon Cavanagh took no steps towards collecting and sifting the statements circulating amongst the people, until after the Archbishop of Tuam had appointed a commission to take evidence respecting the Apparition, and after the commission had met, examined the several witnesses, and forwarded its report to the Archbishop. By this time, the accounts of cures were numerous, indeed almost continual; the body of testimony increased from day to day; and the Archdeacon deemed it his duty, now that the Church, through his Grace of Tuam, had taken cognizance of the matter, to set down the exact particulars of such cures as could be proved to his satisfaction.

The diary opens with the words: *Ad majorem Dei gloriam*, "To the greater glory of God." It is entitled, "An Account of the Miraculous Cures wrought at the gable of the chapel here, where the Blessed Virgin Mary, the Immaculate Mother, appeared on the night of the 21st of August last." A further note specifies that the cures have been wrought on persons who either prayed on the spot, or applied cement or clay taken from the church to the parts of the body affected by pains or wounds.

The following are the cases noted:

1. Delia Gordon, daughter of Mr. P. J. Gordon, of Claremorris: deafness and pain in the left ear. This, the first cure reported, was instantaneous. It occurred on Sunday, the 31st of August. Full particulars of the case, as related to me by Mr. and Mrs. P. J. Gordon, the father and mother of Delia Gordon, and also by the young girl herself, were published in the *Nation* and *Weekly News* of the 7th of last month. The cure was effected by putting into the ear a small particle of cement.

2. A cripple, name not ascertained. He rode on an ass to the very spot, and was able to walk away.

3. A woman, name not stated, living at Carramore, near Knock. She had been suffering from a sore on the hand. The pain ceased instantly.

4. Mrs. Doble, Claremorris.

5. A man named Shallagh, herd to Lord Oranmore.

6. Honora Horan, of the parish of Kilmovee, Co. Mayo. She had been a fortnight unable to speak or swallow food.

7. Mrs. (Martin) Busty, Knock: sore eyes.

8. Mary M'Loughlin, Knock. She had been suffering from pain and stiffness of the knee for many years, and also from a chronic pain in the right side. She drank some of the water taken from the ground at the church gable, and was cured of the pains, which have not since returned.

9. A girl from Claremorris, name not stated. Her hand had been broken, and she was not able to lift it to her forehead. Now she can use it freely.

10. Mrs. (Thomas) Curry, Knock: sore knee.

11. Mrs. Curry's niece. She had been nearly blind; she could not see the steps at the entrance to the church. She visited Knock, and prayed there, and her sight has so far improved that she is able to distinguish objects even at a considerable distance.

12. Patrick Curry: a painful hurt in the arm, caused by a fall from a horse.

13. Lawrence Condron, Jones's Road, Dublin: violent retching.

[I have now before me a letter, written by a Dublin lady, from which I take the following passage:—" You can tell Father Cavanagh that there was a man here in Dublin, living on Jones's Road, by the name of Lawrence Condron, who was very ill, and had a violent retching, and another disease also. A doctor was called in, but he could not stop it with all his medicine. The priest was also called in. The poor man's mother came here, as she leaves us milk, and I gave her a little of the mortar or earth that you sent me, and the moment he took it he was cured, and was here yesterday strong. There are plenty of witnesses of his being cured on the spot."]

14. Patrick Scott, of Ballymoe, a young man who had been a cripple for eight years. He came to the church at Knock on the 27th of November, walking by the assistance of a crutch. He left the crutch after him, and returned homeward bounding with delight.

[A declaration in the following terms is now in my possession:—"I, Patt Scott, parish of Ballintubber, Co. Roscommon, do hereby solemnly declare, that it was at Knock I received power in my leg, which was not of the least use to me for upwards of eight and a half years, being entirely powerless. I could not move or walk without a crutch. I can now walk firmly on it, but it is still short.—Ballintubber, 31st January, 1880."]

The following is an extract from a letter lately written by Patt Scott to Archdeacon Cavanagh, supplying some particulars of his case:—"Dear Father Cavanagh, It is with great pleasure I write an answer to your favor, which I received a few days ago, but must make an apology for so long delaying the particulars you require to know from me. The facts are simply these. Nine years ago I was attacked with a pain in my groin, and for five months no one could tell whether I would live or die. The summer after, I was enabled to move very slowly by means of a crutch, which I continually carried for the last successive eight years, till the day in question. During that time, my leg, from my hip down, was quite powerless, but had feeling. I could not go to my bedside without the aid of the crutch. I never walked on the heel, but simply tipping the ground with the top of my toe, in consequence of a contraction of the sinews. Mrs. —— induced my mother to send me to Knock, that holy place, and on entering the chapel the second time on the same day, I discovered the leg gaining strength. I was so much rejoiced that I determined to leave the crutch after me, as I did, and for the first time in nine years made the effort of walking, independent of the crutch, with both heel and toe, to the astonishment of all the neighbors here, who looked upon it as a very great miracle and curiosity. I forgot to say I carried a stick, and still do. I find I am every day improving, but I shall not feel well satisfied till I pay one or two visits more to Knock. There is no doubt but I derived this great blessing from our Immaculate and Heavenly Queen....

"I am, Reverend sir, respectfully yours,
"PATT SCOTT."

15. John Carney, son of Mr. Thomas Carney, of Eden: instantaneously cured of a very sore and terribly swollen foot by an application of the cement.

16. William Carty had been suffering intense pain from a sore finger. As soon as he placed the finger on the wall, the pain ceased entirely.

17. James Moran, of Kincuin: pain in the side. He had been suffering from it for four years.

18. Mrs. (John Hugh) Fialty, of Cloonlea: acute pain in the right shoulder, arm, and hand; cured after three visits to the church.

19. Mrs. (Martin) Fleming, of Tubber, Ballina: sore leg. In this case the doctors failed to do any good. By bathing the limb in water containing some of the cement a thorough cure was effected.

20. Mary Gallagher, Charleston, Co. Mayo: blindness. She had consulted doctors at home, and also in Dublin, without the least result. After visiting Knock, she was restored to sight.

21. Thos. Conlon, of Shanva here. He was vomiting blood, was in a dying state, and received the last Sacraments of the Church. He was instantaneously cured by swallowing, in a few drops of water, a small piece of the cement.

22. Michael Royan, of Brackloon, Bekan: nearly blind; restored to sight by a visit.

23. Anne Lavin, Castleroyan, parish of Swinford: running evil; had resorted to medical aid with no effect.

24. Maria Crean: evil.

25. Mary Connor, Clonlea: sore and swollen knee.

26. Mary Prendergast, Lessusker. She rode to the church on an ass, being unable to walk, but walked home without any difficulty.

27. Martin Curry, Cloonduce: sore foot; applied to the sore a piece of clay from the church.

28. A young man from Charleston, County Mayo; cured of an evil by a visit to Knock after doctors had entirely failed to help him.

29. A man from Barnacarroll was cured of deafness after he had been a victim to it for five years. The recovery of the sense of hearing was complete.

30. Mary Connell, Wingfield: cured of an eruptive swelling in the head, by going with her mother to the church at Knock, and praying at the spot where the figure of the Blessed Virgin was seen on the 21st of August.

31. Brigid Curry, daughter of Mr. William Curry, of Lecarrow: cured of constant pains in the head, and especially in the eyes and ears.

32. Mr. Joseph Kelly, of Kinclare: chronic headache and megrim, from which he had suffered for a lengthened period.

33. Kate Barrett, Prisen: hacking cough of four years' standing; cured after three visits.

34. Mrs. Kilkenny, of Woodfield: mental derangement, and also a physical ailment that had defied the skill of the doctors.

35. James Burke, Coogue, Pulbog: violent pains in the back and hips.

36. Mrs. (Patrick) O'Brien, of Shanvaghera: restored to health after long indisposition.

37. Mrs. P. Healy: a similar case to the preceding.

38. Owen Mullarkey: ulcer on the face; cured after having lasted thirty years.

39. Mr. Kennedy (father of Miss Kennedy, assistant teacher of the Female National School at Knock): cured of deafness. Some particulars of this case were supplied in one of my former letters.

40. Patrick Kelly, Shammer, Klimovee: epilepsy of a violent type; cured by one visit.

41. Ellen M'Laughlin, Killabeghagh: lameness. She had suffered for three years past with her right foot. She could not touch the ground with it. A number of bones had been extracted from it at different times. She had to be carried on her way to Knock, but, while there, she recovered the full use of her foot, and walked on her return home.

42. A girl named Hughes, the daughter of Andrew Hughes, of Gurtnarah, parish of Claremorris: cured of a pearl on one of her eyes. Her father rubbed the affected eye with some of the cement.

43. A girl named Coleman, of the parish of Claremorris: cured of sore gums (the result of toothache) by washing the part with water containing a portion of the cement.

44. Michael Prendergast, a child two years old, the son of James Prendergast, of Cloonlara, parish of Bekan: cured of a fracture of the skull, the result of a fall.

45. Mrs. (John) Waldron, Lauralia: had suffered from violent retching for more than thirty years; was cured by drinking water in which a piece of the cement had been deposited.

46. Catharine Freehilly, of Island: cured of mental derangement.

47. A young man named Hopkins, second assistant in the National School, Claremorris: cured of epilepsy.

48. John Kilgallen. Coogue, now resident in England, received from his mother a little of the cement, and procured by means of it intense relief from the pain of a broken arm.

49. The mother-in-law of the last-named was suffering from violent pain, the effect of a fall. An application of the cement relieved her.

50. Maria Tully, daughter of Michael Tully, of Churchfield: cured of sore eyes, which had afflicted her for the space of a year and a half; bathed her eyes in water containing a portion of the cement.

51. Michael Moran, Tullarahen: deafness, cured by one visit.

52. Laurence Fleming, parish of Dunmore: cured of deafness.
53. John Kelly, of Ballina: chronic pain in the right side.
54. Michael Langan, a man in the employment of Mr. Little: chronic pain in the foot.
55. Michael MacHale, of Killala: nearly blind; power of seeing much improved.
56. Thady Connor, a herd, of the parish of Kilbridge: lameness; much better since his visit.
57. Brigid Duffy, Tounane, parish of Kilmovee: cured of an evil.
58. Ellen Halligan, of Kilkelly: cured of an evil.
59. Pat. Prendergast, Clarefield, parish of Knock: cured of an evil. This case and the two preceding are recorded as having occurred on the same day—namely, Thursday, the 22d of January.
60. Pat. Boyle, Island: was unable to walk without a stick and a crutch; was cured on his first visit to Knock, and left his crutch behind him.
61. A boy named Kelly from Ballyhaunis: was unable to place his right foot on the ground, or to move about without the help of a crutch. He visited Knock on the 15th of January, and has since been able to walk without the help of a crutch or even a stick.
62. Ellen Morris, Tarman, in the parish of Castlerea: unable to walk at all for a period of two years; completely cured at Knock on the 15th of January.
63. Mrs. Grealy, Ballindreagad: cured of a running evil on the 15th of January.
64. Mr. Conway, brother of Mrs. Curry: cured of blindness; bathed his eyes in water containing some of the cement. He was able to see on the following morning.
65. Richard Kane, of Liscal: sleeplessness and general delicacy of constitution.
66. Martin Concannon, of Kerrane: a megrim.
67. William Heneran, Lakehill: suffered violent pain in his foot, in consequence of the fall of a stone upon it; applied the cement, and obtained relief on the instant.
68. Mrs. Fitzgerald. Swinford: general debility.
69. Miss Glynn, Kilkerrin, housekeeper to Father John Magreal: pains and general debility.
70. Frank Conway, Eden: arm powerless from the elbow; cured by application of the cement.
71. Mary Forestal, Caher, a girl of twelve: was unable to make any use of one of her feet; visited Knock, and returned home quite well.
72. Peter Murphy, Newton, near Claremorris: cured of lameness; used to be unable to walk without a stick.
73. Michael Ansborough, Carramore: restored to sight.
74. Mrs. Kelly, Claremorris: cured of a constant pain in the side.
75. Kate Rodgers: consumption; used to faint every day for a considerable time; is quite restored to health.
76. Mrs. Feeney, hotel keeper, Swinford: violent toothache; cured by an application of the cement.
77. Honora Cussane, parish of Kiltullagh: blindness; cured by visiting Knock. It is stated on the authority of Rev. P. McLoughlin, parish priest of Kiltullagh (Co. Roscommon), that medical men had given up the case.
78. Thomas Moran, of Castles, parish of Kiltullagh, Co. Roscomman: a palsy of the head.
79. Anne O'Donnell, of the parish of Carracastle: blindness and intense pains. She suffered such agony during a period of three years that her mother thought she would find her dead some morning. She is now restored to health and the use of sight.
80. Pat. Boyle, of Garlagh, parish of Crossboyne: epilepsy.

81. Mary Devine, Ballyhaunis, a girl of eleven: lameness and an evil.
82. Michael McNicholas, of Coogue, parish of Knock: blindness.
83. Michael Shaughnessy, parish of Kiltulla: extreme debility. He had been for thirteen weeks unable to turn in bed.
84. Brigid Concannon, of the parish of Glan: right foot powerless; had been unable to move except by the help of two persons; by one visit to Knock was restored to the use of her limbs.
85. Patrick Fallon, Mourneen, Curraleagh: had been for years unable to move unless with a stick and crutch; now walks without using either. He left his crutch behind when leaving Knock.
86. Patrick Browne, Browustown, a boy of about 15: cured of lameness; left his crutch at Knock.
87. John Cawley, a child of five: cured of lameness; left after him at Knock the stick he had been obliged to use.
88. Laurence Madden, of the parish of Clonkeen: had used two sticks in walking; was so far recovered after a visit to Knock as to dispense with one of the sticks.
89. Mrs. (Thomas) Regan, Carracastle: constant pains and general delicacy of long standing.
90. A man, whose name has not been ascertained, received his sight in the church, before all the people, while the *Angelus* bell was ringing on Thursday, the 29th of January.
91. Miss Mannion, of the parish of Roscommon: sight improved by a visit to the church.
92. Martin Noone: paralysis.
93. Mary McLoughlin, Curragh: sore eyes; had been for several years afflicted.
94. Michael Nertney, Tulsk, county Roscommon: restored to sight.
95. Thomas Killeen, of Roslea, parish of Mayo: sight much improved; had been almost stone blind for seventeen years.
[The two cases just set down occurred on Monday, the 2d of February. I was at Knock that day, and happened to be in the church enclosure when Thomas Killeen and Michael Nertney cried out that they began to be able to see. I questioned both of them closely on the spot, and gave the result of my inquiries in a letter written that same evening. Both men convinced me of the truth of their declarations.]
96. Catharine Casey, Deroughal, parish of Aughamore: loss of strength and failure of sight; is now completely recovered.
97. Martin Corcoran, Bushfield, Roscommon: paralysis of the leg.
98. Mrs. Hurley, Roscommon: lameness; much improved.
99. Mary Collins, of Clonbern: blindness.
100. John Flynn, of Cloonmanagh, parish of Kilmovee: an evil; medical remedies had all been tried in vain.
101. John Fogarty, of Crusheen: weakness of the left foot.
102. Pat. Ryder, of Craughwell: epilepsy.
103. Michael Brennan, Ballyhaunis: palsy of the head.

Next week I may give further extracts from the diary, and very remarkable letters from persons cured.

"PERFECT purity," says St. Francis de Sales, "is a virtue which belongs, more particularly, to angels than to men, and in which, nevertheless, Mary infinitely surpasses all the heavenly spirits."

Catholic Notes.

—— The Lenten Conferences at Notre Dame this year on the "Hidden Life of Jesus" have attracted very large audiences.

—— An English pilgrimage to Lourdes is announced for the 2d of June. It will be under the direction of Rev. Lord Archibald Douglas.

—— REV. FATHER LAPONT, S. J., formerly President of St. Xavier's College at Calcutta, has been raised to the Knighthood of the Order of the Indian Empire, for his proficiency in mathematical and physical sciences.

—— THE CONVERSION OF FREEMASONS.—About a year ago, a pious confraternity was established in the diocese of Toledo, Spain, for the purpose of praying for the conversion of Freemasons, and it has since spread over nearly the whole country.

—— The *Pabellon Mexicano* announces the formation of the first circle of Catholic workingmen at Guada Savara, under the name of *Sociedad Fabril.* The aim of these societies may be summed up in two words, "Faith and Progress." The constitutions have been approved by the Archbishop, Monseigneur Labastido.

—— A CHARITY SERMON IN ROME BY AN AMERICAN PRIEST.—By desire of his Eminence, the Cardinal Vicar of Rome, a charity sermon in English was preached in the Church of Gesù e Maria, by Rev. Patrick Toner, pastor of St. Vincent's Church, Plymouth, Pa., on the 3d ult., for the benefit of the Poor Children's Sunday School, under the patronage of the "Circle of the Ladies of the Sacred Heart of Mary." These children are the special objects of the fatherly care of his Holiness. The famous Fra Giovanni sang before and after the sermon, and the choir of St. Peter's was present for the Benediction of the Most Holy Sacrament, which was given by His Lordship, the Bishop of Clifton.

—— DON NICOLA DE PIEROLA, the newly-elected President of Peru, has asked the apostolic benediction of the Holy Father for the commencement and prosperity of his Government in the following letter: "Holy Father:—By the unanimous voice of the people of Peru, I have been entrusted with the supreme magistracy of the Republic, together with all the appointments necessary to the perfecting and purifying of our political institutions, and to secure the triumph of our arms in our war against Chili. While informing your Holiness of my promotion to the highest office in our Republic, so dear to your paternal heart, I renew with most heartfelt satisfaction, the assurances of our faithful allegiance and filial love, which prompt me to kiss the venerable hands of your Holiness, and humbly ask for the apostolic benediction. Given at Lima, Dec., 24, 1879. Nicola de Pierola, President. P. J. Calderon, Secretary of State of foreign relations and divine worship." Don Pierola has for years been the leader of the Catholic party. The former President—a freemason—and his adherents, who had brought the misfortunes of war upon their country, had to fly before the indignation of the people, and seek refuge abroad.

—— WORK OF THE XAVERIAN BROTHERS IN BALTIMORE.—The following Report has just been made to the Honorable Senate and House of Delegates of Maryland by the Joint Committee on Public Institutions, about St. Mary's Industrial School for Boys, near Baltimore, under the direction of the Xaverian Brothers: "Your Committee next visited 'St. Mary's Industrial School for Boys' on the Frederick Turnpike, 1¼ miles from Baltimore, a solid handsome stone structure with all the modern improvements for buildings of this class. Your Committee was much gratified to witness the great economy, good management, and active industry displayed, and of which you will find a fair and truthful exhibit in the Eleventh Annual Report of the Managers which has been placed before you. There are 386 boys in this Reformatory School, all of whom are engaged in useful occupations, the principal of which are shoe-making, printing, basket-making, tailoring and farming. Particular attention is given to the education of the boys, a number of whom are well advanced, with a prospect of future distinction, through the instrumentalities of this noble and charitable Institution, which we believe, in point of management and adaptability, is second to none in the country, and we therefore recommend that a liberal appropriation be made for its support."

—— ST. PATRICK'S DAY brought mingled joy and sorrow to his children in the United States. Everywhere, the old gratitude for his services to Christianity and civilization animated their breasts and gave point to their prayers for their people. Everywhere those aspirations were permeated with the sorrow that not Irishmen alone, but all humanity feels, for the sufferings of the heroic Irish in their own land. To aid them, collections were made; innocent recreations were abandoned and their cost was added to charitable funds for Irish relief. While thousands were giving large sums, there were some even among these gifts more notable for their munificence, as for example that of an unknown Spaniard who once more united "The Shamrock of Erin and the Olive of Spain" by a princely gift of $5,000, or that doubly gracious one of a New York Merchant Prince, Mr. Wm. R. Grace, who, regardless of its cost, offered "to furnish one quarter of the whole cargo required to load the United States ship Constellation; and, further, to give the time of my shipping clerks to classify and attend to the shipment of such donations as may be received by you—thus in part relieving you from the labor necessary to get this vessel's cargo alongside of her and delivered in such shape as will make its proper storage in the vessel easy of accomplishment."—*Catholic Review.*

—— A FLOURISHING CHINESE MISSION.—One of the most flourishing missionary establishments in China, is that of Zi-ka-we, in the province of Kian-nan. First it has a scholasticate, where twenty ecclesiastical students are engaged in the study of Chinese, mathematics, philosophy and theology. Adjoining this, is a novitiate for Chinese lay-brothers. Next comes the seminary for secular priests, and a college with about one hundred native students, some of whom aspire to the priesthood, whilst others are receiving a commercial education to enable them in after life to take charge of the temporal administration of missionary churches, an office which seems to be as regular a vocation of every day life, even as that of the merchant or mechanic. The college itself is furnished with all modern improvements, including observatory, museum, library, laboratory, and philosophical apparatus. It surpasses many of the same size in civilized countries. From the observatory of the college, and but a short distance away, quite a cluster of buildings may be seen; they are the orphan asylum and manual-labor school at Tou-ce-vei, where the orphan boys are taught various trades by the Jesuit lay-brothers. The most remarkable feature of these workshops is a studio for religious pictures and paintings in Chinese style, our Saviour, the Blessed Virgin, and the saints, being represented in Chinese features and dress. The two native brothers engaged here are real artists in their way. All the wants of the mission—clothing, and likewise furniture, both for houses and churches, as also statues and paintings, are supplied from these workshops. The entire establishment forms quite an attraction for European and native visitors coming from Shanghai. It is situated on the right bank of a canal. Near by, on the left bank, is a convent of Carmelite nuns, and a house of "*Religieuses Auxiliatrices*," who have a boarding school, an orphan asylum and a novitiate, besides their establishments at Shanghai.

—ONE OF A BLESSED FAMILY.—Mother St. Francis Xavier, who died recently at the Ursuline Convent, in Quebec, had been a devoted member of the Order for more than half a century. Her name in the world was Miss Annie Barber, and she was a member of that blessed family whose remarkable conversion is perhaps without a parallel in the history of the Church. A correspondent in Canada furnishes the following notice: "Miss Annie Abagail Barber was born in the State of New Hampshire in the year 1811, and was the second oldest daughter of an Episcopal minister, Rev. Virgil Horace Barber, whose father had also received orders in the same church. Her mother, a Miss Booth, was a person of rare endowments, who spent all her leisure moments reading with her husband the writings of the Fathers of the Church, particularly those of St. Cyprian. Thus both husband and wife became well versed in Catholic doctrine, and equally desirous of embracing it; but what was still more extraordinary, they had a mutual desire to follow the evangelical counsels. Their family consisted at this time of four daughters and one son. Mr. Barber, who had removed to New York, was there engaged as professor in the university. After many and severe trials, he relinquished his position and became a member of the Society of Jesus; while Mrs. Barber entered the Visitation Convent in Georgetown, taking with her the three eldest daughters; the youngest was kindly taken in charge by Mrs. Fenwick, mother of the venerable Bishop of that name. The whole family had previously been received into the Church by Bishop Cheverus, in 1817, but it was not until the 2d of February, 1820, on Mr. Barber's return from a visit to Rome, that these two devoted converts pronounced their religious vows together in the convent chapel at Georgetown. A few years later, young Samuel Barber joined his father at the Jesuit College, and three of the daughters became Ursulines—Mary, who pronounced her vows in 1828, and died at the monastery in Quebec on the 9th of May, 1843, a refugee from the devasted convent in Charlestown, Mass.; Anne, the subject of the present notice, and Susan, who made her profession in the monastery at Three Rivers in 1831, and died there in 1837. Mrs. Barber, who took the name of Sister Mary Austin, died at the Visitation Convent in 1860, at the age of seventy, and her son, Father Samuel, died about the year 1850. Father Barber himself died in 1847, at Georgetown College, after having been pastor of Claremont, N. H., where he spent several years, and built the first Catholic church; it was there also that his own aged father became a Catholic, entered Holy Orders, and died a deacon. Mother Josephine Barber is a professed nun of the Visitation Order, and the only surviving member of the family."

Confraternity of the Immaculate Conception
(Or of Our Lady of Lourdes).

" We fly to thy patronage, O Holy Mother of God !"

REPORT FOR THE WEEK ENDING MARCH 24TH.

We have received the following intentions: Recovery of health for 79 persons and 3 families,—change of life for 28 persons and 2 families,—conversion to the faith 18 persons and 6 families,—special graces for 5 priests, 6 religious, 5 clerical students, and 2 persons aspiring to the religious state,—temporal favors for 24 persons and 6 families,—spiritual favors for 32 persons and 7 families,—the spiritual and temporal welfare of 5 communities, 4 congregations, 4 schools and 1 hospital. Also, 41 particular intentions, and 3 thanksgivings for favors received.

Specified intentions: The success of a retreat,—reformation of a poor unfortunate girl,—a young man injured by the cars last August, and now in a helpless and suffering condition,—reconciliation of several persons at variance, and other temporal favors previously recommended,—a happy passage across the ocean for several priests.

FAVORS OBTAINED.

A young man informs us of the conversion of a relative to the true Faith: "A few months ago," he writes, " I sent a petition to you asking the prayers of the Confraternity for the conversion of my uncle, who was at that time a Protestant, and you kindly forwarded me a medal of our Lady for him to wear. I am happy to inform you that he was baptized and received the last rites of the Church on his death-bed." ..... A lady who had recommended the conversion of a Protestant friend informs us that she has since been received into the Church. Several other favors are reported to have been obtained by the use of the water of Lourdes. An infant, thought to be in a dying condition, fell asleep and awoke perfectly well, after taking some of the miraculous water. A lady was suddenly seized with the pains of parturition, caused by the sudden death of her mother, and the most fatal results were apprehended. She took some water of Lourdes that was given to her, made the sign of the cross, and after saying a prayer was instantly relieved, and is now perfectly well.

OBITUARY.

Of your charity pray for the eternal repose of the following deceased persons: Mr. THOMAS MCCABE, whose death occurred at Driftwood, Pa., February 26th. Mr. JAMES MCNELLIS, a native of Co. Donegal, Ireland, who rested in peace on the 1st ult. Mr. THOMAS O'DONNELL, of Benson, Minn., who departed this life the 9th of March. Miss GRACE KEMPS, of Baltimore, Md., whose virtuous life was crowned by a holy death on the 14th ult. Miss AGNES NOLAN, an estimable Catholic of St. Louis, Mo., who departed for heaven on the Feast of St. Patrick. Mrs. ANN CAREY, and Mr. BRYAN HABT, of Waterford, New York ; Mrs. ELIZABETH THOMAS, of Altoona, Pa.; Mr. JAMES BRADLEY, of Philadelphia, Pa.; Mr. FRANCIS DALY, and REBECCA DALY, of Port Carbon, Pa., and Mr. JOHN BOYLE, of Johnstown, Pa., whose deaths are of recent occurrence. MARY COLLINS, FRANK, WILLIAM HENRY and PATRICK MURPHY, of Philadelphia, Pa. And several others, whose names have not been given.

Requiescant in pace.

A. GRANGER, C. S. C., Director.

Youth's Department.

Stupid Hester.

BY THE AUTHOR OF "TYBORNE," "MILDRED'S PRIZE," ETC., ETC.

PERHAPS some of my young readers who were interested in Rosa and Mildred, may like to hear something more about Sister Veronica and her pupils. That dear Sister, for a year previous to her death, was unable to walk, and as I used to stay for weeks together in the extern quarters of the convent, I was allowed to go and sit by her when she was lying on a couch in one of the numerous parlors, or when she was carried in a chair onto the grounds. On these occasions she used to tell me stories of her children during the twenty years and more that she had labored in their service. She and the Mother Superior gave me leave to publish these stories if I thought it would be for the greater glory of God. Of course I do not give the real surnames of the children; and I would here take the opportunity of saying that the convent which I have called St. Agatha's, had in reality quite another name. So with this little preface I will begin my story of "Stupid Hester."

One day Sister Veronica was told to go to the parlor. There she found the Mother Superior and a lady. "This is the First Mistress of the school," said Mother Superior, as she introduced the Sister to Mrs. Reynolds; "and I wished to ask her opinion before I decide on receiving your niece."

"Well, Sister," said Mrs. Reynolds, "I shall be most thankful if you will take this child. Her father, my husband's brother, holds an official post in Hong-Kong, China, and her mother is dead. My husband and I intended to educate her with our own children, but we found it most difficult. My children are all very bright, but Hester *is*—well, the most stupid child *I* ever saw. She will have a nice little fortune when she becomes of age, which falls to her through her mother, and here she is eleven years old, and hardly able to spell; besides, she is so continually in disgrace with Mademoiselle Fibrac, my French governess, that it is more than my husband or I can bear."

"Well, my child," said the Superior, looking at Sister Veronica, "do you feel inclined to take this poor forlorn hope?"

"Yes, Mother: if you approve, I should like to try"; and secretly Sister Veronica's heart yearned towards the motherless child.

Mrs. Reynolds departed, full of joy and thankfulness, and a week later Hester arrived. She was tall of her age, with large features, and a dreamy look in her gray eyes. She was indeed most wofully backward in her studies, and it was found necessary to place her in one of the lower classes, where she towered above the little *dots* of whom the class was composed; even there, she was always at the foot; for all the said dots were very bright, and fought gallantly for the highest places. Hester looked on with an amused smile at their eagerness. The number of times she lost her way about the convent could not be counted. She never *could* understand the different corridors or staircases; she wandered into the kitchen when she was looking for the chapel, and into the laundry instead of the schoolroom. She always mistook one dormitory for another, and as to the alarms of her being lost on the grounds, as old Daniel the gardener said, "it was enough to make a man's hair turn white,"—his hair was a fine iron gray. But Sister Veronica soon perceived that neither scolding nor laughter ever made Hester lose her temper; she was neither passionate, obstinate, nor sullen. She began also to observe in Hester real piety. It was quiet like the rest of her character; in her place in the chapel she would kneel or sit perfectly motionless, and many little signs convinced the watchful Sister that the child's spiritual life was steadily growing.

One of the nuns who was an invalid took Hester in hands, and patiently worked with her at her studies, and with this devoted care the child improved to some extent, but very slowly. So years passed on, and when at fifteen Hester was one of the tallest in the school, she was regarded with considerable contempt by most of the elder girls, and her mistakes and her blunders were a never-failing cause of amusement.

One very sultry day, Fanny Lee and a few of the older pupils were lounging in the garden, rather at a loss for amusement. "I have thought of something," cried Fanny; "do you see Hester Ames with her book?"

"Oh, I suppose she is learning her lessons," said Agnes Doyle; "you know yesterday, when Sister Veronica examined her class in geography, Hester said St. Helena was near Ireland."

A burst of laughter greeted this announcement; as soon as it had subsided, Fanny called loudly to Hester. She obeyed, and came towards the others: "Do you know some one is waiting for you in the parlor?"

"No," said Hester, with a start; "is it—oh, can it be papa!"

"Is he tall, and dark, and rather thin?" said Fanny.

"Oh, yes, yes! that must be him;—that is like him"; exclaimed Hester, the tears of joy starting to her eyes.

"You must not go to the parlor in that dress," continued Fanny; "you know that is never allowed; you must make haste and change it."

Away went poor Hester in a wild search for Sister Lucia, the keeper of the children's wardrobe; of course she looked for the nun in every place where she was *not* likely to be found. Then when the dress was given to her, every button and string that could break or come off did so. At last poor Hester was ready, and rushed down stairs, only to meet with disappointment. There are a great many small parlors at St. Agatha's, as the school brings many visitors, and poor Hester, quite bewildered at the trick played her, could not believe the assurances of the portress that no one had asked for her. The child wandered disconsolately about, and at last took refuge in the chapel, shedding there more bitter tears than any she had ever wept since she entered the school.

Sister Veronica was vexed; she spoke very gravely to Fanny and her companions, and was inclined to punish the former, but Hester interposed. "Oh, Sister, it was all my fault; I ought to have seen that they were in fun; you know I ought not to be so stupid!"

The Sister finally concluded that the best way to make the other girls ashamed was to let Hester's generosity prevail.

Not long after this incident, a beautiful floral exhibition was held in the grounds of Claridge Hall, not far from the convent, and a lady who was well known and trusted by the nuns, offered to take six of the older girls to see it. Both Hester and Fanny were among the number. After passing through the crowded tents in which the flowers were exhibited, the girls and their *chaperone* strayed off to a quiet part of the beautiful grounds, whence a fine view could be obtained; here they discovered a gate leading into a beautifully wooded lane. The children cried out in delight, but soon found the gate was locked; they were quite ready to climb over, but this was beyond Mrs. Rainsforth's powers.

"Well, children," said she, "my eyes are better than my feet; I can see a good way, and as long as you don't go out of sight, you may explore a little, and gather some of that delicious honeysuckle. I will sit on this bench and watch you."

This was no sooner said, than away sprang the eager party, and greatly did they enjoy themselves. The wild flowers were abundant, and each child was busy making up an enormous bouquet.

Suddenly, a strange, hoarse noise struck on their ears, and a sound of rushing feet, accompanied by distressing cries. They came nearer; a mad dog was distinctly heard. With one cry of horror, the children rushed to the gate; all reached it, and clambered over in safety, except Fanny. As she climbed the gate, her foot caught in her dress, and down she went in the road, the dog within a few yards of her, with his glaring eyes, and red tongue hanging out.

Amelia Sutton, Fanny's particular friend, threw herself screaming into Mrs. Rainforth's arms. Hester flew over the gate with a rapidity no one would have given her credit for, and placing herself before Fanny, received the approach of the dog, who immediately attacked her and made his teeth meet in her left arm.

By this time his pursuers had reached the spot, and one man with a hatchet struck the poor animal on the head and killed him. The cries had attracted the attention of those about the grounds, and many gentlemen came running to the spot; among them was a surgeon, and so Hester was carried to the hall, where her arm was immediately cauterized. The Claridge family were absent, and their housekeeper took care of Hester during the operation, while Mrs. Rainsforth had enough to do in looking after Fanny and the other terrified girls. Mrs. Connor, the housekeeper, told Sister Veronica afterwards that she never saw such courage as Hester displayed. While the preparations for the operation were being made, she beckoned Mrs. Connor to her and whispered in her ear, "Crucifix" There was a beautiful little one standing in the room, and Mrs. Connor brought it to her; she held it in her right hand, while the surgeon cut and burnt her left arm, and she smothered her cries into low moans by holding her lips closely pressed to the feet of our Lord's image.

When the arm was bound up, she was brought back to the convent and was laid up for some time. She recovered quickly, however, "owing," the doctors said, "to her extreme placidity"—although her left arm was scarred for life.

Fanny Lee was ill for several days after the accident; the event had, however, an excellent effect upon her; she became a much more pleasing character, and was truly devoted to Hester. It was to Fanny's efforts, after all, that Hester owed much improvement in her studies.

Time passed. Fanny left school, and soon afterwards married. Hester continued at school long after the usual time. Her father talked of coming home, so it was not worth her while to go out to him, and she liked school better than her aunt's house. But her father never arrived; the news of his death came instead. Hester felt it dreadfully; it was the great sorrow and disappointment of her life; she had so fondly loved her father, from whom she had been so long separated, and whose letters had been the chief interest of her life. She remained at the convent till she became of age, and many persons thought she would end by entering a religious order; but she had no religious vocation. Some of the property in which her fortune consisted had risen in value during her minority, so that Hester was really rich; nevertheless, she lived in the very plainest manner.

Fanny Lee, or rather Fanny Markham, was left a widow early in life, with several children. She lived in London, and Hester made her home with her, and spent her time among the poor. "There she is now," added Sister Veronica. She is literally the servant of the poor, and about twice a year takes a short holiday to come to see us and her beloved convent. You know her, and you esteem her. The world thinks her 'odd,' 'rather green,' and 'uninteresting.' The parish priest calls her the 'friend of vagabonds,' and has, after many attempts, given up the hopeless task of trying to prevent her from being 'taken in.' She is a living exemplification of one who 'believeth all things, endureth all things.' She saves many souls, which were to all appearances lost, because of her enduring hope in them—of her patient watching for them."

Far away in a distant land, where the fields were "white unto the harvest," and there was no help, there stands a church and presbytery with schools and convent attached—all built and endowed by an unknown benefactor. Few, very few knew that that was where Hester's fortune was spent, and that she has only a very little left for herself. "So she goes on," said Sister Veronica, and probably will go on till she dies—unknown, forgotten, rather looked down upon.—*Stupid Hester!* But I think she will shine brightly when the Master comes to make up His jewels.

Our Lady and the Young Sailor.

LITTLE B. K. was the son of Jewish parents, and had been carefully instructed in the principles of the Law of Moses. One day, in company with some comrades of his own age, he entered one of the Catholic churches of Paris. It happened to be at a time when they were enabled to witness those beautiful ceremonies attending a First Communion. Who can say what passed within the heart of the little Israelite during that solemn hour? We know, however, that he never forgot what he then witnessed. He even went so far as to express his desire to share in the happiness of those privileged children whom he saw receiving Holy Communion for the first time.

But his hour had not yet come, for his mother, a few days afterwards, had him apprenticed as cabin-boy on board a vessel which was about to sail. She thought thus to destroy the hopes of the child, but "the Spirit of God breatheth where it will." The vessel which bore young B—— met with a violent storm, and was soon a total wreck. But he together with some sailors who had escaped by means of a small boat, were picked up by a vessel which they had the good fortune to meet. But their happiness was not of long duration, for a new storm arose and beat with greater fury upon the vessel, which soon sank. Thinking that his end had come, the poor child closed his eyes and lost consciousness. Once again he was saved, and picked up by another vessel, which also seemed doomed to perish. But, in the midst of the storm, the sailors invoked Mary, Star of the Sea. This prayer addressed to Our Lady made such an impression upon the young lad that he joined his voice with that of the sailors.

Whilst he was thus praying, a heavy sea pitched the vessel to one side, and he was precipitated into the waves. What had become of the sailors? He did not know. As for himself, at first stunned by the shock, he soon recovered his senses and swam desperately. Fatigued and worn out, he was about to give himself up as lost, when he saw, in the distance, a cask tossing about on the waves. Gathering up all his remaining strength, he managed to reach it, and clung to it with desperate energy. It was his plank of salvation. Resting upon this cask, in the middle of the wide ocean, our youthful hero began to reflect. He recalled the scene of the tempest and the touching prayer of the sailors. It was this prayer that saved him; again it ascended fervently from his lips. "Mary, O Holy Virgin," he added, "save me! and I promise thee I shall soon become thy child." He was then picked up by a passing vessel on its way to France, and landed at Rouen. He made all possible haste to return to his family. He reached Paris on foot, and joyfully knocked at the door of his mother's house; but it was closed against him. Two days afterwards, he was found overcome with grief and dying of hunger. A charitable and pious family took him in and cared for him for eight days, and then brought him to the Abbé R——, who finally baptized him and admitted him to his First Communion. And to-day this dear *protegé* of Mary is a fervent Christian. But it may well be that Providence, which has taken him by the hand, has other views in his regard, and may have in reserve for him a place in the ranks of the clergy. Such is at least his desire, and such seems to be his vocation.

THE

AVE MARIA.

A Journal devoted to the Honor of the Blessed Virgin.

HENCEFORTH ALL GENERATIONS SHALL CALL ME BLESSED.—St. Luke, i, 48.

VOL. XVI.   NOTRE DAME, INDIANA, APRIL 10, 1880.   No. 15.

[For the "Ave Maria."]

At Eventide.

MAURICE F. EGAN.

THE tender Mother as she sat among
  The home-made toys that, scattered on the
    floor,
Showed that a young Child played within her
    door,
Took up her weary Son, and softly sung
The low, sad psalms that dreary days had wrung
  From Israel in exile,—now, no more
  She sang triumphant, for her heart was sore,
For on the tune the sword its shadow flung.

She could not gaze upon His golden head
  Or in her hand His dimpled fingers hold,—
Or feel His Heart beat next her Mother-heart,
Without forecasting that His forehead fair
  Should bear the thorns, and His soft Flesh grow
    cold,
  As fiercest pangs through palm and side
    should dart.

GRATITUDE towards Mary is one of the characteristics of the saints, who have all found pleasure in celebrating her greatness. "O Mother of mercy," said St. Anselm to her, "what tongue can express, or what intellect calculate, the number of captives of Satan whom you have restored to liberty by reconciling them with God!" "You are," says St. Bernard, "that generous and compassionate Rebecca, giving your favors not only to the just, represented by Eliezer, but also to the sinners, represented by the camels of that servant of Abraham." "How many benefits has the world received from you!" exclaims St. Bonaventure. "Praise, honor, power, and glory be yours for all eternity!"

On the Appian Way.

SANTA BALBINA.

BY ELIZA ALLEN STARR.

AMONG the photographs of a portfolio, precious mementos of a winter and spring—even to mid-summer—in Rome, is one which invariably holds the eye of the most listless of picture-gazers. There are many others in the portfolio which are larger, many which one might suppose would be more striking, especially to an eye not familiar with Roman scenery; but still, the unlearned as well as the learned, the child of some secluded home on the prairies, as well as the youth who has travelled in Europe before his teens, always pause before this small photograph of "The Appian Way"; that *Via Appia* of the modern Italian, or the *Regina Viarum* of the ancient Roman; and which is as sacred in its associations to the Christian of whatever country or people, as it is interesting to the classical scholar. In truth, we may say that if the *Appian Way* deserved the title of *Regina Viarum*, or "Queen of Ways," from pagan Rome, still more does it deserve this title from Christian Rome. For while the dismantled tombs of the Appian Way beyond the third milestone, give no clue to those whose ashes once rested within; or of their builders, who hoped to perpetuate their names in death, the Christian pilgrim reads, with a thrill of pious joy, on the marble tablet, or tufa wall, the names of saints and martyrs whom he has venerated from his youth, and kneels at the shrines where their sacred relics repose.

The Appian Way, which has defied the ravages of time and the vicissitudes of Governments for two thousand years, was begun B. C. 312, by the censor, Appius Claudius the Blind, "the most illustrious of the great Sabine and Patrician race, of which he was the representative." This magnificent avenue, paved through its whole extent, was carried, by Claudius himself, across the Pontine marshes as far as Capua, and afterwards to Brundusium. Beginning within the present walls of Rome, at the site of the ancient *Porta Capena*, or Capuan Gate, which is now clearly marked for the travellers by a P. C. on the wall of the vineyard between the Church of San Gregorio and San Sisto, it is visible from a distance for miles across the Campagna by the magnificent pagan tombs of Roman patricians, the *columbaria*[*] of their slaves and freedmen, and the cemeteries of the early Christians. It is this avenue of ruins, with stretches of the Campagna on either hand, and mountains on the horizon, which makes the charm of the photograph we have alluded to.

Starting from the Capitol, we cross the Roman Forum, pass through the Arch of Titus, stand face to face with the Colosseum; turn to the right through the Arch of Constantine, to the right again at San Gregorio, pass the rope-walk which invariably marks the populous boundary of a European city, and see on the left the P. C., which tells us that we have reached the old Porta Capena, mentioned by Ovid, Propertius, and Martial. For near it stood the temple of Mars, before which, the armies entering Rome in triumph were obliged to halt; the little temple of Hercules; the temples of Honor and Virtue vowed by Marcellus and dedicated by his son, and also a fountain dedicated to Mercury; and here stood the tomb of that sister of the Horatii, who, coming to the Capuan Gate to meet her sole surviving brother, saw on his shoulders the cloak, wrought by her own hands, of one of the Curiatii to whom she had been betrothed. At this sight, we are told, the maiden cried aloud and wept for him she loved. But her brother, full of wrath at her tears, drew his sword and stabbed her to the heart, saying: "So perish the Roman maiden who shall weep for her country's enemy!" It was at the Porta Capena, too, that Cicero was received in triumph by the Senate and Roman people upon his return from banishment B. C. 57; and not far from this same spot is the *Fountain of Egeria*.

But these localities, distinguishable only to the eye of the close observer, and interesting only to the classical scholar, are almost forgotten in the glow of enthusiasm which kindles at the sight of the fortress-looking church crowning a ridge of the Aventine Hill on the right. Grand in its proportions, solid in its structure, and bearing all the marks of its imperial origin, one must climb the winding, rocky pathway, washed by rains, bordered by wild flowers, and stand in front of the portal with its strip of crimson velvet edged with bullion, to believe it is a church. But its story is one of those which illustrate the empire as well as Christianity, and belongs to the Catacombs as well as to the Appian Way.

In the year 117 after Christ, Alexander I had sat nine years upon the Chair of Peter, to which he was called when only thirty years of age.[*] But this youthful Pontiff had received rare graces from heaven, and this special one, among others, of winning souls to Christ. In spite of the awful persecutions in this early age, Alexander converted many of Rome's noblest senators to Christianity. The most noticeable of these conversions was that of Hermes, Prefect of Rome, whom he baptized, together with his wife, his sister Theodora and her sons, and twelve hundred and fifty slaves, on one of the Paschal days. To all these slaves Hermes gave their liberty, and distributed his immense riches among them, so as to render their freedom a blessing. When the decree against the Christians under Trajan was sent to Rome, Hermes was denounced to the authorities as a Christian, and with Pope Alexander, was committed to prison under the care of the imperial tribune Quirinus. No sooner did the tribune see his prefect in his charge, than he began to expostulate with him: "Why do you resign a post of honor for the chains of the vilest of criminals?" But Hermes replied: "I have not lost my prefecture; I have only exchanged it for a still nobler rank. A terrestrial dignity is liable to all the vicissitudes of earth; a celestial dignity is as eternal as God Himself."

"What," exclaimed the tribune, "can have seduced you, whose wisdom we all admire, to so foolish a doctrine! Do you really believe there will remain anything of us, after this life, save a few ashes which a breath may scatter to the winds?"

"I also," said Hermes, "once smiled at such a hope, and esteemed only this mortal life."

"But," persisted Quirinus, "what can have led you to this change of sentiment? what proofs have you of your present belief? Tell them to me; perhaps I shall believe them in my turn."

Hermes replied: "You have now under your care the very person who convinced me: Alexander!"

At the bare mention of this name, Quirinus uttered a malediction against Alexander, and then, in the same breath, cried out: "O illustrious Hermes, my master, I conjure you to resume your office, your rank. Alexander is an impostor, a miserable magician, whom I have thrust into the

---

[*] *Columbaria*, so called because the walls were filled with small niches for the urns in which the ashes of the dead were kept, these walls having a resemblance to a dove-cote.

[*] Among the portrait-pictures by Fra Angelico is one of Alexander, Pope and Martyr. The beauty of the face is too youthful to be understood, unless we remember the age of Alexander when called to rule the Church of Christ.

lowest dungeon. Is it possible that you have been deceived by this adept in crime? If he is as powerful as is pretended, why does he not deliver himself and you?"

"The Jews," answered Hermes, "said these very words to Jesus Christ, my Master, when He hung upon the cross. And if Jesus Christ had not been horrified at their perfidy, if He had not been certain of their insincerity, He would have come down from the cross, and have revealed Himself to them in all His majesty."

"Ah, well," said Quirinus, with a gesture of disdain, "I will go to this Alexander, and I will say to him: 'Dost thou wish me to believe in thy God? Behold, I triple the number of thy chains; meanwhile, let me see thee, at the hour of supper, in the cell of Hermes. If I see this miracle, I will believe.'" With the proposition on his lips, the tribune actually visited the dungeon of Alexander, and, after having tripled his chains and doubled the guards at the door, left his prisoner.

But no sooner had Quirinus left him, than Alexander extended his arms, chained as he was, and prayed thus: "My Lord and my God, who has seated me on the throne of Peter, Thy Apostle, to You I offer up the passion and the death which await me. But grant me this one favor: conduct me, this evening, to the cell of Hermes, and return me, to-morrow morning, to my own dungeon!"

No sooner had evening come, than a child, bearing a torch, appeared to Alexander, took him by the hand, opened the sealed entrance and conducted him to the cell of Hermes. The two martyrs, thus miraculously reunited, immediately betook themselves to prayer, and in this attitude they were found by Quirinus, when he took the evening repast to Hermes with his own hands.

At first his affright did not allow him to utter a word. He was thunderstruck. "You asked a miracle," they said to him. "The one you demanded has been granted. Believe then in Jesus Christ." But when he had recovered his spirits, he said: "Perhaps this is only one of the exhibitions of your magic."

"What!" exclaimed Hermes; "was it not at your suggestion that the seals of the prison were broken without leaving a trace? You named your own conditions; have they not been kept?"

The face of the imperial tribune showed deep emotion. Some thought was struggling for utterance. At length he said: "I have a daughter, Balbina, whom I had expected to give soon in marriage. But an ulcerous wen has appeared upon her neck, for which no physician holds out the hope of a cure. Heal her, and I will believe in Jesus Christ."

Without a moment's hesitation Alexander replied: "Take this iron chain which is around my neck and lay it upon the neck of thy daughter, and she will be cured."

Quirinus stood as if not quite sure that he ought to leave his prisoners together. Alexander saw this, and said: "Lock the door as usual; to-morrow morning you shall find me in my dungeon."

On the morrow, at the first dawn of day, Quirinus could have been seen at the door of Alexander's dungeon. Nor was he alone. His young daughter, Balbina, miraculously cured, was with him. He opened the door, to find his prisoner within, and casting himself at his feet bathed them with tears, saying: "My lord, I conjure you, intercede for me to that God whose Bishop you are, that He may pardon my past incredulity. Behold my daughter! I have done as you commanded me, and she is cured."

Quirinus was indeed converted. Immediately, at Alexander's request, the Christians under his charge were brought before the Pontiff. Then, at the suggestion of Quirinus himself, the prisoners were brought in, and these, together with Quirinus and Balbina, were baptized. But all this could not transpire without consequences. A secretary in the service of Quirinus reported these events to the Prefect Aurilianus, and the tribune was summoned to his presence to answer for thus becoming the dupe of his prisoner. To the reproaches and threats which were heaped upon him, he boldly replied: "I am a Christian. You may scourge me, strike off my head, burn me—anything you like: but I shall never be other than a Christian. All the prisoners who were in my charge are Christians likewise. I have entreated the Pontiff Alexander, and the patrician Hermes, to quit their dungeons; I have even opened their doors to allow them to escape, but they have refused to do so. They sigh for death as the famished sigh for a feast; now, do with me as you see fit."

"Insolent fellow!" cried the prefect: "your tongue shall be cut out and your body tortured." His tongue was really cut out and his body stretched on the rack. Afterwards his hands and feet were cut off, and, finally, his head was severed from his mangled body, with the order to throw his carcass to the dogs. But the dogs of Rome had finer instincts than their pagan masters; and the body, with the dissevered members, of the tribune of the fortress prison on the slope of the Aventine Hill, remained untouched, when some Christians gathered them up by night and bore them to the Cemetery of Pretextatus on the Appian Way.

As to Balbina, we can well believe what is said of her in the *Acts* of St. Alexander, Pope and Martyr, which are among the few that escaped the burning of the Christian records ordered by Diocletian, and which have been marvellously confirmed by the discovery of the tomb of St. Alexander in Rome on the Nomentan Way, in 1844, 1860 and 1864. In these *Acts* we are told that

Balbina, after living the life of an angel, employing all her goods for the support and nourishment of the persecuted Christians, gave up her soul to God on the 31st of March, in the year 169, on which day her feast is solemnly kept in the fortress Church of Santa Balbina on the Aventine Hill, beside the Appian Way. Her body was laid by the relics of her father, Quirinus, in the Cemetery of Pretextatus. To this day, the Catholic pilgrim in Rome finds himself summoned to her shrine on that day by the *Diario Romano*, and while the dismantled Baths of Caracalla on his left hand, as he ascends the rocky road, proclaim the nothingness of human ambition, on the right a church, of the same era, raises its invincible front under the patronage of the daughter of a Roman tribune, its picturesque tower of brick being one of the marked forms which stand out against the softly undulating lines of the Campagna from a distance. The open timbers of the roof on the interior preserve its ancient aspect. In the choir is an Episcopal chair of great age, all of marble and mosaic; and the tomb of Stefano Sordi, which supports a reclining figure, is adorned with the colored and gold mosaics peculiar to the Cosmatic family. On the wall is a crucifix in relief, from the old crypt of St. Peter's, which is most touching in its expression, so affectionately does our Lord fix His eyes on the Blessed Virgin beside His Cross. Under the high altar is a sarcophagus, containing the relics of St. Balbina and St. Felicitus, surmounted by a gilt crown with palms crossed. Before this sarcophagus, on her feast day, we found, spread out on the marble pavement, a floral carpet, the flowers laid on wet sand, in tasteful patterns, and fringed with long stalks of the white and purple stock-gilly flower. At the corners were pots of pansies, delicate purple and pure white; from all of which we were encouraged, by those in attendance, to draw fragrant mementoes of Santa Balbina, Virgin and Martyr.

Between the Appian and the Ardeatine Ways, which run side by side to each other, and adjoining the Catacomb of St. Callistus, lies the newly discovered, and still only half-explored, Catacomb of Santa Balbina. St. Mark, who was Pope in 336, is known to have greatly enlarged it, and even to have built the basilica where his relics were deposited in this cemetery, whose grandeur is said to be likely to surpass any which have yet been discovered, so numerous, so vast, and so well lighted are the chambers already explored. But there is another cemetery which must draw, still more irresistibly, the feet of one in search of all that concerns St. Quirinus and his daughter Balbina, and this is the Catacomb of St. Pretextatus. It stands on the left side of the Appian Way, between the first and the second milestone outside the walls, extruding under a surface covered with vineyards and prairies, near the site of the circus Maxentius. To which individual of the illustrious family of the Prætextati we owe this Catacomb, has not yet been discovered, but the martyrs deposited in its subterranean beds are perfectly known, thanks to documents of undoubted verity. This cemetery is one to which we shall again call the attention of our readers: but will mention here that in one of the principal chambers is a crypt, containing a sarcophagus in which was preserved, for many ages, the relics of the martyred tribune. On the face of this stone is sculptured, according to the custom of those times, the bust of the person who lay within, clothed in the *lati-clave*, or tunic, with a broad purple stripe, which was a mark of distinction worn by tribunes of senatorial rank. In devotional pictures, Saint Quirinus is represented, sometimes with an arm cut off; sometimes in armor with his horse, as an equestrian tribune; sometimes, too, he is accompanied by a falcon, which refuses to touch the severed tongue of Quirinus, thrown to it for food, or a dog, who refuses to touch the limbs of the martyr, thrown to him in like manner. St. Balbina is represented holding the chain of Pope Alexander which was the means of her miraculous cure. She is invoked for the healing of scrofulous diseases, as well as her father, Saint Quirinus. All the traditions which we have referred to, are observed by ancient pictures in the choir of the noble canonesses of St. Quirinus at Nuyss, not far from Cologne, which is enriched by the relics of the imperial tribune and his daughter. The story of the translation of these relics is too interesting to be withheld. Leo IX, a native of Alsace, and Pope from 1049 to 1055, was earnestly entreated by his sister Pepa, abbess of Nuyss, while on a visit to Rome, to give her the bodies of St. Quirinus and St. Balbina, which he finally consented to do. The relics accompanied Pepa on her return. Arrived one evening at a little distance from Dacksbourg, now Dabo, the mule carrying the relics refused to go on, and the abbess was forced to deposit them on the ground as decently as was in her power. The next morning the relics could not be raised from the ground, with all the strength which could be brought to their rescue. The pious abbess was not one to contend with the manifest will of heaven, and immediately proceeded to build a sanctuary on the spot, which was confided to proper guardians; contenting herself, meanwhile, with carrying to her convent the heads of the Saints, which expressed no unwillingness to accompany her. At two different times, an attempt was made by the nuns of Nuyas to bring the relics, entire, to their convent; but both were defeated by some providential interference. The priory of St. Quirinus, around which a village bearing his name soon sprang up, is still in possession of a large portion of these relics; although Rome has recalled what gives a claim on the veneration of the Catholic pilgrim, in the Church of Santa Balbina on the rocky slope of the Aventine Hill, overlooking the Via Appia.

(TO BE CONTINUED).

'Beth's Promise.

BY MRS. ANNA HANSON DORSEY.

CHAPTER XIII.

AN OLD GATE IS OPENED.

GOING back to "Ellerslie" was no small trial to Mrs. Morley. Its old familiar scenes, clustering with memories of brighter and happier days, saddened her beyond expression. It was but natural that this should be the case; but since she had learned to put self aside, there was no more excessive and morbid yielding to grief; she only clung nearer to the cross, offering the sorrowful memories of the past, with the sorrows and tears of Mary on Calvary, which strengthened and helped her to endure them.

Aunt 'Beth did not look so ill as they had feared to see her; she received them with open arms, smiles and tears blending with her welcome, as she clasped first one, and then the other, to her heart, releasing them only to scan their faces with a loving glance, and fold them in another and closer embrace. Even the old house itself seemed to have put on a festive and rejoicing expression to greet them to its hospitable shelter. It all looked like fairy-land to 'Beth, who had not been to "Ellerslie" since she was a child, and had no remembrance of its attractions; but now as she stood a moment, and cast her eyes over the lovely surroundings, the thought arose in her mind that unhappiness could have no entrance among scenes that embodied so true an ideal of earthly paradise. Everything was such a delightful surprise to her that she did not think of the human lives that had passed their span of tears and smiles, of happy union and bitter separation, under the old grey roof, leaving it finally, with all its brightness and cheer, to join their ancestors in the family vault. Ah, happy it is for the young, that the "shadows" wait for a later day to enter into the pleasures of their life, sparing their dark omens from the morning feast, when the dew is upon its flowers, and its wine-cup is filled to the brim with hopes that sparkle in its sunshine, the bright draught telling no tale of the bitter lees it conceals! And so 'Beth Morley wondered if sorrow could ever find entrance into so fair an eden as "Ellerslie." "I think," she whispered, "I should like to stay here all my life."

After luncheon, Aunt 'Beth had to lie down; the little flush of color in her cheeks, and the brightness of her eyes, which the excitement of their arrival had kindled, made them think she must be in a better condition of health than she really was; but now they saw her pale and languid, and perceived that she was indeed failing.

"My health is perfectly good," she said, having quickly noted the look of concern on their faces; "I only get tired sooner than I used to; but that is because I am getting to be a very old woman. It is my age, but it is not agreeable, I must say, to have your strength drifting away like this—should you think so, my dear?" she asked of 'Beth, who sat on the floor, close to the sofa on which she was reposing.

"It will come back again, Aunt 'Beth," replied 'Beth, with audacious trust in her own prophecy, "and as to being such an antedeluvian as you make out, I don't believe a word of it."

"Oh, I don't give up in the least, you may believe, and don't mean to, my dear. I can't walk about as much as I have been accustomed to, but I've got a sure-footed little mule, as gentle as a lamb and as silky as a kitten, and every morning I get on his back and ride all over the farm, then go to see after my poor friends outside. I don't give up, I assure you!"

"That's lovely, and, if you'll let me, I'll walk along side to-morrow, Aunt 'Beth."

"Yes; that would be pleasant. But I have also a light garden carriage that holds two; sometimes I go in that, and you, my dear Anne, and 'Beth, shall take it by turns to go with me whenever you like. There's a new basket phaeton coming for you, 'Beth, my dear, and the gentlest of horses waiting for it, to drive around in when and where you will; only Lodo must go along at first to take care of you!',

"Oh, mamma, did you ever hear of anything so delightful! A phaeton and horse! And I suppose Lodo is a great New Foundland dog!" exclaimed 'Beth, her face glowing with pleasure.

Mrs. Morley, who was sitting near the window watching the flicker of sunshine and shadow upon the newly-mowed lawn, and inhaling the fragrance of carnations and violets which was wafted in on the summer breeze, turned and caught Aunt 'Beth's eye, and they both laughed.

"Oh, my mamma! how beautiful to see you laugh once more; I am glad I have been so childish, since it has made you laugh, and amused Aunt 'Beth."

Before either of them had time to speak, a neat, pretty girl, with dark skin and great black eyes, her cheeks glowing like a September peach, and her attire fitting her trim little figure to perfection, came into the room holding in her hand a garment that she had been at work on. Dropping a quaint little courtesy to the strangers, she crossed the floor to Aunt 'Beth's sofa, saying, as she held up a long skirt: "Don't you think, mem, it needs a tuck? She's not tall, you know."

"Why yes, Lodo: two tucks would not be out of place. Wait a moment, child. Anne, this is the little girl—you remember; Lodo, this lady is my niece, Mrs. Morley; and this, her daughter and my namesake. I want you to help to make 'Ellerslie' very pleasant for them."

"Yes, mem, I will indeed; and I hope the ladies will like it ever so much," said Lodo, showing her small even teeth in a delighted smile, as Mrs. Morley and 'Beth shook hands with her, and told her how glad they were to see her, and how sure they were that she would be very kind to them." She tripped out smiling, and resumed her work with many pleasant thoughts of the gentle ladies who had spoken so kindly to her, to lighten her task.

"And that is Lodo! No wonder you laughed at me! It was the odd name that made me think of a Newfoundland dog; but why, I'm sure I can't say, only I thought that a nice large dog would be the very thing to make it all complete—the phaeton and horse I mean," said 'Beth, laughing. "I shall take Lodo to my heart! She's the prettiest, quaintest little being I ever saw."

"Yes, that is Lodo. Anne, did you never tell her about Lodo?"*

"No: I believe not. She faded quite out of my mind after I left 'Ellerslie' that time. How she has grown!"

"Who is she? I know she has a history, she looks so like an elf," asked 'Beth.

"She may be one, for aught I know to the contrary," said Aunt 'Beth. "I picked her up on the roadside one day, the raggedest, most forlorn specimen of humanity I ever saw. She bit and scratched my coachman when he lifted her into the carriage, and screamed and struggled all the way home. It was as much as I could do to keep her from jumping out of the carriage window; I had her washed and fed—she was as ravenous as a young kite; then I tried to find out to whom she belonged, but could learn nothing, except that a swarm of gypsies had gone along the road the day before, and I suppose they must have left her somewhere near where I found her. I asked her, her name. She said, 'Lodo, mem, and that's all I know.' I asked her if she had a mamma? 'No, mem: only womens.'

So putting this and that together, I supposed that the gypsies had dropped her in the road to get rid of her, and that they were English gypsies, from the way she always said 'mem,' and I thought it very probable that her mother was an English country girl who had run off and married into the tribe, and afterwards died, leaving her child to their tender mercies. But heaven only knows! Anne, you remember what a little outlaw she was, when you gave her her first lesson in civilization."

"Yes," said Mrs. Morley; "but under it all, I saw a warm, honest little heart, and it helped me to be patient with her."

"Well, as it has turned out, she has been the comfort of my life, but she's like a wild creature about the air and sunshine, and is never so happy as when she's in the woods. I very often send her on errands that give her long tramps under the trees, where she sees her old friends, the birds and rabbits, and has a thousand funny things to tell about them when she returns. She's an odd little person!"

"I wonder if she has ever been baptized?" said Mrs. Morley.

"That I can't tell, nor can she, I fancy. The possibilities are all against it, however. It is one of her freaks to attend service at the Dulaney church over yonder, where I suppose the music and glitter attract her gypsy heart."

"What a romantic little story!" said 'Beth. "Lodo and I will be fast friends, I'm sure."

"And that reminds me," said Aunt 'Beth, "of a very polite note I received yesterday from Mrs. Dulaney, offering a pew in their chapel for the use of my friends; knowing that it was private property, I had written to her, asking if strangers would be permitted to attend, and mentioned that I expected some Catholic relatives who would be glad of an opportunity to attend services there. It is a very polite, well-written note."

"How kind and thoughtful to have taken so much trouble about us, Aunt 'Beth!" said Mrs. Morley, feeling deeply touched.

"Trouble! nonsense, Anne! In the old times there used to be a great intimacy between the Tracys and Morleys—so great that they agreed to have a gate cut in the wall that divides the two estates, which made them very near neighbors indeed, the walk from one house to the other taking only five or six minutes. Before, it was a good half hour's drive round to get there. The gate has not been opened for twenty years, but I'm going to make an effort—if the new people don't object—to have it opened again, which will be very convenient for you and 'Beth, as the chapel is only a few rods from it."

"How nice for you, dear mamma!" said 'Beth. "Now I'm going to get my big hat and stroll around a little. I want to see the hops."

---

* Lodo, in the Spanish Creole dialect of Porto Rico, means dirty. Had Aunt 'Beth known this, she would doubtless have changed it.

"And I will go to my room, so that Aunt 'Beth can get a nap. We have fatigued her, I'm afraid, by making her talk so much," said Mrs. Morley, rising to go.

"Sit still, Anne," said Aunt 'Beth, with a little snap of her teeth. "Don't talk nonsense! When I get to the pass of sleeping in broad daylight, or holding my tongue for fear of talking myself into a fever, I shall consider myself a bad case. I am not sick, and I only lie down now and then to rest myself. Sit still, my child, and let us talk on; I haven't enjoyed anything so much for years: having you two to look at and talk to, makes me feel quite alive again!"

"I'm glad you don't mind talking, for, my dear Aunt 'Beth, I do like to let my tongue run on without hindrance, and, if you like it, I'll talk from morning until night," said 'Beth, kneeling down by the sofa to kiss her.

"Yes, I do like it," said Aunt 'Beth, slowly. "The old house here has been too silent. Sometimes I began to fancy that it was haunted, and I longed for some one to speak to. Mrs. Trott and Lodo couldn't give what I needed, although they did the best they could by faithful service and no end of chatter about domestic matters, that tired me half to death. Oh I'm so glad to have you both here, my dears!"

"And we are pleased also to be with you, Aunt 'Beth; it will do us all good, being together," said Mrs. Morley, smoothing the little thin hand that lay in hers. "I'll stay here, darling, if you are going out," he said to 'Beth.

"I'm going to stay just where I am, dear mamma. The hops can wait," she replied, with a bright smile.

"Ah yes, you were going to look at the hop-vines, and you could not see a lovelier sight, my child; next week we begin to pick them. The hop harvest is the great frolic of the year to the class who hire out, for miles around, but not to their employers."

"Why so?"

"We hire our help in this region by the year, with one arbitrary condition, which is, two weeks' vacation for the hop-picking. Most people are left without help when that time comes, all the hands swarming away to the hop-fields, more for the frolic than for what they earn, although they are paid liberally, for it's a matter of some importance to the growers to get the hops into the drying houses just at the right time. Mrs. Trott and old black Tom are satisfied to be lookers on, so I'm not left entirely to my own resources. I let Lodo enjoy herself at our own hop-picking; she's full of young life, and she makes the most of her frolic. I'm glad you'll see it, my dears; it reminds me of what I've read of gathering in the vintage in France and Italy, and the 'harvest-home' in England and Germany."

"Do they work all the time?" asked 'Beth, much interested.

"From sun rise to sun set, but it is very light work. They are as merry as crickets, and as they pick in squads, they can gossip, and laugh and sing together to their hearts' content. After supper, the flirting and dancing and the real fun begin. Sometimes they dance in a barn, sometimes on the grass by moonlight; it is all very bright and cheerful, and they say there are a great many matches made on these occasions. Children," said Aunt 'Beth, "you have done me good already. Suppose now I had begun to die a-top like an old tree, what a blank my last days would have been! As it is, I am thankful! Weak knees are a great inconvenience, but not half so bad as beginning to die a-top."

"You haven't begun to die anywhere yet, head or feet," said 'Beth, leaning her cheek against hers, "and we'll dance together at the hop-picking! Now," she added, as she rose up, "I smell so many spicy odors, that I'm going out to learn where they come from; I feel quite bewitched, and think perhaps it's all true about the dryads, and naiads, and elfs, and I shouldn't be in the least astonished if I were to meet them roaming about "Ellerslie." They heard her singing a merry little air as she went out on the lawn, where she soon found the carnations and violets, whose pleasant odors had lured her out.

"So much like her father; have you noticed it, Anne?" said Aunt 'Beth.

"Yes: not only in her eyes and countenance, but she has his best qualities of mind and heart," answered Mrs. Morley, gently. Then both were silent—both thinking fond, sad thoughts of him they should never see again on earth; one mingling the prayers in her inmost heart with the tears that welled up from it; the other, enduring like a stoic, the grief that had given her a blow from which she could not recover, and which was the true cause of what she called her " ageing "

It was Sunday morning. The old gate in the wall between "Ellerslie" and "Tracy-Holme" had been opened, and now stood thrown back to admit Mrs. Morley and 'Beth, pioneered by Lodo, on their way to the chapel. It was a beautifully-furnished stone edifice, standing in a grove of ancient elms, Gothic in style, with all its appointments perfect and in the best taste. The high, lancet-shaped windows were of stained-glass from Venice; the altar of purest marble, panelled with *verd-antique;* the tabernacle like carven lace work; an ivory crucifix stood aloft between the two rich windows in the rear, and under it, in full view, a painting of the sinless Mother of Dolors. The furnishing of the altar was of fine lace and massive silver. A niche on either side contained a statue of Mary Immaculate and of St. Joseph, the wisest, the tenderest and holiest of men, as she was the purest and most blessed of women. The chapel was under the patronage of St. Joseph and so named. It was evident that these devout and wealthy Catholics—the Dulaneys—had offered their richest and their best to the service of heaven; there was no grudging or holding back the price apparent in anything; it was the prayer and thanksgiving of their life, built up in visible form—a monument of their faith, which consecrated and crowned their prosperity. A delicate looking young clergyman celebrated Mass, and the music was simply rendered by Mrs. Dulaney, who played upon a small organ, and two young ladies who were visiting her, whose voices were not only pure, but highly cultivated. The congregation was small, and consisted of workmen and workwomen from a paper manufactory recently established in the neighborhood, and the families of the men belonging to the iron works, to whom the opening of the chapel proved an unspeakable boon.

(TO BE CONTINUED.)

Our Lady's Sennight in the Household of Faith.

(CONTINUED.)

Night II.

THE BIRTH TO THE ANNUNCIATION OF THE "ADMIRATION OF ALL THE NATIONS."

AGAIN, the Star-crowned, seated on her throne, attended on either hand by her bending angelic and saintly court, smiles sweetly in the starlight—making the dusky heavens lightsome—and waves her hand as a signal for the celebration of her Birthday by her mortal and immortal children. As the soul-feeding symphonies of the heaven-choirs are caught up by the higher spheres, and in their superhuman delicacy are lost to the grosser mortal ear, we may bid come back to earth, from his place near the feet of the Queen, dear Father Oakley—no longer dying like us, but living—to sing a song of

THE NATIVITY.

"Little children, one with other,
  Put your books and work away:
Come and greet your heavenly Mother,
  'Tis Our Lady's natal day.

"Strip the garden of its treasures;
  Weave a wreath of flowerets gay;
'Tis a day of holy pleasure—
  'Tis your Mother's natal day.

"Though the summer's feast be ended,
  Tho' its bloom have passed away,
Tho' its relics now be blended
  With the tokens of decay;

"Tho' the latest rose has faded,
  And the lily's dazzling sheen;
Tho' the hand of time has shaded
  Spring's and summer's vivid green;

"Yet the wreath we should be twining
  Need not lack its quota bright,
For the aster still is shining,
  Type of Mary's starlike light.

—" Where were all our hopes of heaven,
  Where Redemption's destined way,
But for her in mercy given
  To her parents' prayer to-day?"

The rhythmic flow of these lines reminds one of the author of the "Irish Melodies." It suggests, likewise, another comparison: if Mozart would have bartered all his fame for the honor of being the author of one of the Prefaces of Mass, would not Tom Moore willingly *now* enchange the authorship of all the Odes from Anacreon, the other pagan and Christian poets and philosophers, and the poems of Mr. Thomas Little into the bargain, for the glory he might procure from the writing of this child's hymn on the Virgin's Birth?

"*Et nomen Virginis Maria!*"—We all remember—that have read—what beautiful outpourings of affectionate eloquence these words, "And the name of the Virgin was Mary," evoked from the full heart of St. Bernard. Indeed there is—after the adorable Name—none like it. Trite as it has become, travestied in every possible fashion, curtailed, lengthened, transformed and deformed—in its native simplicity, Mary is yet the favorite name, the sweetest to the eye, the fullest to the heart. Let one of our latest American songsters, who has, in our new land, brought us tidings of a newer, and told them well, give expression to the hallowed name,

MARY.*

"Dear, honored name, beloved for humanties,
  But loved and honored first that One was given,
In living proof to erring mortal eyes,
  That our poor earth is near akin to heaven.

. . . .

"And yet to some the name of Mary bears
  No special meaning and no gracious power;
In that dear word they seek for hidden snares,
  As wasps find poison in the sweetest flower.

. . . .

"But faithful hearts can see, o'er doubts and fears,
  The Virgin link that binds the Lord to earth;

---

* Songs, Legends, Ballads. J. Boyle O'Rielly—p 83.

Which to the upturned trusting face appears
A more than angel, though of human birth."

. . . .

To whom may succeed a singularly pure soul from across the great waters, who in "tasting and seeing how sweet" are all

THE NAMES OF OUR LADY,*

concludes, of the simplest:

. . . .

"*Mary*, the dearest name of all,
The holiest and the best;
The first low word that Jesus lisped,
Laid on His Mother's breast.

"*Mary*, the name that Gabriel spoke,
The name that conquers hell;
Mary, the name that through high heaven
The angels love so well.

"*Mary*,—our comfort and our hope—
O may that word be given
To be the last we sigh on earth,—
The first we breathe in heaven."

Which was doubtless your own privilege, one of sweet name too, whose perfume refreshes yet the Catholic world!

"Cerulean ocean, fringed with white
That wear'st her colors evermore,
In all thy pureness, all thy night,
Resound her name from shore to shore."

The main obeys, but who commands? A singer of Mary's glory whose harp is strung with quivering heart-strings, touched by hands so delicate, yet so firm, we fain would believe the harper is the genius of the ancient Marian Dower, sent by the Saxon scholars and saints of bygone ages of Faith, to wake an echo of the olden glories, and usher in the new reign of the Queen returning to her own. Aubrey de Vere has a charm about his very name that breathes not of these hard material times and manufacturing Britain, but tells of soul-food from the inspiration of the better, nobler past; when chivalry would break a lance in honor of "The Lady," and not stay in breaking the head of one who should deliberately impugn her honor or desecrate her fane. He who has remained mute, with the modesty peculiar to greatness, in this entertainment to Our Lady, shall precede and accompany a gentle American songstress in celebrating

THE PRESENTATION OF THE BLESSED VIRGIN.

"I saw—in countenance a child—
(Three years me thought were hers, no more)
That Maid and Mother undefiled,
The Saviour of the world who bore.

"A nun-like veil was o'er her thrown;
Her locks by fillet-bands made fast;

---

* The Poems of Adelaide A. Procter—p. 342.

Swiftly she climbed the steps of stone;
Into the Temple swiftly passed.

"—Anna and Joachim from far
Their eyes on that white vision raised;
And when, like caverned foam or star,
Cloud hid, she vanished, still they gazed,"

As

"Anna feels her heart grow weak,
And Joachim is pale of cheek."

Eleanor C. Donnelly will continue her

"ANCIENT TRADITION OF THE MOTHER OF OUR LORD."*

". . . . Then, it seems as dark as night,
As the levite takes the child in white
And leads her slowly from their sight.

"O latticed doors! which ope and close
Upon that tiny, virgin rose;
Ye could not hide her if ye chose!"

. . . .

For lo!

". . . . Though the east shall ring her name,
And Mahomet himself proclaim
In these mysterious words her fame:

"'*Speak, Koran! tell how Mary, wise,
Entered the temple at sunrise,
And veiled herself from mortal eyes.*'

. . . .

". . . . Safe behind the latticed screen,
She shall grow up, by men unseen,
A lily pure and most serene.

"And angels shall her playmates be,
To guard the Maiden on whose knee
Shall bloom the Incarnate Deity.

"And after her (the prophets sing),—
Shall eager virgins following
Be brought with gladness to the King!"

Few have been found pure enough to attempt the description of that unfolding of the Lily of Israel from her infantine graces of three years to the ineffable bloom of her maidenhood, that attracted even the admiring eyes of the Holy Spirit. —"Wish me joy, all ye who love the Lord; for when I was little I pleased the Most High." And did she please less when more developed by time and grace? No! But "who is this that proceeds increasing like the sun, and beautiful as Jerusalem?" "And like unto the days of spring, the flowers of roses and lilies of the valleys decked her paths." "Adorned with the necklace" of His Law, "the Lord Himself loved the daughter of Jerusalem!" Oh, God! that some yet diviner Fra Angelico would paint in words those twelve years of "ascension from virtue to virtue,"—the refining of the Tabernacle of pure gold, the divinizing of a creature to bear her Creator and remain an untouched maid!

---

* Out of Sweet Solitude. P. 100.

The best and purest we know, essay to limn the
"Super Omnes Speciosa!" *

"Is any face that I have seen—
Some perfect type of girlhood's face,—
Some nun's, soul-radiant, full of grace,—
Like thine, my beautiful, my Queen?

"Of all the eyes have paused on mine—
And these have met some wondrous eyes,
So large and deep, so chaste and wise—
Have any faintly imaged thine?

"The chisel with the brush has vied,
Till each seems victor in his turn;
And love is ever quick to learn,
Nor throws the proffer'd page aside . . .
. . . .

"And this thou art, a sigh of love—
Love that created as it sighed,
And shaped thee forth a peerless bride,
Dower'd for the spousals of the Dove.

"To set the music of thy face
To earthly measure, were to give
Th' informing soul, and make it live
As thou—God's uttermost of grace."

Aubrey de Vere touches the same train of thought in his "*Mater Salvatoris*": not that she yet was (if we understand his meaning), but was to be, shaped upon His model, to be

"Mother of the Saviour."
"O heart, with His in just accord!
O soul, His echo, tone for tone!
O spirit, that heard and kept His word!
O countenance, moulded like His own!

"Behold, she seemed on earth to dwell!
But hid in light, alone she sat
Beneath the throne ineffable,
Chanting her clear *Magnificat*.

"Fed from the boundless Heart of God,
The joy within her rose more high,
And all her being overflowed,
Until the awful hour was nigh!"

which the archangelic messenger signalled when he proposed the momentous question, the answer to which earth and heaven stood mute to hear. For, continues Canon Oakley,

"Man's redemption hung suspended
On that Maiden's meek consent;
Satan's direful reign was ended
When she breathed her fixed intent:
'Lo! the handmaid of the Lord,
Be it done as saith thy word!'"

We must not anticipate, but celebrate first the holy nuptials of the Queen with holy Joseph. Poets introduce with the pomp of swelling verse the wedlock of poor ordinary mortals—human love and human bond dissolved by death—and seldom even dream of the higher love that welds two souls in one. Who has been found to hymn,

---
* Antiphon—Beautiful above all. Poems, Hill—p. 16.

as deserving, the chaste marriage of virgin with virgin—each knowing the other's vow, and each determined to guard the other's virginity? What lines, burning with angelic fire, could describe the union of these two least human souls in one? Some kindly seraph of the throng recumbent about Mary's throne, strike this hymeneal strain, and sing us of the sweet loves of most holy Mary and Joseph! Earth has seen some feeble reflections and imitations in the emperors, queens and princesses of Catholic ages, but such wholly pure hearts that loved one another with all the tender ardor of most intimate wedlock—and withal for love's sake only—never inhabited, before or since, this corruptible globe. Vestal virgins must hide their crimsoned faces at the contrast of such utter purity; and consecrated priest and cloistered lily-nun are spots upon the sun of light so dazzlingly clear. But none hymns of it, and we must leave cherubs and virtues their spirit-epithalamium.

The awful moment draws near when the maiden must put aside all earthly, and enter upon the life of heaven, in which her career is a continued series of miracles; her days and nights are so jealously guarded by angels that they become to her the ordinary messengers of commands from on high regarding her every motion. If none can be found who may express the remote preparation for her divine destiny, whom shall we find either worthy or capable of giving us a glimpse of the intimate communings of heaven's King—her Bridegroom—with His beloved, to fit her body and soul, proximately, for the work of the Blessed Trinity in her chastest person? Man, beware! thou walkest ground the blessed spirits would bare their feet to tread! Adore in mute stupefaction at the height and depth of mysteries unutterable! At a sign from our gracious Queen, will that unsullied spirit, Adelaide Anne Procter, tell us the story of the divine

"ANNUNCIATION."

"How pure and frail and white,
The snowdrops shine!
Gather a garland bright
For Mary's shrine.
For, born of winter snows,
These fragile flowers
Are gifts to our fair Queen.
From spring's first hours.
For on this blessed day
She knelt at prayer:
When lo! before her shone
An angel fair.
'Hail Mary!' thus he cried,
With reverent fear;
She, with sweet, wondering eyes,
Marvelled to hear.
Be still, ye clouds of Heaven!
Be silent, earth!
And hear an angel tell
Of Jesus' birth;

While she, whom Gabriel hails
As full of grace,
Listens, with humble faith
In her sweet face.
Be still, Pride, War and Pomp,
Vain Hopes, vain Fears,
For now an angel speaks
And Mary hears.

. . . .

"Hail, Mary, Queen of Heaven!'
Let us repeat,
And place our snowdrop wreath
Here at her feet."

This is the "*Mater Admirabilis*" of De Vere:

"O Mother-Maid! to none save thee,
Belongs in full a parent's name;
So fruitful thy virginity,
Thy motherhood so pure from blame.
—Her Son Thou wert; her Son Thou art,
O Christ! Her substance fed Thy growth;
She shaped Thee in her virgin heart,
Thy Mother and Thy Father both!"

(TO BE CONTINUED.)

The Apparitions at Knock.

(CONTINUED.)

THE DIARY OF CURES. ANOTHER HUNDRED CASES. SIGHT, HEARING, AND STRENGTH RESTORED. EXTRAORDINARY CURE OF JEREMIAH SULLIVAN, ETC., ETC.

From "The Dublin Weekly News" of March 13.

104. Michael McNulty, Kilgariff, parish of Ballaghadereen: paralysis of the right arm. He is now so far recovered as to be able to move his right hand to his forehead.

105. Martin Murphy, Ballinafad, parish of Balla: hip-disease.

106. Mary Byrne, Kilmore, parish of Kilmovee: large lump under the tongue. The lump has entirely disappeared.

107. James Acton, Tuam: defective sight.

108. Patrick Alcock, of Kilfree, parish of Gourtin: defective sight.

109. Mary Grady: defective sight. She has recovered the use of one eye.

110. Patrick Fogarty, parish of Crusheen: weakness of the left foot. He has experienced a considerable improvement.

111. Jeremiah Sullivan, parish of Rathharry (Rev. A. O'Leary, P. P.), Clonakilty, county Cork: polypus, or flesh growth in the windpipe. He came to Knock with his father on Sunday, the 1st of February, and got rid of his ailment on the 4th, in the manner about to be related. The following is his statement, as given in his own words to the parish priest:—" I have been suffering from a hoarseness for the last 18 months. I consulted four of the neighboring doctors, one after the other, and to no avail, as none of them was able to ascertain the nature of the disease. Finding myself daily getting worse, I came to the city of Cork, and consulted the most eminent doctor there. On the third day, he found that my ailment proceeded from a flesh growth, or polypus in the windpipe. The conclusion the doctor came to was, that there should be an operation, either externally or internally, either of which would be very dangerous. Hearing of the Apparition of the Blessed Virgin Mary at Knock, I decided on visiting the place. I arrived on Sunday morning, February 1st. Thanks be to God, and to the Blessed Virgin Mary, I coughed off the polypus on the morning of the 4th of February, after my third day's visit here." This account is quite complete in itself. I may, however, add that on the occasion of my last visit to Knock, I met, at Mrs. Byrne's house, a young lady from the city of Limerick, who had come with her brother to the scene of the Apparitions, in the hope of restoring him to health. She told me that one day, while she was in the church, her attention was attracted to Jeremiah Sullivan and his father. They were praying with a fervor of gratitude so intense that she concluded they had come to Knock in the hope of effecting a cure, and that the object of their visit had been achieved. Entering into conversation with them, she learned the full particulars, precisely as I have just laid them before your readers. She described Jeremiah Sullivan as a well-grown, fair-haired, good-looking youth of 17 or 18. She also told me that the polypus was preserved. Considering that it mystified no fewer than four doctors, and that the eminent physician who at last discovered the reason of the hoarseness, thought the cause could not be removed unless by a dangerous operation, it would be of interest to know if the polypus has been examined by any doctors, and, if so, what they have to say about it.

112. John Smith, parish of Virginia (Rev. John O'Reilly, P. P.), county Cavan: general weakness of constitution, loss of appetite, and want of sleep.

113. John Coan, Plougena, county Mayo: paralysis.

114. Thomas Hare, Tuam; paralysis.

115. Bridget Mary McNerny, Cloonfree, Co. Roscommon: blindness of right eye. The eye had been sightless for the space of 18 years. The following letter affords the best evidence on this case that anyone could desire:—"Cloonfree, Strokestown, Feb. 26, 1880.—Dear and Very Rev. Archdeacon:—It is with great pleasure I have to inform you that my eye still continues to improve. I had the great happiness of visiting Knock on the 2d inst. On the following Wednesday, immediately after Mass, I could see my hand for the first time these eighteen years, and thanks to God, every day since my sight is improving. In the year 1861 I received a severe wound in my right eye, the result of a piece of spring steel striking me by accident. All that could be done for me by medical skill was done, but of no avail. After a year's suffering, I completely lost the sight, till the aforesaid date. I purpose, with God's help, to visit Knock on the 25th of March next. Very Rev. Sir, no words could describe the happiness I feel in soul and body since I had the privilege of visiting that valuable time. Thanking you for former kindness, believe me, Very Rev. Sir, your faithful and obliged servant, Bridget Mary McNerny.—Very Rev. Archdeacon Cavanagh."

116. Margaret O'Neill, Dublin: hip-disease. I related the particulars of this cure in a former letter. Miss O'Neill had been suffering from the disease about ten years, and was obliged to make use of an umbrella to assist her in walking. Not feeling any need of the

umbrella after she had visited Knock, she left it there in token of her cure, and I saw it not long ago among the sticks and crutches deposited in the receptacle at the gable. Your readers will remember the published letter of Mrs. O'Neill, expressing her joy and gratitude because of her daughter's cure, and requesting Archdeacon Cavanagh to allow her to make some gifts to the church in token of her own and her daughter's thankfulness.

117. Mrs. Connolly, parish of Castlerea: paralysis. Her body had been entirely powerless for twelve years. She can now move her feet freely, and is nearly able to walk.

118. Thady Kelly, of Banoncolan (Rev. P. Hart, P. P.): paralysis.

119. John Flynn, Clooninemagh, parish of Kilmovee: cured of an evil. All remedies had been tried in vain.

120. Bridget Matilda Dillon; weakness of the heart. The recovery in this case has been complete.

[At this point in the diary I find some further details of the case (No. 20) of Mary Gallagher, Charlestown: blindness, caused by suffusion of the eyes with liquid matter. I have already furnished you with the particulars of this case which I heard given by Father Loftus, the parish priest of Charlestown. It will be seen that the following notes, taken from the Archdeacon's diary, correspond with the statement of Father Loftus in all material points:—"Mary Gallagher was not born blind. Her eyes were affected about two years. The complaint was suffusion of water in the eyes. She could not bear any light, and kept her eyes always closed and downcast. The run of water from them was surprising. I witnessed it myself. The girl's stepmother told me that she was much worse when first brought to Knock than when I saw her. She had been sent to St. Mark's Ophthalmic Hospital, where she remained for nine days; the opinion of the doctors was that she would scarcely ever recover her sight. The run of water from her eyes, which used to saturate her pinafore, has now entirely ceased. She is able to distinguish small objects. Before her visit to Knock, her eyes were never open, unless when opened by force, and then they appeared to be covered with a white scum. The girl's stepmother says that she never saw her eyes until after her return from Knock."]

121. James Carney, Pulbog, Coogue: a very bad sore foot. He had been suffering from it for years.

122. Mrs. P. Carney, Tounaparka, Coogue: intense pain in the middle finger of the right hand. The cure was effected by bathing the finger in water containing some of the cement.

123. Mary Healy, Backs: scrofula.

124. Miss Stuart, Dublin: a nervous affection.

125. Bridget Mary Galvin, Cork: hip-disease. She had consulted several doctors, been five weeks in a Cork hospital, and seven months in one in Dublin, and all to no good purpose. This case has been noticed more fully in one of my previous letters.

126. John Reilly, parish of Kilbride, county Roscommon: paralysis of the right side. As an effect of the disease, his right shoulder rose up so that he could scarcely wear his coat. The shoulder has now gone back to its natural place.

127. Ellen Reay, Limerick: rheumatic gout. She has obtained great relief. During her visit to Knock, the swelling in her hands and feet became much less, and she felt her strength improving.

128. Mary Kate Ryan: fainting fits and involuntary movements of the eyes.

129. Sarah Morrisroe, of Woods, parish of Ballaghy: paralysis. She was suffering from the attack from the 18th of December, 1879, till the 1st of January, this year. On the last named day she visited Knock, and was entirely cured. Mr. Ignatius O'Donel, of Swinford, certifies in the following terms upon her case: "I saw her myself on or about the 22d of December, when she had not the use of her limbs: and on seeing her yesterday, after she had walked seven miles, she did not seem to be a bit tired.—Ignatius O'Donel, Swinford, February 5th, 1880."

130. Mary Phillips, Kiltulla, parish of Bunanadden: paralysis; she left her crutch at Knock.

131. John Noonan, parish of Clomnish, county Fermanagh; a running sore on the face. He had suffered from it for twenty-five years.

132. Pat. Mulloy, of Curry: restored to sight.

133. Mrs. Madden, of Prospect; dry retching. She had been a sufferer for years.

134. A gentleman, whose name is not recorded in the diary, caught cold in his right eye about twelve months ago. He suffered a great deal since, especially at night, and was obliged to give up writing. He placed himself under the care of two eminent medical men—one distinguished as an oculist—but no improvement was effected in the condition of his eye. By bathing it in water containing cement from Knock, he has been entirely cured.

135. Thomas Cochrane, Belfast: blindness of right eye. The sight has been completely recovered.

136. Edward Gibbons, Meelick, parish of Claremorris; mental derangement.

137. Mrs. Armstrong, Claremorris: debility. She had been unable to put her foot to the ground, but now can walk with ease.

138. Pat. Conway, Limerick: lameness. He left at Knock the stick that he had been obliged to use for the past six years.

139. Thomas Dooner, of Rooskey, county Roscommon: evil.

140. Owen Cribin, Bunaconlon: evil.

141. Charles O'Donel, Donegal: constant headache and pain in the shoulder.

142. John McCormick: sore eyes and very defective sight.

143. Pat. Connor: hip-disease. He left his stick at Knock.

144. Andrew Bourke, Kilrush: lameness.

145. Martin Doherty, Ballaghadereen: lameness.

146. Sarah Graham, Ballymote: debility. For four months she had not been able to go to Mass, but now she can walk about on all occasions.

147. Hanora Magrath: sore knees. She had been unable to go on her knees; now she can do so without any difficulty whatever.

148. Alice Dwyer, Kilenaul, Co. Tipperary: blindness of the right eye. She is twenty-nine years old, and had been stone blind of the right eye all her life. The sight is now restored.

149. Bridget Ryan: had pains in all her joints for about eight years, and was unable to move until she was brought to Knock. She is now recovering strength.

150. James Connor, parish of Strokestown: dislocation of the hip, the result of an accident twelve years since. The bones of the hip used to move in and out. He is wonderfully improved, and is confident of complete recovery.

151. Mrs. Noon, Glasgow: defective sight.

152. Daniel M'Carty, Ryden, near Oldham, England: paralysis. He had been unable to bring down his foot any lower than the level of the knee. Since his visit to Knock, he can stretch out the leg.

153. Sarah Pierce, Meath street, Dublin: paralysis.

For fourteen years she was unable to place either of her feet upon the ground; she had to be supported by a chair under each arm, and another at her back, and her legs were bent back beneath this latter. She suffered continually from pains the most intense. The pains are gone, she can now stretch out her limbs, and is improving in health and strength from day to day.

154. Mary Anne Nolan, Cole street, Dublin: paralysis. For years she had been a cripple, moving only by the help of a crutch and stick, and unable to stand erect. She can now not only stand without either crutch or stick, but can move about with very slight support.

155. Belinda Mash, Ballina: dumbness. She had been unable to speak for six years past. She is now restored to the usual power of utterance.

156. Maggie Morley, Lisnaskea: an evil.

157. John M'Mahon, Glasgow: lameness. There were several evils in his leg, and he had been unable to use it for two years, but on his visit to Knock, experienced such an improvement that he left his crutch behind him.

158. Patrick Boyle, Glasgow: heart-disease.

159. John Fox: sore leg; had been five years suffering.

160. Edward Scully, Meath street, Dublin: defective sight and feebleness. He has recovered both his sight and the use of his limbs.

161. John Mooney, parish of Drumlish: nervousness and constant tremor.

162. Anne Keenahan, Moate: sores on the leg.

163. John M'Dermott, parish of Fuerty: running sores on the leg; had been a year in an infirmary without deriving any benefit.

164. Valentine Gillic, Virginia: defective sight of the left eye.

165. Pat. M'Cormick: defective sight. When he came to Knock, he was so nearly blind that he was unable to perform the Stations of the Cross unless led by another person. After a few days, he was able to find his way without assistance.

166. Michael Cull, Bird Hill, Co. Tipperary: blindness. He was stone blind; had been a patient in four of the Dublin hospitals; experienced no improvement; and, when he came to Knock, was unable to move a step without a guide. After a short time, he could see the flame of a candle, and find his way about.

167. Owen Halpin, Mell, Drogheda: deafness. For ten years he had been quite deaf. On the 18th of February, the first day he ever visited Knock, he put a piece of the cement into his ear, and immediately recovered the power of hearing.

168. John Keogh, Loughrea: pearl on the right eye.

169. Teresa Mary Martin (a young girl), Castleblayney, Monaghan: sore knee, caused by a fall a year ago.

170. Rose Anne Ward, a girl of ten: lump in the neck.

171. Bryan Lovet, Longford: an evil of seven years' standing.

172. John Brennan, parish of Kiltimagh: a swelling, the effect of a fall from a horse. For a long time he had been rendered quite unable to do anything towards earning his living. Now he is entirely cured, and able to work as he was before his fall.

173. A daughter of Richard Walsh, of Newport, was restored to sight by bathing her eyes in water containing some of the cement.

174. John Roache, parish of Rooskey, Co. Roscommon: blindness. He received his sight at Knock on the 22d of February, after having been stone blind for seventeen years.

175. Bridget Glynn, Co. Clare: lameness of the right foot.

176. John Brennan, parish of Curry, Co. Sligo: hip-disease. He had been suffering from the disease since November, 1878, and spent three months in hospital without any improvement in his condition. He is now almost as well as ever.

177. John Malley, Co. Clare: deafness, and severe pain in the stomach.

178. Pat. Ryan, Edward street, Limerick: defective sight.

179. Francis Cassidy, Maguire's Bridge: paralysis of the left hand.

180. Lizzie Bryan, Drumtraff, Co. Cork: evil, and swelling in the jaw.

181. Mrs. Healy, Drumtraff: an evil.

182. Thomas Croghan: sore foot.

183. Mary Vesey, Betley, England: lameness. She left her crutch at Knock.

184. James O'Connell, parish of Drumlish: blindness.

185. John Meckin: blindness. He was not entirely blind before his visit to Knock, but his power of vision was very feeble.

186. William Conway, King's County: pain in the heart and stomach, from which he had been suffering for years.

187. Daniel Ren, Queen's County: sore in the leg; had suffered from it for fourteen years.

188. John Shanahan parish of Adare, Co. Limerick: swelling in the right knee.

189. Maria Shields, Loughrea: defective sight.

190. James M'Donnell, Keash: an evil.

191. John Farrell, Castlerea: constant pain and stiffness in the knee.

192. Mrs. Farrell, Clontuskert: pain in the hip and leg; she had been for a long time unable to leave her house.

193. Peter Farrell, Clontuskert: sore leg.

194. Daniel Loughran: constant pain in the heart; he had suffered from it for twenty years.

195. Thomas Doherty: pains in the back and limbs, and general weakness. He had been twelve years subject to these ailments, and had consulted doctors without avail.

196. Henry Bolton, Ennis: stiffness and weakness of the left arm; had been in an infirmary three years.

197. George Culhane, Rathkeale, Co. Limerick: stiff and inflamed knee, the result of a dislocation about seven months ago. The doctors were unable to afford any relief. He is now as active as any man in Ireland.

198. John Finneran, Kilmovee: pains and stiffness in the joints. He spent thirteen weeks in the infirmary of the Swinford workhouse, without any improvement. He resolved to come to Knock, and on his way, he was not able any day to walk more than a quarter of a mile. Now he is able to walk as well as ever.

199. John M'Kenna, Monaghan: defective sight.

200. Dennis Connor, St. John's parish, Limerick: paralysis of the left hand, and lameness, the result of a dislocated ankle. He left his crutch at Knock.

(TO BE CONTINUED.)

LIKE Mary, let us be perfect in our obedience; then, as St. Liguori tells us, we shall please her in a special manner; we shall experience with her, and all the saints, that God is good towards His servants; that He does not suffer Himself to be surpassed in generosity; and that, even in this life, but more especially in the next, He will accomplish in our regard those words of Holy Scripture: "An obedient man shall speak of victory."

Catholic Notes.

——We are indebted to Rev. Father De la Rocque, of Warren, Pa., for kind favors to our travelling agent.

——Longfellow's beautiful poem, "Evangeline," has been translated into Portuguese by a lawyer and man of letters, living at Lisbon. It is prefaced by a short dissertation on American literature.

——VERY REV. FATHER DOANE, Vicar-General of Newark, N. J., has been made a Prelate of the Papal household. His father was the Protestant Episcopal Bishop of New Jersey and his brother is the "Bishop" of Albany.

——The last literary effort of the late Canon Oakley was an article on his "Personal Recollections of Oxford," the proof-sheets of which were revised by him a short time before his death. It has been printed in Time, a London publication.

——DONATIONS.—For Ireland: A Friend, $5; Mrs. Anna Scarlett, $1; A Friend, $5; Mrs. Sallie C. Ridge, $5; Sarah E. Coates, $3. For the needy mission: A Reader of THE AVE MARIA, 50 cts.; Thomas Relihan, $1; A Friend, St. Louis, Mo., $2. A kind-hearted Bishop has sent a set of white vestments; and another good soul contributes a box of flowers and other useful articles.

——A NEW PARISH IN CHICAGO.—The growth of the Church in the city of Chicago has obliged the Very Rev. Administrator to erect a new parish in the southeastern portion of the city. The new parish is bounded by Thirty-fifth street on the north, and Thirty-ninth street on the south, and State street on the west. It has been entrusted to the charge of Rev. Dennis A. Tigh, who has for a number of years distinguished himself by his zeal and ability in the direction of the two parishes of Hyde Park and South Chicago. In the latter place—which he now leaves to a successor, the Rev. F. Van de Laar—he has built a large and commodious church, which, thanks to his exertions, is unburdened with any debt. During the years spent as pastor of South Chicago, he endeared himself to the hearts of all, and it was with unfeigned regret that his late parishioners received the news of his transfer. However, recognizing that his efficiency called him to a wider scene of labor, they are reconciled. Father Tigh still retains the charge of the parish of Hyde Park, where he will reside as before. He has already set about the work of re-erecting a church in his new parish. We have no doubt that in a short time the same evidences of energy and devotedness which characterized his work in his former mission will present themselves even more strikingly in his new sphere of action. We congratulate the good people committed to his charge, and wish both them and him every blessing and success.

——SIGNIFICANT FACTS.—For the first time in the history of this country its chief legislative body recognizes conspicuously the greatest event recorded in the history of the human race, the voluntary death of the Son of God in behalf of fallen men. Ever since England has been a Christian nation, notwithstanding the changes wrought there by the Reformation, the great festivals of the Church have been observed. Good Friday, Easter, Christmas, and other memorable days have not ceased either to be recognized and memorialized by the cessation of ordinary business. In our new struggling and heterogeneous community, it is not strange that the observances of times and seasons have been, up to this period, at least, but partial. Many men whose heads are not yet gray can remember the time when even the festival of the Nativity was passed by without observance, save, perhaps, as a time for family reunions and social delight, and when Good Friday was as completely ignored and forgotten, outside the walls of Roman Catholic Churches and Roman Catholic homes, as was the anniversary of the birthday of Christopher Columbus or of Alexander the Great. But now, not only did the most busy and money-making organization in the United States, the Stock Exchange of this city, close its doors in commemoration of the day, but the Senate of the United States on the motion of the Catholic Senator, Mr. Kiernan of this State, suspends its business, in order, as he said, "to honor the day which the Christian world commemorates as that of the death of our Saviour." These facts are significant and worthy of attention.—Catholic Review.

——BLESSED ALBERTUS MAGNUS.—The Municipal Council of Laningen, on the Danube in Suabia, has issued the following circular, which is addressed to all classes of persons: "Germany has long owed a worthy monument to the man of the most far-reaching mind of the Middle Ages, Albert the Great, a member of the Suabian family of the Counts of Böllstadt. Laningen, the town on the Danube where he was born in 1193, is making every exertion to secure the erection of such a monument for the 600th anniversary of his death, November 15th, of this year. He was the admiration of his age, a walking university, even at a time when there was no university in the whole German Empire; and very appropriately he was styled the Doctor Universalis. In 1245, when he was a public lecturer in Paris, the learned Dominican first introduced into Western Europe the philosophy of Aristotle, with which he became acquainted only through Latin translations from the Arabic, connecting it on one side with Avicenna, and on the other with Moses Maimonides. Demonstrating that the eternal existence of matter is inadmissible, he founded scientific theology, and had St. Thomas Aquinas for his pupil. He rose superior to all the scholastics; for his moral doctrine rests on the principle of free will. Excelling all his contemporaries in acquaintance with the natural sciences, he opened out a new road for himself in physics, as he did in logic and metaphysics, and was the forerunner of Francis Bacon and the modern investigators. His works fill twenty-one volumes, and among them are writings on botany and astronomy. Like the celebrated Gerbert (Pope Sylvester II), he was reputed to be a magician on account of his wonderful learning, and rumor attributed to him the production of an enchanted garden in the middle of winter, while he is reported to have contrived figures which, by means of concealed mechanism, were self-moving. He was Bishop of Ratisbon from 1260 to 1262, and then, having retired to the house of his Order at Cologne, he had a principal part in preparing the plans for that most complete piece of German architecture, the Cathedral of Cologne, which, it is hoped, will be finished during this year. Thus, Albert the Great is the pride, not only of the Suabian Land, but also of the whole German nation; and although his name is aere perennius, still a statue of bronze should commemorate and honor him. This statue will be eight feet high, and will reproduce the likeness drawn by the master hand of his brother Dominican, Angelico da Fiesole, and the entire monument, which will be carried out in conformity with the strictest principles of art, will rise to a height of 25 feet. It will stand in the most conspicuous place of the whole town of Laningen, in front of its noblest building, the Rathhaus.

Favorable circumstances have reduced the cost to the moderate figure of 20,000 marks ($5,000), and it is expected that the unveiling of the monument will take place on the anniversary day. The citizens and the people of the neighborhood invite, with the most profound respect all persons, and especially the educated classes, far and wide, princes, counts, nobles, the clergy who know the greatness of the man who is to be commemorated, to participate in the undertaking and contribute to it. The magistracy of the town will receive subscriptions, and will account for them publicly."

An Appeal for Ireland.

[CORRESPONDENCE.]

DEAR REV. FATHER:—The generosity of America towards Ireland is unbounded, and already larger sums have been collected for the relief of that dear and suffering country than could have been expected. It seems presumptuous, and almost foolish, in an individual to come forward in behalf of needs so well known and so deeply appreciated, and ask for aid, independent of the many admirable agencies now at work; the excuse for it, however, is this: There are wants and griefs which can only be assisted by the secret and delicate ministrations of private charity. Persons who have never known want before, and who occupy positions which make it all but impossible for them to apply for public charity, are enduring incredible privations. If hunger forces them to receive gratefully the dole of Indianmeal which sustains life, unused as they are to live on that food alone, they often sicken and fade away for lack of other nourishment. The want of clothing, too, is bitterly felt, and also the impossibility of making a decent appearance. It is not difficult to imagine what must be the anguish of husbands, wives, and parents who see their loved ones yearning for what might save their lives, and cannot procure it, and who foresee the effects of semi-starvation on the constitutions of the young. Children come to school whose parents are supposed to be above want, and they turn faint and pale over their lessons from hunger.

Some Irish ladies have joined together, with the warm approbation of his Grace, the Archbishop of Dublin, and a cordial understanding with the excellent Duchess of Marlborough, to pursue the double end of enabling the managers of schools to give one meal a day to children in urgent need, and to minister to the necessities of those "ashamed to beg." They have asked me to help them. I cannot refuse to co-operate in such a work. This little bill may run alongside of the great stream of public charity, and reach corners and nooks not otherwise accessible. Will you, dear Rev. Father, receive any donations that may possibly be sent to me for this purpose by some unknown friends in that land where I find, by the kind reception given to my books, that I am not quite a stranger? If anything I have written has ever given pleasure to any of those who will read this letter, will they in return give me the greatest of pleasures—that of helping, even in the least measure, our dear Irish brethren in the Faith?

I remain, dear Rev. Father, very sincerely yours,

GEORGIANA FULLERTON.

AYRFIELD, BOURNEMOUTH, March 14, 1880.

Confraternity of the Immaculate Conception
(Or of Our Lady of Lourdes).

"We fly to thy patronage, O Holy Mother of God!"

REPORT FOR THE WEEK ENDING MARCH 31ST.

The following intentions have been recommended: Recovery of health for 89 persons and 3 families,—change of life for 32 persons and 4 families,—conversion to the faith for 28 persons and 3 families,—recovery of mind for 5 persons,—special graces for 5 priests, 7 religious, and 3 clerical students,—temporal favors for 31 persons and 7 families,—spiritual favors for 26 persons and 7 families,—the spiritual and temporal welfare of 7 communities, 4 congregations, 6 schools, 2 orphan asylums, and 1 hospital; also 14 particular intentions, and 5 thanksgivings for favors received.

Specified intentions: The success of several important enterprises in the interest of religion and charity,—a number of persons in great distress of mind and body,—Catholic education for children whose parents differ in religion,—removal of obstacles to conversions,—the reformation of some intemperate heads of families,—the reconciliation of two friends estranged by a misunderstanding,—several families whose parents are needy, out of work, or in feeble health,—grace for many to make worthy Easter Communions, and to keep their good resolutions.

FAVORS OBTAINED.

A devoted client of Mary writes: "I hope our dear Mother will pardon me for not having written to you before, and thanking her publicly for the grace she obtained for one of my friends and schoolmates when she was very ill last Christmas, and whose speedy recovery seems nothing short of miraculous. I am also indebted to the intercession of Our Lady for the recovery of a sum of money, special protection in sickness, and many other favors, too numerous to mention.". . . . Thanks are returned for the baptism and restoration to health of a child of Protestant parents, recommended last month. A devout Catholic lady in the South informs us that the prayers of the Confraternity and the aid of the Water of Lourdes are often invoked by Protestants in her district. We make the following extracts from her letters: "The woman afflicted with dropsy is gradually recovering her strength. I hope she will become a good Catholic." . . . "A physician being very ill with erysipelas, his wife gave him some of the Water, and placed a blessed medal of Our Lady around his neck; she then commenced to say a prayer for nine days for his recovery. He was at the time in a very precarious condition, being unconscious most of the time, and had been given up by physicians. On the ninth day he began to recover. Nobody expected him to live, and his friends are very grateful for his improvement. The family are Episcopalians."

OBITUARY.

The following deceased persons are recommended to the prayers of the members of the Confraternity: Mrs. CATHARINE CREMINS, of Clontarf, Minn., who departed this life on the 18th inst. Mr. GEORGE PADGET, of Grahamstown, Ky., whose death occurred on the 20th inst. Mr. JAMES BURKE, of New York city, who fell asleep in the Lord on the 22d of March, in the 82d year of his age. Mrs. MARTHA CRIDER, who died at her residence, near Creston, Iowa, on the 23d inst. Mr. WILLIAM BROWN, who breathed his last on the 20th of Septem-

ber, at Terrick-Terrick, Australia. Mrs. MARY A. HARDY, of Cincinnati, Ohio; Mr. MATHEW and Mrs. MARY ROWELS, of Lebanon, Ky.; Mr. PATRICK and Mrs. CATHARINE OSMOND, of Grand Rapids, Mich.; Mr. PATRICK O'MALLEY and EDWARD E. RYAN; Mr. and Mrs. BURKE, JOHN BURKE, and MARY SHUGRUE, of Springfield, Mass., all of whom died some time ago. And several others, whose names have not been given.
Requiescant in pace.
A. GRANGER, C. S. C., Director.

Obituary.

REV. LOUIS GREGORY BROWN, C. S. P.

F. Algernon Brown, who died April 8th, 1878, during Passion Week, has become widely known through the "Five-Minute Sermons." F. Louis Brown was nearly three years younger than his brother, and the events of his life were much the same. He accompanied his brother in his early studies, in his cultivation of music, in his submission to the Catholic Church, in his emigration to America, and in his ecclesiastical career. Both entered the novitiate of the Paulists at the same time, both died at the age of 29, and during Passion Tide. F. Louis, as he was always known in the community and among his friends, was born at Cobham, Surrey, England, March 2, 1851 was ordained priest in St. Paul's Church, N. Y., by Bishop Corrigan, March 8th, 1876, and he died on Wednesday in Holy Week, March 24th, 1880. He was always of a delicate constitution, and began to decline gradually after his brother's death, which was a great shock to him. Soon after that to him most sad event, the symptoms of pulmonary consumption began to show themselves; a hemmorrhage brought him to death's door during the summer of 1879, and since then his disorder made steady progress, until its fatal termination. He was never able to perform any of the heavy labors of the priesthood, but so long as his strength permitted, he devoted himself most assiduously to the training of the choir of St. Paul's Church and the direction of the ecclesiastical chant in the service of the sanctuary. In form and feature he was of an almost maidenly delicacy and beauty, and the modest refinement and gentleness of his character corresponded with his attractive personal appearance. In his last hour he was tranquil and resigned, and, fulfilling all his Christian duties, he peacefully closed his short and quiet life. His body remained in a simple *chapelle ardente* within the house of the Paulists until the afternoon of Good Friday, and was then laid to rest with the remains of his brother who had gone before him. *Requiescat in pace!*—*Catholic Review.*

DEVOTION to Mary manifests, on the part of those that practice it, dispositions that inspire confidence as to their salvation. Sincerely devoted to the Mother, they cannot but be devoted to the Son and anxious to observe His commandments, which can alone lead to life. Filled with the desire of pleasing the Queen of virgins and becoming the objects of her protection, they cannot but vehemently desire to avoid sin, to fly the occasions of it, to correct their failings, and practice virtue.

Youth's Department.

The Four Last Things to be Remembered.

BY REV. J. W. CUMMINGS.

PREPARE for Death—you'll surely die one day;
But when, or where, or how, no man can say.

Fear Judgment—to a wise and mighty Lord
You must account for thought, and deed, and word.

Remember Hell to shun it—dark despair,
Fire, and the worm that never dies, are there.

Look up to Heaven!—if you are firm and true
In serving God, its joys are all for you.

The Unknown Architect.

IN the 15th century, there lived in the Royal abbey of St. Wandrille a lay-brother of the name of Simplician. He was a good religious, who knew all about the growth of cabbages, lettuces, etc., but about anything else, he seemed to be so ignorant, he was never questioned. During the fifteen years since he had left Candebec to enter the convent, he had not set his foot outside the strong gate which closed its entrance, until the Father Abbot entrusted him with a confidential message to the curé of his native city, hoping he had not yet forgotten the way thither. He reached it without trouble, and soon found himself upon the banks of the Seine, whose smiling aspect seemed to chase the wrinkles from his pensive brow. Then, as now, rocks, forests, and fertile hills were imaged on the deep and placid waters of the stream; the castles and monasteries, whose ruins we so much admire, were then in all their splendor, and numberless boats were passing up and down, bearing evidence to the active commerce of those days. France was then enjoying peace under the rule of Louis XII and his minister, Cardinal George d'Amboise. As Brother Simplician went along, the flood of memories, like a mighty tide, came back upon him and gave his steps an unaccustomed celerity. But when he had reached the first houses of Candebec, humble dwellings built against the rocks, over which vines trailed and roses bloomed, where long ago our traveller knew by name many people, he slacked his pace. .... The heat was excessive; the nets were drying in the sun; the people sought the shade, and no one was upon the dusty road. Having reached the presbytery, Brother Simplician was led by a clerk into a low room, where the curé sat reading a great book upon a carved oaken stand. The good priest arose, and received the Reverend Abbot's message with as much joy and respect as if it were a letter from the king. The letter, tied with silk cord and bearing the *fleur-de-lis* seal of the abbey, contained a package of gold coins done up in parchment and inscribed with the words: "An offering to Our Lady of Candebec, to finish her church and to build a spire."

"My good Brother," said the curé, "I will read the Reverend Abbot's letter, and answer it immediately. Wait awhile in the hall, and my clerk will give you some cider."

Brother Simplician would take nothing, and only asked to be allowed to wait in the church until the answer would be ready. This church of Candebec—of which Henry IV, ninety years later, said: "Here is the most beautiful chapel I have ever seen"—was not completed in 1499, and yet, even then, was the pride of the city. The tower had no spire and the grand entrance, closed with wood-work, was under construction; but inside, the four sculptures, the altars, the keystones, the statues niched in the pinnacled recesses, all the rich ornamentation, shone in the sun's rays with colors of gold, azure and purple, which produced a striking effect. Brother Simplician, after kissing the threshhold of God's house, went to kneel in a chapel, where lighted lamps and a silver dove suspended under a ciborium of tracery-work, told of the presence of the Blessed Sacrament. Having finished his prayers, the good Brother went about the church as if he were looking for something. Suddenly he stood still; his eyes cast down upon the flagstones of the floor, caught sight of an inscription traced some years before: "Here lies William Le Tellier, born at Fontaine, near Falaise, architect of this Church of Candebec, over the building of which he presided for thirty years. Died on the 1st of September, 1484. Pray for the repose of his soul." Beside this was another tombstone, that of Roberta, the architect's daughter, deceased before Brother Simplician had retired to the monastery.

The Brother prayed a long time over these stones, wetting them with his tears. Then he sought the sacristy. Upon a large table near the window was a confused mass of pencils, compasses, squares, sketches, figures and notes, and designs, more or less finished, of twenty spires. The Brother examined them all carefully, and murmured to himself: "No: it is not here."

These few words are a revelation in themselves. We will therefore lift the veil of humility with which Brother Simplician had covered up the past, and reveal his history in a few words.

Up to the age of eighteen, he was a gardener, like his father; but gifted with a quick intelligence, exquisite taste, and a strong will, he abandoned his humble occupation to become an apprentice under Master Le Tellier, whose favorite pupil he was. Up with the lark, he was the first in the workshop, where he continued busy as a bee, doing his own task and sometimes that of Colin, his master's son; then he would take a pencil and draw out a plan. According to the custom of the time, he ate at his master's table. Three years thus went by, bright and joyous as a day in spring. After a time he became a master-companion, and to reward his talents and his good conduct, William Le Tellier purposed to give him the hand of his cherished daughter, when the death of Roberta shattered all his hopes of earthly happiness. From that time he thought of nothing but of leaving the world, and he entered the abbey of Wandrille as a gardener, hiding from everyone the secrets of his life and the sorrows of his heart. . . . . His visit to Candebec revived in him many sad memories; but accustomed to control his feelings, when the clerk of the curé came to tell him that the letter was finished, he followed him without betraying the emotions of his soul.

"What do you think of our church," asked the curé, in handing him his letter.

"It is a marvel," answered the Brother; "but it lacks a spire."

"O, that I well know! The whole country is clamoring for one, and I receive many offerings for that purpose; but what we want is a plan; how unfortunate that Master Le Tellier did not leave one! Yet he said to my predecessor: 'That spire is conceived; it will be the most graceful in all the country of Caux'; but, although we have gone over his collection of plans and designs, we have found no trace of it."

"Master Colin will make one," said the Brother.

"Master Colin has drawn more than twenty; but neither he nor I are satisfied with any of them. Nevertheless, he is a good workman and anxious to finish the work of his father and glorify our Lady. But he has not the genius."

Brother Simplician became thoughtful. He made a profound salutation to the curé, and bidding him good-by, returned to his monastery, where he again betook himself to his usual labors. Unfortunately, his thoughts were elsewhere, and soon the Brother cook went to tell the abbot that Brother Simplician had lost his appetite, that he was becoming thin, that he even forgot to water his plants; and, like the practical man that he was, he said: "If he falls sick, how will I be able to supply the table?"

"How long is it since Brother Simplician has been in this way?" asked Dom Gerard.

"Ever since he came back from Candebec; he seems to be under some spell. There, look at him!"

The abbot's window opened on a balcony overlooking the garden. He stepped out, and the cook pointed to Brother Simplician, who, with a stick in his hand, was intently drawing lines in the sand upon the broad walk, while a rascally hen was scratching a border into destruction a few paces off.

"Well, now!" exclaimed the cook; "who ever saw such a thing! Our poor Brother will soon be completely daft, since he allows the hens to skirmish through the Father Abbot's garden."

"Brother Matthew, go and tell him I wish to see him."

A few moments after, the culprit was in Dom Gerard's room, and, on his knees, underwent the following interrogatory:

"Brother Simplician, is it true that you are ill?"

"No, Father; I am quite well."

"Then why is it that you do not eat?"

"Why—I think I eat the same as usual."

"What were you drawing just now upon the ground?"

"Oh, I dare not tell."

"Tell me, I command you."

"Father, I was sketching the spire of the Church of Candebec."

"The spire of Candebec! but there is no such thing."

"It did exist in the mind of Master Le Tellier, Father, and I am trying to recall it."

"Well, I believe the cook is right," thought the abbot; "this is certainly a foolish idea."

"But, my son, how comes it," the abbot continued "that you should dream of planning and building just as an architect would?"

"Because I have been one, Reverend Father," said poor Simplician; "I had resolved never again to think of it. In renouncing my profession, and resuming my first avocation, I had hoped to forget all; but——" and with a voice trembling with emotion, he gave a simple account of his visit to the church, his conversation with the curé, and his whole life. Several times during this recital, Dom Gerard felt the tears flowing over his cheeks. However, he restrained himself, and coldly said to the Brother: "Here, take this sheet and pencil, and draw the spire of Candebec for me."

"I cannot," said Simplician; "a cloud hides it from my view, and I can see it clearly only by going to the Chapel of Barre-y-va. There, upon the wall, my master had traced the outlines; there only will the vision reappear to me. Oh, Father, only allow me to go to Barre-y-va!"

"You shall go to-morrow; but, under holy obedience, say not a word to anyone about this conversation, nor the spire, nor Master Le Tellier."

"I promise, Father. May God reward you—your blessing."

Dom Gerard placed his hand on the head of the religious and blessed him with more emotion than he was willing to manifest.

On the 5th of August Brother Simplician, reciting the Office of Our Lady of the Snow, set out for the Chapel of Barre-y-va. It was such a day as that of sixteen years ago, when he had visited it in the company of Master Le Tellier and his family. Here, after a fervent prayer in the chapel, the pious architect wrapt in meditation, had taken a pencil from his bag and traced a sketch on the outer wall. His pupil looking on, had exclaimed: "O master! what a beautiful spire that will be!"

"Let us go home," William Le Tellier said; "I wish to finish what I have sketched here. This evening you will see it."

But that very evening Roberta was taken ill, and a few days after she died. Brother Simplician was so absorbed in these memories of long ago, that he passed the chapel door in his abstraction. The voice of a blind beggar on the steps recalled him to his senses. He entered the blessed sanctuary; his prayer was not long, for he was in a hurry to examine the wall outside. He came out, drew aside the bushes, and upon the lichen-spotted wall discovered some lines of Master Le Tellier's sketch. These were not much, but they were the spark which a breath would recall to life. The vision was clear and luminous before his eyes, and he hastened to copy these barely visible lines. When he had done this, he returned thanks in the chapel, and hastened back to the abbey, with a firm and rapid step. Tears, regrets, and sad memories vanished. The artist was himself again. His heart palpitated with religious inspiration. He felt the thrill of a masterpiece working itself out in his brain, and as he passed by the Church of Candebec and its unfinished spire, he signed himself, and murmured joyously: "*Sponsa, coronaberis!*" "You shall be crowned, my love!"

After his return to the abbey, Brother Simplician took his plan to the Father Abbot, who examined it carefully, and then looking earnestly at the Brother, said: "If I were to tell you to destroy this plan, my son, even though it should be a masterpiece, what would you do?"

"I would obey you, Father."

"If I should tell you, on the contrary, that this beautiful work shall be preserved; that I will give its execution into the hands of Colin Le Tellier, but that neither he nor anyone else shall know the author's name—yours?"

"I am perfectly willing, Father. Besides, it is not my work: I have only brought out the conceptions of Master Le Tellier."

"Then you give me this plan to make of it a gift, full, entire, and irrevocable, to Our Lady of Candebec?"

"I give it, and promise the profoundest secrecy."

"You may retire, my son; you give me great joy. Go back to your lettuce and beans; pray to God, and forget all else."

Seven years elapsed before the elegant spire with its triple crown of *fleur-de-lis*, its delicate mouldings, its airy lines, received its finishing touches. At last, Colin Le Tellier, who had skilfully directed the work, came to inform the curé that the flowered terminal cross was in its place, and that the solemn blessing could now be given. This grand ceremony was fixed for the 5th of August, the Feast of Our Lady of the Snow. The Abbot of Wandrille, the suzerain of Candebec, was invited to preside. The news soon spread through the convent and caused great rejoicing. Most of the monks—nearly all natives of the country—were to accompany the abbot. On the eve of the Feast, as Brother Simplician was mowing the after-growth in the meadow within the cloister, Dom Gerard came towards him, and asked if he had any wish.

"Oh yes, Father!" said the good Brother.

"Tell me what it is, my son."

"I cannot, because I would have to speak of something about which I have promised never to make mention."

"Well, then, I will speak for you. To-morrow you will come with me to the blessing of the tower of Candebec."

Brother Simplician dropped his scythe, hid his face in his hands and melted into tears. The abbot withdrew, deeply moved.

It was a magnificent feast. The houses of Candebec were adorned with draperies and flowers as on Corpus Christi; all the barks were streaming with flags and pennants; the church was beautifully trimmed with tapestries and garlands. Brother Simplician, who walked along with the religious, neither saw nor heard what was going on around him. From the moment he had caught sight of the spire in the distance, he had looked at nothing else, and his usually impassible countenance was beaming with happiness. As they were entering the church, the abbot looked towards him, and making him a sign to approach, whispered: "Go wherever you wish—I leave you free till the hour of our departure."

Brother Simplician thanked Dom Gerard, and whilst the crowd poured into the church, he betook himself to the stairway of the tower and hastened to the very top, until he stood at the base of the spire and above the bells. These latter were ringing merrily, the church resounded with the sacred chants, and the whole tower vibrated like an immense harp. As he gazed over the surrounding fields, he was seized by a kind of vertigo. He imagined that he felt the motion of waves, and that the church, becoming a ship, was bearing him through space to the eternal port, the object of all his hopes and the reward of all his sacrifices. Evening fell, and in the last moments of a summer sunset, Brother Simplician saluted for the last time the spire of Candebec.

The good religious, the unknown architect, the creator of the triple-crowned spire, had lived to a great age; God in His mercy called him away two years before the Calvinists came to pillage the Church of Candebec. The whole eulogy of Brother Simplician is contained in these words of the Father Abbot on the day after the feast. When he was asked whether the mysterious artist, who had designed the marvellous spire which Colin Le Tellier had only executed according to his own testimony, was an angel or a devil, he replied: "I believe that whatever is beautiful comes from God, and that the man who had the genius to produce such a masterpiece, and to renounce for himself all the praise and the renown of his work, must surely win heaven."

A Good Suggestion.

The *Catholic Standard* of Philadelphia makes the following suggestion to the young folks of the United States, and shows how they may contribute to the aid of the suffering children in Ireland, forty thousand of whom are compelled to stay away from school either from want of sufficient clothing to hide their nakedness, or from want of food:

We make a suggestion specially to the children of our happy country. There are in round numbers ten million of them in the United States. We suggest that *they* take in hand the work of helping the poor, naked, starving children of Ireland. They can *accomplish* it if they *will*. Let every child contribute a penny a week, or, if they can, five cents or ten cents a week, for six weeks, and they will raise a sum sufficient to put those of the children of Ireland who are suffering for want of food beyond the danger of starvation and to furnish such of them as are now naked with clothing.

If but half of the children in the United States —but five million out of ten million— adopt this suggestion, and if the average contribution from each should be ten cents, it would make a fund of five hundred thousand dollars. The schools which the children attend would constitute organizations through which the money might be collected, and the aggregate amounts be sent to one or another of the different relief committees now having members almost everywhere throughout the United States.

It will be a noble work for the children of the United States to engage in.

A Beautiful Comparison.

..... In our conversation we also touched upon religion. He was a Protestant, I a Catholic. When I had answered those current objections which Protestants seem never tired of repeating, a venerable old man, who during our discourse had been seated at a table near by, arose and came over to us, politely requesting us not to take it amiss if he made a comparison for us. I brought forward a chair for the old gentleman, who seated himself between us, and spoke as follows: "I shall leave you to guess to which religion I belong, after you have heard my comparison to the end, and have pronounced which is the right side. I shall appeal to each one of you.

"Two laborers of the district of D—— once passed through beautiful Switzerland on their way to Italy. When they reached the foot of the Alps they felt somewhat uneasy as to how they should make their way across. One of them went and procured a bottle of good wine, put some bread and cheese in his wallet, and brought an iron-pointed mountain staff. 'What's all that for?' asked the other.

"'That I may cross the Alps without accident and reach the beautiful and sunny land of Italy.'

"'Ha-ha!' laughed his companion, 'you are very provident, I see; but I am not going to buy anything, and so shall have no load to carry, and I shall cross the Alps with less trouble and less danger, and shall be in Italy before you.'

"'Every one to his own idea,' replied the other, and they began the ascent. Ah! how light of foot was he that had nothing to carry! He was soon far ahead. But his companion went on his way quietly, taking an occasional sup of wine and a piece of bread, and thus refreshed, he pursued his journey. After proceeding some hours, he finds his fellow-traveller seated on a ledge of rock, weak and tired, and hardly able to rise. 'Ho! friend, I thought you were already in Italy.'

"'Alas!' he answered, 'unless you have the kindness to share your bread and wine with me, I shall never be there.' His companion at once supplied his wants, and they soon arrived together in Italy.

"Which of those two, I ask you, gentlemen, was the more prudent?"

My Protestant friend answered: "Without any question, he that took food with him on his journey."

"Perfectly correct. And thus the Catholic Church is vindicated. She received from Jesus Christ our Lord all the necessaries for the life of the soul, and has kept them pure. Does a man reach some dangerous period of life, he knows where the means are to be found, which will give him strength to overcome the difficulty. Is he tired on his journey, he goes to the table of the Lord, and gains renewed strength. Has he made a false step and hurt himself, he goes at once to the physician (his confessor), who heals him free of charge, and moreover gives him medicine (good advice) to carry with him on his journey. What does Protestantism offer in comparison with this? Thus, gentlemen, you can see for yourselves which side is to be looked upon as the safest and the best." So saying, the old man saluted us politely, and withdrew.

I noticed that my Protestant friend was sunk in profound thought, which seemed to have possession of his whole being, and at last I was obliged to recall him to himself. He is now a Catholic.

A Noble Lad.

Some years ago a pupil of the Polytechnic School, in Paris, found a pair of beads in one of the halls. Indignant at the thought that in that school, then, unhappily, a nursery of infidelity, one should recite the rosary, he assembled his companions together and informed them of his discovery. After the classes, when they went into the court-yard, the beads were hung up in the branches of a tree, and the wretched infidel pupil who had found it ironically cried out: "Let him among our school-fellows who has lost his beads, come forward and take them down, if he dare." Unhesitatingly and bravely a young man, who had always been distinguished in his class, stepped forward, took his chaplet quietly, and said: "I prize this beads of the Blessed Mother highly. Besides, they were given to me by my mother. In remaining a Christian, I do not believe that I have dishonored the school."

"Bravo!" was heard on all sides; "Bravo! he has courage!" An illustrious marshal, an eyewitness of this scene, stretched forth his hand to the young soldier of Jesus Christ, and said to him, with deep emotion: "Bravo! my friend; when one knows how to defend his faith in so worthy a manner, he will likewise know how to stand by his country, and to die for it if necessary."—*McGee's Weekly.*

THE AVE MARIA.

A Journal devoted to the Honor of the Blessed Virgin.

HENCEFORTH ALL GENERATIONS SHALL CALL ME BLESSED.—St. Luke, i, 48.

VOL. XVI.　　　NOTRE DAME, INDIANA, APRIL 17, 1880.　　　No. 16.

[For the "Ave Maria."]
The Angelus.

BY CHARLES WARREN STODDARD.

AT dawn, the joyful choir of bells
In consecrated citadels,
Flings on the sweet and drowsy air,
A brief, melodious call to prayer;
For Mary, Virgin meek and lowly,
Conceivéd of the Spirit Holy,
As the Lord's angel did declare.
　　　　　Ave Maria!

At noon, above the fretful street,
Our souls are lifted to repeat
The prayer, with low and wistful voice—
"According to Thy word, and choice,
Though sorrowful and heavy laden,
So be it done to Thy handmaiden!"
Then all the sacred bells rejoice—
　　　　　Ave Maria!

At eve, with roses in the west,
The daylight's withering bequest,
Ring, prayerful bells, while blossom bright
The stars, the lilies of the night;
Of all the songs the years have sung us,
"The Word made flesh has dwelt among us,"
Is still our ever new delight.
　　　　　Ave Maria!

DEVOTION to St. Joseph was reserved for these latter times. Though founded on the Gospel, God willed that it should not be developed in the first ages of Christianity. One reason why the Church was so tardy in proclaiming St. Joseph's claims to the fullest reverence of her children, was to avoid giving even an indirect encouragement to those early heretics, who asserted that he was the real father of Christ according to the flesh, and who would thus honor St. Joseph by robbing Mary of her glorious title of Virgin-Mother.

The Patronage of St. Joseph.

ST. JOSEPH passed through life unnoticed by men. In the Church founded by his Divine foster-Son, he was, it is true, always regarded with reverence; and yet a public and universal honor was not accorded to him until after the lapse of several centuries, and began in the Greek Church, which appointed his festival to be kept on the Sunday after Christmas. A hymn of praise, found in the collection of sacred hymns of the Greeks, was addressed to St. Joseph by a poet who died towards the end of the ninth century. In the martyrologies of the Latin Church, the name of St. Joseph does not appear before the ninth century. That this devotion to our Saint was introduced into Europe by the Carmelites in the thirteenth century, was the prevailing opinion among Catholic writers; and this opinion had the appearance of truth in its favor; but when the matter was examined more carefully, it became evident that there was not the slightest proof of any devotion to him by the Carmelites before the fifteenth century. The first person of note to raise his voice in favor of devotion to St. Joseph, was John Gerson, chancellor of the University of Paris. In the year 1400, he recommended it in a letter addressed to all the churches, and what he wrote on the same subject to the Duke of Berry and to the arch-chancellor of Chartres was intended for publicity. He maintained it to be probable that Joseph, like John the Baptist, was sanctified in his mother's womb, and urged that at least his espousals with the Virgin Mary should be celebrated by a festival in the Church. He begged the Council of Constance to honor the spouse of the Mother of God, by decreeing a feast day in his honor, and to choose him for the Patron of the Church: this, he said, was the surest means to end the unfortunate schism; so powerful a protector would undoubtedly restore to the holy Church her true Spouse in the person of the lawful Pope; moreover, he composed an office for the festival of the espousals, and a Latin poem in twelve cantos, in honor of St. Joseph.

In the same year—1400—Gerson appeals to the fact that in many parts of Germany, St. Joseph's festival was already kept. Of this fact we have no other proof save this passage of Gerson, but it is certain that the general chapter of the Franciscans in 1399, decided that this festival should be celebrated in the entire Franciscan Order. St. Bernardine of Sienna, who labored earnestly and successfully for the restoration of the spirit bequeathed to his disciples by the seraphic St. Francis, also most zealously promoted devotion to St. Joseph; and Sixtus IV, who was a member of the Franciscan Order, introduced the festival of St. Joseph into Rome in 1481, and adopted it into the Roman breviary. In the beginning of the fifteenth century, the devotion was taken up by the Augustinians, and about the same time by the Carmelites, and by the Dominicans soon after the year 1500. Towards the beginning of the sixteenth century, the festival of the espousals of Joseph and Mary was introduced into Orleans, and afterwards into Chartres. But St. Theresa, promoted devotion towards him who was sharer in the mysteries of the childhood of Jesus, more effectually than Popes and Bishops, generals of orders, and learned men. The zeal with which she was inspired, and with which she recommended devotion to him, was first caught up in Spain and wherever the Carmelite Order exerted any influence; but it soon extended beyond these limits, and when the sixteenth century was coming to a close, the festival of St. Joseph was kept in almost the whole Church. In 1621, Gregory XV ordered the 19th of March to be kept as a holiday, forbidding on it servile work and law proceedings. When Urban VIII, by his Bull of 1642, suppressed several holidays of obligation, he rather reminded the faithful of the precept of his predecessor in regard to St. Joseph's Day. In Austria and its dependencies, devotion to St. Joseph was nothing new in the time of Gregory XV. By a decree issued by Ferdinand III, in January, 1654, it was made a holiday of obligation.

Very likely it was the Carmelites, reformed by St. Theresa, that first took up the idea so strongly insisted upon by Gerson at Constance, and showed a special devotion to St. Joseph as their patron. This devotion began to spread in the seventeenth century, and a special festival was then appointed. Leopold I encouraged it in Austria and the whole of Germany with the greatest zeal, and he succeeded in having the foster-father of our Saviour proclaimed the universal patron and protector of his hereditary dominions and the entire Holy Roman Empire. After having had an understanding with the Bishops on the subject, he received the congratulations of Pope Clement XI; the publication of the decisions was made by the Bishops, and was received with great demonstrations of joy in Vienna and other places. The notice of the forementioned proclamation issued by the town council of Vienna with the view of having the necessary preparations made, is dated February 19th, 1675. The festival, on which we honor St. Joseph as our patron was fixed for the third Sunday after Easter, and when, in the course of time, it had been quite extensively adopted, Pius IX extended it to the universal Church by his decree of September 10th, 1847. At that time there were clear indications of the storm about to burst in 1848. Though short, it was fierce, and an interval of peace followed. When in 1859 the attacks on religion and the Church were renewed, and year by year were growing fiercer and more extended, many pious people directed their hopes to the patronage of St. Joseph, and expressed the wish that the entire Church should call upon him as her patron and intercessor at the throne of God. During the Vatican Council, this sentiment was expressed by a great number of Bishops; and when Rome fell into the hands of its enemies, who had been long and impatiently awaiting the favorable opportunity, the Holy Father, on December 8th, 1870, the festival of Mary conceived without sin, issued a decree in which her chaste spouse was solemnly declared to be the Patron of the Universal Church.

"I am, I am the Lord: and there is no Saviour besides Me," says the Almighty; but until the final separation takes place, it is His will that, as in the case of the angels—the first-born in the spirit world—so should it be also in the case of the glorified of the seed of Adam, that they should be co-laborers in the work of redemption. The angels hover around men with protecting wings, and carry our prayers up to God; the saints by their intercession bring down to us God's grace, which is mighty in the weak, and thus they have a share in the work of the Redeemer, to whom they owe all that they possess. St. Joseph did not wait for the public honors bestowed upon him to pray for all those on whose account the Divine Child who called him father had taken the form of a servant. When the time had come in which the heavenly Father willed to honor the faithful guardian of His Treasure, even in the land of pilgrimage, devotion to our Saint, and the impulse to seek his powerful intercession, made rapid progress, and what was prescribed in the Papal Decree of Dec. 8th, 1870, had already been flourishing in Austria and Germany for two hundred years. But it is deserving of notice why at this particular time the whole Church should place herself under the special protection of St. Joseph.

It is well known that the banner of atheism was first raised in France; and when the municipality of Paris held sway, the French Revolution attempted to set up atheism as the religion of the country. Infidelity sprouted up out of a cess-pool of the most audacious immorality. A new attempt is now being made to set up atheism on the throne of the spirit world. This second immense campaign against the Lord, is equal to the former in its hatred of Christianity, and has much in common with it; amongst other things, the Titans of our day imagine that when they ignore God, He is done away with. But it distinguishes itself in this, that the pretentions of human pride are carried to the verge of madness. Religion is so natural to man, and the denial of God so repugnant to his nature, that it could not acquire any extended influence over consciences except through the bait of liberty; and every revolt against faith that assumed any proportions, was followed as a necessary consequence by the departure of moral restraint and the entrance of vice and crime. We need but a mere glance over the news of the day to be convinced of this. He that thinks it folly to trouble himself about God, and immortality, will quite naturally look upon it as reasonable to live as though God and a future life were mere childish stories; hence the partisans of infidelity are constantly appealing to reason, which they pervert. The assertion that all the miseries of this earth come from belief in God, is no longer new, it is but a result of the socialist maxim: "God is the evil"; and the disciples of Comte obtained great applause with those workmen that set Paris ablaze. But now, the denial of God is praised, as the right and the glory of humanity. Man, they tell us, has a perfect right, without any limitation whatsoever, to be his own priest and god; it is, they consistently add, the first and holiest duty of man to be his own lawgiver. "Belief in God is a degradation to man. To object to atheism is to renounce liberty of conscience."

Whilst infidelity, in the intoxication of its pride, was hurling abuse on every side, Catholics, in search of help, turned to that wonderful Saint in whom men saw only a poor carpenter. Armies had increased to millions, and ingeniously contriving instruments of destruction had carried death farther than the eye can reach, and more effectually than the missiles and the short sword with which the Roman conquered the world. But not in earthly weapons does the Church place her trust. He that was subject to St. Joseph is the Word, by whom all things were made, and without whom was made nothing that was made. As He commanded the waves, and there was a great calm, He can in like manner command the blustering of men when and where He pleases. But all that recommend themselves with confidence to the patronage of Saint Joseph, offer to the Foster-Son a homage of faith and humility, and the more we grow in faith and humility, the nearer the Lord is to us. However, we do not honor the saints solely to secure their intercession, but also that we may gather instruction and encouragement from their example; and we cannot raise our eyes to St. Joseph but they will encounter the Saviour, and the consideration of his virtues, is a consideration of the childhood of Jesus, and His hidden life at Nazareth. When we piously venerate these mysteries so full of grace, Jesus shows Himself tender as a child, though surrounded by the grandeur of the Divinity, and He addresses us in these words: "Have confidence: I have overcome the world!" Yes, let us have courage, for we can encounter no real evil, when in faith and love we place ourselves under the protection of Jesus, Mary, and Joseph.

'Beth's Promise.

BY MRS. ANNA HANSON DORSEY.

CHAPTER XIII—(Continued).

MR. DULANEY, a tall, dignified, white-haired gentleman, had met the party from "Ellerslie" at the chapel door, introduced himself, and conducted them to a pew in the most courteous manner, without the least ostentation or parade of proprietorship. After Mass, and a brief instruction on the Gospel of the day, Mrs. Morley and 'Beth remained, as was their custom, to offer certain private devotions, and a prayer of thanksgiving for the opportunity afforded them of being present at the Holy Sacrifice, and the small congregation had dispersed when they rose to go. They found the Dulaneys waiting for them under the trees. Mr. Dulaney introduced his wife and the Misses Marston—the two young ladies from New York, who were on a visit to them—to Mrs. Morley and 'Beth, welcomed them to St. Joseph's, and begged that they would come whenever they wished, as the chapel door remained open all day. Walking together to the gate, conversing as they went along, Mrs. Morley, having expressed her grateful thanks for the offered privilege, and also for the chapel having been made so easy of access to them by allowing the old gate to be opened, heard how it happened they were able to have the services of a priest all summer. "There are so many priests in our city," said Mr. Dulaney, "in the seminaries, and in charge of parish churches, who are overworked, and not rich enough in this world's goods to be able to get away for change and rest, that my wife and I thought it would be a good plan to find them out, and invite them in turn to "Tracy-Holme" to be cared for, and get back their strength in this pure atmosphere. The gain is all on our side, also the honor in having such guests; and the longer we can keep them, the better we are pleased. Sometimes two or three are here together, and it is so pleasant to see the color coming back to their cheeks and strength to their limbs. They enjoy the country, the fare, the pure air, and the drives, like school-boys on a holiday, and my wife takes care of them as she would of her own sons if they were ailing. Thus it happens that we are enabled to have Holy Mass every day, and what a boon that is for the little we do—a royal boon for that which costs us nothing!"

'Beth and the Misses Marston had gone on together, chatting and laughing; Lodo nad slipped away, and was waiting for 'Beth on the "Ellerslie" side of the gate, behind the white lilacs; she wanted to show her something.

The Dulaney family were quiet in manner, with a sincere kindness of heart expressed in all they said; there was nothing artificial, no pretention nor assumption of any sort about them, which, added to their evident intelligence and natural refinement, gave them the stamp of the best standard of good breeding. Mrs. Morley who had all her life been slow in forming friendships, was most agreeably impressed by her new acquaintances, and felt a desire to know more of them. Again expressing her gratitude, she invited them to "Ellerslie," and told them that but for her aunt's ill health, she would have called when they first came to "Tracy-Holme"—Mrs. Morley really believed what she said; she did not know of Aunt 'Beth's prejudice against "new people," whom she imagined were all alike—vulgar and ostentatious—" but hoped, now that the gate was opened, they would not stand on ceremony," which they promised not to do, and parted at the gate, quite as much pleased with Mrs. Morley and her daughter, as they were with them. They had thought it strange that the old lady of "Ellerslie" had not extended the civilities of the neighborhood to them, and wished that she had been more friendly, as it would have been so much pleasanter; but they were shrewd enough to have some idea of how it was, having heard that Miss Morley was of a very old family and a great aristocrat; but now hearing from this sweet-voiced, gentle lady that she had been an invalid so long, they determined to accept the friendly advances she made and call upon her. In her notes to the Dulaneys about the chapel and the gate, Aunt 'Beth had refrained from saying a word which would have seemed like excusing herself for not having called upon them, as she was asking favors of them, but she determined to go now, that the gate was open, which would enable her to get there without that tired, fainting feeling that sometimes came over her after the least fatigue. Besides, Aunt 'Beth felt a little ashamed of having held herself so aloof, but this feeling she kept secret.

Lodo, hiding behind the lilacs, came forward as soon as Mrs. Morley and 'Beth had got well beyond the gate into the "Ellerslie" grounds; her appearance was so sudden that both started. "I wanted to show you something, mem," she said, looking demurely, from one to the other. but nodding to 'Beth; "will you please to come?"

"I'm sure it's a gnome or an elf," said 'Beth, laughing.

"Yes, dear, go with Lodo; I'll walk home slowly under the beautiful trees," said Mrs. Morley, glad to be left alone just then, for thoughts were crowding into her mind, as she glanced around at the old haunts she remembered so well, that saddened her and filled her eyes with tears.

"There, mem; there it is!" said Lodo, after they had walked a short distance, as, rounding an abrupt turn of a thickly wooded part of the ground, a scene of sylvan beauty was revealed to 'Beth's gaze which more than justified the girl's enthusiasm, and, clasping her hands, she exclaimed: "How lovely! it is like a dream." It was a wild, picturesque ravine, through which a stream dashed, leaping and dancing, over the rocks, into whose foaming waters the sunshine fell in gleams through the great trees that met overhead, transforming all it touched into strange splendors. The very light, sifting through the rich canopy of green, looked as though it shone through emeralds; wild roses clambered over the great grey rocks that cropped out along the sides; the blue periwinkle trailed itself along the crevices, and over the moss; old gnarled roots, covered with lichens and scarlet fungi, and crowned with tufts of feathery grasses; magnificent ferns and dainty asters, added a varied beauty to the place; and as if nothing should be wanting to make it perfect, the calls of the cat-bird, the warbling of the blue-jay, and other feathered songsters, blended their sweet wild notes in unison with the mellow dash of the running stream. "Ellerslie" had been, ever since Aunt 'Beth came into possession, the refuge and safe sanctuary for birds; the sound of a gun was never heard among its bosky shades; and while she would have let a thief who had robbed her go "scot free," she would have visited the extreme penalty of the law on any bird-catcher, who, in spite of her notices to the contrary, had trespassed on her ground to pursue his wanton sport. And the birds seemed to understand that here they were safe, and they built their nests and raised their young from year to year, giving their sweet presence, and sweeter songs, for the privilege of sanctuary. They made their summer homes in every tree, but the ravine was their favorite resort.

"Miss Morley lets me bring my sewing here sometimes, mem, and I just set and listens to the birds and the water, and the rustling leaves, 'till I 'most expect certain to see the 'good people' come out, dressed in green and gold, to have a dance," said Lodo, as she and 'Beth scrambled down over the rocks to a moss-grown seat that had been placed, nearly a hundred years before, about half way down the ravine, just where the best and most perfect view was obtained, by some dead-and-gone Morley who had an eye for the picturesque.

"Oh, Lodo, this is beautiful!" exclaimed 'Beth; "I never saw anything like it in all my life. But who are your friends, the 'good people?' I should think dancing would be a funny occupation for such."

"Only the fairies, mem. Didn't you know there were fairies?" asked Lodo, her great black eyes sparkling with untold mysteries.

"You're the first one I ever saw, Lodo," said 'Beth, with a merry laugh. "I have read about them, but some time you shall come here with me and I will read you some fairy tales out of a book that I have, if you like."

"Oh, mem, that would please me very much. Nobody cares about coming here but me; but if you will let me come with you now and then, I shall be so glad! do you see that bridge way down yonder, mem—it is most covered with ivy, and arches from one side of the ravine to the other?"

"Yes: now I see it. It looks very pretty too; I should like to go over it," said 'Beth.

"Nobody ever goes over it, mem," said Lodo, with a little shudder, "that is, except when they have to."

"What's the matter with it, and why do people have to go over it sometimes? Is it unsafe?"

"No, mem: but when any of the family dies, that's the way they have to take them to the vault over yonder. They're all buried there, and that's the way they all go, over that old bridge," said the girl, as if the very thought had cast a shadow over her wild, sunshiny nature.

"I like that," thought 'Beth, as she folded her hands on her lap, and gazed at the ivy-covered arch; "it gives a mysterious interest to the place, this bridge between life and death; sometimes I shall come here, and dream of those who have been borne across it, and perhaps see white-robed phantoms gliding over."

"There's another place, mem, where we can't see it, a beautiful place on the rocks," said Lodo, thinking that the bridge had made 'Beth sad, because she was silent and thoughtful.

"Oh no: I like this best. The old bridge is lovely, with the water foaming under it, I should not like to be where I could not see it; it is a beautiful picture, Lodo."

"I don't like anything, mem, that reminds me of ghosts, and that always do," answered the girl; "but please don't say anything to Miss Morley; I think she wouldn't like my saying so."

"That reminds me, Lodo, that we've been here long enough; they'll wonder where we are, and maybe wait dinner for us. Aunt 'Beth told me that she always dined early on Sundays; come, let us hurry back; I'm so glad you brought me here," said 'Beth, rising to go.

"I thought you'd like it, mem; Miss Morley's been very good, trying to get school-learning into my head; but the trees and sunshine, and the water and birds, suit me best; I'm more at home with them than with books," said Lodo, as she trudged along with 'Beth, feeling for the first time in her life the pleasure of companionship and sympathy with one so near her own age.

When Mrs. Morley arrived at the house, she found Aunt 'Beth walking slowly up and down the soft velvety lawn, just where a great tree intercepted the sun's rays, throwing them like broken diamonds on the grass. She was waiting to hear how it had fared with 'Beth and her mother among the "Philistines," as she persisted in calling her neighbors in her own mind. She had taken it into her head, crammed as it was with class traditions, that the Dulaneys, having risen from very small and obscure beginnings, must of necessity be ostentatious and vulgar, and she was not only surprised, but well pleased at Mrs. Morley's account of them, and announced her determination of calling upon them the very next day, which she did, and returned home more than satisfied with her visit.

"I declare, Anne, they seem to 'the manor born.' Americans have a wonderful faculty of adapting themselves to circumstances. Here's Lodo; now if she had been an American child, she would by this time, with all the advantages she's had, have manners that would make one believe she had been born to the 'purple and fine linen,' and had always lived in it; but nothing on earth will ever make her more than she is—a little peasant—a good, true, faithful domestic; and, I must confess, I'd rather have her just as she is." Then 'Beth came in, full of enthusiasm about the ravine, her eyes sparkling and her cheeks glowing with the new life she had been breathing in with the pure ozone so plentiful in the atmosphere at "Ellerslie," while Lodo, her heart beating with strange delight at finding some one who loved the wild, beautiful things of nature, which only seemed part and parcel of her own life, tripped upstairs to her own nice little room to take off her Sunday fineries, her ribbons of red and orange, and her necklace of big amber beads, the only thing upon her worth saving when she was found.

Aunt 'Beth, who never did things by halves, intent on showing her good will to her neighbors, invited them and their guests to an early tea on Tuesday, and they had sent an acceptance. Mrs. Morley shrank very much from even so quiet a reunion as this, "but Aunt 'Beth was to be thought of now," she considered; "she needed change, and new, cheerful faces around her—something that would interest her beyond the limits of 'Ellerslie,'" and she determined to put self aside, join the little party, and exert herself as far as she could to make their visit pleasant. It was a small matter, and she did not for a moment think of it as anything meritorious; but it was a sacrifice of self, in a spirit of submission to her cross, and indicated the change that her religion was working in her, making the burden of her great sorrow more easy to bear.

The evening passed delightfully. After tea, Mr. and Mrs. Dulaney, Mrs. Morley and the young priest, Father Hagner, sat round Aunt 'Beth on the veranda, in quiet, pleasant converse. "Ellerslie" and its beauties, the picturesqueness of the old grey house, its magnificent trees of a century's growth, and the velvet smoothness of the lawn, over which the setting sun was now casting long, soft shadows; the time-worn statues gleaming here and there through the shrubbery, as if patiently waiting in their stony silence for a Promethean touch to awaken them to life, were all admired in a way that made Aunt 'Beth sit more erect in her chair, her chin just a little elevated, and with a bright sparkle in her eyes—for if she had a weak spot, it was the pride she took in her lovely old home, and nothing pleased her better than to hear it admired in an appreciative way by persons of taste, which she soon discovered her visitors to be. The Dulaneys had lived abroad two or three years, seeing all that was worth seeing, which, with their own natural good taste, had educated them to the height of admiring a place like "Ellerslie," which, had they been people of vulgar minds, they would have pronounced dingy and old fashioned. This is what Aunt 'Beth thought, as she sat listening to and joining in the pleasant flow of general conversation. "But then," she asked herself mentally, "where did they get their gentle, quiet manners, their refinement, their self-possession? Money can't buy such things; perhaps it is something in their religion. Roman Catholics are strange people, and I can believe their religion capable of working any transformation of character, when I see what it has done for Anne Morley." She was much interested in Father Hagner, and questioned him closely about his health, suggesting remedies, such as a year abroad, a summer in Colorado or Santa Barbara —both beyond his reach,—and ended by inviting him to come over in the morning to look at some fine old paintings of Madonnas and other subjects which were reputed to be by some of the old masters, and had been purchased abroad, ages ago.

Mrs. Dulaney was telling Mrs. Morley of her two boys, Bertie and Paul, whom she was expecting to spend their vacation with her. They were her only children, and it was easy to see that she was proud of them; and Mrs. Morley, thinking they were school-boys, hoped in her heart that the promise of their youth would be fulfilled in their manhood, to reward this good mother's patient care and tender love. The young people who had been wandering through the grounds, returned full of youthful spirits to the house, their hair dressed with roses, and their hands full of violets. 'Beth had made the time pass very pleasantly to them, enjoying the stroll quite as much as they had, and now they promised to sing for her. The wax candles were lit in the music-room, and in a short time their delightful voices were heard blending together, in sweet, harmonious accord, or rising in clear flute-like solo, on the wings of song. Mrs. Morley felt unbidden tears stealing over her cheeks as the strains floated out through the open windows, for they sang the songs of long ago, whose notes were interwoven with the happiest memories of her life. A low breathed invocation to her whose human heart had known sorrow, and been pierced with the sword of grief, soothed her momentary anguish, and no one knew how the beautiful and entrancing sounds had smote and hurt her.

Aunt 'Beth invited her guests, when they were taking leave, to come again. "'Tracy-Holme' and 'Ellerslie' used to be on the friendliest of terms with each other, and now that the gate is open, we must have it so again," she said, holding Mrs. Dulaney's hand. "I am getting to be a very old woman I believe, and it will not be kind to stand upon ceremony with me. If you'll be so good as to come informally, I shall be very glad." And they promised her they would do so. She told them that the hop-harvest was near at hand, and invited them to come over to an afternoon tea, that they might all go and enjoy the sight together. Then they parted, mutually pleased with each other.

"Depend upon it, Anne," said Aunt, 'Beth after they had all gone, "those two pretty girls— cousins, aren't they?—are to marry the two sons, Bertie and Paul, whom they are expecting."

"Are they grown?"

"Oh yes: the oldest is twenty-five, Mr. Dulaney told me, and the second one twenty-three," said Aunt 'Beth. "Indeed, I think it more than probable."

"It may be so. Both girls are extremely pretty and well mannered, and I fancy Mrs

Dulaney would be pleased," said Mrs. Morley.

"One of them, I am sure of," said 'Beth: "the tall, blue-eyed one they call Elaine, for when Violet—the other cousin—began to talk about the young Dulaneys, she blushed like a ' red, red rose,' and didn't say a word."

"Is that a sign, my 'Beth,", asked her mother, winding her arm around her waist.

"Yes, mem," said 'Beth, putting up her rosy mouth to be kissed, and speaking so exactly like Lodo, that Aunt 'Beth, who had just lit her bedroom candle, turned quickly, thinking it was her little maid, and glad that it was not, for what was a bit of fun in 'Beth, would have been pertness in Lodo. They had a little laugh over it, however, and Aunt 'Beth said: "This has been very pleasant indeed, my dears; I have taken quite a fancy to our new friends, and especially to that young priest."

"He is quite interesting, but not to be compared with our old one at home. Oh, I wish you could see Father Thomas, Aunt 'Beth!"

"What! are you a Catholic, 'Beth?" asked the little woman, gravely.

"Not yet, Aunt 'Beth, but I hope to be, when I can be one honestly," said the girl with sudden gravity and gentleness.

"What do you mean by that, child?"

"I can hardly tell you. I don't understand everything that it is necessary for me to believe before I can become a Catholic, and I am waiting for faith, for faith which will make me satisfied in believing without understanding; that is the way it is, dear mamma, and Aunt 'Beth, and it is the first time I have ever said it."

"The grace of faith always comes to the earnest soul," said her mother, pressing her closer to her heart.

"But you say 'honestly,' my love," said Aunt 'Beth.

"Yes: I must believe *all*, not doubting one jot or tittle of what the Catholic Church teaches; until I can do that, I shall remain as I am," she answered, in grave, low tones.

Aunt 'Beth said no more; she kissed them both good-night, and went to her room, thinking that 'Beth's father must have been looking out of her eyes, so strongly did she resemble him as she stood there, giving utterance to her most sacred thoughts.

(TO BE CONTINUED.)

WE serve a Master who lets nothing go to waste; not a drop of the sweat of our brow.— *Frederick Ozanam.*

RELUCTANT blame is the blame which goes to the heart and consciences of the objects of it; and the greatest merit of it is, that while it condemns it does not discourage.—*Sir Arthur Helps.*

Our Lady's Sennight in the Household of Faith.

(CONTINUED.)

NIGHT III.

FIRST VIRGIN-SPOUSE AND VIRGIN-MOTHER.

WHEN now our Queen has returned from her visitation across the mountains, to bless the Baptist and his mother, she will deign to take her accustomed throne, and listen again to her devoted Bards. Let us hear the solution of dear St. Joseph's doubt in O'Reilly's

LEGEND OF THE BLESSED VIRGIN.

" The day of Joseph's marriage unto Mary,
In thoughtful mood he said unto his wife,
' Behold, I go into a far-off country
To labor for thee, and to make thy life
And home all sweet and peaceful.'

"And the Virgin,
Unquestioning, beheld her spouse depart:
Then lived she many days of musing gladness,
Not knowing that God's hand was round her heart;

"And dreaming thus one day within her chamber,
She wept with speechless bliss, when, lo! the face
Of white-winged angel Gabriel rose before her,
And, bowing, spoke, ' Hail! Mary, full of grace;
The Lord is with thee; and among the nations,
Forever blessèd is thy chosen name.'
The angel vanished, and the Lord's high Presence
With untold glory to the Virgin came.

"A season passed of joy unknown to mortals,
When Joseph came with what his toil had won,
And broke the brooding ecstasy of Mary,
Whose soul was ever with her promised Son.
But nature's jealous fears encircled Joseph,
And round his heart in darkening doubts held sway;
He looked upon his spouse cold-eyed, and pondered
How he could put her from his sight away.

"And once when moody thus within his garden,
The gentle girl besought for some ripe fruit
That hung beyond her reach, the old man answered,
With face averted, harshly to her suit:
'I will not serve thee, woman! Thou hast wronged me:
I heed no more thy words and actions mild;
If fruit thou wantest, thou canst henceforth ask it
From him, the father of thy unborn Child'!
But ere the words had root within her hearing
The Virgin's face was glorified anew;
And Joseph, turning, sank within her presence,
And knew indeed his wondrous dreams were true.
For there before the sandalled feet of Mary
The kingly tree had bowed its top, and she
Had pulled and eaten from the prostrate branches,
As if unconscious of the mystery."

Is it not meet that we should imitate the holy Patriarch of the New Law, and sink on our knees in her presence whose is the majesty of more than queen! The mysteries we are about to contemplate are too holy to bear any posture but that of the humblest prostration to adore the God—"the mighty One who hath done great things for".... "His handmaid," and will "show" yet greater "might in His arm," by "exalting the lowly" whom we "must call Blessed":

ANCIENT HYMN.

"Mary! ever blessed Maid,
  Full of heavenly bliss,
Sweetest bud of paradise,
  Flower of gentleness;
Beseech thy Son that in His love
  He grant me this,
His grace, wherever I may be,
  Never to miss!
Ladye! to thee mine orison
  I will begin;
True love of Him, thy sweetest Son,
  Teach me to win;
We live in sad and evil days,
  Night closes in,
But, Ladye, in thy pity save,—
  Save me from sin!

    * * * * * *

"Mine own works, Ladye,
  They bear the ban,
All marred and foolish as they are,
  Of fallen man;
Mother, wilt thou not give thine aid?
  None other can;
Oh! help thou me, full well thou mayst—
  Thou helpest many a man!
Blessed be thy name, Ladye,
  So fair and bright;
My hope rests ever upon thee
  By day and night.
Oh, let me for thy pity plead;
  'Tis a child's right,
Who fain would see his Mother's face
  In heavenly light." *

    * * * * * *

The diviner life proceeds—new lights arising, new ardors burning—the great Priest preparing the Victim—Himself, and no substitute like Isaac's—on the fleshy altar, more unstained than sacrificial stone, of the bosom and heart of the Maid

"'Who hast alone inviolate remained,'†
Sings Holy Church. And I too, Lady sweet,
Can find no word to murmur at thy feet
Melodious as this—which thou hast deigned
To hear so often from a love unfeigned.
Ah! could my heart the melody repeat
(Accept the wish, at least,) at every beat,
And pour a ceaseless worship unrestrained!
Inviolate soul, inviolate body, thine.
Sin could not touch thee, nor the tempter near;
Pain no disease and age no blemish gave;
More Virgin for thy Motherhood divine;

Serene, sublime, 'mid sorrows without peer;
Beauteous in death, untainted in the grave."

Here let us dwell and take our rest—"dissolving in love of the Beloved of God and choice of every truly-wise soul": *Adolescentulæ dilexerunt te nimis.* *

DOMUS DOMINI DOMUS MEA. †

"How bold I grow in this new love,
  To ask thy heart that I may rest
Where thy Creator Spouse, the Dove,
  Has made His dearest, sweetest nest.

    * * * * * *

"That other home is not for me,
  Tho' many a gentle heart might prove
An isle to touch at on the sea,
  My bark were portless should I rove.

"Then let thy bosom be my home.
  And am I bold? 'Tis mine by right!
Thy Son, my Mother, bids me come
  And dwell with Him there day and night."

How they went from inn to inn, and then from door to door, in the city of David, their father, all know; and how there was at last found a grotto stabling the humble ass and patient ox, and a little straw for a bed on that December night. Is all then earthy in this scene—a scene of squalid poverty, and no more? No one to comfort—none on earth? No pity in the sweet heavens?—Listen! some strange commotion! Light breaks on the darkness,—a shining band afar and dimly seen majestically soars in the starlight: somewhat sing they! Nearer, and an impulse makes us join the song:

"Then let us sing the anthem
  The angels once did sing;
Until the music of love and praise
  O'er whole wide earth will ring.

"*Gloria in excelsis!*
  Sound the thrilling song!
In excelsis Deo!
  Roll the hymn along.
Gloria in excelsis!
  Let the Heavens ring;
In excelsis Deo!
  Welcome, new-born King!
Gloria in excelsis!
  Over the sea and land;
In excelsis Deo!
  Chaunt the Anthem grand.
Gloria in excelsis!
  Let us all rejoice;
In excelsis Deo!
  Lift each heart and voice.

    * * * * * *

Gloria in excelsis!
  Sing it, sinful earth!
In excelsis Deo!
  For the Saviour's birth." ‡

---

* "Songs in the Night, by the author of "Christian Schools and Scholars."
† "Quæ sola inviolata permansisti." Hill—P. 55.

* "The youths have loved thee exceedingly"—Adolescen tuli among the Romans might be 32 years old.
† "The Lord's House, my House." Hill—P. 30.
‡ Father Ryan's Poems—P. 168.

Catholics of some education should, from constantly hearing the word in connection with Blessed Mary, and by its analogy with another—"genitor"—understand the import of the properly Latin "*Genitrix*" which is, however, somewhat more comprehensive than "Mother," and can really be applied to our Lord's Mother only in its native force, as implied by Aubrey de Vere in the couplet:

"O Christ! her substance fed Thy growth,
. . . .
Thy Mother and Thy father both!"

Our other favorite Marian lover, Father Hill, says the sweetest things of "his Mother, Sister, Spouse," in

SANCTA DEI GENITRIX.

"Mother of God! My Queen is simply this.
For this elected, the eternal Mind
Conceived her in its infinite abyss,
With the God-man, co-type of human kind.
And she, when came the wondrous hour assigned,
Conceiving her Conceiver, girt Him round,
And held in her Immaculate womb confined
Whom heav'n and the heav'ns of heav'ns cannot bound.
Then brought Him forth, her little One, her own;
And fed her suckling at her maiden breast,
The only pillow of His earthly rest,
And still for evermore His dearest throne.
O Lady! what the worship Faith allows?
The Eternal calls thee Daughter, Mother, Spouse!"

Those who understand something of the language of the Church will enjoy another poetic prayer, redolent of piety as the century from which it dates—the thirteenth:

MARIS STELLA.

"Mary! beautiful and bright
  Velut Maris stella,
Brighter than the morning light,
  Parens et Puella;
I cry to thee, look down on me,
Ladye! pray thy Son for me,
  . *Tam pia,*
That thy child may come to thee,
  Maria!
Sad the earth was and forlorn,
  Eva peccatrice,
Until Christ our Lord was born
  De te Genitrice!
Gabriel's *Ave* chased away
Darksome night and brought the day
  Salutis;
Thou the fount whence waters play
  Virtutis.
Ladye! flower of living thing,
  Rosa sine spina!
Mother of Jesu, heaven's King,
  Gratia divina;
'Tis thou in all dost bear the prize,
Ladye! Queen of Paradise
  Electa,
Maiden meek and Mother wise
  Effecta.

. . . .
Well knows He that He is thy Son,
  Ventre quem portasti;
All thou dost ask Him then is won,
  Partum quem lactasti!
So pitiful He is and kind,
By Him the road to bliss we find,
  Superni;
He doth the gates of darkness bind
  Inferni." *

We conclude our Christmas festivities with a snatch from a sacred sonnet of Maurice Egan, our latest, not least, contribution to American Catholic poets:

. . . .
"O Mother Mary, all our hearts are thine,
In joy and sorrow we give praise to thee;
In this glad time, our hearts we raise to thee,
For Christ's great glory lends its rays to thee;
His love and thy love in our hearts entwine,
Like knotted tendrils of a Tropic vine."

An anonymous Englishman translates of "*Ut sol decoro lumine,*" summing all praise:

"As the sun
    O'er misty shrouds—
  When he walks
    Upon the clouds;
  Or as when
    The moon doth rise,
  And refreshes
    All the skies;
  Or as when
    The lily flower
  Stands amid
    The vernal bower;
  Or the water's
    Glassy face
  Doth reflect
    The starry space;
  Thus above
    All mothers shone
  The Mother of
    The Blessed One."

(TO BE CONTINUED.)

---

* Songs in the Night—P. 168.

GOD comes to holy souls, not so much in heroic actions, which are rather the soul's leaping upward to God, but in the performance of ordinary habitual devotions, and the discharge of modest, unobtrusive duties, made heroic by long perseverance and inward intensity.

It will be part of our amazement when we are judged to see what a life of inspirations we have had, and what immense holiness we might have gained with comparative facility.

Many great saints could have been made out of the grace which has only made us what we are.

The best of us are ungenerous with God; and ungenerosity is but a form of the want of fear.—*Faber.*

On the Appian Way.

SS. NEREO, ACHILLEO AND DOMITILLA.

BY ELIZA ALLEN STARR.

(CONTINUED.)

THE daisies, pink and white, already besprinkled every square yard of green sward within or around Rome; the brilliant crimson anemonies, too, had already spread their corollas in the sunshine; but the sharp air of a March morning, even in Italy, gave a wonderful exhilaration to our spirits as we drove to the stations of the day, on the *Via Appia*. The full blossoming time had not yet come, but still there was a delicate tinge of opening buds along the old vineyard walls and the crevices of the ruins; and here and there, not only a spray of roses (for these blossom the winter long), but of wild mustard and mountain-fringe, swung from their nooks among the broken bricks and crumbling mortar. Santa Balbina raised its fortress-front on the Aventine slope at the right; and still farther on, the ruins of the Baths of Caracalla stood in their unroofed, desolate grandeur against the sky.

To Americans, who have the same idea in locating a church as they have in locating a schoolhouse or a town hall—viz.: the convenience of the parish—the sight of so many churches in a neighborhood absolutely uninhabited, save by those who serve them, is sufficient to prove how carefully Christianity has protected everything connected with her history, early or late. Standing before the Church of SS. Nereo, Achilleo and Domitilla, one of the principal stations of the day, we were carried back to the time when SS. Peter and Paul walked, bound, over this very road to martyrdom: for while passing this spot, according to a tradition faithfully brought down to our own times, Saint Peter dropped one of the bandages which the Christians had put around his ankles, galled by the heavy fetters of the Mamertine prison. The bandage was eagerly secured as a relic of the prince of the apostles, and an inscription served to mark the place where it happened. But the associations most likely to come to mind, are those directly connected with the saints whose names have been given to it. Their story is one—we are sorry to say—not nearly so familiar to Catholics generally as that of anyone of the pagan emperors; and, very often, the story is first learned on this very spot. To go to Rome without knowing something of the Cæsars, the statesmen, and the orators of the Eternal City, would seem ridiculous,—for of what interest can their monuments be to the ignorant? But to go to Rome without knowing anything of her saints, excepting, perhaps, Saint Peter and Saint Paul, is so common that we have ceased to smile at this ignorance; for we can only mourn over the indifference, even of Catholics, to the wonderful charms of the Acts of the Martyrs. While the Bollandist *Acta Sanctorum* for two centuries and a half has been giving to the world one of the most magnificent proofs of the grandeur of these Acts of the Saints in themselves, and their connection with the history and literature of the Christian ages, the Catholics of to-day, and of our country, look upon the reading of the Lives of the Saints as fitted only for monks and nuns, or devotees. The best way to cure such a false notion, is to set them down among the monuments of Christian Rome with nothing but a traveller's guide-book in hand, and they will realize how much they need to read, quite one side of the classics or the popular histories of Rome, to understand them. There are charming histories of the saints, even in our own language, but so long as these are kept on the shelf for pious books, and shunned accordingly, our generation is sure to lose one of the most delightful sources of intellectual culture in art, poetry, and general literature.

But this story of SS. Nereo, Achilleo and Domitilla? Saint Paul in his Epistle to the Philippians (iv, 22), says: "All the saints salute you, especially those who are of Cæsar's household." This epistle is named among those which Saint Paul wrote from his prison in the house of the centurion, still pointed out on the corner of the Corso and the Via Lata, his prison forming a part of the foundation of the beautiful church called Santa Maria in Via Lata. No doubt, therefore, among the very saints of Cæsar's household, whom Saint Paul had in his mind when he wrote this sentence, may be reckoned the parents of the patrician lady, Flavia Domitilla, a niece of the Emperor Domitian, and espoused to Aurelian, a prince indeed, but a pagan. This amiable princess while yet young, had been baptized by Saint Peter, with the other members of her family, more than one of whom had been reckoned worthy to give their blood for Jesus Christ. Among the devoted servants of Domitilla were Nereo and Achilleo, distinguished both for their virtues and their zeal. They had seen, with admiration, the fidelity of their young mistress to her duties as a Christian, and had often said to each other: "Surely the Spouse of virgins has elected this choice soul as His own. Aurelian may try to claim her, but the heavenly Bridegroom will prove a rival too powerful even for a prince." This cherished hope found a sudden expression one day, as they saw the care taken by Domitilla to adorn her person in order to be more beautiful to the eyes of her betrothed. Under an inspiration, as unexpected as it was sincere, they exclaimed: "Consider, O gracious lady, the majesty and the excellence of Him whom you call your Lord, and how far He must excel all the princes of the world; consider, also, the honor of being chosen by Him in an especial manner, as one chooses a well-beloved spouse; and, still further, consider with what a jealous eye this divine Lover will behold any effort on the part of this chosen one to win the praise or admiration of a mere mortal. From the very hour of your baptism, we have believed you one of those specially beloved by Jesus Christ. Can you slight His choice, or hesitate, for one moment, to return Him love for love?"

Never could an arrow from the bow of the skilful archer hit the mark more closely than did these words the conscience of the Christian maiden Domitilla. All the native nobleness of her soul rose up at the sound of these inspired words. Aurelian, prince of the Roman empire as he was, suddenly lost all his charms in her eyes, for she compared him with that type of all beauty, of all excellence, Jesus Christ Himself. Her two faithful servants could not but see the impression made by their words, and they were encouraged to dwell upon the security of those who turn from the short delights of this life, from all the uncertainties of happiness in marriage, from the honors of society, and the grandeur of wealth, to a life humble, retired, full of good works and pious labors, such as a Christian virgin of those days would lead, although of the household of Cæsar. The picture of holy virginity as thus drawn by these servants of God, as well as of her house, completely won Domitilla's heart, and she said, with enthusiasm: "Good Nereo and Achilleo, you who have inspired me to embrace this celestial state, to live like the angels in heaven, hasten to obtain for me all its safeguards and all its merits; obtain for me that veil of the Christian virgin, which the Bishop gives to the true spouses of Jesus crucified."

Trembling with joy, Nereo and Achilleo ran to Saint Clement, who had succeeded Peter, Linus and Cletus, as Father of the faithful, and told him how Domitilla, of the imperial family, had determined to consecrate herself to the service of Jesus Christ. The venerable Pontiff blessed the Lord, and lost no time in discovering her real dispositions. "Have you thought well, my daughter," said the Pope, who had seen so many fair young heads bow under the sword of the executioner, so many tender virgins stretched on the rack until every joint snapped, had seen them devoured by flames, or thrown to the wild beasts in the amphitheatre; "have you thought well of the rude conflict you may be called upon to sustain? and will your courage hold out to win the victory? Aurelian, irritated by your refusal of him, will not fail to accuse you to the emperor as a Christian. To what awful temptations will your faith be exposed, and how can you avoid martyrdom?"

"And is not this to arrive at the highest happiness?" replied Domitilla; "I count little upon my own natural strength, but I expect everything from the all-powerful grace of my Divine Spouse, and persecution will only advance His honor and glory." Saint Clement knew all the merits of this generous reply, and could see that her love of virginity was most sincere; he therefore delayed nothing, but solemnly blessed her, and put the sacred veil on her head.

What Saint Clement had predicted, was not long in coming to pass. Aurelian was enraged by the decision of Domitilla. At first he tried the promise of everything the heart of woman could wish, if she would turn from her resolution; then he threatened her with the imperial anger, and assured her that no influence which he possessed with the emperor should be spared to accomplish her utter ruin, unless she received him again as her affianced husband and fulfilled her promise of marriage. But all this tended only to strengthen her resolution.

As it was not the policy of the Imperial Government to destroy patrician families, but rather to secure them in its own interests, the vengeance of the emperor or of his prefect was not to be vented upon Domitilla first, but rather upon those of her household who had encouraged her rejection of Aurelian. It was, then, to Nereo and Achilleo that the prefect sent his summons; nor did they shrink from the consequences of their advice to Domitilla. In vain were promises, persuasions, and threats lavished upon them; in vain were they scourged with whips, each lash of which was loaded with lead. Their constancy was such even under this torment that the tyrant feared to excite the compassion of Domitilla, and thus rouse her to follow their example. This decided the prefect to send them to Terracina, on the coast between Rome and Naples, with instructions to the consul to proceed against them as Christians. The formalities were gone through with; they were ordered to renounce Jesus Christ, to burn incense to idols—gods of Rome. There it was that the mouths of these servants of Domitilla were opened to declare their faith, and to denounce the superstitions of their countrymen. "How can it be," they exclaimed, "that we, who have been baptized by Peter himself, and instructed in all things concerning our Faith, should acknowledge any other God than the one supreme God, the God of Christians! Blind and most unhappy are they whose eyes are so holden that they do not see Him, who is infinite in His perfections, and who adore in His place divinities they have made for themselves, and thus deify their own base passions! Never can we throw the least grain of incense before the false gods you have called upon us to worship."

For such answers the consul knew there was but one remedy—the torture which ends in death. Stretched upon the rack, their sides were torn with hooks, and the bleeding wounds burned with torches. With every bone out of joint, their ghastly wounds aggravated by pitchy flames, the joy of their faces made the consul so fear its effect upon the bystanders, that he commanded them to be beheaded. Their glorious martyrdom was accomplished on the 12th of May, in the year of our Lord 98. Half a league from Rome, on the *Via Ardeatina*, or Ardeatine Way, which runs nearly parallel with the Appian, was already a Christian cemetery, or catacomb, belonging to the family of Domitilla. In one of the chambers of this underground home of the dead, the bodies of the two martyrs were deposited by a disciple named Auspice. It was in this chamber, and before the very *loculi* (or beds) in which their relics reposed, that Pope Gregory the Great, before the year 600, delivered a eulogy upon their singular merits, exhorting the faithful to imitate those whose venerable bodies they stood so near, and to despise the deceitful allurements of this present life. This eulogy is known as the "Twenty-eighth Homily of Saint Gregory," and we shall see how this eulogy was prized a thousand years after it was uttered by the lips of Saint Gregory in the gloom of the catacomb lying between the Ardeatine and Appian Ways.

But Domitilla? Left to herself amid the seductive influences of a court as corrupt as an emperor's court could well be, did she persevere in her vocation as a spouse of Jesus Christ? To be His spouse—for Domitilla, at least,—did not mean to retire from the world, its troubles and contradictions, as well as its vanities, and to live a life of peaceful contemplation. To be His spouse—for Domitilla, at least,—was to carry His cross, to accept His shame, to share His sufferings. To be His spouse—to Domitilla, at least,—was to choose, not peace, but a sword, and to be a word of contention in the imperial household. But the noble soul of Domitilla rose to the level of her celestial espousals. Not in vain had Saint Peter, prince of the apostolic band, poured over her the waters of regeneration; not in vain had he laid on her tongue the Bread of Angels and the Strength of martyrs; she was no child to need human support at every step. Nereo and Achilleo had merely pointed out to her the way of holy virginity, and the Bridegroom she had chosen could sustain her in the way. If Aurelian should prove implacable, unrelenting in his revenge, Domitilla could be persevering in her refusal of him. Her birth, her youth, her beauty, stood between her and the law for a time, and she was merely sent to the Isle of Ponza, not far from Terracina, in a sort of banishment, from which, it was hoped, she would soon be recalled.

Aurelian, who had never really despaired of winning Domitilla, managed to have two young Christians, well instructed in the faith, but of worldly dispositions, given to Domitilla as attendants. These young women, named Euphrosyna and Theodora, were instructed to persuade the princess that there was not the least harm in listening to the suit of Aurelian, and they began by observing to one another, in a careless way, that all Christians were not called to a life of virginity, that it was quite possible to save one's soul in the state of marriage; and when they had succeeded in drawing Domitilla into the conversation, they added: "If marriage is lawful, why should you, a princess, refuse a prince as your husband, especially when, by accepting him, you may convert him, his family, and all who belong to him?"

The Christian instinct of Domitilla was not to be deceived by this plausible way of putting the case before her, and she replied: "And you, Euphrosyna and Theodora, had you once plighted your troth to two noble princes, would you think of breaking your word to them in order to marry two slaves?"

"Certainly not, unless we had lost our wits!" replied the two girls.

"Then," said Domitilla, "why should I be less wise than yourselves? I have been espoused to the Son of the living God, Christ Jesus, the Creator and Ruler of the world; how can I turn from Him, and all the joys and dignities of an espousal which is for eternity, to marry one who is a mere mortal like myself?"

The beautiful young face of Domitilla became radiant with the joy of her heavenly alliance as she spoke, and Euphrosyna and Theodora, who had only smothered in their souls their love for Christian perfection, were convinced by her direct appeal to their consciences. Still they hesitated. Had they not been charged by the highest authorities in Rome to bring about this marriage? It was worth one more trial to succeed, for they did not ask her to burn incense or to deny her Faith.

"But if you have such confidence in the honor you gain with Jesus Christ by becoming His spouse, ask a favor of Him, and see if He will grant it. We have a brother who is blind; ask your Spouse to give sight to our brother, and see if He will reward your constancy to Him."

"Your brother is not here," replied Domitilla, "and it would delay us to send for him; but you have a mute girl in your service, who can come instantly, and you shall be instantly convinced."

The girl was sent for, and Domitilla immediately besought her Spouse, Christ Jesus, to show to her companions with what favor He regarded the petitions of those who consecrated themselves to Him. As if the voice of Domitilla had instantly penetrated the heavens and reached the ear of her Divine Spouse, the mute girl spoke, and the first use which she made of the gift of speech was to declare herself a Christian! At this astonishing miracle, wrought by the prayers of Domitilla, Euphrosyna and Theodora were overwhelmed with shame and contrition; they threw themselves at the feet of Domitilla, and declared themselves not only Christians, but spouses of Him who had thus rewarded one wholly consecrated to Him.

The news of all this flew quickly to Aurelian; beside himself at being thus foiled in his plans, he obtained an order from the prefect to put an end to the whole affair by setting fire to the house in which Domitilla was living. The two attendants did not fly from her, but their bodies were found the next day by Cæsareo, a Christian deacon, with the body of Domitilla, all in the attitude of prayer, among the ashes and cinders of the mansion.

According to the laws of Rome, the malice of Aurelian could not interfere with the funeral rites of Domitilla. Her precious relics were taken to the family cemetery, where her faithful teachers in the way of perfection had already preceded her. This cemetery, still one of the most beautiful of those near Rome, had been built with a façade of brick which looked out on the Ardeatine Way; the interior, too, had been adorned with all the care which the Roman patrician families were accustomed to bestow on their tombs, and upon its Christian symbols fell the light of day. There was no need of hiding their tombs, Christian as they were, from the Romans of those days, so sacredly were the last resting places of the dead regarded. To this day, the crumbling frescoes on the wall, belonging as they do to the first age of Christianity, claim the admiration as well as the veneration of the pilgrim. The vault of one of its chief passage-ways is covered, in its entire length, with an exquisite design, representing the vine and its branches, that symbol so dear to the early Christian, given to us by our Lord Himself; and among the branches and delicately outlined leaves and clusters of fruit, flit little birds and winged *genii* with baskets of grapes on their heads. The foliage and light tendrils spread over the entire vault, and even the walls, with the suppleness and freedom of nature. In the vestibule are landscapes, in the style of the frescoes at Pompeii, a decoration so rare, that they are thought to exist nowhere among the Roman catacombs excepting in this one of Domitilla, Nereo and Achilleo. Among the symbolical groups in this cemetery, which belong to this first century, the most remarkable is that of Daniel in the lions' den, in which the grouping and execution, but above all the grace and movement in the picture, are worthy of the best days of Roman or Greek fresco. In fact, those pictures at once decide the question of the comparative excellence of Christian decorations during this and the following ages, when persecutions and the misfortunes which they brought to Italy as a punishment, prevented all progress in the fine arts. It was not until Christianity rose superior to all oppression, that her artists regained the dignity and graciousness of outline which belong to these frescoes in the cemetery of Domitilla, painted before the year 100 of the Christian era. It was to this resting place (which the word cemetery really means) that the relics of the young and beautiful Domitilla were taken, under the care of the deacon Cæsareo, and we could even see the spot, far off on the Campagna, as we stood in the clear spring sunshine, before the Church of SS. Nereo, Achilleo and Domitilla, while a little farther on, rose the Church dedicated to the holy deacon Cæsareo.

This ancient foundation, under the title of "*In Fasciola*," or bandage, in allusion to the tradition we have mentioned and the inscription which marked the spot, dates back to a noble matron, Fabiola, who, as some declare, was converted by Saint Jerome; but certainly she, like Saint Marcella, Saint Paula, and many other patrician ladies of Rome, was under his spiritual direction. At her death, about the year 400, she gave her house for a church to be dedicated in honor of SS. Nereo, Achilleo and Domitilla, in sight of whose resting place across the Campagna on the *Via Ardeatina*, the lady Fabiola had lived. In one of those beautiful letters written by St. Jerome to Saint Eustochium, he tells her how Saint Paula, her mother, when on her way to Jerusalem, touched at the Isle of Ponza, "ennobled," as he says, "under Domitian, by the exile of the most illustrious of women, Flavia Domitilla; and visiting the narrow rooms which she occupied during her exile, ending only with martyrdom, felt her soul rise on the wings of faith, and believed that she saw already Jerusalem and the holy places." This enthusiasm seems to have been shared by her saintly companions in Rome, and tell us something of the way in which it came about that Fabiola chose Flavia Domitilla, Nereo and Achilleo, for the patrons of her foundation.

In the year 523, Pope John I rebuilt the church, and soon after the year 795 it was rebuilt a second time by Leo III, and to him we are indebted for its choicest adornments. In the XVIth century, Cardinal Baronius, who took his title from this church, rebuilt it, but took the greatest care to preserve the form of the ancient basilica, and all its precious ornaments were preserved and re-erected. By an inscription on a slab in the tribune (or sanctuary), he entreats his successors to use the same care in their necessary restorations.*

While there is nothing imposing, nothing really beautiful in the exterior of this church, the interior is rich in everything which belongs to antiquity, in everything which can carry the mind back to the primitive ages—even to the very first age of Christianity. The tribune, with its altar, Episcopal chair and stalls, is raised several steps, and surrounded by a screen, inlaid with precious marble. Instead of *ambones*, or small side-pulpits, are two plain reading-desks for the Epistle and Gospel. The altar is inlaid with marble, and above it is a canopy, supported by four pillars of African marble. Below this altar is a marble grating or *transenna* which allows the pilgrim to see the tomb of SS. Nereo and Achilleo, and even to pass through it objects of devotion so as to touch their sarcophagus. This screen, unique in its beauty, reminds one of the *shell pattern* used in needlework even at the present day, and the graceful, open curves, will be found on the 12th of May, the Feast of SS. Nereo and Achilleo, filled with roses, and every beautiful flower and leaf of the season from which the pious visitor is allowed to take what will satisfy his enthusiasm. The Episcopal chair is of unrivalled beauty. The arms are supported by sculptured lions, and the high back rises in a sculptured Gothic point, tipped by a pine-cone and enriched by mosaics. On the back of this chair, Cardinal Baronius caused to be cut, in deep letters, that part of the twenty-eighth homily of Saint Gregory, in which he eulogizes the martyrs Above, on the arch of the tribune, is a mosaic, representing the Transfiguration of Our Lord, who stands in an oval glory, Moses and Elias beside him, and Peter, James and John prostrate at His Feet. As supporters, we see on one side the Annunciation, on the other a Madonna with the Divine Child, and angels near them, with extended wings, in an attitude of admiration. All of these precious decorations are of the time of Leo III, or the VIth century. The basilica has its three naves; on its side-walls are painted the Apostles, all grand figures, with marked characteristics. The altar of the right-hand nave is dedicated to the Blessed Virgin, the left to Saint Domitilla, and on the architrave of the middle nave is found the story, as we have given it, of Flavia Domitilla, Nereo and Achilleo. It is from these that many a traveller has learned it, and has felt a spark of devotion kindled in his heart towards these martyrs of the first age.

Until the sacrilegious invasion of the Lombards in 756, none of the venerated bodies of the martyrs had been removed from the crypts of the catacombs. To quote the elegant expression of Saint Leo, "The crown of martyrs, which encircled the Eternal City, had been preserved intact," until this period; the exceptions numbering only five, according to good authorities. But this Lombard invasion had proved how easily the Church might be rifled of her most cherished relics; and from time to time, as circumstances urged, the most famous were removed and placed under altars expressly dedicated to them, or in places of safety. It was thus that the relics of Saint Domitilla and SS. Nereo and Achilleo, were deposited under the altar of the basilica bearing their name, more than three hundred years after Fabiola gave the foundation. But before they were thus consigned, the people of Rome claimed the right to pay them civic honors, such as Rome had paid to her best patriots. The relics, withdrawn from their original resting places on the *Via Ardeatina*, were escorted in triumph to the Capitol, and the festive procession passed under imperial arches bearing these inscriptions: "The senate and the Roman people, to Saint Flavia Domitilla, for having brought more honor to Rome by her death than her illustrious relatives by their works."—"To Saint Flavia Domitilla, and to the Saints Nereo and Achilleo, the excellent citizens, who gained peace for the Christian republic at the price of their blood." After which the relics were received at the door of the basilica, in which they still rest.

A ride of five minutes brought us to the little square of green grass, set close with daisies, in front of the church that bears the name of Saint Cæsareo of Terracina, the deacon, who rescued the bodies of Saint Domitilla and her companions from the ashes of their funeral pyre. An ancient granite column of beautiful proportions adorns this little piazza, and small as the church is, it won a mention from Gregory the Great, and important events have transpired therein. Here Saint Sergius, of Sicily, was elected Pope in 687; here, Eugenius III, an abbot of SS. Vincenzio and Anastasio was elected Pope in 1145, but was obliged to fly from Rome to Monticello, thence to the Abbey of Farfa, where he was consecrated. The interior of the church, desolate as it now seems, unless visited on a station day, is interesting beyond description. The pulpit is declared to be "one of the most exquisite specimens of church decoration in Rome, covered with the most deli-

---

* "Whoever thou mayest be, cardinal priest, my successor, I pray thee, for the glory of God and the merits of these martyrs, increase nothing, diminish nothing, change nothing, but guard piously the re-established antiquity. So may God, by the prayers of His martyrs, be always your Helper."

cate sculpture, interspersed with mosaic." The marble itself is as fine as alabaster, and the symbols of the evangelists, with the lamb, are treated as harmoniously as flowers among the spiral columns twined with strings of bright mosaic. A niche stands below the pulpit, and on the side, which conceals six marble steps, are round slabs of precious red porphyry let into the creamy white marble. The whole clings to the ancient wall, with its almost effaced frescoes, like a piece of frost-work in a dim forest. The high altar, too, is enriched by the same mosaics of the Cosmati as the pulpit, and small owls peep out from the capitals of the delicately carved pillars. Below the altar is the confession, where the relics of the saint repose, and from which two angels are drawing aside a curtain in marble. In the tribune is a very ancient episcopal chair which has most of its delicate mosaics. The Paschal candlestick belongs to the same order of excellence; but of all the treasures of San Cæsareo, none are more captivating than the reading-desks, standing as they do on the inlaid altar screen, each a simple square of marble resting on an angel's head—no sorrowing angel, but so joyful as to remind one of the everlasting gladness of the hosts of heaven.

There was a piece of embroidery in each of these old churches on their station day, which was unlike anything we saw in Rome, excepting at the *Quattro Incoronati*, and this was an altarcloth of the finest linen lawn, embroidered with silks of different colors in the very *tent* stitch which is so much in vogue among ourselves at this present time; nor will any of this work in our industrial rooms outvie these very ancient altar-cloths, wrought by the hands of nuns, who have mouldered ages ago in their graves. The tinted silks, too, were of exquisite delicacy and have proved that the ancient dyers might venture to warrant their colors. There was something very tender in the bringing out of these delicate fabrics, which harmonized so well with the mosaics of the Cosmati, on all the station days, as if they were among the most prized of the ancient treasures. We touched them reverently, and wished that more of the needle-work of our countrywomen could hope for, or deserve, by the motive for its production, such an immortality as that enjoyed by the frail altar-cloths of the Church of Santa Domitilla, and SS. Nereo and Achilleo, with its neighbor, San Cæsareo, on the Appian Way.

(TO BE CONTINUED.)

OUR sorrows sanctified become our holiest treasures; a life without sorrow would be arid as a garden without rain or dew.

EACH one of us carries in our hearts a germ of sanctity which would blossom forth at the mere bidding of our will.—*Frederick Ozanam.*

The Apparitions at Knock.

THIRD LIST OF MIRACULOUS CURES. CONCLUSION OF ARCHDEACON CAVANAGH'S DIARY. REMARKABLE LETTER OF FATHER MACALPINE, OF BALLINDINE, ETC., ETC.

From "The Dublin Weekly News" of March 20.

I now proceed to complete my extracts from the diary of cures placed in my hands by the worthy pastor of Knock:

201. Patrick Nixon, of the parish of Cappa (Rev. Mr. M'Carthy, P. P.): swelled knee; the result of a heavy fall on flags some time ago. He suffered very much up to the time of his visit to Knock. He had to use two sticks in walking. One of them he left at Knock when returning home.

202. George Fullane, of the parish of Cappa: sore knee. He left his stick at Knock.

203. Thomas Cummins, of Strokestown: sores on one of his hands and feet, and weakness of one arm. The sores have disappeared, and the arm, which used to be very thin, and all but entirely useless, has grown much fuller and stronger.

204. Patrick Bourke, of Loughrea, county Galway: paralysis. He had been five years a cripple, and had been a long time a patient in the Mater Misericordiæ Hospital, without any material improvement of his state. He left at Knock the crutch he had been so long obliged to use.

205. Michael Corcoran, Meath: a cancer. His cure has been quite complete.

206. Lucy Hegarty, of Meath: pain in the left side, and stiffness of the little finger of the left hand. The finger, which had been bent in against the palm of the hand, is restored to its natural straightness, and the pain has ceased altogether.

207. Patrick Donnolly, of 55 Piccadilly-street, Anderston, Glasgow: running evil in the left leg.

208. Thomas Harvey, of Moville: evil in the neck.

209. Mrs. (John) Cassidy had been suffering from a serious illness; she took a drink of water in which a fragment of the cement had been placed, fell asleep, and woke as well as ever.

210. John O'Connor, of Ardagh, near Rathkeale, was for nine years unable to lay his left foot on the ground. He had to use an iron leg, by the help of which he was able to move along very slowly. At Knock he received the use of the limb that had so long been useless, and went away rejoicing. [The iron leg, which O'Connor left after him, was in the receptacle for crutches and sticks at the church when I last visited Knock.]

211. Joseph Barry, Sheriff street, Dublin: had an impediment in his speech, which is now in a great degree removed.

212. Margaret Hecuson: weakness and pain in the chest; a great improvement has been effected.

213. A girl named Staunton, of Killucan: lameness. She came to Knock with a crutch, and left without any such assistance.

214. Margaret Nee, of Moyrus: paralysis. She had been in such an extreme degree deprived of the natural powers of motion that for twenty years she had been unable to go from one place to another except upon her

hands and knees. Since her visit to Knock, her right leg has straightened; she is able to stretch it out and move it freely; the left leg is beginning to extend and become flexible.

215. An exalted dignitary of the Church, who had been suffering from sleeplessness for several weeks together, was cured by having placed under his pillow a piece of the cement from Knock. The night succeeding, he slept profoundly, and has not since been troubled by want of sleep.

[At the point now reached in the diary, I come upon a brief account of the case (No. 4) of Mrs. Catharine Doble, of Claremorris, whose name was inserted in my letter of the 6th inst. Mrs. Doble had been lame for no less than seventeen years. She was scarcely able to touch the ground with her foot, and had to use both a crutch and a stick in order to move the shortest distance. Her recovery at Knock was so complete that she left the crutch and the stick behind.]

216. Joseph Morris, of Castletown-Geoghegan: sore on the leg. His recovery has been quite complete.

217. Michael Martin, of Lissaculleen, county Monaghan: epilepsy.

218. Dominick Rogers, of Ballaghaderrin: lameness. He had been in the habit of using two sticks, both of which he left at Knock.

219. Mary Ryan, of Thurles: had been for ten years unable to go on her knees, or to move one inch without the help of a crutch. Her recovery enabled her to leave her crutch at Knock.

220. Mrs. Smith, Limerick: a running sore on the face.

221. Miss Finegan, of Clifden: sickness of long standing.

222. Mrs. Healy, of Co. Cork: dropsy.

223. Mary O'Dea, parish of Kilmacduagh: blindness of the right eye.

224. Edward Farrell, parish of Rathlin: blindness of the right eye.

225. Pat. Flanigan, Cloontuskert: a heart affection.

226. Mary Quinn, of Mullingar: blindness.

227. John M'Kenna: blindness of ten years' standing. He is quite restored to the use of sight.

228. Joseph Toole, of Innisturk: weakness of the right foot, the result of a compound fracture. He had been hardly able to walk, but now can do so without the slightest trouble.

229. Martin Rorke: sore foot. He had been unable to touch the ground with it for years.

230. Ellen O'Donnell, of Co. Longford: shortness of sight.

231. A daughter of Mr. Mark O'Brien, of Cloonahulty, was suffering so intensely from violent pains in the head that for days together her parents thought her life in imminent danger. She drank some water containing a portion of the cement, fell asleep, and awoke quite well.

Here, for the present, the diary closes. We submit the marvellous record to the judgment and scrutiny of the public, and feel that in doing so we discharge a duty to our readers, and, we may add, to the community at large. No one can say that any part of the evidence in the case has in any degree been withheld from examination. We have given the testimony of the principal witnesses precisely as it fell from their own lips; we have described the scene, the surroundings, and all the material incidents with the utmost fidelity and care; and by publishing without reserve, so far as they could be ascertained, the names and addresses of the persons for whose cures a miraculous character is claimed, we have enabled all concerned to continue the work of inquiry for themselves.

The following letter, regarding the case of Fergus Fallon, referred to in the evidence of Sub-constable Collins, and also included in the diary, will be read with particular interest: —"Ballindine, 14th Feb., '80. My dear Archdeacon—I am in receipt of your letter regarding Fergus Fallon, of Kilcolman. As I was at Knock on the day this man is stated to have recovered the use of his limbs, and hearing that he was in the church, I called him into the sacristy, and made particular inquiries as to how he felt a month previously, and not only that, but for the past twelve months or two years. 'I felt,' said he, 'a month ago, and twelve months ago, just as I felt for the last fifteen years, and that is, that I could not put my foot [I forget which it was, the right or left foot, he said—I think left] to the ground if I got the world.' 'Perhaps,' said I, 'you could have done so had you used the same effort that you do now?' 'No,' rejoined the poor man: 'as sure as if I was this moment going before God, if I got the world for it I could not make an impression with my foot on a print of butter. More than that,' he added, 'the foot was as thin as the small handstick I have in my hand, and since I have come to Knock I find it filling and strengthening. I can now walk with ease without my crutch. I never could do without it before, but I left it outside, and I can do without it now.' I saw him walk, but a little lame. I asked him if he knew Fathers Curran and Corbett. He said yes, and they would bear him out in what he stated of himself as regards his being unable to walk. ... I am, my dear Archdeacon, yours sincerely, P. MacAlpine (C. C.) Venerable Archdeacon Cavanagh."

It will have occurred, no doubt, to many reflecting readers of these letters, that the cases of cures at Knock are very far indeed from being confined to those which have come to Archdeacon Cavanagh's knowledge. This idea is certainly sustained by the following letters which have lately reached me from the counties of Cavan and Longford. The first is from a resident of Mullagh, county Cavan, who furnishes me with his name. He writes:—"Sir—As an eye-witness to a cure effected by cement from Knock chapel, I beg to transmit the facts, through the medium of your columns, for the information of the public. They are as follows:—Mr. James Reilly, a respectable and independent farmer, living in Fartagh, near Mullagh, county Cavan, was suffering for a long time with a disease of a very painful nature in the legs. He tried several remedies, without effecting a cure, when a relative of his wrote to a school-fellow near Knock, who sent some of the cement by post, and no sooner had he applied it to his legs, which were in extreme pain at the time, than he felt relief. He is now walking about his house, etc., though up to the day he applied the cement he could not move through his room without being helped from place to place." The following letter will also invite attention: —"Longford, 6th March, '80. Dear Sir—Reading over the very formidable lists of cures miraculously effected by the visitations to Knock Roman Catholic church, given in your issue of last week, I was forcibly struck by the coincidence of a conversation I had with Doctor Atkinson a few days ago. He assured me positively that a young woman in his dispensary district of Killashee, in this county, who suffered from a cataract on the eye, recently paid a visit to Knock, and returned home perfectly cured. She had been under his care for some time, and he was firmly persuaded she never could have been cured by any human agency. He met her on the road the day on which he related the extraordinary incident to me, and he assured me that her eye was as brilliant and as perfect in shape and movement as it ever was before. I am well aware that Dr. Atkinson is a very clever young man, who bids fair to stand among the stars of his profession, and hence I have the more confidence in his statement. Yours truly, M. Fullman."

At this point, for the present, I close my investigation, but ere long I hope to resume in the columns of your journal the description of this interesting and most important subject.

Catholic Notes.

——The fourteenth centenary of the birth of St. Benedict, founder of the Benedictines, was religiously and joyously celebrated throughout the world by the entire Order on the 6th inst.

——ROYAL PIETY.—King Leopold, of Belgium, immediately after the betrothal of his daughter Stephanie to Rudolph, crown prince of Austria, besought the apostolic benediction for the youthful couple, and received it on the same day by a special telegram from Rome.

——Mr. Cousin, conservator of the Carnavalet Library, has presented that institution with a rare book entitled the "Commentaries of William of Paris on the Epistles and Gospels of the year" (1485). It is bound in swine leather; a chain about 8 inches long, by which it was fastened to the reading-stand, according to the custom of the times, is still an appendage of the book. The fastening of books was a precaution against theft.

——DEATH OF MR. KENELM DIGBY.—The death is announced, after a very short illness, of Mr. Kenelm Digby, in the eightieth year of his age. He was the youngest son of the Very Rev. W. Digby, Dean of Clonfert, who belonged to the Irish branch of Lord Digby's family. Graduating at Trinity College, Cambridge, in 1823, he some time afterwards became a convert to the Catholic Church, and the result of his theological and antiquarian studies was a work called "The Broad Stone of Honor; or, Rules for the Gentlemen of England," published in 1829. Other books from his pen were "Mores Catholici; or, Ages of Faith," "Evenings on the Thames," and "The Epilogue to Previous Works in Prose and Verse." R. I. P.

——CONVERSIONS.—Lord Courtenay, eldest son and heir to the Duke of Devonshire, was lately received into the Catholic Church by Cardinal Manning, and will accompany that eminent Prelate to Rome to be presented to the Holy Father. We have also to record the conversion of Rev. Mr. Compbels and lady. He was rector of the Episcopalian mission established at Lima, Peru. The ceremony of abjuration and baptism was presided over by the Papal Delegate, Monsignor Moceni, who presented Mr. Compbels with a fine portrait of Pope Leo XIII. and Mrs. Compbels with an elegant rosary. Thirteen Ritualists, including five ex-ministers, are reported to have been received into the Church recently at the Brompton Oratory. Mr. G Gilbert Scott, another late convert, was received into the Church at St Mary's, Hampstead.

——AN INTERESTING AND VALUABLE DISCOVERY.—An important and interesting discovery has been made by Father Manirano, O. S. B., who lately found in the Abbey of Subiaco a number of rare MSS; among them are numerous works of Saint Thomas Aquinas, consisting mainly of biographies of saints, and Lenten sermons, together with many "*Questiones disputatas*';

among the latter are three which have never been printed; of these, the first two questions treat of the immortality of the soul. The learned friar has also discovered several MSS, written by the disciples of Saint Thomas, by direction and under the immediate supervision of their great master. The authenticity of all these precious documents has been established beyond doubt by most elaborate and careful researches on the part of the best paleographers.

——CATHOLIC MISSIONS IN AFRICA.—According to recent information, the missionaries of Algiers destined for the apostolate among the negro tribes dwelling around Lake Tanganika, in Central Africa, have fixed their abode at Ouvira, on the farthest northern shore of the lake, for the sake of better communication with their brethren, destined for the Vicariate of Lake Victoria Nyanza. The missionaries of Algiers, established by the Most Rev. Archbishop of that place about twenty years ago, consist of priests and lay-brothers, the latter of whom, on account of savage beasts, and perhaps of more savage men, are often obliged to exercise their skill in the use of fire-arms. This circumstance drew quite a number of veteran soldiers, chiefly from the late Pontifical Army, into the ranks of the brothers; and on the 23d of February, nineteen Belgians, formerly of the Papal Brigade, took ship at Antwerp for Algiers, where they will remain after their arrival until next June, to become accustomed to the African climate. At the expiration of this term of acclimatization, they will depart for Central Africa, under the command of Mr. Joubert, a Breton, and formerly a captain in the Pontifical Army.

——PROPHETIC.—The wonderful changes that have taken place throughout all Europe during the past few years, but especially in Russia, where the Emperor is reduced to such an extremity, that he cannot trust the members of his own family, force us to confess that the predictions of the saintly Pius IX have become a terrible and living reality. On the 24th of April, 1864, in the Church of the Propaganda, this holy Pontiff uttered a solemn protest against the tyranny of the Russian Czar; and on the 30th of July, in the same year, we find him renewing this same protest in a circular letter to the Bishops of Poland. He says therein: "Empire has been given to you by the Most High God, who will examine your works and discover your thoughts; but if you, the servants of His kingdom, do not act according to right; if you do not observe the laws of justice, and conform your actions to His holy will, in speed and terror He will overtake you, and the severest judgments will be visited upon those who are placed as rulers over others: 'for mercy is given to the lowly, but the mighty shall be severely punished.'" The warning voice of the Pontiff was unheeded, and even mocked at by men of this so-called enlightened age. But ah! the times! the changes! What say they now?

——A DUTY OF CATHOLIC CITIZENS.—The *Catholic Universe* is very correct when it urges the necessity of a Catholic vote when faith and morals are concerned in the questions of public interest that come before the people. We have become so much accustomed to seeing both faith and morals disregarded in legislation, that it seems strange to put in the plea of a Catholic vote in the political contests of the day. But the time is rapidly approaching, when the requirements of faith will no longer be disregarded by those who aim at purity in the management of State affairs, and who look upon the commonwealth as simply a *consolidated* individual. We are afraid that too many Catholics do not regard the necessity of carrying their faith with them, even in the discharge of their duty as citizens. We are cautioned against compromising our faith; and as we are to live by faith, it is impossible to be practical Catholics without its exercise in all things. It is easy to conceive what happiness would be granted us in this life, did we all understand thoroughly what it is to be a Christian in the complete sense of the word. All disorders amongst nations, revolutions, upheavals of society, disintegration of social life, estrangement of individuals, corruptions of all kinds, can be traced to the abuse of the maxims and truths inculcated by Him who designed all things and established universal harmony. No infraction of divine law can occur without its corresponding punishment.—*Catholic Columbian.*

———SHIFTING SANDS.—The most casual observer cannot fail to have noticed the change that has taken place among Protestants of late years in reference to religious emblems. Half a century ago, the cross was an object of horror to sectaries; but now it is by no means the distinctive mark of a Catholic Church: in fact, nearly all the sects employ it. Here is what the *South Bend Herald* had to say last week of Easter decorations: "Easter Sunday was duly celebrated in all the churches in commemoration of the resurrection of the Saviour. It is becoming more and more the custom among some of our Protestant brethren to decorate their churches in honor of this great event in the world's history, on the faith of which the whole fabric of the Christian religion rests. In the Presbyterian Church could be seen a representation of the cross, crowned with a wreath of flowers; an image of an angel, with a miniature sepulchre in the background, amidst a profusion of flowers. It was enough to make the bones of old John Calvin and John Knox rattle in their graves, were we to believe the holy horror in which all such emblems were held by the early Protestant churches. But the world moves. This decoration and these emblems were pleasing to the eye, even if they did awaken memories of the fearful struggles of sectarianism in the dead past. But let the dead past bury its dead. In our religious anniversaries, let the hand of the artist be invoked in any way or form to bring more vividly to mind than pen can portray or tongue can tell, the story of Christian love and redemption. With the miniature cross, the angel and the sepulchre, we should not object to the image of Mary and the Child Jesus. Our theology, as well as our secular schools, are falling back on 'the object method' of education."

———A MIRACULOUS OIL FOUNTAIN.—The most ancient church dedicated to our Blessed Lady in Rome is that of "Santa Maria" in Trastevere (beyond the Tiber), already built at the beginning of the third century, by St. Calixtus, Pope and martyr, and dedicated by him to the Blessed Virgin. It stands upon the very spot where, during the reign of the Emperor Augustus, a fountain of oil miraculously sprang forth, and flowed so copiously that its liquid soon reached the Tiber. The pagans considered this event as one of the most notable happenings of the reign of Augustus; but they were unable to fathom its meaning. It was only after a considerable lapse of time that the Christians learned the mystical meaning of the miraculous well. They recognized in the fountain, so marvellously sprang from the bosom of the earth, a type of the Redeemer Jesus Christ, who at that very time was miraculously born of the Virgin Mary. They recognized in it a type of the Incarnate God, Christ Jesus, who, like the good Samaritan, hastened to assist our poor and suffering race, which had fallen under the temptations of the Evil One. He it was, who by His coming, poured the oil of salvation into our wounded souls, and entrusted us for complete recovery to His Church, until He shall return again on the day of final reckoning. The opening from which the oil flowed is still visible in the church, at the steps of the choir, and is about two feet in diameter. Above it we read, "*Fons Olei*"; at the right side, "*Hic oleum fluxit, cum Christus Virgine luxit.*"

Here, when dear Christ of Virgin's womb was born,
A fount of oil sprang forth to hail the natal morn.

At the left side, "*Nascitur hinc oleum, Deus ut de Virgine utroque Oleo sacrato est Roma terrarum caput.*"

Here did the generous earth wide ope and weep,
In joyful unctuous tears,
As Christ from out the Virgin's womb did leap,
And stilled salvation's fears.
O, Rome! twice consecrate art thou!
To rule, by God thou'rt given!
The oil of Faith anoints thy brow,
And breathes its dew to heaven.

The edifice is ornamented, both within and without by beautiful mosaics, and is considered one of the most magnificent churches in Rome.

———JEWISH CONVERTS TO CHRISTIANITY.—The *Archives Israelites* notices a growing tendency among Jewish people all over the world towards Christianity. "How can it be explained," they ask, "that most of our Israelite families have witnessed numerous conversions in their midst during the last fifty years?" Several families, in different countries, are mentioned by name. In Germany, the Loeventhals, and Mendersohns, who at present have not a single member of their family remaining a Jew; the Meyerbeer, and others. In Russia and Poland, Jews, on coming into fortune, very frequently embrace Christianity, and strive to forget their former creed and nationality. The same may be said of many Jewish families of Spanish descent. In England, the Disraelis, and many others could be mentioned. In France, scarcely a member of the Ratisbon, Halevy, and other noted families, now remains a Jew. The writer has disregarded any distinction between Catholic and Protestant converts from Judaism, and has not troubled himself about the motives which, invariably among Protestant Jews, may be set down as worldly and human. Fortunately, this cannot be said of Jewish converts embracing the Catholic Faith. Among the latter may be found many names of men renowned for ability and learning, and of all grades and professions, such as physicians, barristers, and even rabbis, which may easily be concluded from the names, Cohen, Levy, Leffmann, Lehmann, etc. We give here a list of the most prominent Jews who have become sincere Catholics: a Drack, called a deep well of science, whom Gregory XVI made librarian of the Vatican, and whose son, now a priest, is at present engaged in editing an immense work of commentaries on Holy Writ; Rev. Father Liebermann, founder of the Congregation of the Holy Ghost and of the Sacred Heart of Mary, who was declared venerable by Pius IX; Father Herman Cohen, the great Carmelite, who, during the last Franco-Prussian war, fell a victim to his charity towards the French soldiers made prisoners in Germany; the Dominican. Rev. Father Levy, who afterwards gave his life for the Faith in Mesopotamia; the Abbé Olmer at Paris, whose entire family followed his example, two of his sisters entering the religious state; the pious and eloquent Lehmann brothers, both priests; the two Abbés Level, one of whom was Superior of "Saint Louis of the French" at Rome; the famous Father Volt, one of the most eloquent preachers in Austria. To these may be added such names as Rothschild, Miers, Pereire, and others, who have yielded to the divine attraction, and become devoted Catholics.

Confraternity of the Immaculate Conception
(Or of Our Lady of Lourdes).

REPORT FOR THE WEEK ENDING APRIL 7TH.

The following intentions are recommended to the prayers of the Confraternity: Recovery of health for 102 persons and 5 families,—change of life for 30 persons and 7 families,—conversion to the Faith for 42 persons and 8 families,—recovery of mind for 5 persons,—special graces for 3 priests and 4 religious,—temporal favors for 26 persons and 13 families,—spiritual favors for 39 persons and 14 families,—the spiritual and temporal welfare of 5 communities, 2 congregations, 4 schools, and 1 hospital. Also 16 particular intentions, and 4 thanksgivings for favors received.

Specified intentions: The conversion of some well-meaning Protestants using the water of Lourdes,—recovery of a lost situation,—news or return of a number of persons missing,—several intentions recommended by a religious community, as well as all other intentions specified on previous occasions.

FAVORS OBTAINED.

That Our Blessed Lady helps us also in temporal necessities, if her aid is invoked with proper disposition, is shown by the following extracts from recent letters: "I return sincere thanks to yourself and to the members of the Confraternity for prayers that have been answered. God sent me a purchaser for my farm, which has given me a little foothold again." Another correspondent states that by use of the blessed Water of Lourdes she has been cured of neuralgia. We are informed by another person that her husband had been entirely cured of a complaint of the bowels by the same means. "I have been told," says another correspondent, "by the parents of a little boy, who was hurt by a fall about four years ago, that after trying all the doctors for miles around to no purpose, they sent for the Water of Lourdes, which restored him to health the same day."

OBITUARY.

The prayers of the members of the Confraternity are asked for the following deceased persons: Mrs. ELLEN O'NEILL, who slept in the peace of the Lord on the 5th of Feb., at Keokuk, Iowa. Mrs. MARY E. TAGLIABUE, who died suddenly in New York, Feb. 14th. Mr. JOHN CAMPBELL, of Hammond, Wis., whose death occurred on the 5th ult. Mrs. HENRIETTA REDDING, of Altoona, Pa., who breathed her last on Good Friday. Miss C. A. CURTIS, of East Cambridge, Mass., deceased on the 27th ult. Mrs. FELIX O'REILLY, a resident of Co. Cavan, Ireland. Mr. and Mrs. REILLY, of Washington, D. C., both devout Catholics. Mr. JOHN C. SULLIVAN, JAMES CONDRON, and TIMOTHY FARRELL, all of Altoona, Pa.; Mr. JAMES GALLAGHER, of San Francisco, Cal.; Mrs. MARY SMITH, of San Luis Obispo, Cal., all of whom died recently. Miss KATIE STOLL, Mr. JOHN SMITH, Miss HANNAH HIGGINS, Mr. PATRICK LEYDEN, Mrs. BEYER, of Boston, Mass.; Mr. JOHN SMITH, of Chicago, Ill.; Mrs. BROPHY, JOHN DALY, and THOMAS KELLY, of Hudson, N. Y., deceased some time ago.

Requiescant in pace.

A. GRANGER, C. S. C., Director.

Youth's Department.

[For the Ave Maria.]

A Morning Prayer.

BY LADY GEORGIANA FULLERTON.

THESE hands, my God, Thyself hast framed;
　Shall they not toil for Thee?
Shall labor fright them, shall they scorn
　Thy servants still to be?
Whate'er the work assigned to-day
　To each successive hour,
The feeble effort still will need
　Thy all-sustaining power.
Withhold it not, O Lord, and give
　Thy blessing to each task.
To work for Thee, for Thee to live,
　Is all I hope, or ask.

[From "The Catholic."]

The Light-House Keeper's Daughter.

MANY years ago, a little girl lived all alone with her father in a castle that was built on a grand old rock. In this castle was a light-house, and every night the light was brilliantly reflected on the bosom of the deep blue sea.

Little Marie was very delicate, and often unable to leave her bed for many days. The poor child did not have much pleasure in her life at the castle, and—can you believe it?—she had never seen a flower! for nothing but weeds grew by the rocks, and Marie had never lived anywhere else but in this same castle.

Her papa was very kind to her, and every night when she was well enough, he would carry her in his arms, up the narrow, winding stairway that led to the great lamp, and nothing pleased Marie more than to watch her papa light it, and then to see the flame throw its light on the water; it seemed like a fairy tale, she said.

Once when her papa was going away for a few days, Marie said to him: "Papa, will you make me very happy—happier than I've ever been before?"

"Yes, little one, if it is possible for me to do so; how could I refuse my pet anything?"

"Then, dear papa, will you—can you bring me a rose—a lily? Oh, I do want one so much!"

Although she had never seen one, she had often heard her papa speak of them, and had seen many pictures of them in her books. What kind of a flower would he bring her? Would it be a beautiful red rose, a soft white lily, or perhaps some tender little violets? It seemed to Marie as if he never would return; but at last he came, and after carefully fastening the boat to its moorings, he jumped on shore, and hurried to see his little girl. She put her arms around his neck, and whispered: "Dear papa, and my flower!"

"I have not brought you a flower, my child, but I bought you something better instead."

And he gave her a package, which she opened with feverish haste, her hands trembling with anxiety. Alas! it did not contain anything beautiful to her.

The poor, disappointed child burst into tears, and they were indeed very bitter, for they came right from her grieved and aching little heart. She thought that her papa did not understand how much she wanted the flower, and yet she knew he loved her. He did not immediately try to explain to her what the "grains" were, but taking her in his arms, he petted and comforted her until she could listen to all that he had to tell her, and then he informed her that the little grains were flower-seeds, and that, if they were carefully planted, she would one day have a beautiful garden of her own. So her papa found a nice place on either side of the steps, where there was a narrow strip of earth between the grey rocks.

For many days she watched the seeds very eagerly, and took the greatest pains to water the ground where her treasures were hidden; but the constant anxiety lest, after all, she should lose her flowers, proved too great a strain for the delicate child.

She was taken very ill, and was again obliged to stay in bed for a long, long time. Her papa took the most loving care of his pet, and did everything that he could to ease her pain and make the weary hours seem less dull, buying for her many toys—books. and pretty things—and yet one thing more little Marie wanted.

"Papa is so good, so kind, and he loves me so much! Oh, if I had that one flower!" she said to herself.

The beautiful summer had come at last, and one day when Marie was feeling better, her papa said to her:

"Marie, my darling, the air is so soft and warm, and the sky and sea are so blue and calm, that I must carry you out of doors to show you something very pretty; you have never seen anything half so beautiful."

He took her in his strong arms, and carried her down stairs and out on the steps, to the foot of the castle. And what did she see? Flowers, flowers, flowers, everywhere! Roses, lilies, and violets, and, oh, so many others, whose beautiful colors were as brilliant as the rays of the setting sun; and they seemed to smile and nod a joyful greeting to her, as they bowed their heads at the gentle murmur of the breeze.

"Oh, how beautiful, papa! how beautiful!" and a tear softly kissed her pale, wan cheek.

"All this belongs to you, my pet, my darling," and he placed her tenderly by the sweetest of the flowers she so loved.

She inhaled their delicate perfume; she gently carressed them; she softly pressed their tender petals, and when her papa put a garland on her head, and filled her hands with the choicest that he could find, and carrying her back to her room, laid her again on her pretty couch, she seemed like a fairy queen on her throne of flowers. Her papa sat down by her, and taking her hand in his, said to her:

"Last spring, little one, when you asked me for a flower, there was not one to be found. I hunted everywhere, and asked each person I met to tell me where I could find one, but they all shook their heads, and told me that they did not know. But, my dear child, I loved you just as much then as I do now, and when I gave you all those seeds you thought so homely, I knew that I was preparing a happy surprise for you to-day. You had to wait and wait; but by waiting, darling, you have a garden that will last a long time, and instead of having one flower that will fade in a few hours, you have a whole garden full, from which you can gather as many bouquets as you like."

Marie did not forget the lesson of the flower-seed as long as she lived. Children, and grown people also, often ask things of God which, not always receiving at once, they feel badly, and say to themselves, "God does not trouble Himself about me and what I ask Him for." But, children, yes—indeed, yes—He does trouble Himself. Do not forget little Marie and her flowers, The good God keeps in His Heart the remembrance of your prayers; and if you but continue to trust Him and love Him, and give Him your heart, the garden of your soul will be filled with the choicest and most beautiful flowers.

CATHARINE BURTON, an English Carmelite, cherished a very special devotion to St. Francis Xavier, and was signally befriended by him in return. The Apostle of the Indies visited her in her sickness, cured her, comforted her, and fulfilled in her regard all the offices of friendship.

THE AVE MARIA.

A Journal devoted to the Honor of the Blessed Virgin.

HENCEFORTH ALL GENERATIONS SHALL CALL ME BLESSED.—St. Luke, i, 48.

VOL. XVI.   NOTRE DAME, INDIANA, APRIL 24, 1880.   No. 17.

Memorare.

REMEMBER, O Most Blessed Virgin Mary,
That no one ever came to thee in grief,
With sin o'erburdened, or with sorrow weary,
And found not sweet relief.

Then in thy gracious clemency confiding,
Here at thy sacred feet I kneel and pray,
Refuge of Sinners, for thy tender guiding
To help me on my way.

O Mother of my Lord, beloved and cherished,
Virgin all powerful, it can never be
That any lowly suppliant hath perished,
Who placed his trust in thee.

Faith and Reason.

IT is an unquestionable fact that the prevailing tendency of minds outside of the Church, at the present time, is towards infidelity—to unbelief in all and each of the teachings of religion. Anyone considering the spirit of the age in which we live, cannot fail to be struck with the marked antagonism which is made to exist between Reason and Faith. The great vice of these our own days may be said to consist in *pride of intellect*. The one great boast heard on all sides is the supremacy and self-sufficiency of reason. Reason, it is claimed, is the only guide for man in his efforts to attain to a knowledge of truth. Everything taught and inculcated must be brought before the tribunal of reason for its judgment. Even all that religion teaches, all her dogmas and mysteries, must be submitted to reason before acceptance. The Church is condemned, because, they say, she lowers and debases reason—and exacts of her members a blind acceptance of her teachings, however much opposed to reason; she obliges her subjects to sacrifice the wonderful power of intelligence which places man far above the brute, and makes him what he is—the lord of creation. Such being the state of minds, it would seem most fitting that the real relations between Faith and Reason should be understood as set forth by the Church.

St. Paul, in his Epistle to the Romans (xii, 1), says: "I beseech you therefore, brethren, that you present unto God your *reasonable* service." And St. Peter, in his First Epistle (iii, 15), says: "Being ready always to *satisfy everyone that asketh you a reason* of the hope which is in you." These words of the apostles show that the faith which is expected of us is not merely an acquiescence in belief, not a simple submission, but a *reasonable* acquiescence and submission—one therefore in which reason has its part; and were it not thus reasonable, it would not be a virtue. And such has ever been the teaching of the Church. As defined by the late Œcumenical Council of the Vatican: "The Catholic Church has ever held, as she now holds, that there exists a twofold order of knowledge, each of which is distinct from the other both as to its principle and as to its object. As to its principle, because in the one we know by natural reason; in the other, by divine faith; as to its object, because besides those things to which natural reason can attain, there are proposed to our belief mysteries hidden in God, which, unless by Him revealed, cannot come to our knowledge... Not only is it impossible for faith and reason ever to contradict each other, but they rather afford each other mutual assistance. For right reason establishes the foundations of faith, and by the aid of its light cultivates the science of divine things; and faith, on the other hand, frees and preserves reason from errors, and enriches it with knowledge of many kinds." The Church, then, so far from condemning the exercise of reason, rather promotes and encourages its use and development in many ways. But she requires that it be exercised only within its own sphere, with the objects proper to it; that when there is question of divine mysteries, truths supernaturally revealed, which are above reason, then it must yield to faith, and not seek to penetrate that which is placed beyond its province. She holds, and reason itself dictates, that God, being infinitely intelligent, knows truths that are above the reach of finite intelligence; that He can make known such truths to man, and claim a belief in them, though they surpass the understanding. It is permitted to man—the Church admits—to satisfy his reason that such truths have been actually revealed by God. There are always accompanying these revelations what are called the motives of credibility, or the means by which reason may be convinced that they are from God; but once persuaded of the divinity of their origin, reason must bow in submission, and unhesitatingly accept them without further examination.

The Church says to the infidel: "Exercise that reason of which you so proudly boast; listen to its voice; obey its dictates." What does it say to you? It tells you that there is a God, infinite in perfection, the supreme Lord and Master of the universe, upon whom all things depend for their existence, and to whose honor and glory all must be referred. Study the marvellous operations of nature. Consider the wonderful order and harmony existing in that immense universe of things of which this earth of ours is but an atom. Contemplate the expanse above—the heavenly bodies placed therein, whose motions are accomplished with such velocity, and yet with such admirable regularity. Consider the infinite number of stars in the firmament; the variety of seasons which, through such constant and wonderful revolutions, succeed each other in turn, and form part of the course of time. Look out upon that vast territory of land and sea which forms an almost infinite world beneath the celestial world. Study the thousands and myriads of marvels in this terrestrial globe and the world above us; penetrate into the mysteries of the mineral kingdom, with its wondrous laws governing the action of the material elements, as shown in the formation of crystals; study the vegetable kingdom, with its wonderful phenomena; study the animal kingdom, with all its different phases of life and appearances of intelligence; study thyself: study man, with that grand gift of intelligence, placing him at an almost infinite distance above the rest of creation. Study these, and much else which we need not mention. What is the judgment of Reason? Whence comes all this? Will Reason say it is the work of chance? No: all nature proclaims that it is from God, and Reason echoes the voice of nature. Reason declares that the firmament, the heavens, the stars, the earth with all these marvels, have not made themselves, nor established that wonderful order which exists among them; that they have not given motion to themselves, that they do not subsist of themselves, without some supreme intelligence who presides, and has ever presided, over all. Reason requires of you to acknowledge a first cause, a prime mover, a supreme power, from whom all things proceed, who orders all, who disposes all, who animates and sustains all. And this primitive, independent, ever-subsisting power, we call God.

Thus Reason tells you of God: but more than that. Listen again to its voice. It tells you, moreover, that He to whom you owe your being —all that you have and all that you are—that He should be honored as God. That same Reason which brings you to the knowledge of God, leads you further to the knowledge of the worship which you should give to Him and which He has the right to exact of you. He demands, and you owe to Him, a religious worship. Reason dictates that the Creator has a just right to expect and demand from His creatures the homage that belongs to Him; and that, on the part of creatures, they are bound to glorify, as far as lies in their power, that Creator from whom they have received their existence; to believe His teaching, conform to His will, obey His law, offer the homage of their adoration, and devote themselves fully to His service. And in this does religion consist.

Reason, therefore, points out to man the necessity of religion. But inasmuch as there exist a number of religions, contradictory to each other, which have been introduced into the world through the aberrations of the human mind, and one alone can be true—as God, who is truth itself, is one—so it comes within the province of Reason to seek among existing religions that in which is found the one, true, perfect worship of the one only God. Now, amongst these religions you find the Christian religion, and your reason alone discovers in it characters of truth so marked, so striking, that they suffice to convince any sensible, solid, and docile understanding, which does not obstinately persist in imagining difficulties or in lingering over vain disputes.

The Christian religion was founded by Jesus Christ, who, by the miracles alone which He performed, gave proof more than sufficient of the truth of His mission. This new Lawgiver appears upon earth; He preaches His Gospel, which is the Christian law; and to give authority to His preaching, He proclaims Himself sent by God. Evidently if He is from God, if He speaks in the name of God, all that He teaches is true, and we are obliged to subscribe to His doctrine. The impression which Reason produces within us of God, assures us that He cannot bear witness to and confirm falsehood. All that remains for Christ is to prove His mission, and this He does by the miracles which He performs. "The works which I do," He says, "give testimony of Me: if you believe not My words, believe My works." It is certain that miraculous works, being above the powers of nature, can be produced only by the power of God, and in accordance with His will. If, then, Jesus Christ really wrought miracles, and pointed to them in proof of the divinity of His mission, and in support of His claim to be the Messiah sent for the salvation of mankind, the claim cannot be contested, nor can there be any doubt that He has come on the part of God; otherwise, God would be the author of an imposture, in communicating to Him a power which He knew would be employed only to deceive men and abuse their credulity.

Now, a reason which is enlightened and freed from all prejudice, must admit that Jesus Christ wrought a great number of miracles, the principal end of which was to show that He had come from God; it must be admitted that He expelled demons from bodies of which they had taken possession; that He exercised supreme control over the elements, and they obeyed His voice; that He calmed the winds and the waves; that He healed all kinds of infirmities: restored sight to the blind, hearing to the deaf, speech to the dumb, sense and movement to the paralytic, life to the dead; and finally, by a most singular and unheard-of prodigy, He Himself, after having been put to death, and enclosed for three days in the tomb, raised Himself on the third day, living and glorious. Reason must admit all this: it has only to examine the circumstances connected with these facts, their number, the time, the countries, the public places in which they occurred, the multitudes of eye-witnesses, the vast numbers of those who, after hearing the recital of these miracles, embraced the Faith and formed those bodies of Christians so renowned for their zeal and piety; it has but to consider the irreproachable character of the witnesses who beheld them, who related them to others, and made them known to the extremities of the earth; who transmitted them to posterity in their Gospels; who maintained them without ever falsifying themselves, and who, in defence of their truth, sacrificed all that they had, even their very lives. Let Reason make a careful examination of each of these points, and many others which must now be passed over, and it must perforce be convinced that, of all historical facts, there are none better authenticated, none more solidly grounded, none less open to criticism or censure, than these facts, these miracles attesting the divinity of the Founder of Christianity.

Is the exercise of Reason forbidden by the Church? Thus far, Reason alone has led to a knowledge of the truth and divinity of the Christian religion—the religion founded by Christ. Now, it may go still further. Reason finds in the world a number of religions, all professing to be Christian, and claiming to be religions of Christ, and all opposed to each other. There can be but one possessing any right to this claim; there can be but one true religion, for truth cannot be opposed to itself. Here, again, Reason is permitted to exercise its powers and satisfy itself as to which, amongst all these professedly Christian religions, is the one true religion founded by Christ. This true religion must show forth in itself the character and spirit of its divine Founder. It must be *one*, as God Himself is one, all its members professing one and the same faith, and all united under one visible head —the representative of Jesus Christ upon earth. It must be *holy*, as its Founder is holy: holy in its teachings, and holy in the lives of its members, who carry out into practice what it teaches. It must be *Catholic*, or *universal*—everywhere teaching the same doctrine, and spreading throughout the whole known world. It must be *apostolical:* it must have come down to the present time with an uninterrupted succession of pastors from the apostles—those first teachers, sent forth by Christ to make known His religion to mankind. Here are four marks—unity, sanctity, Catholicity and apostolicity—by which Reason may know the true religion. The religion alone that possesses these marks, can claim to be divine. And this it is given to Reason to determine for itself. The Church, then, does not seek to destroy Reason or prevent its exercise; on the contrary, she permits the full exercise of its powers with that upon which it is capable of passing judgment. The Catholic Church lays before Reason her own claims to be divine; she shows that she alone possesses the marks of the true Church; she gives her proofs that she is the one religion established upon earth by Jesus Christ, and that to her care He entrusted the sacred deposit of Truth, with the commission to make it known to mankind until the end of time. And having convinced Reason that she is divine in her origin, that she represents God upon earth, she exercises her authority and claims an acceptance of her teachings, however mysterious they may be. If she is from God, she cannot err; her teachings claim the belief and acceptance of the human mind. Because they are from God, Reason must bow in submission and yield assent; and in this right, reason cheerfully obeys; for it recognizes that it is not the part of finite intelligence to seek to place itself on a level with the Infinite, and endeavor to penetrate His nature.

But, say the rationalists and so-called scientists of the day, we discover by the exercising of our reason—by science—many truths which conflict with the teachings of religion. No: true science and religion can never be found in opposition to each other. Both are from God, who is Truth itself, and can never contradict Himself. Science supposes certain knowledge; its legitimate conclusions are derived from certain principles which make the conclusions themselves certain. Are these so-called discoveries of the present day advanced as certain truths? No: they are as yet but mere theories—some possessing more or less probability, but no certainty; and are they to be put in opposition with the certain teachings of the Faith? When a proposition is certain, the opposite can have not even the slightest degree of probability; it must be absolutely false. Some of these theories are more or less probable, but between them and the dogmas of Faith there exists no contradiction, and none can be made to exist. They may be followed up and developed; and, if ever proved certain, they will be found in perfect harmony with religion. It is said, for example, that science has discovered that the world is much older than religion declares it to be; in fact, there is no computing its age—it must be many millions of years old. Admitting this discovery: does it contradict any dogma of the Faith? No. What does Faith teach in regard to the age of the world? Nothing. It tells us simply that the world was brought forth originally from nothing, by the Almighty power of God. Let Reason seek to discover, if it can, how creation was developed, how long it was engaged in attaining to its present state of perfection; let it dive deep into the depths of the earth and force nature to give its testimony; but let it leave untouched that primitive dogma of Faith, that this world and all things contained therein, owe their existence, originally and primarily, to the infinite act of the will of an Omnipotent God. Again, let Reason occupy itself as much as it will with the theory advanced at the present time of *evolution*, or *natural selection*, or *survival of the fittest*, by which it is sought to establish that the higher and more perfect forms of animal life are but developments of lower and less perfect forms—all evolved from a few primordial forms; but let it leave unassailed that grand, fundamental dogma of religion, that man, as a rational creature, is not himself evolved from these lower forms, but that he came forth directly from the hands of his Creator, endowed with all those natural gifts of soul and body which place him far above the rest of creation, having supernatural gifts added thereunto, to fit him for a supernatural destiny, an eternal union with his Maker. The creation of man, his trial and fall, original sin, the descent of the present human race from one common parent, in whom all have sinned; the Incarnation of the Son of God and Redemption of man; the establishment of Christianity—in which alone man is to find the means by which he may be enabled to attain the supernatural end for which he was created—these are all so many dogmas of Faith, clearly defined, and no legitimate conclusion of real science can ever be found in opposition to them. As the Church teaches: "The shadow of such contradiction arises chiefly from this—that, either the dogmas of Faith are not understood and set forth as the Church really holds them, or that the vain devices and opinions of men are mistaken for the dictates of reason."

In the Church of God upon earth, Reason and Faith go hand in hand, each concerned with its own proper object: Reason seeking to penetrate the natural, and accepting by Faith the supernatural. The children of the Church are called upon to exercise their reason, to develop and perfect the intellectual faculties with which God has gifted them, but without ever losing sight of that God upon whom they depend, and to whom they owe the homage both of Reason and of Faith. They are encouraged in their pursuit after knowledge, they are aided in the search after truth; but at the same time, they are reminded of the supernatural end for which they were created, and which they are to attain by the fulfilment of the duties which they owe to God, to themselves and to their fellowmen. In this way, Faith serves as a light to Reason, preserving it from error, and guiding it in the true path which leads to that eternal abode of happiness, where Faith disappears and gives place to knowledge, and Hope is succeeded by possession and love. Knowledge and love! the two grand faculties of the human soul, there attain to their proper objects: the intellect, in the perfect knowledge of eternal, absolute Truth, and the will in the possession and love of the one supreme, only Good. This constitutes the perfect happiness of the soul rejoicing in the Beatific Vision throughout an eternity.

IN examining, even superficially, those ages which heresy has dared to represent as without the knowledge of the sacred writings, it is easy to convince ourselves that not only churchmen—that is to say, those who made a profession of learning—knew the Holy Scriptures thoroughly, but that laymen, knew them almost by heart, and could perfectly comprehend the numberless quotations with which everything that has descended to us from this period—narratives, correspondence, and sermons—are filled. Those who have ever opened any volume whatsoever, written by the professors or historians of the Middle Ages, must stand amazed before the marvellous power of falsehood, when they reflect that it has been possible, even in our days, to make a large portion of the human race believe that the knowledge of Scripture was systematically withheld from the men who composed, and from those who read the books of that age.—*Montalembert.*

'Beth's Promise.

BY MRS. ANNA HANSON DORSEY.

CHAPTER XIV.

A ROMANTIC ADVENTURE.

THE days at "Ellerslie," although as fair and peaceful as dreamland, were never spent idly. Mrs. Morley went to Mass every morning at six o'clock, and 'Beth accompanied her, being drawn thither by a desire to understand more of the Divine Sacrifice of the altar, and with a secret, indefinite hope that she might receive the gift of Faith, without which—all human reason failing—she must remain outside the one safe Fold. It was very pleasing to the girl to be there at that hour, when the solemn quiet of the sanctuary was broken only by the low voice of the priest, the rustle of his robes as he moved from one side of the altar to the other, and the reverent responses of Mr. Dulaney, who served—except on Sundays—with great recollection and devotion; the only music being the songs of birds that came in fitful strains through the open windows, and the whisperings of the wind in the great trees outside. She always followed the devotion for Mass in her prayer-book, her mind solemnized by the awful significance of the sacred rite; and at the elevation, she bowed her head, while the cry of her heart went up: "Oh, that I could believe!" She did believe without knowing it; but she imagined there must come some wonderful manifestation with the gift of faith—which would be as unmistakable as the sun at noonday—making all things plain; in short, she expected a miracle.

They always found Aunt 'Beth in her great chair on the veranda, awaiting their return, and it made them happy to see her dear old face lighting up at their approach. Although she seemed to grow a little stronger every day since their arrival at "Ellerslie," it was not the old life and strength that they remembered, full of masterful ways, to which everyone willingly yielded, feeling that she was always right; that only showed itself at intervals now, always followed by a langor, which made it but too apparent that her vitality was seriously impaired. But no one must notice it; it did not please her that anyone should show either by sympathy or offers of assistance, that they thought she was failing. She was very busy just now; every morning after breakfast, having settled the affairs of the day with Mrs. Trott, she got into her low garden-carriage, drawn by the donkey, and made the circuit of the farm-lands, especially the hop-fields, to see if the pavilions for the hop-pickers, the great receiving tubs, and the dying houses, were being put in proper order by the workmen. Sometimes when she told Mrs. Morley that she wanted to go outside to visit the sick, or one or two families whose needs she looked after, and invited her to accompany her, "not only" as she said, "for her company, but for her help," she consented readily, only glad to be of use. Lodo had been in the habit of going with her, but in her old practical spirit, fearing that Mrs. Morley might get to brooding over her sorrows if left too much alone, she made use of the little *ruse* as to needing her help. Aunt 'Beth did not know yet how changed Mrs. Morley was, and that an opportunity to do good in some way, or to some body, was a boon above price to her. In their absence, 'Beth practised, studied and read. Sometimes the young ladies from "Tracy-Holme" came over, and spent an hour or two in social chat, or had a game of croquet under the trees, filling the air with the sweet echoes of their young voices and merry laughter. They frequently mentioned the young Dulaneys, Violet rattling on a great deal about both of them; Elaine speaking only of Bertie, who, according to her account, was the handsomest, best and bravest fellow on earth, and evidently her favorite. Violet declared it would be really grand when they came, there would be so much fun: horseback rides, rowing on the lake, fishing-parties, picnics, croquet; "and of course we shall expect you, Miss Morley, to come with us everywhere! You know," she added, reminded by 'Beth's mourning of her great and recent loss, "there will be nothing like gaiety—I mean parties, and all of that sort; it will be only among ourselves, and we mean to have a nice, merry time of it in the woods, on the water, and everywhere."

"You leave 'Ellerslie' out of your plans," said 'Beth, laughingly.

"Don't delude yourself with such an idea. I mean to get round Miss Morley in such a way that she'll give 'Ellerslie' up to my devices, and *you* too," she ran on; "I mean to have a famous time, just as soon as ever our knights arrive, and remember, Miss Morley, we shall expect you to join us in all our expeditions."

"I am sure I shall enjoy them," said 'Beth, "only can't you stop calling me Miss Morley?"

"I shall be delighted to, that is, if you will let us be Elaine and Violet to you; I am the youngest, but I always do the talking, because you know Elaine's in love."

"Oh, Violet!" exclaimed her cousin, her fair face suffused with blushes.

"Is she?" asked 'Beth, not knowing what else to say.

"It is a fact; you'll see for yourself before long," she answered, merrily.

"And you?" queried 'Beth.

"I am not, and don't intend to be for five years to come; I mean to enjoy myself," she answered gaily, singing a snatch of an Italian song about sipping "the bead from life's wine while the sunshine is there."

It was a new revelation to 'Beth, this phrase of young life, and it amused her greatly when she saw that Elaine Marston was not annoyed by her cousin's allusion to her heart affairs. They would not stay to lunch, and throwing on her hat, she walked as far as the gate with them, where they parted with many promises to be very friendly and sociable.

Sometimes 'Beth, by permission, took Lodo with her to spend a morning in the ravine, or "glen," as it was more commonly called, where she read to her something that she knew would please and delight her. Hans Anderson's stories found an answering chord in her wild, untutored imagination, but the "Lady of the Lake" awoke all the dormant romance of her poetical gypsy nature. The girl was supremely happy, and her affection for 'Beth, who had opened such new vistas of happiness to her, was merging into a sort of idolatry.

One morning at breakfast, Aunt 'Beth announced that the basket-phaeton, which she had ordered from New York, had arrived by the early train, "and I want you, my child, to take Lodo, and drive down to the lake in it. Your mother has promised to take a little drive with me."

"Oh dear Aunt 'Beth, what lovely news! How shall I ever thank you?" said 'Beth, her face all aglow with pleasure.

"Don't try to, my child, for the pleasure is mine as much as yours. I don't like to be thanked; you'll enjoy the drive; the road is good, and the bit of country you'll pass through is beautiful. You need have no fears about your horse; he goes well, and is as gentle as a lamb; I brought him up myself, and named him Pegasus, but he is known only as Peg," said Aunt 'Beth, her eyes twinkling with some of their old light. She was very proud of that horse, and always spoke of him with great pleasure. Then she sent 'Beth, with Lodo, round to the coach-house to examine the phaeton, and ordered Peg to be trotted out for inspection. He was a handsome, gentle creature, with a soft, silky, chestnut coat, carried his head well, and stepped so daintily that his feet seemed to spurn the earth. There was spirit enough in his eyes, and from a peculiar way he had of throwing his pretty ears back, it was easy to see what he would have been but for the sobering effect produced by Aunt 'Beth's training.

'Beth was overflowing with delight. Everything was *couleur de rose;* to have such a phaeton and such a horse at command, and to drive about when and where she pleased, seemed to her about the most delightful thing that was ever dreamt of. Aunt 'Beth and Mrs. Morley were about starting off on one of their usual excursions, when 'Beth got back. She threw her arms around Aunt 'Beth, and called her the dearest of fairy-godmothers, kissed her, then lifting her up bodily, carried her out and seated her in her low garden-carriage that stood waiting at the step.

"Oh, my child!" whispered Aunt 'Beth, with streaming eyes, when 'Beth had placed her tenderly upon the cushions, "don't do that again; it reminds me too much of your father; he used to pick me up like a child in his dear strong arms—but there, your mother is coming—she must not see me crying; it would distress her," she said, turning her head away to wipe her eyes and draw her veil over her face. "The light is a little glaring to-day, and a veil is the next blessing to spectacles for old eyes like mine," she remarked to Mrs. Morley, as they drove down the avenue.

'Beth was deeply touched, and she knew now what it was that had been wasting the dear old life away. "Oh," she said, looking sadly after them, "would that she could find help where mamma has found it!" Then, with quiet steps, she went to the drawing-room, where a fine portrait of her father hung, and before which fresh flowers were daily placed. She stood looking up at it until tears blinded her eyes; then throwing herself into one of the great chairs near by, in a perfect *abandon* of grief, she sobbed: "No wonder, no wonder they loved you so, my darling papa! so good so true, so brave, your noble face showing it all as plain as if it were written in a book!" and bowing her head upon her arm, she wept softly, until the emotions, so suddenly awakened, had ceased. She was still sitting in the quiet, shaded room, when she heard the sound of wheels upon the gravel, then the patter of Lodo's feet on the stairs and in the hall, as if she were in search of something, and this reminded her of her drive. She felt so sad that she would have preferred not to go; but now that everything had been prepared for her pleasure, she felt that it would be selfish to disappoint not only Lodo, but Aunt 'Beth, by remaining at home without a reasonable excuse. She rose instantly and went into the hall, and seeing Lodo on the veranda with a lunch-basket in her hand, ready to stow away in the phaeton, she called her, and, saying that she would be ready in a moment, ran up to her room to bathe her face and get a light wrap; then hurried down, threw on her hat, and stepped into the phaeton; Lodo was beside her in a minute, and after spreading the linen carriage duster carefully over their knees, and giving Peg one more affectionate pat, she gathered up the reins with the air of a jockey, and they were off. A light top protected them from the sun; there was nothing to wish for to make their enjoyment complete, either in the clear, bright atmosphere, the balmy air, or the picturesque road over which they rolled without jar or jolt; while Peg, as if conscious of his new finery, and proud of the bright, youthful faces and merry voices of the girls, ambled along with the most satisfied air imaginable, tossing his head now and then with a whinny that sounded very much like a laugh. At last a turn in the road brought them in view of the lake with all its bright glimmer and motion, its flitting sails and picturesque shores on the other side. Before them was a long stretch of level, white sand, the woods coming down almost to the water's edge, showing between their great gnarled trunks, huge, rocky boulders, with a wealth of moss and lichens on their old gray faces.

"Drive close down to the water, Lodo; I feel as though I should like to go right into it!" said 'Beth, taking a long breath as if she were inhaling the refreshment and beauty of the scene.

"Do you, mem? I'd a sight rather go into the woods up yonder."

"There's a boat—oh what a beauty!—fastened to a post, Lodo, and the water is very shallow; can't you drive near enough for me to step into the boat and sit there a little while? oh do, Lodo; I've been used to boats all my life, and there's not the slightest danger, for I can row like a sailor and swim like a frog; papa taught me; and now don't you see how perfectly safe it will be!" exclaimed 'Beth, to whom the sight of the blue bright water had been like a cool draught to a thirsty man.

"Yes, mem: it can be done, I suppose," said Lodo, eyeing the pretty white and scarlet boat askance, as it swung to and fro on the crisp, dancing waves; "I know the bottom's hard, mem, but then I've heard the old fisherman, that brings fish to 'Ellerslie,' say that there's an awful current, whatever that is."

"Now, Lodo, I'll tell you what you will do. I want some ferns, but I don't feel like scrambling about up yonder among the rocks to gather them; I prefer the boat; so drive Peg near enough for me to jump into it and be rocked on the water once more; then you can hitch him somewhere in the shade while you run into the woods and get the ferns for me. I'm sure he'll behave beautifully until you come back; what nicer arrangement could you ask?"

"Yes, mem," said the girl, still hesitating; "but, mem, I don't like the looks of that rope; it's rotten—I know it is!"

"Lodo, if you don't drive me right in, I'll take the reins myself," said 'Beth, in a very positive tone.

"Yes, mem," answered Lodo, her eyes growing larger, and her face a shade paler, as she drove into the clear shallow water, which Peg no sooner felt laving his feet, than he gave expression to his enjoyment by a loud, exultant whinny. Lodo echoed it with a merry laugh, and felt better satisfied when they arrived at the boat, to discover that the water did not reach to his knees, and the sandy bottom was as hard as a floor.

(TO BE CONTINUED.)

On the Appian Way.

SAN GIOVANNI IN OLIO.

BY ELIZA ALLEN STARR.

(CONTINUED.)

STANDING in the shadow of San Cæsario, and looking towards the Campagna, a boy could sling a pebble to the spot where a green lane branches off to the left from the *Via Appia*. This lane, as green and as lonely as many a pasture-lane in New England, leads to the old Latin Gate, now walled up. But although no year of jubilee brings a silver hammer to break through its solid masonry; although no solemnly beautiful procession of Pontiff and his ecclesiastics, no cavalcade of Roman nobles, no chanting penitential confraternity, nor even the host of some sacrilegious invader, ever passes under its arch; the sixth of May of every year finds the heart of Christendom turning towards the small green enclosure directly before the Latin Gate. The grass-grown lane is enlivened, if not thronged, by the pilgrims who may be in Rome on that day, and by lines of students, two by two, from all the colleges of the city. The daisies spread their pink and white disks full under the May sun, and enamel the fresh turf. The perfume from the blossoming vineyards is all around us. There is not, in fact, a lovelier *station* in all Rome than that of "Saint John in oil before the Latin Gate"; nor is there one which has kept more literally to the tradition which has come down to us, unchanged, during eighteen hundred years. The Liturgy of the Church celebrates a special feast, commemorating the event which lends such a charm to this spot, thus giving to the solitude a voice which grand choirs can only feebly echo, whether by anthem or organ-pipes The tradition carries us back to the year 95 of the Christian era, and to the second general persecution of the Church, under Domitian, who was so universally abhorred for his cruelties, his pride and his shameless vices. More cruel than Nero, if we can credit Tacitus, he delighted in making a display of barbarities which other tyrants had the grace to conceal from public view. Rome saw the blood of her noblest families watering her streets by his hand; and he banished, with apparently special ignominy, such pagans as bore a character for extraordinary virtue, and thus seemed to rebuke his crimes. What, then, might not Christians expect?

This general persecution, however, allowed the whole Roman world to compete with its head. At this time Saint John not only still lived, but he was the active shepherd and pastor of all the Asian churches, making Ephesus his home. Here he was arrested; but as if Ephesus was too small to be the scene of such a martyrdom as awaited the beloved disciple, he was sent to Rome and to the emperor for his sentence. When we remember the singular beauty claimed for Saint John by whoever has attempted to portray him, whether in youth or age, and when we remember the venerableness which must have come to him with years, with dignities—above all, with his near personal intercourse with Jesus of Nazareth, and his uninterrupted life with the Virgin Mother of his Redeemer, we fancy, perhaps, that even the brutal emperor must have yielded to the sublime gentleness of the aged apostle. So far from this, however, Saint John seems to have stirred all the savage propensities asleep in the bosom of Domitian. It was not enough to torture that aged frame; the torture must bring ignominy: and as Jesus Christ Himself, in the glory of His perfect age, thirty-three, was scourged by Roman soldiers, so His beloved disciple, when nearly a century old, was called to bear the shame and the torment of the Roman whips.

But the oil and the wine of consolation? how was it to be administered? How were the wounds of that aged flesh to be healed, according to Domitian's ideas of mercy? The baths of the Romans had given rise to the most sumptuous devices, and the costliest marbles had furnished reservoirs for swimming: small seas enclosed in precious red porphyry. Corresponding to these, were hideous cauldrons of iron—not for water, but for oil—boiling oil; and by such a bath were the wounds of the aged apostle to be soothed; the unctuous luxury of the imperial baths only suggesting a more intense torture for imperial victims. As nothing short of the most shameless publicity suited the mind of Domitian, this barbarous sentence was to be carried out beside one of the gates of the imperial city. The one chasm was that opening out on the Via Latina. An immense cauldron, with its boiling liquid, the oil of consolation turned into a torture, was planted a short distance from the gate, just to one side of it, and thus allowed a space for the crowds sure to gather around such a spectacle. Into this bath was thrown the venerable form of the apostle who had outlived his companions around the Divine Master, and in whose memory were stored the dearest traditions of Christianity. We can imagine the horror of Christian Rome at such a wanton outrage; the disgust even of pagans not utterly brutalized. But the horror and the disgust were quickly changed to wonder and to joy, as the snowy head was seen to rise above the boiling oil—above the rim of the cauldron—not only unscathed, but with brow and cheek restored to the freshness of youth, as if having enjoyed a most exhilarating bath. In truth, the martyr came forth from the cauldron, rejuvenated; no longer bent with age, no longer feeble in step, but with the vigor of early manhood. The prodigy struck even the dull senses of Domitian with awe. Instead of another sentence of death, the venerable Apostle was banished to the Isle of Patmos, where heaven awaited him while still on earth to make his solitude glorious. The pen of the aged Evangelist was dipped in rainbows of more than terrestrial brilliancy. Domitian had spared him, only to crown the infant Church with a halo of revelations which surpassed all the prophecies of the Old Law concerning the Messias and His kingdom; while neither poet nor painter can ever hope to rival that vision, in which mingled forms and colors and undying song, dazzle the eye, entrance the ear, and open eternal vistas before the imagination. To Saint John, on his Isle of Patmos, was given that vision of celestial reward which was to light up in after times the darkest hours of the Church of Christ; illuminate prisons as hopeless and as dreary as the Mamertime prison itself; while it would nourish the devout imagination of a Fra Angelico in his studio-cell at San Marco, and sustain the flight of a Dante in his *Paradiso*.

A locality as public as that of the Porta Latina, was not one to be forgotten. The very spot where the immense cauldron stood was quite as likely to be preserved as any other spot in the history of Christianity. To this day the miracle is magnificently kept in mind, not only by the liturgy, but by the Church of Saint John before the Latin Gate, built under the first Christian emperors, upon the spot where a temple to Diana once stood; or rather, it is to be presumed, where the temple of Diana was changed into a temple in honor of the living God. So early as the year 772, this church was rebuilt by Pope Adrian I; and again in 1190, by Celestine III. The last restorations of any note were made in 1685 by

Cardinal Rasponi, and few churches have retained, externally, more of their ancient character. It still preserves its fine *campanile* and the old brick walls of the nave and the aspe, adorned with terra-cotta friezes. The portico is entered by a narrow arch resting on two granite columns; while the entrance door and the altar keep the brilliant, ribbon-like mosaic of the Cosmati, of 1190. Of the ten columns, eight are of plain granite; two are of *porta santa*, fluted, and may have belonged to the temple of Diana itself. The altar-piece is the work of Frederic Zuecheri, and represents Saint John in the cauldron of boiling oil. This was painted by the order of the Cardinal Titular, John Jerome Albani. Near the entrance of this church is a very picturesque marble well, richly adorned with carving, like the well to be seen in the cloister of Saint John Lateran.

But there was an actual certainty involved in this tradition of the martyrdom of Saint John in a cauldron of oil before the Latin Gate, which did not wait until a pagan temple could be appropriated in order to do honor to its claims. Tertullian, Eusebius, Saint Jerome, in their several centuries—Tertullian in the third, Eusebius in the fourth, Saint Jerome in the fifth century—had expressly declared the circumstances attending this martyrdom. But it is not alone to books nor to manuscripts, however precious, that the Church has entrusted her traditions. How many thousands upon thousands were to be instructed, their faith kindled, confirmed, who would never hear of the three great scholars—not even of Saint Jerome! To the monuments of Christian Rome, history, as well as devotion, owes a debt not easily acknowledged in its fulness. The church which rebuilt "Saint Paul's outside the walls," in 1824, not because it was a convenient place for worship, nor certainly because it was a salubrious residence for learned Benedictines, but as a site upon which Christian history had planted its feet, thrown out its banners, and borne testimony to the blood shed by Paul, glorious apostle, "Doctor of the Gentiles"—this same church took possession of the few feet of ground beside the Latin Gate, on which had stood the cauldron of boiling oil. On these few feet of earth, long before the present large Church of Saint John before the Latin Gate arose, not twenty rods from it, a small chapel was built, which was, in some measure, the first memorial erected in Rome to the honor of Saint John the Evangelist. This little chapel was devoutly believed to cover the exact spot on which the cauldron stood. In 1509 it was rebuilt by Benedict Adam Borgognone, Auditor of the Rota for France, under the pontificate of Julius II. Above the architrave to the north side door, he placed his coat-of-arms: three eagles with the motto, *Au plaisir de Dieu;* or, as we might render it, "To the good pleasure of God." Below this is the inscription bearing testimony to the rebuilding: "Benedict Adam, Auditor (of the Rota) for France, dedicated this chapel to Saint John the Evangelist, under the pontificate of Pope Julius II, in the year of our Lord 1509."

Occupying no more space than Domitian's cauldron might have done, this elegant little octagonal chapel was embellished with as much care as a basilica. It was furnished with two doors, one on the north, looking towards Rome, the other on the south, looking towards the Porta Latina. Towards the west was a large barred window, half as high as a man, through which one could look into the chapel and pray when the doors were closed. The altar stood on the east side of the chapel, and was of fine white marble; underneath it was a sort of well, wherein were placed the instruments used in his martyrdom, and other relics of the Saint, such as his venerable hair, which was shaven in so savage a way that the blood streamed from his head under this use of the razor, as well as from his body under the lashes of the Roman whips, all of which is alluded to in the inscription on a very ancient slab of marble still above the north door:

"Here the champion John won the palm of martyrdom, who merited to discern the Word of the Beginning. Here the proconsul had him beaten with clubs and torn with pincers. Boiling oil was not able to inflict any hurt upon him. The oil, the cauldron, thy blood and thy hair, are preserved in this place, which illustrious Rome has consecrated to thee."*

For this reason the altar was hollow, and in the front was an opening in the form of a cross, through which a lamp could be seen, that was kept burning to show the veneration in which the spot was held. The interior walls were adorned with frescoes, which being found, in 1630, greatly discolored and nearly destroyed, Cardinal Francisco Paolucci, renowned for learning and piety, and at that time titular of the Church of Saint John before the Latin Gate, had them repainted by Lazzaro Baldi, a pupil of Pietro da Cortona. These pictures were five in number. The first, arched at the top, serves as an altar-piece, and represents the martyrdom of Saint John in the boiling oil. The one to the left of this represents the Saint holding in his hand the poisoned cup, given to him at Ephesus, from which issues a serpent, as is seen in so many pictures of Saint John, as to be considered

---

* Martyrii palmam tulit hic Athleta Joannes
Principii verbum cernere qui meruit
Verberat hic fuste proconsul forcibe tondet
Quem ferreus oleum ledere non valuit,
Conditur hic oleum, Dolium, Cresor, atque Capilli,
Quæ consecravit inclyta Roma tibi.

one of his special symbols. The third picture represents the Saint conducted from Ephesus to Rome, loaded with chains. Between these two last mentioned pictures is the south door, above which we read in marble,

"In honor of Saint John, Apostle and Evangelist, by Francis, Cardinal Paulutesius, Titular, in the the year 1658."

To the right of the altar-piece, Saint John is seen led into exile; and to the right of this fresco, is the fifth, representing the apostle at Patmos, and writing his magnificent Apocalypse. Between these two last frescoes, is the north door, above which is the remarkable inscription concerning the relics. Finally, opposite the altar, above the iron-grated window, are the arms of Cardinal Paolucci, the last restorer of the chapel, under which we read the favorite motto of Saint John: *Diligite alterutrum*. "Love ye one another."

The chapel is also adorned with stucco ornaments of great beauty, and the doors, as in the time of Benedict Adam, have fine marble jambs. The pavement is formed of terra-cotta slabs, such as were in use among the ancient Romans and are daily drawn from the ruins of antique buildings styled *Taroloni*. Over this is laid a sort of *intaglio* (or impressed) work, in imitation of the stucco which adorns the ceiling and cupola.

All the relics formerly kept in this little chapel are now in the basilica of Saint John in Lateran, to which the Church of Saint John before the Latin Gate was united in 1144 by Lucius II. This act was confirmed by several Pontiffs, his successors, and finally, by Gregory IX, in 1728. Cardinal Guilbert, Archbishop of Paris, titular of the Church of Saint John before the Latin Gate, created Cardinal by Pius IX, of holy memory, December 22d, 1873, has recently renovated this little chapel of San Giovanni in Olio. But this renovation has been accomplished without changing a line of the architecture or of the paintings.

As the small octagonal chapel now stands relieved against the ancient Porta Latina, its angles are finished by delicate pilasters; while, to give it elegance of proportion, above a narrow roof of tiles, rises a wide band of terra-cotta, with arabesque reliefs; this again roofed in steeply like a cupola, surmounted by a cone, and from this springs a slender cross with two little pennons, like flags of triumph. On the feast, which is the sixth of May, this little chapel is always open, and also on the station, when Mass is said in it. On these days, the north door vanishes, and in its place hangs a purple cambric curtain. Lifting or pushing this lightly one side, we see a space barely large enough for an altar, with priest and acolyte, and two or three to assist at the Mass. The small chapel, from the interior, is like nothing in the world so much as a huge cauldron, and we seemed to be in it with Saint John and with that Divine Master to whom he was so dear, and who went down with him into the depths of the boiling, seething, hissing oil, to bring him forth again as from a refreshing bath. The first thought is one of profound veneration, of undoubting faith; and with this comes an exaltation of soul such as must have made Saint John praise God who glorifies Himself in His saints.

Before leaving this spot, consecrated by a deathless martyrdom, we not only touched our rosaries to the altar, to the steps of the altar, to the very pavement under our feet, but we culled a handful of fresh daisies and laid them on the same spots, as we should have touched them to the sides and the floor of the cauldron itself. Then, raising the light curtain, stepped out on the green sward and looked back on this tiniest of chapels, to see it like a picture, framed in by the walls of the neighboring vineyards and the closed Porta Latina; while, beyond, the dismantled Baths of Caracalla rose into the tender atmosphere of that Roman sky.

NOTE.—It gives me pleasure to acknowledge my indebtedness to the erudition of Miss Edes of Rome, translator of Raunard's Life of Saint John, for valuable information concerning the history as well as the frescoes of this interesting chapel, which is only alluded to in the briefest manner in guide-books for travellers. The authorities quoted by her, are: Nibby; Rome in 1838; Venuti; Rona Antica e Moderna; Crescembini: Storia della Chiesa di S. Giovanni avanti Porta Latina, 1763.   E. A. S.

(TO BE CONTINUED.)

Our Lady's Sennight in the Household of Faith.

(CONTINUED.)

NIGHT IV.

MARY'S GREATER BLESSEDNESS—SMILES AND TEARS.

THOSE words of the Hymn to Holy Joseph, "*Miscens gaudia fletibus*"—"mingling joys with sorrows"—are so true a picture of human life, that not only our thrice-blessed Queen had to drink this mingled chalice, but the God of the Heavens, becoming man, drained to the dregs that of which it is required that every man should sip.

Whilst as St. Augustine, in *Sermon I, de Innocentibus*, says, "the mothers mingled their lamentations and the oblation of the infants was passing on to Heaven" from the city of Bethlehem and its environs, the principal object of the tyrant's slaughter was

. . . . "gently pressed
To Joseph's heart, while 'neath the scorching sun,

He fled in terror o'er the desert wild,
To screen from Herod's rage the Mother and the Child."*

Of all those silent years we have not much more in our poets than in the Holy Scriptures. Only one writes of St. John Baptist:

> "The muse of Christian art delights
> To paint thee near Our Lady's knee,
> Her eyes of speaking loveliness
> Turned tenderly, dear child, on thee;
> Whilst stooping, as in sweet command,
> The Infant Christ extends His hand"—

nay, both His arms, and clasps John's olive neck, while with the hearty impulse of unfeigning childhood, He kisses his ruddy lips—as portrayed by a late French artist. But this may be at the parting:

> "But who shall paint, or who shall write,
> The bitter sweetness of that hour,
> When leaving in the Virgin's arms
> The Infant, blooming like a flower,
> Thou, thro' St. Joseph's cottage-door,
> Didst journey to return no more?"

though near Him, says St. Francis de Sales, for twenty-five years: a mortification, the sweet Doctor adds, which surpasses anything recorded of any of the greatest penitents. However, though

> "We know not if thy dreams revealed
> The old home with its rustic door;
> Or showed the Virgin's cool, sweet room,
> The Christ-Child on the sunny floor:
> . . . Well we know thy heart was ne'er
> Deluded by such visions fair." †

After the happy return from the Temple—where sought in sorrow, He was the more joyfully found—but one again lifts the sacred veil of Nazareth's Holy of Holies to see

> "The Heart, that in those secret, holy years,
> Looks thro' the mild eyes of that silent Youth
> So lovingly at Mary, that she fears
> The hour is come, when she must mourn like Ruth,
> Childless and widowed; while each look endears
> That Heart still more to hers, albeit in sooth,
> Her heart and His have ever throbbed as one,
> For He is God, and yet her own, her own, her Son!" ‡

And as, if we cannot visit and dwell upon the holy spots, like St. Jerome of old, we may make, at Cardinal Newman's advice, our spiritual home with the Holy Family; so, if debarred from the actual sight, we may allow ourselves to be transported in happy fancy with Fr. Hill, by gazing

ON A PICTURE OF NAZARETH.

> In dreams no longer, but revealed to sight,
> Comes o'er me like a vision after death,
> That shrine of tenderest worship, that delight
> Of loftiest contemplation—Nazareth.

---
* Emmanuel—Rev. M. Russell, S. J., p. 31.
† Domus Dei—Eleanor C. Donnelly, p. 54.
‡ Emmanuel, p. 82.

> Fair-throned as when creation's King and Queen
> Abode within its walls, it looks around
> As scorning time and change; tho' these have been
> The ruthless masters of its hallow'd ground.
>
> Still smiling as of old, it catches still
> As fresh a morning; basks in such a noon;
> Hears evening's voice as sweetly, softly thrill;
> In glory sleeps beneath a gushing moon.
>
> . . . See upon the slope the very gate
> Where—stop to kiss!—Her lowly footstep fell,
> As daily pass'd the Maid Immaculate
> To fill her pitcher at the well.
>
> That well! where mirrored shone the loveliest face
> That ever woman wore! 'tis there—the same!
> Tho' hating Christ and Jude's banish'd race,
> The Moslems honor there the Virgin's name.
> Give thanks, my soul, give thanks that thou hast seen.
> Make Nazareth all a well of grace; and pray
> To keep its taste within thee—which has been
> The strength of saints. Drink deep, and go thy way."

Refreshed by this sweet draught, we may now speed on without reviewing those long years so heavenly—nay, more than heavenly—that Holy Joseph's hymn will make him in this life happy as the supernals in the enjoyment of God: and thus more blessed even than they:

> "Tu vivens superis par, frueris Deo,
> Mira sorte beatior!"

Those long years!—until Foster-Joseph being laid to rest, Jesus must part from His Mother too:—that Holy Family is broken up, never to be reunited except beyond the stars! For so it is meet that "They should know He must be about His Father's business";* and He must give example, who said: "He who loveth father or mother more than Me, is not worthy of Me."†

The strong and tender poet-priest—Rev. Abram J. Ryan—a Samson Agonistes, from whom, "the Mighty, is come forth sweetness"—tells somewhat of this farewell in a

LEGEND.

> "He walked alone beside the lonely sea,
> The slanting sunbeams fell upon His face,
> His shadow fluttered on the pure white sands
> Like the weary wing of a soundless prayer.
> And He was,—oh! so beautiful and fair,—
> Brown sandals on His feet,—His face downcast
> As if he loved the earth more than the Heavens.
> His face looked like His Mother's—only hers
> Had not those strange serenities and stirs
> That paled or flushed His olive cheeks and brow.
> He wore the seamless robe His Mother made,
> And as He gathered it about His breast,
> The wavelets heard a sweet and gentle voice
> Murmur, 'Oh, My Mother!'—the white sands felt
> The touch of tender tears the while He wept."

We dare not linger over these sweet reveries, nor apply our imagination to figure to ourselves the meditative, but nowise monotonous, life of the

---
* Luke, ii, 49. † Matth., viii, 37.

Mother, while the Son left her alone, to go and preach the Gospel. Tenderest of sons, He had not neglected to show affection to her to whom He gave thirty of the thirty-three years of His life.

Pass the joys; pass the sorrows and temporary anxieties; pass the triumphs in the power and truth of her Son: the attraction and confirmation of human hearts on which He built His Kingdom, "against which the gates of hell should not prevail."

We are transported to Calvary;—and if we have found Mary's devoted bards ever ready to delight her ears with the tripping measures of joy, and the solemn pæans of triumph, we shall find them not less willing to moan with her at sight of the awful woe of the last sacrifice. As our Queen's office at the foot of the cross approaches nearest the priest's, it is fitting that a priest should tell first of

"THE SEVEN DOLORS."

"Sorrow with sorrow loves to dwell,
Mourners their tale to mourners tell—
Who loves the cross, should love thee well,
 My Mother!

". . . How couldst thou hear in patient mood,
The fierce and frantic multitude
Fling on His ear their tauntings rude,
 My Mother?

"I think how once thine arms around
His Infant form in rapture wound,
When all thy hopes with bliss were crowned,
 My Mother!
. . . .
"When wave on wave of sorrow roll'd,
'Twas then our loving Lord consol'd
His mourning son, and said, 'Behold
 Thy Mother!'"*

Aubrey de Vere here is true to all his fame as a tender poet and loving son of

MATER DOLOROSA.

"She stood: she sank not. Slowly fell
Adown the cross the atoning Blood.
In agony ineffable,
She offered still His own to God.
No pang of His her bosom spared:
She felt in Him its several power.
But she in heart His priesthood shared—
She offered sacrifice that hour.
. . . .
"His own in John. He gave. She wore
Thenceforth the Mother-crown of earth.
O Eve! thy sentence too she bore:
Like thee, in sorrow she brought forth."

A poet-priest continues this thought; indeed it is a dear and personal one to us all. But who is this that, "standing over against Him," seeing that He cried out in a loud voice, and expired, said: "Truly this man was the Son of God?" A soldier-like figure, a "centurion" indeed—the first

* Father Frederick Oakley.

fruit of the Passion, and first child of agony brought forth by the new Mother! Let Benjamin Dionysius Hill turn and address, as the centurion did not fail to salute

MATER CHRISTI.

"Mother of Christ—then Mother of us all.
Mother of God made Man, of man made God. *
The thornless garden, the immaculate sod,
Whence sprang the Adam that reversed the fall.
Mother of Christ, the Body mystical—
Of us the members, as of Him the Head:
Of him our life, the first-born of the dead; †
Of us baptized unto His burial. ‡
Yes, Mother, we were truly born of thee
On Calvary's second Eden—thou its Eve:
Thy dolors were our birth-pangs by the tree
Whereon the second Adam died to live—
To live in us, thy promised seed to be,
Who then his death wound to the snake didst give."

Once more, there is sweetness in this gall. It comes only by savoring.

A thought from Dr. Newman: "It is the boast of the Catholic religion that it has the gift of making the young heart chaste." Fr. Russell, translate for us the "How."

"By gazing on the infinitely Good,
Whose love must quell or hallow every other—
By living in the shadow of the Rood;
For He that hangs there is our Elder Brother,
Who dying gave to us Himself as food,
And His own Mother as our nursing Mother."

Which is, however, not yet quite as sweet as the original continuation: "And why is this but that it gives us Jesus for our food and Mary for our nursing Mother."

(TO BE CONTINUED.)

* "Deus factus est homo, ut homo fieret Deus."—St. Augustine.   † Col., i, 18.   ‡ Rom., vi, 4.

———

[*Special Correspondence of "The Pilot."*]

Mass in the Catacombs of Rome.

An announcement recently appeared in the Catholic journals of Rome, to the effect that Mass would be celebrated on the Feast of the Chair of St. Peter, in the Cemetery Ostriano, on the Nomentan Way. The reason of this celebration is, that according to the recent researches of Mariano Armellini, an able pupil of the celebrated De Rossi, the Cemetery of Ostriano is said to contain a chair occupied by Saint Peter, and a baptistry wherein this Apostle administered baptism to the converts to the new religion which he preached in Rome.

Beyond the Basilica of St. Agnes on the Via Nomentana, a large extent of open country, sparsely occupied by vineyards, stretches on the left of the road. In one of these vineyards, you may see a little building resembling a soldier's sentry-box, with a door in it, the roof of which slopes downwards from the door, until it reaches the ground at the back. This is the entrance to the Catacomb or Cemetery of Ostriano.

A long steep stair descending into the earth is revealed to you as the door is opened. The faint daylight that enters by the door is soon lost in the distance. As you descend, with a lighted taper to guide your footsteps, tiers of graves, one above the other, like the berths in an emigrant ship, are seen to open into the walls on each side of you. Some are covered or closed in with marble slabs, bearing inscriptions rudely cut in them, telling the name and age, and occasionally the occupation of the persons whose ashes repose within. Other graves are closed with tiles of red clay; others again, the coverings of which have fallen off, yawn darkly on each side, and as you elevate your taper, the light shines in on the skull and the bones of some early Christian, now mingling with the dust of the brown tufa rock around them. A long and high passage about 5 feet in breadth, with rows of graves on each side reaching from floor to roof, lies before you. At the side of an open grave, from which the bones have been removed, a round piece of open glass, the remains of a phial, is attached to the wall by means of plaster. This was a martyr's grave, and the phial contained his blood gathered by his friends on the day of his martyrdom. In some places, you may still see the dark clots of blood adhering to the glass.

The inscriptions that meet one at every turn furnish a brief but graphic account of what the life of a Christian was in the ages of pagan persecution. On a sepulchral stone is an inscription written in barbarian characters, and terminated by a long palm. It tells its simple story in these words:—"Here Gordianus, Nuncio of Gaul, put to death with his family for the Faith, reposes in peace. Theophila, servant, has made this monument." The outline of the sole of a shoe, enclosing the words "*In Deo*," indicates the duty of walking in the way of the Lord. But it would be a long task to treat of the inscriptions that are found in this catacomb.

In the distance a simple iron chandelier, with three or four wax candles in it, hangs before the entrance to a chapel. The walls of this chapel, as of the others in all the catacombs, are covered with smooth plaster, and adorned with paintings; some fresh and bright in color, others dim, and occasionally so faded that ordinary eyes cannot make out their subjects. Behind the tomb which serves for the altar, on the wall is a picture of the Madonna, of the third century. She is seated, and the Child Jesus rests upon her knees. Her arms are extended like those of the catacombal figures known by the name of *Orantes*, or praying figures. The Greek initial letters of the names of Christ are painted on each side of the Madonna. This painted wall is the back of an arch about three feet in height at the centre. Two *loculi*, or graves, are cut in the wall above the *arcosolium*, or arch; and six tiers of graves rise one above the other, in the side walls of the little chapel. The place is lighted dimly by two candles in brackets, and by the two candles on the altar. The thought of death and of the nothingness of man in presence of his Maker is strikingly inculcated by the two skulls that lie in an open *loculus* or grave to the right, and the whitening bones in other graves around. A more cheerful sight is a beautiful bouquet of flowers—camellias, narcissus blossoms, and large red roses—placed upon the altar.

A monsignor prepares to say Mass. There is no sacristy; the priest robes in the little chapel, the vestments, chalice, etc., being placed upon a grave at the left. The lighted candles on the altar touch the roof of the *arcosolium*. The Holy Sacrifice begins; there is a breathless silence in the congregation, which, including the server, consists of exactly nine persons, and the chapel can afford no space for another; those who come after have to kneel at the entrance to the chapel. There is no altar bell, and the murmur of the prayers by the priest occasionally breaks the great silence. There is a wondrous solemnity about the circumstances in which this Mass is offered up. Here in this little chapel deep delved in the bowels of the earth, one recognizes more clearly the special bond which binds him to the Catholics of the early centuries, and appreciates more keenly the trials and sufferings of his Christian forefathers. There is but little effort required to bring vividly before the imagination the immediate successors of Saint Peter, or the saint himself, standing at this rude and simple altar, and offering up, in presence of the hunted Christians, the self-same Sacrifice that is offered up here to-day.

Towards the conclusion of Mass three English ladies pressed into the already crowded chapel, and one of them, awed by the silence and solemnity of the scene, knelt down. One of the two standing made the important discovery that the priest said "*Ite missa est*," and repeated the fact to her neighbor in an audible whisper. The voice of De Rossi is heard in the gallery without. He is explaining epitaphs, and the topography of the place to the Cardinal Vicar, and his Eminence Cardinal Monaco la Valetta. Armellini is sought for, and found wandering in a gallery far away. A number of people follow him, and the Cardinal and the clergy accompany De Rossi into the Chapel of St. Emerentiana—the foster-sister of St. Agnes, at whose grave she met her death. The Mass is over in the little Chapel of the Madonna, and I, too, pass to the Chapel of St. Emerentiana. Near the entrance stands an American with his two daughters. The old gentleman was evidently desirous of seeing all that was to be seen; but one of the young ladies preferred the upper air and the sunlight. "I can't go down that stair," she said; "the nasty place; I am sorry I came." And all three departed.

The crypt where St. Peter baptized, now called St. Emerentiana, is large and high. Its form is that of an ancient basilica; the altar, standing in a higher arcosolium than that in the Madonna's Chapel, and much larger, is an empty tomb. The chapel is divided into two parts, the part nearest the altar being that reserved for the men, and the part further off for the women. On the left or Gospel side of the altar is the chair on which, according to the opinion of archæologists, Saint Peter sat while teaching and preaching. The marble seat, with arms of the same material, is let into the wall, a shallow niche being formed here. On the other side of a chapel, near the altar, upon a stone pillar is a sort of basin almost filled with oil, on the surface of which a number of tiny lights are floating. This is the revival of an ancient custom referred to by St. Gregory the Great, namely, that of keeping lights burning before the tombs of the martyrs. A document dating from the end of the 6th century, while Gregory occupied the Pontifical throne, refers to this custom. At that time Queen Theodolinda sent her messenger John to Rome in order that he should bring to her some relics of the martyrs buried in the Roman Catacombs; and he likewise brought little phials (*ampollæ*) filled with the oil which burned in the lamps placed at the tombs of the martyrs, and also a list or record of the places whence each phial of oil was taken. This list refers to the present Catacomb, and notes that a certain phial was filled with oil from the lamp which burned before the tomb of a martyr, and near to a chair where St. Peter first sat. St. Emerentiana w-s, it is known, buried near a group of martyrs who were laid in the crypt or chapel of the Apostolic Chair in the Cemetery Ostriano. To-day a picturesquely-dressed peasant woman of the Campagna, dips her finger into the basin of oil, amongst the floating lights, and anoints the forehead of her child with the oil.

Above the altar,—decorated on this occasion with flowers and candles—on the plaster of the wall at the back, are the faint remnants of an inscription half effaced, in red letters, which certainly indicated the name of St. Peter, although all the letters of the name are not clear. Under this is the name of St. Emerentiana. The conjunction of these two names in this chapel, and the historical fact referred to above concerning the burial-place of the latter Saint, have fully confirmed the conjecture of De Rossi, that this cemetery adds another to the many memorials of St. Peter in Rome, and has restored to the science of Christian archæology and to the piety of the faithful one of the most illustrious sanctuaries of subterranean Rome. Here we enter to-day the little underground chapel where the Prince of the Apostles gathered together the Christians of the days of Claudius and of Nero. This chair in which he sat here, may be prior to that bestowed upon him by the Senator Pudens, and which enclosed in gilded bronze, rises above the altar in the apse of the Vatican Basilica.

And as, impressed with new and strange emotions, I came into the open air again, it seemed as if one had returned from the first to the nineteenth century. A cold breeze blew from the snow-covered Sabine Mountains, oranges hung over the garden walls, and students in various colored cassocks passed along the road, on their way to visit this ancient shrine.

Address of the Right Rev. President to the Societies of the C. Y. M. N. U.,

AND TO ALL THE ASSOCIATIONS OF CATHOLIC YOUNG MEN THROUGHOUT THE UNITED STATES.

The Sixth Annual Convention of the Catholic Young Men's National Union will be opened in the city of Washington, D. C., on the morning of Wednesday, May the 12th. All the associations of Catholic young men throughout the country are cordially invited to take part in it.

I sincerely hope that not a single society on the roll of the Union will fail to have its representatives there. They know well that the success of the Union must depend on the energetic and persevering action of the societies composing it,—on their untiring fidelity to the obligations which they undertook by joining it. I appeal to them not to allow any obstacle to deter them from doing their part on this occasion.

In order that the proceedings of the Convention may move smoothly and without the waste of time, attention is earnestly requested to the following points:

1st. That the blanks issued by the National Secretary be returned in time to enable him to present in his report a thorough exhibit of the condition of the Union.

2d. That credentials be made out accurately, so as to expedite the work of the Committee on Credentials, and to facilitate the organization of the Convention.

3d. That, for the same end, timely notice be taken of the final clause of Art. X of the Constitution, requiring prepayment of dues as a condition for representation.

I beg leave to call special attention to the request made in the Address issued by me shortly after the last Convention, that local Societies, or at least local Unions, come provided with a briefly written report of their work during the year,—the special ends aimed at, the means made use of, and the results attained. These reports cannot fail to be a most interesting and useful feature in the Convention, furnishing a large amount of information, which will give mutual edification and encouragement, suggest improvements in plans and methods, and excite all to a noble rivalry in the good work in which we are engaged.

It is to be hoped that there is no society of Catholic young men, whether in or out of the Union, that could fail to recognize the great good which ought to result from such assemblages. It is evidently most desirable that a spirit of fraternal union should be fostered among our Catholic young men, in whatever part of the country they may happen to dwell. From north and south, from east and west, they ought to congregate, with a fraternal charity as Catholic and all-embracing as their Faith. These conventions should be family gatherings, in which the brothers of a widely-scattered yet closely-united family should once a year assemble, in order to keep the affections warm, and the fraternal ties close and strong, which hold them together. And this closer cementing of their bond of brotherhood, must also serve to bind all more devotedly to their common Mother, the Church, who, at the sight of her children thus drawn together by faith and charity, exclaim: "Behold how good and how pleasant it is for brethren to dwell together in unity."

To these gatherings, each society would bring some item of information and encouragement that would benefit all; and from them, each in turn would carry back a renewal of earnestness and a wider experience, that could not but prove of great benefit in its own sphere. Besides the good thus redounding to the societies taking part in the Conventions, the reputation and influence of such assemblages would greatly aid in awakening the spirit of Catholic Faith and activity in places where our young men may stand in need of such encouragement. This is of itself a consideration which ought to have great and convincing weight with every association that has aught of Catholic zeal for the welfare of the Church throughout the land.

These are the objects of the Union and its Conventions, and surely they are objects in which no Association of Catholic young men can fail to be interested. When all are asked to join in action for their furtherance,—when the invitation is sent forth, and the opportunity offered for all to unite as brothers, why should any choose to stand aloof as strangers? Whatever be their special plans and methods, if only they aim at the welfare of our Catholic young men, they come within the scope of the Union, and they cannot but do good and be benefitted themselves by joining hands with their brethren in every part of the country.

To one and all, therefore, whether already in the Union or not yet associated with it, the invitation is extended. I most earnestly trust it may be well received by all, and that it may be my happiness to preside over the largest, the pleasantest, and the most useful Convention yet held by the Catholic Young Mens' National Union.

✠ JOHN J. KEANE,
Bishop of Richmond, President C. Y. M. N. U.

Societies which wish—and all are most cordially invited—to join the National Union, should apply at once.

To become a member, it is only necessary to furnish a certificate or the following form:

To the Secretary of the Catholic Young Men's National Union:
I have examined the Constitution of ———, of ———, and am satisfied it is thoroughly Catholic, and eligible as to membership.
Signed ——————
Bishop or Pastor

Each Society is entitled to three votes, which may be cast, however, by one delegate, but it is very desirable that the full number of delegates should be present. The Secretary, Mr. Juan A. Pizzini, of No. 11 W. Grace St., Richmond, Va., will furnish the badges to be worn by delegates, and will be much pleased to mail to any society desiring them copies of the Constitution and By-Laws, and to give any information wanted. Information regarding hotels, routes, and the like, can be had from Major J. Edmond Mallet, 939 I. N. W., Washington, D. C.

Catholic Notes.

——The late Mr. John Casey, of Erie, Pa., left a gift of $60,000 to Rt. Rev. Bishop Mullen for the completion of the new Cathedral in that city.

——We are under obligations to Rev. Father P. F. O'Reilly, of the Church of the Immaculate Conception, St. Louis, for numerous kind favors, as also for a notable addition to our subscription list.

——The diocese of Columbus mourns the loss of a devoted and efficient young priest in the person of Rev. Martin Walsh, pastor of St. Mary's Church, Urbana, whose death occurred on the 7th inst. R. I. P.

——Specimen copies of *The Illustrated Catholic American*, of which a notice was given in THE AVE MARIA a short time ago, may be had on application to the publishers, Messrs. Hickey & Co, No 11 Barclay St., New York, N. Y.

——CARDINAL NEWMAN.—We are rejoiced to hear from London that his Eminence Cardinal Newman has so far recovered from his late distressing accident—a fall, by which he sustained a fracture of one of his ribs—as to be able to say Mass and preach, which he did at Edgbaston on Easter Sunday.

——EMPRESS EUGÉNIE bequeathed her imperial crown to the Church of Notre Dame de Victoires, at Paris, before setting out on her journey to Africa, where she will visit the spot that was moistened by the blood of her only child. It is needless to add that this crown is of rare value and beauty.

——DONATIONS.—To the Irish Relief Fund (Lady Fullerton's): Teresa M'Gibbon, $1; A Friend, Phœnixville, Pa., $5. For the Needy Western Mission: A Friend, $10; Mrs. J. Mann, $5; Mary A. Keating, $1; Miss F. Lyons, $10; Rose Daley, 50 cts.; C. M., $5.; A Reader of THE "AVE MARIA," $10. The good missionary desires to express his warmest thanks for the aid that has been sent him.

——DEATH OF RT. REV. BISHOP PELLICER.—We deeply regret to announce the death of the amiable and excellent Bishop of San Antonio, Texas, which sad event occurred in that city on Wednesday, the 14th inst. He had been in ill health for a long time, though not incapacitated for work. Mgr. Pellicer was the first Bishop of San Antonio, and received consecration on the 8th of December, 1874. He was beloved by all who knew him, and the news of his death has caused universal regret. R. I. P.

——MINNESOTA CATHOLIC COLONIES.—The fame of the Minnesota Catholic colonies is spreading far and wide. Letters of enquiry have been received this spring from France, Switzerland, Germany and New Zealand. Last week an order—cash enclosed—came to hand from Port Elizabeth, South Africa, for a quarter section of land, and news was received that a party of explorers from Belgium, the forerunners of a large party of colonists, were in Liverpool, *en route* for the Minnesota colonies.—*Northwestern Chronicle.*

——ST. VINCENT'S ABBEY, PA.—A solemn *Triduo* in honor of the fourteenth centenary of St. Benedict, was celebrated at St. Vincent's Abbey, Pa., on the 4th, 5th and 6th inst. Crowds of persons approached the Sacraments in order to gain the Plenary Indulgence attached to the celebration by the Holy Father. The decorations, music, etc. were worthy of the occasion. A lecture on the life and work of St. Benedict was delivered by Rev. Father Mauritius, O. S. B., which was listened to with rapt attention by a large audience. The students of the college gave an excellent entertainment in the evening.

——A TRUE LIKENESS OF OUR BLESSED SAVIOUR.—Messrs. R. W. Carroll & Co., of Cincinnati, Ohio, have recently issued what is purported to be a true likeness of our Saviour. As a work of art, it is excellent, and there are marks of antiquity about it quite unmistakable. It is reproduced on a sheet 27 by 20 inches, with a Latin inscription, which runs as follows: "A true likeness of our Saviour, copied from the portrait carved on an emerald, which emerald the Emperor of the Turks afterwards gave out of the treasury of Constantinople to Pope Innocent the VIII, for the redemption of his brother taken captive by the Christians." The price is 50 cents.

——CATHOLIC INSTINCT.—An illustration of the way in which the Catholic instinct asserts itself in good men, whose antecedents and training would least lead us to expect it, has just been brought to light in the fifth and concluding volume of Mr. Theodore Martin's "Life of His Royal Highness the Prince Consort." It appears that during his last illness, the Prince derived much comfort from a picture of Our Blessed Lady—a copy on porcelain of Raphael's "Colonna Madonna": —"Going through the door," the Queen writes, "he turned to look at the beautiful picture on china of the Madonna which he gave me three years ago, and asked to stop and look at it, ever loving what is beautiful." The next morning (11th of December), as he was being assisted by the Queen from his bed to the sofa, he paused to look at his favorite picture, and said, "It helps me through half the day!"—*Catholic Times.*

——RELICS OF ST. ADALBERT.—On the 11th of March some workmen, while engaged in demolishing the chapel of St. Adalbert, in front of the Cathedral at Prague, struck upon a vault containing a coffin with a corpse, which was thought to be the remains of Saint Adalbert, the Apostle of the Prussians, martyred in 997, and whose body had been taken to Prague thirty years later by Duke Wratislas, of Bohemia. Upon the discovery of the relics, the work was at once suspended, and a committee of historians and archæologists appointed to investigate the matter. When the coffin was opened, in presence of the Archbishop, an oval wooden box was found, which held the bones of the Saint, wrapped up in crimson velvet. Inscriptions of the years 1346 and 1396 referring to different translations of the relics from one church to another, identified them beyond doubt. By order of the Archbishop, the relics were carried in solemn procession to the Church of St. Vitus.

——A REMARKABLE CONVERSION IN THE DIOCESE OF CHARLESTON.—The Rev. J. C. Russell and his family, consisting of five children, were received into the Church and baptized conditionally by venerable Father J. J. O'Connell, O. S. B., on the 31st ult. This distinguished convert has been for the past nineteen years, and up to this time, an eloquent preacher and notable minister of the Methodist E. Church, and has filled the most prominent stations. His conversion has been the result of years of patient enquiry, close study, and fervent prayer. None could witness unmoved the firm and deep piety of this heroic Christian gentleman as he made the profession of Faith at the head of his interesting group of children, and received with them the waters of regeneration. It is to be hoped that his accomplished lady, who assisted with evident emotion, will be shortly numbered among the faithful, and then none of the family will be missing. Few if any could embrace the true Faith in the face of greater difficulties and at greater personal sacrifice than the ex-Protestant minister, who is still in the prime of life and the full vigor of manhood. He will rise in judgment against the many who are as convinced as he, but have not courage to exchange earthly things for the kingdom of God and the salvation of the soul. How terrible must be the accountability of such men! The reverend gentleman resides at present at Fort Mill, York County, S. C., and has resigned his pulpit without reproach or stain on his fair name.— *N. Y. Tablet.*

——THE LATE FATHER GIOVANNI DEL PAPA, the celebrated Franciscan, the news of whose death has caused such universal regret, was born at Lucca in 1842, and when he was still young entered the Order of St. Francis of Assisi. In the April of 1865 he was ordained priest and attached to the Convent of Oriolo. He was well versed in philosophy and theology, and for several years preached with much success. Prince Altieri, who knew Father Giovanni, one day hearing his voice in a choir, was so struck by its wonderful power and sweetness that he proposed to the monk that he should dedicate himself specially to music, and for that purpose proceed to Rome. Having obtained the permission of his Superiors, Father Giovanni went to Rome. Under the direction of the Maestro Capocci, leader of the choir of St. John Lateran, he completed his studies. On the Feast of St. John, four or five years ago, Father Giovanni delighted all those present in the Basilica by his rendering of the *Laudate pueri*, composed by Capocci. From that time forward his fame as an ecclesiastical singer grew and spread abroad. He was named the Cantor of Lateran, and shortly after Pius IX appointed him one of the cantors of the Pontifical Chapel. Several enthusiastic persons, among whom visitors from England were the most prominent, used every effort to induce Father Giovanni to leave his Order to devote himself to the concert hall, promising him immense success and large receipts. But the monk was superior to such blandishments, and repulsed them gently but firmly. His voice was occasionally heard at concerts, but they were always for a charitable object. He was very devoted to the Church; he lived recently in the Franciscan Convent of Ara Cœli, on the Capitoline Hill; and there it was he died of the fever called *perniciosa*, which seems to be an aggravated form of Roman fever. May he rest in peace.

——REFORMATORIES—BIGOTRY.—Everyone knows the necessity of Houses of Correction for boys in our large cities, and almost everyone knows, too, the poor and ineffective, as well as extremely expensive, manner in which such institutions are conducted. Of late years the Xaverian and Christian Brothers have opened Reformatories for boys, the former near Baltimore, Md., the latter near New York. The results obtained by them have been not only incomparably far in advance of the secular Reformatories, but have also proved less expensive, costing only a fraction of what the latter yearly cost the community in which they are established. The reason of the success attending the labors of the Brothers is plain. They have devoted their lives to the service of God for the instruction and reformation of youth, whereas those employed in the State or communal reformatories work for pay. In drawing a parallel, we do not at all wish to disparage the services of the latter, or say that they do not fulfil their duties as well as could be expected; but we do say that the result of their labors for the reformation of youth cannot bear any comparison with those of the Xaverian Brothers and Christian Brothers. The reason is clear. The work of reform and instruction is the ideal, the life-work of the latter. It is with them a labor of love, and teachers or reformers who devote themselves to this unpleasant work merely for a livelihood cannot be expected to do as well. Such has been the success of the Brothers that the State of Maryland and the city of New York wonder at it, and to encourage the good work done in their reformatories have considered it a duty to aid in supporting them. And why should they not? If the Brothers succeed better than others in this important, but most laborious work, why should they not be encouraged? That they should be encouraged, and receive a *modicum* of public aid for the institutions which are doing so much good in keeping the prisons empty, in giving less work for the hangman, in reforming wayward youths and making them Christians and good members of the community, is plain, but bigots do not think so. Only lately a deputation of Protestant ministers waited upon the Maryland Legislature in order to have all aid withdrawn from the good Brothers at St. Mary's Reformatory near Baltimore—an institution that has year after year elicited from impartial members of the City Council a warm approval for the immense amount of good which it has performed—and this at a time when the older communal Reformatory was not only a cause of serious trouble and expense, but also productive of vastly inferior results. Can that be called charity which would rather see wayward or wicked children go to the devil rather than they should be reformed by Catholics? This reminds us of the sad fate of the brilliant but sceptical Gibbons, whose father, seeing that the youth wished to become a Catholic, sent him among German infidels, from whom he eventually imbibed the skeptical opinions that he retained throughout his life. Gibbon's father prevented his son from becoming a Catholic, but by doing so he caused him to live and die an infidel; and these ministerial protesters it would seem would rather see children go to the gallows or die in the penitentiary than be reformed by Catholics! It is gratifying to hear that the protest had the effect of increasing the State aid.

Confraternity of the Immaculate Conception
(Or of Our Lady of Lourdes).

"We fly to thy patronage, O Holy Mother of God!"

REPORT FOR THE WEEK ENDING APRIL 14TH.

The following intentions have been recommended: Recovery of health for 75 persons and 3 families,—change of life for 40 persons and 3 families,—conversion to the Faith for 21 persons and 3 families. Special graces for 5 priests, 8 religious, 5 clerical students, and 2 persons aspiring to the religious state,—temporal favors for 27 persons and 7 families,—spiritual favors for 42 persons and 7 families,—the spiritual and temporal welfare of 9 communities, 5 congregations, and 6 schools,—recovery of mind for 10 persons. Also 28 particular intentions, and 11 thanksgivings for favors received.

Special intentions: Several persons, chiefly widows and orphans, much afflicted in soul and body,—the conversion or removal of some troublesome persons,—grace for several persons to know their vocation,—news from persons long absent from their friends and relatives,—protection of crops,—a person in great difficulty and danger,—the removal of a scandal,—several special intentions recommended by various religious communities,—success of the Forty Hours' Devotion,—a safe journey,—removal of obstacles in the way of religious vocations,—the conversion of several unfortunate priests.

FAVORS OBTAINED.

The worthy rector of a southern mission sends us the following excellent letter, which will be read with interest: "*Deo gratias et Mariæ Matri!* You remember I recommended some time ago the case of an unfortunate young married man, who, while under the influence of liquor, cut a poor fellow down—causing death in a half or three quarters of an hour—and who was under trial for life. Failing to give bond, he was remanded to jail, and at the next regular session of the criminal court, after half an hour's consultation of the jury, was condemned to death. Appeal was taken, and meanwhile whole communities of religious, sodalities and individuals offered up Masses, Communions and novenas for his welfare, body and soul. The poor young man, though raised by the most pious of mothers, had received bad example and turned away from home like the prodigal, at sixteen—home and church alike. Sickness and disease seized upon him; he lost rest, peace, health, courage—all but the new found paradise of his faith, obtained without ostensible miracle, not without extraordinary grace, by the means of the pious prayers of Mary's children. Lately matters were growing worse; his health was being fearfully undermined; he lost the faculty of slight exertion to amuse and employ himself, to keep sorrow from eating his heart out. The final trial was coming off, and I appealed to your charity a third time, asking the prayers of your Society. Thank God, the result was better than we could have expected. The jury disagreed and bail was allowed in the (to us) enormous sum of $4,000. It was impossible to raise it, and we again applied for an abatement within reach of a broken family's means. Again our prayers were heard, and the sum being finally obtained, the young man, at last accounts, was freed, and though much exhausted by anguish, want of food, rest and comfort, is much better off than the convicts at our horrible penitentiary. His disposition towards his religion is now such, that he has turned apostle to exhort others not to delay repentance. To be sure, all is not over yet; but we hope that as we have been favored so far by men and heaven, we may yet be able to satisfy justice for an involuntary murder—done in passion, and in great part in self-defence—by the torments already suffered."

OBITUARY.

The following deceased persons are recommended to the devout prayers of the Confraternity: Mr. CHARLES BOWLING, of New Haven, Ky., who departed this life on the 7th inst. Mrs. ANNE EGAN, aged 87 years, a native of Newpark, Cashel, Co. Tipperary, Ireland, who fell asleep in the Lord at Notre Dame, Ind., on the Feast of St. Joseph. Mrs. MARY ANN BROOKS, an exemplary convert to our holy religion, whose peaceful death occurred at Atchison, Kansas, March 31st. Mrs. JOHANNA KENDRICK, of Schenectady, N. Y., who departed this life on the 16th ult. Miss MARY BARRY, and Mr. GERALD BARRY, lately deceased in Ireland. And several others, whose names have not been given.

Requiescant in pace.

A. GRANGER, C. S. C., Director.

Christmas Collection—Diocese of Fort Wayne, 1879.

Ft. Wayne Cathedral. $625.55	Tipton $20.15
" St. Mary's. 275.00	St. Vincent's, Allen Co. 20.00
" St. Paul's. 96.58	Crown Point 19.00
" St. Peter's. 83.01	Cedar Lake 19.00
St. Mary's, Lafayette. 184.80	Auburn & Missions...... 19.00
St. Boniface's " 100.00	Colfax 18.15
Valparaiso 177.80	Shererville 18.00
Crawfordsville 150.50	Columbia City 17.75
Huntington 116.25	Reynolds 17.00
St. Patrick's, So. Bend 117.25	Chesterton 16.31
Polish Church, " 22.10	St. Anthony's, Benton
St. Joseph's " 16.50	Co................ 16.00
St. Vincent's, Logans-	Rensselaer 15.25
port 80.00	Marion 15.20
St. Joseph's, Logansport 40.95	Reynolds 15.12
St. Bridget's, " 27.00	Covington 14.80
Peru 89.67	Ladoga 15.56
Union City 74.00	Girardot 14.58
Mishawaka 72.00	Attica 14.56
Michigan City 71.62	Harrison & Fulton...... 14.50
Bluffton Roads 65.50	Mary's Home 12.00
Decatur 61.15	Kokomo & Missions...... 13.40
St. John's, Lake Co ... 62.00	Roanoke 11.00
New Haven 55.25	Whitley 10.00
St. Joseph's, Laporte .. 47.92	Clark's Hill 9.99
St. Peter's, " 28.00	Turkey Creek 9.60
Arcola 44.00	Warsaw 9.49
Otis 42.00	Marshfield 8.30
Anderson 41.50	Pierceton 8.45
Avilla 41.50	Leo..................... 7.90
Elkhart 40.00	Remington 7.70
Kentland 36.26	Coal Creek 7.20
Trinity, Benton Co..... 35.00	Westville 6.00
Delphi 33.20	La Crosse 6.00
Lagro 33.00	St. Michael's, Allen Co. 5.94
Muncie 32.95	Pulaski 5.00
Notre Dame 31.85	Mullens 4.00
Lebanon 30.68	Francisville 4.50
Hesse Cassel 32.00	Madeiraville 4.00
Winnamac 30.00	San Pierre 4.00
Plymouth 30.00	Indian Creek 4.00
St. Bridget's & Fowler 30.00	Albion 3.00
Oxford 27.50	Lowell, Lake Co........ 2.00
Goshen 26.05	Lake Station 1.67
Wabash 25.00	Rushes 1.85
Kiassville 25.00	Private donations...... 20.00
Dyer 22.50	Mr. Homann 20.00
Kendallville 22.50	Dispensation fines..... 15.00

✠ JOSEPH DWENGER,
Bp. FORT WAYNE.

Youth's Department.

Barbara's Lesson.

THE winter of 1564 was an unusually severe one in Saxony, owing to the mines being closed early in the season, after a sickly summer and scant harvest.

"Everything works against us," said the miserable miners. "It has been a bad year. What will the next be?"

And there was no hope or consolation for them, such as their fathers had been blessed with in bad times; for Saxony had lost that Faith which can brighten the darkest lot, and sweeten the bitterest cup. The new religion suited them well in prosperity; no more tiresome penance, no more confession, no more carrying the cross, self-denial, and restraint of the passions: Luther had changed all that. But bad harvests, want of work, sickness and trial—had he abolished all these with the old Faith? And were not these crosses ten times heavier under a new religion which knew not how to console?

Christopher Uttman, passing silently amid his murmuring fellow-workmen, gained the shelter of his lowly cottage. Never had it looked more cosy and cheerful, for his neat-handed and industrious wife knew the secret of making a poor home comfortable and even pretty. But now the pleasant picture he looked upon, only made his fears of coming want and misery more keen; for no home can be supported without means, and the small sum in his hand was the last he could expect to touch until the mines reopened in the spring.

"What shall become of us, Barbara?" was his sorrowful greeting to his wife; and he placed on the table the bit of money he had been grasping so tight as he came along, with one thought in his mind. "*My last week's wages!*"

Barbara asked no questions, made no cheering remarks. She knew long before that the mines were to be closed early—and worse still, that there was but little hope of their opening in spring, for the owners talked of abandoning them, as no longer worth working. Thus she could not make any direct effort to cheer her desponding husband. The sweet, peaceful influence of home, the frolics of his two children, who were not old enough to enter into the troubles of their parents, finally brought peace to the father's heart.

"We will trust in God," said his wife as they rose from supper, and making the Sign of the Cross in humble thankfulness for the food of the body and the peace of the soul they yet enjoyed. For Christopher and Barbara were faithful to the holy religion of their fathers, and, though they could seldom practice its duties, the "Reformed religion" being paramount in that district, they still preserved its spirit.

The evening thus ended cheerfully, and while gloom and hopelessness reigned in the neighborhood, the contentment of patient Christian hearts was theirs.

Long after her husband slept, Barbara remained awake, arranging in her thoughts a scheme to be put into practice the very next day. She had great skill in embroidering muslin. Working at first for the mine-owner's wife and daughters, the fame of her beautiful needlework spread by degrees to higher circles, and many a noble dame had availed herself of Barbara's taste and industry, and enriched her heavy brocade dresses with muslin trains, and ruffles, and edgings, whose delicate embroidery looked like fairy work. The young matron now resolved to apply herself steadily to this work, and thus support the family which was deprived of its usual resources.

Barbara arose, as was her custom, before the dawn of day. There was no need to have the morning meal early, as her husband had no longer his daily toil to call him forth punctually; but this little cottage was the home of order and good habits. Besides, she had not forgotten, as too many do, the resolutions made during the sleepless night. As soon as she had put all to rights after the frugal breakfast, she commenced her work. It was a veil at which she had long worked in her leisure hours, and which she now determined to complete as soon as possible, being sure that the lady of the castle would purchase it at a price which would supply food enough for the winter. So day after day, from morning until a late hour of night, she sat at her task, Christopher helping in the domestic duties which she hurried through in the shortest time imaginable, and the neighbors' children amusing her little Karl and Barbara. At first Christopher remonstrated against her unceasing toil; but seeing how her heart was set on it, he at length forbore to pain her by an appearance of want of interest.

It was finished at last, and Barbara surveyed the dainty specimen of her skill with a feeling deeper, tenderer than pride or gratification. The miner held up one corner diffidently between thumb and finger, as if fearful of tearing the thin, almost transparent fabric, on which wreaths and clusters of tiny flowers, buds, leaves and tendrils were wrought so tastefully. He laughed as he remarked the contrast between the pure, graceful thing and his hand so dark and rough with delving in the mine.

"Yet it is the handiwork of a miner's wife," he said, looking with fond pride upon his wife. "Blessed be God who gave me the skill!" was her low-spoken reply.

She was indeed very tired, and only the thought of the large sum she was to receive for it on the morrow served to sustain her. "It will be a joyous Christmas-eve," she said to herself repeatedly.

It was almost noon when she reached the castle, where, being a favorite with the mistress, she was immediately shown into her presence. The lady inquired about her family, and Barbara answered briefly, for she was longing to exhibit her masterpiece which was so carefully covered with a white cloth in the basket she had not let go from her tight hold. Always before she had been timid about showing her work, and the lady's encouraging question as to "what pretty thing she had brought now," was needed to embolden her. This morning, however, the lady made no reference to her basket or its contents; did not even seem to notice it. Had Barbara been less excited, she would have taken warning by this; but in her eagerness she hastened to unfold her beautiful veil, and, with a deeper flush on her cheeks than the long walk had caused, waited, with downcast eyes and throbbing heart, for the customary exclamations of delighted approval. Poor Barbara! How appalling was the continued silence, the deathlike stillness of the room! With a sudden sinking of the heart, she raised her eyes and fixed them imploringly on the lady, who was carelessly looking at the extended veil, without deigning to touch it.

"Certainly it is handsome," were the measured words that fell on Barbara's ear as the knell of her hopes. "You improve very much. But I no longer value muslins. Here is something now worth admiring."

While speaking she had opened a drawer, from which she took a border of Brussels point-lace, and held it out to her grief-stricken companion. She dropped the veil, which she had unconsciously continued to hold, and took the strip of lace in her cold, nerveless hands.

"It is very lovely," she said, in a hoarse whisper. "My work cannot compare with it."

"Could you copy it?" asked the lady. "For a veil in this style I would give you any price you choose to ask."

Barbara made a negative gesture. She could not speak. Mechanically she replaced her veil in the basket, and making a low obeisance, took leave. Still intent on her lace border, the lady scarcely observed her departure. In her selfish longings for novelties, she gave no heed to poor Barbara's disappointment, nor even thought of lightening it by a Christmas present for the little ones awaiting their mother's return.

How that mother returned to them, she never knew. It was quite dark when she stood on the threshhold of her home; she saw her husband come from the inner room, heard him saying the children were snug in bed and he was just going in search of her. She tried to speak, but strength and consciousness left her.

(TO BE CONTINUED.)

Flower-Gardens.

BY L. S. B.

DEAR YOUNG READERS OF "THE AVE MARIA":—How many of you are going to have a garden this summer—a spot of ground all your own, to dig and plant, hoe and weed as you will? Nearly all, I think; for ever since Adam and Eve cared for the first beautiful garden, a little of the farmer and gardener has been born with everyone of us; and the smell of the fresh, moist earth, the bright sunshine, the springing grass and unfolding leaves, the bird-songs and soft air of springtime, bring the farmer to the front, and an out-of-door life, with the beautiful things God seems to be creating afresh for us, is the only one we care for.

And what will you do in your gardens? Be happy in them all day long, like the butterflies? That will be well, for happy children are almost always pretty good; the naughty ones can't manage to be happy very long at a time. But you can do better yet, for you can have in your little flower bed a better meditation book than was ever printed; from the time you sow the first seed, every tiny leaf, every opening bud, can tell you of a loving Father's care for His children; the sunshine that falls as warm and bright on the barefooted boy digging his little plot of ground with patient toil, as on the dainty child of wealth who had only to watch the gardener; the rain that falls on the just and the unjust; the fresh dewy beauty of the mornings; the drowsy mid-days, with the bees buzzing everywhere; the cool peaceful evenings, with the white flowers shining out of the darkness, shadowy and lovely as if they were the spirits of flowers; all the glad, beautiful sounds and sights, if you will open your ears to hear, and eyes to see them, will tell you of the love of the heavenly Father, who is so good to us, His children, and should make you love Him every day more tenderly.

And will you not do something else? Will you not set aside in every garden one little spot, the sunniest and best, that shall be yours to tend with loving care, but every leaf and flower of which shall be reserved for your loving Lord, for the Blessed Virgin Mary, and the dear St. Joseph? All day and all night, our Lord is a willing, loving Prisoner in the tabernacle; we go to Him with our sins and temptations, joys and sorrows, sure of receiving pardon and peace. Surely for all the good gifts He has showered on us all our lives long, and for this last best gift of His Real Presence, we can make His altars beautiful and fragrant with the flowers He has Himself given us. Little children, whom when on earth He gathered in His arms, and blessed, give your hearts to love Him, your hands to work for Him!

If you would all do as I ask, you could keep the altars bright with flowers all the time. You could have little informal "altar societies" of your own, and each one plant his or her favorite flower. It need cost but little, for fortunately the commonest flowers are almost always the prettiest. Poinsettia pulcherrima sounds imposing, and I have known people go into ecstacies of admiration over it; but I would rather have a handful of sweet-peas, with their simple pink and white blossoms, fresh and fragrant as if they had just come from the garden of eden, than all the great, staring poinsettias that ever grew. And I have yet to see in any hot-house a yellow flower with a long name half so pretty as a dandelion or buttercup.

Pansies, pinks, mignonette, nasturtiums, sweet-peas, petunias, phlox, and verbenas are all beautiful, hardy, and easily cared for. Some careful child that likes to pinch and prune, tend and pet her flowers, could have balsams and salvias. You need only plant a morning-glory, and give it a string to twine around, and it will take care of itself, and nothing can be lovelier for the church; the buds on the long sprays will open morning after morning, the delicate blue and white bells looking as fair as if they were swinging in the wind out in the sunshine. And in the country, while your garden-plants are growing, you will have a perfect wealth of blossoming shrubs: lilacs, syringas, roses, snow-balls, apple and cherry blossoms to call to your aid. And the wild flowers, the violets and anemones, all the beautiful host that are planted, watered and tended by no mortal hand, are free to whoever will search out the places where they grow. And it is in the country where flowers are so plentiful, that the churches are oftenest without them.

Many of our native ferns are far more delicate and beautiful than the rare foreign varieties for which the florists ask extravagant prices. If you will take up the ferns with as much earth as possible on the roots and plant them close together in a glass dish, lined with moss, covering the earth when you have finished with mosses of different kinds, you will have as pretty a fernery as you could wish. Give them a frequent sprinkling with water to keep them moist, and they will be contented with very little air or sunshine. Place them on the side altars before the statues of our Blessed Mother and St. Joseph, and see how much more beautiful is the little bit of living growing green that has cost only time and patience than all the artificial flowers you can heap in the vases.

You will also find another use for your flowers. The poor we have always with us, and the sick and the sorrowing, and death comes sooner or later to every home; give your flowers with prayers for the living and prayers for the dead. And be sure that no other garden will ever give you so much pleasure as the little spot you have lovingly given for a garden of the Lord.

An Indian Legend.

There was once a beautiful damsel upon whom one of the good *genii** wished to bestow a blessing. He led her to a large field of corn, and said to her: "Daughter, in the field before us, the corn, in the hands of those who pluck it in good faith, shall have magical virtues, and the virtue shall be in proportion to the size and beauty of the ear selected. Thou shalt pass through the field once, and pluck one ear. It must be taken as thou goest forward; and thou shalt not stop in thy path, nor shalt thou retrace a single step in quest of thine object. Select an ear full and fair, and according to its size and beauty shall its value be to thee as a talisman. The maiden thanked the good *genius*, and then set forward. As she advanced, she saw many ears of corn, large, ripe, and beautiful, such as calm judgment might have told her would possess virtue enough; but in her eagerness to grasp the very best, she left them behind, hoping that she might find one still fairer. At length, as the day was closing, she reached a part of the field where the stalks were shorter and thinner, and the ears shrivelled; she now regretted the grand ears she had left behind, and disdained to pick from the poor ones around her for here she found not an ear which bore perfect grain. She went on, but, alas! only to find the stalks more and more blighted, until in the end as the day was closing, and the night coming on, she found herself at the end of the field without having plucked an ear of any kind. No need that the *genius* should rebuke her folly. She saw it clearly when too late, as how many in all climes and in all ages, in the evening of life call sadly and regretfully to mind the thousands of golden opportunities forever lost, because they were not plucked in their season!

* Spirits.

THE AVE MARIA.

A Journal devoted to the Honor of the Blessed Virgin.

HENCEFORTH ALL GENERATIONS SHALL CALL ME BLESSED.—St. Luke, I, 48.

VOL. XVI.   NOTRE DAME, INDIANA, MAY 1, 1880.   No. 18.

Our Lady's Sennight in the Household of Faith.

(CONTINUED.)

NIGHT V.

BLESSED QUEEN MARY'S LOVERS' COURT.

In the

"Dark days. . . . when the sad Mother met
The sweet St. John, with her dark garments wet
With Precious Blood shed by the Holy One. . . ."; *

she met other, more earthly, and mayhap less fervent lovers, but who, like their prototype, would guard the Holy Mother "in their own home" during the period of her unspoken grief, and afford her the solace of filial, sympathizing affection, by their assiduous attentions to her every queenly wish.

Pretermitting the glorious mysteries ending the mortal career of God's Son and Blest Mary's—and even the years when "sweet St. John" was all in all to her in her bereaved widowhood in Jerusalem, we come to the epoch when the apostolic son removed to Ephesus, and established his See in Asia Minor—taking with him his God-given Mother. Even there the messenger of Christ could not tarry and settle himself down in a comfortable home to fulfil even such high office as the guardianship of Christ's *Genitrix*. While, therefore, the Evangelist goes forth to preach the Gospel and leaves sweet Mother Mary alone at his home, he will not disdain to put her under our tender care, and permit her other sons—the Christian, Mary-loving bards—to assemble about her in the apostolic palace, to attempt to assuage ever so slightly the abiding yearning she feels to "be dissolved and be with Christ." And let not our pious reader be scandalized at the freedom with which her enamored approach the

throne of their Love. Those who have read the life of one we claim as an American saint—St. Francis of Solano, Apostle of the tribes of South American Indians—will remember what the great Doctor St. Alphonsus Liguori also relates in his "Glories of Mary" (Ch. I, Sect. III). The dear San Francisco was a fine musician, and used to attract the poor sons of the forest about him by the sweet sounds of his violin, accompanying his voice in the singing of sacred hymns. He was at the same time passionately devoted to Mother Mary, as all truly poetic and musical souls have ever been, finding in her alone the satisfaction of their hearts in soul-melody and heavenly fancy. This passion for the Lady of his heart, the Saint was accustomed to express by going to sing and play on his instrument before her altar; saying, when asked the reason of such strange devotion: "If earthly lovers can play and sing for their lady-loves, surely I have the best of reasons for serenading my beloved Queen, 'Most beautiful of women,' 'Mother of fair love!'"

Is she beautiful? Answer, her Benjamin!

"O VALDE DECORA!"

"Could I but see thee, dear, my Love!
    That face—but once! Not dazzling bright:
Not as the blest above,
    Behold it in God's light:

"But as it look'd at La Salette:
    Or when, in Pyrenean wild,
It beamed on Bernadette,
    The favor'd peasant child.

"Once seen—a moment—it would blind
    These eyes to beauty less than thine;
And where could poet find
    Such theme for song as mine?

"But if I ask what may not be,
    So spell me with thy pictur'd face,
That haunting looks from thee
    May hold me like a grace."

Or will that exceeding beauty either ever lose its charm, or, compared as she is to the full glorious moon of harvest, be shorn of its splendor like

---

* Maurice Egan—"Preludes"—p. 44.

the waning crescent she spurns with her feet?

"NEVERMORE!"

proclaims her knightly bard, from the watch tower of Sion, the City of God:

"I watched, from the lake, love's planet set
 Toward the mountain's ebon bar;
I said: 'This hour the eyes are wet
 That bid adieu to their love's star.

"'It rose so fair, and shone so bright,
 A twilight spell—so quickly o'er!
For change the cloud or death the night,
 That draws the murmur'd 'Nevermore!'"

Earth's love and earth's lovers! What are ye! Passing like their setting star. Listen to a love and lover unearthly:

"But thou, thy poet's star of love,
 Madonna! if these eyes are wet,
That hail thee beautiful above,
 'Tis not that thou must pale and set.

"'Tis joy that overflows in tears
 From out a heart at perfect rest;
With thee to rule my rescued years,
 O when was bard so deeply blest?

"And keep me true, my dearest Queen!
 That I may sing, as none before,
The sweetest love hath ever been,
 A star that setteth nevermore."

Pure Adelaide had too a Love; and she did love that Love through joy and woe. But grief—world's contact, evil anguish from the tempter—only made it tenderer—subdued. In joy, it sparkled and bubbled like a fountain in the sunshine. Here no low distinctions as of earth: in heaven "they neither give nor are given in marriage, but are as the angels of God." This virgin soul pays her court at this virgin shrine, and lays at Love's feet offering

THREEFOLD.

"Mother of grace and mercy,
 Behold how burdens three
Weigh down my weary spirit,
 And drive me here—to Thee!
Three gifts I place forever
 Before thy shrine;
The threefold offering of my love,
 Mary, to thine.
The Past, with all its memories
 Of pain—that stings me yet;
Of sin—that brought repentance;
 Of joy—that brought regret.
That which has been: forever
 So bitter—sweet—
I lay in humblest offering
 Before thy feet.
The Present: that dark shadow
 Through which we toil to-day;
The slow drops of the chalice
 That must not pass away.
Mother! I dare not struggle,
 Still less despair;

I place my Present in thy hands,
 And leave it there.
The Future, holding all things
 Which I can hope and fear,
Brings sin and pain it may be,
 Nearer and yet more near.
Mother! this doubt and shrinking
 Will not depart,
Unless I trust my Future
 To thy dear heart.
Making the Past my lesson,
 Guiding the Present right,
Ruling the misty Future,
 Bless them and me to-night.
What may be, and what must be,
 And what has been,
In thy dear care forever
 I leave, my Queen!"

Infusing her love—making other lovers for Mary; teaching younger, not more pure, little maidens how to offer joyous gifts on the Great Lady's natal day, this is the one of all she gives the last:

"Give her now—to-day—forever,
 One great gift—the first, the best—
Give your heart to her, and ask her
 How to give her all the rest."

Another lover, with her very name, chosen in later life, as more distinctive than a baptismal name—as it has really become by the renown it has brought—"Marie"—sings well and musically of the

"IMMACULATE HEART."

. . . .

Thy spirit shed that blessed ray,
 O Virgin pure and bright!
Thy radiance brought the beams of day
 O'er earth's unholy night:
The lily-garden's bloom divine,
 Where blemish had no part,
The temple fair, the gleaming shrine,
 Was thy unsullied Heart.

Thy truth, a rare and radiant gem,
 Thy love, with incense-breath
Illumined lonely Bethlehem,
 And perfumed Nazareth.
And thou didst break the spell of wrong,
 And calm the storm of hate,
With magic of thy seraph song,
 O Heart Immaculate!

. . . .

Strong Aubrey de Vere, singing Alexander's world-conquests, the long-buried, fiercest deeds of olden Danes and Saxon feuds on the theatre of their at last subjugated Island-Home, can be delicate as a lady, and gravely sententious withal. She—this Queen so peerless of ours—is to him, as to inspired Church,

Stella Matutina;

or, varied again, represented to us by a

"Pale lily, pearled around with dew";

which, by poet's command, he would have

"Lift high that heaven-illumined vase,

And sing the glories ever new
Of Her, God's chosen, 'full of grace.'"

On the ocean, commanded, as already quoted, as her liveried servant to sound her name to its every shore,

"That fringe of foam, when drops the sun,
To-night, a sanguine stain shall wear:
Thus Mary's heart had strength alone
The Passion of her Lord to share."

Thus does nature in its wildest phase, as in its mildest meadow-face, reflect back to her lovers the features of her who is

"Shining as the sun, beautiful as the moon."

But for whosoever shall lack in love, and remain but coldly indifferent to such charms all but divine, her peerless priest-knight shall make amends:

"My Queen, thou knowest I would bring all hearts
To love thee if I could—and more than mine.
Mine should be last and least. For love of thee,
Unlike all others, breeds not jealousy,
But rather makes its captive moan and pine
(Sure proof that 'tis a passion grace imparts)
To see thee loved thy due. But ah, if all
Of Adam's race should love thee with the love
Of Joseph or of John, 'twere not thy due!
For this no more the many than the few
Suffice; nor would you myriad worlds above
Peopled with souls had never known a fall.

"The gathered love of angels fails no less.
'Tis God's alone can satisfy the claim—
And that (glad thought!) o'erflows the measure's brim.
Yet should I find deficiency in Him
Did He not call thee by the dearest name
Of Mother, and with human lips express
A human heart. But now I may not pine.
The Heart of Jesus loves thee all thy due
(A love the sweeter that there is but one);
And with this Heart, I love thee, and atone
For hearts estranged or lukewarm or half true,
And all the base inconstancies of mine."

Who has ever dared so much? Even in St. Bernard's worship of the first in his heart after the only adorable God, though there is height of expression even to the borders of inspiration, depths of affection even to the melting of the breasts he calls "stony and iron," ardor of love unto burning—an ocean of tenderness—if we have not misinterpreted him, there is yet, a something wanting of the daring familiarity that constitutes the True-Lover, advancing beyond the worshipper, and outstripping the very Son—the mortal Son of her heart. But may not the familiar St. John who leaned and took his love-wakeful repose on the bosom of the Master, as familiarly approach the purest Lady-Mistress, "whom when he shall have loved, he is chaste; when he shall have touched, is pure; when he shall have taken for his own, is ever a virgin,"* like herself! So dares her latest lover, and still trustingly hopes

"TO BE FORGIVEN."

---
* Offic. S. Agnetis. Resp. I Noct.

"I call thee 'Love'—'my sweet, my dearest Love';
Nor feel it bold, nor fear it a deceit.
Yet I forget not that in realms above,
The thrones of seraphs are beneath thy feet.

"If Queen of Angels thou, of hearts no less:
And of mine,—a poet's, which must needs
Adore to all melodious excess
Which cannot sate the rapture that it feeds.

"And then thou art my Mother: God's, yet mine!
Of mothers, as of virgins, first and best;
And I as tenderly, intimately, thine
As He, my Brother, carried at the breast.

"My Mother! 'tis enough. If mine the right
To call thee this, much more to muse and sigh
All other honeyed names. A slave, I might—
A son, I must. And both of these am I." *

* Poems—Hill, p. 33.

(TO BE CONTINUED.)

'Beth's Promise.

BY MRS. ANNA HANSON DORSEY.

CHAPTER XIV—(Continued).

A ROMANTIC ADVENTURE.

'BETH sprang into the boat, and seating herself in the stern, laid her hands on each side of it, and began to rock the light little craft and enjoy herself. "Oh, Lodo! this is splendid! I wish you would get in too, just to see how nice it is; but I suppose you won't, as it is impossible to take Peg and the phaeton in," she cried with childish delight. People living inland, know nothing at all of the passion that persons have for the water who have always been accustomed to it. In the landscape, it is to them like eyes in the human face; there's a blank and a thirst when it is absent, and they see only mountains, fields or plains around them, and long for its refreshment and beauty with a longing that cannot be expressed. So 'Beth's glee was only the joy of meeting an old friend, and she went on rocking the boat until Lodo, afraid that she would upset it, turned Peg's head shoreward, her last words being: "Indeed, mem, you're straining that old rope."

"Oh, Lodo, if I only had oars, I'd row across the lake, and you'd think I was Ellen Douglass! But I'll just sit here and rock, and sing, and paddle my hands in the water to make believe," said 'Beth, while Lodo thanked fortune that there were no oars to lead her dear young lady into more reckless mischief than she was already engaged in. She soon found a shady spot for Peg and the phaeton, and having fastened the reins to a tree, she ran swiftly up into the woods to gather the ferns and other wild-wood beauties that she knew of, determined to make haste back, not sure but that a whale or some other dreadful monster would rise from the bottom of the lake and swallow 'Beth during her absence.

There, all alone with the sweet, dreamy surging of the waves lapping the sides of the boat, and melting with gentle sighs upon the shore, the long bright expanse of blue dancing water stretching away into the distance before her, and the gentle, rocking motion, 'Beth grew thoughtful and dreamy; *en rapport* with nature, she now yielded to its influences as entirely as though she were reading a poem of some master-mind; nor did she know how swiftly the moments had sped until she was aroused by a piercing shriek; starting up, she cast a swift glance around her, and discovered that she was adrift, and quite a distance from the shore, where Lodo stood gesticulating and shrieking in the most frantic way. The old rope had either broken or been too loosely tied to the post and became unfastened, while she was in dreamland, and there she was, without oars, and no help at hand.

"Don't be frightened, Lodo," she called out in brave tones, after having by a sign stilled the girl's shrill screams; "it's lovely out here; no harm can come to me; I'll just drift along until a fisher-boat sees me."

But Lodo only stopped long enough to hear what 'Beth said, then began again filling the air with her piercing cries.

Out there alone, drifting gently on, soft winds blowing back her hair, brightness around and above her, with a sense of freedom from every earthly care and grief, a sweet, restful feeling stole into 'Beth's heart, and she felt that even thus she would be contented to float on and on to the end. But the land-breeze which had freshened, brought Lodo's shrieks nearer, rousing her from her dreamy reverie to a full sense of the situation, and her cheek paled, for she could not really see the end of her adventure. She was not in the least frightened, and but for the thought of the dreadful alarm her mother and Aunt 'Beth would be thrown into if she did not get back in some way, or by some means not yet apparent, she would have laughed at Lodo's childish terror, and looked upon it all as a delightful joke; but the thought of the dear ones at "Ellerslie" gave a gloomy aspect to the affair, and she wondered if she could make herself heard on shore, now that she had drifted still farther out.

"Lodo, Lodo! don't you go back to 'Ellerslie' without me," she shouted through her hands; and a faint "No, mem," came back to her, as the boat, dancing with the waves, floated farther and farther away; not rapidly, but steadily widening the distance between her and the shore. She measured the distance; she was sure it was not more than a quarter of a mile, and, after a moment's thought, made up her mind to swim back, and she found herself wondering what Lodo would do and what extravagance she would commit when she saw her plunge into the lake. She unbuttoned her boots, and unfastened her belt to gather up the folds of her dress, when, looking shoreward once more, she saw a man suddenly emerge from the woods. He looked at that distance like a gentleman, and had a large portfolio under his arm. He had been attracted to the spot by Lodo's shrieks of distress, and stood for an instant looking at her, then at the boat towards which she wildly pointed; he saw no oars, and took in the situation at a glance; it was the work of a moment to fling off coat and vest, and toss them down, divest himself of cap and heavy walking-boots, which he pitched in a heap with them and his portfolio; then he plunged into the lake, and struck out bravely for the boat. 'Beth had watched it all, and was now really terrified. "Suppose he is not a good swimmer; suppose he gets the cramps, and drowns? Oh, I wish I had not been so rash! I wish I had not come to the lake! Why did I not notice the old rope, as wise little Lodo bade me? Oh pity, sweet Virgin Mother, and let no harm come to others through my foolish act!" It was nothing new for 'Beth to breathe an invocation to Our Blessed Lady, whose supreme sorrows, endured with the sufferings of her Divine Son for mankind, ever drew her with tender compassion and reverent love towards her.

She sat perfectly motionless, with folded hands resting on her lap, watching the swimmer's bold, strong strokes, as he dashed the waters aside like a sea-king. Nearer and nearer he came, and 'Beth wondered who he might be; his brown waving hair was cut close, showing a fine broad brow and well shaped head; his eyes were large and dark; his chin round and resolute, and his mouth, slightly open, revealed fine even teeth beneath a long drooping moustache. It was a handsome manly face, exhibiting a grave, tender expression, that would have won a woman's trust among strangers and in distress, if she needed protection or help. Now he is near enough to speak. "How dreadfully embarrassing!" thought 'Beth; "what on earth shall I say to him?"

"You are all right now, madam. I hope you have not been frightened," he said, cheerily.

"No, but I am sorry to be the cause of so much trouble; I'm afraid you are very wet," she replied, without thinking in her confusion of the absurdity of what she said.

"I am used to that," he replied, laughing, as he swam around fishing for the rope, "and have enjoyed my swim amazingly. I feel quite Don Quixote-y swimming out to the rescue of a distressed damsel. Ah, here it is at last!" he said, grasping the rope.

'Beth felt her cheeks crimson; she thought he was laughing at her, and she said: "I was just getting ready to swim back, but you came—"

"Swim! you would have drowned; I'm very thankful I heard that little woman screaming," he said, gravely, all the merriment gone out of his eyes.

"I can swim, I assure you," said 'Beth; "I have many a time swam farther than that; but had you not better get into the boat?"

"I would—thanks!—but you see there are no oars, and I'm afraid we should go on drifting," he answered respectfully, but evidently amused.

"I am very sorry, but what is to be done about it?" she asked, her beautiful eyes full of trouble.

"I'm going to tow you in."

"But you can't swim with one hand!" she exclaimed.

"Yes I can, easily; the boat's a light weight, even with you in it; but perhaps you are Undine, and expect some of your water sprites from the bottom of the lake to come to your rescue?"

"No, I am not Undine," she answered, gravely, again thinking he was laughing at her; "I am only an ordinary mortal, and very grateful for what you have done."

"Don't thank me, please; it makes everything so prosaic," he said, with a nod and a smile; then turning the bow of the boat towards the shore, he wrapped the rope around his strong arm and swam without difficulty, drawing it along swiftly after him. 'Beth thought if he did not get a sudden cramp and go down, or pneumonia, or some other illness, from being so long in the water, she would be more than thankful, since her thoughtless act alone would be the cause of such misfortunes, should they come. "It is quite romantic," she answered, "and I dare say I shall have many a laugh over it all; but, for all that, it is very embarrassing."

At last the shore was reached; Lodo, all smiles and tears, had the phaeton down to the very edge of the water, and the stranger, drawing the boat to the sands, almost beaching her, helped 'Beth in.

"I thank you very much," she said, with gentle courtesy; "but you are so drenched, won't you please get in and let us drive you home? there's plenty of room if one of us sits in the rumble."

"Oh no: a thousand thanks; but I wouldn't get in for the world, to spoil your pretty cushions; besides, I have heaps of dry clothes lying over there. I'll run now and beach my boat until a new rope can be had, then I shall walk home very fast, and be dry by the time I get there."

Won't you have some lunch, then? here's a basket full of cold chicken, bread and butter, jelly, too, I believe; and what's this, Lodo?" said 'Beth, uncovering the basket, and turning things over.

"Claret, mem. I thought you'd like it, and I put in a bottle."

"I am hungry, that's a fact," said the matter-of-fact stranger, frankly; "and if you'll just leave me a bite of something, I shall enjoy it amazingly."

In an instant Lodo was out, taking the basket with her, and spreading a napkin on a large stump; she arranged at least half their plenteous lunch upon it, with plate, knife and fork, and goblet; also, at a sign from 'Beth, the bottle of claret, while their strange friend beached his boat high, and resumed his dry garments, his boots and cap.

"There's your lunch, sir," said Lodo, pointing to the rustic table she had improvised, as he returned.

"Oh, thanks! it reminds me of the Golden Age; but you are not going?"

"Yes, and good-bye, with many thanks," said 'Beth.

"Au revoir," he said, bowing, determined that this should not be their last meeting. He did not tell her who he was, afraid of being formally thanked by her friends for the service he had rendered her; while she refrained from mentioning her own name, lest he should feel compelled by courtesy to call and inquire after her health, and of course be admitted. 'Beth was not ungrateful, but she felt the situation to be an awkward one, and had just enough of the *mauvais honte* of a school-girl left to shrink from seeing him again.

"I'm very hungry, too, Lodo; is there anything left?" said 'Beth, as they were driving homewards. "But oh, Lodo, what made you scream so! I wish you hadn't."

"And if I hadn't, mem, where would you be this blessed minute? It was my screams that brought him; he said so; laws, mem, how could I ever have faced 'Ellerslie' without you!"

"That's true, Lodo; thank you then for screaming; but give me a ham sandwich and a pickle, as I'm just about famished; then some cold chicken; but I won't eat a thing if you don't take something too; that's a good child; stop under the trees here until we eat everything that's left. Oh, it was too splendid out there on the lake! If I had only had a pair of oars! But where are the ferns, Lodo?"

"Well, mem, I think I must have flung them somewhere up there among the trees; I was that scared when I saw you sailing away all alone, by—by—yourself, and I'm so—so—so glad, mem—you're safe!" answered Lodo, bursting into a regular sobbing fit, which relieved her affectionate heart, while 'Beth wiped her tears away, and kissed her, which seemed to make up for everything; after which they finished their lunch and drove dome.

(TO BE CONTINUED.)

A May Sonnet.

BY MARY E. MANNIX.

MADONNA MIA, turn those gentle eyes
In adoration lifted to the Throne,
A moment downward, through the floating skies,
To earth, whence truth and holiness seem flown.
Thou wert His Mother, Mary, and thou art,
Yet on the Cross He gave us sinners thee,
And bade thee guard within thy stainless heart
Such ingrates vile, such lepers white as we.
O Mother loved, loved spite of darkening sin,
That wraps as with a pall this world of woe,
Open thy tender heart and take us in,
Save from the dangers footsore pilgrims know;
Making to bloom these withered souls of ours,
Madonna, in thine own sweet month of flowers.

On the Appian Way.

SAN SEBASTIANO.

BY ELIZA ALLEN STARR.

(CONTINUED.)

RETRACING our steps along the grass-grown lane, we again strike into the Appian Way. Riding southward swiftly, according to the Roman fashion, we soon see the Gate of Saint Sebastian through the Arch of Drusus, that most ancient of all the Roman arches yet standing; and so completely does the eye take in both these objects, that one is never represented satisfactorily without the other. This arch, which is considered, next to the Pantheon, the most perfect existing monument of Augustan architecture, was decreed by the Roman senate in honor of Drusus, second son of the Empress Livia, the favorite wife of Augustus, by her first husband, Tiberius Nero. Drusus died during a campaign on the Rhine in the year 9 before Christ. As Ozanam writes: "At the moment when Drusus was throwing bridges across the Rhine, and cutting roads through the Black Forest, it was time to make haste; for ten years later, a town of Judea would give birth to Him whose disciples were to pass along these roads and complete the destruction of barbarism." The German hordes in their forests baffled the legions of Cæsar, and the body of Drusus was brought back to Rome to be buried by his step-father, Augustus, in the *mausoleum* which he had raised for himself; while the arch bore testimony to his bravery and to the regret felt by the Romans for his untimely death. It is a single, narrow arch, with all the stern, dignified simplicity which characterized the architecture of that period. Formerly, it supported an equestrian statue of Drusus, a seated female figure which represented Germany, and two trophies. To-day, it is one of the most picturesque of all the Roman ruins. Bereft of its statues, the bricks on its summit are bare, except as they are clad by the flowering weeds which make ruins lose half their sadness; and thus we can still see the remains of the aqueduct, by which Caracalla supplied water for his baths. It is through this arch that we catch our first sight of the *Porta San Sebastiano*, with its two semicircular towers of the Aurelian wall resting on a basement of marble blocks. At this famous gate, the Senate and people of Rome received in state the last triumphal procession which entered the city by the old *Regina Viarum*, or Queen of Ways, which we know as the *Via Appia*. This triumph was allowed to Maro Antonio Colonna, after the victory of Lepanto, in 1571; that same victory which Saint Pius V saw, in a vision, at the very time of its accomplishment, and while the faithful were going in procession, before his eyes, through the streets of Rome, chanting litanies for the deliverance of Christian Europe from the power of the Mussulman. As in the triumphs of the old Roman generals, the children of the conquered prince walked in the ranks of the victor, who rode into Rome attended by the nobility, all dressed in great pomp and splendor, preceded by the standard of the victorious fleet.

Looking through the ancient Arch of Drusus at the same time as through the Gate of Saint Sebastian, the eye follows the Appian Way, bathed in sunshine, bordered with vineyards. As we ride over this smiling landscape, it is impossible to realize that on either hand, under this rich verdure of many tints, wind the dark, narrow passages of the Christian catacombs, which Saint Leo the Great called "the crown of martyrs which enriches the Eternal City." But before we reach the entrances to these subterranean cities of the dead, we come to the spot where the *Via Ardeatina* branches off to the right; and here, so close upon the Appian Way, as almost to break its majestic line, stands a church. No parish clusters around it, and no bell brings together on Sundays and festivals scattered worshippers from the vineyards, shepherds in their pointed peasant-hats, sheep-skin overalls and mantles, or shepherdesses, with distaff in hands, in short-blue gowns and the traditional folds of white linen, or *panno*, on the head and shoulders, from tending their flocks on the knolls of the Campagna. It is another of those monuments which stand as witnesses to the traditions of the apostolic age. For here, on the great pagan and Christian highway, Saint Peter, flying from the minions of Nero at the urgent desire of his people, meets his Lord bearing His Cross and hastening towards the city which His Vicar had just left. The Apostle, nothing doubting the presence of his Master, exclaims: *Domine quo vadis?* "Lord, whither goest Thou?" And the answer comes in that deep minor key, so familiar to Peter, and which never failed to enchain him still closer to his Master: *Venio Romam iterum crucifigi.* "I come to Rome to be crucified again." Then Peter knows it is not by flight that he will best serve the necessities of the Church committed to his care; and without a thought of hesitation or of regret, he turns back to imprisonment and to crucifixion. But the place of a meeting so gracious on the part of our Lord, so characteristic on the side of Saint Peter, was not left without a visible proof of this midnight interview between the glorified Head of the Church and His Vicegerent. The stones of the Appian Way kept the prints of the Sacred Feet which stood still, for a moment, as Jesus answered the astonished question of His disciple and His Vicar. The flag-stone, however, on which the impression remained, has been consigned to the keeping of another church more favorable to the safety of this treasure. In this plain little chapel of *Domine quo Vadis*, we see a faithful copy of the original, to which the pilgrim touches devout lips, so strongly is the mind affected by the sacredness of the spot. Two frescoes, one on each hand of this lonely little chapel, keep the exact tradition in mind. On one side is our Lord advancing with a swift step towards Rome; on the other, Saint Peter starting back as if in astonishment, and the keys in his hand as the symbol of his vicarship. But to show the deep hold which this tradition kept over the Roman mind so far down as the 16th century, we find in this chapel a cast of Michael Angelo's Christ bearing His Cross, as met by Saint Peter on the Appian Way. The original, in marble, is on the left of the altar of *Santa Maria sopra Minerva;* and to show how constant has been the veneration to the footprints of those Sacred Feet left on the flag-stone of the Appian Way, the foot of the statue by Michael Angelo in the Church of the Minerva is so worn by the lips of the faithful, that the foot has been sandalled with bronze in order to preserve it.

Those who affect to despise the frescoes on the wall of the *Domine quo Vadis*, and even to think lightly of the cast of the Sacred Feet, still feel their veneration for the spot enkindled by the fact, that Michael Angelo's genius has found honor by a perpetuation of this beautiful tradition.

Soon after passing this wayside monument, for which the Romans have a special veneration as for everything connected with the story of the Prince of the Apostles, we come to the wide-open space covering the site of the Catacomb of Saint Callixtus. Green hillocks mark to the eye the *luminari* which still allow the light of day to pierce into those subterranean chambers. Beyond it, to the west, we see the Catacomb of SS. Nereus, Achilleus and Domitilla, between the Ardeatine and Appian Ways and adjoining the cemetery of Saint Callixtus. The entrance to this last, on the *Via Appia*, is marked forever to the memory by a half-circular ruin, beside which stand two aged cypresses, with the long lines of arches which carried the Roman water-pipes across the campagna in the distance, and the blue hills melting into the sky above and beyond them. On the left of the Appian Way, under what would seem unbroken soda, lies the very ancient Catacomb of Saint Pretextatus, to whose sacred chambers we must descend for some of the most interesting events connected with the Christian *Via Appia*. But leaving both these remarkable cemeteries for the present, we follow the ancient road, until a few tall cypresses point out, even from a distance, one of the spots dearest to the devout pilgrim; in fact, one of the Seven Basilicas, privileged, from the earliest times, to bestow special graces upon those who visited them. For, as the list of Roman basilicas shows, next to the Apostles, Rome venerated the youthful martyrs who won magnificent victories in the Name of Christ, such as Saint Lawrence and Saint Sebastian. The relics of San Lorenzo repose under the altar of his church on the Via Tiburtina, and those of San Sebastiano under an altar of his church, standing in a sort of hallow on the *Via Appia*. The story of the youthful tribune of Diocletian's Guard, born of Christian parents in Narbonne of Gaul, and educated in the polished city of Milan, choosing the career of a soldier, not because of its honors and as a highway to the imperial purple, but because it afforded him an opportunity to succor the persecuted Christians, and to sustain the wavering courage of the martyrs; of the miracles performed to the same end by the Sign of the Cross at his hand; of his profession of Faith, when the time came, face to face with Diocletian, his imperial master, and in the very hall of audience from which he was lead to be stripped of his tribune's armor and to be tied to an olive tree in the imperial court-yard, there to be shot to death, slowly, by the sure arrows of the Mauritanian band of archers; the taking down of the limp body covered with blood, bristling with arrows, and borne to the apartments of a Christian widow of the imperial household, named Irene, who found life feebly asserting itself in the untouched heart of the martyr; the restoration to life only to claim his right to speak the truth of Christ and to denounce the persecutor Diocletian to his face; the appearance of the resuscitated figure of this favorite tribune to Diocletian, from a window overlooking the imperial stairway, to reproach him for his enormities against God and His faithful; the horror of the persecutor, who supposed he saw the disembodied spirit of his victim, and the change of this horror to rage and habitual cruelty, as he ordered the pallid, majestic figure to be struck down with clubs and then thrown into the hideous *Cloaca Maxima*, the vast sewer, through which flowed all the filth of Rome; the vision which came to Lucina, another Christian widow, in her sleep, in which she saw Sebastian, radiant as an angel, in the midst of the horrid sewer, entrusting to her the sacred duty of securing his body and depositing it in care of the Christians; the ready zeal with which she fulfilled the trust, actually rescuing the body and having it conveyed, as a most precious trust, to her own house and vineyard on the Appian Way, about two miles from the gate; all this has come down to us in the verified *Acts of Saint Sebastian*. To this succeeds the story of the holy widow converting her house into a church; of the building of a basilica on this very spot by Constantine, the first Christian emperor, which was consecrated by Saint Sylvester; the renovation of this church in 367 by Saint Damasus, Pope, as an inscription verifies; the formal dedication of this church to Saint Sebastian by Innocent I, before 417; the homily of Saint Gregory the Great pronounced there before 590; its restoration by Adrian I, in the eighth century, and by Eugenius IV, in the fifteenth; and finally, of its entire reconstruction in 1611, by Cardinal Scipio Borghese, from plans by Flaminio Ponzio, precisely as we now see it, with its façade embellished by three round arches of faultless beauty, supported by six antique columns of granite, four of which stand in pairs; and we have a monument which authenticates Christian traditions as well as Christian annals.

But there is a subterranean history connected with this church which is unrivalled in some respects; for the cemetery, or catacomb, of Saint Sebastian is the only one in Rome which has never been closed, which has given uninterrupted testimony to the Church of the Catacombs. Indeed, the word *catacumbus*, applied solely at first to a crypt in this subterranean cemetery, is the origin of our word catacomb, now used for all these underground burial places or chapels. And the existence of this word involves one of the most interesting episodes in the history of the relics of SS. Peter and Paul. The exact date of this event is not stated by our authorities,* but the incident is cited or alluded to in a manner to command a respectful hearing, aside from matters of faith. It would seem that the Oriental Christians, considering themselves the rightful possessors of the relics of the Apostles SS. Peter and Paul, inasmuch as they were countrymen and fellow-citizens, sent deputies to Rome to obtain possession of them. These deputies were divided into two bands, one going to the Vatican hill for the body of Saint Peter, and the other to the Ostian Way, where reposed the body of Saint Paul. They met at the junction of the Appian with the Ostian Way, or where the Church of Saint Sebastian now stands, each with the coveted treasure. But this moment in which their labors seemed to be crowned with success, brought a strange confusion and dismay. Each party setting down its precious burden for a moment, they no sooner attempted to go on, than such a tempest of thunder and lightning surrounded them that, relinquishing their scheme, they took to flight. Meanwhile the Romans, becoming aware of the loss with which they were threatened, pursued the deputies until they came to this spot, to find the relics just as they had been left by the Orientals. No time was lost in securing their new-found possession. A double crypt, lined with marble, was prepared for their reception, which went by the name of *ad catacumbos*.

But this was not the only time in which the prince of the apostles honored the subterranean cemetery of Saint Sebastian. In the first half of the third century, the emperor Heliogabalus, having determined to enlarge the imperial circus on the Vatican hill in order to give the elephants more space, the Christians took alarm, fearing that the excavations might extend to the resting-place of Saint Peter. Remembering the security in which the relics had reposed in the cemetery at the junction of the Appian and Ardeatine Ways, they resolved to entrust them to the same keeping. It was not until 257, when Pope Stephen I, having been discovered in this catacomb, had been put to death upon the spot, that the relics of Peter were again restored to the Vatican Catacomb. To a resting-place thus doubly consecrated, Sebastian charged the pious Lucina to convey his remains, that they might lie at the feet, as it were, of SS. Peter and Paul, as the cemetery at that time seems to have come, as a dower, into the possession of Lucina.

---

* Rome Souterraine: p. 172-4.

The first surprise on passing under the round arches of the portico into the church, is to find ourselves no longer living fifteen hundred years after the Saint, but, as it would be easy to believe, in his own century and generation. It is no longer a matter of mere history that such a man as Sebastian once lived, but of actual personal knowledge. The eye falls as if by instinct on the altar of Saint Sebastian at the left, to see him lying, in marble, scarcely paler than he must have been when laid in his new tomb "at the foot of SS. Peter and Paul." A divine languor, as if he had died from the force of his love of God rather than from the touch of the arrows or the club of the executioner, pervades the whole body, and also the head, which droops heavily towards the shoulder, though resting on his tribunes helmet and armor; while the traces of mortal pain on the face are almost lost in the trance of ecstasy, which must have come when the eyes closed upon the things of earth to open upon the face of God. It is the perfection of manhood, nobly surrendering its strength, not yielding to mortal weakness. This statue, executed by Giorgetti, was designed by Bernini, and is regarded as one of his masterpieces. The inscription on the tablet below the statue is an epitome of the saint's life:

*"The statue of Saint Sebastian, Martyr, whom the Emperor Diocletian ordered to be pierced with arrows because of his Christian Faith, lying under the altar where his body, brought from the catacombs, was laid, as it is seen in the church built in his honor outside the walls of the city, on the Appian Way." Opposite this altar and statue is a case, rich in relics, the pride and consolation of the Franciscan friars. Among these relics is the veritable flagstone on which our Lord left the impression of His sacred feet when He met Saint Peter on the *Via Appia;* also one of the arrows taken from the body of Saint Sebastian when he was removed, apparently lifeless, to the apartments of Saint Irene. The main altar incloses the body of Saint Stephen I, the same who was martyred in the catacomb below. This altar is adorned with four columns of *verde antique*, and has an altar-piece. To the right of the chapel of Saint Sebastian is the opening leading down to the catacomb, or cemetery.

As the Church of San Sebastiano is under the care of Franciscans, it is always a Franciscan who acts as guide to the catacomb. He carries a lighted taper, enclosed in a lantern, to shield it from sudden draughts of air, and from this lights the long, waxen tapers of the visitors. This was our first descent into a catacomb, and it was with a shudder that we saw ourselves going farther and farther into its dismantled passages, from whose crypts and narrow beds the dust of the last martyr had long ago been taken. But traditions and the annals of the early ages of the Church still point to the spot where Saint Sebastian was deposited in peace; where Saint Stephen, celebrating Mass, was discovered by the officers of the emperor, but continued without distraction to the close; then seated himself on his Pontifical chair, and received the blow which crowned him as a Christian martyr, adding the nimbus of sanctity to his triple crown as Pontiff. It is in the centre of the irregular semicircle, on the line of which stood the Pontifical chair of Saint Stephen, that the double crypt, built to contain the relics of Saint Peter and Saint Paul is situated, and which forms a cavity under the altar. To enter this crypt, it was necessary to displace a portion of the altar. This was done so late as 1849, by the architect Perret, when the large plates of marble were found, which, from the time of S. Damasus, in the IVth century, had given the name *Platonia* to the spot. The crypt is still divided into two parts, lined with white marble. It has an opening which communicates with the catacombs. On removing the mortar and nitre from the wall, a painting, very well preserved, was found: our Lord in the centre of a rainbow, and around His head an aureole; on His right, Saint Peter in the attitude of a suppliant; Saint Paul on His left, and on each side of this group a palm-tree in bloom. This seemed to occupy the space opposite the entrance. On the left side wall, M. Perret discovered a figure holding a crown in his hand, and on the same side traces of four other figures also holding crowns. Everything led him to believe that on the opposite side had once been figures enough to complete a group of the twelve apostles. These pictures are judged to belong to the IVth century; and it was precisely at this period that Saint Damasus adorned this venerable crypt with plates of marble, and composed the inscription relating to the deposition of the relics of the apostles:

"Here, if you would know, once reposed saints. If you ask their names, they were Peter and Paul. The East sent disciples we freely acknowledge. By the merit of their blood shed, the saints, having followed Christ to the stars, have attained celestial mansions and the kingdom of the elect. Rome, meanwhile, could defend her citizens. May Damasus recall this to your glory, O new stars!"*

By ascending a stairway, built in the XVIIth century, we come to a corridor which extends be-

---

* Statua S. Sebastiani M. quem Diocletianus Imperator ob Christi fidem sagittis configi jussit jacens sub Altare, in quo ipsius corpus e Catacumbis elatum reconditum in ecclesia ad ejusdem M. honorem ædificata extra mœnia Urbis via Appia.

* Hinc, habitasse prius sanctos cognoscere debes,
Nomina quisque Petri pariter Paulique requiris.
Discipulos Oriens misit, quod sponte fatemur,
Sanguinis ob meritum Christumque per astra secuuti,
Aetherios petiere sinus et regna piorum.
Roma suos potius meruit defendere cives.
Hæc Damasus vestras referat nova sidera laudes.

hind the apse of the basilica of Saint Sebastian. It may be called a gallery from which we can look down into the *Platonia*, and is encrusted with beautiful inscriptions. The one on the right wall is drawn from the revelations of St. Bridget of Sweden, who used to come on foot from her house on the Piazza Farnese,* where it still stands, to spend hours where she could overlook the crypt consecrated by the relics of SS. Peter and Paul. The inscription on the left is by the learned Cardinal Baronius, a religious of the Oratory of Saint Philip Neri, and relates to Saint Stephen, Pope and martyr. To Saint Philip Neri we owe the fervor of religious inspiration which urged Bosio in his explorations of the Roman catacombs; while Saint Charles Borromeo followed in the steps of Saint Philip. Both these Saints, as well as Saint Bridget, had found a favorite place for meditation and prayer, near the subterranean refuge of the great apostles, and near the relics of Saint Sebastian; thus adding the perfume of their own sanctity to that of the age of apostles and the age of martyrs. It is thus that the saints join hands in prayer and good works from century to century; while a Bosio in the sixteenth century and a de Rossi in the nineteenth are associated with them by their enthusiastic labors in the same holy cause.

The Church of Saint Sebastian may be called the advance-guard of Christian Rome and of the Christian monuments; for when we look still farther across the campagna, with its tints of now mingling, then breaking, amethyst and amber, in an atmosphere never to be painted or described, it is to catch the grand outlines of the tomb of Cæcilia Metella and the ragged forms of ruined, desolated pagan tombs, which make the mournful and impressive distance of the Via Appia.†

---

* The house and convent of Saint Bridget of Sweden on the Piazza Farnese, is the venerated possession of the Order of the Holy Cross. E. A. S.

† Among the ruined Palaces of the Cæsars, where we seek in vain a single locality connected with the name of any emperor, rises a small chapel, built on the foundations of the one in which Gelasius II was elected Pope in 1118. The present chapel was built by Urban VIII in 1629, and is dedicated to Saint Sebastian; because it stands on the place where the captain of the pretorian guards was pierced with the arrows of the Mauritanean archers in the imperial court-yard.

(TO BE CONTINUED.)

THE Ark of the Covenant, which, together with many other sacred spoils, was conveyed from Jerusalem to Rome by the Emperor Titus, was subsequently placed in the Basilica of St. John Lateran by Constantine. He deposited in it some very precious memorials, such as the seamless garment of our Lord, the reed which was placed in His hands as a mock sceptre, the pot of manna, the rod of Aaron, and the outer garments of St. John the Baptist.—*Father O'Brien.*

The Month of Mary.

WE have suffered with Mary through the agony of the Passion, and wept with her at the foot of the Cross; but the *Jubilate* of Easter morning has sounded amid Judea's hills, and once more with glad hearts and happy voices, we rejoice with our dear Mother, and welcome the beautiful month of May. The May month, Mary's month, is all hers; every hour of every day should be bound to its fellows with a thought of her love, by an aspiration in her honor; every minute of every hour should be counted as a jewel, to be enshrined in the precious temple of her maternal heart. But in these blooming May days, when all the earth is aglow with light, and love, and beauty; when the dancing steps of the wayside rivulet trip musically over their accustomed paths; when nature rises up in joyfulness, and sits, all clothed in green, upon the mountains, we cannot more fitly add our anthems to the universal hymn of joy than by striking the keynote of our purest source of happiness: that of knowing we are the children of Mary's love. She opens wide her maternal arms, laden with benediction, gathering the blossoms of our prayers into a garland to lay before the tenderness of Jesus, who can refuse her nothing. And how graceful is the thought that we are not alone in our consecration of this beautiful month to the Queen of beauty and holiness! All over the Christian world, in stately cathedral and quaint old abbey choir; in quiet convent chapel and humble village church; in silent oratory and by mossy wayside shrine; in the palaces of kings and the lowly dwelling of the poor; in the hearts of princes and peasants; by the lips of the wise and illiterate; old age and youth; maidenhood and innocent childhood, the songs of Mary are sung; the praises of Mary are sounded in these bright spring days.

A girdle of prayer and devotion and sanctified glory encircles the earth, and Mary is its centre; its gems are rays of light that ascend from many shrines till they blend in an aureola of love about her spotless brow. Can she refuse us aught at such a joyous season, when birds and streams and flowers and sunshine are in sweet accord with the hearts of her devoted children?

The sorrow of the Passion lies behind her; the sea of desolation that rose mountain-high has sobbed itself into the calm repose of her enduring mother-love, and she waits for us with an eager waiting.

Let us go to her, let us fall at her feet; and whatever be the sin and sorrow that have saddened our souls, whatever the consolation or joy that has visited our hearts, who can soften the one or share with us the other, who can weep for our misfortune or smile with our happiness, like the Mother who has known above all women, above all mothers, the consummation of woe, the fulness of joy? Her tenderness is unbounded; her compassion, without limit; her charity, an ever-flowing stream; her patience, inexhaustible; her purity, a living well of sweetness, from which we may drink long draughts of precious waters.

Santa Caterina di Siena.

BY ELIZA ALLEN STARR.

SIENA'S loveliest flower! of her renown
 The everlasting crown!
And yet,
No April violet
In lowliest meadows set,
Was e'er so humble as this maid,
Who blossomed in the shade,
Good Benincasa, of thy house and name;
Whom, still, the Fontebranda burghers claim.

Nor Fontebranda only; nor alone
Dost thou, Siena, raise for her a throne:
For, lo! Imperial Rome,
On her seven hills, crowned by St. Peter's dome,
Names for a patron Benincasa's child.
 The Fontebranda burgher's pride,
To whom the burgher-mothers crowed and smiled.
Stands with patrician Agnes side by side;
Francesca, too, a Ponziani's bride;
 While we, to-day,
With Rome and all Siena say:
For us and ours, O Santa Caterina, pray!
 APRIL 30TH, 1878.

The Ascension.

THE Ascension is one of the four oldest feasts of the Church. St. Augustine believes it to have been instituted by the apostles. It is celebrated on the fortieth day after Easter, because Jesus Christ ascended into Heaven in the presence of His apostles forty days after His Resurrection. In the time of St. Augustine, the feasts of the Passion, Resurrection, Ascension and Pentecost were celebrated wherever the Faith of Jesus Christ was received.

The Ascension may be considered as the end and final accomplishment of all the mysteries of the God-Man. He leaves earth and returns to His Father, after having fulfilled His mission and consummated His sacrifice.

In thus ascending from earth to heaven, He teaches us that we should not attach ourselves to this perishable world; that the earth is not our true country; that we have another in Heaven, whither all the thoughts and aspirations of our heart should be directed. During His life upon earth, our Lord pointed out the way for us; to-day He shows us the goal. We must take the same road if we wish to enter heaven after Him; we must follow His example, if we wish to partake of His recompense and His glory.

Let us celebrate the festival of His Ascension—1st, by ardent desires for our heavenly country, saying with the Prophet: *Alas, how long shall my exile last? How long must I yet live with the inhabitants of Cedar? Oh God of virtue, how admirable are Thy tabernacles! My soul languishes and is straitened with desire to possess Thee.* And with the children of Israel, *Seated on the borders of the river of Babylon, we have poured forth torrents of tears in memory of Sion.*" 2d, by a firm hope of one day reigning with Jesus Christ, saying with St. Stephen: "*I see the heavens opened, and the Son of Man who looks upon me, and holds out His hand towards me.*" He has ascended to His heavenly kingdom, to prepare a place for us; there the members shall one day be reunited with the Head; there is the place of our rest for all eternity.

The Rogation Days.

THE three days following the fifth Sunday after Easter are called *Rogation Days*, or days of supplication and prayer to the Lord of Heaven and earth, that His wrath may be appeased towards the children of men. The origin of this solemnity dates as far back as the fifth century, and by St. Aritus of Vienna and St. Cesaire of Arles, is ascribed to St. Mamertus, Bishop of Vienne in Dauphiny. This holy Bishop was grieved at the sight of the great number of evils which had befallen his diocese, and proposed to his people that solemn processions be made, public prayers offered up, and fasts and other works of penance performed to stay the afflicting hand of God. The people obeyed, and the time was fixed for the three days following the fifth Sunday after Easter, and in a short time this pious solemnity was observed in all the churches of Gaul. The first council of Orleans, held in the year 511, issued a decree expressly ordering its celebration; and we can see from the writings of St. Gregory of Tours, with how much piety and fervor the faithful fulfilled this obligation under the reign of the sons of Clovis. Sometime afterwards it was adopted by the church of Rome, whence it spread throughout the universal Church.

The Rogation Days were at first considered as days of obligation, on which it was not permitted to work, and all were obliged to fast. In after times, the prohibition to work was removed, and the fast restricted to simple abstinence from flesh meat. But there can be no doubt that it is the desire of the Church that these days be passed in a spirit of penance, and prayer; in a spirit of penance, to appease our Lord whom we anger by our sins, and who daily permits us to suffer so many calamities in punishment of our offences; in a spirit of prayer, that we may draw down upon ourselves the blessings of heaven and obtain deliverance from the evils which beset us, or those precious graces which will give us strength to support them and make them tend to our own sanctification.

Maundy Thursday at the Austrian Court.

"MONT," the European correspondent of the Baltimore *Sun*, gives an interesting account of the manner in which the Emperor Francis Joseph and the Empress Elizabeth observe the ancient custom of the *Mandatum*, or "washing of the feet," in commemoration of our Lord's washing the feet of the twelve Apostles. In these days, when faith seems to have died out among the great ones of the earth, and crowned heads have become, in consequence, the oppressors of the people, it is consoling to witness an exception from the general degeneracy; and still more consoling to the Catholic heart is the fact that these exceptions are found among Catholic sovereigns. We have, heretofore, occasionally called attention to the paternal rule of the royal house of Hapsburg, and the marked contrast between its relations with the people and those of the generality of non-Catholic sovereigns; we have chronicled the beautiful and edifying example given by Prince Leopold, heir apparent to the Austrian crown, at a grand festival in his honor at the Court of Berlin, on Carnival night a year or two ago, when he left the party in the height of its joyous festivity at twelve o'clock, because Lent had begun, and was seen early next morning wending his way to Mass; and we have taken note, from time to time, of the happy relationship existing between the people of Austria and the royal family—in striking contrast to the rest of Europe, where a crowned head scarcely dares to show itself in public for fear of assassination. We have now the pleasure of adding another to the many interesting items regarding Francis Joseph and the royal family of Austria. "Mont" writes as follows to the Baltimore *Sun* of April the 13th:

"A correspondent addresses me a pleasant description of the Austrian Emperor's humility in this season when a British Queen goes on a pleasure tour and an ex-Empress on a pilgrimage of love. The Austrian court of late has not been conspicuous for the stateliness of its court ceremonies, or, indeed, for any ceremonies whatever, as the Emperor has been so busily occupied with state affairs that he neglects everything for them. The Empress, though a wonder of beauty and grace, devotes herself entirely to such domesticity as an Empress Queen is allowed to have. One or two state balls alone break the monotony of this imperial devotion to state domestic and affairs. But Holy Week provides an exception of a very peculiar kind to this imperial retirement. On Holy Thursday the Emperor and the Empress washed the feet of twelve poor men and twelve poor women, and afterwards personally waited on them whilst seated at the traditional repast. At ten o'clock in the morning the Great White Hall of the palace was thrown open. This apartment is so called for the reason of its being constructed of pure white marble, decorated with silver ornaments. On three of the four sides galleries are erected as high as the capital of the columns, and in these the *élite* of Vienna assemble on such occasions. Right and left of the entrance, two long, narrow tables are spread—one for the twelve men and the other for the twelve women. These people are selected from the most aged poor of the city. The youngest was eighty-eight years old, and the oldest ninety-seven. No centenarian could be found, as on last year. They were dressed in a costume which is peculiar. A robe in brown stuff like Kentucky jean, trimmed with violet of similar material; the waist is fastened around by a pilgrim's cord, a large white handkerchief around the neck and a broad-brimmed hat. This costume is the same as worn in the days of Maria Theresa, and the male and female are not much different in style. Moreover, the most minute details of the ceremony remain unchanged since those days of that powerful Empress. The chief characters in the ceremony, accompanied each by a relation or two to support their tottering steps, take their assigned places, and the court enters. First comes a numerous group of officers and officials, bearing the chamberlain's key worked on the sleeves of their tunics. I may note that the functions of these gentlemen are merely honorary, and these duties consist in figuring two or three times a year in such ceremonies as this. After them, and immediately preceding their Majesties the Emperor and Empress, comes the grand master of the ceremonies, the Count Hunyady, dressed superbly in the magnificent scarlet and gold uniform of a Hungarian cavalry general. Their Majesties were accompanied by the chief Archdukes and Archduchesses now in Vienna, and they were escorted by their respective suites. The Empress Elizabeth wore a black satin robe, trimmed with black lace, and over this a court mantle, the train of which was borne by two pages of honor. The other princesses and ladies of the court were also robed in black, and form a striking contrast to the tall figure of the Emperor, with his white tunic (on which glistens the Order of the Golden Fleece) and scarlet trowsers. Behind their Majesties, and occupying the fourth side of the hall stand the Emperor's body-guard—German and Hungarian. These guards have all served as officers in the army, and wear magnificent uniforms; the former have a scarlet tunic embroidered with gold, white tight pantaloons, cavalry boots and steel helmets, with white plumes. The Hungarians are clad in light green, with silver facings, scarlet leather boots up to the knee, and a tiger or panther's skin thrown across their shoulders cloakwise. The Emperor stands at one of the tables occupied by the old men. In front of each of these old men there also stands one member of the Imperial family. The Empress occupies a similar position at the other table, and the ladies of honor are the *vis-a-vis* of the old women. The first ceremony performed is the washing of the feet. The Archdukes at one table, the Archduchesses at the other, draw off the right stocking of these poor folks, and the Emperor and the Empress stooping low, wipe the foot with a damp cloth and afterwards dry it. After this comes the banquet, at which the humble guests are served by those hands which hold the sceptre of one of the greatest states of Europe. I need hardly say the *menu* is *maigre* in the most strict sense, and it also dates from the historic days of Maria Theresa. The antiquity of the repast was enjoyable by the old guests and the young lookers on. The first course is served up at each table by twelve *drabans*. These are a body-guard who are on service inside the palace. They wear brilliant scarlet uniforms, with black velvet and gold lace facings, and carry the ancient *hallebard*. Each *draban* brings in a tray, with the dishes on it, and various objects necessary for the feast. The Emperor, bareheaded, himself takes from the tray the plates, dishes, etc., and puts them on the table before each of his old male guests. The Empress treats her guests in a similar way. I must say that this ceremony is rather of the Tantalus order, inasmuch as the viands are served up in four distinct courses before the two dozen guests, but are no sooner served than they are carried off again. The four and twenty invited ones leave the hall hungry, but comparatively rich, for the Emperor and Empress present each of them with a violet silk purse full of gold and silver. On their return home these aged ones find on their modest tables the identical dishes, and even the knives, forks and glasses which excited their admiring tastes at the palace, conveyed by the same *drabans* whom they had seen there. Two little barrels of Hungarian wine, one red, one white, constitute an additional attraction. I need hardly say that many of these aged ones find the feast and the wine conducive of sound slumbers in the winter of their lives. But is it not a princely and pretty picture, that is worthy of our example on more days than Maundy Thursday?"

A Miraculous Cure.

LAST November the *Bulletin Catholique de Montauban* announced that a young novice had been miraculously cured at the fountain of Lourdes, France. The happy recipient of this favor, Sister Theresa of Jesus (Miss Clara Guitard),—who at the time of her admission to the community enjoyed perfect health—had taken a severe cold in October, 1878, which developed a complication of diseases, and finally terminated in pulmonary consumption, which excluded all hope of recovery. The attending physician gave his opinion to this effect. After her cure, which could not fail to create quite a sensation, the Bishop of Montauban appointed a committee of clergymen and physicians to investigate the case. The curé of Beamont, in whose parish the community have their convent, acted as chairman of the committee. The result of the investigation having been submitted to the Bishop, he gave his opinion in the following letter addressed to the curé of Beamont:

MONTAUBAN, Dec. 6, 1879.

MONSIEUR LE CURÉ:—Yesterday I received a visit from the good Sisters of Beamont, who brought me your report. I am much pleased with it, and feel deeply indebted to you and to the honorable gentlemen who assisted you. From the character and intelligence of all concerned in the investigation, its truth is established beyond a doubt. Sister Theresa needs but to be seen, to convince the most skeptical of the supernatural quality of her cure. Blessed be God for the miracles He has wrought at Lourdes, and glory to Mary for her holy intercession, which, by faith, obtains them!

This young religious was confined to her bed for six or seven months; and during four months, milk was the only nourishment she could take. When the physician was apprised of her cure, he could not believe it; he submitted her to a careful examination, but finally was obliged to admit the fact of an entire cure. Is the doctor willing, however, to acknowledge the existence of a miracle? He may, perhaps, do so in his own mind, but he fears to do so publicly, for the sake of science. According to his opinion, the cure of Sister Theresa by a triple immersion in the pond, may be the natural consequence of that violent remedy, which could certainly bring about the transformation stated. This is one more proof to be added to the wonderful effects of hydropathy. But the young Sister did not believe in this effect as attributable to hydropathy; she did not expect anything natural from her immersion; she need not have gone to Lourdes for that purpose. Why did not the doctor prescribe this remedy during the six months in which he had attended her, if he believed in the possible virtue of such treatment? Moreover, he does not, nor can he by any means, positively assert or prove the cure to be an effect of hydropathy. He simply expresses a doubt in the interest of science. "*It may have been the effect of the violent remedy.*" Seriously, could this remedy have been the cause of such a sudden transformation, which gave health at once to a woman ill even to the point of death —nay more, which visibly renewed again the form and substance of a body wasted away by sickness? Consumption, the most obstinate of her many ailments, disappeared immediately. Can this be a merely natural effect? Sister Theresa of Jesus went to Lourdes inspired by the thought that there—if at all—she would recover her health. The Sisters who accompanied her were praying at the grotto, while she, to make her devout supplication, entered the pond, which she left twenty-five minutes later, perfectly cured. Since that time she enjoys an excellent appetite and performs all the duties of a religious life, rising like the others at four o'clock in the morning. If all this can be natural, we must admit that nature has sometimes very singular and unexpected freaks. Once more, let us give thanks to God, and glory to His Blessed Virgin Mother.

Receive, Monsieur le Curé, the assurance of my affectionate attachment.

(Signed) ✠ THEODORE,
BP. OF MONTAUBAN.

The Distress in Ireland—A Touching Appeal.

"Have pity on me, have pity on me ... because the hand of God hath touched me."

WE feel certain that the following fresh appeal for the starving poor in Ireland received a few days since from a well-known missionary priest in that afflicted country, will touch the heart of every reader. No words of ours can add to the force of the pleading, to which we trust there will be a prompt and generous response:

"SEA ROAD, GALWAY, April 8.

". . . . I know of no place where help is more wanted than in this town and county of Galway; and I know of no time when it will be more required than during the months of May and June. Almost everything the poor people had, or received through charity, is exhausted. There is a class of people for whom the Government has done absolutely nothing, and the funds supplied by public charity cannot last long. They are already beginning to fail. If some additional exertion is not made to supply necessary food till June, we shall have the misfortune to see our poor people dying of starvation on the road-side. Already have I seen many of them like living skeletons, scarcely able to ask for the alms necessary to keep them alive; stretching forth their hands for relief where there was none to give them, with the palor of death upon their faces, and the stamp of famine upon every feature. I have seen the starving child go to the starved mother for food, and in heart-rending accents exclaim: 'Mother, I'm dying with hunger and cold.' And what was the answer? 'Child, I would feed you with my blood if I could, and shelter you in my heart; but I have no food to give you but grass, and I have nothing with which to shelter you from the cold but these tattered rags that scarcely cover my poor shivering body.' It is enough to make the heart bleed with compassion.

"Good Bishop McEvilly is doing all that a Bishop can do to aid his poor suffering people, but what can he do against such a tide of misery and distress such as we have not witnessed in Ireland since the famine of '48? You have, no doubt, in America many descended from parents born in this very county, and perhaps town of Galway, and we might ask them who are now above want, and could spare without feeling it, something for their own loved friends in famine-stricken Ireland, and address to them the words of the prophet: 'Have pity on me, have pity on me, at least you, my friends, because the hand of God hath touched me.' Yes, dear father, the hand of God is heavy just now on our dear Irish people, and above all on the people of this county and town of Galway. Their cry of agony is perhaps somewhat stifled by the din of the General Elections, but it is not the less intense for this reason. Will not the readers of THE AVE MARIA spare a little from their superfluities, or even from their legitimate needs, for the starving children of the 'Mary of Nations'? Tell them, that in this case, to give quickly is to give twice. I know most, if not all of them, have contributed already, but they will not refuse to give again, when they learn how great the distress is.

"If Ireland had proved false to her religion and her God, she would not be the famine-stricken Ireland of to-day. The law said: 'You are nothing, apostatize and you will be honored; you are starving, apostatize and you will have plenty; you are slaves, apostatize and you will be free.' But the triumphant children of poor, persecuted Ireland, exclaimed: 'No; you may rob us of our land, our churches and our homes; of our liberties and our lives; but of our Faith, never!' And the words re-echoed through every country on earth, but above all through the great Western Republic, where a home and a welcome, a love and a refuge were opened for the poor persecuted people of Ireland —persecuted on account of their adherence to the 'Faith of their Fathers.' Will the truly sympathetic people of that great Republic forget us to-day in our want? I don't believe it; they are our own flesh and blood; the same blood flows in our veins, the same feelings throb in our hearts.

"Ask the good, kind, generous people who read your widely-extended and influential periodical, who are mostly Irish, and all Catholics, to help us to live just for a couple of months, and hereby win the gratitude and love and prayer of a grateful and loving people, whose earnest supplication will ever be that we may be one in heaven."

Catholic Notes.

——We learn that Mr. Galway, formerly assistant editor of *The Catholic Telegraph* of Cincinnati, has left that city for New York, to fill the same position on *The Catholic World*.

——Mr. J. A. McGee, of *McGee's Illustrated Weekly*, met with a great affliction lately in the death of his eldest son, a bright, interesting lad of five years. We tender the bereaved family our prayerful sympathies.

——We are happy to state that the case of "Richard Gilmour vs. F. W. Pelton, treasurer, etc.," has been decided (14th inst.) in favor of the Bishop. Our school properties are not to be taxed.—*Catholic Universe, Cleveland, Ohio.*

——"There is one sign," says Baring-Gould, "by which you may distinguish the Protestant and the Catholic churches in Germany to-day. The walks in front of the former are generally grass-worn; those in front of the latter are invariably worn smooth by constant use." It is a pregnant observation.—*New York World.*

——A journal of Buenos Ayres informs us that the missionaries of the Congregation of Saint Francis de Sales, delegated by the Archbishop, Monsignor Aneiras, to evangelize the Indians in the Pampas, have recently baptized 1,200 of these pagans. Many officers and soldiers of the regular army in the Argentine Republic acted as sponsors on the occasion.

——"CULTURE."—The "culture," of which we hear so much, may be a sign of better things; but at present, it seems to mean nothing but a worship of the incomprehensible and a new fashion in wall papers. When we hear "cultured" Catholic young ladies descanting on the wonders of foreign cathedrals, and observe that the altars of their parish churches are adorned with hideous artificial flowers, apparently from the cast-off bonnets of a preceding generation, we can only conclude that the world is full of contradictions. But in "cultured" circles an awful gap generally exists between the feminine portion, who find William Morris "so restful," but who never read Faber, and their brothers, who never read anything.—*Catholic Review.*

——AN OLD CATHOLIC CUSTOM—A REBUKE.—We believe it was the *Catholic Universe* that alluded to the old Catholic custom of naming different rooms in even private houses, after favorite saints. This is one of many of those beautiful customs of the ages of Faith, when men really lived in the spirit of Faith and exhibited it in all their daily actions. In our day, we find many Catholic homes without a single religious picture, and some even without the Crucifix. In place of the Blessed Mother of God, we may see the ideal Beatrice, instead of statues of our Saviour, the apostles, or the saints, we will find the representations of the gods and goddesses of the licentious heathens of antiquity. Renowned men of modern times have their effigies every where, but the "Ecce Homo" and the "Mater Dolorosa" are too pious and "fanciful" to occupy a place in the parlor or drawing-rooms. Nothing displays the tender piety of a family more than the decoration of a home with religious pictures.—*Catholic Columbian.*

——THE NUMBER OF JEWS.—The society for the propagation of the Jewish faith, established at Berlin, has published an annual, from which we cull the following statistics: There are at present six or seven millions of Jews dispersed throughout the world. This is about the same number of Israelites that existed in the time of King David. Of these, five million live in Europe; 200,000 in Asia; 800,000 in Africa; 1,150,000 in America. In Europe, Russia has the greatest number—2,621,000. Then comes Austria-Hungary with 1,375,000, of which 375,000 are in Galicia alone. Then comes Germany with 512,000, of which 61,000 are in Ponania; Holland with 70,000; England with 50,000; France with 49,000; Italy 35,000. Spain and Portugal together have 2,000, 3,000 perhaps 4,000; Switzerland, 2,800; Norway, twenty-five. In Berlin there are 45,000 Israelites, nearly as many as in the whole of France. In Asia, India has 20,000; Palestine, 25,000. In Jerusalem they are in the majority, being calculated at 13,5000, whilst the Mussulmans number 7,000, and the Christians 7,000.

——CATHOLIC MISSIONS—The tenth annual report of the Society of Saint Joseph at Mill Hill, England, gives interesting particulars of the labors of this Congregation. The progress of the missionaries among the negroes of the United States, and in the Vicariate Apostolic of Madras, has been favorably noticed by Pope Leo XIII, who in 1878 allotted to them the mission of Afghanistan, and confided to their care the Catholics in the British army of occupation. To assist the good work of the missions, the society has received generous donations from several benefactors. Since the beginning of 1879, twelve priests have departed to various missions; some to Maryland, Kentucky, and South Carolina; others to Madras, where Monsignor Fennelly, the Vicar Apostolic, has sent them to the Gumtoor and Vellore districts. Of the four missionaries that went to Afghanistan, one died of the cholera, of whom a Protestant officer spoke in terms of the highest praise for his zeal and devotion. The Holy Father has just confided the mission of Borneo to the worthy missionaries at Mill Hill, and this new vineyard will soon be tilled by zealous laborers.

——CATHOLIC JOURNALISM.—We learn with great satisfaction, through the columns of *La Civilisation,* that the Holy Father has followed up the warm interest recently displayed by him in the Catholic press, by nominating a commission of Cardinals, under the presidency of his distinguished brother, to examine into a project for creating a new Congregation of Cardinals for press affairs. This commission will, it is stated, "have the character of a central bureau for the Catholic journals of the entire world." The news will give pleasure to Catholics everywhere. It is, above everything, desirable that those who, with journalistic pen, fight our sacred cause, protect our vital interests, resist our multitudinous enemies, and disperse the mists of falsity, should feel that there is a common centre out of which a bond of union will spring. Our purpose even now is definite enough, and our concurrence as close as could be expected; but such an institution as the great and wise Pontiff proposes to plant near himself must inevitably give an impulse to Catholic advocacy and additional strength to Catholic action.—*Catholic Times.*

——RELIGIOUS EDUCATION.—"Through the doctrines of a godless school, my son has become an assassin; be this school cursed forever!" Such was the exclamation of Madame Mlodetzki, a Jewess and mother of the unfortunate young man who expiated on the gallows his attempt against the life of General Melikoff. The sentence was carried into effect on the 3d of March, at Saint Petersburg, the capital of Russia. Could there be a more telling accusation against the modern and infidel instruction of youth than this curse of an unhappy mother? Enough has been said of godless education in this country to induce all fair-minded persons, especially those having at heart the welfare of youth, to approve the action taken not only by the Catholics of our own land but also by those of the whole world, to defend the sacred rights of their children against the machinations of our enemies, who well know that only when faith in God and in His revealed truths has disappeared from the face of the earth, modern revolution will have a chance of success. These wicked men are straining every nerve to exclude the ministers of the Church from the schoolroom, as religious instruction prevents them from so bringing up the rising generation that, when grown to manhood, would be willing instruments in the carrying out of the pernicious designs.

——KNOCK.—It is estimated that there were from 15 to 20,000 pilgrims and visitors to Knock on the 25th ult. The railroads were blocked, and many performed the journey on foot. Several persons, it appears, were favored with celestial visions while praying in the church. A number of new cures are reported to have taken place. Archdeacon Cavanagh has received the following letter recounting a remarkable cure from an English gentleman of birth and position:

——— PARK, 23d March.

MY DEAR SIR: I have the great happiness of being able to inform you that my wife, Mrs. ———, returned here in good health from Knock this day week. She has since enjoyed the same, and is simply not the same person I have known her since my marriage, ten years ago. I quite expected that she would die at Knock, or on the way, and it was very hard for me to allow her to leave in such a state. She suffered dreadfully, and nearly incessantly, for two or three years, from a wound in the chest, and dreadful coughing and retching. All is now gone. She is a new person, and Almighty God has worked a marvellous miracle through the most powerful intercession of Our Lady of Knock and the glorious St. Joseph and St. John the Evangelist. We feel truly humbled and full of gratitude that He should so have blessed us, and will ever be as grateful for His mercy as in us lies. Mrs. ——— will order a handsome statue of St. John three feet high, to be made in Munich, by Messrs. Meyer, as soon as possible; it will be sent to you when finished.

It will take some time to complete the statue, as it will be copied from a sketch of the Saint as he appeared, with mitre and book. I am far from being rich now, as I am only an eldest son, but if I live to succeed to the family estate, and if at that time my wife, Mrs. ——, is still well, I promise to our Lady and SS. Joseph and John to give not less than £200 to improve the Church of Knock, as soon after succeeding as I am able to command the money. I am now obliged to you for your kindness to Mrs. ——, and beg of you to sometimes remember her in your prayers. I remain, Very Rev. Sir,

——Rt. Rev. Bishop Elder entered upon his office of coadjutor and administrator of the diocese of Cincinnati last week. While congratulating the clergy and people of the archdiocese on the possession of good Bishop Elder, we sympathize with those of Natchez, who were devotedly attached to their Bishop, and who feel keenly the parting. The following appreciative notice of Bishop Elder, every word of which we heartily endorse, appeared some time ago in the *Western Watchman* of St. Louis: "The appointment of this eminent ecclesiastic to the important and very responsible office of coadjutor and administrator of Cincinnati, is a most gracious acknowledgment by Rome of splendid talents unostentatiously exercised by one of the most faithful servants of God, of whom our country justly is proud. The appointment of Bishop Elder to Cincinnati stamps the pontificate of Leo XIII as one of progress and careful discrimination. Bishop Elder will be known in history as the typical Bishop of this century. He is now entitled to the rank of confessor and martyr in the Martyrology of the American Church. '*Morti destinatus*,' the refrain in which every episcopal consecration ends, has found its completest fulfilment in the saintly Bishop of Natchez. He has never turned away from danger, never shown his back to death in the performance of duty. He has demonstrated the truth of the martyr policy of the ancient Church, namely, that the most proper place of a Bishop is in the forefront, where disaster and death menace the flock. Bishop Elder loves duty better than life, the good of souls far more than personal safety. The trouble of Cincinnati can be overcome only by a sacrifice, and a sacrifice inspired by supernatural motives; and there is no man in the episcopate of the United States who better represents unselfish devotion to the supernatural than Bishop Elder. He goes to his new post with the spirit of a true shepherd ever ready to lay down his life for his sheep. We hope the people of that vast diocese will appreciate the great sacrifice their new Bishop is making, a sacrifice which has obedience for its only solace, and the glory of God for its only encouragement. With patience and Christian unselfishness, the redemption of that great church is assured."

——Right Rev. Herbert Vaughan, Bishop of Salford, in whose diocese the flourishing city of Manchester is situated, stopped at Dijon, France, on his recent journey to Rome. During his stay, he visited Monsignor Rivet, Bishop of that place, and in the course of conversation gave some very interesting particulars about his see. There are two hundred thousand Catholics in his diocese, of whom one hundred thousand live in Manchester. In this city, there are twenty-three parochial churches, and the number of Paschal Communions is set down at 82,000. Divine Service on Sundays, with sermon, is held five times —of course only one High Mass. The pupils of the cathedral school number about 2,000. Last year the Bishop gave a great mission in his episcopal city, assisted by 72 preachers; Jesuits, Dominicans, etc. The result of this mission was extraordinary; there were no less than fifty-four thousand communicants, and between three and four hundred conversions from heresy. The Catholics of this city have public processions quite frequently; at Pentecost last year, there was one of about ten thousand persons, headed by the cross, with more than a thousand banners floating in the air. Relics and statues of saints were borne along amid the procession, accompanied with solemn chant. It marched through some of the principal streets of the city, not only without being in the least molested, but on the contrary respectfully protected by the police force, who ordered the vehicles to stop, and removed all obstacles in the way. What would Father Faber say, if he had lived to see it? The Catholic schools in the diocese are admirably organized and taught by 600 teachers; they receive an annual remuneration of £61,500 from the Government; a like sum being contributed by the Catholics themselves. The Government inspectors act very generously towards these schools and favor them in many ways. Besides these, there are five priests specially appointed to visit the schools, whose duty it is to see that the children know well the letter and meaning of their Catechism, that they are acquainted with the outlines of Sacred History, go regularly to confession—in fact, to see that their religious and secular education is properly cared for. God's blessing rests on that city, and may it ever remain!

New Publications.

The Miracles of the 16th of September, 1877, at Lourdes. Translated from the French of Henri Lasserre, by a Lady. Dublin: M. H. Gill & Son. 1898.

Many of our readers will remember this beautiful and touching history, which was published in The Ave Maria soon after its appearance in France. It is a full and authentic account of one of the most remarkable cures wrought at Lourdes. The intellect of a cultivated adult may find ample food for reflection in these pages, and the mind of a child will follow the history with delight. We rejoice to see this admirable narrative in book-form, and trust that it may have a wide sale among pious Catholics, and Catholics who are not pious. There is another similar work by Mr. Lasserre, entitled "The Miracle of the 14th of May," which appeared in a previous volume of our little magazine, quite as worthy of being published in more durable form as the present one.

Moore's Melodies. Translated into the Irish Language by the Most Reverend John MacHale, Archbishop of Tuam. New York: Lynch, Cole & Meehan.

Had the illustrious Bishop, whose name appears on the title-page of this little volume, nothing else to recommend him to the love of the Irish people save his successful efforts to preserve and spread the Irish language, that in itself should be sufficient to immortalize his name.

Like all true lovers of country, the Archbishop of Tuam is passionately fond of the ancient language. As an Irish scholar, he is unsurpassed by any living man. He preaches as fluently in Irish as he does in English; and not only in Galway, but likewise in Mayo, the county of his nativity, the sweet tongue of the ancient Erse is still heard as it was spoken three thousand years ago. He has translated into classical Irish, in addition to the work now before us, the first six books of Homer and the Pentateuch. To the venerable Archbishop and the Very Rev. Ulick J. Bourke is due the recent vigorous resuscitation of the Celtic tongue not only in Ireland and America, but also in France and Germany.

To the present volume are added, by way of an appendix, many popular Gaelic melodies and poems. Besides the Irish translation, the original English is given on the opposite page. The book is issued by Lynch, Cole & Meehan, of New York, who are doing much towards the diffusion of the Irish language by means of their Gaelic department in the *Irish American*. The price is only twenty-five cents. It should be in the hands not only of those who have a knowledge of the Irish language, but of every one who wishes to have a memento of the venerable and world-renowned John of Tuam.

——Messrs. Lippincott & Co., of Philadelphia, 715 and 717 Market St., have just published a new and cheap edition of "Nora Brady's Vow," and "Mona the Vestal," by Mrs. Anna Hanson Dorsey. This will be welcome news to many of our readers and other admirers of the gifted author, as these stories, which are among the best she has written, have been out of print a long time. Indeed to most persons they will be entirely new. The first is a thrilling story of the Irish Rebellion of 1848; the second, of the period of the introduction of Christianity into Ireland by St. Patrick. Both are comprised in one neat volume, which will make a very acceptable premium for schools, etc. A more extended notice of these stories will appear in a future number of THE AVE MARIA.

Confraternity of the Immaculate Conception
(Or of Our Lady of Lourdes).

"We fly to thy patronage, O Holy Mother of God!"

REPORT FOR THE WEEK ENDING APRIL 21ST.

The following intentions have been recommended to the prayers of the Confraternity: Recovery of health for 64 persons and 4 families,—change of life for 22 persons and 5 families,—conversion to the Faith for 80 persons and 4 families,—recovery of mind for 3 persons,—special graces for 6 priests, 8 religious, and 8 persons aspiring to the religious state,—temporal favors for 18 persons and 5 families,—spiritual favors for 29 persons and 5 families,—the spiritual and temporal welfare of 6 communities, 5 congregations, and 3 schools. Also 19 particular intentions, and 5 thanksgivings for favors received.

Specified intentions: A blessing on several betrothed couples soon to enter the holy state of marriage,—removal of obstacles to the reconciliation of husband and wife in two families,—reform of several wayward youths,—special protection of several young mothers and their offspring,—favorable decision of a lawsuit for orphan children,—grace for several persons to know their vocation,—a number of persons ruining themselves by intemperance,—success of two claims.

FAVORS OBTAINED.

A devout child of Mary relates two favors which the prayers of the Confraternity are thought to have obtained, namely, the grace of a happy death for a young lady dying with consumption, and who had refused to see a priest; and relief for another lady, afflicted with violent headache. Several cures acknowledge other favors, such as reformation of life, and return to sober and temperate habits, for persons recommended; also the prevention of mixed marriages, the obtaining of situations, etc., etc. The associates are invited to join in thanksgiving. Several cures effected by the water of Lourdes have also been reported to us, of which we give the following particulars: "Last summer," writes a correspondent, "a child next door had a very sore eye. The attending physician told his mother it would not be well for a year. My mother put a few drops of the water of Lourdes on it, and next day it was well. Two or three weeks before, this little boy's mother was very ill with neuralgia, and was not able to raise her head. I gave her some of the Lourdes water, and to the great joy and surprise of all her family, she was able to attend to her household affairs next morning, entirely well."

OBITUARY.

The following deceased persons are recommended to the prayers of the Confraternity: SISTER MARY ALPHONSA (Werning), a member of the Visitation Order at Frederick, Md., who departed for heaven on the 16th ult. Mr. EDWARD SUMMERS, a resident of St. Joseph's County, Ind., whose sudden death occurred on the 21st ult. The deceased was for many years a worthy member of the parish of Notre Dame. Mr. JAMES REYNOLDS, of New Orleans, La., who slept in the Lord on the 22d of March, consoled by the sacred rites of the Church. Mr. DENNIS GREENEY, who died suddenly on the 9th of February. Miss —— STEWART, deceased at Chester, Pa., on the 18th of January. Mr. PATRICK MOLLOY, of Syracuse, New York, who departed this life on the 9th ult. Mr. PATRICK MOORE, a native of Newry, Co. Down, Ireland, whose peaceful death took place on Easter Sunday, at his residence in Chicago. Mr. ROGER PERRY, of New Brunswick, N. J., and Mr. DENNIS SULLIVAN, of Altoona, Pa., whose deaths are of recent occurrence. JOHN, CHARLES and MATILDA BREWER; MALVINA DUGAN LAMBERT and AGNES KREISCH, all of Carroll, Iowa, deceased some time ago. And others whose names have not been given.

Requiescant in pace.

A. GRANGER, C. S. C., Director.

For the Rebuilding of Notre Dame.

Mr. John Canon, $1; Daniel Vaughan, $5; Henry Baker, 50 cts.; Mrs. P. Bartley, $1; Mrs. Mary Lester, $1; Hannah Lyons, $1; Miss Mary Miller, $5; A Friend, $1; Mr. John Cavanagh, $1; P. H. Spelliasy, $1; Daniel Egan, $1; James Egan, $1; A Friend, $1; L. C. McIntyre, $1; Mrs. E. Kendrick, $2.50; Mrs. Isa. O'Reilly, $1; Mrs. Ellen Nolan, $1; Johnnie, Mamie and Jimmey Sullivan, $1.50; Annie Rollman, $1; Philip McMullen, $1; Mary Doherty, $1; Martin Casey, $1; John Bradley, $2; Mary Cunningham; 50 cts.; Dennis Brophy, $1; Edward Devlin, $1; Antoine Draro, 15; George Swartz, $1; Mrs. Reach, $1; Wm. F. Duggan, $1; Mrs. M. E. Foley, 50 cts.

Youth's Department.

To Our Mother.

GLORIOUS MOTHER, from high Heaven,
  Down upon thy children gaze,
Gathered in thine own loved season,
  Thee to bless and thee to praise.

See, sweet Mary, on thy altars,
  Bloom the fairest buds of May;
Oh! may we, earth's sons and daughters,
  Grow by grace as pure as they.

To Our Young Folks.

WE ask all our young folks to read the letter of a good missionary priest, in reference to the famine in Ireland, which may be found a few pages back. It is entitled "The Distress in Ireland—A Touching Appeal." We have a suggestion to make to all our young readers far and wide in regard to it. It is to try and contribute to the relief of the afflicted children of Ireland, who are suffering greatly for want of food and clothing. So great is their need that they are unable to attend school, or even to go to holy Mass. Unless more aid is sent to them soon, they will die in their wretched hovels. Here is a chance to do a good work, and we may be sure that Our Lady, St. Joseph, and St. John, whose wonderful apparitions in Ireland are attested by so many miracles, will not let it go unrewarded. Few, perhaps, will be able to contribute a large sum, but a little from each one will amount to a great deal. Let each boy and girl act as a collector among their young friends, relatives and acquaintances, and raise all the money they can. It should be sent with the names of the donors, which we will publish in THE AVE MARIA week by week. In places where no general collection can be made, let each one send his own gift with the name. The smallest sums will be gratefully received and acknowledged. Money in large sums should be sent by post-office order.

This is the month dedicated to our Blessed Mother, and we know that every young reader of her magazine is desirous to do something in her honor. What could be more acceptable to her—tender Mother that she is—than to succor her afflicted children in Ireland?

Those who deny themselves something in order to contribute to this worthy object, may be sure of a special blessing.

One contribution has been received already, and it is a good beginning.

John J. Ash, $1.

Barbara's Lesson.

(CONCLUSION.)

THE early spring flowers were peeping up from their winter beds when Barbara next crossed the threshold of her cottage. How strange everything seems to the convalescent, going forth the first time after a long illness! It is like a new gift of life. Barbara's sickness had been a prostration from which it was often feared she could not recover, so exhausted had her constitution been from toil, anxiety, and want of sufficient food. During the long, dreary weeks, when, suffering but little pain, yet too weak to lift a cup of broth to her lips unaided, she had been forced to remain inactive, her mind was active and her soul learned much spiritual wisdom. The failure of the work from which she had hoped so much, strengthened while it humbled her. She had built so many castles in the air while laboring day after day on that rejected veil. A hundred times she had handled, in imagination, the large sum she had made sure of receiving for it, considered over and over how judiciously it could be economized so as to last through the entire "bad season"; and, after all, what had skilful work, and anxious planning, and wise resolves done for the little family in whom all her love and care centred? Only added to their distress the burden of her illness.

So it was a wiser Barbara that now stood at the cottage door, receiving draughts of fresh life from the pure, cool air, so welcome after months of confinement to a sick-bed. She watched her husband at work in the garden, which, in past spring-times, had been her care and pride; she smiled at the two little toddlers who were kept busy running to and fro, by their eager desire to be at once with father in the beds and with mother at the door, and withal she was strangely calm and peaceful, free alike from curiosity as to how they had lived through the unprovided winter, and from wonder what was to be done for a living now.

It was in this tranquil frame of mind, resting in her Heavenly Father's arms as free from care as one of her children would be in hers, that a vision seemed to open to her of what she was to accomplish. Was it an inspiration of genius, or a light from heaven? It matters not. All beauty, all taste and skill, whether in designing or executing, come from God.

Barbara turned to re-enter the house. Her watchful husband was beside her in a moment, ready to support the fragile form to the bedroom. But she was not exhausted, as he had feared; her step was steady though slow, and her eyes as she looked up, struck him as full of some new-born hope and conscious power. She allowed him to lead her in, but instead of resting she prostrated herself before the crucifix, saying in a soft tone, "Praised be Jesus Christ!" Her husband devoutly responded, "Forever and ever!" then quietly retired, feeling that she wished to be alone with God.

As they sat at supper that night, Barbara said: "I shall want you to be very busy for me to-morrow, dear husband. I shall need a dozen of nice, round sticks, perfectly smooth, and not thicker nor longer than your middle finger."

"Certainly; you shall have them early in the day, my wife," replied Christopher.

In the morning, when he brought her the sticks, neatly fashioned, he saw that she also had been busy; she had made a small, round cushion, covered with green serge, and stuffed very tight and hard with hay. Taking the little sticks with a grave smile of thanks, she disappeared into the bedroom, while her husband and children betook themselves to the garden. All the week most of her time was spent there in solitude. Christopher asked not for information, she volunteered none; but on the fifth evening, when he came in to supper, she threw herself into his arms, exclaiming:

"Christopher, beloved, thank God with me! See what He has enabled me to do." And she showed him a piece of lace or net, which she had woven on the cushion by means of his little sticks.

Christopher looked at it wonderingly, but as his wife smilingly remarked, to know its value he must wait till it was embroidered. When this had been done, in Barbara's best style, she held it up for his awe-struck admiration. The simple-minded young pair had but one thought; their good Father in heaven had taught her how to make point-lace as exquisite as the manufactured article, which was so costly that only queens could afford it. Her success meant far more than food for the little family. It was the opening of a mine more valuable than that in which the whole village had been so deeply interested. It created an industry, as we would say in these days, promising employment to whole communities. It originated the lace which was to become the widely-sought article afterwards known as *cushion* or *bone-lace*, so-called from the implements used in its manufacture, for the crude wooden sticks were soon superseded by bone-pins. The process has been thus briefly described:

"The lace-maker sits on a stool, and takes a hard cushion on her lap. She lays on the cushion a piece of thick paper on which the pattern has been drawn, and inserts the pins through the paper into the cushion, in places shown by the pattern. Several bobbins are also requisite, on which thread is wound, fine thread being used for forming the meshes or net, and a coarser kind, called gimp, for working the design. The work is begun on the upper part of the cushion, by tying the threads together in pairs, each pair being attached to one of the pins thrust into the cushion. The threads are then twisted one round another in various ways, according to the pattern, the bobbins serving for handles, as well as for holding the material, and the pins serving as knots or fixed points, around which, as around so many centres, the threads may be twisted. The pins inserted in the cushion at the commencement are merely to hold the threads, but as each little mesh is made in process of the working, other pins are inserted to prevent the threads untwisting, and the device on the paper shows where these insertions are to occur."

Such was the invention of Barbara Uttman. It was soon spoken of throughout the world as the most wonderful invention of the age. All the rich dames of the neighborhood were eager to possess some of her rich laces, and as these in turn spread its fame where they went, she was ere long unable to fill the orders, although she had taken all the poor girls of the district into her employ.

The Uttmans, therefore, removed to Dresden, where the husband became a wholesale exporter of the valuable fabric for which his wife was receiving orders not only from the churches and castles of neighboring lands, but from business houses in every part of the globe. But her true heart still clung to the poor village in which God had favored her, and her own hands always worked on laces to be sent thither; for though she had a small branch establishment there, some would order directly from herself. She lived to a good old age, and it is recorded that sixty-four of her descendants were present at her peaceful death.

The Boyhood of Sir Thomas Lawrence.

SIR THOMAS LAWRENCE was born May, 1769, at Bristol, England, and was the youngest of sixteen children. When Lawrence was four years old, he could read the story of Joseph and his brothers with considerable effect. His skill in copying and drawing portraits, even at this age, was so great, that his delighted father, who was an innkeeper, never failed to bring him to the notice of his guests.

When he was six years old, Lord and Lady Kenyon arrived one day at the inn. The host begged permission to introduce to them his little son, whereupon Thomas rushed in, and commenced a lively canter round the room, much to the surprise of the weary travellers. However, they soon became interested in the boy, when they discovered his precocious talents.

"Could you take the portrait of that gentleman?" asked Lady Kenyon, pointing to her husband.

"That I can," answered the boy artist, as he hastened to obtain the materials for his work. In half an hour he finished a portrait, which greatly astonished them, after which he took that of the lady with such success that it was recognized twenty-five years afterwards as her likeness. By such means his talents for recitation and skill in drawing became widely known.

In 1799, Mr. Lawrence and his family removed to Weymouth, and so great was the fame of his son by this time, that in passing through Oxford, he was stopped and beset with applications for portraits. His sitters were eminent men, and his productions were considered marvellous for one so young and uninstructed.

Barrington thus writes of him (in Feb., 1780): "This boy is now nearly ten years and a-half old; but at the age of nine, without instruction from anyone, he is capable of copying historical pictures in a masterly style, and has succeeded in compositions of his own, particularly that of 'Peter denying Christ.' In about seven minutes, he scarcely ever failed of drawing a strong likeness of any person present."

Lawrence worked diligently and regularly, and completed three crayon portraits a week. His plan was to see four sitters a day, to draw half an hour from each, and as long from memory after their departure. At thirteen, Lawrence had become one of the most popular portrait painters in the kingdom; and in his seventeenth year he began to paint in oils. He succeeded in obtaining an interview with Sir Joshua Reynolds, and showed him one of his portraits in oil. Sir Joshua examined the picture with care, and then, turning to the excited boy, said: "Well, now, I suppose you think this very fine, and this coloring very natural." Then Sir Joshua proceeded to speak so kindly, and counsel him so well, that the crestfallen boy was soon reassured, and took his departure with a grateful heart.

Lawrence's progress was now rapid. His graceful manners and pleasing person added greatly to his success. Going to Rome in 1819, he painted a portrait of the Pope, and finished that of Canova. In 1830 he died, just after having been made a Knight of the Legion of Honor.
—*The Young Catholic.*

The Young Prussian.

Frederick, King of Prussia, one day rang his bell, and no one answering, he opened the door, and found his page fast asleep in his elbow-chair. He advanced toward, and was about to awaken him, when he perceived a letter hanging out of his pocket. Curiosity prompted him to know what it was; he took it out and read it. It was a letter from the young man's mother, in which she thanked him for having sent her part of his money to relieve her misery, and telling him that God would reward him for his filial affection. The king, after reading it, went back softly to his chamber, took out a purse full of ducats and slipped it with the letter into the page's pocket. Returning to his chamber, he rung the bell so loudly that it awoke the page, who instantly made his appearance.

"You have had a sound sleep," said the king.

The page was at a loss how to excuse himself, and putting his hand into his pocket by chance, to his utter astonishment he found there a purse of ducats. He took it out, turned pale, and looking at the king, shed a torrent of tears without being able to utter a word.

"What is that," said the king; "what is the matter?"

"Ah! sire," said the young man, throwing himself on his knees, "some one seeks my ruin! I know nothing of this money which I have just found in my pocket."

"My young friend," said Frederick, "God often does great things for us even in our sleep. Send that to your mother; salute her on my part, and assure her I will take care of both her and you."

GOOD always comes out of every evil which God permits on the face of the earth.—*Faber.*

THE
AVE MARIA.

A Journal devoted to the Honor of the Blessed Virgin.

HENCEFORTH ALL GENERATIONS SHALL CALL ME BLESSED.—St. Luke, i, 48.

VOL. XVI.　　　NOTRE DAME, INDIANA, MAY 8, 1880.　　　NO. 19.

[For the "Ave Maria."]

"Abide with Me."

BY ELIOT RYDER.

AT the dawn and close of day,
Silently kneel down and pray:
Thorny is the path of life,
Filled with conflict and with strife;
Mortal man may not control
All the doubts which vex the soul:
Therefore should we pray to Thee—
"Christ, my God, abide with me."

Hours we know of sternest grief,
And in tears we seek relief,
And in agony we cry,
"Why, oh Blessed Lord? oh, why?"
But our grief shall disappear,
And Thy love shall be made clear,
If we bare our hearts to Thee—
"Christ, my God, abide with me."

Blessed talisman of hope,
While in error's night we grope;
Flashing like a spring of light,
Making all around us bright.
Thou canst heal the broken heart,
Thou canst soothe the sinner's smart,
Thou canst make the tempter flee—
"Christ, my God, abide with me."

Oh, Christ, my God! by Thy cross,
Give me strength to bear life's loss.
By Thy earthly life of pain,
Let me live for heavenly gain.
Let me, through the passing years,
Nearer come to heavenly spheres,—
Nearer come to heaven and Thee—
"Christ, my God, abide with me."

Masonry and the Freemasons.

WE must not be satisfied with the assurance given by the Masons that they meddle neither with politics nor religion; that they are true subjects, and permit everyone to be happy in his own way. Such assertions are found in the newspapers and writings which are prepared for the public at large. But it is in a very different strain from this that the "Brothers" express themselves in their lodges when they believe themselves secure from the "Profane" (non-freemasons). Very different also is the utterance of the "Brothers" in those masonic writings and newspapers which are prepared solely for "manifestation to their own members," and are circulated only among the initiated Freemasons. That the Lodge-Brothers may not reproach us with speaking of the "craft" as "the blind might discourse of colors," we will bring forward some passages from the secret writings of the order, and thus offer to our readers the opportunity of judging for themselves concerning the secret bond. Many discourses held in lodges have been already printed, and although the Freemasons endeavor to hide their secrets from the public eye, yet the editor of the *Freemasons' Zeitung* is obliged to confess, that, "partly by persons of frivolous character, but partly also from really treacherous Brothers (so-called), 'the ultramontanes' are constantly informed of everything that transpires among us."

The number of Freemasons, according to their own report, now reaches to "many hundred thousands, and with the non-active members, even to millions." Freemasonry is divided into many grades, and upon a candidate's being received into each separate grade, peculiar ceremonies are observed, of which we shall mention only one, that is but little known.

In a lodge in Sweden a crystal flask is kept, which contains what they call the "Blood of Christ." It is a fluid which consists partly of red wine, and partly of the blood of the Brother last received into the order. At the reception of anyone into a higher grade, a cup half filled with red wine is brought forward. Then the grand master says to the candidate for admission: "Slit open the thumb of your right hand with this pair of compasses, and let your blood flow into this cup." This done, the grand master pours 9 times 9, that is, 81 drops out of the flask into the same cup. The candidate then drinks from the cup, and the flask is refilled with the remainder. Thus he drinks his own blood mixed with the blood of the brother last received. In No. 15 of the *Bauhutte* (Tabernacle) of the year 1877, a Freemason bears testimony that this ceremony is still in use in Stockholm and Berlin; even in our own country, the same monstrosity is said to have taken place. The most revolting feature of the whole affair, is the profanation of the oath, which is repeated at every entrance into a higher grade, in which the Brother is informed that he has hitherto lived as one uninitiated, in delusion regarding the order. On this subject, the Freemason Mosdorf says: "Care must be taken that this trifling with our fellow-men within closed doors, this tampering with the oath and the word of an honorable man, is not at length denounced to the public."

Our Divine Saviour says, "By their fruits you shall know them." The Order of Freemasons has been so long in existence, that we may well ask what have been its works. From these we shall be better able to determine what is the ultimate object of the order, than by listening to the specious phrases concerning its aims, which are gotten up for the uninitiated Brothers and for the general public.

First of all, how does it stand with the so-often praised "brotherly" beneficence? The Lodge-Brothers, for the most part, belong to what are called the better classes, or they could not pay the high admission fees demanded of them. In the lodges, collections for the poor are also taken up, but the amount of these collections must be pitiful indeed. The treasurer repeatedly complains of the inefficacy of his petitions, when he calls upon the benevolence of the Freemasons to come to the aid of the necessitous.

In the year 1877, an extraordinary state of distress afflicted the industrial districts of Saxony. Thousands were entirely without bread. Some fathers of families received only one mark for a week's wages. A relief committee was formed, in which Brother Findel was very active. He wrote to 60 brother-masons, requesting their assistance in promoting the good work. In the *Bauhutte* (Tabernacle), in 1877, No. 24, he communicates the following result of this application: "Of these 60 brothers, one promised help; two declined to contribute in a friendly manner; the others sent no answer at all." In the annual assembly of the "Union of German Freemasons" of the 9th and 10th of September, 1876, it was acknowledged: "Too little comes in; in many lodges the amount of the collection for the poor is very miserable; the brothers who do not frequent the lodges contribute nothing." The beneficence of the Freemasons is not, then it would seem, so great as they would have the world believe it to be.

Nor can beneficence and humanity be the ultimate aim of the Freemasons. For in the furtherance of these, no secret bond is necessary; nor is there any need of holding assemblies within closed doors, still less of taking a frightful oath, or for making any mystery at all.

In all their writings, intended for those who are not Freemasons, the masonic editors constantly assert that Freemasonry is in no way connected with politics or religion; that the lodges do not occupy themselves with any matter bearing on either of these. We will let our readers judge, by some quite recent examples, of the truth of this oft-repeated assertion.

On the occasion of the German war with the French nation, the lodges were in full activity, though not all acting in the same direction. On the 3d of September, 1870, that is, on the second day after the battle of Sedan, the delegates of the united Freemasons' Lodges of Switzerland assembled at Lausanne, and unanimously passed a resolution for a *manifesto* of peace, which the grand lodge 'Alpina' publicly announced. In doing this, it was declared, among other things: "Weak as our voice may be, we protest in the name of humanity against war in general, and against this war in particular. . . . . . against the proceedings by which Governments maintain the power which enables them to dispose of the fate of their subjects, and the peace of all Europe. We demand the imperishable and inalienable rights back again: the right of progress, the right of liberty; relying on the fundamental conditions of all progressive civilization, we pity the people who at the present moment misunderstand them, violate their principles—nay, tread them under foot."

Naturally, such a *manifesto* in the situation that the German lodges actually found themselves in at that time, could not be assented to, and a counter-protest was issued; but we doubt not that the Swiss grand lodges placed their document in the hands of every brother of their lodge who was under arms in that warfare.

When on the 4th of September, 1870, the Gambetta rule began, a rule which was in fact simply that of the Red Lodge, the Italian brothers soon showed their attachment to the French. Brother Garibaldi and his free-troopers fought against the Germans, and even Frappoli, grandmaster of the Italian Great Orient, betook himself to France, in order, as the Freemason sheet, the *Revista* confesses, "to exert himself for the defence of the weaker party."

At the time of the Paris Commune, an uproar took place in every lodge of the grand Orient of France, on which the representatives of 120 masonic lodges proclaimed the inseparable union of the Commune with Freemasonry. Ten thousand Freemasons shouted out, "Long live the Commune! Long live Freemasonry! Long live the Universal Republic!" When the warring powers were deliberating on the conditions of peace, the Orient of Brussels declared that the union of Alsace and Lothringen with their original mother country was a wrong, and stated that it believed itself obliged to support the spontaneous action of the people, while it admonished the Freemasons to work in this spirit.

With regard to the seizure of Rome (20th of September, 1870,) the *Journal de Florence* said: "After the battle of Sedan, our (Italian) Minister still continued undecided as to whether he should seize Rome or not, until a deputation of Freemasons appeared before Minister Lanza with a small strip of paper, on which stood in very laconic words: "If the Government does not order an advance on Rome without delay, a revolution will break out in every city of Italy." Lanza read the paper; and seeing that the signatures consisted solely of the chiefs of lodges, immediately issued orders to General Cadorna to march. The document was made public as well as the names of the signers. It is only necessary to take up the Italian Freemasons' Almanac to come upon those names. We could, moreover, bring forward a whole host of facts to prove that the Freemasons, in spite of their assertions to the contrary, *do* mix themselves up with politics in their lodges. The Freemason journal *Bauhutte* (1874, No 20) speaks thus: "The discussion of religious and political questions is already become customary in Belgium and Italy; and on this account, we have for many years broken off all union with the grand lodges of the former. The latest information, however, places the matter in a different light from that in which it formerly appeared, as a continual warfare exists in that place between the ultramontane and the liberal party, and it is carried on in such a manner that the latter have no resource but to take refuge in their lodges, where they find spiritual support." From this we see that now and then the brothers are right honest. Liberalism, in its warfare with ultramontanism, finds spiritual support in Freemasonry. The political activity among the brothers is, as far as possible, kept secret; but it is otherwise nowadays with religious questions. In regard to this, many Freemasons declare openly for which principles of religion or non-religion Freemasonry is working, and to what goal it tends. This but brings out in greater, relief the audacity, with which, in writings and sheets intended for the public, the lodge brothers still deny that religious questions are treated of in their secret assemblies. In our days socialist democrats have with bold front dared to blaspheme God, and to boast of their unbelief, and Protestant preachers have ventured openly to deny the Divinity of Jesus Christ; so now the Freemasons take courage to creep forth from their concealment, and acknowledge their true colors by proclaiming their unbelief to the world.

We do not mean to assert that all Freemasons are unbelievers; but it is somewhat significant that Brother Maier, Professor at the Real-Gymnazium at Stuttgard, in a masonic periodical dares to assert: "We (Freemasons) are atheists, which means, we do not believe in a personal, self-conscious God." It is to be understood of itself, that such deniers of God offer a favorable opportunity in their masonic sheets for making war against God, and against all positive religion, with the sharpest weapons they have, and for this purpose they bring their (so-named) wisdom to the front. Yes, they do not even shrink from declaring that it is the appointed task of Freemasonry, not only to promulgate the doctrines of unbelief among the brothers of the lodge, but also to tear belief out of the hearts of the people.

In the annual assembly of the Union of German Masons on the 4th and 5th of July, 1874, a resolution was passed, to have essays, poems, and novels, of masonic tendencey, published in the periodicals *Gartenlaube* or *Daheim* purposely for ladies to read. All who do not look on the Catholic Church as the work of God Himself, believe it to be possible to destroy it in spite of its having stood eighteen hundred years. "Ecrases l'infame," that is, "crush the Church," once said the godless Frenchman, Voltaire, who was himself a brother of the lodge. And to destroy the Catholic Church is the object Freemasonry proposes to itself. It is right to state that Freemasonry in the United States is very different from Freemasonry in Europe.

In opposition to the Vatican Council of 1870, counter-councils were held in Italy in secret understanding with all lodges of the world, in order "to set bounds to the over-weening pretensions of Rome." Everyone knows how, either through ignorance or malice, the dogma of Infallibility was misrepresented particularly by the press, and held up to derision. In this respect the secret periodical sheets and publications of the Freemasons everywhere, differed in nothing from the liberal and Protestant newspapers. For instance, the Freemason, Dr. Eimer, in a discourse he delivered in the lodge at Würzburg, called the doctrine of Infallibility a "self-deification." The power of Freemasonry is also shown in the so-called *Prussian Culture-Conflict* (*Culturkampf*). When at the beginning of the struggle, the Protestant unions and a handful of Old Catholics exerted themselves to drive out the Jesuits, many Catholics smiled at it as at an undertaking deemed impossible, but they overlooked the fact that the lodges were working with them.

In the year 1871, a universal hunting down of the Jesuits was prescribed. On the 8th of October of that year, Brother Bluntschli visited his "trusty men" to procure the circulation of a libellous paper, whose purport was to excite a spirit of animosity "against the Jesuits," and drive them out of the country. For this purpose, Brother Findel in the *Bauhutte* exhorts his German brother-Freemasons not only to sign the petitions for driving out the Jesuits themselves, but to obtain as many other signatures as they could.

The Brothers have attained their end, and even more. Those who doubt as to whom we are principally indebted for the culture-conflict (*culturkampf*), should read the following passage taken from the *Rhine Herold*, which was also copied by the *Bauhutte*: "Our object is to point out the 'Last Judgment' passed upon them (the Ultramontanes) by the world. The 'Last Judgment' in which the spirit of Freemasonry sat as judge. They were not mistaken, those vassals of the night, when they awaited so anxiously the opening of the Imperial German Diet, (*Reichstages*) croaking like ravens, and hovering around their nests, looking into the future. They recognized their enemy truly enough when in their daily papers they began to libel the Freemasons and their disciples."

The Freemasons comport themselves as if they were the masters of the world. If the Pope holds a council with his Bishops, the Brothers "in the name of humanity" enter the lists against him. Should two nations be at war, the Freemasons cry "Halt!" when it seems good to them to do so; should no result follow their *dictum*, they summon the princes before their judgment seat, as was the case in 1870 with King William and the crown Prince of Prussia. The forming of public opinion, which is principally effected through the press, is one of the means for attaining the aim of the Freemasons. The same was used in the *Culturkampf*, as Brother Bluntschli will testify for us. It was with the threat of "public opinion" that the Swiss lodges armed themselves, when they desired King William to put an end to the war against France, (*Vgl. Freemasons' Newspaper* No. 39, 1870,) and yet the Brothers complain of horrible calumnies, when from the lodge publications, which the Order, not without reason, orders to be kept secret, we point out what dangers threaten Church and State from this secret band.

The total number of Freemasons in the beginning of the year 1879 amounted to over five millions.

'Beth's Promise.

BY MRS. ANNA HANSON DORSEY.

CHAPTER XIV—(Continued).

WHEN they got back to "Ellerslie," 'Beth went in gaily, determined to put the very brightest face she could on the adventure of the morning, yet feeling a little timid as to its effect on her mother, whom she found with Aunt 'Beth in the lovely summer sitting-room—the windows of which opened to the floor, giving beautiful glimpses of lawn and trees—where they were talking quietly, and sewing for Aunt 'Beth's "dorcas-basket," as she called it, from which a store of warm garments, accumulated during the summer months, were distributed among her needy pensioners when the first frosts came. The air, of the large pleasant room, was perfumed with sweet odors from the flower-beds without; and now 'Beth's laughing, blooming face, her eyes sparkling with the excitement of her adventure, as she came in swinging her big straw-hat in her hand, while her sunny nut-brown hair, broken away from her comb and hanging around her in loose curling tresses, was like a sudden brightness. Both looked up with welcoming smiles, and dropping on the floor before them, she exclaimed, "Oh, mamma, oh Aunt 'Beth, such a lovely time!"

"I was afraid Peg had kept on to Geneva with you, you have been gone so long," said Aunt 'Beth, resting her little hands on her lap, and looking with fond eyes into the bright, happy ones uplifted to hers.

"Aunt 'Beth, Peg deserves golden shoes! and as to Lodo, she's the champion screamer of the United States, and must have a silver trumpet!"

"'Beth dear, how extravagantly you are running on," said Mrs. Morley, smoothing back 'Beth's rebellious curls.

"You won't think so, my darling mamma, when you hear all that has happened since you saw me last." Then, her face dimpled with smiles, she told them of her adventure from beginning to end. Mrs. Morley's face grew a shade paler as she listened, and she took 'Beth's hand, holding it folded in both her own, as if to assure herself that she was indeed safe; but Aunt 'Beth was highly interested, and laughed quite heartily once or twice, especially when the young man appeared on the scene, interrupting the girl to ask, "And what did he say?" and "What did you say?" and when she answered: "I told him I was afraid he was very wet," Aunt 'Beth laughed, and Mrs. Morley also laughed for the first time.

"Very well; since you are so fond of boats, my dear, you shall have one with oars. I have friends in Geneva who will manage it for me. But, 'Beth, your desperate intention to swim ashore frightens me a little, and I am very thankful it was stopped in time to save you from drowning."

"She used to be a splendid swimmer; I think she could have made the distance without difficulty; but I hope there'll be no need to attempt any such risks in the future. But, dear, you have not yet told us the name of the gentleman who came so opportunely to your assistance," said Mrs. Morley.

"I don't know it; he didn't tell his name, nor I mine."

"Well," said Aunt 'Beth, "such primitive simplicity is refreshing. The man must be thanked; you should have thought of that, my dear, for he certainly did you a great service, and saved your mother and me no end of a shock."

"Oh it was so embarrassing, Aunt 'Beth—you can't think—without asking his name. But I gave him some lunch, which he seemed very glad to get, and a bottle of claret too."

"I am glad you gave him something to eat; he must have needed it after his wetting. I wish I could find out who he is, to thank him. I have a sort of presentiment that we haven't heard the last of him. I'll see about the boat, though;—water, I remember, is your favorite element."

"Don't, Aunt 'Beth, please," said Mrs. Morley. "Nonsense, Anne; won't it be better for her to have a boat of her own with oars, than to take some other body's and go drifting off to Jericho in it? There won't always be a man at hand to swim out and tow her in. Besides, she can teach Lodo how to row."

"Aunt 'Beth, Lodo is as much afraid of the water as a cat. I believe she would have a fit if she should be put into a boat," said 'Beth, laughing; "but I can row you and mamma all over the lake."

"We'll see about that," remarked Aunt 'Beth, pulling her little pink ear. "As you can swim, I will not order life-preservers with the boat." The dear old lady was quite agreeably stirred up, and her thoughts turned into a new channel, which cheered and revived her wonderfully.

'Beth was secretely enchanted at the idea of having a boat, but did not say much, as she feared her mother did not quite wish it, and having nothing more to relate, she ran up to her room to change her dress for something lighter, and devote the hour or two before dinner to reading.

Aunt 'Beth put down her work, and going to the house-keeper's room, directed Mrs. Trott to select several fine cauliflowers and send them with her compliments, to Mrs. Dulaney, who had mentioned that, owing to the negligence of the gardener, they had none at "Tracy-Holme."

"Didn't you know that they had all gone to Geneva, Miss Morley? Mr. Dulaney is in New York, and even the priest's gone somewhere. There isn't a soul at home; the dairy-maid was here this morning to borrow that butter-print with the bird cut on it, and she told me," said Mrs. Trott. "She says they're all coming back Saturday, and that there's going to be a double wedding in the family before long, between the two sons and those pretty Marston girls that the old people are so fond of."

"My dear woman," said Aunt 'Beth, "don't gossip with our neighbors' people about their family affairs; I object to it."

"Laws, Miss Morley, I didn't ask her a question! I didn't know nothing about 'em to ask; she just told all she knew without taking breath, while I was getting the butter-print for her, and I wouldn't have thought of it again if you hadn't told me to send the cauliflowers over there, and so I had to tell you!"

"Send them Saturday then, Mrs. Trott," said Aunt 'Beth, a little diverted at the woman's logic.

"I will indeed, Miss Morley. I like the Dulaneys; they're a good lot; but I think it's a great pity they're papists."

"I suppose you mean Roman Catholics?" said Aunt 'Beth, with a snap of her white, even teeth. "Don't forget that Roman Catholics are Christians, and have a right to worship God under their 'own vine and fig-tree,' as much as you Congregationalists have. And remember what St. Paul says—you read your bible every day, and will recollect—he says, 'there's Faith, Hope and Charity, but the greatest of these is Charity,' and I agree with him."

"Yes, ma'am; St. Paul says a great many things hard to be understood; I don't hold with all he has written," answered Mrs. Trott, as she snapped open another egg on the edge of a pan for the cake she was preparing to make.

"You may think what you please about St. Paul, but when we see people fulfilling the Christian law in their daily life, it is reasonable to suppose that they *are* Christians, and I don't think it is right to call them names as if they were heathen; I never do it," said the positive old lady, with a sparkle in her eyes that Mrs. Trott did not observe, being intent on breaking her eggs with great care lest a speck of the yolk should get mixed with the whites.

"I'm only sorry for them that's in the gall and bitterness of error," she answered, with a sniffle.

"We must take care of one thing, Mrs. Trott, and that is, not to let the beam in our own eye make us think it's in our neighbor's; you have forgotten an egg by my count; there, its all right now. Send Lodo to me," said Aunt 'Beth as she went out.

The next day, after an early dinner, the phaeton was brought round, and 'Beth got ready for a drive with Lodo, who was, of course, to hold the reins. They were to go in a different direction from that of yesterday, up towards the hill country, where the roads for quite a distance were good, and the views picturesque.

"Do be careful, my 'Beth, and don't attempt to drive," said Mrs. Morley, who was waiting to see them off.

"No, mamma, I promise; the danger will all be with the young gypsy this time. I shouldn't be surprised if she'd drive me away to some far-off haunt in the woods to see her friends, the 'good-people,' and never bring me back," said 'Beth, with a merry laugh.

"Take care of yourselves, Lodo!" said Mrs. Morley, smiling at 'Beth's light-hearted nonsense.

"Yes, mem, I will surely. Now Peg!" then with a chirrup, Lodo gave the reins a slight shake, and they were off, down the old avenue, out upon the smooth, shaded road, winding through a beautifully wooded stretch of country, past snug farm houses, cultivated fields, and elegant summer homes embowered in trees, until they began to ascend more elevated ground, where the road was steep and narrow. There seemed to be very little travel over it; they met one or two ight country wagons, and now and then groups of rough-looking men, surly-looking fellows, begrimed with coal-dust, skulking along the roadside, who stared at the gay little phaeton and ts pretty occupants with lowering eyes, as it swept past them. 'Beth felt a little timid, and proposed turning back; but Lodo, accustomed to seeing laborers from the iron-works, assured her there was no reason for alarm, explained who the men were, and said what a pity it would be to spoil their drive, but was quite willing to do just as Miss 'Beth said; but "Miss 'Beth," half ashamed of her cowardice, said she might drive on, which the girl did very gladly, until they came to a point which commanded a distant view of the lake, and the gray ivy-draped towers of "Ellerslie," the place where, years before, 'Beth's father turned to look at his old home, which he was never to see again. Lodo drew up under a tree, that 'Beth might enjoy the beautiful view at her leisure, while she pointed out this thing and that, and told her one or two legends of certain localities of the neighborhood that were marked by blasted trees, or a tall chimney from which the house, ruined by fire and tempest, had dropped away—which were conspicuous features in the landscape. Peg, hearing the voice so dear to his half humanized heart, cropped the rich grass at his feet, lifting his head now and then with a toss to give a whinny of approval to whatever she might be saying; then, as if waiting for the merry laugh that always responded to his performance, he quietly resumed his dainty feast—not that he was in the least hungry, but he dearly loved grass that was sweet and juicy, and being somewhat restricted in the use of his favorite luxury by his English keeper at "Ellerslie," he never lost an opportunity to forage on it when chance led him to it, as now.

Lodo having finished her legends, 'Beth dropped into silence, and sat with folded hands gazing far away into the distance. The sun was sinking westward, and the sky was spread with a royal splendor of fire-lit crimson and long dashes of gold with traceries of purple, and aqua-marine between. The air was filled with chattering swallows revelling in fantastic flights, and going through swift evolutions as if they were executing aerial dances with sunbeam and wind; in the distance, fluttered a procession of crows, going home with full crops from their feeding grounds. How still, how bright, how like a poetic spell all this sunlighted space, with the distant water flashing back the brightness! 'Beth did not speak, her heart was filled with memories that carried her thoughts out of the present, with tender, sacred hopes, into the beyond; it was the effect that such scenes always had upon her. But she was aroused from her musing by an emphatic jerk of Lodo's elbow, and a half frightened whisper: "There's some one coming, mem." 'Beth listened, she heard distinctly the rapid hoof-beats of a horse at full speed, and in another moment the rider had turned a curve in the road; but on seeing the phaeton, he suddenly checked his headlong course. 'Beth saw at a glance that the gentleman was her friend of the lake. He approached, and touching his hat, said in a low, hurried voice: "You had better turn back, ladies, at once; there's a strike at the iron-works, and the men are very turbulent. If you are going in the neighborhood of 'Ellerslie,' I will ask permission to ride along side, for presently the road will be swarming with rough men."

"How very kind! yes, we are going to 'Ellerslie'; I am staying there with my aunt, Miss Morley," said 'Beth, her cheek paling. "If you will be so good, we shall be very thankful to have you accompany us."

"Oh lordy, mem! is it a strike?" murmured Lodo, under her breath. She knew something about strikes, and she touched Peg on his flanks with the delicate riding-whip which she carried more for ornament than use, and he started almost on a run, knowing well enough that when he got a hint like that, it meant *go*.

"I hope I haven't frightened you," said the

gentleman; "but I thought we had no time to lose, and at the risk of appearing officious, I dared not go on and leave you up there alone at such a time. Don't thank me, please," he added with the same laugh in his eyes that 'Beth remembered so well, "for the pleasure is all on my side, you know."

"You have a very opportune way of coming to the rescue of distressed damsels. Perhaps you are a guardian angel with your wings folded away under your coat?" laughed 'Beth.

"Perhaps your guardian angel, or mine, had more to do with it than we know," he replied, laughing. "I am simply human."

"And I was almost scolded when I got home yesterday for not knowing your name; it was the first question mamma and Aunt 'Beth—Miss Morley—asked me, after I told them what had happened at the lake. They wanted to thank you for the rescue."

"Oh, now, it is not pleasant to be thanked; it spoils everything, and makes a fellow feel rather cheap, you know," he answered, flushing up to the roots of his hair.

"You want to be mysterious then, and have us speak of you as the mysterious knight, and think that you drop from the clouds?" said 'Beth, wondering at herself for running on so with a stranger, but she was embarrassed at the *rencontre*, and feeling quite desperate, talked in preference to sitting there in awkward silence.

"You could not think that, seeing how glad I was to get your bread and butter. I was as hungry as a kite, and didn't stop until I had eaten everything," he answered.

"You deserved your lunch I'm sure," said 'Beth; "but I can't face Aunt 'Beth this time without knowing who you are; she'd be apt to think you an evil spirit who gets up occasions to appear, and I should never be allowed to go outside of 'Ellerslie' again."

"She might think me a highway robber with better reason, since I still hold possession of her silver forks and spoons, that you so obligingly left with the cold chicken and things," he replied.

"Oh, mem," said Lodo in a low tone, "ask him if he's got 'em all safe, for I've been so worried about them!" 'Beth laughed, for she saw from the suppressed amusement shown in every line of the stranger's face, that this aside had been overheard, and they were going slowly through a stretch of deep sand, where it required no effort to catch every word that was spoken.

"A fine table napkin too, a china plate, and a cut-glass goblet, all of which I have at home, nicely packed, to be delivered, with thanks, to their owner. But jesting aside: I was only waiting, Miss Morley, to be presented at 'Ellerslie' in due form by my mother, Mrs. Dulaney," he said, raising his hat; "but she is visiting with her young friends in Geneva, and I have been obliged to defer the pleasure of calling to inquire after you. I am Bertie Dulaney, at your service."

"How delightful to think of our being neighbors! but how did you find out my name, Mr. Dulaney?"

"I saw you at Mass yesterday morning, and asked Father Hagner at breakfast who you were."

"I've heard so much about you and your brother that you do not seem at all like a stranger. I'm afraid it would make you both vain to know how often you've been wished for, and impatiently expected; and as we are such near neighbors, we can be good friends, after our odd and accidental acquaintance." All feeling of reserve was gone. 'Beth Morley remembered what she had heard of his being engaged to Elaine Marston; what then was to hinder their being on the best and friendliest of terms? They were out of the sand by this time, and among the stones, over which they rattled noisily, with little jars and jolts that precluded any further conversation, which Bertie Dulaney did not object to, for his mind was so full of the beautiful face that had been smiling into his that he was satisfied just to think, and so he had been occupied ever since he had found 'Beth adrift on the lake.

(TO BE CONTINUED.)

On the Appian Way.

SAN SISTO.

BY ELIZA ALLEN STARR.

(CONCLUSION.)

THE return from St. Sebastian, the Catacombs of St. Calixtus and Pretextatus, when once within the Gate of St. Sebastian, gives us, by a wonderful turn in the road, a charming view of San Sisto. As seen from SS. Nereo, Achilleo and Domitilla, to which it is nearly opposite, there is nothing imposing in its appearance; but seen at this turn of the Appian Way within the Gate of St. Sebastian and the Arch of Drusus, the old monastery recovers its prestige, and becomes fixed in the memory of the traveller as one of the most beautiful objects which has met his eye. The foreground, filled in by the irregular vineyard walls and vines, a middle distance is taken possession of by the tapering spires of the cypress, beyond which rises the elegant open campanile of San Sisto; and below this, the tiled roof and rude walls of the ancient monastery, its surface broken only by the oval windows in its storeys. Beyond all this, stretch the ruined palaces of the Cæsars, with here and there a stone pillar among the desolated arches; while the blue of the Roman sky harmonizes the tints in these several distances so subtly that the whole is a picture in itself, asking nothing from the imagination of the artist. The gate opens upon level grounds, and the scarlet poppies, in June and July, show like flames of fire among the grass. There is no desolation here, and the traditions of the place are as green and living as its thick sward. The first home of St. Dominic and his Dominicans in Rome, under Honorius III, there is an aroma of apostolic fervor in the life of St. Dominic within its walls. Its chapter-room was the scene of three miracles by St. Dominic, so startling, so irresistible in their evidence, that these alone would have entitled him to canonization on the plea of *heroic* sanctity.

The history of this church, which is near the Porta Capena and the Fountain of Egeria, in the midst of classic associations, owes its existence, however, to nothing connected with classic antiquity. Wholly Christian in its origin, it takes us back to the persecution inaugurated under Valerian, during which the Church was adorned with so many precious gems in the persons of her virgin martyrs.

The martyrdom of Stephen I, in the Catacomb of Saint Sebastian, on the second of August, 257, seemed to be a signal for every sort of cruelty and wantonness. Not a day passed without the shedding of that blood which is "the seed of the Church." So fierce was the persecution, so sharp-sighted had paganism become, that it was considered unsafe to send the Sacrament of the Holy Eucharist to the sick, dying or imprisoned, by the hands of priests, or of any one likely to be suspected of being a Christian, lest being seized on the way, the Sacred Host should be exposed to sacrilegious insult. It was on such an errand, in place of some venerable servant of God, that a young acolyte, Tarcisius, was hurrying along the Appian Way on the 15th of August, 257, when he was met and rudely accosted by some youths. "Whither so fast, Tarcisius?" Perhaps it was some exaltation of mind visible in the countenance, some recollection of his mien, which excited their malicious instincts. For when he would have passed them, they said: "Nay, tell us where you are going, and on what errand?" And when, conscious of the celestial Presence which he bore on his bosom in the folds of his mantle, he said, "Hinder me not," they cried: "Ha! ha! so you go on some secret errand! Tell us what it is, and tell us what you are guarding under your mantle, or we will find out for ourselves." For a moment, the blue sky must have become suddenly dark before the eyes of Tarcisius; but in another moment all things were clear to his mind as well as to his eyes. He knew that he could not escape from his young tormentors; but he also "knew in whom he had believed"; and he knew that so long as he kept his secret, God would save his trust from the "dogs, raging to devour." He did not strive, neither did he cry out, but was as silent as his Master before His judges, or "as the sheep before his shearers." This, so far from disarming the youthful mob, only irritated them the more, and they fell upon him with sticks, stones and even cudgels. But nothing could unlock those hands folded over his breast, nothing could break the recollected silence of his tongue. When at last death freed him from his responsibility, the pagans unclasped his hands, and searched his mantle, but found nothing. With the last breath of His martyr, Jesus had passed, unseen, through their midst, as He once escaped the fury of his countrymen, when they led him out to the steep brow of the hill on which their city was built, to cast him down. Those older Christians who had followed Tarcisius, at a distance, to see if any evil befell him, now came up, and found the Sacred Host on his person just as it had been given to him. The body of the martyr was lifted carefully, with the Body of his divine Lord still on his breast, and the relics were afterwards deposited with unusual honors in the cemetery of Calixtus. A century later, Saint Damasus, Pope as well as poet, composed for him one of his most beautiful epitaphs:

"Christ's secret gifts, by good Tarcisius borne,
The mob profanely bade him to display;
He rather gave his own limbs to be torn,
Than Christ celestial to mad dogs betray."*

But amid these horrors, the Church did not falter. Calling together the faithful clergy and laity of Rome amid the gloom of some catacomb not as familiar to the pagans as that of Saint Sebastain, a successor to Saint Peter, as well as to Saint Stephen, was chosen in the person of Xystus, or Sixtus, as it is generally written, and the second Pope of that name. This Sixtus, an Athenian by birth, seems to have possessed all the intellectual tastes of his countrymen. In his youth he was devoted to philosophy. It was while entranced by all the fascinations of Athenian subtleties, that a ray of divine light fell upon the pages of Plato and of Aristotle. It was as if the natural truth, the truth attainable by reason, had led him on step by step, through the candor of a soul devoted to truth, until he was prepared to understand the beauty of the supreme and everlasting truth, as revealed by Christ Jesus, and taught by His Church. No sooner had this light broken in upon his mind, than the skies of Greece and its clear air lost their charms for Sixtus, as well as the porticos of the philosophers, where men walked only to

---

* Tarcisium sanctum Christi Sacramenta gerentem,
Cum male sana manus petiret vulgare profanis;
Ipse animam potius voluit dimittere caesus
Prodere quam canibus rabidis coelestia membra.

speak of things pertaining to the soul. The boasted wisdom of these philosophers was now only a twilight compared with the dazzling splendors of the wisdom of God's saints; and he turned from it, without regret, to seek in Rome, at the feet of its persecuted Pontiffs, the knowledge withheld, so often, from the wise and prudent, to be revealed to little ones. In Rome, among men familiar with those interior graces peculiar to the Christians, Sixtus became renowned for his prudence, his sanctity, and for his profound knowledge of everything connected with ecclesiastical discipline. Pope Stephen had chosen him for his Archdeacon, and had confided to him the government of the Church during his own imprisonment in a former persecution. His courage and steadfastness, therefore, had been thoroughly tested. For two years this faithful Pontiff had lent himself to every need of the suffering flock committed to his hand, when a fresh order of Valerian was sent forth, that everywhere, the Bishops, priests, ministers of every grade, should be especially sought out and subjected to tortures even unto death, unless they submitted to the religion of the empire. They were also forbidden to hold any assemblies in their cemeteries. This prohibition was one of the new features in Valerian's persecution. The laws of Rome respected the tombs of the dead to such a degree that even those who had received capital punishment could receive honorable burial—as was permitted to the martyrs—whatever might have been the torments or indignities inflicted upon them, as Christians, while living. It remained for later centuries, nearer our own times, to violate the tombs of the saints and to scatter their ashes to the winds. But not only were Christians allowed to deposit their dead in peace: they were allowed to visit their tombs and to hold in them reunions, which were supposed, or taken for granted, to be similar to reunions held among the pagans in their family tombs. These reunions, as we know, were religious as well as social; but they had been respected by the emperors before Valerian, and thus a refuge had been left open to the persecuted Christians. This was now to be cut off, if possible; and all religious meetings, in any place whatsoever, were forbidden by the emperor. The 6th of August, however, had been appointed by Sixtus as a day of assembly for the Christians, and the place appointed was the cemetery of Pretextatus, where Mass was to be celebrated; this cemetery being one less likely to be watched than that of Saint Calixtus. By some treason or by some misfortune, the assembly was discovered, and Sixtus was arrested by pagan soldiers while preaching to the faithful assembled around him. Conducted to Rome, he was accused of having violated the law. Sixtus replied that he had spared no pains to establish the worship of the true God, and to destroy the superstitious worship offered to idols, declaring that he would die, willingly, in such a cause. There is a tradition that Sixtus was led to the great temple of Mars, and there commanded to sacrifice; and that when he refused, the vast temple shook to its foundations, and a part of the walls and pillars fell in. It is certain, however, that Sixtus was judged worthy of death, and his sentence was to be carried out on the very spot where he had offended the majesty of the law. Thus on the very same day, he was led back along the Appian Way, followed by the two deacons who had assisted his Mass, Felicissimus and Agapitus. On the way to martyrdom, Sixtus was met by his archdeacon, Lawrence. We must suppose him to have been specially dear, since to him had been committed the dispensing of the treasures of the Church among the poor; but evidently he was not one of those discovered in the cemetery that morning. Meeting his venerated Pontiff bound and led as a malefactor, Lawrence exclaims in a transport of grief: "Whither goest thou, O Father, without thy son? Whither goest thou, O priest, without thy deacon?" But Sixtus replied: "Be consoled: a more glorious victory, because a harder combat, awaits thee, my son. In three days thou shalt follow me." This prophecy was literally fulfilled; for, on the 10th of August, the Church celebrates the martyrdom of Saint Lawrence, who said with a smile to his tormentors from his fiery gridiron: "Turn me: turn and eat!"

Passing onward, the procession of soldiers and Christians, surrounding the Pontiff and his deacons, went forward to that same cemetery of Pretextatus which we see to-day, between the first and second mile-stone from Rome, to the left on the Appian Way, opposite the cemetery of Saint Calixtus, its consecrated chambers hidden, as then, under smiling fields and fertile vineyards. Without delay and without courtesy, the Pontiff was led to the very chamber in which he had said Mass, placed in his pontifical chair, and thus seated, his head was struck from his body, his martyrdom being followed by that of the two deacons discovered with him; and blood thus consecrated anew this already sacred place. Saint Sixtus has been called "one of the glories of the catacombs," and to this day may be seen in a chamber of the cemetery of Pretextatus, coarsely cut, and painted in vermilion upon the stone of a *loculus*, or bed, in the wall, the image of a Bishop seated in a chair, and a deacon before him holding a book in his hands. Upon another stone, the chair itself is represented, as if sharing in the veneration of which the martyr was the object; and finally, on the tomb of Gemina, a holy woman, is seen represented, between the figures of SS. Peter and Paul, a portrait, under which is the word SVSTVS. In the IVth century, a small church was built directly over this chamber, in order to mark the precise spot where he suffered. The two deacons were deposited in this cemetery, where their tombs are still to be seen, as well as a fervent petition addressed to them by some pious pilgrims in the III, or the first half of the IVth century. Saint Sixtus himself was carried to the cemetery of Saint Calixtus; and with his body, was taken the episcopal chair on which he suffered, stained as it was with his blood. Around these precious relics were collected those of other holy Popes, martyrs also, until the crypt was called the "Chamber of the Popes." Here, above the chair, which was set upon a marble platform with steps, Saint Damasus, that elegant scholar, poet, as well as Pope and saint, placed an inscription, cut in the characters which were used exclusively by him and which go by his name.* The manuscripts of this Pope contained the inscription which has thus come down to us entire, and has been verified in our own day, by the fragments of the original stone found in the chamber. The inscription contains allusions to circumstances which must have been familiar to Pope Damasus and to the Christians of his day. To us it reads like a biography in brief. The scattered fragments have been brought together with infinite care, so that only seven letters are incomplete, and stand, thus, after fifteen hundred years, in their original place, to the astonishment as well as admiration of the visitor to the catacomb of Saint Callxtus. It may be translated thus:

"At the time when the sword transfixed the tender heart of our Mother, I, the pastor here interred, taught the commandments of heaven. They arrive suddenly, seize me while sitting on my chair; soldiers had been sent, and the people held out their necks to the sword. The aged man, who saw immediately that they desired to receive in his place the crown of martyrdom, was the first to offer himself and to give up his head, in order that the impatient fury of his enemies should touch no other. Christ, who gives in recompense eternal life, manifests the merit of the pastor, and Himself takes care of the flock." †

Saint Cyprian, a contemporary of Saint Sixtus,

---

* These Damascene characters, always 'vermeil dyed,' once known are instantly recognized, not only by their elegant proportions, but by the invariable *triple* ornament at the end of each point; something like the conventional *fleur-de-lis*.

† Tempore quo gladius secuit pia viscera Matris
Ilic positus rector cœlestia jussa docebam ;
Adveniunt subito, rapiunt qui forte sedentem ;
Militibus missis, populi tunc colla dedere.
Mox sibi cognovit senior quis tollere vellet
Palmam, seque suumque caput prior obtulit ipse,
Impatiens feritas posset ne lædere quemquam.
Ostendit Christus reddit qui præmia vitæ
Pastoris meritum, numerum gregis ipse tuetur.

distinctly states that Saint Sixtus was put to death by the sword in the cemetery on the 6th of August, and the *graffiti*, or writing, on the walls leading to this chamber, or chapel of the Popes, invariably invoke Saint Sixtus.

A few words concerning the cemetery of Pretextatus, as seen to-day, will be in place here. We must remember that all the catacombs, with the exception of that of Saint Sebastian, have been re-discovered in our day. That of Pretextatus was discovered by workmen repairing a ruined part of the stages in the cemetery of Saint Callxtus, coming, as they did, unexpectedly, upon a large and beautiful crypt. M. de Rossi, the Bozio of our century, no sooner perceived this through an opening, hardly cleared of rubbish, than running, sliding, creeping on hands and knees, he made his way into the crypt and found himself in an historic sanctuary. On examination, it was found, not cut or dug out of the *tufa* or rock, but built in solid masonry, after the manner of the latest pagan and the earliest Christian tombs. On three sides were niches for receiving sarcophagi, and still bore traces of the marble with which it was formerly faced. The front of the crypt, as seen from the interior of the cemetery, is of beautiful yellow brick, with pilasters in equally fair red brick, and a frieze of terra-cotta. The ceiling, and in fact the whole surface, of this chamber or chapel is painted in fresco. Four garlands run entirely round it from the floor to the *luminare*, which throws a strong light over the chamber. One of these garlands represents roses, another thorns, a third grapes, and the fourth laurel. These garlands are supposed to symbolize the four seasons, and we may say they have never been more gracefully symbolized. Among the three first garlands fly little birds, and from their nests appear the downy heads of their callow young ones. In the last, there are no singing birds, no flowers, no nests; but the laurel represents that period of life which is enlivened by a celestial hope and crowned with the wreath of victory. Below these garlands, and following the arch of the crypt itself, is a harvest field, reapers busy with their sickles, and others binding the sheaves. Within this is represented the Good Shepherd, bearing the lamb on His shoulder, the faithful sheep at His side, with a background of palms, foliage and birds. Through this fresco an opening was made for the last resting-place of some fervent Christian, who still invokes, by the inscription over his tomb, the saints near whose relics he wished to repose. All the letters are not legible, but the visitor can trace out, ... *mi refrigeri Januarius, Agatopus, Felicissim . . . Martyres:* the two last being the names of the deacons martyred with Saint Sixtus. This word, *refrigeri*, was used by the early Christians as an invocation from purgatory, meaning, "refresh me"; in the sense of console, help; so that we have, in this one inscription, a proof of their belief in purgatory, and also in the invocation of saints. The value of this inscription as a testimony to the faith of Christians at so early a period, may well reconcile us to the injury done to the fresco. The elegance of the decorations in this chapel takes us back to an early part of the second century, while the martyrs who have reposed within its walls are among the choicest fruits of the harvests of successive persecutions. The tribune, Quirinus, father of Saint Balbina, whose church overlooks us on our first entrance upon the Via Appia; Saint Januarius, the eldest of the seven sons of Saint Felicitas, martyred in 162 under Marcus Aurelius; Valerian, the husband, and Tiberius, the brother-in-law of Saint Cecilia, martyred under the same emperor, in 177; Urban, the Bishop, who was instrumental in their conversion; and the two deacons of Pope Sixtus II, found here a resting place.

It is on a return from a visit so rich in precious memories as this to the twin-cemeteries of Pretextatus and Calixtus, that we obtain, by a sharp turn in the way, the view we have already described of the Church of Saint Sixtus, or San Sisto, built upon the very spot where Saint Sixtus and Saint Lawrence bade each other so tender, yet so courageous, a farewell. The precise words spoken have come down to us in the genuine Acts of these martyrs, showing how deeply they sank into the hearts and memories of those who heard them. Within fifty years after these events transpired, a Roman matron, named Trigidia, built a church upon this spot, in honor of the Pontiff martyr. His precious remains were taken from the cemetery of Saint Calixtus and deposited here. From the IVth to the XIIIth century, this church had suffered so much, that in the year 1200 Innocent III was obliged to rebuild it altogether, since he had resolved to assemble there all the scattered religious of Rome. In 1488, under the pontificate of Sixtus IV, Cardinal Pierre Ferrici restored it at the Pope's expense. About the same period, another Cardinal, Philippi Buon-Compagni, charged Baccio Pintelli, the celebrated architect of the Sistine Chapel and the Ponte Sisto, to make the small façade, which is still seen on the church. Under the pontificate of Paul V, in the first quarter of the XVIIth century, the Very Reverend Father Séraphin Sicco, General of the Order of Saint Dominic, caused some pictures to be painted there; and Benedict XIII, one century later, completed its embellishment.

It was on the 26th of December, 1216, that Honorius III confirmed the Order of St. Dominic, and in 1217, the same Pope, wishing the young Order to have a house in Rome, gave them the Church of Saint Sixtus on the Appian Way. This, then, was the first home of the Dominicans in Rome and has been ever since in their possession. At this present time, the venerable church and monastery attracts every visitor to Rome, not only on account of its ancient claims upon their regard, but for the frescoes executed on the walls of its renowned chapter-room by Père Besson, himself a Dominican, by the order of Father Mullooly, Prior of San Clemente, the home of the Irish Dominicans in Rome. The principal frescoes represent, with great vividness, the three miracles wrought in this very room by Saint Dominic. The first, is the resuscitating of the son of a holy Roman widow, named Guatonia, who had left her son in his cradle in order to listen to a sermon by the Saint. On her return she found her child dead. In her grief, she took the child in her arms and hurried to San Sisto. Owing to the building being under repairs, the rule of the cloister was not in force, and she carried him to the very feet of Saint Dominic who was at the door of the chapter-room. "She spoke," we are told, "with her eyes rather than with her mouth," but St. Dominic understood her. Withdrawing a little from the door, he prostrated himself in prayer for a moment; then making the Sign of the Cross over the child, returned him, living and well, to his mother. The second was the resuscitating of a mason who was working on the monastery, and who was crushed under a wing of the wall which fell upon him. The monks, greatly distressed at this accident, besought Saint Dominic to have pity on the unfortunate youth. Telling them to draw out the lifeless body from the rubbish, and making over him the prayer of Faith, he restored his broken limbs and crushed body, and gave him to the hands of his brethren in perfect health. The third, was still more remarkable, being the restoration of the young lord Napoleon, who was thrown so violently from his horse to the pavement that his skull was broken, and he died instantly. The news of this disaster came to his uncle, Cardinal Stephen, while he was with Saint Dominic at San Sisto, in company with two other Cardinals, and so afflicted him, that he fell, fainting to the floor. The grief of the uncle so touched the monks, that they begged Saint Dominic to succor the dead youth. The Saint did not refuse, but being vested for Mass, he ordered the body to be brought to the chapter-room. During Mass, he shed floods of tears and was raised from the ground in an ecstasy. The Holy Sacrifice being ended, Dominic went to the corpse, disposed the bruised bones in their broken places, and betook himself to prayer; then rising, and making the Sign of the Cross over the corpse, he cried out, with a loud voice: "Napoleon, I say to thee, in the Name of Jesus Christ, arise!" And at that instant, before all assembled, the young man rose up, well and sound. These beautiful pictures can always be seen, even though the custodian is not near, by looking through the iron gate of the chapter-room. The kindness of Father Mullooly also allows the pilgrim, on the station-days, to climb up the narrow stone-stairs, trodden by so many saints, to the second story, and to look through the oval windows over the campagna beyond. Although the present dampness of the location makes it an unwholesome residence, every facility is given to the traveller to refresh his memory at this fountain of early Christian traditions. Seldom does one pass along the Via Appia without seeing its iron gate swung wide open under its arch of masonry, on which flourishes many a nodding tuft of grass or spray of wild-flowers. The peaceful sunshine and unbroken shadows within the gate always invite one to enter and to gather, as memorials of the place, the daisies or poppies, according to the season, or clutch handsful of the pretty blossoming leek which covers the low-tiled roofs within reach; while the eye takes in the Church of San Cesareo to the right, and, directly in front of the gate, the vast, dismantled, unroofed halls and chambers and banqueting-rooms of the Baths of Caracalla.

From San Sisto, the distance is short to the P. C. on the vineyard wall between the Church of San Sisto and that of San Gregorio which marks the site of the ancient Porta Capena, where the Via Appia, strictly speaking, began. Passing San Gregorio, and the sacred wood of the Camenæ, still a shaded square, and farther on still, the Colosseum, all on the right; to the left the Arch of Constantine and the palaces of the Cæsars, we enter, through the Arch of Titus, on the *Via Triumphalis* of the empire; the tower of the Capitol rising fully to view beyond and above the old Roman Forum; while all these monuments, with their picturesque surroundings of earth and sky, enter into the traveller's recollections of that Appian Way, which can never have so profound an interest for even the classical scholar as for the devout Christian pilgrim.

COLD and contracted, indeed, is that view of a man which regards his understanding alone; and barren is that system, however wide its range, which rests in the mere attainment of truth. The highest state of man consists in his purity as a moral being; and in the habitual culture and full operation of those principles by which he looks forth to other scenes and other times. Among these are desires and longings which nought in earthly science can satisfy, which soar beyond the sphere of sensible things, and find no object worthy of their capacities until in humble adoration they rest in the contemplation of God.—*Abercrombie.*

Our Lady's Sennight in the Household of Faith.

(CONTINUED.)

NIGHT VI.

QUEEN OF LOVE SUBLIME.

SECTION I.—TO HEAVEN ASSUMED: QUEEN OF EARTH.

WE approach the beginning of the end. The apostles may not be there now, as once, transported from the distant confines of earth, to celebrate the death-triumph; but from the ends of the world—more than half broader now than then—her poets shall come to scatter flowers, only less heavenly, on the triumphal car, and, celebrating the "place where they laid her," stand lovingly heartless about the other tenantless sepulchre: their hearts having flown up to "where their Treasure is." But, oh! they entreat: "Let her linger yet a while; and permit us to catch a glimpse of the shining, sinking moon. Sweet Lady-Queen, 'stay with us, because it is towards evening, and the day is now far spent'!"

Her last days and final sleep are thus described for us:

"From her life passed: yet still with her
The endless thought of Him found rest:
A sad but sacred bunch of myrrh
Forever folded in her breast.

"A boreal winter void of light—
So seemed her widowed days forlorn;
She slept, but in her breast all night
Her heart lay waking till the morn.

. . . .

"Love stronger far than death or life:
Thy martyrdom was o'er at last.
Her eyelids drooped; and without strife,
To Him she loved her spirit passed."

Thus Canon Oakley pursues:

. . . .

"So calm was her end that it seemed but a sleep,
Like a phase or a function of vigorous life;
Nor could love find a plea, or make leisure, to weep
O'er a death so unruffled by sorrow and strife."

Coming with the other and older disciples, is one who will not permit himself to be outrun by any, but arrives among "the first to the monument," as elsewhere:

"Yes, Mother of God, tho' thou didst stoop to die,
Death could not mar thy beauty. On thy face
Nor time nor grief had wrinkle left or trace:
It had but aged in God-like majesty.
Mature, yet, save the Mother in thine eye,
As maiden-fresh as when, of all our race,
Thou, first and last, wast greeted 'full of grace'—
Ere thrice five years had worshipt and gone by.
Mortal thy body: yet it could not know
Mortality's decay. Like sinless Eve's,

It waited but the change on Thabor shown.
And when, at thy sweet will, 'twas first laid low,
Untainted as a lily's folded leaves,
It slept—the angels watching by the stone."*

"Could our Lady's fond children have seen her ascending,
With the tokens of homage they witnessed before,
With the light shining round and the meek angels bending,
They too peradventure had dared to adore."†

But still, though

". . . . In secret and silence that Mother of love,
When her work was accomplished, her victory won,
Was translated from earth to her glory above,
To be hailed by the angels and crowned by her Son";

her dear name-sake, "Marie," having been in the secret of the Queen, can give us a glimpse of the glory of that Assumption:

"Lift, radiant East,
Your flaming doors! fling wide your gates of gold;
A Queen would pass beyond your bars, to hold
Her royal feast.

. . . . . .

"Her realm is won:
The radiant crown shall wreathe her sinless brow;
The Mother claims her throne of brightness now,
Beside her Son.

. . . . . .

"Thy body fair
Through gates of gold, beyond the radiant East,
Triumphant passed—the glad, eternal feast
Of love to share!"‡

Thus, finally, was fulfilled the glorious section of the apocalyptic dream, and set upon her throne overlooking all the kingdoms of the world, and inviting, as receiving, the homage of the entire human race, her subjects:

"A woman with light of the sun girded round,
Like a vesture of ambient glory outspread:
With the moon at her feet as a vassal, and crown'd
With twelve stars that mysteriously circle her head." |

SECTION II.—QUEEN OF PURGATORY.

First mere creature with her whole being in bliss—tenderest of all—she turns "those eyes of mercy"—interpreted by St. Bernard to mean the eyes of her Infant Jesus—on those who need most. Our Lady, as special Queen of Holy souls, is fulsomely, not untruly, honored by her appreciative troubadours, singing all her glories in "heaven, on earth, and under the earth."

Hear Aubrey de Vere, as usual rising from some scene of nature, to the imminent supernatural.

"Suddenly through clearing mists, the Star
Of Ocean o'er the billow rose:
Down dropped the elemental war;
Tormented chaos found repose.

───
* Hill—p 50.   † Canon Oakley.
‡ Beside the Western Sea—p. 423.
| Canon Oakley, as above.

"'Star of the Ocean'! dear art thou,
Ah! not to heaven and earth alone:
The suffering Church, when shines thy brow
Upon her penance, stays her moan.

"The Holy Souls draw in their breath;
The sea of anguish rests in peace;
And, from beyond the gates of death,
Upswell the anthems of release."

Founding her story upon an old French legend, Adelaide Procter will cheer us with a narration relating to Mary's office of Queen of Purgatory.

Though the "fettered spirits linger" in Purgatory,

"Yet, on each feast of Mary,
Their sorrow finds release,'
For the Great Archangel Michael,
Comes down and bids it cease;
And the name of these brief respites
Is called 'Our Lady's Peace.'
Yet once—so runs the legend—
When the Archangel came,
And all the holy spirits
Rejoiced at Mary's name;
One voice alone was wailing,
Still wailing on the same.

"I am not cold or thankless,
Although I still complain;
I prize Our Lady's blessing,
Altho' it comes in vain
To still my bitter anguish,
Or quench my ceaseless pain.
. . . . . .
"The evening of my bridal,
Death took my life away;
Not all love's passionate pleading
Could gain an hour's delay.
And he I left has suffered
A whole year since that day.
If I could only see him—
If I could only go
And speak one word of comfort
And solace—then I know
He would endure with patience,
And strive against his woe!"

Thus the Archangel answered:

"Your time of pain is brief,
And soon the peace of heaven
Will give you full relief;
Yet if this earthly comfort
So much outweighs your grief,
Then, through a special mercy,
I offer you this grace,—
You may seek him who mourns you
And look upon his face,
And speak to him of comfort
For one short moment's space.
But when that time is ended,
Return here, and remain
A thousand years in torment,
A thousand years in pain;
Thus dearly must you purchase
The comfort he will gain!

"The lime-trees' shade at evening
Is spreading broad and wide;

Beneath their fragrant arches,
Pace slowly, side by side,
In low and tender converse,
A bridegroom and his bride.
The night is cold and stilly,
No other sound is there
Except their happy voices:—
What is that cold, bleak air
That passes through the lime-trees,
And stirs the bridegroom's hair?
While one low cry of anguish,
Like the last dying wail
Of some dumb, hunted creature,
Is borne upon the gale:
Why does the bridegroom shudder
And turn so deathly pale?
. . . . . .
"Near purgatory's entrance
The radiant angels wait;
It was the great St. Michael
Who closed that gloomy gate,
When the poor, wandering spirit
Came back to meet her fate.
'Pass on,' thus spoke the angel:
'Heaven's joy is deep and vast;
Pass on, pass on, poor spirit,
For Heaven is yours at last;
In that one minute's anguish
Your thousand years have passed.'"*

Whereupon the grand anthem, *Te Deum*, resounds through the vasty vaults at this exhibition of supreme mercy; but as the harsh gates close again upon the tried prisoners of debt, we must intone a prayer for the

HOLY SOULS.

"O Mary, help of sorrowful hearts,
Look down with pitying eye
Where souls, the spouses of thy Son,
In fiery torments lie;
For from the presence of their Lord,
The purging debt they pay,
In prisons through whose gloomy shades
There shines no cheering ray.

"But dark the gloom where smile of thine,
Sweet Mother, may not fall,
Oh, hear us when for these dear souls
Thy loving aid we call!
Thou art the star whose gentle beam
Sheds joy upon the night,
Oh, let its shining pierce their gloom,
And give them peace and light."†

We may continue this cry for mercy,
—For ever still is need while spirits burn,—
and conclude, as does "Marie's"

Requiescant in Pace.

"Mother of pitying love!
On sorrow's flood thy tender glances bend,
And o'er its dark and dreadful torrent send
The olive-bearing dove.
Thy potent prayer shall be
An arch of peace, a radiant promise-bow,
To span the gulf and shed its cheering glow

* The Poems of Adelaide Procter--p. 299.
† Songs in the Night.—A. T. D. --p. 13.

O'er the dread penance-sea.
And on its pathway blest
The ransomed throng in garments washed and white,
May safely pass to love's fair realm of light,
To heaven's perfect rest."

SECTION III.—QUEEN OF MAY—CHOSEN.

We would only choose her now, inaugurate her reign, and send out her heralds to proclaim her coming Feast-month, all her own, all our own. Here is the first Marian herald—no less than a Cardinal, and the grandest of living English prose writers:

"O Mother-Maid, be thou our aid
Now in the opening year;
Lest sights of earth to sin give birth,
And bring the tempter near.

"O Mother, pure and beautiful,
Thou art the Queen of May;
Our garlands wear about thy hair,
And they shall ne'er decay."

The legate of the queenly court would give the reasons for the holding of the Feast-month:—to satisfy our feeble minds, the Church is wise.

"All is divine which the Highest has made,
Thro' the days that He wrought till the days that He stayed;
But I know of one work of His Infinite Hand
Which special and singular ever must stand:
So perfect, so pure, and of gifts such a store,
That even Omnipotence ne'er shall do more.
The freshness of May, and the sweetness of June,
And the fire of July in its passionate noon;
Magnificent August, September serene,
Are together no match for my glorious Queen."

"—O Mary, all months
And all days are thine own;
In thee lasts their joyousness
When they are gone.
And we give to thee May,
Not because it is best,
But because it comes first,
And is pledge of the rest."*

But if even now we cannot assist at the real celebrations of this holy season where the Queen reigns visibly, at least we may kneel before and address her through Father Hill's or our own

"FAVORITE MADONNA."

"Lady Mary, throne of grace,
Imaged with thy Child before me;
Softly beams the perfect face,
Fragrant breathes its pureness o'er me.

"I but gaze, and all my soul
Thrills as with a taste of heaven;
Passion owns the sweet control;
Peace assures of sin forgiven.

"Dream, say they, for poet's eye?
Thou a dream! Then truth is seeming,
Only let me live and die
Safely lost in such a dreaming."

(CONCLUSION NEXT WEEK.)

* Card. Newman. Song for Inclement May, 1850.

Catholic Notes.

—The First Provincial Council of Philadelphia will be opened in the Cathedral of that city on the Feast of the Most Holy Trinity, 23d inst.

—The monastery of Loyola, in Spain, has been unconditionally restored to the Jesuits, who will establish there a novitiate for the province of Castile.

—The Sacred Congregation of Rites declares that an indulgence of one hundred days. may be gained once a day, by a devout and contrite recitation of the *Magnificat.*

—CONTRIBUTIONS.—For the Needy Mission: Two Friends, $3; Mary Campbell, $3; A Subscriber of THE AVE MARIA, $5; A Friend, $10. For the Irish Relief Fund (Lady Fullerton's): A Friend. $10.

—We are under obligations to Very Rev. Father Leo de Saracena. O. S. F., of St. Bonaventure's College, Cattaraugus, N. Y., and Rev. Father Hamel, of the Church of St. Mary of the Angels, at Olean, for kind favors to our travelling agent.

—The pilgrimage of English Catholics to Lourdes has, at the request of Cardinal Manning, been postponed from June until September or October. The Duke of Norfolk will join the pilgrimage, and has asked the members of the Catholic Union to take part in it.

—*The Catholic Union* of Buffalo, one of our ablest papers, has just entered upon the ninth year of its existence. It has always been a bright, vigorous journal, and seems to improve with age. We like to believe that it has the large circulation in the diocese of Buffalo to which its merits entitle it.

—Rt. Rev. Bishop Seidenbusch, O. S. B., of St. Cloud, Minn., and the three Benedictine abbots of this country, Rt. Revs. Alexander Edelbrock, Innocenz Wolf, and Boniface Wimmer, sailed for Europe from New York on the 20th inst., in the steamer Arizona, to be present at the solemn dedication of the newly restored chapel of St. Benedict at Monte Casino.

—Rev. Father Spencer, O. P., Chaplain of the Catholic Protectory at Westchester, N. Y., has been disinherited. His grandfather left the third part of his real and personal estate to him on condition that he would renounce the Faith to which he is a convert, and marry. Father Spencer declines. His father, who is an Episcopalian minister, has refused to see him since he became a priest.

—During the past Lent, the evening sermons given in the parochial churches of Vienna were attended by very large audiences, chiefly composed of men. Foremost among the Lenten preachers was the venerable Father Maximilian de Klinkowstrom, S. J., whose parents were Swedes, and were converted from heresy by Ven. Father Hoffbauer, first Superior of the Redemptorists in Austria. All the members of the Imperial family encouraged, by their example, the devotion of the Viennese.

—PÈRE DIDON.—The famous Parisian preacher, Father Didon, Prior of the Dominicans, before starting for Rome, wrote a letter to the Holy Father, asking him graciously to accept the dedication of his late "Conferences" on Divorce, accompanying the gift by a letter, which the Apostolic Nuncio was commissioned to deliver in his name, and in which, as an humble and faithful son of the Church, he expresses his desire to adhere scrupulously to all Catholic doctrines in his efforts to instil Scripture truths into the minds of the unbelieving.—*Catholic Times.*

—DEATH OF A PASSIONIST PRIEST.—Rev. Father Gabriel Flynn, of the Congregation of the Passion, died on the evening of the 21st ult., at St. Joseph's Passionist Monastery, on the Frederick road, near Baltimore, after a long and painful illness. He was forty-one years of age, a native of Ireland, and had been connected with the Passionist Order twenty years. For the past three years he was stationed at St. Joseph's, and was highly esteemed and widely known as an efficient missionary. The remains were taken for interment to St. Michael's Church, Hoboken, N. J. R. I. P.

—AN INVENTIVE PRIEST.—Father Hartnedy, of Steubenville, O., is a mechanical genius. He brought the old St. Peter's clock from the tower, where it lay corroding for years, to the floor below, and put it in running order, and it now keeps good time. After he got the old clock to running, he went to work and contrived a universal clock, which runs by means of the same machinery. The dial is in the school-room, two floors below the machinery, and shows the time at points all around the earth. This clock, which he calls the universal clock, is run by means of ropes and wheels, requiring considerable mathematical calculation, and Rev. Fr. Hartnedy should be proud of his success. The hours are marked on a dial, and the longitude lines are marked on a revolving disk which revolves with the earth, showing the exact time at every point marked on the disk. We understand that this is the only clock of the kind ever made. Rev. Fr. Hartnedy intends adding the months and dates to the disk as soon as he gets the time.—*Steubenville Gazette.*

—PROGRESS OF THE CHURCH IN CEYLON.—Sir James Longden, British Governor of Ceylon, and lady, recently paid a visit to the Catholic establishments at Jaffna. At the convent of the Sisters of the Holy Family, he was welcomed by Very Rev. Father Pulicani, V. G., and administrator of the Vicariate of Jaffna. A little girl read an address to the Governor, who replied in the following terms: "Rev. Mother-Superior: Receive my congratulations on the good you have done and are doing, and on the progress you have made since my last visit. I have also noticed similar improvements at other points of the island, especially at Kurunegala and at Colombo. I am forced to acknowledge that the Catholics are everywhere animated by the same spirit, and that the education given in their schools is as good as it could be. Nothing, to my mind, can be more hurtful than instruction void of that moral training which assures to our young people the happiness of their whole life. I sincerely wish there were more institutions of this kind in Ceylon." The Governor then visited the little seminary, the orphan asylum, and workshops of Saint Joseph, speaking highly of the condition of affairs and the excellence he witnessed in those institutions. From another part of the island, we hear that Monsignor Pagnani, Vicar Apostolic of Colombo, was splendidly received at Moratuwa, a town of 8,000 Catholic inhabitants, on the occasion of his pastoral visit. He administered the Sacrament of Confirmation to 533 persons, more than 200 of whom were converts from Protestantism and Buddhism.

—KNOCK.—A private letter from Ireland informs us that the wonderful cures at Knock are continuing, and even increasing. The cement from the wall of the famous church has been the means of effecting cures in this country also, it would seem. A correspondent, writing from Massachusetts last week, says:

"I think it only right to make known my cure. I have had weak eyes for about three years, and have been obliged to wear glasses constantly, not being able to see without them. Yesterday a lady friend sent me some of the cement from Knock. I put it in water and applied the water to my eyes. Almost immediately they were cured, and are now quite well. In fact, I write this without the help of glasses. My cure was effected on the Feast of the Patronage of St. Joseph."
The Pittsburg *Telegraph* of a recent date contained the following notice of another alleged cure: "A very remarkable cure of a young man, about eighteen years old, who had been a hopeless cripple from his birth, and who could not walk without the aid of crutches, is said to have been performed at the Catholic church, in Sharon, last week. The following are the particulars as sent by a correspondent of *The Telegraph*, who learned them from Rev. K. O'Brannigan, pastor of the Catholic church: 'It seems that in the parish of Knock, County Mayo, Ireland, the Blessed Virgin and St. John have lately appeared to many persons, and since then some very remarkable cures of various diseases have been effected by prayer and the use of the cement from the walls of the church. Mr. P. McManus, a citizen of this place, but a native of Knock parish, sent for a quantity of the cement, and Jerry McCarty, the young man spoken of above, made application to Rev. Father O'Brannigan for a season of prayer in his behalf. The congregation of the church was notified of the fact, and the young man's request was complied with. The season of prayer lasted nine days, terminating on Thursday last, during which time the cement, which had been procured, was applied. On the last day confessions were made. McCarty abandoned his crutches and is now able to walk with the aid of a cane, and it is said that he is each day recovering more and more the use of his limbs which had heretofore been almost useless to him. We give this to our readers just as it has been related without any comments. The case, which is certainly a strange one, has been the general talk in this place during the past week. The young man is the son of Mr. Wm. McCarty, an employee at the Westerman rolling mill.'"

New Publications.

THE LIFE OF REV. CHARLES NERINCKX: With a Chapter on the Early Catholic Missions of Kentucky, etc., etc., etc. By Rev. Camillus P. Maes, Priest of the Diocese of Detroit. Cincinnati: Robert Clarke & Co. 1880.

This is a very interesting and carefully written biography of one of the heroic men who left all that made life pleasant, to go and preach to the aborigines and pioneer settlers of the Western states. Father Nerinckx was for a long time the associate of our own Father Badin, whose memory is still fresh at Notre Dame and its environs, as in many other parts of the Western world. The author assures us in his preface that "we can vouch for the historical accuracy of the details of our narrative. We got them all at authentic sources, more especially from letters of Rev. Father Nerinckx, many of whose autographs the writer has in his possession." Of Father Nerinckx's first years in Belgium, but little account has been given, because few records have been found of them. His career as an American missionary began with his forty-fourth year, when he was already past what is usually considered as the prime of life. As the author tells us, "the many trials and vigils of his seven years' seclusion in Deudermonde, had somewhat impaired his health; but having an iron constitution and giant strength, he could still hope for a long and laborious exercise of the holy ministry." What Kingsley calls "muscular Christianity" seems to have been quite necessary in those times,—for we read that "In swimming 'rivers, he was often exposed to great danger. Once, in going to visit a sick person, he came to a stream which his companion knew to be impassable. Mr. Nerinckx took the saddle of his friend—who refused to venture—placed it on his own, and then, remounting the horse, placed himself on his knees on the top of the two saddles, and thus crossed the flood, which flowed over his horses back." The form "Mr. Nerinckx" used in this and many other places, reminds us how modern the custom is of calling a priest father on any and all occasions. It must seem strange to Catholics who speak other languages than the English, for the French, for example, rarely address their pastor as *mon père*, except under circumstances which would authorize him in using the reciprocal style, *mon enfant*—in the confessional, for instance, where the penitent appears as the returning prodigal, and these forms have a special significance. For the ordinary purposes of social life, *Monsieur le Curé*, or simply *Monsieur* is sufficient. But in English, a language whose genius is peculiarly opposed to gush or sentimentality, we hear young men of twenty-six addressed as "Father" by their friends, and even by their own parents. But to return to Father Nerinckx, whose patriarchal character gives the title unquestionable propriety as applied to him—the events of his missionary career supply material for 635 highly interesting pages. The anecdote of his returning a colored man's salute, with the remark: "I do not want to be beaten in politeness by a negro," is told of so many distinguished persons, as to make us remark "how men of great minds will agree!" The formation of the Loretto Society is an important era in the religious history of Kentucky, and the simplicity and piety of its beginnings will be found extremely interesting. In fact, up to the close of Father Nerinckx's career by his edifying death in 1824, the interest never flags. Father Maes has performed his arduous task well, and modestly withal. The volume comes in neat and substantial shape, and should be found in the domestic circle of every Catholic family, and on the shelves of every Catholic library.

——*The American Catholic Quarterly Review* for April has the following attractive table of contents: I, Public Education in France—The Ferry Bill, Rev. Aug. J. Thebaud, S. J.; II, The Sixth Nicene Canon and the Papacy, Rev. James F. Loughlin, D. D.; III, The Laws of the Church with Regard to Secret Societies, Rev. C. Coppens, S. J.; IV, American Rationalism, Rev. H. A. Brann, D. D.; V, Anglican Development, A. Featherstone Marshall, B. A., Oxon; VI, The Rehabilitation of Catholic Terms in Dictionaries of the English Language, J. Gilmary Shea, LL.; D.; VII, Notes on Spain, St. George Mivart, F. R. S., F. Z. S., Sec'y L. S.; VIII, A Question on Laughter, H. L. Richards; IX, The Late Encyclical on Christian Marriage, Very Rev. James A. Corcoran, D. D.; X, Epistola Encyclica Leonis Papæ XIII; XI, Translation of the Encyclical Letter of His Holiness Leo XIII; XII, Latin Text and Translation of the Letter of the Archbishops and Bishops of the Provinces of New York, Boston, and Philadelphia to His Holiness Leo XIII; XIII, Book-Notices.

Confraternity of the Immaculate Conception
(Or of Our Lady of Lourdes).

"We fly to thy patronage, O Holy Mother of God!"

REPORT FOR THE WEEK ENDING APRIL 28TH.

The following intentions have been recommended: Recovery of health for 81 persons and 5 families,—change of life for 38 persons and 2 families,—conversion to the Faith for 34 persons and 3 families,—recovery of mind for 5 persons,—special graces for 10 priests and 16 religious,—temporal favors for 44 persons and 6 families,—spiritual favors for 73 persons and 7 families,—the spiritual and temporal welfare of 5 communities, 4 congregations, and 6 schools. Also, 51 particular intentions, and thanksgivings for several favors received.

Specified intentions: A worthy reception of the Sacraments during Paschal time for several persons,—prevention of a marriage between a Catholic and a Jew,—several persons engaged in dangerous avocations, such as mining, railroading, engineering, building, etc.,—a distressed widow,—the spiritual and temporal welfare of several other widows and orphans,—reinstatement into a lost position,—peace of mind for several persons,—a gentleman threatened with apoplexy,—the particular intentions of a missionary among the Indians, and the establishment of a new mission,—success in several enterprises,—several children preparing for their First Communion.

FAVORS OBTAINED.

A Jesuit Father asks us to return thanks for the conversion of five persons, and for the cure of two others. A lady writes that one of her children, who had been afflicted for three years with scald head, was completely cured in one week by applying a few drops of the water of Lourdes every night, making each time the sign of the Cross. Another correspondent reports that a friend of hers has been cured of congestion of the stomach by the use of the water of Lourdes. A gentleman writes that his little daughter who was afflicted with St. Vitus' dance, and who had made use of medicines without any result, was cured in a short time by means of the miraculous water. A devout child of Mary writes: "A short time ago my sister gave some of the water of Lourdes to a person almost blind of one eye. An immediate cure was the result obtained by its application." . . . "Please thank our Blessed Lady," writes a good religious, "for obtaining our request; our petition was granted almost immediately."

OBITUARY.

The prayers of the Confraternity are asked for the following persons: Mr. JULIUS MÜLLER, a native of Würtemberg, Germany, who departed this life on the 5th of March. Miss MINNIE FLANAGAN, of Marengo, Iowa, who rendered her pure soul to God on the 18th of April, in the fourteenth year of her age. Mr. ROBERT MAYTON, who became a convert at his death, which occurred at Monroeville, Ind., on the 15th of March. Mrs. MARY BROWN, of Millville, N. Y. Mr. CHARLES DELAHUNTY, of St. Joseph's, Pa., and Mrs. JOSEPHINE JOHNSON, of Brooklyn, N. Y., recently deceased. Mr. JOHN DENHAM, of Co. Limerick, Ireland. MARY DALY and PATRICK FLYNN, of Philadelphia, Pa. A. BOUCEY, of Danville, Pa.; Mrs. A. MOORE, and P. McENRIGHT, of Decorah, Iowa, who died some time ago.

Requiescant in pace.

A. GRANGER, C. S. C., Director.

Youth's Department.

(For the "Ave Maria.")

May Consecration of the Little Ones to the Queen of Heaven.

I.

IT was a sweet and holy thought,
　At Mary's shrine to lay
The gift with rarest beauty fraught,
　The peerless month of May,
When nature's wealth of joy and love
　Illumes with tend'rest glow,
The fair, unclouded skies above,
　The limpid streams below.
Aye, give, O earth, the glad perfume
　Of thy sweet month of flowers
To her, the Queen of heav'nly bloom,
　And bright, immortal bowers.
And bid the May-time blossoms bear
　Upon their petals bright,
True types of graces gleaming fair,
　Within her crown of light.
To Mary be their homage paid,
　She claims their meed of praise;
And birds that sing in forests glade,
　To her shall chant their lays.
The fountain's murmur of delight,
　The breeze-song, in the leaves,
Each sound that hails the mornings bright,
　Or greets the dewy eves,
Shall swell, with glad, and eager tone,
　The tender tribute-strain
By earth outpoured at Mary's throne,
　To bless her gentle reign.

II.

The spring-tide bloom of human life,
　Fair childhood! blissful time!
Unmarred by storms of care and strife,
　Undimmed by clouds of crime.
Ah! 'tis a sweet and holy thought
　At Mary's shrine to lay
The gift with rarest beauty fraught,
　Life's fair and fragrant May,
For she that Maiden-Mother mild,
　Within her arms will take
Each likeness of her cherished Child,
　And guard it, for His sake.
Ah! tender parents! fondly bring
　To her, your blossoms sweet,
While softly shines their balmy spring—
　Nor dread the summer's heat,
Nor fear the autumn's chilling air,
　The winter's icy blast.
Each bloom is safe in Mary's care,
　Till earthly storms be past.
Dear children, haste, with fond delight,

To deck Our Lady's shrine;
Let roses rare, and lilies white,
Upon her altars twine;
Your sinless hands can fashion best,
The fragrant garlands there,
And well she loves, that Mother blest,
Your spotless wreaths of prayer.
Aye, well she loves, when daylight flees,
And night her shade hath flung,
The tones of tender litanies,
By childish voices sung.
How calm, within the fading light,
Her sculptured figure stands!
And see, amid the blossoms bright,
Her outstretched, loving hands!
That tender gesture seems to say
To each dear little one,
"Sweet child! thy tributes I will lay
Before my King and Son,
And bid Him bless each deed and thought
Thou off'rest at my shrine,
For vainly is all labor wrought
Unblest by love Divine.
Lo! He will cause thy life to grow
Into a goodly tree,
Where wisdom's golden fruit shall glow
Through all eternity."
"MARIE."

SAN FRANCISCO, CAL.

Irish Legends.

I.—THE MASS ROCK.

HE morning sun rose bright and glorious from the calm waters of Clew Bay, casting a ray of golden light along its surface, and lighting up by degrees the more than three hundred islands scattered over its bosom. Here and there, the ripple of the waters might be seen as if tinged with gold, while a tiny little bark is stealing its way to the shore. Gradually the number of little boats increases. Like a spray of gold, the water falls from the oars, but not a sound is heard. They all appear to be making for the same point, under the foot of Croagh Patrick. Through every little valley round the foot of the huge mountain, we can see people quietly wending their way to the same spot, deep in the shade of the sacred hill consecrated by the prayers and footsteps of the great Saint from whom it takes its name. We lose sight of them in a deep valley, where the hill seems to favor their retreat by its varying shadows.

I wonder what they are all doing in that lonely ravine! There is a house, surrounded by trees, in the distance near it, but they are all crowding into a hollow, at this side of the house, while on every neighboring hillock and rock commanding a view may be seen some one anxiously looking about, as if danger were apprehended. Let us steal our way down, and see what is going on. I managed to mingle with the people who were still wending their way in solemn march to the meeting place in the hollow side of Croagh Patrick, and soon fell into conversation with an intelligent-looking old man of the party. Deep furrows of time and care were traced on his fine, noble brow. His once manly frame was wasted away by want. An air of sadness had settled itself on his countenance; his long white hair down to his shoulders, his pallid face, bent body, and tottering limbs, made me take a singular interest in him as he struggled on, trying to keep up with the crowd. "Where are all those people going, my dear man?" I asked him, quietly.

He looked at me rather frightened, and said: "You are a stranger?"

I saw that I had deeply affected the poor man by the question I asked. Big, silent tears trickled down his poor worn cheeks, and he continued: "Ah, sure you won't betray us!" I could scarcely restrain my own tears as I looked at him, and with thrilling interest listened to the old man's story as we travelled together, a little distance from the others, towards the hiding place in the shades of Croagh Patrick. "My dear man," said I, "so far from betraying you, all my sympathies are with you. I feel intensely for you, whatever be the object of your journey."

"Well," said he, "we are going to hear Mass on the lonely mountain side, the canopy of heaven our covering, and the rough rock the altar. We have not heard Mass for the last two months; we got word that the priest would say Mass on the Carrick-au-Affrin (the Mass rock) of Croagh Patrick this Easter morning at this early hour, and, though trembling with fear, we are stealing in to hear it, for the *shaun-na-soggarth* (the priest-hunter) may be on our track. You know that in poor persecuted Ireland, by the unjust and persecuting laws of an alien Government, it is death to say Mass, and a crime to hear it. Still the *soggarth-aroon* (the dear priest) lives among us, shares in our poverty and persecution, and exposes his life for our salvation. In that house yonder among the trees, he lives as a servant, and hears the confessions of those who can steal to him without being noticed. From that house to the quarry we are approaching, there is an underground passage, and in that quarry there is a rough rock which you can see from here; through that passage the priest comes, and on that rock he says Mass, at the risk of his life, on the great festivals of the year." We were just now at the entrance of the quarry; it was deep in the recess of the mountain and surrounded by huge rocks; the one right in front, called the "Mass-rock," was prepared for the solemn Sacrifice; some thousands of people were kneeling in deep silence, when suddenly, at a signal given, two strong men removed a large rock which had concealed the mouth of a cavern that appeared to penetrate into the very heart of the hill. It was the passage to which the old man referred. Immediately a priest in vestments, accompanied by two little boys, came forth in a rather frightened and hurried manner. A deep murmur of suppressed expressions of devotion thrilled through the crowd as the priest commenced the Mass. All now is solemn silence, save the whisper of the sacred words of Sacrifice till the awful moment of consecration, when from the adoring multitude—bent to the ground in adoration—there bursts in the grand old Celtic tongue "*Cead mille failthe!*" a thousand welcomes to Jesus Christ! scarcely had the heartfelt exclamation thrilled upon the air, when another cry is heard from those who had been watching on the hillside. "Save the *soggarth!* the priest-hunters are in view!" O God what a moment of terror! The solemn Sacrifice is not finished, the priest cannot move, and the people will not leave him; they will surround him, as with a wall of brass, by their very bodies, till the last man will die in his defence; the tramp of the soldiers is heard, the people call on the priest to escape; but no: he must consume the sacred species, he must save Jesus Christ from insult; and the people are determined if possible to save him from death. But poor. defenceless people, what can you do before armed soldiers? During the struggle, the Mass is finished. A passage is cut through the crowd, the blood of the faithful defenders sprinkles the altar and the sacred vestments, while the priest is borne away to execution, amidst the sobs and cries of his faithful flock: "*Soggarth aroon! soggarth aroon!*"

II.—THE "SOGGARTH AROON."

The "*soggarth aroon*" was borne away to a mock-trial, to be followed by a cruel death. Scarcely had the wail of woe from his faithful people died away, when another company of armed yeomen came to disperse the congregation. Resistance was useless; they were forced away at the point of the bayonet, with a caution that should they ever again be found there listening to "the mummery of the Mass," they would be condemned to penal servitude for life. Some poor women clung fast to the altar, till their fingers were maimed by blows from the butts of the soldiers' guns, and the sacred spot was sprinkled with their blood. The crucifix and candlesticks that were on the altar were broken up as symbols of superstition; the very graves of the dead were desecrated; two little crosses that marked two tiny graves near the altar were torn up and trampled upon. The people all retired, without resistance, to their cabins on the hill-side and by the sea, with tearful eyes and sorrowing hearts, while their last thoughts and last words were on their "*soggarth aroon.*"

One solitary person remained, unable to move, from fright, fatigue and old age: the good old man who accompanied me to the scene of sorrow. He sat leaning against a rock, with big tears of silent sorrow rolling down his worn cheeks; his pale cold hands were joined over his breast, while his heart was throbbing with unusual quickness, as if he had just recovered from a swoon. I took his cold hands in mine, and endeavored to warm them; I wiped the tears from his cheeks, and, when he was somewhat restored, helped him into a neighboring cabin. When he had sufficiently recovered himself, his first words were, "Is the priest taken?" We told him he was, but that it was hoped he would get off. He burst into tears and said, sobbingly: "There is no chance now for the '*soggarth aroon*'; this is the third time he has been taken. Well, I remember," continued he, as the little children gathered about him and looked wistfully into his tear-bathed face, "well, I remember when he was first taken, thirty years ago; I was then fifty; he was a fine young man, twenty-five years of age, just home from Spain, where he had finished his studies. Full of zeal for the glory of God, he determined to share in the poverty and privations of his poor persecuted people, to live among them in the holes and hiding-places of the mountain, and, if necessary, to die for them. His love was not lost on the good, grateful people of Mayo; they loved him as a father, and would die in his defence. One, however, was found to be a traitor: he went to the major—the head of the yeomen—and told him that there was a priest in the neighborhood, that he had his hiding-place among the rocks of Croagh Patrick, and that he would deliver him into their hands for a sum of money. The bargain was struck, and the blood-money given. The traitor feigned to be sick, and sent for the priest, while around and within the traitor's house, the priest-hunters lay in ambush to catch him, and get the promised price for his head. The poor priest came at the call of duty, little thinking of the treason that awaited him. The moment he entered the house, two strong men pounced upon him and seized him as their prisoner. 'I came here to attend a sick man,' said the priest, calmly; 'allow me to do my duty, and then I will go with you where you wish.' 'There is no sick man here,' they said. 'But I was sent for,' replied the priest; 'in that room there is a sick man in bed; allow me to attend him.' They did so in order to have a laugh at him; the priest went over to the bedside of the traitor, and put his hand on his forehead; it was cold in death. Bending over the bed where the traitor lay, the holy priest took, unperceived, the particle of the Blessed Sacrament which he carried in his bosom as a Viaticum for the dying, and reverently consumed it; then having said a prayer for his enemy, turned calmly to his persecutors, and said: 'I am too late for this poor man: *he is dead!* do what you wish with me now.' The two men who had seized him on his entrance, fell paralyzed on the floor, and the priest walked quietly away to his hiding-place in the mountain, thanking God for his miraculous escape. For ten years he was heard of no more in public; the faithful Catholics alone knew his hiding-place, and used to bring him food from the little they had for themselves; and two or three times a year they used to go stealthily to confess to him in his hiding-place in the rock, and whenever he could safely do so, he said Mass on that rock now sprinkled with the people's blood. The second time was just ten years ago to-day, Easter Sunday; he had hardly finished Mass, when the priest-hunters, who had been long watching for him, seized him at the foot of the altar, tore the sacred vestments from his body and trampled on them, broke the chalice on a stone and put the pieces in their pockets; then stripping him naked, they fastened him to the altar, tore his back with a hundred stripes, till his blood flowed in torrents, sprinkling the altar, the grotto, the pavement, everything around; the people, in the mean time, being dispersed by an armed band of soldiers, could not help him.

"When the bloody work was done, they threw him his blood-stained clothes,—told him that should he be ever again caught saying Mass, he would be tried by court-martial and executed as a traitor. One by one, the people stole back to see about their *soggarth;* they found the place around sprinkled with his blood, the ornaments of the altar that were not worth taking away, scattered about in broken fragments; they traced him to his hiding-place in the rock by his blood, that marked the stones and reddened the soil; they found him, exhausted from sufferings, hunger and loss of blood; he was on the verge of death; every comfort that poor people could give him, they gave; but what had they to give—poor, persecuted, poverty-stricken peasants? By degrees, he recovered; his increasing energies he spent on them, hearing their confessions, consoling and advising them, though he was not able to leave his grotto; it took a whole year to recover him. About this time a Catholic family of some means came to live in that respectable house in the trees, and they, having secured a hiding-place for him in the house, and made an underground passage from it to that hollow in the hill, where the Mass-rock is now situated, took him into their house even at the risk of their lives and property. There he has lived for the past 20 years, dressed in every kind of garb that could conceal him; there many strange things have happened which I cannot now tell you."

The little children who had been all attention during this narrative, looked again wistfully into the old man's face, and tried to coax him to tell them the "*wonderful things*" that happened in the big house. "No, my little children," said he, "I cannot tell you now; my heart is too full of sorrow at what will soon happen to the *soggarth aroon;* he will be hanged till he is half dead; then his body, still quivering with torture, will be cut down; his heart and hands, still palpitating, will be torn out and cast into the fire, while his murdered body will be quartered and exposed to the gaze and mockery of the *sassenach*."

One of the little children, a bright, curly-headed boy, who had been listening with more than usual attention to everything that was said, now put in his silvery voice, and asked: "But why did they take the holy priest? did you see the man that God struck dead? why did they beat the priest? and why are they going to murder him? who are these wicked men? and won't you tell us all the wonderful things that happened in the big house?" By this time the poor man's face was bathed in tears which were still flowing down his pallid, worn cheeks. One of the little ones, a cherub-child of five, crept into his lap, and wiping away the tears, said: "Oh, don't cry, and we'll not ask you to tell us any more!"

"Dear little children," he said, "I will tell you all another time, but I must now shed tears." Who is it that, speaking of tears, so truly says:

"Tears that trickle down our eyes,
They do not fall to earth and dry;
They soar like angels to the skies,
And, like angels, cannot die;
For, oh, our immortality flows in each tear,
Sounds in each sigh.

"But, ah, the tears that are *not* wept,
The tears that never outward fall,
The tears that grief for years has kept
Within us—they are worst of all;
The tears our eyes shall never weep
Are deeper than the tears that flow."

(TO BE CONTINUED.)

For the Suffering Irish Children.

James Smith, $11; Joseph Smith, $10; G. Woodson, 50 cts.; Joseph Henry, $1; H. Dunn, 50 cts.; D. G. Taylor, 70 cts.; Alexis Campeau, 60 cts.; Jose Chaves, 25 cts.; Anthony Van Mourick, 46 cts.; G. Van Mourick, 25 cts.; Marshal Olds, 10 cts.; Harry Snee, 5 cts.; Willie Ayres, 10 cts.

THE AVE MARIA.

A Journal devoted to the Honor of the Blessed Virgin.

HENCEFORTH ALL GENERATIONS SHALL CALL ME BLESSED.—St. Luke, i, 48.

VOL. XVI.   NOTRE DAME, INDIANA, MAY 15, 1880.   NO. 20.

Mary in the Upper Chamber—The Christian Faith is Founded upon her Testimony.

BY NICOLAS.

MARY was not left upon earth in vain after her Divine Son's Ascension into heaven. She had to accomplish a great work; one that was to prepare the way for the work of God; namely, the work of the Christian Faith. And here I purpose to manifest an ancient truth in a new light as regards Mary; that is to say, I would point out that Mary co-operated in the formation of the Christian Faith in the Upper Chamber, just as efficaciously as she co-operated in the work of the Redemption upon Calvary, and in the work of the Incarnation at Nazareth.

For, in order to make us feel more deeply what we owe to Mary, and to maintain her honor as the Mother of God, and in order to unite our devotion to her indissolubly with the devotion we render to Jesus Christ, it has pleased God that, as we owe Jesus Christ to the consent she gave, so we should owe our knowledge of Him to the testimony she alone could give. Thus, by an admirable unity of design, Mary is assigned the same place in the dispensation of faith as that she holds in the dispensation of grace. It corresponds to the place she held, when she brought forth the Author of grace and faith Himself; for He has made her the sole witness of the truth of that great mystery, in which she alone co-operated.

This valuable train of thought has been suggested by one of the lights of the Church in the present day, His Eminence Cardinal Wiseman. It is one particularly adapted to affect Protestants, and such as are offended by the devotion paid to the Blessed Virgin. For, as in opposing that devotion, they take their stand upon the ground of pure faith in Jesus Christ, the best way of overcoming their opposition is to make them see that they owe that very faith to Mary; that so, by means of devotion to Mary, as the Mother of our Faith, they may be inspired with devotion to Mary, the Mother of God. They would realize the full sanctity and dignity of her Divine Maternity, if they saw what importance it confers on her testimony to the mysteries of our Faith,—a testimony upon which the whole edifice of Christianity rests. We will endeavor to make clear this beautiful and important fact, which has hitherto been overlooked. As it is a new perception of the truth, it needs to be brought home to the mind carefully and deliberately.

The grand Mystery of our Faith is the Incarnation of the Word of God. The whole of Christianity is summed up in the Divinity of Jesus Christ; His doctrine, His works, His life, and His death, derive their whole value from His Godhead. Christian doctrine is but an empty sound, Redemption vanishes away, the Cross falls, if the Crucified was not God; if He was but a righteous man, or a saint, or a prophet, one more or less closely united to God, and not very God Himself.

Now, Jesus Christ can only be called truly God in so far as He was the Son of God, made Man in the Mystery of the Incarnation. He did not become God after His conception; He was not man made God, but God made man, by the operation of the Holy Ghost, in the womb of the Blessed Virgin Mary. What He became that instant, He will be for evermore. This His origin, His entrance into the world, is the standard by which we must judge of all that follows. For this reason, the unbelieving Jews, who were ignorant of this Mystery, in vain saw Him work miracles—give sight to the blind, and hearing to the deaf; raise the dead to life, make devils tremble, and rule both the storm and the sea. They cried, indeed: "*A great Prophet is risen up amongst us*"; they would willingly have made Him their king, but as soon as it was a question of adoring Him as their God, they brought forward the plea of His birth as an obstacle: "*Is not this the carpenter's son?*" they said; "*and they were scandalized at Him.*"* And even after His Godhead had been made manifest in such a striking manner by His Resurrection and Ascension, by the prodigies which marked the preaching of His apostles, by the conversion of the world and the triumphant reign of the Cross, no more definitive argument by which to establish the doctrine of that Godhead, when contested, can be found; no more indelible seal of its decisive and positive nature, than the Divine Conception of Jesus Christ, and the dignity of a Virgin-Mother of God, as it is upheld and proclaimed in Mary. Thus the Conception of the Son of God in Mary's womb—the Incarnation, in a word—is the great initial mystery of Christianity. It is to Mary, after God, that we owe this great blessing. Her sanctity it was which drew God down to her; He waited for her consent, and by the intervention of her charity, she has never ceased to exercise her influence over all those consequences which have ensued from her Divine Maternity. But besides all this, the Incarnation, being made a blessing to us only by means of a faith which is able to appropriate it to itself, and consequently being a blessing only to those who have any knowledge of it, it follows that the author of that knowledge is, in a certain sense, the author of the blessing.

Now, this author, this witness, to whom it has pleased God we should owe our knowledge of the Mystery of the Incarnation, is the same Virgin, to whom we owe, under God, the Incarnation itself. And these two obligations which God chose that we should owe to Mary, reciprocally demonstrate each other's importance. For it would be impossible to make us feel more forcibly how the Incarnation depended upon Mary, than by making the very knowledge of it, after it had taken place, depend upon Mary also; since, without that knowledge of it, the whole Mystery of the Incarnation would be to us a dead letter. We cannot, then, disregard this knowledge, when we see that it is necessarily founded on Mary's co-operation in the Mystery itself, and is, as it were, an extension of her maternity.

Every one must admit, from the consideration of all these points, what dignity, what importance, this her prerogative of being the fundamental witness of the Christian Faith, gives to the Blessed Virgin. But the truth of this statement will be contested, or at least it will be brought within narrower bounds. The number of other witnesses to the Divinity of Jesus Christ, with which the Gospels abound, independently of Mary's testimony, will be brought forward; the Apostles' profession of faith, even before they were enlightened by the Holy Spirit; and lastly, above all, the knowledge of all things (most unquestionably, therefore, the knowledge of the Saviour's Divinity) with which the descent of the Spirit of Truth filled their souls to overflowing. In answer to these objections, let us consider that two things are evident, when we examine the Gospels: first, that the Mystery of the Incarnation was known when they were written, for the Evangelists either relate it or allude to it; secondly, that it was unknown, even to the Apostles, during the lifetime of Jesus Christ.

It was impossible for those who had any personal knowledge of our Lord, and who saw His wonderful works, not to be impressed by the feeling of His Divine Nature, and, above all, the Apostles. They had been privileged to be the witnesses of His Transfiguration and of His Resurrection; they were the confidants of His love, the conquests of His grace, the heralds of His glory; they must have been so penetrated with the idea of His Godhead, as to be ready, one and all, to exclaim with Peter: "*Thou art the Christ, the Son of the Living God!*" But after all, their faith arose from an impression wrought upon the mind; it was true faith certainly, but a faith deficient in the historical knowledge of that Mystery of the Incarnation, a history which was to be its dogmatic foundation.

The Jews, too, even though they were ignorant of the Mystery of the Incarnation, were, without doubt, to blame for not believing in the Godhead of Jesus Christ. They had the evidence of His own solemn declarations, supported by the holiness of His moral teaching and the power of His miracles. That supernatural sanctity and power could not be at the command of falsehood and wickedness. And this rational argument for the ground of our faith suffices, and will always suffice to convince or reason, and to put incredulity to flight. Still, even side by side with this argument, it must be owned that the argument supplied by the knowledge of the history of the Incarnation of the Word, is still a valuable exposition of the Godhead of Jesus Christ. It surrounds Him with a dazzling brightness, displaying His Divine filiation, and making visible, so to speak, His pathway from heaven to earth.

God did not permit the Godhead of Jesus Christ to be manifested all at once with that splendor with which the revelation of the Mystery of His Incarnation would have clothed it, in order that the faith of the Jews might be exercised; but He gave them at the same time quite enough evidence of it by all they saw of Him and of His works, during His immediate presence among them. The same reason made Him choose to pass for Joseph's Son, which made Him say to His disciples after His glorious Transfiguration:

---

* Matthew, xiv, 25. Mark, vi, 2.

"*Tell the vision to no man, until the Son of Man be risen from the dead.*"[*] Jesus Christ, in thus choosing obscurity, was acting according to a plan already laid down; a plan to which the Blessed Virgin admirably conformed herself. But future generations were to be spared this trial of their faith. Deprived of His actual presence, they were not required, like the Jews, whilst in ignorance of the Incarnation, to believe that Jesus, the apparent Son of Joseph and Mary, was nevertheless the Eternal Word; and throughout the whole dispensation of the successive lights and shadows of our faith, the distinct and absolute knowledge of the Incarnation of the Word, in the immaculate womb of the Blessed Virgin Mary, has been published to the world, now no longer blest with the vision of the Word Himself in person. And thus too the Church, gratefully responding, imprints three times in the day upon the lips and hearts of the faithful, and rings out to the four winds, the good news of the Annunciation and the Incarnation, wherein the whole of Christianity consists and is substantially summed up.

We must not, therefore, confuse the faith of contemporary believers in our Lord with that of those who came after. The object of their faith was the same, that is to say, His Godhead; but the former had in His Godhead an implicit and virtual belief; in the latter it is an explicit and doctrinal faith. The Apostles indeed possessed both kinds, but, during the lifetime of Jesus, their belief was implicit only. Conscious as they were of His Divinity, they professed their belief in it, although unable to give an account as to how He came to possess that Divine Nature. Later on, they learned this, and have given us the history in the Gospels, drawn up during the course and towards the close of their apostolate. In them the Mystery of the Incarnation of the Word, as it was announced by the angel, and as it was accomplished in Mary, is revealed; and it is there laid down as the foundation of the knowledge of Jesus Christ. The doctrine of the Son of God made Man results from several other passages in the Gospels and Epistles; and St. John, in the sublime exordium of his Gospel, openly proclaims the eternal generation of the Word, and His Incarnation. But the full meaning of every one of these passages seems brought out by the history of the Annunciation, the fundamental and the most explicit of all passages relating to this doctrine. The rest are but commentaries upon it; without it they would be to us simply an enigma. And the Church, in the prayer in which she commemorates this the foundation of our faith, adds to Mary's words: "*Ecce Ancilla Domini, fiat mihi secundum verbum tuum*"; the "*Et Verbum caro factum est,*" of St. John; thus considering it as forming part of, and completing, that great saying of the Most Blessed Virgin.

Now, it has pleased God that there should be but one witness to the truth of this fundamental mystery, upon which the whole doctrine of the Apostles hangs; that one person only should be our guarantee with regard to those details, which chiefly characterize it; and this sole witness, this one only guarantee of our faith, is Mary.

This is an indisputable fact. Mary was alone with the angel when the great Mystery was announced. It was from her only that the Apostles could receive the knowledge of it, and transmit that knowledge to us: and if, says St. Ambrose, St. John speaks of this mystery more clearly, and after a more sublime manner than the rest of the mysteries of the Incarnate Word, it is because he was more closely connected with her, who was the very Temple in which those heavenly mysteries were accomplished: "*Mirum non est præ cæteris Johannem locutum esse mysteria divina, cui præsto erat aula cœlestium sacramentorum.*"[*] Moreover, in order to make Mary's office more conspicuous, as the witness to the fundamental mystery of our faith, God chose that she should be the faithful and mute depository of that mystery, during the whole time of her Son's life upon earth; He chose that she should keep the secret inviolably during all that number of years. "God chose," says Calvin, "that the treasure of this exalted mystery should be made over to the charge of the Virgin, and be as though buried in her heart, in order that shortly afterwards, when the fitting time was come, it might be communicated to all the faithful." Thus it is that all the faithful owe to Mary the knowledge of the Mystery of the Godhead of Jesus Christ. Even as she, in concert with Almighty God, kept it secret, so she also has been the means of making it known to all.

To appreciate the greatness and worth of Mary's testimony, it will be useful to consider for a moment that wonderful discretion, which sealed her lips for so long a period, and under circumstances when her silence was peculiarly meritorious. When the angel struck Zachary dumb to punish him for his incredulity, and to prevent him from revealing, before the proper time was come, the announcement which had been made to him of the miraculous conception of Christ's Forerunner, this privation of speech did not prevent him from making known to the people, by signs, that he had had a vision.

In Mary's case such a precaution was useless. The angel did not even bid her keep the secret. She, who was inspired by the grace of the Word

---

[*] Matthew, xvii, 9.

[*] Lib. de Inst., 'v, 7.

Himself; she whose soul was guarded by humility, faith, patience, fidelity and circumspection, and all other virtues, never allowed the glorious trust committed to her to escape her custody, nor any mention of it to transpire, until that distant day when it pleased God that she should publish it to the world. She has just beheld an angel; she has heard him salute her as "*blessed amongst all women*"; she has learned the great secret of God, the accomplishment of all His promises, the fulfilment of all the ancient hopes of Israel, the salvation of the universe; she is told that this great marvel is to be accomplished in her, and that immediately, by means of a most great and glorious prodigy. Without loss of her virginity, she is a mother, and the Mother of God; she is the Sanctuary of the Holy Ghost, the Spouse of the Most High, the living Tabernacle of the thrice Holy Trinity:—and yet of all this she breathes not one word. No trace of emotion upon her countenance betrays the Mystery, upon which hangs the destinies of the world; a Mystery which lies enfolded within herself. She attends just as usual to the most commonplace necessities of her state; in the eyes of her companions, she is no less humble; she is no less submissive to her spouse, St. Joseph. No one sees any difference in her; she is as calm and as simple as ever. The God now so closely concealed within her, will one day be made manifest to the whole universe. The heavens, angels, and the very stars, will proclaim His Birth and His glory. Prophets and saints will receive Him in His Temple; the Apostles, and great wonders on earth and in heaven, will herald His work to the very ends of the world. All the great ones of the earth, all the saints, wise men and kings, all people, will acknowledge Him, and pay homage to His greatness. And all this Mary knew; the angel had announced it to her; the Holy Spirit will presently inspire her with words of prophecy, which allude to her secret without betraying it; and still she is self-controlled, and still she is silent. Her silence will be unbroken for a yet longer space of time; even after many eloquent signs have spoken, and thus, as it were, set her free. She will speak last of all; and when she speaks, much that seemed an enigma will be solved by her words, and those words will be made the foundation of the Christian Faith as well as its crown. Mary's testimony is thus rendered doubly valuable from her silence, her humility and her magnanimous reserve, which so well befitted the Mother of that God who so humbled Himself as to become her Child.

Two circumstances, diametrically opposite to one another, which occurred whilst our Lord was as yet unborn, demonstrate in a more especial manner the merit of Mary's discretion. The first was when Joseph, her spouse, being ignorant of the Mystery of the Incarnation, conceived suspicions against her good fame, and would have put her away; the second was when her cousin Elizabeth humbled herself in her presence, and proclaimed her to be the Mother of God. Who is there that does not admire Mary's heroic patience upon the first of these occasions? She was the Mother of the Holy of Holies, whom she then bore within her womb; she was a Virgin, and so highly did she esteem her chastity, that sooner than relinquish it, she would have put aside the honor of the Divine Maternity; and yet she knows that in his heart her chaste spouse suspects her to be fallen into the lowest abyss of shame. One word would have sufficed to reinstate her again. But had that word been spoken, Mary knew how highly it would have exalted her in Joseph's eyes; it would have revealed the heavenly secret; it would have made her a witness in her own cause; and so her humility, her discretion, her confidence keep her silent. She left it to God rather to send His angel to make known to Joseph the mystery of her glorious innocence. And when that heavenly messenger came, she obtained, all the more meritoriously in that she was not aware of it, the fullest, the noblest, and the most holy justification.

Upon the second occasion, Mary's discretion was tried by honor, not by shame. She went to visit her cousin Elizabeth, and, during the interview, which was rendered so intimate by the connection between the two mysteries by means of which both had become mothers—the one Mother of the Word, the other of His Forerunner— Mary merely saluted Elizabeth. She left it to the Holy Spirit to reveal her Divine Maternity, and even then, she entered into no explanation of it, but gave all the glory to God.

It may be objected that, however much we may admire Mary's discretion, as it was manifested upon the two occasions we have been considering, nevertheless the revelation of her Divine Maternity made by the angel to Joseph, and by the Holy Spirit to Elizabeth, prevented her from being the sole confidant of the Mystery, and that henceforward, the secret having been divulged, we no longer owe the knowledge of it to Mary alone. And to add to this objection, the still more public proclamation might be cited, made by the angels in the sky, when the Child-God was born; and later on, the testimony of the shepherds, of the star, of the wise men, and of Simeon.

But these objections have no weight whatever. All these circumstances, all these marvellous testimonies to the *native* Divinity of Jesus Christ, not only do not diminish the debt we owe to Mary, but rather add to it; for once more, it is to her, and to her alone, that we owe our knowledge of the fact. Elizabeth, who was already in declining years, died shortly after; the angels winged their flight to heaven again; the shepherds returned to their solitudes, and the wise men to the East; the star disappeared from the sky, and Simeon closed his eyes in peace; the halo of glory which shone over Bethlehem was quenched by the wrath of Herod, and for a space of thirty years there remained only the obscure household of a carpenter, in which, to all appearance, Jesus was the Child and Mary the wife. Mary alone survived all these earlier witnesses to the Divinity of her Son. She survived Joseph also, who disappears from the scene when Jesus entered upon His public life. She is therefore our only witness, not only as regards the Divine Incarnation, but also with regard to the Visitation, to the Nativity, to the Adoration of the Wise Men, to the Presentation in the Temple, to the Flight into Egypt, to the Wisdom of Jesus amidst the Doctors, and finally, to the first thirty years of the life of our God upon earth.

This is expressed in the Gospel itself, with its characteristic sobriety and depth, when speaking of the great testimonies borne to Jesus during His Birth and Infancy, it repeats three times: "*And Mary kept all these words, pondering them in her heart.*" "that is to say," observes Calvin, a second time, "that this treasure was entrusted to her to keep within her heart, until the fitting time came when it was to be made manifest to others."* And the intention of this remark made in the Gospel, is the more notable, because, as Grotius observes, it is made by St. Luke, who is more especially the Evangelist concerning these mysteries, and who evidently wished thereby to designate Mary as his authority: "Quod ideo videtur a Luca expressum, quia *ipsam* habebat harum narrationum *Auctorem.*" †

(CONCLUSION NEXT WEEK.)

* Calvin. Comment. upon the Harmony of the Gospels, p. 49. † Grotius, Annot. in quatuor Evangelia.

THE CATHOLIC CHURCH is a city to which avenues lead from every side, towards which men may travel from any quarter, by the most diversified roads, by the thorny and rugged ways of strict investigation, by the more flowery paths of sentiment and feeling; but arrived at its precincts, all find that there is but one gate whereby they may enter, but one door to the sheep-fold—narrow and low, perhaps, and causing flesh and blood to stoop in passing in. Men may wander about its outskirts, they may admire the goodliness of its edifices, and of its bulwarks, but they cannot be its denizens and children if they enter not by that one gate of absolute, unconditional submission to the teaching of the Church.—*Cardinal Wiseman.*

An Offering of the Most Precious Blood.

BY MARCELLA A. FITZGERALD.

TO atone for the Faith that falters
  When shadows around us lower,
For the Hope that, half despairing,
  Turns from Thy mercy's power;

For the Charity grown so niggard
  Of gold to the hungry poor,
Trustless and cold and wary,
  No longer the fair and pure;

For the wrongs that are crying for vengeance,
  All crimes or hidden or known,
For the insults deep and bitter
  Cast at Thy Altar Throne;

For the sins of the whole wide world,
  We offer, Thee, Lord, to-day
The ransom Thy Son, our Saviour,
  Came down to the earth to pay.

The Precious Blood shed at His scourging,
  That flowed from His brow thorn-crowned,
That sprinkled thy streets, O Sion
  Making them holy ground.

That fell from His hands extended
  On the arms of the cruel Cross,
From His sacred feet nail-riven,
  To save us from endless loss.

That sprang in a living torrent
  When the keen lance rent apart
His holy side, and opened
  A path to His Sacred Heart.

Take, then, this gift we offer,
  The gift beyond price we bring,
The atonement made for us, Father,
  By Thy Son, our Lord and King.

MOSSY WOODLAND.

OUR great Washington said, "Be careful not to encourage the supposition that morality can be maintained without religion."

THERE is nothing more touching to a kind and generous heart than to see one, to whom it has refused compassion, withdraw silently, and never ask it again. The prayer or appeal that is never repeated is almost always remembered with regret.—*M. A. T.*

'Beth's Promise.

BY MRS. ANNA HANSON DORSEY.

CHAPTER XV.

HIGH-TEA AT "ELLERSLIE."

MRS. DULANEY and the Marstons returned home on Saturday evening, and, to their delight, found that the "boys,"—as they were usually spoken of by their parents—had come; Bertie arrived the day after they went away to Geneva; and after the first loving welcomes were over, and the joyful excitement had somewhat subsided, he was roundly taken to task by the girls for not having immediately joined them there, for which delinquency he had no better excuse to offer than that he "was too happy to find himself at home once more, to want to start right off again." What his adventures had been, and how he had spent his time, he did not relate, even when his mother told him how sorry she was that he had been so lonely in the empty house, without a soul to speak to, and forbade another word of reproach being uttered to the poor, dear fellow!

Paul Dulaney came up from New York, with his father, in the afternoon train. They were all together once more, and it would not be too much to say that a happier reunion had never taken place.

They were all at Mass on Sunday; and 'Beth thought Mr. Dulaney held his head a trifle higher, and wore a proud look of content on his face, as he walked up the aisle with his two tall handsome sons, one of them fair, the other dark—both plainly dressed and looking, every inch, gentlemen. Their demeanor was reverent and devout; born Catholics, the principles of their faith, fostered by a religious education, had "grown with their growth, and strengthened with their strength," and had become a second and higher nature, which to question or doubt would have seemed to them little short of madness; or to shrink from confessing openly, a base betrayal of true manliness and courage.

Father Hagner's face wore a troubled look, as did many of the poorer members of the little congregation, and well they might. He had been up at the iron-works, among the turbulent strikers, exhausting himself in a, so far, vain attempt to convince them of their mistake, and restore order. Their own priest was some thirty miles away, in another part of his mission, but had been telegraphed for, in the hope that, having labored among them for many years, and being regarded by them as a faithful friend, he would be able to influence them to give up their unreasonable demands. Father Hagner gave a short instruction; his heart was full of the misery, and perhaps crime, impending over the misguided men at the "iron-works," but the only allusion he made to the affair was after Mass, when he requested those present to say a decade of the rosary with him, that peace might be restored, which they did fervently—some of them with half stifled sobs—who had husbands and sons engaged in the strike. 'Beth glanced at the Dulaney pew just then, and saw a chaplet in the hands of each of its occupants, as they knelt aiding in the rosary. There was no sham in these young men; had one noticed, one would have seen that they did not make a merely meaningless sign with their fingers on their shirt front, when they made the sign of the cross, but did it in a decorous and earnest way not to be mistaken; and that they were not ashamed to pause and use the holy water at the door, turning their face towards the altar, and bowing their heads as they crossed themselves with the blessed drops.

The Dulaneys were out under the old trees waiting to greet Mrs. Morley and 'Beth, and introduced their sons, Bertie and Paul. They all walked together to the gate, in pleasant converse, where they separated with kindly expressed hopes of meeting again very soon, each turning their respective ways, yet not all, for Bertie Dulaney asked Mrs. Morley's permission to attend her and 'Beth to their own door.

"Mr. Dulaney is afraid, mamma, that I shall run myself into some sort of danger between here and the house, and thinks he had better be at hand," said 'Beth, laughing, while a delicate flush stole over her face.

Then Mrs. Morley told Bertie how glad she was of an opportunity to thank him for his good services to her daughter, and how sincerely grateful she was to him. He treated it all as a trifle, was slightly embarrassed, and turned the conversation from himself as quickly as he could do so, without appearing rude. He was sorry to find the way so short between the gate and "Ellerslie house," and made his bow reluctantly at the door, thinking his acquaintance was yet too recent for him to go in, as Mrs. Morley politely invited him to do. Then, half angry with himself for not accepting her invitation, and prolonging his interview with 'Beth, he walked slowly homeward, his mind full of a thousand little touches of dress and personality that made her his ideal of poetic girlhood.

"He's a fine, manly fellow," Mrs. Morley told Aunt 'Beth. "He has a frank, truthful look in his eyes, and although his manner is quiet, it is easy to see that he is full of spirit. His life, doubtless, has been all sunshine."

"I wouldn't give a snap of my finger for a young man without spirit; nor do I think that too much sunshine is good for them, Anne. Without difficulties and trials in some shape or other, what's to bring out, and strengthen the good that's in them? I should hate Adonis himself, if he had nothing but his beauty and grace to recommend him. I always feel when I see a pretty, simpering man, with his hair curled by a barber, and his gloves fitted on by a milliner, as if I should like to dress him up in petticoats and set him down to a spinning-wheel, though I doubt if any of that sort are capable of doing anything as useful as making yarn," said Aunt 'Beth.

"Dear Aunt 'Beth," said Mrs. Morley, amused at this tirade, "the world's full of strange people— no two alike—all differing in temperament and intellect."

"That is true. I should like to have the managing of some of them for a little while. The fact is, Anne, my temper's on edge; I've been hearing more about those miserable fellows up yonder at the iron-works, since you went to church. Gibbs, Elder & Co's. factor—a man I've always known and respected—called to tell me about the strike, and after a good deal of beating about the bush, what do you suppose his errand was? simply to beg of me, in the name of his employers, to let it be known that I would extend no assistance to the families of such of the strikers as live in the neighborhood of 'Ellerslie.' I told him to say that I was not a person to be dictated to, and while they might be sure I would offer no encouragement to the misguided men, I would not let their wives and children, who are innocent, suffer for bread. They are the ones who should suffer. By their own foolish act, they have taken the bread out of their children's mouths, the fools! at a time, too, when the whole country seems to be running into bankruptcy! I'm going to drive up the road after dinner to see Robin Goode, or rather Bad, for I know he's one of the ring-leaders; he and his always come to me in their troubles; now I shall go to him, to see if I can put some common sense into his head."

"But will it be safe, dear Aunt 'Beth, for you to go alone? Won't you take one of the men along?"

"No; that would not do at all. I'm not in the least afraid. The misfortune is this: they know that if the worst comes to the worst, I won't let the women and children starve, or themselves either, for that matter; I mean those of them who live in this neighborhood; knowing this, will help to demoralize them still more, and make them hold out longer. I'll take Lodo along, and see Robin Goode; he's in the rolling-mills, and is a sort of speech-maker and political leader among the hands, and I'll give him a ta'k that will make his hair stand on end," said Aunt 'Beth, bringing her little hand down upon her knee with strange energy.

"Are all the strikers Catholics?" inquired Mrs. Morley.

"A great many of them are, and a great many others are Methodists and Nothingarians; but they have all got the devil in them now, alike. Come, my child, there's the dinner-bell. But where's 'Beth?" she said, rising from her sofa and taking Mrs. Morley's arm.

"She went up to her room to have a conference with Lodo, who asked for a catechism a day or two ago, and has been studying it. 'Beth hears her say what she learns, and answers her questions. You do not object, dear aunt?" answered Mrs. Morley.

"Not I. Why should I, Anne? She's more than half pagan, and I shall be very glad if you can make a good Christian of her, poor little waif!" said Aunt 'Beth, taking her high-backed chair at the head of the table, saying, "Now, my dear Anne, let us be cheerful as well as thankful for the good things provided for us."

Aunt 'Beth honestly thought she was saying grace; the words were the outcome of her heart's fulness, expressing exactly what she felt. Mrs. Morley, and 'Beth—who had now taken her place at table—crossed themselves, and in their hearts asked God's blessing on the bounties of His providence, without attracting her attention, which was at that moment engaged in giving directions to Lodo about a certain jelly she wished brought from the store-room.

Dinner over, true to her word, Aunt 'Beth, taking Lodo along, drove two miles up a cross-cut road to Robin Goode's cottage. He was standing in his shirt-sleeves at the stile, his arms folded on top of it, his old battered hat slouched down over his eyes, looking moodily at the ground, in deep thought. Had he seen in time who was coming, he would have gone off to the woods and hid himself, but he did not even hear the carriage wheels until they stopped quite near him, and a voice said: "Good day, Robin." Then lifting his head, he saw "old lady Ellerslie," as the plainer classes around the country called her, and he knew that he would have to stand and listen to whatever she might have to say to him. He knew at once that, as ailing as she had been for a year past, she never would have driven so far and on Sunday too, unless she had meant to give him a piece of her mind about the "strike," a thing which years of kindness on her part towards him and his, gave her a right to do.

"Will you 'light, ma'am, and go in? my wife's in there, and will be main proud to see you," he said, taking off his old hat, revealing a large head covered with black grizzled hair, and a face showing both force and honesty of purpose.

"Not to-day, Robin. I have come to have a talk with you, and I want you to go up the road a little way with me, that we may not be intarrupted," she said, in her quick, decided way. "There's nothing that anybody could say that would make any difference, ma'am," he replied, in a surly tone, as he leaped the stile and walked alongside the low carriage, while Lodo drove slowly under the shade of the great trees on the edge of the woods until "old Lady Ellerslie" bade her stop. "I'll hold the reins, Lodo, and you can go into the woods a little while. I wish to speak to Robin alone."

"I'll keep in sight of them," thought the girl, as she skipped out of the carriage, "and if anything happens, I can scream again."

But nothing happened, except that Aunt 'Beth poured out her vial of wrath upon Robin Goode's head. The substance of what she said was this: Did he know what a state the country was in? Did he know that they had stopped building railroads everywhere on account of the times? Did he know that the iron manufacturers all over the country were closing, or working their mills on half time? Did he know that in the city of New York over sixty thousand workmen of various crafts had been cast adrift in one week, and were literally without bread, and without a prospect of work ahead, because their employers had failed? As it is there, so it is elsewhere through all the length and breadth of the land. Had he ever considered who furnished the capital and took all the risks of manufacturing on a large scale? Did he reflect that, while workmen were engaged in "strikes" for a few pennies more or less on their wages, their employers were obliged to contract their operations and reduce their expenses throughout, or fail. "And here," she continued, "Gibbs, Elder & Co., without profit to themselves, are willing to keep their mills running, only reducing your wages five per cent., until the times mend. I tell you Robin, you and your fellow-workmen are in the wrong; and seeing this, I tell you plainly that if you keep on, none of you need expect assistance from me, for you'll bring all that you may have to suffer upon yourselves. I'll shut up 'Ellerslie' and go away, and you can all burn it down if you choose.—Just wait a moment, Robin, I shall soon be done. There's no telling what a thousand or more lawless men, out of work and wanting bread, would be ready to do; I should not feel safe at 'Ellerslie,' where I was born and have lived in peace all my days, if this goes on; and I want to know this: if you can't live on a few cents less a day, how much better can you live *on nothing at all?* You are all digging a pit for your feet, and will be sorry for it, I fear, only when it is too late; I read the papers, Robin Goode; I know what a panic there is throughout the country, such as was never known before; and I have come up here to warn you, and beg you, and your fellow-workmen through you, to stop in time, and accept the terms offered by your late employers."

The energetic and excited little woman, whose generous heart was moved with the most charitable intent towards the misguided men engaged in the "strike," would not have hesitated to have said to them, all, and even more than she had said to Robin Goode, had they been on the spot; nor could they have silenced her either by scowls or threats, such was her indomitable will and courage when she felt that she had a duty to perform; but there was no one there except Robin Goode, and she hadn't given the great rough fellow a chance to get in a word edgeways, although he had several times attempted to do so, for he had enough to say on his side of the question too. She had not come up there to argue with him, she told him, but to tell him the plain truth, and if he wouldn't heed it, he'd have to take the consequences. "But I hope you will heed, Robin, for the sake of those youngsters of yours, and your hard-working, patient wife, whose health is not what it used to be, and for she sake of the little one sleeping out yonder on the hill-side, who died in my arms, Robin."

The veins swelled like cords in the man's throat, a dark glow mounted to his face, and as he turned away, he dashed his rough, hairy hand across his eyes, for well he remembered his fair haired little daisy, whom of them all he had loved best, and whose death had nearly broken his heart. Aunt 'Beth beckoned to Lodo, and in another moment, they were driving homewards. She thought she had said enough, and that it would be better to leave him while his feelings were softened, to think over what she had said.

"I don't know that I've done any good!" sighed the fearless little woman, after relating all that had passed to Mrs. Morley and 'Beth, as she sipped her tea; "but I've given him something to think about. Oh dear, will things ever come straight? The world's full of great wrongs that will never be righted until the judgment day!"

"Dear Aunt 'Beth, if all tried as you do, there would be fewer wrongs and less suffering," said Mrs. Morley, tenderly.

'Beth, who had slipped away from the veranda where they had been taking tea, now came back with a bunch of spicy old-fashioned pinks, interspersed with sprigs of thyme, in her hand, which she offered Aunt 'Beth, who held them to her face, inhaling their aroma with evident satisfaction.

"How did you know I liked them, child?"

"By seeing you every day, more or less, going about with a little posy of pinks and thyme in your hand, smelling them every few minutes," said 'Beth, with a loving smile at the dear old face.

"They always refresh me, no matter how languid I may be feeling; there's a sentiment and a memory about these old-fashioned flowers that make them very dear to me," said Aunt 'Beth. "But I think I'll lie down a little while, although

I don't feel half as tired as I thought I would. To-morrow, you know, the hop-pickers begin, and I want to have the Dulaneys and those two bright girls over to an afternoon tea. Afterwards we'll all go and see the pickers at work; it is really a very pretty sight. Are you going to church this evening?"

"For a little while," Mrs. Morley answered. There was no regular afternoon service, but she loved to go and kneel before the Adorable Presence, close by the feet of the holy Virgin Mother, who had suffered in her sacred and sinless heart every wound and every pang endured by her Divine Son. There she rested her weary, aching heart; there she could weep in silence the tears that relieved and soothed,—tears without sin or revolt against the divine will, such as the Master shed at the tomb of Lazarus. 'Beth generally went over to meet her mother at the chapel door, sometimes going in to kneel and pray for the gift of faith, that she might enter into the one safe Fold which her heart now longed for. She had been reading steadily, and thinking deeply over, some books that Father Thomas had given her, one especially, which proved, by Scriptural evidence alone, the Divine origin and dogmas of the Catholic Faith.* "There could be no mistake here," she thought, as she carefully compared it with her own Bible, finding it all exactly the same as in her mother's Catholic version. She often stole away to spend a half hour in the chapel reciting the rosary, a devotion whose sacred mysteries had taken strange hold on her heart from the moment she had comprehended their meaning. But these things belonged to 'Beth Morley's hidden life; no one knew the grave, deep thoughts that exercised her mind, seeing her always so bright and full of life. The tabernacle of her pure heart was open only to heaven.

Next morning's sun rose fair and unclouded, and 'Beth was awakened from her dreams by the noise of a slight cough in her room. She opened her eyes, and was for a moment or two on the border-land between sleeping and waking, when she saw Lodo standing near the foot of her bed, her great black eyes wild with suppressed delight.

"Oh, mem, they're here!" she exclaimed, a broad smile showing her pretty white teeth.

"Who? what?" asked 'Beth, sitting up and pushing back her hair; "you don't mean the 'strikers'?"

"The hop-pickers, mem; nearly a hundred—mostly young people,—and there'll be such fun! and only think, mem, I'm to go two whole days! You can hear them now, if you listen."

* Bishop Becker, of Delaware, in his reply to Bp. Lee, of the Protestant Episcopal Church, is the author of a small book of this kind, one of the strongest, most convincing and indisputable works in proof of all that the Church teaches, that one could read.

'Beth listened, and heard a distant and cheery hum of voices, with blithe sounds of laughter and scraps of song mingled together, so in harmony with the sunshiny brightness of the day, that she felt quite exhilarated.

"It sounds awfully jolly! I should like to go with you, Lodo," she said, laughing.

"You'll come, mem, after a while, to look at us; I must go now: I just ran in to tell you, mem."

"Thank you, you little elf; but stop a minute. Put on that sun-down in your hand: I want to see how you look in it," said 'Beth.

Lodo put her rough straw-hat, with its red ribbon streamers, on her head, which, with a bright blue calico skirt, a loose white sacque belted in by a white apron, and a string of large red beads around her throat, completed the attire, in which she looked very pretty.

"Do they all dress in this manner?" asked 'Beth, smiling her approval.

"Mostly, mem."

"I'm sure they don't look so though. Now run away. You'll have to tell my fortune, little gypsy, when I come over to-day," said 'Beth.

"I think I could, mem, if all signs are true," said Lodo, nodding her head as she went out.

"What can she mean?" thought 'Beth, as the rose hue deepened in her face; "how absurd the little witch is! No doubt she has built up quite a romance about me in her own mind."

When Mrs. Morley came in, she found 'Beth dressed, and after the "good-morning" embrace, they went as usual to Mass. They caught a glimpse, here and there, of the hop-fields as they walked along, and heard distinctly the pleasant hum arising from them.

"It reminds me of the Italian vintage," said Mrs. Morley, sadly, remembering but too vividly with whom she had enjoyed one of the most picturesque sights of that sunny land.

But presently all else was forgotten, for as they knelt in their pew, Father Hagner, robed for Mass, came in from the sacristy, attended by one of the young Dulaneys—'Beth did not look to see which of them—and the Divine Sacrifice began.

When they got back to "Ellerslie," they found Aunt 'Beth quite elated. Robin Goode had paid her an early visit, and from his talk, she thought he was giving in; but he promised nothing positive, except to deliver a letter she had written to Gibbs, Elder & Co., and ask to have a conversation with them.

Mrs. Morley was astonished as well as cheered to see how much good the stirring up of things was doing the dear old lady of "Ellerslie;" she was much better, undoubtedly; her prostrated nerve power was stimulated; it had received a new impetus, and she began to feel that she no longer "cumbered the earth," like a dead tree. The fine weather, so necessary for the hop-gathering, the presence of so much life and stir, quite revived her; it was her festival season as well as theirs—one which she had always enjoyed; and now, to add to her happiness, Mrs. Morley and 'Beth, her only living kindred, were under her roof, ready to enjoy it with her.

"Now, 'Beth," she said after breakfast, "everybody's a-field except Mrs. Trott; we'll have a cold early dinner to-day; but there's to be a high-tea for the Dulaneys you know, and I shall want your help."

"I am yours to command, my queen," said 'Beth, kneeling before the little woman's chair, her arms about her, her bright, beautiful face uplifted to hers. "I can break eggs, I can whip them up to a froth that you can slice with a knife; I can sift flour, cream butter, and do such lots of things as would astonish you! can't I, mamma?"

"Yes: I recommend her as assistant, Aunt 'Beth," said Mrs. Morley.

"Oh, child, you are so like your father!" said Aunt 'Beth, with quivering lip. Then there was a brief silence, broken presently, when she had quite recovered her voice, by her telling 'Beth that she wanted her to put fresh flowers in the vases, and whole wax candles in the *candelabras* and sconces. "Cut the flowers at once, my child, before the sun begins to burn them, and they'll keep fresh; then go at the candles; and when that's done, I'll tell you what next. There'll be plenty of things to do to keep you busy for hours; meantime, you and I, Anne, will wash dishes."

It was indeed a busy day throughout—a day, 'Beth thought, to be marked with white, and remembered. The arrangements for the "high-tea" were all perfect; the old silver, the quaint old china as thin as egg-shells, with flowers, and rare cut-glass that sparkled like diamonds, with dainties of various sorts, and vine-wreathed fruits interspersed over the length and breadth of the solid mahogany table that was black with age, and so polished that every article on it was reflected as in a mirror, made a fair spectacle in the antique dining-room where the panelled walls were hung with time-shadowed portraits, and the windows opening to the floor, were draped with Virginia creeper and clematis. 'Beth was invited to preside, but preferred to serve, while her mother and Aunt 'Beth were to take the head and foot of the table. 'Beth was in an ecstasy of delight at the success of her arrangements, and at the approval they received; she flitted around, giving a last touch to this, or moving another thing to a more effective place, training a vine here, or placing another half-blown rose there, until at last, finding nothing more to be done, she hurried away to make her toilette.

Never had 'Beth Morley looked lovelier. Her simply made, close-fitting dress of black English crape, displayed the symmetry of her lithe, graceful figure. A cluster of half-opened white roses, at the throat, relieved the sombre hue of her toilette. Loose open sleeves revealed the beauty of hands and wrists as lovely as those of a Grecian statue, and her nut-brown curling hair, with its tinge of gold, crowned her as with a diadem. Her mother had pinned a white rose among the loose curls at the back of her head; that was all; and her utter unconsciousness of her attractions but enhanced her loveliness.

Presently the Dulaneys, with Elaine and Violet Marston, arrived, and were duly welcomed; hats and wraps were laid aside, and a great deal of gay chat among the young people ensued. But the afternoon tea was the first thing in order, and it was not long before they were summoned to it by the little lady of "Ellerslie" herself, who led the way to the dining-room, and directed each of her guests to their respective places. Mrs. Trott had brought in the steaming tea urn, the hot muffins, French rolls, broiled sweet-breads, and other dainties, and there was nothing more to be done but for every one to sit down and enjoy the hospitable feast so bountifully set before them.

When 'Beth began to hand around the tea-cups, with a demure air, Bertie Dulaney pushed back his chair, and sprang up, exclaiming:

"Oh, now, I declare that won't do. Miss Morley!" may I not wait too?"

"Yes," said Aunt 'Beth, "I'll be glad if you will. There's a salver on the side-board. I only bargain that you do not break anything."

It made them all very merry, and his efforts to do every thing in a waiter-like style, his dread of letting something slip or of upsetting hot tea on somebody's back, were highly amusing. He was at once dubbed "Jeems," and his father's and brother's calls upon him were incessant. Father Hagner, much to Aunt 'Beth's regret, was not present; he had gone up to the iron works again to see what he could do. The two amateur waiters were complimented on their new accomplishment after tea, and were then made to sit down, while Paul Dulaney and Elaine Marston served them in due form, and were kept busy by their unnecessary demands amidst much merry chatter and chaff.

(TO BE CONTINUED.)

THE following are said to have been the last words of Charles Carroll, of Carrollton, the Catholic signer of the Declaration of Independence: "I have lived until my ninety-sixth year, I have enjoyed continued health, I have been blessed with wealth, prosperity, and most of the good things this world can bestow—public approbation and applause—but what I now look back on with great satisfaction to myself is, that I have practiced the duties of my religion."

Our Lady's Sennight in the Household of Faith.

(CONCLUSION.)
NIGHT VII.
QUEEN OF MAY, AND HEAVEN, AND ALL.

THE worshippers throng from all the nations; shouts of gladsome triumph prelude the coming *Festa:*—the throne of more than ever gracious Mary is set on an altar of deep blue:—the starry-torches are lit in wheeling constellation of the sky; the moon bends meek her silver crescent to the lovely feet. Higher Heaven's doors,

"... On golden hinges turning,"

spread wide their jewelled valves, and all but angelic tongues are mute as the royal *cortège* flashes through and conducts the Queen of Heaven. The bards attend, and, as the heavenly music ceases, tune their varied instruments, and twine their wreaths of flowers for angels to weave in living garlands all about the throne and her who sits thereon.

Who more worthy than St. Bernard to please the Queen and gain her favor—as he is interpreted to speak by Dante Alighieri—master mystic of all the ages!

"O Virgin Mother, Daughter of thy Son!
Created beings, all in lowliness
Surpassing, as in height above them all;
Term by the eternal counsel preordained;
Ennobler of thy nature so advanced
In thee, that its great Maker did not scorn
To make Himself His own creation;
For in thy womb rekindling shone the love,
Whose genial influence makes now
This flower of germin in eternal peace:
Here thou to us, of charity and love,
Act as the noonday torch, and act beneath,
To mortal men of hope a living spring.
So mighty art thou, Lady, and so great,
That he who grace desireth, and comes not
To thee for aidance, fain would have desire
Fly without wings. Not only him who asks,
Thy bounty succors, but doth freely oft
Forerun the asking. Whatsoe'er may be
Of excellence in creature, pity mild,
Relenting mercy, large munificence,
Are all combined in thee...."*

---

* The vision of Dante Alighieri—Rev. H. F. Cung., p. 566. *Purgatorio* and *Paradiso* abound in verses laudatory of the Blessed Virgin in all her offices. Cf., for some examples among hundreds, Purg., C. VII, C. VIII; Parad. C. XXIII; and C. XXXI; whole C. XXXII, and C. XXXIII; Tasso's "Gierusalemme Liberata"—the other greatest Catholic epic—devotes over fifty stanzas of Canto II to a relation of the profaning of a shrine of Our Lady—by orders of Aladine, advised by the apostate Wizard Ismeno—and the rescue of the sacred image by Sophronia and Olinda; who, being condemned to be burned alive, are wrested from the pile by the Amazonian Clorinda.— Finally, the English writer Brydge's "Hymn of the Calabrian Shepherds" is a fine specimen of earnest Italian devotion to Our Lady.

While Gabriel now, with archangelic seven, advances, and the angels bend around, repeating, as fittest praise, the God-taught "*Ave*," kneel we, and tell

"Our Beads":

the modern mystic, and Mary lover, Abram S. Ryan, leading one choir of the throng:

"Sweet, Blessed Beads! I would not part
With one of you, for richest gem
That gleams in kingly diadem:—
Ye know the history of my heart.

. . . .

"Ah! time has fled, and friends have failed,
And joys have died;—but in my needs,
Ye were my friends! my blessed Beads!
And ye consoled me when I wailed.

"For many and many a time in grief,
My weary fingers wandered 'round
Thy circled-chain, and always found
In some Hail Mary sweet relief.

"Ye are the only chain I wear,
A sign that I am but the slave,
In life, in death, beyond the grave,
Of Jesus and His Mother fair." *

The last bead is counted, and all are seated, by the waved permission of Gabriel, the master of the Marian ceremony; at a sign from the throne, a disembodied spirit advances from his station at Mary's feet, and holds discourse—aided by the promptings of St. Dominic—on the

"HOLY ROSARY."

"Instruction's aid and learning's substitute,
And shattered senses' guide and supplement,
Eyes to the blind and language to the mute,
Unschool'd devotion's free and ready vent:
So plain, that all its force may understand;
So rich, that none its plainness need despise;
So trite, that all its service may command;
So precious, that its riches all may prize.
Prayer of the lips and heart in one combined;
For while the lips to God their homage yield,
Pass in array before each heavenward mind
Th' historic scenes on sacred page revealed:
The joys of Mary and her Son: the train
Of sorrows strewn along the dolorous way;
And glories linked in one unbroken chain
With that which crown'd the Resurrection-Day!"†

As this is a May-day of all nations, the child of the eldest daughter of the Church—himself an humble son of the eldest daughter of the Father —surely has a double right to be heard in this "chosen abode" of hers, "in the full assembly of saints"‡—and heard in the music of his native tongue as he sings the

"HYMN A LA VIERGE."§

"Ainsi la myrrhe parfumée
Qu'enhale un brasier devorant,
S'élève à demi consumée,
Et vole en nuage odorant.

---

* P. 187.   † Canon Frederick Oakley.   ‡ Eccus. xxiv. 15.
§ Ch. Nodier-Noel de la Place, 460.

Des flots d'encens et de cinname
Roulent dans sa mobile flammé,
L'or, l'emerande et le saphir,
Et le feu pur qui la colore
Fait pâlir celui dont l'aurore
Emaille les cristaux d'Ophir.

Ainsi cette Vierge ingénue,
Pleine de grâce et de beauté,
S'élance, et plonge dans la nue
Son front rayonnant de clarté.
Le chœur mystérieux des anges
Mêle le bruit de ses louanges
Aux concerts des mondes ravis;
Le terre frémit devant elle
Et sous les pas de l'immortelle
Les cieux abaissent leurs parvis.

. . . .

Hélas! ces héros éphémères
Qu'élèvent de sanglants pavois,
Sont inexorables aux mères!
Ils ne comprendraeint pas ta voix;
Mais Dieu, dans son amour immense,
Permet que ton pouvoir commence°
Où finit celui des humains.
D'un seul regard tu le désarmes,
Et l'on dit que l'une de tes larmes
Eteint la foudre dans ses mains."

Except the *Niebelungen*—from their very name, hidden back in the dim twilight of unlettered ages—the poems of Ottfried, or Otfrid, a monk, are the oldest German composition, in verse. Ottfried flourished in the time of Charlemagne, when there was scarcely a distinction of Frank and Teuton, about A. D. 800; and it is from his metrical paraphrase that the English poet Coleridge translates the delicious fragment quoted in our article, "Our Lady and Some Non-Catholic Poets." * And this was only a morsel of the exquisite tidbits extracted from the honeycomb of the old monkish devotees of Mary the Virgin. If we followed up the traditions, and by their light delved in the mines of the olden "Minnesingers," the troubadours of Germany, and their Catholic descendants, we should find the most unalloyed gold, growing virgin-pure in the hearts of the Java, Voralberg and Teutonic Alps. We would willingly revive these beautiful spirits, and let them repeat their thousand-year love-ditties, if time served and we had not already written on the testimony of Protestant Germany,† and were not ample specimens made public through the pages of our excellent contemporary, *Alte und Neue Welt*. Our

SPIRITUAL LECTURE

will now be rendered by the gifted author of "Beside the Western Sea," who stints not her talents in the praise of her dearest namesake. As it is meet and just, the glorious "*Salve Regina*," the composition of Adhemar of Montell, Bishop of Puy and spiritual chief of the first crusade, a thousand years now dead, shall be taken up in chorus by united choirs of the Heavens, the earth, and purgatory.* To end our May-day, let us hear the legend of the "*Salve*,"

"THE MARTYRS OF SANDOMIR."

" *Salve Regina!*" . . . .

The first sweet day of smiling June was gliding to the west,
The warbling bird had ceased his tune and sought his leafy nest;
And, gathered in their eden home, monks gave willing ear
To one who read, from holy tome, the list of martyrs dear.
Why changed that clear and quiet voice to awesome murmur soon?
He read—O eager band, rejoice!—' The second day of June';
(At dawning of the morning sun within that very year)
The nine and forty martyrs won their crown at Sandomir,—
At Sandomir, 'twas their abode, and 'twas their record fair,
For never martyr's blood had flowed to bless the vineyard there.
"'Tis Heaven's message unto us,' the holy Sadoc said;
'An angel's hand hath written thus the warning thou hast read.'
Submissive to that summons sweet, for combat to prepare,
They sought their hidden God's retreat, and knelt in vigil there;
And when the herald beams of light unbarred the golden east,
They decked the shrine for holy rite and shared the nuptial feast.
And while the soft auroral sun stole through the arches dim,
The soldiers of the Cross begun their ne'er omitted hymn:
'*Salve Regina!*' thus they sang; but at its op'ning strain,
What wild, discordant tumult rang, in mock'ry of refrain?
Rejoice, ye soldiers of the Lamb! the glad release is nigh,
And yours is now the martyr's palm, the robe of royal dye.
In rushed the ruthless Tartar horde, with wild, demoniac yell;
And calmly, 'neath the savage sword, those Christian heroes fell:
Nor ceased their holy *Salve* strain, for as each voice grew still,
Another rung the glad refrain, with glad ecstatic thrill;
And with the swiftly-flowing blood, the heavenward floating breath,
The music poured its pulsing flood upon the place of death;
And when, save one, that martyr-throng had passed the crimson sea,
One voice completed, clear and strong, the wondrous melody:
It was the dauntless leader's tone that last and longest rose,
That bore the sacred prayer, alone, unto its tender close.

---

* Dante's Purgatorio, Canto VII.

---

* THE AVE MARIA, Aug. 9, 1879.
† Ib., Nov. 8-15, 1879.

'*O dulcis Virgo!*' thus he sang, and with that latest breath,
His freed, exultant spirit sprang beyond the gates of death." *

. . . .

When now the last word, "*Maria*," last, including all, has been chanted, the precentor's voice proclaimed the verse: "*Ora pro nobis*," the mighty unison responding: "*Ut digni efficiamur*," and the poet-priests have sung together the "*Oremus*": let the rocks and caves, the eternal hills and snowy peaks of the mountainous western lands, all inanimate things, resound with this

"ECHO TO MARY."

"Who gently dries grief's falling tear?
    Maria.
Of fairy flowers which fairest blows?
    The Rose.
What seekest thou, poor plaining dove?
    My Love.

"Rejoice, thou Morning Dove!
Earth's peerless Rose, without a thorn,
Unfolds its bloom this natal morn,†
 Maria, Rose of Love!

"What craves the heart, of storms the sport?
    A port.
And what the fever'd patient's quest?
    Calm rest.
What ray to cheer when shadows slope?
    Hope.

"O Mary, Mother blest!
Through nights of gloom, thro' days of fear,
Thy love the ray by which to steer,
 Bright Hope! to port of rest.

"Desponding heart, what gift will please?
    Heart of ease.
What scent reminds of a hidden saint?
    Jess'mine faint.
What caught its hue from the azure sky?
    Violet's eye.

"O Mary, peerless dower!
A balm to soothe, love's odor sweet,
A glimpse of heaven in thee we greet—
 Heart's ease, Jess'mine, violet flower!

"Of Mary's love who must secure?
    The pure.
What lamp diffuses light afar?
    A star.
When is light-winged zephyr born?
    At morn.

"My eyes, with watching worn,
Will vigil keep till day returns,

---

* We would beg that this Polish legend of their apostle may serve as a tribute from the Catholic, persecuted land—whose language has been all but destroyed with its nationality—to the Queen very dear to their bleeding hearts.
If we quote no translations from the other most Catholic and ever-persecuted—now, alas! starving--nation, Ireland, it is because their beautiful language has become unfamiliar to her sons' tongues and our—nearly half—Irish-American poets sing sweetest in English.

† This translation--Nativity of the B. V. M., Sept. 8, 1877,-- is from *The Catholic World*, the original having appeared in the Spanish *Revista Cattolica* of Las Vegas, New Mexico.

To see thy light my spirit yearns,
 Mary pure, Star of Morn!
"Whose name most sweet to dying ear?
    Maria.
On heavenly hosts who smiles serene?
    Their Queen.
What joy is perfected above?
    Love?

"Welcome, thou spotless Dove!
Awake, my soul, celestial mirth!
This day brings purest joy to earth!
 Maria, Queen of Love."

Blessed Andrew Bobola.

BLESSED ANDREW BOBOLA, of the Society of Jesus, beatified by our late Holy Father, Pius IX, sealed his fidelity to the Holy See by a most cruel but glorious martyrdom. Sprung from one of the most ancient and noble families of of Poland, Andrew Bobola had labored full thirty years in his native land with indefatigable zeal, and had led a great number of schismatics back to the Church. At an inroad of the Cossacks into the district of Pinzk, the holy man fell into their hands not far from Ianow. At first these fanatical adherents of schism sought to win their prisoner over to their side by persuasion and promises; but when they perceived that all such attempts were in vain, they beat and scourged him most unmercifully. Then they bound him fast to a saddle, and dragged him to their captain in Ianow. The latter imperiously ordered him to renounce the communion of Rome. The noble confessor answered: "I am a Catholic priest; I was born in the Catholic Faith, and mean to die therein." This fearless answer put the Cossack in a rage. He drew his sword, made a blow at the head of the confessor, and inflicted a deep wound on the hand which the holy man raised to protect his head. A second blow of the sword fell on his left foot, wounding him so painfully that he fell to the earth. Whilst he lay extended on the ground, a soldier knocked out his right eye. He was then dragged into the court-yard of Ianow and there for a long time burned with torches. The barbarians tore the skin from his head, his hands, and his back, and in addition to other indescribable tortures, drove splinters under the nails of his hands and feet, and tore out his tongue by the roots through a large gash which they made in his neck. After having thus dreadfully abused and mutilated the holy confessor, they left him. One of the commanders coming shortly afterwards to the scene of murder, and perceiving that life still remained, gave orders to put an end to his sufferings. Two strokes of the sword terminated his martyrdom, which took place on the 16th of May, 1657.

[*From* "*The Catholic Union.*"]
Mariolatry.

THE word, as applied by Protestants speaking of the Catholic Faith, and used as it always is in that case with a sinister meaning, is a highly objectionable one.

"Catholics complain that they are accused of Mariolatry: and yet 'The Devotion and Office of the Sacred Heart,' p. 262 (Dublin, 1855), contains this clause from a prayer: 'I reverence you, O sacred Virgin Mary! and *together with* the Holy Trinity, bless and praise you *infinitely*.' If the Catholic worshipper thus blesses and praises Mary, how could he bless and praise God any more?"

These words occur in a highly respectable New York contemporary, and we cannot let them pass unnoticed.

Catholics certainly do object to be accused of Mariolatry, because the accuser manifests a total ignorance of the Church's teaching. Theologians divide devotion, veneration, and adoration, and style them in technical language: *latria*, the highest kind of adoration, which is paid to Almighty God alone; *hyperdulia*, or super-service, which is offered to our Blessed Lady as the Mother of God; and *dulia*, or simple service, which is rendered to the saints. Therefore, the word Mariolatry, composed as it is of Mary and *latria*, and implying that supreme adoration of Our Lady which has never been, and never can be, authorized by the Holy Church, is a highly objectionable term. We do not know the book quoted from, nor are we certain that it bears an *imprimatur;* we cannot therefore verify the quotation, or compare it with the context. Turning, however, to a work, not indeed written at Dublin, in 1855, but by St. Justin, the Greek Doctor and Martyr, about 155, some seventeen hundred years before the other, we find these words in the original Greek: "Ali' te kai ton par' auton Vion Elthonta kai . . . . excomoioumenoa gathon aggelon straton, Pneuma te to prophetikan debometha kai proskunoumen, logo kai alatheia timontes." (Justin, Apol. i vulg. ii. p. 48.)

Here the holy angels are spoken of in conjunction with "Him and the Son, who came forth from Him; and the prophetic Spirit; whom we adore and venerate, honoring them in word and in truth.". We do not suppose that Protestants will assert that within forty years of the death of St. John, the beloved disciple, many Romish corruptions had crept in, yet the passages quoted from that period, and from our own, are almost identical.

The Church, though frequently mentioning our Blessed Lady in prayers to the Adorable Trinity, has ever been careful to separate, and keep clearly defined and distinct, the cultus of the Mother of God from that God Himself. The Breviary and the Missal are the authoritative office-books of the Church, and faithfully reflect her spirit and mind in authentic forms of prayer and praise. These therefore are the proper books to quote, and not any ephemeral manual, authorized or unauthorized, which is not used and recognized by the whole Catholic Church throughout the world. The Anglican Keble nearly expressed the teaching of the Church when he wrote—

"*Ave Maria!* thou whose name,
Almost adoring love doth claim."

She stands alone in all the solitary grandeur of the star-like glory of her immaculate conception. To no other mortal, as Origen, in the third century remarks, was it said Kecharitomene— "for Mary alone is salutation reserved" (Hem. VI, in Lucam). The words actually used in the Angelic Salutation were probably the Syriac maliat taibuto, which are translated from the Peshito "full of grace," words that occur nowhere else in that version. Luther, with a true Protestant dread of honoring the Mother of God, translated the Du holdselige! "thou gracious one," and says with impious frivolty he could not otherwise translate them or the Germans would not understand the expression. "Du bist voll Gnaden?" what German would understand what was said: full of grace? He might think of "a barrel full of beer, or a purse full of gold" (Sendbrief Erlangen, edit. 1855, vol. XX, p. 112). Thus had it ever been with Protestants; they cannot understand the plenitude of divine grace that filled our Blessed Lady at the moment of her Immaculate Conception, and ever preserved her from sin; consequently our devotion to her is an enigma and a stumbling-block.

FATHER DE RAVIGNAN, S. J., one of the greatest orators that France has ever produced, was accustomed to begin his celebrated Conferences at Notre Dame, in Paris, with the Sign of the Cross—that famous Sign of the Cross which seemed so peculiarly his own, and which he made with such pomp and stateliness. He could not endure that others should curtail the Christian sign. "What!" he would say, "is the Cross a plaything, a scarecrow? you all seem to want to play with it, or else to be rid of it. It should not be so; put away all fear and shame. A Christian should be proud to display his standard; and, for the honor of Christ, the Sign of the Cross should not be used without some formality."

Found Faithful.

THERE was found, in the cell of one of these noble confessors,* a relic precious for the Church of Paris; it is the last testament of M. Bécourt, curé of Bonne-Nouvelle. This monument of priestly generosity and fealty witnesses so well to the true sentiments of the priest towards his persecutors, that it should be reproduced verbatim:

PRISON OF THE CONDEMNED,
Thursday, May 24, 1871.

I send to my good mother, my last, respectful, and affectionate salutations. A remembrance to my father, who died in 1840.

Adieu, dear mother, good sister and good brother. Adieu, Mgr. d'Arras. May Mgr. d'Arras deign to comfort them . . . .

I desired to be a curé in Paris: that is the occasion of my death; it is an old presentiment, and perhaps a punishment.

Adieu to Dugny (where he had been curé); to the poor as to the rich. Believe, all of you, in my love in our Lord Jesus Christ. Adieu! adieu!

I ask pardon of God. . . . . of my mother, for my faults . . . . of my brother and sister, for my harshness . . . of my parishioners, for my defects . . . . of my penitents, for my poor direction. I ask pardon for certain oppositions which self-love has caused me to make in respect to two curés, M. Hanicle and M. Barot. I ask pardon of all those whom I have offended and scandalized. I pardon everyone, without the least feeling of enmity, those who by imprudence shall have caused my arrest and my death. To Heaven, parents and friends; to Heaven! Pardon, my God, pardon! May those who are enemies to-day, become friends to-morrow! and may Paris become a city of brothers, who love each other in God! All to God! all for God! May God be loved! May all my parishioners believe the word of a dying man. I prepare myself as if I were going to mount the altar.

Let the parishioners and the children know that *I die because I willed to remain at my post, and to save souls by not leaving Paris.* May every one pray for me! . . . . Will God receive me? I beg to be recommended to prayers everywhere. Pray for the repose of the soul of the unhappy curé of Bonne-Nouvelle, so sinful in his life. At the beginning of our troubles, in the month of September, I offered myself as a sacrifice for Paris. God has remembered it. *May my blood be the last shed!* Mgr. Daveluy, my subdeacon at my first Mass, was martyred in Corea, in 1865. I die in the faith and union of the Holy Church. May Dugny, may Puteaux be converted! I pardon, I pardon with Jesus Christ upon the cross. . . . . I die aged fifty-seven years and —— days. If I had only profited by them!

FRIDAY, MAY 25, half-past six in the evening.

I die in the love of God, with submission to His holy will, trusting in Mary, notwithstanding my sins. My relatives, my friends, my parishioners, and even those who do not know me personally, pray for me! I will pray for you, if God brings me to His holy Paradise.

<small>* Histoire de la Commune de Paris en 1871. Par M. l'Abbé Vidieu.</small>

For two days I make my sacrifice from hour to hour. Happy he whom Faith sustains in this terrible moment!

God wishes always our greatest good for eternity. If He had wished to work a miracle. . . . He has not wished it. Everything as He wills.

One of my brethren having a consecrated Host, I have received Communion as Viaticum.

"See," says Louis Veuillot, "a poor priest who is about to be killed. He has nothing to hope for from man except a cruel and immediate death. He hopes for no help from the world; his humble memory needs no reparation. Henceforth his only business is with God. He confesses to God. One cannot imagine more entire conditions of sincerity.

"He has lived fifty-seven years, he has been a curé; he has served last a large parish. See how he has mingled with the world, what he has done, what disturbs his last moments, in what manner he receives that cruel and unjust death. He names all those whom he has known, in order to embrace them for a last time. Not one word, and plainly not one movement of his heart, against anybody. He falls assassinated, as if he were dying by accident, and thinks of those who treat him thus, only to pardon them. You have here the priest."

Catholic Notes.

——Rev. Fathers Igoe and Barr, of Renovo, Pa., have our best thanks for kind services to THE AVE MARIA.

——CATHOLICITY IN ROUMANIA.—The mission of the Franciscan Fathers in Roumania embraces 27 parishes, attended by 38 priests; it is subdivided into three districts, numbering in all 70,000 Catholics, each district being governed by a dean. The superior of the mission is Mgr. Fidelis Dehm, O. S. F., who resides at Jassy.

——THE HIGHEST PRICE EVER PAID FOR A PICTURE IN MODERN TIMES was for a Murillo's "Assumption," which brought in France $125,000 two centuries after it was painted. Correggio's "Saint Jerome," executed by him for a price equivalent to about $200, could have been sold to the King of Portugal about two centuries after the artist's death for $90,000. When the French took possession of Parma, the duke offered $200,000 for the privilege of retaining the painting; the offer was refused, and the treasure was sent to Paris.

——We are glad to see the evident signs of prosperity attending the career of our esteemed contemporary, *The Home Journal*, of Detroit, Mich., which has been recently enlarged to nearly double its former size. *The Home Journal* has a wide field that is peculiarly its own, and in which it has hitherto done good service. It therefore deserves encouragement. The present enlargement is an indication that Mr. Walter Savage, the editor and proprietor, will spare neither pains nor expense to advance the status of the paper in a measure commensurate with the support which it receives. We hope his efforts will be appreciated. Mr. Savage deserves praise for his energy and persevering effort. He has our best wishes for continued prosperity.

——HOW THE HOLY FATHER IMPRESSES NON-CATHOLICS.—Not long ago, Mr. Waddington, late President of the French Ministry of State, had an interview, lasting more than two hours, with the Holy Father. Although a Protestant, the French politician could not find words to praise the deep penetration, the keen judgment, the extreme kindness and graceful demeanor of our great Pontiff. "If our statesmen," said he, "could only listen to Leo XIII as I have done, and if they would follow his counsels, I think political difficulties would be more easily avoided, and many great problems would appear less difficult of solution." The same impression of the charming presence of the Holy Father has been felt by the new French ambassador at Rome, General Desprez, who replaced Marquis de Gabriac.

——RELIGION IN SOUTH AMERICA.—Three Lazarist Fathers and one lay-brother lately arrived at Asuncion, the Capital of Paraguay, and the Sisters of Charity will soon be installed there also. Monsignor di Pietro, Papal Nuncio, is manifesting a decided ability in the arrangement of the affairs of the Church of Paraguay, which had been greatly disturbed both by civil and foreign wars. Finding a most virtuous and exemplary native priest in a little hamlet, hidden within the depths of a primeval forest, he consecrated him Bishop, thus bringing Paraguay back again to association with the Holy See. Then the Nuncio thought of establishing a seminary for native priests, of whom there are now but twenty-four in the country. The Government looks with a favorable eye upon this social and religious revival, and is giving full support to its maintenance and advancement. Thus we see in Chili, Buenos Ayres, Paraguay, and Peru, most encouraging signs that at last the thraldom of secret societies, which for decades of years has kept these unhappy countries in revolution, is about to give way to the salutary influence of our holy religion, the only source of true peace and happiness among the nations.

——A SCOTTISH SHRINE OF MARY.—".... About three miles further up the Spey from Fochabers, is situated 'Chapel Well,' which for centuries has been famed as a holy well. Diseases, especially of the eyes, are said to be cured by bathing with its sacred waters. The well is a still pool of water, coffin-shaped in appearance, and lies at the foot of a small eminence, where, in Catholic ages, stood a chapel dedicated to 'Our Lady of Grace,' to which pilgrimages were made. The old historian, Father Blackhall, tells us how the 'Lady Aboyne,' in the 17th century, travelled from Deeside to pay her devotions at this chapel and well of 'Our Lady of Grace,' and perhaps this title arose from the many graces obtained at this venerated spot. The ruins of the chapel had almost disappeared from the green knoll above the well, and as the plough was advanced upon it, the Laird or Squire of Orton, on whose estate it stands, enclosed the knoll, planted it with shrubs, and erected a neat mausoleum, in the form of a chapel, as a sepulchre for his family. The well, however, remains in a nice little field outside the laird's enclosure, and surrounded with some venerable trees. The month of May is the great season for visiting 'Chapel Well,' and especially the Sundays, the first Sunday being the greatest day of all, when hundreds assemble at the well from dawn to dusk."—*Catholic Visitor.*

——McGEE'S ILLUSTRATED WEEKLY continues with unabated ardor the good work of giving beautiful pictures and interesting reading-matter to the, we hope, constantly increasing number of its readers. Among the choice morceaux in the first May number, is one of Miss Eleanor Donnelly's poetic gems, "Before the Crucifix," an elaboration of St. Teresa's motto, "To suffer or to die," and of that of St. Mary Magdalene de Pazzi, "To suffer, yet not die." One such poem is of itself worth a year's subscription to any periodical. The prose articles of this number of the *Illustrated Weekly* are excellent, especially the editorial on "Religion and Natural Science," which is illustrated by a well-conceived cartoon occupying the first page of the paper. The other illustrations are outer and inner views of Holyrood Palace, Edinburgh, with a portrait of the unfortunate Mary, Queen of Scots; her cabinet in Holyrood Palace, into which her bedchamber opened; the bedchamber itself, in which some of the leading events of her troubled reign took place—among them the murder of her foreign secretary, Riccio; her first interview with the coarse and ruffianly John Knox; her marriage to Lord Darnley, and afterwards to the Earl of Bothwell; the beautiful interior of the Abbey Church, etc. A full-page portrait of St. Thomas Aquinas graces the number, and a half dozen well chosen scenes depict some of the results of the famine in Ireland. These, with some miscellaneous pictures taken from British Columbia, complete the illustrations of the May number of this excellent periodical.

——THE AVE MARIA BELL—A TOUCHING REMINISCENCE.—"At half-past eight in the evening, that is to say, two hours after the *Ave Maria,* one of the large bells of Santa Maria Maggiore rings the *Smarrita.* What is the *Smarrita?* you will ask. Old Romans well remember the tale, and we will let them relate the touching narrative to you. One day, not so very long ago, an English traveller ventured to enter the labyrinth of the catacombs, unaccompanied even by a guide or '*custode*' of the place. In those days the catacombs were less frequented than they are now, and the curious visitors, who were anxious to wander at leisure in those subterranean passages, never bethought themselves to provide for their safety by engaging a *cicerone.* The Englishman, who had penetrated into the underground galleries by the entrance near the Appian Way, very soon lost himself in the dangerous labyrinth, and the more eagerly he sought an issue, the more difficult did he find it to recognize his position. After long weary hours of fruitless search, when he was just abandoning himself to his despair, considering that all further attempts would be vain, a low, distant sound penetrated through the silence and darkness which surrounded him, and brought a ray of hope to the lost man's heart. He recognized the chime of the *Ave Maria,* cheered up, and allowing himself to be guided by the sound, he groped his way perseveringly in the direction whence it came; and shortly after, arriving at the extremity of one of the galleries, he found an issue leading into some forsaken drains, not far from a narrow lane beside the Pincian Hill. The bell which had saved him was one of St. Mary Major's. The grateful Englishman offered as thanksgiving a rich gift to the basilica, upon condition that from that time, every evening, the same bell would be made to toll at the precise moment when he had been returned to life and light. Rome is full of such touching records and commemorations. It is the city of traditions, and every step upon its sacred ground is hallowed by remembrances."—*Roman Correspondence of The Catholic Times.*

——"EDUCATION" *vs.* EDUCATION.—"S.," the San Francisco correspondent of the Baltimore *Sun,* a daily newspaper that has established a first-class reputation for the trustworthiness of its news, the excellence of its correspondence, and, above all, the freedom of its pages from the debasing matter usually found in newspapers, writes as follows under date of April the 18th: "The Baltimore *Sun* gives correction to our public-school system that is appreciated here. By confining education to the head, while entirely neglecting the hand and the heart, we are raising a nation of helpless men who know no way to earn a living. Of 400 applicants at an intelligence office here, asking employment, 382 answered, 'I want some light occupation; I have a good public-school education, and consider myself qualified for almost any kind of clerking, shop-keeping, copying or superintending; but I have no trade and no special training for anything, though I think I could assist in teaching school, or something of that sort.' This is almost verbatim from one and all; of the 382, not 20 were placed and retained. No doubt the turnout of most public schools is about the same in this respect. Finding ourselves in the way of being asked for counsel, we invariably advise young men, instead of wasting time, trusting for something to turn up that will convert public-school learning into gold, to roll up their sleeves and learn some handicraft; never have we found one to do it; invariably, they say: 'I do not feel that, with my education (tossing the head proudly), I ought to come down to be a common mechanic. In fact, I am not fit for work; never was taught to expect such stooping; I despise work, anyhow.' Here is, in brief, a fair exhibit of the mischief our common-school system is doing. The funny caricatures representing men with giant heads and pigmy limbs, fairly picture the race of men now crowding the walks of life. We pray the Baltimore *Sun* to continue to urge the inseparable combination of instruction to the head that plans, the hand that executes, and the heart that humanizes. For the first time, our school-board of examiners have, within the past few months, only in one case, however, advanced a lady teacher, whose examination rated her No. 3, to two grades higher, on the ground of her success in imparting what she knows to her pupils. Hitherto merit was measured only by what the applicants knew; no account being taken of their power of imparting it. It is to be hoped that the common sense of this innovation will strike your school-boards."

—PERSONAL.—"A Reader, St. Augustine, Pa."—Enquire of any priest. A copy of "The Faith of Our Fathers" would be useful to you. Any large catechism will instruct you on the point. Write again, if you do not find what you wish for.

New Publications.

"THE IRISH LOURDES." THE APPARITION OF THE BLESSED VIRGIN, at Knock, Co. Mayo, Ireland. By Sister Mary Francis Clare. New York: Lynch, Cole & Meehan. Price, 25 cents.

Of all the sad signs of the age in which we live, infinitely the saddest is the acknowledgment on the part of mankind that God's presence is felt in our midst no more. It is the boast of our century that it has disenchanted the universe, and that never again can credence be given to the fictions of former ages. And, as far as it goes, the boast is just; but still it might be more comprehensive. We have rid ourselves of the magic of fable, but we have also rid ourselves of the magic of faith. And still, incredulous as our age is, and undeserving as it is of any special favors on the part of Divine Providence, still never, perhaps, in the history of the Church has there been a time in which God's power and love have so conspicuously shone forth as the present.

Wonderful apparitions have been seen, and innumerable miracles have been performed; but the alleged apparitions at Knock surpass anything yet recorded; first, as to their number and variety; and secondly, as to the number of individuals who witnessed them. Already hundreds of extraordinary and seemingly well-authenticated cures have been effected, not only by persons visiting the humble little chapel at Knock, but even by the application of the cement taken from the wall on which the Blessed Virgin, St. Joseph and St. John appeared; and God only knows what favors and blessings may follow. The gifted and indefatigable Nun of Kenmare, whose devotedness to the suffering poor has endeared her to every Irish and Catholic heart, has added another to her many valuable contributions to Catholic literature by the publication of this little work, which has the threefold merit of being complete, reliable and timely.

—We have received from the publisher, James Sheehy, of 33 Barclay street, N. Y., a copy of a new work by John O'Kane Murray, entitled Lives of the Catholic Heroes of America. It is a large and handsome volume, containing entertaining biographies of twenty-four famous personages connected with the early history of the American Church. Four are Americans, ten French, three Spanish, three Irish, one Belgian, one Russian, one Italian, and one English. The author says: "I hope the work, in spite of its many shortcomings, will be found to combine variety, interest and instruction. The Catholic discoverers, explorers and missionaries of America were men unsurpassed in all that constitutes heroic greatness. The perusal of their lives cannot fail to elevate the mind and give a healthy stimulus to deeds of virtue." The book is full of interest from the first chapter to the last, and no better or more appropriate one, we think, could be put into the hands of the youth of our country. The author deserves the thanks of the Catholic public, especially, for the good work he has done in promoting an interest in the study of our Catholic heroes and heroines. We hope the author will give us another volume like this on the lives of the men of our own times. Criticism is disarmed before a work which provokes nothing but approval.

NORA BRADY'S VOW; AND, MONA THE VESTAL. By Anna H. Dorsey. Philadelphia: J. B. Lippincott & Co.

These two fascinating tales of Ireland merit the hearty reception which we predict for them at the hands of those to whom they are dedicated; namely, "To the Irish people, brave and unconquered, bearing like martyrs oppressions to which they will not submit like slaves."

"Nora Brady," says the author, "is not a fictitious character, although the name is an assumed one." Certainly her admirable traits, her heroic charity, are worthy the emulation of all, whatever their country or station in life. In fact, Nora performed nothing beyond what faith requires, "for our justice must exceed that of the scribes and pharisees." It is, after all, the faith reflected in her deeds that we praise, as it is the faith of the Irish people which has raised them above their oppressors. Their calamities, and the patience with which they are endured, exhibit the power of faith, the distinguishing virtue of the Irish people.

The classical account of "Mona the Vestal" is too full of charming history, of lively, graceful portraiture, reflecting the times when St. Patrick defied the pagans at the court of Tara, to be passed lightly over by those who love the land of the Saint, or the faith he established there. The book is a rare acquisition to our Catholic literature.

Confraternity of the Immaculate Conception
(Or of Our Lady of Lourdes).

"*We fly to thy patronage, O Holy Mother of God!*"

REPORT FOR THE WEEK ENDING MAY 6TH.

The following intentions have been recommended to the prayers of the Confraternity: Recovery of health for 66 persons and 4 families,—change of life for 38 persons and 3 families,—conversion to the Faith for 65 persons and 48 families,—recovery of mind for 8 persons,—special graces for 72 priests, 9 religious, and 10 clerical students.—temporal favors for 51 persons and 4 families,—spiritual favors for 92 persons and 4 families,—the spiritual and temporal welfare of 5 communities, 4 congregations, and 3 schools. Also, 69 particular intentions, and 15 thanksgivings for favors received.

Specified intentions: Preservation of several youths from the vice of intemperance,—restoration of property to its rightful owner,—preservation of live stock from plague and disease,—particular graces for a number of parents,—several Catholic children frequenting public schools, and grace for their parents to fulfil their duties towards these children,—sales, resources, employments and other temporal favors,—reconciliation of several parties at variance,—an innocent man who has been slandered,—liquidation of a just debt,—two persons at the point of death,—recovery of one subject to convulsions,—protection from enemies.

FAVORS OBTAINED.

We publish the following extract from a letter received some time ago: "Please return thanks to Our Blessed Lady for a special favor. A friend of mine was suddenly taken with the pains of parturition on Sunday evening last. The doctor was sent for, who pronounced her case a very critical one. The next day, my wife went to see her, but the sufferer was so exhausted from pain that she scarcely recognized her visitor. Upon calling a second time, my wife offered her some of the Lourdes water, which she took thankfully; both then recited a few Hail Marys. Shortly after my wife's departure, the patient fell into a profound sleep, which lasted until 7 o'clock next morning. She went again to see her next day, and found her sitting up sewing, all danger of a miscarriage having vanished. The convalescent said that the pains ceased after taking the blessed water, and that she felt as well as she had ever been in her life."

A similar case, where both mother and child owe their safety to the use of the water of Lourdes, has been reported to us by a zealous promoter of THE AVE MARIA, living in one of the Western States. Two persons have requested us to return thanks for the settlement of a lawsuit pending for the last eight years, the agreement being to the satisfaction of both parties.

OBITUARY.

The prayers of the members of the Confraternity are requested for the following deceased persons: Mr. WILLIAM ANDREWS, of Palmyra, who departed this life a short time ago. Mrs. P. FLYNN, of Purissima, Cal., whose death occurred on the 17th of April. Mr. HORDMAN, of High Grove, Ky., recently deceased. And several others whose names have not been given.

Requiescant in pace.

A. GRANGER, C. S. C., Director.

Youth's Department.

Irish Legends.

(CONTINUED.)

III.
THE OLD MAN'S STORY.

"WELL, little children," said the old man recovering from his sad thoughts; "you wish to hear more about the '*soggarth aroon*,' and where I was when he was taken, and if I saw him; and you wish to hear all the wonderful things that happened in that big house while the holy priest was living there. I will tell all I can to-day, but I must come back some other time and tell you more."

The old man was now seated outside of the little thatched house on a stone-seat, where they had placed him to recover from the weakness which the sad thoughts of the past and fears of the future had brought on him. Around him were the little children, looking eagerly into his face, anxious to hear the wonderful things he had to tell. Before him stretched an immense tract of country from the charming town of Westport; at his feet, away by the lordly Nephin, arose the wide-extended plains of Mayo; while the lovely isle-studded bay lay smiling before him.

"Look, children," said he, pointing to a house among the trees bordering on the bay; "that house was once mine; there I lived in happiness with my wife and family forty years ago. I had ten children; had not too much to live on, but still I managed to support them respectably and comfortably, and we were happy. There I concealed the poor *soggarth* from the persecuting *sassenach*, till I found that it was impossible to secure him longer. When danger threatened him, when the hell-hounds that sought his life were on his track, I and my son rowed him off in my own boat in the midst of a stormy night, to Clare Island. I knew that nothing could happen to us while I had the minister of God and God Himself with us. We landed him safely on the other side, safe from the hands of his persecutors. But I suffered for it myself. I was thrown out of my little holding, without time or mercy, by those who called themselves the owners of the soil. Well I remember the fearful December evening when the bailiff with his men came to eject me and my sick wife and helpless family; everything of any value was taken to be auctioned for the rent which I could have paid if they had given me time, even unjust as it was. But no: no time, no mercy was given to me, because I had shown mercy to a persecuted priest and enabled him to escape. My furniture was taken, and they left us but a few rags to cover us; the fire was extinguished, and we were thrown out in the yard to perish; the roof was taken off the house lest we might again find shelter there. The cries of agony from my little children perishing with cold, the moaning of the night wind through the trees, the ruined home where we were once so happy even in our poverty, the snow falling fast around us, the blank, hopeless future before us,—all crushed my heart; but above all, the look of resigned agony and despair of my poor sick wife with her little infant on her breast. O God, it was a fearful thing to see that pale sick woman's misery! It was too much for me, I had to sit down and cry with the rest. But what was I to do? I could not see my wife and child dying; so I took off my coat and rolled it round both. She sat on the ground and leaned against the roofless wall; as I tried to shelter her from the piercing cold I felt the throbbings of her breaking heart; I saw the tear of silent sorrow steal down her poor cheek; up to this, sorrow had choked her utterance, but now, looking at me through her tears, she sobbed out: 'Musha, Pat, avourneen, don't deprive yourself of your coat for me this cold, wintery night, I have not long to live; spare yourself for the sake of these little children, for ———,' she never spoke more, she was unable to finish the last word; the tears and sufferings of her desolate children were too much for her to bear; her heart broke within her at the sight. She would have said with her last breath: 'Forgive their persecutors and my murderers'; and indeed, I do. Words cannot tell the scene that now followed. The dying child sought the nourishment of its tender years from the breast of a dead mother; the little ones gathered round to kiss her poor, cold, tear-bathed face; those who were more advanced in age, sat with me and cried till the morning dawn broke on the scene of misery. The neighbors, who had been kept away during the ejection at the point of the bayonet, came one by one, and mingled their tears with ours; the child died on its mother's breast, and both were buried in the same grave. The little orphan children who were unable to work were taken in charity, to live with strangers almost as poor as themselves. The heart that so loved them would throb for them no more; the voice that consoled them was silenced in death; the arms that caressed them are mouldering in the grave; the four that were able to work, had to go to earn their bread, till at length they laid by enough to take them to America. Where they are now, I don't know; for a while they sent their poor father just what kept him alive; they have now, no doubt, children of their own and forget him; the five little ones that were thrown on the charity of others, are all dead. I am now left alone.

"One by one they're gone before us.
They have faded fast away;
But we know they're watching o'er us
In that bright eternal day.
They are watching for us only
Where no pain can ever be;
The last and dearest left us lonely
To feast on God eternally.

. . . .

"Sweet the rest when all is over,
Land of light and life and joy,
Where the Saviour's smiles discover
Endless bliss without alloy."

"But," said one of the children, "you have not told us anything about the *shaun-na-soggarth*, the priest-hunter, or where he was struck dead, or what happened the priest on Clare Island!"

"Oh, my little children," answered the old man, "I cannot tell these things now, it is too late. I have to go to that little house before it gets dark," pointing to a thatched cabin in the distance, "and I'm not well able to speak further."

"Oh do!" said all the little voices together, "stop with us to-night, and tell us the stories to-morrow."

The old man consented; the shades of evening were now falling; Croagh Patrick was covering its lofty head with its cloudy "night-cap," Clare Island was no longer to be seen, and the islands of Clew Bay were fading from view. The distant plains that extended for miles round the monarch of mountains, had all disappeared. Nothing was now to be seen, save here and there the glimmering light from the surrounding cabins, and the twinkling stars that came out one by one in the distant heavens. It was nature's resting-time, and the inmates of this hospitable house also retired to rest, but the little ones could scarcely sleep, thinking of all the lovely stories they were to hear on the following day.

(TO BE CONTINUED.)

A Famous Work of Art.

IN the glittering court of Elizabeth of England, was a page, named Conrad von Gemmingen a member of an old and noble Bavarian family. At that time it was customary for young nobles to serve as pages in foreign courts, that from their early years they might learn the noble carriage and the knightly manners that became their future station. The queen seemed to be particularly pleased by the guilelessness, the candor, and the fine figure of the German youth. One day when she made her appearance at a court-festival in all the splendor of her royal robes, covered with diamonds and precious stones, the noble boy seemed to be dazzled and overpowered by the splendor. Noticing this, the queen smiled and asked the page: "Do these stones please you?" When he answered "Yes," she continued: "And would you like to be yourself the possessor of this finery?" And as he replied to this question also with a candid "Yes," she said, smiling: "Then, Conrad, as soon as ever you become a prince, I will make you a present of this finery as a token of my good will."

Many years passed by. The queen had entirely forgotten the German page and her promise. Conrad von Gemmingen had gone back to his native country and entered the Church. Admitted after a time amongst the canons of Eichstätt, it came to pass that, in 1593, he was named coadjutor to the Bishop Kaspar von Seckendorf, and in 1595 was made Bishop of Eichstätt, and thus successor of St. Willibald. In this manner the condition laid down by the queen of England was really fulfilled; her little page was a prince of the Holy Roman Empire. Then Bishop Conrad called to mind the circumstance of his youth mentioned above, and made up his mind to recall her promise to the memory of the proud queen, who was now pretty well advanced in years. He therefore sent a messenger to inform her that he was now Bishop of Eichstätt and had a place amongst the princes, and to remind her of her royal word. Elizabeth, although head of the Protestant Church and an enemy of the Catholic religion, was yet too proud to let herself be accused of not keeping her word. She sent at once to the Bishop the admired finery, in which glittered numbers of pearls and diamonds. Greatly rejoiced at the almost unhoped for present, the Bishop determined to offer up the treasure to the Lord of lords and the Kings of kings. He therefore ordered a monstrance to be made, in which all these pearls and precious stones of the royal robe should form part.

And this is the origin of the Eichstätt monstrance, the celebrated ornament of the cathedral of that place, which at the beginning of this century was sacrilegiously stolen by state robbers. The accounts remaining at Eichstätt give us some idea of the magnificence of this article, which was destined to be a throne of the Eternal Wisdom. Its cost was 150,000 florins; the gold alone was worth 14,000 florins; the large diamond, 7,000 florins; the large pearls, 1,500 florins; the smaller ones in the hands of the Child Jesus, 1,000 florins; and each of the pearls in the crown that surrounded the luna, 100 florins. Thus were the jewels of the Protestant queen of England turned into ornaments for the King of kings.

"That is a Boy I Can Trust."

I once visited a large public school. At recess a little fellow came up and spoke to the master, and as the boy turned to go down the platform, the master said: "That is a boy I can trust; he never failed me." I followed him with my eye, and looked at him when he took his seat after recess. He had a fine, open, manly face. I thought a good deal about the master's remark. What a character had that little boy earned! He had already got what would be worth more to him than a fortune. It would be a passport into the best store in the city, and, what is better, into the confidence and respect of the whole community.

I wonder if the boys know how soon they are rated by older people! Every boy in the neighborhood is known, and opinions are formed of him; he has a character, either favorable or unfavorable. A boy of whom the master can say, "I can trust him; he never failed me," will never want employment. The fidelity, promptness and industry which he shows at school are in demand everywhere, and are prized by everybody. He who is faithful in little, will be faithful also in much. Be sure, boys, that you earn a good reputation at school. Remember, you are just where God has placed you, and your duties are not so much given you by your teachers or your parents as by God Himself. You must render an account to them, and you will also be called to render an account to Him. Be trusty—be true.—*N. Y. Tablet.*

How a Church was Built.—On the seacoast near Calais is a large village; its inhabitants are poor fishermen, who live by their labor. They had no church, and the distance to the nearest house of God was considerable; but how were they to erect a church? They laid the matter before a naval officer, a man with a truly Christian heart and of excellent and lofty sentiments. "My friends," he said to them, "you can have a church in a short time. Here is my plan: Lay a fish aside in every boat *pour le bon Dieu* (for the good God), and sell all these fishes at the highest price that you can get for them for the benefit of your church. Begin this very day, and you will soon be able to lay the corner-stone of your church." The suggestion was carried out faithfully. In the town there was quite a demand for the fishes *pour le bon Dieu;* they always sold at a high price. The emperor stopped on a journey at Calais and heard of the circumstance, which so edified him that he said: "I must also add my little fish"; and the emperor's fish was a note for a thousand francs. Thanks to those fishes *pour le bon Dieu*, the church was built. It is not a magnificent specimen of architecture, but it answers its destination, and is much visited.

THE AVE MARIA.

A Journal devoted to the Honor of the Blessed Virgin.

HENCEFORTH ALL GENERATIONS SHALL CALL ME BLESSED.—St. Luke, i, 48.

VOL. XVI.　　　　NOTRE DAME, INDIANA, MAY 22, 1880.　　　　NO. 21.

Mary in the Upper Chamber—The Christian Faith is Founded upon her Testimony.

BY NICOLAS.

(CONCLUSION.)

THUS the heart of the Blessed Virgin is our Lord's first Gospel. In that virginal heart, now consecrated by a whole life of silence, of humility, and of holy reserve, we read, transcribed by St. Luke, the account of the great event of the Incarnation of the Son of God. To that event, as to their basis, all the other events and all the other evangelical mysteries refer. Whence the beautiful saying of St. Ildephonsus, when he calls the Virgin Mary, "God's Evangelist, under whose discipline the Word made a Child was brought up." *

But another more specious objection, the chief objection, yet remains to be considered. After our Saviour's Ascension, when the Apostles assembled in the Upper Chamber, and received the Holy Ghost, all things were made known to them, as their Divine Master had foretold, and as we see from their writings, as well as the words they uttered. The Spirit of knowledge flooded them with a vivid light, which transformed them into the Doctors of nations, and made them penetrate instantaneously all the highest mysteries of the Christian Faith, of which they have continued to be the everlasting oracles. Now, can we suppose that He would have allowed them to remain ignorant of the chiefest of all these mysteries? And did they not therefore obtain the knowledge of it from this heavenly revelation, and not from the Blessed Virgin? The answer to this objection is to be found in the general dealings of God's providence, and the conduct

* Serm. de Assump.

of the Apostles themselves confirms it. For it is an invariable characteristic of the order of Divine Providence never to do anything that is useless or superfluous; never to cast away the natural means which come readily to hand, and which God Himself has formed, in order gratuitously to substitute supernatural agents, which would usurp their place. God makes all things serve to His own ends; in His works, grace never dethrones nature; on the contrary, it exalts it, enriches it, and crowns it. When therefore grace, when celestial virtue, intervenes, all it does is to raise the natural elements it finds already there; it fills them up where they are wanting, it completes their resources, it perfects their worth. This beautiful truth needs no further development, it only requires to be pointed out. It speaks for itself; and the constant realization of it is the grand characteristic of the Christian religion.

It follows, then, that the Holy Spirit, when He came down upon the Apostles, doubtless taught them a great number of things. Those poor fishermen, upon a lake in Judea, were transformed into lights of the nations. But, however vast and prodigious was the knowledge He imparted to them, He did not disdain any of those natural means by which they might acquire information; He did not dispense them from any of them. They were supernaturally instructed only in things they had no other means of knowing; but they were merely assisted, helped, and directed concerning things they could learn in a natural manner, such as the *fact* of the Incarnation.

And, indeed, it must not be supposed that the Evangelists were inspired, in such a sense, as that the *facts* they relate were directly revealed to them by the Holy Spirit. It was no such thing. For as they possessed natural means of information, they were only inspired in so far as they needed assistance in the employment of those means. This they themselves declare: "Forasmuch as many have taken in hands," says St. Luke, "to set forth in order a narration of the things that have been accomplished among us; according as they have delivered them unto us, who from the beginning were eye witnesses and ministers of the word; it seemed good to me also, having diligently attained to all things from the beginning, to write to thee, in order, most excellent Theophilus, that thou mayest know the verity of those words in which thou hast been instructed." Thus we see that inspiration, far from taking the place of "diligent" enquiry into the facts, in the Gospel, is rather, on the contrary, set aside by the writer in his character as an historian. Most certainly, as Grotius observes, there is no doubt but that God directed His Evangelist in this pious research: " Dubitandum non est quin piam diligentiam Deus direxerit"; but this divine assistance merely seconded and completed the ordinary conditions of human certitude.

And in this was manifested great wisdom. For inspiration by itself would in fact have been ineffectual in a world which disbelieved in its existence. Incredulity then, as indeed in all times, required natural, palpable proofs—proofs which could withstand criticism, which could be brought to bear upon the question, which could be discussed and twisted this way and that; and which, having won their way triumphantly against all the attacks of false science and impiety, from Julian down to Voltaire, and from Celsus to Strauss, would first force men to believe in their historical veracity, and then in the fact of their inspiration.

This alliance of natural and supernatural elements in the Christian Faith, analogous to the alliance between the humanity and divinity of its Author, Christ Jesus, had been preordained by Him, as He declared to His disciples, when He said: " When the Paraclete cometh, whom I will send you from the Father, the Spirit of Truth who proceedeth from the Father, He shall give testimony of Me: *and you shall give testimony, because you are with Me from the beginning.*"* This passage shows us plainly the two kinds of testimony instituted by Jesus Christ in the establishment of Christianity: namely, the Divine testimony of inspiration, and the human testimony of the Apostles. And it would even seem as though our Lord, by abstaining from acting directly Himself upon the world, and by making use of men, and of men so thoroughly human, so to speak, as were the Apostles, in order to convert the universe, chose more especially to invest the divinity of His work with a human, natural, and historical aspect.

The Apostles were faithful to this economy of their Divine Master. When they were most strongly inspired, and when miracles attested the truth of their preaching, they always appealed to their having been actual *witnesses* of the facts of the life of Jesus Christ. St. Peter brings it forward perpetually; and St. John, even after the marvels that attended the apostolic preaching, wrote: " That which we have *heard*, which we have *seen with our eyes*, and *our hands have handled* . . . . we do bear witness of and declare unto you. . . . That which we have *seen*, we declare unto you." * . . .

But the conduct of the Apostles, when they elected the successor of Judas, most fully manifests the truth of this proposition, as well as the consequence we would derive from it. The conditions of this election were thus laid down by St. Peter: " Wherefore of these men who have companied with us, all the time that the Lord Jesus came in and went among us; *beginning from the baptism of John, until the day wherein He was taken up from us*, one of these must be made a *witness* with us of His Resurrection." Evidently the testimony " *de visu.*" Natural and historical testimony was not replaced by inspiration in the Apostles' case. Thus Jesus checked the gift of inspiration, where knowledge could be obtained by ordinary means; and the Apostles exercised those means to the full. But they circumscribed human testimony within certain limits; it was to commence "*from the baptism of John until the day wherein Jesus was taken up to heaven.*" That is to say, it was confined to the three years of our Lord's public life; the only part of His life with which they were acquainted.

And now amongst those who companied with the Apostles, who is there that can testify of the thirty preceding years of the Saviour's life; of the prophetic mysteries of His Childhood, of the glorious mystery of His Birth, and, above all, of the great and fundamental mystery of His Divine Conception; in a word, of the Incarnation? Happy the soul that can pour out this wealth of knowledge into the apostolic treasury! One only can bestow it, and that one is manifestly the Blessed Virgin—*Mary, the Mother of Jesus*, who, as the sacred historian tells us, was in the Upper Chamber, "*persevering in one mind with the Apostles.*" This mention of her is all the more significative in a certain sense, inasmuch as the historian is St. Luke, the special Evangelist of those earlier mysteries. He would thereby have us to understand that it was Mary who gave testimony concerning them; Mary, who, as he says in his Gospel, "*had kept all these things in her heart.*" This is the opinion of St. Anselm: " Notwithstanding the descent of the Holy Ghost," says he, " many great mysteries were revealed to the Apostles by Mary." *Plura tamen incomparabiliter per Mariam revelabantur.* †

And indeed God, who, as we have already said,

* St. John, xv, 26.
* St. John I. Ep. 1, 1–3.
† Lib. de Excel. Virg.

utilizes all that is good in human means; who employed, whilst He purified at the same time, the unspiritual testimony of the Apostles; who inspired them to replace the testimony of the apostate Judas by the election of a witness of the same standing in the order of time; would assuredly not have set aside the testimony of the holiest, the best informed, and the most faithful of His creatures. He would not have disdained the witness of her whom He chose to be His Mother. No: we are rather led by the clearest and most logical process of induction, to consider Mary's testimony as an extention of her Divine Maternity.

In the room at Nazareth we see her co-operating with the Holy Spirit in the Incarnation of the Son of God; in the Upper Chamber at Jerusalem we behold her co-operating with the same Spirit of Truth, in the manifestation of this great Mystery. At Nazareth she prepared a home for God in her chaste womb; and by the operation of the Holy Spirit, the Incarnation of the Word is wrought therein; at Jerusalem she affords the Church her testimony concerning this Mystery, and again by the operation of the Holy Spirit, the Apostles are enabled to apprehend it. At Nazareth, the Holy Spirit overshadowed her, and the consent she gave caused her to become the Mother of our God; at Jerusalem, the same Spirit came upon her, and the testimony she bore caused her to become the Mother of our Faith. "Thy voice, O Mary," says a pious interpreter (the same voice which in the Visitation filled Elizabeth with the Holy Spirit, and with the knowledge of the Divine Maternity), "was the voice of the same Spirit speaking to the Apostles. So that all those mysteries which required any supplement, or confirmation, or witness, were made clear to them, developed, and confirmed, by thy holy mouth, as by a faithful interpreter of the Spirit of Truth."*

Of a truth, then, our Faith, founded, as St. Paul says, upon the testimony of the prophets and apostles, is yet more particularly founded upon the testimony of the Blessed Virgin, whom the Church so justly hails as their Queen. Thus, contrary to the maxim: "*Testis unus, testis nullus,*" the Word of words is confirmed before the whole world, and for evermore, by one chief witness, namely, the Blessed Virgin Mary.

Remove this one testimony, and it is not one single link merely which will be wanting, but the principal rivet which sustains the weight of the whole evangelical chain. Not only would a breach be made, but the very basis would be taken away. So that what would be contrary to nature in the physical order, thus constitutes the economy and, as it were, the equilibrium of our Faith. We seem to see a pyramid resting upon its point. Faith in the great Christian mystery, throughout the whole world and throughout all ages, rests upon one point; that is, upon one witness, upon one voice, upon that same voice whose *Fiat* had determined the accomplishment of the mystery.

What a sublime and incomparable position this apostolic character gives Mary in the economy of our Faith; and in what a magnificent manner it reacts again upon her prerogative as the Mother of God, whence indeed it derives all its value!

The apostles, who, as they tell us themselves, were witnesses of the last three years of our Lord's life only, nevertheless, confess the anterior events which they did not behold, such as the Nativity and the Incarnation, just as positively as they speak of the Transfiguration and the Resurrection, which they did see. Indeed it is from the former part of the history of Jesus upon earth, that they derive the notion of the *Word made flesh,* which pervades their whole doctrine, and which could have rested upon Mary's testimony only. Now, what gave this testimony its great weight? what was it that so added to the value of what they themselves had seen, as to induce them to make this testimony the foundation of their whole doctrine? None of those things which attested their own witness. Neither miraculous powers, nor supernatural gifts, nor the pledge of martyrdom, unless indeed it were the keen martyrdom of sorrow: Mary's life had been a quiet one; she was to die at last in peace. It was her supereminent sanctity, her dignity as the Mother of Jesus, which alone constituted the value of her testimony. And that sanctity and dignity were the only warrant the Apostles had for their faith in the mystery of the Incarnation, and consequently they are the only surety of the faith of the whole universe in Christianity.

So that the Christian universe, whether consciously or unconsciously, renders Mary's sanctity and dignity a homage proportioned to its faith in the Incarnate Word, inasmuch as belief in the Word Incarnate can proceed only from belief in the Blessed Virgin Mary.

PROTESTANTS would hear, with no little surprise, devotion to our Lady mentioned as a means of increasing their faith in our Lord, seeing that in their ignorance they assume that the one devotion is inimical to the other; whereas, on the contrary, says the Catholic theologian, the practice, so peculiar to Catholics, and at the same time so universal among them, of uniting themselves with Mary in the contemplation of Jesus, unspeakably elevates their contemplation of His Divine Majesty.

---

* Vox tua, O Maria, fuit Apostolis vox Spiritus Sancti, quidquid supplementi opus erat, vel testimonii, ad confirmandos singulorum sensus quos acceperant ab eodem Spiritu, et religioso ore tuo perceperunt.—*Rupert. Lib. I. in Cantic.*

May Thoughts on the "Magnificat."

BY THE REV. MATTHEW RUSSELL, S. J., AUTHOR OF "EMMANUEL."

JESUS TACEBAT. Not alone
When at the last hour He would atone
By silence for our sinful speech—
Like lesson He was wont to teach
Throughout His toilsome exile here.

And she, most near to Him, most dear,
Learned well that lesson. Few the words,
Which, sweet as innocent song of birds,
Fell from Our Lady's lips; and they
Back into silence sank away,
Unnoted, save a phrase or two
Which Holy Writ keeps ever new.
Once only did her soul flow o'er:
When at her cousin's cottage door
Her grand *Magnificat* outburst.
And mark how calmly from the first
High her exulting spirit soared:

"My soul doth magnify the Lord,
Who from on high hath deigned to bless
His lowly handmaid's lowliness.
Lo! henceforth generations all
Shall blessèd and thrice blessèd call
Me, unto whom the Mighty One
Hath in His might, such great things done."

Oh! God be praised, who laid our lot
Within that Church which grudges not
The title thou thyself didst claim.
Yes, "Blessed Virgin," is the name
Which Christian hearts with joy bestow,
Thy prophecy fulfilling so.
We were before thy prophet-soul
When God the future did outroll,
Distinct and clear before thine eye
In that meek hour of ecstasy.
Of *us* thou thoughtest, not of those
Who blame each word of praise that flows
From loving hearts in prayer to thee—
Who coldly carp and chide, while we
As God's true Mother bless thy name,
And thee for our own Mother claim.

If scandals, heresies, *must* come,
'Tis well that sign there should be some
For all, and not a learned few,
To mark the false creed from the true,
Plain to all simple hearts and pure.
Thou, Mary, art that sign secure!
Scarce other "Note" faith's instinct needs
Than the Hail Mary and the Beads.
How, then, dares Heresy to raise
A standard which itself betrays—
This jealousy of her who bore
The Lord whom we and they adore?

Yes, all who love the Crucified,
Must cherish her who stands beside;
To us in that dread moment given
As Mother, and who now in heaven,
Mother of Jesus glorified,
Within His Heart and at His side
Forever holds a mother's place.
Hail, Queen of Heaven! Hail, full of grace!

Nor let the impious slanderer say
That Mary's clients turn away
The worship due to God alone,
And lift a creature to His throne.
Was e'er the vilest fanatic
Duped by this hideous lying trick?
The simplest crone that tells her beads,
—Her cross the only book she reads—
Knows well that she upon whose breast
The Babe divine doth sweetly rest,
Is still a woman meek and mild,
Though Jesus, Jesus, is her Child!

They, too, who raise this parrot-cry
Of a besotted bigotry,
Know well, themselves—for o'er and o'er
We've stooped to them—we adore
One only God, of lords the Lord,
Eternal Trinity, whose word
Made all created things to be,
And, foremost of mere creatures, Thee!
Thee, Mary, whom God raised so high,
That saint and angel come not nigh!

Nay, they who Mary's prayers disdain,
If they the Christian name retain—
(Those wretched souls who half deny
Themselves, their Maker, we pass by)—
Believe, or to believe pretend,
That God once deigned on earth to send
His Son, co-equal God, to be
Our bloody ransom on the Tree;
And they believe that God as man,
Living and dying, wrought this plan—
True Man, True God, both then and now,
And His true Mother, Mary, thou!
Ye, then, who love the Child, for shame!
Blaspheme no more the sacred name
Of Mother, nor presume to part
Whom God forever heart to heart
Hath joined as Son and Mother.

                    Thou,
O Mother of my God, wilt now,
And always to my dying day,
Be unto me a mother. Pray

That never till the day I die
May I by word or deed deny
The love which fills my heart and mind
For thee, true Mother of mankind!
And when thy Son the sign has given,
Take me, O Mother, home to heaven.

'Beth's Promise.

BY MRS. ANNA HANSON DORSEY.

CHAPTER XV—(Continued).

OUT in the hop-fields, with the sun-rays slanting through the tops of the trees beyond, tinging the delicate green of the vines still left clinging to the high poles around which they had grown and interlaced themselves, with a fleck of gold on every tremulous leaf; the scene was a gay and busy one. Men cut the vines close to the roots, after which the poles were drawn out of the earth, the vines still clinging around them, and borne away to the pavilions, where they were set leaning against the large wooden bins, into which the blossoms were tossed as fast as the deft fingers of the pickers could gather them. When filled, the bins were emptied into wagons, and the hop-flowers hauled away to be spread out in the drying-house. The endless variety of color, and shades of color, in the cheap, pretty dresses of the women and young girls; their healthy, cheerful faces, as they sang or chattered over their work; the merriment and rustic flirtations that went on in the pavilions where young men and girls worked together; the flitting here and there of bright spots of color as, on some errand or other, they ran among the green aisles formed by the vines yet uncut, to pavilions where friends or relatives were busy, made a gay spectacle, full of artistic tints and pretty grouping, all rendered brighter by the peculiarly clear atmosphere and the golden radiance of the westward sloping sun. The old lady of "Ellerslie" had a pleasant nod and a kind word for her busy harvesters, as she, with Mrs. Morley and her guests, walked slowly here and there over the field, observing and enjoying that which was novel and pleasant to some of the party, while she pointed out and explained everything that seemed to interest them. The young people went off together, and somehow, after a little while, 'Beth found herself alone with Bertie Dulaney, the others having lost themselves among the hops. She immediately proposed going in search of them, which he agreed to, leading her all the time in an opposite direction to that in which he had last seen them; nor did they see each other again until, slowly sauntering home after sunset through the now quiet and deserted hop-fields, he exclaimed: "They have got back before us, Miss Morley! How on earth did we miss them! They are sitting there on the veranda as composedly as if we had not been lost. Let us be very dignified with them."

"Perhaps they'll think *they* are the ones to put on injured airs," said 'Beth, laughing, and wondering what Elaine Marston would think of her lover's desertion; "we'll begin, though, and tell them we've been looking for them ever since they gave us the slip."

"I'm only afraid they'll see at once that I am shamming, and that instead of reproaching them, I am much more inclined to thank them for the very happiest hour of my life," said Bertie Dulaney, in a low voice, as he looked down into the fair, sweet face uplifted towards his.

A delicate rose tint overspread 'Beth's face, that mysterious sign by which heart answers heart plainer than words can tell, and she awoke to the half consciousness of a new and indefinable sentiment, which startled her, for was not this man, who had awakened it, betrothed to Elaine Marston? What, then, did he mean by seeming to prefer her companionship, whenever they were all together, to that of Elaine? why did he say so many things to her whenever an opportunity offered, which might mean a great deal or nothing? These thoughts rushed through 'Beth Morley's mind, and aroused her pride and a sense of what was due to herself. "If he thinks he can amuse himself by carrying on a flirtation with me under the very eyes of the girl he's engaged to, it is time he should begin to find out his mistake," she thought, as, shaking off her momentary embarrassment, she said, laughingly: "I shall make them ashamed of themselves."

But when reproached, they all declared that they had looked everywhere for them, and not seeing a trace of them, had hurried home, expecting to find that they had returned.

"Yes!" said Violet, her red lips pouting, while dimples lurked in her cheeks, betraying how much more she was disposed to laugh than to scold: "I am the one who has been the most ill-treated and neglected, for do you know, 'Beth,—you told me to call you so—that while I stopped to pick off a few hops with Lodo, those two, Paul and Elaine, deliberately walked away! I didn't care, though, for I dote on Lodo, and I did really enjoy picking hops. She said I nipped them off as fast as the best of the pickers, and as a reward for my usefulness, I'm invited to the dance they're going to have in the barn to-night."

"Indeed, Miss Morley, I told her twice that we were going," said Elaine to Aunt 'Beth, "and thought she had started with us, until I looked round and missed her; then we went back, but everyone was gone. Is not that so?" she said, appealing to Paul Dulaney.

"It happened exactly so; but I beg your pardon, Violet; I really thought you were coming," he replied.

"Trotting on behind like Mrs. Bacon's poodle! No, I thank you! I have lived to learn that three is an awkward number," said Violet, tossing her pretty head.

'Beth glanced at Elaine, whose eyes had so happy a light in them, and whose lips wore so joyous a smile that she wondered if Violet could possibly mean that she had been carrying on a flirtation with Paul Dulaney, and intended to punish them both by giving a hint of it to his brother, to whom she was engaged? She thought things might grow disagreeable if this went on, and wishing to have a few minutes to herself to try and shake off the disagreeable impressions that had chilled and made her uncomfortable, she proposed that they should have some music, and went into the music-room to light the candles, telling them she would call them when she had finished, and refused their pleasantly-offered assistance. As she struck a match, she heard the quick scrape of another, and saw that Bertie Dulaney had followed her—despite her wishes—to help her to light up. She could not be rude enough to tell him he should not, nor did she feel that it would be quite delicate to put on an air of resentment, for which she would be unable to give an explanation should one be asked. Then she determined to show a simple indifference, and make no change in her manner towards him, now at least.

"How kind you are! I was just wondering if I could reach the candles in that sconce without climbing on a chair. I believe it is just within reach of your arm, Mr. Dulaney; thank you very much," she said, flitting about lighting the long wax candles in *candelabras*, on brackets, in the sconces and upon the piano, until the beautiful old room was flooded with a white mellow radiance. "Now you may open the piano, while I uncover the harp"; running her long, pretty fingers over the strings, she added: "Will you please tell them to come in?"

"In a moment, Miss Morley," he said, standing just before her; "did I not hear something said about going to see a dance in the barn?"

"Yes: the girls were speaking of it."

"May I be your escort?"

"I do not think of going, Mr. Dulaney. I think that sort of gaiety and my dress are not in harmony," she said, coldly.

"Pardon me! I see," he answered, quickly.

"But do not refer to it, please, lest my not going should interfere in some way with their enjoyment. You will all enjoy the fun, I'm sure, for these country people *dance*, I hear, and take steps, and throw their heart into their heels with prodigious antics."

"I shall take no pleasure in it, if you are not there; as it is, may I stay here until they get back? I'm awfully tired."

"I'm afraid not, Mr. Dulaney," said 'Beth with something of *hauteur* in her expression, as she thought of Elaine. "Will you, or shall I, tell the girls and your brother that everything is ready?"

He bowed and went out, without another word, to do her bidding, while she remained standing where he had left her, with a shadow more of perplexity than anger on her countenance. "I have heard and read of men-flirts," she thought, indignantly, "but if Mr. Dulaney chooses to forget that he's an engaged man, and expects to amuse himself, it shall not be at my expense. I am so disappointed in him!"

The young people came in laughing and chatting; then there was a flutter over the music books, and a little playful *badinage* about the selections to be made, until finally, all being ready, sweet sounds filled the room and floated out, entrancing the ear and heart of the party on the veranda. Harp and piano united in a concert of rare harmonies, and the round, full-voiced notes of alto and high clear soprano blended in wonderful passages of melody, now brilliant, now tender, now gay, now sad, and the moments slipped by, winged with music to which an angel might have paused to listen. Both, Elaine and Violet had voices of rare sweetness, flexibility and compass, which had been cultivated by the most skilful teachers, but never had they sung with such expression and effect as to-night, while their sweet, unaffected readiness to oblige, and their genuine enjoyment in having given so much pleasure, greatly enhanced the delicious treat.

But it was time for those who were going, to start for the barn where the hop-pickers were holding their revel. Mr. Dulaney, Elaine, with Violet and Paul, went, the girls declaring that they meant to dance, if they were invited by the rustic beaux, and gave permission to the two gentlemen to select partners from among the belles of the occasion. Bertie Dulaney told them he "would come presently," and Elaine, apparently well satisfied, went with Paul, and Violet with Mr. Dulaney. It was growing a little chill, and Aunt 'Beth proposed going into the music-room, to which they readily agreed, and found the change very agreeable, particularly Mrs. Dulaney, who had already felt one or two twinges of neuralgia, the only ill that her flesh seemed heir to. 'Beth drew a low *tabouret* close to her mother, and sat leaning upon her knee, almost clinging to her, as if for safety, for there had come into her heart a strange feeling of unrest, and weariness. Aunt 'Beth, well pleased with the brave, hansome young fellow who had been so good to 'Beth, made Bertie Dulaney come to her sofa, and had he been vain or conceited, he would have been made to feel himself quite a hero by all the kind, pleasant things she said to him; his mother listening, and beaming with fond pride, while he, flushing and laughing, declared:

"Any other fellow would have done the same; really now, Miss Morley, you are giving me more praise than I deserve; it was all accidental, you know; but I'm very glad I happened to be of service." After a little while he got away from the sofa, and went across the room to join Mrs. Morley and 'Beth, and was soon engaged in a pleasant conversation with the former, in which the girl took no part except when addressed, answering courteously, but with an air of reserve which was perfectly incomprehensible to him. Had he offended her? What had he said or done? Why was she so strangely changed towards him? He could not imagine. Hurt, and feeling a little nettled by what he considered a caprice, he got up, saying he believed he would go and look at the dancers; then bowed himself out and went away, his head bared to the cool night air as he sauntered through the shrubbery, wondering if it were indeed true that all women were fickle and capricious, as he had often heard, and if it could be that this one, on whose purity and truth he would have been willing to stake his life, was of that sort. After going a short distance, he heard the voices of the party he was going to meet, laughing and talking merrily, advancing towards him; but he was in no mood to join them, and making a quick turn, he crossed the field and taking the path which led to the gate— now never closed—between "Ellerslie" and his home, he was soon on the other side. As he was passing the chapel, a sudden impulse seized him. It was his turn to serve Mass the next morning, and he had the door key in his pocket. "This sort of thing wont do, losing my head and getting into a fever over nothing; I'll go in here a little while to say my beads and cool off"; and obeying the good impulse, he unlocked the chapel door and went in. The sanctuary lamp cast a faint glimmer of light over the altar and shrine of Our Lady; all else was in shadow: here was the august Presence which whispers to the tempest-tossed passions of life: "So far shall ye come, and no farther"; and here was the silence in which the whispers of the soul could best be heard. Kneeling down reverently, his rosary in hand, the brave, sweet nature of Bertie Dulaney, which had been so suddenly stirred into a passion of resentment and pain, yielded to the holy influences of the place, and he went forth more calm than when he entered.

When his mother and the rest of them got home from "Ellerslie," the servant told them, when they inquired if he had come, that he had been in some little time and had gone immediately to his room.

The "Ellerslie" hops were all gathered into the drying house, and the crowds of merry pickers had moved on to "fresh fields, and pastures new," leaving Aunt 'Beth time to attend to other things in which she was growing more and more interested. This was the "strike," and the disposition of the strikers, and the misery that impended over them if they continued stubborn. She made several expeditions with Father Hagner among the hills to see some of the rough men engaged in the trouble, to talk over and argue the case with them. They felt a great respect for the brave little woman who showed no fear of them, and whose only object in seeking them in their poor homes, was their own good—they were sure of that—however much her ideas and their own might differ. They gave welcome also to the gentle young priest, and listened to all he had to say, without, however, giving way in the least to his good counsels; "for," said they, "his business and ours are two different matters; our business is to grub for the body, his is to see after the soul; and it's plain as day, if the bread is taken from us, the soul and body won't hold together; so nothing's left for us but to fight our own battle." The good priest who had been engaged in missionary work among them for many years, had hastened there as soon as ever he knew how matters stood, and after first conferring with Gibbs, Elder & Co., and finding that their demands were fully justified by the emergencies of the hour, he lost no time in going among his people, exhorting, arguing and expostulating with them day and night, and there began to appear a faint hope that things would take a more favorable turn, as the unreasonableness of the stand they had taken was made more apparent to their understanding. Besides, a long, bitter winter was at hand, and what, then, if they held out? This latter consideration was doing its work in their own minds, although no one had yet ventured to speak it out. It would have seemed too much like "giving in."

After the "high tea" at "Ellerslie" on the evening described, 'Beth had kept within doors for a day or so, practising, reading, sewing a little for the "Dorcas-basket," and spending all the intervening time with her mother. The young people at "Tracy-Holme" were having riding and boating-parties, or some merry expedition or other every day, but to their great disappointment, 'Beth excused herself from joining them for reasons which seemed good to herself, reasons dictated by honor as well as a regard for her own peace of mind. They were all so kind and pleasant, that she was glad to have a tangible excuse for declining to go once or twice, in the fact that

Aunt 'Beth and Father Hagner were off together on their well-meant expeditions, and her mother would be left quite alone. One morning, when after vainly entreating her to go on a fishing-party to the lake, the Marstons hastened away that the others might not be kept waiting, 'Beth, feeling that they had not taken her refusal to go, very kindly, and dissatisfied with herself, put on her hat and taking up a book she had been reading, determined to go and spend an hour or two in the "glen." Everything was lovely; the place itself was a poem with its great whispering trees; the sun-rays piercing the green shadows here and there; the clear torrent dashing over the rocks with a sound full of music and refreshment; birds flitting from tree to tree, with outburst of fitful song, and the shy chipmunks running in and out of their hiding-places, their bright eyes peering about with curious glances, then suddenly scampering up the trees to saw off with their nimble teeth a few more hickory nuts for their winter store. It was no use, 'Beth thought, to attempt to read dry print, with all this living movement of beauty and brightness around her, and she laid her book down on the moss, and with her hands folded idly on her lap, fell to dreaming waking dreams, into which a certain sadness entered. She had been disappointed in Bertie Dulaney whom she had thought almost as perfect and brave as Roland; he had proved himself a trifler, and, according to her views, unprincipled; and she felt, too, the disrespect shown to herself in having made her the object of his attentions, and breathed tender words to her, when he was engaged to be married to Elaine Marston. While she sat there thinking how bitter a thing it was to be disappointed in a character which had seemed to be possessed of every virtue, and determining to guard against credulity in future, she heard footsteps on last year's leaves, and turning her head saw Bertie Dulaney standing within a few feet of her.

"I hope that I have not startled you, Miss Morley," he said, lifting his hat.

"No, only surprised me. I thought you were out on the lake with the others."

"No: I felt no interest in going; in fact, Miss Morley, I staid at home hoping to see you."

"A poor exchange, Mr. Dulaney," she answered coldly, as she rose up.

"Not so. I do not know how I have offended you; and I wanted to hear it from your own lips, how and when I was so unfortunate," he said, in grave, gentle tones.

"You have not offended me, Mr. Dulaney," she answered, looking down. How could she tell him what was in her mind? Every delicate womanly instinct forbade it. She felt the awkwardness of her position, which she could neither explain nor ignore.

"I am glad to hear that, and hope we shall be friends again," he said; "but I shall not think so if you go away as soon as I come."

"I left mamma quite alone, and I have been here some time already," she said, looking into his face for the first time, and noting its grave lines and the puzzled expression in his eyes; then she hastened to add: "I suppose you will drive down to the lake shore presently to meet the girls?"

"No: there's no necessity for me to do so. They are paired off, so that I should only be in the way."

"I do not understand," said Beth. "Who went?"

"My father and Violet in one boat, Elaine and Paul in mine, the one you floated away in, you know."

"Who rows?" she asked, wishing he had not referred to her adventure.

"They have men to row; while they, it is supposed, will catch fish; but there will be few or none caught, at least in one boat."

"Why?" she asked, for want of something better to say.

"Lovers are never very successful anglers I fancy—I mean my brother Paul and Elaine; you know they are engaged!"

"No, I did not know it. I thought he was engaged to Violet," said 'Beth, feeling how utterly she had misjudged him; her heart, at the same time, relieved of a great weight.

"They have been engaged ever since they left school, and are to be married in December. As to Violet, she's fancy free, and he'll be a smart fellow who captures her, she's such a little flirt. She declares that she intends to amuse herself, for a year or two, in flirting to her heart's content, before she settles down."

"They are very lovely girls, Elaine especially," said 'Beth, from whose heart the last cloud had drifted. She had found her Roland again.

"And my brother, Miss Morley, is one of the best and noblest fellows living," he said, warmly.

Then they fell to talking of other things, wandering down to the glen together instead of going back to the house, and presently they sat down on a ledge of rock to watch the fantastic dance of the brook as it foamed along through the great ferns and blue flags that grew in wild luxuriance along its rugged edges; and there he told her all that he had been longing to say since the day he first saw her drifting so helplessly away on the lake.

It was a new tale to 'Beth Morley, and had taken her so by surprise that she could not answer him; but he saw that she was not offended, and when he urged her to give him at least a hope that she would some day accept him, she only said: "You must let me think; I cannot decide all at once you know." Her voice was not steady, and when he asked her if he might continue to visit her on the same old friendly terms while he awaited her decision, she told him "yes," and did not withdraw her hand which he had taken to help her to rise, and which he would have liked to hold, but presently she gently withdrew it and began to talk of indifferent matters.

A strange, quiet sense of happiness had stolen into 'Beth Morley's heart; nature was sweetly unfolding there, that old yet ever new mystery by which soul is attracted to soul, finding their counterpart through a pure and exalted sentiment. She did not speak of what had passed to her mother, she wanted to be quite sure of herself first; now she was only conscious of a serene contentment in Bertie Dulaney's presence, and a feeling of pride in having won his love. 'Beth did not know these signs for all that they meant, or she need not have waited "to think," before she could answer him. As her love of the beautiful in nature always winged her thoughts heavenward, so now this pure, new-born sentiment seemed to draw her by an irresistible force to the feet of the sweet Virgin of virgins. To kneel alone in the silent chapel, when only the shadows of the leaves outside were dancing on the wall—when only the last golden tints of the setting sun vied with the sanctuary lamp in shedding a fairer radiance around the holy place—when only the last song of the birds from their leafy covert broke the silence—to kneel there and commend herself to her care, to ask her guidance in this new and bewildering phase of her life, and say some decades of her rosary, seemed to 'Beth to be the natural outgrowth of the strange happiness that brooded in her heart.

Well for her, indeed, that this devotion to the Blessed and Immaculate Virgin had sprung up in her soul, almost at the moment she first became acquainted with it! Was it a grace born of that consecration of her to Mary by her mother at her birth? Has it ever been known that one so placed under our Blessed Lady's protection was abandoned? Does she not keep watch over them with jealous eye to deliver them out of the snares and pitfalls which the great adversary, and the world, seek to weave around them? Well was it for 'Beth that she had this holy refuge to fly to, when the dark days drew nigh!

(TO BE CONTINUED.)

As light precedes darkness, so consolation is offered to us before our trials. Jesus was transfigured before the three apostles whom He had chosen to witness His sufferings and His agony. In that moment of glory He spoke of the ignominious death that awaited Him, and of the sufferings of His Passion.—*P. Boylesve.*

The Tyrannical Suppression of Educational Institutions in France.

IT is just thirty-five years since a few hot-headed zealots in the royal court of France succeeded, by scheming and misrepresentations bereft of all sense of honor, of justice and of fair-play, in suppressing the houses and educational institutions conducted by the Jesuits in that beautiful but sadly misgoverned country. A secret embassy was first sent to Pope Gregory XVI with the view of procuring the legal suppression of the Society of Jesus in France, but the Holy Father promptly answered its misrepresentations by saying that he could not accede to its requests; he referred the ambassador, M. Rossi, to the then Superior-General of the Order, the Very Rev. Father Roothaan. Failing here, M. Rossi, in order to cover his defeat probably, had recourse to a base stratagem. If he was not responsible for it, the French Government certainly was, for it lay between the ambassador and the Government. The Holy See refused to grant anything to M. Rossi and while the French Jesuits,—prominent among whom was the renowned and much-beloved orator of Notre Dame, Father de Ravignan,—were making representations of the real state of affairs to their General, from whom they had received no orders, and who was awaiting their answer to some recommendations made by him, the French Government caused the following paragraph to be inserted in the official paper, the *Moniteur*, of July the 6th, it having previously appeared in the *Messager*:

"The King's Government has received despatches from Rome. The negotiation with which M. Rossi was charged has proved successful. The Jesuit Association will cease to exist in France, and is about to disperse voluntarily. Its houses will be closed, and its novitiates will be broken up."

As soon as the paragraph in the *Moniteur* became known at Rome, no less astonishment was felt there than at Paris, and certainly the greatest surprise was felt by those whose names were involved—the Holy Father himself, and Cardinal Lambruschini, the Papal Secretary of State. M. Rossi was called upon for an explanation. The envoy extraordinary seemed astonished, and replied that he had never written anything of the kind; and he remarked that the passage was not in the official part of the *Moniteur*; it was a mere newspaper paragraph, to which no importance should be attached. He would, however, write to his Government to have the mistake set right. He spoke to the Cardinal Secretary and to several members of the diplomatic body to this effect.

But the pretended mistake was not set right, and the French Minister, M. Guizot, when spoken to, maintained the truthfulness of the paragraph in the *Moniteur*, which he said M. Rossi had sent, and that the Government was prepared to uphold it and have it carried out to the letter wholly.

So, with base trickery, wholly unworthy the name of diplomacy, the Society of Jesus had its houses broken up and its schools closed, but—mark well the sequence—in a very short time, less than three years afterwards, the throne and crown rolled in the dust: with the cry from the infuriated populace of "Down with the Ministers!" the throne disappeared, and was seen no more.

So much for the rotten *monarchy* of France. The so-called "*Republic*" of to-day seeks to follow in its footsteps. Let it beware that it meet not with a like fate as a result of its unconstitutional measures in despoiling Frenchmen of their God-given rights. Already ominous signs appear on the horizon, and fearful rumblings are heard. The Paris correspondent of the Baltimore *Sun*, in a recent letter to that paper, gives the following description of the present state of affairs in unhappy France:

"Just now the primary question agitating the hearth-and-home people of this continent, is one of the gravest, because embracing the two most important features of social and domestic life, to wit: Religion and politics combined. Let me note this from a political point on the spot, and totally divested of any personal leanings, extenuating nothing, nor setting down aught in malice. The first thing that excites one's surprise is to see in this fag-end of the nineteenth century and in the boasted home of 'liberty, equality and fraternity,' a general proscription of large bodies of citizens, simply on account of their private organizations, with which the Government and the State have absolutely nothing to do. This surprise is by no means lessened, when we find a ministry calling itself progressive and liberal to an extreme degree, making use of the rusty and mouldy enactments of despotic kings and local and corrupt legislatures of the last century, thus eagerly grasping at the worn weapons of royalty to fight the clerical crusade of republicanism. . The antique names 'Bourbon, Parliament of Paris, the Year X,' and other obsolete and fossilized authorities, are invoked and acted on by men who profess themselves to be the champions of regenerated, progressive France, and the shining lights of that looked-for period when, as Victor Hugo says, 'there shall be no more frontiers and no more fighting.' I have mentioned organization as the chief offence of these proscribed citizens, for, as regards doctrine, morals, and civic life, the non-authorized orders of French men and French women are neither more nor less Catholic and French than the vast bulk of the population of the country. It is, then, simply as 'societies' that these people are expelled, because a religious order would cease to be one if the idea of society is eliminated. Practically, these societies or orders have as much right to exist as the '40 Immortels' of the French Academy, for the claims of literature, championed by this illustrious body, are not more urgent than the demands of charity, instruction and learning, assisted by the organizations whose very existence is now condemned. The absurd—I say absurd to any common-sense observer—and antiquated fears of the unseen powers of the Jesuits, for instance, ought certainly not to weigh much in the formation of any opinions now prevailing on this subject. So far as I have seen, they are very much like other people, doing and saying things wise, and the reverse of wise occasionally, but in no way worthy of being placed above the law, outside the law, or below the law. These proceedings of the present French ministry are, from a political point of view, absolutely unintelligible. Socially speaking, they are a mistake of the first order. To set class against class, family against family, town against town, province against province, and all this for no object whatever, excepting to gratify a traditional spite and to chase away a traditional bugbear, seems reducing social politics down to the very zero of rashness and incompetence. Coming hither from Belgium, these views have been forced upon me by the prevalence in all circles of conversation on the present strife, and its being engendered by the revengeful and evidently short-sighted cabinet of France. The predictions as to the future consequences of this social revolution are startling. The disturbance in every family looking to a moral education of youth—and an economical education, too,—is beyond description. You hear it in the railway trains, at the depôts, in the hotels and on the streets. It is the question of the hour, and to pass it over would be as if one were deaf from prejudice and blind through ignorance. Of course at the present moment it would be hard to speculate on the issue of all this unnecessary provocation to internal revolution. The optimist view is that though for the moment suppressed as organized bodies, the religious orders as individuals will exercise throughout the country as much influence as ever—heightened, indeed, by the persecution 'of which they are the object. What is this influence? Take these orders in their respective spheres, and we find, as I have said, that charity and learning constitute their very essence and their only influence. Why oppose such? Simply to gratify, as I have said, certain traditional spite and the advancement of certain vain-glorious political demagogues and opportunist 'statesmen' who are already preparing ballot-boxes for the next election. One would hardly credit anybody of politicians with such a weak attack as this, and the ministry themselves seem to think so, for they will, it is said, forbid the councils-general, which are, perhaps, the truest mouthpieces of France, discussing the question on the opening of these council sessions next week. But a fact has just been made public which will cause them more anxiety than any action of the councils-general: the Archbishop and Bishops are about to sign collective protests against the enforcement of the obsolete royal laws named, just as they did against the passing of 'clause 7.' The Archbishop of Paris will lead the van in this public episcopal remonstrance. The Pope himself has publicly declared, in presence of the whole pontifical court, that the Church would energetically maintain the civil rights of the Catholic religion in France, adding, moreover, that this ecclesiastical action in reality tended to the peace, concord and prosperity of the country. As for the orders themselves, they seem unanimously resolved not to sue for an authorization of which, according to M. Dufaure himself, they have no need. Several meetings have been held by members of Senate and the heads of the orders threatened by the late decree, and the most emnent legal opinion of the country will be obtained as to the strict rights of the members of these orders as French citizens. Such is the resistance now preparing, and which will be incorporated in a series of resolutions before the session of the Chambers which opens on the 21st instant. It is said that M. de Freycinet has given utterance to the intention of the Government being reconciled to all the orders save and except the Jesuits, and they say, 'Well, to be persecuted is part of our expectations!' Thus you will see from what sources this country is again internally tortured—by Frenchmen. Where will it end? Where it has ever ended, in the victory of morality, right and order."

[*From The "Catholic Review."*]

Renan Blessing the Church.

M. EARNEST RENAN has been playing the part of the Prophet Balaam; called to London to curse the Roman Catholic Church, he has ended by blessing it. Dean Stanley, it was said, had invited Rénan to deliver his discourses in the nave of Westminster Abbey, where, at the invitation of the Dean, the Pantheist Max Müller had already held forth. But there is a point beyond which even English Protestantism refuses to go; and the outburst of indignation at the proposal of Dean Stanley to make the Abbey a theatre for Rénan, was sufficiently strong to induce him to change the programme, and to arrange for Rénan to deliver his lectures in a hall, where all sorts of things are given. However, it may be said that some of Dean Stanley's own sermons in the Abbey, which he has so horribly desecrated, are more obnoxious to Christians than were M. Rénan's discourses. He is a man of great learning and he possesses a most happy facility of speech. He spoke in French—but the London *Times* gives admirable translations of his discourses. We cannot give space for even a summary of his lectures—but we think it worth while to mention some of the points which he made, and to quote some of his words. He described most eloquently how the Church came to recognize Rome as its capital, and to acknowledge the Bishop of Rome as its head; and what he said on this matter, based upon the facts, going back as far as the days of Saints Peter and Paul, and of Pope Clement, would be well worth the study of such *pseudo savants* as Dr. Irenæus Prime and Dr. Leonard Bacon. But let us quote a few sentences:

"Every victory of Rome was a victory of reason." .... The reference was to Clement of Rome. Lost, as it were, in the *penumbra* of a very remote age, and reminding one of the head of an old worn-out fresco by Giotto, still recognizable by its golden aureole and by some vague traits of a pure and sweet glory, Clement was one of the grand figures of nascent Christianity. Everything leads us to believe that Clement was of Jewish origin. He seems to have been born at Rome of one of those Palestinian families which for a generation or two had dwelt in the capital of the world. The extent of his knowledge in cosmography and history, argue a pretty careful education. It was generally admitted that early in life he had been in personal relations with the Apostles, especially with Peter, although, perhaps, we are without any very decisive proof as to this. What could not be doubted was the high rank he held in the wholly spiritual hierarchy of the Church of his time, and the unique authority he enjoyed. His approval carried the weight of law. All parties laid claim to it and were even anxious to shelter themselves under his authority. He was the first type of a Pope presented in Church history. His lofty personality, made greater still by legend, was, next to that of Peter, the holiest image extant of primitive Christian Rome. His venerable countenance was for all following centuries that of a mild and grave lawgiver, a perpetual sermon of submission and respect. Already the idea of a certain primacy of this Church was coming to light. The right of warning other churches and settling their differences was yielded to Rome. Like privileges—so at least it was believed—had been accorded to Peter among the disciples. But a closer and closer bond of union between Peter and Rome was forming. Serious dissensions were rending the Church of Corinth. The Roman Church was consulted as to those troubles, and answered by an epistle which has been handed down to us. It bears no name, but one of the oldest Christian traditions attributes it to Clement. M. Rénan proceeded to give an analysis of this document, which showed, he said, how little the Corinthian Church had changed since St. Paul's time. Then was the same spirit of pride, of disputation, of levity. The main opposition to the hierarchy was rooted in the Greek temper, ever capricious, undisciplined, not knowing the secret of reducing a crowd to the condition of a flock. Men, women, and even children were in full revolt. Transcendent doctors, priding themselves on gifts analogous to the old, speaking with tongues and the discernment of spirits, despised the Presbyters and aspired to their places. *The Roman Church which spoke through Clement was that of order, of subordination, of rule. Its fundamental principle was humility, submission—worth more than the subtlest gifts.* Clement's epistle was the first manifest in the Christian Church of the principle of authority. A great outcry was raised some years ago about a saying of a French Archbishop once senator. "My clergy is my regiment." Clement had said the same long before, as M. Rénan proved by a striking quotation from his epistle.... "Peter and Paul had been the two chiefs, the two founders of the Church of Rome. They were the two halves of an insuperable pair, two luminaries, like sun and moon. What the one taught the other taught also; they were ever as one, they battled with the same enemies, both were victims of the perfidies of Simon Magus. At Rome they lived like two brothers; the Church of Rome was their joint creation. The supremacy of this Church was thus founded for the ages to come." ... "He called on his audience to behold the true miracles of nascent Christianity. It deduced order, hierarchy, authority, obedience from the free subjection of men's wills; it organized the crowd, it brought anarchy under discipline. How was this miracle, the spirit of Jesus, with which His disciples were powerfully inoculated, wrought it, that spirit of sweetness, of self-denial, of forgetfulness of the present, that unique pursuit of inward joys which kills ambition, that sublime preference given to children, the words incessantly repeated as those of Jesus, 'Let him who would be first among you, be servant of all.' The impression left by the Apostles did not contribute less to the result. The Apostles and their immediate vicars wielded an uncontested sway over all the Churches. But the Episcopate was deemed the heir of the Apostolic powers. The Apostles remained alive, and governed after their death. The idea that the president of the Church holds his mandate from the members of the Church who have nominated him, was not met once in the literature of that time. The Church thus escaped, *in virtue of the supernatural origin of its power*, the decrepitude inherent in all delegated authority; a legislation and executive authority might spring from the crowd, but sacraments, dispensations of heavenly grace, have nothing to do with universal suffrage. Such privileges came from Heaven." . . . "The Church was all the world's affair, not that of an aristocracy of inspired Phrygian pietists or Gonostic searchers after 'deep things.' Catholic opinion was the impregnable bulwark against which the countless heresies hurled themselves in vain. To confute a heretic, no reasoning was required; it was enough to show that he was outside the Catholic pale; and the rule afterwards formulated by Vincentius of Lerins, 'Quod semper, quod ubique, quod ab omnibus traditum,' was already the test of truth." . . . "The learned lecturer proceeded to argue that even the spirit which in 1870 proclaimed Papal Infallibility, was already very clearly recognizable from the close of the second century. The fragmentary Muratori Canon, for instance, written about 180, shows us some determining for the Churches the Codex of Scripture. Irenæus refutes all the heresies in the authority of what Rome believed, which Church he styles 'the greatest, oldest, most illustrious, possessing by unbroken succession the true traditions of the Apostles Peter and Paul, the Church to which, in virtue of its primacy,' all the rest of the Church was bound to have recourse.' "The immense charities which this very wealthy Church distributed throughout the world, greatly helped to consolidate her authority." . . . "You have wished me to recall your thoughts to the grandeurs of Catholicism, at its best epoch. I thank you for so doing. Bonds of childhood, the strongest of all bonds, attach me to Catholicism, and I am often tempted to say of it what Job said, at least in our Latin version, 'Etiam si occiderit me, in ipso separabo.'"

Thus it is that this modern Balaam was compelled to bless instead of cursing the Church into which he was baptized and which gave him the education which in later days he has so sadly misused. Perhaps God may yet have mercy upon him, and bring him back to the fold from which he has strayed.

God will demand of me an account of how I have used all that He confided to me, body, soul, intelligence, will, senses, health, strength, worldly goods, natural and supernatural gifts. Every thought, every desire, every word will be examined and judged. Recompense or punishment will be awarded. I must render an account of every useless word that I have spoken.—*P. Boylesve.*

[*From "The Dublin Nation."*]

Further Apparitions at Knock.

WE have received the following narrative from a well-known dignitary of the Irish Church, whose name we are prepared to give privately, though not allowed to publish it. We may assure our readers that there is nothing less likely than any shade of credulity in our very reverend correspondent's character or temperament; and this is one reason why we look upon the document which we publish below as one of the most remarkable we have ever read. The very reverend gentleman, writing to the *Weekly News*, says:

As your paper may well be esteemed "The Gazette of Our Lady of Knock," I send you this marvellous narration. I have the most entire confidence in the good sense and high virtue of my dear child, Bridget Hough. I have known her since her infancy, and I can attest that one more reliable for truth and judgment could hardly be found in the county. She is just twenty years old. The only changes I have made in the dear child's manuscript is in italicizing portions of two or three sentences that appeared to possess a striking demonstrative value. Continuity of view and unchanged impressions for hours together—objects remaining visible and unvarying at different distances and different times—numbers of person, on some of the occasions, beholding precisely the same appearances at the same moments—if you make all the things beheld to be simply *unreal*, and yet be obliged to *attribute to them all the effects of reality*, in the identity of impressions, constancy of impressions, and harmony of testimony, the miracles performed on the senses and minds of the multitude must be greater and more numerous than those every day recorded as happening at Knock. Here we speak of the impressions on the mind, and say nothing of the unquestionable facts of the cures. In fact, human testimony is not worth a straw if so many could have a uniform delusion regarding obvious manifestations. I may add that a companion of Bridget Hough, who went to Knock at the same time, worn away with three running sores, came back with her, and came back *perfectly cured*.

[LETTER.]

Very Rev. Dean:—To comply with your wishes, I undertake to give you, Rev. Father, a true and exact account of the visions I saw at Knock, as far as I can remember. The first vision I saw, and the first time, was on Good Friday, about twenty minutes past three o'clock. I saw our Blessed Lord, nailed to the Cross, with the two thieves, one at each side of Him, His Blessed Mother at His right side, with her hands and eyes lifted up, and turned towards the people as if she was praying for them; Mary Magdalen at the foot of the Cross, with her hands raised as if she was trying to put them round the Feet of our dear Lord. At the head of the Cross was a lamb; away from the lamb, at the other side of the Cross, were two moons-like (I mean the very shape), but of the purest white: I could not describe them better. *I saw that vision the rest of the day.* I left the church for a little time, and came back in the evening to spend the night there. About half-past eight, I saw, on the opposite gable of the church, our Blessed Lord as if taken down from the Cross. I saw all the wounds opened—with His right hand laid down on His Heart—the left hand stretched out from Him, with the lamb laid on it, and turned towards the people. At first when I saw Him, the crown of thorns was pressed on the forehead and raised a little. I looked at our Blessed Lord in this position for about an hour and a half. The next thing I could observe then was a light getting in through the gable of the church, and immediately a star appeared at the other end of the church. Then the people got awfully excited. Every time I looked at our Blessed Lord I thought His holy eyes were fixed on myself alone, until this time, when the people got excited. Then He turned away His head and looked at the people. After looking at them for about five minutes, He turned to me again, and continued to do (as far as I can remember) about sixteen times successively. When He turned to me again, after the first time He looked at the people, I could see the crown of thorns pressed down, with the Blood streaming down from the wound. His Heart appeared to me then to be open in two, with the Precious Blood flowing from it. I could discern also, at the left side, a large open wound. At about a foot above our Blessed Lord's head, a red door appeared; it was closed when first I saw it, and then opened. I could see nothing inside but all darkness. Then, outside, was something long, and very white. It moved slowly in, until it went inside the door. Then the most brilliant light shone all over His body and on the whole gable, and His Sacred Body appeared to me to be vanishing, by degrees, until I could see nothing but the wounds and Face. His Sacred Face appeared then more plump and joyous-looking than before. He smiled three times. I should smile myself in return. I then fainted, and was taken out in the air. When I went next day to the church, I could see the wounds and shadow as plain as ever.

Easter Saturday I saw our Blessed Lord and His Holy Mother with the chalice in His hand, as if administering the Blessed Sacrament. *I saw that all day.* Then on Easter Saturday night, nine of us got a privilege to remain in the Church all night. We all knelt round the altar of Our Blessed Lady. All lights were out except what were on this altar. There appeared on the crown that was on the statue, stars going round. We all got excited. At first we thought it might be the reflection of the lights, so we came to the conclusion to quench all the lights and remove the lamp that was burning opposite the altar. Then, immediately, the statue got the most brilliant white, and the crown was removed from her head, and Our Lady bent out over us, with her hands joined together, as if she was praying for us. We then put back the lights and the lamp, and put the crown on again, and immediately the stars appeared the same as before.

On Easter Sunday, on the same place, appeared to me the Blessed Virgin, St. Joseph and the Child—about the age of twelve years—in front of St. Joseph, with the Saint's right hand on His shoulder. *I could see that vision all day.* I went out to go round the church to pay my rounds; when I came back I could see them as plain as ever. When I went to the door of the church, I turned round again to see whether I could discern it from the door as plain as near the altar, where I had been, and I could, just as plainly; but before I could turn again, I fainted, and was taken away.

On Easter Monday morning, before I left for home, I could see the shadows of each of those visions in each place, where I saw them first plainly.

I hope you will excuse any errors you may see in this writing. I may have committed some, for I always get too excited when I reflect on it.—I remain, my dear Dean, your obedient child,

BRIDGET HOUGH.

We are authorized to state that Miss Hanna Pasley, 9 Grafton-street, Dublin, also witnessed some of the visions described in the foregoing remarkable communication.

Catholic Notes.

—We could mention a place where a Presbyterian minister sent a bouquet for the Blessed Virgin's altar one day during May, and even preached twice in his church on Our Lady. They were *moving* sermons, for the congregation, we are told, left the church. He isn't there any more.

—One of the Boston papers reports that a party of infirm persons sailed from that city for Knock on the 6th inst. Others are to follow later on. The same paper states that a blind woman who attends St. Mary's Church was recently cured by the application of the water of Lourdes.

—Our best thanks are due to Very Rev. Father Quigley, V. G., of Charlestown, S. C., and the Rev. pastors of St. Patrick's, St. Mary's, and St. Joseph's Churches, in the same city, for kind favors to our travelling agent. We are also under obligations to Rev. Father Garvey, of the Church of the Annunciation, Williamsport, Pa., and Rev. Thomas McGovern, of Danvill.

—We have sent the following sums to Ireland this week: $19.55, care of Lady Georgiana Fullerton; $290, to Rev. Father Edward Murphy, S. J., Sea Road, Galway—$127 of which is the Children Fund; and $100 to Most Rev. Archbishop MacHale. Nearly fifty dollars more have been received since the above remittances were made. We thank our readers in the name of the Blessed Virgin and the suffering poor of Ireland for their generous response to the appeal.

—Miss Kate Hand has sent $2 for the Needy Mission. An estimable lady in New York has also been good enough to send us for the same object a fine set of red vestments, a confession stole, an alb, and a quantity of altar linens. The grateful missionary desires us to state that he intends to offer a novena of Masses for the intentions of his benefactors on the nine last days of this month. The generosity of the contributors and the gratitude of the recipient in this case are admirable.

—Among the contributions received last week for the starving poor of Ireland, one deserves special mention. A little boy sent a dollar, and the remitter informed us that it was the sum total of what he had been saving for the purchase of a coveted tool chest. No donation that ever passed through our hands has gladdened us more than this. God bless that dear child! How pleasing to the infinitely loving Heart of Jesus and the tender, Immaculate Heart of Our Blessed Mother must that act be! It will not be without its reward even in this world.

—A SINGULAR OCCURRENCE.—In our last we mentioned the fact of the huge cross of St. Laurence O'Tool's Church having blown down. The particulars are rather strange. The cross was lifted out of the socket in which it rested and carried outward by the wind, alighting on its base on the curbstone, where it was found standing without even a chip being struck off its *contour*. A gentleman, who was standing near by when the solid stone took its flight, incontinently fled, thinking the day of judgment had come.—*Western Watchman.*

——Paris.—We make the following extract from a welcome letter received last week from Paris. It shows that the great mass of French Catholics are sincerely pious, and that the threatened dangers to religion from the reigning Government in that country are not so imminent as most people imagine: "In all the churches I visited, I found everywhere pious and recollected worshippers. In no one, however, have I been more edified than in the provisory Chapel of the Sacred Heart on Mt. Martre, and at Notre Dame des Victoires. There I saw piety such as I have never seen before in my life. I still feel impregnated with the atmosphere of devotion reigning there. One would remain in that blessed place the whole day. What touching canticles I heard there! One is moved to tears in spite of himself. France cannot perish while such fervent piety reigns in the hearts of her children. If the Government was only better, beautiful days would come again for this unhappy country. So far, however, no one would suspect anything extraordinary against the Church; priests, seminarists, religious Brothers and Sisters of various descriptions, move freely in the streets in their religious dress. You find them everywhere. May God in His mercy avert the dangers that threaten them!"

——Congress did a wise and sensible thing the other day when, by an unanimous vote of both Houses it accepted as a gift to the nation the desk upon which Thomas Jefferson wrote the Declaration of Independence, and ordered it to be placed among the treasures of the nation. As a country grows in age, it prizes more and more the mementoes and memorials of its youth, and it is natural that it should gladly treasure them up and hand them down to coming generations as articles to be cherished and, to some extent, venerated. This desire to preserve the relics of the great and the good is common to all mankind. But the same gentlemen who accepted with thanks this relic of Thomas Jefferson, or at least many of them, have doubtless often scoffed at the veneration which we, poor benighted and superstitious Papists, pay to the relics of our saints, and the regard in which we hold the places in which they labored, the clothes which they wore and the articles which they handled. Thomas Jefferson was an able man and a good patriot, albeit he was tainted with the pernicious notions of the French Revolution. It is well to preserve mementoes of him, when they are connected with the great events of his life. But those who do so can scarcely, with good grace, sneer at Catholics who, from the foundation of the Church until this moment, have sought to preserve with pious care the relics and mementoes of God's saints and martyrs.—*Catholic Review.*

——An Inviting Shrine.—The beautiful devotion of the Sacred Heart, so deeply rooted in the parish of St. Joseph de Levis, P. Q., by the unremitting efforts of its pastor, has lately produced a new effect which gladdens all hearts. It is the miniature shrine dedicated to Our Lady, and lately blessed, that nestles against the sanctuary and is shaded by its walls. It is built on the rock, like its namesake across the ocean—the far-famed Sanctuary of Notre Dame du Puy (in France)—and, by its appellation, recalls the native place of the departed foundress, whose memory will be forever blessed. Facing the entrance is a tiny Gothic altar, whose slender turrets enshrine a beautiful statue of Our Lady of the Angels, while a host of gilt needlets, flashing in the sun, look like a battalion in bristling armor, doing duty before its Sovereign. The diagonally-parted vault, with its delicate streak of blue in the centre setting off the white and gold, has a pleasing effect; each curve having for sole ornament a carving on wood, representing one of our Blessed Mother's symbolical names; the star, the anchor, and the virginal Heart being entwined with roses. A beautifully finished case for church vestments, which runs the whole width of the wall, with two confessionals on the opposite side, and a centre chandelier, form as yet the only furniture of the little oratory; but there is a stillness about the place and an atmosphere of peace which invite us to prayer. The chapel, although private, may be visited by adorers to the shrine of the Sacred Heart, either by the outer door opening on the convent-chapel yard, or by the inner sanctuary doors which lead to it. From her graceful throne, Our Lady of the Angels will greet the visitor with a smile, and in return for his *Aves*, open to him the door to her Son's residence—the dwelling-place of His Sacred Heart. Of the crowds of visitors which the coming celebration of Saint Jean Baptiste will gather into Quebec, not a few, we hope, will wend their way to the shrine, on the opposite shore of the St. Lawrence, before they bid adieu to the old city. Many a pilgrim, no doubt, will recall a tie to the shrine by the little mite which he contributed towards its erection. There he will be repaid for the trifling cost and trouble of the excursion, in finding, like the Magi, the Divine Child and His Mother.

——First Communion, and May Procession at the Academy of the Oblate Sisters of Providence (Colored), Baltimore, Md.—We have from time to time taken pleasure in calling attention to the edifying Order of the colored Oblate Sisters of Providence, in Baltimore, and the noble work performed by them, at their Academy and Orphanage, for the higher instruction of the young people of their race, and the succor and protection of colored orphans. Since the establishment of the colored Sisters was first opened in Baltimore, where the Order was founded, the good nuns have been a source of edification to all who have known them, and now that such a multitude of the colored race have been thrown upon society suddenly and unprepared, with few to take an interest in their real welfare, such an interest as calls for sacrifices either personal or pecuniary, we know of no undertaking so deserving of warm encouragement and support as that of the colored Oblate Sisters of Providence. Their Order has begun a work whose ultimate magnitude no one can predict. The field is large, and daily increasing in magnitude. There is a glorious apostolate in it, and who will may aid it and become a participator in its merits and its work for the salvation of souls. On Sunday, the 9th of May, there was a beautiful May procession of girls, from 3 to 20 years of age, at the institution above-named. Nearly a hundred girls, with crowns of flowers on their heads and in white dresses, with colored sashes and long white veils, moved in procession through the garden of the Academy, along Chase street and Greenmount Avenue. The May Queen was personated by Mary Jane Callahan. Four girls carried a statue of the Blessed Virgin in the procession, and all had flowers in their hands. The statue of our Blessed Lady in the garden was crowned by the May Queen, after which the procession went into the chapel where the flowers were laid on the Blessed Virgin's altar and May devotions were held. Hymns and anthems were sung by the girls, and Rev. John R. Slattery delivered a discourse. Twenty of the girls made their First Communion and renewed their baptismal vows. Rev. Father Early, of Charlestown, now on a visit to Baltimore, and Fathers De Ruyter and Leeson took part in the services.

——THE STARVING POOR OF IRELAND.—It will be remembered that several weeks ago a statement from the Duchess of Marlborough went the rounds of the newspapers to the effect that the wants of the famine-stricken poor in Ireland were nearly relieved, and that in a short time no further aid would be needed, or something to that effect. But the actual state of the case, as described by eye-witnesses, is not so encouraging. Mr. James Redpath describes in a recent letter a ride in the parish of Islandeady, in the county Mayo, which he visited in conducting his investigations of the Irish famine for the New York *Tribune*. He gives a vivid glimpse of the destitution of the Irish peasantry —all the stronger as he makes no effort at picturesque description, but gives rather a catalogue of effects than an artistic picture. We quote:

"There were still more dreadful scenes in the other cabins. I know no farmer in the East or West who keeps his cattle in such foul stables. And yet children and infants, and mothers and stalwart workingmen—not beggars, but honest fellows, willing and eager to work—have been born and reared and married in these dreadful dens, none of them having any floors save the cold black earth; none of them having windows larger than two feet by eighteen inches, and nearly all of them having cows or horses or donkeys in the same room, undivided by either a stone wall or a partition of any kind. Heaps of oozing muck at the doors! The last cabin filled me with dismay. It was dark and dirty and small. There were little heaps of what is called 'bog deal' and furze, as fuel, and a little peat fire. 'Bog deal' is the roots of ancient fir trees that have been preserved in the moist bogs. No one remembers when the fir trees grew. They disappeared a generation ago. An old woman, at least seventy years old, with white hair, discolored by the smoke of the cabin, and clad in foul rags, with her bare feet on the wet floor, haggard and hideous from want, sat on an old rickety chair and told me she had been twice married—once to a man named Conway, once to a man named Flynn, and that she had two sons, one by each husband, in the United States. They had not written to her for years. One of these sons lives in Scranton, the other in Philadelphia. Her granddaughter, a beautiful young girl of fourteen or sixteen, was working with a spade in the garden. Though beautiful now, twenty years hence, if she lives here, she will be ugly and wrinkled like the rest. On Sunday I saw an old man and woman, with their young son, sitting around a basket, the lid of which, inverted, held their dinner. There was a saucer in it. It held salt water—common salt dissolved. The rest of the meal consisted of cold potatoes; that was all. I recalled it as I saw the little children of one of these hovels crowded around the pot with the cold Indian meal porridge. When I went back to the hotel, a Castlebar banker told me that 'there was far less distress than was talked about, and that Ireland had never been better off.'"

——DONATIONS TO THE IRISH RELIEF FUND (LADY FULLERTON'S), from the school children of Sinsinawa Mound, Grant Co., Wisconsin; School District No. 5: M. Carey, 10 cts.; Nellie Carey, 10 cts.; Cecilia Carey, 10 cts.; Emma Carey, 10 cts.; Bertha Carey, 10 cts.; Mary Barnning, 10 cts.; Benny Barnning, 10 cts.; Bridget Murray, 25 cts.; William McCabe, 10 cts.; Patrick White, 10 cts.; Maggie Murray, 20 cts.; Annie Murray, 20 cts.; Mary Murray, 10 cts.; Danny Driscoll, 10 cts.; Benjamin Miller, 10 cts.; Herman Miller, 10 cts.; Mary Williams, 10 cts.; Regina Williams, 5 cts.; Wennella Williams, 10 cts.; Walter Murray, 10 cts.; Rosa Hoppman, 10 cts.; Benjamin Hoppman, 10 cts.; Lizzie Brotz, 10 cts.; Charlie Cain, 10 cts.; Lizzie Cross, 10 cts.; Ellen Williams, 10 cts.; Felix Scolen, 10 cts.; Minerva Williams, 20 cts.; Christina Hoppman, 10 cts.; Willie White, 15 cts.; Jennie White, 10 cts.

——CONTRIBUTIONS FOR THE SUFFERING IRISH.— Some Friends, $10; Henry O'Neil, $1; A Reader of THE AVE MARIA, $1; John Murrin, $5; Miss Kate Hand, $8; A Reader of THE AVE MARIA, $1; Miss Libbie T. Kress, $1; Mrs. Ann Johnson, $1; A Subscriber of THE AVE MARIA, $1; Charles Christmas, $1; Mrs. Eliza Christmas, $1; A Friend in Fall River, $2; John Hanlon, $1; Miss Bridget Hughes, $1; Mrs. Bridget Sheridan, $1; Mr. Thos. Sheridan, $1; Mrs. Johannah Sullivan, $1; Miss Julia Herlihy, $1; Miss Catharine Herlihy, 50 cts.; Mary Danahy, 25 cts.; Katie Danahy, 25 cts.; Mrs. Edward Ring, $1; A Friend, $1; Mrs. C. Brown, $5; A Subscriber of THE AVE MARIA, $10; Mrs. Lawrence Finn, $5; A Friend, $1; Peter and Lizzie McKenna, $5; A North of Ireland Convert, $5; William Cullinane, $1; A Child of Mary, $2; Thomas Relihan, $1; A Client of Mary, $5; Mrs. Kate Harrington, $1; Maria Navarre, $1; Miss Mary Duffy, $1; M. Geary, $2; H., Springfield, Ill., $2; One of the Macs, $5; A Reader of THE AVE MARIA, $5; Miss N. A. Leary, 50 cts.; A Reader of THE AVE MARIA, $2; Michael Sullivan, $5; Ellen Horen, $1; Mary Stewart, $2; Friends, Salem, Mass., $12.50; Michael Weaver, $1; Two Friends, Waterloo, Wis., 50 cts.; A Friend, Lancaster, Pa., $1; Sisters of Providence, St. Mary's, Viga Co., Ind., $15; Michael Egan, $5; John Sullivan, $2; Thos. Parker, $2; Thos. Holland, $1; David Toling, $1; James Burke, $1; A Friend, $1; Mrs. Nolan, $1; Jean Nolan, $1; Thos. Duffy, $1; John McMahon, $1; Patrick Curran, $5; A Friend, $1; Mrs. J. M. Higgins, $2; Thos. Cain, $5; Henry Cain, $5; Mrs. J. Murphy, $5; Mrs. Conlon, $1; Charles Murray, $1; Mark Toole, $10; Christopher C. Fletcher, $5; Mrs. H. C. Gibson, $6; Mrs. Tillie Luther, $1; Jacob C. Luther, 50 cts.; Enoch Short, 25 cts.; Mrs. Mary P. Kaylor, 25 cts.; James and Miss Lizzie O'Flaherty, $2; A Friend, $2.

New Publications.

STUMBLING-BLOCKS MADE STEPPING-STONES ON THE ROAD TO THE CATHOLIC FAITH. By Rev. James Moriarty, A. M. People's Edition. Price, 30 cents.

It is enough to announce the publication of this cheap edition of Father Moriarty's work, which has been received with such general favor, and for which the demand has been so great as to call for a third edition. It has already been noticed in these pages.

THE CATECHISM OF PERSEVERANCE. By Monsignor Gaume. Translated from the Tenth French Edition. In Four Vols. Vol. II. Dublin : M. H. Gill & Son.

We are pleased to announce the appearance of the second volume of this valuble work. Those engaged in the instruction of the young, and those seeking instruction in the Catholic religion for themselves, will find this work most useful. It is too well known to require at our hands more than a mere announcement of its translation into English.

—— We are indebted to a kind friend in Dublin for a copy of "The Illustrated Record of the Apparitions at the Church of Knock," published by T. D. Sullivan, 90 Middle-Abbey street, Dublin.

Confraternity of the Immaculate Conception
(Or of Our Lady of Lourdes.)

REPORT FOR THE WEEK ENDING MAY 12TH.

The following intentions are recommended to the prayers of the members this week: Recovery of health for 19 persons and 3 families,—change of life for 9 persons and 2 families,—conversion to the Faith for 16 persons and 2 families,—recovery of mind for 5 persons,—special graces for 20 priests, 11 religious, and 10 clerical students,—temporal favors for 28 persons and 6 families,—spiritual favors for 28 persons and 8 families,—the spiritual and temporal welfare of 3 communities, 2 congregations, and 1 school; also, 16 particular intentions, and 4 thanksgivings for favors received.

Specified Intentions: Rain for a certain district,—the success of a retreat,—means to pay a debt,—removal of obstacles to a religious vocation,—cessation of enmity between two persons,—removal of scandals,—the success of a mission,—restoration of sight for several persons,—four persons in great spiritual danger.

FAVORS OBTAINED.

"Some time ago," says a worthy mother, "I wrote you, asking prayers for my son who was then given to intemperance. Now he has taken the pledge, and is doing well. Thanks to God and our Blessed Mother!" .... Another correspondent writes: "You recollect, no doubt, my receiving some water of Lourdes on the 14th ult. I began a novena to the Immaculate Mother of God on the 26th, and ended it on the 4th inst., St. Monica's Day. My ear had been troubling me very much, and appeared to be getting worse. It gave me great pain. On Tuesday morning it began to discharge, and broke on the last day of my novena, and has continued to free itself ever since. As for hearing, I have not heard so well in a long time. I ask you to give thanks for so signal a favor." Another lady asks us to return thanks to Our Blessed Lady for the return to a Christian life of a Freemason, who had not received the Sacraments for eighteen years.

OBITUARY.

The prayers of the Confraternity are requested in behalf of the following deceased persons: Mr. CHAS. A. MCINTYRE, who departed this life at East Cambridge, Mass., on the 30th ult. Miss MARY FRANCES MCMANUS, deceased at Buffalo, N. Y., on the 20th of March. Mrs. ELIZABETH MIRGON, who died suddenly at Columbus, O., on the 30th of April. SISTER MARY ALEXIUS (Hannigan), who calmly expired at Frederick, Md., on the 1st of May. MARY ELIZABETH MCBRIDE, of New York, who breathed her last in Rome, Italy, on the 12th ult., in the 85th year of her age, fortified by the Sacraments. SISTER MARY ISIDORE, of the Sisters of the Holy Cross, who slept in the Lord at St. Mary's Academy, Notre Dame, Ind., May 11th. And others, whose names have not been given.

Requiescant in pace.

A. GRANGER, C. S. C., Director.

Youth's Department.

A Child's May Offering.

BY M. A. A. G.

FAIREST roses, purest lilies,
For our lovely Queen of May;
Pansies purple, violets humble,
Give to her their charms to-day;
Heliotrope, devotion breathing;
Stars of Bethlehem, sweet and gay;
Mignonette, and myrtle wreathing,
Jonquilles, tulips' bright array;
Every bud and every blossom
Seems its beauteous Queen to greet:
See, the wealth of floral treasure
At our peerless Lady's feet!

The Story of Robin Redbreast.

A TRIAL IN OLD-WORLD BIRDLAND.

BY ETHEL TANE.

"WHICH of our tribes do men love better?" asked the king of the Nightingales. He spoke to Robin Redbreast.

It was April; the spring flowers were unveiling their delicate faces all over the land, and the Nightingale king had just come off his long journey from the South.

Robin's dark eyes twinkled. "Ask the House-Sparrows," said he.

Perhaps some of the sparrows overheard this question, and answered; for really they do seem settled everywhere. Anyhow the rumor of it was passed from beak to beak all through the forest and along the winding meadow streams; it even reached the city, and was chattered about on every housetop, for town-birds are terrible gossips.

"Which does mankind love more, Philomel or Robin?" The whole country side rang with this question. As the home-coming Nightingales crossed the moors, the Whinchat's sharp query stopped them; when they rested by the pleasant water-courses, the Reed Warbler's gentle voice came up from among the rushes—she was busy building her nest, but stopped to put the question of the hour; the Woodpecker forgot his scared insects in the rotten bark under his formidable bill, and allowed them a period of peace; even Jenny Wren had her word on the subject. It was time to stop this fuss.

"We will have a trial year," said the king of the Nightingales, "and both strive to win the hearts of men after our separate fashions. The House-Sparrows shall be witnesses,—Robin was right; they *do* hear everything—and the owl shall be judge."

So a deputation from all the smaller feathered tribes was despatched to the Owl's fortress, once a lordly castle, but now ruined and ivy-grown. They selected a bright noon-day, for at this hour the bird of wisdom sits at home and ruminates. By night he goes in search of his prey, and, possibly, might have given them an unpleasant reception.

"The Nightingale king has spoken well," said the Owl, graciously. "This question of pre-eminence in human love has troubled even me—so many voices debate it all day among the branches near. Again, I say, he has chosen well to put the matter to a legal test. I consent to preside at the proposed trial, and appoint it to be held here twelve calendar months from the date of this present speaking."

He ceased. The deputation bowed their heads and retired, well pleased.

Gaily the seasons chased each other round their familiar old planet, and shaped anew its never-dying beauty. When all had made their circuit, a great stillness fell on the country for many leagues around the Owl's fortress. Not a bird warbled in the woodlands or chirped on the hedgerows; all were gone to the court of judgment in the Baron's ancient dining-hall.

A massive stone bench ran round the chamber, broken in many places. On this, at the upper end, the Owl perched as on a dais; to his right and left, deputations from the Nightingales and Redbreasts; before him, on the floor, the Sparrow witnesses grouped round a sharply-pointed fragment of stone designed to be the witness-stand for each of them in turn. The general public covered the floor, thronged the rafters, crowded the empty window-frames. What a sea of glossy heads and restless round eyes!

The witness first called, lived at the large country-house of a rich old merchant, who, after making many thousands of pounds in a dingy city warehouse, had come to end his busy life on this beautiful demesne, the former property of a spendthrift nobleman. He was a sensible man and a kind one. He had no children, but many friends; neither he nor his wife cared much for books, yet they were never idle. Farming the neglected land, and caring for the equally neglected people upon it—from these two sources they drew plenty of business and pleasure. Their crops were generally heavy, their beasts always gained prizes at the exhibitions—best of all, their tenants' cottages were models to the whole region round, and every man on the estate knew that his landlord loved him. So you see, dear children, the merchant made a good use of his well-earned holiday.

"And what does he think of the Nightingale?"

"He calls him a wonderfully fine singer, my lord, but he is too gouty to go out and listen to him often."

The next witness owned a nest beneath the thatched roof of a tiny cottage, standing all by itself in a green lane. Here a young girl lived with her grandmother. Half a mile beyond, the lane melted into open chalk downs, for centuries mere sheep-walks, but now covered every harvest time with tall, yellow corn. The undulating plain swept away to the very horizon. At one spot only a group of ancient oaks rooted in an exactly hoof-shaped hollow broke the sameness of the vast cornfield. The ploughman never invaded this miniature valley; underbrush unfolded the huge oak trunks; wood strawberries ripened there, and a chorus of music came out from the coppice in spring—sweet, thrilling songs from the hearts of happy Nightingales. That part of the downs is called "The Devil's Jump," and tradition whispers that Satan's own hoof printed the odd-shaped little hollow. Miles away, on the other side of the nearest market town, a similar one exists, and it is said that the Father of Evil leaped at a bound from one spot to the other.[*]

Very, very few people came to the cottage in the lane. The grandmother sat all day in her arm-chair, knitting, or dozing, or telling her beads; she could do nothing else. The little maiden kept the house in order, and fed the poultry. It was a very quiet life. Her chief pleasure was the letters which often came from over the sea, directed to her or grandma, in a certain sprawling boyish hand. These were written by her sailor brother. Sometimes, on golden May evenings, when grandma was safe in bed, and the round red sun still peered over the downs, this lonely little girl stole up there to hear the Nightingales sing, and read again her dear brother's latest letter. Their songs seemed like echoes of her loving thoughts about him.

The third witness was a remarkable bird, indeed, for he lived under the same roof with a famous poet. At this announcement, the eye of

---

[*] If my little readers should ever visit Devizes, an old town in Wiltshire, England, they would hear this story and see the "Jump."

all the Nightingales grew larger with expectation.

"Your master," queried the judge, "how stands he affected towards Philomel?"

"His love for him is a poet's love."

The judge inclined his head; he knew how much these few words meant. But whence came the mischievous sparkle in the Sparrow's eye?

The fourth witness was from a large farm-house where a flock of rosy children lived, who sometimes talked about the Nightingale in the summer.

Number six (a brisk, perky bird) gave a suburban address.

Number seven had his home under the eaves of an almshouse; and number eight lodged just above one of the windows of a children's hospital. None of the last four had anything to say about Philomel, and the judge proceeded to re-examine all eight witnesses on behalf of Robin Redbreast.

"I've no great love for master Robin," said witness number one; "but I won't deny that master and mistress like him better than any other bird that flies. In the winter they throw us all out a good meal of crumbs three times a day, but Robin is the only one allowed to eat his victuals in with them. Master says that Robin always tries to make the best of things; sings away in the cold instead of moping, and trusts his human friends."

"And the lonely little maiden of the cottage?"

"Well, Robin's trilling songs certainly never bring tears to her eyes—tears of joy, my lord judge, you understand—as the Nightingales sometimes do on those May evenings. But through the chilly autumn days and the long, dreary winter, I see her nodding at him out of the cottage window, while he hops about the garden, or comes up on the sill itself. Then grandma laughs and nods too, and they both feed him. Year in, year out, she would miss him more, I fancy, he is so much more faithful than the Nightingales."

Now the poet's Sparrow rose and all held their breath. Shall I tell you why? Because in a matter like this, a true poet interprets aright the heart of man. This witness would really settle the question. But he merely bowed and asked to be allowed to give his testimony last. So the next witness, he from the farm-house, jumped on the stand almost before he was called, to protest that Robin Redbreast was the delight of the children's eyes, and one of their greatest amusements.

What said the city Sparrow? Alas! neither Philomel nor Robin was ever seen or heard in the squalid alley where that poor bird had been hatched. It was different with him from the suburbs. Mr. Robin was a frequent visitor on his master's trim lawn, though none of the shyer songsters would venture so close to town, and of course the family were devoted to him in consequence.

And the poor old people in the almshouse? And the little sick children, shut up in their hospital? In all these dull lives, Robin Redbreast was a living picture, an animating poem, a bright bit of romance. Both witnesses seemed quite breathless with sympathetic excitement when their eulogy was done.

But the climax came when the poet's bird mounted the witness stand. Hooked on one of his claws, all could see a scrap of crumpled manuscript paper.

"One day, last June," said the Sparrow, "I hopped into my master's study when he happened to be out of the room. Imagine my surprise to find among his papers a deliberately worded verdict on the question which has agitated Birdland so long. Allow me to read it to the court:

'Thou art the bird whom man loves best,
The pious bird, with the scarlet breast,
  Our little English Robin:
The bird that comes about our doors
When autumn winds are sobbing.
Thou art the Peter of Norway boors;
  Their Thomas in Finland,
  And Russia far inland;
The bird which, by some name or other,
All men who know thee call their brother.'"

It was enough. The Owl gave judgment; the court rose; the great question was never mooted in Birdland any more; for though the poet has been dead near thirty years, his verdict lives on, and if you open the works of William Wordsworth, you may read it for yourself.

But though the Owl was so wise, there was one line in the verdict he never understood. Why was Robin called "The pious bird"?

That title of his dates back to the times when people were so penetrated with Christian Faith, that they found reminders of God and the saints everywhere. They could not see the graceful clematis, for instance, embowering the thorny hedges or veiling the jagged rocks, without thinking how pleasant a shelter it would have made for the Holy Family when they fled into Egypt. Perhaps the beautiful vine was thus favored. They had more faith and imagination than geographical knowledge, and they named it "The Virgin's Bower." The restless weeping-willow seemed to be always shuddering at itself. It was therefore supposed to have given the wood from which the Cross was made. Robin suggested one of the sweetest fancies of all. Before the first Good Friday, he was clad altogether in sober brown. But he had been on Calvary, and had striven with his little beak to loosen one of the nails that fastened Jesus to the Cross. Some drops of the Precious Blood stained the compassionate bird's breast, and lo! Robin bears the crimson memorial there to the end of time.

Irish Legends.

(CONTINUED.)

IV.

THE SHAUN-NA-SOGGARTH.

"AND now, dear children," said Paudhrig O'Malley—as they called the old man—"are you ready for the stories?"

Six little silvery voices eagerly answered in the affirmative, and six little beaming faces looked up anxiously at good old Paudhrig as he sat again on the stone seat outside the cottage-door on the slope of Croagh Patrick, commanding a magnificent view of nearly all Connaught. Many other children from the neighboring cabins had now gathered round; and many grown people, too, had come to hear the wonderful things that had happened in times gone by, from the oldest man in the neighborhood, good Paudhrig O'Malley, so that he had quite a little congregation about him.

It was a lovely morning; the cloudy night-cap of Croagh Patrick had already disappeared; the whole surrounding country, sea and land, was bathed in light; nothing could be more beautiful than the isle-studded bay, nothing more enchanting than the sun-lit plain; it looked like fairyland. All agreed to change their position to the top of the hill, and, if necessary, to carry the old man with them. It was great sport for the children. They gained the summit in about half an hour; some refreshments were brought along, as they determined to remain there all day. Having made the old man comfortable in the centre of the group, they all sat round him on the ruins of St. Patrick's Chapel, which are still to be seen there. The little ones gathered at his feet, whilst others leaned against the crumbling walls of St. Patrick's cell, to enjoy the magnificent landscape while listening to the story.

"Is it any wonder," said Paudhrig, "that St. Patrick should pray for and bless Ireland from this spot? Is it any wonder that years of persecution and rivers of blood have never been able to efface the effect of that prayer? Why should we not have here a lasting monument of his presence and of his prayers, instead of these crumbling walls, now almost level with the ground!"

"Yes," said one of the little ones at his feet; "but won't you tell us the stories?"

The dear little child did not understand the good old man's outburst of faith and patriotism; but the stories themselves are an interesting record of both, so he began by again pointing out to them the house near the bay that was once his own.

"In that house," said he, "my dear little children, the wreck of which I related to you last evening, there lived afterwards *Shaun-na-soggarth.*"

"But why," said an inquisitive, bright little boy, "is a priest-hunter called *Shaun-na-soggarth* (John of the priest)?"

"Because," said the old man, "in the richness of our grand old Celtic tongue, *Shaun-na-soggarth* may mean, John, the servant of the priest, or the friend of the priest, or the persecutor of the priest, according to circumstances. And these circumstances have settled its meaning, and afterwards every priest-hunter was called *Shaunna-soggarth.* This fellow was first called *Shaundhu* (Black-Jack), because he was a dark, downlooking rascal. When I was thrown out of that house for harboring the priest, *Shaun-dhu* went to the agent and offered to take the house and farm, and pay more than I was paying for them, if the house was repaired for him. The agent declared that he would never again allow a papist into that house or any other house on the estate. *Shaun-dhu* then went to the Protestant Church in Westport, received the Protestant sacraments, and pretended to conform to the Protestant religion, in hopes of securing the house and land, which he did, when the house was repaired. His next step was to betray the holy young priest that came to replace poor Father Hurley, who died of want and cold in Clare Island. I have already told you how he feigned sickness, and sent for the priest, whose hiding place the Catholics knew, and also how God struck him dead, and paralyzed the two wretches who laid sacrilegious hands on the good priest. For ten days he lay dead, without a hand to move him; the paralyzed yeomen were unable to stir; they died of starvation at the very door; the rest fled. The stench from the bodies of the priest-hunters at last attracted attention. They were discovered as they had been struck by God—one on the bed where he had lain down in perfect health a few days before; the others at the door—who were found to have gnawed their own flesh before they died, and all with the mark of God's vengeance on them. They were buried, and for ten years priest and people were unmolested. No one ever occupied that house since; it is said to be haunted by a black dog, whom the people call 'Black-Jack.' The howling of the black dog is heard distinctly as he rattles his chains through every part of the house during the long winter nights. Many of the old people say they have seen him with eyes of fire and mouth of flame; whether it be the devil or the priest-hunter, no one can tell."

"And," said one of the children, "what happened to the men that ran away,—did the devil take them also?"

"O Jemmy, why do you say that!" said his good little sister Maggie.

"Why do I say that?" said the boy; "why, what does God Almighty keep a devil at all for, if it be not to take away such bad men as those!"

"My dear children," said the old man, "God does not employ the devil to punish people; He simply permits him to torture them forever when they die in mortal sin. We should all pray even for our persecutors, that they may not die enemies of God; and God has promised to hear our prayers, especially those of innocent little children, because He loves them so much. Indeed," continued the old man, "one of these very priest-hunters was converted, and became a good, fervent Catholic, through the prayers of his little child. Well do I remember the occasion on which the priest, poor Father Mulligan, who is now in the hands of his enemies, when he was going away to the wretch who would have betrayed him, asked me, and two or three neighbors who were near his hiding place, to go and guard the Blessed Sacrament for him, and to remain there praying for him till his return. It was a little hut in a hollow of the mountain, surrounded by rocks, just big enough for his bed and table and chair, and for a rude stone altar where he sometimes said Mass, and always preserved the Blessed Sacrament for the sick. Around this altar we were kneeling and praying for the safety of the priest while he was away. One woman was crying bitterly, and I heard her say to a sweet, innocent-looking little child, 'Agnes, go there and pray for your father; I cannot pray; Jesus is there and He will hear you.' This was the wife and child of one of the very persecutors of the priest, who, like *Shaun-dhu*, had given up his religion. The little innocent did exactly as she was told: went over to the altar, and said in her own simple way: 'Dear Jesus, are you there?'

"Immediately a sweet voice from the tabernacle answered: 'I am, My child.'

"'Dear Jesus, will you please save the priest and convert my father?'

"The tabernacle door opened, and the little stone hut was filled with a supernatural light; on the rough rock, which served as an altar, the Holy Infant appeared, surrounded by glory, and looking lovingly at the little child, said: 'Child of My Heart, I will.'

"We all fell down in adoration. How long we were there, I don't know; but towards evening, Father Mulligan came, and found us all still on our knees in prayer, even the little child, who, seeming unconscious of the favor she received, ran to the priest and said: 'O Father! we had such a lovely 'Holy Infant,' like what you have at Christmas, but alive; and the place was all filled with light! oh, it was so lovely!' We were just telling the priest all that had happened to her, when a poor man, bathed in tears and sobbing bitterly, cast himself on his face at the door. All looked at him in wonder and fear, not knowing what to say, till the poor woman who had been crying, exclaimed: 'O John! are you coming to persecute the priest even here?'

"'No,' said he, sobbing, 'but to ask his pardon and yours, and forgiveness from my God.' All was over; the man was converted by the prayers of his child; the priest was saved, the victory of the day was won."

The little children listened with breathless astonishment to this wonderful story; and as the evening shades were falling, and the old man standing up to go away, they all asked him to tell them more about the Holy Infant. But it was too late; he remained, however, to tell them what he could about little Agnes, the 'Child of the Holy Infant,' promising to tell them more some other time.

(TO BE CONTINUED.)

For the Suffering Irish Children.

The Catholic Pupils of St. Mary's Academy, Notre Dame. Ind., $60; Patrick Galerty, $1; Mrs. Galerty, $1; Mrs. Mullen, $1; Kate Galerty, 50 cts.; Mary Galerty, 50 cts.; Collected from children, 82 cts.; Patrick Ceahan, $1; L. Nicon, 25 cts.; M. Bannan, 25 cts.; E. Davey, 25 cts.; E. Trainor, 25 cts.; R. I. Dennis, 25 cts.; Miss Emily Harper, $1; Margaret McKessy, 50 cts.; Annie Beer, 50 cts.; Miss B. Rhine, 25 cts.; Ellen Hesmey, $1; Mary McTarr, 25 cts.; Dehlia Galerty, 25 cts.; Mrs. Spalding. 50 cts.; A Friend, 25 cts.; Mrs. Gorman, 50; Mary Kellady, 57 cts.; Mrs. Judge Morris, $5; A Friend, 25 cts.; Mrs. Chas. F. Mayor, $1; Mary McQuany, $1; Mary McCann, $1; Ann Downy, $1; A Friend, 50 cts.; John McKenna, 50 cts.; Mrs. Lizzie McHale, $1; Wm. C. McKenzie, $1; Mrs. K. Guilfoy, 50 cts.; A Friend, 19 cts. ($25 collected by Mrs. Galerty and Miss Kate Galerty); A little Boy's "pile," saved to buy a tool chest, $1; Joda McMahon, 10 cts.; Mamie McMahon, 10 cts.; George Tourtillotte. 25 cts.; Charlie Young, $1; Charlie Droste, $1; Eddie O'Donnell, $5; Marshal Olds, $1; Mrs. Hannah Driscoll, $1; Helen and Annie Crosson, $2; Frank Mattes, 95 cts.; W. Hanavin, $1; Hattie Murphy, $1; Daisy O'Hara, $6.25; Frank O'Hara, $5; N. N., 2 cts.; Bollina Simpson, 50 cts.; Chlotilda Simpson, 50 cts.

We desire to inform our young folks that we have sent $127 of their contributions to the good missionary, Father Murphy, S. J., for distribution among the suffering children of Co. Galway. Next week, we expect to send fifty or one hundred dollars more.

May our Blessed Lord, who has said that what we do for the needy He accepts as done for Himself, and our Blessed Mother, whose compassionate heart burns with love for her poor children, abundantly reward every donor!

THE AVE MARIA.

A Journal devoted to the Honor of the Blessed Virgin.

HENCEFORTH ALL GENERATIONS SHALL CALL ME BLESSED.—St. Luke, 1, 48.

[For the Ave Maria.]

Veni, Sancte Spiritus.

BY CHARLES KENT.

COME, O come, most Holy Spirit,
  From the heaven we would inherit,
    Shedding down one ray divinely;
Come, of poorest love paternal,
Come, O source of gifts supernal,
    Light of hearts that sink supinely.

Thou, of solacers completest,
Thou, of soul-loved guests the sweetest,
    Sweet repose in dereliction;
Heavenly rest 'mid toil and anguish,
Healing shade for those who languish,
    Comforter in dire affliction.

Light benefic! Light divinest!
Fill the inmost heart, Benignest!
    Of Thy faithful Thee adoring:
Hide Thy grace, celestial Spirit—
Naught is left in man of merit,
    Naught but needs his soul's abhorring.

Wash the guilt that soul imbruing,
While its barren drought bedewing;
    Heal the blains about it squandered;
Bend each will most stern and rigid;
Warm each bosom cold and frigid;
    Guide aright what steps have wandered.

Give Thy faithful strength abiding,
In Thy heavenly grace confiding,
    Shadowed by Thy sevenfold splendor;
Give them virtue's worth immortal;
Give salvation at death's portal,
    Endless joys Thy praise to render.

ALL perfection consists in docility to the inspirations of the Holy Ghost.—*Faber.*

Feast of Our Lady, the Help of Christians.*

EVER since our entrance upon the joys of the Paschal season, scarcely a day has passed without the Calendar's offering us some grand Mystery or saint to honor; and all these have been radiant with the Easter sun. But of our Blessed Lady, there has not been a single Feast to gladden our hearts by telling us of some mystery or glory of this august Queen. The Feast of her Seven Dolors is sometimes kept in April,—that is, when Easter Sunday falls on or after the 10th of that month; but May and June pass without any special solemnity in honor of the Mother of God. It would seem as though Holy Church wished to honor, by a respectful silence, the forty days during which Mary enjoyed the company of her Jesus, after His Resurrection. We, therefore, should never separate the Mother and the Son, if we would have our Easter meditations be in strict accordance with truth,—and that, we surely must wish. During those forty days, Jesus frequently visited His disciples, weak men and sinners as they were: could He, then, keep away from His Mother, when He was so soon to ascend into heaven, and leave her for several long years here on earth? Our hearts forbid us to entertain the thought. We feel sure that He frequently visited her, and that, when not visibly present with her, she had Him in her soul, in a way more intimate and real and delicious than any other creature could have.

No Feast could have given expression to such a mystery; and yet the Holy Ghost, who guides the spirit of the Church, has gradually led the faithful to devote the entire month of May to the special honor of Mary, the whole of which comes, almost every year, under the glad season of Easter. No doubt the loveliness of the May month would, some time or other,

---

* Adapted from the Liturgical Year, by Dom Guéranger.

suggest the idea of consecrating it to the Holy Mother of God; but if we reflect on the divine and mysterious influence which guides the Church in all she does, we shall recognize, in this present instance, a heavenly inspiration, which prompted the faithful to unite their own joy with that of Mary's, and spend this beautiful month, which is radiant with their own Easter joy, in commemorating the maternal delight experienced, during that same period, by the Immaculate Mother when on earth.

To-day, however, we have a Feast in honor of Mary. True, it is not one of those Feasts which are entered on the general Calendar of the Church; yet it is so widely spread, and this with the consent of the holy See, that our *Liturgical Year* would have been incomplete without it. Its object is to honor the Mother of God as the *Help of Christians*,—a title she has justly merited by the innumerable favors she has conferred upon Christendom. Dating from that day, whose anniversary we have so lately celebrated, on which the Holy Ghost descended upon Mary in the Cenacle, in order that she might begin to exercise over the Church Militant her power as Queen,—who could tell the number of times that she has aided, by her protection, the kingdom of her Son on earth?

Heresies have risen up, one after the other; they were violent; they were frequently supported by the great ones of this world; each of them was resolved on the destruction of the true Faith; and yet, one after the other, they have dwindled away, or fallen into impotency, or are gradually sinking by internal discord; and holy Church tells us that it is "Mary alone who destroys all heresies throughout the whole world."* If public scandals or persecutions, or the tyranny of secular interference, have, at times, threatened to stay the progress of the Church, Mary has stretched forth her arm, the obstacles were removed, and Jesus' Spouse continued her onward march, leaving her foes and her fetters behind her. All this was vividly brought before the mind of the saintly Pontiff, Pius the Fifth, by the victory of Lepanto, gained, by Mary's intercession, over the Turkish fleet, and he resolved to add one more title to the glorious ones given to Our Lady in the Litany: the title he added was, "*Auxilium Christianorum*," *Help of Christians*.

Our present century, the 19th, has had the happiness of seeing another Pontiff, also named Pius, institute a Feast under this same title—a Feast which is intended to commemorate the help bestowed on Christendom, in all ages, by the Mother of God. Nothing could be happier than the choice of the day on which this Feast was to be kept. On the 24th of May, in the year 1814, there was witnessed in Rome the most magnificent triumph that has yet been recorded in the annals of the Church. That was a grand day, being the anniversary of the date whereon Constantine marked out the foundations for the Vatican Basilica, in honor of the Prince of the Apostles; Sylvester stood by and blessed the Emperor, who had just been converted to the true Faith: but important as was this event, it was but a sign of the last and decisive victory won by the Church in the then recent persecution of Diocleasian. That was a memorable day whereon Leo the Third, Vicar of the King of kings, crowned Charlemagne with the imperial diadem, and, by his apostolic power, gave continuance to the long interrupted line of emperors: but Leo the Third, by this, did but give an official and solemn expression to the power which the Church had already frequently exercised in the newly constituted nations, which received from her the idea of Christian government, the consecration of their rights, and the grace that was to enable them to fulfil their duties. That was a joyous day, whereon Gregory the Ninth took back to the City of Peter the Papal throne, which had been pent up at Avignon for seventy and years; but Gregory the Ninth, in this, did but fulfil a duty, and his predecessors, had they willed it, might have effected this return to Rome, which the necessities of Christendom so imperatively called for.

Yes, these were all glorious days; but the 24th of May, of 1814, surpasses them all. Pius the Seventh re-entered Rome amidst the acclamations of the Holy City, whose entire population went forth to meet him holding palm branches in their hands, and greeting him with their hosannas of enthusiastic joy. He had been a captive for five years, during which the spiritual government of the Christian world had suffered a total suspension. It was not the Allied Powers, who had made common cause against his oppressor, that broke the Pontiff's fetters; the very tyrant who kept him from Rome, had given him permission to return at the close of the preceding year; but the Pontiff chose his own time, and did not leave Fontainebleau till the 25th of January. Rome, whither he was about to return, had been made a part of the French Empire five years previously, and by a Decree in which was cited the name of Charlemagne. The city of Peter had been reduced to a head-town of a department, with a Prefect for its administrator; and, with a view to making men forget that it was the City of the Vicars of Christ, its name was given as a title to the heir-presumptive of the Imperial crown of France.

What a day that 24th of May, which witnessed the triumphant return of the Pontiff into the Holy City, whence he had been dragged, during

---

* Gaude, Maria Virgo! cunctas hæreses sola interemisti in universo mundo. (Office of the Blessed Virgin; Matins, vii. Antiphon.)

the night, by the soldiers of an ambitious tyrant! He made the journey in short stages, meeting on his way the allied armies of Europe, which recognized his right as King. This *right* is superior, both in antiquity and dignity, to that of all other monarchs; and all, no matter whether they be heretics, schismatics, or Catholics, must admit it, were it only on the strength of its being an historical fact.

But what we have so far said is not sufficient to give an adequate idea of the greatness of the prodigy thus achieved by Our Lady, the Help of Christians. In order to have a just appreciation of it, we must remember that the miracle was not wrought in the age of Sylvester and Constantine, or of St. Leo the Third and Charlemagne, or of the great prophetess Catharine of Sienna, who made known the commands of God to the people of Italy and to the Popes of Avignon. The age that witnessed this wondrous event was the 19th, and that, too, when it was under the degrading influence of Voltairianism, and there were still living the authors and abettors of the crimes and impieties that resulted from the principles taught in the 18th century. Everything was adverse to such a glorious and unexpected triumph; Catholic feeling was far from being roused as it now is; the action of God's providence had to show itself in a direct and visible manner; and to let the Christian world know that such was the case, Rome instituted the annual Feast of the 24th of May as an offering of acknowledgment to Mary, the *Help of Christians*.

Let us, then, give thanks to the Blessed Mother of God on this feast of the twenty-fourth day of May, which has been instituted in commemoration of the twofold blessing she thus brought upon the world—the preservation of the Church, and the preservation of society. Let us unite in the fervent acclamations of the then loyal citizens of Rome, and like them, sing with all the glad joy of our Easter *Alleluia*, our greetings of *Hosanna* to the Vicar of Christ—the Father of that dear Land, our common Country. The remembrance of St. Peter's deliverance from prison, and his restoration to liberty, must have been vividly in the minds of that immense concourse of people, whose love for their Pontiff was redoubled by the sufferings he had endured. As the triumphal chariot, in which he had been placed, came near the Flaminian Gate, the horses were unyoked, and the Pontiff was conveyed by the people to the Vatican Basilica, where a solemn thanksgiving was made over the tomb of the Prince of the Apostles.

Let us now read the account, as given in to-day's Liturgy, of the great event that prompted the institution of our Feast:

The Faithful have frequently seen it proved, by miraculous intervention, that the Mother of God is ever ready with her help to repel the enemies of religion. It was on this account that, after the signal victory gained by the Christians over the Turks in the Gulf of Lepanto, through the intercession of the most Blessed Virgin, the holy Pope Pius the Fifth ordered that to the other titles given to the Queen of Heaven in the Litany of Loretto, there should be added this of *Help of Christians*. But one of the most memorable proofs of this her protection, and one which may be regarded as an incontestable miracle, is that which happened during the Pontificate of Pius the Seventh. By the intrigues and armed violence of certain impious men, the Pontiff had been driven from the Apostolic See of Peter, and was kept in close confinement, mainly at Savona, for upwards of five years. During this period, by a persecution unheard of in any previous age, every possible means was resorted to in order to prevent his governing the Church of God. When lo! suddenly and to the surprise of men, he was restored to the Pontifical Throne, to the great joy, it might be almost said, with the concurrence, of the whole world. The same thing happened also a second time, when a fresh disturbance arose and compelled him to leave Rome, and go, with the Sacred College of Cardinals, into Liguria. Here again, the storm that threatened great destruction was appeased by a most prompt interference of God's providence and the Pontiff's return to Rome filled Christendom with new joy. Before returning, however, he would carry out an intention, which his captivity had hitherto prevented him from doing: with his own hand, he solemnly placed a golden crown on the celebrated statue of the Mother of God that was venerated at Savona under the title of *Mother of Mercy*. The same Sovereign Pontiff, Pius the VII, who was so thoroughly acquainted with every circumstance of these events, rightly attributed their happy issue to the intercession of the most holy Mother of God, whose powerful help he himself had earnestly besought, besides urging all the faithful to obtain it by their prayers. He therefore instituted a solemn feast in honor of the same Virgin-Mother, under the title of *Help of Christians*. It was to be kept, every year, on the twenty-fourth of May, the anniversary of his own most happy return to Rome. He also sanctioned a proper Office for this feast, in order that the remembrance of so great a favor might ever be vividly in the minds of the faithful, and secure the thanksgiving it deserved.

I have lifted up mine eyes to the mountains, from whence help shall come to me: my help is from the Lord, who made heaven and earth.* Thus prayed the Israelites of old; thus also prays the Church—though, for her, the help is nearer and comes more speedily. The Psalmist's petition has been granted:—the heavens have bowed down, and the Divine Help is now close by our side. This Help is Jesus, Son of God and Son of Mary. He is unceasingly fulfilling the promise made us by His Prophet: *In the day of thy salvation, I have* HELPED *thee.*† But this King of kings has given us a Queen, and this Queen is Mary, His Mother. Out of love for her, He has given her a throne, on His right hand, as Solomon did for his mother Bethsabee;‡ and He would have *her*, also, to be the *Help of Christians*. It is the Church that teaches us this, by inserting

* Ps. cxx, 1, 2. † Is. xlix, 8. ‡ III Kings ii, 19.

this beautiful title in the litany; and Rome invites us, on this day, to unite with her in giving thanks and praise to our Blessed Lady of Help, for one of the most signal of her favors.

Our supplications to thee, O Help of Christians! are thus earnest, because our wants are great; but we are not, on that account, the less mindful of the special honor that we owe thee at this holy season of hope, when the Church contemplates the joy thou hadst in presence of thy Risen Jesus. She congratulates thee on the immense happiness that thus repaid thee for thine anguish on Calvary and at the Sepulchre. It is to the Mother, consoled by and exulting in her Son's triumphant Resurrection, that we offer this sweet month, whose loveliness is so in keeping with thine own incomparable beauty, dear Mother! In return for this homage of our devotion, pray for us, that our souls may persevere in the beauty of grace given to them by this year's union with our Jesus; and that we may bē so well prepared for the Feast of Corpus Christi, as to merit to receive all the graces necessary to perfect the work of our Paschal Regeneration.

'Beth's Promise.

BY MRS. ANNA HANSON DORSEY.

CHAPTER XIV.

IF SHE HAD ONLY KNOWN!

THE days sped brightly and swiftly for 'Beth Morley; every moment seemed rounded with a full, quiet happiness, which she sought neither to analyze nor define. She asked no questions of the future; she was satisfied to know in her very heart that Bertie Dulaney loved her, and was ever shyly conscious that the thought of him made a strange, tender vibration in it of chords never before awakened, although the words were still unspoken that would have made him "the happiest fellow on earth." What this new mystery was, she did not ask herself. The young people at "Tracy-Holme" and 'Beth were oftener together now, and several times she had joined their excursions; but whether riding or walking, whether roving through the glen or gypsying in the woods, whether at "Ellerslie" or at "Tracy-Holme," Bertie Dulaney always managed to be by her side; and while he made himself agreeable to others of the party, he was watchful of her every movement. To put his hand upon her bridle rein if they were riding, to guide her horse away from the rough or dangerous places of the road; to press back, heedless of his own hurt, the wide, thorny vines that obstructed her path when they were all in the woods or in the glen; to find her music for her in the evening, or turn over the leaves when she was at the harp or piano; to move her chair out of range of the night breeze as it drifted in through the open windows, and a thousand other little unobtrusive services, gave unmistakable evidence of how his mind was occupied and filled with the thought of her. Every morning found him at "Ellerslie" on some pretence or other—either a message from the girls, or a book, or a rare flower from his mother's conservatory, which he always gave 'Beth with her love; or a piece of new music which he had ordered from the city, thinking she "would like it," and try it for him. It looked very much as if he were trying to throw dust in the eyes of Mrs. Morley and Aunt 'Beth; but nothing was farther from his thoughts than an intention to cover up and make a secret of his love; he only thought it would be better so to act until she gave him the right—by accepting him—to speak out and declare that she, of all the world, was his choice.

One morning, Aunt 'Beth with her knitting, and Mrs. Morley with some light needle-work in hand, were together in the summer sitting-room, talking over the latest news of the "strike," about which the heart of the dear old lady of "Ellerslie" continued to be much troubled. She had just said: "I hear that the amount of wages lost by the strike is over twenty thousand dollars. Only think, fifteen hundred men, all told, literally without bread and without work, and winter so near!"

Just at this moment, 'Beth and Bertie Dulaney ran in, both radiant and evidently full of some new plan. He had met her in the grounds as he was on his way to invite her to go with him to the lake for an hour's row.

"There's nothing I should like better this perfect day, but—what a horrid little word that is!—I must hear first what mamma and Aunt 'Beth have to say about it," she said, when he told her what he had come for, her face beaming with pleasure at the very thought of a row.

Bertie Dulaney made his bow, said pleasant things to the two ladies, then proferred his request, and, as he had hoped, they interposed no objection to 'Beth's going.

"Pull the bell beside you, Mr. Dulaney; we'll have the phaeton prepared, for of course you can't walk to the lake," said Aunt 'Beth, with a little nod that made her white curls dance.

"Oh no, no, Miss Morley! my own trap is ready; I only ran over to see if Miss 'Beth would like to go; then I meant to drive round," he exclaimed.

"If you don't mind, we'll go in the phaeton," said 'Beth; "otherwise we can walk."

"I am delighted! I have been fairly pining for a drive in it. Will you let me hold the ribbons?"

"Oh, no! Peg does not like strangers, and there's no telling what he might do if you attempted to drive," said 'Beth, laughing.

"Of course you know all about boating, Mr. Dulaney?" said Mrs. Morley.

"Yes, indeed, Mrs. Morley; I am more at home in a boat than anywhere else, I assure you. I can pull an oar very steadily," he answered.

"So can I, mamma, you know; and if I see he's not skilful, I'll take the oars from him and give him the tiller-ropes; so don't be uneasy, dearest," said 'Beth, gaily. How bright and happy she looked, and with what proud, loving eyes he regarded her, almost forgetful that others might be observing him! In a few minutes the wheels of the phaeton were heard on the gravel, and a prolonged whinny from Peg announced that he was ready and waiting for them.

"The sun gets very hot towards noon, Mr. Dulaney; you'll get back in time to avoid it?"

"Oh yes, indeed! Mrs. Morley; have no fear."

"And don't let 'Beth row; it will overheat her," she added.

"She shall not touch an oar, now that I have your orders, Mrs. Morley," he replied, bowing himself out, looking so full of life and happiness, and withal so handsome, that Aunt 'Beth remarked, "I think, Anne, that is as fine a young fellow as I have seen for many a long day."

"Yes," said Mrs. Morley, "he is very attractive. His greatest charm is his genuine and unaffected manner. But better than all, he is a devout Catholic Christian."

"He has a good safeguard if he is that," said Aunt 'Beth, looking thoughtfully out at the flicker of sunshine and shadow among vines that hung trailing over the windows. "But it has struck me, Anne, that he is very much taken with 'Beth, and since I have got over some of my nonsensical ideas about new people, I think it would be a very suitable thing."

"I have observed it too; but I think, perhaps, that having been thrown together in the country here, they only enjoy each other's society, as most young people who have the same tastes do, without there being anything particular in it. I hope —I hope to keep 'Beth a few years longer," said Mrs. Morley, gravely.

"We must not be selfish, Anne. We must remember that the young have their lives to live out, even as ourselves before them. Human nature is human nature; it is like the seasons: the blossoming of trees and the falling of the leaves, or the rising and setting of sun, moon and stars; it has its laws even as they have, and we cannot control them."

"You are right, dear Aunt 'Beth; I can only commend my child to the care of our dear Lord and His Blessed Mother; and although it will be a great trial to me when she decides to marry, I shall not refuse to sacrifice whatever it may cost me to secure her happiness."

"That's right, my dear. 'She's ower young to marry yet,' the old song goes, and we must not begin to borrow trouble until we see 'signs and portents.' But do you know that I am very much in love?" said Aunt 'Beth, her eyes twinkling.

"Aunt 'Beth, what can you mean!"

"I'll tell you; it's with your young priest over yonder," laughed Aunt 'Beth, her white curls vibrating. "You know I've been driving up and down with him to see some of the strikers that I know, and have watched him and listened to him in their poor abodes, until my old eyes have run over at his earnestness, his compassion, his pleadings, and patient reasoning with them, despite their oftentimes rude and threatening behavior, and I have thought that surely the Master Himself was there in his person."

"As He was," murmured Mrs. Morley.

"Do you know, he would give his very life to avert the misery, and suffering, and possible crime, that these men are bringing upon themselves! I heard him tell them so, and I saw one lift his huge fist to give him a blow that would have killed him, 'because,' the ruffian remarked, that he wanted them to put their necks under the heels of the rich, and would hear no more of his hypocritical talk. He swore, and used such language that my blood ran cold; but Father Hagner stood waiting until his rage had expended itself, then went on, and finished what he had begun to say. And he has told me some things about his belief, too, that have surprised me," said Aunt 'Beth. "*That* is the sort of a pastor that I believe in, a man who thinks only of the good of his people, and not of his own comfort and profit and convenience—one who, like Christ, is ready to die that others may live and be saved."

"There are thousands like him in the Catholic priesthood," said Mrs. Morley.

"There are some, doubtless. That Irish priest up at the iron works is another of that sort. I have seen these two since the strike putting self entirely aside for some higher motive than ordinary; and seeing, you know, my child, is believing."

"Their motive, dear Aunt 'Beth, is not inspired by nature, but by the pure love of God, and in obedience to the spirit of their holy Faith," said Mrs. Morley, gently.

Aunt 'Beth dropped her hands in her lap, and fixed her eyes on Mrs. Morley's face as if something had suddenly dawned upon her mind urging her to speak, but she only said: "It must be a good faith that lifts man above the littleness and the grovelling weaknesses of nature. But there are good people in all sects, I believe."

Lodo came in for some directions about a piece of work she had in hand, interrupting the conversation, which was not resumed after she had heard about the seams and fells and gores that had been puzzling her, and gone back to the housekeeper's room. Aunt 'Beth thought an agreeable book would be a pleasant change, and because she knew that it would interest and entertain Mrs. Morley, she asked her to read a few pages aloud from an old volume she had hunted up on the library shelves that morning, the "Memoirs of the Duchess d'Abrantes," who was the wife of Junot, one of Napoleon's brave generals; and she was not disappointed, for in no book that has been written of those times has there ever been given such graphic details of the strange and wonderful events of the first Empire, including all, from the revolution to St. Helena.

We will follow 'Beth and Bertie Dulaney to the lake. It is not an idle love story we are writing, but one of as severe a trial and suffering as can enter the life of a pure, true-hearted woman. But to appreciate it, 'Beth's promise, made to her mother when she was "fancy free," untried, and strong in power of will, must be remembered. 'Beth had made up her mind that very morning, that the next time Bertie Dulaney should plead for a favorable answer to his suit, she would frankly give it, for it had become very clear to her own heart that she returned his preference, and to keep him in suspense, she thought, would be like the merest coquetry and trifling on her part, and altogether unworthy of her. Daily she had taken the affair to the Blessed Virgin, and asked her safe guidance; she had viewed it in every aspect, and could see no reason why it should not terminate happily. She did not want to marry for a year or two; she could not leave her mother while her heart was so sore with the grief of her loss; but she felt they would be very happy engaged, and sure of each other's love. Then there was no objection that could be urged against him by either her mother or Aunt 'Beth. He was a good Catholic, a civilian; he had fine qualities of mind and heart, and they both admired and had the most friendly feelings toward him, and Aunt 'Beth had got over her foolish old world notions about new people. Then 'Beth thought of an old verse she had once read, which had made so great an impression upon her mind, that she had long ago formed her ideal from it. Again and again, she whispered:

> "What is noble? To inherit
> Wealth, or fame, or high degree?
> There must be some other merit
> Higher yet than these, for me.
> Something nobler far must enter
> Into life's majestic span,
> Something to create and centre
> True nobility in man."

And she had found her ideal in Bertie Dulaney, her knight "*sans peur sans reproche.*"

But while driving to the lake, the subject so near both their hearts was not approached. 'Beth felt a little conscious and was more quiet than usual; but he was so happy to have her all to himself that he talked of a thousand pleasant things, thinking only of the bright present, for she had not repulsed him and he was full of hope. His servant was on the sands waiting with the oars, which were kept with fishing tackle and other things in a boat-house a short distance off; he had already laid a plank from the shore to the boat, and, giving up the oars, he took the phaeton and Peg in charge, until they should come back. 'Beth waited only long enough to give Peg a treat of sugar, and hear his grateful whinny, then giving her hand to Bertie Dulaney, who had stood by watching her, she ran over the sands with him, and sprang into the boat; in another moment they had pushed off, he rowing, she holding the tiller-ropes. How bright and fair it all seemed to them, not even the shadow of a cloud drifting by!

"This is really lovely," she said, in merry tones, "and I believe you *do* know how to row."

"I shall always know how to row, if you are at the helm," he said, regarding her fondly.

"I might run you upon a reef," she answered.

"I'm quite willing to risk it."

"Did you ever see anything so beautiful! The deep blue of the sky and the calm deep blue of the water make it seem as if we were floating in the air. Won't you stop rowing a moment and just let us float?"

"Gladly," he answered, resting on his oars; "this is where I found you, you know, and just here I want you to tell me something that I wish above all things in life to hear, and upon which my future very much depends." He was very grave and was speaking from his heart. "I need not tell you again that I love you," he resumed, "you know that. Now I want to know from your own pure, honest heart if you think you can ever care enough for me to be my wife?"

'Beth was trailing her hand in the water leaning a little over the side of the boat, her large hat shading her face, except her purely moulded chin and part of the cheek that was towards him, into which a faint, delicate glow had stolen; her eyes were fixed upon the sun-lighted ripples, as if expecting an answer from the blue depths; for now that the decisive moment had come, and her heart was stirred by its own happiness, she hesitated, she had not courage to put into words what it urged her to say. She loved him with a pure womanly love, and he was worthy of all that he asked for, yet how could she break through her maidenly reserve to tell him so?

"Won't you tell me?" he asked; "you know I may have to go away, perhaps to-night, or to-morrow. I am expecting orders every day."

"Orders! what do you mean?" said 'Beth, lifting her head and looking at him with a startled look in her eyes.

"Orders to join my ship. I belong to the Navy, you know?"

"No, I did not know it," she faltered, her voice tremulous and faint, her face very white, the color gone even from her lips, while her heart felt as if it had suddenly turned to ice.

"But I will not go: I will ask for longer leave. 'Beth, darling, are you ill? Forgive me if I have said anything to pain you."

"It is only a slight faintness," she said, gently. "I think, if you please, I should like to go back. I am sorry, so very sorry that I cannot answer you as you wish. Oh, how I wish we had never met!" and without being conscious of what she was doing, she wrung her hands, her face white with a strange, hopeless sorrow. It had been so sudden, this death-blow to her bright, sweet dreams. But her promise to her mother, which she had called God to witness, must be kept. Oh, if she had only known!

"But why? why?" he urged. "If you care in the least for me, I'll wait, wait patiently, gladly, wait as long as you wish."

"It can never be," she faltered. "There is a reason I cannot explain. You must not ask me."

"A reason? But you have known for weeks that I loved you! Why did you not tell me at first that there was a reason against it? why, when I have been hopeful and happy, did you not let me know that it would all come to nothing in the end? I couldn't have believed that you would be so false," was the protest of his outraged heart.

False! when her heart was almost breaking! How could she tell him of that promise and perhaps ruin his career in the profession he had chosen, by causing him in the first flush of feeling, to resign? No: swayed by the nicest sense of honor she would hold her peace and suffer his reproach; her promise must be kept, even though the sacrifice of her earthly happiness should shadow her whole after life.

"I cannot explain," she said at last, "but I ask you to believe one thing. I had no design of deceiving or trifling with you."

"To believe that, I must know just one thing, and I beg you, for God's sake, to answer me truly; it will not be so intolerable for me to bear, if you will only tell me, that but for this one 'reason' you would have accepted me," he plead.

"If it will comfort you—yes. Try and think kindly of me as I shall of you," she said.

"I don't know what this reason may be, but I am satisfied for the present. But I tell you, darling, that no reason shall separate us. Almighty God disposes of human events, and our Blessed Lady compassionates her suffering children; to Them I will appeal with ceaseless prayers against this terrible injustice, this blow which has fairly unmanned me. I will never give you up," he replied, meaning every word he said.

"We must not see each other again. Your best happiness will be in forgetting me," she said.

"You may not think so now, but you will by-and-by, find somewhere in the world one who will make you forget all this disappointment——"

"I want only you," he interrupted, "and there is a whisper in my heart even now, assuring me that I shall yet win you. God only knows what it is that has so suddenly risen between us. He only knows whether it be a reason sanctioned by religion, or if it be only a caprice of some overstrained idea of duty; I don't know, but whatever it is—after what you told me just now—I won't abide by it. Will you promise one thing?" he asked, eagerly.

"You will not ask that which I cannot promise, I know. What is it?"

"Promise me that if at any time or moment, that this reason shall cease to exist, you will let me know, by a word and a line, even if I am at the ends of the earth. You can always learn where I am by inquiring at the Navy Department. Will you promise this?"

"Oh, it would be a vain promise! that 'reason' will only end with my life," she said, with a choking sensation in her throat.

"But promise me!" he insisted.

"I promise as you wish, then, but it is then as I say," she replied.

"And you'll be true to me, 'Beth?"

"Yes, I will be true to you. Will you please say no more! All is said now, and the sooner we part, the better for both of us."

Had the girl's strange sorrow transformed her and made her suddenly old that she could speak so calmly and without reserve, while her heart was wrung with unutterable pain? The boat had been floating farther out and farther into the sunshine; the blue waters rippled and laughed around them; nothing of the brightness had changed since just a little while ago they had pushed off from the shore happy and full of hope—nothing except their own young lives into which a sudden darkness had fallen. They were both silent on the way back. Bertie Dulaney saw that it would be useless to urge an explanation, but he trusted her, and knew that the "reason," whatever it might be, was in her own mind imperative, else why let it bring such bitter pain to them both?

(TO BE CONTINUED.)

WHEN there is question of a sacrifice to be made, of an affection to be withdrawn, for example, let us not wait till God Himself acts directly. When it is we who work, God lends His grace, and the sacrifice is made without too much anguish.

Corpus Christi.

BY MARY E. MANNIX.

SMILING the morn, and parting May
  Upon the threshold stands,
Casting the wreath of blooms away
  That fills her virgin hands.

Dropping them softly, flower by flower,
  Before the altar shrine,
Where waits, through many a patient hour,
  The King of Love Divine.

June roses hasten into bloom,
  And lily blossoms white,
Tell to the air, in soft perfume,
  The depth of their delight.

Speed, lagging soul! haste, wanderer home,
  And find your welcome here,
The joyous feast of Love has come,
  The sweetest of the year.

The Feast of the Blessed Sacrament.

FOR a long time, the Feast of the Blessed Sacrament was celebrated only on Holy Thursday, the day on which the Church commemorates the institution of this great Mystery. In the year 1216 Robert, Bishop of Liege, established a particular festival in honor of the Blessed Sacrament, which was celebrated the following year in the Church of St. Martin at Liege. It owed its origin to a miraculous vision with which the Blessed Juliana, a religious of Mount Cornillon, had been favored some time previous. Pope Urban IV afterwards published a Bull making this festival universal throughout the Church; and this decree was confirmed by Clement V in the general council of Vienna, held in the year 1814.

On this day, the Adorable Body of our Lord Jesus Christ is carried in solemn procession, in order to make reparation, in some manner, for the ingratitude and forgetfulness of careless Christians, and the outrages of heretics and impious men. With what tender devotion should not the faithful sanctify a festival on which Jesus Christ gives us such great proofs of His love; and in which He manifests, in a striking manner, according to the expression of the council of Trent, His divine magnificence and His infinite mercy!

To-day, this God, our Saviour, is exposed on our altars, there to give audience to those who wish to offer their vows and prayers; with what confidence and respect should we not present them! To-day, this God of goodness is borne along through our midst, dispensing everywhere His graces and His blessings; with what recollection should we not follow Him, in order to testify our gratitude and love! This bountiful God invites the faithful to approach His Sacred Table, where He gives Himself for the food and nourishment of our souls; with what holy joy should we not present ourselves at this celestial banquet!

All-powerful as God is, what more could He do for us? He descends upon our altars; He permits Himself to be carried among us; and what more touching invitation could He give to follow him, to accompany Him, to make known our wants? Is it because He seems to do too much for us, that we believe ourselves dispensed from making a return?

How great is the happiness of Christians to have a God who communicates Himself to them with so much goodness! What love can equal that of Jesus Christ? Not content to pour out His Blood in order to wash away the sins of men, He must needs also discover the wonderful secret of nourishing their souls with His own substance, and of immolating Himself daily for their sakes. It is in the adorable mystery of the Eucharist that Jesus Christ gives Himself to us in such an ineffable manner. Has He not a right, then, to expect our homage and our gratitude in return?

How dear should not this festival be to every Christian heart! What modesty, recollection and faith should we not show in the presence of our Lord Jesus Christ! How great should be our care to purify our hearts, in order that He may deign to make them His sanctuary! Let us place no limits to our love for Jesus Christ, since He has not limited His love for us.

WHEN you find in a book counsels and precepts which may be useful to you in your household or daily avocations, you hasten to copy the *recipe* and consult it as an oracle. Do as much for the guidance of your soul; preserve in your memory, even write down, the counsels and maxims which you hear or read; then, from time to time, consult this collection, which will please you all the better for being your own work. Now, this collection of thoughts will be your own; you have chosen them because they pleased you. They are counsels which you have given yourself—moral *recipes* which you have discovered, and the efficacy of which you perhaps have proved.—*Golden Sands.*

Polyglot Academy at the Vatican.

IN the grand hall of the Consistory—a witness of the indefectibility of the Church, on account of the great number of persons who have assembled therein from all parts of the world, to prostrate themselves at the feet of the Vicar of Jesus Christ, and, consoling him in his imprisonment, give a solemn and public attestation of their devotion and their love;—in this historic hall, all the languages resounded on the 18th ult. to celebrate the exaltation of Leo XIII to the Chair of Peter; to bear testimony to his glorious achievements, his exalted designs, the sanctity of his life, his unwearied zeal in promoting the welfare of society, the increase of sound and healthful studies, and the greater splendor of our holy religion.

This wonderful and unrivalled spectacle was presented by the students of the Greek and Urban Colleges of the Propaganda, which, owing their origin and prosperity to the Roman Pontiffs, wished, on this occasion, to give a mark of reverential and filial gratitude to the reigning Pontiff.

In former years, visitors to the many wonders of the Eternal City never failed to be present at the Exposition of the Academy of Languages given by the students of the Propaganda within the Octave of the Epiphany. Here they heard with delight young men from all quarters of the globe singing in their native tongues the praises of the Wise Men of the East, and the glories of the Divine Infant, and, like the people who, of old, were astonished and confounded in mind, when they heard the apostles speaking divers languages, "they were all amazed, and wondered, saying, ... how have we heard, every man our own tongue wherein we were born? .... we have heard them speak in our own tongues the wonderful works of God." (Acts, Chap. ii.) Here also they beheld with surprise and admiration, sitting side by side in peaceful and fraternal union, the frank and independent American, the dusky Negro, of Abyssinia, and his scarcely less dark complexioned brother of Egypt; the swarthy sons of Chaldea, Persia, Kurdistan and India; the sallow natives of China, Syria, Arabia and Armenia; the stern looking Pole, Illyrian, Albanian and Russian; the phlegmatic German, and his neighbors from Switzerland, Belgium and Holland; the lighthaired Dane, Swede and Norwegian, with the fair countenances and the bright, merry eyes of the children of the British empire and colonies; all together on the same social level, presenting a visible and living monument of the unity and Catholicity of our holy Church, whose mild and gentle rule, received from its Divine Master, the King of heaven and earth, is alone capable of captivating the minds and hearts of persons of so many different and contrary dispositions and characters, of rendering them subservient to the teachings of the Gospel, and of firmly uniting them in one and the same true, grand and unchangable old Faith.

This year, on the occasion referred to, forty-nine poetical compositions were recited, in as many different languages, in presence of his Holiness Leo XIII, the Cardinals, a great number of Archbishops, Bishops and Roman Prelates, the Diplomatic corps, the Generals of Religious Orders, the members of the Roman nobility, all the students of the Urban and Greek colleges of the Propaganda, and a representation from all the foreign ecclesiastical colleges. The Academy opened with an elegant introduction in Italian, recited by Rev. Michael Camiliere, a student from Smyrna; this was followed by the singing of the "*Oremus pro Pontifice nostro Leone*," a masterpiece by Maestro Mustafà, rendered by the Pontifical choir, with an ability which it alone possesses. Then the first part of the poetical compositions was begun in the Asiatic and African tongues in the following order, with the names and countries of the students who recited them: Hebrew, Mr. Anthony Delenda, of the Island of Santorin; Ancient Chaldaic, Rev. Thomas Ando, of Alkosch, Mesopotamia; Modern Chaldaic, Mr. John Ando, of Alkosch, Mesopotamia; Tamulico, Mr. Joseph Rodrigo, of Colombo, Island of Ceylon; Theban Coptic, Mr. David Assaad, of Mt. Libanus; Menfitic Coptic, Mr. Gabriel Mobarak, of Mt. Libanus; Gallas, Mr. John Baptist Farag, of Nubia; Arabian, Mr. Stephen Issa, of Mossul; Durchan idiom, Mr. Daniel Surur, of Meren, in Central Africa; Turkish, Mr. James Magar, of Ancyra; Curdic, Rev. Joseph Gharib, of Diarbekir; Ilario, Mr. Arthur Morzal, of Rigna, in Central Africa; Cingallan, Mr. Joseph Rodrigo, of the Island of Ceylon; Tartaric, Mr. Paul Tersian, of Kutaja, in Asia Minor; Ancient Armenian, Mr. Avedis Arpiaran, of Eghin, in Armenia Major; Modern Armenian, Mr. George Tersibaschi, of Ancyra; Persian, Mr. Isaac Kudabasci, of Khosrova, Persia; Syriac, Mr. Joseph Siriani, of Aleppo; Ethiopian, Mr. Arthur Morzal, of Central Africa; Amarico, Mr. Daniel Surur, of Central Africa; Akkà, Mr. John Baptist Farag, of Nubia.

At the conclusion of the first part of the exercises of the Academy, the Pontifical choir intoned the "*Civitas Jerusalem noli flere*," another masterpiece of Cher. Mustafà, which resounded with wonderful and surprising effect throughout the venerable hall; poems were then recited in the languages of Europe in the following order: Ancient Greek, Mr. Theodore Delioan, of the Island of Lesbos, in the Ægean Sea; Modern Greek, Cæsar Coti, of the Greek colony of Corgese, Corsica; Georgian, Michael d'Antonio, of Gori; Celtic, Alexander McDonald, of Nova Scotia; English, Martin Kehoe, of the Diocese of Marquette; German, Bernard Slump, Leugerich, Hanover; French, Adolphus Paquet, St. Nicholas, Canada; Icelandic, Otto Ortwed, Copenhagen; Swiss, Ignatius Weber, of Basle; Bulgarian, Isidore Stoikoff, of Bulgaria; Rumenian, Augustine Bunea, of Transylvania; Albanian, Joseph Bianchi, of Sappa; Polish, Leo Kiszakiewiez, of Galicia; Swedish, Henry Wang, of Kongsringer; Irish, Francis Fox, of Creggan, Ireland; Flemish, Hubert Minkenberg, Schaffhausen, Germany; Illyrian, Vitus Putizza, of Gradaz; Russian, Angelus Glarinich, of Stolaz; Danish, Peter Schreiber, of the Prefecture Apostolic of Denmark; Dutch, Walter Kittelwesh, of Baal in Holland; Spanish, Reginald Corbet, of the Vicariate-Apostolic of Colombo; Hungarian, Victor Barach, of Topolya, Hungary; Latin, Abraham Erninian, of Constantinople; Ancient Sclavonian, Vladimir Paslanski, of Galicia; Portuguese, Charles Olyzer, of Macon, United States; Scotch, Robert McCloskey, of Glasgow; Ruthenian, Nicholas Nyczay, of Galicia. Finally, William O'Reilly, of Trim, Ireland, recited an Italian poem, entitled, "The Propaganda at the feet of Leo," which was remarkable for its beauty and purity of thought and its fine delivery. Hymns were also sung by students in the Chaldaic, Arabic, Turkish, Kurdistanic, Cingalian, Armenian, Syriac, Greek, Georgian, Rumenian, Bulgarian and Ruthenian idioms, after their various manners, and with the amusing modulation of voice peculiar to their respective countries. The Academy terminated with the "*Apparuit*" of Baini, executed by the Pontifical choir.

When we consider the disastrous decline of orthodox studies, and how an impious, absurd, and sophistical literature is corrupting the minds and poisoning the fountains of healthful knowledge and true science, we feel a just pride in pointing to this immortal Palladium—the Papacy,—under whose sheltering wings learning, science, the arts and civilization have a safe refuge and an earnest encouragement. And this inspires us with the hope that the time is not far distant when the light of the true Faith will penetrate and disperse the darkness which envelops the minds of so large a portion of mankind; and that, seeing clearly, and acknowledging that they have been deceived and deluded by false and fallacious theories, they will place themselves under the rule of that one, true, and holy Faith, which alone can give to the world true peace, the only possible prosperity, and the only liberty which can elevate the dignity of man.

THE longer the Church battles with the world, the more venerable she seems to become, and her victories of grace more brilliant.—*Faber*.

Protestant Testimony that Honor is Due to the Blessed Virgin.

BISHOP BULL, "On the Invocation of the Blessed Virgin" (Catholic Safeguards, Vol. II, p. 205), says: "The Blessed Virgin Mary was the only woman who took off the stain and dishonor of her sex, by being the instrument which brought That into the world which should repair and make amends for the loss and damage brought to mankind by the transgression of the first woman Eve. By a woman as the principal cause we were first undone; and by a woman, as an instrument under God, a Saviour and Redeemer is born to us, and the Blessed Virgin is that woman."

Dr. Hickes, "On the due Praise and Honor of the Blessed Virgin Mary" (Catholic Safeguards, Vol. II, p. 202), says: "If the names of other saints are distinguished in miniature, hers ought to shine with gold, especially if we consider that she, of all the daughters of Israel, had the honor to be chosen by the Holy Trinity for the Mother of God. What shall be done to the woman whom the King of kings delighteth to honor? Certainly, if we were to hold our peace, and refuse to praise her among women, the very stones of the Church would cry out of the wall, and the beam out of the timber would answer it. If what the woman did, who poured forth a box of precious ointment upon the Head of our Saviour, was to be spoken of as a memorial of her wheresoever the Gospel was preached throughout the whole world, surely that Most Blessed Virgin, who had the honor to bring forth and educate the Son of God, ought to have a festival, and be mentioned with all due reverence in all the churches of the saints."

Mrs. Jameson (Introduction, p. xx) says: "With Christianity, new ideas of the moral and religious responsibility of woman entered the world. ... We are to suppose that for the exaltation of the male sex, Christ appeared on earth as a man; and for the consolation of womankind, He was born of a woman only, as if it had been said: 'From henceforth no creature shall be base before God, unless perverted by depravity.' (Augustine, Oper. Supl. 238, Serm. lxiii.) Such is the reasoning of St. Augustine, who, I must observe, had an especial veneration for his mother Monica, and he is desirous to prove that through the Virgin Mary all womankind were henceforth elevated in the scale of being. And this was the idea entertained of her subsequently. 'Ennobler of thy nature,' says Dante, apostrophising her, as if her perfections had ennobled not merely her own sex, but the whole human race: '*Tu sei colei che l' umana natura nobilitasti.*'"

Some Italian Feast-Days.*

As to the religious feast-days of these people, in spite of what is sometimes displeasing to our taste—which is more difficult to please than theirs—in their opinion they are splendid, and there is not in these mountains a single inhabitant, even among the poorest, who does not contribute to their splendor by a little offering, brought voluntarily and joyously throughout the year. After having assisted at the different offices of the day in the church, after having prayed with all their heart and sung with all their might the *Tantum ergo* during the Benediction, accompanied, that day, by noisy detonations (no stranger than the roar of cannon by which the most civilized people in the world celebrate their national feasts), when the great doors are opened, and the crowd come forth beneath the starry sky, everybody is then seen searching for the best place to watch the *Foochetti* which are to follow. Families gather together; young and old, all are there; the girls place themselves near their mothers upon the grass or upon the benches prepared beforehand; the young men gather around. No one thinks of dancing or of the public house. Soon the dark blue of that beautiful night grows bright, and then, at each rocket which rises, applause and cries of joy are heard. This public gaiety, which causes no disorder, gives the sensation of a true recreation, free from all evil and all fatigue, and one feels happy in seeing these poor, intelligent, laborious and Christian people enjoy themselves in peace.

I cannot express how much these fireworks (for which all the Italians have taste and skill), which furnish all this population with a pleasure so innocent and so gay, have always seemed to me superior to those diversions more or less dangerous or gross, which everywhere else, in towns or villages, are indispensable ingredients of the popular feasts.

Seated on my terrace during these lovely summer nights, how many times have I seen all these villages, concealed in the mountain, by turns illuminated, and the rockets mount upward, while the distant noise of the explosions was heard! The same *fête* often was celebrated in two or three different localities; then fire answered to fire, rocket to rocket, and all these lights my heart rejoiced to see, for they signified that a joyous and healthful *fête* was bringing gayly to a close, for all, from the rich to the poorest, a day which had been filled with the thought of God and the remembrance of the saints.

* From "Souvenirs d'Italie et d'Angleterre." Par Mme. Augustus Craven.

The days spent in this retreat will never be effaced from my memory. They abide there, with the joys and pains which filled them, colored by that enchanting light which sheds over everything in Italy its incomparable charm. But while transcribing to-day the pages which enclose these memories of a time already so far distant, and while recalling all, which, I desired or feared, and all which has since been accomplished, more than ever I renew here that wish, formed erewhile, at the same time as the wish of seeing the material prosperity of this beautiful country developed: Oh! may it never acquire anything at the expense of *that thing most precious* which it already possesses! May *Progress*, whatever it may be, and however it is accomplished, be even more powerless to obscure in souls the divine sun of the faith, than it would be to alter the radiant light of the sky and the immutable beauty of nature!

Apparitions.

Rev. Dr. Mahar in "The Catholic Universe."

THE accounts that have come from Knock, Ireland, of apparitions of the Blessed Virgin in that place, have led to extraordinary manifestations of devotion on the part of Catholics, and, as usual, manifestations of incredulity and sneers on the part of those who are not of the Church. Even among Catholics, there are found some who throw doubt on these wonders; then, again, there are some among us who possess no devotion worth speaking of; and, being associated frequently with Protestants, would like to be freed from the necessity of defending their brethren who believe in the facts that are narrated of such places as Lourdes, La Salette, and Knock. It would be a great relief to these Catholics if the saints never appeared, or miracles were never worked, and these weak children were not called to defend anything but mere possibilities of things yet untold—possibilities of which they could have the shaping. Such Catholics simply steer from Scylla into Charybdis; for when they once admit that the apparitions of Lourdes, La Salette and Knock are delusions, they are forced to the conclusion that Catholics are blind devotees, running after a jack-of-the-lantern as a light from Heaven; for there can be no denying that Catholics, as a rule, accept as genuine these apparitions.

We have no patience with this class of Catholics. Their faith is weak and their courage also; they have nothing of Confirmation except its indelible mark. You may say that these wonders are not articles of Faith. This is not to the point. Faith does not alone make known to us the things that are contained in the Deposit, but throws light upon countless facts in our daily life as well. It makes God present to us, brings the saints and angels near to us, makes us mindful of what has been done by God to man, and causes us to see His hand where those who have no faith, or whose faith is dead, do not see beyond the natural powers God uses as His agents. Those who have little of the spiritual life, whose thoughts are seldom or never on the things of God, who never have His name upon their lips, who manifest no sign of their belief in Him, except when circumstances demand an explicit *yes* or *no*, naturally enough receive an account of a miracle or an apparition as a tale from some remote unexplored country of whose inhabitants we know no more than the fact of their existence. To a faithful people, God and His angels and saints are ever present and near; to the unfaithful, they are beyond the distant stars, with an interminable, almost impassable, abyss between. Mark those who do not believe in these apparitions, and you will find they are persons who do not invoke a saint, nor pray for the departed souls of their fathers and mothers.

Nor is there any reason to be afraid to profess before Protestants a belief in these wonders. There are many accounts of apparitions in the Old Testament and in the New. Non-Catholics accept these. What reason, in the name of common sense, can there be to make us believe that with the closing of the last page of the Bible God has ceased to manifest His wonders to men? On the contrary, if we find God and His messengers continually appearing in the history of His chosen people and in as much of the history of the Church as is contained in the inspired books, why not for that very reason expect the same providence to be shown in the history of religion now? Why should we expect the story of four thousand years to be reversed? If Divine messengers have appeared four hundred and ninety-nine times, why not the five hundredth? The utter silliness of the reasoning that induces the belief that the age of miracles has past away, is beyond comprehension and is utterly impossible, except to those whose faith has also past away. It is not because there is in these apparitions a confirmation of the doctrine of the intercession of saints that non-Catholics object, but simply because of the miraculous part involved. This is clear from one fact alone—that they object not only to miracles that are attributed to the intercession of the saints, but also to all other miracles as well.

It is true that the Church is cautious about receiving accounts of miracles and apparitions. It is true that she wishes such statements to be sifted by a proper tribunal before her final sanction is given to them. All that is the caution of law, and does not prevent individuals from knowing with certainty of such apparitions and turning them to proper account. There is such a thing as certainty in matters of religion without at all an act of homage to the declarations of the Church. To illustrate this in the particular we are speaking of, take the case of the death of a saint. Numbers of persons have appreciated his sanctity, are certain that he is in heaven, and gather about his tomb to invoke his intercession. The Church makes no difficulty against this, in fact supposes it in her legislation regarding canonizations. After the death of St. Alphonsus Liguori and miracles were wrought through his intercession, those who witnessed these wonders were certain of his sanctity, though they were not required nor allowed till about fifty years afterwards to call him saint. No one, therefore, can sanction his incredulity by adducing the cautious prescriptions of the Church. We need not be afraid of falling under the conviction of superstition by accepting miraculous facts. It would be interesting to find where such accounts as these of Knock have proved false or unfounded in any one instance in the history of the Church. If there were such instance, suspicion might be reasonable. Besides, we must not forget that we ought to fear, lest by casting doubts on these manifestations, we may be only using our efforts to defeat the good Almighty God intends to effect by such wonders.

A Beautiful Catholic Custom.

A correspondent of the *Catholic Review*, writing from Tucson, Arizona, gives the following description of a beautiful custom of the Church not often witnessed in this country:

"I witnessed a ceremony here the other day not often seen, I think, in the United States. I was at the seven o'clock Mass last Sunday. As the priest retired from the chancel he stopped a moment, and, turning towards the congregation, simply said: 'I am called to bring the Blessed Sacrament to a dying person. It will be taken immediately.' He said this so quietly that I, not noticing him at the time, understood not what he said. I looked up, and perceived that he had said something, from his having turned to the congregation; but what it was, I did not know. After a few moments, I saw an altar boy advance from the sacristy, bearing a large, heavy silver processional crucifix. He was followed by a number of other boys, all in surplices, one with a censer, others bearing lighted candles; then came the priest appropriately robed. Soon I saw persons passing candles around among the congregation, and then they lighted one from another. The ciborium was taken from the tabernacle, a passage way through the broad middle aisle, crammed with people, was made, the procession started, a little boy preceding ringing a bell; then the whole congregation followed, most of them with candles, passing out through the plaza on to the principle streets, making a grand display. I understood then that it was some distinguished member of the congregation who was dying, and that demonstration was a tribute of respect to him from his old fellow-parishioners. The men all followed with heads uncovered. All persons we met (save an occasional non-Catholic, of whom there were very few in the street at that hour Sunday morning) knelt as they met the procession, and when the Host passed, rose and followed in the train. I found now we were leaving the main street, and that we finally halted in a small side street, before a one-story, miserable little mud house. Over the door an attempt had been made at ornament by festooning there a piece of new white sheeting about four or five yards in length, rising in the middle over the door like a painted arch, and the ends falling at each side of the door. On this white ground a piece of pink muslin about six inches wide was pinned, meeting at the top in the form of a painted arch, and reaching down at each side. In the folds of pink at the top was nestled a figure of a white dove. The procession filled the street for a long way each side of the house. As the priest entered the house, the ringing of the bell ceased, and there was nearly ten minutes of perfect silence. The vast crowd outside, all kneeling right in the street, joining in prayer for the dying person inside. Nothing I ever experienced in my life seemed more solemn than this scene at that moment. The fleeting character of this world, the reality of eternal life, the justice and mercy of God, the doctrine of redemption, and the proof of faith, all here practically at work. Each one of us had brought before him in the most tangible manner that inside of this poor hut an immortal soul was fitting itself for an eternal life. How small it made all worldly things seem! At last, there is the bell: the priest emerges with his train. A soul is shriven—most likely, a soul is saved. To have been at the battle of Waterloo, is thought to have assisted at a grand affair. Here was a drama to which that was nothing. All returned to the church, received the blessing, and dispersed.

Catholic Notes.

—The death is announced by cable of Cardinal Pie, the illustrious Bishop of Poitiers.

—The Holy Father lately bestowed his Apostolic Benediction on *The Catholic Messenger* of Parkersburg, W. Va.

—This week we are enabled to send $150 more to Ireland: $100 to Rev. Father Murphy, S. J., Sea Road, Co. Galway; and $50 to Sister Xavier, Presentation Convent, Michelstown.

—A night-school for newsboys has been established in New Orleans, under the auspices of the Society of St. Vincent de Paul, and the Sisters of Mercy. The average attendance is sixty-nine boys.

—The Holy Sacrifice of the Mass was recently celebrated in the Tower of London for the first time since the Reformation. A number of the Catholic guardsmen there obtained this permission.

—Rt. Rev. Fintan Mundwiler, O. S. B., of St. Meinrad's Abbey, Spencer Co., Ind., was installed as Abbot—vice Rt. Rev. Bishop Marty—last week, by Rt. Rev. Bishop Chatard of Vincennes.

—Subscriptions are being made in the north of France to meet the expenses required to sustain the resistance in favor of religious congregations. Large sums have already been raised for this purpose.

—The coronation of the statue of Notre Dame des Victoires with the imperial crown lately presented by the ex-Empress Eugenie, will soon take place. This crown will adorn the statue only on the greater festivals.

—All Catholics and all lovers of poetry will hear with regret of the death of Mrs. Coventry Patmore, the second wife of the author of "The Angel in the House," and, like her gifted husband, a convert to the Catholic religion. R. I. P.

—On the occasion of the celebration of the Feast of St. Paul of the Cross, Founder of the Congregation of the Passion, Rev. Father Fidelis (Kent Stone) preached an eloquent sermon in English on the life and labors of the Saint, in the Church of SS. John and Paul on Monte Celio, Rome.

—The Carthusian monks of France, who manufacture a celebrated brand of liquor, and who pay the Government one million francs a year, and annually distribute five millions of francs among the poor, threaten, in consequence of the recent religious decrees, to remove to England.

—A society paper in England, announcing the Rev. Joseph G. Sutcliffe's late reception into the Church, at St. Dominic's, Haverstock Hill, says that a further secession of Ritualists may speedily be looked for; among whom are likely to be one or two very prominent men, and a considerable sprinkling of Protestant Sisters of Mercy.

—The distress in Ireland appears to be greatest in Co. Galway. The Rev. Father Malony, of Kinvara, writing to a friend in this country under date of the 17th ult., says that the people of his parish, which comprises five hundred and fifty families, are in dire want, with no hopes of succor, except through charity, till the middle of July. He states further that if relief is not afforded, actual starvation will be the result.

—The attacks of anti-religious publications against the clergy and the members of charitable communities have already begun to bear fruit by the most revolting deeds in some parts of France. Two Sisters of St. Vincent de Paul, while passing through one of the boulevards at Rennes not long since, were insulted by a drunken workman, who cried out, "Away with the nuns! away with the priests!" On the same day, a priest, carrying the Viaticum to a sick person, was also molested.

—On the 16th of April, the anniversary of the death of Bernadette (Sister Mary Bernard), a solemn service was held in the parochial church of Lourdes, which was attended by so large a concourse of people that sufficient room could not be found within the sacred precincts to hold all. The greatest devotion and recollection prevailed, all deeply regretting the loss of both the priest and the child who are the glory of the city, and whose names will be forever associated with Our Lady of Lourdes.

—We witnessed a touching act of Faith on Tuesday afternoon last. As the *Angelus* bell rang, a laborer, dinner-pail in hand, was approaching the Cathedral. He raised his hat, evidently reciting the *Angelus*, and when opposite the main Cathedral door, he reverently knelt on the step, and thus in the open street finished his devotions. Then making a grave and reverent sign of the cross, he replaced his hat and walked off, with no seeming concern for the passers-by. —*Catholic Universe.*

—We regret deeply to announce the death of Miss Annie W. Gibson, of Crompton, R. I., who has been a contributor to THE AVE MARIA from its inception in

1865. She was a graceful writer, a devoted friend, and a fervent Catholic. Her death, which happily occurred during this month devoted to Our Lady, of whom she was a fervent client, was calm and peaceful. Like her brother, the revered pastor of Crompton, Miss Gibson was a convert to the Faith, and cheerfully submitted to many sacrifices for its sake. R. I. P.

—CONVERSIONS TO THE FAITH.—The conversions of members of the Church of England to Catholicity still progress in remarkable numbers. Amongst the latest converts are the Rev. Horace S. Wilcocks, Plymouth, and the family of the Rev. Leonard Fish, a city clergyman. Mr. H. C. Cobbold, a leading Suffolk gentleman, has, with his wife and family, also come over to the Catholic Church. The more unobtrusive families who are daily being gathered into the fold are to be numbered by the hundred.—*Dublin Freeman.*

—The daily papers of the 19th inst. contained the sad announcement of the death by accident of Rev. Father H. Kaetz, pastor of Seymour, Wis. He was driving to another parish near by, in company with some clerical friends, when the vehicle broke and started the horse on a run. Father Kaetz jumped out and struck on the back of his head. He was brought to Green Bay, where examination proved that the spinal cord was fractured and the brain injured. He lived only about five hours after the accident. The deceased was 27 years old. R. I. P.

—THE ENGLISH PILGRIMAGE TO LOURDES.—The English pilgrimage to convey the banner of St. George to the basilica of Our Lady of Lourdes will leave England for Lourdes early in June. About nine days will be occupied going and returning. Cardinal Manning will place himself at the head of the pilgrimage. Four hundred noblemen and gentry of the United Kingdom have already sent in their names to Cardinal Manning's secretary as desirous to join the pilgrimage. It is expected to be the most noteworthy movement of the kind witnessed in England since the Reformation.

—A NOBLE SOUL.—Among the many whole-souled responses to our appeal for the starving poor in afflicted Ireland, was the following, which does honor to the writer's true Christian charity. Here is one who feels that the love of our neighbor is the measure of our love of God: "Enclosed I send you five dollars for the poor starving people of Galway, Ireland. I have a large family of my own to provide for, but that touching appeal in THE AVE MARIA would take the last cent I had. I give it with all my heart, and hope it may relieve some poor soul whose prayers for me and my family will be worth more than all the money I could make during the rest of my life. Pray for me."

—FATHER BURKE, O. P.—Catholics everywhere will rejoice to hear that the eloquent Dominican, Father Burke, has recovered from his protracted illness, and is again in the pulpit. An Irish correspondent writes of him: "We are happy to say that the great Dominican, of whose unrivalled genius and power as a public orator, his fellow-countrymen at home and abroad are so justly proud, is almost himself again. He looks as strong as ever. That his recovery may prove complete and permanent, and that he may be spared to the Church for many a long year to come, will be the prayer, we feel assured, of all who read these lines. He pronounced an eloquent and interesting panegyric on the life and labors of St. Catharine of Sienna, one of the glories of the Dominican Order, in the Church of St. Savior, in Dublin on the 30th ult., the Feast of the saint. He spoke with the earnestness and the ardor of a devoted client, and in glowing and animated language set forth the austerities and mortification of her early life, the struggles and trials through which she had to pass, and finally, the triumphant issue which crowned her efforts."

—THE MARQUIS OF RIPON.—A Catholic, in the person of the Marquis of Ripon, will now, for the first time in the history of British India, rule as Viceroy in that most populous portion of the possessions of the Queen, having almost as many subjects of the crown as there are co-religionists of his Excellency in the length and breadth of Christendom. The appointment of the noble Marquis to the vice-regal throne at Calcutta, will be welcomed as an event of exceptional interest in all parts of the Catholic world. His selection as Lord Lytton's successor does signal honor to Mr. Gladstone, who, as the author of the ill-considered pamphlet, published a few years ago, under the title of "Vaticanism," may be said to have acted in this instance not only with courage, but with magnanimity. Lord Ripon's nomination to the office of Governor-General is like an acknowledgment on the part of the Prime Minister that in questioning as he did, in his mistaken argument, the loyalty of Catholics, he was guilty of an error of judgment. Elsewhere we offer our meed of recognition to the noble service done to the crown during the last four years by the retiring Viceroy; but while we would, as alone befits him, welcome the coming, we would, in the same breath, speed the going Governor-General of India, bidding him with our whole heart God-speed on his setting forth to assume his grand and resplendent responsibilities.—*Weekly Register.*

—THE FIFTH CENTENARY OF ST. CATHARINE OF SIENNA.—The fifth centenary of the death of St. Catharine of Sienna, which occurred on the 30th of April, was celebrated at Rome with great pomp and tender devotion by the Roman people, who thus showed their gratitude to this Saint for the part she had in persuading Gregory XI to return from Avignon to his Apostolic See of Rome. A solemn Triduum was celebrated in the Church of S. Maria Sopra Minerva, by the Dominican Fathers, in honor of this illustrious heroine of the Church, and glory of the Dominican Order. Solemn High Mass was sung each day of the Triduum, and ceremonies appropriate to the occasion were held in the afternoon, closing with the Benediction of the Blessed Sacrament. On the Feast itself, Pontifical Mass and Vespers were celebrated by Mgr. Salina, Bishop of Chalcedony, *in part. inf.* Panegyrics extolling her virtues were delivered by some of the most eloquent preachers of Italy, amongst whom might be noted Father Vincent Lombardo, who compared St. Catharine to Deborah, of Scriptural renown, because like her, endowed with wisdom, armed with the shield of fortitude, and with her heart inflamed with a motherly love, she conciliated the inimical factions of those times, overcame the many difficulties placed in the way of her exalted designs, rendered vain the efforts of the enemies of the Church and of society, and persuaded Pope Gregory to return to Rome. The church, which was filled each day with a devout assemblage, was most beautifully adorned, and a hundred and fifty lights, placed in pleasing order, produced a wonderful effect throughout the vast edifice. Nearly a thousand communicants partook of the Bread of Life on the Feast and preceding days. On this occasion, the shrine containing the urn, where the body of St. Catharine reposes, was restored and overlaid with beautiful marble. The chapel which contains the walls of the room wherein St. Catharine died, was also restored.

—A STRIKING CURE.—We take the following

notice of another remarkable cure at Knock from a recent letter of an esteemed friend in Dublin. Our correspondent says: "A striking case of cure at Knock has come in my way. The parish clergy will report regularly on it to Father Cavanagh, P. P. of Knock and Archdeacon. Being in the neighborhood myself last Sunday (2 May), I walked to the spot, Longwood, a post-town, Co. Meath, saw the individual, and had confirmation there of the report from priest, doctor, and neighbors. Anne Grady was born in November, 1862, and when three years old, began to have epileptic fits. At first they occurred only about once a fortnight, but gradually multiplied, and at last came on some twice or thrice a day, and even at night. She fell twice into the fire, used to disturb the congregation at Mass by screaming, even during the elevation, and wore out her poor mother with trouble, care and anxiety. Her grandfather had vainly tried every means within his power to effect a cure; at length, on Ash-Wednesday of this year, she was put into the work-house hospital at Trim—about 7 miles off. Meantime, her father, a laboring man, had collected enough for a journey to Knock. He had no means of his own, and his cabin is so poor that no light comes in but by the door; so he collected from compassionating acquaintances, and his wife, with Anne, started by train (after removing the sufferer from Trim work-house on Easter Sunday) the following Tuesday. From the moment of starting, no more fits have occurred. Slight weaknesses came on twice since, but she did not fall; she has sense and strength now, can be trusted by herself out of the house, and makes herself useful. Calling at the place some few days before Sunday last, I found she was absent at a distance, and occupied in planting potatoes. She bears the marks of a burn on her neck, and has a purple blotch on the forehead; she is thin and wasted, but sensible, full of piety, and most grateful to the Blessed Virgin Mary."

—THE CHURCH IN BULGARIA.—Rev. Thomas Brzeska, Superior of the Mission of the Resurrectionists, at Adrianople, Bulgaria, publishes a long letter in the *Missions Catholiques*, dated Dec. 17th, of which we give here a brief epitome. He states that the revival of nationalism, threatened for a time the existence of the Catholic Church in Bulgaria. He and his priests, however, lost no time in visiting the most exposed Catholic settlements, and succeeded in persuading the inhabitants not to emigrate. Many Russian emissaries had been travelling through the land, inducing the people to do so, promising great advantages, and frightening them with a massacre to be enacted by the Turks after the departure of the Russian troops. The efforts of these emissaries had been partly successful, but a large number of the emigrants, either disappointed in their expectation, or overcome by homesickness, returned to their native soil. One of the chief motives of the adhesion manifested by the Catholic Bulgarians, is the gratuitous education bestowed by the Catholic priests and religious—among the latter chiefly Sisters—upon the Bulgarian youth. The expenses for it are partly defrayed by the Roman Propaganda, partly by the Society of the Propagation of the Faith, at Lyons. The schismatics leave no means untried to pervert their Catholic fellow-citizens, but these can boast of quite a number of confessors, who, reduced almost to beggary by the malice of their enemies, did not flinch or give way in the least. One of these confessors, a wealthy Catholic farmer at Novo Selo, had his fine grist mill totally destroyed, and afterwards 15 head of cattle wantonly killed by musket shots; yet he bore all this in the spirit of Christian meekness, and although very much reduced in circumstances, he neither laid his complaints before the court nor asked alms of the Catholic missionaries, but remained firm in his convictions, exhorting his friends and neighbors by word and example to do the same. Another Catholic boldly rebuked two schismatic priests for their attempt to weaken the resolution of a body of peasants to remain firm, and confessed to be a Catholic, which glorious example saved the entire village from apostasy. The writer remarks also that the Turkish Governor, Réouf Pascha, who is a Greek by nationality and religion, and his counsellor, Vassa Effends, an Albanian Catholic, are treating the Catholic missionaries with the greatest courtesy and have given them most valuable assistance. In conclusion, he gives some interesting details on the material state of the mission, thanks the members of the Propagation of the Faith for the alms already received, and assures them of the benefit of prayers and Masses said by the missionaries for the spiritual and temporal welfare of their benefactors.

——$1 received from Eliza Kenny for the Needy Mission; the same from Elmira C. of M., and from two friends.

——CONTRIBUTIONS FOR THE SUFFERING IRISH.—Two Friends, Chelsea, Mass., 75 cts.; Lawrence Gagan, $1; Mamie T. Gagan, $1; Mr. George Powers, $1; Mrs. A. Carr, $1; Mr. Michael Hoolahan, $1; Eliza Kenny, $1; James Durkin, $1; B. C. Durkin, $1; Mrs. Benson, $1; Peter Kevenny, $1; John Lynch, $1; Mary Hughes, $1; Mrs. P. McDermott, 50 cts.; Mary Shaughnessy, 50 cts.; Abbey Shea, 50 cts.; Lizzie McDermott, 50 cts.; Mrs. Densy, Jr., 25 cts.; Mrs. Densy, Sr., 25 cts.; Mrs. Costello, 25 cts.; Mrs. St. Joseph, $2.50; Katie McCarthy and Mrs. Catharine McCarthy, $11; A Poor Invalid, $1; C. F. Collins, $1; E. H. Collins, $1; James D. Simpson, $1; Convent of Notre Dame, San Francisco, Cal., $25; A Friend, $5; E. M. O'Dowd, $1; Julia Govern, $1; A Friend, St. Louis, Mo., $3; A Friend, St. Louis, Mo., 90 cts.; A Friend, Kansas City, Mo., 65; A Friend, Shasta, Cal., $1; A Friend, 10 cts.; Mrs. T. McMahon, $1; Miss A. McCarthy, $1; Dennis Murphy, $1; Dennis Howe, $1; James Manging, $1; Matthew Nagle, 50 cts.; John Lynch, $1; Wm. Daley, $1; John Flaherty, $1; John Danehee, $1; Michael Ryan, $5; Daniel O'Connell, 50 cts.; Owen McMahon, 50 cts.; Owen Riley, 50 cts.; P. M. Kane, $5; Mrs. P. M. Kane, $5; J. J. Kane, $1; P. M. Kane, Jr., $1; Mary E. Kane, $1; Alma M. Fowler, $1; Mrs. A. Fowler, $1; Mrs. E. Gormly, $1 ($32.10 collected by Miss Annie McCarthy); Mrs. Margaret Benson, $5; Frank Mattes, 20 cts.; A Friend, $2; Addie Murphy, $1; Edward Quigley, $1; M. O'Farrell, $1; Mrs. D. Hyland, $3.50; Hannah Lyons, $1; D. E. Mitchell, $1; M. Mitchell, $1; J. H. Mitchell, $1; James Mitchell, $1; John Nugent, $1; Mrs. John Nugent, 50 cts.; P. Donahue, $2; Peter Flynn, $1; John Brown, 50 cts.; M. T. Roony, $1; Mrs. John Roony, $1; John Roony 50 cts.; Hugh M. Roony, $1; Wm. Martin, 50 cts.; Mrs. C. S. Roony, 75 cts.; Mrs. Darcy, 50 cts.; R. Millar, $1; M. W. Roony, $1 ($16.25 collected by Mr. D. E. Mitchell); Mrs. Kohencamp, $1; Mrs. Redicker, $1; Miss Maggie Redicker, 10 cts.; Miss Galvin, 50 cts.; Mrs. Mary Speicher, 25 cts.; Mrs. Mary Smyth, 25 cts.; Mrs. Buolion, 10 cts.; Mrs. Golbach, 50 cts.; Mrs. Hogan, 25 cts.; Mrs. Fisher, 50 cts.; A Friend, $1; Mrs. H. J. Smith, 50 cts.; Mrs. Gels, 14 cts.; Mrs. M. G. Egler, 25 cts.; Mrs. Glienarth, 50 cts.; Mrs. L. Langenbacher, 25 cts.; Mrs. Lofink, 25 cts.; Mrs. N. Denmarck, 25 cts.; Mrs. Fisher, 25 cts.; Mrs. Luoff, 25 cts.; Mrs. Hannah Boyle 50 cts.; Mrs. Kate Benz, 50 cts.; Mrs. Kate Egler, 25 cts.; Mrs. Albert Mahler, 25 cts.; Mrs. Jno.

Fishbach, 25 cts.; Mrs. Kate Urban, $1; Mrs. Mary Ward, 25 cts.; Mrs. Krelley, 50 cts.; Mr. Anton Feldung, 25 cts.; A Friend, 50 cts.

Confraternity of the Immaculate Conception
(Or of Our Lady of Lourdes).

"We fly to thy patronage, O Holy Mother of God!"

REPORT FOR THE WEEK ENDING MAY 19TH.

The following petitions have been received: Recovery of health for 39 persons and 2 families,—change of life for 22 persons and 2 families,—conversion to the Faith for 19 persons and 3 families,—temporal favors for 9 persons and 11 families,—spiritual favors for 36 persons and 4 families,—the spiritual and temporal welfare of 3 communities, 1 school, and 1 asylum; also 24 particular intentions, and 3 thanksgivings for favors received.

Specified intentions: Two persons ruining themselves by intemperance,—a young man who is the cause of great grief and anxiety to his mother,—a person who has become paralyzed,—recovery of health, or a happy death for several persons,—grace of perseverance for one who has given up his intemperate habits,—the prevention of marriage between a virtuous young lady and an unworthy man,—the conversion of several well-disposed Protestants,—recovery of stolen property,—a Catholic about to marry out of the Church,—conversion to the Faith, and the temporal welfare of a non-Catholic gentleman of advanced age; spiritual and temporal favors for his daughter, a convert.

FAVORS OBTAINED.

A gentleman of Iowa writes: "My daughter's child was cured of a running sore in the ear, which was not only painful, but also emitted a disagreeable odor. By the application of a few drops of the Water of Lourdes.".... A lady in California says: "Thanks to Our Blessed Lady, my child has been restored to perfect health." A gentleman informs us that since invoking the prayers of the Confraternity, he has been able to sell a property which before he had vainly endeavored to dispose of.

OBITUARY.

The following deceased persons are recommended to the prayers of the Confraternity: Mrs. C. McLane, of Pottsville, Pa., deceased last week. Miss Annie Dunn, of Boston, Mass., whose death occurred on the 2d inst. Mrs. Lydia Gallagher, who breathed her last at Gibson's Station, Ohio, on the 13th of April. James Donahoe, of Chicago, Ill., who departed this life on the 18th of May. Mrs. Mary Flanagan, who died at Altoona, Pa., on the 1st inst, after receiving the consolations of religion. Mrs. J. Smith, who rested in peace at Kingston, Canada, on the 30th ult. Mr. Thos. Fallon, of San Francisco, Cal., who departed for heaven Jan. 1st. Thomas Brady, who slept in the Lord at East New York, N. Y., on the 13th inst. M. D. Wise, John and Edmund Dowling, Mr. Joseph Fox and Mrs. Eliza Nolan, of Lockport, Ill., lately deceased. Sister Gabriel; Mr. Augustine Foger, Patrick Eneight, John Ward, John Heffernan, Daniel Dalton, Catharine Hickey, Alice Dwyer and Patrick Rossiter, recently deceased. And some others, whose names have not been given.

Requiescant in pace.

A. GRANGER, C. S. C., Director.

Youth's Department.

The Blessed Sacrament.

BY EVA.

MY SAVIOUR on the altar lies
In chains of love for me:
The Sovereign Lord of earth and skies,
A Mighty God is He.

The Heavens tremble at His nod,
The Angels prostrate fall:
But He is here our loving God,
The Sovereign Lord of all.

The God of love, the God of life,
A hidden God is He;
The King of Glory from above
Has come to dwell with me.

I am not worthy Thou shouldst come;
But whither shall I go?
My Lord! my God! my only Love!
Thee only do I know.

Come, then, within this heart of mine,
It languishes for Thee;
Come, Thou, celestial Bread Divine,
My Jesus, come to me!

A Son's Gift, and what Came of It.

LURHEIM, a small town in Germany, was distinguished for the thrift and steadiness of its inhabitants. Free from the extremes of great wealth and hopeless poverty, a peaceful contentment reigned in its well-ordered homes. Worth was respected there, as opulence is in more sordid communities; and a mutual confidence made intercourse among the various families as genial and unrestrained as if they were all akin.

In this happy community we have only to make the acquaintance of one family, a very small one, for it consisted only of father and son. It had once been a large circle, but death had broken the links, year after year, until it was reduced to three; some years of quiet resignation to the divine will that had thus reduced it on earth only to reunite it in a better world, and then the last and dearest link of the chain was broken, the Christian mother went to her reward. There was no longer a family circle; the aged father, the youthful son, child of his old age, felt themselves like solitary waifs surviving a wreck. They were all in all to each other now, and if the Wagner household had been formerly dear to all, it was still more affectionately regarded now.

John Wendelin Wagner had often been mayor of the borough, and might still have retained that office, but after the death of his beloved wife he felt unequal to the duties it entailed on one so conscientiously strict in fulfilling them. However, he did not deem himself released, either by advanced age or bereavement, from the duties of a good citizen. His advice, valuable as the fruit of long experience and disinterested devotion to the general good, was at the service of all, and the farm which he cultivated with his son, was made to contribute its full share to any projects of religion or charity which demanded it.

When winter put a temporary stop to the work of the farm, the father and son did not spend their time in idleness. They were both skilful in plaiting straw, and they busied themselves in making straw hats which found a ready sale. Fridolin, as the son was called, was not, on the whole, so industrious a worker as his father. He mused and sang a good deal over his work, shook his head sometimes at the result, and evidently thought his productions common-place. The old man knew what was passing in his mind. Often a tear stole down his cheek as he secretly watched him, and thought of the ingenious and tasteful ways he had admired in the boy's mother in the first years of their married life. He had become accustomed to them, perhaps; but now he observed the same gifts naturally unfolding in his young companion, and though a good deal of time seemed wasted in trials and experiments, not for all the worth of the hats would he have said a word to prevent it; that the boy was thus amused was enough for the fond parent.

The result of Fridolin's endeavors was finally a hat which was the marvel of everybody. How had he dyed the straw of so many different tints? The bright red which was plaited around the crown and looked like a fine ribbon, though pretty, was nothing strange; to dye that color was easy; but the garland of so many shades, and so cunningly intermixed that at a little distance it resembled a wreath of fresh culled flowers, was really a marvel of taste and skill both in the coloring and the plaiting of the straws. In the middle shone distinctly the name of *John Wendelin Wagner* in the natural hue of the straw, such a pure golden contrast to the gay colors around it. It was his birthday present to his good father, who smilingly read off his full name, as he embraced the ingenious donor, and expressed much delight at the unique gift.

"However," said he, "I do not wish to wear so elegant a hat, unless my son has its fellow, you understand?"

Fridolin colored with innocent pride. He lost no time in obeying his father's hint, by plaiting a hat for himself, bearing his name in full, *Mathias Fridolin Wagner*, in the midst of a garland; but it must be confessed that this garland was inferior to the first, and that the band of green straw beneath it showed to poor advantage beside the hat surrounded with red. Wendelin bantered him on the difference, affecting to believe that his skill had exhausted itself in its first essay; but the good son only laughed and shook his curly head, he knew well that his motive was not misunderstood.

But these times of virtuous and peaceful enjoyments were suddenly ended. War threw its lurid shadow over Flurheim. A French army which had long been ravaging that part of Germany, descended on the defenceless town, and, in revenge for some real or pretended insult, devastated the borough and drove many of the inhabitants into the forests and mountains, threatening them with a terrible fate if they presumed to return. Among these were the aged Wagner and his son. Less afflicted than their companions, who had been torn from family as well as from home, they encouraged these with pious sentiments of trust in an overruling Providence; but oh, the misery and suffering of those forced marches! the brutal insults, the continual fear of straggling bands of the enemy who were prowling in every direction, these were harder to endure than even the bodily pain of hunger, thirst and fatigue. In a few days the little company of fugitives had become scattered, some seeking to return to their desolate families by circuitous routes, others flying in desperation, they knew not, cared not whither. The Wagners, finding themselves alone, considered what course to adopt, and decided to seek a distant town where some of their kindred dwelt, far remote from the scene of war. Full of faith and resigned to the divine will which allowed these calamities, they pursued their way, but a fresh misfortune was in store for them, and the most grievous that could befall, for it separated this fond parent and child. Captured, and accused of being spies, they were torn apart and subjected to many hardships ere they became free.

And now the plan they had formed was of necessity abandoned. Wendelin, knowing that his son was ignorant of the route they had intended to follow, deemed it most likely that, if alive and free, he would seek to return to his native town. The noble-hearted Christian accordingly turned his feeble steps in that direction, but fortunately met with a generous workman, who, learning the stranger's history, persuaded him to accept the shelter of his poor home until peace was restored. "Believe me, dear sir," said the workman earnestly, "you would sink on the road, alone and unaided. Besides, much of Flurheim has been destroyed, perhaps your house with the rest. Your son is young and vigorous; in the worst case he can care for himself, but how could he help you in such times?"

Wendelin, accustomed to listen to reason rather than to feelings, saw the wisdom of this advice. He had some scruples as to the propriety of accepting the generous offer of a home from one who evidently had to work hard for a livelihood; but finally he consented to go with him to his abode, which, if poor in earthly wealth, proved to be rich in kindness and hospitality.

Meantime how had it fared with Fridolin? When he found himself again at liberty, his first thought was, as his father had foreseen, to return home. Alas! in time of war, when one is forced to leave home, the return is very difficult. The poor youth, obliged to make many turns to hide from the invading army whose spies and stragglers seemed to be everywhere, found himself at last in a part of the country that was quite strange to him. While raising his heart to God for help and direction, he noticed a thriving homestead at some distance. With renewed hope he set forward. The farmer and his family were at supper when the weary traveller stood at the door; ere he could make known his necessities, he was cordially invited to partake of the plentiful repast. Then, after his hunger was partly satisfied, he told in a brief but touching manner of his misfortunes, the greatest of all being his uncertainty as to his father. The good youth melted into tears as he thought that death might ere this have been that father's fate, and the farmer's wife and daughter sympathized in his tears.

"Not so," said the sturdy farmer. "You will see him again, be sure of that, but to be candid with you, it will not probably be until the war is ended. As you are a farmer's son, you will feel at home with us for the present, and in God's good time all will come right."

Fridolin thus became an inmate of this happy household. The kind farmer, to gratify his longing after his beloved father, caused inquiries to be made by his servants when they took the grain to market, and two or three times they brought back some idle rumors which caused their master and Fridolin to set off to a distant village, sure that they were on the track of the aged wanderer, but only to return disappointed.

Grateful for the warm, active sympathy of his new friends, the youth did not allow the grief which he constantly felt to interfere with the prompt and careful fulfilment of the duties which fell to his share. One less prudently raised would have felt many additional hardships. Fridolin, accustomed to orderly and industrious habits, fell into the ways of the energetic farmer as if by instinct. His steady conduct was a source of wonder to the household. He was so young, so pleasant in manner, so quick and ingenious in whatever he undertook, that it seemed a mystery how he could unite with all this such patient application to the farm work. Truly he must have had a good father, said the farmer and his wife in their frequent conversations about this strange inmate of their home. They agreed between themselves that should the lost parent not be found, the good youth should always remain with them as their own. In this benevolent project they were encouraged by the priest of their parish who knew from report of the Wagner family, and was quite charmed with his new parishioner.

Nearly a year had passed ere peace was finally proclaimed. Fridolin, scarcely able to wait till the country was cleared of the troops and once more safe to peaceful travellers, set out in quest of his father. He took the direct road to Flurheim, and travelling from early dawn expected to reach it by nightfall. In the afternoon he came to a wayside shrine of the Blessed Mother, and pressed as he was for time, Fridolin knelt to salute her with the Angelical Salutation, and then to ask her blessing on his filial quest. While he prayed, an exclamation of surprise caused him to turn his head. Beside him stood a woman eagerly inspecting his straw-hat which she had picked up from the ground. A few questions from each proved that this was the wife of the artisan in whose house dwelt the owner of a similar hat. In less than an hour Fridolin was clasped in his father's arms.

The next morning they set out for Flurheim. It was scarcely more than the wreck of the pretty town they loved so well. The Wagner farm had fared better than most properties in the vicinity, and they could easily have taken up the old life, so free from care and anxiety. But Fridolin had other thoughts. He became the restorer of his native village, the benefactor of his impoverished townsmen by establishing a manufactory of fancy straw-hats, like those which had providentially led to his reunion with his father. The trade flourished, and the venerable Wagner blessed the wonderful results of his son's ingenious little invention, which had once seemed but a boy's caprice.

THE mind and the heart are like a house in which we take lodgers. Let us beware, then, of the thoughts to which we give hospitality.

Irish Legends.

V.

THE MARTYRED PRIEST.

GLOOM of sadness has settled over Croagh-Patrick. It is but three months since poor old Paudhrig O'Malley told his last story on the summit of the holy mount; and oh, how many changes have taken place since! The old man's prediction about the holy priest, Father Mulligan, have been fulfilled; all his fears are realized. Having brought him before a court-martial, he was accused of high treason, and immediately condemned to be hanged and quartered. The execution was carried out with incredible barbarity in presence of a mocking multitude—the parts of his mangled body, being exposed for days in order to deter any other priest from succeeding him in his sacred ministry, were thrown into a common sewer. That very night as the good lady, Mrs. O'Donnell, of Belleview, who had sheltered him in the "big house," as the people called it, was at her prayers in "the priest's room," the glorified soul of the martyred priest appeared to her, told her where the remains of his body had been thrown, and asked her to have them buried in consecrated ground. The good, pious lady, who had been so kind to him in life during twenty years, did not forget him in death. In the middle of the night, a fine moonlight night of July, she sent her men, at the very risk of their lives and of hers, to take up the sacred remains of the holy priest from the sewer where they had been thrown. They easily discovered them by means of a heavenly light that shone brightly above them like a pillar of fire. They brought them to the consecrated spot where he had so often celebrated the Holy Mass, and buried him there in the dead of the night, between the graves of the two little angel children who had so often served him during the Holy Sacrifice. No cross marked his grave, for the altar was his cross; no epitaph adorned his tomb, for the tears and sighs and prayers of a grateful people were his epitaph; no fresh flowers were strewn on the earth that covered him; it was already reddened with the blood of his faithful flock, and day after day will be moistened with the bitter tears of one who had loved him during life and still loves him in death, the good, kind, hospitable lady, who at the risk of her property and her life, had sheltered him, and between whose grandchildren, Dermot and Charley O'Connor, he is now reposing.

Poor Father Mulligan's body is now in repose and his soul is in heaven. What priest is to replace him and guide and comfort the poor, abandoned flock, now straying without a shepherd on the bleak slopes of Croagh-Patrick? God, "who tempers the wind to the shorn lamb," will provide them a shepherd.

"Weep not for Saints who ascend, to partake of the joys of the sky;
Weep not for spirits who bend with the worshipping spirits on high;
Weep not for the spirit now crowned with the garland to martyrdom given,
Oh, weep not for him who has found a home and a refuge in Heaven!"

VI.

THE BANSHEE'S WAIL.

We must now pass on to another scene of sorrow. Scarcely had the wail of woe ceased to reverberate through the rocks and crags of Croagh-Patrick for the holy priest who had so long loved and guarded his flock, and at last gave his life for them, than other and very different sounds were heard. From the depth of every lake and creek, where St. Patrick had chained the demons of pagan Ireland, monsters bound forth, rattling their chains in triumph. *Lug-na-demon*, on the north side of the hill, where the saint had confined the demons with the serpents and toads and everything venomous of the land, re-echoed with horrible noises as if all hell was rejoicing over the death of the people's "*soggarth aroon.*" But this infernal triumph cannot last long, for priest after priest will be found to walk in the blood-stained foot-prints of their martyred brothers, and give up their lives for their people, their country, and their God. Of all the voices that were heard round Croagh-Patrick, the most pitiful, the most heart-rending, was the wail of the Banshee round the cottage of Paudhrig O'Malley. Scarcely had he heard of the martyrdom of the holy priest, whom he loved so well, than he took to his bed, from which he never rose; and scarcely was he on that poor bed, where good Mrs. O'Donnell had for years supported him, than the Banshee's wail was heard day and night in mournful tones, indicating, as the people said, that poor Paudhrig had not long to live. Many of the old people said that they saw her counting her long gray hairs and shedding bitter tears from her eyes reddened with grief. Whatever may be in this Banshee story, poor Paudhrig O'Malley was on his death-bed; the neighbors all gathered in to see him, and among others, the lady who had been so kind to him, Mrs. O'Donnell, of Belleview, or, as the people called her, "the black lady of the big house," as she had been in mourning for many reasons for the last twenty years. The little ones also came, who had heard the good old man so often telling the stories of the past century. He was now going on ninety years of age; he would probably have lived longer, but for the shock he received at the death of the good, holy priest.

Life was fast ebbing away; but still his memory was fresh and his intellect bright. Some of the little children, who were all crying round his bed, asked him to tell them, before he died, the story of the little child to whom the Holy Infant appeared, and the wonders that happened in the big house; but the poor old man, with the sad tear in his eye, and love for the little children still in his heart, told them that he was not now able, but that the good lady who had herself witnessed all the wonders of the big house, and heard from the holy priest himself the story about little Agnes of the Holy Infant, would tell them all. His last hour had come; there was no priest near, but God was with him; and in the peace of God, and surrounded by all who loved and prayed for him, poor old Paudhrig O'Malley gave up his soul to God. They buried him near the Carrig-au-Affrin, where he had for eighty years so often knelt and prayed.

"Passed away, but only waiting
Joyfully on yonder shore,
Waiting to receive the loved ones,
Ne'er to part for evermore."

VII.

THE MARTYR-CHILD.

Scarcely had the last sod been placed on the grave of Paudhrig O'Malley, when the pitiful wail of the "*Cœiné*" was again heard, and many a story was told about the "Patriarch of Croagh-Patrick." The wild wail that accompanied his funeral, resembling in its variety and pathos the weird moaning of the "Banshee," again resounded from every rock and crag in the plaintive, expressive accents of the grand old Celtic tongue: "Paudhrig avourneen, Paudhrig aroon!" Among the many stories that were told concerning the old man was that of the martyr-child, Agnes, who used to be his continual companion praying before the Blessed Sacrament in the priest's hiding-place. Whenever the priest went out on his perilous journeys to attend the dying, Paudhrig and Agnes were sure to remain watching and praying till his return. On one occasion, poor little Agnes was alone in the lonely cavern of the mountain-side, where was hidden in the recesses of the rocks the rude residence of the priest and of the "hidden God." She had her little hands joined before her breast, bending like a lily before the rough stone altar where she knew the Holy Infant reposed, and where she had often seen him in His Infant form, and received His Infant caresses. The dear, innocent child, now just ten years old, had no thought of danger; her thoughts and her heart were with Jesus in the tabernacle. She had gone to confession that morning and was to receive her First Communion the next day; all her thoughts were intent on this supreme moment of her life, when suddenly the priest-hunter made his appearance. One of those bandogs of the law, anxious to obtain the "five pounds" reward offered for the priest's head, having traced him into the very recesses of the mountain, stood before the trembling child with his panting bloodhound. "Where is the priest?" said he, roughly.

"There is no priest here, sir," said the child, calmly rising from her knees and standing between the tyrant and the altar. He took her by the hair and pulled her away from the altar in order that he might rob the tabernacle of the little silver box in which the Blessed Sacrament was preserved. The child, strengthened by God, throwing her arms round the tabernacle, exclaimed, "You shall not touch Jesus Christ!" He seized her again by her golden locks and holding her up, exclaimed, "Come, tell me where the priest is, or I'll beat you to death," at the same time striking the innocent child a terrible blow on the shoulders.

"O sir," she replied, "I can't tell you: I don't know!" Stroke after stroke fell on the quivering body of the poor little innocent, till at last, thinking she was dead, as she hung in his hand by the hair a bleeding mass of wounds and blood, he threw her aside and went to rob the tabernacle. As he was forcing open the door, a feeble voice from the dying child was heard: "Ah, don't touch Jesus Christ!" Opening the pyx, the traitor threw the Blessed Sacrament upon her bleeding body, saying: "There's Jesus Christ for you!" and putting the sacred vessel in his pocket, started with his bloodhound on the track of the priest.

(TO BE CONTINUED.)

For the Suffering Irish Children.

Edward Howard, 25 cts.; James Bannister, $1; Aloysius Kelly, $1; Fred. Farrelly, 25 cts.; A Friend, $1.50; Miss Nora McGetrick, $1; Miss Delia McGetrick, $1; A Friend, $1; John McVoy, Jr., $1; Alphonsus McVoy, $1; Angela McVoy, 60 cts.; Frank McVoy, 45 cts.; Eugene McVoy, 47 cts.; Nellie Weadley, 15 cts.; Kittie Weadley, 15 cts.; Mamie Banantine, 20 cts.; Josie McVoy, 25 cts.; Alfie Banantine, 5 cts.; Theodore Banantine, 5 cts.; Mary McVoy, $2.13; (Children of Mary's Relief Club, for Lady Fullerton, $12); Mrs. Margaret Warlaumont, $2; Mary Schnöbelen, 50 cts.; Joseph Schnöbelen, 25 cts.; Lizzie Schnöbelen, 25 cts.; Maggie Schnöbelen, 25 cts.; Henry Schnöbelen, 25 cts.; Lucy Schnöbelen, 25 cts.; Francis Schnöbelen, 25 cts.; Stella M. Agnew, 50 cts.; George R. Agnew, 50 cts.; Mervina A. Agnew, 50 cts.; A. Lee Agnew, 50 cts.; Mary McInerney, $1; John McInerney, $1; Thomas McInerney, $1; Julia McInerney, $1; William McInerney, $1; A Friend in New York, $3; Mrs. W. Downey, $1; A Reader, 50 cts.; Mary E. M., 50 cts.; Thomas F. M., 50 cts.; N. W., 10 cts.; Mary G. Kearney, $1; Mary Shilue, $1; James M. Shilue, $1; W. S. Shilue, 50 cts.; E. A. Shilue, 50 cts.; John Fitzgerald, 50 cts.; F. Fitzgerald, 50 cts.; A Friend, 50 cts.

THE AVE MARIA.

A Journal devoted to the Honor of the Blessed Virgin.

HENCEFORTH ALL GENERATIONS SHALL CALL ME BLESSED.—St. Luke, i, 48.

VOL. XVI.　　　NOTRE DAME, INDIANA, JUNE 5, 1880.　　　No. 23.

"Ring on, Sweet Angelus!"

BY MALCOLM DUNCAN.

WHEN the day begins to break,
　And the sleeping flowers awake,
There is joy in every humble heart where love of
　　you doth dwell;
　For you exorcise all pain,
　As the morning comes again,
And the cares of earth fast vanish at the pealing
　　of a bell,
　　Ring on, Sweet Angelus!

When, amid the day's turmoil,
Weary plodders cease their toil,
And the sun is just above us with its benison
　　and balm;
　Then a myriad of notes,
　From a host of feathered throats,
Vie with you in adding harmony to all the noon-
　　tide calm,
　　Ring on, Sweet Angelus!

When the dews begin to fall,
Like a fond good-night to all
We hear you—sweet reminder of a Mystery divine!
　Calling faithful ones to pray,
　Giving peace to end the day,
And soothing every penitent who lingers at a
　　shrine,
　　Ring on, Sweet Angelus!

As we hear your brave tones ring,
All the heavens seem to sing,
And the very world is jubilant with praises and
　　with prayer;
　And we lift our thoughts on high,
　Far above the starry sky,
While the mists of sin are scattered by the music
　　in the air!
　　Ring on, Sweet Angelus!

The Nature, Excellence and Advantages of Devotion to the Sacred Heart of Jesus.

BY REV. EDMUND J. O'REILLY, S. J.

TO the Heart of Jesus we owe intense affections of love and gratitude. These affections, when conceived, rest on a solid foundation. They spring from a deeply imbedded root. That root, that foundation is no other than our Faith, called by the holy Council of Trent the root and foundation of all justification, and consequently, we may infer, of all true Christian piety. These affections spring from our faith, developed and applied. We are, through the mercy of God, Catholics; and, as Catholics, we believe most firmly whatever the Holy Catholic Church believes and teaches. But our faith may be more or less explicit, more or less lively. Again, though our faith is raised above reason, it is by reason we are led to faith, and reason afterwards combines with faith, and aids us to deduce from it much that is helpful in our service of God. Faith and reason never really disagree, though faith teaches many things which reason alone would not discover. With the assistance, then, of faith and reason, let us consider the nature, the excellence, and some of the advantages of devotion to the Sacred Heart of Jesus.

First of all, we may ask, what is *the object* of this devotion? By object I mean, not exactly the end, or aim, or result of the devotion, but the thing to which it is directed. The object of the worship and honor—that which is worshipped and honored—is the Bodily Heart of our Lord—His Heart of flesh. Our Lord's Body, and every part of It, is entitled to supreme adoration, that adoration which is due to God alone; because, through the hypostatic or personal union of the Divine Word, the Second Person of the Blessed

Trinity, with an individual human nature, *the Man Jesus is God.* The humanity is indeed most really distinct from the Divinity. The two natures are in nowise confounded, nor fused into one; but the human nature belongs to the Divine Person. That particular human nature is His as much as my human nature is mine; it is a second, additional nature acquired by the Eternal Son of God. Ever since the stupendous Mystery of the Incarnation was effected in the womb of Mary, that human nature has been, and now is, and ever will be, truly the Human Nature of the Son of God, comprised, if we may so speak, within the range of His Divine Personality. It would be irrational to proclaim *that Man* to be God, to honor *that Man* as God, and yet to exclude from the honor thus paid the nature in virtue of which He is Man. What is true of the whole nature is true of its parts, the soul, the body, and the constituent portions of the body. We do not, and we may not, even mentally, *separate* our Lord's Humanity from the Divine Person, nor one part of His Humanity from the rest. We do not, and we may not, view, for instance, His Heart as something standing by itself, removed from His Body and His Person. Christ is a whole, not to be divided. But we may fix our attention specially upon one part; we may direct our thoughts and our feelings to one part for a time. Take the case of an artist, or any other observer, gazing on a large and complicated picture, he knows the picture is one, and he does not think of taking it to pieces, he would value it comparatively little in a state of dismemberment; yet he confines his view to some portion of the picture, and this often for no very brief space; he studies and admires this more immediate object of his inspection, not as a whole, but as a part which he could not sufficiently study and admire without this concentration and temporary narrowing of his attention. It is the same with a building; it is the same with landscapes, trees, and flowers; our powers of contemplation are limited, and must be concentrated in order to their thorough exercise. Our affections, too, are unable to take in at once the whole array of the objects which respectively belong to them: among those whom we love equally or unequally, whether naturally or supernaturally, we are forced to comparatively forget one while we are engaged with another.

The Heart of Jesus, then, is the object of this devotion—the Human Heart of Jesus, comprised in His humanity, united with the Divine Person, part of that wonderful whole—the Incarnate Son of God—not separable, even in our minds, from the rest of that whole, but specially dwelt upon as the immediate term of our appreciation, of our worship, of our love. But why the Heart of Jesus? why the Heart rather than any other portion of the humanity of Christ? Is there a motive for this selection?

No doubt there is a motive for the selection of the Heart; a motive which our reason recognizes, when once our faith has taught us who and what Christ our Lord is; when once we understand, as far as we can understand, the Incarnation, the Life of Christ, His Passion, the Redemption which He has wrought, the innumerable benefits He has bestowed upon men; a motive which our Infallible Guide, the Catholic Church, has recognized and acted upon in the sanction she has given to the worship and love of the Sacred Heart; a motive which our Lord has indicated in the Gospel. Divine faith, developed and applied by reason, affords this motive for honoring, in a special manner, the Heart of Jesus, and cultivating devotion towards it.

We find that, from the most ancient times of which we know anything, the human heart has been looked upon as the seat of our affections, and thus has come to be their symbol, their representative. To speak of the heart in a moral sense, is to speak of the affections, the highest as well as the lowest, the best and the worst. Even those affections which are the most bound up with intelligence, nay, intellectual acts—acts of the understanding, as distinct from the will—are sometimes attributed to the heart; and all this, not only in common intercourse, or in profane poetry or prose, but in the Sacred Scripture. There is scarcely a book in the Bible that does not contain one or more, often very many more, expressions to this effect. There are seventy-one books in our canon of the Old and New Testament, and in sixty-three of these the heart is spoken of in its moral signification. In the Gospel, among other passages, we have our Lord's testimony concerning Himself: "Learn of Me, because I am meek and humble of Heart." He, elsewhere, blames two of the disciples for being "slow of heart to believe." (Luke, xxiv, 25.) Again, He says (Matt., xv, 19), "From the heart come forth evil thoughts, murders, adulteries, fornications, thefts, false testimonies, blasphemies." But not to multiply particular illustrations, we may safely say there is the voice of the whole human race, confirmed by that of God, for the reference of various human sentiments to the heart. All men are agreed in viewing the heart as the symbol of all kinds of human affections, most of all of love. The heart is the symbol, the representative, figuratively the source, of all virtuous and vicious actions of the human will.

The Heart, then, of our Lord stands for the whole of His human virtues, sentiments, affections, and, above all, His love for us. The object of our worship is our Lord's Heart of Flesh as part of His Sacred Humanity, hypostatically united to His Divine Person, and, therefore, entitled to supreme adoration, while the motive, the ground, the reason for selecting especially this part as the object of our honor, and devotion, and love, is Its embodiment of our Lord's virtues and affections; and this manner of viewing the Heart is based on the common consent of mankind ratified and approved by Christ and by God. It would, therefore, be a great mistake to exclude from our worship the real Bodily Heart of Christ and to substitute a *mere* symbol, a sort of phantom. It would likewise be a great mistake in the opposite direction to view this object of our honor and love merely as a portion, *some* portion, *any* portion, of our Lord's Sacred Body. It is His physical Heart. It is, at the same time, the legitimate symbol of all that can attract us, all that can instruct us in His Humanity. Nay, more, it may be taken, and sometimes is taken, as a symbol of His Divine love for us, that eternal uncreated love which preceded and originated the Incarnation. However, the love and virtues of Christ as man are more obviously signified and symbolized by His Sacred Heart. Christ is truly God, but He is also truly Man. He is as truly a human being as any of us, as any of the millions of our race that are scattered over the globe. He is our model in His exterior conduct, He is our model in His interior sentiments as manifested by His outward actions, or ascertainable by legitimate inference from whatever natural or revealed knowledge we have of human nature. Behold here, then, the motive for dwelling especially on the Sacred Heart.

We come next to *the excellence* of that devotion. This excellence already shows itself in the nature of the devotion, as described. This excellence is inseparable from the excellence of Jesus Christ Himself. It is one with His excellence. The Heart of Jesus embraces the whole moral being of Jesus as Man. No bodily substance is in itself capable of affections or any kind of spiritual acts. But we view the Heart of Jesus as living, as animated by His Soul which is the real seat of all His human spiritual acts. We take in all the virtues of that most holy Soul. We are warranted in this by the voice of all men, and by the language of our Lord Himself.

munications to holy souls. These the Church, in some instances, recognizes and receives with favor, but never proposes to the belief of the faithful. Much less does she place them on the same footing with the Scripture and those public divine traditions which, together with the Scripture, have come down to us under the Church's guardianship from Christ and His Apostles, and constitute, so to speak, the storehouse whence our doctrines of Catholic Faith are drawn. So it is with the revelations received by Blessed Margaret Mary. They are trustworthy, they are in a high degree profitable; they afford us a reliable assurance of the excellence of devotion to the Sacred Heart. But we have for it a higher sanction still—the teaching and action of the Church herself in the institution of this festival, and the encouragement she affords us to cultivate the devotion at all times. Although the holy religious spoken of was employed by our Lord as an instrument for promoting the honor and worship of His Heart, this honor and worship does not rest on her word. It has an independent foundation in the doctrine of the Incarnation and Redemption.

This devotion is, of course, eminently supernatural. Still, it is eminently accommodated to our nature. Such is, throughout, the character of the supernatural order of things—of the Christian dispensation—of the Catholic religion. It perfects, and does not destroy nature. Our divine religion is not cold, abstract, repulsively formal. It has its forms, as all that is well ordered must have; but it is congenial to our natural being, which comes from the hand of the same omnipotent, all-wise, and all-bountiful Creator. Some would say that it is the craving of our nature which seeks to turn spiritual objects to its own account, and thus leads us into abuses. Grant, for a moment, that the craving of our nature has its share in the work. What then? Is that craving illegitimate? Is our whole nature so bad that whatever it desires must be wrong? But this use, this application of spiritual objects is not to be, by any means, principally attributed to our nature, though most fully in accordance with it. No: God has willed it, and His Church tells us so. His Church tells us how which indeed, even in its present form, is becoming old, though still comparatively modern. Devotions in themselves quite sound and solid are none the worse of this sort of newness; for newness and freshness are closely allied, and a legitimate novelty conduces to interest and fervor.

Neither is there anything narrow or weak in this devotion. The Heart of our Lord is surely noble in all Its affections, the noblest that ever beat in human breast. The noble Heart of the God-Man is far from being little. It has nothing in it small, or low, or trivial. There is not anything weak in this devotion. Some may connect the idea of affections, specially sensible, tender affections, with that of weakness. It is true there are affections and sensibilities which involve weakness; but this is not so with all sensible affections. What would become of mankind if all of them had to be condemned? Assuredly an unfeeling man or woman is no object of admiration or approval. St. Paul, speaking of a moral corruption that is to come "in the last days," enumerates among the vices of those whom he denounces that they shall be "without affection." (2 Tim., iii, 3.) On the other hand, let not those be alarmed who find themselves devoid of devotional *feeling*, though they would desire to have it, those for whom the Sacred Heart does not *seem* to have any attraction. Let them not be alarmed, because neither virtue nor prayer is dependent on sensibility, though it is a sweetening help to both. There are affections besides those which we call feelings —affections most pleasing to God—affections, namely, of the will. Dry they may be, devoid of sweetness, affording no soothing comfort, but not the less genuine and profitable on that account. Love, and sorrow, and gratitude, and desire, in a word the most complete devotion of the will, may exist without feeling. Indeed, mere superficial sensibilities, not having a deep source in the understanding and will, are worth but little. It is otherwise when they are, as it were, an overflow from those higher powers of the soul, though even then they are of but secondary importance. So much for the *excellence* of devotion to the Sacred Heart.

The chief *advantages* of devotion to the Sacred Heart are not far to seek. They are, to no small extent, apparent in what we have seen of the nature and excellence of the devotion. This devotion brings us into close union and contact with Jesus Christ. It helps to engage our minds with the thought of Him. It draws us towards Him. It enables us to realize Him more thoroughly. It rivets our attention on the examples of virtue which His human life affords. It endears to us all His teachings. "Learn of Me, because I am meek and humble of Heart." A common meaning given to these words is, that we are told to learn from the meekness and humility of our Lord's Heart to be ourselves like unto Him in these virtues. There can be no doubt that such is His desire and our duty; and it is fair to infer so much, at least, from the words. But is this their whole meaning? is this their direct meaning? Many, and not without reason, deny that it is so. Our Lord does not say, Learn of Me to be meek and humble of heart; nor does He say, Learn to *imitate Me* who am meek and humble of heart; but Learn of Me, *because* I am meek and humble of heart. Learn what? Learn everything that our Lord teaches. He had just said: "Take up My yoke upon you"; then, after the words in which He commends His meekness and humility, He says: "And you shall find rest to your souls, for My yoke is sweet, and My burden light." The whole yoke of Christ, the whole burden He places upon us, may be, and ought to be borne cheerfully, because He is meek and humble of Heart. His meekness and humility commend His whole teaching, His whole discipleship. He is not a hard task-master, He is not an oppressive exacter. He may demand of us occasional sacrifices, but what sacrifices did He not make for us! The great sacrifice of Calvary, and so many other afflictions and privations during His whole mortal life. And, then, what rewards has He not in store for us in the next life, and even in this, as a return for the little He requires us to endure. The knowledge and love of that meek and humble Heart will smooth our difficulties and sweeten our toils, greater or less as they may be.

This devotion blends itself with all the actions of those who thoroughly practice it, and thus serves as an admirable antidote to that secularist spirit which seeks to segregate religion from learning and from all temporal pursuits. The apostles of that dangerous system do not universally condemn religion; but would keep it apart from the interests of life, and drive it into a corner of its own. They would have us spend most of our days in forgetfulness of that God, in whom, according to St. Paul, in the Acts (xviii, 28), "we live, and move, and be." The devotion to the Sacred Heart combines with all our actions, and helps us to comply with the direction contained in those other words of St. Paul: "All whatsoever you do in word or in work, all things do ye in the name of the Lord Jesus Christ" (Col., iii, 17). This devotion, again, openly practised, involves a noble profession of devotedness to Jesus Christ in contradiction to that war which is made on Him and His Name. Our Lord is persecuted now as truly in Christian countries as He was in Judea when He said: "Saul, Saul, why persecutest thou Me?" (Acts, ix, 4). In Rome itself the most barefaced blasphemies are uttered and published against Him with impunity. The same is true in a greater or less degree of many countries. The Church, also is undergoing a fearful persecution in many parts of the world; and we cannot see when or where this persecution will end. The world, that world which our Lord so strongly denounced, is up and stirring, and banded well against Him, both openly and secretly. This is, then, a time when all Catholics ought to make the most uncompromising profession of their religion, of their fidelity to it, of their love for it, and for God, and for Jesus Christ. The enemies of our faith, many at least among them, scoff at devotion, and we glory in it—we glory in sound, solid, truly Catholic devotion, such as that towards the Sacred Heart, warranted to us by the Church, not in apocryphal fictions, even where they are otherwise innocent. We glory only in what is really wisdom, though the world may call it folly.

The warmth of this devotion is, likewise, a great consolation to us. In an inclement season, when storms are raging, and rain and snow falling, those who are safely sheltered in well built and well provided houses enjoy their security doubly, as contrasted with the bleak misery from which they are protected, and make much of the comforts by which they are surrounded. So it ought to be with us in the house of God—the Holy Catholic Church. We should gather round the Heart of Jesus a truly sacred and invigorating fire, the source of inestimable spiritual delights. We should make much of our safety, of our comfort, of our enjoyment as contrasted with the chaos of confusion and spiritual ruin by which the Church and we are encompassed without—not in a spirit of hatred against our enemies —not in a spirit of uncharitable triumph. No: we should desire to bring into this holy dwelling those who have the misfortune to be outside of its walls, and to make sharers of its blessings those who are fruitlessly within.

THE wonderful efficacy of the Rosary is daily demonstrated in all those who make use of the recitation of it, for the obtaining of special graces. Its sweet consolation soothes the broken-hearted, and cheers the grieving ones; it enlivens faith, inspires hope, and inflames charity. How sad, to think that countless numbers, claiming the Blessed Virgin for their mother, are so negligent in the recitation of the Rosary, that they do not even know how to recite it! The young of both sexes regard it as a sign of illiteracy to be caught at this devotion. Parents should begin early to make a contrary impression on the minds of their children, by having the daily exercise of the Rosary, at which the whole family should assist and answer to the prayers.—*Columbian.*

'Beth's Promise.

BY MRS. ANNA HANSON DORSEY.

CHAPTER XVI—(Continued).

HOW different the going back to "Elleralie" from their drive down to the lake! 'Beth felt that she had grown older, that a long, long time must have passed since she had met Bertie Dulaney that morning under the trees. But she felt that she must keep her trouble to herself; her mother should never be pained by knowing the sorrow that her promise had brought her, and she would bear it with courage for her sake. "But why?" was the refrain that kept up its sad echo in her heart, "why could not some one have told me? why, and how did it happen that Bertie Dulaney's profession was never spoken of, nor even hinted at? Oh, if I had only known!" It was not many days before she learned the reason.

As they turned into the avenue at "Elleralie," and the moment of their separation drew near, he turned and looked into her drooping eyes, into her face on which a shadow rested, and said: "Are you sure there's no little word you can say that I can hang a hope upon? It all seems so like a dream, I can't believe it."

"I cannot deceive you, I would not, Mr. Dulaney; I have said all there is to say," she answered, lifting her clear truthful eyes to his. "There's nothing left for us but to part and forget."

He helped her out of the phaeton, and clasping her hand closely, held it for a moment, as if it were hard to give her up, then dropping it, he walked rapidly away to go and hide himself out of sight where he could rally his manhood, his courage, and endurance to his aid, and it is not strange that his steps turned towards the chapel, which was generally deserted at that hour, and that kneeling there he reviewed his brief, happy dream, his dreary disappointment, and laid his heart bare before Heaven, asking strength and help to accept and bear his trial. He wanted to bear it like a man. He knew that he would have a struggle for it, that he would be tempted to seek forgetfulness in associations and scenes whose allurements he had always withstood; and there was nothing left for him but to place himself anew under the protection of the Blessed Virgin, and ask her to guide and succor him through the inexplicable and bitter strait in which he found himself. He shrank from joining the family party at lunch, because he knew that his brother and the girls would ask no end of questions as to how he had spent the morning, and how 'Beth was, and why he did not persuade her to come over with him; all interspersed with chaff and sly hints, which under other circumstances would have amused him, but would now be positive torture; and going round to the stable, he had his horse saddled, and telling the groom that he was going to the post-town, mounted, and dashed off into the road.

'Beth had gone up to her room with a heavy step, after Bertie Dulaney had left her, and, locking her door, she threw herself upon her bed and gave vent to her pent-up emotions by a passionate fit of weeping. "Let this strange, unforeseen sorrow that has come into my life, hurt only me, sweet and compassionate Mother! let mine be all the pain, and help me, thou to whom I was given when I first drew breath, that I may be strong and patient to bear my cross," she whispered between her sobs, knowing how futile human sympathy would be even if she confided her sorrow to any one. 'Beth's head ached; and it was no pretence when she declined going down to tea on that account. She was glad to be alone, after her mother and Aunt 'Beth, alarmed at her absence, had both come up to suggest no end of things for her relief, and gone away, hoping that she would fall asleep, and awake quite restored.

"I can't imagine what it is; she says she did not row, and they were not out long; but she certainly looks ill," said Mrs. Morley.

A night's rest will bring her round; so don't fret, Anne, my dear. Women will have headaches as long as the world stands. Come, I'm going to look after my bees. Lodo says that some of them have made honey as clear as crystal," and getting on their hats, they went off to inspect the hives.

Aunt 'Beth was getting back her old strength and courage; there was a faint color in her face, and the ring that they all liked to hear in her voice. Lodo believed "it was the strike at the iron works that had done it, because it took her out of herself and stirred her up." It helped, no doubt; but having her kindred with her, and enjoying 'Beth's youth and fine spirits, proud of her beauty and loving her with a strange tenderness, besides feeling responsible for Mrs. Morley's well-being and comfort, had from the first a good effect upon her, a mental stimulus which soothed while it invigorated.

The next morning 'Beth was down to breakfast, a little pale and quiet, as might have been expected after a headache, but "quite well," she told them. She busied herself among the flowers as usual, re-arranging fresh ones in the vases with beautiful taste, practised an hour or two, but sick at heart through it all; then she came and sat with her mother, reading aloud from the entertaining "Memoirs of the Duchess d'Abrantes," or talking with her, as she seemed most inclined, and the day passed much as other days, except that the cloud which had thrown its sudden shadow over her life gave her an indefinite sort of feeling that yesterday had been very long ago. She lay thinking all night instead of sleeping, and, looking squarely into the face of her trial, she made up her mind that, with God's help, she would do her best to live out her life without failure of the behests of such of its duties as lay before her. That which had happened was unforeseen, and, as it seemed unavoidable, there was neither blame nor reproach to be attached to anyone in the case; there was no help for it, and nothing to be done except to leave everything in the bands of God, and bear the sting it had given her in silence until such time as He should see fit to heal it. She felt that the hurt of what had happened would abide with her, but she hoped the Mother of Sorrows would help her to bear it without bitterness. The remembrance of the pain inflicted on Bertie Dulaney, and the sudden destruction of his hopes, sharpened the edge of her grief; but it was unforeseen; it was past, and would have to drift along and go down out of sight with other wrecks that are swept away on the current of life.

One day Mrs. Morley and 'Beth returned from a short drive and found the old lady of "Ellerslie" walking up and down, under the trees, in front of the house, where the lawn grass, kept evenly and closely shaved, was like velvet. It was her favorite place for that sort of exercise, and she had been there some time, wondering when they would get back. She turned quickly when she heard the wheels approaching, and stood watching them as they drove up.

"You drive very well, my child, and Peg looks as proud as if he had taught you," she said to 'Beth, when she drew up at the carriage step.

"He's such a knowing sort of a 'beastie,'" answered 'Beth, who had got out and stood smoothing his long nose with her soft hand, "that I should not be surprised if he did have some such thought. Mamma was a little bit afraid though, just at first."

"Yes; but my confidence increased as we went on, and I quite enjoyed it," said Mrs. Morley.

"I am glad of that," said Aunt 'Beth, who had called Lodo to drive the phaeton round to the stables, knowing how much it would delight her, and Peg trotted off with one of his absurd whinnys, which she answered with a ringing laugh, a duet so ridiculous as to amuse them all.

"Let us sit here a little while, Anne, it is so lovely, and it will rest you before going up. Pull that low chair forward, 'Beth darling, for your mother, and sit you here by me—there," said Aunt 'Beth, smoothing the girl's shining hair; then she put her hand under her chin, and holding up her face, looked tenderly, yet with scrutinizing glance into it. "Too pale! where are your roses? Fie upon you, to let one headache drive them away!"

"But I am very well, dear Aunt 'Beth,—indeed, I am, and my roses will come back by-and-by," she answered. "Have you been lonesome since we went away?"

"I might have been, but the Dulaneys have been over. I wondered what had become of them all, but it seems that they've had some trouble within a day or two which quite depressed them," said Aunt Beth, still fondling and smoothing the bright head at her knee; "and they told me something that surprised me very much."

"Something pleasant, I hope, as well as surprising," said Mrs. Morley. 'Beth's heart stood still; what was coming?

"Not so pleasant as one could have wished, for that handsome, delightful son of theirs, Bertie, went away, most unexpectedly, Tuesday evening. But that is not the strange part of it. It turns out that he is a naval officer, a lieutenant, and went to join his ship, which is ordered to China. I thought it was very remarkable that we had not had the slightest intimation of his belonging to the navy, and could not help expressing my surprise. Did you suspect it, Beth?"

"No," she answered, quietly.

"Mrs. Dulaney explained their silence on the subject by saying that they were all so happy to have him home again, after an absence of years in various parts of the world, that they had entered into an agreement among themselves, and made him promise too, not to refer to his profession in the remotest way during his leave, that they might be able to cheat themselves into the delusion that he belonged to them and would never go away again; and then,' said she, 'when Mrs. Morley and her daughter came, in deep mourning for their sad loss, which we had read of in the New York papers, we thought there were still greater reasons for making no allusion whatever to ships, or the sea, or the profession, lest it should revive painful thoughts in their hearts. But indeed, Miss Morley, I miss him dreadfully, and his going away was so sudden! I didn't dream of such a thing until he came down at tea-time and told us he had been packing his trunk to go away by the New York train that night to join his ship. We were so grieved that his father and I begged him to resign; his father even offered to make him perfectly independent by settling his portion upon him if he would only consent, but he said he loved the career he had chosen, and did not think it would be honorable to resign without some very important reason; he said, dear fellow! that he was sorry to grieve us by refusing, and hoped we'd both forgive him. And so, Miss Morley, we had to submit, he seemed so cut up and sorry.' Then I said what I could to comfort her, for tears were streaming from her eyes all the time we were talking. Mr. Dulaney had left us together and joined the young people in the music-room, to avoid the subject which his wife said he felt very keenly."

"I am very sorry for them," said Mrs. Morley, glancing at 'Beth, who sat looking down at the dancing, flickering shadows of the leaves on the grass, her face quite pale, and about her lips and the corners of her mouth a rigid, drawn expression in place of the smile that usually dimpled them.

"I liked the young fellow very much," continued Aunt 'Beth, "and his going off in that way is incomprehensible, as his leave, his mother told me, would not expire for two weeks. Young people are so capricious nowadays, there's no counting on them from one day to another. I suppose he found it dull here after roving all over the world. Did he tell you he was going away that evening—the day, you know, that you drove to the lake, 'Beth?"

"No——, but, mamma, do you not feel chilly? I'll go up and get your shawl," said 'Beth, hurrying in; she felt that she could bear to hear no more about Bertie Dulaney and his going away, so she went upstairs and, after bathing her head, sat down at the window to compose her mind.

"But," continued Aunt 'Beth to Mrs. Morley, "I suppose he must have got his letters by the afternoon mail ordering him off. He would never have been so discourteous as to go without saying good-by to us had he been known it in time. Only think of his mother not seeing him again for three years! I must go over in the morning to see her."

It was all plain to Mrs. Morley; a sudden pang had wrung her heart while Aunt 'Beth was talking, and her eyes had almost involuntarily sought her child's face, where she saw a confirmation of her fears. She remembered the promise she had urged her to make before coming to "Ellerslie," hoping to shield her life from possibilities which had so bitterly darkened her own. She had watched Bertie Dulaney's devotion to 'Beth; the signs of his love were unmistakable to her keen perception, and she likewise noted that 'Beth accepted, and was pleased with his attentions, and happy in his society. She was sure that he had offered himself the day they went to the lake, and that 'Beth had discarded him when he revealed his profession to her. She remembered the joyousness of their going, and the silence of their return, and how 'Beth had gone directly up to her room with slow steps, making no allusion whatever to their drive afterwards, and, to crown all, his sudden departure, and the pale quiet which had since then settled upon her face, as if some insidious disease were eating away the springs of her life.

"Oh, if I only *knew* that it were not so, and that she does not care for him," thought the poor mother, "I should be so thankful! Oh, my child, my child! has a sorrow like this come into your young life! But who could foresee it?" Very tenderly she spoke to, and kissed 'Beth that night, but made no reference to what was troubling her; she felt that she had no right to intrude on a confidence that was so carefully guarded, and on a pain that she had no power to soothe.

"Wake me in time to go to Mass with you, dear mamma," said 'Beth, as her mother turned to go into her own room. She had not been to Mass since that day on the lake, or near the chapel to say her beads; she had feared meeting Bertie Dulaney, not dreaming that he had gone away that very night. But she could go now, and she felt that there, at least, she could pray for courage to bear her cross at the very feet of Him who alone could give her help. Her life and its duties were before her; she could not let this strange trial, which seemed to have dropped upon her from the clouds, prey upon her mind until she grew morbid and helpless to rise superior to it. She had made a solemn promise, which, having appealed to God to witness, she must keep faithfully, and with His help and the help of the Blessed Virgin Mother, outlive without vain regrets all that had happened to disappoint and embitter her existence. Henceforth she must look forward, and in time "let the dead past bury its dead." These were the thoughts that were gradually—not all at once—evolved in her heart from the pain of the blow that had stricken it, showing a pure, sound nature and a true, noble will, which would in time, with the blessing of Heaven, reward her efforts with success.

Mrs. Morley never made but one attempt to sound 'Beth's silence. Some two weeks later, when they were alone one evening in the dusk, wandering arm and arm amongst the flaming sumachs and the great spicy chrysanthemums, whose white and crimson flowers filled the air with pungent aromas, she said:

"'Beth, my child, will you tell me something?"

"Anything that I can tell you, dear mamma—yes," said the girl, with a startled look.

"Did Bertie Dulaney ever tell you that he cared for you?"

"We will not speak of him, dear mamma, if you please," she answered, speaking low.

"Tell me then, my 'Beth, tell me this: are you happy? Answer me truly, my child."

"I have you, precious mamma, why should I not be? You and I are all to each other," she said, clasping her mother close in her arms.

And Mrs. Morley never referred to the subject again. Even if it were as she supposed, it was better for 'Beth to suffer an early disappointment like this, than live to endure such agonies as had come to her own lot, she thought, and tried to be content, hoping that time would wear off the sharp edge of the trial, and that 'Beth would yet find happiness that would more than compensate her for all. How often she wished they had not come to "Ellerslie," or that they had come earlier, or deferred it later, thereby avoiding Bertie Dulaney; but how could they, when Aunt 'Beth had so much need of them, and how could the wildest imagination ever have dreamed of such a thing as had happened in the course of real, everyday life? Then she thought it would be better to go home. They had stayed longer already than they had intended, and as Aunt 'Beth was now quite well, there was no reason why they should not return; she was sure the change would be good for 'Beth, and knew that Father Thomas would cheer them and give them enough to do to divert her mind from its sadness. She mentioned it to 'Beth one morning on their way from Mass, who said: "Yes, mamma, I shall be glad to get home. I'm afraid it is getting too frosty for you up here." Oh, how tender and loving she was to her mother, redoubling her attention to every little need, guarding her own words and looks lest she should ever suspect the sacrifice she endured for her dear sake! being willing rather to die than add even a feather's weight of care to her heart which had already been so long and so sorely stricken.

Aunt 'Beth opposed their going away from "Ellerslie" until after Christmas. "What shall I ever do without you both?" she asked again and again. Of course it was a pain to them to leave her, but they told her it was necessary, although neither of them could explain why. Certain business letters from her lawyer reached Mrs. Morley one morning really demanding her personal attention, a tangible and practical reason, to which Aunt 'Beth was satisfied to yield. That night she slipped a little package into 'Beth's hand when she kissed her "good-night," and whispered: "Your father's last Christmas gift, my child. I found it in his chest—that time, you know, when his things came home—marked for his 'little 'Beth' and took it out to keep for you, until the first wild grief of our hearts had subsided a little. It is a beautiful locket, set round with large pearls. You must wear it for his dear sake. I will speak to your mother about it tomorrow, and I know she will be glad of what I did."

"I am so thankful to get it! I have often wished for some little personal memento of my dear father, and this is like a message from him," said 'Beth, pressing it close to her heart.

"Yes, it is a message; 'For my dear little 'Beth' is on the wrapping in his own hand-writing; not that you were really little, my dear, but he very often expressed his love by using this diminutive." Aunt 'Beth kissed her tenderly, and then said: "It was a great disappointment to me, your not fancying Bertie Dulaney, my child. He used to remind me of your father somehow, and it would have suited so well for you to have lived at 'Tracy-Holme' until you came into possession at 'Ellerslie.'"

"Aunt 'Beth, I had no idea that you were so romantic! I am going to follow exactly in your footsteps, and never change my name," said 'Beth, with a little laugh that veiled the sudden heartache she felt. Good-night, darling! I suppose mamma is sound asleep."

(TO BE CONTINUED.)

Safe in the Fold.

(Sent to a Postulant in a Convent of Mercy.)

BY ELIZA M. V. BULGER.

"He calleth His own sheep by name."—*John*, x, 3.

Safe at last within the fold,
Sheltered from the storm, the cold!
   How like a dream
   Doth it now seem,
That wild and dreary desert wold!

O Pastor kind! O Shepherd true!
There is no friend on earth like You;
   'Twas Love divine,
   Not worth of mine,
That placed me 'mid the chosen few.

How weary was I when you came!
Despair had well-nigh quenched Hope's flame;
   But your dear Voice
   Bade me rejoice;
You sought me, calling me by name!

No more a wanderer will I roam,
'Mid winding pathways far from home,
   For Saviour, dear,
   Your presence *here*
Will guard me through the years to come.

Safe in the sheltering fold at last,
Down at Your feet, dear Lord, I cast
   My thankful heart,
   From You to part
No more till life itself is past.

But there's a pasture still unseen,
The fields of Heaven forever green;
   Come, kindly guide,
   The way is wide,
Time and eternity between!

Sanctuary of Our Lady of "La Barca" in the Town of Muggia, Corunna.

BY REV. JOACHIM ADAM.

FROM the very beginning of the world, men desired to see realized the idea of Redemption, which Divine Mercy allowed to be hoped for even at the very moment when He fulminated that terrible sentence against our first progenitor and his race. There, in the same place where sin was committed, resounded the first promise of a Saviour; there, appeared the first light of hope to him who had disinherited himself of his right to heaven; and there, side by side with the great figure of the Messiah, who had to repair all with His Blood, was seen the figure of the wonderful woman whose destiny was to wage war against the enemy of the human race, crushing his head by the Fruit of her womb. From those remote times, that admirable figure, that abyss of grace, that mark of all the ages—Mary, according to the language of St. Bernard, instead of vanishing from the memory of men, became more known in proportion as the prophecies were proclaimed.

Jeremias, moved by the Holy Spirit, enthusiastically exclaims: " Rejoice ye in the joy of Jacob, ... for the Lord hath redeemed Jacob, and delivered him out of the hand of one that was mightier than he.... and they shall come, and shall give praise in Mount Sion ... for the Lord hath created a new thing upon the earth: *A woman shall compass a man!*" (Jerem., ch. 31.)

Isaias also, divinely inspired, penetrates the distant future, and cries out: "There shall come forth a rod out of the root of Jesse, and a flower shall rise up out of his root, and the Spirit of the Lord shall rest upon him.... Behold a Virgin shall conceive, and bear a Son, and He shall be called Emmanuel." (Is., ch. 7, 14.)

We will not detain ourselves longer at present in quoting other prophecies of the Old Testament, for the reason that in other parts of our narrative we shall occupy ourselves with them, whilst relating pious legends. We wish only to remind our readers that the idea of a Virgin-Mother was the incessant theme of the prophecies of the Old Testament.

After four thousand years had elapsed since the promise made in Eden, the fulness of time having arrived, the divine oracles were fulfilled. The daughter of Juda, the illustrious stem of the House of David, the precious child, object of the sighs and desires of the patriarchs and prophets, was born in Nazareth—a daughter to Joachim and Anne, who for a long time had lamented her barrenness. As reward of their great virtues and perfect conformity to the will of God, they deserved to possess her who was to be the greatest and holiest of all creatures after her Son—conceived without stain of sin, all pure and immaculate. Her name is Mary, which means "Star of the Sea." In fact, she is the star that guides us to a port of safety. The angel proclaimed her *full of grace*; the mother of the Baptist pronounced her *blessed amongst women;* the martyrs in the amphitheatre of Rome uttered the name of Mary after that of Jesus on the very spot where abject slavery had but a moment before bowed to a cruel tyrant with that exclamation, "*Morituri te salutant!*" "those about to die, salute thee."

One day St. Bridget asked the Blessed Virgin what occupation she had in heaven; to which our Lady made answer, "I ask mercy for the wicked and miserable." Throughout the entire world, the salutary effects of her protection are felt; but Spain, privileged above other nations, testifies to her protection with thousands of temples and monuments erected to her honor. Among these is the celebrated Sanctuary of "La Barca"—Our Lady of the Bark, where a stone is seen moving at certain times without any apparent cause.

The town of Muggia, pertaining to the province of Corunna, and to the archbishopric of Santiago, is 13¼ leagues distant from the former, and 10 leagues from the latter. It is protected on the north by a high rock covered with sand. Here stands the celebrated Sanctuary of Our Lady of "La Barca." The stone of which I speak, stands in a parallel position with regard to the other rocks about it, and moves by itself. A great deal has been said and written concerning this wonderful phenomenon; some criticize the reverence and faith of those who see in this fact the miraculous workings of Divine Providence, yet very unwisely, since so-called scientists and wise ones have thus far failed to otherwise explain how the motion is caused. We have tried to get authentic information concerning the Sanctuary of Our Lady of "La Barca" and the movement of the stone. We are indebted to the writings of D. Luciano Ros, a professor of law, who has made every possible research to satisfy the curiosity of the devotees of this sacred shrine. He states that the Blessed Virgin appeared upon the moving stone to St. James; some writers have tried to prove that she appeared to the Apostle at Saragossa; perhaps she may have appeared in both places.

Upon this rock, looking towards the sea, and moving itself at certain times, it is said that the Blessed Virgin appeared, and that the miraculous motion is a token of respect for Our Blessed Lady. Unbelievers attribute it to superstition, but we do not assert that the movement of the stone is miraculous; it may be caused by some effect of nature unknown to us. We shall occupy ourselves first by speaking of the Sanctuary, small indeed in size, but celebrated by the many miracles wrought therein.

It has been asserted by some that this hermitage was founded in the year 35 A. D., while others place it in the 16th century. Our author admits neither of these assertions, but proves the apparition of the Blessed Virgin to St. James. Listen to his argument: "Many writers have ventured to explain this apparition. The Armenian Breviary is supposed to have been written A. D. 636; in it we find that St. James entered into Galicia, where he preached and ministered for a time, till the Blessed Virgin appeared to him, and commanded him to return to Jerusalem, which he did."

Some will oppose this proof, on the ground that it does not make mention of Muggia; but no town of this ancient kingdom, nor "Tria Flavia," (the Padron of to-day) where the apostle resided and performed numerous miracles, lay claim to such a privilege. Walfrido, who wrote in the middle of the eleventh century, refers to the apparition in these words: "*In Mari Callaico Artebrarum, apparuit B. V. Maria Beato Jacobo, in cymba lapidea.*" "In the sea of Galicia, in the promontory Artabra, on a boat of stone, the Blessed Virgin Mary appeared to St. James the Apostle." In many pictures, the apostle was represented kneeling in the garb of a pilgrim, before the image of Our Lady of "La Barca." Philip V, approving the Constitutions of the Royal Congregation of St. James in 1742, after speaking of the antiquity of Duyo on Cape Finistere, says: "Finally, at a very short distance from this place is venerated the sacred spot on which the Blessed Virgin, while yet in her mortal life, appeared to the Apostle St. James, in whose memory there still remains a memorial of that Queen, under the name of 'La Barca.'"

Have we forgotten the recent apparition of the Blessed Virgin at Lourdes? No Catholic questions it, since it happened in our own days, and is a visible sign. Why, then, should we not give the same credence to Our Lady of "La Barca"? To believe this apparition false, it should have been proved so at the time it is said to have happened; but there were present those who could contradict such a proof; if it was invented afterwards, why do not the writers of those centuries say anything against the falsity? What interest could they have had in asserting that the Blessed Virgin appeared at Muggia rather than at any other place? By tradition, the Apparition of Our Lady to St. James was preserved fresh in the memory of those living in those days, and if we deny the value of tradition, we deprive ourselves of one of the best means of ascertaining many ancient and true events.

We cannot assert the antiquity of the first hermitage, though it is believed to be built in the same spot where the present sanctuary of "La Barca" stands. History and tradition keep profound silence concerning the origin of this name or title. The faithful gave the name of Bark (Barca) to the stone where the Blessed Virgin is said to have appeared, and probably for this reason the same name was given to the image and sanctuary. The sanctuary is situated in the district of the township of Muggia, in the ancient kingdom of Galicia, province of Corunna and in the diocese of Santiago, at the foot of the mountain Corpino, in a place called "Las Cruces," at a distance of 555 metres from the town, and about 50 from the sea.

Towards the end of the fourteenth and the beginning of the fifteenth century, a question arose to determine the parish in which the said sanctuary should be situated; the Archbishop of Santiago finally decided to place it under the supervision of the parish priest of Muggia. By these documents, we see that the chapel existed in the twelfth or thirteenth century. The present chapel, in which many have been restored to health, was not erected till the year 1710.

The image is small, being only twenty inches high, with the Holy Infant on the right arm; our sovereign Lady is sustained by a cherubim on a bark, with two angels rowing and another at the rudder. The Popes have enriched the sanctuary with spiritual blessings. Clement XI, in 1718, granted a Plenary Indulgence to those who would visit the sanctuary. Pius VI, in 1777, granted a similar indulgence, and many partial ones. The principal celebration is held on the Feast of the Holy Name of Mary, which falls on the Sunday within the octave of her Nativity.

Now we shall relate something of the stone, its movement, and the cause of it. We have not visited this wonderful place, but we will follow our guide, the learned Mr. Roa.

"The stone of 'La Barca,'" says he, "seen without the light of faith, is as the sacred wood of the Cross, contemptible or indifferent to profane eyes. This shapeless mass near the sea is distant N. W. from the chapel 54 metres, placed upon rocks with a convex shape and with three points. It is very close to another stone which it touches in its movements. Its circumference is a little more than 109 feet. Viewed from the lower part, it seems to be separated from the rock where it rests, and no contact is noticed except where it has the point of prop. When it moves, you can observe with some difficulty that it has a point or socle where it turns, and that is in the under rock. We have observed the following phases: 1st, It has its point of prop from east to west in a semicircular shape. 2d, That the movement takes place in an oblique direction. 3d, That it moves spontaneously without the action of any known motor, without any person upon it; sometimes with many people upon it, it can be moved from north to south; other times, twenty men or more cannot move it. When it moves, you can increase its motion by applying force. 4th, That it does not communicate its motion to another rock which it touches. Finally, I do not consider the sun nor the moon, heat or cold, the sea or the tide as the causes of its movement. These are the principal results we have been able to find out after careful investigation."

Some hold that a certain quantity of the sea-water penetrates into the stone and causes the motion; others attribute it to the changes in the weather; again others assert that the stone being in equipoise, can be moved only by a strong force; others think it one of those oscillating stones to which the Celts paid divine honors; finally, the people in general believe that the movement is miraculous. It is absurd to say that the waters of the sea can move it, for they have no way of approaching it; neither can we attribute it to the changes in the weather, since the movement would necessarily be in accordance with the variations of the atmosphere, but the contrary is the case. If it is because the stone is equally balanced, how is it that it sometimes moves, when alien force is applied to it, and at other times not?

The above quoted author Mr. Roa, does not pretend to assert that the motion is miraculous, but he does not dare to deny it, and says only that thus far no one has been able to explain the real cause of it. But we can assert that not only men extremely pious, but also of those liberal minds, have recognized a supreme power in the motion of the stone; amongst them we may mention the illustrious Jovellanos in his oration before the institute of natural sciences, 1846.

We will finish these remarks concerning Our Lady of "La Barca" and the mysterious stone, by quoting once more Mr. Roa: "His Eminence Cardinal Garcie Cuerte, Archbishop of Santiago, came to the Sanctuary of Our Lady of "La Barca" on the 15th of July, at 6 o'clock p. m., he went to see the stone of "La Barca," accompanied by a large concourse of people, and in spite of a great force of men applied, the stone remained immovable. At 7 o'clock on the following morning his Eminence was going to the chapel to say Mass, when two persons had the curiosity to go and try the stone, and observing that it moved, they ran to inform the secretary of the Cardinal who went to see its movements, and said, 'Do you know that to-day we are celebrating the Feast of Our Lady of Mount Carmel?' This remark of the secretary confirms the pious belief, that the stone moves on all feasts of Our Lady and even on many Saturdays. The Cardinal learning the fact, and the noise of the stone being heard, his Eminence went to see it. He observed it moving, now with persons upon it, now without them and with very little force. This wonderful occurrence must have moved his Eminence, since in the Parish Book he testified the above fact and signed his name."

Let us hope that Our Lady of "La Barca" will move the hearts of some obstinate sinners, more hardened than the mysterious stone of Muggia.

[*From the London Weekly Register.*]

Germany and the Holy See.

The negotiations between the Vatican and the German Government are wisely kept secret because of the intricate nature of their subject. From what has already been published, we may judge that great advances have been made towards obtaining the freedom of the Church from the May Laws; but in consequence of the stubborn attitude assumed by some statesmen at Berlin, there are still vast difficulties barring the way to peace. The steps towards conciliation, definitely made public, are, that in regard to the vacant places of priests, now numbering nearly nine hundred, the right has been given to the Bishops to name candidates for them, subject to the approval of the Government; that the Bishops are submitting lists of three candidates for each vacant cure, and that the Holy See is negotiating with the Government in support of such lists furnished by the Bishops exiled on account of the May Laws, since those Bishops were, and remain, approved by Rome, and that the Prussian Cabinet is considering the advisability of suspending the May Laws, at least for a time. It is to be noted that the letter of concession was addressed by the Holy Father to Mgr. Melchers, Archbishop of Cologne, so that, in accepting the message, the Government had to receive it from the hands of one of the exiled Bishops. The move of conciliation thus made by the Holy See is in no sense, as has been falsely asserted, the granting of the main point of the May legislation; it is merely the conferring on the State a privilege of *veto*, which has been given again and again to the civil power in various countries. For another false rumor—that Leo XIII, unlike Pius IX, is prepared to go any length for the sake of peace with the European Governments—the best answer is to be found at Berlin itself; and it is an answer that applies equally to the taunt that the Catholic deputies, the Centre party, were willing to sell themselves body and soul, in their voting power, to appease the Government. The current report at Berlin is that Prussian politicians are causing the halt in the negotiations, because Rome gives only the prospect of conciliation, and does not make a compromise—an impossible compromise—between the May Laws and the conscience of the clergy. At the same time the Government takes umbrage at the action of the Catholic party, which, both in the Landtag and in the Reichstag, has refused to sell that liberty of action without which political life becomes a culpable slavery. Berlin gossip, coming sometimes from high sources, maintains that the party of the Centre has its orders secretly and individually imparted from Rome, and that by opposition on all questions, and alliance with the Socialists, the Catholics hope to worry the Government into submission. Of course such a rumor is nothing but an ignorant and malicious falsehood. The truth appears clearly in one glance at the policy of the Centre. Going back to last year, the Tariff Bill was passed with the substantial help of Catholic votes, because it was believed to be of service to the home-trade of the country, and because in all that is truly serviceable the Catholic party were and are willing to support a Government which is inclined to redress their wrongs. Such a method of judgment guided their vote on the army budget, which they opposed through a real, as opposed to a boastful, patriotism, in order to lessen the burdens of a people crushed under tax and conscription. The Drink License Bill parted them again from the Government; upon such a question, whether in Germany or in England, the Catholic vote would be utterly distinct from all calculations of policy. The Polish Question made another divergence between the Centre and the Government. The Railway Question and the Provincial Police Bill were subjects of more purely local interest, but we may judge by analogy from the rest that the vote of the Centre was merely given to the side that seemed most just and beneficial in their judgment; that it would willingly have been given in union with the Government if that were possible, and more willingly because of the attempted reconciliation; but that even reconciliation in prospect could not bias Catholic judgment so far as to make it blind to the actual fitness or unfitness of the measures under discussion. The great accusation thrown in the face of the Catholic Deputies is that they are in alliance with the Socialists. The calumny is so unreasonable, so monstrous, that the wonder is, not so much that it has come into being, as that anyone free from the most ignorant prejudices can be found to believe it. Yet there are Prussian statesmen who show themselves beyond the pale of reason by declaring that the Church is herself rendering peace impossible by the alliance of Catholics with the enemies of all order. The foundation of this slander is simple. The Catholic vote was given against the rigorous anti-Socialist measures, since it was clear that the tool then used with iron harshness for the repression of Socialism might be used to-morrow for the repression of Catholicism. This reason was plainly stated at the time. Nor is the real attitude of the Centre unknown, for even now the Press of our own country is openly stating that the fearful strength of Socialism in Germany is due to the destruction of ecclesiastical teaching authority and religious belief. In other words, it is due to the persecution of the Catholic Church. The hesitating German Government itself knows full well that the abrogation of the May Laws would be as great a blow as it could aim at Socialism.

THERE is but one real antagonist of the world, and that is the faith of Catholics: Christ set that Faith up, and it will do its work in the world, as it has ever done, until He comes again.—*Cardinal Newman.*

THE Holy Scriptures are a sublime fragment-truth which Protestants took with them when they left the Church. The soul that seeks a full knowledge of the truth, can never consider itself in possession of it simply because it has the Bible. Objective confirmation of the truth is necessary safely to repose in the faith. —*Countess Hahn-Hahn.*

Catholic Notes.

—An interesting festival was recently held at Montserrat, to celebrate the thousandth anniversary of the famous miraculous statue of Our Lady preserved there.

—Mgr. Massaja, Vicar-Apostolic of Abyssinia, who was thrown into prison there, has been released through the intervention of Leo XIII with the Christian powers.

—Rev. Henry M. Roth and Rev. Charles Lemper were elevated to the dignity of the priesthood by Rt. Rev. Bishop Dwenger on the 23d ult., in the Cathedral of Fort Wayne.

—We are under obligations to Rev. Father Brady, of the Church of the Annunciation, St. Louis, Mo.; also to Mr. McCloskey, of Fall River, Mass., for kind services to our travelling agent.

—A Sister of St. Vincent de Paul died lately in France, at the civil hospital in Versailles, in the ninety-first year of her age, having been an attendant of the sick there for over seventy years.

—A fearful famine is devastating Persia, on account of which a great many Christians have left that country. The extent of this plague may be judged from the fact that wheat is sold for the equivalent of $800 a bushel.

—The publishing house, Herder, of Freiburg, has lately received a special mark of encouragement from Leo XIII, who presented its managers, Hutter & Rees, with a silver memorial medal stamped with a bust of his Holiness.

—We are glad to have another $200 to send to Ireland this week. The one who wished some time ago to send us a suit of clothes for some poor sufferer, may do so. Doubtless we shall hear of a chance during the summer to send it free of cost.

—A most valuable historical curiosity has been discovered by a peasant in France. It consists of a piece of gold chain, part of a necklace, bearing on one side the monogram of Queen Bathilde, wife of Clovis II, and on the other the head of Christ with an inscription.

—THE PASSION PLAY—"The Passion Play," which takes place every ten years at Oberammergan (Bavaria), was commenced on the 17th of May; at the first representation 5,000 persons were present; a great number of strangers, among whom were many English and Americans, assisted at this world-renowned play.

—Gambetta's aunt (Rose Gambetta) died lately at Nimes. She was the housekeeper of a priest, Canon Ailhaud, and preferred working thus, to asking her unworthy nephew for help. "I pray God to enlighten and convert him," said she, "but I will ask nothing from him."—*Indo-European Correspondence.*

—During the Octave of the Feast of Our Lady of Consolation at Luxemburg, as many as 36,933 pilgrims visited the shrine of the miraculous picture. The Octave closed with the usual grand procession, swelled, as in past centuries, by thousands of the Children of Mary from all parts of the Grand-Duchy of Luxemburg and the neighboring countries.

—ROYAL FAITH.—The imperial family of Austria assisted on Whit-Sunday at a touching family feast. Mary Valeria, the youngest of the imperial princesses, received Holy Communion for the first time, in the chapel of the palace. Their majesties the Emperor and Empress also approached the holy table with their daughter, thus giving to all families a sublime example, which is truly worthy of imitation.

—Two more cases of cure in proof of the reality of the apparitions at Knock, have come under the notice of a London priest, and are reported in the *London Universe.* One is that of a child whose eyes had been diseased from birth, who, taken to Knock by her mother, returned perfectly cured; and the other case, that of a man, declared by medical men to be hopelessly suffering from cancer in the face, was cured after a *triduo*, during which cement from the chapel at Knock was applied.

—An antique Catholic pectoral cross was dug up last week by a laboring man, now employed on a building job at Hampstead, this relic being disinterred in the neighborhood of the Addison-Road, at Kensington. The object in question is a little cross, which he at first thought was only pewter, and which appeared to have belonged to a rosary. On closer inspection, however, it turned out to be a pectoral cross of silver, bearing on one side the legend, "*Caritas Christi urget nos,*" and on the other a well-executed figure of the Blessed Virgin with the Divine Infant in her arms.—*London Weekly Register.*

—CATHOLIC MISSIONS IN AFRICA.—Nineteen missionaries are occupied in the missionary field of equatorial Africa. Five of these have established themselves at Ouganda on the Nyanza, since February 1879; they were received at the court of the powerful King Nitesa, who aided them to the full extent of his power. Four are at Oujiji, on the Tanganika, and occupy the thickly populated country of Ouroundi. The ten others, who left Zanzibar last year, are at present establishing new stations in this same region of the Great Lukei. Another expedition, consisting of more than twenty members, with Father Guyot at their head, will soon leave France to take part in this difficult but very promising mission.

—A poor Irish woman went to a venerable priest in Boston last week, and asked him to forward to Ireland her help for the famine sufferers. "How much can you spare?" asked the priest.

"I have a hundred dollars saved," she said, "and I can spare that."

The priest reasoned with her, saying that her gift was too great for her means; but she was firm in her purpose. It would do her good to know that she had helped a little; she could rest happier thinking of the poor families she had saved from hunger and death. The priest received the money with moistened eyes.

"Now, what is your name," he asked, "that I may have it published?"

"My name?" said she, counting over her money; "don't mind that, sir. Just send them the help—and God will know my name."—*Pilot.*

—A GRACEFUL OFFERING TO IRELAND.—The generous and enterprising Catholic publisher, Mr. P. O'Shea, of New York, has in press for immediate publication a new volume of poems by Miss Eleanor C. Donnelly. It is intended as a premium book for schools and colleges, and is offered as a gift to the Irish Famine Fund. Mr. O'Shea generously gives his services as publisher free of all charge. The volume, which is to be entitled, "Legend of the Best Beloved, and Other Poems," will be published in a rich octavo volume, in a style that shall be worthy of the sacred cause to which it has been so generously devoted. The volume will be printed on heavy toned paper with a red border-line, and will be elegantly and uniquely bound with chaste and appropriate symbolic decoration. Terms to clergymen colleges and academies, and to all who order six or more copies, $1; to others, $1.50. All orders should be addressed to Mr. P. O'Shea, No. 37 Barclay St., New York.

—About a year ago an eight-page weekly journal, called the *New York Catholic*, was started in New York city. It had a brief life of fourteen numbers, when, through lack of support, it was forced to suspend. These fourteen numbers contain, complete, the excellent story of "Sybilla: a Tale of the Days of St. Patrick," by Wm. Collins; much matter of practical use to Catholics; choice information about and selections from Catholic literature; and perhaps more actual news concerning the Church than was ever before published in one paper during the same length of time. The editor has on hand several hundred copies of each issue, and will send a set of the paper to anyone sending him 25 cts. in postage stamps. This sum is little more than sufficient to pay the postage on the paper, and affords a splendid opportunity to obtain a large amount of excellent Catholic reading matter for a small sum. Address, Eliot Ryder, Cobleskill, Schoharie Co., N. Y.

—The modest but learned religious, R. P. Dom Berengier, O. S. B., has received a most consoling recompense from his Holiness Pope Leo XIII, for a work on the missions of his order, by a brief, which we take pleasure in reproducing:

"To our beloved son, Theophilus Berengier, Religious of the Order of St. Benedict.

"Dear son, health and apostolic benediction:—We have received the homage of your letter with a copy of the volume you have published under the title of *La Nouvelle Nursie*. We praise, beloved son, the thought you have had to make known, for the glory of God's name and the edification of the faithful, the apostolic labors to which the Benedictine monks with constancy devote themselves in Western Australia, in order to spread there the reign of Christ. We have no doubt but that it will be agreeable to us to read your work, if at any time the cares of our pontificate should give us the leisure to do so. Meanwhile we express to you our gratitude; we implore from the bottom of our heart, the aid and the protection of the Lord for your *confrères*, who are laboring with so much zeal in those distant countries, that their labors may produce each day more abundant fruits, and we grant with pleasure, both to you and to them, as a pledge of the heavenly favors, and of our paternal affection, the apostolic benediction.

"Given at Rome at St. Peter's, on the third day of April, 1880, in the third year of our pontificate.

"LEO XIII. POPE."

—English-speaking Catholics everywhere will learn with regret the news of the death of the veteran Catholic publisher, Mr. John Murphy, of Baltimore, which sad event occurred at the Carrolton Hotel in that city, on the 27th ult. Mr. Murphy was born in Ireland, but came to this country when only ten years of age. After securing a common school education, at the age of sixteen he went to Philadelphia and learned the printing business. On attaining his majority he went to Baltimore, and in 1835 assumed the superintendence of a job-printing establishment. In 1837 he formed a partnership with William Spalding, and they conducted the printing business together until 1639, when the firm was dissolved, and the business was continued by Mr. Murphy, who then combined with it the publishing and stationery business. His publications were chiefly standard Catholic books. The "Proceedings of the Plenary Council of Baltimore," which he published in 1866, were executed in such superior style that Pope Pius IX, to whom a copy had been sent, conferred on Mr. Murphy, with his blessing, the honorary title of Printer to the Pope. The deceased was a man of great worth, and was highly esteemed by all who knew him. R. I. P.

—LOURDES.—"Through the kindness of Rt. Rev. Eugene O'Connell, D. D.," says *The Catholic Sentinel*, "we have been favored with the perusal of a letter written by a gentleman who visited Lourdes whilst making the tour of Europe, and who imparts to the Bishop the following interesting evidence of a miracle performed there. The writer (who is a scion of one of the noblest families in Ireland) was accompanied by his wife, and records the fact of meeting at Lourdes Dr. Doxons, who was at first incredulous regarding the miracles, but—as he candidly admitted to the writer—he could not but be convinced when he saw with his own eyes the flames of a taper pass harmlessly through the fingers of Bernadette when she was in a state of ecstacy. The writer also made the acquaintance, whilst at Lourdes, of the Curé de Chagny, who, after being totally blind for eighteen years, was miraculously and instantaneously cured at the Grotto, on the Feast of the Assumption, in 1873. The grateful Curé returns every year to Lourdes on this festival to celebrate at the Grotto his Mass of Thanksgiving for this singular favor. The writer saw him and heard the relation from his own lips. A *religieuse* of the Convent of the Immaculate Conception in Lourdes, saw the Curé de Chagny when he arrived at Lourdes in a blind and paralyzed condition, and was present at the Mass when he was miraculously cured. She received Holy Communion from the Curé on the following day, when he celebrated Mass for the first time in eighteen years.

—PROTESTANTS INVITING A CATHOLIC BISHOP TO PREACH TO THEM.—Right Rev. Bishop Keane, of Richmond, received some time ago a letter from a number of the old citizens of Boydtown, Mecklenberg Co., Va., requesting him to make them a visit. They had never seen a Roman Catholic priest or Bishop, and wished to know what he looked like, and what he could say of his church. They had, no doubt, heard of the Bishop's doings in other parts of the State, and they determined, if possible, to see and judge for themselves. The Bishop cheerfully accepted the invitation, although the visit involved a carriage ride of twenty miles from the nearest point on the railroad. He found a carriage waiting for him when he arrived at the station, and he reached the town on Saturday night, where he was most hospitably entertained by some of the leading citizens. At eleven o'clock the next day, a meeting was held in the court house, which was crowded by an eager and, of course, very curious congregation who listened respectfully and intently while, for more than an hour, the good Bishop explained to them, in his most happy and attractive manner, the principles and doctrines of the Catholic Church, and refuted the popular objections against her. The rest of the day he spent in friendly intercourse with the people, explaining points of Catholic doctrine and practice, answering the numerous questions asked him. Being urged to give them another address that night, he did so, and the house was again crowded. The interest grew, and the people then insisted that he should stay over Monday, and give another lecture Monday night. He consented and spent all day Monday as he had spent the previous day. At night the court house was again crowded, and the Bishop spoke for two hours and a quarter. The next morning he bade his new friends good-by, and returned to Richmond. Some of the people said they were fully convinced, and wanted to join the Church at once; and all were disabused of prejudices and misunderstandings regarding Catholicism. The good Bishop has a wonderfully attractive manner which secures for him a cordial welcome among all classes. He is doing a great work in Virginia.

—THE FRENCH GOVERNMENT AND THE JESUITS.—The French Jesuits, fearing that the hour of exile from their native land is fast approaching, are preparing new homes abroad; among them are some in Spain, Africa, and the East. The principal new foundation, however, is to be established in the little principality of Monaco, situated on the northern coast of Italy. Here two large colleges, capable of accommodating 2,000 students, are in process of construction, and will be completed by the 2d of November next. The land was purchased some time ago. The Superior-General of the Order is supervising the plans and directing the enterprise. The number of Jesuits who perhaps before long may be exiled from France, is about 1,480; they conduct 56 colleges spread over 44 departments. The intended blow may, however, be averted. The *Decentralisation*, a Catholic journal published at Lyons, assures its readers that the Jesuit College of St. Joseph, in St. Helena street, Lyons, will not be closed, come what may; and the same journal asserts that this fact can be affirmed of all other Jesuit schools in France. Should this be the case, we may ascribe it to the determined and able opposition of the French Catholics to the unjust proceedings of the Government. This movement first started in the Provinces of Flanders and Hainault, where 25 delegates presented a document to the prefect of Lille (Department du Nord), covered with thousands of signatures loudly protesting against the expulsion of the Jesuits and other religious Orders. The same has been done at Ronbaix, Tourcoing, Armentiers, and other places. The valiant Bishop of Angers, Mgr. Freppel, openly declared before the congregation in his Cathedral that the entire clergy and all good Catholics of the land would rally around the Jesuits and defend their rights. Not only in France, but even from other parts, objections are raised against the unworthy designs of the French radicals. Thus the British Government has taken the lead, objecting to the expulsion of religious belonging to the British empire. The same has also been done by Spain; and it is asserted, on good authority, that even Germany and Russia will do the same in behalf of their subjects. Among the Jesuits of Russian nationality is the prince Gagarin, a blood relation to the Czar himself. The members of other non-authorized communities of men number 5,917 belonging to 397 congregations; all the superiors of these different bodies will hold a council in which resolutions setting forth a decisive line of action are to be passed. The late decision of the French ministerial council, declaring all congregations of women without exception to be authorized, may be viewed as a step towards reconciliation; meanwhile collections are being taken up everywhere for the maintenance and defence of Catholic schools, and in the diocese of Nimes alone 55,000 francs (about $11,000) have been contributed in less than a week for this noble purpose. All measures of resistance to the radical Government are directed and organized by a committee of Catholic senators and legislators established in Paris.

——$1 received from B. W. Litzinger for the Needy Mission; $2 from J. C. Burke; $1 from A Friend; $1 from a poor Missionary; $20 from "Michael."

——CONTRIBUTIONS FOR THE SUFFERING IRISH.—Mrs. Powers, 50 cts.; Nellie Clare, $1; John Kelley, $1; Mrs. John Hartnett, $1; John Curran, $1; Patrick Casey, $2; Bernard McNulty, $1; John Kelley, $1; Mrs. Kelley, 50 cts.; Mrs. Curran, 50 cts.; J. Barret, 50 cts.; R. Crowe, 50 cts.; A Reader of THE AVE MARIA, $1; Mrs. Coffee, $1.50; Mrs. Ellen Powers, $1; Mrs. B. Montgomery, $1; Mrs. Elizabeth Clements, 25 cts.; Mary A. Noe, 50 cts.; Bettie Logsdon, Lou Logsdon, 50 cts.; Emma Clements, 25 cts.; J. Keenan, $2; A subscriber of THE AVE MARIA, $1; A Reader of THE AVE MARIA, $3; J. C. Burke, $2; Ella Murphy, 50 cts.; Robert M. Anderson, $10; D. H., $1; Ellen Donovan. $2; Mrs. Donovan, 50 cts.; Mary A. Dias, $20; Thomas J. Holton, $1; John F. Bawmann, $1; Mrs. B. Conroy, $1; Mr. H. L. Richards, $5; A Friend, $4. The following donations, amounting to $57.50, were received from Barclay, P., and were collected by Mr. Patrick Shevlin: P. T. Lynch, $2; Thomas Carmody, $1; Michael Cummiskey, $1; Andrew Kelliher, $1; Lawrence Collins, $1; Stephen Murphy, $1; Thomas Moran, $1; Michael McMahon, $1; Nicholas Falsey, $1; James Driscoll, $1; Mrs. Frank Waples, $1; William Murray, $1; Patrick Burns, $1; William Melvin, $1; Thomas Dobbins, $1; Michael Degnan, $1; Frank Lapoint, $1; Patrick O'Neal, $1; Mrs. Patrick Ryan, $1; Mrs. Rodger Harvey, $1; James Glynn, $1; William Stuthers, $1; Mrs. Ellen McAndrew, $1; Daniel Collins, $1; James Carroll, $1; Mark Welsh, $1; Patrick Shean, 75 cts.; Mrs. Thomas Finn, 50 cts.; James Reynolds, 50 cts.; James Kiney, 50 cts.; P. J. Carroll, 50 cts.; John Cummiskey, 50 cts.; John Sweeney, 50 cts.; John Ryan, 50 cts.; James Sweeney, 50 cts.; John Donnelly, 50 cts.; John Rafferty, 50 cts.; Patrick White, 50 cts.; Mrs. John McMahon, 50 cts.; Daniel O'Brien, 50 cts.; Patrick McGelver, 50 cts.; Thomas Leonard, 50 cts.; Peter Deegan, 50 cts.; Dennis Carroll, 50 cts.; Patrick Carroll, 50 cts.; Thomas Finn, 50 cts.; Mrs. Gaffey, 50 cts.; Mrs. Thos. Guthery, 50 cts.; John Carey, 50 cts.; Patrick Cain, 50 cts.; Owen Creighton, 50 cts.; John W. Carroll, 50 cts.; Mrs. Breen, 25 cts.; Mrs. Kinney, 25 cts.; John Singen, 25 cts.; Henry Myer, 30 cts.; Patrick Farrell, 50 cts.; James Sheridan, 50 cts.; John Kelly, 50 cts.; Miles McNally, 50 cts.; James Larkin, 50 cts.; Edward McCabe, 50 cts.; Patrick Horrigan, 50 cts.; Lawrence McAnelly, 50 cts.; Thomas Farrell, 50 cts.; Martin Roach, 50 cts.; Patrick McGrath, $1; John McVeney, $1; Ellen Toughy, $1; John North, $1; Thomas Gaffey, $1; Mrs. D. Oheron, $1; John Murphy, $1; Patrick Lamey, $1; Michael Scollins, $1; Edward McDonnell, $1; Patrick Adams, 50 cts.; Patrick Shevlin, 70 cts.

New Publications.

PEARLS FROM THE CASKET OF THE SACRED HEART OF JESUS. A Collection of Letters, Maxims and Practices of the Blessed Margaret Mary Alacoque, Religious of the Order of the Visitation. Edited by Eleanor C. Donnelly. New York, Cincinnati and St. Louis: Benziger Brothers.

This little book, neat and just the right size to be made a *vade mecum*, will be very acceptable to all the devout clients of the Sacred Heart, during this month especially. It consists of various letters written by Blessed Margaret to different persons; of little notes of counsel to nuns, which will prove consoling to many troubled hearts; of maxims, of which we subjoin a single specimen: "Be troubled at nothing, not even at your defects; be humbled on their account, but correct them peaceably, without being discouraged or cast down"; and, finally, of Blessed Margaret's practices and prayers to the Sacred Heart. The editor displays her good taste in this little work, as in everything that comes from her pious and gifted pen.

"ONLY A WAIF." R. A. Braendle. "Pips." New York: D. and J. Sadlier & Co.

The aim of this interesting story is to create sympathy for the class indicated by the title; to correct the prevalent impression that certain avocations necessitate vicious habits; to illustrate the truth that "Honor and shame from no condition rise," and to show that under circumstances the most adverse, the truly virtuous heart may maintain its purity and innocence.

—*Donahoe's Magazine* for June contains several articles of much interest. The contents of this popular periodical are always varied and attractive.

Confraternity of the Immaculate Conception
(Or of Our Lady of Lourdes).

"We fly to thy patronage, O Holy Mother of God!"

REPORT FOR THE WEEK ENDING MAY 26TH.

Prayers are asked for the following intentions: Recovery of health for 21 persons,—change of life for 18 persons and 3 families,—conversion to the Faith for 22 persons and 3 families,—special graces for several priests and religious,—temporal favors for 19 persons and 3 families,—spiritual favors for 16 persons and 8 families,—the spiritual and temporal welfare of 3 communities and several schools; also 2 thanksgivings for favors received, and 25 particular intentions.

Specified intentions: A person afflicted with inflammatory rheumatism,—employment and situations for several persons,—cure of a lady suffering from cancer,—cure of one whose lower limbs are paralyzed,—a profitable sale of property,—a young man grievously tempted,—recovery of a paralytic,—a poor cripple,—restoration of harmony in a family,—means of paying debts,—happy death or restoration to health of a number of invalids,—several persons ruining themselves through intemperance,—the removal of some scandals,—return of a father to his family,—that a person at the point of death may receive the last Sacraments.

FAVORS OBTAINED.

A correspondent writes: "There have been several remarkable cures and favors obtained here. One is that of a young lady who had the hip disease and was obliged to go around on crutches. She made a novena to Our Lady of Perpetual Succor; and since a week ago last Saturday morning, she needed the crutches no longer."... "Another young lady had an abscess on her jaw, and several of her attendant physicians said that it would have to be cut out, and would necessitate the removal of a part of the jaw-bone. She began a novena, and applied the water of Lourdes, and before the conclusion the abscess had entirely disappeared."..... "Please return thanks to Our Lady," writes another person, "for the prayers of the Confraternity have been heard; both my brothers have obtained good situations."

OBITUARY.

The following persons, as well as several others whose names have not been given, are recommended to the prayers of the Confraternity: SISTER MARY OF ST. GERTRUDE, of the Sisters of the Good Shepherd, who went to her reward on the 20th ult., in the eighteenth year of her religious life. Mr. JOHN W. KELLY, of Baltimore, who died a beautiful death at San Francisco, Cal., on the 3d ult., in the seventy-ninth year of his age. Mr. GEORGE A. BERGAN, an ecclesiastical student, whose death occurred on the 15th ult. Miss ANNIE W. GIBSON, of Crompton, R. I., lately deceased.

Requiescant in pace.

A. GRANGER, C. S. C., Director.

Youth's Department.

Lucy's Dream; or, How the Eleven Promises Came True.

"OH, dear me! I quite forgot!" exclaimed little Lucy Cooper, as she sat up in her white-curtained bed, where she had been trying to compose herself to sleep for the last half hour; "I quite forgot the practice I drew at the commencement of the month of June, and to-day is the last day, and the day of my First Communion. I must ask Madame to let me run down to the chapel for five minutes"; and so saying, she jumped out of bed, and, dressing herself like lightning, crept softly to the other side of the room, where the nun who had charge of the dormitory was engaged in saying her night-prayers. The rustle of the dress attracting the nun's attention, she turned round, and on seeing the little white figure at her side, exclaimed: "Why, Lucy! not gone to bed yet?"

"Oh yes, dear Madame! I have been to bed; but, somehow, do what I would, I could not sleep; when, all of a sudden, I remembered I had not accomplished the practice I drew at the commencement of June, and this is the last day, and the day of my First Communion. Do, dear Madame, let me go to the chapel, just for five minutes!"

"What is your practice, and why cannot you say it by the side of your bed?"

"It is the little chaplet of the Sacred Heart to be said in presence of the Blessed Sacrament, to thank God for the promises He made to the Blessed Margaret Mary. Do let me go, please; I won't stay more than five minutes!"

The nun felt very much inclined to refuse, but her kind heart was touched by the pleading face, and she said: "Well, come back directly when you have finished, and don't make a noise."

Lucy could not make out what made the stairs creak so much, as she crept down as quietly as she could. The light in the corridor guided her down the stairs, but as she reached the last step, it was put out, and everything would have been pitch dark if it had not been for the dim light that shone through the glass door of the chapel at the end of the corridor. As she groped along, the little white pussy came to pay her a visit, and would persist in getting under her feet. Of course its tail got trod upon, which sent it running off, squeaking as though it wished to wake the whole house. However, no one came to the rescue, and Lucy arrived in safety at the chapel door. "Come, dear angels," she said, as she entered, "come, and help me to say my chaplet well." As she walked up the aisle of the lonely chapel, with its many shadows, a feeling she could have scarcely explained came over her, but she turned her heart with confidence to our dear Lord in the Blessed Sacrament, and knelt at the very spot where she had received the sweet Jesus for the first time that morning. Then quickly taking her beads and bending her head in adoration she commenced: "Soul of Christ," etc.; then came the aspirations, Jesus, meek and humble of Heart, make my heart like unto Thine! Then ten times, Sweet Heart of Jesus, be my love! Sweet Heart of Mary, be my salvation! When she got to the middle, she raised her head to gaze on the silent tabernacle in which reposed the sweet Jesus, whom she was adoring, when, behold! the sanctuary no longer appeared the same; the many shadows had changed to golden lights, which not only played around the altar, but likewise filled the whole chapel and then escaped through the arched windows and disappeared, she knew not where. As she knelt, lost in amazement, a soft, and gentle voice whispered in her ear: "Come, finish your chaplet, and then I shall explain to you the meaning of all this splendor." With childlike curiosity she turned to look at the speaker, but a hand was laid upon her eyes, and the voice continued: "Finish your chaplet first." Somehow or other, Lucy did not feel at all frightened, and being used to obey, continued her prayer with all her former fervor. As she did so, the sweet voice by her side joined in, and his every word seemed to increase her devotion. When the last aspiration was ended—"May the Sacred Heart of Jesus everywhere be praised!"—the hand was raised, and Lucy beheld a brilliant angel, robed in deep red garments; but these were nearly hidden by the snow-white wings of downy feathers. "Look, little one," gently breathed forth the spirit in accents so soft that they seemed to pierce her soul through and through with heavenly delight: "look at this beautiful rose," and he showed her a rose of snowy whiteness; "see what a lovely thing your aspirations have made! It is going to ascend now to Jesus;" and he gently breathed, and the rose was wafted heavenward. When the beautiful rose had disappeared, the angel again turned to Lucy and said: "Although I have never shown myself to you before, we have long been friends, for every day I have joined with you in your fervent prayer; and now the Sacred Heart of Jesus allows you to take a journey with me to-night, in order that you may see how faithfully He fulfils those promises you have been thanking Him for; so let us just ask His blessing and start at once."

"But, dear Angel," objected Lucy, "I promised my mistress to stay only five minutes, and I am sure it is now half an hour since I left the dormitory."

"I have settled all that with your mistress, so fear nothing."

After a few minutes' silent prayer, a soft and shining cloud surrounded them, and Lucy felt herself gently raised far above the chapel, until she seemed lost amid the twinkling stars. The moon was shining in all her splendor, and the wide world appeared entangled with the golden rays which she had seen darting from the tabernacle. For some time they travelled on in silence, but at last Lucy found courage to address the beautiful spirit by her side: "Are you my guardian angel?" she said, in a low whisper.

"No, little one: I am the angel of the Sacred Heart of the loving Jesus; my office is to aid all those who honor that ever Adorable Heart."

"Oh, dear Angel!" cried the little girl, "how happy you must be to have such a glorious mission! How I wish it were my lot to share it with you, ever so little!"

"And so it is your lot, my little one; and the lot of every loving soul; you will see that, as we journey together. There, now, we are going to enter that house just below, so we must descend;" and the cloud dropped gently until they were level with the window of the top story. On entering, a sad spectacle met their eyes: a room almost bare; in one corner stood an old bedstead, on which lay a sick woman; by her side sat a young girl, whose head was buried in her hands, hot tears were streaming from her eyes and fell upon her work, which lay neglected on her lap. The angel gently approached the young girl, and after standing over her for some minutes, whispered something in her ear. She instantly dried her tears, and, taking her chaplet from her pocket began to slowly seek strength from the Sacred Heart of Jesus. The angel joined in and Lucy followed his example. As each aspiration fell from their lips, three beautiful roses were formed which the angel breathed heavenward as he had done the first. Then a golden light shone through the apartment and pierced the young girl's heart; on the golden stream were written these words: "I will grant grace to all according to their state in life." Thus strengthened, the young girl took up her work, and with a fresh ardor, resumed her tedious task. The angel's work was done, and so they departed. Lucy was so impressed with what she had just seen that she did not speak to her companion for some time, but continued to thank our dearest Lord for all His mercies. At last, however, on looking below on the numerous houses which lay beneath, she perceived that many of them were surrounded by a soft mysterious light, and that others were enveloped in total darkness; so, thinking she would very much like to know what it meant, she ventured to ask: "Why, dear Angel, do some of the houses shine so brightly while others look as black as night?"

"The houses which are encompassed by the bright light, my little one, are those on which rest the special blessing of the Sacred Heart. You know the divine Saviour Himself, has promised to bless the house in which a picture or statue of the Sacred Heart is held in veneration. If we entered each of those dwellings, we should find there an image of that divine Heart loved and honored. However, we must content ourselves by visiting only one, where we shall see another of the grand promises fulfilled."

This time they entered a house of better appearance than the last. A happy family circle were seated at different parts of the room enjoying a quiet chat. Just as Lucy entered with the angel, a clock struck nine, and the angel whispered to the father of the family, who rose at once, saying: "Come, children, we must not forget our devotions for the month of June." At these words, they all rose, and clustered round a little altar at the end of the room. The eldest daughter lit the tapers, during which one or two servants joined the circle, and the pious father took his beads, and all followed his example. Lucy watched to see if the roses would appear, and she was not disappointed, for as one rose-leaf after another escaped from the lips of each person present, a pretty garland was soon formed by the celestial spirit, who sent it whither he had sent the others. At the beginning of the prayer, one little boy kept turning his head, and instead of beautiful white petals, Lucy noticed withered ones fall to the ground; but a look from the angel had chased away all distractions, and the child's rose, although smaller than the others, joined in with the rest. By-and-by a stream of light glided through the apartment, and Lucy's heart filled with pleasure in making out these words, written upon each ray: "I will put peace in their families."

Almost before the little girl was aware, they were once more many miles further on their journey. At one time, fields, woods, and meadows lay beneath them, and then all at once, the smoky atmosphere would predict that they were approaching some busy town or city. "O, dear Angel, what a large place! where are we?" cried our little friend.

"It is the city of New York; there is much work to be done here," said the angel with a sigh; "but now that the devotion to the Sacred Heart is taking root, we may hope for the salvation of countless souls. Even now the city numbers thousands of faithful Catholics."

They had now been travelling for many hours; daylight had long appeared, and the sun was already far above the horizon. The angel spoke to Lucy: "I must not forget, my little one, that your nature is not the same as mine; you must be getting very hungry; take a little of this cordial," and he presented her a little flask. Lucy was very glad, for she was beginning to feel faint. The liquor was very refreshing, and most wonderful, for it satisfied both her hunger and thirst, and so revived her strength that she felt as though she could go on to the end of the world. This time their mission lay in the best part of the city, and entering a lofty mansion, they found themselves in an elegantly furnished room. A little girl of about ten years of age was seated by the window, an open book was in her hand; but the far-off gaze betrayed that her thoughts were very far away from her lesson, and on coming nearer, Lucy perceived that her eyes were filled with tears. At the same time as Lucy and the angel, entered another little girl who approaching the first, exclaimed: "Come, Katie! put away that book; I am sure no one will have the heart to expect a lesson to-day. See, here is a telegram saying that papa and our new mamma will be here this forenoon, so we must put on smiling faces, my dear," she said, trying to force a laugh, "and at the same time, not forget to keep our good resolutions. Who knows," she continued—choking back her tears, and looking up to a portrait, which, by the likeness to herself, Lucy could tell was that of her own mother—"perhaps this new mamma will not be so dreadful after all, it always seems to me that when we dread a thing very much, it turns out just the opposite of what we expected."

"It is all very well for you to talk, Mary," rejoined her sister, "but I can never go and meet her; I am sure she will be as cross as she can; Miss H —— says stepmothers always are," and here came a fresh burst of tears.

"That is not altogether true, Katie, and even if she is cross, we must try and make her kind. Come now, before we go down stairs to meet them, let us finish our novena, and I am sure we shall find new strength to go through this dreadful interview."

The two little girls knelt down before their altar, and as they did, the angel left the room and glided down the stairs. As he reached the hall-door, a carriage drew up, out of which stepped a lady and gentleman. "Where are the young ladies?" was the gentleman's first inquiry, while a decidedly vexed expression passed over his face at not finding his daughters there to meet him.

"I do not think they expected you quite so soon, sir," was the servant's reply; "but I will call them at once."

The angel here whispered a little word to the lady, who stopped the servant, saying: "No, no;

take me to their room," and then, turning to her husband, she continued: "It is better that I should take them by surprise, for then the meeting will not be so hard."

"Well, do as you like, my dear, only do not spoil them too much. I will meet you at lunch in a quarter of an hour," and he turned away to give some orders to the coachman.

The servant led the way upstairs until they reached the room which Lucy and the angel had left a few moments before. As she placed her hand on the handle, the lady stopped her, saying: "I will go in alone," then, opening the door very quietly, she entered unperceived by the inmates. The chaplet was not quite finished, and so she stood still, first looking at the children, and then at the portrait of their mother. As those eyes met hers, a tear sprang to her eye and she half turned as though inclined to leave the room, but in an instant the angel's wings were around her, and she once more turned towards the children. When the last aspiration was ended, the younger little girl added with childlike simplicity: "Sweet Jesus, please give us the grace to love our new mamma even if she is cross."

"Let us run down stairs," observed the other, "or else we shall be too late, and that will never do." They had just risen to their feet, when the lady advanced and gently laid a hand on the shoulder of each, saying, in a winning voice: "And who told you your new mamma would be cross, my children?"

Had the angel himself appeared on the scene, the children could not have been more startled; but soon recovering from her surprise, Katie flung her little arms around the lady's neck, exclaiming: "Oh no! you are not cross, and we will love you very much!" The embrace was warmly returned, and the stepmother only released herself to fold the elder one to her heart. In those few moments what a load had been taken off three hearts, and how Jesus had consoled them in their trouble!

A few minutes more and the wide ocean lay beneath and a clear blue sky above. Lucy had never seen anything so grand; she crept close to the angel for fear of falling into the vast expanse. He perceived her fears and whispered gently: "God is everywhere, fear nothing." These words not only reassured her, but induced her to talk to the beautiful spirit. So she began: "Dear Angel, can you see God, and all the beautiful angels and saints who live in heaven?"

"Yes, little one: I never leave the throne of God."

"How is that?" continued the little girl; "we keep travelling, and yet you never leave the throne of God!"

"God is everywhere, my child; we live in Him, and He lives in us," and, as usual, at the name of God, the angel's voice shook with tender emotion.

"Oh, where do all these dear little birds come from? But no, they are not birds. What pretty flowers! Are your brothers and sisters in heaven throwing them down upon us, dear Angel? Look! look! how fast they come!" exclaimed little Lucy, as they were literally covered with a shower of roses.

"They must be coming from some ship in distress," said the angel, as he gently blew them off, while at the same time, quickening his speed, he continued: "Do you see that black cloud in advance of us? It is the Angel of Death, and I want to overtake him, or else I may be too late to do my work."

The black cloud was not travelling very fast, so they soon came up to it, and as they did, the beautiful Angel of the Sacred Heart lowered his head, and slightly touching a golden harp that hung by his side, a sound sweeter than any earthly music, played upon the air, and he sang in accents clear and silvery these words: "May the Divine Heart of Jesus conquer everywhere!"

Lucy gave a start, for, instantly, a sound of music, grand and deep, coming from the black cloud, vibrated through the air, and a voice as though of distant thunder let fall these words: "Fear nothing, brother, for It has conquered me! Speed onward; I must wait until your mission of charity is completed."

A little further on, the sky was not so clear nor the water so smooth, and presently one flash of lightning mingled with the golden rays, which—as my little readers will remember—Lucy always saw encompassing the wide world; then dreadful peals of thunder rent the air. The angel enveloped Lucy with his wings so that she could hardly see what was going on around, but by degrees she managed to pop her head over the top, and she soon perceived that they were descending towards a spot on the angry waves which seemed as though on fire. As they approached nearer, loud shrieks were heard, and voices loudly calling for help. But what was most surprising, one little flower after another kept popping through the flames, and fluttered round the angel until he breathed it heavenward. The angel cared neither for flame nor lightning, but passing right through to the burning vessel—for such it was—a touching spectacle presented itself. Amid a panic-stricken multitude, a faithful few were seeking refuge in the Sacred Heart of Jesus. A Catholic priest knelt in the middle of the deck, surrounded by about twenty persons, who were apparently unconscious of the burning timber around, or of the dreadful death awaiting them; but by means of the little Chaplet of the Sacred Heart, were seeking refuge from Him who had promised to be their refuge in life and particularly at the hour of death. As the words "Sweet Heart of Jesus, be my love! Sweet Heart of Mary, be my salvation!" ascended to heaven, soft and gentle notes, which seemed to bid defiance to the storm, could be heard above the roaring and foaming of the waves, entoning the fourth promise of our Divine Saviour: "I will be their refuge during life, and above all at the hour of death." In another moment, the Angel of Death descended, and the burning vessel rapidly sunk. All sounds had ceased, but that of the fearful storm. But the Sacred Heart of Jesus was waiting on the eternal shores to greet those whose last act had been one of confidence in His mercy.

(CONCLUSION NEXT WEEK).

Irish Legends.

(CONTINUED.)

VIII.

THE CHILD OF THE HOLY INFANT.

THE bleeding child lay in the corner of the priest's hiding place, pouring out her life blood, shed for the love of "Jesus in the Sacrament," and still pouring out her fervent, innocent prayer for the priest and his pursuers—that the former might be saved, and the latter converted. Five years before she prayed and was heard; and now again, her prayer—her dying prayer—was heard; for this time also the priest was saved, and this time also the priest-hunter was converted. The Holy Infant again appeared to her, and wiping away the flowing blood from her wounds and the tears from her eyes, said, in accents more than heavenly: "Child of My Heart, I have heard your prayer. The priest is safe, and the priest-hunter converted; but I will take you to Myself."

The little child arose upon her knees; the Holy Infant took the particle of the Blessed Sacrament that had been thrown from the pyx, and with His own sacred hands gave her Holy Communion. He kissed her in love, and she died in the peace of God.

"The Lover of children her youth has forgiven;
She faints in her joy; is this death? it is heaven!
To her home in it soareth the innocent dove
Her first, last Communion—thus dying of love.
She's the youngest whose glory streams out on our sight
From her home where she sparkles with martyrdom's light.
Robed in red, with white lilies less white than her brow,
Poor little Agnes will pray for us now."

IX.

THE POWER OF PRAYER.

You may imagine the surprise of the priest when, on his return to his poor little hut in the cavern, he found there the blood-stained body of the innocent child whom he had left to keep company with Jesus; when he had found the tabernacle robbed and Jesus gone. It was indeed too much for him; he who had borne so much, was completely unnerved at the sight of the martyred form before him; he sat down and wept. He knew that the priest-hunter was on his track, but he cared more for the loss of the Blessed Sacrament and of the little innocent who had guarded It, than for his own safety. The priest-hunter was indeed pursuing him, and in a few moments stood before him, not to capture him, however, but to ask his pardon. Before the penitent, now bathed in tears, had time to speak, the priest, standing up, said: "Tyrant, if you want me, I am here; but where is the Blessed Sacrament?" and then pointing to the dead child, he continued, "Is that your work?"

The man, now transformed from a wolf into a lamb by the prayers of the child he had murdered, was unable to speak, and could only cast himself at the feet of the priest in tears. After recovering from his first outburst of sorrow, he confessed his crime, and received absolution.

That night, the beatified soul of the martyred child appeared to the priest, and told him not to mourn for her, as she was with Jesus whom she so loved in heaven; assuring him, at the same time, that the Blessed Sacrament was not lost, but that she had received It from the Holy Infant Himself as her First Communion and Viaticum.

They buried the little martyr near the Carrig-au-Affrin, on the side of Croagh-Patrick.

"In the world, little Agnes, how short was your stay!
From its joy's and its sorrows you soon passed away.
Sleep in peace, gentle maiden, for happy thy lot,
By those who have loved you you'll ne'er be forgot."

(TO BE CONTINUED.)

For the Suffering Irish Children.

A. Van Mourick, 25 cts.; H. Snes, 20 cts.; A Child of Mary, $1; One who loves Mary, $1; Mrs. Edward Norton, 50 cts.; E. T. D. 25 cts.; Ellen Noone, $1; Mary Campbell, $1; Annie Whalen, 50 cts.; Carrie Weysenberg, 10 cts.; Katie Ryan, 25 cts.; Agatha Ryan, 25 cts.; Patrick Ryan, 25 cts.; Mary Anne Ryan, 25 cts.; Mary Lee, 25 cts.; Eddie Lee, 25 cts.; Robert Lee, 25 cts.; Michael Lee, 25 cts.; Katie McVey, 10 cts.; Addie McVey, 15 cts.; Lizzie Farrell, 10 cts.; N. N., 35 cts.; Children of the Sodalities of the Convent of the Visitation, Ottumwa, Iowa, $5.50; A Sympathizer, $2; A Subscriber of THE AVE MARIA, $10.

——$50 more have been sent to good Father Murphy, S. J., this week.

THE AVE MARIA.

A Journal devoted to the Honor of the Blessed Virgin.

HENCEFORTH ALL GENERATIONS SHALL CALL ME BLESSED.—St. Luke, i, 48.

VOL. XVI. NOTRE DAME, INDIANA, JUNE 12, 1880. No. 24.

[For the "Ave Maria."]
"O Maria, Speranza Mia!"

BY CHARLES WARREN STODDARD.

As southward o'er the watery way,
 The wanderer takes his aimless flight,
Thou art his pilot-cloud by day,
 His guiding-star by night.

Thy smile athwart the Tempest's wrath,
 Beguiles his spirit to repose;
Thy tears compel his desert-path
 To blossom as the rose.

Yet false his life, as thou art truth,
 And sad his days, as thou art sweet;
Oh! be the loadstone of his youth,
 And draw him to thy feet!

'Beth's Promise.

BY MRS. ANNA HANSON DORSEY.

CHAPTER XVII.
HOW 'BETH FOUGHT OUT HER BATTLES.

THE Indian summer was dying away in gray mists when Mrs. Morley and 'Beth left "Ellerslie"; biting frosts and rude winds had despoiled the trees of their richly-tinted leaves, which were strewn over the mossy earth in grotesque patterns, and bright patches of color like fantastic designs in a kaleidoscope; the song birds had taken flight, and even the swallows, always the last to go, began to shiver and decide it was time for them to move southward. The old lady of "Ellerslie" felt disconsolate, and the spacious house with its wide halls, high ceilings and silent chambers seemed to her at times filled with whispering echoes, that made it feel more lonely, although it was only the sobbing and sighing of the winds she heard. But sometimes the wind has a voice that speaks strange words to the heart and memory. She wondered the first day or two, while the rain beat and lashed her windows, and she could see nothing beyond the mist that enfolded "Ellerslie," how on earth she would be able to fill the void in her daily life, now that 'Beth and her mother were really gone; but when the storm gave place to blue skies and sunshine, she found so much to occupy her, so many outside claims upon her attention and sympathy, that she had no time for sadness; without going out of the way to seek it, there was work enough for her to do; and, as was her habit, she did it with a will, turning neither to the right nor left until it was accomplished. And Lodo, ever on the alert for her comfort, kept the fire always bright upon the hearth, and fresh flowers from the conservatory upon the table. Her writing-desk, work-basket and books were always just exactly where they ought to be; and when Aunt 'Beth was in the mood for it, she would rejoice to bring in her sewing, and, on the slightest encouragement, talk over the summer and all that had happened, Mrs. Morley and 'Beth being the central figures, both of them encircled by the girl's grateful affection and vivid fancy in such an aureole of brightness, that while her own eyes glistened more and more, and her sewing dropped idly in her lap as she went on, the heart of the old woman of "Ellerslie" warmed up and felt gladdened almost as much as if those they talked of had dropped in unexpectedly and paid them a brief visit. But we must follow them. It was a cold gray morning with a drizzling rain when the train ran into the station at Washington. The gas was still burning in the public waiting-room, and the few travellers who were there, waiting for the ticket-office to open, intending to leave by the outgoing train, were huddled around the stove, or regaling themselves with hot coffee and other comfortable things at the lunch table, served by a drowsy, untidy woman, who yawned audibly every few moments. Mrs. Morley, overcome with fatigue, reclined on their shawls, her head sometimes on 'Beth's shoulder—who would so place herself, whenever she stirred, as to support it—and had slept through the night, undisturbed by the motion and rumbling of the train as it dashed on and on, ever into the dark, except when now and then the red glare from large smelting furnaces at no great distance from the railroad, cast a lurid and uncanny light upon it, making the few passengers who were awake almost think they had caught glimpses of an inferno, to which the night gloom, that followed as they plunged on, was a relief and rest. 'Beth held her mother's hand in her soft, warm clasp, but she did not sleep; her thoughts were too full of memories of her unclouded dream of happiness, which, but for the pain its sudden vanishing left with her, seemed as unreal as any dream. Her youth and strength, while it helped her in one way, intensified her unhappiness in another. She wanted to bear her trial with courage and patience, but there were times when she rebelled and thought she might have been spared so cruel an experience, an experience which she sometimes imagined was more like a malicious ruling of fate than the ordering of a divine and merciful Providence. Oftentimes she wondered why she had been—as it seemed to her—so unnecessarily tortured. And so she had been fighting her battle out, all alone, for days and weeks, praying for help, and ever wondering if God, who had permitted so heavy a blow to fall upon her, would not some time reveal His purpose, and make it plain to her; if He would only do this, how easy a task to be resigned! She would have been so thankful to forget; but did people ever forget—she questioned—that which had dried the fountain of gladness in their heart, turning life into an arid desert without oasis or flower? She could not tell. The lines that had fallen to her were strange and untried, and she was sure only of one thing, her womanly pride, which would enable her, at least, to conceal her cross, instead of moping weakly and inviting the pity and comments of the curious. But even this would not, could not satisfy the higher craving of her heart, which was, not to forget Bertie Dulaney, but to remember him without pain, as one altogether worthy of being remembered, and think of her lost happiness without a single bitter regret. She knew there was a long and sorrowful struggle before her, into which no human help could enter, and which she would have to bear alone. "Catholics," she argued, "find consolation in the practice of their religion; even my mother's broken heart was solaced and her life made endurable by it; but what can help me? I am not a Catholic, and my sorrow is so different from most other sorrows, and seems so undeserved and unnecessary, that I cannot see how God can pity sufferings which He might have averted! Oh, Father! couldst Thou not have spared me! Oh Mary, my Mother! couldst thou not have led me by another and less thorny way!"

And so it had been going on in 'Beth's mind, over and over again, ever since the first numbness and surprise of her grief had gone by, while outwardly she was always composed and had made the days pass as usual in the sweet home-life at "Ellerslie." She had gone every morning with her mother to Mass, and tried to pray; sometimes she went alone towards evening to say her beads, and ask help of that pure, sinless Heart which had been pierced with the sword of grief; but a cloud seemed to hang between her and the devotion she had so loved, until *Paters* and *Aves* became, as it were, a vain repetition of words that went no farther than her lips. She played and sang, and gathered flowers for the vases every day; she talked, and even laughed sometimes; drove about with chattering little Lodo, up and down through the beautiful country which was flaming and glowing with variegated and gorgeous autumnal tints; she gathered ferns, which, touched by the frosts, looked like stately golden palms, and a store of scarlet, bronze, and green leaves, dashed with crimson and yellow, to press and make into winter bouquets—bright memories of "Ellerslie"—for her Washington home; she went over hill and dale, everywhere except to the lake, which she avoided, feeling that there her bright dream had gone down out of sight, like something with a mill-stone about its neck. The sense of duality that had come into her life since that day, bewildered her sometimes and made her wonder which was the real, which the unreal state.

And now, all through the weary night of their journey home, the same thoughts had been ringing their sad changes through 'Beth's mind as she sat looking out into the blank darkness, until the first faint shadowy streaks of dawn fringed the horizon with its solemn light. She watched it flickering, broadening, flushing like the inside of a sea-shell, deepening into crimson, and at last bursting into golden splendor, and she closed her heavy eyes, wondering if light would ever rise for her. There was nothing sentimental or romantic in 'Beth Morley; she had all the attributes of a fine, noble nature; and when her strange trial had come upon her, like a bolt out of a cloudless sky, she was full of the blithe gladsomeness of untried girlhood; and now—although she was unconscious of the fact—the ordeal through which she was passing was developing and refining through "pain's furnace heat," as well as strengthening all her higher and better qualities, and leading her, step by step, nearer and nearer to the open portals of that divine Faith wherein alone the weary heart can find its true rest, its best solace.

"Dear mamma, how soundly you slept! Here we are in Washington, and there's dear old Andy watching every window as the cars slip by, and looking very blue because he doesn't see us, we being on the wrong side," said 'Beth, beginning to gather their wraps.

"I believe I have slept all night," said Mrs. Morley, now fully awake. "But you, my darling!"

"Oh, I've been dreaming, too!" said 'Beth, in cheerful tones; "and there was the loveliest sunrise! I thought we were going to have a splendid day, and here's a Scotch mist to welcome us home."

By this time the train had stopped, and the weary, sleepy passengers were thronging out with carpet-bags, baskets, bundles and babies; and Andy, who stood on the platform scanning every face that appeared, and looking more miserable each moment, suddenly beheld the two he was waiting for in the door-way of the last car, and his old brown face broke into smiles of welcome as he bustled past and around every obstacle that lay in his way to help them down, and tell them how glad he was to see them home once more. "And, ma'am, how proud I am to see you lookin' so well, is mor 'n I can tell you; and as for young missis, it 'pears to me she's growed taller, but she aint so rosy-like as she was; I s'pose travellin' all night's what done it; here's the *coupé* jest a step from here, my ladies," said Andy, as, loaded with wraps and hand-bags, he led the way to the carriage and handed them in. "Pull the robe round you good, missis: it's right down cold; but we'll soon be home," continued the faithful old servant, as he tucked the robe around their feet and deposited the shawls and cloaks on the front seat. In another minute our tired travellers were being driven rapidly home, where welcoming dusky faces greeted them at the door; within, bright fires threw out a cheerful glow, and a hot breakfast awaited them; afterwards a long, quiet rest. 'Beth, when alone in her own room, could but contrast her going away with her coming home. She went, filled with bright anticipations, her heart bubbling over with the joyousness of a wholesome, happy nature, her outlook into the future undimmed by even the shadow of a cloud, or a dream of the least thing sorrowful; she had come back no longer a merry girl, ready to catch and enjoy every fleeting pleasure; she seemed to herself to be years older, a saddened woman, bearing a secret grief for which she thought there was no healing, no help.

But happily for 'Beth Morley, there was no lack of occupation in these first few days at home; unpacking trunks, assorting and arranging things, and assisting her mother in getting their domestic affairs into the right grooves, gave her no time for sad thoughts. Then one or two visits with her mother to the dear grave under the old trees on Georgetown Heights, which they found had been tended by their faithful old servant with scrupulous care, where great white chrysanthemums and a few late roses shed fragrance, and the grass was still green above the quiet resting-place of their unforgotten dead.

After a few days the Brandts and some others, old navy friends brought to Washington by duty, began to drop in of evenings, glad beyond words to see Mrs. Morley, who now, for 'Beth's sake, received visitors and exerted herself to entertain them in her own graceful, quiet way. Father Thomas took an old-fashioned early tea with them once, "in honor of their return," he said, and had many things to tell them; some sad enough, others mirth-provoking. He noted Mrs. Morley's improved looks, but there was a something in 'Beth's countenance and manner which gave him infinite concern, the more so as he could neither define it nor ask its meaning. He was glad to hear all they had to tell him about "Ellerslie" and its brave old chatelaine, whose energy and courage when the "strike" began delighted him, and whose amiable paganism and untiring benevolence combined, amused and greatly interested him, as did also Mrs. Morley's account of the Dulaneys and the beautiful chapel at "Tracy-Holme," of their hospitality to the overworked clergy during the summer months, which was rewarded a thousandfold by having a daily Mass and other devotions at St. Joseph's during the whole season.

"That is admirable!" said Father Thomas, "and I engage your good offices, 'Beth, to get your friends to put my name upon their invalid list for next summer. I should enjoy it highly—I mean a visit to the good Dulaneys, and to "Ellerslie" too, remember! Aunt 'Beth would refresh me beyond measure, so you must be sure, my child, to put in a good word for me."

"Never fear about an invitation; Aunt 'Beth is quite well acquainted with you, Father Thomas, and nothing would delight her more than to have you for a guest; I know you'd get on famously together," said 'Beth; "the difficulty will be on your part if you don't go to 'Ellerslie' next summer."

"Well, my child, my present mind is fixed upon going if I'm invited, unless war, pestilence, or famine give me a counter-invitation to stay with my people. Good-night," said Father Thomas, shaking hands. 'Beth went to the hall door with him, and the last sound Mrs. Morley heard was his genial laugh as he went out.

Among the letters brought by the postman next morning, was one of large size, edged and sealed with black, the seal covered with heraldic devices, and large enough for an escutcheon; it was a portentous looking missive, and Mrs. Morley opened it wondering what it might reveal.

She soon knew. It was from Rome, from the Prince Sforza-Piccolomini, announcing the death of Madame the Princess, his wife, from an attack of Roman fever.

"Oh, poor *bonne-mère!*" exclaimed Mrs. Morley, her eyes filling with tears as the remembrance of all Mrs. Hamilton's well-intended kindness and generosity rushed through her mind; "she is dead, 'Beth; died among strangers in a strange land; you never knew her, my child, but she was very good to me and my brothers."

"I am sorry, dear mamma; I have always hoped to know her for that very reason; but there's something else in the envelop; what can it be?" said 'Beth, taking it from the table where her mother had placed it; "it seems to be a letter, mamma."

"The dear, kind heart, thinking of me to the very last!" said Mrs. Morley, opening it. It was a communication from the Roman lawyer who had drawn up the last will and testament of her highness the Princess Sforza, relating to certain bequests to her granddaughter, Anne Morley, *née* Hamilton, among which were the portraits of her parents, Col. and Mrs. Hamilton, with all the costly furniture and silver belonging to her Boston residence, and last of all the beautiful old home among the Berkshire Hills. It was drawn up in duly legal form, and so worded that the testator's meaning could not be misunderstood in the smallest particular. Having a good knowledge of Italian, Mrs. Morley had no difficulty in reading the document; she was informed that Madame the Princess had settled a handsome life annuity on her husband, and left him to do with it as he pleased, as also all the elegant and costly appointments of the old family palace in Rome and of the villa near Perugia; the balance of her fortune she had left to be divided equally between a New England college and a public library in Boston.

"I shall be very glad to have the portraits of my father and mother, but all the rest will only add to my cares. As to the Berkshire Hills' property, it seems simply embarrassing; for we shall, sometime, live at "Ellerslie"; your dear father wished it, and his wishes will, under all circumstances, be sacred to me. Aunt 'Beth also spoke to me about it, and would have us make it our home even now, that she might enjoy it a little while with us. I can't think what I shall do, unless—unless—" Mrs. Morley did not say what, but her face had suddenly brightened as some idea, which was evidently pleasant, flitted into her mind like an inspiration, and did not flit away again, for she held it, and sat turning it over and over, while her hands dropped upon the papers in her lap, and she forgot everything else except the castles she was building—not in Spain —but among the beautiful Berkshire Hills. 'Beth went up to her room intending to put on her wraps and hat and run off to pay Father Thomas a visit; she really felt no interest in the Roman news, or in the legacy itself, only so far as it gave pleasure to her mother who, she imagined, had already formed some plans about a portion of it. Before she was quite ready, Mrs. Morley came up and asked her to wait a few moments for her, as she was going to deposit the Roman papers in her lawyer's care, and they could walk together, and afterwards call on Father Thomas, where the *coupé* would meet them, and then take a short drive.

(TO BE CONTINUED.)

The Conversion of an Infidel through the Intercession of the Blessed Virgin.

BY THE LATE REV. FATHER J. P. DONELAN.

THE remarkable conversion which we are about to relate will, doubtless, be viewed by many as a mere human affair—an effect of sudden impulse or fanaticism. There are those into whose hands these pages will fall who will treat the whole matter lightly and pass it by as another fiction, and, perhaps, censure the writer for giving the facts to the public. But there are higher and holier motives for proclaiming to the world this striking proof of God's mercy. In giving publicity to this wonderful conversion, in stating minutely each fact as it transpired, and every circumstance attending the conversion of Mr. M——, the writer is guided by a fervent wish to promote the glory of God, to show forth His mercies, and to proclaim His goodness. He desires to show to the world the efficacy of prayer, of the intercession of the saints and angels, and first, and above them all, of Mary the ever 'Blessed and Immaculate Mother of God. What the thoughtless or the prejudiced may think or say of his efforts, the writer neither heeds nor cares. Conscious of the truth of what he states, and impelled by no other aim than to testify to the wondrous ways of God, he sends forth this testimony to seek its way into the hands of all. Should any censure, so let it be; if any approve, let them return thanks to our Heavenly Father who continues to manifest His mercies in such wondrous ways. If these facts shall be read by any who love and venerate the glorious Mother of God, they will but serve to strengthen that filial trust in her protection. With the subject of this narrative, let such exclaim: "Would that every heart were filled with love for Mary, the refuge of sinners and the Mother of my God!" It is also to give an additional motive for this devotion that the following pages are written. Let them be read attentively, for the writer, as well as numerous other eye-witnesses, is ready to substantiate every circumstance here related.

Mr. M——, at the time our narrative begins, was confined to his room by the illness of which he subsequently died. His body was exceedingly emaciated, but his mind remained remarkably strong and vigorous. All who ever heard him declaim against Revealed Religion, or who knew him during his days of health, agree in pronouncing him a man of unusually strong argumentative powers. In the district, at least, where Mr. M—— was most known, his opinions on the subject of religion need not be mentioned. They are as familiar to his acquaintances, and indeed to a great portion of the people, as the history of any fact. During a long and eventful life, forty years of which he had openly professed himself an infidel, he had gloried in the wild and senseless theories of Voltaire, of Rousseau, of Paine, Diderot, D'Alembert, Bolingbroke and Kneeland. Following in the track of such demoralizing leaders, his naturally strong intellect succeeded to no inconsiderable extent, in compiling a system partaking of the inconsistencies of one, the absurdities of another, and the horrid blasphemies of all. This system he had openly professed and strenuously endeavored to inculcate during five and thirty years. Possessed of an inventive genius and a fluency of words, it is not to be wondered at that few were found to enter the arena of dispute with him; and to convince him was impossible, so strongly was he wedded to his own peculiar views. Not an apparent discrepancy in the Bible had escaped him; no difficulty, no seeming contradiction, or prophecy, in either the Old or the New Testament but was as familiar to him as the Commandments are to a Christian. He had studied the sacred volume for the express purpose of culling such passages, and most fearful was the use he made of his ill-directed talent. He would set forth in his intercourse with the young men, many of whom looked upon him as their leader in infidelity, the strongest arguments and most plausible theories against the truths of the Gospel. For several years, he was accustomed, after the duties of the day were over, to argue against the Christian religion in presence of an assemblage of persons who, attracted by the bold originality of his manner and by the novelty of his views, would gather around his door or in some public place. His chief aim was to instil his principles into the minds of the young, and too fatally did he for years succeed. Many, corrupted by his irreligious teaching, are now suffering the dread consequences; many there are who, during the long period of thirty or forty years, learned from him to blaspheme the God of Truth and to deny His sacred revelations. Some remain there, and others are scattered in different parts of world, while—how shall it be said!—no few have already passed the confines of time, and are now in eternity. It was long, and indeed the constant custom of Mr. M——, to seek interviews with the sick and the dying; and then, while performing some friendly office, to distil the poison of his infidelity into the very soul of the death-stricken victim. No Christian minister could be more zealous for good than was this misguided individual in disseminating his blasphemous principles. Strange infatuation! frightful wanderings of the human intellect! And yet, the writer of this narrative entertains not the slightest doubt as to Mr. M——'s sincerity. He had become impressed with the belief that all religious authority was an unauthorized restraint on human liberty; that the mind of man should tower above all dependence on others for guidance; and being naturally of an ardent temperament and possessing a heart ever sensibly alive to the necessities of others, he considered it his duty to destroy, as far as possible, the results of religious education in those around him; hence his unceasing exertions against revealed religion, and his equally strenuous efforts to elevate human reason to the throne of the Deity. Against his character in a moral point of view, no one could speak; a kind father, he labored to support his family, and reared them in respectability; in nothing but religion was he opposed to them; and, strange as it may appear to some, he was not opposed to his children's joining the Catholic Church. While he was willing that they should enjoy their own opinions, he never permitted them to introduce the subject of religion in his presence; and if perchance in an unguarded moment, or when they beheld him slowly sinking beneath the effects of disease, they introduced the subject, it would serve only to elicit from the father a tirade against the professors and the doctrines of revelation.

During the spring of 1846, Mr. M—— was attacked with a severe bronchial affection, which in a few months proved fatal. His once robust and hardy constitution rapidly yielded to the inroads of disease; and, trusting with apparent, and no doubt sincere, reliance to his erroneous principles, he looked on death as the termination of all his sufferings. To the earnest entreaties of his family and friends, whenever they ventured to broach the subject of preparing for death, he would reply in his usual style, assuring all of his perfect resignation, of his trust and entire confidence in the god whom he worshipped, of his willingness to abide the consequences of his belief, and his settled conviction of the truth of his opinions on the subject of Rational Religion.

Many visited him during the time of his illness, but few dared to speak to him on pious subjects through a natural and very justifiable dread of exciting him against religion. So excitable were his feelings and vehement his manner on this point, that not unfrequently in disproving Christianity and supporting his own views he would become speechless from fatigue. The few who ventured to introduce the subject of religion, succeeded in nothing but in calling forth his reiterated opposition, and a renewal of his entire confidence in the sufficiency of reason and morality for man's security. When questioned on the immortality of the soul, on his prospects beyond the grave, or his views of eternity, he would reply that a future state was absurd, that the soul's immortality was a mere fiction, and that the doctrine of future rewards and punishments was the offspring of designing legislators. Nothing seemed capable of altering his views on these points. He treated Christianity as a fable; the history of its Divine Founder was but one of the many chimeras by which the human mind was enslaved; the sacred truths contained in the written word of God were but ill-arranged contradictions, while reason was the only Deity, and was alone deserving of man's adoration. On one occasion, in reply to the repeated request of a pious Catholic lady for permission to introduce a priest into his room, he answered, with emphasis: "Not only one, but a host of priests, that they may see how an infidel can die!" Such were his feelings, and such the vain boastings of this child of error. "See how an infidel can meet death," was his frequent remark; and when, on another occasion, he was exhorted to think of the frightful eternity into which he was about to enter, he replied, with much apparent sincerity: "That change which you call eternity, but which I call the simple dissolution of all human organization, has no terror for me: I am not afraid to die, for that ends all my sufferings and all my being; no Christian can meet death with less of fear than I now experience its slow but sure progress." O, loving Saviour, how frightful are such sentiments! As he himself remarked afterwards when suing for mercy at the foot of the cross, "how vague and undefined is the idea an infidel forms of the state beyond the grave! No faith enlivens the dreary blank, the horrid gloom brooding over the last moment; no gleam of cheering hope dispels the dread, the fearful doubts, which at times rack the infidel's soul, despite the boasted security which lends a seeming but a fatal calmness; no heavenborn charity points the spirit above, nor lifts the soul upon the wings of prayer, as, looking from the window of the eyes, it gazes on the past, the present, or the future. All is gloom, is wild and cheerless doubt." Ah! who can believe it is all of death to die? Who can place his hand upon his heart and say he is prepared to meet that change which knows no change? to set out upon that perilous journey, which ends—where? "The chamber where the good man meets his fate" may indeed be called the dwelling place of angels, for it is there the gates of a happy eternity are opened to him; it is there that the vision of the heavenly Jerusalem first bursts upon his view, and the spirits of God welcome home another soul ransomed by the blood of the Lamb. But no such cheering truths cluster around the dying infidel; no angel is there to point the doubting and the trembling soul to a better world; no bright visions of God and of His angels open to his view; no star of hope rises 'mid the storm, to guide the wanderer home, or cheer the departing spirit in that awful gloom; all is dark and frightful uncertainty; all is doubt; and though the parting soul may still persist, this perseverance can arise from nothing else than wilful obstinacy or a frightful yet well-merited, judgment of God. Child of error, stay thy wayward course! change thy wicked thoughts while yet lingering this side the grave—if so it be that God may still pardon thee. But if thou wilt not, and persevere in thy infidelity, one step more, and all is lost for ever! One awful moment, and it will be too late! There is no return—no change—no hope! Lo! even now the angels of God are waiting for thee. See, from the happy shores of Canaan, they are beckoning to thee. Thy Lord waits for thy return; thy Saviour lives to make intercession for thee; thou hast a Mother in heaven, the Mother of God, who pleads to her Divine Son for thee, and the recording angel is ready at Heaven's command to blot forever thy faults from the register of death. "Why will ye persist, O house of Israel!" "As I live, saith the Lord, I will not the death of the sinner, but rather that he be converted and live." "Turn to Me, O Israel, and though thy sins be as red as scarlet, I will make them white as snow." "Oh house of Israel, why will ye die!"

Praised and glorified forever be the mercies of our God, who was pleased to manifest these consoling assurances so openly and so wonderfully to the subject of our narrative! What but the power of God could so effectually operate the change which filled men and angels with joy? But to resume our subject. Yielding to the request of the afflicted family, a Catholic clergyman from a neighboring city, having previously been invited by the resident clergyman of the parish, visited Mr. M——. Not unaware of the peculiar circumstances of the case, and being an entire stranger to the sick man, the clergyman had no other resource than to recommend the object of his mission to the special care of God, through the hands of Mary, the Blessed Mother of our Lord. This he did, and the result proved that the Church is guided by a spirit of truth when she so sweetly addresses the Mother of God as the "Refuge of Sinners." On being introduced into the room, he found the sick man reclining in a chair, apparently much exhausted from conversation. The sufferer reached forth his hand, and feebly, yet with much earnestness, welcomed his visitor. There was no violence of feeling manifested by Mr. M—— during this, nor indeed during any of the subsequent visits made by the priest. On this occasion, the subject of religion was not introduced. They spoke of various topics—of questions of history, of the leading political and stirring events of the day, and after the lapse of an hour, the clergyman retired. Nothing of any particular interest marked this visit, or the time which intervened between it and the following one. It is but just to remark that the resident clergyman of the place had previously visited the sick man, and was received by him in the same friendly manner; and although the efforts of that zealous priest met with no encouragement on the part of Mr. M——; although to all the tender invitations of religion, and its most touching truths, he replied in his usual manner, we may confidently believe that these visits had their effect. During these interviews, we may safely say the good seed was planted, which subsequently fructified a thousand-fold. On one occasion, in his remarks to that reverend gentleman, Mr. M—— used language which he immediately regretted; for although deeply wedded to his own views, he seldom forgot, when in conversation with clergymen, the respect due to them. How earnestly did he afterwards ask pardon of God and of the good priest for this offence! And may we not hope that, as the words produced no other feeling on the mind of the clergyman, than pity for the momentary forgetfulness that caused them, kind Heaven heard them not, or, hearing, excused them?

(TO BE CONTINUED.)

"I returned from Babylon to Jerusalem, from a foreign country to my home, from isolation to society, from division to unity, from unrest to peace, from a lie to truth, from the world to God. . . . The exit from the dark cavern in which I lived was on the summit of a mountain, and by many a dark labyrinthine way I reached it. And now I stood on the top of that mountain, in the open air, in a bracing atmosphere, under a boundless canopy of stars, reflected in an equally boundless sea. And a voice said to me: 'This is the Church of Christ,' and I fell down in adoration. . . . I have found God in His revelation, and I believe."—*Countess Hahn-Hahn on her Conversion.*

To One who Painted a Picture of Our Lady Immaculate.

BY J. W. S. N.

HERE dear Saint Luke's rare privilege thine own
  To limn the features of the Mother-Maid,
As bright they glowed in Nazareth's sweet shade
When Mary's arms were Jesus' safest throne;
When on His ear fell softest mother-tone
  That of the earth a very heaven made:
Did those mild eyes that Jesus' mirror-ray'd
Upon thee dwell,—then had the artist grown
  Strong 'neath the inspiration of the gaze
That charmed the Babe Divine with its pure grace;
  Then had St. Luke's remembrance, clear, been thine.
Well, after many hopeful, prayerful days,
  Thy soul will win its envied treasure-place,
And Mary's presence on thee brightly shine.

[*From "The Catholic World."*]

Canova.

ONE hundred and twenty years ago, God bestowed a rare gift on Italy. He gave to that ever-favored land a man who stood foremost in his art, who outstripped his immediate predecessors—victims of the terrible decay and corruption into which sculpture and painting had fallen,—and who even to-day is not surpassed in the strength and power of his genius and the number and kind of his works. He was a Christian gentleman, "without fear and without reproach." His name was honored among men. The very children in the streets cried: *Ecco il nostro gran Canova!* "Behold our great Canova!" To-day, in Italy, a visitor will meet many traces of his master-hand. To-day, in America, how many know him? How many realize the influence he exerted over art, ennobling and purifying it? Few indeed. He has not been shown to us that we may appreciate him. So, in the earnest desire to win for him a recognition of his admirable qualities as man and as artist, we give this little sketch of Antonio Canova.

The once powerful republic of Venice claimed among its former and more splendid dependencies, the province of Treviso. Within this province is situated the little village of Possagno. It is secluded from public observation by the hills of Asolano which surround it. Here, hidden by the obscurity of the village, among a simple people, unspoiled by any contact with an aristocratic and wealthy luxuriance, was born on the morning of All Saints' Day, November 1st, 1757, one upon whose career the eyes of all Europe would rest as the greatest artist of the present age; and not alone of the present, but, perhaps, all things being considered, the greatest also of a preceding age. We say advisedly, all things considered. Any one who will carefully study the history of art in Italy to the time of Michael Angelo, and from that period through its decline till Canova appeared, as a true renovator, will appreciate the force of our observation.

Antonio Canova was the only child of Pietro, a stone-cutter, and Angela Zardo, who, according to one of Canova's biographers, was nowise distinguished from the women of her native hamlet. Shortly after his father's death, which occurred three years later, the young Antonio was deprived of his mother's care. She formed a second marriage, and removed to her native town, Crespano. She naturally desired to carry her son to her new home; but his grandfather, Pasino Canova, pleaded so earnestly to keep the boy with him that it was finally settled that he should remain part of the time with Pasino, who proved a faithful guardian, and the other part with his mother, now Angela Sartori.

Possagno, although insignificant compared with Venice and the more celebrated cities and towns of Italy, held nevertheless resources of its own. The country was rich in the fertility of its soil, while the wool of its sheep gave occupation, and even wealth, to many. But its own peculiar value consisted in the abundance of a kind of soft stone which, because of its readiness to yield to the chisel, was much used in ornamental carving, altars, and such like. The grandfather of our Antonio was a simple mason and stone-cutter. He was, perhaps, a little of an architect and sculptor, but very far from being an artist. That he loved his work, however, and labored faithfully in it, is sufficiently attested by the number of stucco, soft-stone, and sometimes marble carvings of his workmanship in the churches and on the altars of Possagno and the neighboring villages. They show tolerable power of execution, and neatness of design, and evince at once the capability of the man, whose talents, while being in no way great, were sufficiently of importance to prevent his being hidden in mediocrity; and in a limited sphere, far from great cities, they caused him to be employed in works rather above their and his own suitable occupation. The remarkable good-humor and intelligence of Pasino gave him a degree of ascendency over his equals, amongst whom he was very popular. Such was the man who, for the present, was to be the guardian of Antonio, who gave him his first lessons in the use of the chisel —that chisel which was afterwards to astonish the world by the superiority of its work.

Before taking up our young sculptor's life, with the commencement of his labors, we will devote a few words to her whom Canova ever warmly cherished, and who was to him a loving and sympathetic mother. This was Caterina Ceccato, the wife of Pasino, the boy's devoted grandmother. She watched his growth with the most affectionate solicitude, and by her tender care supplied the loss of his mother; for, as will be seen, the arrangement made at the time of Angela's second marriage could not continue.

The native worth of men is deepened and brought into strong relief by the tender influence of a true mother. She holds the power to mould the strong nature, to soften its asperities, to render it more docile to the control of religion, to combine the mastery of a large intellect with the simplicity of a child's heart. And this is especially true of a man of genius. His character cannot be rounded and complete unless the mother's gentle influence has worked its will. Talents and virtue mutually lend a noble dignity to each other. Voltaire, with his wonderful gifts, was one-sided; he wanted a mother's love and piety. Byron had all the elements of true greatness, had they been mingled wisely; to him was denied the judicious and patient affection ever ready to prompt and to mould. Deprived of both parents, Canova, more fortunate than many, found a second mother in Caterina. She directed his childish acquirements as far as she was able; she opened to him the way to virtue, and at last had the happiness of seeing the object of her earnest solicitude prove himself worthy of it. On his side, Canova was permitted to enjoy one of the purest pleasures a genuine man can taste—that of ministering to his grandmother's wants in her old age. Upon her husband's death, as soon as his means permitted, Canova brought her to Rome to reside with him; and we are told that many of his friends long remembered how earnest were his efforts to soothe her declining years. Canova had sculptured the bust of Caterina in the native dress of her province, which was the same as that of Titian's mother, as seen in the pictures of that master. This bust he kept in his own apartments. Showing it one day to a friend, he said with deep feeling: "That is a piece which I greatly value; it is the likeness of her to whom I owe as much as it is possible for one human being to owe to another" adding with a smile, "you ladies are usually solicitous about appearances; you see my grandmother is dressed nearly as Titian's mother is represented by that artist; but, unless affection renders me a partial judge, my relative is by far the finer old woman."

The extreme poverty of his relatives made it necessary for the lad to be early taught some trade. It was natural, therefore, that the grandfather should have regarded Antonio as his destined assistant and successor; accordingly, before his bent showed itself, just as soon as his hand could hold and manage a pencil, the old man began to initiate his grandson into the principles of drawing; later, although still in tender years, the little fellow commenced to mould in clay, and at last was permitted the use of the chisel. Thus, early in life, long before his real art career had been entered upon, Canova acquired a dexterity in the mechanical use of the tools which afterwards gave him the great advantage of being able to execute the rapid conceptions of his genius with corresponding facility.

It would seem that the arrangement made upon the second marriage of our young Antonio's mother proved a total failure. During the half years he spent in his step-father's home he was constantly in trouble with him. He openly averred he did not love him: were his mother alone, he declared, he would work for her and live with her, as he loved her very dearly, and was very proud of his little half-brother, Giovanni Baptista Sartori. She had her husband now; she did not need him. The secret of this boyish sensitiveness and pride might be found in his devotion to his clay and chisel. He was constantly moulding and cutting, much to Francis Sartori's disgust; yet we find no evidence of his neglecting the duties and tasks required from him. When with his grandfather, Antonio's daily labor was naturally in the workshop, and here he was always to be found, except when his grandmother's legendary lore allured him away to her side. Indeed, his enthusiastic and ardent mind was as often swayed by the good old matron's tales and ballads as by his favorite employment. Thus constituted, the sports of the village boys held little attraction for him.

At his mother's, all was different. Francis Sartori has been reputed as a good, pious man, but probably had very little sympathy with his step-son's earnest love of his art. The outbreak was not long deferred, and it came in this wise: Antonio, then twelve years of age, had begun to rough-hew a statue of his own design; it was intended to represent the Blessed Virgin, his Madonna, as he called her. The Feast of Corpus Christi was drawing near, and the boy was very anxious to finish his statue, as his cousin, Betta Blasi, and several of her young companions, who were Children of Mary, had promised, if it were very nice, to decorate it for the feast. Then they did not doubt but that their pastor would permit them to bear it in procession. He worked very steadily, but only after his daily tasks were finished and his time his own. One morning, after Antonio had retired to a neglected part of the little garden, where an old arbor served him for a workshop, Francis Sartori came to him, evidently in great anger; he sternly demanded what he was doing. "This," replied the boy, quietly, pointing to his statue, which stood upon a stool.

"And is this what I bade you to do?" asked his step-father.

"I have done my work, and it is only when I have finished it that I come here."

Francis, whose anger against the poor lad had probably some jealous origin, then broke out into a torrent of abuse hardly consistent with the character of piety given him. Finally taking a stone, he hurled it at the stool; the force of the blow caused the statue to fall from its pedestal, and it was shivered in pieces. At this Antonio, who had borne his step-father's outburst in silence, broke into a fit of passionate weeping; the sight of perhaps his first real piece of work lying broken at his feet proved too much for the little fellow; still sobbing, he cried out: "If it is in this way you are going to treat me, I will not remain here another day." Then collecting almost tenderly the bits of his Madonna, he put them into a bundle and left. Going through the house, he wished to say good-by to his mother; this Francis forbade. So Antonio left Crespano and walked to Possagno, where his grandfather warmly welcomed him. His story told, the old man blamed him for quarrelling with his step-father, and, much to the boy's astonishment, set off for Crespano to consult with the mother. It was then decided that he should live altogether with Pasino, spending Sundays at his step-father's. Antonio's joy at this arrangement was great; he immediately set to work at his statue again, with the determination to make a second, larger and better than the other; thus early revealing an all-important trait in a true genius—perseverance and love of hard work. For, whatever may be the common notions respecting the all-powerfulness of native gifts in the production of great works, unceasing, arduous industry gives the best assurance of perfection in the end. That perfection stands upon too high an eminence to be gained at a bound; the height may only be reached by patient toil and devoted self-denial, and many who envy the genius which gains the steep, shrink from the labor that the struggle entails.

Antonio's Madonna has quite a little history of its own, which is worth giving.

Pasino, who had thus far been the lad's teacher, could be of no assistance here, for the old man had only sculptured leaves and mouldings, and had always followed his model strictly with the help of a three-legged compass. Now, it chanced that there stood in a niche in the corner of the market-place at Possagno a Madonna which was held in great esteem by the people, and was probably a spot where pilgrimages were frequently terminated; be this as]it may, this statue, partly on account of the homage paid it, and partly for lack of better material, served our young sculptor as his model; He took from it, however, only the general attitude and the drapery. The face seems to have been inspired by a picture after Raphael which had belonged to his father. For six weeks Antonio labored hard and steadily; then his work was finished; loud were the praises on all sides; for his grandfather, in his simple delight, proclaimed the statue a *chef-d'œuvre*. The good parish priest, who, it would seem, was a connoisseur, was invited to see the already famous Madonna. He examined it carefully, smiling a little, perhaps, at the eagerness with which the grand-parents, cousins, and friends of the boy awaited his verdict. And now it comes: "No, it is not a *chef-d'œuvre*, but it shows remarkable promise. My child," he said, turning kindly to Antonio, "you have the germ of a great talent, but it depends upon your own earnest, faithful labors to be developed."

Beyond all the lavish praise he had received did these words satisfy the young sculptor, for none knew better than himself the faults of his work, and none felt more keenly than he his powerlessness at the moment to do better. Emboldened, however, by the kindness of the priest, the boy, while thanking him, said: "But, Reverend Father, please to grant me a great favor which will encourage me so much."

"Speak, my child," returned the priest; "if this favor depends upon me, it certainly shall be granted to you."

Then said the boy: "Father, I would like to offer to God and to the Blessed Virgin this first work of my hands. And perhaps, if this poor little statue is not too unworthy of such an honor, you will place it in one of the chapels of the church?"

"My boy," replied the priest, cordially, "that is a very happy thought of yours—to offer to God and His Holy Mother the first fruits of your talent, never forget, my child, that talents and genius are God's gifts; we must not allow them to make us proud in ourselves, but must give all the glory to God alone. Think often of this, my little friend, and ever try to keep faithful to the inspiration that prompted you to-day to offer to God your first efforts, henceforth, before you begin any work, implore His assistance, and say from your heart these words of the Psalmist: 'Not to us, O Lord, not to us, but to Thy Name be the glory,' and you will see all your efforts crowned with success. In the earnest hope that you, my boy, will follow these counsels, and will never lose sight of the glory of God, I will willingly accord to you the favor you have asked, but I attach one condition; it is that you will promise, when you become a great artist, to replace this statue by another more worthy of your talent, and above all more worthy of the One to whom you offer it to-day. Will you promise?"

"Yes, Father, yes, I promise it with all my heart," cried the boy, filled with deep emotion; "and if I ever become a real artist, I will give part of my work to ornament this church where I was baptized, and where I made my First Communion."

"May God hear your promises and bless them. In His Name I bless you, my child."

The boy fell on his knees, all around him knelt also, and the priest, making the Sign of the Cross over Antonio, pronounced those exquisite words by which our holy Mother Church conveys her blessing to her children.

The next day our artist's Madonna was taken to the church and placed in the chapel of the Blessed Virgin. There the young Children of Mary assembled to cover it with flowers and jewels, according to the Italian custom. So lavish were they in their decorations that the little statue itself was completely hidden; on Corpus Christi it was borne in procession; after the festival was over it was placed in a niche upon a pedestal which Pasino had himself prepared, and under which his little grandson engraved this inscription:

To the Blessed Virgin Mary,
The humble offering
of her
Faithful and devoted servant,
Antonio Canova, of Possagno.
1770.

We shall see later how much more than well Antonio kept his promise, and may we not be very sure that the fidelity of the boy and the man to his good pastor's advice won for him the remarkable success which marked all his efforts, and enabled him to attain to so high a degree of excellence as artist and as Christian?

The natural beauty of the scenery in the province of Treviso, and the refreshing breezes from the Alps, caused many of the Venetian nobility to build their summer villas in the neighborhood of Possagno and other obscure villages of this province. Among these noblemen was a certain Signor Giovanni Falieri, belonging to the patrician family Falieri of Venice. Signor Falieri, who often had occasion to employ Pasino Canova, held the old man in high regard for his many good qualities. Becoming acquainted with his grandson, he took the boy under his especial patronage. Stories are related of the manner in which his attention was first called to the boy's genius. Whatever truth may be attached to these anecdotes, it is very certain that Antonio early excited his patron's interest—excited it by gifts that promised much, by an ardent passion for an art in every way worthy of being cherished, and by the excellent virtues of his heart. An opportunity occurring at this time, Signor Falieri showed practical interest; he placed the boy under the instruction of Bernardi Torretto, nephew of the sculptor Torretto, the elder, and himself one of the most skilful artists of Venice. He was then residing at l'agnano, at a short distance from Falieri's villa. Torretto quickly discovered the genius of Canova, and was very earnest in the direction of his pupil's studies; while the boy's gentle manners and docile disposition soon gained the master's heart. He remained with Torretto about three years, when the latter died, leaving Canova, who had only received the first instructions in his art, without any guidance for his future career. The boy returned to his grandfather and to the obscurity of the workshop; but he was not forgotten. Falieri, his kind patron, sent for him to come to Venice and recommence his studies under Torretto's nephew, likewise a sculptor. The Falieri palace was opened freely to him, and every expense to be incurred in his studies was to be defrayed by his generous friend.

One of the most strongly marked characteristics of Canova was his love of independence, his dislike to accept too freely of another's bounty if it could be avoided. This characteristic early showed itself in the resolution he took, upon his arrival in Venice, of devoting half the day to the mechanical part of his art for some remuneration. While, therefore, we do not depreciate the great generosity of Signor Falieri towards his young *protégé*, we cannot but admire the firmness with which Canova adhered to his resolution; and though the reward of his labors was a mere pittance, the true spirit of independence exhibited by the lad (while he never once forgot his debt of gratitude to Falieri) is worthy of imitation. He remained not quite a year with Ferrari, the nephew of Torretto; and now, from this his fifteenth or sixteenth year, we may follow the real art career of Antonio Canova.

Hitherto the genius of this great mind had had no natural outlet. True, Canova was always working at his favorite employment in some form or other, but there was no decided aim; he was ambitious, yet for what he himself knew not. As we learn from one of those very few confidential letters he wrote in after-life of this period, his mind seemed to be oppressed with feelings which he could neither comprehend nor subdue. He seemed to be urged forward by them to a high imaginary goal of perfection. In his own expressive words: "I often felt as if I could have started on foot with a velocity to outstrip the wind, but without knowing whither to direct my steps; and, when activity could no longer be supported, I would have desired to lie down and die." This is a strong picture—the picture of a mind gifted with extraordinary powers, yet not knowing how to wield its own faculties. At times Canova would suddenly examine his drawings or his last model, and as suddenly turn from them, evidently seeking in vain for something still beyond him. We see in this dissatisfaction with himself, this longing after excellence, after some hardly-descried eminence, the workings of a mind above its situation, held back not alone by lack of necessary information, but also by the crudity of those other qualities of the mind whose full maturity is needed to control and counterbalance the imagination of the boy. At Venice this inquietude began to leave him; he was no longer depressed by hopeless wishes; his aim was now clear and decided. He threw himself with all ardor into the almost vast arena of study opening before him. Still, at this time, while his taste is constantly improving, and all through his life and art career, even in the fullest development of every faculty of his gifted mind, he will never find himself satisfied. This no real artist can ever be. Many dark hours of self-abasement in the realization of failure are before Canova; but these hours will be for him the irritation indicating growth, and he will come out from them quickened and invigorated with new determination to reach his ideal of excellence.

Canova remained in Venice about eight years. The first year of this period was passed under the nephew of Torretto; he worked also with great success at the Academy of Arts, and he carved of white marble two baskets of fruit and flowers for the Farsetti family, to whose kindness he owed the privilege of devoting much time of study in the gallery of their palace. So earnest and unremitting were his exertions that in four years' time the young Antonio became sufficiently skilled in his profession to present himself before the world. He therefore set up his first studio in a vacant cell at the monastery of the Augustinian Friars attached to the Church of San Stefano. Here, and later in San Maurizio, he worked till 1780,* in which year he left Venice for Rome.

For the reason that we could not, within the limits of this sketch, undertake a critical review of Canova's works, and because our idea is more a general notice or study of the sculptor and his manner of working than any extended consideration of the same, we will be content to mention only one or two of the ten pieces executed by

---

* Quatremère de Quincy gives October, 1779; Cicognara, December, 1780. The evidence is in favor of the latter authority.

him while at Venice. We will then pass with him to Rome, first, however, touching on his method of study. The statues of Orpheus and Eurydice were his first after the baskets already spoken of. His last work before leaving Venice was the group of "Dædalus and Icarus." Both Quatremère de Quincy in his *Canova et ses Ouvrages*, and Memes in his *Biography*, give an exhaustive criticism of this group, which may be said to mark the boundary line between the style of the student and the remarkable degree of perfection of reality and ideal which he afterwards attained.

In order, however, to judge fairly of Canova's reformation in the method of study for artists, and to estimate its value correctly, it is of the utmost importance that we realize the condition of sculpture not only during the time immediately preceding Canova, but more particularly from that of Michael Angelo—whose death was followed by a rapid degeneracy in art—through the long period of decline lasting even to our Antonio's days. It is beyond our power here to give anything like an adequate sketch or description of those times; the careful reader must search for himself to justify our statement that Canova was a true reformer where reform was needed; we shall be content to say that one great cause of the decline may by found even in Michael Angelo's days: what that great master noticed in the art of his period was a timidity of execution, but a great fidelity to nature; this needed only deeper expression and freedom of the imagination. To combine these would have been to restore art to its days of pristine glory, such as we have now only glimpses of in what is left us from the time of Phidias; this was what Michael Angelo in the commencement of his career promised. But to his vigorous perception the simplicity of the Greek sculpture seemed poverty; he resolved on a bold style which should appeal to the imagination alone. From the simple and natural he advanced with rapid strides to the forced and exaggerated; hence, while his works may be sublime, it is not the sublimity that connects itself with our sympathy. Rarely, if ever, are such muscular exaggerations met in nature; true art should always be the highest ideal of nature, not exaggerated but perfected. The consequence of this neglect to follow nature was rapid decline. Michael Angelo's immediate successors, in following his example and receding more and more from nature, became more and more exaggerated; defects which his great genius alone could conceal were in their hands a fruitful source of corruption. Other influences, too, were at work; men's minds were drawn more towards intellectual and scientific studies. During the seventeenth century, the genius of the time was turned to philosophical and mathematical researches. Some among those who still clung to art were sensible of its degeneracy, but they either failed to discover the secret, or, discovering it, lacked courage to reform; or the times and the patronage were against their efforts. So novelty, at the expense of simplicity and the perfected ideal of nature, was the characteristic of the days of corruption and decline in art.

Canova realized this, and, early perceiving that he could not rest his hopes of excellence upon the imitation of the masters, resolved "to begin the art where the art itself had begun." In a word, he was both gifted and courageous enough to put aside the preconceived ideas of study, which his sound judgment showed him were false; and, like the Greek, he studied nature earnestly and faithfully. In this he went diametrically opposite to the schools of his day, where the sound maxim of Ghiberti, "that since sculpture consists in imitating truth, we should begin by imitating with truth," was wholly disregarded. Canova estimated nature truly, and, although he could not yet entirely appreciate her full value, he felt he was on the right road in taking her simply for his model. The end proved him correct; for in his works he has united the classic simplicity of the Greeks with the perfection of nature and the ideal beauty of the imagination. All through his course of study, even to a late period in life, Canova devoted a large portion of time his to anatomy, which he justly regarded as "the secret of the art." Anatomical knowledge alone would, however, have rendered him merely theoretical, had he not united with it (as every artist should) the practical power gained from constant observation and sketches. He termed the studies made when watching the crowds of people in the streets, the animated gestures during conversation, or the display of all passions wherever witnessed, *il scolpir del cuore* —the sculpture of the heart. His quick glance and ready memory enabled him to catch and retain those fugitive expressions of muscular action never to be perceived in the artificial movements of academical models. The advantages of the warm Italian climate, where the lower classes are so little solicitous about clothing, furnished abundant material for these accidental studies.

(CONCLUSION NEXT WEEK.)

How can they preach to the heathen to leave all things and take up the cross, who have made little or no sacrifice themselves? How can one feel an enthusiasm for a cause for which he has sacrificed nothing?

The Passion Play at Oberammergau.

THE correspondent of *The London Daily News* gives the following telegraphic account of the first public performance of the Passion play at Oberammergau on May 17th:

"The rush is so great that all tickets for the first day's performance were sold yesterday by 5 o'clock, and at 7 last evening the public crier went round the village with the announcement that, in order not to disappoint those who had travelled far, and been unable to get places, there would be a second representation on Tuesday. The unreserved seats, which numbered close on three thousand, were full at a very early hour in the morning, although the play did not begin until 8 o'clock. One could not help noticing the preponderance of English and Americans in the reserved seats. English was almost the only language that was spoken. I hardly think that there were 10 per cent. of Germans. Shortly after 8 o'clock, the loud boom of cannon, fired from a neighboring elevation, announced that the play was about to commence. All eyes were turned towards the stage, and the chorus, attired in splendid robes, advanced in a grave and stately manner, singing in very fair voices three or four verses, beginning with the words, 'Though the angel of God is just, still He does not wish the death of the sinner'; while the chorus are singing the last verse they divide in the middle, falling back on either side and disclosing the central stage. As the last note is heard, the curtain rises, showing a fine tableau, representing the expulsion of Adam and Eve from paradise. When the curtain drops on the first tableau, the chorus resume their original position, and continue singing until another tableau is shown in the same way. Then comes the first scene, the chorus retiring. It is the entry of Christ into Jerusalem. The effect is very fine indeed. Our Saviour, riding on an ass, sits sideways, followed by His disciples and people and children with flowers. Josef Maier, who represents Christ, filled his part admirably, so that the eyes of the audience of nearly 5,000 people were riveted on him. The sun was shining brightly at the time, lighting up the beautiful robes of the performers, and rendering the scene charming in the extreme. The Saviour then dismounts, drives out the money-changers from the temple and overturns their tables. Then follows a tableau, also well set, representing the conspiracy of Joseph's brethren. I may remark that all the subjects of the *tableaux vivants* are taken from the Old Testament, and each time are followed by a fulfilment from the New Testament. The second scene, remarkable for its gorgeousness, was the Council of High Priests and others of their order, discussing what punishment should be dealt to the man of Galilee. The scenes which followed were striking representations of the acts and sufferings of our Lord up to the crucifixion. This last scene was very effective and beautiful, and was performed in a really wonderful manner. The audience was almost breathless with the seeming reality of the representation. The figure looked as if it was actually nailed on the cross; blood was on both hands and feet, and even with a good opera-glass one could not possibly detect how Josef Maier could remain so long in this position. The crucifixion scene lasted twenty-one minutes, and was carried out in every detail, even to piercing the breast with a spear, blood rushing out of the wound. The actions of the performers were represented on the one hand with such earnestness, and on the other with such intense simplicity and devotion, that one's eyes were fixed to the spot. After the body was taken down and buried in the sepulchre, a short time elapsed, when the entrance-stone fell, and Christ appeared, clad in silver gauze, for but a moment."

The correspondent of *The Telegraph* says:

"Josef Maier acted, or rather moved, the part of Christ with a calm, earnest, and dignified manner, and the words he had to utter were delivered in a deep rich voice, which fell upon the ear with a strange smoothness and sweetness. Every movement he made was quiet and graceful. The actresses were by no means so good as the men. The chorus sang indifferently, although the Choragus, the sole tenor, and bass members of the Schutzgeister were admirable. The spectacular effect of the procession with the cross was grand, owing to the new and correct Roman soldier costumes. The acting of Judas was magnificent. The crucifixion scene was terribly realistic, causing a profound and painful impression. The performance was perfect and infinitely better mounted than in former years."

Another correspondent writes:

"Josef Maier is a tall, thin man, about five feet eleven, with long, shiny black hair and beard, and a pale face. His eyes are small and his nose wants boldness, but his expression is gentle and devotional. He has been much petted by visitors, especially the English, and has received many presents. Next in importance is Gregor Lechner, who plays Judas, and has played this character for the last thirty years. Caiaphas is represented by the burgomaster, Johann Lang, and Pilate by Thomas Pindel. I mention these last three characters because they are very important—Judas having by far the longest speaking part in the drama. Judas is inclined to be a little stagey, and to play to the audience. Caiaphas and Pilate could not be represented with greater force or dignity, and the meekness, propriety, and grace of Josef Maier are beyond all question. What strikes a spectator like myself, accustomed to dramatic performances of all kinds and in all countries, is the quiet dignity of the whole performance. It is not an unreasonable estimate to put down the summer visitors to Oberammergau at 300,000."

Catholic Notes.

——An Italian exchange always speaks of us as *Ave Maria di New-York*.

——Count Joseph Stolberg, son of Joseph von Stolberg, lately entered the Dominican Order at Venlo.

——A new Catholic paper, called *O Brazil Catholico*, has been recently established in the capital of Brazil.

——A great famine, occasioned by an exceptionally serious inundation, reigns in the mission of western Tong-King; it has already made many victims.

——Mgr. Chevalier, of the Society of Foreign Missions, Bishop of Hierapolis and Vicar-Apostolic of Mayssour, died recently at Bangalore. R. I. P.

——Mr. de la Rivière, the son of a wealthy patrician family which figures prominently in the history of the German republic, has entered the fold of the Catholic Church.

—The municipality of Rome has paid a tribute to the memory of Father Secchi by erecting, on the promenade, of the Pincio a statue representing the great astronomer in the attire of a member of the Society of Jesus.

—The Rev. Thomas Jones, late Anglican pastor of Walkerville, two miles above Windsor, Ont., was received into the Church on the first of May, together with his wife and two children, by the Rt. Rev. Mgr. Bruyère, V. G., assisted by the Very Rev. Dean Wagner, of Windsor.

—A man in West Alexandra, Ohio, having felled an oak, about six feet in girth, found, in a cavity in its centre, a German Catholic prayer-book, folded in cloth, which crumbled to the touch. The date of printing was 1729, and enough was read of some writing in French on the blank leaves, to learn that the book belonged to a French soldier.

—The cause of Catholic elementary education progresses favorably in Belgium. Catholic schools are continually being opened amid the applause of the people, both in the towns and in the country. At Louvain the "Dernier des ecoles Catholiques," founded three years ago, has been most successful, being powerfully aided by the University students. A great sensation has been caused at Charneux by a school-mistress, who had been over the communal school since 1862, sending in her resignation, notwithstanding very advantageous offers made to her by the civil authorities, in order to take charge of the Catholic girls' school.—*Catholic Telegraph.*

—The miracle of the liquefaction of the blood of St. Januarius took place at Naples as usual on the 2d of May. The vials containing the miraculous blood were carried in procession the preceding day to the Church of St. Chiara and placed opposite the relic of the head. After forty-five minutes of prayer, it partly dissolved, a portion remaining hard. On returning to the cathedral, the blood was found hardened, but afterwards the greater portion dissolved, and it was replaced in this condition. The next day—Sunday—when the blood was exposed to the veneration of the people, the hardened portion dissolved. Towards evening it was altogether liquefied. In the morning the blood was found hard, and somewhat increased in volume, and after eleven minutes of prayer, it dissolved altogether. The phase of the blood dissolving with a portion remaining hard has been observed frequently.

—Rev. George Steiner, a well-known priest of the diocese of Fort Wayne, departed this life at Alberquerque, New Mexico, on the 1st inst. He had been in ill health for some years and was several times at the point of death; but it was hoped that rest and a change of climate would restore his strength and prolong his career of usefulness. God ordained otherwise and took him to Himself. In the death of Father Steiner the diocese loses one of its most devoted and efficient priests. He was remarkable for his genial disposition and good-heartedness, and was endeared to all who knew him. He bore his prolonged illness with exemplary resignation and preserved his wonted cheerfulness to the very last. The Catholics of Huntington, Ind., of whom Father Steiner was the beloved pastor, and the clergy of Fort Wayne, will not soon forget the example of his devoted life. R. I. P.

—THE REMARKABLE CONVERSION OF TWO ANGLICAN CLERGYMEN.—In the year 1849, two Anglican clergymen, both of them Oxford men, set off from English shores on a pilgrimage, or, as they probably termed it, a tour to Jerusalem. While crossing the sea, a Protestant Bible which they had in use fell overboard; and this little incident was afterwards recognized by the two travellers to be of some prophetic significance, for, on reaching the Holy Land, their religious creed underwent a great transition. Arriving at a monastery where they announced themselves, in the "lingo" of the High Church School, as Catholic priests, they were asked to celebrate Mass, an invitation they were honest enough to refuse, making at the same time further explanations of their ecclesiastical position. Whether the good monks were up to the subtleties of our modern English controversy may perhaps be a matter of doubt; but they knew very well how to define their own position, and very effectually too; for, in the end, the two Anglican clergymen submitted to the Holy Roman Church. Thirty years have passed since then: and one of these converts so favored in the place and the circumstances of their conversion, is the Rev. Father J. H. Wynne, the respected head of the Catholic mission at Bournemouth, and the other is the Right Rev. James Laird Patterson, who has just been raised to the Episcopal rank, under the title of Bishop of Emmaus, a little village almost within the shadow of which he received the grace of conversion to the Faith.—*Catholic Times.*

—THE NEW CHAPEL OF ST. PAUL OF THE CROSS IN ROME.—Through the munificence of Prince Alexander Torlonia, the Passionist Fathers of Rome have had the consolation of seeing the chapel dedicated to their Founder, St. Paul of the Cross, elegantly finished. It is remarkable, both on account of the great value and magnificence of the marble employed in its construction, and the beauty of the frescoes. The monoliths of oriental alabaster which form the two busts of the columns lateral to the altar are very rare. These monoliths, together with all the alabaster of the chapel, were the gift of Pius IX, of sacred memory, who had a great love for the Order. The altar is much admired on account of the precious stones from which it is formed, particularly the six agates on the candlesticks, which were on exhibition at the last Exposition of Vienna. On Sunday, the 25th ult., the body of the Saint was exposed to the veneration of the faithful, and in the afternoon was carried in procession to the new chapel. An immense number of people assisted. The Passionist Fathers preceded, vested in their sacerdotal robes, followed by several mitred abbots and many Bishops. Cardinal Howard closed the procession. When the chapel was reached, hymns of praise were sung by the choir, under the direction of Capocci, after which Cardinal Howard blessed the multitude. All immediately pressed forward to the urn, which contained the body of the Saint, to secure some of the flowers with which it was covered. The concourse of the faithful was so great that the legal act of depositing the body under the new altar could not be commenced till nightfall. This function took place in the presence of Mgr. Lenti, Vicegerent of Rome, assisted by the notary of the vicariate and by proper witnesses.

—THE SUFFERING IN IRELAND.—We make the following extract from an Irish letter received last week just after going to press. The writer is a priest: "I cannot keep my tears from falling on the very paper on which I am writing as I think on what I have seen and heard of in and about Galway. In a national school, on one of the Galway islands, the inspector asked one of the children where were his brothers and sisters, that they were not at school?' The child hesitated, being ashamed to tell the cause of their absence. 'Tell me, my boy,' said the kind inspector, ' what keeps them at home; I am not going to blame you nor them if they cannot come.' 'Sir,' said the boy, bursting into tears, '*they have nothing on them.*' The good man, who was all sympathy and kindness, so felt for them that he visited their little house, without a second room, without a chimney, and found the children just as their little brother described them with *absolutely* ' nothing on them,' crawling *naked* round the dying embers of a miserable turf fire, shivering with cold, and slowly dying of want. Seven children had to sleep on one wretched bed of straw, covered with a blanket: no, not even that, but with some miserable dirty rags fastened together. . . . Famine fever has already visited the islands of Galway; sixty cases are reported; perhaps before this letter reaches you, many of the poor famine-stricken people will have died the most agonizing of all deaths—famine. Unless our poor people are helped to get through the 'starving months,' June and July, there is little chance for them. Even *ten cents* enables one poor person to get through a day. It would make your heart bleed to see the big tear of silent, heartfelt gratitude on the face of these poor people even for a half-penny; and to see the poor mother remaining hungry herself to bring the morsel of bread to her starving children at home."

——INDIAN MISSIONS IN THE WEST.—On the Feast of the Blessed Trinity, two Indian children—a boy and a girl—of the Indian mission schools of Devil's Lake Agency, received their First Communion. The boy—Luke Hepan, *i. e.*, the second male child—is about eighteen years old; he was one of the first scholars to enter the Indian mission school when it opened there in the fall of 1874; he was baptized April 2, 1876, by Rev. Louis Bonin; he is fairly educated, and a trustworthy and promising young man. The girl is named Thecla Wakanhditaninkiye,—*i. e.*, she who causes lightning to appear,—is about sixteen years of age, and was baptized by Rt. Rev. Bishop Marty, O. S. B., on the 30th of June, 1878; from that time up to the present she has been a constant attendant at the mission school. The poor children were both proud and happy over this most notable event of their lives, and their joy was entered into and appreciated by their schoolmates and all others, both whites and Indians, who witnessed the ceremony. In the afternoon, the children renewed their baptismal vows and were enrolled in the Confraternity of Our Lady of Mount Carmel. The work of Christianizing the Indians is going on slowly but surely, and it is consoling to see that the efforts and sacrifices made in their behalf are crowned with success. An excellent example is being set before these Indians by numerous members of their own tribe, which cannot fail to be productive of much good, and eventually of many conversions. Two weeks ago, General McNeil, United States Indian Inspector, visited the Agency in order to look into the conduct of affairs. He found everything in the best possible condition; before leaving, he said: "I shall be pleased to report most favorably on the state of affairs at Devil's Lake Agency. Never, in the course of my experience, have I found an agency in such perfect order in every particular; and I have heard less complaints against the agents than ever before." These expressions were most deserved, and undoubtedly very gratifying to the excellent agent, Major James McLaughlin, as the good services of an honest Indian agent are seldom appreciated.

——FOR THE NEEDY MISSION:—50 cts. from James Molloy; $10 from Mrs. Isabella Mann.

Confraternity of the Immaculate Conception
(Or of Our Lady of Lourdes).

" We fly to thy patronage, O Holy Mother of God!"
REPORT FOR THE WEEK ENDING JUNE 2D.

The following intentions are recommended to the prayers of the members this week: Recovery of health for 30 persons,—change of life for 19 persons and 1 family,—conversion to the Faith for 28 persons and 4 families,—special graces for several priests, religious, and clerical students,—temporal favors for 15 persons and 8 families,—spiritual favors for 28 persons and 8 families,—recovery of health, or a happy death, for 3 persons,—the spiritual and temporal welfare of 6 communities; also, 13 particular intentions, and 4 thanksgivings for favors received.

Specified intentions: Grace for 2 persons to choose a suitable state of life,—success in business enterprises, —safe delivery,—peace and harmony in a family,—a family much afflicted by sickness and death,—removal of obstacles to a religious vocation,—a family and several persons given to intemperance,—grace for several persons to make good confessions,—removal of scandals, —means for a number of persons to pay their debts,— complete recovery of a little boy, whose life was miraculously preserved some time ago by the application of the water of Lourdes,—success in studies and examinations,—prevention of a threatened lawsuit,—a parish without a priest,—return of a father to his family,—safe voyage and return of a Bishop.

FAVORS OBTAINED.

A lady writes: " Please return thanks to Our Lady of Lourdes for the cure of a case of deafness and running ears by the water of Lourdes. The case had baffled the skill of two physicians." . . . Another person writes: " Please return thanks to our Blessed Lady for the return to the Faith of my two brothers, who had not practised their religion for three years." . . . A gentleman says: "On a former occasion, I asked the prayers of the Confraternity for the conversion of my wife to the true Faith. This request—thanks to Our Blessed Lady!—was speedily granted."

OBITUARY.

The following deceased persons are recommended to the prayers of the Confraternity: Mr. JOHN MURPHY, of Baltimore, Md., who departed this life on the 27th ult. Mr. PETER HAND, of New Orleans, La., whose death occurred on the 4th of February. Mrs. SHANNON, of Riverside, Conn., deceased on the 19th of May. Mr. M. KING, who was killed in the mines of Minnesota. CATHARINE QUINN, who breathed her last on the 30th ult. REV. FATHERS CARNEY and MOONEY, of New York. Mrs. M. H. BRENNAN, of Roxbury, Mass. JOHN and VINCENT CASSIDY; Mrs. E. SLICK; Mrs. M. A. O'KANE; Miss K. FINDLEY; Mrs. A. BEDE; MARY, JAMES, THOMAS, and MAGGIE DUGGAN; ELLEN and MICHAEL MCDONALD; ANN and ELLEN GRIEVES, CATHARINE RAFFERTY; ANN DOYLE; JOHN FITZPATRICK; Mr. and Mrs. VANDERHOFF; Mrs. M., ANNA, CHARLES and WM. KUHN; NANCY STEWART; L. CARROLL; MARGARET COUGHLIN; Mrs. C. SUBDEVILL; Mrs. S. CAMPBELL, and Miss K. HYDE. And some others, whose names have not been given. .
Requiescant in pace.

A. GRANGER, C. S. C., Director.

Youth's Department.

Lucy's Dream; or, How the Eleven Promises Came True.

(CONCLUSION.)

NOW the scene was again changed, and the angel was travelling very quickly. So fast did they go, that the objects over which they were passing were quite undiscernible; all that Lucy could tell was that they were no longer over the wide ocean, but that a very large city lay beneath. Houses, streets, horses and people, all seemed running into each other, just as the fields and trees appear to do to the passengers of an express train. Gradually, however, the angel slackened his speed, and Lucy was very glad, for her poor little head could scarcely stand such rapid movement. Now that she had time to breathe, she turned to her companion, and said: "Dear Angel, you will not be angry if I tell you I am getting very tired?"

"Angry, my poor little one? nothing pleases the good God or His angel so much as simplicity. Take a little more of this cordial," and he once more gave her the wonderful little flask, which again renewed her strength.

The night was now far advanced, but the moon was shining in all its splendor, and the rays of glory grew brighter and brighter. By the time they reached the earth, the streets were quite forsaken, and everything reposed in the quiet stillness of deserted midnight. Suddenly, however, sounds of noisy mirth resounded on all sides, and such a twirling and whirling, and so much dazzling light, that it was hard to know what was going on. Lucy wondered what the angel wanted in all this bustle, for he usually visited houses of peace; however, she thought the best thing she could do was to find out what it all meant; so before we relate what was the angel's business here, we must tell what she saw. The place where they stood was a large and lofty hall, brilliantly illuminated, though not with the rays of the Sacred Heart, for there was not so much as a single one here. The ball-room, for such it was, was crowded with people who were dancing and twirling to their heart's content. The angel glided noiselessly amongst the dancers, until he came to a certain spot where he suddenly stopped short, and then gently touched the floor with the tip of his wing. On came the gay dancers; but for a long time no one crossed the spot. One, two, three minutes passed, and a crowd had collected round a young man who had fallen. How the accident had happened, no one could find out. The angel knew and Lucy guessed, but they did not come forward to explain matters, so the wise people of the world were left in ignorance. Unseen the angel caused the patient to be carried from the room to his home, where the outstretched arms of a tender mother were ready to receive him. The angel did not enter, but simply made the sign of the cross over the house, and sped on his way. Soon the white cliffs of sunny France were lost to sight, and nothing was visible but the blue sky and the shining waters. Now and then a ship which looked like a speck upon the vast expanse passed beneath; but no sound was heard and everything bespoke perfect calm, even the gentle ripple of the waves broke not the stillness, for Lucy and the angel were very high above the waters. Everything seemed so heavenly and Lucy felt so happy that she again addressed her companion: "Dear Angel, do tell me why you made that poor man fall, and why you did not stay with him; perhaps he will die, and I should not think he is very well prepared."

"When the Sacred Heart converts a sinner it is not always done all at once, my little one, and sometimes sinners are so hardened that the merciful Heart of our Redeemer has to use violence. This young man will not die; and we are going to pay him another visit as we return." Then the angel went on telling many a secret about the Sacred Heart, which Lucy never forgot, and which he will tell to us if we only ask him. As they were thus chatting together, a sound of gentle music fell upon their ear, and instantly the angel unfolded his beautiful wings, took his golden harp, touched it softly, and sung: "May the Sacred Heart of Jesus be praised and loved everywhere!" when another sound as sweet as the first, replied: "And may the devotion to the Immaculate heart of the ever Blessed Mother of God be spread throughout the universe!" Lucy looked to see where the sound came from, but all that she could see was a very soft white cloud lined with azure blue. When the cloud had vanished out of sight Lucy asked the angel who had sung the answer to his aspiration. "It was the Angel of the Immaculate Conception, my little one."

"I wish, dear Angel," continued Lucy, "I could see all the beautiful spirits that you see."

"Do not wish what is not the will of God, my child. You are very happy, are you not?"

"Oh, how could I be otherwise? I never felt so happy in my life."

Presently the angel and Lucy arrived at a busy seaport town, but did not linger there; travelling onwards, they came to a mighty city. A large and massive cathedral towered aloft in the very centre of the city. However, lofty though it was, the golden rays which still encompassed the wide world did not enter through the many windows, but a damp mist seemed to hang over the place. Many other churches could be seen at short distances, but it was only a very few which were lit up by the hallowed light. The noise and bustle of the place would be hard to explain; the streets were crowded with people, yet each one seemed intent with his own affairs. Lucy noticed that the angel appeared very sad, and that as he passed over the numerous churches which were enveloped in the black mist, he always covered his face with his wings. Somehow the place seemed familiar to her, and she was sure she had seen a picture of that large cathedral in her atlas-book. "Oh, yes!" she exclaimed, half aloud; "it is St. Paul's Cathedral, is it not, dear Angel? Then we are in England—papa's native country?"

"Yes, my child; and I suppose you can guess why everything looks so black here, although the sun shines on this city as it does on every other."

"It must be," replied Lucy, "because it is Protestant. Poor England! do you think will it ever be converted?"

"That is known to God alone, my little one; but the angels see many things which give them great hopes; above all things, the relics of the many saints which lie beneath its sod make it very dear to the Sacred Heart. And then, the ever Blessed Virgin never ceases to intercede that the Holy Sacrifice may once more be offered in the many churches which in days gone by belonged to the true Faith."

By this time the multitude had become lessened and the noise and bustle had almost ceased, for they had reached one of those pretty and pleasant suburbs which surround busy London. The angel showed Lucy a large white house at the back of which lay a spacious garden. "It is there we are going to make our next resting-place," he said, as they approached the spot. Everything around was perfectly still; all that could be heard was the gentle rustle of the leaves and the cheering sound of numerous little songsters who seemed as though trying to keep time with the distant din of the not very true notes of school-pianos. Lucy could tell at once that they were in the vicinity of an establishment for young ladies. On entering the enclosure, beneath a mulberry-tree they found a young nun sitting, busily engaged with a piece of work; in fact, so absorbed was she, that she did not perceive the approach of a fairy-like little creature who was tripping down the garden-walk, until two arms were thrown around her neck and she was greeted with these words: "Here I am at last, Kate! only don't begin to scold, or else I will run off directly."

"So your conscience tells you you deserve a scolding, then, Miss May?" replied her elder sister, at the same time returning her affectionate salute. "Come now, what have you been doing during the last two months?"

"Oh, I have been enjoying myself most delightfully, though I must say I have not been very good," was the quick reply. "There, don't look so scandalized! I have come on purpose to tell you the whole story, and then I'll do just as you tell me, for I am fairly entangled in a net in which my conscience does not feel very comfortable." And she began as follows: "When mamma left home at the end of April, I begged her to let me leave the convent and stay at home to take charge of the house, at the same time making all sorts of promises, and indeed I intended to keep them. Well, the first week passed off very nicely, when one fine morning Alida Smith paid me a visit, and you know she is just the one both you and mamma have always warned me against. When I first entered the drawing-room, I was very guarded as to the conversation, but after a time she became so amiable and pleasant, that before I was actually aware of it, she had prevailed upon me to accept an invitation to a croquet party that very evening. After she had gone, my conscience told me many times to send an excuse, but I had not the moral courage, and so 7 o'clock found me in a circle of fashionable Protestants instead of in my usual place at the May Benediction. Of course that evening I made many friends and was invited to I don't know how many houses. The first afternoon had passed away so pleasantly that I could not resist another, and then another, and so on till the end of the month. Old nurse often remonstrated, but I only laughed at her fears, and as she did not say anything to papa, and as I always managed to get home before he came from the city, I was suffered to go on without interference. At the beginning of June, I received a letter from mamma telling me not to forget to either send or take a bouquet to the church every day during the month. There was a great deal of good advice in the letter, which made me think seriously for a little while, but it was soon forgotten. In accordance with her wish, however, I sent the flowers every day, though I did not go near the church myself, except on Sundays to Mass, until Wednesday, which was the last day, when I could find no one to take the flowers. At first I thought, 'Oh, never mind!' but something urged me to set off and perform the act of devotion. On arriving at the presbytery, who should open the door but the good old Father himself! so you may be sure I did not get off scott free, but had to follow him into the parlor, and there give an account of my proceedings. He was as kind as usual, but nothing would do but that I must go to confession there and then, and receive Holy Communion this morning, after which he made me promise to come and put myself under your direction, so here I am," she said with a merry laugh, "waiting for you to pass judgment on the poor little culprit."

"I don't think," replied her sister, "that it is quite such a laughing matter as you seem to think, May dear; and the only way to get away from your new acquaintances is to stay here until mamma comes back."

It was very easy to see by the expression of May's face that this decision was not only unexpected but decidedly hard to relish, and, as no answer came, her sister rose, saying, "Come: it is the Sacred Heart which has led you so far, let us go and ask Him to give you strength to do what I am sure is the best means to renew your former fervor."

After following for a few minutes in silence, May objected. "But if I stay here, who will take care of papa and the boys?"

"The same person who has been doing so for the last two months, and I do not think that person's name is May," rejoined her sister, with a smile.

"Well, I suppose you are right, Sister; but certainly it is very hard to stay shut up in a convent during the holidays. It is all very fine for you who are a nun, but I like to have a little freedom sometimes."

"Now, May, you know you are only talking nonsense; mamma will be back next week, and then you can go home as soon as you like."

They had reached the chapel door, and on entering, were followed by Lucy and the angel. Dart after dart escaped from the holy spot where Jesus resided, piercing without difficulty the heart of the young man religious, but it was not quite the same with poor little May's. Somehow they could not find a welcome there, but were forced to return to their home in the silent tabernacle. The sisters knelt down side by side beneath the soft twinkling of the sanctuary lamp. The angel took his place by May and whispered softly in her ear. She bent her head, but still Lucy could see that her heart kept close shut. After a few minutes' silent prayer, the elder sister drew forth her chaplet, the angel inspired May to do the same. The first aspiration was scarcely uttered before May's heart was entirely melted.

"Now, Lucy," said the angel as they were once more started on their journey, "we must make haste back to France and finish the conversion of the young man you were so zealous about a little while ago, and then we will return to America and finish our work, for we have something more to do there yet."

They travelled on very fast, only delaying now and then as they passed by some shrine or chapel. They soon arrived at Paris, and Lucy became so interested with all that she saw, and it was so strange to hear the people talking in a language that she did not understand, that before she was aware of it they had entered a house. For some time she could not make out what kind of a room they were in, for it was almost entirely dark. At last she perceived that they were close to a sick bed, by the side of which sat an elderly lady: she was gazing absently on the patient, for her hand grasped a chaplet and her lips were silently moving, sending forth at the same time one snow white leaflet after another. When the last roseleaf had united itself to its predecessors, a pale soft light enveloped the patient, and Lucy recognized the victim of the ball. Presently he awoke with a start, crying out in the English tongue: "Mother, mother, the scapular! the scapular! Oh, mother, I have had such a dream!" he rejoined, in a calmer tone. "It seemed to me that I was falling into a deep pit, and all I could see was the scapular you wanted me to put on the other day floating far above my head, while a voice mockingly resounded in my ear, 'Catch hold of it if you can, and you will be saved!' But my efforts were all in vain, and I was sinking faster and faster into the pit, when all at once your beads appeared in sight and gently drew it within my reach; I grasped it and awoke." A tear of thanksgiving fell from the mother's eye, while she took from under the pillow a scapular of the Sacred Heart, and, placing it around the neck of her son, said in a voice full of emotion: "May I send for the priest now, William?"

At these words a dark frown passed over the young man's countenance, but grace conquered, and, covering his face with his hands, he replied: "Yes, yes, or it may be too late." The Christian mother waited not another minute, but knowing well what a silent power the crucifix has to draw forth tears of contrition, laid it gently on the bed, while she herself went to summon the priest. The angel with his little companion kept watch until the dear old lady returned with him who was to finish the great work of the conversion of a sinner.

On their journey, Lucy learned from the angel that they were now going back to the country of her birth, where she should see the remaining two promises accomplished.

"But, dear Angel, are there not three more?" she inquired.

"Why, my little one," answered her conductor, "have you already forgotten how almost miraculously your own convent chapel has been built and embellished? Is that not proof enough that the sweet Jesus aids visibly every undertaking made in His name?"

"Oh, yes, so it does!" cried the little girl, quite delighted at the thought. "Is it you who have inspired so many good people to offer their little contribution in order to adorn our chapel?"

"Ah, that is my secret, Lucy," said the angel.

When they were once more over the broad plains of the New World, they continued travelling for some time, passing by turns over forests, fields, and large cities, until the cloud began by degrees to descend and at last alighted on a building of noble aspect. The day had not yet begun to dawn, and the house would have been enveloped in darkness had it not been for one dim light which glimmered through a side window: thither the angel directed his course, and in a trice they were within the building. Everything was quite calm and still, and a very holy feeling came over Lucy as they drew near the tiny light, for she perceived they were in the presence of the Holy of Holies. For a few moments the angel prostrated himself in lowly adoration; then moved towards the door, which at that moment gently opened, and a priest entered dressed as though for a journey. He knelt down before the Blessed Sacrament, and as he did so, the angel reverently lowered his head until it almost touched the tabernacle door, when he breathed forth in low accents: "Divine Master, grant him what he asks." The words were no sooner uttered than a ray of light darted from the tabernacle and pierced the young priest's heart. On it Lucy could trace the promise our dear Lord has made, "That all priests who practice devotion to His Sacred Heart, should have the power to touch the hearts of the most obdurate sinners."

In a few moments the priest rose and left the chapel, the angel and Lucy following close behind. Descending a number of stairs, they found themselves in a large hall lighted only by a lantern which a man held in his hand.

"I have come for you, as you wished," he said, addressing the priest; "but I fear you cannot do any good, for he is the very picture of despair."

"Is the poor man so much worse, George?"

"Yes, Father; the doctor says he cannot last until to-morrow night."

These few words exchanged, the door was quickly unfastened and they left the house. First they walked up one street and then down another until they came to a dark, dismal-looking house, which Lucy could think was no other than a prison. She shuddered as she entered, but the angel told her not to fear for nobody would harm her. Passing through a long narrow passage, they came to a low iron door. Their guide took out a large bunch of keys which made a great noise and unlocked the door. He then made way for the priest, saying, "I will return in a quarter of an hour." Before the good Father entered the cell, he made the sign of the cross over it, and called his guardian angel to his assistance. The place was not quite dark, for a lantern was suspended from the ceiling, so that Lucy could see at a glance what it contained: a straw bed and one stone seat. Moans came from the bed, and as the priest stepped forward, the poor prisoner tried to rise to see who it was.

"You are suffering, my friend?" began the priest, as he seated himself on the stone seat.

"Yes, I am suffering," was the response; "but what is that to anyone? No one cares for me."

"Yes, some one cares for you. I care for you, or else I should not have come at this hour."

At these words the poor man raised himself as best he could and looked steadfastly at the priest, saying: "It is no use trying to make me go to confession, for I *won't* go," and then he turned his back to the priest, who, however, was not discouraged, but instead of arguing with the dying man, he drew forth his chaplet, and, in a low voice, addressed himself to the Sacred Heart.

"What are you doing?" inquired the sick man, when he found that the priest still remained.

"Praying, my friend."

"What for?" asked the other, with a hollow laugh.

"For you."

"Oh! and what kind of a prayer are you saying?"

"Jesus, meek and humble of heart, make his heart like unto Thine!"

At the moment the priest had begun to pray, Lucy had perceived the angel spread his wings over the sufferer, and every now and again whisper in his ear.

"Yes, I remember, I remember," murmured the dying lips. The priest thought the man was wandering in his mind, but, however, the tone had changed for the better.

"What do you remember, my friend?" he ventured.

"I remember that sermon, and it is the only one I can remember. It touched me at the time, but many years have passed, and now my heart must be like a stone. Oh, no! there is no mercy for me, there is no mercy for me!"

"There is mercy for every soul until it is buried in hell," rejoined the priest in a grave and solemn tone; then softening his voice, he said: "My friend, repeat once after me these words, 'Jesus, meek and humble of Heart, make my heart like unto Thine!'" The angel now whispered more than ever, and almost against himself, the dying man repeated the words of the priest, and then burst into tears.

"It is enough, Lucy, we may go now," said the angel. When again in the open air, the cloud upon which they rested ascended higher and higher until they were at a greater distance from the earth than they had ever been before.

"Now, Lucy," said her guide, "I have brought you up so high because what you are going to see belongs more to heaven than earth," and he made her a sign to look up. She did so, but all that she could discern was a soft luminous cloud which was descending very slowly from the sky. Presently soft strains of music reached their ears, which by degrees came nearer and nearer. The angel now touched Lucy's eyes, and the soft cloud unfolded, and behold: they were at the feet of a majestic Lady who held in her arms a Child of surpassing beauty. The angel prostrated in lowly adoration, and Lucy did the same. In fact, she dared not look up again, until she heard a sweet voice call her by name. Raising her eyes, the Lady beckoned her to come forward. She did so. The lovely Child smiled upon her and pointed to His pierced Heart which was exposed to view. As she gazed upon that loving Heart, a cry of joy escaped her, for, behold, her own name appeared engraven in letters of gold. Presently it sunk deep into the wound, and another was seen on the surface. It was the name of some one she loved dearly. In a moment it was replaced by another, and then another, until the vision slowly ascended and she could no longer discern the names written on the Heart. However, when it had withdrawn to a short distance, it stopped once more, and the angel told her to look very attentively. She did so, and behold, one little rose after another fluttered like tiny birds around the angel, who blew them very gently towards the vision, where they rested at the feet of the Divine Infant. The Holy Child raised His little hand and blessed each one as it approached Him, then pressing it to His Sacred Heart, He gave it to His Mother who let it fall towards the earth. The luminous cloud now once more encompassed the vision and it was soon lost to sight. Lucy and the angel were again alone; they continued their journey for some time, until at last Lucy recognized the cross which topped her own convent gate. One moment more, and they were again in the chapel whence they had started; when boom! went the large bell as it began to toll out the morning *Angelus.* Lucy gave a start and looked around her on all sides; it was broad daylight, but the angel was no longer to be seen. "Dear me! what does it all mean? where has the angel gone?"

"What angel? and what are you doing here, my little lady?" said the kind Sister, who had just finished ringing the *Angelus.* Lucy had now rubbed the sleep out of her eyes, during which operation the whole truth had flashed to her mind.

"I must have been dreaming, Sister," she said; "but oh, I have had such a lovely dream! I've been dreaming about the Sacred Heart and a beautiful angel. Do help me to get back to bed without waking anybody, and if you promise not to tell anybody you found me here, I'll tell you all about my dream the first time we meet." The good Sister took her up in her arms and carried her to the dormitory where the soft bed was very acceptable after having spent the night on the hard floor.

Lucy never forgot her dream, and her little companions noticed that from the day of her First Communion, prayer became her special delight, and that if any of them were in trouble she would exclaim, "Say your chaplet of the Sacred Heart and all will come right." But she kept her dream a secret, only telling it to the Sister who found her in the chapel, and to the prefect who had given her permission to leave the dormitory.

Perhaps some of my young readers do not know how to say the chaplet of the Sacred Heart, which is so richly indulgenced, and, at the same time, is so appropriate a prayer to be said during the Holy Sacrifice of the Mass, when so many children do not know what to do. Take your beads, or if you have no beads, use your fingers, and instead of the Creed say:

"Soul of Christ, be my sanctification!
Body of Christ, be my salvation!
Blood of Christ, fill all my veins!
Water from Christ's side, wash out my stains!
Passion of Christ, my comfort be!
O good Jesus, listen to me!
In Thy wounds I fain would hide,
Ne'er be parted from Thy side.
Guard me should the foe assail me;
Call me when my life shall fail me!
Bid me come to Thee above,
With Thy saints to sing Thy love,
World without end. Amen."

Then in the place of the "Our Father" say: "Jesus, meek and humble of Heart, make my heart like unto Thine!" Then ten times: "Sweet Heart of Jesus, be my love!" Once, "Sweet Heart of Mary, be my refuge!" End the chaplet by the three following aspirations: "Sacred Heart of Jesus, have mercy on us!" "Immaculate Heart of Mary, pray for us!" "May the Sacred Heart of Jesus every where be praised!" To each of these aspirations there are three hundred days' indulgence attached.

And now before I finish, I have a favor to ask of each little one who may read this story. It is that the first chaplet of the Sacred Heart they say will be offered up for my intention; and I promise them in my turn that they shall never be forgotten in my daily prayers.

For the Suffering Irish Children.

Aloysius Mukautz, $1; Thecla Mukautz, 25 cts.; Blanch Mukautz, 25 cts.; Mary Lynch, 20 cts.; Bernard Lynch, 10 cts.; William Lynch, 10 cts.; Nora Lynch, 10 cts.; Alice Monaghan, 25 cts.; Albert Monaghan, 25 cts.; Frank Ridley, 10 cts.; Joseph Tobin, 25 cts.; Charles Tobin, 25 cts.; Henry Wessner, 10 cts.; Emma Wessner, 5 cts.; Mary Agnes Dooley, 25 cts.; Mrs. Byron, $1; Eddie Byron, 10 cts.; Teresa Byron, 10 cts.; A Reader, $1; Addie Missel, 20 cts.; Tillie Missel, 30 cts.; Bridget Eagan, 50 cts.

THE AVE MARIA.

A Journal devoted to the Honor of the Blessed Virgin.

HENCEFORTH ALL GENERATIONS SHALL CALL ME BLESSED.—St. Luke, I, 48.

VOL. XVI.   NOTRE DAME, INDIANA, JUNE 19, 1880.   No. 25.

The Conversion of an Infidel through the Intercession of the Blessed Virgin.

BY THE LATE REV. FATHER J. P. DONELAN.

(CONTINUED.)

ONE week passed between the first and second visits of the priest. During the interval how fervently was the prayer of faith addressed to the throne of grace for this lost one of the tribe of Israel! Christians of various denominations united in supplicating God in his behalf. All felt an interest in his conversion, for all had known and grieved over his errors. The Sisters of Charity gathered their orphan charge around the shrine of Mary, and bad them pray for him. The pure and fervent prayer went up from cloistered innocence, and the matin and the evening office was chanted in his behalf. The spotless Lamb was immolated on the altar to plead for mercy and for pardon for this wandering child of error; for all knew that the Lord loveth mercy, and heareth the cry of the swallow for food; all knew that His mercies endureth from end to end, and His goodness even unto everlasting. Cheering thought! consoling truth! How wonderful are Thy ways, O God of our fathers! how great Thy mercies! how exalted Thy views! Let heaven and earth proclaim Thy glory, and let all that is within us and around us bless Thy holy name! How omnipotent is prayer! what can it not operate! From what dangers of soul and of body can it not rescue man! How often was the arm of God, already uplifted to strike the rebellious Jews, held back by the prayers of Moses, or permitted to fall only in blessings upon His people! The troubled waters roll back their sullen waves and serve as sentinels to cover the retreat of the Israelites; and again, at the prayer of Moses, the sea, the earth and elements are embattled against the hosts of Pharaoh; the flinty rock gives forth its gushing streams to cool the travellers in the wilderness; the brazen serpent is an instrument of mercy, and the prayer of faith is answered by manna from heaven. A mother's prayer is heard in heaven, as Agar weeps for her boy Ismael in the wilderness of Bersabee: for her child is faint and she cannot bear to see him die; she turns in anguish from him, and lifting up her voice she weeps. Oh, the power of prayer! It brought an angel from heaven in that hour of trial, and the miraculous waters bring back to life the drooping form of her boy Ismael. David sinned, Magdalen was a sinner, and the thief upon the cross was guilty; yet the supplications of the one stayed the avenging sword of justice, the tears of the "sinful Mary" blotted out her offences, and paradise was the reward of the good thief's prayer. It was this consoling assurance that encouraged the good to pray for Mr. M——. The charity of God urged them; they hoped, and, thanks to God! they did not hope in vain.

Whatever the motives by which he was actuated, whether the grace of God had already begun to operate in his heart, or through mere human motives, as personal regard, certain it is that Mr. M—— expressed his surprise during the week that the strange clergyman had not called again. How natural it is for man at all times to love sympathy! but it is particularly in sickness, in suffering, and in trials that kindness and attention are appreciated. A kind expression, a gentle look, or a word of sympathy, is never entirely useless; would that they were more common! It was very probably this motive that actuated Mr. M—— in asking why his reverend visitor stayed so long away. It was for this precisely the clergyman was waiting; most anxiously had he watched the current of affairs, and inquired of all who could inform him, the result of his first apparently accidental visit; and on being informed of the inquiry on the part of his patient, he lost no time in repairing to his bedside.

Behold him, then, a second time in the sick

man's room. How anxiously every throb of his heart beats with earnest, yet half-doubting hope! The invalid smiles a welcome, and presses his hand in token of its sincerity. As yet, not one word of religion is introduced; the approaching end of all his sufferings, the calmness and fortitude with which a disciple of reason can die, and the beauteous order of nature, which teaches the young to provide for the old, the strong to protect the weak, and the departing to look to an honest name and the tranquillity of the grave as the reward of a good life—such was the theme of his conversation; and as he proceeded, it must have been evident to all that he was sincere. He remarked how different was his situation—calm, collected, and prepared—from the death of many whom he had known professing Christianity. They seemed terrified and appalled at the gloom of the grave, and what they foolishly believed the judgment-seat of God; while he—and as he spoke he placed his hand on his heart and raised himself in bed—could look on death with calm composure, and smile at its approach. For him there were no fears of judgment, for his God was always with him; Reason, free, untrammelled reason, was the only deity in whom he believed; there was no other God, no judgment-seat, but the tribunal of man's own conscience. He expressed in unbounded terms his pity for the deluded followers of "priestcraft," as he styled revelation, and lauded to the skies the ennobling principles of "The Age of Reason." The voluminous books of Voltaire were a fortress for the protection of human rights, while the other heroes of infidelity were the true apostles of mind, the supporters of truth against the inroads of error.

It seemed impossible to change the current of conversation. Whatever was said, he would turn to the advantage of his own opinions. Many little stratagems were used to effect this purpose, but all in vain. To oppose him, or to argue against his views, was only to excite him to still more frightful language, or to irritate his feelings and thus thwart the desired object. Silence, or even an apparent acquiesence in as much of his opinion as was not too evidently opposed to Divine Truth was the only means left to follow. After an hour or more passed in this manner, the clergyman, who had during the time whispered many a silent prayer to heaven in his behalf, requested to be left alone with the sick man. All present looked amazed; they obeyed, apparently unconscious of what they were doing. The clergyman closed the door, and, advancing towards the sick-man's bed, gazed for a moment at him, then threw himself upon his knees, as he leaned with extended arms towards him. "Unfortunate man," exclaimed the priest, "why do you continue to outrage the mercies of God? Think of that awful eternity before you! think of that God whom you blaspheme and deny, but who has sent me here to save you from ruin!"

"There is no God," angrily replied the infidel; "you have no God!"

"There is a God," the clergyman answered, still kneeling: "and He sends me here to-day. Let me ask His mercy for you?"

"Fool, then, as you are," said the infidel, as the fire flashed fearfully from his eyes; "fool, then, as you are, pray, but pray loud, or else your Bible God will not hear you."

The priest lifted his eyes to Heaven, and thought of her, the Refuge of Sinners, the Mother of God, and prayed for mercy through her hands. The lovely words of St. Bernard gushed from his heart and from his lips; and the prayer went up: "Remember" etc. Eternal God, how sudden a change comes over the sick-man's soul! While yet pronouncing the words of the prayer, a stifled groan is heard, a sigh, as if from the very soul, and, at the close of the "Remember," as the priest looked towards him for whom he had been praying, what were his feelings, what his surprise, to find him shedding tears, his hands clasped in prayer, and to hear those expressive words: "Mary, standing at the foot of the cross of Jesus, pray for me! Jesus, my God, have mercy on me!"

Surprised and alarmed, the clergyman gazed upon the scene; but a moment passed, and he was clasped in the sick man's arms. A flood of tears was streaming from his eyes; his countenance was changed, sorrow and joy, grief and hope, were blended there; a mild and gentle calm had replaced the stern, determined look which had characterized him through life, and a smile of delight beamed through all his tears: "O God of mercy!" he exclaimed, what have I done to deserve this favor at Thy hands? Jesus, Saviour! my Lord and my God, what is this? Oh! heaven of heavens! and all that they contain, thank my Saviour for me! Oh, Mary, standing at the foot of the cross of Jesus, pray for me! Oh! Jesus dying on the cross for me, have mercy on me! Oh! Mother of God, pray for me! My Mother, the Refuge of Sinners, and the cause of my salvation, thank my God for me! Oh! angel that has always been with me, thank my Saviour for me!"

These, and many similiar aspirations, proclaimed the wondrous change effected in Mr. M——. "And is it possible," asked the clergyman, "that God has manifested His mercies to you so wonderfully?"

"Yes, Father," replied the happy convert; "yes, I feel a change in all my views. From the moment you commenced that prayer, I seemed transported out of myself. God has been pleased to show me my error. The Blessed Mother of my Saviour seemed to stand before me, and with a mild countenance, point to her Divine Son upon the cross beside her. I looked, and Jesus, my Saviour, smiled upon me, and I could not repress my feelings as I cried out: "Oh, Mary, standing at the foot of the cross of Jesus, pray for me! Oh, Jesus, dying on the cross for me, have mercy on me!"

"Since this is so," said the priest, with tears of joy, "let us return thanks to our good God for His mercy and His goodness."

"Do so, do so, Father," rejoined the sick man; "do so, and I will unite with all strength." And the priest knelt and recited in thanksgiving to God the *Te Deum*, the Litanies of Jesus and of the Blessed Virgin. What a joyous scene! how fervently did they pray—the converted infidel, and the priest of religion! how earnest the petitions, how strong the faith of the recent convert! "Have mercy on me!" would he reply as the petition went up to Jesus, his Redeemer; with eyes turned towards Heaven, and hands uplifted, while every feature of his countenance glowed with love and hope, commingled with fear: "Have mercy on me, oh Jesus! have mercy on me! Mother of God, my Mother, pray for me! look upon your child; he owes his salvation to your prayers with Jesus for him. Oh Blessed Mother, look upon me! thou knowest that I love thy Divine Son, but do you love Him for me! Would that every heart were filled with love for Mary, the Refuge of Sinners, and the Mother of my God!"

He earnestly entreated to be permitted to make his confession immediately; but fearing that the excitement of the past few moments might be injurious to him, the clergyman proposed to delay the confession for a time in order to leave him alone with his God. But much to his surprise, he found that Mr. M—— was as calm and tranquil as a child. There was a total change not only in feeling and in mind, but in appearance and in action. There was indeed an earnestness of expression, but it was as calmly dignified as if from long reflection; there was indeed a glow upon his cheek, and joy sparkling in his eye, but it was the smile of gratitude to God, and the eye bespoke the settled feelings of the heart. So earnest were his wishes to be allowed forthwith to make his confession, that the clergyman consented. What the fervor and contrition which marked that penitential act, it is not ours to know; it is locked up in the impenetrable gloom of the past; but may we not hope that He who has entrusted to His Church the power of binding and of loosing in the court of conscience, ratified in Heaven the ministrations of His representative here below?

Who can express the joy, the wonder of the family, when, on calling them into the room, they for the first time discovered the change that had been operated? Tears and sighs, and expressions of amazement were heard from all sides. "Come to my arms, my children," he exclaimed, as he embraced them most affectionately; "come to your father's arms, dear children, and join me in thanking God for His mercies to me. Your father is saved, he is a Christian; he believes as you do, he thinks as you do; your God is his God, and the Blessed Virgin, your Mother in heaven, is his Mother also: she has snatched me from ruin; but for her, I would have been lost forever. Tears choked the utterance of his delighted family, and they could articulate but brief expressions of their joy and gratitude. "Praises be to Jesus!" "Glory to God!" and "Thanks to Our Blessed Lady!" were repeatedly heard from weeping wife and daughters; their prayers had been heard, their dearest earthly wishes granted; their hearts teemed with emotions which words could not express, and they could only weep their gratitude to the Father of mercies. They now beheld that father, whom they had never heard speak of religion but to oppose it, a fervent believer in its saving truths. How often, from early childhood up to the present moment, had they heard him protest against the attributes of God—at one time accusing Him of partiality, at another arraigning His authority, now denying His existence, and again defying human reason! but now, through the mercies of that same insulted Being, they heard that parent proclaiming the goodness and the power of God, imploring His pardon, professing his entire belief in all the attributes of the Divinity, and repenting from his soul the follies and the errors of his ways. Well might they weep, for when through very excess of joy the tongue can no longer perform its office, the deep well-springs of the heart give forth their tribute, and the eyes bespeak the thoughts the lips would fain utter.

As the evening was now far advanced, the clergyman, after explaining the nature and efficacy of Extreme Unction, deemed it advisable to comply with the sick man's request, and accordingly he prepared to administer this consoling Sacrament. Let the reader picture to himself this interesting scene. There, stretched upon a bed of sickness and of death, was the ransomed child of error who had for so many years been lost, but was now found; the redeemed one, who had wearied his soul in the ways of infidelity, but now an humble suppliant at the cross of Jesus; his eyes uplifted to heaven, or resting on the little crucifix which he held firmly grasped in both hands, as he would lift it up before him, then press it to his lips, and again repose it upon his bosom.

At his head knelt his wife, the partner of his toils and troubles through life, she who had so long prayed for his conversion and grieved over his wanderings. Around his bed were kneeling his pious daughters mingling their tears and prayers with his. How earnestly and how often had they asked this favor from Heaven! How many fervent Communions had they offered in his behalf! And the blessed boon had come, their prayers were granted. It was hard, indeed, to part with their father, but to part with him thus—to see him die a Christian, ah! there was joy in the sorrow! and here they knelt to thank their God, and bless the hand that reflected the painful blow. Some pious friends were also kneeling there; they had called to inquire after his condition, and, hearing the joyful news, they mingled with the little group now gathered around his bed. The priest of God slowly repeated the appointed prayers, and ere he proceeded to the unctions, he addressed both to the sick man and to those present a few words explanatory of the immediate ceremonies. He reminded them of the venerable antiquity of this Sacrament, of its necessity, and the divine authority for its institution recorded in the fifth chapter of the epistle of Saint James; he spoke of the consoling assurances attached to its faithful observance. The promise of truth was given that the prayer of faith, united to the "anointing with oil in the name of the Lord" should save the sick man, that the Lord "should raise him up." And that in case any stain of sin still defiled the sick man's soul, and the frailties of human nature still rendered him displeasing to Heaven, the grace of the Sacrament would wash them all away, through the merits of the Blood of Christ. "If he be in sins, they shall be forgiven him." What a consoling reflection for the dying Catholic! how admirably calculated to encourage him in that trying moment, when earth fades away, and the unseen visions of eternity are about to open before him! when the curtain shall fall, and the veil which conceals an unknown world shall be removed! Such did it prove to Mr. M——. He listened with edifying attention to the explanations given, and when the clergyman proceeded to anoint the different senses, he repeated in English what the Church required him to pronounce first in Latin. "*By this sacred unction, and through His most gracious mercy, may our Lord remit unto thee all sins of which thou hast been guilty through the sense of seeing*"—and so of the rest. As the sign of the cross was formed upon his eyes, his ears, his mouth and hands and feet, the sick man responded "Amen," in a tone which bespoke the emotions of his heart. All looked on with wonder and were highly edified, as they beheld him thus captivated by the grace of God. The calm resignation now depicted on his countenance was far different from what had characterized him during the first part of his illness: it was the calm tranquillity breathed upon the soul by a hope in God. Tears were in his eyes, but they were the tears of an humble and a contrite heart, they were tears like those which Magdalen shed when "she wept and was forgiven." Every expression that escaped his lips was an aspiration to God; he prayed earnestly for pardon; he called on Heaven in accents and in language which filled all present with amazement. For several moments after he was anointed, he poured forth such an earnest, such a pious strain of thanksgiving and of humble petition to God, that a stranger would have concluded that he had always been accustomed to piety. And why should we wonder? Was it not the work of God? If the ministering angel touched Isaiah's hallowed lips with fire, why need we wonder that another angel brought from above the inspiration which spoke through this recent triumph of the Cross? The ways of God are deep and mysterious. "Thy ways are not My ways, and thy thoughts are not My thoughts; for as far as the heavens are above the earth so far are My ways above thy ways and My thoughts above thy thoughts." "Who hath known the mind of the Lord, or who hath been His counsellor?" "Oh! the depth of the knowledge of the wisdom of God! How incomprehensible are His judgments! how unsearchable His ways!" Here was another evidence of the power of God. Like another Saul, our convert had been, at least in one sense, a persecutor of the people of God; and even while yet glorying in his pride of intellect, he is stricken down in the midst of his career, and now humbly asks, "Lord, what wilt Thou have me to do?" The wolf has become a lamb, the reviler adores, and the goodness, the power and the mercies of God stand avenged before His enemies. Glorious victory! more effectual in proclaiming the attributes of God than the creation of a world; for in that His power and wisdom are manifest, while in this His mercy and His patience stand proclaimed. The Good Shepherd had indeed found the sheep that was lost, and had brought it home rejoicing; the prodigal had returned to his Father's house, and there found a secure asylum. The wearied spirit, like the dove of the deluge, had sought in vain for a spot whereon to rest, and now it was returned to the ark, where a more than Moses had welcomed it home. Another sinner had been converted; there was joy before the angels of God, and earth was sharing in the festival of heaven. "Glorious things are said of the City of God!" where such charity for man is found. Who would despond, or who despair, since grace and mercy may still be found?

(TO BE CONTINUED.)

LET us converse about God so long as we have a tongue; let us be astir for God so long as we have limbs left. We are not of such great value that we should be always be husbanding ourselves for better times.

Ave Maria Sine Labe Concepta.

Hail, Mary, our Mother! Hail, Virgin the purest!
Hail, Mary, the Mother of mercy and love!
Hail, Star of the Ocean, serenest and surest
That ever shone brightly in heaven above!
'Mid the shadows of death stretching down o'er the nations,
Thy children have always rejoiced in thy fame;
Oh! how proudly we witness in our generations
The last crowning halo that circles thy name.

Tradition, which, joined with its sister evangel,
God placed upon guard at the door of His bride,
Tradition, which beams like the sword of the angel,
As, flame-like, it "turneth on every side,"
Tradition shoots up o'er the ages victorious—
Its summit in heaven, its base upon earth—
Like a pillar of fire, far-shining and glorious,
And shows thee all sinless and pure in thy birth.

As fair as the rose 'mid Jerusalem's daughters,
As bright as the lily by Jordan's blue wave,
As white as the dove, and as clear as the waters
That flowed for the prophet and circled his grave;
As tall as the cedar on Lebanon's mountain,
As fruitful as vine-tree in Cades' domain,
As straight as the palm by Jerusalem's fountain,
As beauteous as rose-blush on Jericho's plain;

As sweet as the balm-tree diffusing its odor,
As sweet as the gold-harp of David the king,
As sweet as the honeycomb fresh from Mount Bodor,
As sweet as the face veiled by Gabriel's wing;
The silver-lined sky o'er the garden of Flora,
The rainbow that gilds the dark clouds within view,
The star that shines brightest, the dawning Aurora—
More chaste than the moon, and more beautiful too.

The glass without stain, and the radiance immortal,
The ever-sealed fount in the city of God,
The garden enclosed, on whose sanctified portal
None e'er but the King of the angels hath trod:
The sign that appeared in mid-heaven—a maiden
With the moon 'neath her feet, and twelve stars on her head,
Sun-clothed, going up from the desert to Eden;
Such Mary, the Queen of the living and dead.

Oh! such are the words of the saints now in glory,
Whose voices are heard o'er the dark waste of time,
Like sentinels set through the centuries hoary,
Proclaiming her free from original crime;
Of the prophets and pontiffs, and doctors and sages,
Who once in this dark vale of misery trod,
Like lamps hanging out on the mist-covered ages
To light up the ways of the city of God.

We see by their light with a swelling emotion
The bark of the Church, as it onward doth ride,
Through tempest and gloom, where the Star of the Ocean
Doth brightly illumine its path o'er the tide;
Where clouds become thicker and hurricanes fiercer,
And threaten to shut out its radiance from view,
We see through the darkness the figure of Peter
As he points it out still to the sailors and crew.

We hear the loud ring of the multitude's pæan
By the nations in triumph exultingly sung,
From the cliffs of the North to the distant Ægean,
As Celestine silenced Nestorius' tongue:
In Ephesus' temple—the temple of Mary—
The Fathers hold council by Peter's command,
In Ephesus' streets, long expectant and weary,
The crowds stand with joy-bells and torches in hand.

We see the grand figure of Cyril before us,
Where John, her adopted, before him had trod,
As Pontiffs and people swell loud the glad chorus,
That Mary, our Mother, is Mother of God.
And oh! that we've witnessed the last shining lustre,
That Star of the stars, in her diadem set,
The first in existence, last placed in the cluster,
To shine through a long line of centuries yet;

There were journeys by land, there were ships on the ocean,
That bore Judah's princes to Sion's bright walls;
The people have heard with a thrilling emotion
The voice of the high priest, as on them it calls.
Oh! bless them, dear Mother, we pray with emotion,
And bless this green island that looks up to thee;
For this, dearest Mother, is gem of the ocean,
And thou art Immaculate, Star of the Sea.
—*Catholic Standard.*

'Beth's Promise.

BY MRS. ANNA HANSON DORSEY.

CHAPTER XVII—(Continued).

HOW 'BETH FOUGHT OUT HER BATTLES.

THE city of Washington was again full; all had returned from their summering in Europe, or among the mountains, or at the Virginia Springs, or Saratoga, to their stately, pleasant homes; and the friendly autumn visiting, so different from the wild visiting whirl of the season, had begun. Old acquaintances and many new ones, among whom were some of the leading Catholic ladies of the city, called upon the Morleys who received calls although not visiting themselves. Among these was an old schoolmate of Mrs. Morleys when she was at Madama de Villier's boarding institute, the only one of her companions with whom she had been intimate or had held any correspondence,—a Mrs. Spencer, whose husband had just been appointed one of the judges of the Supreme Court. Mrs. Justice Spencer was a cultivated, elegant woman, well fitted for her distinguished position, and possessed of virtues and traits which made her a good wife and mother, and shed a happy lustre over her home life. She paid due "tribute to Cæsar" in discharging her social duties punctiliously and systematically, as the wives of men in high official life in Washington are expected to do; but her true happiness was found in the society of her husband and children and a small circle of intimates whom she had culled here and there from among the cultivated and fashionable people who thronged around her, and taken to her warm heart for this or that trait or quality by which she discerned they were congenial with her own tastes and requirements. It was a great happiness to her to meet Mrs. Morley, although her sympathetic heart was deeply touched by the pathos of her quiet, patient sorrow, which neither of them referred to; and Mrs. Morley was well pleased to renew the old friendship. It struck this worldly-wise lady that 'Beth was the most lovely and *spirituelle* looking creature she had ever seen, but that she was too pale, too quiet, and she rushed to the conclusion that her health was really suffering from wearing heavy mourning and confining herself to so secluded a life, an opinion in which Captain Brandt, who was one of Mrs. Spencer's greatest admirers, fully agreed, and hoped that she would succeed in bringing her, by degrees, into society. "It is not natural for a beautiful young girl like 'Beth Morley to be mewed up like a disconsolate old maid," said the old captain; "but you'll have to manage like a diplomat, madam, to succeed, for Mrs. Morley, who's an angel, if there ever was one upon earth, has got to be—to be—so extremely pious, you know—a Roman Catholic—that I shouldn't be surprised any day to hear that mother and daughter had gone into the nunnery over there in Georgetown and taken the black veil, hang me if I would! I know if poor Morley could tell us his thoughts he'd say they'd grieved enough, and didn't want that beautiful girl of his hid under a bushel."

"I see that I shall have to feel my way very carefully. I wouldn't for all the world pain them, even by an effort to do them good. Meantime I agree with you, Captain, and shall do my best," said Mrs. Spencer.

But 'Beth's reply to Mrs. Spencer's persuasions and invitations was: "You will please excuse me, just this time. No; I don't mean to bury myself; I mean to go into society, but not now; and when the time comes, dear Mrs. Spencer, you shall be my *chaperone*, if you will take me. Yes: I am sure it would interest me, and perhaps I should enjoy it in a way; but I really cannot imagine anything just yet in the gay world that would not give me pain instead of pleasure by its very contrast."

"Very well, my dear, I'll wait on condition that you'll sometimes come to me, in a quiet way."

"Yes, I promise that, for you are mamma's old friend, but that is not all; I'll come because I love you myself, dear Mrs. Spencer," said 'Beth, with her winning smile.

"Give my love to your mother, and tell her I don't know such a gad-about as she is; here I have missed her three successive times, and I want her to send me word when I may expect to find her at home before I come again," said Mrs. Spencer, laughing, as she held 'Beth's hand in the friendly pressure of her own, and kissed her affectionately.

"Yes: mamma has many errands."

"I understand," interrupted Mrs. Spencer; "but indeed, my dear, I think that going so much as she does among the poor and miserable is not good for such a sensitive creature as your mother. I've heard all about it, you see."

"Mamma will certainly not agree with you, and please, dear Mrs. Spencer, do not say anything like that to her, it would pain her, I think."

"No, dear; depend upon it I will not," she answered, as she went out the hall door to her carriage.

And 'Beth went on the even tenor of her way, bravely fulfilling each daily duty that presented itself whether great or small; she was neither moody nor unduly silent; she conversed cheerfully with friends, and never allowed her secret pain to throw a moment's shadow over the tender, confiding intercourse between her mother and herself. The feeling that she was living two separate existences in one, each a distinct individuality, one unreal and like a phantasmagoria, the other weary, heavy, and smarting with pain, grew upon her. It was a strange sort of a life, and while the quiet endurance of it saved her mother from sharing her pain, and veiled her bruised heart from curious eyes, it brought her no comfort, no peace or resignation, no help; and she knew now that supports like these could only come from a Divine Source. She went often to the old church; it was restful to her tired young heart to kneel where no disguise was needed, where her inner life lay open before God, who she hoped would one day pity her; and where she could ask succor of her who had known sorrow above all sorrows, while she bowed at her feet, bedewing them with her tears. And although there was a certain degree of consolation in this, 'Beth knew that something was yet requisite to obtain the help she craved, and it dawned upon her that, to attain it, she must throw off the trammels of self, the bewildering mists of human reasoning, and humbly yield all to a supernatural faith in the Truth, as revealed by Almighty God to His Church. And she wished that she could; it was as if a hand which she could not reach was stretched out to help her. She had resumed her visits to Father Thomas, and many were their long talks together over her difficulties, but she had not yet unbosomed herself fully to him. With the keen eye of experience, and from long observation of every phase of human nature, he had discerned that there was a something that had brought sorrow into the life of this once light-hearted, laughing girl; but she was reticent, and although he would have been glad to know what it might be, thinking, if he did, it would be the possible lever by which he could remove her difficulties and break down the partition wall that kept her outside the one true Fold. He did not feel free to question her as to a temporal affair about which she was not inclined to speak; and, after all, perhaps he was mistaken. He could see plainly that her cheerfulness was only assumed, that there was neither life nor spirit in it, but he determined to seem not to notice, hoping that she would voluntarily confide in him, if her trouble was of a nature that he could by any possibility relieve.

"Beth, my child," he said, after one of their long conferences, as with a weary sigh she rose to go, "I cannot understand why you hold back. You believe: you admit that you do; you are convinced that the Catholic Church is divinely founded, that she is one, undivided, universal and holy; the conservator of all Truth; you do not doubt her dogmas; what, then, is it, I ask in the name of God, that prevents your entrance into her safe fold? It must be pride. You aspire to understand the mysteries of Faith which you believe; could you do so, what need of faith? Those mysteries which are divine are to be accepted without hesitation or doubt, because God, who is the eternal Truth, has given them to His Church through His only Son, who sealed His divine mission by the death of the Cross, and confirmed it by His glorious resurrection and the coming of the Holy Ghost. You have always believed this and received it as a Christian doctrine; can you understand it? can you comprehend the Trinity, which is the greatest mystery of all? You have accepted these great truths without question all your life; you believe that Jesus Christ is truly the Son of God, and yet you hesitate to receive the Faith He established, because you cannot understand its dogmas, founded and taught by His very word! Do you expect to understand, as you do natural things, how these wonderful miracles of the power and love of Almighty God are wrought? I tell you, my dear child, you are trifling with the grace of God, and if you go on, it may be withdrawn from you."

"But what am I to do?" she asked, piteously.

"Do? Come like a little child and say, 'Dear Lord, I submit myself to Thee! I am willing to put all human reasoning and pride under foot I desire only the Truth and Thy grace; I believe and willingly accept that which my feeble, human understanding cannot grasp; grant me faith, grant me courage, and enlighten my spirit!' Do this, my child. Stop reading and puzzling your brain over what is no human problem, but that which no mere human science can ever reach, can ever measure, or fathom—Faith—the 'believing without having seen,' for which the soul will receive eternal benedictions! You shut yourself out from help, from consolation, and, in the end, from hope itself, by standing and waiting, with folded hands, for a miracle."

"I will try; I only dread the doubts that will come afterwards, and perhaps make me give up," she said, in a low voice. Father Thomas had never spoken so to her before. Her heart—prepared by suffering, and finding naught that earth could offer sufficient to impart the peace, the true rest she so eagerly longed for—received his words like seed sown in good soil.

"That is a temptation, my child: Almighty God is too generous to abandon those who throw themselves with simple, confiding trust upon His mercy. Ask the help of Our Blessed Lady of Succcor, who, ever watchful over the souls for whom her Divine Son surrendered His life, ever jealous of the heritage won at such bitter cost, stands only waiting your approach, to lead you, my child, to Him. Put aside, then, the littleness of intellectual pride; by a supreme effort, throw off whatever impedes your true progress, and in a spirit of docility and humility accept the great grace, the great boon that is offered you 'without money and without price,' yet, in value, more inestimable than the universe. Remember who it is that stands at the door of your heart asking admittance, and close it no longer against Him, whose Sacred Heart suffered unto death for our transgressions."

"But I am not ready: my own heart, my own life must be changed."

"Undoubtedly, my child; but that cannot be all at once. It is only the *will* that can be changed—the free will—at first. True religion is a principle that cannot be worked out except by gradual progression, fighting our way inch by inch against ourselves for the love of God. Submit the will and intention to our Lord; be docile like a little child that is led by the hand learning how to walk, a short tottering step at a time; like the same child learning the rudiments of speech and letters, and the uses of life from his mother, in whose love he confides and to whom he clings for support, feeling certain that she understands all that he fails to comprehend, and happy in her safe guidance. The soul will have its battles to fight so long as breath animates our clay; but, fed and strengthened by the Divine Sacraments of our Holy Mother the Church, we shall gradually—if faithful—learn the science of the saints and walk in new raiment."

"I will see you again, Father Thomas; I begin to see that I myself am the only impediment. You have been very patient and kind with my ignorance all through these two years of reading and disputing," said 'Beth; then hesitating as if half inclined to go, and yet half inclined to speak, her lips quivered, and she was about turning away, when Father Thomas said: "What is it, my child?"

"Would it not seem a very mean thing, Father Thomas, for me to take this step just now, as if I —I just did it because I am unhappy? Father, I have had a great trial, and I want to be sure that human motives, after all, are not urging me to seek consolation by becoming a Catholic."

"Another temptation, my dear child. Consider how long you have been preparing yourself for this step. The trial you speak of must be of recent occurrence, therefore not your motive in the beginning; a Catholic by baptism, and at heart, and only held back by flimsy reasons, why should you not bring your wounds where they can be best healed? Does not a hurt child run straight to the arms of its mother? do not the sick resort to a physician? does not our Lord Himself invite His children who "are weary and heavy laden" to come to Him for rest and refreshment? Whatever your cross may be, my child, bring it to Him: He will help you to bear it; never fear that He will turn from you, for His Sacred Heart bore the weight of all human grief, and He beholds in the poor human heart, bruised with anguish, the image of His own, and is touched with an infinite pity that straightway seeks to heal its wounds."

"I will delay no longer: this moment I am ready to submit; this moment, Father Thomas, I ask to be received into the Church," said 'Beth, kneeling at the good priest's feet. There was no nervous emotion, no excitement either in her countenance or manner; her face was calm and pale, her eyes grave and earnest, her hands folded on her breast in an involuntary attitude of submission.

"God be thanked, my child, for this victory over yourself!" said Father Thomas, much affected, as he blessed her; then bidding her rise he added: "I will go at once into the Church; you will find me in the confessional."

And 'Beth Morley took her first step; she entered the confessional with new emotions, in which no feeling or thought of self mingled; and grace was given her which made the way plain before her. The lions that she had so dreaded in the path leading hither, shrunk away out of sight, and a sweet calm, as refreshing as a fountain in the desert, fell with the holy absolution upon her heart. She remained some time in church, offering her thanksgiving before the Divine Presence of the Altar and to the compassionate Virgin of virgins whose intercession, she loved to think, had guided and obtained this grace for her. Not yet, but soon, on the Feast of the Immaculate Conception, she was to receive Holy Communion. 'Beth had no ecstatic emotions, such as she had dreamed of; but her heart was softened, and down in its very depths she felt satisfied at what she had done, and also experienced a thankfulness tempered with humility which made her accept willingly, and believe fervently, all that the Catholic Church believed and taught now and henceforth. She felt that now, indeed, she had something to cling to like an "anchor, sure and steadfast," hope's own symbol. A little while ago, when her mind tossed to and fro, revealing her own weakness, and she felt all powerless—even when aided by pride and a strong will to keep up her courage—how darkly the shadows fell around her! but now how different it would be! so different! for now, come what might of sorrow or pain, she could go with firm trust, as a child to its father, for help and solace; and little by little, as the days wore on, a certain peace stole into her heart, which made its hidden grief more endurable, until she began to hope that, after all, the bitterness of it would pass away, and resignation take its place.

On the eve of the Immaculate Conception, 'Beth went into her mother's room, and after ascertaining that she was not asleep, knelt down, resting her arms on the side of the low bedstead, and leaning over, kissed her.

"Beth, my darling, this is very sweet, but why are you not in bed? I hope you are not feeling unwell?" said Mrs. Morley.

"No, mamma, I am perfectly well, but I have something to tell you which I had intended to defer until to-morrow morning, something that you will be glad to hear. I am at last a Catholic, and will make my First Communion to-morrow morning. We are now one in Faith, dear mamma, and I want your blessing and your forgiveness for the faults of my life by which I may have pained or distressed you," she answered, in sweet, grave tones.

"How thankful, oh my God! how thankful! now do I feel that Thou art no longer angry with me for my long unfaithfulness, since my child is restored to her heritage of Faith which, through my fault, she had nearly lost!" raising her eyes heavenward, and folding her hands, while an expression of almost rapture lit up her face. "Yes, my child, I bless you: bless you from the depths of my very soul; and as to forgiveness—it is I who should ask yours, you have never pained me; you have always been the dearest and best of children, dutiful, and obedient, my stay and my comfort."

"Thank you, dear mamma, your words make me very happy. It is after midnight, the great Festival is already here, and in a few hours we shall, kneeling together, receive the Bread of Life. Let us rest a little while now, that we may rise with the dawn, refreshed and strengthened for the great Feast."

"Good night, then, my daughter; this happiness will be refreshment enough even if no sleep comes." Once more mother and daughter embraced each other, and separated with hearts full of inexpressible gratitude and peace to await the supreme moment when Jesus Christ would give them Himself, the pledge of eternal life.

(TO BE CONTINUED.)

[From "*The Catholic World.*"]

Canova.

(CONCLUSION.)

OUR readers should bear in mind that we write of no one portion of Canova's life, but simply describe his method of study as begun in early years, continued and perfected to his death. The amount of hard work he accomplished seems almost incredible; but who, except those who give themselves to just such hard work through years of long and painful pupilage, could effect what Canova did? The number and kind of his works bear witness to his life. His daily sketches and studies from life, his constant and faithful comparisons of his ideal with nature, his earnest and skilful adaptation of anatomy to his art, show the secret of his success. He did not even dread the use of the dissecting-knife, in so far as it was necessary to a more perfect harmony of the human body to his work. When he was fairly on the road of his profession his daily labors ran thus:*

He devoted the first hours of the morning, while his mind was fresh and vigorous, to composition or modelling. He sketched upon paper the outline of his thought, corrected and retouched it. Having at length satisfied himself with the design of his work as it would appear in painting, his next object was to examine and recompose it according to the principles of sculpture. For this he modelled the sketch in clay or wax; the arrangement of every individual part was carefully studied. The model in this condition had served the masters before him as the only guide for the statue; not so Canova. This model was the first step to the real one, which he made of the same size as the marble to be carved. † With what skill and care it was finished those who have seen any of the original marbles may readily imagine from their perfection. When this model was completed so thoroughly that Canova knew it would prove an unerring guide, then, but not till then, was the manual labor of the marble confided to the workers in his employ. Many times, too, not content with this, he would block out the masses of marble himself. And to the labor entailed by such a course is traced the origin of the disease that caused his death. The last touches were given by the master-hand alone, that the marble might seem to glow, as it were, with all the silent attributes of beauty and life; and even in these last touches he did not fail to compare his work with a living model.

It is difficult to-day, when the study of nature in her highest forms is so earnestly inculcated, to realize the impression made on men's minds by Canova's works in that age of mannerism which has just preceded us—that age of forced and exaggerated expression, which, without the genius of a Michael Angelo to conceal its gross errors, was a total failure. To see a man stand forth, convinced in his judgment that Nature is his true teacher, and to adopt her principles, not servilely, but with a breadth and nobility of purpose, is indeed a grand sight. And when we remember the wonderful mutual harmony between the natural and the ideal, as evinced in the compositions which emanated from Canova's master-mind, we can hardly praise him enough for his courageous efforts to replace Art in her own genuine sphere. Many of our readers may not admire Canova's works, but even these cannot fail to pay their tribute to the man himself, and to appreciate his efforts to recall the wandering steps of his loved mistress and direct them towards their highest goal—the perfection of the ideal and the real. A hair-breadth beyond that perfection, and the downward path is rapid; and while we readily admit that Canova was not faultless, his imperfections are almost lost in our earnest admiration of the fidelity with which he accomplished his work. With his birth the fulness of time had come; God gave the work into his hands, and nobly did he perform it.

Never yet has man or nation undertaken any needed reform or attempted to establish any needed laws, but instantly the mass of people springs up and defies them; Canova was not exempt from the bitterness of his labors. This, however, is hardly the place to repeat all the comments and opposition with which ignorance and prejudice assailed him; enough to say that the generosity with which he received these attacks, though suffering inwardly from their ignoble pettiness, sooner or later disarmed the crowd, who then did him justice. We might add that he was ill-fitted for such opposition because of his modest reserve, being retiring and diffident

---

* For the details of Canova's daily labors we are greatly indebted to the *Biography* of the sculptor by Memes. Among the other works consulted may be mentioned Cicognara, De Quincy, and Boucion.

† It is only in this manner that the real effect of the full-sized statue which the sculptor is planning can be gained. Michael Angelo, late in life, became sensible of his error in not having followed this plan; and Vasari in his *Vita de' M. Angelo,* says that towards the close of this master's life, he began to study his compositions with more care, making his models for statues, and even architectural ornaments, the full size. He then placed them at their proper height, in order to observe the true effect of the future work.

almost to an extreme; still, his high purpose bore him up, and in his moments of discouragement, when he doubted if, in face of so much opposition his views could be correct, he subjected them to the severest examination. He hastened to the Capitol or the Vatican, and confronted them with the antique, and the result enabled him to be constant to his method and patient with his opponents.

We now pass with Canova to Rome—Rome, the mother and mistress of the world; kind friends had opened the way, and in 1781 our young artist found himself on the road which was to lead to great after-success. When he arrived in Rome in 1780, he was courteously received by the Venetian ambassador, Cavaliere Juliani, to whom he carried letters; this nobleman, when he had paid to the young Canova all the dues of hospitality, wished to be assured if the lad showed any promise of the future sculptor. He was a generous protector, and, should Canova stand the trial, he would prove a firm friend. So Juliani caused the model of "Dædalus and Icarus" to be transported from Venice; he then invited artists and connoisseurs of renown to inspect its merits; among these may be mentioned Volpato, Battoni, Puccini, Cades—or Cadef, as the Italians write the name—and Gavin Hamilton, an English painter, and author of *Schola Italicæ picturæ*. Canova's trepidation, it may be imagined, was extreme; it would almost seem as though his whole future depended upon the decision of these men; he afterwards acknowledged that this was one of the most trying periods of his life. According to Cicognara, the guests stood around the group and gazed at it in silence; they did not dare to censure what commanded their deepest admiration, though at wide variance with the style then followed; the simple beauties of the group so faithful to nature seemed like poverty of effect when compared with the work from the schools of that day. Hamilton broke the silence; he cordially embraced the trembling artist; he congratulated him on the talent exhibited by the group; he exhorted him to follow the course he had adopted, and, by strenuously adhering to nature, unite its exact and beautiful imitation with the simplicity of taste and ideal of the ancients. Rome, he added, abounded with specimens of their grand work, to the study of which he urged the lad to devote himself.

One of the guests present passed a severe censure on the group, which Canova overheard, and which pleased him more than any direct praise. This guest had observed that the group must have been copied from models executed by the application of some soft material to the living form, so impossible did it seem that the chisel alone could have produced so striking a representation of nature; when, in truth, this group was the result of Canova's severe study of the human form, unassisted by any mechanical means.

The merits of the young sculptor being thus recognized by all present, Juliani proved the sincerity of his promises of patronage, and the work for which Canova's studies had prepared him now began. The ambassador's manner of showing his interest was both delicate and gratifying—by employing Canova on a large piece of statuary, the choice of the subject to be left to the sculptor. By providing the material, and, when the work was finished, if no other purchaser appeared, by considering it as belonging to him on payment of its full value, he relieved his *protégé* from all embarrassment of poverty, and yet left him independent.

Rome inspired Canova with fresh ardor; he made profound and severe studies from the antique, without ever neglecting his observation of nature. His principal works at this time were the "Theseus and Minotaur," a small "Apollo," and a "Psyche;" these were in marble. His fame now rose rapidly, and in 1792 he was employed on the tomb of Ganganelli, Clement XIV; then followed with incredible celerity the group of "Cupid and Psyche," "Adonis and Venus," the "Magdalen kneeling," and many others. Such was his power and versatility; yet still to the severity of his own previous training is due this rapidity of conception and execution.

The revolutionary frenzy which spread over Europe at the close of the eighteenth century, filled Canova with consternation; he cared nothing for politics, but, unable to endure these scenes of anarchy daily enacted in Rome in 1797-98, and the outrages committed on his loved Pontiff, Pius VI, which he was powerless to avert, he left his studio, gave up his numerous works, and retired to his native town, Possagno. Here he remained in quiet more than a year, studying and painting in oils; charming stories are related of his reception at Possagno, which he had left a poor, nameless youth, and to which he returned just before he had reached the zenith of his fame. Betta Biasi, his cousin, and the heroine in his Madonna *fête*, who was then married, formed a sort of conspiracy (so runs one of the stories) with all the inhabitants of Possagno; it was carried out in this wise: Canova, who had first visited Crespano, went thence to his native hamlet; he made the journey on foot, and what a walk that must have been; how vividly that other walk in the far past must have come before him! Then, a little boy, his future all unknown, returning to his grandfather, his broken statue in his bundle, his heart heavy with grief, and denied his mother's parting kiss; afterwards the years of labor, the moments of discouragement that were as years which had intervened, the hopes that trembled in the balance with the fears; and now the success that was crowning his efforts, his mistress, Art, smiling so kindly upon her lover. Absorbed, probably, in such thoughts, he kept his way; and as he neared the town, a crowd of youngsters who were in ambuscade burst upon him. They overwhelmed him with their greetings of joy and admiration, while their hearty *Evvivas* filled the air. The sculptor stopped, overcome by emotion, but they respectfully urged him to advance. Canova always had a sincere repugnance to any kind of public demonstration and popular acclamations or honors; imagine, then, his astonishment when twenty steps more brought him to a turn in the road, and he perceived that it was actually covered with *immortelles*, laurel-branches, and roses! To the right and left of this triumphal path were the inhabitants of Possagno, Crespano, and neighboring towns; they had all assembled to greet him; the village bells were sounded, the old men and women joined the procession, and with triumphal music and songs they conducted him to his old home, Pasino's house; for they were proud of the man who had gone forth from among them and had so nobly distinguished himself; to them he was as a prince, and for a prince they could not do more.

The affairs of the Holy See having assumed a more settled aspect, Canova returned to Rome and attained a still more brilliant renown. He soon after visited Germany for the benefit of his health, upon which his severe labors were telling. It was at this time he executed the "Perseus with Medusa's Head." This remarkable piece was so truly classical in its beauty that, by the order of Pius VII, it was placed on one of the *stanze* of the Vatican hitherto reserved for the most precious relics of antiquity; this great privilege was supplemented by the illustrious Pontiff requesting Canova's presence at the Vatican, and there publicly embracing him, with genuine earnestness an honor accorded only to sovereigns (yet, in his art, was not Canova a sovereign?) On this occasion he received from the hands of the Pope the investiture in two of the Roman orders of knighthood, and was also nominated Inspector-General of Fine Arts, in Rome and the Pontifical States. In the same year (1802) Napoleon invited Canova to Paris; he desired to see this great artist, whose praises resounded on all sides; he also desired to obtain some of his work. But Canova, while he admired the conqueror of Egypt, the vanquisher of Italy, he could never forgive the author of the treaty of Campo Formio; therefore, though Napoleon's offers were brilliant, Canova remained faithful, and, had it not been for the intervention of the Sovereign Pontiff himself, Napoleon would have been refused; he went then as ambassador of the Holy See. Twice afterwards, in 1810 and 1815, he visited Paris; on his last visit he was charged with a special mission—namely, the recovery of the spoils taken from Rome by the order of the First Consul. What better man could have been chosen for this task than he who so loved the art treasures of which Rome had been despoiled, and who had so mourned their loss? And what a joy to his heart when his efforts proved successful and Rome's treasures were restored?

As a result of the first two visits, he executed a colossal statue of Napoleon, a bust of Josephine, and another of the Empress Marie Louise. His conversations with Napoleon are full of interest. After his third visit to Paris, in 1815, he passed over to England, and there, in London, saw for the first time what he termed the finest Greek antiquities the world possesses—the Elgin Marbles; his delight at the sight of them was intense. "These statues, these fragments," he exclaimed, "will produce a great change in art." Upon his return to Rome, he labored harder than ever, not alone in relation to his own improvement, but also to establish the style of Phidias, as shown in the Elgin Marbles; and as Cicognara remarks, he himself acknowledged that a visible improvement and the highest efforts of his chisel were to be found in the works which he executed subsequently to his visit to London. On his return, in 1816, he was enrolled among the Roman patricians with the title of Marquis of Ischia, and to this dignity was assigned the annual pension of three thousand crowns; thus his name was inscribed in the Golden Volume of the Capitol; so many were the honors he received that we may not pause to enumerate them; through all he showed the same simplicity and unassuming modesty, united with untiring zeal and hard labor. Religion ever possessed a strong influence over Canova, and to it he untiringly devoted his whole spiritual life.

It was his great wish now to show some appreciation of all that had been done for him, and he proposed a colossal statue of "Religion," to be finished in marble at his own expense. The model, upwards of twenty feet in height, was completed—a grand and imposing figure—but, from some unknown cause, obstacles from Cardinals and princes were thrown in the way of the execution in marble of a work destined to commemorate the return of the head of our holy Church from banishment. A copy from an engraving made of the model was—probably after Canova's death—executed by the order of Lord Brownlow for his home in England. Under the masterly engraving we have just mentioned, drawn by the sculptor's request in the strong hope that he might still accomplish his desire, were inscribed these words: "Pro felici reditu Pii VII,

Pontificis Maximi, Religionis formam sua impensa in marmore exculpendam Antonius Canova libens fecit et dedicavit"—In memory of the happy return of our Sovereign Pontiff, Pius VII, Antonio Canova joyfully executed and dedicated this statue of Religion, finished in marble, at his own expense.

The model of this statue of Religion (which had already filled Italy with admiration at its excellence) gave evidence of its being one of Canova's finest designs, and it is greatly to be regretted that he was never permitted to finish the marble, and enjoy the keen pleasure of offering it according to his heart's desire; the difficulties placed in his way are not a little puzzling, so we will pass them over in silence.

The hour was come for Canova to fulfil his promise made in early youth to the good priest of his native village; he had not forgotten it, but was biding his time; faithfully had he labored to cultivate to the utmost God's gift to him, and now, in the full strength of his power, he would return that gift to God. He had, with the single exception of his half-brother, the Abbate Sartori Canova—to whom he was devotedly attached—no family ties; so he resolved to devote his remaining years, his time, energy, and property, to the building of a beautiful church at Possagno, which should contain some of his best pieces. His plan was to unite in this one temple all the beauties of the Parthenon of Athens and the Pantheon of Rome: he labored incessantly upon all the means necessary for carrying this wonderful enterprise into execution, and at last, in the summer of 1819, all his plans being matured, he went to Possagno to arrange for the beginning of his operations. He confided the direction of his plans to Giovanni Zardo, surnamed Fantolin, an architect of Crespano; he wished to associate in his great project all the inhabitants of Possagno; even the young girls were filled with enthusiasm, and almost rivalled the workmen in the ardor with which they labored—they having persuaded Canova and their parish priest to permit them to carry the lighter stones and other materials needed, and to this work they devoted their free hours on working days and their holidays; it was a genuine labor of love to these good people of Possagno, and a generous emulation possessed them. Canova, however, formed a contract with them and the workers, and right royal was he in the payment of gratuities and wages; on one occasion, as he offered a gratuity to the young girls, and they had all received his gift, his face was noticed to beam with the conscious feeling of doing good, and he afterwards remarked that "this was one of the few days of real existence"; "yet," he continued, "how little did it cost me to make so many human beings happy! After all, the true value of money is to be estimated by the quantity of happiness which it may purchase for others; in this light riches are indeed desirable."

On the 11th of July, 1819, the corner-stone was to be laid; on that day an immense concourse of people assembled not only from the neighboring towns but even from Venice. Canova, after having heard Mass in the humble little church where his Madonna was, and which his magnificent structure was to supersede, habited in the robes of his office as Knight of Christ, headed the procession and proceeded to the spot; there, amidst the joyful acclamations of the crowd and the music of the Church, the solemn rite of blessing the corner-stone, in the perfect ceremony of the ritual, was concluded. How Canova's deepest emotions must have been stirred at that moment, —a moment which witnessed the beginning of the end of all his labors, the crown of all his works, the final consecration of all his great gifts to the glory of God, to whom he had first promised them when as a mere lad he knelt at his pastor's feet and listened to his kindly encouragement!

The work was pushed rapidly forward, and each autumn found Canova at Possagno, encouraging the workmen and directing the building, while in the winter at Rome he accepted new commissions, that there might be no lack of the necessary funds. The following extract from his will, made shortly before his death, proves how near and dear to his heart was this work: "To the honor and to the probity of my brother, and sole heir, I confide the obligation of continuing, completing and embellishing in all its parts, without the least reservation and in the shortest time possible, the temple of Possagno, according to the plans established by me and communicated to him; to which objects if the funds appointed prove insufficient, all my effects and property are to be sold till the necessary sums be obtained."

His constitution was shattered and his physical energy giving way, still he labored on indefatigably; nor do any pieces executed by him at this time show any diminution of his power as a sculptor. For his new church he made a group called "The Pietà," which unfortunately never got beyond the model. It has been cast, however, we believe, in plaster, and is in the church it was intended to adorn in marble.

In 1822 Canova, were it possible, was even more diligent; but the end was drawing near. In September he made his usual visit to Possagno, and superintended, with active and unwearying earnestness, the work of the builders. On the 1st of October he visited the Falieri villa—a spot dear to him, recalling youthful associations. Thence he passed to Venice. Here his disorder, which had been the source of great suffering all summer, returned with increasing violence. His stomach failed of its usual functions, and his days were now numbered. He retained to the last full possession of all his faculties, and bore his intense sufferings with the heroism of a Christian. On the 12th of October his friend Signor Aglietti told him that his death was very near. Canova received the news with perfect serenity, saying simply: "Ecco noi veniamo a questo mundo a far la nostra rivista e poi—sic transit gloria mundi"—Lo! we come into this world to play our part, and then vanishes the glory of the scene. But he added a moment later, "Beato, beato che l'ha fatto bene"—Happy, happy he who has played it well! He then made his confession with deep earnestness, and in the evening Extreme Unction and the Viaticum—those last sacraments given him to prepare and sustain his soul when it should come into the awful presence of its God—he received with all his wonted fervor, increased, perhaps, by the solemnity of the thought that he was dying. After this he remained quietly resting and waiting, saying a few words occasionally. It was noticed that he many times repeated: "Prima di tutto convien fare il proprio dovere"—First of all we ought to do our duty. What a deep impression would not the silence of that chamber, broken only by the hardly-restrained emotion of his friends or the dying words of the sculptor, have made upon a stranger! At last the time fixed in God's eternal decrees came. Those around him heard him utter rapidly several times: "Anima pura e bella"—Pure and beautiful spirit; and a moment later he expired calmly and quietly, his face suddenly growing more and more highly radiant and expressive. This was on the morning of the 13th of October, 1822, when Canova was in his sixty-fifth year.

A post-mortem examination revealed a combination of troubles, including paralysis of the stomach. The remote origin seems to have been in the depression of the right breast, occasioned by the bearing against the head of the trapano, an iron instrument in constant use among sculptors.

His funeral was grand and imposing, and was in no way a heartless ceremony. Before the remains were conveyed to Possagno Venice desired to pay public honor to the man who had commenced his career under her shelter. The feeling which found vent there was something almost incredible. It is only when we remember who and what the man whom they were honoring was that we can understand the depth of reverence, respect and love shown his remains. The multitude of all ranks stood uncovered and bending as the coffin was slowly borne to St. Mark's, conducted by the professors and pupils of the Art Academy. Over this vast concourse, perfect silence prevailed, broken only by the solemn pealing of the *requiem* or the almost deep whisper of the response. Yet the most remarkable tribute, after the religious ceremony, was that paid by the Academy in their great hall, whither the remains were borne when the services at St. Mark's were ended. The walls were draped in black, and around them were hung engravings or drawings of Canova's works. The hall was filled with the most distinguished men of Venice. There, in the darkened room, with a solitary funeral torch placed at the head of the bier, the president of the Academy delivered with the eloquence of truth an oration on the life and works of him whose remains were in their midst. And it is recorded that when the orator touched on the private virtues and sincere friendship of the man whose memory they were honoring, he was unable to proceed, being overcome with emotion. In that pause one spontaneous burst of responsive feeling from the audience completed the oration.

On the following day the bier was borne to Possagno, where the people greeted it with sobs and tears, and where, amidst every show of deep feeling, the body of Antonio Canova was consigned to its final resting-place. The Venetian Academy obtained his heart, and, having enclosed the precious relic in a vase of porphyry with suitable inscriptions, placed it in the hall of the Palace of Arts. The Venetian artists selected Canova's own model for the tomb of Titian (which had not been used), and erected it in marble in honor of the man they so dearly loved and appreciated. But not alone in Venice was his memory held in such high esteem. Throughout all Europe the tidings of his death were everywhere received with expressions of sadness and a sense of a loss not easy to replace.

What more can we say of this illustrious man? If we have forborne to find fault, to criticize his works, to pull to pieces his execution that we might discover his imperfections, it is because in a sketch like this they seem wholly lost in the grand sum of his excellences.

Great private virtues, apart from his profession, were his. Benevolence, gratitude, single-heartedness, sincerity of friendship, and a splendid generosity distinguished him. His purse, his chisel, his interest, were always at the command of those who lived in intimacy with him. His acquirements were those of an artist and a man of taste. He was adverse to taking pupils, and never would receive them, though he was always ready to assist and show interest in any promising artist. He rarely wrote on the subject of art, but to the memory and note-books of his friends, and an occasional letter, we owe our knowledge of his practical methods, and these sources are both authentic and ample.

One trait of Canova's—an admirable one, well worthy of imitation—may be seen from a remark of his when he was urged to refute certain injurious expressions that had appeared against him in some of the literary journals. With noble candor he replied: "Le me opere sono in pubblico, e il pubblico ha tutto il diripto di giúdicarle; ma io mi sono proposito di non rispondere a qualunque critica osservazione altrimente, che coll' impiegare ogni studio per miglio fare".— My works are before the public, and that public has every right to pass judgment upon them; but for my own part, it is my resolve not to reply to any critical observation whatsoever, otherwise than by exerting every effort to do better.

And again, an English nobleman, although admiring the simplicity and purity of the style shown in the group of "Pheseus and the Minotaur," objected to it, because it was, as he said, "too cold." The sculptor listened in silence to the critic's remarks. Some time after, he produced that exquisite group of "Cupid and Psyche," in which the latter is recumbent, and the former bending over her as she just awakes. To the Englishman's expression of surprise and delight, Canova simply replied: "Preferisco costantemente di rispondere a quanto convenevole osservato piú tosto collo-scarpello, che colle parole"— I always prefer to answer a judicious observation with my chisel rather than by words.

A nature like his was highly susceptible to love, and twice he was on the point, according to Cicognara, of entering the married state, but was deterred, perhaps, by the feeling which Michael Angelo so well expresses: "Art is jealous, and requires the whole man to herself." Art was his mistress and absorbed his all. His heart, however, was never entangled by a low or unworthy passion. All his sentiments accorded with the lofty character of the man.

He had sculptured with his own hand fifty-three statues, thirteen groups, fourteen cenotaphs, eight great monuments, seven colossals, two groups of colossal statues, fifty-four busts, twenty-six basso-relievos. He besides painted twenty-eight oil-paintings, and left in his portfolio a large number of studies, architectural designs and models. Memes divides his works into three classes or distinct orders, thus:

I. Heroic compositions.
II. Compositions of grace and elegance.
III. Sepulchral monuments and relievos.

Canova was very affectionately attached to Pius VII, and bequeathed to him in respectful terms, the privilege of selecting from his whole possessions, whatever might be most pleasing or agreeable to him; desiring in this manner to testify his love and devotion to the occupant of the Holy See. Leo XII, in 1826, caused a fine monument to be placed in the entrance-hall of the new museum at Rome, in honor of Canova, and beneath it is this inscription: "Ad Ant. Canova—Leo XII, Pont. Max."

Catholic Notes.

——The death is announced by *The Indo-European Correspondence*, of Rt. Rev. Dr. Fennelly, Bishop of Thermopylæ and Vicar-Apostolic of Madras. R. I. P.

——We are indebted to Rev. Father Doherty, pastor of the Church of the Immaculate Conception, Kansas City, Mo., for numerous kind favors to our travelling agent and a notable addition to our subscription list.

——The Berlin *Tageblatt*, speaking of the conference held by the Trappist, Father Francis, with the Catholic workmen of that city, says that the German Trappists, expelled from Prussia, have been invited by the English Government to Zululand, to civilize the country.

——At the English College, Valladolid, Spain, Mass is sung every Saturday by the students as an act of reparation to the Blessed Virgin, for the insults offered her by fanatical English soldiers, who dragged her image through the streets of the city three hundred years ago.

——Reports from Russia state that insects are destroying everything in several provinces of that unfortunate country, and that a terrible famine is threatening. Thus continues the fulfilment of the prophecy of Pope Pius IX, of saintly memory, "The hand of God will weigh heavily on Russia."

——It was estimated that on the occasion of Cardinal Newman's sermon at the Brompton Oratory during his recent visit to London, there were present at least two hundred of the sons and daughters of the men and women who, thirty years ago, were led over to Rome by the advocacy of the leader of the Oxford movement.

——The work of covering the cupola of St. Peter's continues with all possible speed. It is divided into sixteen enormous sections, thirteen of which are already covered. It is estimated that it will take a couple of years to finish the remaining three. The sheets of lead necessary to cover each section, weigh nearly one thousand pounds.

——On the 6th inst., the Sunday within the octave of the Sacred Heart, Messrs. Thomas McNamara and Nicholas Irmen, scholastics of the Congregation of the Holy Cross, made their religious profession in the Church of Our Lady of the Sacred Heart, at Notre Dame. The Very Rev. Father Provincial of the province of Indiana presided at the impressive ceremony.

——The works at Cologne cathedral have been renewed since the winter with great activity, and it really seems, in spite of adverse prediction, that the building will actually be finished at last. Works of restoration are being carried on at the same time as the works of completion, especially beneath the south tower, whose foundations have to be renewed while its summit is being finished.

——The venerable Bishop of the Islands of Madeira some time ago placed his diocese under the protection of Our Lady of Lourdes, and since then his zealous efforts for the spiritual welfare of his flock have been crowned with wonderful success. The number of confessions and Communions in the little chapel dedicated to Our Lady of Lourdes within a year amounted to nearly 8,000.

——The Milanese Society for Promoting Catholic Interests has succeeded in obtaining the signatures of no less than 500 prelates to a petition drawn up for presentation to the Holy See by the Archbishop of Udine; the object of which is to solicit the extension to priests in general of the privilege already enjoyed by the clergy of Spain and Portugal of celebrating three Masses on All Souls' day, in behalf of the souls in Purgatory. Amongst the supporters of this important petition are many Italian, French, German, and English Bishops.

——NON-CATHOLIC OPINION OF A GREAT CATHOLIC CHARITY.—The *New York Staatszeitung*, a German newspaper which generally manifests a decidedly hostile attitude to the Catholic Church and her institutions, has lately published an article highly eulogistic of the New York Foundling Asylum, in charge of the Sisters of Charity. Want of space permits us to give only an outline of the article: "The asylum, located on 68th St., between 3d and Lexington Avenues, is one of the finest edifices of New York city. The building was begun in 1872, and is not yet entirely completed. The principal building covers an area of 90 by 60 feet, and is five stories high. Up to date, $330,000 have been expended in the construction of the work. The foundlings are received in a cradle, placed in the basement, under the archway of the main stairs. The parlor and the residence of the physician are on the first floor; on the second floor are the Sisters' quarters, the clothesrooms and working rooms; the dormitories and infirmary occupy the other three stories. The play-rooms, dining-hall and class-rooms, and also the bathing-rooms are in other buildings adjoining. The number of children supported by the institution at present is 1,622. About 1,000 of these children are boarded out in trustworthy families, the board varying from $8 to $10 per month. Among the children, are 247 below 6 months, 212 aged between 6 and 12 months, 422 below 1 and 2 years, 532 from 2 to 5 years, and 209 over 5 years of age." The reporter of the *New York Staatszeitung* has only words of the highest praise for the exquisite neatness, mild and prudent administration, and the spirit of tender charity shown by the good Sisters towards these poor and abandoned children.

——A POET'S REPARATION.—There is a pleasant bit of history, never yet in print, of the way in which Mr. Longfellow came to write his poem of "Monte Cassino." Premising that Father Boniface, now the Prior, and formerly for many years the Librarian, of the monastery on Monte Cassino, which was founded by St. Benedict himself, is an American by education, and therefore quite familiar with our literature, the story runs thus: When Mr. Longfellow published his translation of Dante in 1867, he copied from Benvenuto, in a note to the 75th line of Canto XXII of "Paradiso," an account of what Boccaccio had "pleasantly narrated" to the said Benvenuto about a visit he once made to the old monastery and to its library, which, he says, he found "without door or fastening," with "the grass growing upon the windows and all the books and shelves covered with dust"; while he was assured by one of the brethren of whom he made inquiry as to why those precious books were so vilely mutilated, that "some of the monks, wishing to gain a few ducats, cut out a handful of leaves, and made psalters which they sold to the boys, and likewise of the margins they made breviaries which they sold to women." In due time Mr. Longfellow's volume found its way to Monte Cassino, and the monks there read what they had always considered as Boccaccio's slander, with a sort of indorsement by one of the distinguished names in modern literature. In the course of three or four years thereafter, Mr. Longfellow himself, in travelling through Italy, made his way to the famous monastery upon the mountain, where he was hospitably entertained over night (as his poem records), and in the morning was shown the treasures of the library with its ancient manuscripts—four thousand flat ones, and no less than forty thousand in rolls—not kicking about the floor, with their edges clipped, as Boccaccio had said, but carefully preserved through all the ages as bright and clean as when they were finished by the patient monks, centuries ago. After his return home, Mr. Longfellow did "poetic justice" in its best sense by writing the delightful account of his visit above mentioned, a copy of which he sent to "the urbane librarian," Father Boniface.

——THE CITY OF JERUSALEM.—During the last few decades, the city of Jerusalem has enjoyed great material prosperity, verifying the prophecy of Isaias: *Jerusalem shall be built anew*. In 1852, an old Mahometan hamlet on Mount Sion, and a Protestant college on the Jaffa road, were all that could be seen outside of the ramparts. At the present time, however, the holy city is surrounded on every side by splendid suburban villas, and religious and industrial establishments, reminding one more of European civilization than of oriental semi-barbarism. Russians, French, English, Germans, Austrians and other Europeans, and of course Americans, are all vieing with each other in settling the land of promise, and no less than 20,000 Jews alone have been added of late to the population; in fact, the old city inside the walls, will be nothing less in the course of time than what the cities of London, or Paris, Vienna, or Berlin now are. Many new buildings, chiefly religious establishments, have been erected outside the ramparts, and the grand cupola of the Church of the Holy Sepulchre has been entirely rebuilt. Among the religious houses recently erected by Catholics, is a large Carmelite Convent on Mount Olivet, built by the Princess La Tour d'Auvergne; the residence of the Latin Patriarch and his Cathedral; a hospice inn for French pilgrims, and a school of the Christian Brothers. In the town itself is a hospice for the Austrian pilgrims, and another built by the Missionaries of the Holy Land, capable of receiving 200 pilgrims; the Church of St. Anne, splendidly rebuilt by the French, and in charge of the Missionaries of Algiers, who have erected here a novitiate for their missions in Africa and Syria; also the Church of the Flagellation, the Ecce Homo Church, and a female orphan asylum, in charge of the Sisters of Our Lady of Sion. The joyous peal of church bells, but ten years ago so hateful to Turkish ears that the sound of a bell from a Christian spire was a certain signal of destruction to the house, and almost certain death to the inmates, can now be heard at every hour of the day, ringing out their gladsome peals to the ears of Christian and Mussulman alike, tolling the knell and downfall, as it were, of the creed and race of that wonderful city, which ranks second only, in the eyes of the sons of the prophet, with Mecca and Medina in the cradle lands of Islamism.

——THE LATE DR. O'CALLAGHAN.—We find, in one of the New York daily papers, the following notice of Dr. Edward O'Callaghan, who died recently in that city. The attendance of a large number of distinguished Catholics, laymen and clergymen, at the funeral services in the cathedral, witnesses the high regard in which Dr. O'Callaghan was held: "Dr. O'Callaghan was born in Mallow, County Cork, Ireland, in 1799, and after receiving a classical education, studied medicine both in Dublin and Paris. He arrived in Quebec in 1843, and, after practising medicine for a number of years, became engaged in politics. In 1834 he settled in Montreal as editor of the *Vindicator*, the organ of the Nationalists, and was elected a member of the Assembly of Lower Canada in 1836. He was prominent in the insurrection headed by Papineau in 1837, and, on its failure, fled with his chief to Albany. Dr. O'Callaghan settled in this city in that year, and practised medicine until 1848, when he was appointed keeper of the historical manuscripts in the office of the Secretary of State at Albany. Two years previously he had published the 'History of New Netherlands, or New York Under the Dutch.' Being commissioned by the Legislature to write the 'Documentary History of the State of New York,' he was twenty-two years engaged in the task, which was completed in 1870; during that period, also, he published 'Documents Relating to the Colonial History of the State of New York,' translated several volumes of Dutch records in the Secretary of State's Office, and also 'Jesuit Relations of Discoveries'; wrote the 'Origin of the Legislative Assemblies of the State of New York' and 'Voyages of the Slavers, St. John and Arms,' and edited Wilson's 'Orderly Book,' the 'Orderly Book of Gen. John Burgoyne,' and 'Journals of the Legislative Councils of New York.' He likewise published 'A List of the Editions of the Holy Scriptures and Parts Thereof, Published in America Previous to 1860,' 'Historical Manuscripts Relating to the War of the Revolution,' and 'Laws and Ordinances of New Netherlands from 1638 to 1674.' In 1870 he was invited to New York by Mayor Oakey Hall, to edit the archives of the city of New York, upon which he was employed for several years. Dr. O'Callaghan was a member of the Catholic Union and of the Historical Society, to which he contributed many papers. He was also honorary member of several learned societies in Europe. He spoke French, Dutch, and German with fluency. For some years previous to his death, Dr. O'Callaghan suffered greatly from inflammatory rheumatism, and was incapacitated for literary labor." May his soul rest in peace.

—CONTRIBUTIONS FOR THE SUFFERING IRISH:—Mrs. Isabella Mann, $10; J. J. L., $1; M. F. F. B., $5; A Child of Mary, $1; Miss M. McCloskey, $1; A Reader of THE AVE MARIA, $1; S. Buckley, $1; Mrs. E. Wall, $2; Mrs. Anna Vaughan, $2; A. H. Wagner, $1; Mr. and Mrs. Devoughs, $1; Mr. and Mrs. James O'Neill, $1; A Friend, 50 cts.; Mr. Dillehunt, 25 cts.; Mr. John McFarland, 50 cts.; A Friend, 25 cts.; A Friend, 25 cts.; Kate Kane, $1; Annie Brannagan, 25 cts.; Mrs. McLaine, 20 cts.; Mrs. T. Regan, 50 cts.; Mrs. Grimes, 50 cts.; Mrs. M. Dunn, $1; Rose Kiley, 50 cts.; Some Friends, 50 cts.; A Poor Reader of THE AVE MARIA, $2; Katie Clarke, $1; A Friend. $1; A North of Ireland Convert, $5; A Subscriber of THE AVE MARIA, Malden, Mass., $1; S. Girardot, $1; A Life Subscriber of THE AVE MARIA, $10; A Friend, $2; Mrs. Coady, $1; Leonard Mitchell and family, $4; A Friend, 50 cts.; A Reader of THE AVE MARIA, $1; Salmon Falls, N. H., $2; Miss Lizzie Kromp, relatives and friends, $11.5.

New Publications.

LACORDAIRE'S LETTERS TO YOUNG MEN. New York: P. O'Shea, No. 37 Barclay Street. Price, $3.

To comment upon a volume like this is much like trying to select a bouquet of flowers where all attract by the splendor of their hue and the delicacy of their perfume. One is, however, attracted by three blossoms, as it were, amid this rich parterre: the simplicity of the writer; his unostentatious and practical piety; and the beauty of his friendships.

The simplicity of the soul of Lacordaire finds a fit vehicle in the beauty and directness of his diction in these letters. Having quitted a profession in many respects the most opposed to the Christian life, he carries its practicality alone to the walls of the monastery. Singularly free from either a dreamy scholasticism or a vain enthusiasm, qualities often found among those won from the intellectual world to a religious life, he exhibits throughout the volume a practical wisdom, which is rendered beautiful by the ardor of his piety. His friendship was a jewel worth the possession of a monarch. The tender words thus recorded, whether breathing only the sentiments of the affections or the gentle reproof, are alike charming. The Anglo-Saxon character lacks the effusive grace of the Latin race. The Saxon when he feels deeply, cares only to conceal that feeling. Lacordaire, educated in all the traditions of his race, expresses without reserve all the warmth of his soul, and bares to his friends a heart filled with the deepest emotions of piety and love.

No review can do justice to these letters, but if this slight notice shall cause one of our readers to procure the book, we can assure him not only a rich literary repast, but the possession of a mint from which he can draw at will sterling coin, current not only in this world, but in the City of God.

THE MIRACULOUS MEDAL. Its Origin, History, Circulation, Results. By M. Aladel, C. M. Translated from the French, by P. S. Illustrated. Baltimore: John B. Piet, No. 174 W. Baltimore St.

This work, a goodly 12mo. of nearly 350 pages, we took up with the intention of giving it only a cursory perusal, but on reading a few pages found it so entertaining and instructive that we could not lay it aside until we had finished it. It gives a very accurate account of the revival of devotion to the Blessed Virgin in the beginning of this century, of her appearance to Sister Catharine Labouré in 1830, of the medal that was shortly afterwards struck in honor of the Immaculate Conception, together with its wonderful circulation, and the extraordinary cures and conversions that have been effected by its means. There are also some edifying chapters on the Dogma of the Immaculate Conception, as also on Our Lady of La Salette, Lourdes and Pontmain. The accounts of some miracles recorded are so interesting, that we would like, if space permitted, to quote them in full. The story of the conversion of M. Ratisbonne, which is given in detail, is admirably told. The history of the medal in the late wars, both in this country and in Europe, is full of interest and edification.

The whole volume is well calculated to increase devotion towards the Holy Mother of God, and to excite anew confidence in her power and intercession.

—The Cæcilia for June comes promptly to hand, and, as usual, contains a number of well chosen articles bearing on the cause it so ably advocates, viz.: the restoration of liturgical music. Among them, we would draw special attention to a discourse on Church Music by Rt. Rev. Bishop Ulathorne, and "Schools for Ecclesiastical Chant," by Rev. U. O., O. S. B.; also a translation from the French, entitled "On the Duty of the Clergy to foster Church Music." The Cæcilia Society is active and hopeful, under the direction of its energetic President, Prof. Singenberger.

We may hope to see the day when the senseless and profane compositions so often heard in our choirs, will give place to the solemn old Gregorian Chant, or, at least, to harmonized music composed expressly for the Church, and having a due regard to the dignity and solemnity of the divine Offices.

Confraternity of the Immaculate Conception
(Or of Our Lady of Lourdes).

"*We fly to thy patronage, O Holy Mother of God!*"

REPORT FOR THE WEEK ENDING JUNE 9TH.

Prayers are asked for the following intentions: Recovery of health for 28 persons,—change of life for 16 persons and 2 families,—conversion to the Faith for 17 persons and 1 family,—special graces for 4 priests, 9 clerical students, and several lay persons,—temporal favors for many persons,—spiritual favors for 22 persons and 4 families,—the spiritual and temporal welfare of 3 families, 19 persons, and several religious communities,—recovery of sight for four persons,—recovery of mind for 6 persons,—recovery of hearing for 2 persons; also 4 thanksgivings for favors received, and 13 particular intentions.

Specified intentions: The successful issue of a number of lawsuits,—grace of a happy death for several persons,—peace and harmony in some families,—protection of a family from the incursions of the Indians,—means to erect a chapel and other necessary buildings,—financial prosperity of several business men,—a person in great distress,—profitable sales of property,—grace of sobriety for a young man,—a number of persons given up to intemperance,—suitable members for a novitiate, and light to discern their vocation,—return of a young man to his home,—resources, situations, employments, etc., for many persons and families,—grace to know their vocation for several persons,—a poor man sentenced to be hanged,—removal of the cause of strife between a husband and wife,—success in studies, etc., etc.

FAVORS OBTAINED.

A gentleman of Montreal writes: "My little boy Frankie was very ill with brain fever which produced convulsions. He was unable to eat anything for five days. I had two doctors attending him for a week, but despite their efforts he was sinking very fast. On Saturday last, I obtained some of the water of Lourdes from the Director of the Christian Brothers' School, and gave the child a drop on a spoon; this was on Saturday night. On Sunday morning he sat at his place at the table, and ate his breakfast as usual. He is completely cured. No medicine could have procured such a result. Thanks be to God, and blessed be the Holy and Immaculate Virgin Mary! To say that I am grateful, is but a poor expression of my feelings. Frankie is my only son, and the thought of losing him nearly broke my heart." A lady asks us to return thanks to Our Lady of the Sacred Heart for the return of her brother to our holy Faith which he had abandoned for a long time.

OBITUARY.

The following deceased persons are recommended to the prayers of the Confraternity: Mr. JAMES S. BANNOCK, of Chicago, Ill., who breathed his last on the 27th ult. Mr. W. MURPHY, of the same city, deceased on the 17th ult. BRIDGET McHUGH, who departed this life at Beloit, Kan., on the 29th of May. CATHARINE DOBE, of Fremont, Ohio, whose death occurred on the 4th inst. Mrs. K. HENNEBOY, of Chicago, Ill., who rested in peace on the 25th of May. EDWARD PFEIFFER, who slept in the Lord on the 17th of April, at Richfields, Wis. And some others, whose names have not been given.

Requiescant in pace.

A. GRANGER, C. S. C., Director.

Youth's Department.

St. Aloysius Gonzaga.

BY REV. MATTHEW RUSSELL, S. J.

ALOYSIUS, dear young Saint!
  Help at thy hands I come to claim;
It cheers me, when my soul is faint,
  To think of thee, to name thy name.
I yearn to thee as to a brother,
  A brother gone to God before—
I love thee next to Mary Mother
  In Him whom she and thou adore;
I love but Him and her above thee,
And more thou wouldst not let me love thee.

The hoary saints of mien austere,
  Rapt eye and venerable form,
We think of them with reverent fear—
  They cannot win a love so warm
As thou with thine unwrinkled brow,
  Thy youth fulheart and youthful face,
That smile that gleams upon me now,
  And all thy noble, modest grace.
For ah! too quickly home thou hastedst—
Thy twenty twelvemonths were not wasted.*

Thy sun went down before its noon,
  That should have lit up noon and even—
A few short hours it shone, but soon
  Its mild light faded from our heaven.
The ripe fruit could not keep its hold;
  Its rich load snapped the bough in twain—
God would not wait till thou grew old,
  To clasp thee to His breast again.
So young, yet old in sainthood hoary,
Closed, high-born angel! thy brief story.

And here is one who fondly bears
  Deep in his heart thy sacred name,
And wears the habit that he wears
  Partly that thou hast worn the same:
Brother to little Stanislaus,
  Ignatius' child as thou and he—
Oh! by the love such kinship draws,
  Act a true brother's part to me.
Though sins on sins unworthy prove me,
Dear Aloysius! try and love me.

I pray as thou thyself hast prayed,
  While thou didst linger here below;
And, as the saints then lent thee aid,
  Thou'lt help me in thy turn, I know.
Ah! help me, help me in my need—
  Help me to work, to love, to pray—
Help me! I need thy help indeed:
  Turn not thy sweet young face away.
Turn not away thy face, dear Lewis,
But turn it, beaming kindly, to us.

* St. Aloysius died at early dawn of June 21, 1591, aged twenty-three years, three months, and eleven days. He received his First Communion at the hands of St. Charles Borromeo. His confessor was Venerable Cardinal Bellarmine, who testified that he had never mortally offended God. St. Aloysius is the patron of youth.

"What is the Good of Obeying?"

Translated from the French for "The Ave Maria."

WHAT is the use of obeying? How many times does that question come to the lips of a child? And is it not usually thus that he receives, at least at the bottom of his heart, the commands of his parents and teachers? I was like others when I was young; I rebelled very often against the gentle laws, whose importance and wisdom I did not understand; and when I could see no further than the end of my nose, I would have put myself at the helm and guided my bark at the risk of making shipwreck at the very beginning of my imprudent course. What a fine thing it would be to govern one's own self! Did I not know better than any one else what suited my needs and tastes? And the adventurous opinions of youth, are they not preferable a hundred times over to the learned and prosy ideas of that superannuated old woman whose name is Experience?

Such as I was at that time, I resembled most children of yesterday, to day, and forever; but when I had reached my twelfth year, I was vividly impressed by the recital of a little drama, whose hero I knew, and I learned then how useful implicit obedience without discussion or remark may be.

It was Sunday morning; while waiting for the appointed hour for Mass, desirous of making the most of my time, I clambered along the top of a high wall which separated the yard from the garden, hoping, at the risk of breaking my legs and arms, to reach a large branch of *acacia* which hung over the old wall. I confess that it was one of my favorite exercises, though it had often been forbidden me.

"Have done, master Albert!" cried my old nurse, who had just come in from the market. "See how you are ruining your best trousers! not to speak of the accidents which happen often to those who least expect them; you are in a fair way to make a cripple of yourself for life."

My mother opened her window. "How disobedient you are, child! How many times have I forbidden you those imprudent climbs!"

"Oh, he will only be happy when he has put us all in mourning!" replied Annette, who never wanted for a word. "Let him go and see the poor little Coussinet boy, and he will learn what it may cost to disobey one's parents."

"What do you mean?" asked my mother, anxiously. "Has anything happened to the child?"

"Ah, madame! it makes one's very hair stand on end, only to think of it. God grant it is all a heap of lies and gossip, such as one is accustomed to hear on market-days: but the milk-woman told me herself that she saw him when she arrived with her wagon before the train passed."

I listened with all my ears; Matthew Coussinet, although several years younger than I, was my favorite playmate on account of his extreme gentleness. He always let me have my own way. My mother herself, knowing him to be perfectly well-bred, preferred to see me with him rather than with many of the other boys of my age. Then Mr. Coussinet, Matthew's father, who had been a soldier, knew so many nice stories about the African wars! It was from thence that he had brought his comrade, as he called in his good-humored way his wooden leg, and I never wearied of hearing him tell of the Kabyles and of Kabylia.

"Just think, madame," said Annette, in a choked voice, "the whole express train passed over the poor little fellow's body yesterday. His father had forbidden his going on the track, and he bettered himself a great deal by his disobedience!" she added, somewhat sarcastically, glancing in my direction.

"After Mass, we will go to these poor people," said my mother, much agitated, while I remained motionless under the window.

The road to the Coussinets was charming. Always in the shade, along a hollow in the wood, above which stout chestnut trees interlaced their leafy branches, forming thus a natural arch of deepest green. On the banks, hollies with shiny leaves were busy ripening their red berries in the June sun, and according to the season, there were either violets or wild strawberries to be picked. Usually I climbed a hundred times to the attack, only, it would seem, in order to have the pleasure of rolling down again as often; thus, ordinarily, we were a long time on the road, but that day my mother could hardly keep up with me.

I had seen Matthew three days before. He was helping his brother to turn the hay to dry in the sun. His black eyes sparkled like diamonds above cheeks which were like red roses; and it seemed as if I still heard him shout as we parted, "I hope I shall see you soon again, Albert."

Again! and the end had come; my poor playmate! In spite of myself I slackened my pace as we approached the end of our walk. Certainly I hoped for nothing; yet I did not wish to remove all hope just yet.

And here is the little house with the brown Persian blinds, with its little vine which climbs up to the roof. How I tremble! My mother feels obliged to take me by the hand. I look at her and see that she is very pale too.

On the door-step Mother Coussinet sits tranquilly; her husband is smoking his pipe inside the door. We can discover nothing by appearances. A few steps off, the goat is grazing.

Oh, wonderful to think of! Here comes Matthew, running to meet us. There are the very bright eyes that I feared never to see again; his curly hair is filled with bits of hay. The fellow doubtless has been rolling in the stacks, while I was mourning over his death. "Ah! you can be happy in thinking you have made me nicely anxious," I began. But he threw himself about my neck, and said: "Hush, Albert! mother knows nothing of it yet; father will tell you all in a moment."

"I might well say wonderful! yes indeed, a miracle of obedience on the one side, and on the other, a miraculous recompense awarded to the docility of a child.

"Yesterday evening at about six o'clock," began Mr. Coussinet, after he had led us into the adjoining field some distance from the house, "I found that I was a little late in shutting the gate; I hurried, because I knew that the express train was due, and that there was no time for joking with that. As I shut the second gate I heard the train; the locomotive issued from the tunnel at lightning speed. 'Papa, papa!' cried a little voice which made me shudder. My God, may I be punished for my carelessness! The child had followed me as he often did; in my preoccupation I had neither seen nor heard him, and I had shut him in upon the track. I saw him, pale and distressed, running up and down like a poor frightened bird, crying 'papa, papa,' in a voice which I shall hear until the Judgment day.

"The key had fallen from my hands, and I could not stoop to pick it up. I stood like one paralyzed with fright. Impossible even to try to climb over the barrier gate. The child held out his little arms without knowing what he did, and the monster with its great red eyes was advancing to devour him. The noise made me giddy; everything grew dim, and my mouth was closed, but at the bottom of my heart I prayed as I never prayed in my life. 'My God! my God! my God!' that was all, but it was enough, it seems, for our heavenly Father. At that moment a ray of intelligence shot through my soul; without stirring, still paralyzed in body, but free in mind, I saw what was to be done. 'Down, down, boy! flat on your face on the ground!' I cried, in a voice which was heard above the noise of the engine and the smoke.

"Oh, Madame! the child was so accustomed to obey! his mother had brought him up so well; never has he known what it is to resist. But there, I confess, obedience was difficult. Never mind! the poor little angel, without taking a step forward or back, without attempting a movement hardly, stretched himself out at full length!

"Madame," continued Mr. Coussinet, after a moment of silence, during which I could hear the beating of my heart, "I counted eighteen cars as they passed over the body of my child! I cried and gnawed like a mad dog; one, two, three, my God! my God! four, five, six! . . . . They passed over my heart, every one! When it was over, I was like a dead man; I could not see clearly. Then suddenly it grew bright around me, and I heard a little voice cry:

"'Papa, papa, open the gate quick, for fear another train will come.'

"'I rubbed my eyes; surely I had died with the child, and the good God had taken us both to paradise.

"But no! It was indeed he, my child, so pale, with his curly head and bright eyes. I felt of him; I felt of him all over; he was whole and sound.

"Madame, I doubt if Almighty God ever received thanksgiving such as mine. And to think that, as good luck would have it, his mother had been off in town since morning. Oh, the poor woman, she would be dead if she had seen it as I saw it! . . . . a mother's heart, you know is not very strong. But, hush! there she comes. I shall tell her guardedly this evening, when I am more calm, and when she has seen the child play about all day, as usual."

"But do you think Matthew can keep the secret so long?" asked my mother, drawing her hand across her eyes.

"He? oh yes! I rely on his word as I do on the curate's. That child there would let himself be cut in bits before he would disobey. He is not like most children, who require so much reasoning, *and why? and how? and what for?* and all such questions. So," he continued, modestly but proudly, as he caressed the little boy's curly head, "I can well say that after God, who is the Master of life and death, it is to himself that he owes his rescue. If he had reasoned and argued when I cried to him, he would have been killed. But he believed that his father could not be wrong. Didn't you boy?"

"Of course," replied Matthew, without a moment's hesitation; "parents are always right."

My mother looked at me; I felt myself getting red up to my very ears, and to conceal my embarrassment, I hugged Matthew.

"He is a little hero, isn't he?" I said to my mother on the way home, as she asked me why I was so serious.

"He is a docile child," she replied simply. "Obedience saved his life."

"I am going to try to be obedient," I said, kissing the hand which stroked my forehead.

Young friends, I kept my word, and I always get on well. Try it yourselves, and see how well you, too, will succeed.

Irish Legends.

X.

THE STORY OF THE "BIG HOUSE."

O doubt, little children, you are all anxious to hear the wonders that happened in the big house; but we must first tell you something about that big house itself, over in the trees near the Mass-Rock, with its underground passage, its shady walks, its prison-like walls and mysterious appearance."

This was said by the black lady of the big house, about three months after the death of Paudhrig O'Malley, to the children to whom she had promised to finish the tales he had been telling them on the top of Croagh-Patrick. She had now come and gathered the little children about her to fulfil her promise.

"Well, more than twenty years ago," said she, "I was robbed of all my property in the south; my house was taken and my estate confiscated, because I would not change my religion and become a Protestant. But as I was a widow, and had a daughter just married to a Mr. O'Connor of this province, I got a miserable barren tract of land here on the bare slopes of Croagh-Patrick, with that wretched house which you call 'the big house,' instead of my rich land and splendid castle in the south. I had no choice but to accept it, or have nothing. They said I should go to 'Hell or to Connaught,' and that I would get nothing else. I was a 'harmless papist.' Just this time twenty-one years ago, I came with my daughter Kathleen, and her four children, Dermot and Charlie, Ellen and Mary;. poor O'-Connor, their father, had also lost all his property because he would not conform to the Protestant religion; he would not come with us, but went off to join the Austrian army. My dear husband had been dead just twelve months; he died in Spain; I came here in mourning, and for one reason or other I never changed that mourning. I have been always 'the black lady of the big house,' though the house is not very big. I had to get it repaired; to have that wall built round the grounds, and many of those trees planted. Though it was a sad change for me, God had His own wise ends in it. I was scarcely a month in the house, when poor Father Mulligan got that terrible torturing at the Mass-Rock which poor Paudhrig told you of with tears in his eyes. I took the holy priest into my house and risked my life for him. I gave him a room and the means of saying Mass every morning. For twenty years he was the blessing and consolation of my house. I had that underground passage made for him to come safely through to the Mass-Rock on the great feasts and say Mass for the people. My two little grandchildren, Dermot and Charlie O'Connor, used to serve his Mass, when they grew up, and dear Ellen and Mary always assisted at it. They are all gone from me now; I'm alone; even the holy priest has been torn from us. We have but just wept over his martyred remains."

The good old lady could tell no more; tears choked her utterance. All "the wonders of the big house" must be told at another time.

" Down time's silent river their fair names shall go,
A light to our race towards the long coming day;
Till the billows of time shall be choked in their flow,
Can we find names so sweet for remembrance as they;
And we will hold their memories forever and aye,
 · A halo of glory that ne'er shall decay
So long as her children to Ireland are true,
O'Connor of Connaught, O'Donnell aboo."

(TO BE CONTINUED.)

It is told of a certain Dominican friar, that on his death-bed he was observed to make many gestures of reverence, as though in the presence of some persons of great dignity. Those who stood by asked him the cause of these gestures. "This house," he replied, "is full of angels, and our Blessed Lady is here, whom let us salute." The Fathers hearing him speak thus, intoned the *Salve Regina*, which being ended, he smiled and said, "Oh how acceptable was your salutation to Mary! As she listened to you she smiled."

For the Suffering Irish Children.

Tommy Kean, 25 cts.; Johnny Kean, 25 cts.; Mrs. Crowley, 25 cts.; Patrick Crowley, 10 cts.; Catharine Crowley, 10 cts.; John Crowley, 25 cts.; Clara Crowley, 10 cts.; Philip Connell, Jr., 15 cts.; Joseph Connell, 10 cts.; John Connell, 10 cts.; Charlie Gatze, 25 cts.; Mrs. Burns, 25 cts.; Mrs. Flanigan, 25 cts.; Mrs. J. Kennedy, 25 cts.; C. Miller, 25 cts.; Mr. Stouch, 25 cts.; Katie Ott, 10 cts.; Mrs. Foley, 10 cts.; Mrs. Little, 10 cts.; Mrs. D. Crowley, 25 cts.; J. Gardner, 25 cts.; Mrs. M. Foley, 10 cts.; Martin Crowe, 25 cts.; Charlie Gatze, 25 cts.; John Wester, 25 cts.; Mary A. Hartnett, 10 cts.; J. Hartnett, 25 cts.; G. A. Reil, 10 cts.; Mrs. J. Long, 25 cts.; Mrs. J. Horrigan, 25 cts.; Mrs. D. Barnes, 25 cts.; James Rodgers, 25 cts.; Dannie Dorcy, 10 cts.; Mrs. M. Connell, 25 cts.; Mrs. E. Connell, 25 cts.; Mr. P. Connell, 25 cts.; Miss A. Connell, 25 cts.; Martha Connell, 25 cts.; Alexis Campeau, 10 cts.; James Hayes, 50 cts.; Mrs. McVeill, 50 cts.; Mrs. A. Jackson, 50 cts.; Mrs. Keating, 25 cts.; Mrs. Brown, 25 cts.; Mrs. Connoty, 25 cts.; Mrs. McCarty. 25 cts.; Mrs. Fox, 25 cts.; Charlie McVeill, 25 cts.; Mrs. Hampton, 25 cts.; Mrs. Tighe, 25 cts.; Mrs. House, 25 cts.; Mrs. Snither, 25 cts.; Mrs. Mahen, 25 cts.; Mrs. McCann, 25 cts.; Mrs. Donnelly, 25 cts.; Mrs. Flunegan, 25 cts.; Mrs. Kealler, 25 cts.; Joseph O'Hara, $5.15; Mary O'Hara, $5.10; A Friend, $15.

THE AVE MARIA.

A Journal devoted to the Honor of the Blessed Virgin.

HENCEFORTH ALL GENERATIONS SHALL CALL ME BLESSED.—St. Luke, i, 48.

VOL. XVI.   NOTRE DAME, INDIANA, JUNE 26, 1880.   No. 26.

The Pilgrimage of St. Anne of Auray.*

INTRODUCTION.

THE borough of St. Anne is situated in the parish of Pluneret, three leagues from the city of Vannes in Brittany; it was in ancient times a small hamlet, called *Keranna*,† from the devotion which had given it existence. A chapel, under the invocation of St. Anne, seems to have been founded here in the early ages of the Church, since tradition tells that it was destroyed about the close of the seventh century, when the country was desolated by the cruel wars which followed King Judicael's death, and the Church of St. Anne was left to decay.

However this may be, at the date when our history begins, 1622, nothing of the ancient chapel remained but some shapeless stones entirely hidden beneath the soil, and vague memories which still nourished the piety of the neighborhood. A remarkable phenomenon contributed to keep alive the veneration for the sacred ruins. They were in the middle of a wheat-field, called Bocennen or Bocenno, which, though easily dug with a spade, had never admitted the passage of a plough across it; the experiment had often been made, and always failed: the team, on reaching the spot, would rear up and draw back in affright, and if still urged forward, the terrified animals endangered the plough in leaping aside; hence it became a custom, in sending any one to plough the Bocenno, not to forget the warning which had grown into a proverb: "Take good care of the site of the chapel." These repeated events seemed to prove that the Saint, formerly honored there by the fathers, intended to be known to the children, and the oldest men had inherited a fixed belief from their ancestors, that the chapel would one day rise from its ruins.

I.
DISCOVERY OF THE STATUE.

A simple laborer of the village of Keranna was the instrument whom it pleased God to select for the accomplishment of His designs,—according to the sacred laws by which His providence delights to reveal to the lowly and humble, what is hidden from the great and the mighty ones of this world.

Yves Nicolazic was of a poor family, and had long held the farm of Bocenno under the house of Karloguen; he was one of those rare characters whose tastes and habits so incline to virtue that it may be said to have been born with them. From infancy, most punctual in the discharge of his moral and religious duties, he had now reached the age of forty-three, mature both in years and virtues. His neighbors usually chose him as umpire in their differences, being convinced that he would a thousand times rather suffer a wrong than injure another. This habitual goodness was the more solid, inasmuch as it rested on a deep foundation of faith and piety, sustained by the love of prayer. Watchful to gain profit for heaven from every hour of the day, he recited his rosary as he went along the road. His devotion to the Holy Souls made him take delight in offering his actions for their solace and relief. His parents had implanted in his infant heart a special love for the most Blessed Virgin and St. Anne, which he always cherished, never separating in his thoughts the daughter from the mother. Such was the man on whom St. Anne was about to lavish the most astonishing favors, and who was to be the agent in a work so important that the greatest princes would have coveted the honor.

Time passed on, and he felt his devotion to his holy patroness increase more and more; it was the forerunner of the marvels about to take place. The first of these was a light of extraordinary brightness, which appeared suddenly in his house

---
* Translated and abridged for THE AVE MARIA from the Historical Work of Père Martin, S. J.
† Ker Anna, that is, village of Anna.

at midnight, and seemed to proceed from a torch borne by a solitary hand. The phenomenon lasted, he said, while one might recite the *Pater* and *Ave* twice. Six weeks later, the same prodigy was renewed in the Bocenno field, on Sunday, about an hour after sunset, but the light did not last so long, and the mysterious hand was not visible. Nicolazic could only account for it by supposing that his lately deceased mother was thus reminding him to pray more frequently for her, which he was careful to do; but he was soon undeceived.

One evening, his brother-in-law and he had gone as usual, about an hour after sunset, by different roads to seek their cattle, and in returning with them had to pass near a spring, which then flowed scantily along the grass, but afterwards became the beautiful fountain of St. Anne. The two men met here and had commenced speaking, when their cattle suddenly started back in terror, and could not be urged forward. What could be near the well? They advanced to see what was hidden by the foliage, when, to their amazement, they beheld, standing on the edge of the rill, a lady of majestic aspect: her robe, which was dazzling in its whiteness, swept the ground, and she was surrounded by a light at once so soft and bright that it illuminated the whole scene. The first impulse of the men was to fly; but when, ashamed of their childish timidity, they returned, all had disappeared.

The prodigy was soon renewed, and during the ensuing fifteen months, Nicolazic never passed three weeks without a vision. Whenever he was returning later than usual from his fields, a torch, held by an invisible hand, lighted his way, and was never agitated by the night breeze. Often the Saint herself appeared to him, near the lone spring, or in his house, or in the barn beside some old carved stones, which his father had years before raised out of the ruins of the buried chapel. In these apparitions, St. Anne always, wore a robe of dazzling whiteness; she was always upborne on a cloud, and held a torch in her hand; she maintained silence, but her majestic aspect was blended with sweet graciousness, and the light which seemed to penetrate her surroundings, reminded the good laborer of the light which had enraptured the Apostles on Mount Tabor. Twice he heard delicious music, that seemed to rise from the sacred ruins, and beheld a brightness proceeding from them and extending even to the village.

Although these visions had a sensible effect on Nicolazic, increasing his devotion to the Saint so that every thought of her filled him with tender emotions, still he dreaded their recurrence, fearing illusion, and resolved to reveal all to some one who could advise him; he therefore addressed himself to one of the Franciscan Fathers who had not long before been invited to Auray, and were already held in the greatest esteem by all. Father Modestus saw no reason to doubt the wonderful things which Nicolazic revealed to him, but prudently contented himself with advising him to be still more attentive to his duties, to have some Masses celebrated, and to visit, in order to implore more light from heaven, the Church of the Holy Ghost and also a votive chapel of Our Lady of Nazareth which was then much venerated along the whole coast. Nicolazic obeyed, and his prayers were answered in the following manner:

It was the vigil of St. Anne's feast, July 25th, 1625. Nicolazic was returning home from Auray, where he had probably been to confession, preparing for the festival. Walking leisurely along, saying the rosary, as was his habit, he had reached the stone cross, afterwards called *Nicolazic's Cross*, when he beheld his holy patroness, radiant mid the twilight gloom, borne on a cloud, and holding her flaming torch. As he proceeded quietly on his way, she withdrew a little from the road, and followed his steps till he reached his home. Much impressed by the length of time the vision had lasted, and more than ever anxious to know what God required of him, he withdrew to the barn where, stretched on the hay in a corner, he continued his prayers, with no thought of sleep. It was within an hour of midnight when he heard a singular noise; raising himself a little, he plainly heard the footsteps of a multitude and a confused murmur of voices, as of many persons approaching from every direction and in great excitement; running out to learn the cause he saw nothing, and heard the noise no longer. He went as far as the meadows, but all was calm and lonely as befitted the hour, the air scarcely rustling the leaves of the trees.

Returning to the barn, he resumed his chaplet with fresh ardor. Suddenly the barn is illuminated, and a voice asks if he never heard of a chapel that once stood in the Bocenno, and ere he could reply a radiant lady, majestic and amiable, appeared before him.

"Yves Nicolazic, fear not. It is I—Anne, the mother of Mary. Go, tell thy pastor that in the midst of the field called the Bocenno, there was, even before the village had an existence, a celebrated chapel, the first one erected to my honor in Brittany. Nine hundred and twenty-four years ago, this very day, that chapel was destroyed, and I desire that it be rebuilt by thy efforts. God wills that my name be venerated here again."

Thus spoke the lady, in the dialect of the country, and all vanished.

The first feeling of Nicolazic was more of joy than surprise. He had heard her voice, which he could never forget, she had told him her name, and shown her confidence in his zeal; to doubt of success would be a crime; and so rejoicing in the honors his patroness would shortly receive, and through his means, he fell into a peaceful sleep.

His waking thoughts were quite different. His heart sank within him when he reflected on the difficulties to be surmounted, how the rector would receive the message, what the neighbors would say, the astonishment of some, the ridicule of others, the incredulity of all. He would be esteemed a visionary, perhaps an impostor; and how was he, a poor laborer, to collect money to build and maintain a chapel? For six weeks he resisted the inspirations which allowed him not a moment's peace. He fled from everybody lest he should be questioned as to his trouble, but he could not fly from himself. The Saint took pity on his weakness. Appearing again, and addressing him in a severe voice, she bade him inform his rector, and consult some worthy neighbors, under pain of her indignation; terrified at this, he betook himself next morning to the presbytery, where, asking to be heard in confession, he related all that had occurred in two years.

The rector of Pluneret, Don Sylvestor Roduez, was of anything but a credulous turn of mind. Attributing these extraordinary things to a disordered brain, and highly amused at the part which concerned himself, he soon dismissed Nicolazic and what he called his extravagances. The poor man's humiliation now seemed complete, but this was only the first step in his rugged road.

His holy mistress, as he was accustomed to call the Saint, came on the following night to console him, and, reproving his want of confidence, encouraged him to rise above the world's opinions, and to meet, with more firmness, the opposition which was only beginning; but even this favor did not determine him to proceed. The fear of passing for an idiot was insupportable; he wished to obey, but could not summon resolution. Seven weeks passed. The Saint appeared again, and compassionating him, promised that he should now enjoy palpable proofs of her care. Emboldened by her goodness, he cried out, involuntarily:

"My good mistress! can anyone believe me when I say there has been a chapel on a spot where I never saw one, and where no trace of it remains? And then, who am I, that I should find any person willing to bear the expense of the new one?"

"Take courage, and do what I ask," replied St. Anne. "Thou shalt have enough to begin with, and I shall find not only enough to complete it, but to do many great things besides, at which all will be astonished."

These words made a lasting impression on the hearer, filling him with the liveliest confidence and joy. With fresh courage he sought the rector next morning. Don Roduez was at home, and willing to spare him a few moments, but at the mention of the new apparition he lost his temper, and it would not have been prudent to continue the subject. Nothing daunted, Nicolazic presented himself before the curate, Don Jean Thominec, but was even more coldly received there. But this double humiliation could not shake his trust, and now almost daily there were new marvels. He saw descending on the Bocenno sometimes burning torches, again showers of bright stars; and often he was suddenly transported thither from his house, to hear melody so entrancing that it seemed to him a foretaste of heavenly harmonies.

One evening in particular—it was the first Monday in March, 1625, five days before his great discovery—he saw from afar the Bocenno all on fire, and found himself immediately in the midst of the blazing light, and heard again the steps of a throng as if hurriedly gathering around the sacred spot, while a concert arose of such sweetness that he was beside himself with delight. It seemed to him not to last quite half an hour, but on reaching home he found it had detained him three hours, for the servants were asleep and his sister tired of watching for him. He never could speak of that evening's vision without shedding grateful tears. He was not the only one favored by the Saint that night: about nine o'clock, three persons returning to Pluvigner from the market of Auray, saw in the Bocenno, a majestic lady, radiant with light; but she had appeared more distinctly to her trusted servant, commanding him to speak again to his pastor, and assuring him that she would soon give to all unmistakable signs of the truths he advanced, the chief sign being a light that would cause the discovery of a holy image once venerated there.

The first measure now adopted by Nicolazic was to take into confidence an upright neighbor, named Lazulit, who willingly accompanied him in this visit to the rector.

(TO BE CONTINUED.)

No joy is ever half so sweet as that which has been earned by pain, and especially by suffering incurred from unselfish devotion and unflinching fulfilment of duty.

ONE of the poets has versified an Arab story, wherein is told how an angel wrote in a resplendent book the names of those who loved his Master; but the chief to whom he came in vision did not know the Lord of the angel, and he begged to have his name written as one who loved his fellow-men; and lo! when the angel brightened the tent and showed the golden book, his name stood first.

[For the Ave Maria.]

Rhyme of the Friar Stephen.
[A. D. 1334.]

BY ELEANOR C. DONNELLY.

I.

AMONG the records of the ancient Tartars,
The old Franciscan chronicles that show
The sainted lives of those monastic martyrs
Who fell in Asia centuries ago;

We come upon a strange and thrilling story,
Like some rare, gorgeous blossom ripened fast,
Arising in its oriental glory
From out the dust and debris of the past.

The legend of the holy martyr, Stephen,
Is full of solemn truth for all who read;
—Attend, ye self-reliant ones! for even
The best and wisest may its moral heed.

A young Hungarian, fair, and brave, and gifted,
Led by the spirit to the wilderness,
In the first blush of life,—his heart uplifted
Above the snares of earth's false happiness,—

The little Stephen, in his childhood, found him
Before the gates of one of those old haunts
Of Friars Minor in the desert: 'round him,
He saw, aglow with heaven's blest romance,—

The simple cloisters, cool and dim and quiet,
Wherein the monks were pacing grave and good;
—A limpid fountain in the midst, and, nigh it,
The little chapel with its cross of wood.

Some milk-white doves were near the fountain feeding:
The boy approach'd, and watched them, tender-eyed;
Then knelt before the monks, enraptur'd, pleading,
"Oh! take me in, and let me here abide!"

And so they took him in from want and danger,
In all his childish innocence and grace,
In that fair morning-hour, the little stranger
Among the good Franciscans found his place.

And there abode; a pupil first, but later,
A novice in his flow'ring youth profess'd.
—Devoted heart and soul to his Creator,
His ardent fervor distanced all the rest.

For in his bosom burned the mighty fires
That only glow in apostolic men;
"Now, God be with our Stephen!" said the friars,
"For in *his* zeal, Saint Francis lives again!"

Alas! beneath the pure and thornless flowers
Of the first Paradise, the serpent crawled:
And the young Adam, peerless in his powers,
Bemoaned his fate in Satan's snare enthralled.

And since that dark, primeval day of sorrow,
No flesh can glory in its strength untried;
The weakness of the creature can but borrow
The grace and courage by its Lord supplied.

II.

A noble visage, a persuasive bearing,
A form as fair as that of fabled prince;
A self-devotion that was almost daring,
A golden tongue to argue and convince;

A mind enrich'd with study and reflection,
The fiery passions held in stern control;
And, over all, supreme in chaste election,
The pure vocation of the virgin soul,—

These were the gifts the youthful Friar Stephen
Brought from the desert in his manhood's dawn,
When, in submission to the will of Heaven,
He journeyed to the Convent of Saint John.

The poor old convent on the rich environs
Of Islam's stronghold, magical Seráy,
The mighty city where the fairest syrens
Of luxury and pleasure held their sway:—

Oh! what a field for an apostle's labors,—
Oh! what a soil to sow with heav'nly seed!
Only to save the souls of these dear neighbors,
Where is the monk that would not work and bleed?

—The eyes of Stephen glow with holy fire—
His heart throbs quickly 'neath his russet gown;—
He sees the sunlight on the lofty spire
Of mosque and palace in the Moslem town.

And down he knelt among the monks, and, pressing
His brazen crucifix upon his heart,—
"O Fathers! give to me," he cries, "your blessing.
And let me straightway to my work depart!"

"Nay, nay, my son!" the holy Prior urges,
"Be not too rash or hasty in thy zeal,—
Thro' yonder town such foul corruption surges,
Its giant force might make an angel reel:

"And thou art young, and passionate, and eager,
And needest all the strength that God can lend;
Refrain thyself in prayer,—and in the rigor
Of holy penance, a brief season spend."

"What sayest thou, good Father? must I idle
These precious moments in a selfish prayer,
While, like the music calling to a bridal,
I hear the voice of souls that call me *there?*

"That cry to me, '*Bring hither thine evangel,
Oh! come to us, and help us!*'—Must I wait?"
—Alas! the while he pleaded, like an angel,
Within his breast self-trust was waxing great!

Who could resist his zeal? who so censorious
As to mistrust the brave and gifted friar?
Lo! in the end, the golden tongue, victorious,
Had bent the wiser will to its desire.

And forth he went,—the convent-cell was cheerless,
The monks were strange, the cloister stern and gray,
And down he went, all confident and fearless,
Into the fatal city of Seráy.

Into the fiery furnace of destruction,
That vast volcano of seductive sin,
Whose gorgeous flowers, growth of rank corruption,
Enchanting, veiled the rottenness within.

It was some feast-day of the great Mahomet,
And all the beauteous city was abroad,

And thro' the streets the children of the Prophet,
Were chanting loudly, "Allah is our God!"

And oh! the splendor of that wondrous vision!
Bewildering as some enchanted scene,
The lovely gardens, streets, and groves Elysian,
The gilded villas set in flow'ring green.

And right and left, a hundred fountains playing,
And bright-winged birds disporting in the trees,
And garlands of the fairest blossoms swaying
From door to door, with ev'ry passing breeze.

While thro' the long, cool vistas of the bowers,
The groups of dancing-girls were whirling fair,
Voluptuous houries, crowned with blushing flowers,
And glittering with gold and jewels rare.

It seemed a portal of the Moslem heaven,
That strange, seductive city of Seráy,—
And never had the guileless eyes of Stephen
Gazed on a scene so marvellously gay.

Reared in the desert's virginal seclusion,
Screened from temptation's sight and sound and snare,
How could he meet this magical illusion,
Save with the arms of penance and of prayer?

—Back on his spirit rush'd the Prior's warning—
But all to late, for, in his ardent breast,
The fiercest passions rose in reckless scorning,
And writhed, like serpents 'round an eagle's nest.

Thoughts and temptations, ne'er before imagined,
Swept in a torrent thro' his burning brain;—
Before him pass'd the oriental pageant,
Bewitching music wooed him with its strain.

And looking, he forgot his lofty mission,
And listening, remembered not the cries
Of souls that called him (in his morning's vision)
To bring to them the Gospel of the Skies!

As one who walks in an enchanted slumber,
And leaves the past in blank oblivion,
So, walking thro' that throng, too vast to number,
The monk forgot the Convent of Saint John.

Till on a sudden, thro' the screen of flowers
That curtained in the song and laughter sweet,
A bell rang sharply from the convent-towers,
And on his startled ears, reproachful, beat!

III.

Oh! sad awaking of the tortured spirit!
Oh! wretched fate of the presumptuous soul!
A stainless life, with all its grace and merit,
Debased and blacken'd in the fiend's control!

With bended head, and footstep slow, uneven,
His heart's strange anguish written on his face,
Back to his convent went the hapless Stephen,
And 'mid the waiting brethren took his place.

A change was over all,—the simple choir
Looked bare and homely to his altered eyes;
The chant, the psalms, the lecture seemed to tire
After that glimpse of Moslem paradise.

No more before his desk, in chaste emotion,
He led the Sacred Office, brave and fair;
Or in his stall, with tenderest devotion,
Poured out his soul in efficacious prayer.

Mechanical, he went and came,—a phantom
That wore the young apostle's face and form,
But in his duties spoke and wrought at random,
—A heart of ice which nothing seemed to warm.

But in the nights when all the rest were sleeping,
And that unnatural calm was swept away,
He paced his cell with groans and bitter weeping,
And wandered back, in thought, to old Seráy.

Once more he heard the plash of perfumed waters,
Amid the groves with bird and blossom bright;
Once more he looked on Islam's lovely daughters,
The airy dancers of a day's delight.

Around him breathed the wierd, bewitching sweetness
Of Eastern music. Mosque and villa fair,
The Moslem town in all its strange completeness
Of palaces and people, glittered there.

What could he do, but flee in fear and trembling
To cast himself before the Prior's feet,
And laying bare his soul, without dissembling,
The shameful story, shuddering, repeat?

Oh! then began the strange and awful combat
Of light and darkness,—paradise and hell!
The wounds of Christ, the magic of Mahomet,
Besieging in their turns that citadel.

And it was Lent, and all the monks in choir
Besought the Lord with discipline and prayer,
To look in mercy on the tempted friar,
And save him from the madness of despair.

Woe to the man who in his own poor powers,
Hath put his trust in battle with the fiend,—
For well we know that broken staff of ours
Hath often pierced the hand that on it leaned!

The anxious days momentous dawned and darkened,
The demon raged,—the angel hid his face,
Before the crucifix, no longer hearkened
The hapless Stephen to the voice of grace.

For, in the hour when all the holy friars
Were gathered at the Maundy-Thursday Mass,
The young monk, mastered by his mad desires,
Fled, like an evil shadow, o'er the grass;

Fled, like a traitor, to that Moslem city,
Infested with its unbelieving horde,
The very day, (O angels! weep in pity!)
Whereon a Judas once betrayed his Lord!

IV.

Amid the wond'ring children of the Prophet,
The young apostate stood, and loudly swore,
"All glory be to Allah and his Prophet,
I am a Christian and a priest no more!"

Then, issuing from grove and garden shady,
The joyous Moslems take him by the hand,
And lead him to the footstool of the Kadi,
Who smiles upon him with approval bland.

The Imaums flock around him; soft reposes
The Kadi's hand upon his jewelled sword,
"To-morrow, brother, in the Mosque of Roses,
Thou shalt renounce the Christ thou hast adored!"

And on the morrow, true to that sad saying,
The Mosque of Roses shows a wondrous sight;
A mighty crowd, within its wall, is swaying,
And all its perfumed air is full of light.

And high above them all, his monk's attire
The cynosure of ev'ry eager eye,—
Beside the Kadi stands the fallen friar,
To speak aloud his sacrilegious lie.

Alas! alas! on that tremendous morrow,
The Christians in their churches, full of woe,
(On that Good-Friday, full of mortal sorrow,)
The Passion of Our Lord, were chanting low.

The while the priest the sacred words pronouncing,
Beheld the page, with blinding tears, grow dim,—
Within the Mosque, a Christian was renouncing
The Blessed Christ who bled and died for him!

—They tore the sacred habit from his shoulders,
And cast it at the Kadi's feet disgrac'd;—
A scarlet robe of silk was 'round him folded,
And, on his head, a jewelled turban placed.

Upon his feet they fastened golden sandals,
A chain of pearls upon his bosom bold,
And, over all, they cast a gorgeous mantle,
Magnificent with 'broideries of gold.

And thro' the city ran the rapt'rous criers,
"Rejoice! ye sons and daughters of Seráy!
The mighty high-priest of the Christian friars
Hath trampled on the Cross of Christ to-day!"

V.

Then went there forth a marvellous procession
Of all the grace and glory of the town,—
And, in the midst, beneath the shining crescent,
The young apostate with his jewelled crown.

And high above the flags and floating banners,
(The target of derision and dislike),
The sacred habit of the Friar Minors
Was lifted on a mocking soldier's pike!

Oh! then the hearts of the unhappy Christians
Were broken by that last most bitter blow,—
And, right and left, the scandalized Franciscans
Their faces hid with sobs and groans of woe.

Dear Lord! thro' all the impious ovation,
Thro' all the blare of trumpet, roll of drum,
Those sobs, those groans, those broken exclamations
Unto the guilty ear of Stephen come.

He sees the blush upon the dear old faces,
He hears them mourning for *his* awful sin,—
A strange compunction, last of all his graces,
Incipient, stirs his sobered heart within.

—They bring him to a banquet fit for princes,
They set before him food, and bid him dine;
He neither eats nor drinks: in silence, winces,
Whene'er they tender him the sparkling wine.

At last, alone, within his gorgeous dwelling,
He falls upon the floor in strangest wise,
His burning heart within his bosom swelling
And tears, in torrents, gushing from his eyes.

Then, drawing (from the folds of his attire)
His ivory tablets, slowly writes thereon:
"*The sinner Stephen, the apostate friar,
Sends greeting to his brethren of Saint John;*

"Like Judas I have sinned, but not like Judas,
Do I despair of mercy or of heaven:
For, by the help of Him who hath renewed us,
I shall repair the scandal I have given!

"I pray ye, therefore, brothers, do not harden
Your hearts against me, nor my plea deny,
But send to me a priest with hope of pardon
That I may make my peace before I die."

Late in the night, a Moslem mercenary
Stole with the tablets to the convent-door,
And ere the dawn, within that monastery
The friars sang *Te Deum* o'er and o'er!

The lost was found, the dead to life had risen,
A halo hovered o'er the Moslem town;
Above the Cross, the torture, and the prison,
They caught the glory of the martyr's crown!

The while, within his closet's dark recesses,
The weeping Stephen kneels before the priest,
With trembling lips his heinous crime confesses,
And feels once more his guilty soul released!

VI.

All brightly glowed the glorious Easter morning,
The dew-drops sparkled upon old Seráy,
And, crown'd with jewels, like a bride's adorning,
The Mosque of Roses, in the sunlight, lay.

From far and near, in jubilant elation
The Tartars flocked; for it was rumored loud
That Friar Stephen in a grand oration
Would there address the mighty Moslem crowd.

Ten thousand Mussulmans the vast enclosure
Delighted thronged; and thro' that sea of men
The Friar made his way with strange composure
And mounted to the tribune once again.

Oh! how they cheered him as he towered above them,
Clad in his scarlet robe adorned with gold;
What passionate emotions seemed to move them,
As through the mosque their shouts of triumph rolled!

But lo! a hush,—a stillness as from heaven,
Upon the tempest falls;—'tis Stephen cries,
"All glory to the Cross of Christ be given!
And may Mahomet perish with his lies!

"I believe in Jesus Christ, my Lord and Master,
The Son of God, the Saviour of the world!
But on Mahomet, on the foul impostor,
Anathema! anathema! be hurl'd!"

And straightway tearing off his scarlet vesture,
He cast it from him in their startled sight,
And stood before them, with triumphant gesture,
Clad in the habit of the Minorite!

With glowing face and arms outstretched to heaven,
A victim eager to be sacrific'd,
"Tho' I have sinned," cried out the happy Stephen,
"I am a Christian, and would die for Christ!"

But then, O saints and angels! what a vision!
—Like cruel tigers thirsting for his blood,
With shouts of fury and of mad derision,
The Moslems fell upon him where he stood,—

And tore him from the tribune, scourged and smote him,
Pluck'd out his beard with fierce satanic ire;
Unto the place of torture, raging, brought him,
And lit the flames that fed the fatal pyre.

—Six days and nights, amid those torments dire
(A patient miracle of life in death),
By God sustained, despite of scourge and fire,
The martyr lived, and witnessed to his faith!

Till, in the end, enraged at his endurance,
Upon th' intrepid friar rushed his foes;—
Hope had its meed, and love its sweet assurance,
And Stephen sank beneath those deadly blows.

What tho' his lifeless body cold and prostrate,
Lay crush'd and bleeding 'mid the embers faint?
—The angels welcomed Stephen, the apostate,
Transformed to Stephen, the Franciscan Saint!

His grievous sin sublimely expiated,—
The robes of shame forever cast aside;
In Christ's dear grace and favor reinstated,
The martyr reigned,—and God was glorified!

'Beth's Promise.

BY MRS. ANNA HANSON DORSEY.

CHAPTER XVIII.
HOW IT FARED WITH 'BETH. NEW TRIALS.

AS Father Thomas had told her, all the dread that had filled 'Beth's mind of being tormented by doubts after entering the Church, was only a temptation. Now that the final step was taken, and poor human reason had submitted its arrogance and its littleness in a docile and humble spirit to the divine behests of Faith; now that she had received the life-giving Sacraments, and with them that solace and help which they alone can impart, 'Beth Morley only wondered why she had so long kept aloof. "What a coward I have been," she thought, "to have allowed such flimsy reasons to frighten me! Where are the clouds, the uncertainty and regrets I so much dreaded? Gone, even as the shadows of night before the newly risen sun. I feel just like a long lost child who has found its mother; like one tossed upon the wild seas without rudder or compass, who suddenly finds himself in a safe port where no tempest can harm him. Ah, how patient our dear Lord has been with my foolishness! And by what strange paths His Blessed Mother, to whom I was offered at my birth, and afterwards in baptism, has led me back to the one true Fold from which I was so far astray! My soul is more than satisfied!"

And so it was, indeed. In becoming a Catholic, Beth had entered a new life wherein she found those divine helps which, if they did not remove, gave her renewed strength and patience to bear her cross. And none too soon did she shelter herself in this safe refuge, this holy place of "sanctuary," in the very bosom of the Church, where she would find solace in coming trials, for she had yet to bear in the near future a more consuming grief and anxiety than she had ever known. Happily and mercifully is the future hidden from us! To foresee either a great joy or a great sorrow would unfit us in the interval for the duties of daily life, for shuddering with affright and grief at the approaching tribulation, or intoxicated with joy and exultation at the coming happiness, how could we bear the intolerable waiting for the fulfilment of either? Let us be thankful for the veil that falls between, secure in our trust in the all-wise Dispenser of human events, who cares for us in weal and woe, and leads us through the dark and through perils undreamed of, when all human help fails.

'Beth kept her sorrow out of sight, not allowing even its shadow to fall upon the dear life so dependent for its earthly comfort upon her. She was always pleasant and affable to friends and acquaintances, and while there was no affectation of exuberant spirits, the graceful amenities of social intercourse suffered nothing at her hands. Sometimes Mrs. Morley, who had, ever since their return from "Ellerslie," grown keenly observant of every change that came into 'Beth's face, noticed a sad introverted look in her eyes, and a drooping, weary expression about the lines of her mouth which would disappear the moment she was spoken to, or when any sound or movement near her awakened her from her brief reverie, showing how perpetually she was on guard to conceal her heart's secret. Mrs. Morley, we must remember, had only surmised what had happened between 'Beth and her lover, but the more she thought of the affair, the more fully she was convinced of the truth of her surmises, and with this certainty arose the question: "Was it not unreasonable to exact from my child a promise which has evidently destroyed the happiness of her young life, that happiness which I only sought to guard against the bitter griefs I have myself endured? And how sweetly and readily she promised, what I—selfishly and maybe weakly —exacted! Then, after all, how strangely we went to meet the very thing I would, above all others, have tried to shun! But how could we know? Had some enemy designed the affair, it could not have been more fatal to her unsuspecting and pure heart." But what could Mrs. Morley do, except to wish she had not required that "promise" which, she feared, had brought such unhappiness to 'Beth? She was not even sure of it, but she would have been glad had the "promise" never been required by her or made by 'Beth; but in this uncertainty what could she do? 'Beth had not given her her confidence even when she afforded her the opportunity to do so at "Ellerslie," and she would doubtless evade the subject if again spoken to; besides, Mrs. Morley not being by any means certain that it was as she suspected, if 'Beth *had* a secret that her womanly pride or delicacy made her wish to conceal, she felt that she had not even a mother-right to claim the knowledge of it. And so she had to wait, only to wait, the hardest thing on earth to do when one is filled with care and anxiety about the termination of any matter upon which hangs the well-being of ourselves or of those near and dear to us. 'Beth's efforts to be cheerful made her sad; for under it all she noted the indefinable signs of a heart ill at ease. She could do nothing but offer herself and child anew to the most Holy Virgin, and implore her aid and intercession for a happy termination to an affair which had cast a shadow between them and continued to give her great anxiety and unhappiness. "Oh, fatal promise!" she often whispered when alone, and thinking it over; "would that I could undo it! Would that I had never required it! I thought it would save her from the blows that have fallen upon me, from misery and heart-break, and now see what has come of it! So much, dear Lord! for not leaving things in Thy merciful hands and taking the future into our own!"

"A charming, agreeable girl," was the verdict of society on 'Beth Morley, "one of great elegance and taste, but almost too much dignity of manner for one of her age; however, her beauty atones for that; and as the shock of her father's death probably lent this gravity to her character, it is more interesting. She will have lost it by the time she makes her *début* next winter."

But there were times when, despite her prayers, her courage, and her brave effort, 'Beth grew sad and sorrowful; when she felt weary and discouraged; when the woman's heart within her grew chilled; when thoughts of the sudden and untimely frost that had fallen upon and blighted her beautiful flowers of hope, and awakened her so rudely from her brief, bright dream of love, swept over her. "It is my cross," she would whisper, "and I must bear it to the end. I would not have chosen it—oh no! But, dear Lord, do Thou help me! I am only human, and very weak!" Then she would seek and find refreshment in the Sacraments, and so go back, almost·solaced, to the stir and duties of her daily life.

She had once or twice promised Mrs. Spencer to come to her sometimes "in a quiet way," and one evening a note came from that lady claiming her presence the day following. "Nobody is to dine with us," wrote Mrs. Spencer, "except Captain and Mrs. Brandt, and an English gentleman, a member of Parliament, I believe, who has brought letters of introduction to my husband, and had to be invited to dinner. I have not seen him, but suppose he is reserved and awkward like the rest of his countrymen, and he may be as old as the hills, for the Judge was in such haste to keep an appointment with the President, that I hadn't time to ask a question about the coming guest. Do not send an excuse, as I shall be not only disappointed, but very angry with you."

"You see, mamma, this would quite break up our plans for a quiet evening together," said 'Beth, handing the note to her mother: "what shall I do?"

"Go, my dear, by all means; it would not do to decline when Mrs. Spencer makes such a point of your coming. It would seem impolite, I think. As to myself, I have letters to write that have been hanging over me for weeks, which will keep me busy until you get back."

"I'm very fond of Mrs. Spencer, but I don't feel at all inclined to leave you alone. However, I'll go on one condition, since you wish it, mamma," said 'Beth.

"And that?" questioned Mrs. Morley.

"And that, dear mamma, is that you will see Dr. Milner about those attacks of short breathing that you have; I notice them quite often. You seem to think they are nothing, and perhaps they are, but I shall be happier when Dr. Milner tells me the same thing. Will you see him to-morrow?"

"Yes, my child, if I get time. I have a great many things to attend to to-morow. The "Little Sisters of the Poor have agreed to receive old Mrs. Wright, and I shall have to see about moving her there, for she's very infirm, and seems to depend upon me so much that I promised to go with her and see her comfortably settled. Then there are several other things that will require my personal attention and keep me occupied all day. But I will see the Doctor the day after, if it will make you happier, my child."

"That will depend on what he says, dearest mamma; not that I think you are ill, but I fear you are not so well as you ought to be, and you are such a busy little mother nowadays that you take no thought or care of yourself, so I mean to look after you myself," said 'Beth, smoothing her mother's hair with gentle, caressing touches, then she stooped over and kissed her, and went away to answer Mrs. Spencer's note, accepting her invitation to dinner.

In a rich mourning silk of exquisite fit and style, with square *corsage*, filled out with puffs of illusion, a black velvet band around her white throat from which suspended the pearl locket—her father's last gift—a bunch of lilies of the valley fastened among the wave's of her beautiful hair and another at her waist, 'Beth looked very lovely. And so thought her friend, Mrs. Spencer, who met and embraced her as she entered the drawing-room, where Captain and Mrs. Brandt and Judge Spencer also gave her warm greeting, after which she was introduced to Mr. Neville, their stranger guest. Until that moment, 'Beth had forgotten all about him, but the impression left upon her mind by Mrs. Spencer's note had been that he was an old or middle aged man; that he was a member of Parliament, and a friend of

Judge Spencers, having made it seem more probable. But so far from this, Mr. Neville was a tall, fine-looking man of about thirty, and his face was one of the best types of Saxon comeliness, strong, intelligent and high bred. His manner was quiet and a trifle awkward, but his kindly eyes and agreeable expression made one sure of the *noblesse oblige* of his character. The young Englishman, who had from choice spent much of his grown-up life in the northern regions of Europe, outside and beyond the beaten track of tourists, and had only a year before returned home on the death of an uncle whose heir he was, thought he had never seen so lovely a woman as 'Beth Morley; her grace of manner and modest self-possession seemed to him the perfection of fine breeding and a sweet, womanly nature. And after his reserve had thawed a little under the genial influence of his agreeable entertainers and their friends, his conversation proved him to be a man of great intellectual culture and observation. Captain Brandt, in his delight at having 'Beth there, "shining," as he declared, "like a bright particular star," surpassed himself, and was so absurdly agreeable that the evening passed merrily away, and Mr. Neville who had led her out to dinner, found himself chatting with her as unreservedly as if he had known her for years; and she, later on, listened with absorbing interest to certain things he was telling her about those far northern lands he had visited.

"I hadn't an idea that he was young, and handsome, and agreeable," said Mrs. Spencer, in a low tone, to Captain Brandt, nodding her head towards them. "I declare, I am delighted! They really look as if they were made for each other, don't they, Captain?"

"It's a match, madam! We shall hear wedding bells before long, or I'm no prophet! Gad! I wish poor Morley could have been spared to see her grown to be such a beauty!" he answered with a grin of delight, as he stuck his glasses on his nose to take a nearer survey of the unconscious pair. As the Judge and Mr. Brandt were deep in a game of whist on the other side of the fire place, there was nothing to interrupt the confidential conversation which ensued between Mrs. Spencer, and the captain, who, out of apparent possibilities, evolved a little plot over the details of which they smiled with a look of extreme satisfaction, their glances and occasional nods in the direction of 'Beth and Mr. Neville plainly indicating the subject that interested them, if any one had been at leisure to have observed them. When 'Beth bade "good-night" and told Mrs. Spencer how much she had enjoyed the evening, Mr. Neville inquired "if it were permissable for him, a stranger, to ask leave of Miss Morley to call upon her!"

"Certainly," said Mrs. Spencer, who still held Beth's hand.

"Have I your permission to call, Miss Morley?" he inquired, as he turned towards her and bowed.

"Mamma and I will be happy to see you, Mr. Neville," she answered in quiet tones, then went up stairs to get her wraps. When she came down, Mr. Neville was waiting at the bottom of the staircase to hand her to the *coupé*. With a quiet "thanks" and "good-night," 'Beth drew herself back on the cushions, the door was closed, and she was, in another moment, on her way home, with no other thought of the handsome Englishman in her mind except that "he had been a great traveller, and was very polite." After this, followed an episode in 'Beth Morley's life which was entirely unlooked for, and which pained her gentle, generous nature not a little. Mr. Neville called with Mrs. Spencer the following day, and was introduced to Mrs. Morley, on whom he evidently made an agreeable impression, and was invited by her to repeat his visit. 'Beth gave him quiet welcome, but exchanged only a few words with him, devoting herself to Mrs. Spencer who was giving her glowing accounts of a foreign *prima-donna*, who, she had just heard, was engaged for the week following to sing in opera at Ford's Theatre.

"I shall make the Judge engage a boy for the whole time, and I shall expect you to go with me every evening, 'Beth," she said, as she got up to leave.

'Beth laughed and said: "Music is always a great temptation to me, but I cannot promise; thank you all the same though."

"I shall come and carry you off bodily, so it will be best for you to yield with a good grace, and make your *toilette* regularly for the occasion. It's delightful here, but I shall have to hurry Mr. Neville off, to show him the lions of the Senate and House, who by the time we get to the Capitol will be roaring and shaking their manes at each other. Good-by, darling. Don't discourage her by a word, Anne, about the opera," said Mrs. Spencer, as she gave Mrs. Morley a good-by kiss.

Mr. Neville availed himself of the invitation Mrs. Morley had given him to "call again." He came once or twice with Mrs. Spencer, then feeling better acquainted, and always welcome, his visits became more frequent and were made alone. A cluster of lilies of the valley were left for Miss Morley every day, and be quite frequently now brought "rare sweet violets," difficult to find just at this season, which he simply offered and she as simply accepted.

Meantime Mrs. Morley had consulted Dr. Milner, and 'Beth's mind was set at rest about her mother's health. "There's a little functional trouble, that's all," the Doctor had told 'Beth; "her nerves have not recovered from the shock of three years ago, and she must be careful not to overtax them, my child. I have told her all about it, and given her remedies which will relieve her, with care and a due amount of rest."

"Oh, Doctor, what you say is such a relief! I am so thankful! I was afraid mamma had heart-disease," said 'Beth, while tears of relief filled her eyes.

"Your mother'll live to be an old woman, my dear; but she must be careful, or with those nerves of hers she may be a very suffering one," he said, standing a moment at the hall door.

"She *shall* be careful, if I have to keep her in a cage like a delicate canary," answered the girl, with something of her old glad spirit in her tones. The Doctor laughed and hurried away to a consultation whose verdict would be life or death to the suffering patient.

Aunt 'Beth, far away at old "Ellerslie," had so missed them, that to satisfy the hunger of her heart she had taken to writing long letters, one of the things she had hated to do all her life. But it was a solace now for her to sit down and make her pen talk for her; it relieved her loneliness, and she could say all that was in her mind without being interrupted or argued with, which to one of her positive temper, was—as she confessed—a great satisfaction. And as she received two letters a week, one from Mrs. Morley and a long cheerful one from 'Beth, her mind, what with her correspondence and other duties, was very agreeably occupied. The "strike" had ended in December, to her great joy and relief, and the Dulaneys had come back to spend Christmas at "Tracy-Holme," where with Paul and his young wife, Violet, and a party of friends from New York, they had a gay time. "'Ellerslie' gave a dinner," Aunt 'Beth wrote, "and we had a grand old-fashioned time, with wood fires blazing, plenty of egg-nogg, holly wreaths and mistletoe, the 'fatted calf'—although there was no prodigal to partake of it—roast turkey, and every other thing that was ever thought of for Christmas feasting. I only wanted you two to make the feast a festival!" The next astonishing piece of news Aunt 'Beth's letters brought was that, in the spring, Lodo was to be married to a young farmer she had met at the hop-picking, and they were going out to settle in the far West, she believed, on some uncleared land he had bought, a very wilderness which Lodo thought would be a new paradise to her, where she could live, work, and sleep in the open air, under the trees, if so minded; and giving herself no uneasiness about Indians, or scalping-knives, or wild beasts. The next letter came to 'Beth, telling her that the Dulaneys had taken their second flight back to the city, and things had fallen again into their usual winter quiet. "They gave me, before they went," she continued, "a fine photograph of my favorite Bertie, which you will find in the enclosed envelop. I thought you might like to see it, knowing what friends you were last summer."

'Beth hesitated about looking at it. "What harm can it do? my looking at it can alter nothing," she argued; then she opened the envelop and took it out. It was, indeed, a faithful likeness, true to the life, only there was a sterner expression on his countenance than she remembered ever to have seen there, and he was in full uniform. She did not trust herself to look at it twice, but handed it with the letter to her mother. She sat up late that night to write to Aunt 'Beth, and returned the photograph with the simple remark that, "It was excellent, and they were glad to see that Lieut. Dulaney was looking so well."

"If she would only open her heart to me!" thought Mrs. Morley, when she noted the sad far-away look in 'Beth's eyes, as she sat with her fair, long hands clasped about her knees, gazing out into the dim, wintry twilight; "If I could only know what she is thinking of this very moment, how quickly all might be remedied, if things are as I suspect them to be! But hoping to spare me, she will never admit it, or break that promise which I so unwisely required, even if my supposition is true."

'Beth had not referred to the picture except to say that she had written to Aunt 'Beth and returned it. The sight of it had revived memories and regrets which had been slumbering and, she had hoped, overcome; but she sought her usual strong help in the Sacraments, and took up her cross anew, looking forward with hope into the future. She had enough to do; Father Thomas, who necessarily had much suffering brought to his notice, had recommended several worthy and extreme cases of want to Mrs. Morley's benevolent attention, which she, with 'Beth's willing assistance, undertook to provide for. The sight of sufferings greater than our own is a wholesome panacea, which, if it does not heal, prevents our brooding and pining over them; while the very effort to relieve and solace those to whom destitution, sickness and grief have brought almost despair, is in itself a sacred balm for our own sore, weary hearts. Nothing was allowed to interfere with the time apportioned to the duties of charity and the works of mercy which they had assumed; they were either not at home, literally, or if they were, too much engaged to see company if visitors called; and Mrs. Spencer not unfrequently missed seeing both Mrs. Morley and 'Beth, when she had come full of the world's news, and almost beside herself with delight at the success her cherished plan seemed to promise, and of which her fine tact told her, it would be impolite to refer to at present; for Mr. Neville had made her his confidant, and continued his attentions to 'Beth, who neither repulsed nor encouraged them, but always received him in a friendly way, partly because he was Mrs. Spencer's friend and because she really liked him and found his conversation agreeable and full of information. Meantime society had made a lion of Mr. Neville, who was invited, courted and *fêted* with the most distinguished attention; but Mr. Neville was not fond of this sort of thing, and responded to it all only so far as absolute politeness required. The beauty of American girls would have fascinated and lured him into the very whirl of the season, had he not seen one—'Beth Morley—who far surpassed his ideal and whom he meant to win if possible; and it leaked out—through Mrs. Spencer or Captain Brandt—that the handsome Englishman was already very much in love with a young lady whom he had met in Washington, nobody could tell where, and her name was vainly guessed at, which made the report more piquant and mysterious, while some few believed it, and others discredited it entirely.

(TO BE CONTINUED.)

The Conversion of an Infidel through the Intercession of the Blessed Virgin.

BY THE LATE REV. FATHER J. F. DONELAN.

(CONTINUED.)

BEFORE receiving the Holy Communion Mr. M—— requested his family to collect all his infidel books, papers and manuscripts, and burn them. Had they, who were commissioned with this grateful task, yielded to his wishes they would have burned them in the public streets as a testimony of his conversion to Christianity; but it was deemed sufficient to burn them in private, as he publicly mentioned the fact on many occasions. How strong an evidence this of his sincerity! None but a mind radically changed could be brought thus to give up the cherished sources of all its arguments and boasted theories; but the grace of God was triumphant here, and like the humble penitents mentioned in the Acts of the Apostles when appalled by the punishment inflicted on the Sons of Sceva, he too came "confessing his sins," and committing his wicked books to the flames.

On this occasion Mr. M—— received Holy Communion: his preparation for it had been truly edifying; not a moment had been lost since his conversion; his wife and daughters had each in turn read and prayed by his bed, while no few among the many who visited him performed the same pious office. He longed for that Sacred Food, that last and perpetual memorial of Christ's Passion and suffering, in which the soul feasts upon the Food of angels. He prayed most earnestly to be a partaker of that "Sacred Banquet in which Christ is received, His Sacred Passion commemorated, the soul is filled with grace, and a pledge of future glory is given to the worthy receiver." And his pious wishes were gratified. On questioning him concerning this sacred dogma, the clergyman found him thoroughly instructed; as if by intuition, he possessed a thorough knowledge of the subject, the dispositions required, the manner of receiving the Holy Communion, and even the ceremonies peculiar to this holy act, and an entire faith in the sacred Mystery. Thus encouraged, the priest prepared to administer the Holy Communion as Viaticum. On this occasion many were present; nor were they all Catholics, although all were in tears, so edifying and affecting was the scene. Words can ill express the piety manifested by Mr. M—— at this important moment. All were kneeling, while the half-suppressed sob and the silent tear told eloquently the feelings of those present; it was a holy and a joyful moment. As the priest rose from his knees and elevated the Sacred Host before the sick man's eyes, he raised himself in the bed, and crossing his hands upon his bosom, exclaimed, with tears in his eyes: "Lord, I am not worthy that Thou shouldst enter under my roof, say but the word and my soul shall be healed! My heart is ready, O God! my heart is ready! Even as the hart panteth after the streams of living waters, so does my soul thirst after Thee, O God! When shall I come and appear before my God! How good Thou art, my Saviour and my Redeemer! What have I in heaven but Thee? and beside Thee, what do I desire on earth? What shall I render to the Lord for all that He hath done unto me? I will thank my God; I will praise and glorify His holy name. Pardon me, O my Lord and my God, for all my transgressions against Thee and Thy Church. I believe Thou art my Redeemer, and that in the last day I shall rise to meet Thee. Oh, my Saviour and my God, why art Thou so good to me? I am not worthy to be called Thy child, but let me call Thee Father! No matter what Thou doest unto me, I will love Thee still. Punish me, condemn me, afflict me, I will call Thee Father. What have I done to deserve this so great favor, that Thou shouldst come to me upon my bed of sickness! I have blasphemed Thee, I have been Thy enemy, and is this Thy revenge? Come, Lord Jesus, come quickly! My soul hungers and thirsts after Thy Holy Sacrament, I am Yours and You are mine." These and many other similar aspirations did he pronounce, as still holding his hands crossed upon his breast, he kept his eyes steadfastly fixed upon the consecrated Host. Strength seemed to be given him for the time; his voice, though feeble, was distinct, save when either his own tears for a moment obstructed his utterance, or the sobs of the kneeling group interrupted him. Not a word was spoken save by the sick man, who was thus holding sweet converse with his Lord. Any interruption of so sacred a colloquy would have been deemed almost sacrilegious by those present, and the clergyman himself, though not unused to trying scenes, stood lost in wonder and amazement. The Sacred Viaticum was placed upon the sick man's tongue; he folded his hands and reposed himself in prayer upon his pillow, the appointed ceremonial was finished, and all continued to kneel in silence lest they should call back to earth the thoughts of this child of God. A brief half hour passed in thanksgiving for the blessings which Heaven had bestowed upon the family, and the clergyman journeyed homeward rejoicing and grateful.

It is not necessary to recount the different visits of the succeeding two weeks. Let it suffice that each was marked by some incident of interest and edification. Numbers, daily and hourly, flocked to see this example of God's goodness, and nearly all were moved to tears by the fervor of his piety and the unction of his words. So great was the curiosity excited by this conversion, that several from the city of Washington visited him to assure themselves of its reality. To one of these Mr. M—— remarked, that he wondered much why men did not believe in the truths of Christianity. "For me," he continued, "even were I to try, I could not now reject my belief in all its doctrines. I have tried the world, I have been an atheist and an infidel; I have sometimes thought myself happy, I was sincere in what I said, and spoke freely what I believed, yet how different are my feelings now from those which I formerly had! Everything around me and within me has changed; I always loved my family, but I never loved them so dearly as now. I now look upon my children and my wife with different eyes: they were always kind and dutiful to me, but, till I became a Catholic, I never appreciated their tenderness; and here," said he, raising his little crucifix, which he constantly kept either in his hand or on his breast, "here is now my sign, here is my model; by this I was redeemed, under this sacred banner I have enlisted, and under this I will live and die. O Jesus, dying on the cross for me, have mercy on me! Mary, standing at the foot of the cross of Jesus, pray for me!"

Referring to some misunderstanding which had formerly existed between him and another for some real or imaginary cause, he observed: "How different is the morality taught by religion from that which the followers of reason practice! Even in my own case—the last and worst of all mankind, the most unworthy being in existence—how is it manifested! For years I have proudly kept aloof from *him*, foolishly supposing that reason and honor dictated the step; nay, had I met him, there have been moments when my heart would have gloated over his death; his very name I hated; but now, how different is my case! Oh God of mercy! how freely do I forgive him, and earnestly beg him to forgive me! I, a worm of the earth; I, a sinful man and the greatest of sinners! Were he here now, how affectionately would I embrace him and ask his forgiveness! for all is changed: as I hope to be forgiven I forgive all in him. Glorious system of Divine Revelation! glorious Religion! sublime Morality! the false apostles of infidelity never conceived it; it must have come from God; the Deity alone could suggest it, the Christian alone can practice it. I always admired it in others, but attributed it to human motives; I now feel my error; Oh, God, forgive me! Thou who hast died for me, and prayed for those who crucified Thee, I thank Thee! I forgive also all who ever injured me, and ask pardon of all whom I have injured!"

We must not suppose that Mr. M—— was hurried away by impulse of feeling, or that the fervent expressions which thus came from his very soul were the effect of religious excitement or enthusiasm. To be convinced of the reverse, it was but necessary to see and hear him, while living, speaking on the subject of religion; to mark his tranquil manner and the calm and sweet smile depicted on his countenance. Now that he has gone, that the sound of his voice is hushed forever in the grave, his sincerity and earnestness of purpose, the settled and firm conviction which actuated him can be found by every honest mind in his uniform deportment, in the traits which characterized him before and after his conversion; then, all was firm, determined resolution; in his denunciations of Christianity, even when most vehement, he was remarked for his consistency. Where real merit was due, and he so believed, it was accorded. Between the deserving and the guilty, the really sincere and the base pretender, errors of judgment, and human frailties, a settled determination of malice and momentary weakness, he was quick to discriminate and sure to make every allowance. After his conversion to Christianity, the same noble traits were observable in him; the errors of his former life he condemned indeed as the effects of pride of intellect, ambition of being known and noticed; but in others, he bewailed them as misfortunes which we should weep over rather than condemn. He spoke of the professors of infidel opinions as persons whom we should pray for rather than despise; of their errors he spoke in terms of unmitigated abhorrence, but of themselves, he spoke in true

Christian charity; no hour of the day or night passed without bearing to heaven his earnest supplications in their behalf, for the snare of the fowler had been broken, his soul had been rescued from danger, and he wept as he thought of those still detained in the bondage of their error. There was no wild outbreaking of feeling, no violence of expression; all was calm, all was tranquil, and the fervent outpourings of spirit, by which his inmost soul was made known, fell upon the ears of all who heard them as the accents of one standing on the verge of eternity; they still come back upon their memories like echoes from that other world where all is truth, all is stern reality. Some may condemn, and others doubt them; but of such we can only say, in the words of our Divine Redeemer: "Ye know not of what spirit ye are."

On the afternoon of a day in June, a messenger was despatched to Washington to request the immediate attendance of his confessor, for he was rapidly sinking, and he desired once again to see his reverend friend. In a short time the priest was at his bedside, for he had frequently promised the sick man to be near him in his last agony. A smile of joy lighted up the countenance of the sick man as the priest entered the room. To every exhortation to place his reliance on the merits of his Saviour and to keep his mind calmly bent on God, he would reply in a feeble whisper, or by raising his crucifix to his lips and kissing it with emotion; he was observed to weep, and when encouraged to hope for pardon, he replied: "Jesus wept for me in the garden, and may I not weep for my sins at the cross?" When asked if he desired to receive once more his Lord in the Holy Communion, he raised his hands in an attitude of supplication, and smiling through his tears, replied: "Did the people of God sigh for their altars and their homes? Does the wounded bird seek its nest or the wounded hare its burrow? So does my thirsting soul long for her Food to strengthen her in this journey of death." Sublime answer! bespeaking the faith of the Christian and the hope inspired by true philosophy. Holy Communion was then administered; he was supported by one of his daughters, as at this time he was too feeble to raise himself in bed. It was generally known that he was approaching his end, and accordingly several persons had assembled to witness his last moments; among those present were professors of different religions, yet all with one accord knelt and prayed. Hard indeed must have been the heart so prejudiced as not to melt with mingled sympathy and joy at so moving a spectacle. Every breath of the dying man was a prayer, and every prayer was a tribute of gratitude to God. Calm as a sleeping child, he lay with his hands still holding his crucifix and beads, his eyes raised to heaven and his thoughts intent on God. To every petition of the Litany for a dying person he replied calmly and earnestly; to every aspiration he smiled assent, and for every prayer which the minister of God recited he looked—for he could not speak—his gratitude. No troubled heavings of the bosom or fearful wanderings of the eye gave reason to fear that he was tormented by doubts or assailed by temptations; hard and long was his death agony, and the violence of his bodily sufferings forced a groan from sinking nature, but the soul, the immortal soul, was calm; no fears but the salutary dread of judgment disturbed him, no doubt harrassed him, no dangers appalled him. He had made all his temporal arrangements, and had bestowed his dying blessing on his family and friends; he had taken leave of all earthly things and now he was composed to die. The shades of death were gathering around him, and the night of eternity was fast setting in, yet a bright star of hope was rising to his view. The enemies of his salvation were doubtless assaulting him, but in his hand, and in his heart, and on his lips, was his shield of protection, the cross of Christ and the name of Mary. The cold sweat of death dampened his brow, and his spirit was breathing its last earthly vow to heaven, but the angels of God were hovering around his pillow, and the smiles of his Blessed Mother were resting on her child. In that awful moment, when the tide of life was ebbing fast, and the heart was ceasing its pulsations, then was Mary his Mother there; he had loved her in life, he still loved her in death; even as the lamb frightened at the coming storm seeks shelter in the fold, so did the departing spirit now seek refuge in the bosom of its God. The sacred names of Jesus and of Mary were ever on his lips as they were ever in his heart; his eyes would rest with intense emotion first upon his crucifix, then upon the little group, his wife and children whom he was about to leave alone and unprotected, and a tear would steal from his eyes. The prayers for a departing soul were said, and though his voice failed him his lips still moved. "Depart, Christian soul, out of this world," said the minister of God in the sweet yet peculiar words of the Ritual, as he held the cross before the eyes of the dying man; "Depart out of this world in the name of God the Father Almighty, who created thee; in the name of Jesus Christ, who redeemed thee; in the name of the Holy Ghost, who sanctified thee; in the name of the angels, archangels, thrones, and dominations, cherubim and seraphim; in the name of the patriarchs and prophets, of the holy apostles and evangelists, of the holy martyrs and confessors, of the holy monks and hermits, of the holy virgins, and of all the saints of God; may thy place be this day in peace, and thy abode in holy

Zion!" Let the body return to the earth, and the spirit go back to the God who gave it; go forth, Christian soul! The resplendent company of the angels will meet thee at thy departure; the court of Apostles will receive thee, the triumphant army of martyrs will conduct thee, crowds of joyful confessors will encompass thee, choirs of holy virgins will go before thee; a happy rest in the bosom of the patriarchs will be thy portion; Jesus Christ, thy Saviour and thy Judge, will appear to thee with a mild and cheerful countenance, and give thee a place among those who are to be in his presence forever; go forth, then, Christian soul, to meet thy Saviour and thy Judge; thou art not alone, angels are hovering o'er thee, Mary is near thee, she will be thy solace, thy refuge, thy shield; go: thou art not friendless and lone, thou wilt not be unprotected in that strange, distant land; let not thy spirit tremble nor thy soul grow sad with fear, for thy Mother will meet her child there, her name will be thy passport, her bosom thy rest; lift up thy heart with joy and thy soul in gladness, for thou hast loved her on earth, and thou shalt love her in heaven.

(CONCLUSION NEXT WEEK.)

Address of Cardinal Alimonda.

THE following address, by his Eminence Cardinal Alimonda, was delivered to the Catholic youth of Genoa on the occasion of their late reunion:

I have heard it rumored abroad, and the rumor has been repeated even by well-meaning persons, that the Catholic youth wish to act as priests—to speak to the people, and teach them as if they were priests. I am acquainted with you, my young friends, and I know that, in your religious fervor, your submission to ecclesiastical authority is such that you await its orders in every grave affair. I am confident that you are, and always will be, faithful soldiers of our holy religion. In truth, I was surprised at the report which was noised abroad, and answering, I said: "*Nil sub sole novum*."—There is nothing new under the sun. Laymen, young and old, have not been found dilatory in occupying themselves deferentially with those things that pertain to religion, and it was a mercy of God. Ermas Ieroteo, Athenagoras, Justin, Clement of Alexandria, Arnobius, Lactantius, Tatianus, Æneas of Gaza, Boethius, Marcellinus, the two Procopius, Cassiodorus, Eginhardt, Stephen of Cologne, Nithard, and numberless others of this class, were simple laymen, but they spoke and wrote volumes, and worked openly in favor of religion as if they were priests. They fought the great battle of the first centuries, which was to cause the triumph of the cross over the assaults of paganism; blessed by the clergy, and miraculously sustained by Divine Providence, they became illustrious champions of our holy Faith. Would to Heaven, my dear friends, that the spirit of those noble men might be revived in your ranks, and that in many of you, I could salute, returned to life, an Athenagoras with his apology of Christianity, a Clement of Alexandria with his exhortation to the pagans, and a Lactantius with his divine institutions! Would that I could see you performing the laborious work which they generously undertook for love of Jesus Christ!

We stand in need of this active and intrepid intervention of the Catholic laity in the public affairs of the Church. "*Nil sub sole novum*." The Church at its birth was scantily supplied with priests, but God raised up valorous laymen to meet the want. Now, priests are again scarce; an effeminate and irreligious education extinguishes vocations for the ecclesiastical state, and the few who desire to embrace this career encounter a merciless barrier which detains them: God calls them to the sanctuary, and the Government drives them to the barracks. Behold, the Church impoverished of its ministers, inconsolably deploring her loss! Courage, therefore, my young friends; ascend as far as you are allowed to go; supply the scarcity of levites, and console the sorrow of our common mother for the loss she suffers. The necessity of performing this work is great; therefore, let vigilance and vigor characterize your work. Providence sends you, and we, your elder brothers in the Church, extend a hearty welcome to you, our younger brothers, and we greet you with the salutation of King Alexander to Jonathan, calling each one of you with the name of friend: "*Aptus es ut sis amicus noster*"—You are worthy to be our friend.

Cardinal Newman at Oxford.

From "The Liverpool Catholic Times."

We gave last week an account of the reception of his Eminence Cardinal Newman at Oxford, and also a report of the sermons which he preached in the Church of St. Aloysius. Events of greater interest have seldom transpired, even in our great historic University. We must be permitted to attribute a very deep meaning to the festival of Cardinal Newman's "return home." Oxford must be regarded as the "home" of his Eminence in a sense which is at once tender and intellectual. We all know how sympathetically he has written of his associates and brother-workers at the University; how almost pathetically he has spoken of his own pain in quitting the scenes of so much happiness; and how admirably he has united personal respect for his old friends with the desire to convert them to the true Faith. This respectfulness and this earnestness were so warmly appreciated by those who best knew him that, at Oxford, the Fellows of Trinity— of which College he was once a scholar—unanimously elected him to be an Honorary Fellow, in the autumn of the year 1878. A Cardinal is, therefore, now an Oxford Fellow; and, as we have said, we cannot but regard such a combination as having a deep meaning for all Englishmen.

The sermons which we reported were singularly felicitous in their fitness to the place and time. The sermon in the morning was on the doctrine of the Blessed Trinity, and was in the Cardinal's happiest vein of simple eloquence. We may regard it as a Christian essay on the true attitude of the Christian intellect, quite as much as a sermon on the Divine Mystery. Humility—intellectual humility—was insisted on as the only fitting attitude in which the intellect can ever hope to "find out God." And we all know that intellectual humility is the rarest of all graces at our universities. It is because men will worship their own brains, instead of bowing to the authority of the Divine Church, that they get into inextricable confusion on all the mysteries and all the dogmas of Christianity: instead of believing, because God is God, they disbelieve, because they cannot judge Him. "If we attempt to look at the sun," said Cardinal Newman, "we are blinded"; and yet everybody knows that "the sun is the very source of heat of light, and of growth, and of all that we are in a certain sense." Yet Protestantism, and free-thought, and every revolt of the reason, insist upon private judgment when facing the Truth; nor will they accept one single dogma of the Church except it seem to commend itself to human brains; whereas Cardinal Newman wisely replies: "If God would be good to us, He must tell us something about Himself; and if He tells us something about Himself, He must tell us a mystery." But a mystery can only be accepted on the authority of the Power which declares it; and just here it is that "modern thought," as it is foolishly called—for such thought is no more modern than is pride—declines to accept Authority or to acknowledge Power, unless both be meekly submissive to its own caprice. At Oxford there is no belief in Church Authority, but only belief in individual interpretation, so that every undergraduate, as well as every tutor, has to fall back on himself as a last resource. Cardinal Newman points out, that in regard to Divine truths, we must accept them on the authority of a Divine Teacher and that we offend against logic as well as common sense when we presume to examine into the Intellect of the Infinite.

The second sermon of Cardinal Newman was a sort of corollary of the first, being intended to show that the supreme authority of the Church necessarily involves a supreme pastor, a supreme authority. His Eminence pointed out that this supreme pastorate and authority was developed externally, that is, visibly, with the growth of the visible communion of Christians. It was impossible for St. Peter to "guide a flock of sheep till that flock existed; and that would continue some time, of course a considerable time." As his Eminence observed, "it was not a question at first of the structure of the Church, but a question of the existence of it." And as soon as the "structure" was completed, the authority was developed with the structure. This is a very simple statement of the "theory of development" which some years ago puzzled our Protestant friend. There was no development whatever in doctrine, only a development in the sphere of its exercise. And just as Protestantism, being but human, has developed downward, be getting sects, contradictions and vast schisms; so Catholicity, being divine, has developed upward, begetting increase of numbers and of power. While his Eminence was preaching at Oxford, there were at the same time many Anglican clergymen preaching in the same city and university, who were all at discord with one another as to Christian doctrines; and this must continue to be so as long as Protestant opinions oppose the divine teaching of the Holy See. It is now more than thirty years since the distinguished "Dr. Newman" gave in his allegiance to the Holy See: all that time he has quietly yet earnestly begged his old friends to come and join him. Only a few have responded, but all those who have not done so have gone backward in peace and in usefulness. The Catholic Fellow of Trinity seems to have renewed his invitation in his recent visit to the scenes of his first labors.

Catholic Notes.

——We are heartily grateful to Rev. Father Dunn, of St. Patrick's Church, Kansas City, Mo., for kind favors to our travelling agent.

——The "Imitation of Christ" has been translated into forty-six different languages, and the editions it has passed through are counted by thousands.

——*The Post* of Montreal, a daily Catholic paper, has suspended for lack of support. This is not creditable, considering that Montreal has a Catholic population of 25,000.

——The Trappist Order mourns the loss of its venerable Superior-General, Very Rev. Father Francis Regis, who died recently in the seventy-third year of his age. He was a native of France. R. I. P.

——The firm of John Murphy & Co., of Baltimore, will be continued under the same name by Mr. Frank Murphy, eldest son of its deceased head. We heartily wish Mr. Murphy a long and successful career.

——"Maybe there isn't any God for the United States," said a Canadian Mayor to Bob Ingersoll not long since, "but there's one for Canada; and you can't have any hall in this town in which to defame Him."

——A Jesuit Father has discovered in Santiago de Compostella, a city of Spain, a manuscript of the middle of the twelfth century, which, if genuine, antedates by nearly three centuries the earliest Basque manuscript hitherto known.

——Rev. Father John Walsh, the devoted and beloved pastor of St. John's Church, Altoona, Pa., we are pained to announce, departed this life on the morning of the 8th inst., in the 61st year of his age and the 33d of his priesthood. R. I. P.

——The generosity of our readers enables us to send $220 more to Ireland this week, as follows: $100 to Most Rev. Archbishop Croke, $50 to Rt. Rev. Bishop MacEvilly, of Galway, and $70 (children's collection) to Rev. Father Murphy, S. J. The whole sum forwarded up to the time of writing amounts to $979.55.

——Revs. Alexander M. Kirsch, James Rogers, Joseph Scherer and Paul Kollop, all members of the Congregation of the Holy Cross, were elevated to the dignity of the priesthood last week at Notre Dame, by Rt. Rev. Bishop Dwenger, of Fort Wayne. Messrs. Patrick Moran, Nicholas Irman and Thomas McNamara, C. S. C., also, received minor orders.

——Rev. Mother de Pazzi, the beloved Superior of the Presentation Convent at St. John's, Newfoundland, lately celebrated her silver jubilee. The occasion was duly observed by the pupils of the school and the members of the community. We share in the good wishes offered to the venerated religious, and hope that it may be long before the time comes to speak in praise of her beautiful virtues.

——A ship-load of emigrants from Connemara, Ireland, sailed from Galway on the steamer Austrian, on the 11th inst., for Boston, *en route* to Minnesota, where land has been set apart for them and other provisions made. The ship is specially chartered for the trip, and contains fifty families of about eight persons each. The people were entirely destitute in the old country; the problem of their transportation from Ireland to their Minnesota homes, was solved by Rev. Father Nugent, of Liverpool, and Bishop Ireland of Minnesota.

——The diocese of Fort Wayne mourns the loss of another young and efficient priest in the death of Rev.

Martin Noll, which occurred on the 14th inst. He had lately been appointed pastor of Lafayette. Ind. Up to the time of his death, which was caused by a stroke of apoplexy, Father Noll's health had been excellent. Among other sacerdotal virtues for which he was distinguished and which caused him to be highly respected by all who knew him, was his charity to the poor, who always found in him a father and friend. R. I. P.

———THEN AND NOW.—A Madras paper, having unearthed a relic of the grotesque Protestant bigotry of the last century, contrasts it with the views of to-day:

On the 27th of January, 1747, the Court of Directors of the Hon'ble East India Company wrote to the Governor and Council at Fort St. David as follows :—"... We strictly forbid your suffering any Romish Church within our bounds, or any of their priests to dwell among you. nor that religion to be openly professed ; and in case any Papists have crept into places of trust in our service, they must be immediately dismissed."

On the 29th of April, 1880, the *Madras Times* announces that the Marquis of Ripon, a "Papist," has been appointed Viceroy of India.—*Indo-European Correspondence.*

———SHRINE OF THE SACRED HEART IN CANADA. —In consequence of the Plenary Indulgence granted by Pius IX, of happy memory, for a visit to the Shrine of the Sacred Heart, at St. Joseph de Levis, P. Q, Canada, during the Feast and Octave, numbers of adorers repaired thither to pay homage to the Divine Heart and offer up their petitions. The beautiful shrine remained decked as on grand occasions all the while. On entering the pious precincts, the visitor feels himself in a vivid manner in presence of that loving Heart which delights to dwell with the children of men. The necessities of all, but particularly of those affiliated to the work of erection, were recalled by the members of the community during the favored days, and besides the daily prayers and other good works performed according to promise, a number of thanksgiving Masses have been sung during the past year in behalf of benefactors both living and dead.

———FALLEN AT THEIR POSTS.—The operations of the Society for the Propagation of the Faith are so vast and cover so wide a field, that the official records march but slowly into line. One list religiously compiled and preserved—that of the Negroes who have fallen in the strife—only appears long after the events to which it refers. For instance, the necrological catalogue for 1878 was not complete before the 15th of February last, and mayhap it is even yet imperfect; but it nevertheless enshrines the names of 85 missionaries who have laid down their loads and gone to rest in the very midst of their labors. The congregations which furnish most sacrifices are the Society of Foreign Missions and the Society of Jesus. Others contributing are the Congregation of the Holy Spirit, the Lazarists, the Marists, the Augustinians of the Assumption, the Priests of St. Sulpice, etc. The graves of the dead are as wide apart as China, Japan, the Indies, Cochin China, Africa, and all parts of America, and most of them closed their eyes in savage and barbarous regions, destitute of the commonest comforts. Of course they had one and all the glorious consolation of duty done and purpose of life fulfilled, and that compensated for every trial.

———ADVICE TO EARNEST PROTESTANTS.—"If earnest Protestants desire to hinder the spread of the Roman Catholic Church," says the New York *Times*, "they should attack, not the Pope, but the arguments of Rationalism. The Protestant clergy do not seem to be aware of the formidable warfare which is now waging against revealed religion. The defenses which were effective against the noisy artillery of Paine, are useless against the noiseless and ceaseless sapping and mining with which Rationalism attacks them. Orthodox Protestantism shuts its eyes to the fact, that science and literature are in the hands of its enemies ; it refuses to perceive that the ground on which it stands is slipping from under its feet; that Germany, which, at the call of Luther, accepted the infallible Book in place of the self-styled infallible Church, has now rejected the Book, and that the new Reformation, which reforms Christianity out of existence, is spreading all over the Protestant world. The result will not be the permanent triumph of Rationalism, but a Roman Catholic revival which will make that Church far stronger than she has been at any time since the Reformation. When men clearly see that Protestantism is a failure, they will accept the Infallible Church rather than the empty sentimentalism of Rénan."

———WHAT A PRIEST HAS TO SAY ABOUT KNOCK.— We clip the following paragraph referring to the apparitions at Knock, from a letter written by an Irish priest to a gentleman in St. Paul. It appeared a week or two ago in the *Northwestern Chronicle:* " Allow me to give you my own experience of Knock. I went there on a pilgrimage last Tuesday, May 11th. I confess I was sceptical about the certainty of the cures and apparitions, and resolved to see with my own eyes, and judge with my own reason, about those matters. The first thing which struck me was the various crutches and bandages left by those who had been cured there. They were of various patterns, some the former property of the rich and some that of the poor. It is hard to suppose that so many persons—hundreds—had conspired to deceive. I went into the church, and the sight that struck my eyes was one worthy of the ages of faith. The crowd, filling the church to inconvenience, were all engaged in saying the Rosary most fervently. I knelt down inside the altar rails, and joined in the prayers. I looked at the window (one side of the Blessed Virgin's altar) and I saw on it a bright, mellow light, such as one sees in pictures, as the halo surrounding saints. I watched the light for an hour; strange to say, though to me most vivid. only comparatively few saw it. It could not have been the effect of the sun. It appeared at night as well as during the day, and it was quite unlike the light produced by the sun. I went to the outside of the window and there was no halo or light there ; it was entirely on the inside. Nor could it have been produced by the lamp and candles, as when they had been removed, it still continued to appear. That is all I saw, but three other persons in the church declared they saw, as distinctly as I, the light, *under that light* an apparition of our Lord with His head resting on the shoulder of some person, in tears and grief, as if He was consoling, by much familiarity, some penitent sinner. The three so favored were surprised that I did not see this apparition, as I was that everyone else did not see the light. The ways of God are inscrutable. There are pilgrims coming from all parts of the world to visit Knock."

———MAY DEVOTIONS IN CHINA.—On the 16th of March, 1853, Father Milfait, a missionary, set foot on the island of Hong Kong, which had long been forsaken, in order to proclaim anew the glad tidings of Redemption to its pagan inhabitants, and the few

Christians to be found there. The good priest was a zealous and devoted servant of Mary; on her intercession he placed the greatest reliance in his dangerous undertaking. After spending some time in instructing the Christian families scattered through the country, and making himself master of the language, he turned his attention to the heathens. The month of May was nearing. Like a true servant of Our Lady, he would not let her month pass by without offering her his homage and entreating her intercession for the conversion of the benighted idolaters. In a cabin, open to wind and weather he had an altar erected, surmounted by a picture of the Immaculate Conception. The altar and the picture were surrounded with flowers and crowns. Morning and evening the Christians were gathered together to say their beads, and throughout the day families came in turn to offer their prayers to the Mother of God. Hardly had the devotion begun when, to the delight of the missionary, the first fruits began to appear. On the very first day a young man entered the cabin: He had heard of the Christian religion and had travelled hither to be instructed in it; and when he crossed the threshold and saw the beautiful picture of the glorious Virgin, he instantly fell upon his knees and saluted the Queen of Heaven with many reverences. When the missionary heard of his desire to become a Christian, he placed him under the instruction of a catechist who was master of the language, and the neophyte showed such zeal that he seemed to forget all else. During the course of his instruction, he cast himself at least twenty times a day before the image of Mary. He said to the missionary, "Father, sin is in my heart, but you will drive it out by baptism." On Pentecost, the missionary baptized him, and he immediately hurried back to his family to inform them of his happiness and to invite them to share in it. But this was not the sole fruit of the devotion; five idolaters were converted, and one apostate reconciled, and after ten months, the missionary had the happiness of baptizing forty-three pagans, and had seventy-three anxiously awaiting the same grace.

—CONTRIBUTIONS FOR THE SUFFERING IRISH:—Terence McKernin, $1; James Brady, 50 cts.; Peter McNulty, 50 cts.; Mary McDonald, 50 cts.; Martin Higgins, 50 cts.; Michael Sullivan, 50 cts.; Miss Mary O'Brien, $1; Mr. John Mahoney, Sr., $1; Mrs. E. R. Parker, $2; H. Beh n, $1; Henry and Mary Raway, $3; Peter and Margarette Dunn, $5; A Subscriber of THE AVE MARIA, Kennedyville, Md, $5; Mrs. E. Wall, $2; A Friend, $5; Mrs. C. G. Sacra, 50 cts.; A Reader of THE AVE MARIA. $5; A Friend, $50; Dennis Mulherin, $1; A Friend, $2; Bridget Sullanin, 50 cts.; J. M., $2; James Fitzpatrick, $1; Mrs. E. Dillon, $1; H. M. and T., 35 cts.; A Friend, $1; Mrs. Maria Navarre, a package of dry-goods.

Acknowledgments.

ST. JARLATH'S, Tuam, June 3, 1880.

REV. DEAR SIR:—Your very kind letter, conveying £20 ($100) for the relief of our poor people, has duly reached me.

Wishing you and the charitable readers of your excellent little magazine every blessing in this life and the life to come,

I remain, Rev. dear sir, faithfully yours,

✠ JOHN MACHALE.

PRESENTATION CONVENT, Mitchelstown, Ireland.

DEAR REV. FATHER:—I hasten to thank you for the £10 you so kindly sent for the relief of our poor, hungry children. Our Rev. Mother desires me to express her gratitude to you, and say that the benefactors shall have the prayers of the large number of our children (from one to two hundred) who have to be provided with food and clothing. She only hopes to be able to continue to relieve them during the long summer between us and the harvest, which is always late in this locality.

With renewed thanks, I remain, dear Rev. Father,

Your very grateful and most respectful,

SISTER MARY XAVIER.

Confraternity of the Immaculate Conception
(Or of Our Lady of Lourdes).

"We fly to thy patronage, O Holy Mother of God!"

REPORT FOR THE WEEK ENDING JUNE 16TH.

The following intentions are recommended to the prayers of the members this week: Recovery of health for 7 persons,—conversion to the Faith for 14 persons,—spiritual favors for 14 persons,—temporal favors for 7 persons,—recovery of sight for 4 persons,—recovery of mind for 4 persons,—change of life for 8 persons;—also 16 particular intentions, and 2 thanksgivings for favors received.

Specified intentions: Successful rebuilding of an edifice, destroyed by fire,—employment for 2 persons,—success of a lawsuit,—conversion of a dying man,—success in business.—cure of 4 persons addicted to intemperance —conversion of an unruly child,—removal of obstacles to a vocation,—prevention of a mixed marriage, and the spread of a disease,—profitable sale of land,—protection of crops in a certain locality,—successful examination.

FAVORS OBTAINED.

We take the following extract of a letter of recent date: "Rev. Father! My little grandson was affected with St. Vitus' dance. I gave him the blessed water you sent me, according to direction; thanks to our Divine Lord and His Blessed Mother! the boy is now fully recovered. I can say with St. Bernard, that I never knew our Lady to refuse me anything I asked."

OBITUARY.

The following deceased persons are recommended to the prayers of the Confraternity: MICHAEL CASHMAN, Esq., of Glanmire, Cork, Ireland, who departed for heaven on the 23d of May, at the venerable age of ninety. His life was not only blameless, but signalized throughout by deeds of charity and devotedness. Mrs. SARAH J. CORBENY, whose death occurred in Chicago, on the 1st inst. G. E. MURPHY, of Columbus, O. Mrs. MULLIN and Mrs. GILBRIDGE, of Boston, Mass. Mrs. SHEEHAN, of Oil City, Pa. Mrs. J. GANNING, of Sinsinawa, Wis.; PATRICK, ELLEN and BRIDGET RYAN, of Keenesville, Ont., who died some time ago. Miss E. GABRIELLA, Mr. VICTORY, THOMAS FITZGERALD, CHARLES MCCABE, Mrs. C. BARRETT, Mrs. MARTIN DOLAN, Mrs. R. A. BERRY, Mrs. GOODWINE, HANNAH ALLEN, DANIEL GALVIN, BRIDGET COYLE and sister, JOHN R. ENOS, Dr. B. STEVENS, M. MALLON. And several others, whose names have not been given.

Requiescant in pace.

A. GRANGER, C. S. C., Director.

Youth's Department.

Lucy's Consolation.

BY SUSAN L. EMERY.

HE sat beside baby Margaret's sick couch, and softly turned the pages of her book, and read with eyes that often left the page to seek the baby's face. Her eyes were swollen and heavy, and she was pale with watching. Mamma was ill in the next room, and baby was very ill here beside her, and papa was far away.

That morning Lucy had heard the doctor say to nurse, "I have hardly any hope for baby." And nurse had cried out sorrowfully: "Oh, my poor lady! it will break her heart."

Lucy wondered wearily that afternoon how hearts felt when they broke. It did not seem to her that hers was breaking, but never had it been so heavy. The book she was reading was full of stories about saints, and of miracles they had wrought, such as restoring sight to the blind, healing the sick, and even raising the dead. Why would not some pitying saint cure mamma and baby Margaret?

Lucy fell upon her knees, and prayed, speaking the names as they rose to her memory, from the stories she had just been reading: "St. Elizabeth of Hungary, St. Antony of Padua, St. Stanislaus, St. Aloysius, dear Blessed Mother, ask our dear Lord Jesus to heal my mother and little baby, and to bring papa home right away." And then suddenly nurse's voice broke in upon the prayer: "Miss Lucy, run quick: tell the doctor to come; baby is worse!"

She caught a glimpse of the tiny face grown yet more white and rigid than it had been before; then she seized her hat and ran out of the house and along the street. How fast she ran! yet to her anxious mind her flying feet seemed heavy as lead and clogged and stumbling.

"Dear Mother pray! Dear saints, pray! Dear, dearest Lord Jesus, have mercy!" she sobbed, with panting breath. The doctor was gone a mile from home, so she ran on. Through her blinding tears she hardly saw the houses as she passed; but presently a well-known voice cried to her: "Lucy, where are you going, child? For me?" and the doctor's horse stopped beside her, and his hand was held out to her to lift her into the chaise. "What is the matter?" he asked; "were you going for me?"

"Yes, yes," she answered. "The baby is worse; I think she is nearly dead, nurse says to come."

The kind old doctor's eyes grew moist, as the little girl broke into a passion of tears. "You must save baby! you must save baby!" she said.

He put his aged hand that had felt so many fluttering, failing pulses, softly over Lucy's young hand that had seldom known any touch but of the well, and strong, and living, until these last long, painful weeks. "Only God can save," he said, pityingly; "only God can cure."

She did not look at him after, nor speak; again and again in listless fashion, like a kind of accompaniment to the horse's hurrying hoofs, she repeated to herself the words, "Only God can save, only God can cure."

It was a short drive, yet, before the chaise reached her home, she felt as though she had said those words a thousand times, and as though she would never have any other words to say. They went up the stairs together and were turning towards the room which Lucy had left, when nurse spoke from mamma's door, and they went to meet her; her face told all.

"No need to go there now," she said, while the tears ran down her cheeks; "the little lamb is past all pain. It's my lady wants you now."

She and the doctor went to mamma together. Steadily Lucy went back to the baby's room. Little Margaret lay there, in the place where she had left her, but the warm coverlid was gone, and one white sheet covered the tiny figure. The face that had been so drawn and pinched with suffering was very quiet now, the eyes were closed, and the look was placid and gentle and very fair to see. Some one had closed the shutters, and only a tiny ray of light fell with the cool gray shadows over the peaceful scene. The baby hands were folded upon a spray of lilies, not more white nor beautiful than that face stamped with the wondrous sign of death.

Death! This then was death; Lucy had never before been in the presence of that mysterious power. She knelt by the couch and gazed and gazed; sixty minutes ago, she had touched that child, had kissed it, prayed beside it, and begged all the saints to pray for it; sixty minutes ago, she had believed her prayers could save it, now it dead now. Nothing could bring it back, nobody could make it open its eyes or smile or cry again; only a baby, yet not all the strength of earth could make it weep or wake. If hearts only *would* break! if, instead of that hard tearing pain in hers, it only *would* break, and let her die too! She thought of papa, happy papa, who did not know their sorrow yet; unhappy papa, who must know it when his long-looked-for letters came from home. She thought of mamma, whose little baby was gone from her now, to those other little baby-sisters who in like manner had been taken.

And mamma's grief and papa's grief joined themselves to Lucy's and weighed her down to the very ground. "St. Elizabeth of Hungary, St. Antony of Padua, St. Stanislaus, St. Aloysius, dearest Mother! ask our Lord to give baby Margaret back to us again."

How she came to say those words she hardly knew; they sprang to her lips like an over-flowing tide that would have its way; and all her heart went with them in an intense power of faith and intercession. God, who first gave life to baby, could, and surely would, give life to her again, and restore her to them.

The doctor found her kneeling there as he looked into the room on his departure. "My little child," he said, "who left you here? this is too sad for you."

She raised to his such a grave, calm, holy face, that for many a day after he wondered over it. "I would rather stay here," she said; "God will comfort us."

Then left alone again with her beloved dead, she prayed the same prayer steadily, in unshrinking faith; "God could not help but hear," she said. Praying, she watched. Those blue-veined lids would open soon; those eyes that papa called his "sweetest violets" would look lovingly at her; those lips would part and smile; those hands would catch the lilies folded in them, would press them close, and press out all their sweet perfume. Soon, very soon, God would answer her earnest praying, and she would snatch the living baby, well and strong, from this white bed of death, and carry it in triumph to mamma. God, the good God, and His strong holy saints, were listening to her, and would not refuse her cry.

Hark! footsteps on the stairs, men entering; who are these? She cannot comprehend it. Surely they have not come to take the baby from her. And then she hears nurse speaking: "Go, my precious; leave us with baby for a little while."

She knows now, she knows it all; they will put baby in a coffin, like Agatha, and Rose, and Julia. All the saints, and God Himself, have refused to hear her prayer, she thinks; and there bursts from the child's lips such an irrepressible bitter cry, that the stony men exclaimed, "God pity her!"

She fled fast from them, she put nurse from her as if nurse had been a child herself; earth and heaven held but one refuge for her—her mother's arms, and no one should keep her from them any longer.

"Mamma! mamma! you must take me. O why must a little child like me suffer so!"

Just now you would not have believed mamma could lift her hand or head; but mother-love is marvellously strong. At the sound of that heart-rending cry, she raised herself, and held out her arms, and gathered the weeping, exhausted creature to her breast. "My darling! my precious child! you shall—" but here she paused, startled and amazed. This was no ordinary case of grief; no ordinary sense of sorrow had put that strained, despairing, deserted look in the eyes of a little girl. It was the look of one to whom the very light of life has grown dim, and for whom all hope and joy in life have died. Had Lucy been homeless and an orphan and outcast, then she might have looked like this.

"Lucy! what has happened? Is there worse news? Your father?"

"Yes," answered Lucy, and her lips were white and stiff, and her voice was strange, "*much* worse; my Father—my Father in Heaven—would not hear me; the saints would not answer me: they would not raise the dead."

She drew herself back from the close clasp of her mother's arms; she stared at her with wide unchildlike eyes. "Where *is* our Father," she said, "when He does not hear?"

Mamma folded her closer, closer to her; mamma's sad face grew suddenly, gravely glad.

"Oh, my darling!" she cried, "God is here. He did hear you, you may be sure of that. Let us lie still and rest a little while, and then I will tell you. You are utterly worn out now. He is here, and He listens to you, and loves you, as surely as I am here."

Too exhausted for further questioning or longer struggle, Lucy lay there; and through the gathering summer twilight, just as those other words, "Only God can save, only God can cure," had haunted her, so now, but like a sweetly chiming bell, she seemed to hear, over and over, "God is here: He did hear you; lie still and rest."

It was mamma's own baby who had died; it was mamma's own Father in Heaven who had let her baby die. And yet as Lucy lay there, close to that wounded mother-heart, which God had chosen to smite so often and so hard, Lucy's sore heart grew calm again. What did it mean?

By and by, mamma spoke.

"Lucy!"

"Yes, mamma."

"Would God hear your prayers for baby first, or would He hear its mother's prayers—its own mother's?"

"Mamma, of course he would hear yours."

"And I," said mamma, softly, "would not have my baby—not one of my babies—here again for all the joy their love and life could give me."

"Then that was why He would not hear me," exclaimed Lucy; "you did not want it; and don't you suffer like me, then?"

"Suffer!" Lucy did not need an answer when she saw her mother's face.

"It is as if they pulled my heart out of me, child," she said. "When my first baby died, I thought I should die too. But I never would have dared to pray as you have done. Let God take them when He choses, for He knows best."

Lucy had not thought of that. Oh no! she could not desire that; but mamma spoke again. "Once I told the priest that my sorrow was too great to bear. And then he said to me that if I saw it rightly, I would know I was a happy mother, for my babies were surely and safely gone to heaven, and I had given saints to God, and I could pray to them as to any saints. That is my comfort. I cannot tell you any more, it is too beautiful. God must teach us things like these."

That evening Lucy stole into baby's room again. She was lying in the tiny casket, but it was not terrible to see. A crucifix was at the head, and blessed candles burned there, and rare sweet flowers made the place like our Lady's altar on a festal day. Lucy knelt fearlessly beside it. "Answer my prayer. Make me see too, dear Lord!" she prayed. "Teach me those things that are too beautiful to tell."

No strong vision came to her; but her mother's words and her own prayers grew plain to her; this little child for whom she had prayed so long and hard, was alive now and glad forevermore in the presence of God. Had she come back to life here, she would have had to die again. Now baby Margaret was forever free from death and pain and sin.

It was a very quiet Lucy whom papa met when he came home from his long journey; yet it was a very happy Lucy too. She spoke little of herself to others, but often as she went slowly to and fro through the streets where once her feet sped gayly, she said below her breath, to her angel perhaps or to that little loving sister-saint above: "I am glad the good God lets us suffer; it is sweet to suffer; it makes the eyes of the soul see beautiful, blessed things."

Loss is often gain, and often to have our prayers refused is God's kindest answer to them. Suffering and sorrow are the royal highways by which the chosen people go to endless joy in heaven.

A Repentant Sinner.

After the Revolution that disgraced the close of the last century, a chaplain was called to attend a soldier very severely wounded. The priest found a man whose countenance showed the greatest serenity. He said to the wounded man: 'My friend, I was told that your wounds were very serious." Smiling sadly, the soldier answered: "Reverend sir, will you raise the bedclothes a little from my chest?" The priest complied, and then drew back with a shudder, for he perceived that both arms were gone.

"What!" exclaimed the soldier, "you stand with horror at such a trifle! Raise the covering from my feet, then." The priest did so, and saw that his feet had likewise been carried away 'Ah!" he said, greatly moved, "how I pity you poor fellow!"

"Oh no," answered the mangled form of humanity; "I suffer only what I earned for myself Not long since, in an insane fury, I chopped off all the limbs of a crucifix, so that the image of my Redeemer fell to the ground; and in the next battle my own arms and legs were carried off by cannon balls. As I treated Him, so has He treated me. But thanks be to God for punishing me in this world for my crime, that He may spare me in the next, as I hope and trust He will in His exceeding great mercy!"

Yes, God is just. And yet there are men that with smiling countenances continue to heap crime upon crime. To them it seems but a trifling matter to insult this Sovereign Being. But how they will open their eyes when they see Him at the Judgement!

A Youthful Martyr.

An orphan boy, twelve years old, Arab by origin, and whose baptismal name was Peter, was placed some time ago with a family of farmers in the environs of Orleansville. He tended flocks, which occupation brought him in contact with the Arab shepherds of the neighboring tribes. These solicited him many a time to renounce the Christian religion. They promised to receive him into their tribes, to nourish him, to give him money, to find him a situation, and the like, but without avail. "What! I renounce my religion," he replied, "to become a Mussulman again? no, never!" Seeing that they gained nothing by their promises, they had recourse first to threats, then to blows; but all in vain. At last, taking hold of him they threatened to kill him if he did not comply with their request; but his reply was: "Never will I renounce my religion!" Summoned once more to apostatize, he refused to do so, and they then cut off his head. The news of the child's martyrdom soon reached the colonists by whom he was employed, and these brave people erected a modest monument to his memory, with the following inscription: "Here lies the body of Peter, who died a martyr for the Faith of Christ." Mgr. Lavigerie has ordered an inquest to be made for the purpose of gathering the facts of this child's martyrdom.

BOSTON, the "Hub of the Universe," as it is called, derives its name from a Catholic monk of the 7th century.